ROMANS

Zondervan Exegetical Commentary on the New Testament

ROMANS

ZONDERVAN
Exegetical Commentary
ON THE
New Testament

FRANK THIELMAN

CLINTON E. ARNOLD
General Editor

ZONDERVAN ACADEMIC

Romans
Copyright © 2018 by Frank S. Thielman

Published in Grand Rapids, Michigan, by Zondervan. Zondervan is a registered trademark of The Zondervan Corporation, L.L.C., a wholly owned subsidiary of HarperCollins Christian Publishing, Inc.

Requests for information should be addressed to customercare@harpercollins.com.

Zondervan titles may be purchased in bulk for educational, business, fundraising, or sales promotional use. For information, please email SpecialMarkets@Zondervan.com.

ISBN 978-0-310-10403-2 (hardcover)
ISBN 978-0-310-55554-4 (ebook)

The author wishes to acknowledge with gratitude the use of the Thesaurus Linguae Graecae and the material in it copyrighted by the TLG and the Regents of the University of California in the research for this book.

Cover design: Tammy Johnson
Interior design: Beth Shagene

Printed in the United States of America

25 26 27 28 29 30 31 32 33 34 35 36 37 38 /TRM/ 22 21 20 19 18 17 16 15 14 13 12 11 10 9 8 7 6

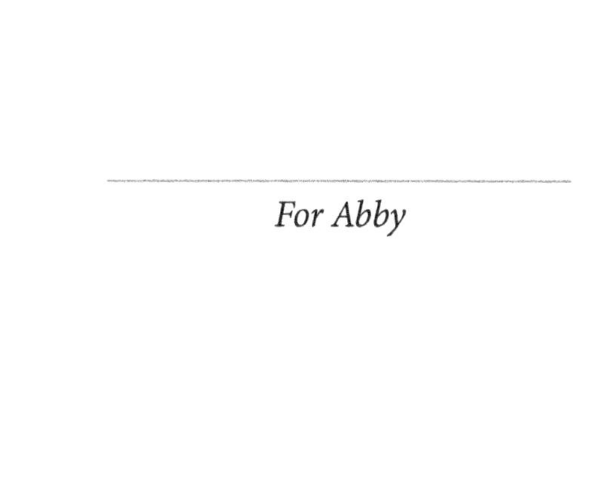

For Abby

Contents

Series Introduction

This generation has been blessed with an abundance of excellent commentaries. Some are technical and do a good job of addressing issues that the critics have raised; other commentaries are long and provide extensive information about word usage and catalogue nearly every opinion expressed on the various interpretive issues; still other commentaries focus on providing cultural and historical background information; and then there are those commentaries that endeavor to draw out many applicational insights.

The key question to ask is: What are you looking for in a commentary? This commentary series might be for you if

- you have taken Greek and would like a commentary that helps you apply what you have learned without assuming you are a well-trained scholar.
- you would find it useful to see a concise, one-or two-sentence statement of what the commentator thinks the main point of each passage is.
- you would like help interpreting the words of Scripture without getting bogged down in scholarly issues that seem irrelevant to the life of the church.
- you would like to see a visual representation (a graphical display) of the flow of thought in each passage.
- you would like expert guidance from solid evangelical scholars who set out to explain the meaning of the original text in the clearest way possible and to help you navigate through the main interpretive issues.
- you want to benefit from the results of the latest and best scholarly studies and historical information that help to illuminate the meaning of the text.
- you would find it useful to see a brief summary of the key theological insights that can be gleaned from each passage and some discussion of the relevance of these for Christians today.

These are just some of the features that characterize the new Zondervan Exegetical Commentary on the New Testament series. The idea for this series was refined over time by an editorial board who listened to pastors and teachers express what they wanted to see in a commentary series based on the Greek text. That board consisted of myself, George H. Guthrie, William D. Mounce, Thomas R. Schreiner, and Mark L. Strauss along with Zondervan senior editor at large Verlyn Verbrugge, and former Zondervan senior acquisitions editor Jack Kuhatschek. We also enlisted a board of consulting editors who are active pastors, ministry leaders, and seminary professors to help in the process of designing a commentary series that will be useful to the church. Zondervan senior acquisitions editor Katya Covrett has now been shepherding the process to completion, and Constantine R. Campbell is now serving on the board.

We arrived at a design that includes seven components for the treatment of each biblical passage. What follows is a brief orientation to these primary components of the commentary.

Literary Context

In this section, you will find a concise discussion of how the passage functions in the broader literary context of the book. The commentator highlights connections with the preceding and following material in the book and makes observations on the key literary features of this text.

Main Idea

Many readers will find this to be an enormously helpful feature of this series. For each passage, the commentator carefully crafts a one- or two-sentence statement of the big idea or central thrust of the passage.

Translation and Graphical Layout

Another unique feature of this series is the presentation of each commentator's translation of the Greek text in a graphical layout. The purpose of this diagram is to help the reader visualize, and thus better understand, the flow of thought within the text. The translation itself reflects the interpretive decisions made by each commentator in the "Explanation" section of the commentary. Here are a few insights that will help you to understand the way these are put together:

1. On the far left side next to the verse numbers is a series of interpretive labels that indicate the function of each clause or phrase of the biblical text. The corresponding portion of the text is on the same line to the right of the label. We have not used technical linguistic jargon for these, so they should be easily understood.
2. In general, we place every clause (a group of words containing a subject and a predicate) on a separate line and identify how it is supporting the principal assertion of the text (namely, is it saying when the action occurred, how it took place,

or why it took place?). We sometimes place longer phrases or a series of items on separate lines as well.

3. Subordinate (or dependent) clauses and phrases are indented and placed directly under the words that they modify. This helps the reader to more easily see the nature of the relationship of clauses and phrases in the flow of the text.
4. Every main clause has been placed in bold print and pushed to the left margin for clear identification.
5. Sometimes when the level of subordination moves too far to the right—as often happens with some of Paul's long, involved sentences!—we reposition the flow to the left of the diagram, but use an arrow to indicate that this has happened.
6. The overall process we have followed has been deeply informed by principles of discourse analysis and narrative criticism (for the Gospels and Acts).

Structure

Immediately following the translation, the commentator describes the flow of thought in the passage and explains how certain interpretive decisions regarding the relationship of the clauses were made in the passage.

Exegetical Outline

The overall structure of the passage is described in a detailed exegetical outline. This will be particularly helpful for those who are looking for a way to concisely explain the flow of thought in the passage in a teaching or preaching setting.

Explanation of the Text

As an exegetical commentary, this work makes use of the Greek language to interpret the meaning of the text. If your Greek is rather rusty (or even somewhat limited), don't be too concerned. All the Greek words are cited in parentheses following an English translation. We have made every effort to make this commentary as readable and useful as possible even for the nonspecialist.

Those who will benefit the most from this commentary will have had the equivalent of two years of Greek in college or seminary. This would include a semester or two of working through an intermediate grammar (such as Wallace, Porter, Brooks and Winbery, or Dana and Mantey). The authors use the grammatical language that is found in these kinds of grammars. The details of the grammar of the passage, however, are discussed only when it has a bearing on the interpretation of the text.

The emphasis in this section of the text is to convey the meaning. Commentators examine words and images, grammatical details, relevant OT and Jewish background to a particular concept, historical and cultural context, important text-critical issues, and various interpretational issues that surface.

Theology in Application

This, too, is a unique feature for an exegetical commentary series. We felt it was important for each author not only to describe what the text means in its various details, but also to take a moment and reflect on the theological contribution that it makes. In this section, the theological message of the passage is summarized. The authors discuss the theology of the text in terms of its place within the book and in a broader biblical-theological context. Finally, each commentator provides some suggestions on what the message of the passage is for the church today. At the conclusion of each volume in this series is a summary of the whole range of theological themes touched on by this book of the Bible.

Our sincere hope and prayer is that you find this series helpful not only for your own understanding of the text of the New Testament, but as you are actively engaged in teaching and preaching God's Word to people who are hungry to be fed on its truth.

Clinton E. Arnold, general editor

Author's Preface

C. E. B. Cranfield compared trying to explain Paul's argument in Romans 9–11 to ascending the North Wall of the Eiger, perhaps the steepest and deadliest technical climb in the Alps.[1] If that is true of Romans 9–11, the challenge of explaining the whole letter is daunting indeed. Cranfield thought that his own magisterial commentary had failed "to come anywhere near" doing the letter justice.[2] If my commentary does anything at all to help its readers understand Romans, it will only be through God's gracious provision of many helpful friends.

I would like to thank Clint Arnold and Tom Schreiner for inviting me to contribute this volume to the ZECNT and to thank Clint and the editorial board for the helpful suggestions they offered for the manuscript's improvement. I also owe an enormous debt to George Guthrie for help with the diagrams and to Chris Beetham at Zondervan, whose careful editorial work was invaluable. I am grateful to Timothy George, Dean of Beeson Divinity School, and to the Samford University board of trustees for granting me two semester-long sabbaticals, one at the beginning and one at the end of the project, that allowed me to concentrate fully on Romans.

Other friends and family also helped in many ways. My colleague Paul House and my brothers, Sam and Nathan, through a number of enjoyable conversations helped clarify my thinking about Romans, especially its relationship to the Old Testament and its practical application to the Christian life. Nathan and his wife Margaret opened their home near the Duke University libraries to me. My mother, Dorothy Thielman, invited my family and me to visit her often, and her home provided a quiet place to work. Each of my children, Jonathan, his wonderful wife Emily, and my daughters Sarah Jane and Rebekah, took an encouraging interest in the work and helped in practical ways. Fellow members of the small prayer and Bible-study group that have helped nurture my wife, Abby, and me spiritually for many years faithfully prayed for my work on this commentary. I am deeply grateful for their kind interest and support.

In human terms my greatest debt of gratitude, however, is to Abby, my best friend,

1. C. E. B. Cranfield, *A Critical and Exegetical Commentary on the Epistle to the Romans*, 2 vols., ICC (Edinburgh: T&T Clark, 1975–79), 2:445. Cranfield got the image from the Swiss New Testament scholar Ernst Gaugler, *Der Römerbrief*, 2 vols. (Zürich: Zwingli, 1945–52), 1:327.

2. Cranfield, *Romans*, 1:x.

constant companion, and coworker in the advancement of the gospel. Without her help, wise counsel, and unconditional love I probably could never have written much of anything, and certainly not a commentary on Romans.

My hope for this commentary is simply that it will play the role of a footman, opening the door to Romans and then quickly stepping out of the way so that others might "enter" the letter itself, sit at the feet of the apostle Paul, and in the apostle's voice hear the voice of God.

Frank Thielman
Lent 2017

Abbreviations

Abbreviations in this volume, and the explanations of them below, generally follow the *SBL Handbook of Style*, 2nd ed. (Atlanta: SBL Press, 2014) and the *Checklist of Editions of Greek, Latin, Demotic, and Coptic Papyri, Ostraca and Tablets*. Abbreviations for books of the Bible, the Apocrypha, the Pseudepigrapha, the Apostolic Fathers, and classical texts do not appear below, but appear in the *SBL Handbook of Style*.

AB	Anchor Bible
ABD	*Anchor Bible Dictionary*. Edited by David Noel Freedman. 6 vols. New York: Doubleday, 1992
AHR	*American Historical Review*
AnBib	Analecta biblica
ANF	*The Ante-Nicene Fathers*. Edited by Alexander Roberts and James Donaldson. 10 vols. 1885–1887. Repr., Peabody, MA: Hendrickson, 1994
ANRW	*Aufstieg und Niedergang der römischen Welt: Geschichte und Kultur Roms im Spiegel der neueren Forschung*. Edited by H. Temporini and W. Haase. Berlin: de Gruyter, 1972–
AThRSup	Anglican Theological Review: Supplementary Series
BBR	*Bulletin for Biblical Research*
BDAG	Danker, F. W., W. Bauer, W. F. Arndt, and F. W. Gingrich. *Greek-English Lexicon of the New Testament and Other Early Christian Literature*. 3rd ed. Chicago: University of Chicago Press, 2000
BDF	Blass, F., A. Debrunner, and R. W. Funk. *A Greek Grammar of the New Testament and Other Early Christian Literature*. Chicago: University of Chicago Press, 1961
BDR	Blass, F., A. Debrunner, and F. Rehkopf. *Grammatik des neutestamentlichen griechisch*. 18th ed. Göttingen: Vadenhoeck & Ruprecht, 2001
BECNT	Baker Exegetical Commentary on the New Testament
BETL	Bibliotheca Ephemeridum Theologicarum Lovaniensium
BHT	Beiträge zur historischen Theologie

BJRL	*Bulletin of the John Rylands University Library of Manchester*
BNP	*Brill's New Pauly: Encyclopaedia of the Ancient World*. Edited by Hubert Cancik. 22 vols. Leiden: Brill, 2002–2011
BNTC	Black's New Testament Commentaries
BR	*Biblical Research*
BZNW	Beihefte zur Zeitschrift für die neutestamentliche Wissenschaft
CBQ	*Catholic Biblical Quarterly*
CEB	Common English Bible
CEJL	Commentaries on Early Jewish Literature
CGELNT	*The Concise Greek-English Lexicon of the New Testament*. Frederick William Danker. Chicago: University of Chicago Press, 2009
CJ	*Classical Journal*
CurTM	*Currents in Theology and Mission*
Douay-Rheims	The Douay-Rheims translation of the Vulgate. American edition of 1899
EBib	*Etudes bibliques*
ECC	Eerdmans Critical Commentary
EDEJ	*The Eerdmans Dictionary of Early Judaism*. Edited by John J. Collins and Daniel C. Harlow. Grand Rapids: Eerdmans, 2010
EDNT	*Exegetical Dictionary of the New Testament*. Edited by Horst Balz and Gerhard Schneider. ET. 3 vols. Grand Rapids: Eerdmans, 1990–93
EKKNT	Evangelisch-katholischer Kommentar zum Neuen Testament
Eng.	Most English editions of the Old Testament
ESV	English Standard Version
ETL	*Ephemerides Theologicae Lovanienses*
ExAud	*Ex Auditu*
ExpTim	*Expository Times*
FC	Fathers of the Church
FRLANT	Forschungen zur Religion und Literatur des Alten und Neuen Testaments
HALOT	*The Hebrew and Aramaic Lexicon of the Old Testament*. L. Koehler, W. Baumgartner, and J. J. Stamm. Translated and edited under the supervision of M. E. J. Richardson. Study edition. 2 vols. Leiden: Brill, 2001
HCSB	Holman Christian Standard Bible
Heb.	Hebrew text of the Old Testament
HNT	Handbuch zum Neuen Testament
HNTC	Harper's New Testament Commentaries

HThKNT	Herders Theologischer Kommentar zum Neuen Testament
HTR	*Harvard Theological Review*
HTS	Harvard Theological Studies
HUT	Hermeneutische Untersuchungen zur Theologie
IBC	Interpretation: A Bible Commentary for Teaching and Preaching
ICC	International Critical Commentary
IGUR	*Inscriptiones Graecae Urbis Romae*. Edited by Luigi Moretti. Rome, 1968–90
Int	*Interpretation*
JAAR	*Journal of the American Academy of Religion*
JBL	*Journal of Biblical Literature*
JETS	*Journal of the Evangelical Theological Society*
JRS	*Journal of Roman Studies*
JSJ	*Journal for the Study of Judaism in the Persian, Hellenistic, and Roman Periods*
JSNT	*Journal for the Study of the New Testament*
JSNTSup	Journal for the Study of the New Testament Supplement Series
JSPSup	Journal for the Study of the Pseudepigrapha Supplement Series
JTC	*Journal for Theology and the Church*
JTS	*Journal of Theological Studies*
KEK	Kritisch-exegetischer Kommentar über das Neue Testament (Meyer-Kommentar)
KJV	King James Version
LCL	Loeb Classical Library
LEH	Lust, Johan, Erik Eynikel, and Katrin Hauspie, eds. *Greek-English Lexicon of the Septuagint*. Rev. ed. Stuttgart: Deutsche Bibelgesellschaft, 2003
LNTS	The Library of New Testament Studies
LSJ	Liddell, H. G., R. Scott, and H. S. Jones. *A Greek-English Lexicon*. 9th ed. with revised supplement. Oxford: Clarendon, 1996
LSJSupp	Liddell, H. G., R. Scott, H. S. Jones, R. McKenzie. *Greek-English Lexicon Revised Supplement*. Oxford: Clarendon, 1996
Luther	Luther, Martin. *Biblia, das ist, die ganze heilige Schrift, Deutsch*. Wittemburg, 1545
Lutherbibel	*Die Bibel*. Translated by Martin Luther. Rev. ed. Stuttgart, 1999
LXX	Septuagint
MGS	Montanari, Franco, Madeleine Goh, and Chad Schroeder. *The Brill Dictionary of Ancient Greek*. Leiden: Brill, 2015
MM	Moulton, J. H., and G. Milligan. *The Vocabulary of the Greek Testament*. London, 1930

MT	Masoretic Text
NA$^{24, 25, 26, 27, 28}$	*Novum Testamentum Graece*, Nestle-Aland, 24th–28th eds.
NAB	New American Bible
NAC	New American Commentary
NASB	New American Standard Bible
Neot	*Neotestamentica*
NET	New English Translation
NETS	*A New English Translation of the Septuagint*. Ed. A. Pietersma and B. G. Wright. New York: Oxford University Press, 2007
NICNT	New International Commentary on the New Testament
NICOT	New International Commentary on the Old Testament
NIGTC	New International Greek Testament Commentary
NIV	New International Version
NJB	New Jerusalem Bible
NLT	New Living Translation
NovT	*Novum Testamentum*
NovTSup	Supplements to Novum Testamentum
NRSV	New Revised Standard Version
NSBT	New Studies in Biblical Theology
NT	New Testament
NTS	*New Testament Studies*
OCD	*Oxford Classical Dictionary*. Edited by S. Hornblower and A. Spawforth. 3rd ed. Oxford: Oxford University Press, 1996
OT	Old Testament
OTP	*Old Testament Pseudepigrapha*. Edited by J. H. Charlesworth. 2 vols. New York: Doubleday, 1983, 1985
PG	Patrologia Graeca [= Patrologiae Cursus Completus: Series Graeca]. Edited by J.-P. Migne. 162 vols. Paris, 1857–1886
PGL	*Patristic Greek Lexicon*. Edited by G. W. H. Lampe. Oxford: Clarendon, 1968
PGM	*Papyri Graecae Magicae: Die griechischen Zauberpapyri*. Edited by Karl Preisendanz. 2nd ed. Stuttgart: Teubner, 1973–1974
PNTC	Pillar New Testament Commentary
PSI	Pubblicazioni della Società italiana per la ricerca dei papiri greci e latini in Egitto. Florence, 1912–
P.Cair.Zen.	*Zenon Papyri, Catalogue général des antiquités égyptiennes du Musée du Caire*. Edited by C. C. Edgar, O. Guéraud, and P. Jouguet. Cairo, 1925–40
P.Fay.	*Fayum Towns and their Papyri*. Edited by B. P. Grenfell, A. S. Hunt, and D. G. Hogarth. London, 1900

P.Flor. *Papiri greco-egizii, Papiri Fiorentini*. Supplementi Filologico-Storici ai Monumenti Antichi 3. Edited by G. Vitelli and D. Comparetti. Milan, 1915

P.Lond. *Greek Papyri in the British Museum*. Edited by F. G. Kenyon, H. I. Bell, W. E. Crum, and T. C. Skeat. 7 vols. London, 1893–1974

P.Oxy. *The Oxyrhynchus Papyri*. Edited by B. P. Grenfell, A. S. Hunt, et al. London: Egypt Exploration Fund, 1898–

P.Rev. *Revenue Laws of Ptolemy Philadelphus*. Edited by B. P. Grenfell. Oxford: Clarendon, 1896

P.Ryl. *Catalogue of the Greek and Latin Papyri in the John Rylands Library, Manchester*. Edited by A. S. Hunt, J. de M. Johnson, V. Martin, C. H. Roberts, and E. G. Turner. Manchester, 1911–52

P.Tebt. *The Tebtunis Papyri*. Edited by B. P. Grenfell, A. S. Hunt, J. G. Smyly, E. Lobel, M. Rostovtzeff, C. C. Edgar, J. G. Keenan, J. C. Shelton, and A. Verhoogt. London and Leiden, 1902–

REB Revised English Bible

RevScRel *Revue des sciences religieuses*

RTR *Reformed Theological Review*

SBLDS Society of Biblical Literature Dissertation Series

SBLTT *Society of Biblical Literature Texts and Translations*

SBT Studies in Biblical Theology

ScEs *Science et esprit*

SD Studies and Documents

SEÅ *Svensk exegetisk årsbok*

SEG Supplementum epigraphicum graecum

SIG *Sylloge Inscriptionum Graecarum*. Edited by W. Dittenberger. 4 vols. 3rd ed. Leipzig: Hirzel, 1915–24

SJT *Scottish Journal of Theology*

Smyth Smyth, Herbert Weir. *Greek Grammar*. Rev. Gordon M. Messing. Cambridge: Harvard University Press, 1956

SNTS *Studiorum Novi Testamenti Societas*

SNTSMS Society for New Testament Studies Monograph Series

SP Sacra pagina

StPatr Studia patristica

SUNT Studien zur Umwelt des Neuen Testaments

TANZ Texte und Arbeiten zum neutestamentlichen Zeitalter

TB Theologische Bücherei: Neudrucke und Berichte aus dem 20. Jahrhundert

TDNT *Theological Dictionary of the New Testament*. Edited by G. Kittel and G. Friedrich. Translated by G. W. Bromiley. 10 vols. Grand Rapids: Eerdmans, 1964–76

THKNT	Theologischer Handkommentar zum Neuen Testament
TLNT	*Theological Lexicon of the New Testament.* C. Spicq. Translated and edited by J. D. Ernest. 3 vols. Peabody, MA: Hendrikson, 1994
TNIV	Today's New International Version
TNTC	Tyndale New Testament Commentaries
TOB	Traduction Œcuménique de la Bible
TPINTC	TPI New Testament Commentaries
TUGAL	Texte und Untersuchungen zur Geschichte der altchristlichen Literatur
TynBul	*Tyndale Bulletin*
Tyndale	*The Newe Testament dylygently corrected and compared with the Greke.* William Tyndale. Antwerp, 1534.
UBS[5]	*The Greek New Testament*, United Bible Societies, 5th ed.
WBC	Word Biblical Commentary
WH	Westcott, B. F., and F. J. A. Hort. *The New Testament in the Original Greek.* Cambridge: Macmillan, 1885
WTJ	*Westminster Theological Journal*
WUNT	Wissenschaftliche Untersuchungen zum Neuen Testament
ZECNT	Zondervan Exegetical Commentary on the New Testament
ZNW	*Zeitschrift für die neutestamentliche Wissenschaft und die Kunde der älteren Kirche*
ZPE	*Zeitschrift für Papyrologie und Epigraphik*

Introduction

Rome in the Mid-First Century

When Phoebe arrived in Rome in AD 57 carrying Paul's letter to the Christians there, she entered the nerve center of a vast empire stretching from southern Britain, Gaul, and Spain in the west to Syria in the east, and from the Danube River in the north to the Mediterranean coast of Africa in the south.[1] The emperor, the senate, and the Roman military viewed every place they controlled in this massive area as subservient to the interests of the city of Rome. In the eyes of those who ruled Rome, the gods had given these lands and their peoples to the Romans in order to serve them. Avitus, the Roman prefect of Germany in AD 58, explained the situation to a German leader who appeared before him one day and pled for a homeless tribe of Germans who were starving, asking if they could use a strip of their own ancestral lands along the Danube River that the Romans had left vacant. No, they could not have the land, said Avitus, because the Romans were better than this tribe and the gods had decreed that the Romans should control their ancestral territory (Tacitus, *Ann.* 13.56.1).[2]

What were the goals that the Roman senate and people wanted those whom they had conquered to serve? At least in the late 50s AD, the goals seem to have been primarily the honor and survival of Rome's own citizens and their descendants, preferably in comfortable, entertaining surroundings. The narrative of the Roman historian Tacitus that describes the Roman reconquering of Armenia in AD 58 illustrates those goals and how Rome accomplished them. In that year the Armenian king Tiridates I attempted to retake his people's ancestral lands, occupied by Rome in the first-century BC. In response, the powerful Roman general Corbulo, believing that "the grandeur of Rome" was at stake, assembled a large army, and encouraged his troops "to strip of his home this vagabond foe . . . to secure alike glory and spoil"

1. Chris Scarre, *The Penguin Historical Atlas of Ancient Rome* (London: Penguin, 1995), 51, 53.

2. According to Tacitus, Avitus then offered to make the strip of land a personal gift to this German intermediary, who had supported Rome's cause in the past. The offer, however, was "spurned . . . as the price of treason." See Tacitus, *The Annals and the Histories*, trans. Alfred John Church and William Jackson Brodribb; ed. Moses Hadas (New York: Random House, 2003), 273.

for Rome (Tacitus, *Ann.* 13.34, 39).[3] Corbulo invaded the fortress town of Volandum, murdered every adult in it, and auctioned off as slaves those who were left alive (Tacitus, *Ann.* 13.39). Presumably, they were children.

He then moved on to the Armenian capital Artaxata where the population simply opened their gates to the Roman soldiers, offering to give them all their property. Tacitus, writing as a loyal, upper-class Roman about sixty years after the event, states concisely and with no emotion what happened next: "The city was fired, demolished and levelled to the ground" (*Ann.* 13.41).[4] Corbulo could not spare the troops to provide an occupation force for the city, Tacitus explains, and, in any case, "If . . . the place were left untouched and unguarded, no advantage or glory would accrue from its capture."[5] The thunderstorm that descended on the city shortly after the Romans torched it confirmed that its destruction was the right thing to do: "Heaven was wroth against it."[6] The thunderstorm reference seems intended to extinguish any twinge of misgiving about the brutality of Corbulo's strategy with the reassurance that Jupiter was on the side of Rome. His temple had stood for centuries on Rome's Capitoline Hill, but his thunderbolts could reach Armenia.

Back in Rome, the following year, the emperor Nero invented something he called "the Great Festival" at which a series of plays celebrated the eternal existence of the Roman Empire (Suetonius, *Nero* 11).[7] As part of the festivities, the Roman historian Suetonius says that Nero handed out lavish gifts to people, "1,000 assorted birds daily, and quantities of food parcels; besides vouchers for grain, clothes, gold, silver, precious stones, pearls, paintings, slaves, transport animals, and even trained wild beasts."[8] Perhaps among the slaves (listed here between paintings and transport animals) were some of the Armenian children whose parents had been murdered a few months before in Volandum. The anguished face of a young boy taken as war booty under the emperor Marcus Aurelius about a century later and depicted on a triumphal arch in Tripoli, Lybia, vividly expresses the sort of human pain that stands behind the throwaway comments of elite historians such as Tacitus and Suetonius.[9]

Rome was populated with a large number of slaves, many of them war captives or their descendants, from foreign lands. Nero's advisor Seneca urged elite slave owners like himself not to be too upset "if a captive, suddenly reduced to servitude still retains some traces of his freedom and does not run nimbly to mean and toilsome tasks, if sluggish from inaction he does not keep pace with the speed of his master's horse and carriage, if worn out by daily vigils he yields to sleep, if when transferred

3. Tacitus, *Annals and the Histories* (Church and Brodribb), 261, 264.
4. Ibid., 265.
5. Ibid.
6. Ibid.
7. Suetonius, *The Twelve Caesars*, trans. Robert Graves, rev. Michael Grant (Harmondsworth: Penguin, 1979), 218.
8. Ibid., 218–19. For the date, see Edward Champlin, *Nero* (Cambridge: Harvard University Press, 2003), 69–72.
9. See the photograph in Jerry Toner, *Popular Culture in Ancient Rome* (Cambridge: Polity, 2009), 66.

to hard labour from service in the city with its many holidays he either refuses the toil of the farm or does not enter into it with energy . . ." (*Ira* 3.29.1).[10]

No one knows how many slaves lived in Rome in the late 50s, but the number was high enough that the sales tax on them figured into Nero's tax reform plan for the city in AD 56 (Tacitus, *Ann.* 13.31). The conditions in which slaves lived varied widely according to the temperament of their owners and the work they were assigned, but verbal, physical, and sexual abuse, some of it extraordinarily brutal, was the norm.[11] Seneca, writing a few years before Paul wrote Romans, urges Stoic restraint in the treatment of the slave. "Why are we in such a hurry to flog him at once, to break his legs forthwith?" (*Ira* 3.32.1 [Basore, LCL]).[12] There is no need, he goes on, to "call for the whip in the midst of dinner, all because the slaves are talking" (*Ira* 3.35.2 [Basore, LCL]). In the time of Nero, recalcitrant slaves (e.g., those who resisted sexual abuse) were flogged or tattooed on face or forehead.[13] Two skeletons found, among hundreds of others buried when Mount Vesuvius erupted in AD 79 about a hundred and fifty miles southeast of Rome, probably give some idea of what a slave's life was like. They are of a fourteen-year-old girl and a baby, perhaps that of her master. Her bone structure reveals "a lot of running up and down stairs or hills" and her teeth show that she suffered from extreme malnutrition.[14]

It is no wonder that many slaves yearned for their freedom, and a number of them attained it through a master's willingness to release them or through saving enough money to purchase themselves. Such former slaves—freedmen and freedwomen–retained some responsibility to their master, but, once freed, it was possible for them to gain significant amounts of wealth and social status. In AD 56, the same year that Nero revoked the sales tax on slaves, the Roman Senate had serious discussions about "the irreverent spirit" that some in "the freedmen class" were showing to their former masters (Tacitus, *Ann.* 13.26).[15] Some, the senators had complained, had gotten carried away with their freedom and were treating their former masters as their equals, even, in some cases, threatening them with violence. Should not power be given to former masters to retract the freedom of surly freedmen?

In its solution to the problem, however, the senate realized that giving masters the power to retract the freedom they had once given to a slave would pose a greater risk to civil order than a few rude freedmen. Many freedmen held important positions in the

10. See Toner, *Popular Culture*, 72. The quotation is from Seneca, *Moral Essays*, trans. John W. Basore, 3 vols., LCL (Cambridge: Harvard University Press, 1928–1935).

11. William V. Harris, *Restraining Rage: The Ideology of Anger Control in Classical Antiquity* (Cambridge: Harvard University Press, 2001), 317–36; Toner, *Popular Culture*, 70–74. Martial, *Epigrams* 12.58: "Your wife calls you one for slave girls and she herself is one for litter boys. You make a pair, Alauda" (trans. D. R. Shackleton Bailey, 3 vols., LCL [Cambridge: Harvard University Press, 1993]).

12. Cf. Toner, *Popular Culture*, 70.

13. C. P. Jones, "Stigma: Tatooing and Branding in Greco-Roman Antiquity," *JRS* 77 (1987): 139–40.

14. Andrew Wallace-Hadrill, *Herculaneum: Past and Future* (London: Frances Lincoln, 2011), 130 (quoting archaeologist Sarah Bisel).

15. Tacitus, *Annals and the Histories* (Church and Brodribb), 257–58.

governmental, religious, and military structure of the city—indeed, quite a few knights and even senators, says Tactitus delicately, "derived their origin from no other source" (Tacitus, *Ann.* 13.27).[16] To threaten such people with a return to slavery at the whim of a former master would create more problems than it solved. Instead, it was decided, slave owners should think long and hard before granting freedom to their slaves. They should give it only to the deserving, since once given it could not be retracted.

This debate and the senators' eventual resolution to it says much about the social fabric of Rome in the late 50s. First, it demonstrates one of the primary expectations that masters had of their freedmen: freedmen were a public sign of their masters' status and of the honor to which they were due. Freedmen were to remain bound to them as clients, enhancing their honor by respectfully calling on them in the morning both to receive something from their master and, in turn, to receive assignments from the master that would benefit him and his household in various ways. Freedmen would often accompany their former masters when they traveled through the town on important business, and a large number of clients in the retinue of a wealthy person was an important sign of the dignity that he possessed.[17] The problem under debate was generated apparently when a few freedmen became so wealthy and so invested with honor themselves that they could afford to ignore or even insult their former masters.

Second, in its solution to the problem the senate indicates how reliant the city was on the massive number of former slaves that were then playing critical roles in the city's governance. Many people in Rome at the time of Paul's letter had experienced the degradation of slavery, and many others had risen out of slavery to possess a measure of freedom and dignity that could sometimes rival even the wealthy freeborn population. Movement between the social classes was not impossible, but class structure was rigidly preserved, and everyone was protective of the honor that their social status gave them.[18] The higher one lived on the social scale, the more benefits one was expected to distribute to others and the more honor one received in return.[19]

Most people, whether slave, freedman, freedwoman, or freeborn, were just trying to survive. Although access to the forum, the amphitheater, the circus, and the theater was surprisingly available across the social classes (though seating was strictly arranged according to one's class) and food was sometimes freely distributed (at least to citizens), life seems to have generally been stressful and short.[20] Only seven

16. Ibid., 258.

17. John E. Stambaugh, *The Ancient Roman City* (Baltimore: Johns Hopkins University Press, 1988), 159.

18. For a fascinating account of a family that worked hard to move from slavery to freedman and freedwoman status, then to become Roman citizens, then to the recognition of their year-old daughter as a Roman citizen, finally to becoming prominent citizens of Herculaneum, and carefully preserving all the documentation to prove who they were, see the account of Lucius Venidius Ennychus in Wallace-Hadrill (*Herculaneum*, 142–45, 232–36).

19. On the gift-honor cycle in Paul's culture and the sometimes vicious competition for honor, see John M. G. Barclay, *Paul and the Gift* (Grand Rapids: Eerdmans, 2015), 24–39, 432–34.

20. On the distribution of food, see Stambaugh, *Ancient*

percent of people reached the age of sixty, about a third of children died before their first birthday, and half died before they reached age five.[21] *Expositio*, the abandonment of infants in a relatively safe place in the overoptimistic hope that they would be raised by someone else, was a common form of "birth control," at least for healthy infants.[22] Those born with some disability were sometimes simply thrown away, as were children of slaves born under an unlucky star or with a weak constitution (Seneca the Elder, *Contr.* 10.4.16).

Not everyone approved of this. Musonius Rufus, a Stoic philosopher who lived in Rome about the time that Paul's letter arrived in the city, criticizes the relatively well-off, "who are not even able to use poverty as an excuse" for exposing "children . . . so that the earlier-born ones may be better off" (Lecture 15B).[23]

As the routine abandonment and murder of children indicate, the fight to survive could be ruthless. Jerry Toner argues that the nonelite in ancient Rome viewed survival as a "zero-sum game" in which another person's success depleted the amount of luck available to everyone else, and so working to damage a neighbor's success could aid one's own survival.[24]

The following grave inscription, which shows up more than once, reveals how stressful the struggle to survive was for most people: "Bones reposing sweetly, I am not anxious about suddenly being short of food. I do not suffer from arthritis, and I am not indebted because of being behind in my rent. In fact my lodgings are permanent–and free!"[25]

Where did people, in fact, live? Most people in Rome in the mid 50s lived in *insulae*, "islands," that is, large apartment blocks that could reach five stories, but more typically seem to have been three and four stories high.[26] Shops usually occupied the first floor and sometimes contained within them an upper mezzanine level that provided living space for the shop owner and his family, although that space would "certainly" have been "low and dark."[27]

The same was probably true of the lower-rent apartments in the upper levels,

---

Roman City, 133–35. On the stress of nonelite existence and the mental health problems it generated, see Toner, *Popular Culture*, 54–91.

21. Toner, *Popular Culture*, 62, 75.

22. John Eastburn Boswell, "Expositio and Oblatio: The Abandonment of Children in the Ancient and Medieval Family," *AHR* 89 (1984): 12–16.

23. Translation is by Cynthia King, *Musonius Rufus: Lectures and Sayings*, rev. ed. (n.p.: CreateSpace, 2011), 63. Thanks to Toner (*Popular Culture*, 18) for bringing this passage to my attention.

24. Toner, *Popular Culture*, 14.

25. Nicholas Purcell, "Life in the City," in *The World of Rome: An Introduction to Roman Culture*, ed. Peter Jones and Keith Sidwell (Cambridge: Cambridge University Press, 1997), 148. The inscription memorialized a freedman named Ancarenus Nothus and was found at a columbarium on the Via Latina. See E. Courtney, *Musa Lapidaria: A Selection of Latin Verse Inscriptions*, American Classical Studies 36 (Atlanta: Scholars Press, 1995), 174–75, 386–87.

26. Martial, *Epigrams* 1.117.7; Juvenal, *Satires* 3.199. Martial and Juvenal were writing in the late first and early second century, but probably reflect conditions that also existed at an earlier time. Cf. James E. Packer, "La casa di via Giulio Romano," *Bullettino della Commissione Archeologica Comunale di Roma* 81 (1968–69): 127.

27. Russell Meiggs, *Roman Ostia* (Oxford: Clarendon, 1973), 251. Cf. James E. Packer, "Housing and Population in Imperial Ostia and Rome," *JRS* 57 (1967): 81, and idem, "La casa di via Giulio Romano," 147.

which had the added problem of being difficult to escape in a fire. Juvenal describes someone on the first floor of an apartment building "shouting 'Fire!'" but the person up on the third floor doesn't "know anything about it. After all, if the alarm is raised at the bottom of the stairs, the person protected from the rain by only a little roof tile—where the gentle doves produce their eggs—will be the last to burn."[28] There were no kitchens, so people either bought hot food from nearby shops or cooked over outdoor grills.[29] There was generally no heating system, and Martial, writing in the late first century, could complain that his third-floor apartment on Rome's Quirinal Hill was "a cubbyhole shut in by a window that doesn't quite close, in which Boreas himself would not care to pass the night" (*Epigrams* 8.14.5 [Bailey, LCL]). Boreas was the god of the north wind.

Light was provided by windows onto the street or an inner courtyard, and access to water and latrines for the whole apartment block was sometimes available on the ground level.[30] The Insula of Serapis and the Insula of the Charioteers in Ostia, together with a public bath between them and shops and courtyards on either end, formed their own neighborhood.[31] Although they are from a later period than Paul's letter and from Rome's port town about fifteen miles away, they probably give an accurate, general impression of what many neighborhoods in Rome were like in Paul's time.[32] The archaeological remains of something very much like this apartment-complex neighborhood also showed up in Rome in the 1940s when the Metro stop at the Termini train station was being constructed. Although it comes from the time of Hadrian (emperor, AD 117–38), like some of the the insulae in Ostia it probably reflects how people lived in an earlier period. Here a vast house, clearly the home of the wealthy owner of the surrounding property, existed with rental apartments above it, shops across the street, and a bath complex designed to accommodate the residents of the neighborhood.[33] Those who occupied the lower rent rooms in the upper floors of such neighborhood apartment buildings would have spent little time in their apartments.[34] Instead, they would have been outside as much as possible and in constant interaction with others. "Life had an inevitably communal nature in such surroundings," says John Stambaugh; "people leaned out the windows and looked into the street and into other apartments."[35]

28. Juvenal, *Satires*, 3.197–203 (trans. Susanna Morton Braund, LCL [Cambridge: Harvard University Press, 2004]).

29. Stambaugh, *Ancient Roman City*, 178.

30. Meiggs, *Roman Ostia*, 239–40.

31. Stambaugh, *Ancient Roman City*, 178, 321 (plate 30).

32. After the great fire of Rome in AD 64, Nero introduced reforms in the way *insulae* were constructed (Tacitus, *Ann.* 15.43; Suetonius, *Nero* 16.1). The remnants of an *insula* built just after the fire can still be seen near the Trevi Fountain. On this, see Antonio Insalaco, "Vicus Caprarius: l'area archeologica," *Forma Urbis: Itinerari nascosti di Roma Antica* 8 (2003): 4–19.

33. Andrew Wallace-Hadrill, "*Domus* and *Insulae* in Rome: Families and Housefuls," in *Early Christian Families in Context: An Interdisciplinary Dialogue*, ed. David L. Balch and Carolyn Osiek (Grand Rapids: Eerdmans, 2003), 13–14.

34. Packer, "La Casa di Via Giulio Romano," 147, speaks of the state of extreme squalor in which people must have lived on the fourth and fifth floors of the early second century *Insula dell' Ara Coeli* (as it is now called), still visible in Rome's Piazza d' Aracoeli near the Capitoline Hill. He estimates that on these floors forty-eight people would have been packed into an area of about 138 square meters (about 1485 square feet).

35. Stambaugh, *Ancient Roman City*, 178.

It was probably this social interaction, leading to social networking, that made life bearable for most Romans. There were not only family groups but numerous larger, more powerful groups that individuals could join and from which they could receive help. There were clubs and trade guilds, always with particular religious associations, in which people helped one another and banded together to accomplish goals that benefited the group's members.[36] In Rome, people with similar occupations tended to occupy the same neighborhood, and it is probable, with the volatile housing market, that people with common interests were sometimes able to occupy the same apartment block or, if numbers were smaller, the same floor in a particular block.[37] It is easy to imagine such groups meeting in the larger spaces of an apartment block. Perhaps, if their numbers were high enough or some within their membership were wealthy enough, they could eventually manage to build their own building in which to have their meetings.

At least by the late first-century BC, the Jews of Rome, who lived together primarily in the neighborhood across the Tiber River (Trastevere), were able to build their own "Synagogue of the Hebrews," followed by synagogues named after the emperor Augustus and his powerful son-in-law, Marcus Agrippa. These two officials may have either sponsored the construction of the buildings or at least given permission for their construction to a group they favored.[38] Sometime in the second half of the first century, perhaps about the time that Paul's letter arrived in Rome, the Jews a few miles away in Ostia may have finished building their own synagogue, patterning it after the meeting buildings for clubs in Ostia.[39]

Christianity in Rome in the Mid-First Century

Paul's letter to the Romans is itself the earliest concrete evidence of Christianity in Rome, but by the time Paul wrote the letter in the mid 50s the city's Christian community was already famous (1:8) and known for its stability (16:19; cf. 15:14).

36. George Hope Stevenson and Andrew William Lintott, "Clubs, Roman," *OCD* 352; Bradly S. Billings, "From House Church to Tenement Church: Domestic Space and the Development of Early Urban Christianity–the Example of Ephesus," *JTS* 62 (2011): 51–58. It is true that *collegia*, or clubs, were sometimes forbidden (e.g., Suetonius, *Jul.* 42.3; *Aug.* 32.2), but A. Andrew Das has effectively argued that they were left alone as long as they did not create civil unrest (*Solving the Romans Debate* [Minneapolis: Fortress, 2007], 181–85).

37. Billings, "From House Church to Tenement Church," 560–62.

38. Harry J. Leon, *The Jews of Ancient Rome*, updated ed. (Peabody, MA: Hendrickson, 1995), 11, 140–41; Peter Richardson, "Augustan-Era Synagogues in Rome," in *Judaism and Christianity in First-Century Rome*, ed. Karl P. Donfried and Peter Richardson (Grand Rapids: Eerdmans, 1998), 20–22. Cf. Billings, "From House Church to Tenement Church," 554–55.

39. Anders Runesson, "A Monumental Synagogue from the First Century: The Case of Ostia," *JSJ* 33 (2002): 198–203, 205–9. On the likelihood that this building was originally constructed to serve as a synagogue and strongly hints at the existence of similar synagogue buildings in Rome in the first century, see Stephen K. Catto, *Reconstructing the First-Century Synagogue: A Critical Analysis of Current Research*, LNTS 363 (London: T&T Clark, 2007), 52–61. At this point, however, the first-century date of the Ostia synagoguge is not entirely clear. See Edward Adams, *The Earliest Christian Meeting Places: Almost Exclusively Houses?*, LNTS 450 (London: Bloomsbury, 2013), 129.

Paul had never been there, although he had often wanted to go (1:10–13; 15:22–23; Acts 19:21), and he says nothing about how Christianity arrived there.

The only other city in Italy for which there is evidence of Christianity in the fifties is Puteoli (Acts 28:13), about a hundred and thirty miles south of Rome and its busiest coastal port in the mid-first century. It was the place where the grain shipments from Egypt arrived and was well known for funneling products and ideas from the eastern Mediterranean region to Italy. It is the only other city besides Rome where it is certain that a large Jewish community existed (Josephus, *J.W.* 2.104; *Ant.* 17.328). Some Jews also lived in Pompeii, and it is now reasonably clear that by AD 63 Christianity existed there too. Yet Pompeii was less than thirty miles from Puteoli, and it is easy to see how Judaism and eventually Christianity could reach Pompeii from the busy port just to its northwest.[40] Christianity probably entered Italy and made its way to Rome, therefore, by following Judaism along the important east-west trade route that ran through Puteoli.[41]

Some of the "visitors from Rome, both Jews and proselytes" who were in Jerusalem for the pilgrimage festival of Pentecost shortly after Jesus's death and resurrection may have brought the gospel back to Rome (Acts 2:10–11; cf. 2:41). In addition, in 16:7 Paul greets Andronicus and Junia and describes them as fellow Jewish Christians who were both well-known apostles and followers of Christ before him. There is no reason to think that they were latecomers to the Roman Christian community, and if they immigrated to Rome from Judea sometime in the 30s or 40s they may have helped spread the gospel there.[42] Everything, then, points to the origins of Christianity among Jews in Rome in the first half of the first century.

This receives some confirmation from brief and more ambiguous references to Jewish Christianity in Rome in Acts and in Suetonius's *Life of Claudius*. Acts 18:2 says that when Paul arrived in Corinth he "found a Jew named Aquila, a native of Pontus, recently come from Italy with his wife Priscilla, because Claudius had commanded all the Jews to leave Rome." Luke makes no reference to the conversion of Aquila and Priscilla under Paul's teaching in Corinth, and their willingness to support Paul's missionary efforts by offering him hospitality and work implies that they were already Christians when they lived in Rome.[43]

Suetonius adds some detail to this account of Claudius's expulsion when, in the course of reeling off a series of actions that the emperor Claudius took with respect

40. On the whole question of Christianity in Pompeii, see Bruce W. Longenecker, *The Crosses of Pompeii: Jesus-Devotion in a Vesuvian Town* (Minneapolis: Fortress, 2016), and for the presence of Judaism there, see idem, 256–57.

41. Peter Lampe, *From Paul to Valentinus: Christians at Rome in the First Two Centuries*, trans. Michael Steinhauser; ed. Marshall D. Johnson (Minneapolis: Fortress, 2003), 7–10. In light of Bruce Longenecker's argument (*The Crosses of Pompeii*), however, Lampe is too skeptical about the existence of Christianity at Pompeii.

42. Cf. Karl-Wilhelm Niebuhr, "Roman Jews under Nero: Personal, Religious, and Ideological Networks in Mid-First Century Rome," in *The Last Years of Paul: Essays from the Tarragona Conference, June 2013*, ed. Armand Puig i Tàrrech, John M. G. Barclay and Jörg Frey, WUNT 352 (Tübingen: Mohr Siebeck, 2015), 70.

43. Lampe, *From Paul to Valentinus*, 11–12.

to foreign people groups he blurts out, "Since the Jews constantly made disturbances at the instigation of Chrestus, he expelled them from Rome" (*Claud.* 25.4 [J. C. Rolfe, LCL]). It is true that Suetonius speaks here of "Chrestus," not "Christus," and that he writes as if "Chrestus" were himself in Rome creating trouble, but in light of Luke's comment about Aquila and Priscilla it seems likely that Suetonius's statement is a garbled reference to social discord in Rome's Jewish community created by the preaching of the gospel of Jesus Christ.[44] If Paul arrived in Corinth in late 49 or early 50 as many scholars believe, then Claudius probably gave his order of expulsion in 49, a date that is corroborated by the fifth-century Christian apologist Paulus Orosius.[45] It is clear, therefore, that Christianity in Rome took root primarily among the Jewish population of the city and was well established by the time Paul wrote Romans.

If Christianity in Rome originated with Rome's Jewish community, however, then why did Paul address his letter primarily to gentiles (1:5–6, 13; 11:13; 15:15–16)? Had the expulsion of Jews under Claudius so decimated the Roman Christian community of its Jewish Christians that a group once mainly Jewish had now become dominated by gentiles? Had a small group of Jewish Christians trickled back into Rome after Claudius's death in 54 and created the tensions over observance of Jewish customs that dominate 14:1–15:7?

Although many interpreters of the letter answer these questions affirmatively, the evidence for this reconstruction probably will not bear the weight placed on it.[46] Claudius "commanded all the Jews to leave Rome" (Acts 18:2), but it is unlikely that he rigorously enforced his command.[47] To expel every Jew from Rome would have involved displacing tens of thousands of people and would have surely made a greater ripple in the historical record had it been strictly enforced.[48] Tacitus never mentions the expulsion, and despite the claim of Orosius that Josephus gives its date (*Historia adversus Paganos* 7.6) no extant text of Josephus contains any reference to it. Dio Cassius refers only to Claudius's prohibition of Jewish meetings in AD 41 and adds that an expulsion would have created too much disorder because of the vast numbers of Jews in the city (*Roman History* 60.6.6).

The evidence suggests that Claudius issued both the edict in AD 41 and the edict in AD 49 from a need to appear to the public as Rome's strong bulwark against

44. For the arguments on one side and the other, see, respectively, e.g., Erich S. Gruen (*Diaspora: Jews amidst Greeks and Romans* [Cambridge: Harvard University Press, 2002], 39) and Das (*Solving the Romans Debate*, 150–58). Das has the most persuasive case.

45. Orosius claims he got the date (the ninth year of Claudius's reign) from Josephus who, however, says nothing about the expulsion in any of the extant editions of his works. On the dates of Claudius's expulsion order and Paul's arrival in Corinth, see Das (*Solving the Romans Debate*, 158–61), Gruen (*Diaspora*, 41), Robert Jewett (*Romans*, Hermeneia [Minneapolis: Fortress, 2007], 18–20), and Craig S. Keener (*Acts: An Exegetical Commentary*, 4 vols. [Grand Rapids: Baker, 2012–15], 3:2705–8, 2760–63).

46. Barclay, *Paul and the Gift*, 456.

47. On this view, Luke gave a precise description of Claudius's actual command: "all" [πάντας] Jews were to leave. Luke does not say that all Jews actually left, however, only that Aquila and Priscilla left because of the command.

48. Das, *Solving the Romans Debate*, 163–64.

foreign influences. He seems to have had little will to enforce the edict of AD 49 consistently once it had served its rhetorical purpose.[49] Some Jewish Christians, such as Aquila and Priscilla, left the city as a result of the edict, but it is not at all clear that the ethnic composition of the Christian community in Rome significantly changed as a result of the number of Jews who left.

It seems more likely that the Roman church was mainly gentile when Paul wrote to it because the numbers of gentile Christians in Rome had simply increased over time. It is probable that many of these gentiles were first attracted to Judaism, like so many other gentiles in Rome in the first century.[50] The gospel, grounded as it was in Judaism but with its focus on reaching out to all nations, would have been intelligible and attractive to such gentiles, and it seems logical to expect that their numbers would increase (cf., e.g., Acts 8:26–39; 10:1–48; 16:14–15; 17:4, 12). The tensions evident in 14:1–15:7, moreover, certainly had an ethnic component (cf. 15:8–9), but the distinction between the weak and the strong may well not have followed strictly ethnic boundaries.[51] Just as there were many non-Jews in Rome in the mid-first century who followed some Jewish customs, there were undoubtedly more Jewish Christians in Rome than just Prisca and Aquila (16:3–4) who, like Paul, believed they were free from the constraints of the Jewish law (cf. 1 Cor 9:19–23). What probably joined them all together right across their ethnic differences and their differences about the Mosaic law's interpretation was their knowledge of the Mosaic law and of the Scriptures generally. "I am speaking to those who know the law," Paul says in Romans 7:1.

Still, it is likely that when Paul's letter arrived in Rome most Romans who knew about Christians viewed them as a separate group from the Jews.[52] Certainly by the time Nero shifted the blame for the great fire of Rome from himself to the "Christians" only seven years after Paul's letter arrived, he viewed them as a distinct type of human being (*genus hominum*) with a particular name (*Christiani*), and their numbers were large (Suetonius, *Nero* 16.2; Tacitus, *Ann.* 15.44).

This ethnically diverse body of Christians probably met in several different places in the city.[53] Paul's concluding greetings (16:3–16) seem to presuppose at least five individual groups of Christians: those who met in the house of Prisca and Aquila (16:5), those associated with the household of Aristobulus (16:10), those associated with the household of Narcissus (16:11b), the brothers and sisters "with" Asyncritus, Phlegon, Hermes, Patrobas, and Hermas (16:14), and the saints "with" Philologus, Julia,

49. Gruen, *Diaspora*, 39; idem, "The Jews of Rome under Nero," in Tàrrech, Barclay, and Frey, *Last Years of Paul*, 96–98, 102–3.

50. On non-Jews in Rome following Jewish customs, see Leon (*Jews of Ancient Rome*, 250–56), who cites, for example, Josephus (*Ant.* 20.195) and Seneca the Younger (in Augustine, *The City of God* 6.11).

51. Cf. A. J. M. Wedderburn, *The Reasons for Romans* (Minneapolis: Fortress, 1988), 32, 50–54, 59–60; Richard N. Longenecker, *Introducing Romans: Critical Issues in Paul's Most Famous Letter* (Grand Rapids: Eerdmans, 2011), 134–35, 144–47; idem, *The Epistle to the Romans: A Commentry on the Greek Text*, NIGTC (Grand Rapids: Eerdmans, 2016), 9.

52. Cf. Das, *Solving the Romans Debate*, 197–98.

53. Lampe, *From Paul to Valentinus*, 359–65.

Nereus, Nereus's sister, and Olympas (16:15). Apart from Herodion (16:11a), who probably belonged to the household of Aristobulus, it is unlikely that the other people named in the list belonged to any of these groups since they are not named with them. It is also unlikely that they formed a single group, since they are scattered among the other groups. Peter Lampe was correct, then, to conclude that Paul's greetings assumed at least seven separate clusters of Christians who met in different places.[54]

This fits the pattern of many of the so-called titular churches of Rome (the *tituli*), twenty of which go back to the third and fourth century.[55] Their designation as "titular" derives from the inscription that would have stood over the main entrance of the private building, whether a house or an apartment block, designating the owner of the property where the church met in its earliest existence. It is not that any of these churches can be reliably correlated with house churches of the first century but simply that the pattern they reveal of Christians meeting in various places in the city on private property is similar to the pattern of clusters of Christians meeting in privately owned or rented accommodation that appears in Romans 16.[56]

The titular churches of Rome also reveal the probable geographical concentrations of Christians in the city, and this in turn hints at the social standing of the earliest Roman Christians.[57] Lampe proposed sensibly that ancient Roman Christians lived mainly in the sections of the city where two or more of these churches exist within a few hundred yards of each other, especially if other factors point to the same places. His analysis concluded that most Christians probably lived in three sections of Rome: the region across the Tiber, the area around the Porta Capena and along the Appian Way, and the Aventine Hill.[58] The trans-Tiber region was known for its immigrant population, especially its Jewish element, and the Porta Capena where the Appian Way entered the city was the obvious entry point to the city for immigrants from the east.[59] The Aventine Hill, standing between these two sections, formed a kind of bridge between them.

The Aventine was a pleasant residential area in antiquity, just as it is today, but the other two areas were densely populated, economically distressed neighborhoods.[60]

54. Ibid., 359.

55. Ibid., 360–65.

56. Adams, *Earliest Christian Meeting Places*, 99: "It is now generally accepted that the *tituli* were a post-Constantinian phenomenon."

57. Lampe, *From Paul to Valentinus*, 41–47.

58. The churches that led Lampe to this conclusion can easily be located on a map of modern Rome. For Trastevere, see Santa Cecilia, San Crisogono, and San Callisti. For the area around the Porta Capena, see Santi Nereo e Achilleo (the current name of Titulus Fasciolae) and San Sisto Vecchio (the current name of Titulus Crescentianae). For the Aventine, see Santa Sabina and Santa Prisca.

59. It was "the oldest and most prestigious of Roman roads, the one on which its armies marched down to Campania and from there the length of south Italy, to the conquest of Sicily, North Africa, and eventually (from Brindisi) the whole of the eastern Mediterranean" (Amanda Claridge, *Rome: An Oxford Archaeological Guide* [2nd ed.; Oxford: Oxford University Press, 2010], 356).

60. For this paragraph, see Leon (*Jews of Ancient Rome*, 136–39) and especially Lampe (*From Paul to Valentinus*, 38–40, 48–61).

The trans-Tiber region, or Trastevere, was dominated by warehouses and populated by dock and warehouse workers as well as by those employed in the brickyards just to the north, in the area around the Vatican hill. Trastevere was notorious for its putrid smell because hides were tanned there and the tanning factories used urine from public latrines to cure the hides.[61] Juvenal, writing about sixty years after Paul, could describe the Porta Capena area as dominated by Jewish beggars (*Satires* 3.12–16). It was the gateway into the city at the end of Italy's most important road from the south, and so it too was dominated by people who earned a living loading, unloading, and transporting goods.

It is easy to imagine many of Rome's Christians as relatively poor, hardworking people with roots in the East and speaking Greek as well as or better than Latin. Some of them could have tended shops in large apartment blocks owned by a master or patron and slept and kept a few belongings, perhaps with their families, on a small mezzanine level above their shops or in rooms behind them.[62] Others might have slept in small apartments on the third or fourth floor of an apartment block, walking down three or four flights of stairs and through narrow, winding streets to their work on docks or in warehouses along the Tiber, or in smelly tanning operations further back from the river, or in the Vatican brickyards to the north.[63] If their master or patron were Jewish or a gentile who observed some of the Mosaic law, perhaps they were allowed to rest on Saturday when, at least during Augustus's rule, not only Jewish but some gentile shop owners closed their shops.[64] If some gentiles were still doing this in Paul's time and some of those shop owners were Christians, they could have been among the people Paul describes in 14:5 who considered "one day" as special over "another."

On Sunday, before it was light and shop owners had to get their retail space ready for another day, perhaps one or two of them opened the shop to provide space for Christians in the neighborhood to meet together for prayer, the reading of Scripture, the Lord's Supper, and collections for the needy.[65] Or perhaps someone made space available on Sunday evening in one of the upper story rooms of an apartment building.[66] If the Christians who belonged to the households of Aristobulus and Narcissus

61. Martial, *Epigrams* 6.93.1–7; Juvenal, *Satires* 14.201–2. The excavations beneath the ancient titular church of Santa Cecilia revealed eight circular basins that were either used in the tanning of leather or for storing grain and date back to the time of Augustus (Lampe, *From Paul to Valentinus*, 50; n.a., *The Basilica of Santa Cecilia in Rome* [Rome: Basilica di Santa Cecilia, 2001], 42–43).

62. Cf., respectively, the early second-century AD Insula dell' Ara Coeli in Rome (Packer, "Housing and Population," 77; idem, "La Casa di Via Giulio Romano," 147; Claridge, *Rome*, 263–64) and the first-century AD "House of the Wattlework" in Herculaneum (Wallace-Hadrill, *Herculaneum*, 261–71).

63. Cf. Packer, "Housing and Population," 81; idem, "La Casa di Via Giulio Romano," 147; Lampe, *From Paul to Valentinus*, 50–51.

64. Cf. Horace, *Satires* 1.9.67–72; Ovid, *Ars* 1.415–16; Leon, *Jews of Ancient Rome*, 12; Das, *Solving the Romans Debate*, 111–12.

65. Cf. 1 Cor 11:17–34; 14:26; 16:2; Acts 2:42; Did. 14.1; Justin Martyr, *1 Apol.* 61, 67. For Christians meeting before work, while it was still dark, see Pliny the Younger, *Ep.* 10.96.7. On the variety of places where the earliest Christians may have met for worship, see Adams, *Earliest Christian Meeting Places*, 137–97.

66. Cf. Acts 20:7–9.

were slaves or freedmen and freedwomen who worked within the households of wealthy Roman families (see the commentary on 16:10–11), it is possible to imagine them living in large apartment blocks on the Aventine Hill, overlooking the Tiber or the Circus Maximus. Such apartment blocks might easily have had courtyard space large enough for a fairly large gathering of Christians to hear the long letter from the apostle Paul recently brought by Phoebe, one of his coworkers (16:1–2). It would not have been a burden for Christians from Trastevere and the Porta Capena area to make the half-hour walk up the Aventine Hill to join others who lived there to hear the letter read. A sympathetic insula owner or manager might have allowed it.[67]

It is also possible to imagine that someone rented space in a bath complex in the Porta Capena area or a warehouse along the Tiber in Trastevere for groups of Christians from various communities to come together to hear the apostle's letter. About a century after Paul's letter came to Rome, Justin Martyr told the Roman prefect Q. Junius Rusticus (urban prefect from 163–68) that he lived "above the baths of Myrtinus" and that it was a place of assembly for Christians.[68] A few decades later still, the person who spun the tales in the *Acts of Paul* imagined him arriving in Rome and renting a warehouse outside the city as a place for teaching other believers.[69]

Whether Paul envisioned his letter read aloud at many different times to a number of small gatherings of Christians throughout Rome or a few times to larger groups, he seems to have thought of himself as speaking to a large, diverse crowd. His letter is addressed "to all who are in Rome, dearly loved by God, called to be holy" (1:7), and in the greetings at the end of the letter he urges the whole group to greet certain smaller groups of believers or individuals that he knows personally or by reputation (16:3–16).

Some of these were Jewish Christians, many were probably gentiles, some had Latin names, some Greek, and judging from the names themselves (e.g., Urbanus, Herodion, Persis, Asyncritus, Phlegon, Hermes, Hermas) many had slavery, with all the violence that entailed, somewhere in their background. In addition, Paul explains the gospel so frequently in the letter with the help of an unbelieving Jewish interlocutor (e.g., 2:17–29; 9:19–20; 11:1) that it is difficult not to think he imagined a few unbelieving Jews in the audience. It is true that this interlocutor was a fictional pedagogical device intended primarily to aid in Christian instruction, but Paul, writing from Corinth, was familiar with a situation in which unbelievers and inquirers walked off the street and into the places where Christians assembled (1 Cor 14:16, 23, 25), and it is likely that he imagined this happening in Rome also.[70] The letter is

67. On the level of autonomy sometimes given to "supramenial" slaves, see Bruce Longenecker, *The Crosses of Pompeii*, 273–74.

68. L. Michael White, *Texts and Monuments for the Christian Domus Ecclesiae in Its Environment*, vol. 2 of *The Social Origins of Christian Architecture*, HTS 43 (Valley Forge, PA: Trinity Press International, 1997), 42–43; Adams, *Earliest Christian Meeting Places*, 72–74, 171–79.

69. White, *Texts and Monuments*, 47–48; Adams, *Earliest Christian Meeting Places*, 146–55.

70. Stanley Kent Stowers, who argues convincingly that the interlocutor is a device for insider instruction, is willing

designed primarily to strengthen and unify Roman Christians in all their diversity, but it's explanation of the gospel is so clear and detailed that it must have functioned as a first step in discharging Paul's desire, indeed obligation, to preach the gospel to Greeks, barbarians, wise, foolish, Jew, and gentile in Rome (1:14–16).

The Setting of Romans in Paul's Ministry

When Paul wrote Romans, he had preached the gospel in a meandering line (κύκλῳ) from Jerusalem in Judea to Illyricum, the Latin-speaking area directly across the Adriatic Sea from Italy (15:19). He felt that his work in the east was complete, and he was now setting his sights on Rome and then, with the help of the Roman Christians, Spain (15:23–24). But before he made his way west, he told his audience, he must first complete an act of service to poverty-stricken Jewish Christians in Jerusalem (15:25). The mainly gentile Christians in Macedonia and Achaia had contributed to this relief aid, and delivery of it would show that gentile believers in these regions understood their spiritual indebtedness to Israel (15:26–27).

This travelogue meshes tightly with the narrative of Paul's travels in Acts 19 and 20. There Luke says that sometime during his three years in Ephesus, "Paul resolved in the Spirit to pass through Macedonia and Achaia and go to Jerusalem, saying 'After I have been there, I must also see Rome'" (Acts 19:21). It is clear from Paul's Corinthian correspondence that his path from Ephesus to Macedonia and Achaia was complicated, and Luke does not describe the complexities, but Luke and Paul agree that he ended up in Macedonia and finally "Greece" (Acts 20:1–3) or "Achaia" as Paul calls it.[71] While Paul was in Macedonia, he may have also traveled west to neighboring Dalmatia (cf. 2 Tim 4:10), which was part of the province of Illyricum and the northern end of Paul's meandering line of gospel proclamation according to Romans 15:19. If so, Luke omits that detail, perhaps to keep the focus on Paul's eastward movement toward Jerusalem.

According to Luke, Paul spent three months in "Greece," and when he departed on his journey to Jerusalem he took with him a group of people from a variety of cities in Macedonia, Galatia, and Asia (Acts 20:3–4). Luke does not say why this geographically diverse group accompanied Paul, but it is easy to determine this from Paul's Corinthian correspondence. There he plans for individuals from each of the churches that contributed to his collection for the poor in Jerusalem to accompany him on the journey (1 Cor 16:4; 2 Cor 8:19; 9:4). All this makes it virtually certain that Paul wrote Romans during the three-month stay in Greece described in Acts 20:2–3.

---

to say that "interested unbelievers would certainly not be excluded" (*The Diatribe and Paul's Letter to the Romans*, SBLDS 57 [Chico, CA: Scholars Press, 1981], 182).

71. C. K. Barrett, *Acts*, 2 vols., ICC (London: T&T Clark, 1994–98), 2:919–20, 946.

The city from which Paul wrote, moreover, was clearly Corinth. Phoebe, whom Paul commends in 16:1–2, and who probably carried the letter to Rome, was from Cenchreae. This town was "the port of Corinth" and only seven miles to its southeast, on the Saronic Gulf.[72] It was the port through which Paul himself passed when he left Corinth for Syria (Acts 18:18). Paul also sends greetings from Gaius and Erastus (Rom 16:23), and although these were not uncommon names, it seems likely they refer to the same people mentioned elsewhere with these names who were involved with Paul's ministry and had associations with Corinth (Acts 19:22; 1 Cor 1:14; 2 Tim 4:20).

A good case can be made that Paul's three months in Corinth spanned the winter months of AD 56–57. This is the date one reaches by correlating the information about Paul's movements in Acts 18–20 with the most likely date for the year during which L. Junius Annaeus Gallio was proconsul of Achaia. At some point toward the end of his first stay in Corinth, Paul appeared before Gallio (Acts 18:11–17). An inscription from Delphi (in Achaia) and dated almost certainly to AD 52 calls Gallio the friend and proconsul of the emperor Claudius.[73] Proconsuls typically served for one year, beginning exactly halfway through the year (July 1), and under Claudius they sailed from Rome for their overseas assignments on April 1. Gallio, then, must have sailed from Rome to Achaia in the spring of AD 51 and, if he was a typical proconsul, left office at the end of June AD 52. All this means that Paul probably appeared before him in Corinth sometime during AD 51–52.

It is reasonable to think of this happening shortly after Gallio arrived in midsummer AD 51. Jewish opponents of Paul brought him before Gallio, hoping that the proconsul would punish Paul for "persuading people to worship God contrary to the law" (Acts 18:13). Gallio summarily dismissed the case, making it clear that he had no intention of getting involved in the internal affairs of Corinth's Jewish community (Acts 18:14–17). Had Gallio been in Corinth more than a few months, the Jews would likely have known he would not hear such a case and would not have wasted their efforts on an accusation doomed to failure.[74]

Luke says that after his encounter with Gallio Paul stayed "many days longer" in Corinth and then sailed for Syria (18:18). It is not clear whether Luke counted these "many days" within the "year and six months" Paul stayed in Corinth during

72. Philo, *Flaccus* 155 (trans. F. H. Colson and G. H. Whitaker, *Philo*, 10 vols., LCL [Cambridge: Harvard University Press, 1929–1962]). Corinth also had a port on the other side of the isthmus, Lechaion, just a few miles to the north on the Gulf of Corinth. Cenchreae was the obvious place of departure for points east. See Keener, *Acts*, 3:2787–88.

73. On the Gallio inscription, see Robert Jewett, *A Chronology of Paul's Life* (Philadelphia: Fortress, 1979), 38–40; Colin J. Hemer, "Observations on Pauline Chronology," in *Pauline Studies: Essays Presented to F. F. Bruce on His 70th Birthday*, ed. Donald A. Hagner and Murray J. Harris (Exeter: Paternoster, 1980), 6–9; Rainer Riesner, *Paul's Early Period: Chronology, Mission Strategy, Theology*, trans. Doug Stott (Grand Rapids: Eerdmans, 1998), 203–7; and Eckhard J. Schnabel, *Paul and the Early Church*, vol. 2 of *Early Christian Mission* (Downers Grove, IL: InterVarsity Press, 2004), 1192.

74. Riesner, *Paul's Early Period*, 209.

his first visit (Acts 18:11), nor is it clear whether "many days" refers to several weeks or months, or even a year.[75] The flow of the narrative gives the impression, however, that Luke included the Gallio incident within the year and six-month total and that the "many days" was a relatively short period of time after the Gallio incident–enough to show that the Roman proconsul did not impede Paul's work in Corinth, but not a matter of "months" or a "year."[76] Otherwise Luke would have used those calendar terms, just as he did in 18:11, rather than "days."[77]

If Paul left Corinth for Syria in the late summer or early autumn, before the harsh winter months made sailing on the Mediterranean risky, then he left in the latter half of the year 51 and probably spent the winter months of 51–52 in Caesarea, Syrian Antioch, and traveling overland through southern Galatia (Acts 18:22–23).[78] He eventually came to Ephesus, probably in the spring of 52 (Acts 19:1), and spent about three years there (Acts 19:10; 20:31), leaving sometime in the spring or summer months of AD 55. Paul stayed longer than he had originally planned in Macedonia, something that Luke does not mention (Acts 19:21; 20:1–2) but is implied by Paul's reference to preaching in Illyricum (Dalmatia) in Rom 15:19 (cf. 2 Tim 4:10) and by the composition of 2 Corinthians from Macedonia. He then arrived in "Greece" (Acts 20:2), and it was from there, in the winter months of AD 56–57, that he wrote Romans.

Paul's Purposes in Writing Romans

Why would Paul write such a long letter, most of it devoted to a closely argued presentation of the gospel, to Christians in a city he had never visited (1:10, 13; 15:22)? Like the argument of Romans itself, the answer to this question is complex.[79] It is best to begin, however, with the reasonably clear statement that Paul gives near the letter's opening about his purpose for writing. Paul says in 1:13 that he wants to come to Rome to have "some fruit" among the Roman Christians since they are (primarily) gentiles and God has made him a messenger of the gospel to the gentiles (cf. 1:5–6).[80] People from all walks of life live in Rome ("Greeks . . . barbarians, . . . sophisticated . . . foolish"; v. 14), and no shame is attached to the gospel's proclamation, he explains, so he is enthusiastic about announcing God's good news there (v. 15–16a).

75. Hemer thinks it refers to nearly a year ("Observations," 8).

76. Cf. Keener, *Acts*, 3:2780.

77. Cf. Acts 27:7 for Luke's use of the phrase to refer to a relatively short period of time most appropriately measured in days.

78. For this and what follows in this paragraph, see Eckhard J. Schnabel, *Der Brief an die Römer: Kapitel 1–5*, Historisch Theologische Auslegung: Neues Testament (Witten: Brockhaus, 2015), 19–20.

79. For surveys of the extensive debate over the purposes of Romans, see, e.g., Karl P. Donfried, ed., *The Romans Debate*, rev. and exp. ed. (Peabody, MA: Hendrickson, 1991); Wedderburn, *Reasons*, 1–21; Longenecker, *Introducing Romans*, 94–128.

80. Cf. Barclay, *Paul and the Gift*, 456–57.

If Paul had stopped there, it might be legitimate to question whether anything about Paul's purpose in writing the letter can be gleaned from such statements: he is describing why he wants to come to Rome, not why he wants to write to the Romans.[81] But he immediately launches a detailed description of the gospel that he has just said he wanted to preach in Rome ("for it is the power of God for salvation to everyone who believes"). This explanation extends to 15:13 and contains pastoral advice about how the Roman Christians should live in their own context on the basis of the gospel (12:1–15:13). Paul's letter, then, does for the Romans what Paul says he wants to do for them when he arrives in Rome: it preaches the gospel to them and discusses the implications of the gospel for their day-to-day lives.

It may seem odd that Paul wanted to preach the gospel to people who were already his brothers and sisters in the faith, "full of goodness, filled with all knowledge, and able to admonish one another" (15:14), especially since he was "eager to preach the gospel where Christ [had] not been named" so that he might not build on another's foundation (15:20).[82] The Roman Christians seem not to have had a particular apostle to whom they were attached, however, and it is likely that Paul considered them to be part of his apostolic responsibility since most of them were gentiles (1:5–6; 11:13; 15:14–16). Although there was nothing amiss in the form of the gospel they believed (1:8, 12; 16:19), they still had pastoral needs that he believed it was his responsibility to address. They needed to see how the gospel they held in common with Paul was relevant to the challenges of day-to-day life in the cultural context in which they lived (12:1–13:14) and to their own internal divisions over the interpretation of the Mosaic law (14:1–15:13).[83] Gospel-based advice about these issues was probably the "spiritual gift" that Paul says he wanted to share with the Roman Christians in order to strengthen them when he finally visited them (1:11).[84]

He also hoped that his visit to them, when it finally happened, would be an occasion for the Roman Christians to encourage him (1:12). Paul had two specific forms of encouragement in mind. First, he wanted the Roman Christians' heartfelt support for his extension of the gospel westward to Spain (15:24). When Paul said he wanted "to be sent on" (προπεμφθῆναι) to Spain by the Romans, he used a term that probably means he hoped they would outfit him with "companions, food, money, and perhaps a means for travel by sea."[85] Second, he wanted the Roman Christians' prayers for the success of his relief project for the poor among the Christians of Jerusalem (15:30), a

81. Cf. Wedderburn, *Reasons*, 97 (discussing M. Kettunen, *Abfassungszweck des Römerbriefes*, Annales Academiae Scientarum Fennicae: Dissertationes Humanarum Literarum 18 [Helsinki: Suomalainen Tiedeakatemia, 1979]).

82. See, in particular, Günther Klein, "Paul's Purpose in Writing the Epistle to the Romans," in Donfried, *Romans Debate*, 32, 39–40.

83. Cf. Longenecker, *Introducing Romans*, 142–45.

84. Cf. Erwin Ochsenmeier, "Romans 1,11–12: A Clue to the Purpose of Romans?," *ETL* 83 (2007): 395–406, who emphasizes Paul's purpose of strengthening the church at Rome in the face of suffering, particularly persecution from the wider, unbelieving society in which it was located.

85. The quotation is from Arland Hultgren, *Paul's Letter to the Romans* (Grand Rapids: Eerdmans, 2011), 552.

project that demonstrated the tight spiritual bond between Jewish and gentile Christians and reminded gentile Christians that the foundation of their faith lay in Israel's ancient biblical traditions (15:27).

Paul's commission to take the gospel to the gentiles and his conviction that Israel's traditions remained important for gentile Christians, then, were at the forefront of his thinking when he wrote Romans. His commission as apostle to the gentiles led him to believe that he should offer pastoral counsel based on the gospel to the Roman Christians and led him to hope that they would support the next major phase of his ministry as he moved westward to Spain.

The completion of his project to provide relief from the predominantly gentile churches in Macedonia, Achaia, and Galatia to needy Jewish Christians in Jerusalem formed a fitting end to the first phase of his missionary efforts, encompassing the territory from Jerusalem to Illyricum. It was also the most recent reason why his long-anticipated visit to Rome had been delayed yet again, and in practical terms the reason why the letter became necessary. In light of Paul's personal absence from Rome, the letter was an effort to provide spiritual encouragement to the Romans on the basis of the gospel and to ask for their support both for the extension of the gospel to those in the west who had never heard it and for the extension of the practical, loving effects of the gospel to Jewish Christians in need.

Romans contains such a lengthy, detailed explanation of the gospel Paul preaches because Paul had never been to Rome, and although he assumed that he and his Roman audience shared the same faith (1:12), he also knew that his understanding of the gospel was sometimes misrepresented by his opponents (3:8, 31; 6:1, 15; 7:13). Writing from Corinth, he may have remembered that five and a half years earlier, the charge leveled against him before the proconsul Gallio was that he persuaded "the people to worship God contrary to the law" (Acts 18:13; cf. 21:21, 28). Especially to a group who, whether Jewish or gentile, had embraced the gospel in a Jewish context, Paul probably wanted to explain his own understanding of the gospel in a nuanced way that showed how, despite some controversial elements (e.g., 5:20; 7:5–6), it nevertheless honored Israel's Scriptures and traditions (1:2–3; 3:10–19; 4:1–25; 9:4–5, 6; 15:8–12).[86]

In summary, three main reasons and one subordinate reason prompted Paul to write Romans. First, he wanted to exercise his apostolic calling to proclaim the gospel to the nations in the multicultural context of Rome, especially in the sense that he wanted to use the gospel to encourage and strengthen the city's Christians in their faith. Second, having finished the work God called him to accomplish in the east, he

86. On Paul's efforts in Romans to defend his gospel against criticism, see especially Peter Stuhlmacher, "Paul's Understanding of the Law in the Letter to the Romans," *SEÅ* 50 (1985): 88–89; idem, *Paul's Letter to the Romans: A Commentary*, trans. Scott J. Hafemann (Louisville: Westminster John Knox, 1994), 8–10; Wedderburn, *Reasons*, 108–23; and Longenecker, *Introducing Romans*, 145–47, 153–54.

wanted to ask for the support of the Roman Christians in his effort to take the gospel west to Spain. Third, he wanted to ask for the Roman Christians to support with their prayers his theologically and practically important task of bringing alms from his predominantly gentile churches in Macedonia, Achaia, and Galatia to poverty-stricken Jewish Christians in Jerusalem.

These three reasons all revolve around Paul's understanding of the gospel, and so it was important for him to explain the gospel at length and in a nuanced way that put to rest common Jewish misunderstandings of its relationship to Israel's traditions. This defense of his gospel against accusations that it was at odds with Israel's Scriptures and disrespectful toward Judaism was an important, although subordinate, purpose for the letter. The result of these concerns was Paul's longest, most influential letter. It explained the gospel fully and applied its principles to the day-to-day lives of believers in the competitive, complex, and often dangerous capital of the Roman Empire.

IN DEPTH: The Text of Romans

Just how long was Romans? Surprisingly, by the mid second century Romans was circulating in two forms: the sixteen-chapter form that appears in modern editions and a fourteen-chapter form that is no longer preserved in any extant ancient manuscript or version of the text.[87] The fourteen-chapter form of Romans is only known from indirect witnesses to it. The most important of these witnesses is Origen, who seems to attribute the short edition to Marcion. He says in his commentary on Romans, written in the mid-third century, that Marcion, who flourished about a century earlier, "completely removed" the doxology from the end of Romans (16:25–27), "but he also cut up (*dissecuit*) everything from the place where it is written 'But all that is not from faith is sin,' [14:23] to the end."[88] It is not entirely clear whether *dissecuit* here means that Marcion merely edited the last part of the letter or "cut it away" entirely, but in either case it is fairly clear that Origen was familiar with a short version of Romans that he attributed to Marcion.[89]

In the next sentence, however, Origen says that he also knows about copies of Romans uninfluenced by Marcion that have the doxology (16:25–27) after

87. There is also some evidence of a fifteen-chapter form for the letter. The manuscript 𝔓46 (the second or third-century Chester Beatty Papyrus II) locates the doxology between 15:33 and 16:1, and the fourteenth-century manuscript 1506 puts it after 14:23 and omits 16:1–24 entirely. This evidence, however, is much less substantial than the evidence for an early fourteen-chapter form of the letter.

88. Origen, *Commentary on the Epistle to the Romans, Books 6–10*, trans. Thomas P. Scheck, FOC 104 (Washington, DC: Catholic University of American Press, 2002), 307.

89. Harry Gamble Jr., *The Textual History of the Letter to the Romans*, SD 42 (Grand Rapids: Eerdmans, 1977), 22–23; Jason D. BeDuhn, *The First New Testament: Marcion's Scriptural Canon* (Salem, OR: Polebridge, 2013), 304–5.

14:23. This statement matches the extant manuscript evidence. A large number of ancient manuscripts of Romans place the doxology immediately after 14:23, exactly where Origen says he sometimes found it in copies that predate his own time (the 240s). T. W. Manson crisply stated the implications of all this:

> It is very unlikely that any thinking person with the complete text of Romans as far as 15:13 before him would have thought of putting the doxology at 14:23. The natural inference is that when the doxology was attached to 14:23, it was attached to a form of the text which ended at that point.[90]

If this is right, then it seems likely that Marcion did not create the fourteen-chapter version of Romans but inherited it. The text of Marcion's Romans that Origen had before him was missing chapters fifteen and sixteen, and *dissecuit* does not mean that Marcion "cut up," or edited, this section of Romans but that he "cut it away." If this is right, then Marcion, who certainly tampered with the rest of Romans, nevertheless started with a previously abbreviated edition.

This approach to Origen's witness receives support from other sources also, two of which are particularly impressive.[91] First, Tertullian, who wrote the treatise *Against Marcion* never mentions that Marcion cut out these chapters and never quotes from Romans 15–16 himself. It seems likely, then, that Tertullian only knew a fourteen-chapter form of Romans.[92] Second, an early fourteen-chapter form of Romans seems to stand behind an Old Latin summary of the contents of the letter found in the magnificent eighth-century Codex Amiatinus, perhaps the most valuable manuscript of the Vulgate.[93] This summary jumps directly from a reference to 14:15–17 to a description of 16:25–27, indicating that its author was working with a text of Romans that attached the doxology directly to chapter fourteen.

In addition, Ulrich Schmid has plausibly argued that if Marcion's abridged version was the original fourteen-chapter version, its influence would have disrupted more than the textual tradition of the letter's last two chapters.[94] Tertul-

90. T. W. Manson, "St. Paul's Letter to the Romans–And Others," in Donfried, *Romans Debate*, 8. Certainly the great historian of early Christianity, Theodore Zahn, qualified as a "thinking person," and he thought that Paul had originally written 16:25–27 after 14:23 (*Der Brief des Paulus an die Römer*, 3rd ed. [Leipzig: A. Deichertsche Verlagsbuchhandlung, 1925], 615). From the perspective of the letter's argument, however, it is, admittedly, difficult to see how Zahn can be right.

91. On this and other Latin evidence, see Gamble, *Textual History*, 16–22.

92. Cf. Gamble, *Textual History*, 106.

93. On Codex Amiatinus, see Bruce Manning Metzger, *The Text of the New Testament: Its Transmission, Corruption, and Restoration*, 2nd ed. (New York: Oxford University Press, 1968), 77.

94. Ulrich Bernhard Schmid, "Marcion and the Textual History of *Romans*: Editorial Activity and Early Editions of the New Testament," in *Biblical Quotations in Patristic Texts*, vol. 2 of *Papers Presented at the Sixteenth International Conference on Patristic Studies Held in Oxford 2011*, ed. M. Vinzent, L. Mellerin, and H. A. G. Houghton, StPatr 54 (Leuven: Peeters, 2013), 103–8.

lian complains that his own copy of Marcion's Romans is riddled with deletions, and it is hard to imagine that the heretic left, for example, 2:3–11, 4:1–25, and 9:1–11:36 intact. The lack of any significant disruption in the textual history of Romans at these very un-Marcionite points in the text is evidence, argues Schmid, that Marcion's edition of the letter did not have a large impact on the letter's transmission. It was at least not large enough to consider it the source of the dramatic variations in the text surrounding the doxology (16:25–27). The doxology wanders from one place to another across the manuscript tradition, disappears entirely from some manuscripts, and shows up twice in others.

All of this raises the question of how a short form of Romans rose to such early prominence in the manuscript tradition. This question has been heavily debated over the last century and a half, resulting in a wide variety of suggestions. Was Paul himself responsible for the short form, with chapters fifteen and sixteen perhaps composed by someone trying to make Paul look less controversial than he actually was?[95] Did part of a letter from the otherwise unknown Christian Tertius (16:22) become attached somehow to the original short form of Romans?[96] Did Paul write two forms of the letter, a fifteen-chapter form sent to Christians in Rome and the same letter, with chapter sixteen as a "covering note," sent to Christians in Ephesus?[97] Did the first collection of Paul's letters, supposedly ending with Romans, lose its final two pages and accidentally produce a form of the letter ending at chapter fourteen?[98]

Perhaps the simplest way to account for the fourteen-chapter form of the text is to imagine with J. B. Lightfoot that early in the letter's history an attempt was made to universalize it. The last two chapters with their lengthy discussion of Paul's travel plans, their commendation of Phoebe, and their extensive list of personal greetings would have been deleted along with references to Rome in 1:7 and 1:15.[99]

Codex Boernerianus (G) may testify to a form of the text like this. Instead of "to all who are in Rome, dearly loved by God" (πᾶσιν τοῖς οὖσιν ἐν Ῥώμῃ ἀγαπητοῖς θεοῦ) in 1:7, it omits any reference to Rome and has "to all who are in the love of God" (πᾶσιν τοῖς οὖσιν ἐν ἀγάπῃ θεοῦ). At 1:15, similarly, Codex

95. F. C. Baur, *Paul: The Apostle of Jesus Christ* (1873–75; repr., Peabody, MA: Hendrickson, 2003), 1:369–81.

96. W. H. Ryder, "The Authorship of Romans XV. XVI.," *JBL* 17 (1898): 184–98.

97. Manson, "St. Paul's Letter," 13. Is the fourteenth-century manuscript 1506, which has a blank half page where 16:1–23 belongs, evidence for such a version of Romans? See the description of 1506 in Lampe, *From Paul to Valentinus*, 154.

98. Schmid, "Marcion and the Textual History of *Romans*," 99–113.

99. J. B. Lightfoot, *Biblical Essays* (London: Macmillan, 1893), 315–20. See, more recently, Larry W. Hurtado, "The Doxology at the End of Romans," in *New Testament Textual Criticism: Its Significance for Exegesis*, ed. Elden J. Epp and Gordon D. Fee (Oxford: Clarendon, 1981), 192. Cf. Gamble, *Textual History*, 115–18.

Boernerianus speaks of Paul's desire "to proclaim the gospel also to you" (καὶ ἐπ' ὑμῖν εὐαγγελίσασθαι), again omitting any reference to Rome. No doxology appears after either chapter fourteen or chapter fifteen. Instead, at the top of the page where chapter fifteen should begin, the manuscript leaves five and a half lines blank and then reproduces chapters fifteen and sixteen, concluding not with the doxology but with a grace benediction similar to 16:20b, "The grace of our Lord be with you all. Amen." Either the scribe left a blank for the doxology, which for some reason he did not copy, or (and this seems more likely), he copied a fourteen-chapter manuscript of Romans until he reached its end and then supplied chapters fifteen and sixteen from a separate manuscript. Up through chapter fourteen, Codex Boernerianus may preserve a copy of the abbreviated and universalized text of Romans that gave rise to all the later confusion.

An Outline of the Letter's Structure and Argument

I. The Letter Opening (1:1–7)
   A. Paul Describes Himself (1:1–6)
   B. Paul Describes the Roman Christians (1:7a–e)
   C. Paul Greets the Roman Christians (1:7f–g)
II. The Thanksgiving and Intercessory Prayer Reports (1:8–10)
   A. Paul Thanks God for the Romans' Well-Known Faith (1:8)
   B. Paul Prays Fervently That He Might Be Able to Visit the Roman Christians (1:9–10)
III. Why Paul Wants to Visit the Roman Christians (1:11–15)
   A. The Primary Reason Stated: Paul Wants Their Faith to Be Strengthened (1:11–14)
   B. The Primary Reason Restated: Paul Wants to Preach the Gospel to Them (1:15)
IV. Why Preaching the Gospel in Rome Is Appropriate (1:16–17)
   A. The Universal Reach of the Gospel (1:16)
   B. The Faith-Centered Nature of the Gospel (1:17)
V. God's Wrath against Human Sin Is a Demonstration of His Righteousness (1:18–32)
   A. Paul States His Thesis: God's Righteousness Revealed in His Wrath (1:18)
   B. Why God Reveals His Wrath against Human Impiety and Unrighteousness (1:19–23)
   C. How God Reveals His Wrath against Human Impiety and Unrighteousness (1:24–31)
   D. Paul Summarizes His Thesis: Human Beings Have Brazenly Disobeyed God, So God's Wrath against Them Is Justified (1:32)
VI. Jews Are Also Subject to God's Wrath (2:1–3:20)
   A. God as an Impartial Judge Not Merely of Gentiles but of Jews Also (2:1–16)
   B. God as an Impartial Judge Even of Jews Who Teach the Law and Possess Circumcision (2:17–29)
   C. Objections to Paul's Understanding of God's Impartial Judgment (3:1–8)
   D. Scripture's Testimony That Everyone Is under Sin (3:9–20)

VII. The Death of Christ Demonstrates God's Righteousness and Excludes Human Boasting (3:21–31)
   A. The Death of Christ Demonstrates God's Righteousness (3:21–26)
   B. God's Righteousness Excludes Human Boasting (3:27–31)
VIII. The Scriptures Show That Righteousness Comes by Faith Rather Than by Works (4:1–25)
   A. Abraham Was Justified neither by His Works nor by His Circumcision but by Faith (4:1–12)
   B. The Link between Abraham's Faith and God's Faithfulness to His Promise to Abraham (4:13–25)
IX. Justification by Faith Brings Peace and Reorients the Believer's Existence (5:1–8:39)
   A. Justification by Faith Rescues Believers from God's Present and Future Wrath (5:1–11)
   B. Christ's Obedience Overwhelms the Effects of Adam's Disobedience (5:12–21)
   C. Union with Christ's Death and Resurrection Initiates a New Life (6:1–23)
   D. Union with Christ's Death and Resurrection Frees Believers from the Law (7:1–6)
   E. The Goodness, Yet Inability, of the Law (7:7–25)
   F. God's Solution to the Human Plight (8:1–39)
X. Israel's Present Rejection of the Gospel Does Not Imply the Failure of God's Word (9:1–11:36)
   A. Paul's Anguish over Israel's Rejection of the Gospel (9:1–5)
   B. The Scriptures Describe God's Choice of His People as Free and Surprising (9:6–29)
   C. Unbelieving Israel Is Culpable for Rejecting the Gospel (9:30–10:21)
   D. Still, God Has Not Cast Off His People (11:1–32)
   E. A Concluding Statement of Astonishment and Praise (11:33–36)
XI. Exhortation to Live in a Way That Is Consistent with the Gospel (12:1–15:13)
   A. A Mind Transformed and Renewed by God (12:1–2)
   B. Community without Competition (12:3–8)
   C. Loving One Another and Remaining Steadfast in a Hostile Environment (12:9–13:14)
   D. The Strong Should Show Love for the Weak (and the Weak for the Strong) (14:1–15:13)
XII. The Purpose of Paul's Letter in the Context of His Apostolic Vocation (15:14–33)
   A. Paul's Purpose in Writing the Letter, Especially 12:1–15:13 (15:14–16)
   B. Paul's Past Apostolic Labors (15:17–21)
   C. Paul's Future Plans (15:22–29)
   D. Paul's Appeal to the Romans to Pray for His Ministry in Jerusalem (15:30–33)
XIII. Paul's Concluding Greetings, Warnings, and Ascription of Praise to God (16:1–27)
   A. Paul's Commendation of Phoebe (16:1–2)
   B. Paul's Greetings to Friends in Rome and Others Whom He Knows by Reputation (16:3–16)
   C. Paul's Warning, Greetings from Third Parties, and Concluding Doxology (16:17–27)

Selected Bibliography

Adams, Edward. *The Earliest Christian Meeting Places: Almost Exclusively Houses?* LNTS 450. London: Bloomsbury, 2013.

Aletti, Jean Noël. *God's Justice in Romans: Keys for Interpreting the Epistle to the Romans*. Trans. Peggy Manning Meyer. Subsidia Biblica 37. Rome: Gregorian and Biblical Press, 2010.

Allen, R. Michael. *Justification and the Gospel: Understanding the Contexts and Controversies*. Grand Rapids: Baker, 2013.

Ambrosiaster. *Commentaries on Romans and 1–2 Corinthians*. Trans. Gerald L. Bray. Ancient Christian Texts. Downers Grove, IL: InterVarsity Press, 2009.

Anderson, Gary A. *Charity: The Place of the Poor in the Biblical Tradition*. New Haven: Yale University Press, 2013.

Badenas, Robert. *Christ the End of the Law: Romans 10.4 in Pauline Perspective*. JSNTSup 10. Sheffield: JSOT Press, 1985.

Bailey, Daniel P. "Jesus as the Mercy Seat: The Semantics and Theology of Paul's Use of *Hilasterion* in Romans 3:25." PhD diss., University of Cambridge, 1999.

Barclay, John M. G. *Paul and the Gift*. Grand Rapids: Eerdmans, 2015.

Barclay, John M. G., and Simon J. Gathercole, eds. *Divine and Human Agency in Paul and His Cultural Environment*. London: T&T Clark, 2008.

Baur, F. C. *Paul: The Apostle of Jesus Christ*. Translated by Allan Menzies. 1873–75. Repr., Peabody, MA: Hendrickson, 2003.

Bavinck, Herman. *Reformed Dogmatics*. Edited by John Bolt. Translated by John Vriend. 4 vols. Grand Rapids: Baker, 2008.

Beale, G. K. *We Become What We Worship: A Biblical Theology of Idolatry*. Downers Grove, IL: InterVarsity Press, 2008.

Becker, Adam H., and Annette Yoshiko Reed, eds. *The Ways That Never Parted: Jews and Christians in Late Antiquity and the Early Middle Ages*. Minneapolis: Fortress, 2007.

Bell, Richard H. *The Irrevocable Call of God*. WUNT 184. Tübingen: Mohr Siebeck, 2005.

———. *Provoked to Jealousy: The Origin and Purpose of the Jealousy Motif in Romans 9–11*. WUNT 2.63. Tübingen: Mohr Siebeck, 1994.

Bird, Michael F., and Preston M. Sprinkle, eds. *The Faith of Jesus Christ: Exegetical, Biblical, and Theological Studies*. Milton Keynes: Paternoster, 2009.

Bjerkelund, C. J. *PARAKALÔ: Form, Funktion und Sinn der parakalô-Sätze in den paulinischen Briefen*. Bibliotheca Theologica Norvegica 1. Oslo: Universitetsforlaget, 1967.

Blaschke, Andreas. *Beschneidung: Zeugnisse der Bibel und verwandter Texte*. TANZ 28. Tübingen: Francke, 1998.

Bockmuehl, Markus. *Revelation and Mystery in Ancient Judaism and Pauline Christianity*. Grand Rapids: Eerdmans, 1990.

Bruce, F. F. *The Letter of Paul to the Romans*. TNTC. Leicester: Inter-Varsity, 1985.

———. *Paul, Apostle of the Heart Set Free*. Grand Rapids: Eerdmans, 1977.

Bultmann, Rudolf. *Theology of the New Testament*. Translated by Kendrick Grobel. 2 vols. New York: Scribner's, 1951, 1955.

Burke, Trevor J. *Adopted into God's Family: Exploring a Pauline Metaphor*. NSBT 22. Nottingham: Apollos, 2006.

Byrne, Brendan. *Romans*. 2nd ed. SP 6. Collegeville, MN: Michael Glazier, 2007.

———. *'Sons of God'-'Seed of Abraham': A Study of the Idea of the Sonship of God and of All Christians in Paul against the Jewish Background*. AnBib 83. Rome: Biblical Institute Press, 1979.

Calvin, John. *The Epistles of Paul the Apostle to the Romans and to the Thessalonians*. Trans. Ross Mackenzie. Edinburgh: Oliver & Boyd, 1960.

———. *Institutes of the Christian Religion*. Trans. Ford Lewis Battles. 2 vols. Library of Christian Classics. Philadelphia: Westminster, 1960.

Campbell, Constantine R. *Paul and Union with Christ: An Exegetical and Theological Study*. Grand Rapids: Zondervan, 2012.

Campbell, Douglas A. *The Deliverance of God: An Apocalyptic Rereading of Justification in Paul*. Grand Rapids: Eerdmans, 2009.

———. *Framing Paul: An Epistolary Biography*. Grand Rapids: Eerdmans, 2014.

———. *The Rhetoric of Righteousness in Romans 3.21–26*. JSNTSup 65. Sheffield, UK: Sheffield Academic Press, 1992.

Carson, D. A., Peter T. O'Brien, and Mark A. Seifrid, eds. *The Paradoxes of Paul*. Vol. 2 of *Justification and Variegated Nomism*. 2 vols. Grand Rapids: Eerdmans, 2004.

Clarke, Andrew D. A *Pauline Theology of Church Leadership*. LNTS 362. London: T&T Clark, 2008.

———. *Serve the Community of the Church: Christians as Leaders and Ministers*. Grand Rapids: Eerdmans, 2000.

Cranfield, C. E. B. *The Epistle to the Romans*. 2 vols. ICC. Edinburgh: T. & T. Clark, 1975–79.

Chrysostom, John. *The Homilies of S. John Chrysostom, Archbishop of Constantinople, on the Epistle of St. Paul the Apostle to the Romans*. Translated by J. B. Morris. Vol. 7 of *A Library of Fathers of the Holy Catholic Church*. Oxford: John Henry Parker, 1841.

Cohen, Shaye J. D. *The Beginnings of Jewishness: Boundaries, Varieties, Uncertainties*. Hellenistic Culture and Society 31. Berkeley, CA: University of California Press, 1999.

Collins, John N. *Diakonia: Re-interpreting the Ancient Sources*. New York: Oxford University Press, 1990.

Dahl, Nils Alstrup. *Studies in Paul: Theology for the Early Christian Mission*. Minneapolis, MN: Augsburg, 1977.

Das, A. Andrew. *Paul and the Jews*. Library of Pauline Studies. Peabody, MA: Hendrickson, 2003.

———. *Paul, the Law, and the Covenant*. Peabody, MA: Hendrickson, 2001.

———. *Solving the Romans Debate*. Minneapolis, MN: Fortress, 2007.

Davies, W. D. *Jewish and Pauline Studies*. Philadelphia: Fortress, 1984.

De Roo, Jacqueline C. R. *Works of the Law at Qumran and in Paul*. New Testament Monographs 13. Sheffield, UK: Sheffield Phoenix Press, 2007.

Deichgräber, Reinhard. *Gotteshymnus und Christushymnus in der frühen Christenheit: Untersuchungen zu Form, Sprache und Stil der frühchristlichen Hymnen*. SUNT 5. Göttingen: Vandenhoeck & Ruprecht, 1967.

Dibelius, Martin. *Die Geisterwelt im Glauben des Paulus*. Göttingen: Vandenhoeck & Ruprecht, 1909.

Dodd, C. H. *The Epistle of Paul to the Romans*. London: Collins, 1959.

Donaldson, Terence L. *Paul and the Gentiles: Remapping the Apostle's Convictional World*. Minneapolis, MN: Fortress, 1997.

Donfried, Karl P., ed. *The Romans Debate*. Rev. and exp. ed. Peabody, MA: Hendrickson, 1991.

Downs, David J. *The Offering of the Gentiles: Paul's Collection for Jerusalem in Its Chronological, Cultural, and Cultic Contexts*. WUNT 2.248. Tübingen: Mohr Siebeck, 2008.

Dunn, James D. G. *The New Perspective on Paul*. Rev. ed. Grand Rapids: Eerdmans, 2008.

———. *The Partings of the Ways between Christianity and Judaism and Their Significance for the Character of Christianity*. London: SCM, 1991.

———. *Romans 1–8*. WBC 38A. Dallas, TX: Word, 1988.

———. *Romans 9–16*. WBC 38B. Dallas, TX: Word, 1988.

———. *The Theology of Paul the Apostle*. Grand Rapids: Eerdmans, 1998.

Dunn, James D. G., ed. *Paul and the Mosaic Law*. 2nd ed. Grand Rapids: Eerdmans, 1996.

Epp, Eldon Jay. *Junia: The First Woman Apostle*. Minneapolis, MN: Fortress, 2005.

Esler, Philip F. *Conflict and Identity in Romans: The Social Setting of Paul's Letter*. Minneapolis, MN: Fortress, 2003.

Fee, Gordon D. *God's Empowering Presence: The Holy Spirit in the Letters of Paul*. Peabody, MA: Hendrickson, 1994.

———. *Pauline Christology: An Exegetical-Theological Study*. Peabody, MA: Hendrickson, 2007.

Ferguson, Everett. *Baptism in the Early Church: History, Theology, and Liturgy in the First Five Centuries*. Grand Rapids: Eerdmans, 2009.

Fitzmyer, Joseph A. *Romans*. AB 33. New York: Doubleday, 1993.

Gagnon, Robert A. J. *The Bible and Homosexual Practice: Texts and Hermeneutics*. Nashville, TN: Abingdon, 2001.

Gamble, Harry, Jr. *The Textual History of the Letter to the Romans*. SD 42. Grand Rapids: Eerdmans, 1977.

Garlington, Don. *Faith, Obedience, and Perseverance: Aspects of Paul's Letter to the Romans*. Eugene, Ore.: Wipf and Stock, 2009.

Gathercole, Simon. *Defending Substitution: An Essay on Atonement in Paul*. Grand Rapids: Baker, 2015.

———. *Where Is Boasting? Early Jewish Soteriology and Paul's Response in Romans 1–5*. Grand Rapids: Eerdmans, 2002.

Georgi, Dieter. *Remembering the Poor: The History of Paul's Collection for Jerusalem*. Trans. Ingrid Racz. Nashville, TN: Abingdon, 1992.

Godet, Frederic. *Commentary on St. Paul's Epistle to the Romans*. Translated by A. Cusin. New York: Funk & Wagnalls, 1883.

Gore, Charles. *St. Paul's Epistle to the Romans: A Practical Exposition*. 2 vols. London: John Murray, 1899.

Gruen, Erich S. *Diaspora: Jews amidst Greeks and Romans*. Cambridge, MA: Harvard University Press, 2002.

Hahne, Harry Alan. *The Corruption and Redemption of Creation: Nature in Romans 8.19–22 and Jewish Apocalyptic Literature*. LNTS 336. London: T&T Clark, 2006.

Harris, Murray J. *Slave of Christ: A New Testament Metaphor for Total Devotion to Christ*. NSBT 8. Downers Grove, IL: InterVarsity Press, 1999.

Hays, Richard. *Echoes of Scripture in the Letters of Paul*. New Haven: Yale University Press, 1989.

———. *The Moral Vision of the New Testament: Community, Cross, New Creation*. New York: HarperCollins, 1996.

Hengel, Martin. *Between Jesus and Paul: Studies in the Earliest History of Christianity*. Translated by John Bowden. Philadelphia: Fortress, 1983.

Hodge, Charles. *Commentary on the Epistle to the Romans*. 1886. Repr., Grand Rapids: Eerdmans, 1950.

Hübner, Hans. *Gottes Ich und Israel: Zum Schriftgebrauch des Paulus in Römer 9–11*. FRLANT 136. Göttingen: Vandenhoeck & Ruprecht, 1984.

Hultgren, Arland. *Paul's Letter to the Romans*. Grand Rapids: Eerdmans, 2011.

Jewett, Robert. *A Chronology of Paul's Life*. Philadelphia: Fortress, 1979.

———. *Romans*. Hermeneia. Minneapolis: Fortress, 2007.

Johnson, Luke Timothy. *Reading Romans: A Literary and Theological Commentary*. Reading the New Testament Series. Macon, GA: Smyth & Helwys, 2001.

Joubert, Stephan. *Paul as Benefactor: Reciprocity, Strategy and Theological Reflection in Paul's Collection*. WUNT 2.124. Tübingen: Mohr Siebeck, 2000.

Käsemann, Ernst. *Commentary on Romans*. Translated by Geoffrey W. Bromiley. Grand Rapids: Eerdmans, 1980.

———. *Exegetische Versuche und Besinnungen*. Göttingen: Vandenhoeck & Ruprecht, 1960.

———. *New Testament Questions of Today*. Translated by W. J. Montague. Philadelphia: Fortress, 1969.

Kim, Seyoon. *The Origin of Paul's Gospel*. Grand Rapids: Eerdmans, 1981.

———. *Paul and the New Perspective: Second Thoughts on the Origin of Paul's Gospel*. Grand Rapids: Eerdmans, 2002.

Knox, Wilfred L. *St Paul and the Church of the Gentiles*. 1939. Repr., Cambridge: Cambridge University Press, 1961.

Koch, Dietrich-Alexander. *Die Schrift als Zeuge des Evangeliums: Untersuchungen zur Verwendung und zum Verständnis der Schrift bei Paulus*. BHT 69. Tübingen: Mohr Siebeck, 1986.

Kooten, George H. van. *Paul's Anthropology in Context*. WUNT 232. Tübingen: Mohr Siebeck, 2008.

Kraus, Wolfgang. *Der Tod Jesu als Heiligtumsweihe: Eine Untersuchung zum Umfeld der Sühnevorstellung in Römer 3,25–26a*. Neukirchen-Vluyn: Neukirchener Verlag, 1991.

Kümmel, Werner Georg. *Römer 7 und das Bild des Menschen im Neuen Testament: Zwei Studien*. TB 53. Munich: Kaiser, 1974.

Kuula, Kari. *The Law, the Covenant, and God's Plan*. 2 vols. Publications of the Finnish Exegetical Society 85. Göttingen: Vandenhoeck & Ruprecht, 2003.

Lagrange, Marie-Joseph. *Saint Paul: Épître aux Romains*. 3rd ed. *EBib*. Paris: LeCoffre, 1922.

Lambrecht, Jan. *The Wretched "I" and Its Liberation*. Louvain Theological & Pastoral Monographs 14. Louvain: Peeters, 1992.

Lampe, Peter. *From Paul to Valentinus: Christians at Rome in the First Two Centuries*. Translated by Michael Steinhauser. Edited by Marshall D. Johnson. Minneapolis: Fortress, 2003.

Leenhardt, Franz J. *The Epistle to the Romans: A Commentary*. Translated by Harold Knight. Cleveland: World, 1957.

Légasse, Simon. *L'épître de Paul aux Romains*. Lectio Divina Commentaries 10. Paris: Cerf, 2002.

Leon, Harry J. *The Jews of Ancient Rome*. Updated ed. Peabody, MA: Hendrickson, 1995.

Lietzmann, Hans. *Der Brief des Apostels Paulus an die Römer*. 3rd ed. HNT 8. Tübingen: Mohr Siebeck, 1928.

Lightfoot, J. B. *Biblical Essays*. London: Macmillan, 1893.

———. *Notes on Epistles of St Paul from Unfinished Commentaries*. London: Macmillan, 1895.

Livesey, Nina. *Circumcision as Malleable Symbol*. WUNT 2.295. Tübingen: Mohr Siebeck, 2010.

Loane, Marcus L. *The Hope of Glory: An Exposition of the Eighth Chapter in the Epistle to the Romans*. Waco, TX: Word, 1968.

Lohse, Eduard. *Die Brief an die Römer*. KEK. Göttingen: Vandenhoeck & Ruprecht, 2003.

Longenecker, Bruce W. *Remember the Poor: Paul, Poverty and the Greco-Roman World*. Grand Rapids: Eerdmans, 2010.

Longenecker, Richard N. *The Epistle to the Romans: A Commentary on the Greek Text*. NIGTC. Grand Rapids: Eerdmans, 2016.

———. *Introducing Romans: Critical Issues in Paul's Most Famous Letter*. Grand Rapids: Eerdmans, 2011.

———. *Paul, Apostle of Liberty: The Origin and Nature of Paul's Christianity*. Grand Rapids: Baker, 1976.

Luther, Martin. *Lectures on Romans: Glosses and Scholia*. Edited by Hilton C. Oswald. Vol. 25 of *Luther's Works*. Saint Louis: Concordia, 1972.

McFadden, Kevin W. *Judgment according to Works in Romans: The Meaning and Function of Divine Judgment in Paul's Most Important Letter*. Minneapolis: Fortress, 2013.

Meyer, Heinrich August. *Hand-book to the Epistle to the Romans*. Translated by John C. Moore and Edwin Johnson. New York: Funk & Wagnalls, 1884.

Michel, Otto. *Der Brief an die Römer*. 14th ed. KEK 4. Göttingen: Vandenhoeck & Ruprecht, 1978.

Moo, Douglas. *The Epistle to the Romans*. NICNT. Grand Rapids: Eerdmans, 1996.

Morris, Leon. *Romans*. PNTC. Grand Rapids: Eerdmans, 1988.

Murphy-O'Connor, Jerome. *Paul: A Critical Life*. Oxford: Clarendon, 1996.

Murray, John. *The Epistle to the Romans*. 2 vols. NICNT. Grand Rapids: Eerdmans, 1959–65.

Nickle, Keith F. *The Collection: A Study in Paul's Strategy*. SBT 48. London: SCM, 1966.

Norden, Eduard. *Agnostos Theos: Untersuchungen zur Formengeschichte religiöser Rede*. Leipzig: Teubner, 1913.

Oakes, Peter. *Reading Romans in Pompeii: Paul's Letter at Ground Level*. Minneapolis: Fortress, 2009.

O'Brien, Peter T. *Introductory Thanksgivings in the Letters of Paul*. NovTSup 49. Leiden: Brill, 1977.

Origen. *Commentary on the Epistle to the Romans, Books 1–5*. FC 103. Translated by Thomas P. Scheck. Washington, DC: Catholic University of America Press, 2001.

———. *Commentary on the Epistle to the Romans, Books 6–10*. FC 104. Translated by Thomas P. Scheck. Washington, DC: Catholic University of America Press, 2002.

Ortlund, Dane C. *Zeal without Knowledge: The Concept of Zeal in Romans 10, Galatians 1, and Philippians 3*. LNTS 472. London: T&T Clark, 2012.

Pelagius. *Pelagius's Commentary on St Paul's Epistle to the Romans*. Translated by Theodore de Bruyn. Oxford Early Christian Studies. Clarendon: Oxford, 1993.

Penna, Romano. *Paul the Apostle: A Theological and Exegetical Study*. 2 vols. Translated by Thomas P. Wahl. Collegeville, MN: Michael Glazier, 1996.

Pierce, C. A. *Conscience in the New Testament*. SBT 15. London: SCM Press, 1955.

Piper, John. *The Justification of God: An Exegetical and Theological Study of Romans 9:1–23*. Grand Rapids: Baker, 1983.

Puig i Tàrrech, Armand, John M. G. Barclay, and Jörg Frey, eds. *The Last Years of Paul: Essays from the Tarragona Conference, June 2013*. WUNT 352. Tübingen: Mohr Siebeck, 2015.

Räisänen, Heikki. *Jesus, Paul and Torah*. JSNTSup 43. Sheffield: Sheffield Academic, 1992.

———. *Paul and the Law*. WUNT 29. Tübingen: Mohr Siebeck, 1983.

Reasoner, Mark. *The Strong and the Weak: Romans 14.1–15.13 in Context*. SNTSMS 103. Cambridge: Cambridge University Press, 1999.

Ridderbos, Herman. *Paul: An Outline of His Theology*. Translated by John Richard De Witt. Grand Rapids: Eerdmans, 1975.

Riesner, Rainer. *Paul's Early Period: Chronology, Mission Strategy, Theology*. Translated by Doug Stott. Grand Rapids: Eerdmans, 1998.

Sabou, Sorin. *Between Horror and Hope: Paul's Metaphorical Language of 'Death' in Romans 6:1–11*. Paternoster Biblical Monographs. Milton Keynes: Paternoster, 2005.

Sanday, W. and A. C. Headlam. *The Epistle to the Romans*. 5th ed. ICC. Edinburgh: T&T Clark, 1902.

Sanders, E. P. *Judaism: Practice and Belief 63 BCE–66CE*. London: SCM, 1992.

———. *Paul, the Law, and the Jewish People*. Philadelphia: Fortress, 1983.

Schlatter, Adolf. *Romans: The Righteousness of God*. Translated by Siegfried S. Schatzmann. Peabody, MA: Hendrickson, 1995.

Schlier, Heinrich. *Der Römerbrief*. HTKNT 6. Freiburg im Breisgau: Herder, 1977.

Schnabel, Eckhard J. *Der Brief an die Römer: Kapitel 1–5*. Historisch-Theologische Auslegung: Neues Testament. Witten: Brockhaus, 2015.

———. *Der Brief an die Römer: Kapitel 6–16*. Historisch-Theologische Auslegung: Neues Testament. Witten: Brockhaus, 2016.

———. *Paul and the Early Church*. Vol. 2 of *Early Christian Mission*. Downers Grove, IL: InterVarsity Press, 2004.

Schrage, Wolfgang. *The Ethics of the New Testament*. Translated by David E. Green. Philadelphia: Fortress, 1988.

Schreiner, Thomas R. *The Law and Its Fulfillment: A Pauline Theology of Law*. Grand Rapids: Baker, 1993.

———. *Romans*. BECNT. Grand Rapids: Baker, 1998.

Schubert, Paul. *Form and Function of the Pauline Thanksgivings*. BZNW 20. Berlin: Töpelmann, 1939.

Scott, James M. *Adoption as Sons of God: An Exegetical Investigation into the Background of* ΥΙΟΘΕΣΙΑ *in the Pauline Corpus*. WUNT 2.48. Tübingen: Mohr Siebeck, 1992.

———. *Paul and the Nations: The Old Testament and Jewish Background of Paul's Mission to the Nations with Special Reference to the Destination of Galatians*. WUNT 84. Tübingen: Mohr Siebeck, 1995.

Seifrid, Mark A. *Christ, Our Righteousness: Paul's Theology of Justification*. NSBT. Leicester: Apollos, 2000.

Shedd, William G. T. *A Critical and Doctrinal Commentary on the Epistle of St. Paul to the Romans*. 1879. Repr., Grand Rapids: Baker, 1980.

Sprinkle, Preston M. *Law and Life: The Interpretation of Leviticus 18:5 in Early Judaism and in Paul*. WUNT 2.241. Tübingen: Mohr Siebeck, 2008.

———. *Paul and Judaism Revisited: A Study of Divine and Human Agency in Salvation*. Downers Grove, IL: InterVarsity Press, 2013.

Stanley, Christopher D. *Arguing with Scripture: The Rhetoric of Quotations in the Letters of Paul*. New York: T&T Clark, 2004.

Stott, John. *Romans: God's Good News for the World*. Downers Grove, IL: InterVarsity Press, 1994.

Stowers, Stanley Kent. *The Diatribe and Paul's Letter to the Romans*. SBLDS 57. Chico, CA: Scholars Press, 1981.

———. *A Rereading of Romans: Justice, Jews, and Gentiles*. New Haven: Yale University Press, 1994.

Stuhlmacher, Peter. *Paul's Letter to the Romans: A Commentary*. Translated by Scott J. Hafemann. Louisville: Westminster John Knox, 1994.

———. *Reconciliation, Law, and Righteousness: Essays in Biblical Theology*. Translated by Everett R. Kalin. Philadelphia: Fortress, 1986.

Theissen, Gerd. *The Social Setting of Pauline Christianity: Essays on Corinth*. Translated and edited by John H. Schütz. Philadelphia: Fortress, 1982.

Theodoret of Cyrus. *Commentary on the Letters of St. Paul*. Translated by Robert Charles Hill. 2 vols. Brookline, MA: Holy Cross Orthodox Press, 2001.

Tholuck, Friedrich August Gottreu. *Exposition of St. Paul's Epistle to the Romans*. Translated by Robert Menzies. Philadelphia: Sorin and Ball, 1844.

Thorsteinsson, Runar M. *Roman Christianity and Roman Stoicism: A Comparative Study of Ancient Morality*. Oxford: Oxford University Press, 2010.

Twelftree, Graham H. *Paul and the Miraculous: A Historical Reconstruction*. Grand Rapids: Baker, 2013.

VanLandingham, Chris. *Judgment and Justification in Early Judaism and the Apostle Paul*. Peabody, MA: Hendrickson, 2006.

Wagner, J. Ross. *Heralds of the Good News: Isaiah and Paul "In Concert."* NovTSup 101. Leiden: Brill, 2002.

Watson, Francis. *Paul, Judaism, and the Gentiles: Beyond the New Perspective*. Rev. and exp. ed. Grand Rapids: Eerdmans, 2007.

Watt, Jan van der, ed. *Salvation in the New Testament: Perspectives on Soteriology*. NovTSup 121. Leiden: Brill, 2005.

Wedderburn, A. J. M. *The Reasons for Romans*. Minneapolis: Fortress, 1988.

Westerholm, Stephen. *Justification Reconsidered: Rethinking a Pauline Theme*. Grand Rapids: Eerdmans, 2013.

———. *Perspectives Old and New on Paul: The "Lutheran" Paul and His Critics*. Grand Rapids: Eerdmans, 2004.

Wilckens, Ulrich. *Der Brief an die Römer (Röm 1–5)*. EKKNT 6.1. Zürich: Benziger, 1978.

———. *Der Brief an die Römer (Röm 6–11)*. EKKNT 6.2. Zürich: Benziger, 1980.

———. *Der Brief an die Römer (Röm 12–16)*. EKKNT 6.3. Zürich: Benziger, 1982.

Wilder, Terry L., ed. *Perspectives on Our Struggle with Sin: 3 Views of Romans 7*. Nashville: Broadman & Holman Academic, 2011.

Wilk, Florian, J. Ross Wagner, and Frank Schleritt, eds. *Between Gospel and Election*. WUNT 257. Tübingen: Mohr Siebeck, 2010.

Wilson, Walter T. *Love without Pretense: Romans 12.9–21 and Hellenistic-Jewish Wisdom Literature*. WUNT 2.46. Tübingen: Mohr Siebeck, 1991.

Wright, N. T. *Justification: God's Plan and Paul's Vision*. Downers Grove, IL: InterVarsity Press, 2009.

———. "The Letter to the Romans." Pages 393–770 in vol. 10 of *The New Interpreter's Bible*. Edited by Leander E. Keck. 12 vols. Nashville: Abingdon, 2002.

———. *Paul and the Faithfulness of God*. Vol. 4 of *Christian Origins and the Question of God*. Minneapolis: Fortress, 2013.

———. *Paul: In Fresh Perspective*. Minneapolis: Fortress, 2005.

Yinger, Kent L. *Paul, Judaism, and Judgment according to Deeds*. SNTSMS 105. Cambridge: Cambridge University Press, 1999.

Zahn, Theodore. *Der Brief des Paulus an die Römer*. 3rd ed. Leipzig: Deichert, 1925.

Zerbe, Gordon M. *Non-Retaliation in Early Jewish and New Testament Texts: Ethical Themes in Social Contexts*. JSPSup 13. Sheffield: JSOT Press, 1993.

Ziesler, John. *Paul's Letter to the Romans*. TPINTC. London: SCM, 1989.

CHAPTER 1

Romans 1:1–7

Literary Context

Romans 1:1–7 is the longest letter opening in the Pauline corpus.[1] The expanded elements focus on Paul himself (1:1, 5) and the message to which his identity was so closely tied (1:2–4). He seems especially concerned for his Roman readers to know why he considers it appropriate to write such a letter to them (1:5–6) and that the gospel he will proclaim in the letter has its foundations in the Scriptures that both he and they consider authoritative (1:2–4).

Paul himself is a "slave of Christ Jesus," an expression that in a Jewish context underlines Paul's authority to speak for God just as Moses and the prophets spoke for him. God summoned him as his emissary to the non-Jewish peoples of the world (1:5), and did so to communicate "good news" (εὐαγγέλιον), a term that in Greco-Roman contexts connoted an official message of world-wide importance. Despite his never having visited Rome, then, he has a responsibility to take the gospel there also. It was a large and socially diverse city that needed to hear the gospel (1:14–15), and most of the Christians there were gentiles who fell within Paul's divinely given mandate (1:6, 13; 11:13; 15:15–16).

In the letter's next section Paul will explain that he plans to exercise his mandate to take the gospel to the gentile Christians in Rome by visiting them (1:9–13; cf. 15:23, 29, 32). At the letter's conclusion he will explain his desire for the Roman Christians to support his future travels to Jerusalem and to Spain in the service of his calling (15:24–28, 30–31). Paul's need for their support of these plans made a substantial letter of introduction a sensible move.

Here at the beginning, however, he hints that the letter is more than an introductory description of his gospel. It is also a way of fulfilling his apostolic responsibility to his Roman readers (1:6). In it he will explain more fully the gospel he briefly outlines in this introduction, and he hopes that this letter will prompt the Roman Christians themselves to continue to respond to the gospel obediently.

1. Samuel Byrskog claims that "no other known letter from the Greco-Roman or traditionally Jewish environment contains such an extensive letter opening" ("Epistolography, Rhetoric and Letter Prescript: Romans 1.1–7 as a Test Case," *JSNT* 65 [1997]: 38).

Paul probably had in mind the practical impact his proclamation of the gospel in the letter would have on the disunity that had affected Roman Christianity. Some gentile believers there had adopted an attitude of arrogance toward Jewish unbelievers (11:18), and people within the Roman Christian community were divided over matters of diet and Sabbath observance (14:1–15:7). The whole community needed to hear again the gospel that transforms one's thinking and, in the process, eliminates boasting in any humanly conceived badge of honor (12:2–3), whether one's ethnic group (3:27–30), one's special piety (4:1–8; 11:5–6), or even one's good judgment in embracing the gospel (11:17–21).

- **I. The Letter Opening (1:1–7)**
  - **A. Paul Describes Himself (1:1–6)**
  - **B. Paul Describes the Roman Christians (1:7a–e)**
  - **C. Paul Greets the Roman Christians (1:7f–g)**
- II. The Thanksgiving and Intercessory Prayer Reports (1:8–10)

Main Idea

God had summoned Paul to be an emissary of the joyful news that, in Christ Jesus, God is fulfilling the biblical promise to claim the whole world for himself. Those who have responded to that joyful news in faith are God's people, and they too have a summons from God to live in a way that is consistent with their commitment to the good news of God's love, grace, and peace.

Translation

Romans 1:1–7

1a	Sender	**Paul,**
b	Description	slave
c	Possession	of Christ Jesus,
d	Description	called
e	Purpose	to be an apostle,
f	Description	set apart
g	Purpose	for the gospel of God,
2a	Time	which he promised beforehand
b	Agency	through his prophets
c	Place	in the holy Scriptures

3a Reference	concerning his Son,
b Expansion	who was born from David's offspring
c Reference	according to the flesh
4a Expansion	who was appointed Son of God in power
b Reference	according to the Spirit of holiness
c Time	from the resurrection of the dead,
d Apposition	Jesus Christ our Lord,
5a Agency	through whom we received grace and apostleship
b Purpose	for the obedience of faith
c Place	among all the gentiles
d Purpose	on behalf of his name
6a Association	among whom you are also called
b Agency	by Christ Jesus.
7a Recipients	**To all who are in Rome,**
b Description	dearly loved
c Agency	by God,
d Description	called
e Purpose	to be holy,
f Greeting	**grace to you and** **peace**
g Source	from God our Father and the Lord Jesus Christ.

Structure

The structure of Paul's letter opening follows the basic three-part pattern of most ancient Greek letters. The sender's name appears first in the nominative case, the recipient's name appears next in the dative, and then a brief word of greeting: "Apollonios to Thoonis greeting" (Ἀπολλώνος Θοώνει χαίρειν).[2] Sometimes each element of this basic three-part form received elaboration, depending on the letter's purpose. In a letter of extraordinary importance from a high official, such as the emperor, the name of the sender might receive considerable elaboration. The purpose for this was to emphasize the authority that the person writing the letter possessed to articulate the perspectives and give the instructions contained in the letter.[3] The name of the recipients might also receive some elaboration that emphasized their own official

2. John L. White, *Light from Ancient Letters*, Foundations and Facets (Philadelphia: Fortress, 1986), 102 (no. 62).

3. See White, *Ancient Letters*, 133 (no. 88); Byrskog, "Epistolography," 36; Jewett, *Romans*, 97.

standing and responsibility, or, in personal letters, their relationship to the letter's sender.[4]

People sometimes expanded the greeting into two parts. Instead of the simple, "Greetings!" (χαίρειν) they sometimes wrote "many greetings and continual good health" (πλεῖστα χαίριν καὶ διὰ παντὸς ὑγιαίνιν) or, in places where the Semitic languages were spoken they might say, "Greetings [χαίρειν] and good peace [εἰρήνην ἀγαθήν]."[5]

A comparison of the opening of Romans to these conventions is instructive. First, Paul's elaborate emphasis on his authority at the letter's beginning shows that he wrote in an official capacity and in order to carry out a mandate.[6] Second, Paul also elaborated on the description of the letter's recipients in ways that showed their own status and responsibility. Just as God called Paul to be an apostle, so God had called them to be holy.[7] Third, like many other letters from his time, Paul offered a two-part greeting, the second part of which spoke of the well-being of his readers. Instead of a colorless expression of greeting and good health, however, Paul articulated a highly distinctive two-part prayer that his readers might experience the "grace" (χάρις) and "peace" (εἰρήνη) that come from having God as their Father and Jesus Christ as their Lord (1:7).[8] Paul modified the standard greeting in this way in all his extant letters and probably did this because these concepts were of such great importance to his understanding of the gospel.[9] Their importance is particularly visible, however, in his letter to the Romans (see the comments below on 1:7).

The letter opening, then, can be divided into three parts: a lengthy description of Paul himself (1:1–5) that blends into a much shorter description of the recipients (1:6a–7e) and Paul's brief but distinctive letter greeting (1:7f–g). Paul's description of himself also falls into three parts: a claim to divine authority to preach the gospel (1:1), a digression on the nature of the gospel (1:2–4), and a return to Paul's divine authority to preach the gospel (1:5), with an emphasis on his special assignment to take the gospel to the gentiles (1:5c).

The digression on the gospel at the center of this framework focuses on the close connection between the gospel and the Jewish Scriptures and on how this connection is especially evident in the central role that "Jesus Christ our Lord" plays in the gospel (1:2–4). The parenthetical nature of this description of the gospel, together with its

4. See, e.g., White, *Ancient Letters*, 116 (no. 76), 141 (no. 90), 143 (no. 91), 145 (no. 93), 153 (no. 98).

5. See, e.g., White, *Ancient Letters*, 120 (no. 81), 141 (no. 90), 153 (no. 98); 2 Macc 1:1; cf. 2 Bar. 78:2 (in Syriac).

6. Cf. Jewett, *Romans*, 97; Jeffrey A. D. Weima, *Paul the Ancient Letter Writer: An Introduction to Epistolary Analysis* (Grand Rapids: Baker, 2016), 14–19.

7. Cf. Byrskog, "Epistolography," 37.

8. Judith M. Lieu, "'Grace to You and Peace': The Apostolic Greeting," *BJRL* 68 (1985): 168.

9. 1 Tim 1:2 and 2 Tim 1:2 add "mercy" (ἔλεος) to the two other terms (cf. 2 Bar. 78:2).

distinctive vocabulary, syntax, and emphases, have led many interpreters to speculate that Paul incorporated a widely used piece of Christian liturgy at this point.[10] Paul's personal identity was so closely tied to the gospel itself (1 Cor 9:16; Phil 1:15–18), however, that a digression on the gospel in the midst of a self-description should not be a surprise, and even if he used traditional language here he did so because it expressed what he wanted to say.[11]

The length and structure of the letter's opening, then, sets the tone for a document of immense *gravitas*. It communicates that the letter's author is the official messenger of God himself and that the message he brings concerns the fulfillment, through the Lord Jesus Christ, of God's purposes for the world. These purposes require an obedient response of faith not just from Jews but also from gentiles. Because the Christians in Rome have believed the gospel, God has also summoned them to live in a distinctive way within the unbelieving world.

Exegetical Outline

➡ **I. The Letter Opening (1:1–7)**

- **A. Paul Describes Himself (1:1–6)**
  1. Paul Is a Slave of Christ Jesus (1:1a–c)
  2. Paul Is Called to Be an Apostle (1:1d–e)
  3. Paul Is Set Apart for the Gospel That Comes from God (1:1f–g)
  4. The Gospel Was Promised by the Writing Prophets (1:2)
  5. The Gospel Is about God's Son as Described in the Scriptures (1:3–4)
  6. Paul Was Given the Task of Urging the Gentiles to Believe This Message (1:5)
  7. Transition: The Roman Christians Fall within Paul's Apostolic Responsibility (1:6)
- **B. Paul Describes the Roman Christians (1:7a–e)**
  1. God Loves the Roman Christians as Part of His Family (1:7a–c)
  2. God Has Summoned the Romans to Be His People (1:7d–e)
- **C. Paul Greets the Roman Christians (1:7f–g)**
  1. Paul Prays That the Roman Christians Will Experience Grace and Peace (1:7f)
  2. This Grace and Peace Will Come to Them from God, Who Is Their Father and from Jesus Christ, Who Is Their Lord (1:7g)

10. See, e.g., Ulrich Wilckens, *Der Brief an die Römer (Röm 1–5)*, EKKNT 6.1 (Zürich: Benziger, 1978), 56–61; Joseph A. Fitzmyer, *Romans*, AB 33 (New York: Doubleday, 1993), 229–30; Jewett, *Romans*, 97–98; Longenecker, *Romans*, 64.

11. On the second point, see Cranfield, *Romans*, 1:57–58, and N. T. Wright, "The Letter to the Romans," in *The New Interpreter's Bible*, ed. Leander E. Keck, 12 vols. (Nashville: Abingdon, 1994–2002), 10:416–17.

Explanation of the Text

1:1 Paul, slave of Christ Jesus, called to be an apostle, set apart for the gospel of God (Παῦλος δοῦλος Χριστοῦ Ἰησοῦ, κλητὸς ἀπόστολος, ἀφωρισμένος εἰς εὐαγγέλιον θεοῦ). Paul identifies himself to his readers as an authoritative spokesperson for Christ Jesus, summoned by God for the special task of proclaiming a joyful and important message from God to all humanity.

Ancient Greek letters typically began with the name of the sender, and Paul follows this custom here. He then describes himself further with three phrases.

First, he is a "slave [δοῦλος] of Christ Jesus."[12] In the OT, those who spoke for the Lord, such as Moses and the prophets, were sometimes called "slaves" of the Lord, and that is probably how Paul uses the term here.[13] He is a slave of Christ because he speaks for Christ.

Second, he is "called to be an apostle" (κλητὸς ἀπόστολος).[14] The adjective "called" (κλητός) could be used to describe someone "summoned" to a particular task (Homer, *Iliad* 9.165; *Odyssey* 17.386; Judg 14:11 [LXX]), and God has summoned Paul to fulfill the task of an "apostle" (ἀπόστολος). For Paul, apostles were envoys—people whom someone or some group had sent on a specific mission (2 Cor 8:23; Phil 2:25). He also used the term of a particular group of envoys to whom God had assigned an authoritative role in defining the gospel and overseeing the spread of its message (Gal 1:17, 19; 2:6–10). This group seems to have had a particularly close connection to the visible Jesus, primarily through knowing him prior to or shortly after his resurrection. This close association with Jesus's visible, earthly ministry seems to have been a requirement for those fulfilling the role of apostle in this special, authoritative sense (1 Cor 9:1; 15:7; cf. Acts 1:21–22). Paul considered himself to be the last and least of these apostles: unlike others, the resurrected Jesus had appeared to him after the ascension and at a time when Paul was zealously persecuting Jesus's followers (1 Cor 15:8–9; cf. Gal 1:13–17; Phil 3:6; Eph 3:8; 1 Tim 1:12–15). Paul did not believe, however, that this made him less authoritative as an apostle or less able to adjudicate what did and did not constitute authentic Christianity (2 Cor 11:13; Gal 1:1–2, 11–12; 2:14). God had graciously given him his apostolic role, and with this gift came all the power and authority necessary to complete the task (1 Cor 15:10; 2 Cor 12:12; Eph 3:4, 7–8).

Paul focused his own apostolic work on taking the gospel to non-Jewish peoples (Rom 11:13; Gal 1:1, 15–16; cf. Eph 3:1, 5, 8). This kind of apostleship often meant traveling with the gospel to distant places (Rom 1:5–6, 13–14; 1 Cor 4:9, 11; 9:5; 1 Thess 2:1–2, 7) and frequently entailed suffering (1 Cor 4:8–15; 1 Thess 2:1–2, 9; cf. Eph 3:1, 13; 6:20). Paul placed apostles at the foundation of the church (Eph 2:20) and at the head of the list of gifted people Christ had given to the church for its edification (1 Cor 12:28–29; Eph 4:11; cf. Eph 3:5).

12. Cf. Phil 1:1; Titus 1:1. The translation "slave" (cf., e.g., NAB) is potentially confusing, since this term covers in English a wide variety of social institutions that involve various levels of oppression, and Paul does not intend to communicate that his service to God is oppressive. "Slave," however, does capture connotations of living under an all-encompassing authority that other renderings such as "servant" (e.g., NIV, ESV) and "bondservant" (NASB) may miss. It is necessary for the student of the Greek text to see the range of Paul's usage of the noun, and for this purpose "slave" is perhaps the most versatile translation (cf., e.g., 6:16–17, 19–20).

13. For Moses, see, e.g., Neh 9:14; Ps 105:26 (LXX 104:26); Mal 4:4 (LXX 3:24); and Dan 9:11. For the prophets, see, e.g., Ezra 9:11; Jer 7:25; 25:4; Ezek 38:17; Dan 9:6, 10; Amos 3:7; Zech 1:6. Cf. Josephus, *Ant.* 5.39; 11.90.

14. Cf. 1 Cor 1:1.

For Paul, they played an important, authoritative role in shaping the church's growth into what God intended the church to become (Eph 2:21; 4:13). For this reason, his apostolic calling to take the gospel to the gentiles meant overseeing gentile believers whom he did not personally know through his letters. This element of his apostolic calling led him to write Romans (Rom 11:13; 15:15; cf. Eph 1:1; 3:1–2; Col 2:1).

Third, Paul describes himself as "set apart for the gospel of God" (ἀφωρισμένος εἰς εὐαγγέλιον θεοῦ). The participle "set apart" (ἀφωρισμένος) is in the perfect tense, emphasizing that God's action of setting Paul apart continues to shape who he is.[15] The genitive θεοῦ is a "genitive of source," describing the origin of the gospel.[16] This is who Paul is: he is a person that God has dedicated to a particular purpose (cf. Acts 13:2; Gal 1:15), and that purpose is the proclamation of the "gospel" (εὐαγγέλιον) that comes from God. This term referred in Greco-Roman antiquity to extraordinarily happy news, often of a political sort. According to an inscription from 9 BC found in Priene, just south of Ephesus in Asia Minor, "The birthday of the god was for the world the beginning of the joyful messages [εὐανγελίων] which have gone forth because of him."[17] The "god" in this case was the Emperor Augustus, and the "joyful messages" were the glad tidings of peace and prosperity that he had supposedly brought to the Roman world. Paul and his readers would have known this use of the term and would perhaps have understood the Christian gospel to stand in contrast to this Roman "gospel."

The more important context against which to explain Paul's use of the term, however, is the appearance of the corresponding verb "proclaim good news" (εὐαγγελίζω) in the LXX. There the verb often refers, just as it does in the Greco-Roman world generally, to the good news of victory in battle (e.g., 1 Sam 31:9; 2 Sam 1:20; Ps 68:11 [LXX 67:12]) or to the glad tidings that the transfer of political power from one king to another has gone in one's favor (1 Kgs 1:42–43).[18] In several places in the prophets, however, the verb refers to the announcement of the joyful message that the arrival of God to rescue Israel from a disaster of their own making is imminent (Isa 40:9; 52:7; Joel 2:32 [LXX 3:5]; cf. Isa 60:6; 61:1). "I am here," says the Lord in Isa 52:6–7, "like season upon the mountains, like the feet of one bringing glad tidings [εὐαγγελιζομένου] of a report of peace, like one bringing glad tidings [εὐαγγελιζόμενος] of good things, because I will make your salvation heard, saying to Sion, 'Your God shall reign'" (LXX). Paul also understood the gospel as the happy news that God had come to rescue people from the disastrous situation into which sin had plunged humanity. Paul had in view, however, not only the salvation of Israel but of everyone who believed (1:16–17).

1:2 which he promised beforehand through his prophets in the holy Scriptures (ὃ προεπηγγείλατο διὰ τῶν προφητῶν αὐτοῦ ἐν γραφαῖς ἁγίαις). The writing prophets promised the happy news that God commissioned Paul to proclaim.

This is the first of two phrases that describe the gospel to which Paul has just referred in 1:1, and it only makes explicit what the term "gospel," set in its biblical context, has already implied. When Paul speaks of what God has promised, it is sometimes difficult to tell what portion of Scripture he had in mind (Rom 9:4; 2 Cor 1:20; Eph 2:12). He usually

15. On the perfect, see especially Robert Crellin, "The Semantics of the Perfect in the Greek of the New Testament," in *The Greek Verb Revisited: A Fresh Approach for Biblical Exegesis*, ed. Steven E. Runge and Christopher J. Fresch (Bellingham, WA: Lexham, 2016), 430–57.

16. Fitzmyer, *Romans*, 232.

17. Gerhard Friedrich, "εὐαγγέλιον," *TDNT* 2:724.

18. Cf. the one appearance of the noun in the LXX in 2 Sam 4:10 and the use of the feminine noun εὐαγγελία in 2 Sam 18:20, 22, 25, 27; 2 Kgs 7:9.

refers, however, to the promises God gave to Abraham (Rom 4:13–14, 16, 20–21; 9:9; Gal 3:16–19, 21, 29) or to the patriarchs (Rom 15:8; Gal 4:23, 28). Elsewhere he speaks of "the promise of the Spirit" (Gal 3:14 NRSV) and of "the promised Holy Spirit" (Eph 1:13). These phrases probably refer to statements in the biblical prophets that one day God would restore the fortunes of his people, dwelling among them and pouring out his Spirit on them (Isa 32:15; 44:3; Ezek 11:19; 36:26–27; 37:14; Joel 3:1–2). This is the same general period to which Isaiah and Joel referred when they prophesied the future announcement of good news (Isa 40:9; 52:7; 60:6; 61:1; Joel 2:32). It seems likely, then, that when Paul spoke of the gospel as "promised beforehand through his prophets," he was thinking of passages such as these.

1:3 concerning his Son, who was born from David's offspring according to the flesh (περὶ τοῦ υἱοῦ αὐτοῦ τοῦ γενομένου ἐκ σπέρματος Δαυὶδ κατὰ σάρκα). The gospel that Paul was summoned to proclaim is about the Messiah of Jewish expectation, God's fulfillment of his promise to David and his chosen royal deliverer.

This is the second of the two phrases that further describe the gospel, and in this phrase Paul both continues the theme of the gospel's close connection to traditional Jewish expectations and becomes more specific about the gospel's content. In the OT, Israel's king was sometimes portrayed as the "son" of God in the sense that God had chosen him to be his king, just as an adoptive father chose to adopt a son (Ps 2:7; cf. 2 Sam 7:12–14; Ps 89:26–27).[19] It was natural, then, to think of the Messiah, Israel's royal deliverer, as God's "son" (e.g., 4Q246 2.1; Mark 1:1, 11).[20] Paul, like other early Christians, certainly believed that Jesus's divine sonship involved more than his fulfillment of traditional expectations for a uniquely chosen Jewish king, and Paul will make that clear in his next phrase. First, however, he affirms the agreement of the gospel with these widely known, traditional expectations.

Jesus was born, Paul continues, "from David's offspring" (ἐκ σπέρματος Δαυίδ). The prophet Nathan had told Israel's great king David that the Lord would give him "offspring" (LXX, σπέρμα) on his throne forever (2 Sam 7:12–13, 16; cf., e.g., Ps 89:3–4, 19–37, 49; 132:11–12), and the writing prophets later applied this promise to their expectation that God would send Israel a royal deliverer. This future king would be like David (Jer 30:9; Ezek 34:23–24) and would be descended from David's ancestral line (e.g., Isa 9:6–7; 11:1–10; Jer 23:5–6; cf. 2 Sam 7:16). Not surprisingly, then, the expected Messiah was called "son of David" at least as early as the first-century BC (Pss. Sol. 17:21). Belief in the Davidic descent of the Messiah was also widespread during Jesus's time (e.g., Mark 10:47–48; 12:35; John 7:42; cf. Mark 11:10). The NT frequently affirms that Jesus fulfilled this expectation (Matt 1:1, 6, 17, 20; Luke 2:4, 11; 3:31; Acts 13:22–23; Rev 5:5; 22:16; cf. Acts 15:16). Paul himself affirms it again in Romans 15:12 (cf. Isa 11:10) and 2 Tim 2:8.

He is "David's offspring," Paul adds, "according to the flesh" (κατὰ σάρκα). Some interpreters give the phrase a negative connotation, taking it to mean either that Jesus's divine nature is more important than his physical descent from David or that Jesus identified with human beings in the trouble that they brought on themselves because of their rebellion against God.[21] It is more likely,

19. See James D. G. Dunn, *Romans 1–8*, WBC 38A (Dallas, TX: Word, 1988), 11; Hans-Joachim Kraus, *Psalms 1–59*, trans. Hilton C. Oswald (Minneapolis: Fortress, 1993), 131–32.

20. Cf. Fitzmyer, *Romans*, 233; Longenecker, *Romans*, 63.

21. For the first position, see, e.g., Dunn, *Romans 1–8*, 13 (and cf. Jewett, *Romans*, 105–6). For the second position, see Wright, "Romans," 417–18.

however, that Paul uses the phrase in a neutral way. The basic meaning of the phrase "according to the flesh" in Paul's letters seems to be that something is considered from only a human angle and therefore incompletely. Sometimes this has negative connotations (e.g., 8:4–5; 1 Cor 1:26; 2 Cor 1:17; 5:16; 10:2–3; 11:18; Gal 4:29), and sometimes it is neutral (4:1; 9:3, 5; 1 Cor 10:18; Col 3:22; Eph 6:5). Here, with no discernable negative connotations in the context, it only emphasizes that Jesus's physical descent from David is not all there is to say about his divine sonship. The phrase merely points forward, then, to the second angle from which Paul looked at Christ's divine sonship.[22]

1:4 Who was appointed Son of God in power according to the Spirit of holiness from the resurrection of the dead, Jesus Christ our Lord (τοῦ ὁρισθέντος υἱοῦ θεοῦ ἐν δυνάμει κατὰ πνεῦμα ἁγιωσύνης ἐξ ἀναστάσεως νεκρῶν, Ἰησοῦ Χριστοῦ τοῦ κυρίου ἡμῶν). The gospel is also about the Messiah in his role as the powerful Son of God, a role that shows him acting just as Yahweh did in former times. This is a role he has filled since the dramatic change of the ages began when he became the first to rise from the dead.

Paul here lets the other shoe drop: he has said who Jesus is "according to the flesh," and now he describes Jesus "according to the Spirit of holiness" (πνεῦμα ἁγιωσύνης). When Paul speaks of the Holy Spirit elsewhere, he modifies the noun "spirit" (πνεῦμα) with the adjective "holy" (ἅγιος), but here, instead, his modifier is the genitive-case noun "holiness" (ἁγιωσύνης). Some interpreters have taken this odd expression as evidence that Paul is referring to Christ's spirit, which is holy.[23] When Paul brings the word "spirit" into close connection with the concept of holiness, however, he usually refers to the Spirit of God (e.g., Rom 5:5; 9:1; 14:17; 15:13, 16; 1 Thess 1:5–6). Without clear contextual indications that something else is happening here, it is best to take this use of the expression in the same way. "Holiness" (ἁγιωσύνης), then, is an "attributive genitive" and functions like an adjective, but with more emphasis.[24] This is not merely the "holy Spirit" but the Spirit that makes people holy by setting them apart as God's people (cf. 2 Thess 2:13).

Paul is probably describing the outpouring of God's Spirit that would characterize the time of Israel's restoration according to the prophets (Isa 32:15; 44:3; Ezek 11:19; 36:26–27; 37:14; Joel 3:1–2; cf. Acts 1:4–5; 2:33; Gal 3:14). According to Ezekiel, this is a time when God will put his "Spirit" within his people (36:26–27; 37:14; cf. 11:19) and will at the same time "cleanse" (37:23; cf. 36:29) them from their wrongdoing and "sanctify" (37:28) them. Some Jews of the Second Temple period continued to hope for this coming of "the Spirit of holiness" as part of Israel's restoration (1QS 4.21; T. Levi 18.11; cf. 18.6–7). Paul seems to be saying here that with the resurrection of Jesus, this much-anticipated time has started to arrive. His unusual way of speaking of the "Spirit of holiness," then,

22. Among ancient interpreters, see especially Theodoret of Cyrus, *Commentary on the Letters of St. Paul*, trans. Robert Charles Hill, 2 vols. (Brookline, MA: Holy Cross Orthodox Press, 2001), 1:45, and, more recently, L. W. Hurtado, "Jesus's Divine Sonship in Paul's Epistle to the Romans," in *Romans and the People of God*, ed. Sven K. Soderlund and N. T. Wright (Grand Rapids: Eerdmans, 1999), 225–27; Gordon D. Fee, *Pauline Christology: An Exegetical-Theological Study* (Peabody, MA: Hendrickson, 2007), 243.

23. E.g., Heinrich August Meyer, *Hand-book to the Epistle to the Romans*, trans. John C. Moore and Edwin Johnson (New York: Funk & Wagnalls, 1884), 34; W. Sanday and A. C. Headlam, *The Epistle to the Romans*, 5th ed., ICC (Edinburgh: T&T Clark, 1902), 9; Fitzmyer, *Romans*, 236; Longenecker, *Romans*, 74–75.

24. Maximilian Zerwick, *Biblical Greek*, Scripti Pontificii Instituti Biblici 114 (Rome: Pontifical Biblical Institute, 1963), 14–15; Daniel B. Wallace, *Greek Grammar Beyond the Basics: An Exegetical Syntax of the New Testament* (Grand Rapids: Zondervan, 1996), 87.

could be an intentional effort to use a more Semitic idiom common in places where this Jewish hope flourished.[25] It may also rise from an effort to express the idea that God's eschatologically given Spirit brings with it the holiness that is a necessary characteristic of God's restored people.

Viewed from this perspective, Jesus "was appointed Son of God in power" when he rose from the dead. For Paul to say that Jesus "was appointed" (ὁρισθέντος) Son of God does not mean that he had not been God's Son prior to this point.[26] Paul can speak of God the Father sending his "Son" into the human condition (Rom 8:3; Gal 4:4), and so he is unlikely to have said here that Jesus became God's Son only after he was born from David's offspring. The term Paul uses here (ὁρίζω) basically referred to marking something out, determining something, or delimiting it (Luke 2:22; Acts 2:23; 11:29; 17:26; Heb 4:7). In Acts it refers to God "marking out" Jesus or "appointing him" to be judge of the world (Acts 10:42; 17:31). The Acts 17:31 reference is particularly instructive, since it says that God provided proof that he had given Jesus his role as judge by raising him from the dead.

Here in Romans 1:4 Jesus's resurrection from the dead also marks him out for a particular role. Like the term "judge" in Acts 17:31, the term "Son of God" here refers to Jesus's function: from the time of his resurrection he began to function as "Son of God in power." The resurrection is the critical point of demarcation because it signals the change of the ages from the time when sin and death conspired with the law to keep human beings locked in their sinful condition to the time when God began to transform the world to remove the corrosive effects of sin, including death. Jesus was the first person to experience this eschatological resurrection into an immortal body (1 Cor 15:20), but his resurrection anticipates a general resurrection of God's people to a similarly immortal existence (1 Cor 15:21–23). So, "dead" (νεκρῶν) here is plural and "from" (ἐκ) means "from the time of."[27]

Paul finishes his description of the gospel by identifying the Son of God with great specificity. He is Jesus, the one who is both "Christ," the "anointed" (χριστός) king of Israel and "Lord" (κύριος). Paul has explained at length what it means that Jesus is Christ. In addition he now adds to this term the title that the LXX uses to describe Yahweh himself, something of which Paul was fully aware (Rom 10:9, 13; cf. Joel 3:5 LXX). To use the words of Richard Bauckham, this means that for Paul Jesus was "included in the unique identity of the one God of Israel."[28]

1:5 through whom we received grace and apostleship for the obedience of faith among all the gentiles on behalf of his name (δι᾽ οὗ ἐλάβομεν

25. On the Semitic coloring of the phrase, see Fitzmyer, *Romans*, 236.

26. Earlier interpreters worked hard to avoid this impression and sometimes stretched "appointed" (ὁρισθέντος) to mean "declared" or "made manifest." See, e.g., John Chrysostom, *The Homilies of S. John Chrysostom, Archbishop of Constantinople, on the Epistle of St. Paul the Apostle to the Romans*, trans. J. B. Morris, vol. 7 of *A Library of Fathers of the Holy Catholic Church* (Oxford: John Henry Parker, 1841), 11; Ambrosiaster, *Commentaries on Romans and 1–2 Corinthians*, trans. Gerald L. Bray, Ancient Christian Texts (Downers Grove, IL: InterVarsity Press, 2009), 4; Martin Luther, *Lectures on Romans: Glosses and Scholia*, ed. Hilton C. Oswald, vol. 25 of *Luther's Works* (Saint Louis: Condordia, 1972), 148. The term comes close to this meaning when it is used to speak of "defining" words (e.g., Plato, *Gorg.* 475a; *Republic* 505c; Aristotle, *Nicomachean Ethics* 1104b; LSJ 1251, s.v. ὁρίζω IV.3), but in the available literature it never clearly means "declare" or "make manifest."

27. Cf. Ambrosiaster, *Romans*, 4; Pelagius, *Pelagius's Commentary on St Paul's Epistle to the Romans*, trans. Theodore de Bruyn, Oxford Early Christian Studies (Clarendon: Oxford, 1993), 60; Wright, "Romans," 419.

28. Richard Bauckham, *Jesus and the God of Israel* (Grand Rapids: Eerdmans, 2008), 184. For Paul's inclusion of Jesus within the divine identity via his use of the name "Lord" (κύριος) for Jesus, see Wright, "Romans," 419; Bauckham, *Jesus and the God of Israel*, 186–232; and Fee, *Pauline Christology*, 558–85.

χάριν καὶ ἀποστολὴν εἰς ὑπακοὴν πίστεως ἐν πᾶσιν τοῖς ἔθνεσιν ὑπὲρ τοῦ ὀνόματος αὐτοῦ). Paul received as a gracious gift from God the assignment to go to the world's non-Jewish peoples and urge them to respond obediently to the message of the universal lordship of Jesus.

The phrase "through whom" (δι' οὗ) connects the description of Paul's vocation that follows to the full name for Jesus that he has just used ("Jesus Christ our Lord"), and this is significant. It is precisely in his role as the Messiah and Lord, sovereign not only over Jews but over all the earth, that Jesus gave Paul the mission of proclaiming the gospel to the gentiles. Paul's use of the plural "we received" (ἐλάβομεν) does not mean that he wanted to include in his purview other apostles (some of whom, likewise, God called to go to the gentiles).[29] This is an "epistolary" or "literary" plural (cf. 2 Cor 7:2–16; 10:1–11:6; Col 4:3; 1 Thess 2:18).[30] As the second half of this verse will show, Paul focuses in this letter on his own mission to the gentiles, a mission God graciously gave him. The God-given nature of his mission explains why he felt he had both the authority and the duty to pen the letter (11:13; 12:3; 15:15).[31] "Grace" and "apostleship," then, both refer to Paul's call to be an apostle to the gentiles (1:1), a vocation that he considered to be a gift from God (cf. 1 Cor 3:10; Gal 2:9; Eph 3:2, 7).

Paul received this gift for the purpose of (εἰς) bringing gentiles to "the obedience of faith . . . on behalf of his name." The phrase "on behalf of his name" or "for the sake of his name" (ὑπὲρ τοῦ ὀνόματος αὐτοῦ) probably refers to the name "Jesus Christ our Lord" that Paul has just used and that emphasizes the lordship of Jesus over the universe. Paul knew that one day every knee would bow and every tongue would confess that Jesus bore the name above all names, that he was "the Lord Jesus Christ" (cf. Phil 2:10–11). He probably understood his work as apostle to the gentiles as serving this ultimate goal by establishing communities that "named" Christ as Lord in corporate worship (Rom 15:20).

The phrase "the obedience of faith" (ὑπακοὴν πίστεως) is more difficult. Does the accent fall on obedience, which is then qualified as "faithful" obedience?[32] Does it fall on faith as the obedient response to the gospel?[33] Does Paul perhaps intend to emphasize both ideas equally?[34] Paul is summarizing the apostolic work that God called him to do, and this work involved much more than issuing an initial call to the gentiles to believe the gospel (1:11, 13; 15:16, 18). It is likely, then, that Paul used this phrase to refer both to the obedience of believing the gospel (cf. 10:16; 11:23, 30–31) and to the obedience that arises from the powerful reign of God's grace in the believer's life (5:21; 6:1–23; 7:5–6; 8:4, 7–9).[35]

29. See, e.g., Origen, *Commentary on the Epistle to the Romans, Books 1–5*, trans. Thomas P. Scheck, FC 103 (Washington, DC: Catholic University of America Press, 2001), 75; Chrysostom, *Romans*, 11; Ambrosiaster, *Romans*, 4; Sanday and Headlam, *Romans*, 10; Dunn, *Romans 1–8*, 16.

30. A. T. Robertson, *A Grammar of the Greek New Testament in Light of Historical Research*, 3rd ed. (London: Hodder & Stoughton, 1919), 407.

31. See especially Ernst Käsemann, *Commentary on Romans*, trans. Geoffrey W. Bromiley (Grand Rapids: Eerdmans, 1980), 14.

32. Don Garlington, *Faith, Obedience, and Perseverance: Aspects of Paul's Letter to the Romans* (Eugene, OR: Wipf & Stock, 2009), 10–31; Longenecker, *Romans*, 80–82, 97–98. Cf. the NIV's "the obedience that comes from faith" and the CEB's "faithful obedience."

33. E.g., John Calvin, *The Epistles of Paul the Apostle to the Romans and to the Thessalonians*, trans. Ross Mackenzie (Edinburgh: Oliver & Boyd, 1960), 17–18; Cranfield, *Romans*, 1:66–67; Klaus Haacker, *Der Brief des Paulus an die Römer*, THKNT 6 (Leipzig: Evangelische Verlagsanstalt, 1999), 28.

34. E.g., Douglas Moo, *The Epistle to the Romans*, NICNT (Grand Rapids: Eerdmans, 1996), 52; Thomas R. Schreiner, *Romans*, BECNT (Grand Rapids: Baker, 1998), 35. Cf. the TNIV's "faith and obedience."

35. Barclay, *Paul and the Gift*, 492.

1:6 Among whom you are also called by Jesus Christ (ἐν οἷς ἐστε καὶ ὑμεῖς κλητοὶ Ἰησοῦ Χριστου). Those to whom Paul writes this letter are among the gentiles to whom God commissioned Paul to preach the gospel since Christ Jesus had also summoned them.

Paul now begins to make the transition from the description of himself as the sender of the letter (1:1–7) to the description of the letter's recipients (1:8), and he drops the first hint of the letter's purpose. If God commissioned Paul to call the gentiles to lives of obedience, beginning with faith in the gospel, and if the Romans are gentiles, then Paul's commission applies to them as well. Paul implies, then, that his readers are predominantly gentile, an impression that other references in the letter confirm (1:13; 11:13; 15:15–16).

He also implies that although his readers are already believers, they nevertheless need to continue to respond to the gospel with the obedience that arises from faith. The phrase "called [κλητοί] by Christ Jesus," reminiscent as it is of Paul's own claim that he was "called [κλητός] to be an apostle" (1:1), certainly refers to a call in the past to which the Romans have already responded (cf. 8:30; 9:24; 1 Cor 1:9; 7:17–24; Gal 1:6; 5:13; 1 Thess 4:7). It probably also refers, however, to the present call of Christ Jesus in the form of the gospel that Paul is about to recount so fully in this letter (cf. Gal 5:8; 1 Thess 2:12; 5:24).[36] This is a call to which the Roman Christians, like all the gentiles who hear Paul's proclamation, should respond with faith and obedience.

1:7 To all who are in Rome, dearly loved by God, called to be holy, grace to you and peace from God our Father and the Lord Jesus Christ (πᾶσιν τοῖς οὖσιν ἐν Ῥώμῃ ἀγαπητοῖς θεοῦ, κλητοῖς ἁγίοις· χάρις ὑμῖν καὶ εἰρήνη ἀπὸ θεοῦ πατρὸς ἡμῶν καὶ κυρίου Ἰησοῦ Χριστοῦ). Paul identifies his readers as people in Rome whom God loves and has summoned to be his people. He prays that God, who is the Father of all believers, and Jesus Christ, who is the Lord of the universe, would freely bless them and grant them peace.

Paul's identification of his readers focuses on two characteristics that align them closely with the Israel of the Jewish Scriptures. First, they are "dearly loved by God" (ἀγαπητοῖς θεοῦ). The Mosaic law stipulates that God loved the patriarchs and so chose Israel to be his people (Deut 4:37; 10:15; cf. 7:8; 23:5), a concept that Paul himself affirms later in Romans (11:28). The idea that God loves Israel is such an important part of its identity (e.g., Isa 5:7; 41:8; 43:4; 44:2; 60:10; 63:9; Jer 31:3; Hos 11:1) that "beloved" (ἠγαπημένος) is one of its common biblical names (e.g., LXX Deut 32:15; 33:5; 33:26; Jer 11:15; 12:7). The term "dearly loved," which Paul uses here, has a particularly tender quality. It often expresses the love of family members for one another, of a father for an only son or daughter, for example, or of a mother for the man who has married her daughter and whom she wants to welcome into the family (e.g., Gen 22:2, 12, 16; Judg 11:34; Tob 10:12).[37] The Roman Christians are not simply God's people, then, but also part of a metaphorical family. God is their "Father," as the second half of the verse says, and, as Paul will say later in the letter, they are God's adopted children (8:14–15, 19; 9:26; cf. 8:29).

Second, the Roman Christians are "called to be holy." God also constituted Israel to be "a holy nation" (ἔθνος ἅγιον; Exod 19:6 LXX), and urged

36. Most English translations have "called to belong to Christ Jesus" rather than "called by Christ Jesus," but as the similarly constructed phrase "loved by God" (ἀγαπητοῖς θεοῦ) in the next verse shows, the genitive-case noun should be taken as a subjective genitive rather than a genitive of possession. See Cranfield, *Romans*, 1:68, and BDAG 549, s.v. κλητός.

37. Cf. BDAG 7, s.v. ἀγαπητός 1.

them in the Mosaic law, "You shall be sanctified [ἁγιασθήσεσθε], and you shall be holy [ἅγιοι], for I am holy [ἅγιος], I the Lord your God" (Lev 11:44 LXX; cf. 19:2). To be "holy" in such contexts meant to be separate from other peoples. "You shall be holy [ἅγιοι] to me, for I the Lord your God am holy [ἅγιος], who has separated [ἀφορίσας] you from all the nations to be mine" (Lev 20:26 LXX). This separation was both something that God accomplished at his own initiative and something that required a distinctive way of life described for God's people in the Mosaic law. Israel's holiness was both a reality created by God and a summons given by God to his people. The Roman Christians too have been set apart at God's initiative to live in a way that separates them from other people. When God "called" them to be holy he summoned them for a particular purpose, just as when he "called" (κλητός) Paul to be an apostle he also "set" Paul "apart" (ἀφωρισμένος) for the task of proclaiming the gospel to the gentiles (1:1).[38]

The second half of the verse transforms the standard epistolary greeting into a prayer that the Roman Christians would receive "grace" (χάρις) and "peace" (εἰρήνη). Although these words appear in all thirteen Pauline letters, they take on special importance here because both words are so significant in the rest of the letter.[39]

At least for Paul, "grace" (χάρις) was God's freely given favor (3:24; 5:15; cf. 12:3, 6; 15:15), given apart from any worth in the recipient, whether that worth was linked to ethnicity, social status, or effort (4:4, 16; 11:5–6).[40] God's grace was demonstrated in overwhelming abundance in the atoning death of the Lord Jesus Christ (3:24–26; 5:17, 20), and God gave it to all who were willing to receive it (5:17) through trusting that Christ's crucifixion had atoned for their sin. This gift, and the trust through which people received it, initiated a distinctively Christian mode of existence (5:2; cf. 5:21; 6:14–15) characterized, in practical terms, by the welcoming, loving acceptance of others across the boundaries of ethnicity, social status, and effort.[41]

It was natural, then, for Paul to link the grace of God with "peace" (εἰρήνη), both peace with God (5:1) and peace with other believers (14:19). In Romans, peace comes to God's people in the final day (cf. 2:10), after God, in his role as judge, has declared he will not punish them (2:10; 5:1). Paul can call God "the God of peace" (15:33; 16:20) because God took the initiative in reconciling his people to himself in the atoning death of Christ (3:25–26; 5:9–11), and this reconciliation with God leads to life (8:6), joy (14:17; 15:13), and reconciliation with others (14:19). "Peace" is a characteristic of eschatological existence (2:10), and in Paul's thought this period of existence has already started for those who have faith in Christ (5:1; 14:17).

The application of these truths to the Roman Christians is a critically important part of the letter's purpose, and so here at the beginning Paul prays that "grace" and "peace" might be theirs.

38. Cf. Cranfield, *Romans*, 1:70. *Pace*, e.g., Käsemann, *Romans*, 16, and Moo, *Romans*, 55, who place the emphasis on status rather than conduct.

39. The two words also appear in the greeting sections of 1 Pet 1:2; 2 Pet 1:2; 2 John 3; and Rev 1:4.

40. This definition is dependent on Barclay, *Paul and the Gift*, 331–574.

41. On this, see ibid., 493–519.

Theology in Application

In the letter opening, Paul placed special emphasis on his authority to interpret the gospel for others. He then began to define the gospel as the fulfillment of the Jewish Scriptures. It is appropriate to begin the study of Romans by thinking through what this opening paragraph teaches about the apostolic authority of Christian Scripture and about the deep indebtedness of those Scriptures to the sacred texts of Judaism.

Romans as Authoritative Christian Scripture

Paul opens Romans with a heavy emphasis on his authority. This is clear from the astonishing length of the opening itself and the amount of space within it that Paul spends describing himself in authoritative terms. He is a spokesperson for Jesus, the anointed King. God has summoned Paul and set him apart for a critically important task, and that task is the proclamation of joyful news of worldwide significance from the one God. Within this self-description, the terms "apostle" and "apostleship" play an important role (1:1, 5). Paul knew that the Roman Christians were familiar with these terms because two of their number, Andronicus and Junia, were also "apostles" (16:7).

"Apostles" carried authority in the early church because of their close ties to the earthly ministry and resurrection of Jesus, and the early Christians considered them foundational to the church's existence. In Paul's three lists of spiritual gifts that include "apostles," they always come first (1 Cor 12:28, 29; Eph 4:11). In Ephesians, apostles and prophets form the foundation on which the church is built (2:20; cf. Rev 21:14), and "the mystery of Christ," hidden from other generations, has now been revealed to Christ's "holy" apostles and to prophets by the Spirit (Eph 3:4–5). In both references, the term "apostles" comes before "prophets," and in the second reference the adjective "holy" shows the apostles' unique importance.

These rhetorical hints of their importance are matched by their function as the gatekeepers and interpreters of the traditions about Jesus. The apostles mediated in the dispute that led to the Jerusalem Council. Their decision at the Council prevailed, and their letter describing their decision circulated as an authoritative document among the churches (Acts 15:1–29; 16:4). The apostles James, Cephas, and John gave to Paul and Barnabas "the right hand of fellowship," confirming their agreement with the gospel Paul preached (Gal 2:9), and Paul himself boldly passed a negative verdict on Cephas's behavior in Antioch because it deviated from the "truth of the gospel" (Gal 2:14).

Although Paul was hesitant to use his apostolic authority outside the boundaries of churches he and his coworkers had founded (2 Cor 10:13–16), he nevertheless believed that he had the authority to do this if necessary. Since he understood his own calling to concern especially the establishment of churches among the gentiles, he believed it was appropriate for him to exercise his apostolic authority in the predominantly gentile Christian community at Rome, both by writing to them and later by visiting them.

The authority of apostolic writings became increasingly important among Christians as the apostles aged and passed away and false teaching began to proliferate (2 Pet 1:1, 12–15; 3:2). By the late second century, Christians had made the link between the witness of the apostles and the written deposit of that witness in their writings, now considered Scripture:

> Since, therefore, the tradition from the apostles does thus exist in the Church, and is permanent among us, let us revert to the Scriptural proof furnished by those apostles who did also write the Gospel, in which they recorded the doctrine regarding God, pointing out that our Lord Jesus Christ is the truth, and that no lie is in Him. (Irenaeus, *Against Heresies* 3.5.1)[42]

The apostles, in other words, continued to play their traditional foundational role in guiding the theology of the church through their writings and the writings of their followers.[43]

This means that Paul's opening statement of authority remains permanently important for the church. His letter was not merely authoritative at one time among an ancient group of Roman Christians but remains authoritative for the church. As the written witness of the apostle, it is Scripture, and it serves as a touchstone for claims about what Christians should believe. Romans is not merely an account of "Paul's" gospel, but since Paul writes as an apostle his account of the gospel must be the church's account as well. John Chrysostom, writing in the fourth century, said that when Paul's letters were read aloud in worship he heard a "spiritual trumpet" and could almost see Paul and converse with him.[44] The weighty tones of Paul's self-introduction in 1:1–5 should also come to Christians today as a clear call to pay attention to Paul as he delivers this authoritative message in his capacity as an emissary of Christ Jesus.

Romans as a Witness to the Continuing Authority of Israel's Scriptures for Christians

Paul's letter opening also emphasizes the profound connection between the gospel and the Jewish Scriptures. The biblical prophets promised the gospel beforehand (1:2). Jesus is a descendant of David (1:3), and one can only know who David is and

42. *The Ante-Nicene Fathers*, ed. Alexander Roberts and James Donaldson, 10 vols. (1885–87; repr., Peabody, MA: Hendrickson, 1994), 1:417.

43. See also, e.g., Justin, *Dialogue with Trypho* 103.8.

44. Chrysostom, *Romans*, 12.

why one of his future descendants would be so important by reading about these subjects in the Jewish Scriptures.[45] The eschatological significance of Jesus's close association with the Spirit and of Jesus's leading role in the general resurrection of the dead only makes sense in a Jewish context where the Jewish Law, Prophets, and Writings are "holy Scripture."

As Romans proceeds, it will often take the form of a fictional dialogue with an interested but unbelieving Jewish person about how the gospel Paul is articulating can be consistent with the Scriptures that both he and Paul consider authoritative. Paul's insistence on putting his description of the gospel in such terms is a testimony to the importance of the Jewish Scriptures to a trustworthy understanding of Christian theology.

At the same time, Paul also makes clear in 1:2–4 that the way the people of God should interpret the Jewish Scriptures has changed with the arrival of "Jesus Christ our Lord." Just as the Scriptures are necessary for understanding his full significance, so he is necessary for understanding their full significance. With the arrival of Jesus, what had been simply the Scriptures became, in a sense, the Old Testament.[46] It is "old" not in the sense that it was wrong and needed correction or was so anchored in its own time that it was no longer relevant, but in the sense that its witness to God and his purposes was incomplete. The Old Testament needed the gospel to give it focus and to complete its story line. Paul will say later in the letter that "Christ is the goal of the law, with the result of righteousness for everyone who believes" (10:4), and his meaning there is similar to the implications of 1:2–4 here. The law, and all the Old Testament, reach their goal in Christ and in the inclusion of gentiles as full members of God's people. This means that the way the Jewish Scriptures functioned previously has ended. They continue to function as authoritative Scripture for the church but in a different way than they did for ancient Israel.

From early times, people associated with the Christian church have struggled to keep this apostolic perspective on the Jewish Scriptures. Sometimes, as with the second-century heretic Marcion, they have marginalized the Old Testament and tried to repudiate the church's Jewish roots. As recently as the early twentieth century, serious theological thinkers have admired Marcion and argued that the retention of the Old Testament represents "a religious and ecclesiastical crippling."[47] At other times, as with the second-century Ebionites, they have tried to make Christianity into a reformed version of Judaism, interpreting Jesus as little more than a prophet like Moses or a Messiah who provided an example of how the Mosaic law

45. Peter Oakes, *Reading Romans in Pompeii: Paul's Letter at Ground Level* (Minneapolis: Fortress, 2009), 152.

46. Francis Watson, *Text and Truth: Redefining Biblical Theology* (Grand Rapids: Eerdmans, 1997), 179–85.

47. Adolf von Harnack, *Marcion: The Gospel of the Alien God*, trans. John E. Steely and Lyle D. Bierma (Durham, NC: Labyrinth, 1990; orig. German ed., 1924), 134.

should be kept.[48] Christians in more recent times have also sometimes downplayed the differences between Christianity and Judaism in an otherwise laudable effort to foster religious dialogue and understanding.

Christians should avoid both tendencies. They worship the Jewish Messiah who is also king and Lord not just of the Jewish people but of the universe. This truth means that for Christians the Jewish Scriptures are God's authoritative word, but they remain authoritative because the New Testament completes their story line. Christians should never forget their debt to Judaism, recognizing that there is much to learn from dialogue with those who follow its teachings and that the horrific treatment of Jews through the centuries by powerful people calling themselves Christians has made the issues surrounding this dialogue quite complex. The burden for sensitivity here lies heavily on Christians. At the same time, faithfulness to the gospel and honesty in the dialogue require that Christians articulate what they believe: the one God, whom both Jews and Christians confess, has focused his gracious plan for all creation on God's Son, Jesus the Davidic Messiah.

48. See H. J. Schoeps, "Ebionite Christianity," in *Early Christianity and Judaism*, ed. Everett Ferguson, David M. Scholer, and Paul Corby Finney, Studies in Early Christianity 6 (New York: Garland, 1993), 125–26; Ray A. Pritz, *Nazarene Jewish Christianity*, Studia Post-Biblica (Leiden: Brill, 1988), 19–21.

CHAPTER 2

Romans 1:8–17

Literary Context

Paul now explains how the apostleship to which God called him and the gospel for which God set him apart (1:1–7) affect the Roman Christians to whom he is writing. He has already hinted in 1:5–6 that his apostolic commission covered the Romans: they were among the gentiles for whom God gave him the gift of apostleship. His assignment involves calling them to the "obedience of faith" along with other gentiles.

There is an important difference, however, between the believers in Rome and Paul's other letter audiences, and that difference explains the reason for these two paragraphs. Paul did not lay the "foundation" for the gospel in Rome (15:20). A famous and stable Christian community had existed in Rome for many years (1:8; 15:14, 23; 16:19). Paul needed to clarify at the start, then, that he understood the Romans not only to be his "brothers and sisters" in the faith (1:13) but to be fellow believers who could offer him encouragement just as he, in his role as an apostle, could encourage them (1:12). Paul will briefly mention the ways in which they can encourage him later in the letter (15:24, 30–32), but the letter itself was his effort to encourage them. He needed to make clear to them, then, that the gospel God commissioned him to preach had an important contribution to make to the strengthening of their faith (1:11) and could yield fruit among them, just as it had among gentiles elsewhere (1:13).

The particular "fruit" Paul had in mind and the particular form in which this "strengthening" would take place begin to emerge toward the end of the passage in the language of social division. The gospel, Paul says, is for everyone: gentiles, Greeks, barbarians, sophisticated, foolish, and Jew (1:14–16). People from all these groups and more lived in Rome, and the gospel collapsed the barriers between all of them. Some of these barriers had made their way into the Roman church (11:18; 12:3; 14:1–15:7; cf. 16:17), and Paul believed that God had called him to proclaim the gospel in Rome in such a way that its implications for their dissolution became evident (11:13; 15:15).

The letter is a proclamation of this gospel and an application of it to the Roman believers in advance of the visit to Rome that Paul at last could see on the horizon (1:13; 15:23–24, 28–29, 32). This paragraph makes the critical transition from the stated reasons for Paul's apostolic concern for the Roman church to the actual proclamation of the gospel in Rome via the letter. It ends, then, with what most interpreters correctly understand as the letter's thesis statement, 1:16–17. The opening sentences of the letter have been moving toward this statement.[1] We have learned that God set Paul apart for the proclamation of the gospel (1:1). We have also learned that the gospel concerns God's Son, Jesus Christ (1:4, 9), and the obedience of faith among the gentiles. Paul and the Roman Christians hold in common this faith and the obedient response to which it leads (1:8, 12). But what precisely is the gospel? What does it do for the one who believes it?

Paul answers these questions in compressed form in 1:16–17. Most of the rest of the letter will be devoted to explaining what this compressed statement means (1:18–11:36) and how it applies to the socially divided Roman church (12:1–15:13).

I. The Letter Opening (1:1–7)
➡ **II. The Thanksgiving and Intercessory Prayer Reports (1:8–10)**
III. Why Paul Wants to Visit the Roman Christians (1:11–15)
IV. Why Preaching the Gospel in Rome Is Appropriate (1:16–17)
V. God's Wrath against Human Sin Is a Demonstration of His Righteousness (1:18–32)

Main Idea

Paul is thankful for the well-known commitment of the Roman Christians to the gospel and expresses his thanks to God in prayer. At the same time, he prays earnestly that he might be able to visit Rome to exercise his call to proclaim the gospel in that massive, cosmopolitan city. He is eager to do this because the gospel is about God's power to save every human being who believes its message, regardless of his or her social, ethnic, or cultural location.

Translation

Romans 1:8–17

8a	Assertion	**First, I thank my God**
b	Means	through Jesus Christ
c	Reference	concerning all of you
d	Cause	because your faith is proclaimed in the entire world.

Continued on next page.

1. Cf. Dunn, *Romans 1–8*, 37.

Continued from previous page.

9a	Oath	For **God is my witness**
b	Relationship	whom I serve
c	Sphere	in my spirit
d	Sphere	in the gospel of his Son
e	Content	that I make mention of you unceasingly
10a	Restatement	always in my prayers asking
b	Content	if I might succeed in coming to you
c	Time	somehow
d	Time	at last
e	Means	by the will of God.
11a	Desire	For **I long to see you**
b	Purpose	in order that I might share some spiritual gift with you
c	Purpose	so that you might be strengthened
		that is, more precisely,
12a	Expansion	to be encouraged together with you
b	Means	through one another's faith
c	Restatement	both yours and mine.
13a	Assertion	Now **I do not want you to be unaware, brothers and sisters,**
b	Content	that I have often planned to come to you (but have been hindered until now)
c	Purpose	in order that I might have some fruit
d	Place	among you also
e	Comparison	just as [I] also [have] among the rest of the gentiles.
14a	Assertion	**I am a debtor**
b	Reference	to Greeks and
c	Contrast	to barbarians,
d	Reference	to the sophisticated and
e	Contrast	to the foolish,
15a	Result	hence my eagerness, as far as depends on me, to proclaim the gospel
b	Place	also to you who are in Rome.
16a	Explanation	For **I am not ashamed of the gospel,**
b	Explanation	for **it is the power of God for salvation**
		to everyone who believes,
c	Restatement	to the Jew first, and also to the Greek.
17a	Explanation of 16b	For **the righteousness of God is revealed**
b	Sphere	in it
c	Means	from faith to faith,
d	Verification	just as it is written,
		"But the one who is righteous by faith will live." (Hab 2:4)

Structure

In 1:8–17 Paul continues to follow a common pattern in Greco-Roman letter openings with a reference to the well-being of the letter's recipients. Although most ancient letters did not include a reference of this type, it was often there and sometimes took a religious shape with the sender claiming that if the recipient were well he or she would give thanks to the gods.[2] Paul frequently included a similar section near the beginning of his letters, and he typically used it to anticipate elements of critical importance in the rest of the letter.[3]

Here in Romans Paul's thanksgiving prayer report expresses his gratitude that the faith of the Roman Christians is well-known (1:8), and this gives way to an intercessory prayer report that focuses on Paul's long-standing desire to visit the Roman Christians (1:9–10). Paul next explains at length why he wants to visit them (1:11–17), and this explanation can be divided into two parts.

In the first part (1:11–15) Paul explains that his desire to visit Rome is grounded in the nature of the apostolic call that was the focus of the letter greeting. It is a call to share his spiritual gifts in Rome (1:11b) and to see the gospel bear "fruit" among all kinds of people there (1:13d), whether cultured or rustic, gentile or Jew (1:14).[4] This part begins and ends with a statement of Paul's strong desire to exercise his apostolic call among the Roman Christians (1:11a, 15a).

Between these statements, Paul qualifies this desire in three ways. First, he corrects any notion that he thinks his visit to Rome will be one sided—they will encourage him just as he will encourage them in the faith (1:12). Second, he makes clear that he would have visited them earlier, but God hindered him from doing so (1:13). Third, he explains that his strong desire to visit Rome arises from his conviction that the gospel cuts across the humanly imposed social barriers of culture and education (1:14).

2. David Pao argues persuasively that no "thanksgiving" convention existed in ancient epistolary practice but that Paul adapted and creatively expanded the "health wish" (*formula valetudinis*) that often appears in ancient letters. He did this because giving thanks to God as a form of worship was so important to his theology ("Gospel within the Constraints of an Epistolary Form: Pauline Introductory Thanksgivings and Paul's Theology of Thanksgiving," in *Paul and the Ancient Letter Form*, ed. Stanley E. Porter and Sean A. Adams, Pauline Studies 6 [Leiden: Brill, 2010], 101–27). Cf. Weima, *Paul the Ancient Letter Writer*, 51–53.

3. Second Corinthians, Galatians, and Titus are the clear exceptions (cf. 1 Tim 1:12). Paul often follows a thanksgiving prayer report (Rom 1:8; 1 Cor 1:4–9; Phil 1:3–6; Col 1:3–5; 1 Thess 1:2–5; 2 Thess 1:3–4; 2 Tim 1:3–5; Phlm 4–5; cf. 1 Tim 1:12–14) with an intercessory prayer report (Rom 1:9–12; Phil 1:9–11; Col 1:9–14; 2 Thess 1:11–12; Phlm 6). These reports always anticipate important themes in the rest of the letter. On this, see Paul Schubert, *Form and Function of the Pauline Thanksgivings*, BZNW 20 (Berlin: Töpelmann, 1939), 180, and Peter T. O'Brien, *Introductory Thanksgivings in the Letters of Paul*, NovTSup 49 (Leiden: Brill, 1977), 262, 271. For this pattern in everyday correspondence of the period, see, for example, the intercessory and thanksgiving prayer reports in the letters of Isias and of Dionysios to Hephaistion (White, *Ancient Letters*, 65–67, nos. 34 and 35). Cf. Marie-Joseph Lagrange, *Saint Paul Épître aux Romains*, 3rd ed., *EBib* (Paris: LeCoffre, 1922), 12.

4. For understanding "barbarians" (βάρβαροι) and "fools" (ἀνόητοι) as "rustics," see Jewett, *Romans*, 131.

In the second part (1:16–17) Paul assumes that some people might question whether the gospel—with a message that cuts across social boundaries—is appropriate for the city of Rome, whose ethos glorified those boundaries and the power structure they represented (see the introduction). Paul explains why this implicit objection to bringing the gospel to Rome is not valid, and the result is the thesis statement of the letter. In two dense sentences, Paul explains what the gospel is and what it does. It turns out to be good news for every individual who believes its message, whether Jew or Greek.

The structure of 1:8–17, then, follows a stair-step pattern. The bottom stair is Paul's thanksgiving and intercessory prayer report, stating Paul's gratitude for the Roman's well-known faith in the gospel and his fervent desire to visit them (1:8–10). The second stair states the reason why Paul is so eager to visit Rome (1:11–15). The top stair, and the climax of the passage, states the reason why Paul would bring a message that treats all human beings alike to a place whose power and prestige rest on making social distinctions between human beings. This reason involves giving a compressed definition of the gospel (1:16–17). Most of the rest of the letter is devoted to unpacking the meaning of this climactic statement (1:18–15:13).

Exegetical Outline

➡ **II. The Thanksgiving and Intercessory Prayer Reports (1:8–10)**
- **A. Paul Thanks God for the Roman Christians' Well-Known Faith (1:8)**
- **B. Paul Prays Fervently That He Might Be Able to Visit the Roman Christians (1:9–10)**

III. Why Paul Wants to Visit the Roman Christians (1:11–15)
- **A. The Primary Reason Stated: Paul Wants Their Faith to Be Strengthened (1:11–14)**
  1. First Clarification: Their Faith Will Encourage Paul Also (1:12)
  2. Second Clarification: Paul's Delay Is Not Due to Lack of Enthusiasm (1:13)
  3. Third Clarification: The Universal Reach of the Gospel Obligates Paul to Visit Rome (1:14)
- **B. The Primary Reason Restated: Paul Wants to Preach the Gospel to Them (1:15)**

IV. Why Preaching the Gospel in Rome Is Appropriate (1:16–17)
- **A. The Universal Reach of the Gospel (1:16)**
  1. God's Saving Power Comes to Everyone Who Believes the Gospel (1:16a–b)
  2. God's Saving Power Is for Both the Jew (First) and the Greek (1:16c)
- **B. The Faith-Centered Nature of the Gospel (1:17)**
  1. The Gospel Reveals the Righteousness of God to Every Human Being Who Believes It (1:17a–c)
  2. It Does This in accord with the Biblical Principle That the One Who Has Faith in God Becomes Righteous and Therefore Lives (1:17d)

Explanation of the Text

1:8 First, I thank my God through Jesus Christ concerning all of you because your faith is proclaimed in the entire world (Πρῶτον μὲν εὐχαριστῶ τῷ θεῷ μου διὰ Ἰησοῦ Χριστοῦ περὶ πάντων ὑμῶν, ὅτι ἡ πίστις ὑμῶν καταγγέλλεται ἐν ὅλῳ τῷ κόσμῳ). Paul is thankful to God for the encouragement that the very existence of a faithful Christian community in Rome is to a vast number of Christians in other places.

In English, Paul's expression "first" (πρῶτον μέν) hangs in the air because there is no corresponding "and second . . . ," but in ancient Greek letters and discourses, this idiom was not unusual. It was a way of launching a topic with several subpoints, and these points did not necessarily receive further enumeration (cf., e.g., 1 Cor 11:18; 2 Clem. 3:1; Plato, *Letters* 7.337b–c).[5] Paul's second point may come into the discourse at 1:13 when he says, "Now [δέ] I do not want you to be unaware, brothers and sisters, that I have often planned to come to you."[6]

Like many ancient Greek letters, Paul begins on an upbeat note of joy and thanksgiving, but his thanks to God is far from merely conventional. Ancient letters that included this element typically focused on the physical well-being of the recipient and the sender. Paul typically focused instead on God and what he had done in the lives of the letter's recipients through Jesus Christ, just as he does here (cf., e.g., 1 Cor 1:4–8; Phil 1:4–6; Phlm 4–5).[7] Such theocentric expressions of thanksgiving anticipated the important theme of giving thanks to God in worship that he would develop a few paragraphs later (cf. 1:21).[8]

The cause of Paul's thanks to God was the fame of the Roman Christians' "faith" (πίστις). Much later, close to the letter's end, Paul will say that the report of the Roman Christians' "obedience" (ὑπακοή) has reached everyone, and that this has given him cause for joy (16:19). The similarity of the two statements shows that Paul made a close conceptual connection between the Romans' obedience and their faith. The Romans' faith in the gospel has led to lives of obedience to God (cf. ὑπακοή πίστεως in 1:5), and Paul is thankful to God that this is widely known.

Paul enjoyed both hearing and passing along reports of the faithfulness of believers in various parts of the world because these reports encouraged other believers by providing examples for them to follow (2 Cor 8:1–5; 9:1–4; 1 Thess 1:6–8; 2 Thess 1:3–4) and by providing a reason to praise God (2 Cor 9:11–14). Paul believed that other Christians took encouragement from the knowledge that even in Rome, the greatest city in the world as they knew it, there existed a vibrant community of people who had believed the gospel. This is why he thanks God.

1:9 For God is my witness whom I serve in my spirit in the gospel of his Son that I make mention of you unceasingly (μάρτυς γάρ μού ἐστιν ὁ θεός, ᾧ λατρεύω ἐν τῷ πνεύματί μου ἐν τῷ εὐαγγελίῳ τοῦ υἱοῦ αὐτοῦ, ὡς ἀδιαλείπτως μνείαν ὑμῶν ποιοῦμαι). Paul remembers the Romans constantly in prayer, and he says this not merely to be polite but because it is true. The God whom he serves when he proclaims the gospel can testify that this is so.

Letters from Paul's time frequently mention near the beginning that the writer continually

5. BDAG 893, s.v. πρῶτος, 1.b.β.

6. Origen entertained this possibility (*Romans 1–5*, 78).

7. Pao, "Gospel within the Constraints of an Epistolary Form," 120–21.

8. Ibid., 121–22, 125–26.

remembers the recipient, and sometimes that this remembering takes the form of prayer.[9] Paul follows this convention, but, perhaps because he wants to stress that what he has said is no formality, he calls God as his witness that it is true (cf. Phil 1:8).[10]

Paul describes God as one whom he "serves," and the word he uses (λατρεύω) refers to cultic service or worship (e.g., Rom 1:25; cf. Exod 20:5 LXX; Matt 4:10//Luke 4:8). This service did not consist of outward rituals, such as circumcision (cf. 2:29; Phil 3:3), but in inner conviction that expresses itself in outward obedience. Paul will say later in the letter that this kind of worship is the reasonable human response to God's merciful character as the gospel reveals it (12:1). For Paul it meant proclaiming the gospel in places like Rome (cf. 1:1, 5; 15:16), and for the Roman Christians it meant "offering" their "bodies as a sacrifice that is living, holy, and acceptable to God" (12:1).

1:10 always in my prayers asking if I might somehow, at last, succeed in coming to you by the will of God (πάντοτε ἐπὶ τῶν προσευχῶν μου, δεόμενος εἴ πως ἤδη ποτὲ εὐοδωθήσομαι ἐν τῷ θελήματι τοῦ θεοῦ ἐλθεῖν πρὸς ὑμᾶς). Paul prays fervently that God's will for his apostolic work might include, finally, a visit to the Roman Christians.

The word Paul uses for "asking" (δεόμαι) means to plead for something and has an air of urgency about it (e.g., Ps 29:9 LXX [30:8 Eng.; 30:9 Heb.]; Isa 37:4 LXX; Jdt 8:31; Acts 8:22, 24), especially when combined with the emphatic expression "if . . . somehow, at last" (εἴ πως ἤδη ποτέ).[11] Paul was communicating to the Romans the great strength of his desire to visit them. As the prayers themselves show, if this is to happen God must remove any hindrances, including the hindrance of further work for Paul in the region stretching from Jerusalem to Illyricum, work that up to this point took priority over Paul's own desire of many years to visit Rome (15:19, 22–23).[12] So, if Paul is to visit Rome, it must be the will of God (cf. 15:32).

1:11 For I long to see you in order that I might share some spiritual gift with you so that you might be strengthened (ἐπιποθῶ γὰρ ἰδεῖν ὑμᾶς, ἵνα τι μεταδῶ χάρισμα ὑμῖν πνευματικὸν εἰς τὸ στηριχθῆναι ὑμᾶς). Paul prays to visit Rome because he has a strong desire for God to use the gifts God has given him to bolster the Roman Christians' commitment to the gospel.

Paul used the term "for" (γάρ) in its logical sense to give the reason why he prays constantly that he might be able to visit the Roman Christians.[13] He did this because he had a strong desire to see them. The verb "long for" (ἐπιποθέω) is an emphatic word that elsewhere in biblical Greek could refer to the longing of a nursing infant for its mother's milk (1 Pet 2:2) or to a deer's instinct to find water (Ps 41:2 LXX; 42:1 Eng.; 42:2 Heb.).[14] In the Pauline corpus the word almost always refers to a longing or desire related to other people, usually a desire to be with them (Phil 1:8; 2:26; 1 Thess 3:6; 2 Tim 1:4). This strong term combines with Paul's oath (1:9a), the reference to his "spirit" (1:9b), the double reference to his constant prayer ("unceasingly," "always," 1:10a), and the emphatic expression of his

9. See, e.g., White, *Ancient Letters*, 39 (no. 16) and 65 (no. 34).

10. Cf. 1 Thess 2:5, 10; 2 Cor 1:23, also places where Paul suspects that his readers may not believe what he says.

11. On the meaning of "ask," see BDAG 218, s.v. δεόμαι b, and for the expression "if . . . somehow at last," see Acts 27:12; Rom 11:14; Phil 3:11 (εἴ πως) and Phil 4:10; Philo, *Confusion* 196; 2 Clem. 13:1 (ἤδη ποτέ).

12. Illyricum occupied an area along the eastern coast of the Adriatic Sea.

13. "For" can also be used, as it is in v. 9a, simply to carry the discourse along. See BDAG 189–90, s.v. γάρ 2.

14. *TLNT* 2:59.

hope to visit them (1:10b–d) to communicate an urgent, heartfelt desire to come to Rome.

The purpose for the visit, which Paul describes in the next clause, is that he might share "some spiritual gift" (τι . . . χάρισμα . . . πνευματικόν) with the Roman Christians (1:11b). The term translated "gift" (χάρισμα) here refers to something that is "freely and graciously given" or "a concrete expression of grace."[15] Paul's apostleship was such a gift (1:5; 12:3; 15:15–16; cf. 1 Cor 12:28–29; Eph 3:2, 7–8; 4:11), as were other ministries and abilities that God gave to believers for their mutual edification (Rom 12:6–8; 1 Cor 12:28–31; 1 Tim 4:14; 2 Tim 1:6). In 1 Corinthians Paul connects these freely given gifts with the work of the Spirit (12:1, 4–11), and so the expression "spiritual gift" (χάρισμα . . . πνευματικόν) is not unexpected, although it is unique in the Pauline corpus.

In a way that is consistent with the note of mutuality Paul sounds throughout 1:11–12, he does not say he wants to "impart" (KJV, ESV, TNIV, NET), "convey" (NJB), or "bring" (REB) a spiritual gift to them, but to "share" (NAB, NRSV) with them a gift he has. Theodoret of Cyrus, writing in the mid-fifth century, but still much closer chronologically and culturally to Paul's Greek than any modern interpreter, put it this way: "His words are redolent of a humble attitude: he did not say 'to give' [ἵνα δῶ] but *to share* [ἵνα μεταδῶ] I give some of what I received."[16]

The word "some" (τι) diplomatically avoids the impression that Paul thinks he has perfectly diagnosed the Roman Christians' need in advance of his visit and knows precisely how to address it.[17] He is confident that when he arrives among them he will be able to share a spiritual gift with them, but he does not know precisely what form this will take.[18]

The verb "strengthen" (στηρίζω) appears in one other place in Romans (16:25) and several times in the Thessalonian correspondence (1 Thess 3:2, 13; 2 Thess 2:17; 3:3) but nowhere else in Paul's letters. In the Thessalonian letters Paul uses it to express his hope that this young and persecuted Christian community will persevere in their commitment to the gospel (cf. Rom 16:25). It seems likely that here too Paul refers to the strengthening of the Roman Christians because he knew that faith in the gospel was an ongoing commitment in need of encouragement.

This is the only one of Paul's six uses of the verb that is in the passive voice ("be strengthened" [στηριχθῆναι]), something that most translations miss but is nicely preserved in the NAB ("so that you may be strengthened"). The passive contributes to the deferential tone of the passage, slightly diminishing the role of Paul himself and leading to the next thought in which Paul clarifies what he says to remove any misunderstanding that only the Romans and not Paul himself will benefit spiritually from his visit.

1:12 that is, more precisely, to be encouraged together with you through one another's faith, both yours and mine (τοῦτο δέ ἐστιν συμπαρακληθῆναι ἐν ὑμῖν διὰ τῆς ἐν ἀλλήλοις πίστεως ὑμῶν τε καὶ ἐμοῦ). Paul clarifies that what he said in 1:11 should be understood in the sense that both he and the Roman Christians will encourage one another as each benefits from the other's commitment to the gospel.

The phrase "that is, more precisely" (τοῦτο δέ ἐστιν) introduces not a correction of 1:11 but

15. BDAG 1081, s.v. χάρισμα; Gordon D. Fee, *God's Empowering Presence: The Holy Spirit in the Letters of Paul* (Peabody, MA: Hendrickson, 1994), 488.

16. Theodoret of Cyrus, *Commentary on the Letters of St. Paul*, trans. Robert Charles Hill, 2 vols. (Brookline, MA: Holy Cross Orthodox Press, 2001), 1:48 (PG 82:56).

17. Cf. Jewett, *Romans*, 124.

18. Moo, *Romans*, 60; Jewett, *Romans*, 124.

a more detailed explanation of what it meant (cf. "Aristotle," *Mag. mor.* 1.1.11 1182b; cf. Philo, *Flight* 189; Josephus, *Ag. Ap.* 1.82).[19] Paul wanted to avoid any misunderstanding that he would only fill the role of encourager and the Roman Christians would only fill the role of the encouraged.

He communicates his desire for mutual encouragement in three ways. First, he affixes to his characteristic term "encourage" (παρακαλέω) a preposition that means "together with" (σύν) to show that he will experience encouragement together with them. Second, he says that their faith will be an encouragement to "one another" (ἀλλήλοις). Third, the conjunction he uses to join "yours" (ὑμῶν) and "mine" (ἐμοῦ) "serves to unite complements" and so emphasizes the equity between the two parties: he will be encouraged by their faith just as their faith will be encouraged by his.[20]

How will their "faith" encourage each other? It is likely that Paul uses the term "faith" here in the way he uses it in 1 Thessalonians 3:1–10 where he says that he sent Timothy to Thessalonica "to strengthen" (στηρίξαι; cf. Rom 1:11) the new believers in their faith in light of the persecution they were enduring (3:2).[21] He then describes how Timothy returned from this visit with the good news of the Thessalonians' "faith and love" (3:6). Paul and his coworkers, he continues, "were encouraged [παρεκλήθημεν] about you because of your faith [διὰ τῆς ὑμῶν πίστεως]" (3:7 NIV). Here the Thessalonians' "faith" is their steadfast commitment to the gospel despite the hardship they had been experiencing (1 Thess 3:2–3). In Romans, too, "faith" can refer to a trust in and commitment to the promises of God, a commitment that can either "be weak" (ἀσθενέω) or "grow strong" (ἐνδυναμόω) but, ideally, is unwavering (Rom 4:19–20). Here in 1:12, then, Paul says that he will be encouraged by the Romans' unwavering commitment to the gospel, just as he hopes they too will be encouraged by the steadfastness of his commitment.

1:13 Now I do not want you to be unaware, brothers and sisters, that I have often planned to come to you (but have been hindered until now) in order that I might have some fruit among you also just as [I] also [have] among the rest of the gentiles (οὐ θέλω δὲ ὑμᾶς ἀγνοεῖν, ἀδελφοί, ὅτι πολλάκις προεθέμην ἐλθεῖν πρὸς ὑμᾶς, καὶ ἐκωλύθην ἄχρι τοῦ δεῦρο, ἵνα τινὰ καρπὸν σχῶ καὶ ἐν ὑμῖν καθὼς καὶ ἐν τοῖς λοιποῖς ἔθνεσιν). Paul wants his Roman readers to understand that his desire to visit them has actually given birth, more than once, to concrete plans that did not materialize. The hindrances that previously prevented his coming, however, are now gone, and the time has nearly come for Paul to proclaim the gospel among the Roman Christians, just as he has done among other gentiles.

Paul's conjunction "now" (δέ) resumes the theme of his strong desire to visit the Romans in order to strengthen them (1:9–11), a theme from which Paul had deviated briefly to explain that he would also benefit from the visit (1:12).

Paul sometimes used the phrase "I do not want you to be unaware" (οὐ θέλω ὑμᾶς ἀγνοεῖν) to correct his readers when he knew or suspected that they misunderstood something (11:25; 1 Cor 10:1; 12:1; 1 Thess 4:13 ["we"]; cf. 1 Cor 11:3). Ancient letters sometimes used phrases like this, however, to emphasize the author's aim in writing the letter or to highlight the circumstances surrounding the

19. *Pace*, e.g., J. B. Lightfoot, *Notes on Epistles of St Paul from Unfinished Commentaries* (London: Macmillan, 1895), 248; Fitzmyer, *Romans*, 248, and the translation "or rather" in the NJB, NRSV, and REB.

20. On τὲ καί, see Herbert Weir Smyth, *Greek Grammar*, rev. Gordon M. Messing (Cambridge: Harvard University Press, 1956), §2974.

21. Cf. Haacker, *An die Römer*, 33–34.

letter's composition.[22] That is how Paul uses the phrase here (cf. 2 Cor 1:8; Phil 1:12).

Here Paul's overall aim in the letter and his circumstances as he writes are both in view. His circumstances come to the fore in the phrase "until now" (ἄχρι τοῦ δεῦρο), which hints that his long-awaited visit to Rome is within reach. His goal in writing is probably closely connected with the purpose he articulates here for his upcoming visit: he hopes when he arrives to see "some fruit" (τινὰ καρπόν) among the Roman Christians through the proclamation of the gospel among them (1:15; cf. Phil 1:22; 4:17). "Fruit" (καρπός), then, does not refer to new converts but to the profit that the Roman Christians, and especially the gentiles among them, will receive from understanding more fully the implications of the gospel for their lives (cf. Phil 1:22; 4:17).[23]

1:14 I am a debtor to Greeks and to barbarians, to the sophisticated and to the foolish (Ἕλλησίν τε καὶ βαρβάροις, σοφοῖς τε καὶ ἀνοήτοις ὀφειλέτης εἰμί). The message God summoned Paul to preach is good news for all humanity, of whatever social class, and Paul is duty-bound to proclaim it to everyone.

Paul frequently used the metaphor of debt in a moral sense (Rom 8:12; 13:7–8; 15:27; 1 Cor 7:3; Gal 5:3). It was clearly a live metaphor for him (Rom 4:4; 13:7; Phlm 18) and implied a real sense of obligation, usually an obligation toward God (Rom 8:12; Gal 5:3) or toward others because of one's relationship to God (Rom 15:1, 27). Paul can speak elsewhere of preaching the gospel as a "necessity" (ἀνάγκη) laid on him: it is no ground for boasting because he must do it (1 Cor 9:16). Here, then, he means that he is obligated to people to proclaim the gospel to them because God has given him this commission (cf. Rom 1:1, 5).

From the perspective of Greco-Roman culture, Paul's description of those to whom he was obligated is surprising. Roman culture was tightly organized along the lines of social class. Those born into certain families and with access to education in older forms of Greek philosophy and rhetoric occupied the most powerful positions in this structure. Being "sophisticated" or "wise" (σοφός), "powerful" (δυνατός), and "of noble birth" (εὐγενής) went together (1 Cor 1:26). Slaves and those without an understanding of Greco-Roman culture were the weakest, most exploited members of society and were widely despised by those above them on the social ladder. They were "foolish" (μωρός), "weak" (ἀσθενής), "low" (ἀγενής), and "despised" (ἐξουθενημένος) (1 Cor 1:27–28). When Paul uses the term "Greeks" (Ἕλληνες) here, he does not mean natives of Greece in the first century (whom upper-class Romans generally disliked) but people educated in the ancient Greek way of life as first-century upper-class Romans understood it. In other words, he means people who stood at the top of the Roman social ladder.[24]

"Barbarians" (βάρβαροι) stood at the bottom of the same ladder.[25] They were foreigners in the ancient Greek sense of people who were innately inferior, uneducated, and naturally suited only for

22. See White, *Ancient Letters*, 207. See also the examples in ibid., 24 (no. 1), 34 (no. 11), 48 (no. 22), 81 (no. 45), 88 (no. 52), and especially, 157 (no. 101), 158 (no. 102), 164 (104b), 174 (no. 110), and 181 (no. 114).

23. Cf. BDAG 510, s.v. καρπός 2. For the metaphorical use of "fruit" to refer to the effects of persuasive discourse, see Plato, *Phaedr.* 260d.

24. See Benjamin Isaac, *The Invention of Racism in Classical Antiquity* (Princeton: Princeton University Press, 2004), 381–405; Jewett, *Romans*, 130–33; and James R. Harrison, "Paul's 'Indebtedness' to the Barbarian (Rom 1:14) in Latin West Perspective," *NovT* 55 (2013): 315–36.

25. Cf. Plato, *Theaet.* 175a: "Rich men and beggars, kings and slaves, Greeks and foreigners [βάρβαροί τε και Ἕλληνες]" (Plato, *Complete Works*, ed. John M. Cooper [Indianapolis, IN.: Hackett, 1997], 194).

slavery. "'Tis meet that Greeks should rule barbarians" (*Iphigeneia at Aulis* 1400), said Euripides, and Aristotle quoted the line in support of his notion that "barbarian and slave are the same in nature" (*Politics* 1252b).[26] Since Aristotle also thought that slaves were naturally inferior to their masters "in intelligence" (τῇ διανοίᾳ 1252a; translation mine), it is easy to see how being "barbarian" might be equated with being "foolish" (ἀνόητος). Intervening years did nothing to soften this attitude, and it was commonplace among the Roman upper classes in the first century.[27]

For any upper-class Roman among Paul's first readers, the thought of the apostle being under some "obligation" to barbarians must have seemed absurd.[28] Barbarians were obligated to serve the Romans as slaves, as their ill breeding dictated. For Paul, however, the gospel cut through all this and leveled the social landscape. The gospel insisted that all humanity stood before God on equal terms: all had rebelled against him (1:18–3:20) and all received the free offer of a right standing and relationship with him through the atoning death of Christ (3:21–4:25; cf. Gal 3:28; Col 3:11). Paul's apostolic commission was to preach this gospel, and so he was under obligation to all.

1:15 hence my eagerness, as far as depends on me, to proclaim the gospel also to you who are in Rome (οὕτως τὸ κατ' ἐμὲ πρόθυμον καὶ ὑμῖν τοῖς ἐν Ῥώμῃ εὐαγγελίσασθαι). Paul was ready to visit Rome because of his apostolic commission to preach the gospel to everyone, whatever their social standing.

As Paul has already clarified with the expressions "by the will of God" (1:10) and "[I] have been hindered" (1:13), the way he carries out his commission from God is subject to God's direction. This comes out again in the way Paul formulated the expression "my" (κατ' ἐμέ). The phrase he uses consists of a preposition (κατά) with an emphatic form of the first-person singular pronoun as its object (ἐμέ), and since it stands in the attributive position (between the article and the adjective), it probably indicates possession (cf. 2 Esd 6:11). The same phrase is sometimes used in Greek literature, however, to mean "as far as depends on me" (e.g., Euripides, *Iphigeneia at Aulis* 931; Demosthenes, *On the Crown* 247.9; "Demosthenes," *Against Polycles* 13.7). Since Paul has just emphasized that only divinely arranged circumstances prevented his frequent plans to visit Rome from materializing (1:13), the phrase probably also carries something of that nuance here (cf. Tyndale, KJV, NJB).[29] Paul is eager to come to Rome, and if it were up to him he would have been there by now.

The term "hence" (οὕτως) reveals that the reason for his eagerness lies in what he has just said: the gospel is for everyone, whatever their social standing. There was no better place to reach a cross section of humanity than Rome. According to John E. Stambaugh's study of the social fabric of the city, "we must conclude that Rome in the early principate was one of the most densely populated cities the world has ever known—as crowded, probably, as modern Bombay or Calcutta."[30] During the first centuries BC and AD, moreover, a "large influx" of "merchants, teachers, tourists, and slaves from all over the empire poured into the city that had now assumed its proper role as imperial capital."[31]

26. Quoted in Isaac, *Invention of Racism*, 177–78.

27. Jewett, *Romans*, 131.

28. Except in the sense perhaps that Romans were obligated to civilize barbarians. On this, see Harrison, "Paul's 'Indebtedness,'" 315–19.

29. Cf. Käsemann, *Romans*, 20.

30. Stambaugh, *Ancient Roman City*, 90.

31. Ibid., 91.

1:16 For I am not ashamed of the gospel, for it is the power of God for salvation to everyone who believes, to the Jew first, and also to the Greek (Οὐ γὰρ ἐπαισχύνομαι τὸ εὐαγγέλιον, δύναμις γὰρ θεοῦ ἐστιν εἰς σωτηρίαν παντὶ τῷ πιστεύοντι, Ἰουδαίῳ τε πρῶτον καὶ Ἕλληνι). Paul is eager to preach the gospel in Rome because he is not ashamed of its cross-centered, socially unifying message that God is willing and able to save each person who believes it.

The conjunction "for" (γάρ) links Paul's statement that he is not ashamed of the gospel to what he has just said about his eagerness to preach the gospel in Rome. Rome was the seat of power and Greco-Roman culture in Paul's world, and most people derived what power they had from their social connections with people higher up the social, political, or economic ladder. In such a context, the message of the early Christians, with its focus on one who had been crucified and on elements that were common to all humanity (3:21–26), might appear shameful. Paul is not ashamed of it, however, because (γάρ) through the gospel God has demonstrated his power to bring people "salvation" (σωτηρία). As he says elsewhere, "The message of the cross is foolishness to those who are perishing, but to us who are being saved it is the power of God" (1 Cor 1:18 NIV). The terms "salvation" (σωτηρία) and "save" (σῴζω) in Romans refer primarily to the rescue of God's people from his present and future wrath against the impious and wicked (see 1:18; 2:5; 5:9–10; cf. 1 Thess 5:9) and the rescue of his people from the decay that sin has brought into the world (8:24; cf. 8:21–23). There is a sense in which salvation has already come to anyone who believes the gospel (8:24; cf. 1 Cor 7:16; 9:22; 2 Cor 6:2; Eph 2:5, 8; Titus 3:5; 2 Tim 1:9). There is also a sense in which salvation still lies in the future (5:9–10; 10:9–10, 13; 11:26; 13:11; cf. 1 Cor 1:18; 3:15; 5:5; 15:2; 2 Cor 2:15; 1 Thess 5:8–9). Here the focus is on the present availability of salvation to the believer who, through trusting the gospel, can escape God's wrath, which is presently under way (1:18).

This salvation is both universal in its reach and individual in its application, something communicated by the singular form "everyone" (παντί) and then emphasized with the phrase "to the Jew first, and also to the Greek." The gospel comes to the Jew first because God entrusted Israel with his word (3:2). He also gave them "the adoption as sons, and the glory, and the covenants, and the legislation, and the worship, and the promises, whose are the fathers, and from whom is the Messiah, as far as the flesh is concerned" (9:4–5; cf. 11:17–18; 15:27).[32] Even so, the gospel comes with its saving power not merely to one ethnic group, however privileged in other ways, but to all humanity, and so even the Greek is included in its reach (cf. 1 Cor 1:24).

"Greek" (Ἕλλην) here is roughly equivalent to "gentile" (ἔθνος), although Paul was perhaps thinking of Greco-Roman culture, the form of gentile culture best known to Greek-speaking Jews. Paul may have had Greek culture especially in mind in the description of human impiety and unrighteousness in the letter's next section (1:18–32; cf. 2:9, 10; 3:9).

1:17 For the righteousness of God is revealed in it from faith to faith, just as it is written, "But the one who is righteous by faith will live" (δικαιοσύνη γὰρ θεοῦ ἐν αὐτῷ ἀποκαλύπτεται ἐκ πίστεως εἰς πίστιν, καθὼς γέγραπται, ὁ δὲ δίκαιος ἐκ πίστεως ζήσεται). Paul now explains why God

32. The negative counterpart to the priority of the Jew in salvation is that apart from the gospel, condemnation also comes to the Jew first, then to the Greek (2:9–10).

is able, through the gospel, to save everyone who believes. He states that the way the gospel works to save every believer corresponds with what the Scriptures say about how one receives life.

The gospel saves because (γάρ) "the righteousness of God" (δικαιοσύνη . . . θεοῦ) is revealed in it. This phrase or its equivalent appears seven times in Romans (here in 1:17; 3:5, 21, 22, 25, 26; 10:3), but, on the most generous count, only three times elsewhere in Paul's letters (1 Cor 1:30; 2 Cor 5:21; Phil 3:9) and three times outside the Pauline corpus in the NT (Matt 6:33; Jas 1:20; 2 Pet 1:1). The expression, then, is distinctive of Romans and important for understanding the letter's argument.

As the "In Depth" look at righteousness language in Romans explains, however, exactly what this phrase expresses is a matter of intense discussion among interpreters. Its next use at 3:5 unambiguously refers to a characteristic of God himself (that he is righteous), and since Paul has just emphasized in 1:14 and 16 that God's saving power is available to everyone equally without regard to race or culture, a reference to God's righteousness fits the immediate context here also. As a righteous judge, God treats everyone alike (cf. 2:11; 3:26).[33]

A more active sense for the expression also fits the immediate context well, since in the next sentence Paul will use a closely parallel phrase to say "the wrath of God is revealed." Just as "the wrath of God" is described as an activity in 1:18–32, "the righteousness of God" most naturally refers to an activity also—to the powerful, saving activity Paul has just described in 1:16 (cf. Ps 97:2–3 LXX [98:2–3 Eng. and Heb.]).[34]

In addition, the phrase can refer to a positive verdict that God renders in a judicial sense and therefore to a righteous status he gives people. He declares people to be righteous, and so they receive "righteousness" (δικαιοσύνη) from him as a gift (3:21–22, 25–26; cf. 1 Cor 1:30; Phil 3:9). This reading also makes good sense here because, as Paul's supporting quotation of Habakkuk 2:4 shows, he is concerned with the connection between the faith of an individual and that person's "righteous" (δίκαιος) status.[35]

Is it likely that Paul intended the expression here to cover all three of these meanings? Normally, such a "thick" reading of a brief expression would seem oversubtle, but since 1:16–17 is a tightly packed summary of what is to come in the letter, Paul was probably thinking of all these meanings at this point.[36] Paul will explain in 3:21–26 that the death of Christ is the means by which God's saving righteousness rescues sinners from condemnation by giving them righteousness, but doing so in such a way that God's righteous character remains intact. Here Paul anticipates that fuller explanation of

33. Origen, *Romans, Books 1–5*, 87.

34. See, e.g., Adolf Schlatter, *Romans: The Righteousness of God*, trans. Siegfried S. Schatzmann (Peabody, MA: Hendrickson, 1995; orig. German ed. 1935), 20–24; C. K. Barrett, *The Epistle to the Romans*, rev. ed., BNTC (Grand Rapids: Baker, 2011), 30; Jewett, *Romans*, 142. Some interpreters, e.g., C. H. Dodd, *The Epistle of Paul to the Romans* (London: Collins, 1959), 38–40; Käsemann, *Romans*, 24–30; Schreiner, *Romans*, 64–68, believe that the active element in the concept of God's righteousness implies not only that God saves believers but begins to transform them so that they become righteous. Although Paul does use righteousness language to describe the new life of the believer in chapter 6 (vv. 7, 13, 16, 18, 19, 20), he does not derive the righteousness of the believer either from God's saving righteousness or from the righteousness that God gives as a free gift. Cf. Moo, *Romans*, 74–75.

35. Chrysostom, *Romans*, 30; Luther, *Romans*, 151–52; Philip Melanchthon, *Commentary on Romans*, trans. Fred Kramer (St. Louis: Concordia, 1992; orig. Latin ed. 1540), 70; Cranfield, *Romans*, 1:97–99.

36. As N. T. Wright says, Paul writes "symphonically, hinting at themes yet to be stated in full" (*Justification: God's Plan and Paul's Vision* [Downers Grove, IL: InterVarsity Press, 2009], 181). See also Frank Thielman, "God's Righteousness as God's Fairness in Romans 1:17: An Ancient Perspective on a Significant Phrase," *JETS* 54 (2011): 35–48.

how the gospel is God's saving power for everyone who believes.[37]

Paul next says that the righteousness of God is revealed "from faith to faith." This expression is also ambiguous. A number of interpreters believe that it is simply an emphatic way of saying that the righteousness of God is revealed by faith alone or, as the NIV puts it, "by faith from first to last" (cf. REB: "Beginning in faith and ending in faith").[38] The Greek idiom "from (ἐκ) X to (εἰς) X," however, where X represents the same term is relatively common and does not ever seem to mean "emphatically X."[39] Instead, the idiom has a distributive quality, just as "from X to X" has in English. "From sea to sea" (ἐκ θαλάττης εἰς θάλατταν) means from one sea to another. "From treachery to treachery" (ἐκ προδοσίας εἰς προδοσίαν) means from one act of treachery to another act of treachery. "From strength to strength" (ἐκ δυνάμεως εἰς δύναμιν) means from one level of strength to another. "From death to death" (ἐκ θανάτου εἰς θάνατον) and "from life to life" (ἐκ ζωῆς εἰς ζωήν) probably mean from a source of death to an instance of death and from a source of life to an instance of life.[40]

Here, then, "from faith to faith" (ἐκ πίστεως εἰς πίστιν) likely refers to the movement of faith from one time to another (from faith in the former era to faith in the new era) or from one person to another (from the faith of one to the faith of another).[41] Since Paul's emphasis in the immediate context lies on the link between a person's faith and that person's righteousness regardless of their social status, the phrase probably refers to the faith that every righteous person has in common with every other righteous person. The righteousness of God is revealed, then, wherever faith in the gospel is found.[42]

Paul concludes his thesis statement with a supporting quotation from Scripture that lends its authority to the connection he has just made between righteousness, the gospel, and faith. The principle that the righteousness of God is powerful enough to save wherever faith in the gospel is found, Paul now says, is consistent with (καθώς) the witness of Scripture.[43] The Scripture to which he refers is Habakkuk 2:4, also quoted in Galatians 3:11 in support of the link between righteousness and faith, but with the added, polemical thought that "no one is justified before God by the law." In neither place does Paul follow exactly the text of any known form of Habakkuk 2:4. Every other independent witness to this text from antiquity has a personal pronoun in the phrase so that it refers either to God's faithfulness, or to the faithfulness of the righteous one, or to God's righteous one (who is faithful).[44] Paul, then, must have known the text in a form that had

37. Cf. Sanday and Headlam, *Romans*, 24–25.

38. See, e.g., Barrett, *Romans*, 31.

39. Charles L. Quarles, "From Faith to Faith: A Fresh Examination of the Prepositional Series in Romans 1:17," *NovT* 45 (2003): 5–13.

40. These occurrences of the idiom are, respectively, from Plutarch, *Alcibiades* 30.1.1; *Galba* 14.2; Ps 83:8 LXX (84:7 Eng.; 84:8 Heb.); and 2 Cor 2:16 (both) and are discussed fully in Quarles, "From Faith to Faith," 6–13.

41. For the first interpretation, see Origen, *Romans, Books 1–5*, 87; Theodoret of Cyrus, *Letters of St. Paul*, 1:50; Chrysostom, *Romans*, 30; Quarles, "From Faith to Faith," 18–21. For the second interpretation, understanding the first occurrence of faith as a reference to God and the second as a reference to the believer, see Ambrosiaster, *Romans*, 9; Dunn, *Romans 1–8*, 43–44; Wright, "Romans," 425. Luther (*Romans*, 153), Calvin (*Romans*, 28), and Melanchthon (*Romans*, 70–71) thought the phrase referred to degrees of faith.

42. Cf. Pelagius, *Romans*, 63.

43. Cf. the use of the same introductory formula for Scripture in, for example, 2 Kgs 14:6; 23:21 LXX; Tob 1:6; Mark 1:2; Acts 7:42; Rom 2:24; 3:4, 10; 4:17; 8:36; 9:13, 33; 10:15; 11:8, 26; 15:3, 9, 21.

44. See, respectively, (1) the MT (although this is disputed) and the LXX (manuscripts S, B, Q, V, and W*); (2) Heb 10:38, 1QpHab 7.17–8.3, and 8ḤevXIIgr 17.29–30; and (3) the LXX (manuscripts A and C). Thorough discussions of this evidence appear in Moo (*Romans*, 76–77n65) and Fitzmyer (*Romans*, 264–65).

a personal pronoun. By dropping it, he focused attention on the terms "righteous," "faith," and "shall live."[45]

It is unclear whether the phrase "by faith" (ἐκ πίστεως) modifies "the one who is righteous" (ὁ . . . δίκαιος) or "will live" (ζήσεται). Does Paul want to emphasize that righteousness comes by faith or that faith is the path to life?[46] From the perspective of the syntax, it seems more likely that "by faith" modifies the verb "will live." Some argue that there is no doubt that the corresponding phrase in the Hebrew text of Habakkuk 2:4 means this and that had Paul meant "the one who is righteous by faith shall live" he would have put the prepositional phrase between the article and its adjective (ὁ δὲ ἐκ πίστεως δίκαιος ζήσεται). From the perspective of the letter's overall argument, however, Paul's emphasis lies on how righteousness comes to those who have faith.[47] In his next use of righteousness language and faith language together (3:21–26) the verb "live" does not appear, and all the emphasis falls on "the righteousness of God through faith in Jesus Christ to all who believe" (3:22; cf. 3:26).

The problem probably arose because Paul made his point using a quotation. He clearly felt free to modify Habakkuk 2:4 to some extent to bring out the point he wanted to make, and so he left out the personal pronoun; yet, he was unwilling to take the more drastic step of rearranging the prepositional phrase.[48] Even so, his emphasis lies on the connection between faith and righteousness, a connection that he has just mentioned in 1:17c and will explain in greater detail in the climactic paragraph of 3:21–26.[49] Faith in God's provision of Christ's atoning death as the means for dealing with human sin brings righteousness to the believer, and this righteousness allows the believer to live.

What does it mean to say that the believer "will live"? It means, first, that he or she will escape the wrath of God on the final day and instead have "eternal life" (2:5–8; 5:17–18, 21; 6:22–23; 11:15). It means, second, that he or she is united to the crucified and risen Christ, is indwelt by the Spirit, and is therefore able to "live" in the present in a way that anticipates to some extent this future eternal life with God (6:2, 4, 10–11, 13, 22; 8:2, 6, 10, 13).

IN DEPTH: Righteousness Language in Romans

Romans contains the highest concentration of righteousness language in the Pauline corpus. The words "righteousness" (δικαιοσύνη), "justify" (δικαιόω), "righteous" or "just" (δίκαιος), "righteous requirement" (δικαίωμα), "justification" (δικαίωσις), and "righteous judgment" (δικαιοκρισία) appear a total of sixty-four times in the letter, but only forty-nine times in the other Pauline letters combined. Clearly, to understand Romans one must understand how Paul uses these terms.

45. Eduard Lohse, *Die Brief an die Römer*, KEK (Göttingen: Vandenhoeck & Ruprecht, 2003), 82.

46. See, on one side, e.g., the ESV, NRSV, and Fitzmyer, *Romans*, 265, and, on the other side, NAB, REB, and Cranfield, *Romans* 1:101–2.

47. Francis Watson, "By Faith (of Christ): An Exegetical Dilemma and Its Scriptural Solution," in *The Faith of Jesus Christ: Exegetical, Biblical, and Theological Studies*, ed. Michael F. Bird and Preston M. Sprinkle (Milton Keynes: Paternoster, 2009), 154–62.

48. He also kept the lightly adversative conjunction "but" (δέ), although it plays no role in the flow of his own syntax.

49. Cf. his use of Gen 15:6 in the same way in Rom 4:3, 22.

The meaning of this language, however, is hotly disputed. Human rebellion against God means that people are unrighteous, and to have peace with God they need to be righteous—this much is uncontroversial. But what does God do to provide them with righteousness? Does he "impute" righteousness to them by giving them something that is alien to them when he gives it and remains alien to them throughout their natural lives?[50] Does he give them a righteous status?[51] Does he "make" them righteous by beginning a process in them that will eventually result in righteousness of character?[52] Does he give them both a status of righteousness and a transforming power?[53] Does he both call people into a relationship with himself and sustain them in that relationship?[54] Does he both acquit and vindicate them?[55] Does he declare that they are presently within God's family, something that he will ratify on the final day based on the way they have lived in the meantime?[56]

In the same way, no one disputes that God is also connected with righteousness in a positive sense in Romans, but when Paul speaks of "the righteousness of God" in his summary of the gospel (1:17) what does he mean?[57] He might be saying that (1) God is himself righteous, or that (2) God engages in righteous activity, or that (3) God gives righteousness to people, or (4) some combination of these.[58] If, as many interpreters believe, the phrase means that God engages in righteous activity, is the activity righteous because it is "right" according to a particular standard in a forensic context,[59] or is it right from the perspective of loyalty to one's relationship to another, particularly to God's covenant relationship with Israel?[60]

Sorting all this out in detail is impossible within the pages of a relatively concise commentary, but it is helpful at the beginning to grasp the basic parameters of the language and to summarize the findings of the more detailed exegesis that follows.[61] We can do this in three steps.

50. Luther, *Romans*, 151–52, 257, 259–60.

51. Cranfield, *Romans*, 1:97–99.

52. *TLNT* 1:336.

53. Käsemann, *Romans*, 24–30.

54. James D. G. Dunn, *The Theology of Paul the Apostle* (Grand Rapids: Eerdmans, 1998), 344.

55. Mark A. Seifrid, "Paul's Use of Righteousness Language against Its Hellenistic Background," in *The Paradoxes of Paul*, vol. 2 of *Justification and Variegated Nomism*, ed. D. A. Carson, Peter T. O'Brien, and Mark A. Seifrid (Grand Rapids: Eerdmans, 2004), 52–53.

56. N. T. Wright, *Paul: In Fresh Perspective* (Minneapolis: Fortress, 2005), 57, 111–12, 121–22, 148, 158–60; idem, *Justification*, 90–92.

57. Cf. 3:5, 21, 22, 25, 26; 10:3.

58. See (1) Origen, *Romans, Books 1–5*, 87, and Pelagius, *Romans*, 63; (2) Stephen Westerholm, *Perspectives Old and New on Paul: The "Lutheran" Paul and His Critics* (Grand Rapids: Eerdmans, 2004), 285–86, 293; (3) Ambrosiaster, *Romans*, 9, and Chrysostom, *Romans*, 30; and (4) Sanday and Headlam, *Romans*, 24–25; Cranfield, *Romans*, 1:97–99; and Moo, *Romans*, 83.

59. Mark A. Seifrid, *Christ, Our Righteousness: Paul's Theology of Justification*, NSBT (Leicester: Apollos, 2000), 36–47.

60. Dunn, *Romans 1–8*, 41; cf. Wright, "Romans," 403; idem, *Fresh Perspective*, 25, 29–30, 37, 53, 77, 96, 119; idem, *Justification*, 178, where Wright adds the idea that the phrase also implies God's establishment of justice within his creation.

61. See also Thielman, "God's Righteousness as God's Fairness," 35–48.

First, it seems important to remember that Paul was writing to an audience that was mostly unknown to him in a large city where Greek was widely spoken and understood but was not the native tongue. In this situation Paul probably did not assign to his righteousness language eccentric meanings. He may have used this language in surprising ways, but he probably did not use it in ways that were at the same time unusual and subtle. In the Greco-Roman world, "righteousness" was

> the state that distributes to each person according to what is deserved; the state on account of which its possessor chooses what appears to him to be just; the state underlying a law abiding way of life; social equality; the state of obedience to the laws.[62]

One could be law-abiding without being fair, but the "just" (δίκαιος) person was both.[63] In the late-fifties AD, possibly within months of the time Paul wrote Romans, Nero seems to have been minting coins in Alexandria that depicted the goddess known in the Latin-speaking world as *AEQUITAS* ("Equity," "Fairness") under the Greek label ΔΙΚΑΙΟΣΥΝΗ ("Righteousness"). She stands upright, arm outstretched, with evenly balanced scales dangling from her right hand.[64] Average people, who slapped coins like this down on a counter to buy their food and drink or dug into their coin purses to pay their rent, probably understood Paul's concept of "righteousness" first in terms of "fairness."

It was particularly important for judges to be just and fair. According to Aristotle, "to go to the judge is to go to justice; for the nature of the judge is to be a sort of animate justice."[65] In legal contexts, then, to "justify" meant to deem something to be right, to give someone justice, or to render a legal decision.[66] When applied to people, this could sometimes have a positive sense, as it does

62. Pseudo-Plato, *Definitions* 411d–e, on "justice" (δικαιοσύνη) (Cooper, *Complete Works*, 1679). Closer to the time of Paul, see Arius Didymus, *Epitome of Stoic Ethics*, ed. Arthur J. Pomeroy, Texts and Translations 44; Greco-Roman Series 14 (Atlanta: SBL Press, 1999), 50–51. Paul was no philosopher, but he would have been aware that this understanding of "justice" was widespread.

63. Aristotle, *Nicomachean Ethics* 1129a 33–34. What counted as "fair" or "deserved" was culturally determined. "All men agree that what is just in distribution must be according to merit in some sense, though they do not all specify the same sort of merit but democrats identify it with the status of freeman, supporters of oligarchy with wealth (or with noble birth), and the supporters of aristocracy with excellence" (Aristotle, *Nicomachean Ethics*, trans. W. D. Ross [London: Oxford University Press, 1925], 1131a 26–29).

64. The image continued to appear until the reign of Diocletian, often with the explanatory Greek label. On all this, see Wilhelm Koehler, *Personifikationen abstrakter Begriffe auf römischen Münzen*, part 1 (Königsberg, Prussia: Hartungsche Buchdruckerei, 1910), 17; J. G. Milne, *Catalogue of Alexandrian Coins* (Oxford: University of Oxford, Ashmolean Museum, 1971), xxxi; and Thielman, "God's Righteousness as God's Fairness," 42.

65. *Nicomachean Ethics* 1132a 20–22 (Ross).

66. See MM 162–63, s.v. δικαιόω, who point out that in legal contexts "the word was good vernacular" in the first-century AD. Dionysius of Halicarnassus (*Ant. rom.* 10.1) describes how in ancient times Roman law was made by kings on a case-by-case basis, "and what was declared just by them, this was law" (καὶ τὸ δικαιωθὲν ὑπ᾽ ἐκείνων τοῦτο νόμος ἦν; transl. mine).

when the historian Polybius says that people can learn from well-written historical accounts who is "likely to pity us, feel indignation at our wrongs, and defend our cause [τὸν δικαιώσοντα]" (3.31.9).[67] Sometimes it could have the negative sense of punishing someone for a crime, as it does when Josephus speaks of those "condemned [δεδικαιωμένων] for pulling down the golden eagle" that Herod the Great had affixed to the Jerusalem temple (*Ant.* 17.206 [R. Marcus and A. Wikgren, LCL]).[68]

Second, Paul also assumes throughout Romans that at least some of his readers are familiar with the Jewish Scriptures, and many of his readers would have been familiar with the use of righteousness language in the LXX.[69] The LXX use of these terms overlaps largely with their use in other Greek literature, but there is a stronger emphasis on the active and positive use of the words "righteous" and "righteousness." The LXX often describes God as righteous because he takes up the cause of people, particularly the poor and oppressed, including Israel.[70]

Two examples, easily multiplied, illustrate this emphasis. In Isaiah the Lord's unjustly treated Servant confidently announces:

> The Lord became my helper; therefore I was not disgraced, but I have set my face like solid rock, and I realized that I would not be put to shame, because he who justified [ὁ δικαιώσας] me draws near. Who is the one who contends [ὁ κρινόμενος] with me? (Isa 50:7–8 LXX; cf. Rom 8:33–34).

Similarly, the psalmist praises God for rescuing his people:

> The Lord made known his deliverance [σωτήριον]; before the nations he revealed his righteousness [δικαιοσύνην]. He remembered his mercy to Iakob and his truth to the house of Israel. All the ends of the earth saw the deliverance [σωτήριον] of our God. (Ps 97:2–3 LXX [98:2–3 Eng.]; cf. Rom 1:16–17)

Even here, however, the common Greco-Roman understanding of righteousness as impartial legal justice is not far away. Isaiah's Servant did nothing wrong, and God justifies him in court (Isa 50:8–9). The psalmist similarly concludes his celebration of God's saving righteousness with the statement that God "will judge the world with righteousness [ἐν δικαιοσύνῃ] and peoples with uprightness [ἐν εὐθύτητι]" (Ps 97:9 LXX [98:9 Eng.]).[71]

67. *The Histories of Polybius*, trans. Evelyn S. Shuckburgh, 2 vols. (London: Macmillan, 1889), 1:192.

68. *Josephus*, trans. Henry St. J. Thackeray et al., 13 vols., LCL (Cambridge: Harvard University Press, 1926–65). See LSJ 429, s.v. δικαιόω III.1; G. Schrenk, "δίκη, κτλ.," *TDNT* 2:211; and Seifrid, "Paul's Use of Righteousness Language," 45–49.

69. Peter Stuhlmacher, *Reconciliation, Law, and Righteousness: Essays in Biblical Theology*, trans. Everett R. Kalin (Philadelphia: Fortress, 1986), 92n18.

70. Schrenk, "δίκη, κτλ.," *TDNT* 2:195–96, 212–14.

71. The term translated "uprightness" here (εὐθύτης) typically meant "straightness" (LSJ 716, s.v. εὐθύτης) and could be used metaphorically in legal contexts to refer, for example, to "the supreme righteousness [εὐθύτητα] of the divine and

Third, Paul's use of righteousness language in Romans falls within these parameters, with a surprising twist that stands at the center of the gospel.[72] The first use of righteousness terminology comes in the letter's thesis statement in 1:16–17 where Paul defines the gospel as "the righteousness of God" (1:17). As interpreters have often noticed, the context of the phrase shows that Paul intended to connect it with God's saving activity: the gospel powerfully saves everyone who believes (1:16) because the righteousness of God is revealed in the gospel (1:17).

Although it is less commonly noticed, the context also emphasizes God's impartiality and fairness, notions firmly connected with righteousness in both the Greco-Roman world generally and in the LXX. Just prior to speaking of "the righteousness of God" Paul has emphasized that the gospel comes equally to everyone whether Greek, barbarian, or Jew (1:15–16). It is significant that Origen, in the earliest extant commentary on Romans, took the phrase in 1:17 as a reference to God's fairness based on this context:

> The righteousness of God is revealed in the gospel through the fact that with respect to salvation no one is excluded whether he should come as a Jew, Greek or barbarian. For the Savior says equally to all, "Come to me, all you that labor and are burdened."[73]

This mid-third century Greek speaker, then, understood "the righteousness of God" to be God's impartially distributed saving power.[74] This tilts the scales heavily in favor of interpreting the phrase this way.

As the argument of Romans unfolds in the next two chapters, the understanding of God as a righteous God in the sense that he is just and fair receives repeated emphasis. God's "righteous decree" that the wicked deserve to die (1:32; cf. 2:26) is something everyone can perceive. On the day when he pours out his wrath on the wicked, he will do so after rendering a "righteous judgment" (2:5) that is tempered by forbearance, kindness, and patience (2:4) and yet is fairly applied to each person according to his or her deeds (2:6; cf. Prov 24:12; Ps 62:12). God does this without taking the privileges of ethnicity or education into account (2:13). His justice, then, will be perfect: everyone else might lie, but God's judgments are true and just (3:4–5).

This is exactly the picture of God that Paul's readers would expect him to

blessed law" (Dio Chrysostom, *Borysthenic Discourse* [*Or.* 36] 23 [Cohoon and Crosby, LCL]).

72. Cf. Westerholm, *Perspectives Old and New on Paul*, 261–96.

73. Origen, *Romans, Books 1–5*, 87.

74. Origen's commentary on Romans is preserved mainly in Rufinus's early fifth-century Latin abridgment, but there is no reason to think that Rufinus tampered with Origen's meaning at this point.

uphold. Those familiar with the LXX might remember Solomon's prayer of dedication for the temple. It assumes that as a just judge God's business was "condemning the guilty by bringing their conduct on their own head, and vindicating the righteous [LXX: τοῦ δικαιῶσαι δίκαιον] by rewarding them according to their righteousness [δικαιοσύνην]" (1 Kgs 8:32 NRSV; cf. 2 Chr 6:23; Prov 17:15; 18:5; 24:24; Isa 5:23).[75] Similarly, people in the Greco-Roman world assumed that God or the gods were just and were unwavering in their commitment to justice.[76] "If the gods changed their judgments and left unchastised one whom they decided to chastise," said one early second-century AD philosopher, "they could neither govern the world well and justly [δικαίως] nor produce a reasonable justification for their change of mind."[77] In Romans 1:16–3:20 Paul operates within the same basic understanding of the relationship between God and justice.

At the same time, however, Paul has described every human being as wicked and therefore unable to survive God's judgment on the final day. Everyone, both Jew and Greek, is under sin (3:9), and no one is righteous, not even one (3:10; cf. 3:20; Ps 142:2 LXX [143:2 Eng., Heb.]). If Paul's righteousness language were to continue to operate within the most common uses of that language in the Greco-Roman world, therefore, it is quite difficult to see how anything he says up to 3:20 could qualify as "good news." The idea that God is a just God is small comfort to the wicked that have fallen afoul of his justice, and Paul argues that this includes everyone.

The surprising twist comes in 3:21–26 where Paul suddenly uses righteousness language in a puzzling way and then resolves the puzzle by reference to the atoning death of Christ.[78] The puzzle begins in 3:21 where Paul speaks of the appearance of "the righteousness of God apart from the law." What will the standard of righteousness be if it is not keeping the law of God (cf. 2:13)? Paul answers this question immediately when he says "the righteousness of God" comes "through faith in Jesus Christ" (3:22). Rather than the law, the standard of

75. Westerholm, *Perspectives Old and New on Paul*, 265–66. Thanks to F. Gerald Downing ("Justification or Acquittal? A Critical Examination of Judicial Verdicts in Paul's Literary and Actual Contexts," *CBQ* 74 [2012]: 305) for bringing many of these references to my attention.

76. See, respectively, Aelius Theon, *Progymnasmata* 126.23 ("because he is just, the God would not permit those who reverence him to be unprovided for" [James R. Butts, "The Progymnasmata of Theon: A New Text with Translation and Commentary" (PhD diss., The Claremont Graduate School, 1987), 537]) and Appian, *Civil Wars* 3.2.13 (the gods will help anyone who prosecutes Caesar's murder because "of the justice of his [the prosecutor's] cause" [Appian, *Roman History: The Civil Wars, Books 1–3.26*, trans. Horace White, LCL 4 (London: William Heinemann, 1913)]).

77. Ilaria Ramelli, *Hierocles the Stoic: Elements of Ethics, Fragments, and Excerpts*, trans. David Konstan, Writings from the Greco-Roman World 28 (Atlanta: SBL Press, 2009), 65.

78. For the perspective on Paul's righteousness language developed here, see Westerholm, *Perspectives Old and New on Paul*, 273–84.

righteousness, then, is reliance on Jesus Christ. Paul explains that this unusual form of righteousness entails the justification of the sinner (3:24). Up to this point in the argument, Paul has used righteousness language, including the verb "justify" (δικαιόω), to refer to doing what is right (3:5, 10) and to the declaration that those who do what is right are righteous people (2:13; 3:4, 20).[79] Now, suddenly, Paul says that God declares sinful people to be righteous people. Paul had just affirmed that God cannot lie (3:4), so how can he say that God's righteousness is displayed in declaring unrighteous people to be righteous? Why does that not portray God as a liar?

Paul reveals that he knows what a strange set of statements he has made in 3:21–24 by his emphatic use of terms for grace—those who have sinned and fallen short of God's glory are "justified freely by his grace" (v. 24; δικαιούμενοι δωρεὰν τῇ αὐτοῦ χάριτι). It is only because God is such an abundantly gracious God that he is willing to declare righteous those who are unrighteous (cf. 5:17).[80]

This focus on God's grace in the context of Paul's definition of God's righteousness also shows that Paul is using the verb "justify" or "declare righteous" (δικαιόω) in a specific sense that is slightly different from the way he used that verb in 2:13. In 2:13 God will declare those who do the law to be righteous because they are innocent of wrongdoing and therefore do not deserve punishment. In 3:24 those whom God declares righteous are guilty of wrongdoing and deserve punishment but will not receive what they deserve. The two instances of justification have this in common: both lead to an escape from punishment. In 2:13, then, justification means a correct declaration of innocence and release from punishment. In 3:24, justification means only release from punishment. God is not pretending that unrighteous people are actually righteous when he justifies sinners in 3:24. Rather, he is declaring only that they will not receive the punishment they deserve.[81]

This is the place where the death of Christ figures so importantly into Paul's thinking on justification. God can only be just himself and at the same time "justify" the ungodly because of the sacrificial death of Christ (3:25–26). In his death

79. That the verb "justify" (δικαιόω) can refer to declaring someone to be in the right or vindicating someone seems clear from, e.g., Luke 7:29, 35; 16:15.

80. Cf. Westerholm, *Perspectives Old and New on Paul*, 280–81.

81. "'Justifying the wicked' is refusing to authorize and execute the expected punishment; it is not uttering a false verdict of 'not guilty'" (Downing, "Justification as Acquittal?," 303). Downing argues that when justification language is used in ancient courtroom settings it does not refer to "acquittal" in the way that term is used in legal settings in the modern Western world. It simply refers to releasing someone from punishment. His argument is largely convincing. It is not clear, however, that Paul's justification language is always juridical, even when he is talking about the final judgment. For example, God can be declared righteous or his judgments and actions vindicated (e.g., Luke 7:29; Rom 3:4). In Rom 2:13, then, God is probably both declaring doers of the law to be just and releasing them from punishment, whereas in 3:24 God only releases sinners from punishment.

Christ was the metaphorical "mercy seat" (ἱλαστήριον), the place God had provided for meeting with the representative of his people (Exod 25:22) and atoning for the sins of his people on the Day of Atonement (Lev 16:2, 13–15). Paul does not say precisely how Christ's death was a "proof" of God's righteousness (3:25). Paul could have reasonably understood the sacrificial goats in the Day of Atonement ritual, however, as substitutionary sacrifices. He also develops the notion of Christ's substitutionary death for the ungodly in 5:6–8. It is very likely, then, that he believed the substitutionary nature of Christ's death allowed God to remain just even as he withheld punishment from the sinful.[82]

God's righteousness is also displayed in this arrangement because it shows him to be impartial and fair. He holds all accountable to the same standard and finds them guilty of violating that standard (3:19). In doing this, he makes no distinction based on social privilege but treats people alike simply because of their humanity (3:9, 20). The justifying effects of Christ's atoning death are similarly available through faith and to "all who believe," without "distinction" (3:22). This is how a "human being," any human being, is justified (3:28). Greek and barbarian, cultured and rustic, Jew and gentile can all receive the good news and experience peace with God through "the abundance of grace and the gift of righteousness" (5:17) that God has provided them in the death of Christ (1:14–17; 3:22, 29–30; 4:11; 9:30–33; 10:4, 10–13).

God's righteousness, then, encompasses his honesty and impartiality as a judge but also his saving power in the sense that the LXX often uses the concept. God rescues his people, now viewed not as Israel but as everyone who believes the gospel, through the atoning death of Christ. The thought is similar to the idea expressed in Psalm 65:

> O you who hear prayer, to you shall all flesh come. When iniquities prevail against me, you atone for our transgressions. . . . By awesome deeds you answer us with righteousness, O God of our salvation, the hope of all the ends of the earth and of the farthest seas. (65:2–3, 5)

Since "righteousness" (δικαιοσύνη) referred to justice, fairness, and equity, and when applied to God could refer to his saving power, it is not surprising that Paul could also use the term to refer to the upright behavior that should characterize believers (6:13, 16–20). Nor is it surprising that he could mingle this idea with references to the saving power of God.

He does this first in 5:21 by personifying "grace" and saying that it reigns

82. On the substitutionary nature of at least the live goat in Lev 16:20–22, see Simon Gathercole, *Defending Substitution: An Essay on Atonement in Paul* (Grand Rapids: Baker, 2015), 37, and on substitution in Rom 5:6–8, see idem, 85–107.

"through righteousness for eternal life."[83] "Righteousness" (δικαιοσύνη) here is identical to the "life-giving justification [δικαίωσις]" that came through Christ's death in 5:18 (cf. 10:4, 10). The abundant grace of God, seen most clearly in his justification of sinners, is therefore a power that reigns over those who have received it. When Paul goes on to speak of "righteousness" as a power to which believers submit their abilities, it is certainly a personified ethical quality that stands opposed to unrighteousness, sin, uncleanness, and lawlessness and that leads to sanctification (6:13, 19), but it is also a power, similar to God's personified grace in 5:21.

This does not mean that "righteousness" in 6:13, 16–20 is identical to "justification" (as it was in 5:21) or emerges organically out of justification. An initial justification does not plant a seed of righteousness that begins a process whereby the justified person becomes increasingly righteous.[84] That justification is a juridical decision rather than a transformative process is clear from Paul's willingness to describe it as something that has happened in the past: believers have "been justified" (δικαιωθέντες) by faith and by Christ's sacrificial blood (5:1, 9; cf. 8:30). Moreover, if justification had started a process of becoming righteous, there would have been no need to follow the statement that grace reigns through "righteousness" (5:21) with the rhetorical question, "Should we remain in sin that grace might increase?" (6:1). If Paul had intended to say in 5:21 that God's grace was making believers more righteous in the ethical sense, it would be obvious that once they believed the gospel of justification they would not remain in sin.

So, the righteousness of Romans 6, although a powerful work of God in the believer's life, is nevertheless a *consequence* of God's justifying grace. Those who are graciously freed from the penalty of "death" they deserve (1:32) begin immediately to live the "life" justification makes possible (5:18; 8:10), and living this new life entails submitting to God (cf. 8:4, 7–9) or, as Paul puts it in 6:13, offering one's self to God, and one's members, as weapons to "righteousness."[85] The first step in the reign of grace in the life of any believer, then, comes with the judicial release of that believer from punishment ("justification" [δικαίωσις] in 5:18 or "righteousness" [δικαιοσύνη] in 5:21). Once that has happened, the reign of grace continues in that person's life as he or she submits to God and becomes increasingly more "righteous" in the ethical sense. This leads, in turn, to what Paul calls "sanctification" (6:19, 22).

83. Cf. Barclay, *Paul and the Gift*, 497: "The language of 'reigning' (βασιλεύω) figures grace as a counteracting power whose authority replaces that of sin; far from offering a license for sin, the Christ-gift establishes an alternative regime of power."

84. *TLNT* 1:336.

85. Cf. Käsemann, *Romans*, 177; K. Kertelge, "δικαιοσύνη," *EDNT* 1:327; Schreiner, *Romans*, 324, 331; Brendan Byrne, *Romans*, 2nd ed., SP 6 (Collegeville, MN: Liturgical Press, 2007), 194; Barclay, *Paul and the Gift*, 494–500.

Theology in Application

In his thanksgiving and intercessory prayer report Paul both emphasizes the importance of mutual encouragement among Christians and summarizes the gospel that forms the basis for this mutual encouragement. His emphasis on mutual encouragement urges believers to see their faith not merely in terms of their own relationship to God but also as a means of encouraging other Christians to remain faithful to the gospel. His summary of the gospel particularly emphasizes that God's saving power is for all who believe, apart from any worth that they have in themselves.

Faithfulness to the Gospel as an Encouragement to Other Christians

In Paul's thanksgiving prayer report to his Roman readers in 1:8, he expresses gratitude that people everywhere know about the Roman Christians' faith (cf. 16:19). That this is not mere flattery is clear from the way this theme emerges later in the letter and from time to time elsewhere in Paul's correspondence. Later in the letter he expresses thanks to Prisca and Aquila, coworkers who are now among the readers of this letter in Rome, for risking their necks for him and for their work among the gentile churches (16:3–4). He was also clearly thankful for the hard work of Tryphaena, Tryphosa, and Persis (16:12) and to Rufus's mother for being a mother to him (16:13). Writing to the Thessalonian Christians several years earlier, he had expressed his gratitude that their "faith in God has become known everywhere" (1 Thess 1:8 NIV). The conversion of the Thessalonians from worshiping idols to serving the "living and true God" and to trusting that his Son Jesus would rescue them from God's wrath was well known to Christians in Macedonia and Achaia and served as an example to them (1 Thess 1:7, 9–10).

Paul's gratitude for the Roman Christians' faith, then, is a reminder to all believers of two important truths. First, when Christians faithfully persevere in their commitment to the gospel in spite of hardship (1 Thess 2:14; Phil 3:17; 4:9; 2 Tim 1:8; 2:3; 3:10–15) or give practical help to others even when it is personally costly (2 Cor 8:1–6) or negotiate their way through the godless landscape of a pagan culture in a way that manages to bear witness to the gospel (1 Cor 10:31–11:1), the reverberations of their faithfulness give it a value far beyond each of these particular situations. Such expressions of one's faith serve as examples to others to be faithful too.

Second, Christians who seek to be faithful can learn how to be faithful from watching others whose faithfulness is exemplary. Having relationships with other, more mature Christians in the church and learning the accounts of faithful Christians of the past are necessary components of Christian discipleship. Like Paul, all Christians should cultivate a thankful spirit for the faith of other believers.

The Socially Unifying Implications of Justification by Faith

This passage also summarizes the gospel, especially in the pithy thesis statement of 1:16–17. In the thirty-seven words that comprise this summary, the verb "believe" (πιστεύω) appears once and the noun "faith" (πίστις) appears three times. Salvation, Paul insists in 1:16, is a matter of faith in the gospel. As he will imply in 1:17 and says explicitly later, this means faith that the death of Jesus has atoned for human sin, making it possible for God to remain just and, at the same time, to release from their just punishment those who have faith in him (3:22, 25, 26).

A critical consequence flows from this way of understanding salvation. If salvation comes to the one who believes, then it is not earned by one's behavior or awarded to one's social group; it is, rather, a free gift of a gracious God (3:24; 4:4, 16; 11:5–6). Salvation comes entirely from God to those who rely on God for it. Wherever the church deviates from the principle that a right standing with God is a free gift of God's grace, received by faith, it deviates from what Paul elsewhere calls "the truth of the gospel" (Gal 2:14).

This emphasis, moreover, persists throughout the letter as Paul unfolds his thesis statement (2:9–10, 28–29; 3:9, 22–24, 29–30; 4:9, 12, 16–17; 10:12; 11:11–12, 25–27, 32) and bears important practical fruit toward the letter's conclusion when Paul uses it to try to ease social tensions among the Roman Christians (11:13, 18; 14:1–15:13). The gospel affirms the fundamental unity of human beings across the ever-present dividing lines that sinful human beings impose on their societies.

The gospel is basically about the relationship between God and human beings as human beings rather than the relationship between God and Israel, God and Rome, God and slaves, God and free people, God and men, God and women. It certainly has something to say about and to each of these groups, but what it says flows from the principle that they all have something fundamental in common with one another. Everyone in those groups is God's human creature, and since God is righteous he treats them as equals.[86] They all share with their common ancestor Adam the plight of rebellion against their Creator (5:12–19; cf. 1 Cor 15:22). Moreover, as God's promise to Abraham had already demonstrated (Gen 15:5–6; 17:5; cf. 22:18), God's gracious answer to this common plight is available to all, through faith, regardless of the social group to which they belong (Rom 4:16–25; cf. Gal 3:5–9, 14, 16, 18, 29). Union with Christ and the presence of the Spirit dissolve barriers between human beings (1 Cor 12:13; Gal 3:28; Col 3:11), and Christians are part of a "new creation" where "neither circumcision nor uncircumcision means anything" (Gal 6:15; cf. Col 3:10; Eph 2:15; 4:13, 24).

86. This emphasis on the essential unity of humanity cuts against the grain of much social theory in antiquity. For the common use of ethnic stereotyping and protoracism in antiquity to support ideas of the superiority of one people over another, see Isaac, *Invention of Racism*.

The church of every age needs to be attentive to this element of the gospel. When social and ethnic divisions creep into the church, they are symptoms of a profound misunderstanding of who human beings are before God and of God's own character. Laying claim to some group privilege either implies that one's own group deserves God's favor more than another group, which is false, or that God is unjust and will show favoritism to one's group despite its faults, which is also false (Rom 2:23; 11:18).

Human beings are, without exception, sinful (3:9), and God is, without fail, impartial (2:11). If anyone survives "the day of the wrath and the revelation of the righteous judgment of God" (2:5), it will be because God has found a way to justify the ungodly and to remain just at the same time, not because God has found something deserving in one ethnic or social group or because he has suspended his righteousness. "What do you have that you did not receive?" Paul asks the divided Corinthian church, "and if you received it, why do you boast as if it were not a gift?" (1 Cor 4:7 NRSV). A church divided along social and ethnic lines or one that refuses to welcome certain social and ethnic groups (Rom 14:1, 3; 15:7) is a church that has seriously misunderstood the gospel.

CHAPTER 3

Romans 1:18–32

Literary Context

In 1:18–32 Paul begins to unpack the dense thesis statement that concluded the letter's solemn and authoritative introduction (1:16–17). That thesis statement had summarized the gospel as the saving power of God for everyone who believes (1:16). The gospel can save those who believe, Paul said, because the righteousness of God is being revealed in it (1:17). Because the righteousness of God stands parallel to the saving power of God in this statement, we might think that God's righteousness and his saving power are virtually identical. God's righteousness is a broader concept than this, however, and Paul demonstrates another important element of it in 1:18–3:20.

God's righteousness includes the visitation of wrath on all who are impious and unrighteous, without regard to the cultural and ethnic context from which they come. We can only appreciate the aspect of his righteousness that leads to the salvation of everyone who believes if we also appreciate the aspect of his righteousness that leads to the condemnation of everyone who sins.

Paul explains this condemning element of God's righteousness in three steps in 1:18–3:20. First, in 1:18–32 he argues that God is fair to pour out his wrath on everyone who has rebelled against him because God has shown his immortality, power, and divinity through his creation and has reasonably expected that people would glorify and thank him for what he has made. Instead, however, they chose to worship the creation itself, and so God gave them over to the consequences of this disastrous choice. In anticipation of his second step, Paul has purposefully described human wickedness and God's just punishment of it in 1:18–32 in a way that will draw an imaginary, unbelieving Jewish dialogue partner into agreement with him.

Second, in 2:1–3:8 he turns to this imaginary dialogue partner and makes clear that he is not exempt from God's wrath. He might imagine himself to be free from the quintessentially gentile sins Paul has just described (especially idolatry and homosexuality) and he might think that his knowledge of the law and possession of circumcision will protect him from condemnation, but this is not true. God's righteousness demands that he judge human beings without regard to their cultural location: neither Jew nor Greek will escape his wrath if they have sinned.

Third, in 3:9–20 Paul makes clear for his dialogue partner that nothing he has said in 2:1–3:8 implies that anyone will escape God's wrath on the "day of wrath" (2:5). In fact, all have sinned. "There is no one righteous, not even one" (3:10). The righteousness of God, then, is not merely his saving power, but his fairness in judging people strictly according to what they deserve and without regard to their cultural or ethnic context. Viewed from this angle, God's righteousness can only mean that he must condemn every human being as a sinner.

All this sets the stage, however, for Paul's explanation in 3:21–26 of how God's righteousness is also his power for the salvation of all who believe. God's righteousness can mean both his fairness in condemning the sinner and his saving power on behalf of the sinner because of the atoning death of Christ. Those who trust in the sufficiency of Christ's death to atone for their sin have escaped punishment in God's court. Since this acquittal is by faith rather than by any obedience to or knowledge of the Jewish law, it cuts, like God's judgment, across ethnic lines and shows God to be righteous in his treatment of all human beings in the same way (3:27–30). God's righteousness, conceived as God's fairness, is preserved both through the atoning nature of Christ's death and through the availability of that atonement to everyone who believes, whether Jew or non-Jew.

Main Idea

When God punishes human rebellion against himself, he acts as a righteous judge both in deciding to punish human beings and in the way he executes the punishment. They cannot plead ignorance in their defense, since he holds them responsible for acting in accord with the truth about himself that he has clearly shown to them in creation. They also cannot plead that his punishment is too harsh, because he has handed them over to the consequences of their own choice to rebel against the truth he has revealed.

Translation

Romans 1:18–32

18a	Explanation	For **the wrath of God** **is revealed**
b	Source	from heaven
c	Disadvantage	against all the impiety and unrighteousness
d	Source	of human beings
e	Description	who stifle the truth
f	Sphere	in unrighteousness.
19a	Basis of 18a	For **what is knowable about God is visible**
b	Identification	to them,
c	Basis of 19a	for **God has made it visible**
d	Identification	to them
20a	Explanation of 19c	for **his unseen attributes are clearly seen**
b	Cause	because they are perceived
c	Means	through what is made
d	Time	from the time of the world's creation
e	Restatement	(that is, his eternal power and divinity)
f	Result	with the result that they are without excuse.
21a	Concession	For, although they knew God,
b	Basis of 20f	**they did not glorify or**
		thank him as God
c	Contrast	but **they were rendered futile**
d	Sphere	in their reasoning processes
e	Contrast	and **their foolish heart was darkened.**
22a	Concession	Claiming to be wise,
b	Assertion	**they became fools**
23a	Assertion	and **they exchanged the glory of the incorruptible God**
b	Contrast	for the likeness of the image of corruptible humanity and
c	List	birds and
d		quadrupeds and
e		reptiles.
24a	Result	Therefore, **God handed them over**
b	Simultaneous	in the lusts of their hearts
c	Object	to the uncleanness
d	Description	of the dishonoring of their bodies among themselves.

25a Basis **They exchanged** **the truth that came from God**
b Contrast for a lie

c Expansion and **revered and served** the creature rather than
d the Creator,
e Description who is blessed forever, amen.

26a Basis of 25a–c Because of this **God handed them over** to dishonorable passions

b Explanation of 26a for, the fact is, **their females exchanged** **their natural sexual role**
c Contrast for a sexual role contrary to nature.

27a Parallel And **males,** likewise,
b abandoned the natural sexual role of the female and
c Contrast **burned in their strong desire for one another,**
d Explanation males with males "accomplishing" what is obscene and
e receiving by way of return the recompense
f Sphere in themselves
g Explanation that was necessary ⮨
for their error.

h
28a And just as they did not deem it worthwhile to acknowledge God,
b Asssertion **God handed** **them** **over**
c Sphere to a worthless mind,
d to do things that are not fitting,
29a Description filled with all
List
[1] unrighteousness,
[2] cunning,
[3] greed,
[4] malice;
b Description full of
List
[5] envy,
[6] murder,
[7] strife,
[8] treachery,
[9] mean-spiritedness,
c Description, List [10] rumormongers,
30 [11] slanderers,
[12] God-detesting,
[13] bullies,
[14] arrogant,
[15] braggarts,
[16] contrivers of evil,
[17] disobedient to parents,
31 [18] senseless,
[19] faithless,
[20] heartless,
[21] ruthless.

Continued on next page.

Continued from previous page.

32a Concession		Although they know full well	the righteous decree of God
b Content			that those who practice such things are worthy of death,
c Assertion	**they not only**	**do them but also applaud those who practice them.**	

Structure

The beginning of 1:18–32 links the passage back to 1:17 and shows that the section is designed to explain the righteousness of God in terms of the wrath of God. Since God's righteousness implies his fairness and impartiality, it is essential for Paul to show that God's wrath toward the impiety and unrighteousness of human beings is fair, and the structure of 1:18–32 emphasizes that element of his wrath.

Paul organized the passage loosely, as the many different attempts to describe the details of its structure show.[1] It unfolds in four parts: a brief introduction (1:18), two main parts (1:19–23, 24–31), and a brief conclusion (1:32).[2] After the introduction (1:18), which announces the theme that the righteousness of God is revealed in the wrath of God, the first main part of the passage (1:19–23) focuses on *why* God reveals his wrath against human beings. This part explains that God had good reason for doing so because he had made the truth about himself clear to human beings, and they intentionally suppressed that truth.

Paul explains this point with a tightly reasoned series of subordinate clauses. He maintains that God can justly punish human beings for their impiety and unrighteousness "because" (διότι) the knowledge of God is visible to them (1:19). The knowledge of God is visible to them "for" (γάρ) God made it visible to them. God made it visible "for" (γάρ) it is obviously present in the world God made (1:20). God made knowledge of him obvious in the world "with the result that" (εἰς τό + infinitive) human beings have no excuse. They have no excuse "because" (διότι) they knew who God was and what he had done but failed to glorify and thank him, allowing their thinking instead to become pointless and their interior lives to become dark (1:21). Paul concludes the opening section by summarizing the result of this human refusal to acknowledge God: instead of worshiping the incorruptible God, they worshiped his corruptible creation. In other words, they became idolaters (1:22–23).

1. See the wide variety of approaches surveyed by Wiard Popkes, "Zum Aufbau und Charakter von Römer 1.18–32," *NTS* 28 (1982): 490–91.

2. Cf. Jewett, *Romans*, 149–50.

The second main part of the passage (1:24–31) focuses on *how* God has revealed his wrath against human beings, and the emphasis falls again on God's fairness. God hands people over to their idolatry (1:24, 26, 28), and he does this in response to the human exchange of worshiping the Creator for worshiping the creature (1:23, 25) or to the human failure to deem God worth knowing (1:28). God's abandonment of people to their sin, in other words, corresponds perfectly to their own choice to abandon him. The punishment is neither too harsh nor too mild but perfectly fits the nature of the crime.

The crime is serious, however, and so the punishment is certainly harsh. Devoid of the truth that God had revealed to them, human beings were left to their own foolish and confused thinking, and this in turn led to all manner of sexual (1:26–27) and social (1:29–31) mayhem. The rhetoric of this section is difficult to reproduce in English but contributes to a sense of evil run amok. Sin tumbles over sin with dizzying speed, and the human desire to rebel against God seems to be the only unifying principle of this otherwise chaotic activity. The assonance of repeated initial "a" and "as" sounds in 1:27 and 31, the popping "p" sounds in 1:29, and the skillful wordplays, for example, in choosing words for "envy" (φθόνου) and "murder" (φόνου) that differ from one another by only one letter in 1:29 all contribute to the speed, intensity, and horror of what Paul describes.[3] Three times the solemn phrase "God handed them over" (παρέδωκεν αὐτοὺς ὁ θεός) tolls like a bell above the cacophony of human wickedness (1:24, 26, 28).

The passage ends (1:32) with a summary statement intended to demonstrate the culpability of human rebellion against God, its extreme character, and the ultimate nature of God's penalty for it. Despite their knowledge that impiety and unrighteousness deserve to be punished with death, human beings not only engaged in them in all their horrendous variety (cf. 1:28–31) but gave their approval and encouragement to others who did so (1:32).

3. See Dunn, *Romans 1–8*, 54; Jewett, *Romans*, 149.

Exegetical Outline

→ **V. God's Wrath against Human Sin Is a Demonstration of His Righteousness (1:18–32)**
   - **A. Paul States His Thesis: God's Righteousness Revealed in His Wrath (1:18)**
   - **B. Why God Reveals His Wrath against Human Impiety and Unrighteousness (1:19–23)**
      1. God Has Revealed Himself Clearly to Human Beings (1:19–20)
      2. Human Beings Did Not Glorify or Thank God (1:21–23)
   - **C. How God Reveals His Wrath against Human Impiety and Unrighteousness (1:24–31)**
      1. God Handed Human Beings Over to the Results of Their Sexual Sin (1:24–27)
         a. Introduction: worship of the creature resulted in the dishonoring of humanity (1:24–25)
         b. Explanation: worship of the creature resulted in unnatural sexual relations (1:26–27)
      2. God Handed Human Beings Over to Their Pointless Way of Thinking (1:28–31)
         a. Introduction: The effect on the mind of rejecting God (1:29)
         b. Explanation: Vices that result from a worthless mind (1:30–31)
   - **D. Paul Summarizes His Thesis: Human Beings Have Brazenly Disobeyed God, So God's Wrath against Them Is Justified (1:32)**

Explanation of the Text

1:18 For the wrath of God is revealed from heaven against all the impiety and unrighteousness of human beings who stifle the truth in unrighteousness (Ἀποκαλύπτεται γὰρ ὀργὴ θεοῦ ἀπ' οὐρανοῦ ἐπὶ πᾶσαν ἀσέβειαν καὶ ἀδικίαν ἀνθρώπων τῶν τὴν ἀλήθειαν ἐν ἀδικίᾳ κατεχόντων). God's wrath is an expression of his righteousness because it is fair: he brings it against human beings who know the truth about him but intentionally stifle that truth.

A few English translations (e.g., NIV, NAB, REB) leave out the conjunction "for" (γάρ) that links 1:18 to the preceding discourse.[4] At one level, this is understandable since it is reasonably clear that Paul begins a new section with this sentence, a section that begins to explain the thesis he has just uttered in 1:16–17. The link between 1:18 and 1:17, however, is too crucial to the flow of the argument to leave unexpressed. The phrase "the wrath of God" (ὀργὴ θεοῦ) stands parallel to the expression "the righteousness of God" (δικαιοσύνη θεοῦ) in 1:17, and the "for" shows that Paul considers the revelation of God's wrath to clarify, in some way, the meaning of "the righteousness of God."

Commentators frequently understand the "for" as introducing a contrast, either to the saving righteousness of God in 1:16–17 (which saves people from God's wrath) or to the emphasis at the end of 1:17 on "faith" (apart from which people experience God's wrath).[5] It makes the most sense, however, to think of the "for" as introducing a further explanation of the righteousness of God.[6] The

4. Among commentators, see Longenecker (*Romans*, 200–201), who thinks that "for" simply indicates a transition to new, traditional material.

5. See, respectively, e.g., Frederic Godet, *Commentary on St. Paul's Epistle to the Romans*, trans. A. Cusin (New York: Funk & Wagnalls, 1883), 99, and Cranfield, *Romans*, 1:108.

6. Markus Bockmuehl, *Revelation and Mystery in Ancient Judaism and Pauline Christianity* (Grand Rapids: Eerdmans, 1990), 138–41; Jewett, *Romans*, 151–52.

wrath of God, as Paul explains it in the following paragraphs, shows that God is equitable and fair. He reveals it against creatures who continue to stifle the truth that he has clearly demonstrated to them.

The present tense of the verbs "is revealed" (ἀποκαλύπτεται) and "stifle" (κατεχόντων) is important for two reasons.[7] First, it shows that God's wrath is not merely something that will happen in the future on "the day of . . . wrath" (2:5) but is something that takes place in the present.[8] Second, it shows the righteousness, or equity, of God's wrath. Just as human beings stifle the truth about God in the present, so God reveals his wrath against them in the present.

It was not immediately obvious within Paul's larger Greco-Roman cultural context that the human behavior he describes in 1:21–22 and 1:24–31 represented the outpouring of divine wrath. People could have understood the homosexual behavior described in 1:26–27 as morally neutral as long as it did not violate conventions of social status, and they might have traced the list of social evils in 1:29–31 back to a lack of education.[9] Even those who agreed with Paul that homoerotic behavior was against nature would not have seen the dishonor it brought to those who engaged in it as the wrath of God. Similarly, people might have thought that the social ills in 1:29–31 deserved divine wrath in the afterlife (cf. 1:32), but to see the ills themselves as God's wrath was something new. Understanding the truth about these behaviors required God's revelation of it, and Paul's use of the present passive "is revealed" (ἀποκαλύπτεται) means that God makes this truth known through the proclamation of the gospel.

The terms "impiety" (ἀσέβεια) and "unrighteousness" (ἀδικία) may loosely anticipate the focus of the rest of the passage on the sins of human beings directly against God and against other human beings.[10] The adjective "all" (πᾶσαν) applies to both vices and hints that Paul intended them to cover, in a sweeping way, all human sin.[11]

1:19 For what is knowable about God is visible to them, for God has made it visible to them (διότι τὸ γνωστὸν τοῦ θεοῦ φανερόν ἐστιν ἐν αὐτοῖς· ὁ θεὸς γὰρ αὐτοῖς ἐφανέρωσεν). Some knowledge of God is available to all human beings because God himself has made it clear to them.

The initial "for" (διότι) introduces a detailed substantiation of Paul's claim that human beings "stifle" the truth about God (1:19–21).[12] Since they cannot stifle a truth they do not understand, Paul asserts that some knowledge of God is available to them. The adjective "knowable" (γνωστός) means "known" elsewhere in the NT (e.g., Luke 2:44; Acts 28:28). It can certainly mean "knowable" in other literature (e.g., Plato, *Republic* 510a; Epictetus, *Diatr.* 2.20.4), however, and that must be what Paul means here since he would not have said, in effect, "What is known . . . is known."[13]

7. On the word "stifle," see BDAG 532, s.v. κατέχω 1b. See also Fitzmyer, *Romans*, 278.

8. Jewett, *Romans*, 151; Kevin W. McFadden, *Judgment according to Works in Romans: The Meaning and Function of Divine Judgment in Paul's Most Important Letter* (Minneapolis: Fortress, 2013), 21–24, argues persuasively against reading this as a futuristic present (and therefore a reference to future judgment) on the basis that Paul explains the revelation of God's wrath in terms of God's present judgment of handing people over to their sins (1:24, 26, 28).

9. See David M. Halperin, "Homosexuality," *OCD* 720–23; Roy Bowen Ward, "Why Unnatural? The Tradition behind Romans 1:26–27," *HTR* 90 (1997): 284; Otto Michel, *Der Brief an die Römer*, KEK 4; 14th ed. (Göttingen: Vandenhoeck & Ruprecht, 1978), 105; and Epictetus, *Diatr.* 1.18.1–14.

10. A reading that goes back as far as Origen, *Romans, Books 1–5*, 90.

11. Cranfield, *Romans*, 1:112; Fitzmyer, *Romans*, 278.

12. BDAG 251, s.v. διότι 3.

13. So most commentators, but see, especially, Lagrange, *Romains*, 23. Cf. BDAG 204, s.v. γνωστός 2.

Paul implies by this statement that human beings cannot know everything about God. They can only know as much about him as God allows them to know, but he has allowed all human beings to know enough to hold them responsible for worshiping him and treating one another justly. Has God made this knowledge visible simply "to them" (most translations) or has he made it evident "within them" (NASB, cf. KJV)? The prepositional phrase at issue here (ἐν αὐτοῖς) can certainly mean "within them," but it is also another way of simply expressing the dative case in Greek and can just as easily mean "to them" (cf. 2 Cor 4:3; 8:1).[14] If it means "within them," it anticipates Paul's later claim that people have "the work of the law written in their hearts" (2:15; cf. 1:32).[15] Paul's focus in the immediate context, however, is on the knowledge of God that is visible in what he has created (1:20, 25), and so "to them" is a better rendering.

1:20 for his unseen attributes (that is, his eternal power and divinity) are clearly seen because they are perceived from the time of the world's creation through what is made, with the result that they are without excuse (τὰ γὰρ ἀόρατα αὐτοῦ ἀπὸ κτίσεως κόσμου τοῖς ποιήμασιν νοούμενα καθορᾶται, ἥ τε ἀΐδιος αὐτοῦ δύναμις καὶ θειότης, εἰς τὸ εἶναι αὐτοὺς ἀναπολογήτους). God is just to hold human beings responsible for knowing his power and divinity because they can easily derive this knowledge from the natural world around them.

This sentence explains (γάρ) what Paul meant when he said in the last clause of 1:19 that God made what is knowable about himself visible to human beings. The syntax of the sentence is complex but reasonably clear. The phrase "his unseen attributes" (τὰ . . . ἀόρατα αὐτοῦ) stands in apposition to "his eternal power and divinity" (ἡ . . . ἀΐδιος αὐτοῦ δύναμις καὶ θειότης), and the expression "because they are perceived" translates an adverbial participle of cause (νοούμενα) that modifies the main verb "are clearly seen" (καθορᾶται).[16] The prepositional phrase "from the creation of the world" (ἀπὸ κτίσεως κόσμου) and the dative phrase "through what is made" (τοῖς ποιήμασιν) both modify the participle, which comes directly after them (νοούμενα). The prepositional phrase should be taken temporally (cf., e.g., Heb 4:3), telling the time from which it was possible to perceive God's unseen attributes, and the dative phrase should be taken as a dative of means or instrument, expressing how it is possible to perceive them.[17] The final accusative and infinitive construction (εἰς τὸ εἶναι . . .) describes in a climactic way the result of the whole complex statement.[18]

God himself is invisible (Col 1:15–16; 1 Tim 1:17; Heb 11:27), but Paul maintains that God made his invisible attributes of eternal power and divinity known to people. Because of this, they could "clearly see" what was "unseen." This clear vision of the invisible God's attributes happened when they perceived his eternal power and divinity by means of his creation. Paul does not explain exactly what in the visible creation provides knowledge of these attributes of the invisible God. Another Hellenistic

14. BDF §220 (1). Cf. the phrase "for the likeness" (ἐν ὁμοιώματι) in 1:23 and "for a lie" (ἐν τῷ ψεύδει) in 1:25. Commentators often observe that the phrase in 1:23 reflects the Hebrew syntax of Ps 106:20 (*bĕtabnît*), but it is also good Greek.

15. See, e.g., Calvin, *Romans*, 31; Meyer, *Romans*, 57.

16. See NET and the discussion of the adverbial participle of cause in Wallace, *Greek Grammar*, 631–33.

17. On the dative of means or instrument, see Wallace, *Greek Grammar*, 162, and, with reference to the dative expression here in this verse, see C. F. D. Moule, *An Idiom-Book of New Testament Greek*, 2nd ed. (Cambridge: Cambridge University Press, 1959), 44.

18. See, e.g., Cranfield (*Romans*, 1:116), Longenecker (*Romans*, 210 [who also sees an element of purpose in the clause, "so that people would be without excuse"]), and Wallace (*Greek Grammar*, 592–94).

Jew from roughly the same period, however, could say that human beings themselves are "made . . . in the image of his own eternity [ἀϊδιότητος]" (Wis 2:23 NRSV). The "power" (δύναμις) evident in the activity of fire, wind, the stars, and rushing water, he continues, should lead people to perceive (νοέω) "how much more powerful [δυνατώτερος] is he who formed them" (Wis 13:4). "From the greatness and the beauty of created things," he continues, "their original author, by analogy, is seen [θεωρεῖται]" (Wis 13:5 NAB).[19] It seems likely that Paul had similar ideas in mind here.

1:21 For, although they knew God, they did not glorify or thank him as God but they were rendered futile in their reasoning processes and their foolish heart was darkened (διότι γνόντες τὸν θεὸν οὐχ ὡς θεὸν ἐδόξασαν ἢ ηὐχαρίστησαν, ἀλλ' ἐματαιώθησαν ἐν τοῖς διαλογισμοῖς αὐτῶν καὶ ἐσκοτίσθη ἡ ἀσύνετος αὐτῶν καρδία). People had no logical defense before the threat of God's wrath because they knew that God deserved honor and thanks for his gifts in creation, but they refused to worship him. This unreasonable rebellion distorted their reasoning powers in other areas.

Just as with the beginning of 1:19, the "for" (διότι) here shows that what follows substantiates something Paul has just said, in this case the words "they are without excuse" (1:20). His explanation unfolds in three steps. First, he summarizes what he has just said in 1:19–20 about God making himself known to human beings. He does this using a classic example of the adverbial participle of concession, "although they knew God" (γνόντες τὸν θεόν).

Second, he identifies specifically the offensive behavior that he described in broad terms as "impiety and unrighteousness" in 1:18 and that he hinted at in the statement "they are without excuse" at the end of 1:20. The problem is that human beings, despite their knowledge of God, "did not glorify or thank" God. From a Jewish perspective, the mighty works of God, not least in the creation he has made, should prompt all people groups to glorify him. In other words, they should enhance his reputation by praising him (Ps 89:8–10; 1 En. 36:4; cf. Rom 15:6, 9). The proper response to the good gifts God had provided everyone through his creation, moreover, was thanksgiving (4 Ezra 8:60; 1 Tim 4:3), a sentiment that was not absent from Greco-Roman philosophical thinking (e.g., Epictetus, *Diatr.* 1.16.20; 4.1.103–5).[20]

Third, their decision not to acknowledge God as the Creator distorted their thinking. The expression "were rendered futile" translates a verb (ἐματαιώθησαν) used in the LXX of behavior that is foolish because it accomplishes nothing, is disobedient to God, and brings his punishment (1 Sam 13:13; 1 Chr 21:8). The LXX uses it twice in the third-person aorist passive, just as it is used here, to describe Israel becoming "pointless," "useless," or "worthless" (ἐματαιώθησαν) through the worship of idols that were also "pointless," "useless," and "worthless" (ματαίων).[21] Israel, in other words, began to resemble the gods that it worshiped. Paul does not say that explicitly here, but in a context that will soon turn to an indictment of idolatry (1:23), this idea probably informed his choice of words.[22] Idols themselves are foolish—they can neither see nor think—and the reasoning powers of those who worship them become similarly dysfunctional (Isa 44:9–20; Pss 115:4–8; 135:15–18; Wis 15:14–17).

19. See also 1 En. 2:1–5:6.

20. On 4 Ezra, see Käsemann, *Romans*, 42, and on Epictetus, see Jewett, *Romans*, 157.

21. 2 Kgs 17:15; Jer 2:5.

22. See the discussion in G. K. Beale, *We Become What We Worship: A Biblical Theology of Idolatry* (Downers Grove, IL: InterVarsity Press, 2008), 209–11.

1:22 Claiming to be wise, they became fools (φάσκοντες εἶναι σοφοὶ ἐμωράνθησαν). Precisely when they asserted their own wisdom, the irrational human beings who refused to worship the Creator made fools of themselves.

The expression "claiming to be" (φάσκοντες εἶναι) was fairly common Greek for describing claims that had no reasonable basis and were untrue: "You are in the wrong there too," says Socrates to Dionysodorus, "for you assert that there is [φάσκων . . . εἶναι] no such thing as making a mistake" (Plato, *Euthyd.* 288a).[23] The verb "claim, assert" (φάσκω) often carried the connotation of asserting something that had no sound rationale to substantiate it.[24] The claim of which Paul speaks here, then, both stands in contrast to Paul's carefully reasoned argument and itself substantiates Paul's case that the failure of human beings to worship the Creator has affected their reasoning ability.

The participle "claiming" (φάσκοντες) is an adverbial participle of time, emphasizing through its present tense that human beings were made foolish while they were making claims to the contrary.[25] The picture is of babbling fools whose topic for the day is their own wisdom.

1:23 and they exchanged the glory of the incorruptible God for the likeness of the image of corruptible humanity and birds and quadrupeds and reptiles (καὶ ἤλλαξαν τὴν δόξαν τοῦ ἀφθάρτου θεοῦ ἐν ὁμοιώματι εἰκόνος φθαρτοῦ ἀνθρώπου καὶ πετεινῶν καὶ τετραπόδων καὶ ἑρπετῶν). Human foolishness took the form of an irrational exchange of the worship of the glorious and eternal God for images of his mortal creatures.

The "and" (καί) is epexegetical, identifying more precisely the foolishness of 1:22b. This foolishness consisted fundamentally of an irrational exchange of the most senseless and damaging kind. Human beings traded away the "glory" of the "incorruptible" God. God's "glory" (δόξα) refers to his renown (cf. 1 Macc 2:51), power (cf. Gen 45:13 LXX), and honor (cf. Isa 35:2 LXX) manifested in many ways, but in this context Paul was probably thinking of its manifestation in the creation: "The whole earth is full of his glory," cry the seraphs in Isaiah (6:3).[26] If something is "incorruptible" (ἄφθαρτος), it does not wither and die, like the crown of celery that victorious athletes wore for a moment but that quickly wilted in the hot Mediterranean sun (1 Cor 9:25). What is "incorruptible" retains its beauty and vitality forever. This is true of God, Paul says, and so, by implication, is true of his glory. Human beings should have glorified and thanked God for his immortal glory since they were the beneficiaries of it (1:21), but instead they worshiped something else.

Paul designed his description of what human beings worshiped instead of God to emphasize the ridiculous nature of the exchange. Human beings worshiped "the likeness of the image of corruptible humanity." The wordiness of the phrase is a rhetorical move called *pleonasm*, which multiplies words to "enrich the thought."[27] Here, Paul is communicating just how far human beings had moved from the worship of the incorruptible God. According to Genesis 1:26 (LXX), human beings were made in the "image" (εἰκών) and "likeness" (ὁμοίωσις) of God, but here Paul speaks not even of people worshiping other people but of people worshiping "the likeness of the image" of other people, something God had expressly forbidden in Deuteronomy 4:16

23. W. R. M. Lamb, trans., *Plato: Laches, Protagoras, Meno, Euthydemus*, LCL 165 (Cambridge: Harvard University Press, 1977). See also, e.g., Plato, *Charm.* 173b; *Republic* 347e.

24. In addition to the references to Plato in the previous note, see Acts 24:9; 25:19.

25. So correctly NAB ("While claiming to be wise"). On the adverbial participle of time in the present tense, see Wallace, *Greek Grammar*, 625–26.

26. On all this, see *TLNT* 1:364–66.

27. Smyth, *Greek Grammar*, 681 (§3042).

(LXX).[28] In contrast to God, moreover, human beings are "corruptible" (φθαρτός), that is, they wither and die quickly. As if this were not enough, people moved ever further from God as they gave their worship to a variety of animals. Paul's list follows an order that matches the animals' habitats from high to low, moving from the heavens ("birds") to just above the surface of the earth ("quadrupeds") to the surface of the earth itself ("reptiles")—ever further, in other words, from God.[29]

Paul describes idolatry here in ways that Hellenistic Jews typically used to describe gentile religions (e.g., Wis 11:15; 12:24; 13:10; 14:12–21; 15:18–19; Let. Aris. 135–38).[30] But, just as he did in 1:22, here in 1:23 he also uses language that would easily recall for anyone familiar with the Jewish Scriptures in Greek, Israel's own apostasy at the time of the exodus when they too worshiped the likeness of a quadruped at the foot of Mt. Horeb (Ps 106:20 [LXX 105:20]; cf. Jer 2:11). He may be preparing just such a reader for the turn that the argument will take in this direction at 2:1.[31]

1:24 Therefore, God handed them over in the lusts of their hearts to the uncleanness of the dishonoring of their bodies among themselves (Διὸ παρέδωκεν αὐτοὺς ὁ θεὸς ἐν ταῖς ἐπιθυμίαις τῶν καρδιῶν αὐτῶν εἰς ἀκαθαρσίαν τοῦ ἀτιμάζεσθαι τὰ σώματα αὐτῶν ἐν αὐτοῖς). Because human beings knowingly refused to honor God as the Creator, God revealed his wrath against them by handing them over to dishonorable conduct.

The term "therefore" (διό) reaches back to the entire section stretching from 1:19 to 1:23 with its description of why God reveals his wrath against humanity. Now Paul describes *how* God reveals his wrath, and, again, the focus lies on the fairness of the punishment. Not only does the crime merit punishment, but it merits precisely the punishment God gives. God hands people over to the consequences of their knowing refusal to acknowledge him as God.

The phrase "God handed them over" (παρέδωκεν αὐτοὺς ὁ θεὸς) appears here for the first time in the section, and this concept will become the section's dominant theme (1:26, 28). In a broad sense, God hands people over to the consequences of their basic sin of refusing to acknowledge him as their Creator: the human response to God's revelation of himself as Creator has been dishonorable and irrational, and it results in the dishonorable and irrational behavior Paul is about to describe.

In a narrower sense, God hands people over "in the lusts of their hearts to . . . uncleanness" (ἐν ταῖς ἐπιθυμίαις τῶν καρδιῶν αὐτῶν εἰς ἀκαθαρσίαν). The phrase "in the lusts of their hearts" (ἐν ταῖς ἐπιθυμίαις τῶν καρδιῶν αὐτῶν) refers to the context of God's action. He hands them over while they are engaged in the illegitimate desires that originated with their refusal to acknowledge him.[32] He hands them over "to uncleanness" (εἰς ἀκαθαρσίαν). The expression "to hand someone over to something" was often used in judicial contexts (e.g., Matt 10:17; 20:19; 24:9; Luke 21:12; 24:20; Acts 8:3), and so Paul assumed that the punishment he described here was a judicial punishment.[33] Paul pictures God as a just judge giving to people precisely what they deserve. He could use the terms "lust"

28. Cf. Käsemann, *Romans*, 45.

29. Cf. Deut 4:17–18, although the order there is different.

30. Cf. Haacker, *An die Römer*, 51.

31. Cf. Wright, "Romans," 433, although he locates the argument's turn at 2:17.

32. See Cranfield, *Romans*, 1:122, who understands the syntax of "in the lusts of their hearts" (ἐν ταῖς ἐπιθυμίαις τῶν καρδιῶν αὐτῶν) by analogy to the phrase "to follow the passions of your heart" (πορεύεσθαι ἐν ἐπιθυμίαις καρδίας σου; NJB) in Sir 5:2. Cf. Robert A. J. Gagnon, *The Bible and Homosexual Practice: Texts and Hermeneutics* (Nashville: Abingdon, 2001), 232.

33. See BDAG 762, s.v. παραδίδωμι 1b.

(ἐπιθυμία) and "uncleanness" (ἀκαθαρσία) together elsewhere with sexual connotations (Gal 5:16, 19, 24; Eph 4:19, 22; Col 3:5; 1 Thess 4:5, 7), and as 1:26–27 shows they carry those connotations here.

The next phrase (τοῦ ἀτιμάζεσθαι τὰ σώματα αὐτῶν) could be either a purpose clause ("so that their bodies would be dishonored," NASB), a result clause ("as a result, they did vile and degrading things," NLT), or an epexegetical clause ("to impurity, to the dishonoring of their bodies," ESV). It is difficult to decide between these options, but since the pattern in the next paragraph (1:26–27) involves a general description of what God hands people over to (shameful passions) followed by a specific description (homosexual activity), Paul probably follows that same pattern here. The epexegetical option, then, is best.[34] The uncleanness to which God has handed over idolatrous human beings is specifically the mutual dishonoring of their bodies.[35] Here, too, the fairness of God's punishment is clear: just as they have dishonored him, so he has handed them over to their dishonorable conduct toward one another.

1:25 They exchanged the truth that came from God for a lie and revered and served the creature rather than the Creator, who is blessed forever, amen (οἵτινες μετήλλαξαν τὴν ἀλήθειαν τοῦ θεοῦ ἐν τῷ ψεύδει, καὶ ἐσεβάσθησαν καὶ ἐλάτρευσαν τῇ κτίσει παρὰ τὸν κτίσαντα, ὅς ἐστιν εὐλογητὸς εἰς τοὺς αἰῶνας· ἀμήν). God handed human beings over to their refusal to worship him because they chose to abandon the truth about God that he had revealed to them and instead worship "gods" that were a sham.

"They" translates a compound relative pronoun (οἵτινες), a word that denotes "a person or thing in general, or . . . the *class, character, quality,* or *capacity* of a person (less often a thing)."[36] Here, the term points back to "them" (αὐτοῖς) at the end of 1:24 and communicates that Paul is about to say what it was about human beings that prompted God to hand them over to the dishonoring of their bodies. The reason Paul gives for God's action is an emphatic summary of what he has already said in 1:18–23. The verb "exchanged" (μετήλλαξαν) is repeated from 1:23 (ἤλλαξαν), but now with a preposition (μετά) that intensifies its meaning: people completely abandoned the truth God had revealed to them about himself (1:19–20).[37] God revealed the truth about himself as Creator to them, but they knowingly exchanged this truth for a lie—the lie that the images they "revered and served" were actually gods who would respond to their worship with salvation and blessing. This was a common Jewish view of non-Jewish religious practices (e.g., Isa 44:20; Ep Jer 6:8, 34–38, 47; cf. 1 Cor 8:4; 10:19–20; Gal 4:8), but they were also practices to which the Jews themselves had sometimes fallen prey (e.g., Jer 2:26–28). The thought of idolatry was so repulsive to Paul that he utters a common Jewish benediction, praising the Creator in defiance of the idol worship he has just described.[38]

1:26 Because of this God handed them over to dishonorable passions, for, the fact is, their

34. For the same syntax elsewhere in Paul, see Rom 11:8; 1 Cor 9:10; 2 Cor 8:11. For the same conclusion on somewhat different grounds, see Gagnon, *Homosexual Practice*, 233–34.

35. Cf., e.g., William G. T. Shedd, *A Critical and Doctrinal Commentary on the Epistle of St. Paul to the Romans* (1879; repr., Grand Rapids: Baker, 1980), 126; Jewett, *Romans*, 168–69, and, in addition to the ESV, the NRSV and NET.

36. Smyth, *Greek Grammar*, 561 (§2496); cf. Wallace, *Greek Grammar*, 344.

37. See Smyth, *Greek Grammar*, 366 (§1648) on the addition of a preposition to a verb to "mark the completion of the action of the verbal idea."

38. Cf., e.g., Gen 9:26; Ps 41:13; Tob 3:11; Rom 9:5; 2 Cor 1:3; 11:31; Gal 1:5; Eph 1:3; 1 Pet 1:3, and the comments of Friedrich August Gottreu Tholuck, *Exposition of St. Paul's Epistle to the Romans*, trans. Robert Menzies (Philadelphia: Sorin and Ball, 1844), 65; Dunn, *Romans 1–8*, 63–64, and Jewett, *Romans*, 171.

females exchanged their natural sexual role for a sexual role contrary to nature (διὰ τοῦτο παρέδωκεν αὐτοὺς ὁ θεὸς εἰς πάθη ἀτιμίας· αἵ τε γὰρ θήλειαι αὐτῶν μετήλλαξαν τὴν φυσικὴν χρῆσιν εἰς τὴν παρὰ φύσιν). Because human beings dishonored God, God gave them over to dishonorable relationships with one another. For example, he gave them over to unnatural sexual behavior among women.

Paul now specifies what he meant when he spoke in 1:24 of "lusts," "uncleanness," and of bodies being "dishonored." The exchange of a natural for an unnatural sexual function corresponds with the exchange of the truth God had revealed for the lie of idolatrous worship. The righteousness of God is revealed in the wrath of God (1:17–18) in part because the way God reveals his wrath demonstrates his fairness.[39] When people trade away the God of creation for other gods, they also trade away the design of God's creation for a parody of that design. God has responded to the exchange of the truth about himself for the lie of idolatry by handing people over to this other sort of exchange.

The expression "sexual role" (χρῆσις) literally meant "use" but is commonly found in circumlocutions for sexual intercourse. Plato could speak of "the use of what belongs to Aphrodite" (ἡ τῶν ἀφροδισίων χρῆσις) and simply mean "sexual intercourse," and Xenophon could refer to sexual activity (in this case male homoerotic activity) as "the use of the body" (ἡ τοῦ σώματος χρήσιν).[40] Here Paul refers to women filling a sexual role that is "contrary to nature" (παρὰ φύσιν). He does not explicitly say that this is homoerotic activity, but Plato, Ovid, Plutarch, and Pseudo-Phocylides could all refer to female homoerotic activity as unnatural, and Paul's next sentence makes this meaning likely.[41]

1:27 And males, likewise, abandoned the natural sexual role of the female and burned in their strong desire for one another, males with males "accomplishing" what is obscene and receiving by way of return, in themselves, the recompense that was necessary for their error (ὁμοίως τε καὶ οἱ ἄρσενες ἀφέντες τὴν φυσικὴν χρῆσιν τῆς θηλείας ἐξεκαύθησαν ἐν τῇ ὀρέξει αὐτῶν εἰς ἀλλήλους, ἄρσενες ἐν ἄρσεσιν τὴν ἀσχημοσύνην κατεργαζόμενοι καὶ τὴν ἀντιμισθίαν ἣν ἔδει τῆς πλάνης αὐτῶν ἐν ἑαυτοῖς ἀπολαμβάνοντες). God also gave human beings over to unnatural, homosexual intercourse among men. This shameful conduct carried its own punishment of dishonor.

The sense of balance and fairness in the revelation of God's wrath continues as Paul turns from female to male homoerotic behavior. Just as women exchanged their natural sexual role for unnatural behavior, so men have done something similar. Now, however, the language is more emphatic. Instead of simply exchanging what is natural for what is unnatural, males "abandoned" females, "burned" with "strong desire" for other males, and worked at "obscene" behavior.

The language of "'accomplishing' what is obscene" (τὴν ἀσχημοσύνην κατεργαζόμενοι) is deeply ironic. Although the verb Paul uses (κατεργάζομαι) could certainly refer to "committing" sin (Rom 2:9; 7:15, 17, 20; 1 Cor 5:3), he also often uses it to mean "achieve," "accomplish," "bring about," "produce," "create" (e.g., Rom 15:18; 2 Cor 12:12).[42] In a context where he speaks of receiving payment as a return for some activity (τὴν ἀντιμισθίαν . . . ἀπολαμβάνοντες), it seems likely that he uses the

39. Cf. Gagnon, *Homosexual Practice*, 235.

40. See Plato, *Laws* 841a (Cooper, *Complete Works*, 1502); Xenophon, *Symp.* 8.28; and BDAG 1089, s.v. χρῆσις 3.

41. Mark D. Smith, "Ancient Bisexuality and the Interpretation of Romans 1:26–27," *JAAR* 64 (1996): 239–40. For the relevant texts, see note 46 below.

42. BDAG 531, s.v. κατεργάζομαι 1–2; MGS 1096, s.v. κατεργάζομαι 1 E.

expression in the second, positive sense yet does so ironically.[43] Homoerotic behavior, he argues, is labor whose reward is a punishment.

What punishment does Paul have in mind? Interpreters have suggested a wide variety of proposals, but the most likely idea sticks close to the present context.[44] Paul understood homoerotic sexual activity to be "dishonorable" (cf. τοῦ ἀτιμάζεσθαι, 1:24; πάθη ἀτιμίας, 1:26) and "obscenity" (ἡ ἀσχημοσύνη). The context indicates that the dishonor lay in the inconsistency of this activity with what was "natural" (φυσικός, 1:26–27). "Natural" means neither "without passion" nor "culturally normal" but "what is obvious from the operation of the physical world" (cf. 2 Pet 2:12).[45] Paul thought that the eternal power and divinity of the Creator were obvious from the physical world and led clearly to the conclusion that people should glorify and thank the Creator (1:20–21). In the same way, Paul probably considered the "natural" character of heterosexual activity to be obvious from the physical anatomy of male and female and from the role of heterosexual intercourse in the production of children.[46]

When human beings chose to revere and serve the creature rather than the Creator (1:25) and irrationally failed to glorify and thank God, their reasoning powers became futile and blurry, and they were shown to be foolish (1:21–22). In the same way, Paul considered homoerotic sexual activity to be foolish at an obvious level: it used the human body in a way contrary to its natural design, and it could accomplish nothing. Because of this, those who engaged in it dishonored themselves, and this is the sense in which they received "in themselves" the recompense for their sin.[47] At the level of human relations, this was equivalent to worshiping the creature rather than the Creator (1:25).

1:28 And just as they did not deem it worthwhile to acknowledge God, God handed them over to a worthless mind, to do things that are not fitting (καὶ καθὼς οὐκ ἐδοκίμασαν τὸν θεὸν ἔχειν ἐν ἐπιγνώσει, παρέδωκεν αὐτοὺς ὁ θεὸς εἰς ἀδόκιμον νοῦν, ποιεῖν τὰ μὴ καθήκοντα). God justly handed people over to the worthless way of thinking that resulted from their decision to consider God worthless.

For the third and final time, Paul says that God handed human beings over to their own rebellion against him, and once again God's response is perfectly commensurate with the crime. Paul communicates this in two ways. First, he does this through the grammar of the sentence. The opening conjunction "and" (καί) connects the balance between crime and punishment in this verse with the expression of the same balance in 1:26–27. The next word, translated here "just as" (καθώς), ac-

43. Cf. Gagnon, *Homosexual Practice*, 238–39.

44. For a survey of proposals and for the solution described here, see Gagnon, *Homosexual Practice*, 259–70, and cf. David E. Fredrickson, "Natural and Unnatural Use in Romans 1:24–27: Paul and the Philosophic Critique of Eros," in *Homosexuality, Science, and the "Plain Sense" of Scripture*, ed. David L. Balch (Grand Rapids: Eerdmans, 2000), 216–18.

45. For the first two ideas, see, respectively, Fredrickson, "Natural and Unnatural Use," 199–207, and Jewett, *Romans*, 177.

46. Although many people in the Greco-Roman world seem to have viewed homoerotic activity as "normal," some, like Paul, thought of it as unnatural. See, e.g., Plato, *Laws* 636c, 838e–839a, 841d; Plutarch, *Mor.* 990d; Ovid, *Metam.* 667, 728–35, 758; Philo, *Abraham* 135–37; *Spec. Laws* 2.50; Pseudo-Phocylides, 190–92. *Pace* Ward ("Why Unnatural?" 284), Paul differs from many of these texts in valuing mutual and frequent sexual pleasure among heterosexual married couples (1 Cor 7:2–5; Eph 5:31). On this point, cf. Jewett, *Romans*, 176.

47. Cf. Fredrickson, "Natural and Unnatural Use," 216–18, where, however, Fredrickson argues that the dishonor lay not in homosexual behavior but in yielding to passion. For the connection between dishonor and the use of the body against nature, see the comments of Chrysostom (*Romans*, 47–50), whose thought world was close to Paul's.

complishes the same purpose by communicating correspondence and balance.[48]

Second, Paul uses a skillful play on words to connect the contempt with which human beings treated God with God's punishment of handing human beings over to their own attitude. They tested the idea of acknowledging God and found it "not qualified" (οὐκ ἐδοκίμασαν) for their approval. The mind that works this way, however, is itself obviously "unqualified" (ἀδόκιμον) for anything worthwhile. God punished human beings, then, by giving them over to the worthless mind that found him worthless (cf. 1:21).

As a result of this punishment, human beings did "what was not fitting" (ποιεῖν τὰ μὴ καθήκοντα), an expression that emphasized failure to fulfill one's obligations. A woman hired to work in a winepress was under contract to do "everything that is required" (ποιοῦσαν πάντα ὅσα καθήκει), and Stoic philosophers could write treatises called "Concerning Duty" (περὶ τοῦ καθήκοντος).[49] The human mind was supposed to glorify and thank God (1:21), to reverence and serve him (1:24), and when it did so, it made reasonable and good decisions about how to live. The list of horrors that Paul gives next shows what happens when God hands people over to a mind that has strayed far from these obligations.

1:29–31 filled with all unrighteousness, cunning, greed, malice; full of envy, murder, strife, treachery, mean-spiritedness, rumormongers, slanderers, God-detesting, bullies, arrogant, braggarts, contrivers of evil, disobedient to parents, senseless, faithless, heartless, ruthless (πεπληρωμένους πάσῃ ἀδικίᾳ πονηρίᾳ πλεονεξίᾳ κακίᾳ, μεστοὺς φθόνου φόνου ἔριδος δόλου κακοηθείας, ψιθυριστάς,
30καταλάλους, θεοστυγεῖς, ὑβριστὰς, ὑπερηφάνους, ἀλαζόνας, ἐφευρετὰς κακῶν, γονεῦσιν ἀπειθεῖς,
31ἀσυνέτους, ἀσυνθέτους, ἀστόργους, ἀνελεήμονας). Minds unqualified for anything worthwhile produce a wide variety of wicked behaviors, all of them examples of the human failure to do one's duty to God and others.

The participle "filled" (πεπληρωμένους) describes the state of those whom God handed over to a worthless mind—the "them" (αὐτούς) of 1:28. Its perfect tense hints that a complex history of bad behavior has reached a saturation point that now defines humanity.[50] The list begins with "unrighteousness" (ἀδικίᾳ), and this term recalls "the impiety and unrighteousness [ἀδικίαν] of human beings" in 1:18, a phrase that summarizes human sin and the reason for the revelation of God's wrath. The twenty other vices Paul lists all fall under the general heading of "unrighteousness."[51] They all stand in contrast to the perfect fairness and justice of God that Paul has been describing throughout this passage.

The vice list has twenty-one elements and can be divided into three parts. The first set, of four vices, is general in nature and emphasizes the depth and breadth of human depravity. Each of these four general vices describes an evil that people are willing to do to others in order to satisfy themselves: unrighteousness (ἀδικίᾳ), cunning (πονηρίᾳ), greed (πλεονεξίᾳ), malice (κακίᾳ). The list begins with the adjective "all," and the "-ia" sound at the end of each of the four words in Greek produces a rhythmic and rhyming sound that emphasizes the

48. So Wilckens (*An die Römer [Röm 1–5]*, 111), Moo (*Romans*, 117), NET, and TNIV. The meaning "because" or "since" (e.g., BDAG 494, s.v. καθώς 3; NASB, NAB, NRSV, ESV) for the Greek term used here is unusual.

49. See MM 312; Diogenes Laertius, *Lives of the Philosophers* 7.4 (Zeno); Cranfield, *Romans*, 1:129; Brad Inwood, "Panaetius," *OCD* 1104; Ramelli, *Hierocles the Stoic*, xxvii.

50. On the perfect, see Crellin, "The Semantics of the Perfect," 451, 454–55.

51. Cf. Wilckens, *An die Römer (Röm 1–5)*, 113; Dunn, *Romans 1–8*, 67–68. Jewett (*Romans*, 184) argues against this view.

sweeping nature of the list. The dative case with verbs of filling is rare in Greek, and Paul probably chose it here for its rhetorical effect when the words were pronounced.[52]

The second set, of five vices, continues the idea that human beings are full of evil, but Paul uses a new word for "full" (μεστός)—this time an adjective—and the list becomes more specific: envy (φθόνος), murder (φόνος), strife (ἔρις), treachery (δόλος), mean-spiritedness (κακοήθεια). Again, the rhetoric of the sentence is impressive, especially in the soundplay "phthonou-phonou" that begins the list, and this underlines again the gravity of the human problem. Here too, each vice describes an evil that human beings use to hurt others.

The third set, of twelve terms, completes the list. Rather than referring to vices, these words refer to people who practice vices. Syntactically, then, this part of the list is related neither to the participle "filled" nor to the adjective "full" but reaches back to the pronoun "them" (αὐτούς) in 1:28. So, the wrath of God is revealed as God hands people ("them") over to the social chaos of a world populated with people like themselves, people that Paul will now categorize according to the sort of villainy they practice. With the exception of "God-hater" these are again social sins, nearly all of them verbal in nature. The first term (ψιθυριστής) is derived from the verb "whisper" (ψιθυρίζω) and means "one who offers derogatory information about someone in a tone of confidentiality" (cf. ψιθυρισμός in 2 Cor 12:20).[53] The "slanderer" (κατάλαλος), the "God-hater" (θεοστυγής), the "bully" (ὑβριστής), the "arrogant" person (ὑπερήφανος), and the "braggart" (ἀλαζών) often reveal their vices through speech.[54]

The last two vices depart from the theme of speech and stand together rhetorically through their two-word construction. The "contriver" (ἐφευρετής) of evil is someone bent on "discovering" ways of doing harm (cf. ἐφευρίσκω, "discover").[55] "Disobedient to parents" reflects the Greco-Roman notion that duties (τὰ καθήκοντα; cf. τὰ μὴ καθήκοντα in 1:28) to parents stood next only to duties to God and country and, in Jewish thought, second only to responsibilities to God.[56] Among these duties was obedience, unless extraordinary situations dictated otherwise.[57]

The final set of four terms ends the list in a rhetorically powerful way reminiscent of its beginning. Like the four terms at the beginning, these final four words have an "a" sound in common, although now the sound is at the beginning rather than the end of each word. The rhythmic assonance this produces emphasizes the relentless nature of human rebellion, and the words themselves produce the terrifying picture of human beings acting like the lower animals, devoid of the humanizing qualities of understanding (σύνεσις), affection (στοργή), and mercy (ἔλεος), and constrained by no sense of loyalty to a commonly agreed norm of behavior (συνθήκη).[58]

1:32 Although they know full well the righteous decree of God that those who practice

52. The genitive is much more common, but the required "-as" ending on the first three words would have clashed with the initial consonants of the words that follow them. On the dative with verbs of filling, see Smyth, *Greek Grammar*, 347 (§1508[b]); Wallace, *Greek Grammar*, 170–71.

53. BDAG 1098, svv. ψιθυρισμός and ψιθυριστής.

54. For the translation "bully," I am indebted to Jewett, *Romans*, 187.

55. See *CGELNT* 157.

56. See, e.g., Ramelli, *Hierocles the Stoic*, 83; Philo, *Decalogue* 106–7; and, on the whole issue, the definitive treatment of Peter Balla, *The Child-Parent Relationship in the New Testament and Its Environment* (Peabody, MA: Hendrickson, 2005).

57. For the rare exceptions to the general rule, see Musonius Rufus's essay, "Must One Obey One's Parents under All Circumstances?," in Cora E. Lutz, *Musonius Rufus: The Roman Socrates* (New Haven: Yale University Press, 1947), 100–106.

58. On "faithless," see LSJ 265, s.v. ἀσύνθετος II, and BDAG 146–47 and MGS 326, both s.v. ἀσύνθετος.

such things are worthy of death, they not only do them but also applaud those who practice them (οἵτινες τὸ δικαίωμα τοῦ θεοῦ ἐπιγνόντες, ὅτι οἱ τὰ τοιαῦτα πράσσοντες ἄξιοι θανάτου εἰσίν, οὐ μόνον αὐτὰ ποιοῦσιν ἀλλὰ καὶ συνευδοκοῦσιν τοῖς πράσσουσιν). In summary, God's wrath reveals his righteousness, or fairness, because human beings are well aware of God's just penalty of death for those who practice unrighteousness but have made a considered choice to defy this truth and to encourage others to do the same.

The compound pronoun translated "they" (οἵτινες) is in the nominative case and so begins a new sentence. It reaches back to "them" (αὐτούς) in 1:28 and introduces what follows as a summary description of those who practice the twenty-one vices Paul has named in 1:29–31. "They are the ones who" know the divine penalty for their conduct and yet not only practice these things but also applaud others who do the same.[59]

The term "righteous decree" (δικαίωμα) is reminiscent of the letter's thesis statement in 1:16–17 and brings to the surface the leitmotif of 1:18–32 that God is a righteous God whose wrath against humanity is fair and equitable. God's own righteousness, revealed in the penalty of death for the sins Paul has just described, forms the contrasting background for the main point of the sentence. Human beings have rebelled against God, "knowing full well" (ἐπι + γνόντες) the gravity of what they are doing. This emphasis explains how Paul can imply that approving evil is worse than doing it. To say that people applaud evil implies that human wickedness is not a matter of thoughtless actions committed in the heat of passion but of cool calculation, in defiance of the truth they know about God (1:18–19, 21, 28).[60]

How can Paul say that human beings generally know God punishes human unrighteousness with death? The idea that people who were wicked and offended God deserved death, whether in this life or in a form of suffering after their physical death, was widely believed in antiquity, and Paul assumed this general knowledge here (e.g., Deut 30:15–20; Plato, *Republic* 1.330d–e; Pss. Sol. 15:10–11; Luke 23:41).[61] Later he will explain the nature of death as a penalty for sin in more profound terms and describe the solution to this problem as union with the crucified and risen Christ (5:12–8:39).[62] Here he simply wants to show that human beings have enough access to the truth about how God punishes unrighteousness to be held justly responsible for the punishment they receive.

Theology in Application

The main theological teaching of this passage lies in what it says about the justice and equity of God's wrath. Although "the righteousness of God" in 1:17 is much more than simply a reference to God's fairness, it certainly includes that notion, and this first section of Paul's explanation of the gospel focuses on God's fairness in bringing his wrath against human beings.

59. Max Zerwick and Mary Grosvenor, *A Grammatical Analysis of the Greek New Testament*, 5th ed. (Rome: Pontifical Biblical Institute, 1996), 461; Zerwick, *Biblical Greek*, 68–69 (§§215–17).

60. Cf. Cranfield, *Romans*, 1:135, quoting Apollinarius (fourth-century AD)

61. Cf. Meyer, *Romans*, 71–72; Lagrange, *Romains*, 34; Wilckens, *An die Römer (Röm 1–5)*, 115.

62. Cf. Dunn, *Romans 1–8*, 69.

The Reasonableness of God's Wrath

Paul maintains that at some point in the distant past human beings faced a choice of whether to act in accord with what they knew to be true and worship the Creator of the natural world or, instead, to worship the creation itself. Their fateful decision to worship the creature rather than the Creator, therefore, was indefensible (1:20) and justifiably brought God's punishment.

The form in which God's wrath is being revealed against this ongoing rebellion, moreover, is itself just, since it is commensurate with the crime. Just as it was irrational not to conclude from the creation that a powerful, eternal God was its maker and instead to claim in effect that creatures made themselves, so God's punishment of this rebellion affected the ability of human beings to think clearly about God, his creatures, and how they should relate to one another. They became "futile" in their reasoning powers and "their foolish heart was darkened" (1:21). They called foolishness wisdom (1:22) and traded the truth for a lie (1:25). They refused to give God their stamp of approval, and so God gave them minds that could not distinguish between the worthwhile and the worthless (1:28).

This inability to think in accord with the truth about God, his creation, and the way creatures should relate to one another worked itself out in practical terms in a wide variety of social ills. Paul probably highlighted homoerotic sexual activity because it was such a clear example of human beings, blinded by passion, engaging in activity that was contrary to nature and ended in dishonor and futility. The social ills Paul fires off in rapid succession in 1:29–31, similarly, describe a society that does not function because its individual members are blinded by their own passions and have therefore lost the ability to think clearly and act rationally for the good of the whole. In summary, human beings have suppressed the truth about God; this has led to impiety and unrighteousness; and the unrighteousness is itself the outpouring of God's wrath in the present on those who richly deserve precisely this punishment (1:18).

The Reasonableness of Paul's Argument

In applying this passage to the contemporary church it is important to avoid a possible misunderstanding about it. Paul is not claiming that every human being who does not believe the gospel thinks and lives in the confused and morally reprehensible way he describes here. As the structure of the larger argument of Romans reveals, Paul is purposefully offering a sweeping assessment of humanity as a way of drawing a fictional interlocutor (2:1) into agreement with him so that he can show this interlocutor that he too falls under the same indictment. Paul knew that some unbelievers had a better understanding of God and a higher moral standard than what he describes here, and Paul will bring those people to the attention of his interlocutor later in the argument (2:14–15).[63] For now, he focuses on what was often the case in Greco-Roman society rather than what was always the case.

The passage speaks most directly to the issue of God's fairness in punishing people by turning them over to the consequences of their sin. The notion of God punishing people at all is profoundly offensive to the modern imagination, at least in the West, and various efforts have arisen, even within Christianity itself, to avoid the idea. The notion of God's wrath against impiety and unrighteousness, however, is both clearly taught in this passage and is part of the fabric of the Bible's picture of God. In the Bible generally, just as in this passage, God's wrath is a critical component of his righteousness. It is not "right" or "just" in biblical terms for someone who is stronger to stand on the sidelines and watch while wicked people oppress the weak.

In his account of the Rwandan genocide of 1994, Philip Gourevitch tells the story of how, after Hutu Power militias had mercilessly slaughtered at least eight-hundred thousand Rwandan Tutsi children, women, and men merely because they belonged to a different social group, many of the perpetrators of the genocide escaped over the border to Goma, Zaire. When they arrived, befuddled international-aid agencies treated them as needy refugees rather than as fugitive murderers. Gourevitch reports that an acquaintance of his who knew the complexities of the situation arrived in the city during this time. He stared at the volcanic mountain that overshadowed the refugee camps and promised God that if the volcano erupted and wiped out the killers he would start going back to church.[64] At such moments, the often unpopular doctrine of the wrath of God seems much more appealing. In situations such as the Rwandan genocide, it seems only right that the One who is both powerful and just should step in, rescue the weaker party, punish the oppressor, and restore justice.

Isaiah 59 offers just such a picture of God's righteousness and wrath. It portrays a society that has run amok because it has denied the truth about God and his requirements for treating others with compassion and justice. Injustice prevails in court, and violence rules in the street (59:4, 6). "Their feet run to evil, and they are swift to shed innocent blood" (59:7; cf. Rom. 3:15). The victims of this oppression realize that they are themselves not innocent and so are hesitant to call upon God to bring them justice: "We hope for justice, but there is none; for salvation, but it is far from us. For our transgressions are multiplied before you, and our sins testify against us" (Isa 59:11–12).

At this point, the Lord himself takes the situation in hand, "displeased . . . that there was no justice . . . and . . . no one to intercede" (59:15–16). He puts on the armor of warfare, the "garments of vengeance for clothing" (v. 17), and, upheld by "his righteousness" (v. 16), brings salvation to the oppressed. This picture of God's salvation involves repaying his adversaries with wrath according to their deeds

63. Godet, *Romans*, 100.

64. Philip Gourevitch, *We Wish to Inform You That Tomorrow We Will Be Killed with Our Families: Stories from Rwanda* (New York: Picador, 1998), 166–67.

(v. 18), but it also ends on a note of hope for those adversaries. Eventually, people from west to east will fear the Lord (v. 19), and "a Redeemer will come to Zion, to those in Jacob who turn from transgression" (v. 20).[65]

Paul's picture of God's wrath also ends in hope, as we already know from 1:16–17. Ultimately, God's righteousness, which includes his wrath, leads to the salvation of everyone who believes the gospel, whether Jew or Greek (cf. 11:26–27).

Thinking about God and Treating Others with Love and Justice

Romans 1:18–32 also teaches that a close link exists between how people think about God and the judgments they make about how to act. The truth God revealed about himself to humanity through creation and for which he held them responsible was that he was the Creator of everything and they should have thanked and worshiped him for what he made. Paul put all this into the past tense because he wanted to depict a situation in primordial history in which people had a correct, although rudimentary, understanding of God and his creative power and then abandoned it. After abandoning the one true God, humanity's situation became much more complex.

There is no clear correspondence today, anymore than there was in Paul's time, between societies that are just and societies where most people worship one God as creator of all things. Paul has set up the argument so that his interlocutor, who turns out to be a Jewish man in 2:17, will imagine that Jewish society is more just than gentile society, but Paul's larger point in 1:18–3:20 is that this is not, in fact, the case. Similarly, it would be hard to argue that there is more justice, say, in Islamic societies, Jewish neighborhoods, or heavily Christianized areas where a large proportion of people worship one creator God than in other more secular or polytheistic societies. What data could possibly prove such a claim? Often those most affected by injustice have no voice and leave no objectively measurable data behind. The terrible truth is that some of the most horrific societal acts of mass murder in recorded history—the Holocaust, the Rwandan genocide, efforts at "ethnic cleansing" in Bosnia—have taken place within countries where the society's governing authorities and the church's institutions were closely allied.[66]

Paul's argument implies, however, that individual Christian congregations and individual Christians, wherever they are located, should be more just than the societies in which they live, and that this justice begins with their worship of the one God.

65. The translation of Isa 59:19 is fraught with difficulty, but the interpretation adopted here reads the verse through the lens of Ps 102:15 and 113:3–4. See Shalom M. Paul, *Isaiah 40–66: Translation and Commentary*, ECC (Grand Rapids: Eerdmans, 2012), 511.

66. Timothy Longman, *Christianity and Genocide in Rwanda*, African Studies (Cambridge: Cambridge University Press, 2010), 1–30.

Paul does not say this directly in 1:18–32, but the portrait of how believers should live that appears near the end of Romans turns out to be almost the mirror image of the portrait of unbelievers developed here.[67] There, God restores the capacity of believers to think rationally about himself. Instead of futile thinking, idolatry, and dishonorable conduct, believers now give to God "reasonable worship" (12:1–2), and they treat others honorably, whether they are believers or unbelievers (12:10, 17). Haughtiness and strife are replaced with humility and harmony (12:3–8, 16; cf. 13:13), violence with a refusal to retaliate even against persecutors (12:14, 17–21), and an empty and foolish claim to wisdom with a refusal to be wise in one's own sight (12:16). Unrestrained debauchery is replaced with a realistic appraisal of the eschatological urgency of the times (13:11–14), and a refusal to glorify the Creator is replaced by a united company of believers from a wide variety of cultures glorifying God with one voice (15:6, 8–12).

Romans 1:18–32, and its counterpart in Romans 12:1–15:13, challenge the church to be a society that lives in the way God intended human beings to live when he created them. Only by living out this positive alternative to the proud, self-absorbed, exploitative, and violent way of life that dominates so much of the fallen world around it will the church bear a credible witness to the truth of the gospel.

67. Beale, *We Become What We Worship*, 216–22.

CHAPTER 4

Romans 2:1–16

Literary Context

In Romans, Paul wants to show that the gospel is for everyone without exception. He is obligated to proclaim the gospel to Greeks, to barbarians, to wise, to the unlearned—and to Jews. If the good news of God's saving righteousness in Jesus Christ is for everyone, then the bad news that all stand under condemnation apart from God's righteousness is also for everyone. Thus, in 1:18–32 Paul explained that God is revealing his wrath against all humanity for its ungodliness and unrighteousness. Paul explained this in such a way, however, that some Jewish unbelievers might well assume he was only describing gentiles, not Jews. After a long description of the idolatry and sexual immorality of gentiles, for example, the Wisdom of Solomon takes comfort that these vices have not misled Israel (11:15–14:31; 15:4–5). Whereas God poured out his wrath on the wicked Egyptians and the "accursed race" (σπέρμα . . . κατηραμένον) of Canaanites, he gave blessing to Israel and merely chastened them as a father would discipline a son (11:1–14; 12:3–11, 19–22; 15:1–6; 15:18–16:29):

> For they were killed by the bites of locusts and flies, and no healing was found for them, because they deserved to be punished by such things; but your sons were not conquered even by the teeth of venomous serpents, for your mercy came to their help and healed them. (16:9–10)

In Romans 2:1–29, therefore, Paul wants to show that the good news of God's saving righteousness is not merely for impious and wicked gentiles but for Jews also, because they stand as much in need of God's saving power as gentiles. Paul does this by emphasizing God's fairness in judging the whole world impartially, Jews included. It is not enough to condemn evil, to possess the Mosaic law, to teach the law to others, or to carry the physical mark of circumcision in order to avoid God's wrath and receive eternal life on the final day. As an impartial judge, God focuses on what one does, not on the social group to which one belongs.

In 2:1–29 Paul constructs a Jewish interlocutor with two different approaches to how he will survive the coming day of God's wrath. On one hand, in 2:1–3b and

2:17–24 this interlocutor seems unaware that he too is a sinner who falls under the indictment of what Paul has just said in 1:18–32. In these sections of the argument, Paul wants to point out that his interlocutor's view of his own obedience to the law is far too optimistic.[1] On the other hand, in 2:3c–16 and 2:25–29 the interlocutor seems to think that his Jewishness alone, evident particularly in his circumcision, will rescue him from God's wrath despite his sin.

It is true that Paul does not specifically call his fictional debating partner a Jew until the beginning of the next subsection (2:17), and for this reason some interpreters think that Paul's opponent is not Jewish at all or at least that Paul intends to make no distinction between Jew and gentile at this point.[2] The evidence that he refers to a Jewish debating partner, however, is too weighty to make this more general reading convincing. Paul refers to "the Jew first and also the Greek" in 2:9–10; he introduces the "law" into the argument in 2:12–16; and, as C. John Collins has pointed out, he uses a common Old Testament strategy in 2:14–15 of indicting Israel by comparing their sinfulness to gentile piety.[3]

In 2:1–16, then, Paul exposes as unbiblical and un-Jewish his interlocutor's hard-hearted attitude toward his own sin and God's mercy. His interlocutor, like the gentile, is unrighteous, and since God is an impartial judge the interlocutor stands as firmly under the sentence of condemnation as any gentile.

V. God's Wrath against Human Sin Is a Demonstration of His Righteousness (1:18–32)

➡ **VI. Jews Are Also Subject to God's Wrath (2:1–3:20)**

A. God as an Impartial Judge Not Merely of Gentiles but of Jews Also (2:1–16)

B. God as an Impartial Judge Even of Jews Who Teach the Law and Possess Circumcision (2:17–29)

C. Objections to Paul's Understanding of God's Impartial Judgment (3:1–8)

D. Scripture's Testimony That Everyone Is under Sin (3:9–20)

VII. The Death of Christ Demonstrates God's Righteousness and Excludes Human Boasting (3:21–31)

1. On this element of Paul's argument, see particularly Simon Gathercole, *Where Is Boasting? Early Jewish Soteriology and Paul's Response in Romans 1–5* (Grand Rapids: Eerdmans, 2002), 197–215.

2. E.g., Franz J. Leenhardt, *The Epistle to the Romans: A Commentary*, trans. Harold Knight (Cleveland: World, 1957), 73–74; Schlatter, *Romans*, 48; Luke Timothy Johnson, *Reading Romans: A Literary and Theological Commentary*, Reading the New Testament Series (Macon, GA: Smyth & Helwys, 2001), 37–41. Cf. Longenecker, *Romans*, 245–46.

3. On the third element, see C. John Collins, "Echoes of Aristotle in Romans 2:14–15: Or, Maybe Abimelech Was Not So Bad After All," *Journal of Markets and Morality* 13 (2010): 142. Collins gives as examples of this OT motif Josh 2:1–4; Ruth 1:14; 1 Sam 7:1–2 (cf. Josh 9:17); 2 Sam 15:18–22; 1 Kgs 17:8–16, 24 (cf. 18:36–37); Jer 38:7–13 (cf. 39:15–18); Jonah 1:16; 3:5–10.

Main Idea

Here Paul explains that doing what is good, not merely condemning those who are bad, will count on the day of judgment, and the doing, not the hearing of God's law, leads to justification on that day. Paul demonstrates this in the service of his overall point that God will not favor Jews over gentiles on the day of judgment but will treat all in the same way, condemning the wicked among the Jews just as he condemns the wicked among the gentiles.

Translation

(See pages 121–23.)

Structure

Paul has been speaking in the third-person plural up to 1:18–32, but in 2:1a he suddenly speaks directly, in the vocative voice and in the second-person singular, to a fictional interlocutor. The passage falls into three main parts.

In 2:1b–5 Paul assumes that his fictional interlocutor has joined him in condemning the ungodly and unrighteous people of 1:18–32. He points out that having such an attitude toward others at the same time that one is oblivious to one's own sin and impending judgment reveals a heart hardened toward God's kindness, forbearance, and patience, and positions one directly underneath the Damocles's sword of God's coming wrath.

In 2:6–11 Paul explains how he can say this with such assurance and why his interlocutor should agree with him: they both know that God is an impartial judge. Paul states this principle at the beginning (2:6) and end of this paragraph (2:11) in language that echoes the biblical text that both he and his interlocutor accept as authoritative. Sandwiched between these two expressions of the principle is a carefully arranged explanation of it. Paul first explains the principle simply from the perspective of the "works" that form the criterion of God's judgment, using both positive (2:7) and negative (2:8) expressions. He then explains the principle from the same perspective but with the issue of ethnicity introduced, and again uses positive (2:10) and negative expressions (2:9), this time in reverse order.[4] The whole paragraph follows a chiastic pattern and progresses from a simple statement of God's impartial judgment according to works to the more specific point that God's impartiality implies the exclusion of ethnicity as a criterion of God's judgment.

4. Among many interpreters who structure the passage along these lines, see especially Jewett, *Romans*, 194.

Romans 2:1–16

1a	Inference	Therefore, **you are without excuse, O man**
b	Description	everyone who judges.
c	Sphere	For in that which you judge the other,
d	Explanation of 1a	**you condemn yourself,**
e	Explanation of 1c–d	for **you—the one who judges—practice the same things.**
2a	Assertion	Now **we know that the judgment ...**
b	Agency	pronounced by God on those who practice such things
c	Object	**... is according to truth.**
3a	Rhetorical Question	And **do you, O man think this:**
b	Description	who judges those who practice such things and does them yourself
c	Content	that *you* will escape the judgment pronounced by God?
4a	Rhetorical Question	Or **do you despise the abundance**
b	List	of his [1] kindness and
c		[2] forbearance and [3] patience,
d		not knowing that the kindness of God is trying to lead you to a complete change of mind?
5a		But in accord with your hardness and unchanging heart
b	Assertion	**you are treasuring up wrath for yourself in the day of the wrath and**
c	Expansion	**the revelation**
d		of the righteous judgment
e	Agency	of God
6a	Description	who will render to each person
b	Manner	in accord with his or her works: (Prov 24:12; Ps 62:12)
7a	Explanation	on one hand eternal life to those who seek glory and

Continued on next page.

Continued from previous page.

b	List	honor and
c		immortality
d	Means	by endurance in good work; but,
8a	Alternative	on the other hand, there will be wrath and anger for those characterized by selfish ambition and
b	Description	who are disobedient to the truth but obedient to unrighteousness
9a	Restatement (of 8a)	affliction and distress on every human life who works at what is bad,
b	Expansion	the Jew first and also
c		the Greek; but
d	Alternative	glory and honor and peace
10a	Object	to everyone who works what is good,
b	Expansion	the Jew first and also
c		the Greek.
11a	Explanation of 2:6–10	For **there is no partiality with God.**
12a	Explanation cont.	For **as many as have sinned …**
b	Sphere	apart from the law
c	Result	**… will also be destroyed**
d	Sphere	apart from the law,

e	Restatement/Contrast	and **as many as have sinned ...**
f	Sphere	in the law
g	Result	**... will be judged**
h	Sphere	through the law.
13	Explanation of 2:11–12	For **it is not the hearers of the law who are righteous before God, but the doers of the law will be justified**
14a	Explanation of 2:13	For whenever gentiles do the things of the law,
b	Description	who do not have the law by nature,
c	Assertion	**they are a law to themselves**
15a	Explanation	in that [1] they show the work of the law written in their hearts,
b	List	[2] their conscience bearing witness with them and
c		[3] their thoughts among one another accusing or even defending
16a	Time	on the day when God judges the hidden things of human beings
	Standard	according to my gospel,
b	Agency	through Christ Jesus.

In 2:12–16 Paul introduces the issue of the Mosaic law into the argument to explain that Jewish possession of the law does not nullify the principle that God will make no distinction between Jew and gentile on the day of judgment. Doing the law, not possessing the law, will lead to justification on that day. Gentiles too have a moral compass that functions as a form of God's law. It sometimes agrees with the Mosaic law and sometimes leads them to righteous conduct. Because of this, God will be able to judge people justly on the final day apart from the question of whether or not they possess the Mosaic law.

Exegetical Outline

VI. Jews Are Also Subject to God's Wrath (2:1–3:20)

➦ **A. God as an Impartial Judge Not Merely of Gentiles but of Jews Also (2:1–16)**

1. Paul Addresses a Fictional Jewish Interlocutor (2:1a)
2. Paul's Interlocutor Stands in Danger of Judgment (2:1b–5)
3. This Is True Because God Is an Impartial Judge (2:6–11)
   a. Paul states his theme (2:6)
   b. Positive explanation (2:7)
   c. Negative explanation (2:8)
   d. Negative explanation, with an ethnic element (2:9)
   e. Positive explanation, with an ethnic element (2:10)
   f. Paul restates his theme (2:11)
4. Jewish Possession of the Mosaic Law Makes Jews No More Likely Than Gentiles to Be Acquitted at the Final Judgment (2:12–16)
   a. Only doers of the law will be justified (2:12–13)
   b. Gentiles can be doers of the law as well as Jews (2:14–15)
   c. God will hold Jews and gentiles to the same standard at the final judgment (2:16)

Explanation of the Text

2:1 Therefore, you are without excuse, O man—everyone who judges. For in that which you judge the other, you condemn yourself, for you—the one who judges—practice the same things (Διὸ ἀναπολόγητος εἶ, ὦ ἄνθρωπε πᾶς ὁ κρίνων· ἐν ᾧ γὰρ κρίνεις τὸν ἕτερον, σεαυτὸν κατακρίνεις, τὰ γὰρ αὐτὰ πράσσεις ὁ κρίνων). The one who has applauded the outpouring of God's wrath on the ungodly in 1:18–32 but then imagines that God will excuse his own ungodliness stands self-condemned.

Paul has been speaking in the third person, but now suddenly shifts to the second-person singular and, using present tenses, addresses a single person directly. It is as if he steps out of the page and looks directly at the individual to whom he speaks. This was a common rhetorical device among philosophers both when they taught their disciples orally and in their writings.[5]

"Therefore" (διό) normally draws an inference from something that precedes it (1:24; 4:22; 13:5; 15:22), and although the connection here is not entirely clear (cf. 15:7), the inference is probably that the person to whom Paul suddenly turns belongs to the group he has just described in 1:18–32. Like them, this person is "without excuse" (ἀναπολογήτους, cf. 1:20), although now, in the context of judgment (κρίνω) and condemnation (κατακρίνω), this expression takes on more of a legal nuance.[6] Paul's interlocutor, like the people described in 1:18–32, knows who God is, what he requires, and that the penalty for an impious and vicious way of life is death, but this person "practices" these death-deserving deeds anyway.[7] He is also someone who has just joined Paul in "judging" (κρίνεις) or "condemning" (κατακρίνεις) the unrighteous people described in 1:18–32. Paul has sprung a rhetorical trap on his interlocutor.

Who is this person? Paul becomes more explicit about his identity in 2:12, 17, 23, and 25. He is addressing a Jew who possesses the Mosaic law, the ethical and legal code of Israel that separates them from the nations. Sometimes Paul's interlocutor believes that he is basically obedient to the law, and Paul seeks to show him that he too is a sinner (2:1–3b, 17–24). Yet most of Paul's argument assumes that his interlocutor expects God to hold him to a different standard than the gentiles. He thinks God will condemn the unrighteous among the gentiles to the death they deserve (1:32) but will treat his own people Israel more leniently because of his covenant with them.[8]

Such an attitude did not characterize all Jews, nor was it unique to them.[9] The profound awareness of personal sin in the Prayer of Manasseh (9–14; cf. Sir 39:5) and Paul's correction of the ethnic boasting of gentile believers later in Romans itself (Rom 11:13–36) is enough to demonstrate this. Paul is concerned at this point in his argument, however, to show that "all—both Jews and Greeks—are under sin" (3:9). It made sense, then, to set up a dialogue with a Jew who thinks he will be treated more leniently than gentiles on the final day of judgment either because God will show him

5. Stowers, *Diatribe*, 85–93.

6. See LSJ 117; *CGELNT* 28, both s.v. ἀναπολόγητος; and the use of the term in a legal context in Dionysius of Halicarnassus, *Ant. rom.* 7.46.4.

7. The repetition of the term πράσσω in 1:32 and 2:1 (πράσσοντες, πράσσουσιν, πράσσεις) emphasizes the similarity between the conduct of the interlocutor in 2:1 and those deserving of death in 1:32.

8. *Pace* both Stanley K. Stowers (*A Rereading of Romans: Justice, Jews, and Gentiles* [New Haven: Yale University Press, 1994], 37, 100–104), who argues that Paul addresses only gentiles in 2:1–16, and Gathercole (*Where Is Boasting?* 197–215), who argues that Paul's interlocutor is a Jew who boasts primarily in his obedience to the law.

9. So, correctly, Stowers, *Diatribe*, 112.

favoritism despite his disobedience or because he thinks of himself as actually obedient to the whole Mosaic law.[10]

That both attitudes could exist side by side within the Judaism of Paul's time is clear from the Wisdom of Solomon.[11] There, the author emphasizes how the idolatrous Egyptians who enslaved God's people were punished justly and harshly for their sins but that when God's people sinned, he dealt with them more mildly (Wis 11:9–10; 12:20–22; 15:1–6; 15:18–19:22):

> For even if we sin we are yours, knowing your power; but we will not sin, because we know that we are accounted yours. (Wis 15:2)

Paul's use of the present tense throughout the sentence (κρίνων, κρίνεις, κατακρίνεις, πράσσεις, κρίνων again) and the expressions "in that which" (ἐν ᾧ) and "the same things" (τὰ . . . αὐτά) drive home the interlocutor's intense lack of self-perception.[12] He habitually judges others for wicked actions that match his own conduct. Paul hopes to open this person's eyes to what is actually taking place in all this: he is engaged in self-condemnation (cf. Matt 7:1–5) and stands exposed, without any credible defense (ἀναπολόγητος).

2:2 Now we know that the judgment pronounced by God on those who practice such things is according to truth (οἴδαμεν δὲ ὅτι τὸ κρίμα τοῦ θεοῦ ἐστιν κατὰ ἀλήθειαν ἐπὶ τοὺς τὰ τοιαῦτα πράσσοντας). When God renders his verdict of judgment against those who do evil, his standard of judgment is the truth about their conduct, not whether they have joined him in condemning others.

The phrase "now we know that" (οἴδαμεν δὲ ὅτι) introduces a description of knowledge that the author shares with his audience (Rom 3:19; 8:28; 1 Tim 1:8), and here his "audience" at the rhetorical level is his interlocutor. It was a common conviction among Jews that God judged people according to reality rather than appearance.[13] As Proverbs 24:12 (LXX) puts it:

> Be aware that the Lord is familiar with the heart of everyone, and he who formed breath for all, he knows everything, he who will render to each according to his deeds.

God, who sees into the human heart (cf. 2:16), has no trouble piercing through the hypocrisy of those who condemn others for the same conduct that they "practice" (πρασσοντας; cf. 1:32). The negative verdict he renders (κρίμα) matches the truth of what the defendant has done (cf. 2:5–6).[14] This strict truthfulness stands in contrast to human thinking, which suppresses the truth that it knows about God and exchanges it for a lie (1:18, 25).

2:3 And do you, O man who judges those who practice such things and does them yourself, think this: that *you* will escape the judgment

10. Stowers (*Rereading Romans*, 101) plausibly argues that Paul sets up a dialogue with a stock character of ancient moral reasoning, the "pretentious person . . . who hypocritically pretends to moral virtue and arrogantly criticizes others even though he does the same kind of things" (cf., e.g., Epictetus, *Diatr.* 2.21.11–12; Plutarch, *Curios.* 515D). Stowers believes, however, that the fictional dialogue is with a gentile rather than a Jew.

11. For discussion of this text and others where these themes come together, see Gathercole, *Where Is Boasting?*, 163–82.

12. Jesus uses the same phrase (ἐν ᾧ) twice to perform exactly the same function in Matt 7:2. The present tenses are probably "customary" presents, on which see Smyth, *Greek Grammar*, §1876 and Wallace, *Greek Grammar*, 521–22, 523n26.

13. Cf. Dunn, *Romans 1–8*, 80.

14. The term "judgment" (κρίμα) in the translation is not the act of judging but the product of judging (as the -μα ending indicates), and the phrase "pronounced by God" renders a subjective genitive (τοῦ θεοῦ). This judgment, then, is a "verdict" (see Godet, *Romans*, 115). Paul uses the term twelve times, almost always of a negative verdict (Rom 2:3; 3:8; 5:16; 13:2; 1 Cor 11:29; 11:34; Gal 5:10; 1 Tim 3:6; 5:12).

pronounced by God? (λογίζῃ δὲ τοῦτο, ὦ ἄνθρωπε ὁ κρίνων τοὺς τὰ τοιαῦτα πράσσοντας καὶ ποιῶν αὐτά, ὅτι σὺ ἐκφεύξῃ τὸ κρίμα τοῦ θεοῦ;). The one who practices the very wickedness he condemns is hardly an exception to the rule that God will condemn the wicked!

The phrase "those who practice such things" (τοὺς τὰ τοιαῦτα πράσσοντας) appears for the second time since its use in 1:32 to describe those who "practice" the vices listed in 1:29–31. Paul's imagined Jewish interlocutor would perhaps consider himself innocent of the sort of idolatry and sexual irregularity described in 1:19–28. If he is honest with himself, however, he could not escape the indictment of many of the sins in 1:29–32. Cunning, greed, malice, envy, strife, mean-spiritedness, arrogance, disobedience to parents, and faithlessness at least are common to human existence and society. Later Paul will accuse his interlocutor of stealing, adultery, and handling goods stolen from gentile temples (2:22).[15] Paul's interlocutor must admit, then, that he is among "those who practice such things."

Paul uses the verb "consider" (λογίζομαι) more often than any other New Testament author, and he uses it in Romans more than anywhere else.[16] He can use it with its most basic meaning, "count" (e.g., Rom 4:4), or with its less frequent meaning "hold (an opinion), think" (e.g., Rom 3:28).[17] Here it seems to have something of both meanings. His interlocutor thinks that he will escape God's judgment by an odd calculation: he joins God in condemning unrighteousness (2:1a), but he practices unrighteousness himself (2:1b); he knows that God is impartial (2:2), but he somehow thinks he will nevertheless escape God's condemnation (2:3).

Paul sets this up as a rhetorical question to expose its folly. God cannot both render judgments "according to truth" (2:2) and allow someone who practices unrighteousness (2:1b) to escape condemnation. The ridiculous nature of his interlocutor's position is accentuated by the emphatic second-person singular pronoun (σύ, "you"). Paul asks his interlocutor if he thinks that somehow he is an exception to the rule of God's impartial judgment. The conclusion should be obvious: he is not an exception.[18]

2:4 Or do you despise the abundance of his kindness and forbearance and patience, not knowing that the kindness of God is trying to lead you to a complete change of mind? (ἢ τοῦ πλούτου τῆς χρηστότητος αὐτοῦ καὶ τῆς ἀνοχῆς καὶ τῆς μακροθυμίας καταφρονεῖς, ἀγνοῶν ὅτι τὸ χρηστὸν τοῦ θεοῦ εἰς μετάνοιάν σε ἄγει;). If Paul's unbelieving Jewish interlocutor snubs God's patience with his continued wickedness, then he must be unaware that there will come a day of reckoning whose wrath God, in his mercy, is trying to spare him.

Paul now formulates a second rhetorical question that amounts to another guess at what his interlocutor could be thinking. The coupling of one rhetorical question to another with the particle "or" (ἤ) is not unusual in Paul, especially in polemical contexts. When Paul does this elsewhere, the second rhetorical question approaches the same issue from a slightly different angle, just as it does here (1 Cor 9:6; 11:22; 2 Cor 3:1).[19] Paul and his interlocutor agree that God is rich in "kindness" (χρηστότης), "forbearance" (ἀνοχή), and "patience" (μακροθυμία). God is often said to have these

15. Gathercole, *Where Is Boasting?*, 211–12.

16. It occurs forty times in the NT, thirty-four of which are in Paul and nineteen of which are in Romans.

17. See BDAG 597–98, s.v. λογίζομαι.

18. So correctly Meyer, *Romans*, 82. Paul does not mean "you, of all people" (Jewett, *Romans*, 200; cf. Sanday and Headlam, *Romans*, 55), which would imply that his interlocutor is more wicked than the gentiles whom he judges. Paul's point is rather that his interlocutor is no less wicked than they are.

19. BDAG 432, s.v. ἤ 1dβ.

qualities in ancient Jewish and early Christian literature. They are frequently used in descriptions of his generous willingness to forgive the offenses of people or to endure their transgressions in order to give them time to realize the disaster that awaits them if they do not repent (Exod 34:6 [LXX]; Ps 24:7 [LXX; 25:7 Eng.]; Pr. Man. 7, 11; Wis 11:23; 15:1; Let. Aris. 188, 194; T. Gad 4:7; Rom 3:26; 9:22; Eph 2:7; Titus 3:4; 1 Pet 3:20; cf. 2 Bar. 21:20).[20]

If Paul's interlocutor views God's forbearance with contempt, then he must not realize its purpose: God, in his kindness, is trying to lead him to "a complete change of mind" (μετάνοια).[21] The verb "lead" (ἄγει) is a "conative" present, referring to action that the subject is attempting to accomplish.[22] It effectively portrays God as desiring the repentance of those from whom he is withholding the final expression of his wrath. As 2 Peter 3:9 puts it, "the Lord . . . is patient [μακροθυμεῖ] toward you, not wishing that any should perish, but that all should reach repentance [μετάνοιαν]."

The theological belief expressed here is, again, something that Christians and Jews shared (e.g., Let. Aris. 188; Wis 12:10) and that Paul expresses because he thinks his interlocutor should agree with him on this point. The rhetorical question seeks to show that the interlocutor thinks in a way that is inconsistent with what a Jewish person should believe about God.

2:5 But in accord with your hardness and unchanging heart you are treasuring up wrath for yourself in the day of the wrath and the revelation of the righteous judgment of God (κατὰ δὲ τὴν σκληρότητά σου καὶ ἀμετανόητον καρδίαν θησαυρίζεις σεαυτῷ ὀργὴν ἐν ἡμέρᾳ ὀργῆς καὶ ἀποκαλύψεως δικαιοκρισίας τοῦ θεοῦ). The stubborn insistence of Paul's Jewish interlocutor that he is a special case, not subject to God's condemnation of the unrighteous, will only make his condemnation that much more severe on the final day.

The conjunction that begins the sentence (δέ) is adversative. It states the reality that stands in contrast to the delusional thinking of Paul's interlocutor. The condition of the interlocutor's heart is the origin of the bizarre notion that he can get away with the very sins he condemns in others (cf. Matt 15:18–20; Mark 7:20–23): it is "in accord with" (κατά) his "hardness" (σκληρότης) and his "unchanging" (ἀμετανόητος) heart that he thinks this.[23] Paul's language recalls biblical descriptions of Israel's need to turn away from their hardheartedness and impenitence (LXX Deut 10:16; Psa 94:8 [95:8 Eng.]; Jer 8:6). The interlocutor's own unresponsiveness to God means that while God's impending judgment hangs over him like Damocles's sword, he continues to "accrue a treasure" (θησαυρίζω) of divine wrath (cf. Pss. Sol. 9:5; Jas 5:3).

In the Old Testament, the day of God's wrath not only dawns for gentiles (Isa 13:9, 13; Ezek 38:18–19, 23; Zeph 3:8) but also, in an ironic way, for Israel because of Israel's wickedness (Zeph 1:15, 18; 2:2–3).[24] This is exactly Paul's point here. It now becomes clear that when Paul spoke in 1:18 of God's eschatological wrath being "revealed (ἀποκαλύπτεται) against all the impiety and unrighteousness of human beings," he meant

20. On the theological importance of Exod 34:6–7 throughout the OT, see P. R. House, "God's Character and the Wholeness of Scripture," *Scottish Bulletin of Evangelical Theology* 22 (2004): 4–17.

21. BDAG 640–41 and *CGELNT* 230, both s.v. μετάνοια.

22. Smyth, *Greek Grammar*, §1878; Wallace, *Greek Grammar*, 534–35.

23. For the use of κατά here to mean "because," cf. 2:7 ("because of persistence in good work" [καθ' ὑπομονὴν ἔργου ἀγαθοῦ]). See BDAG 512–13, s.v. κατά 5aδ.

24. Marvin Sweeney, *Zephaniah*, Hermeneia (Minneapolis: Fortress, 2003), 99.

all human beings without exception. This is the sense in which the "revelation [ἀποκαλύψεως] of the righteous judgment [δικαιοκρισίας] of God" is righteous—it is fair, measured out to all on the same basis, and without partiality.

2:6 who will render to each person in accord with his or her works (ὃς ἀποδώσει ἑκάστῳ κατὰ τὰ ἔργα αὐτου). God's character as a righteous judge will be revealed on the future day when he pours out his wrath because he will judge people by their actions, not by the social group to which they belong.

This relative clause describes the basis for Paul's statement that on the day of wrath God's judgment will be "righteous."[25] Its wording is almost identical to the last clause in both Proverbs 24:12 LXX and Psalm 61:13 LXX (62:13 Heb.; 62:12 Eng.), and it differs from Proverbs 24:12 only in a change of the verb tense that shifts the time of God's repayment from present-day life to a future judgment.[26]

The clause expresses a well-known dictum in Judaism and tends to show up in three contexts. First, it appears in places where the emphasis falls on God's commitment to help the defenseless against the bullies that oppress them (Ps 62:11–12; Prov 24:10–12; Sir 16:11–14; cf. Job 34:10–11, 28; 1 En. 100.7). Second, it occurs in texts where the emphasis falls on God's ability to see through pious verbiage to the condition of the heart (Ps 62:4b; Prov 24:12a; cf. Job 34:11, 21–25; Jer 17:10). Third, it occurs in passages like this one that emphasize the justice with which God judges the unrighteous deeds of both Jews and gentiles (Pss. Sol. 2, 17; cf. Job 34:11, 19).[27]

Divine judgment according to works also appears frequently in early Christian texts (2 Cor 5:10; 11:15; 2 Tim 4:14; 1 Pet 1:17; Rev 2:23; 20:12–13), including later in Romans (14:10–12).[28] It is not, then, a feature of Paul's indictment that separates Christianity and Judaism or Pauline theology and Jewish theology but a basic truth, affirmed in the Scriptures that Paul and his unbelieving Jewish interlocutor shared and on which, Paul believed, they should agree.[29]

How can this feature of biblical and Pauline theology cohere with the equally biblical and especially Pauline conviction, articulated most forcefully in this letter, that no one is innocent of wrongdoing and that if God judged people strictly according to their works, no one would escape punishment? Paul will shortly say that "there is no one righteous, not even one" (3:10) and, alluding to Psalm 143:2, that "by works of the law no flesh will be justified before him" (3:20). Basing his argument on Abraham's relationship with God in Genesis 15:6, he will claim that justification comes "to the one who does not work but believes on him who justifies the impious" (4:4) and that the person is blessed "whom God counts righteous apart from works" (4:6).[30]

The difficulty becomes even more pressing in several statements that follow 2:6. In 2:7–10 and 13 Paul says that God will repay those who do good with eternal life, glory, honor, and peace and will justify (δικαιόω) the doers of the law. In 2:27 he envisions an uncircumcised person who "will judge" the Jew, presumably on the final day, because he has kept the law whereas the Jew has not kept it. To put the problem in a nutshell, how can Paul say both that God will justify those who do the law

25. See the helpful synopsis in Dunn, *Romans 1–8*, 85.

26. So also, Jewett, *Romans*, 204.

27. On the Jewish background, see especially Dunn, *Romans 1–8*, 85.

28. On Rom 14:10–12 as a "judgment of works" despite not mentioning the term "works" (ἔργα), see McFadden, *Judgment according to Works in Romans*, 111.

29. On this, see especially Gathercole, *Where Is Boasting?*, 124–34.

30. Cf. 9:12, 32; 11:6.

(2:13) and that God will justify people apart from works of the law (3:28)?

Interpreters have proposed many solutions to this conundrum, two of which are especially common:

1. Paul speaks in 2:6–10, 13, 27 of the good works that inevitably follow from faith and that God will repay with eternal life (cf. Rom 14:10–12; 1 Cor 4:4–5; 6:9–11; 2 Cor 5:10; Gal 5:21; Eph 6:8; 2 Tim 4:8).[31]
2. In order to demonstrate God's impartiality, Paul says that in principle God will repay eternal life to those whose good works merit it (2:6, 10, 13), but he does not mean that anyone will actually receive eternal life in this way.[32]

Although the arguments for both approaches are almost equally convincing, the second approach is more in line with Paul's purpose in 2:1–29 and is probably correct. Paul is articulating a theological principle that he believed to be true, that he shared with his imaginary Jewish interlocutor (who probably represented many other Jews), and that illustrated the impartiality of God (2:11). This principle is that God does not judge people on the basis of their intellectual grasp of his requirements or their possession of a physical mark such as circumcision but on the basis of whether they obey what they know about his requirements (2:7, 10, 13) from the heart (2:26, 29). The critical criteria at the judgment will be their inner disposition toward him and the way of life it produces. God will not render judgment based on what people possess, know, or hear. Nor will his judgment take into account the social group with which they identify.

Paul does not say in this section of his argument that anyone will actually be found whose inner disposition and outward actions are so fully synchronized with what God requires that they will be justified on this basis (2:13) and able to condemn others without hypocrisy (2:27). The gentiles of 2:14–15 who have God's law written on their hearts only obey it occasionally, not always.[33] It is clear from this passage that Paul believed if anyone were found to have reached this high standard of devotion to God, God would declare them just (2:13) and give them eternal life, glory, honor, and peace on this basis (2:7, 10). It is equally clear from the immediately subsequent argument, however, that Paul did not believe anyone fulfilled this lofty requirement, at least as he had described it in this passage, apart from the gospel. If there is not even one righteous person (3:10), it is clear that "the doers of the law" who "will be justified" (2:13) is, as McFadden has argued, "an empty set."[34]

The gospel that Paul begins to explain in 3:21 demonstrates that there are actually, as Paul writes, many righteous people, made righteous not by living in perfect conformity to the law but by their faith in the gospel (cf. 1:17; 5:19). Additionally, those who have this faith have experienced the transforming power of God's grace in their lives. Rather than sin reigning there, God's grace reigns "through righteousness for eternal life" (5:21).[35] In

31. See, e.g., Godet, *Romans*, 117–18; Sanday and Headlam, *Romans*, 56–57; Schreiner, *Romans*, 114–15; Gathercole, *Where Is Boasting?*, 124–35; Barclay, *Paul and the Gift*, 463–64.

32. See, e.g., Charles Hodge, *Commentary on the Epistle to the Romans* (1886; repr., Grand Rapids: Eerdmans, 1950), 49–50, 53–54; John Ziesler, *Paul's Letter to the Romans*, TPINTC (London: SCM, 1989), 83–84; Moo, *Romans*, 142; McFadden, *Judgment according to Works in Romans*, 139–53; and cf. Longenecker, *Romans*, 266–72.

33. Moo, *Romans*, 153.

34. McFadden, *Judgment according to Works in Romans*, 126. McFadden credits Lee Irons with this helpful phrase (see idem, 126n20). Cf. Calvin, *Romans*, 47; Hodge, *Romans*, 54; Moo, *Romans*, 142, who points out that Paul is not speaking hypothetically here despite the tendency to refer to this view of Paul's argument as "the hypothetical view." Paul believed that if anyone kept the law perfectly, they would be justified on this basis.

35. On the power of God's grace in Paul's thought, see especially Barclay, *Paul and the Gift*, 493–519.

the end, therefore, God's present declaration that those who believe the gospel are righteous—that they are "right with" him—will be confirmed by a future judgment according to works in which their confession of the gospel is found to be consistent with what they have done (14:10–12; 2 Cor 5:10).

Paul was probably thinking as he wrote 2:7, 10, 13, 14–15, 26–27, and 29 of the Christian who would survive the judgment, not because he or she had completely fulfilled the law but because of Christ's death and resurrection. He was probably also thinking of how the believer's justification would, in fact, be confirmed not by perfect obedience to the law but by the transformation in their way of life produced by their experience of God's grace and the power of the Spirit (6:1–23; 8:1–17; and 12:1–15:7). This realization probably shaped the way he phrased his argument in 2:1–29, especially his description of those who seek "glory and honor and immortality" (2:7; cf. Rom 8:18, 21; 9:21; 1 Cor 15:42, 50–54), those who do "what is good" (2:10; cf. 12:2), and those who have experienced "circumcision of the heart ... in the Spirit and not the letter" (2:29). This phrasing is probably what has made it so hard for interpreters to decide whether Paul is speaking here of a justification on the basis of works that no one will actually experience or a justification according to works that believers, justified on the basis of Christ's death, do experience. It is best to interpret the passage, however, according to its place in Paul's argument, and at this point Paul's focus is on God's impartial indictment of all humanity, as his summary of this part of his argument in 3:9–20 shows.

2:7–8 on one hand, eternal life to those who by endurance in good work seek glory and honor and immortality; but, on the other hand, there will be wrath and anger for those characterized by selfish ambition and who are disobedient to the truth but obedient to unrighteousness (τοῖς μὲν καθ' ὑπομονὴν ἔργου ἀγαθοῦ δόξαν καὶ τιμὴν καὶ ἀφθαρσίαν ζητοῦσιν, ζωὴν αἰώνιον· τοῖς δὲ ἐξ ἐριθείας καὶ ἀπειθοῦσι τῇ ἀληθείᾳ πειθομένοις δὲ τῇ ἀδικίᾳ, ὀργὴ καὶ θυμός). God will judge people on the final day according to the goals they have set, whether the eternal goal of a life focused on others or a goal of self-service. One group will receive eternal life; the other group will experience God's intense anger.

Paul now elaborates on what he meant when he said in 2:6 that God would render "to each person in accord with his (or her) works." The two clauses that comprise 2:7–8 are neatly balanced (μέν ... δέ), and this balance emphasizes the fairness of God's future judgment. The shift from the singular ("to each" [ἑκάστῳ]) to the plural ("to those ..." [τοῖς ...]) also emphasizes God's fairness. He treats each person, and all people, impartially.

The first clause states the positive side of God's future "righteous judgment" (δικαιοκρισίας, 2:5). "Eternal life" at the end of the clause is the direct object of the verb "will render" (ἀποδώσει) in 2:6 and refers to complete, never-ending victory over death (5:21; 6:22–23). God will render "eternal life" on the final day of judgment to those who "seek glory and honor and immortality" by means of "endurance in good work." Both the present tense of the participle "seek" (ζητοῦσιν) and the term "endurance" (ὑπομονήν) emphasize the steady, consistent way of life characterizing those who will receive eternal life. The term "endurance" in particular is often followed by a noun in the genitive case that names some hardship as its object, such as war (ἡ ὑπομονὴ τοῦ πολέμου; Polybius, *Histories* 4.51.1), sufferings (ὑπομονὴ ... παθημάτων; 2 Cor 1:6), pain (ὑπομονὴ λύπης; Pseudo-Plato, *Definitions* 412c), or difficult work (ὑπομονὴ πόνων; Pseudo-Plato, *Definitions* 412c). Paul's focus, therefore, is on the effort involved in enduring. Here the object of endurance is "good work" (ἔργου ἀγαθοῦ), a collective phrase that seems to sum up what Paul meant by the plural "works" (ἔργα) in 2:6 when that term is understood in a positive sense. In sum, Paul tells his interlocutor that only those who persevere in what is good will receive eternal life on the final day when God will judge the world with equity.

This would not have been controversial within a Jewish context. Over and over again the Old and New Testament Scriptures, as well as the Jewish literature generally from the Second Temple period, assert that when the day of reckoning comes, God will give life to those who do what is good (e.g., Lev 18:5; Deut 4:1; 5:33; 30:6, 11–20; Ezek 18:5–9; Wis 5:15; 6:18; 1 Macc 7:36; Pss. Sol. 9:4–5; T. Jos. 18:1; 4QMMT C 26–32; Matt 25:46).[36] Paul knows that in reality this principle becomes effective for someone only through "the obedience of faith" (1:5; 16:26) by which people trust that God has graciously forgiven their sins (4:7–8) through the redemptive and reconciling death of Christ (3:24–26) and then, transformed by this grace, begin living in obedience to God (6:17). Here, however, he leaves this gospel-centered outworking of the principle in unexplained and uncontroversial terms for the sake of argument. His interest lies in showing that God's judgment according to this criterion on the final day will be impartial.

Paul's next clause describes a second group whose fate stands opposite (δέ) the first group. Just as the first group will receive "eternal life" (ζωὴν αἰώνιον), so this group will receive "wrath and anger" (ὀργὴ καὶ θυμός). The terms "wrath" and "anger" are in the nominative case and so cannot be direct objects of the verb "will render" (ἀποδώσει) in 2:6. That verb has now become too distant to control the second clause, and Paul either intended the reader to supply the expression "there will be" (ἔσται) or he intended the nominatives as exclamations, "Wrath and anger!"[37] These two terms frequently appear together in the LXX as a description of the Lord's anger against those who oppose him (e.g., Deut 9:19; 29:22; Ps 89:7–8 [90:7–8 Heb. and Eng.]; Isa 10:5; 13:9). They are coupled together in these passages to express the intensity of God's anger, and that was Paul's intention here also.[38] Paul describes the group that will receive God's wrath on the final day in two ways.

First, they are characterized by "selfish ambition" (ἐριθεία). Paul expresses this with an article and a prepositional phrase in the same way that he will later speak of "the one who has faith in Jesus" (ὁ ἐκ πίστεως Ἰησοῦ, 3:26) or "the people of the law" (οἱ ἐκ νόμου, 4:14).[39] The term "selfish ambition" (ἐριθεία) occurs seven times in the NT, and those passages are concerned with self-promotion (Phil 1:17; 2:3), divisiveness (2 Cor 12:20; Gal 5:20), and envy (Jas 3:14, 16). Prior to its occurrence in the NT, the term is rare and shows up in political contexts where it refers to a self-promoting ambitiousness that works not for the common good but for the advancement of one's own power and prestige (Aristotle, *Politics* 1302b 4; 1303a 14).[40] It is possible that Paul thought of this vice as a contrast to seeking "glory and honor and immortality" (δόξαν καὶ τιμὴν καὶ ἀφθαρσίαν; Rom 2:7). In the Greco-Roman world, "immortal glory

36. On judgment according to works in Judaism and early Christianity, see Kent L. Yinger, *Paul, Judaism, and Judgment according to Deeds*, SNTSMS 105 (Cambridge: Cambridge University Press, 1999), 19–140; Gathercole, *Where Is Boasting?*, 37–160; and Chris VanLandingham, *Judgment and Justification in Early Judaism and the Apostle Paul* (Peabody, MA: Hendrickson, 2006), 18–174.

37. Godet, *Romans*, 119; Jewett, *Romans*, 207.

38. Cf. Cranfield, *Romans*, 1:149. The attempt of Godet (*Romans*, 120) and Meyer (*Romans*, 88) to distinguish between the two terms is ill advised. On their meaning, see Harris, *Restraining Rage*, 50–70.

39. Godet, *Romans*, 119; Meyer, *Romans*, 86.

40. Hermann Büchsel, "ἐριθεία," *TDNT* 2:660–61; *TLNT* 2:70–71; BDAG 392 and MGS 819, both s.v. ἐριθεία.

and honor" (ἀθανατον δὸξαν καὶ τιμήν; Polybius, *Histories* 2.70.5 [transl. mine]) were sometimes conferred on those who acted in the interest of the wider community (cf. Polybius, *Histories* 5.9.10; 1 Macc 2:51, 64).

Second, the recipients of God's eschatological wrath are "disobedient to the truth but obedient to unrighteousness" (ἀπειθοῦσιν τῇ ἀληθείᾳ πειθομένοις δὲ τῇ ἀδικίᾳ). This phrase is reminiscent of Paul's description in chapter 1 of the "unrighteousness" (ἀδικία) of those who suppress "the truth" (ἀλήθεια), particularly the truth about God (1:18, 25). Paul had probably intended his fictional interlocutor to identify those people with gentiles, but now this interlocutor learns that he is guilty of the same unrighteousness and deserves the same penalty. In retrospect, then, 1:18–32 had not merely described gentiles but all humanity, including Jews.[41]

2:9–10 affliction and distress upon every human life who works at what is bad, the Jew first and also the Greek; but glory and honor and peace to everyone who works what is good, the Jew first and also the Greek (θλῖψις καὶ στενοχωρία ἐπὶ πᾶσαν ψυχὴν ἀνθρώπου τοῦ κατεργαζομένου τὸ κακόν, Ἰουδαίου τε πρῶτον καὶ Ἕλληνος· δόξα δὲ καὶ τιμὴ καὶ εἰρήνη παντὶ τῷ ἐργαζομένῳ τὸ ἀγαθόν, Ἰουδαίῳ τε πρῶτον καὶ Ἕλληνι). God will not make a distinction between the Jewish individual and the gentile individual when he punishes evil and does good to those who persist in what is good.

Paul repeats what he has just said in 2:7–8 but with three differences that emphasize his overall point and fill out its meaning. First, he reverses the order in which he describes the two groups and what they will receive from God, producing a "chiastic" (A-B-B'-A') sequence. This means that the nominative-case terms "wrath" (ὀργή) and "anger" (θυμός) at the end of 2:8 stand adjacent to the nominative terms "affliction" (θλῖψις) and "distress" (στενοχωρία) at the beginning of 2:9. As a result, a grim list of four items describing the punishment God will measure out to those who deserve it on "the day of . . . wrath" (2:5) stands at the rhetorical center of 2:7–10. This places the emphasis on the disaster that will come to those who do evil on that day.

Second, Paul had referred to the two groups in the plural in 2:7–8, but he now reverts back to the singular of 2:6, an emphasis that is especially clear in the expression "every human life" (πᾶσαν ψυχὴν ἀνθρώπου).[42] This places the focus on the individuality, and therefore the inescapable nature, of the judgment.

Third, he now explicitly states what has been his point all along, that the Jew who does evil will not escape God's condemnation. The day of God's wrath will reveal his "righteous judgment" (2:5), which means that God's judgment will be fair. The Jew does have priority over the gentile in ways that Paul has hinted at in 1:16 and will explain more fully in 3:2 and 9:1–5, but this priority does not mean that God will judge the Jew in a different way than he judges the gentile.

2:11 For there is no partiality with God (οὐ γάρ ἐστιν προσωπολημψία παρὰ τῷ θεῷ). Because God is impartial, he takes no account of one's social group in his work as judge.

The term "partiality" (προσωπολημψία) appears for the first time in extant Greek literature in the NT (Col 3:25; Eph 6:9; Jas 2:1; cf. Acts 10:34; Jas 2:9; 1 Peter 1:17), and within that body of literature this is its earliest use. The term is probably derived from the expressions "to regard the face" (*nakar panim*; LXX, ἐπιγινώσκειν πρόσωπον or θαυμάζειν πρόσωπον) or "to lift up the face" (*nasa*

41. Cf. Cranfield, *Romans 1–8*, 1:140–42.

42. Wilckens, *An die Römer (Röm 1–5)*, 127.

panim; LXX, λαμβάνειν πρόσωπον or θαυμάζειν πρόσωπον) in the Hebrew Scriptures (e.g., Lev 19:15; Deut 1:17; 10:17–18; 16:19; Ps 82:2; cf. 2 Chr 19:7). This expression often appears in instructions to judges to render impartial judgments that are untainted by bribery and that are the same for high and low alike.[43] The basis for this approach was the fair judgment of God himself. In a way that continues to be consistent with the OT, Paul asserts that the equity of God's judgment extends beyond Israel to all the nations of the earth (Pss 67:4; 96:10; 98:9; Isa 11:4).[44]

2:12 For as many as have sinned apart from the law will also be destroyed apart from the law, and as many as have sinned in the law will be judged through the law (ὅσοι γὰρ ἀνόμως ἥμαρτον, ἀνόμως καὶ ἀπολοῦνται· καὶ ὅσοι ἐν νόμῳ ἥμαρτον, διὰ νόμου κριθήσονται). Paul can say that God is impartial because the criterion he will use for judgment on the day of his wrath is not whether one falls within the circle of people marked out by the Mosaic law but whether one has sinned.

This verse, once again, states why (γάρ) Paul can say that there is no partiality with God. It introduces a paragraph (2:12–16) that repeats the point he made in the previous paragraph (2:6–11) about God's impartial judgment on the basis of works. Now, however, Paul makes this point by reference to the Mosaic law and its function of distinguishing between Jews and gentiles. This follows naturally from his reference to Jew and Greek in 2:9–10.

The two occurrences of the relative adjective "as many as" (ὅσοι) emphasize the universality and equity of God's judgment. The criterion of the judgment is not whether one has access to the Mosaic law, as Jews did, but whether one has sinned. Paul does not call the law here specifically "Mosaic" or "Jewish," but that he is speaking specifically of the Jewish law is clear from his assumption that some people sin even though they are "without the law" (ἀνόμως; cf. 1 Cor 9:20–21). All human beings have access to "what is knowable about God" (1:19; cf. 1:28), "the truth that came from God" (1:25; cf. 2:2, 8), and "the righteous decree of God" (1:32). Everyone can discern, to some extent, the difference between "the good" and "the evil" (2:6, 9–10; cf. 1:29–30). To the Jews alone, however, belongs the giving of the law (9:4; cf. 3:2; Eph 2:12), and in this law they have a record of God's will, a basis for deciding the best course of action, and "the embodiment of knowledge and truth" (2:18–20). The law, then, was the feature of Jewish life and culture that distinguished God's people from other peoples. It was "holy," and its commandments were "holy and righteous and good" (7:12). So, to be "in the law" (ἐν νόμῳ)—that is, within (ἐν) its sphere of influence—was a blessing (cf. 3:2; 9:4).[45] For purposes of surviving the day of wrath, however, possessing the law would not matter.[46] The question would only be whether one had sinned.

Paul connected "the law" with "sinning," and that connection probably explains why he introduces the two words into his argument together here. He believed that sin and God's just penalty for sinning, death, were present in the world be-

43. See E. Lohse, "πρόσωπον, κτλ.," *TDNT* 6:779–80; Dunn, *Romans 1–8*, 88–89.

44. *Pace*, e.g., Dunn (*Romans 1–8*, 89) and Jewett (*Romans*, 209), who hold that the broadening of the concept of God's impartial judgment to cover the nations is a new emphasis of Romans.

45. On the use of ἐν here in a locative sense, see Moo, *Romans*, 146n10.

46. Paul's point is not that Jews would be judged more severely than gentiles because of their possession of the law, as some older commentators thought (e.g., Tholuck, *Romans*, 77), but only that they and the gentiles are equally sinners and would be destroyed on the day of God's wrath with equal justice.

fore the giving of the law at Mount Sinai (5:12–14). When God introduced the law into an already sinful situation, however, it made sin worse. This happened both at the national level, with Israel (5:14, 20), and with every human being at the individual level (7:7–11). The fault for this lay not with the law (7:12–13) but with sin and sinful human beings who had displayed a tendency to sin since the time of Adam's transgression (7:7–25; cf. 5:12, 14, 18, 19).

The verb "sin" could refer simply to missing a target (e.g., Herodotus, *Histories* 1.43.2), making a mistake (e.g., Dio Chrysostom, *Homer* [*Or.* 53] 3), or breaking the law or custom of a particular social group (e.g., Acts 25:8). In the LXX and NT, however, it most often refers to action that is intentional and morally culpable and therefore an offense against God (e.g., Ps 50:6 LXX [51:6 Heb.; 51:4 Eng.]; Luke 15:18, 21; 1 Cor 8:12).[47] Since both gentile and Jew know what God requires, God can charge both with sin on the final day. Whether one possesses the Mosaic law on that day will be of no advantage.

2:13 For it is not the hearers of the law who are righteous before God, but the doers of the law will be justified (οὐ γὰρ οἱ ἀκροαταὶ νόμου δίκαιοι παρὰ τῷ θεῷ, ἀλλ οἱ ποιηταὶ νόμου δικαιωθήσονται). Belonging to the people group that has the Mosaic law will not matter when God judges the world. It is not merely having heard the law read that will exempt one from punishment but doing what the law commands.

The "for" (γάρ) attaches this sentence to the one before it and alerts the reader that Paul is about to give the reason for what he has just said. The reason was an axiomatic truth within Judaism and early Jewish Christianity: hearing, reading, or studying the law is not what counts before God, but obeying the law (Jas 1:22–25; Josephus, *Ant.* 20.44; m. Avot 1:17; 3:18; cf. Matt 7:24–27; 23:3; Luke 11:28).[48] The phrase "righteous before God" (δίκαιοι παρὰ τῷ θεῷ) refers to the way God views someone. Just as he can consider a certain principle to be "righteous" (2 Thess 1:6), so he can consider a person to be "righteous," and the person whom he considers righteous is not the one who merely hears (and does not obey) the law.

To make clear whom God considers righteous, Paul shifts to a verbal construction whose meaning is similar to the phrase "righteous before God." Those who do the law, he says, "will be justified" (δικαιωθήσονται). In other words, God will declare them what they already are—righteous and therefore exempt from punishment—because of their obedience to the law.[49] The verb is future because the declaration will happen on "the day of the wrath and the revelation of the righteous judgment of God" (2:5), and it is passive because God, as judge, will make the declaration. Because God is a just judge (2:5), he will declare to be righteous only those who actually are righteous (Exod 23:7; Deut 25:1; 2 Kgs 8:32; 2 Chr 6:23; Isa 5:23).[50]

As Paul will say clearly in 3:9–10, everyone, both Jews and gentiles, are under sin, and no one at all is actually "righteous" (δίκαιος) because they keep the law. Although in principle God would declare righteous those who had done the law, in Paul's thinking this involved such complete obedience to God that no one had achieved that standard. Later Paul will speak of "the law of faith" (3:27) by which God will justify gentiles and Jews (3:28) and claim that

47. See Ernest De Witt Burton, *A Critical and Exegetical Commentary on the Epistle to the Galatians*, ICC (New York: Charles Scribner's Sons, 1920), 436–43; G. Stählin, "ἁμαρτάνω," *TDNT* 1:293; BDAG 49–50, s.v. ἁμαρτάνω.

48. Lagrange, *Romains*, 48; Dunn, *Romans 1–8*, 97; Haacker, *An die Römer*, 64.

49. Westerholm, *Perspectives Old and New on Paul*, 267–69.

50. Ibid., 264–65.

those who walk according to the Spirit fulfill the law (8:4). It would not be outside Paul's lexicon to say that the doers of the law will be justified and to mean by this that those who have "obeyed the gospel" (10:16) have done the law, in this specialized sense, and so been declared righteous by God. That thought may have been in the distant background when Paul wrote 2:13, and it may come closer to the surface briefly in 2:16 where Paul speaks of the gospel as the standard of judgment on the final day. But Paul's primary concern here in 2:14 is to argue for God's impartiality in judging people on the basis of what they do rather than what they possess, and there is no indication that the law here is anything but the Mosaic law, which promises life to those who do it (10:5; cf. Lev 18:5).

2:14 For whenever gentiles, who do not have the law by nature, do the things of the law, they are a law to themselves (ὅταν γὰρ ἔθνη τὰ μὴ νόμον ἔχοντα φύσει τὰ τοῦ νόμου ποιῶσιν, οὗτοι νόμον μὴ ἔχοντες ἑαυτοῖς εἰσιν νόμος). Gentiles who from time to time do what the Mosaic law requires, despite having no access to the Mosaic law, show that merely hearing the Mosaic law read every Sabbath in the synagogue is not a necessary prerequisite for keeping God's law and being justified.

Once again, the term "for" (γάρ; cf. 2:11, 12a, 13a) shows that Paul is giving support to something he has just said, in this case his statement in 2:13 that it is not the hearers but the doers of the law who will be justified. The law in 2:13 is the Jewish law, the revelation of God's will that sets the Jews who live by it apart from the gentiles. This means that gentiles cannot fall into the category of "hearers of the law." They fall "by nature" (φύσει) outside the boundaries of those who hear the law read Sabbath by Sabbath.[51]

The dative case expression "by nature" could easily go with "do" (ποιῶσιν) rather than "have" (ἔχοντα), and most commentators and translators take it this way.[52] When a justification is given for this, it is usually said that if Paul had intended to say the gentiles "do not have the law by nature" he would have placed the expression "by nature" before "have." Gathercole has persuasively shown, however, that this is a red herring: Greek prose writers from Paul's period reveal no hesitation in placing "by nature" after the verb that the expression modified or at the end of a clause.[53] Moreover, Paul's use of the term "nature" elsewhere to identify the group to which one belongs rather than to one's behavior supports taking "by nature" here with "have" rather than "do" (2:27; Gal 2:15; 4:8; Eph 2:3).[54] These gentiles, then, do not have the law because they were born outside Judaism (cf. Eph 2:11–12, 14–15).

Despite not having the law, they sometimes "do the things of the law" (τὰ τοῦ νόμου ποιῶσιν). If anyone had taken the sweeping description and condemnation of human sin in 1:18–32 to mean that humanity could never do what was right, this statement corrects them. Not only do human beings generally have some knowledge of God (1:19–21) and his "righteous decree" (1:32) but sometimes they do it. That they do not always do it is indicated by the "whenever" (ὅταν; cf. NET) that introduces the present subjunctive verb "do" (ποιῶσιν). This temporal particle can also simply mean "when" (e.g., 11:27; 1 Thess 5:3), but it refers most basically to action that may happen, often to

51. S. J. Gathercole, "A Law unto Themselves: The Gentiles in Romans 2.14–15 Revisited," *JSNT* 85 (2002): 32–33, 35–37.

52. See, e.g., Longenecker, *Romans*, 274–75; Tyndale, KJV, NIV, NRSV, ESV.

53. See, e.g., Wis 13:1; Ign. *Eph.* 1:1; and Josephus, *Ant.* 8.152 (Gathercole, "A Law unto Themselves," 36).

54. Gathercole, "A Law unto Themselves," 36–37. Cf. Cranfield, *Romans 1–8*, 1:156–57; Schreiner, *Romans*, 121, 123; Jewett, *Romans*, 213–14.

action that is repeated.[55] Paul probably uses it here to emphasize the idea that gentiles only "do the things of the law" from time to time, a reading that is confirmed in 2:15 where their thoughts mainly accuse and only occasionally defend them.

When they do what God requires without having the Mosaic law to guide them, gentiles show that they have an instinctive sense of right and wrong. The idea that some people felt instinctively what was right to do and could therefore function as "a law to themselves" (ἑαυτοῖς εἰσιν νόμος) was a traditional Greek philosophical notion by Paul's time, although it was construed in various ways. Aristotle thought that some people were so virtuous they did not need laws, "for they are themselves a law" (αὐτοὶ γάρ εἰσι νόμος; *Politics* 1284a 13 [H. Rackham, LCL]). The Stoics thought that living virtuously was synonymous with living in accord with nature (Arius Didymus, *Epitome of Stoic Ethics* 5b3; cf. Aristotle, *Rhetoric* 1375a; Philo, *Joseph* 29). Philo believed that ethnic tradition could function as an unwritten, willingly obeyed law, which was particularly praiseworthy (*On the Special Laws* 4.150), and so on.[56] Paul commits himself to none of these specific ideas, but their presence in the ancient literature does show that the general notion of an innate, unwritten law was in the air and that Paul's use of it here is likely.[57] Paul uses the notion to serve his general point that being a "hearer of the law" was not necessary for doing the law, and so being a Jew gave one no advantage over being a gentile on the day of God's wrath.

2:15 in that they show the work of the law written in their hearts, their conscience bearing witness together with them and their thoughts among one another accusing or even defending (οἵτινες ἐνδείκνυνται τὸ ἔργον τοῦ νόμου γραπτὸν ἐν ταῖς καρδίαις αὐτῶν, συμμαρτυρούσης αὐτῶν τῆς συνειδήσεως καὶ μεταξὺ ἀλλήλων τῶν λογισμῶν κατηγορούντων ἢ καὶ ἀπολογουμένων). Three characteristics of their moral consciousness show that gentiles have a form of God's law: the essence of the law is within them, they have a conscience, and they can engage in moral reasoning about the actions of others around them.

The indefinite relative pronoun (οἵτινες) introduces a more detailed description of what Paul meant when he said that gentiles are "a law to themselves."[58] The NASB gets this exactly right with its translation, "Gentiles . . . are a law to themselves, *in that they* . . ." (emphasis added).

He can say that they are a law to themselves because they have "the work of the law" (τὸ ἔργον τοῦ νόμου) inscribed in their hearts. This phrase is similar to the expression "works of the law" (ἔργα νόμου) that Paul uses eight times in Galatians and Romans, always in an adverbial prepositional phrase and always negatively, to describe how a person is not justified or does not receive God's Spirit (3:20; 3:28; Gal 2:16 [3x]; 3:2, 5, 10; cf. Rom 3:27). In that phrase the plural "works" seems to refer to the individual duties the Mosaic law requires. Here, however, the singular "work" carries the nuance of what the law is driving at or trying to accomplish. Aristotle counsels the forensic orator in the difficult position of defending someone who has violated the written law that it is often effective in such cases to appeal to the universally accepted "unwritten [ἄγραφον] law." The justice of this law runs deeper than the written law and actually accomplishes what the legislator who formed the written law was driving at, for "the written law . . . does not do the work of the law" (τὸ ἔργον τὸ τοῦ

55. BDAG 730–31, s.v. ὅταν 1aα.

56. See also Michel, *An die Römer*, 118n20; Fitzmyer, *Romans*, 310–11; Niebuhr, "Roman Jews under Nero," 84–85.

57. *Pace* Gathercole, "A Law unto Themselves," 37–40.

58. On the use of the indefinite relative pronoun in this sense, see BDAG 729–30, s.v. ὅστις 2b.

νόμου, *Rhetoric* 1375b [J. H. Freese, LCL]; cf. Appian, *Civil Wars* 1.1.13).[59]

This meaning for the phrase makes sense here too since Paul is trying to show in the surrounding context that gentiles who are not born into the society of Israel with its God-given law nevertheless occasionally do "the things of the law" (2:14). They sometimes do what the Mosaic law was driving at with its commands, but they do this without actually having those commands spelled out for them in a legal code.

They are able to do this because this point or goal of the law is "written in their hearts" (γραπτὸν ἐν ταῖς καρδίαις αὐτῶν). This phrase is similar to Jeremiah 38:33 LXX (31:33, Heb. and Eng.) where the Lord says, "I will write [my laws] on their hearts" (LXX: ἐπὶ καρδίας αὐτῶν γράψω [νόμους μου]). We should be cautious, however, about concluding from this similarity that Paul speaks of "new covenant" gentile Christians that fulfill Jeremiah's prophecy (Jer 38 [31]:31–34). Paul certainly knew Jeremiah's prophecy (cf. 11:27; 1 Cor 11:25; 2 Cor 3:6), and its language may have influenced his language here, but he does not cite that text or give any clear indication that he is alluding to it.[60] Ancient Greek thinkers commonly expressed the belief that humanity was bound by certain universally acknowledged moral standards, "which, though unwritten [ἄγραφοι], bring upon the transgressor a disgrace which all men recognize" (Thucydides, *History of the Peloponnesian War* 2.37.3 [Charles Forster Smith, LCL]). Veneration of the gods, honoring parents, avoiding sexual contact between children and parents, and returning good to those who do one good, according to Xenophon's Socrates, are among those laws (*Mem.* 4.19–24; Demosthenes, *On the Crown* 275).[61]

Paul next introduces two genitive-absolute constructions that interpreters have taken in various ways. The most likely understanding of the syntax sees these two constructions as providing two further pieces of evidence, in addition to the law written on their hearts, that gentiles have a moral standard to which God justly holds them accountable.[62]

First, their conscience functions as a moral compass. Since the conscience in antiquity referred to a knowledge that one shared with one's self, it is possible for the conscience to "bear witness together with" (συμμαρτυρέω) one's self, and that is probably Paul's meaning here.[63] Gentiles have a conscience that is capable of alerting them that what they have done is wrong, or, by the absence of a painful conscience in a given situation, of confirming that their conduct was correct.

Second, their moral deliberations with each other yield accusation and, occasionally, defense of one another. It is not clear whether the phrase "among one another" (μεταξὺ ἀλλήλων) refers to conflicting thoughts within individuals or to moral judgments that one individual makes about others. If it refers to conflicting thoughts, then the conjunction "and" (καί) functions in an epexegetical way and the whole phrase explains how the conscience works.[64] The ancient "conscience," however, was not a forum for internal debate but an internal knowledge of the morality of one's actions, usually a painful knowledge of past wrongdoing. It

59. See also the note appended to Freese's translation of the phrase. On the link between Romans 2:14–15 and this passage in Aristotle, see Collins, "Echoes of Aristotle in Romans 2:14–15," 130.

60. As Fitzmyer points out (*Romans*, 311), the language is also close to Isa 51:7 LXX.

61. Hermann Kleinknecht, "νόμος, κτλ.," *TDNT* 4:1027–28.

62. C. A. Pierce, *Conscience in the New Testament*, SBT (London: SCM, 1955), 85.

63. Jewett, *Romans*, 215–16.

64. See, e.g., Cranfield, *Romans* 1:162; Moo, *Romans*, 153; Fitzmyer, *Romans*, 311.

is more probable, then, that the "thoughts among one another" to which Paul refers are the reasoned decisions that gentiles make about the moral quality of the actions of others around them.[65] These moral judgments sometimes accuse and sometimes even defend the conduct of others.

IN DEPTH: Paul's Understanding of the "Conscience"

Ancient Greek speakers used the term "conscience" (συνείδησις) in both philosophical discourse and in everyday conversation to refer to an internal awareness of the morality of one's actions, usually of a retrospective knowledge of wrongdoing.[66] In Paul's thinking, everyone, including unbelievers, had a conscience (2:15; 1 Cor 10:29; 2 Cor 4:2). Paul's own conscience could bear witness that he told the truth (Rom 9:1) or acted with pure motives (2 Cor 1:12; cf. 2 Tim 1:3), and he could appeal to the conscience of other believers to confirm what he knew to be true of his own motives and conduct (2 Cor 5:11; cf. 4:2). Such uses of the conscience could make it a helpful guide to right conduct in morally ambiguous situations (1 Cor 10:23–11:1; cf. Rom 13:5).

Paul did not think, however, that the conscience was infallible. It could become desensitized by behavior that violated it (1 Cor 8:7, 8, 12; 1 Tim 4:2; Titus 1:15; cf. 1 Cor 4:4) or take misguided offense at the behavior of others (1 Cor 10:29). When Paul says, "I am not aware [σύνοιδα] of anything against myself, but I am not thereby acquitted," he is acknowledging that God, not the conscience, is the final arbiter of what is right or wrong. That is why he continues, "It is the Lord who judges me" (1 Cor 4:4).

Paul believed that only God knew infallibly the intentions and motives that led people to take certain actions. Human beings are too fraught with a tendency to despise others and excuse themselves to know whether even their own motives are right. That is probably why Paul counseled even believers never to repay evil for evil (12:17), never to seek vengeance against those who harmed them (12:19), and not to pass judgment against or despise a fellow believer who disagreed with them (14:10–12). In the end, only God's judgment of the intentions that produce moral or immoral action is pure and just enough to guarantee that a particular punishment or exoneration is justified (2:16; cf. 1 Kgs 8:39).

65. See Meyer, *Romans*, 94; Sanday and Headlam, *Romans*, 61–62; and especially Jewett, *Romans*, 216. Cf. Dunn, *Romans 1–8*, 102.

66. Pierce, *Conscience in the New Testament*, 29–53; *TLNT* 3:332–35.

2:16 on the day when God judges the hidden things of human beings according to my gospel, through Christ Jesus (ἐν ἡμέρᾳ ὅτε κρίνει ὁ θεὸς τὰ κρυπτὰ τῶν ἀνθρώπων κατὰ τὸ εὐαγγέλιόν μου διὰ Ἰησοῦ Χριστοῦ). Paul's gospel teaches that God will judge human beings through the Messiah Jesus, and the future day on which he does that will reveal that God has used no different standard of judgment with the gentiles than he has with the Jews.

The connection of this verse to 2:14–15 is not obvious. In 2:14–15 Paul presupposes that gentiles show in the present that they are a law to themselves by their internal law, their conscience, and their moral reasoning. In 2:16, however, he seems to say that the thoughts of accusation and defense at the end of 2:15 take place in the future, during the final day of judgment, for although "judges" (κρίνει) is present tense the phrase "in the day when" (ἐν ἡμέρᾳ ὅτε) throws the present judgment into the future (cf. 2:5).

No solution to the problem is compelling, but perhaps the most straightforward reading sees Paul making a shift from the present display of moral consciousness among gentiles in 2:15 to the final day in 2:16 when God will judge gentiles based on their obedience to what they knew to be right. Perhaps he was returning to the thought of final justification by works that he left behind in 2:13, or perhaps he expects his readers and hearers to understand that God will bring the internal deliberations he has described in 2:14–15 into the open on the final day.[67] In either case, his point is clear: the final day will bring to light the existence of an internal moral standard among the gentiles by which God can judge them, a moral standard that for the purposes of a just judgment is identical to the law that the Jews possess in written form. The God who knows "the hidden things" within people will have no trouble judging people by conformity to an internal law (cf. 2:28–29; 1 Cor 4:5; cf. 1 Kgs 8:39).

Paul is not ready to present the gospel's solution to human sin in full, but he anticipates that solution here. For those who stand condemned before God on the final day, that condemnation will take place according to the standard laid out in the Mosaic law for Jews and the law written on the heart for gentiles. But there is more to be said about the final day of judgment. Judgment on that day will take place "through Christ Jesus," God's anointed king (2 Cor 5:10; 2 Thess 1:5–10; 2 Tim 4:1; cf. Pss. Sol. 17:29). It will take place according to the standard of the "gospel," "the law of faith" as Paul will describe it in 3:27. On that day God "will justify" (δικαιώσει) both the circumcised and uncircumcised on the basis of their faith in the gracious God who provided redemption for them through the atoning death of Christ (3:30; cf. 3:24–26).

67. For the first explanation, see Godet, *Romans*, 126; Meyer, *Romans*, 95–96; Sanday and Headlam, *Romans*, 62; and Longenecker, *Romans*, 280–81. For the second explanation, see Dunn, *Romans 1–8*, 105–6; Schreiner, *Romans*, 125.

Theology in Application

The complexities of this passage should not obscure the straightforward nature of its primary point, expressed clearly and concisely in 2:11: "There is no partiality with God." It is a point that has important implications for the way Christians think about and treat unbelievers and a point that should prompt all Christians to examine the state of their own hearts.

Paul's fictional interlocutor in 2:1–16 is an unbelieving Jew, but Paul reveals later in the letter that the attitude his interlocutor displays here has also infected gentile Christians in Rome. Some of these gentile Christians have become arrogant in their attitudes toward Jewish unbelievers who, they observe, were branches broken off the tree of God's people so that gentile Christians could, as they saw it, take their place (11:18–19). Paul warns these Roman gentile Christians that their haughty attitude reveals an unhealthy presumption that God will continue to be merciful to them because they are somehow better than unbelieving Jews.

Christians, then, are not exempt from the warning implicit in 2:1–16. The church needs to be vigilant that it does not comfort itself in its own sinfulness by pointing fingers at others who are supposedly more sinful. This kind of warning to God's people runs throughout Scripture.

God's Impartiality and Its Implied Warning in the Prophets and the Gospels

The impartiality of God is a fundamental theological principle, affirmed throughout the Bible, and it is a principle that the biblical prophets often articulated as a warning to God's people against complacency in their relationship with God. Amos begins his prophecy, for example, with a severe indictment of the nations surrounding Israel and an announcement of the judgment they will experience because of their wickedness (Amos 1:2–2:5), but then the longest of his opening oracles of judgment is reserved for Israel itself (2:6–16). The story of Jonah begins with an account of this Israelite prophet fleeing from the Lord across the sea in disobedience and, in so doing, bringing trouble on an obviously more pious group of gentile sailors who, in the end, turn to the Lord (Jonah 1:1–16). The story continues with the wicked idolators of Nineveh believing God, much to Jonah's dismay (3:5; 4:1).

Matthew's Gospel opens with gentile astrologers "from the east" trekking to Jerusalem to worship the Jewish Messiah, Jesus, an event that "troubled" the Jewish king Herod "and all Jerusalem with him" (2:1–3). A few paragraphs later, when "Jerusalem and all Judea" (3:5) go into the wilderness to listen to the preaching of John the Baptist, the prophet urges them, "Do not presume to say to yourselves, 'We have Abraham as our father,' for I tell you God is able from these stones to raise up children for Abraham" (3:9). Jesus recalls the story of the Ninevites' repentance and applies it to the scribes and Pharisees (Matt 12:38–41; Luke 11:29–30, 32). He then goes further to say that "the queen of the South will rise up at the judgment with this generation and condemn it, for she came from the ends of the earth to hear the wisdom of Solomon, and behold, something greater than Solomon is here" (Matt 12:42; cf. 16:4; Luke 11:31).[68]

These passages show that God is often at work in the hearts of unbelievers in surprising ways to draw them to himself. The proper response of God's people to unbelievers is not to stand in judgment over them as a group but to humbly seek to lead them to the gospel, communicating clearly that Christians, as much as anyone, need God's continual forgiveness for sin through the sacrificial death of his Son Jesus.

The Human Tendency to Excuse One's Self but to Condemn Others

There is, therefore, something especially tragic in the occasional sweeping statements of older interpreters on Romans 2:1–16 that Jews made their religion "a matter of public opinion," or that Paul was warning people against "the Pharisee . . . always present in each one of us."[69] It is perhaps a confirmation of the depth of human depravity that the very people whose sacred literature shows them to be intensely aware of the dangers of complacency and hypocrisy have become, in the eyes of these interpreters, prime examples of that very sin. Amos, Jonah, John the Baptist, Jesus, and Paul were all Jews, and when they articulated this motif they were speaking in the first instance to other Jews, warning them not to be complacent in their election.[70] Paul was doing this in front of a predominantly gentile audience in Rome in order to instruct them in the gospel, but the fictional dialogue he carries on here is an inner-Jewish dialogue.

The passage reveals how important it is for those who claim to be God's people to examine the condition of their own disposition to God. Do we merely take comfort in condemning the sins of others? Is it possible that our own hearts are hard and impenitent, quick to identify the sin outside us but blind to our own guilt? "I am not aware of anything against myself," Paul tells the Corinthians, "but I am not thereby acquitted [δεδικαίωμαι]. It is the Lord who judges me" (1 Cor 4:4). Paul knew that even the believer because of the continuing, pernicious power of sin could deceive himself or herself into thinking that all was well when it was not.[71] Romans 2:1–16 should prompt Christians to examine their own hearts to see if they are hard and unrepentant, distracted by the sins of others from their own need to acknowledge and turn from sin (cf. 2 Sam 12:1–15; Matt 7:1–5; Luke 6:37–38).[72]

68. On the whole theme, see Collins, "Echoes of Aristotle in Romans 2:14–15," 142.

69. See, respectively, Charles Gore, *St. Paul's Epistle to the Romans: A Practical Exposition*, 2 vols. (London: John Murray, 1899–1900), 1:94–99; Leenhardt, *Romans*, 74.

70. Cf. Oda Wischmeyer, "Römer 2.1–24 als Teil der Gerichtsrede des Paulus gegen die Menschheit," *NTS* 52 (2006): 356–76.

71. Cf. Matt 7:21–23; 22:11–14; 25:11–13, 44–46.

72. For parallels to this idea in the Jewish and Greco-Roman worlds, see W. D. Davies and Dale C. Allison Jr., *Matthew*, 3 vols., ICC (London: T&T Clark, 1988–97), 1:668–71.

CHAPTER 5

Romans 2:17–29

Literary Context

After speaking of God's impartiality in an abstract way for several sentences (2:6–16), Paul now suddenly snaps back to the diatribe style and once again addresses his fictional interlocutor.[1] The strong suspicion that Paul conceived this interlocutor as a Jew emerged in 2:9–10 where he spoke of God's impartial judgment of "the Jew first and also the Greek" and in 2:12–16 where he began to divide humanity into those who possessed the law in writing and gentiles for whom the law was written on the heart. Now Paul becomes explicit, finally addressing his interlocutor as a "Jew."

The point of the new section is identical to the point of the previous section. Paul wants to demonstrate to his Roman readers, by means of this fictional dialogue with a Jew, that Jews as well as gentiles are transgressors and that their Jewishness gives them no privileges over gentiles on the day of judgment. Just as condemning the unrighteous person and possessing the Mosaic law will not permit Jews to escape God's judgment (2:1–16), so teaching the Mosaic law and possessing physical circumcision will count for nothing on that day (2:17–29). Keeping the law from the heart, not making judgments based on it, possessing it, or teaching it to others, will bring praise from God. The difference in the two sections lies in the way Paul makes his point: now he focuses on the failure of Jews to fulfill their vocation of being a light to the gentiles (2:17–24) and shows that physical circumcision is not the defining boundary of the people of God (2:25–29).

Paul's goal in the section is to show that even the Jew falls under the searching indictment of 1:18–32 and that God extends no privilege to the Jew on the day of judgment because of possession of the law and circumcision. That these are Paul's points becomes clear in the next section where he begins with the rhetorical question, "What, then, is the advantage of the Jew, or what is the benefit of circumcision?" (3:1) and shortly thereafter utters the statement, "We have already charged that both Jews and Greeks—all—are under sin" (3:9). Paul believes that in the previous section

1. On the diatribal characteristics of the passage, see Stowers (*Diatribe*, 96–98), who notes the close stylistic parallels between the passage and, for example, Epictetus, *Diatr.* 2.19.19; 3.7.17; 3.24.41 and Seneca, *Ep.* 77.17–18.

(2:1–29) he has dismantled the idea that despite a hard and impenitent heart the Jew will survive the day of judgment (2:3–16, 25–29), and he has reminded the Jew that, like the gentile, he is a sinner (2:1–2, 23–24).

Main Idea

Neither knowing the law so well that one can teach it to others nor possessing physical circumcision will exempt the Jew from God's judgment of the sinner. Only doing what God requires, from the heart, will bring praise from God on the final day.

Translation

Romans 2:17–29

17a	Condition/List	But	if you	[1] call yourself a Jew and	
b				[2] rely on the law and	
c				[3] boast in God and	
18a				[4] know his will and	
b				[5] discern what is important,	
c	Cause			because you are instructed from the law.	
19a	Condition/List	And,		likewise,	
b			[if] you are persuaded that you are yourself		[1] a leader of the blind,
c					[2] a light to those in darkness,
20a					[3] an instructor of the foolish,
b					[4] a teacher of infants,
c					[5] having the embodiment of knowledge and truth in the law.

21a	Rhetorical Question	[1] **You who**	**teach the other person—**	**do you**	**not teach yourself?**
b	Rhetorical Question	[2] **You who**	**preach not to steal—**	**do you**	**steal?**
22a	Rhetorical Question	[3] **You who**	**say not to commit adultery—**	**do you**	**commit adultery?**

b	Rhetorical Question	[4] **You who detest idols— do you rob temples?**
23	Rhetorical Question	[5] **Do you who boast in the law dishonor God through ⤶ transgression of the law?**
24a	Result/OT Quotation	For "the name of God is blasphemed
b	Sphere	among the gentiles
c	Cause	because of you" (Isa 52:5)
d	Comparison	just as it is written.
25a	Explanation	For, on one hand,
b	Assertion	**circumcision is beneficial**
c	Condition	if you practice the law,
d	Contrast	but, on the other hand,
e	Condition	if you are a transgressor of the law,
f	Assertion	**your circumcision becomes uncircumcision.**
26a	Condition	If, … therefore, … the uncircumcised person keeps the just ⤶ requirements of the law,
b	Rhetorical Question	**will not his uncircumcision be counted as circumcision?**
27a	Result	And **the one who is by nature uncircumcised but**
b	Result/Concession	**carries out the law will judge you**
c	Description	who transgress the law
d	Contra-expectation	despite the letter and circumcision.
28a	Explanation	For **the one who is a Jew in what is visible is not a Jew,**
b	Restatement	nor **is circumcision in what is visible,**
c	Restatement	in the flesh
29a	Contrast	But **the Jew in secret is a Jew,**
b	Restatement	**and circumcision of the heart is circumcision,**
c	Sphere	in the Spirit and not the letter,
d	Assertion	whose praise is not from human beings but from God.

Structure

This section is devoted to the question of Jewish identity: What makes a Jew a Jew and therefore part of the people who will survive the final day of judgment? It begins and ends, therefore, with explicit references to "the Jew" (2:17, 28, 29), and Paul brings his fictional Jewish interlocutor back into the argument in order to make his case. Internally, the section falls into two paragraphs.

The first paragraph (2:17–24) raises the problem posed by the Jew whose detailed knowledge of God's will and commitment to Israel's vocation to be a light to the gentiles goes unmatched by obedience and actually brings the name of God into disrepute. The paragraph consists of fifteen elements (2:17–23) and a closing quotation from Scripture (2:24).[2] The fifteen elements describe Paul's interlocutor with three lists of five characteristics each, and the whole list of fifteen exerts a powerful rhetorical force, using anacoluthon, polysyndeton, and asyndeton.[3] The list begins with a lengthy protasis ("if" clause), the first part of what was to be a conditional sentence, but the list becomes so long that no corresponding apodosis ("then" clause) emerges (anacoluthon).[4] Paul punctuates the first list of five items with more conjunctions than the syntax needs (polysyndeton); the second list of five items has only one, light conjunction (asyndeton); and the final list of five items consists of a series of pithy rhetorical questions. The resulting rhetorical effect is exasperation at the wide gap between the privileges that Paul's interlocutor claims for himself as a Jew and this interlocutor's failure to live up to the responsibility such claims entail.

The second paragraph (2:25–29) focuses on circumcision, and Paul assumes that his fictional Jewish interlocutor regards physical circumcision as the defining mark of the Jew. Again, Paul's point is that Jewishness and circumcision do not consist of outward, visible marks but instead entail carrying out the law from the heart. Paul views this heartfelt obedience to be something a gentile can do. The paragraph concludes with the radical and climactic claim that it is possible for someone who is physically uncircumcised to carry out the law more faithfully than someone who is physically circumcised.[5] The highly compressed Greek of the lengthy final sentence (2:28–29) lends the statement an emphasis that is appropriate for its climactic claim.[6]

In both paragraphs Paul believes he is arguing from the perspective of the Scriptures that both he and his interlocutor regard as authoritative. The first paragraph ends (2:24) with a quotation of Isaiah 52:5. The second paragraph ends with a reference to circumcision of the heart, a concept that the Bible uses in addressing Israel's need to rely not on the outward trappings of being God's people but on willing trust in and obedience to God (Deut 10:16; 30:6; Jer 4:4; 9:25–26).

2. Cf. Jewett, *Romans*, 219–21.

3. BDF §§460 and 467.

4. Wilckens (*An die Römer [Röm 1–5]*, 147) comments, probably correctly, that the broken syntax matches the disjunction between the interlocutor's privileges as Jew and his obedience.

5. Andreas Blaschke, *Beschneidung: Zeugnisse der Bibel und verwandter Texte*, TANZ 28 (Tübingen: Francke, 1998), 411: "Vv. 28f. circle back to v. 17 and form, at the same time, the provocative high point of the argument" (my transl.).

6. Dunn, *Romans 1–8*, 119.

Exegetical Outline

VI. Jews Are Also Subject to God's Wrath (2:1–3:20)

A. God as an Impartial Judge Not Merely of Gentiles but of Jews Also (2:1–16)

➡ **B. God as an Impartial Judge Even of Jews Who Teach the Law and Possess Circumcision (2:17–29)**

1. What Does It Mean to Be a Jew? Obedience, Not Merely Knowledge of God's Will (2:17–24)
   a. Five characteristics of the Jew's relationship to God and his will (2:17–18)
   b. Five characteristics of Israel's calling to be a light to the gentiles (2:19–20)
   c. Five rhetorical questions that reveal the disparity between knowledge and practice in Paul's Jewish interlocutor (2:21–23)
   d. A biblical proof of Israel's failure to be a light to the gentiles (2:24)
2. What Does It Mean to Be a Jew? Circumcision of the Heart, Not Physical Circumcision (2:25–29)
   a. Disobedient circumcision is worthless (2:25)
   b. Obedient uncircumcision is circumcision (2:26)
   c. Obedient uncircumcision shames disobedient circumcision (2:27)
   d. The reason: being a true Jew is a matter of the heart (2:28–29)

Explanation of the Text

2:17–18 But if you call yourself a Jew and rely on the law and boast in God and know his will and discern what is important, because you are instructed from the law (Εἰ δὲ σὺ Ἰουδαῖος ἐπονομάζῃ καὶ ἐπαναπαύῃ νόμῳ καὶ καυχᾶσαι ἐν θεῷ καὶ γινώσκεις τὸ θέλημα καὶ δοκιμάζεις τὰ διαφέροντα κατηχούμενος ἐκ τοῦ νόμου). Paul's fictional interlocutor makes impressive claims about being a Jew and knowing what God wants people to do.

With the conjunction "but" (δέ) Paul signals that he is turning directly to his fictional interlocutor again for the first time since 2:5, and here he refers to him explicitly as a Jew. Paul lists five characteristics of his Jewish interlocutor, and this is the first of three lists of five in 2:17–23.[7] The first characteristic (i.e., that Paul's interlocutor claims the name "Jew") stands as a heading over the entire paragraph down to 2:24 and contrasts with the phrase "among the gentiles" in that final sentence. In the first century the term "Jew" (Ἰουδαῖος) could have a geographical reference ("Judean"), a political reference ("citizen of Judea"), or a religious reference ("Jew").[8] Here, Paul intends a religious reference: his Jewish interlocutor defines himself as one who knows the will of God as the Jewish law reveals it. He therefore should have shown to the gentiles the character of the one God who created the heavens and the earth (Exod 19:5–6).[9] Instead, the name of God is blasphemed among the gentiles

7. Jewett, *Romans*, 219–21.

8. Shaye J. D. Cohen, *The Beginnings of Jewishness: Boundaries, Varieties, Uncertainties*, Hellenistic Culture and Society 31 (Berkeley, CA: University of California Press, 1999), 70.

9. For this understanding of Exod 19:5–6, see Douglas K. Stuart, *Exodus*, NAC (Nashville: Broadman & Holman, 2006), 422–24, and Christopher J. H. Wright, *The Mission of God: Unlocking the Bible's Grand Narrative* (Downers Grove, IL: InterVarsity Press, 2006), 329–33.

because of the interlocutor's unfaithfulness to keep the law and receive the blessings it promised to those who kept it.[10]

The next four items in the first list focus on the interlocutor's relationship to God and his law. He "relies on" (ἐπαναπαύομαι) the law, an expression that can refer elsewhere to leaning on something for support either physically (2 Kgs 5:18; 7:2, 17; Ezek 29:7 LXX) or metaphorically (1 Macc 8:11). In Micah 3:11 (LXX) the word probably means what it does here: Israel's leaders, priests, and prophets were acting unjustly but "were relying [ἐπανεπαύοντο] on the Lord, saying, 'Is the Lord not with us? No harm shall come upon us.'" In the same way, Paul's interlocutor is relying for security from God's wrath on possessing and knowing the law but, fatally, without obeying it (Rom 2:21–24). This is also the sense in which the interlocutor boasts in God. Paul can speak of boasting in God in a positive sense (e.g, 5:2–3, 11; 15:17). Here, however, the boast has a negative connotation, similar to that found in 2:23 where Paul portrays his interlocutor as boasting in the law. As the next item in the list ("and know his will") shows, boasting in God here refers to reliance on an intellectual knowledge of God's will. Since the interlocutor does not couple this knowledge with obedience, his reliance on it is misplaced.[11]

The fifth and final item in the first list defines more specifically how well Paul's interlocutor knows God's will. The circumstantial participle "are instructed" (κατηχούμενος) indicates the cause of the interlocutor's ability to know God's will, and its present tense shows that the law provides a ready resource for making ethical decisions.[12] "Happy are we, O Israel," says Baruch in describing the Mosaic law, "for we know what is pleasing to God" (Bar 4:4).[13]

The phrase "discern what is important" (δοκιμάζεις τὰ διαφέροντα) refers to deciding in ambiguous situations what the best course of action would be from God's perspective (cf. Rom 12:2; Eph 5:10; Phil 1:10; 1 Thess 5:21). Because the law provides an ever-present resource to the interlocutor, its instruction equips him to distinguish the bad from the good and the good from the best.

2:19–20 And, likewise, [if] you are persuaded that you are yourself a leader of the blind, a light to those in darkness, an instructor of the foolish, a teacher of infants, having the embodiment of knowledge and truth in the law (πέποιθάς τε σεαυτὸν ὁδηγὸν εἶναι τυφλῶν, φῶς τῶν ἐν σκότει, παιδευτὴν ἀφρόνων, διδάσκαλον νηπίων, ἔχοντα τὴν μόρφωσιν τῆς γνώσεως καὶ τῆς ἀληθείας ἐν τῷ νόμῳ). Paul's fictional interlocutor knows that his vocation as a Jew is to teach the nations the will of God.

Paul begins his second list of five characteristics with another second-person singular verb that continues the lengthy apodosis of his conditional sentence: "[If] you are persuaded . . . ." The verb translated "you are persuaded" (πέποιθας) is in the perfect tense, perhaps indicating the settled nature of the interlocutor's persuasion.[14] The verb "be convinced" (πείθω) is often followed by "that" (ὅτι) and only rarely, as it is here, with an accusative and infinitive construction.[15] This unusual syntax, cou-

10. Cf. the exegesis of 2:17–24 in Wright, "Romans," 445–48.

11. For the conceptual connection between boasting and reliance in Paul, see also Phil 3:3 and the comments of J. Zmijewski, "καυχάομαι, καύχημα, καύχησις," *EDNT* 2:227.

12. *TLNT* 2:293. On the circumstantial participle of cause, see Smyth, *Greek Grammar*, 458 (§2064).

13. As quoted in James D. G. Dunn, *The New Perspective on Paul*, rev. ed. (Grand Rapids: Eerdmans, 2008), 124.

14. On the perfect tense, see Crellin, "The Semantics of the Perfect," 451, 454–55. Cf. Longenecker, *Romans*, 302.

15. This is the only instance of the construction in the NT. For a rare parallel outside the NT, see Aeschylus, *Seven against Thebes* 444–45 (πέποιθα δ' αὐτῶι ξὺν δίκηι τὸν πυρφόρον ἥξειν κεραυνόν, "But I trust that the fire-bearing thunderbolt will

pled with the use of "yourself" (σεαυτόν) in a role that is not immediately clear, make this a difficult clause to translate. It is best to see "yourself" as an accusative of respect.[16] A wooden translation of the whole clause, then, would run, "[If] you are convinced, with regard to yourself, that you are a guide for the blind . . . ." Jesus criticized the scribes and the Pharisees with irony as "blind guides" (ὁδηγοὶ τυφλοί; Matt 23:16, 24; cf. 15:14) in a context where the subject is their efforts to cross sea and land to make proselytes to Judaism. Since Paul here is also talking about the relationship of Jews to gentiles (2:24), the "blind" are probably gentiles, and the notion that Jews should provide guidance for them must have been common currency in some Jewish circles.[17]

This becomes even more probable with the next phrase, "a light to those in darkness" (φῶς τῶν ἐν σκότει), which, together with the notion of leading the blind, recalls Isaiah 42:6–7 (LXX) and the role of the Lord's Servant in providing "light to nations" (φῶς ἐθνῶν) and opening "the eyes of the blind" (ὀφθαλμοὺς τυφλῶν).[18] Some Jews probably identified with the Servant and sought to fulfill this task (cf., e.g., Wis 18:4; T. Levi 14:3–4; Sib. Or. 3:194–95; 5:238), and Paul imagines an interlocutor who is among this group but who does not himself keep the law that he knows and teaches.[19] He was supposed to provide light for those whose "foolish heart was darkened" (1:21) but failed in this task (2:24).

The next two characteristics of Paul's interlocutor are roughly synonymous. He is an "instructor of the foolish" (παιδευτὴν ἀφρόνων) and a "teacher of infants" (διδάσκαλον νηπίων). The opposite of being foolish for Paul was to "understand what the will of the Lord is" (Eph 5:17), and an "infant" was someone who had not progressed far in his or her understanding of spiritual things (1 Cor 3:1). Both "fools" and "infants" needed to understand the truth (2 Cor 12:6; Eph 4:14–15). Paul probably did not intend to distinguish sharply between an "instructor" (παιδευτής) and a "teacher" (διδάσκαλος). The two terms could be used interchangeably in the first century of the philosopher's role in educating his pupils (Epictetus, *Diatr.* 1.9.12, 18). Here, too, Paul may have in mind what his interlocutor, as a Jew, should be doing for those whom Paul has described in 1:18–32. He should be instructing those with "foolish hearts" (1:21) and who think they are wise but are actually fools (1:22; cf. 1:28, 31).

Paul's next phrase, like the participial phrase at the end of 2:18, explains the role of the law in the interlocutor's knowledge of God's will.[20] He is able to teach those who are ignorant because he has the law, which provides the "embodiment" (μόρφωσις) of truth and knowledge. The term "embodiment" could refer to "shaping" something, such as fruit trees so that they bear more fruit and are easier to harvest (Theophrastus, *Caus. plant.* 3.7.4), or it could refer to the "form" that resulted from shaping something, such as a sign of the zodiac (Ptolemy, *Tetrabiblos* 2.8.1).[21] The word only appears twice in

justly come to him" [*Aeschylus*, trans. Herbert Weir Smyth, LCL (Cambridge: Harvard University Press, 1922)]). See Meyer, *Romans*, 99.

16. Cf. Sanday and Headlam, *Romans*, 65. The accusative here, then, would function in the same way as the dative in Aristophanes, *Knights* 770 (κεἰ μὴ τούτοισι πέποιθας, lit., "And if you are not persuaded with respect to these things . . ."). Thanks to Jewett (*Romans*, 225) for this reference, although I take the Greek quite differently.

17. Cf. BDAG 1021, s.v. τυφλός 2aβ.

18. See also Isa 49:6 and Zech 8:23 (Gathercole, *Where Is Boasting?*, 201n21).

19. On the currency in the Second Temple period of the idea that Israel should be a light to the nations, see Gathercole, *Where Is Boasting?*, 193, 201.

20. Moo, *Romans*, 162.

21. Cf. Johannes Behm, "μορφή, κτλ.," *TDNT* 4:754.

biblical Greek, once negatively to refer to the mere form of something, as opposed to the substance (2 Tim 3:5), and here, where it is used positively of the organized presentation of truth and knowledge in the law.[22] In Hellenistic Jewish literature, "wisdom" (σοφία) was sometimes said to take shape in the Mosaic law (Sir 24:23; Bar 4:1), and, although Paul speaks of "truth" and "knowledge" rather than wisdom here, he was probably expressing the same idea.[23] Once again, Paul was probably thinking of what should have been his interlocutor's role in teaching the truth to those who had exchanged the truth of God for a lie (1:25).

2:21–23 You who teach the other person—do you not teach yourself? You who preach not to steal—do you steal? You who say not to commit adultery—do you commit adultery? You who detest idols—do you rob temples? Do you who boast in the law dishonor God through transgression of the law? (ὁ οὖν διδάσκων ἕτερον σεαυτὸν οὐ διδάσκεις; ὁ κηρύσσων μὴ κλέπτειν κλέπτεις; ὁ λέγων μὴ μοιχεύειν μοιχεύεις; ὁ βδελυσσόμενος τὰ εἴδωλα ἱεροσυλεῖς; ὃς ἐν νόμῳ καυχᾶσαι, διὰ τῆς παραβάσεως τοῦ νόμου τὸν θεὸν ἀτιμάζεις;). Paul's interlocutor teaches God's law to others and takes pride in obeying it, but actually he disobeys the law and brings God into disrepute.

The next five characteristics are formulated as rhetorical questions. Many commentaries, editions, and translations (e.g., NA[28], NJB, REB, ESV, NET) express only the first four sentences as questions and formulate the fifth sentence as a statement that is then confirmed by the Scripture quotation in 2:24. It is true that the first four sentences begin with a participle whereas the last sentence begins with a relative clause.[24] It is also true that the "for" (γάρ) in 2:24 is understood most naturally as giving support for a preceding statement rather than for a question.[25] The last sentence in the series (2:23), however, is structured basically like the previous four sentences with a phrase that describes the subject of the verb coming first and then the second-person singular verb inserted at the end.[26] The "for" in 2:24, moreover, could introduce support for the statement *implied* by a preceding rhetorical question. It seems best, then, to think of all five sentences in 2:21–23 as rhetorical questions (NIV, NASB, NAB, NRSV). The last question (2:23) does stand apart from the other four questions as a summary of their overall point: those who boast in possessing and knowing the law dishonor God by transgressing the law.[27]

The first question stands like a heading over the others and is reminiscent of Jesus's advice in Matthew 23:2–3: "The scribes and the Pharisees sit on Moses' seat, so do and observe whatever they tell you, but not the works they do. For they preach, but do not practice."[28] Paul then gives three examples of how his interlocutor fails to practice what he preaches. The first two, stealing and adultery, come from the Decalogue, although their order is reversed, which shows that we should not read too much into this. Paul is not, for example, thinking of the second table of the law in these first two items and the first table of the law in the third item, as Godet thought.[29]

The third item has provoked much debate. It is not immediately clear how detesting (βδελυσσόμενος)

22. BDAG 660, s.v. μόρφωσις. Theodoret of Cyrus explains the term here as a "stamp" or "picture" (χαρακτήρ), and Chrysostom seems to view its meaning as a "picture" (εἰκών). See *PG* 82:73 and *PG* 60:434 respectively. The law, then, gives clear and visible shape to knowledge and truth.

23. Dunn, *Romans 1–8*, 113.

24. Lagrange, *Romains*, 54.

25. Cranfield, *Romans*, 1:170; Dunn, *Romans 1–8*, 113.

26. Jewett, *Romans*, 229.

27. Cf. Käsemann, *Romans*, 69.

28. Wilckens, *An die Römer (Röm 1–5)*, 150.

29. *Romans*, 128.

idols is inconsistent with robbing temples; rather, detesting idols and robbing temples could easily flow out of the same ideology. Does Paul mean that although his interlocutor repudiates idolatry, he is nevertheless often irreverent in his behavior and attitudes?[30] Does he mean that his interlocutor has made an idol of the Mosaic law?[31] Does he accuse his interlocutor of dishonoring God by robbing the temples of the gentiles and showing disrespect for their religions?[32] It is more likely that Paul had in mind the prohibition of Deuteronomy 7:25:

> The carved images of their gods you shall burn with fire. You shall not covet the silver or the gold that is on them or take it for yourselves, lest you be ensnared by it, for it is an abomination [LXX: βδέλυγμα] to the LORD your God.

As the frequent occurrence of "temple robbery" in vice lists from antiquity shows, profiting from goods stolen from temples was common.[33] Paul is probably pointing out here that the Mosaic law prohibited temple robbery because of the danger that it might lead those who possess such materials into idolatry (cf. 1 Cor 10:14, 20). His point, then, is that his interlocutor detests idolatry but opens the door to this very vice by profiting from the sale of items taken from gentile temples.[34]

Paul is not accusing all Jews of stealing, adultery, and temple robbery. His Jewish interlocutor is a work of fiction, created by Paul to get a point across about the gospel to those reading this letter. This Jew is hardhearted, impenitent, and ignorant of God's merciful ways (2:4–5), yet he is proud of God's law (2:23) and eager to condemn those who violate its commands (2:1). He is, then, an ideal illustration of the point Paul is making at this stage of his argument: God is impartial in his treatment of humanity. If he were to give preferential treatment on the day of judgment to one group over others, he would give it to the Jews (1:16; 2:10), yet like everyone else they will stand condemned before him on that day unless they trust in God himself to rescue them through Christ Jesus, his Son.

Paul's final rhetorical question summarizes the other four questions and ends this third and last series of five items. When Paul says that his interlocutor "boasts" (καυχάομαι) in the law, he means that he is proud of his obedience to the law. Many students of the law must have both understood that they were sinners and begged the Lord for forgiveness for their sins even as they boasted in the law in the appropriate sense of expressing joy at the wisdom and understanding the law could provide to those who studied it diligently (Sir 39:5–8). All Jews, in other words, were not like Paul's Jewish interlocutor. That some Jews were too optimistic, from Paul's perspective, about their ability to keep the law, however, is also clear. The rich man who asked Jesus how he could inherit eternal life was optimistic that he had kept the commandments (Mark 10:19–20). Luke says, moreover, that Jesus told the parable of the Pharisee and the tax collector to "some who trusted in themselves [τοὺς πεποιθότας ἐφ' ἑαυτοῖς] that they were righteous [δίκαιοι], and treated others with contempt" (Luke 18:9). Josephus thought that Jews rarely sinned (*Against Apion* 2.178); an unknown Hellenistic Jew of the period could say "children of the Hebrews alone are invincible where virtue is concerned" (4 Macc 9:18), and an author of the Sibylline Oracles

30. Cranfield, *Romans*, 1:169–70; cf. Shedd, *Romans*, 55.
31. Fitzmyer, *Romans*, 318.
32. Edgar Krentz, "The Name of God in Disrepute: Romans 2:17–29 [22–23]," *CurTM* 17 (1990): 429–39; Jewett, *Romans*, 228–29.
33. See the evidence assembled in Krentz, "Name of God," 433–34n22. See also Schreiner, *Romans*, 132.
34. So, among many others, Gottlob Schrenk, "ἱεροσυλέω," *TDNT* 3:256; Käsemann, *Romans*, 71; Dunn, *Romans 1–8*, 114–15; Schreiner, *Romans*, 133.

could say that the Jews "alone are pious" (5:281).[35] If the boast of Paul's interlocutor was a boast in his obedience to the law, then Paul wants him to take a more serious look at himself.

By his transgression of the law, Paul continues, his interlocutor dishonors God. The Greek tragedians speak of dishonoring the gods and mean by this that the gods have been offended or insulted (e.g., Aeschylus, *Seven against Thebes* 1018–19; Euripides, *Children of Hercules* 78; *Madness of Hercules* 608–9; Sophocles, *Antigone* 76–79). The term "dishonor" (ἀτιμάζω) can also refer, however, to shaming someone, an extraordinarily serious offense in the honor-shame culture of ancient Greece and Rome (cf. Acts 5:41; Jas 2:6).[36] As Paul's quotation of Scripture in 2:24 shows, this is the way he uses the term "dishonor" here. His interlocutor has exposed God to public ridicule by breaking the very law that he relies on, teaches to others, and boasts in obeying.

2:24 For "the name of God is blasphemed among the gentiles because of you," just as it is written (τὸ γὰρ ὄνομα τοῦ θεοῦ δι ὑμᾶς βλασφημεῖται ἐν τοῖς ἔθνεσιν, καθὼς γέγραπται). The ridiculous hypocrisy of Paul's interlocutor subjects the God in whom he boasts to ridicule among non-Jews. This means that Paul's interlocutor is re-creating in himself the situation that led Israel into exile and brought dishonor to God's name in times past.

This is the letter's second explicit quotation from Scripture (cf. 1:17), and in an unusual move Paul places the citation formula at the end of the quotation rather than at the beginning. This has the effect of integrating the language of the quotation tightly into what Paul has just said in 2:23.[37] The quotation tells the reason why (γάρ) Paul can say that his interlocutor's transgression has dishonored God, and it makes clear that this dishonor is not just a matter of insulting God himself but of sullying his worldwide reputation. The second-person plural "you" (ὑμᾶς) contrasts with the second-person singulars in the surrounding context and broadens Paul's indictment beyond his interlocutor to Israel generally.

The nature of the quotation itself reveals how Paul can do this. Its wording is close to Isaiah 52:5 LXX ("Because of you, my name is continually blasphemed among the nations" [δι᾽ ὑμᾶς διὰ παντὸς τὸ ὄνομά μου βλασφημεῖται ἐν τοῖς ἔθνεσιν]). In its context in the LXX, this means that Israel is responsible for the blasphemy of God's name among the nations because, as Isaiah 50:1 says, their "iniquities" and "transgressions" led to their exile among the nations.[38] Because of the suffering of God's people in exile, the nations now ridicule Israel's God, who, the gentiles imagine, was not strong enough to protect his people.[39]

It is a theme that appears more than once in Scripture. At the end of his long prayer of confes-

35. For these and other examples, with careful analysis of the relevant passages, see Gathercole, *Where Is Boasting?*, 163–82. Translations are quoted from Gathercole.

36. LSJ 270; BDAG 148, both s.v. ἀτιμάζω. Cf. Lysius, *Speeches* 2.27 and the third-century BC papyrus P Ptr II.4(6): "It is a dreadful thing to be insulted [ἀτιμάζεσθαι] before a crowd" (MM 89).

37. Christopher D. Stanley, *Arguing with Scripture: The Rhetoric of Quotations in the Letters of Paul* (New York: T&T Clark, 2004), 147.

38. Schreiner, *Romans*, 134–35; Mark Seifrid, "Romans," in *Commentary on the New Testament Use of the Old Testament*, ed. G. K. Beale and D. A. Carson (Grand Rapids: Baker, 2007), 612–13. This point supplies a sufficient answer to the arguments of Richard Hays (*Echoes of Scripture in the Letters of Paul* [New Haven: Yale University Press, 1989], 45) and Stanley (*Arguing with Scripture*, 147–48) that Paul's quotation represents a "stunning misreading" (Hays) of this text within its original literary context in Isaiah.

39. Although the LXX differs from the MT by making explicit that Israel is to blame for the defamation of God's name among the nations, the thought is present in the MT also. See John N. Oswalt, *The Book of Isaiah: Chapters 40–66* (Grand Rapids: Eerdmans, 1998), 363–64.

sion, Daniel acknowledges that Israel is in exile because of their own sins but urges God to ease his peoples' plight "for your own sake" and "because your city and your people are called by your name" (Dan 9:17, 19). Ezekiel prophesied similarly that because Israel's sin had led to their exile and thus to the profaning of God's "holy name" among the nations, God would bring Israel out of its exile, restore them to their land, purify them, and give them both a new heart and his Spirit (Ezek 36:16–38). God's "name" in these texts is a way of speaking of his reputation, and so it makes sense that Paul would bring the reference to God's name in Isaiah 52:5 LXX forward to the beginning of the quotation.

Paul has now circled back to the idea in 2:19 that God called Israel to be a light to the gentiles. As the intervening sentences have shown, Paul's interlocutor has not fulfilled this vocation because, despite his knowledge of the law, he has disobeyed it, and like Israel of old his disobedience has led the gentiles to dishonor God. Zechariah pictured ten people from the nations desperately clutching at the robe of one Jew with the plea, "Let us go with you, for we have heard that God is with you" (Zech 8:23; cf. Isa 2:2–3; Mic 4:1–2). Paul's fictional interlocutor has instead led gentiles to ridicule his God because of his disobedience to the law. Paul may have been thinking of the ridiculous conduct of the interlocutor he had created. He blindly condemned in others the very sins that he committed himself (2:1) and fancied himself a teacher of the very virtues that he violated (2:21–22).

2:25 For, on one hand, circumcision is beneficial if you practice the law, but, on the other hand, if you are a transgressor of the law, your circumcision becomes uncircumcision (περιτομὴ μὲν γὰρ ὠφελεῖ ἐὰν νόμον πράσσῃς· ἐὰν δὲ παραβάτης νόμου ᾖς, ἡ περιτομή σου ἀκροβυστία γέγονεν). Not the physical rite of circumcision but doing what God requires is what makes someone a member of the people of God.

The "for" (γάρ) connects this paragraph not so much to 2:24 as to the thought of the whole previous paragraph (2:17–24). Circumcision was a surgical procedure performed among Jews on male infants who were eight days old and on male converts to Judaism. It involved the removal of skin around the male sexual organ. The procedure was commanded in the law as an "everlasting" (*'olam*; αἰώνιος) sign of God's covenant with Abraham and his descendants (Gen 17:10–14) and continued to be an integral part of Jewish ethnic identity in the first century. Paul will equate being a Jew with circumcision when he speaks in the same breath of "the advantage" (τὸ περισσόν) of being a Jew and the "benefit" (ὠφέλεια) of circumcision (3:1). From the Jewish perspective, to be male and to be uncircumcised or to have a "foreskin" (ἀκροβυστία) was synonymous with being a gentile (cf. Gen 34:14 LXX; Acts 11:13; 1 Cor 7:18).[40] Paul's point here is similar to his point in 2:17–24, although instead of focusing on the law generally he focuses on this one distinguishing commandment of the law. Just as mere knowledge of the law in 2:17–24 brought no benefit to Paul's Jewish interlocutor because he disobeyed the law, so Paul says here that circumcision brings no benefit unless it goes hand in hand with obedience to the law.

What is this benefit? Since Paul says that transgression of the law metaphorically turns the circumcised Jew into someone who is uncircumcised, the benefit of circumcision must be membership among the Jewish people. Their advantage is access to God's word in the Mosaic law, with its promises

40. BDAG 39, s.v. ἀκροβυστία 3.

that God would be faithful to his people (3:1–4; cf., e.g., Deut 4:31).[41]

The implication of Paul's statement that circumcision is beneficial if one keeps the law, however, is that physical circumcision is not part of the law's "just requirements" as Paul will describe them in 2:26. This is a radical idea for a Jew, but it is conceptually similar to Jeremiah's criticism of "those who are circumcised merely in the flesh" and of "all the house of Israel," which are "uncircumcised in heart" (Jer 9:25–26; cf. Lev 26:41; Deut 10:16; 30:6).[42] Israel's Scriptures recognized that possession of a physical mark was not the essential element in belonging to the people of God. God required his people to keep the whole law, and that is something Paul's interlocutor has not done. A few paragraphs later in his argument Paul will make clear that no one else has done this either (3:9–20).[43]

2:26 If, therefore, the uncircumcised person keeps the just requirements of the law, will not his uncircumcision be counted as circumcision? (ἐὰν οὖν ἡ ἀκροβυστία τὰ δικαιώματα τοῦ νόμου φυλάσσῃ, οὐχὶ ἡ ἀκροβυστία αὐτοῦ εἰς περιτομὴν λογισθήσεται;). God would count an uncircumcised gentile who did what he required as possessing the necessary mark of belonging to God's people.

Jews could sometimes refer to gentiles simply as "the uncircumcision" (ἡ ἀκροβυστία; lit., "the foreskin"; cf. 3:30; 4:9; Col 3:11; Eph 2:11), and Paul adopts this terminology here, indicating that he inhabits the same rhetorical and symbolic world as his interlocutor. Paul imagines an uncircumcised gentile who keeps "the just requirements of the law" (τὰ δικαιώματα τοῦ νόμου). Elsewhere in Romans where Paul uses similar language to speak of God's "just requirement" (δικαίωμα), he also has in mind an obedience to God that gentiles as well as Jews can give and that, as in this use of the term, does not entail the literal observance of certain commands of the Mosaic law (1:32; 8:4). Paul, then, continues his radical approach to physical circumcision. The expression "will be counted" (λογισθήσεται) is a divine passive, and its future tense probably looks forward to the final day of judgment (2:5, 16): on that day God "will count" as "circumcision" (περιτομή) the "uncircumcision" (ἀκροβυστία) of anyone who keeps the requirements that God makes of all humanity.[44] The conditional nature of this sentence is important. Paul does not say that any uncircumcised gentile actually keeps the law's just requirements well enough to be counted among God's people but only imagines a situation in which this is the case.[45]

2:27 And the one who is by nature uncircumcised but carries out the law will judge you who, despite the letter and circumcision, transgress the law (καὶ κρινεῖ ἡ ἐκ φύσεως ἀκροβυστία τὸν νόμον τελοῦσα σὲ τὸν διὰ γράμματος καὶ περιτομῆς παραβάτην νόμου). On the day of judgment, a gentile who kept the law would put to shame a Jew who transgressed it.

Since the rhetorical question in 2:26 functioned as a statement, the "and" (καί) that begins this new sentence connects the following statement to it and

41. Cf. Cranfield, *Romans*, 1:172. The verb "becomes" (γέγονεν) is what Wallace (*Greek Grammar*, 574) calls an "intensive perfect," which emphasizes the present results of a past action and is often best rendered in English as a present (as in the ESV).

42. On the unprecedented nature of Paul's perspective on circumcision, see John M. G. Barclay, "Paul and Philo on Circumcision: Romans 2.25–9 in Social and Cultural Context," *NTS* 44 (1998): 536–56.

43. Cf. Moo, *Romans*, 168–69.

44. On the future tense, see Godet, *Romans*, 130; Meyer, *Romans*, 102; Moo, *Romans*, 169n17. *Pace* Jewett, *Romans*, 233, who sees it merely as a logical future.

45. Cf. Longenecker, *Romans*, 315.

brings the thought to a climax: an uncircumcised gentile who kept the law would be, from God's perspective, circumcised (2:26) *and in fact* would judge the Jewish transgressor of the law (2:27).[46] The future tense verb "will judge" (κρινεῖ) points to the final judgment (2:5, 16) and appears at the front of the sentence to place emphasis on this astonishing thought.[47]

The attributive use of the prepositional phrase "by nature" (ἐκ φύσεως) refers to what something is by birth or naturally. Paul's near contemporary Philo, for example, could speak of people failing to exercise and so losing the strength they have by nature (τήν ἐκ φύσεως ἰσχύν; *Sacrifices* 86) and of the natural defenses of animals (τὰς ἐκ φύσεως παρασκευάς; *Creation* 85). Baby boys, of course, have a "foreskin" (ἀκροβυστία) by birth whether they are Jewish or gentile. Paul is using the term "foreskin" (or "uncircumcision"), however, in the same sense that he used it in 2:26a to refer to the gentile, the person whom Paul's Jewish interlocutor defines as different from himself because he has a foreskin.

Paul imagines a gentile who "carries out" (τελοῦσα) the law, a term that often refers to fulfilling the intention of something, such as Scripture (Luke 18:31; 22:37; Acts 13:29), and is fitting for a gentile who keeps the law but remains, by definition, uncircumcised (cf. Jas 2:8). Paul's interlocutor, by contrast, is a transgressor of the law despite possessing "the letter" and circumcision. The prepositional phrase translated "despite the letter and circumcision" (διὰ γράμματος καὶ περιτομῆς) should be understood circumstantially rather than instrumentally (cf. 4:11; 8:25; 14:20), indicating the conditions under which the transgression takes place.[48] "Letter" here refers to the specific, written revelation of God in Scripture, one of the privileges of the Jew that Paul will enumerate in 3:2, although there he will call the Scripture "the oracles of God" (cf. 9:4; Eph 2:12).

As C. John Collins has pointed out, the motif of gentiles putting Jews to shame through their superior piety is common in the Old Testament (Josh 2:1–4; Ruth 1:14; 1 Sam 7:1–2 [cf. Josh 9:17]; 2 Sam 15:18–22; 1 Kgs 17:8–16, 24 [cf. 18:36–37]; Jer 38:7–13 [cf. 39:15–18]; Jonah 1:16; 3:5–10) and in the teaching of Jesus (Matt 12:40–42; Luke 11:31–32; cf. Matt 8:10–11; 21:43; Mark 12:9; Luke 7:9; 20:16). It should always be understood as part of a prophetic critique within Judaism.[49] Paul does not "play to gentiles" here.[50] Just as in 2:25–26, Paul's approach recalls Jeremiah 9:25–26 where the prophet compares Israel to other nations that practice circumcision and says what they all need is actually circumcision of the heart.[51]

2:28 For the one who is a Jew in what is visible is not a Jew, nor is circumcision in what is visible, in the flesh (οὐ γὰρ ὁ ἐν τῷ φανερῷ Ἰουδαῖός ἐστιν, οὐδὲ ἡ ἐν τῷ φανερῷ ἐν σαρκὶ περιτομή). Being a Jew is not a matter of physical circumcision.

Paul now says why (γάρ) he can make the astonishing claim that a foreskinned gentile who keeps the law will judge Paul's circumcised interlocutor who transgresses the law. Paul's Greek is unusually

46. It is also possible (NASB, NET) to see v. 27 simply as a second rhetorical question connected to the first question with "and" (καί).

47. For this construal of the grammar and logic, see Meyer, *Romans*, 103.

48. *Pace*, Bernardin Schneider, "The Meaning of St. Paul's Antithesis 'The Letter and the Spirit,'" *CBQ* 15 (1953): 199. See BDAG 224, s.v. διά 3c.

49. See Collins, "Echoes of Aristotle in Romans 2:14–15," 142, and the comments in the "Theology in Application" section on 2:1–16.

50. "Paul appeals to or plays to Gentiles": Nina Livesey, *Circumcision as Malleable Symbol*, WUNT 2.295 (Tübingen: Mohr Siebeck, 2010), 108.

51. Simon Légasse, *L'épître de Paul aux Romains*, Lectio Divina Commentaries 10 (Paris: Cerf, 2002), 209.

compressed, but its meaning becomes clear if the verb "is" (ἐστιν) in the first half of the sentence is mentally supplied in the second half and if the subject of each clause is mentally repeated so that it also becomes the predicate of its clause. The result could be paraphrased this way: "The visible Jew is not [a Jew], nor [is] visible, fleshly circumcision [circumcision]."[52] The term "visible" is the opposite of "hidden," as 2:29 shows (cf. Mark 4:22; Luke 8:17), and Paul explains precisely what he means by this term when, in the second clause, he places the prepositional phrases "in what is visible" (ἐν τῷ φανερῷ) and "in the flesh" (ἐν σαρκὶ) in apposition to one another. The outward, physical rite that Paul's interlocutor regards as the boundary of Judaism is not the real boundary marker after all.

2:29 But the Jew in secret is a Jew, and circumcision of the heart, in the Spirit and not the letter, is circumcision, whose praise is not from human beings but from God (ἀλλ' ὁ ἐν τῷ κρυπτῷ Ἰουδαῖος, καὶ περιτομὴ καρδίας ἐν πνεύματι οὐ γράμματι, οὗ ὁ ἔπαινος οὐκ ἐξ ἀνθρώπων ἀλλ' ἐκ τοῦ θεοῦ). The true Jew and the true circumcision are invisible characteristics, gifts of God's Spirit, not of the Mosaic law. On the final day, God will look into the heart to determine who belongs to his people, not at the outward trappings of Judaism that matter to human beings.

Paul now gives the antithesis to his description of the merely visible, physical Jew. Once again, the compressed Greek needs to be filled out with the verb "is" (ἐστιν) in the clauses separated by "and" (καί) and by the repetition of the subjects "Jew" (Ἰουδαῖος) and "circumcision" (περιτομή) in the resulting predicates of each clause.[53] The Jewishness of the Jew is something "in secret" (ἐν τῷ κρυπτῷ; cf. Matt 6:4, 6), and circumcision is "of the heart" (καρδίας) and is therefore similarly something that cannot be seen (cf. Deut 30:6; Jer 4:4; 9:25–26). Paul's point is virtually identical to the point he makes in 1 Corinthians 4:5 to an audience of gentile believers who, like his fictional Jewish interlocutor, have also been judging people by outward appearance rather than by spiritual criteria:

> Do not pronounce judgment before the time, before the Lord comes, who will bring to light the things now hidden in darkness and will disclose the purposes of the heart. Then each one will receive his commendation from God.

Paul's contrast between "the Spirit" and "the letter" does not oppose a spiritual to a literal interpretation of circumcision.[54] This is instead the language of salvation history.[55] "Circumcision of the heart in the Spirit" refers to the future circumcision of the heart that Deuteronomy says God himself will accomplish for his people after their exile when he restores their fortunes (30:6; cf. Ezek 11:19; 1Q504 4.10–14; Jub. 1:23; Odes Sol. 11:2).[56] It stands in contrast to the period presided over by "the letter," the Mosaic law, and particularly the Decalogue, which, apart from God's eschatologically given Spirit that enables his people to keep its precepts, only generates further rebellion against God (4:15; 5:13, 20; 7:6; 2 Cor 3:3, 6–11).

The reality that Paul describes here will only be fulfilled among Christians (7:6; 8:1, 4, 7; 13:8–10), but he is not yet ready to develop that idea.[57] Here he speaks only of an imagined group of gentiles

52. Lagrange, *Romains*, 56; Cranfield, *Romans*, 1:175.

53. Lagrange, *Romains*, 56; Cranfield, *Romans*, 1:175.

54. As Theodore of Mopsuestia thought (Schneider, "St. Paul's Antithesis," 179).

55. See Schneider's persuasive argument to this effect ("St. Paul's Antithesis," 193–207).

56. Blaschke, *Beschneidung*, 131–33, 153; Hultgren, *Romans*, 130.

57. A. Andrew Das, *Paul and the Jews*, Library of Pauline Studies (Peabody, MA: Hendrickson, 2003), 183.

who are more Jewish than his equally fictional Jewish interlocutor because God has transformed their hearts so that they do what he requires. Paul's interlocutor has to concede the point that because of the emphasis that Scripture places on circumcision of the heart, if such gentiles existed anywhere, they would indeed put him to shame on the day of judgment.

Theology in Application

Paul's belief that circumcision was irrelevant to membership in the people of God was radical, but the theological grounding he gave for it was thoroughly biblical. The Bible often insists that ritual should be an aid to serving God in the weighter matters, not a replacement for this more important mode of service.

The Bible's Warning against Replacing Obedience with Ritual

The Scriptures frequently assert that God is far more concerned that his people practice justice and mercy than that they observe various sacrificial rituals. Psalm 50 is an especially clear statement of this concern. It pictures the just Creator of all the earth calling his people together in the presence of all he has created and testifying against them (Ps 50:1–7). "Not for your sacrifices do I rebuke you," God begins; "your burnt offerings are continually before me" (50:8). God is not that interested in these things. It is not as if he is hungry and needs "to eat the flesh of bulls" and "drink the blood of goats" (50:13). Rather, God wants his people to be thankful and faithful to him and to trust him to deliver them in the day of trouble (50:14–15). In other words, he is not a petty deity that human beings can bribe with sacrifices but the one God who wants to be in a personal, heartfelt relationship with those whom he has created. Similarly, God is not impressed with people who recite his statutes and take his covenant on their lips but are pleased with thievery, keep the company of adulterers, and slander others behind their backs (50:16–20). God wants his people to be thankful to him for all he has done for them and, out of these thankful hearts, to live in the way God has charted for them (50:23).

God complains in this Psalm that his people know sacrificial procedure well and enjoy discussing and practicing it, but, in the process, their gratitude to him has grown dim and they have forgotten his commitment to justice.

At the beginning of Isaiah, God indicts Israel in the same way. They have paid inordinate attention to sacrificial ritual and the religious calendar at the same time that they are practicing "iniquity" and their "hands are full of blood" (Isa 1:10–15). God has had enough of their sacrifices (1:11) and their mixture of solemn assembly with iniquity (1:13). His people need to "learn to do good; seek justice, correct oppression; bring justice to the fatherless," and "plead the widow's cause" (1:17; cf. Hos 6:4–6; Amos 4:4–5; 5:21–25; Mic 6:6–8).

Jeremiah rebukes Judah for the same obtuseness to the deepest concerns of God, but focuses attention on Judah's overreliance on the presence of God's temple in their midst:

> Will you steal, murder, commit adultery, swear falsely, make offerings to Baal, and go after other gods that you have not known, and then come and stand before me in this house, which is called by my name, and say, "We are delivered!"—only to go on doing all these abominations? (Jer 7:9–10; cf. 7:3–4)

Following a pattern that Paul also follows in 2:17–29, Jeremiah distinguishes between obedience to the commands in the Mosaic law that address ritual issues and obedience to more important commands:

> For in the day that I brought them out of the land of Egypt, I did not speak to your fathers or command them concerning burnt offerings and sacrifices. But this command I gave them: "Obey my voice, and I will be your God, and you shall be my people. And walk in all the way that I command you, that it may be well with you." (Jer 7:22–23)

Just as Paul's interlocutor might have asked him how he could distinguish between obeying the law and obeying the command to be circumcised, so Jeremiah might have been asked how he could make this division between commands about sacrificial ritual and obeying God. Did not God command his people to perform sacrificial ritual? Like Paul, Jeremiah subordinates ritual to matters of justice such as stealing and adultery.

Authentic Obedience to God

Those who claim to be God's people today need to heed Paul's instruction as much as ever. It is possible to make a talisman out of nearly any religious ritual or concept, whether it is a set of doctrinal affirmations, a certain code of conduct, or a particular configuration of political positions. It is possible to know much about theology, church history, biblical exegesis, church polity, liturgical procedure, the precise meaning of various confessions of faith, and to enjoy thoroughly discussing all this but to be wicked in God's eyes. "To the wicked God says: 'What right have you to recite my statutes or take my covenant on your lips?'" (Ps 50:16).

It would be appropriate for all of us who study Romans closely and enjoy teaching its profound, beautifully expressed, and often controversial argument to others to ask ourselves the question that Paul asks his interlocutor in 2:21: "You who teach the other person—do you not teach yourself?" Because this interesting ancient text is also God's word, every interpreter and teacher of it at some point needs to reckon personally with its message. How grateful am I to God for what he has done for me through Jesus Christ? Do I express this gratitude in a life characterized by the humility, love, endurance, and concern for the well-being of others that Paul describes in 12:1–15:13? If Psalm 50 and Romans 2:17–29 are any indication, God is more concerned about the way I answer these questions than he is about any of the interpretive technicalities that make this text so enjoyable to study and to teach.

CHAPTER 6

Romans 3:1–8

Literary Context

Since announcing the basic message of his gospel in 1:16–17 as the revelation of God's righteousness, Paul has been explaining what God's righteousness means. Paradoxically, God's righteousness involves both the impartial salvation of "barbarians," Greeks, and Jews on one hand (1:16; cf. 1:14); on the other hand, it involves the punishment of the unrighteous for their ungrateful rebellion against God and their vicious treatment of their fellow human beings (1:18–2:29). So far, Paul's primary focus has been on the punishment of the wicked, and he has made the case that this punishment is fair because the wicked richly deserve it (1:19–21; 2:6, 8–9) and because it is impartial (2:11). God punishes not only gentiles for their idolatry with all its accompanying sins (1:18–32) but Jews also since they too are sinners (2:1–29).

Paul recognized that this second element of God's righteousness—that it means the impartial punishment of Jews alongside gentiles—was the most difficult part for biblically literate people to accept because the Scriptures single out the Jewish people as God's special possession and object of his love, mercy, and faithfulness (e.g., Exod 19:5–6; Deut 4:32–39; 1 Kgs 8:52–53). Paul therefore emphatically insists that God will punish Jews who disobey him no less than gentiles who disobey him. He makes his case so forcefully that he ends chapter two with the astonishing picture of an uncircumcised gentile keeping the law and receiving a more favorable judgment from God in the end than a circumcised Jew who breaks the law (2:26–27).

Paul knew that his explanation of God's righteousness along these lines generated an important set of questions. Has Paul left Jews with any advantage? Does his argument imply that the tables have turned and Jews are actually at a disadvantage when compared to gentiles? Paul answers these questions in 3:1–20. In 3:1–8 he discusses whether Jews have any advantage over the other nations. Then, in 3:9–20 he discusses whether gentiles are in a better position than Jews with respect to God's judgment.

These questions come up again in 9:1–11:36. There Paul will again address the question of whether his explanation of God's righteousness means that Israel has lost the advantage that, according to Scripture, God gave to it. In 9:1–11:36 Paul will be more concerned than he is here with exactly what the Scripture promised Israel and how these promises can be fulfilled in light of his gospel's explanation of salvation history. Here in 3:1–8 his concern is restricted to the issue of whether God is fair in punishing his people with his wrath since God promised to be faithful to them.

Except for the brief intrusion of actual opponents in 3:8, Paul's argument advances in this section by means of a fictional dialogue with a Jewish interlocutor, just as it did in 2:1–29. The interlocutor and his positions are not necessarily representative of Judaism generally but are devices constructed by Paul to make his argument clear for his audience in Rome.[1]

V. God's Wrath against Human Sin Is a Demonstration of His Righteousness (1:18–32)

VI. Jews Are Also Subject to God's Wrath (2:1–3:20)

A. God as an Impartial Judge Not Merely of Gentiles but of Jews Also (2:1–16)

B. God as an Impartial Judge Even of Jews Who Teach the Law and Possess Circumcision (2:17–29)

➡ **C. Objections to Paul's Understanding of God's Impartial Judgment (3:1–8)**

D. Scripture's Testimony That Everyone Is under Sin (3:9–20)

VII. The Death of Christ Demonstrates God's Righteousness and Excludes Human Boasting (3:21–31)

Main Idea

Paul's case that God will judge Jews impartially alongside gentiles on the final day does not mean that God is unfaithful to his word and that there is actually no advantage in being a Jew. The Jew's advantage lies in his or her access to God's will in the law, not in exemption from punishment for breaking the law. Israel's unfaithfulness in breaking the law and subsequent punishment, then, does not entail God's unfaithfulness to Israel. In addition, God is not unjust to punish sinners, even if that punishment enhances his reputation as righteous and true. To say that would imply that God should not punish those who do evil because his punishment produces a good result! This is a position Paul would never support in any form.

1. Cf., e.g., Paul Achtemeier, "Romans 3:1–8: Structure and Argument," in *Christ and His Communities: Essays in Honor of Reginald H. Fuller*, ed. Arland J. Hultgren and Barbara Hall; AThRSup 11 (Cincinnati: Forward Movement, 1990), 81–83.

Translation

Romans 3:1–8

1a	Rhetorical Question	**What, then, is the advantage of the Jew, or**
b	Restatement	**what is the benefit of circumcision?**
2a	Measure	**Much in every way!**
b	Explanation	For, first of all, that **they were entrusted with the oracles of God.**
3a	Rhetorical Question	**What, then?**
b	Condition	If some were unfaithful,
c	Rhetorical Question	**will their unfaithfulness cancel**
d	Contrast	**the faithfulness of God?**
4a	Exclamation	**Certainly not!**
b	Assertion	**Rather, let God be true and every human being a liar,**
c	Comparison	just as it is written,
	OT Quotation	"So that you may be justified
d	Sphere	in your words and
e	Restatement	win
f	Time	when you are judged." (Ps 51:4)
5a	Condition	But if our unrighteousness demonstrates the righteousness of God,
b	Rhetorical Question	**what shall we say?**
c	Rhetorical Question	**The God who inflicts his wrath is not unjust is he?**
d	Assertion	**(I speak in a human way.)**
6a	Exclamation	**Certainly not!**
b	Rhetorical Question	**Otherwise, how will God judge the world?**
7a	Condition	But if the truthfulness of God abounded
b	Means	by means of my lie
c	Purpose	for his glory,
d	Rhetorical Question	**why am I too still judged as a sinner?**
8a	Rhetorical Question	**And we should not do bad things that good things may come should we?**
b	Comparison	As we are slandered and
c	Repetition	as some claim that we say.
d	Assertion	**Their condemnation is just.**

Structure

In 2:1–29, and especially from 2:17 onward, Paul has been addressing a fictional Jewish person who has provided a counterbalance to his position on the impartiality of God's judgment. This was a common teaching device in a form of Greco-Roman philosophical discourse often called the *diatribe*. Now, in 3:1 for the first time this constructed debating partner talks back. Such an intrusion into the dialogue by the fictional dialogue partner was also common in the Greco-Roman diatribe and often took the form of a question, as it does here.[2]

The subsequent argument continues to advance by means of rhetorical questions, but interpreters are divided over which parts of the dialogue belong to the fictional interlocutor and which parts come from Paul himself.[3] Although Paul raises objections to his argument with questions in 3:3, 5, and 8, the way he formulates the questions (using μή) already anticipates the negative answer he will give to them. There is perhaps an interlocutor somewhere behind these questions, but because Paul formulates them this way they seem to function more as statements from Paul himself than forcefully posed objections from the fictional interlocutor. Still, the interlocutor seems to materialize concretely again in the first-person singular in 3:7 and wants to know why "I" am condemned as a sinner if "my" lie enhances God's reputation. All this means that Paul was probably not using his questions to construct a dialogue along the lines of a set pattern and that trying to find such a pattern is probably a red herring in interpreting the passage.

A more helpful way to organize the passage is by means of the subjects Paul discusses, and this method yields two principle sections, 3:1–4 and 3:5–8. In 3:1–4 the topic is the faithfulness of God. As the references to the "oracles of God" in 3:2 and "the faithfulness of God" in 3:3 show, Paul is concerned in this section to show that God has been and will be faithful to what his word says about his people. The first benefit of being a Jew is that God has entrusted the Jews with his law (3:2). It is true that the Jews have been unfaithful to this law, but their unfaithfulness to God does not mean that God will be unfaithful to them (3:3). Unlike human beings, God does not lie (3:4).

Paul's quotation of Psalm 51:4 (50:6 LXX; 51:6 Heb.) at the end of the first section (3:4) sets the stage for the concern of 3:5–8. The Psalm asserts that in any lawsuit over the justice of God's judgment, God will always triumph. In 3:5–8 Paul's interlocutor will foolishly put God's activity as a judge on trial, and as Psalm 51:4 promises,

2. Stanley Kent Stowers, "Paul's Dialogue with a Fellow Jew in Romans 3:1–9," *CBQ* 46 (1984): 710–13.

3. See, for example, the differing outlines in Stowers, "Paul's Dialogue," 715, and Jewett, *Romans*, 241. Some interpreters (e.g., Longenecker, *Romans*, 332–34) believe that the questions come not from an opponent, whether fictional or otherwise, but from Paul himself. In the end, however, there does not seem to be much difference between Paul posing the questions to himself and Paul putting the questions on the lips of an interlocutor whom he has created.

the interlocutor's case against God goes nowhere. Although we can assume that the interlocutor in this section is still Paul's Jewish debating partner from 2:1–29, he emerges clearly only in 3:7, and his Jewishness is not an issue. The question deviates from whether God can be faithful to his word and punish the Jewish sinner (3:1–4) to whether God can be righteous and punish anyone at all. Paul opened the door to this broader perspective in the first section when he spoke of the falsehood of "every human being" (3:4).

The central problem of 3:5–8 appears in the questions in 3:5 and 3:7, and the reasoning behind the problem is odd (3:5d). A righteous judge who wants people to consider him righteous must punish the sinner who appears in his court. Similarly, since lying is a sin, to call a liar a sinner is to tell the truth. The objector claims, however, that as an unrighteous person and a liar he has aided a righteous and truthful God by demonstrating that God is righteous and truthful. God therefore should not punish or judge him. Paul spends little time on this idea but merely swats it down with two simple observations: if the objector were correct, righteous judgment would be impossible (3:6b) and evil would become indistinguishable from good (3:8a).

Paul probably addresses the twisted form of moral reasoning he mentions in 3:8a ("We should not do bad things that good things may come should we?") because people had accused him of thinking this way. This "slander" (3:8b), however, probably did not arise from Paul's teaching on the wrath of God. Instead, it arose because of his teaching (which will emerge later in Romans) on God's gracious justification of the unrighteous (6:1, 15). Paul mentions it at this point in his argument because, like the other odd teaching he describes in the second section (3:5, 7), it concludes that a good result justifies evil conduct.

This second section of 3:1–8 digresses from the more substantive issue raised in 3:1–4, and so Paul will return to that issue at the beginning of the next section in 3:9. Paul has shown in 3:1–4 that his teaching on the impartiality of God's judgment does not threaten the privileged place of Israel in salvation history. God has been and will be faithful to his own "oracles" concerning Israel. When it comes to God's judgment, however, have the gentiles surged ahead of the Jews so that they are actually at an advantage over them? If a gentile can keep the just requirements of the law and receive praise from God on the final day, as Paul argued in 2:25–29, then such a conclusion is certainly possible. Some gentile Christians in Rome seem to have actually drawn this conclusion (11:17–19). Paul will address this idea in the next section, and 3:9 will form a transition to that next stage in his argument.

Exegetical Outline

VI. Jews Are Also Subject to God's Wrath (2:1–3:20)

A. God as an Impartial Judge Not Merely of Gentiles but of Jews Also (2:1–16)

B. God as an Impartial Judge Even of Jews Who Teach the Law and Possess Circumcision (2:17–29)

➦ **C. Objections to Paul's Understanding of God's Impartial Judgment (3:1–8)**

1. Is God Faithful to What His Word Says about His People? (3:1–4)
   a. The Jews retain the advantages given to them by the word of God, including the Mosaic law that God entrusted to them (3:1–2)
   b. The Jews' unfaithfulness to that trust did not result in God's unfaithfulness to them (3:3–4)
2. Is God Righteous and True If He Punishes the Wicked? (3:5–8)
   a. God is not unrighteous when he punishes the unrighteous because he is a righteous judge (3:5–6)
   b. The liar cannot escape God's truthful judgment as a sinner because that would imply no distinction between right and wrong (3:7–8)

Explanation of the Text

3:1 What, then, is the advantage of the Jew, or what is the benefit of circumcision? (Τί οὖν τὸ περισσὸν τοῦ Ἰουδαίου, ἢ τίς ἡ ὠφέλεια τῆς περιτομῆς;). If what Paul has just said in 2:25–29 is true, then it seems God does not consider the Jewish people his unique, covenant people.

Paul places a natural question on the lips of his fictional Jewish interlocutor. Since (οὖν) Paul has just made the case that the real Jew and real circumcision are spiritual matters of the heart, not matters of outward observance, and since he has taken the further step of implying that the outward observances are not necessary at all, he seems to have ignored God's unique, covenantal relationship with Israel. Circumcision played a prominent role in this covenant (Gen 17:9–14). If an uncircumcised gentile could keep the just requirements of the law better than a Jew (2:26), then what became of the "everlasting covenant," inscribed in the "flesh" by circumcision, that God made with Abraham and his descendants (Gen 17:13)?

The term translated here "advantage" (περισσός) is an adjective that most often means "extraordinary" or "abundant," but preceded by the neuter, singular article and followed by a genitive noun can mean "the excellence of" or "the advantage of" something (cf., e.g., Let. Aris. 161.1). Paul has already implied that being circumcised in the physical sense "benefits" (ὠφελεῖ) the Jew as long as he does what God requires (2:25a–c). Now, the double rhetorical question provides a transition to a brief explanation of that advantage.

3:2 Much in every way! For, first of all, that they were entrusted with the oracles of God (πολὺ κατὰ πάντα τρόπον. πρῶτον μὲν [γὰρ] ὅτι ἐπιστεύθησαν τὰ λόγια τοῦ θεοῦ). Jews do retain important advantages over gentiles, despite their lack of any soteriological advantage over them. The gift of God's law, together with the responsibility of sharing that gift with the nations, is one of those advantages.

Paul continues the question-answer style common in the philosophical teaching of the period by answering his fictional interlocutor's question. He forcefully insists that no one should understand his argument to mean that the Jews have lost their advantage with God. "Much in every way" is hyperbole intended to emphasize the more nuanced truth for which Paul is arguing. To speak precisely, Jews do not have an advantage "in every way" (κατὰ πάντα τρόπον) as 2:1–29 has shown. Nevertheless, they do have important advantages that fall short of any soteriological privilege.[4] The "for" (γάρ) connects the advantage Paul is about to describe to the statement he has just made that Jewish advantages are many. He follows it with "that" (ὅτι), producing a somewhat awkward sentence that serves as a reminder of the occasional and oral nature even of Romans.[5] Another reminder comes in the expression "first of all" (πρῶτον μέν), whose form (μέν) signals that it should be followed by other items in a list (cf., e.g., Sir 23:23; 2 Macc 14:8; Jas 3:17; Heb 7:2; Josephus, *Ant.* 5.133; 6.34). Paul, however, goes no further in listing advantages than this "first" item.[6] Other advantages will come much later (Rom 9:3–5; cf. Eph 2:12), but here he focuses on a single advantage that was closely related to his previous argument.

Paul's fictional Jewish interlocutor was someone who heard the law read in the synagogue (2:13), was instructed by it in how to make good choices (2:18), and knew it well enough to teach it to others (2:19–20). It makes sense, then, that Paul thought first of "the oracles of God" when he began to describe the advantages of being a Jew. As early as the third-century BC, Greek-speaking Jews could call the law of God "the oracles" (τὰ λόγια) of God (Deut 33:9–10 LXX; Isa 5:24 LXX [sg.]; Ps 118:11 LXX [119:11 Eng.]; Let. Arist. 158, 177; Acts 7:38; Philo, *Decalogue* 16). That is probably what Paul intended by the expression here.[7]

Paul frequently uses the verb "believe" (πιστεύω) in the passive voice to speak of being "entrusted" by God with the task of preaching the gospel (1 Cor 9:17; Gal 2:7; 1 Thess 2:4; 1 Tim 1:11; Titus 1:3). His comment that the Jews "were entrusted" (ἐπιστεύθησαν) with God's law probably refers in a similar way to Israel's calling to be a light to the gentiles (Isa 42:6–7), a role that Paul had already subtly referred to in 2:19–20 and 24.[8] God had selected Israel, out of all the nations of the earth, to receive his law (Deut 4:8; Ps 147:19–20), and Israel's obedience to the law would set it apart as "a kingdom of priests" (Exod 19:6), presumably mediating the character of God to the rest of the world.

3:3 What, then? If some were unfaithful, will their unfaithfulness cancel the faithfulness of God? (τί γὰρ; εἰ ἠπίστησάν τινες μὴ ἡ ἀπιστία αὐτῶν τὴν πίστιν τοῦ θεοῦ καταργήσει;). Paul insists that the unfaithfulness of some Jews to their covenant responsibility to obey the law and be a light to the gentiles does not mean that God will be unfaithful to his word concerning them.

It is difficult to know how to puncuate these two questions. Is the first question simply a transitional expression that moves the discourse along to the more substantive question ("What then? If some did not believe, does their unbelief nullify the faithfulness of God?" [NET; cf. NASB, HCSB]), or

4. Hultgren, *Romans*, 135.

5. On the awkwardness of the sentence, see Cranfield, *Romans*, 1:178. "For" (γάρ) is omitted in a significant set of manuscripts (B D G Ψ 81 365 1506 2464), and this omission is probably a result of the awkwardness of the sentence.

6. BDAG 630, s.v. μέν 2c. When Paul uses the expression in Rom 1:8 and 1 Cor 11:18, other items follow (although they are not enumerated).

7. Ambrosiaster, *Romans*, 23; Chrysostom, *Romans*, 81; Theodoret of Cyrus, *Letters of St. Paul*, 1:60; Légasse, *Romains*, 213–14, 232 n136. *Pace*, e.g., Meyer (*Romans*, 111–12), Moo (*Romans*, 182), and Schreiner (*Romans*, 149), who believe Paul refers primarily to the promises of God and, e.g., Dunn (*Romans 1–8*, 130–31) and Fitzmyer (*Romans*, 326–27), who believe that Paul refers to all the Scriptures.

8. Cf. Wright, "Romans," 453.

does the first question state the problem ("What if some were unfaithful?") and the second question deny a suggested consequence of the problem ("Will their unfaithfulness nullify God's faithfulness?" [NIV; cf. KJV, NRSV, ESV, NAB]). In Greek, it is simply a matter of whether to put the question mark after "for" (γὰρ) or after "some" (τινες). The decision is difficult, but the first option is probably best. "What then?" (τί γάρ;) was commonly used in philosophical discourse as a transitional expression (e.g., Xenophon, *Mem.* 2.6.2; Epictetus, *Diatr.* 1.12.18; Justin, *Dialogue with Trypho* 1.3), and Paul definitely uses it this way in Philippians 1:18.[9]

If this is the correct punctuation, moreover, then the two questions are probably Paul's own questions, intended to carry the argument forward from his perspective rather than objections that his fictional interlocutor raises.[10] This is clear from two considerations. First, the question is set up to expect a negative answer (μὴ . . . καταργήσει;), and therefore an answer that assumes Paul's standpoint.[11] Second, Paul's reference to the unfaithfulness of "some" Jews implies that others have been faithful, and this seems more in line with his own convictions (cf. 11:1–5) than with those of his interlocutor.[12]

The expressions "were unfaithful" (ἠπίστησάν), "faithlessness" (ἀπιστία), and "faithfulness" (πίστιν) combine with the expression "were entrusted" (ἐπιστεύθησαν) in 3:2 to form a skillful play on words that cannot be reproduced in English. Although usually the verb translated here as "were unfaithful" (ἠπίστησάν) means to disbelieve or distrust something (2 Macc 8:13; Luke 24:41; Acts 28:24), very rarely it can mean to "disobey" or "be unfaithful" to someone (Euripides, *Children of Hercules* 1024; Xenophon, *Anab.* 2.6.19; 2 Tim 2:13).[13] This more unusual meaning is the one Paul intended here, as the contrast between Israel's faithlessness and God's faithfulness and reliability shows.

This is a biblical contrast and appears, among many other places, in the Song of Moses (Deut 32:1–43). This song contrasts God who is "a God of faithfulness" (v. 4; LXX πιστός; Heb. *emunah*) and a loving, nurturing father, to Israel who are "children in whom is no faithfulness" (v. 20; LXX πίστις; Heb., *emun*). The Song of Moses was in Paul's mind when he wrote Romans, and he refers to it explicitly later in the letter when he describes God's response to Israel's faithlessness. In that later passage he says that God remains faithful and merciful to unbelieving Israel because he is making them jealous of the gentiles who are responding to the gospel in faith and seem to be taking over Israel's unique relationship with God (Rom 10:19; 11:11–15; cf. Deut 32:21). Paul probably had this more elaborate line of thought in mind here in 3:3. This is one way in which the unfaithfulness of some "will not cancel [καταργήσει]" (cf. REB) the faithfulness of God, and the outworking of this scenario in the eschatological future (11:12, 15) explains why the verb "cancel" (καταργέω) is in the future tense.[14]

3:4 Certainly not! Rather, let God be true and every human being a liar, just as it is written, "So that you may be justified in your words and win when you are judged" (μὴ γένοιτο· γινέσθω

9. Cf. Meyer, *Romans*, 112n3; Lagrange, *Romains*, 62; Cranfield, *Romans*, 1:179–180; BDAG, s.v. τίς 1007 (1.a.α.ℶ), and the helpful discussion in Jewett, *Romans*, 244, although he comes to different conclusions.

10. See also, e.g., Stowers, "Paul's Dialogue," 715. *Pace*, e.g., Jewett, *Romans*, 241.

11. Moo, *Romans*, 184n33.

12. Légasse, *Romains*, 214.

13. G. Barth, "ἀπιστέω, κτλ." *EDNT* 1:121; Légasse, *Romains*, 232n141.

14. E.g., Godet, *Romans*, 134; Jewett, *Romans*, 245; *pace*, e.g., Käsemann, *Romans*, 80.

δὲ ὁ θεὸς ἀληθής, πᾶς δὲ ἄνθρωπος ψεύστης, καθὼς γέγραπται, Ὅπως ἂν δικαιωθῇς ἐν τοῖς λόγοις σου καὶ νικήσεις ἐν τῷ κρίνεσθαί σε). It is a basic axiom that God keeps his word, and this is true even if it implies that everyone else must be considered a liar. Scripture itself testifies to this when it portrays an unfaithful man confessing that God was just to condemn him for his unfaithfulness.

Paul emphatically rejects the idea that the unfaithfulness of some Jews to their covenant with God could cancel God's faithfulness to them. The expression "certainly not!" (μὴ γένοιτο) was an interjection used for putting a thought as far away from the discussion as possible. Depending on the context, it could mean, "Perish the thought!" (e.g., Aeschylus, *Seven against Thebes* 5; Plutarch, *Lyc.* 20.6; Luke 20:16), "Far be it from me!" (Epictetus, *Diatr.* 1.2.35; 1.5.10; 1.8.15), "Far from it!" (Epictetus, *Diatr.* 1.5.10), or, as here, "Certainly not!"[15] Paul uses it in 1 Corinthians (6:15) and Galatians (2:17; 3:21; 6:14), but most frequently in Romans (3:6, 31; 6:2, 15; 7:7, 13; 9:14; 11:1, 11), and his use of it often closely parallels its use in the *Discourses* of the Stoic philosopher Epictetus.[16] Both Paul and Epictetus use the expression, for example, to reject a position and at the same time to initiate an explanation of why the position should be rejected. In Paul this subsequent discussion tends to focus on a certain topic such as "righteousness" (3:4–5) or "judgment" (3:6–8), and the same pattern occurs in Epictetus, although not as consistently (Epictetus, *Diatr.* 1.29.9–11).[17]

The term "rather" (δέ) sets up a contrast between the idea that God could be unfaithful and the next phrase, which explains God's faithfulness more fully. Instead of being unfaithful, God is "true" (ἀληθής), and since the context is one that emphasizes faithfulness to God's word (3:2), the truthfulness of God probably refers to his reliability to do what he has said he would do (cf. 9:6).

The phrase, "let God be true" (γινέσθω . . . ὁ θεὸς ἀληθής) posits the reliability of God as axiomatic. Older commentators sometimes stumbled over the meaning of the expression "let God be" (γινέσθω . . . ὁ θεὸς) because the verb in this expression (γίνομαι) more commonly means "become" rather than "be." Since it was thought that God could not "become" any truer than he already was, the verb was commonly explained as if it meant "appear" and Paul was thought to be saying, "Let God appear to be true, even if every human being appears to be a liar."[18] Others thought that perhaps Paul meant to say God would be "revealed" as true as history unfolded, and this interpretation shows up in a slightly different form in more recent commentators who think Paul is referring to the final day, which will show that God is true.[19]

It is better, however, to view the verb here simply as equivalent to the verb "be" (εἰμί) and as stating a proposition: "God must be true, even if this means that, by definition, everyone else is a liar."[20] The great mathematicians of the third and second-centuries BC used the third-person singular imperatives of the verbs "become" (γίνομαι) and "be" (εἰμί) interchangeably in this way when they were proving geometrical theorems (Apollonius, *Conica* 4.8; Archimedes, *To Eratosthenes*, proposition 3). Paul probably uses the third-person singular im-

15. The translations from Epictetus belong to W. A. Oldfather, *Epictetus: Discourses, Books 1–2*, LCL (Cambridge: Harvard University Press, 1925). The other translations are mine.

16. Abraham Malherbe, "μὴ γένοιτο," *HTR* 73 (1980): 231–40.

17. Malherbe, "μὴ γένοιτο," 236–38.

18. E.g., Tholuck, *Romans*, 96; Shedd, *Romans*, 64.

19. E.g., Godet, *Romans*, 134; Meyer, *Romans*, 113–14; cf. Käsemann, *Romans*, 80–81; Dunn, *Romans 1–8*, 133; Jewett, *Romans*, 245.

20. E.g., Moo, *Romans*, 186n45.

perative of the verb "become" (γινέσθω) in a similar way here: "If we posit that God is true [as we must], then this remains true even if every human being is a liar."

Paul's phrase "every human being is a liar" alludes to Psalm 116:11 (115:2 LXX), and he may have had in mind the contrast in that Psalm between the psalmist's perception, in his distress, that everyone was false and his certain knowledge, now that the Lord has rescued him (Ps 116:1–9 [114:1–9 LXX]), that the Lord is "gracious," "righteous," and "merciful" (Ps 116:5 [114:5 LXX]). The Psalm testifies to God's faithfulness to protect the psalmist in accord with his commitment to him even when "every human being" fails to tell the truth. The suggestion that "every human being [is] a liar" also anticipates Paul's claim a few sentences later that everyone, whether Jew or Greek, is under sin (3:9) and begins to broaden the perspective beyond the unfaithfulness of some Jews to the sinfulness of everyone.

Paul takes Psalm 51:4 (50:6 LXX; 51:6 Heb.) as proof of this point. It makes more grammatical sense to take the two verbs of legal action in this quotation as passives (KJV, RSV, ESV, NET, NASB, NAB) than to take one (δικαιωθῇς) as passive and the other (κρίνεσθαι) as middle with an active force (NIV, NJB, NRSV, HCSB).[21] If this is correct, then this fragment of the Psalm confesses that God must "be judged" to be in the right in the matter of David's sin with Bathsheba (Ps 51:1–4a). When his punishment of David goes under review in the court of right-thinking human opinion, God wins the case: he is found to be right and true even when he must punish his people for their sins.

3:5 But if our unrighteousness demonstrates the righteousness of God, what shall we say? The God who inflicts his wrath is not unjust is he? (I speak in a human way) (εἰ δὲ ἡ ἀδικία ἡμῶν θεοῦ δικαιοσύνην συνίστησιν, τί ἐροῦμεν; μὴ ἄδικος ὁ θεὸς ὁ ἐπιφέρων τὴν ὀργήν; κατὰ ἄνθρωπον λέγω). God is not unjust to punish those who sin, even if their sin results in the demonstration and verification of his righteousness.

Paul's quotation of Psalm 51:4 not only proves his point but raises an additional problem that Paul formulates in two questions. The quotation speaks of the demonstration of God's righteousness as a result of human sin. Paul has also argued that God's eschatological judgment of the world will show his righteousness because it will be an impartial judgment of "the Jew first and also the Greek" (2:9–10). If the unrighteousness of the Jew (or, for that matter, any human being) demonstrates God's impartial righteousness, then it enhances God's reputation. But is God acting righteously when he punishes someone who enhances his reputation?

As Lagrange says, "The objection is somewhat strange since the sinner scarcely intended to play a helping role in demonstrating the justice of God."[22] Paul's disclaimer, "I speak in a human way" (κατὰ ἄνθρωπον λέγω), shows that he understood the weakness of this objection to his case for God's impartial judgment (cf. 6:19; 1 Cor 9:8; Gal 3:15). As 3:8 shows, however, Paul was aware of bizarre and slanderous misrepresentations of his teaching. Here, then, he probably anticipates an objection to his argument that he suspects could arise despite its rather silly logic.[23]

The first-person plural reference to "our [ἡμῶν] unrighteousness" is another hint (together with the statement "all human beings [are] liars" in 3:4) that Paul's thought is moving toward his conclusion in 3:9 that all human beings are under the power of sin.

21. So, correctly, Calvin, *Romans*, 61; Sanday and Headlam, *Romans*, 72; Dunn, *Romans 1–8*, 134; BDAG 568, s.v. κρίνω 2 b.

22. *Romains*, 65 (my transl.). Cf., e.g., "Ambrosiater" (*Romans*, 25): "This is absurd!"; Tholuck (*Romans*, 97): "Insolent sophistry"; F. F. Bruce (*The Letter of Paul to the Romans*, TNTC (Leicester: Inter-Varsity Press, 1985], 91): "So foolish to Paul that he apologizes for mentioning it."

23. Cranfield, *Romans*, 1:183–84.

3:6 Certainly not! Otherwise, how will God judge the world? (μὴ γένοιτο· ἐπεὶ πῶς κρινεῖ ὁ θεὸς τὸν κόσμον;). God is not unrighteous for punishing those who sin and who, as a by-product of their condemnation, enhance God's reputation for righteousness. The reason for this is obvious: for the God of the Scriptures to judge the world at all, he must judge it justly, and this involves exonerating the innocent and condemning the guilty.

Just as with 3:3–4, Paul's rejection of the position suggested by the previous rhetorical question was already clear from the way he formulated the question (using μή), but his rejection now becomes emphatic with the expression "certainly not!" (μὴ γένοιτο). Paul's reasoning is brief and to the point: he will waste no more time than necessary refuting this less than theologically compelling position. The conjunction "otherwise" (ἐπεί) often appears in rhetorical questions that explain the reason for a particular position, sometimes, as here, when a daft question prompts the explanation, or when explanation itself is painfully obvious (e.g., Xenophon, *Mem.* 2.7.14; 1 Cor 5:10; 4 Macc 1:33).[24]

Paul backs up his denial that God is unjust in punishing the unjust by appealing to a principle Jews would have accepted as axiomatic: God will judge the world. Paul knows that in a Jewish context God's judgment of the world is always just. God "practices steadfast love, justice, and righteousness in the earth" (Jer 9:24) and judges the peoples of the earth justly and equitably (Pss 9:8; 96:10, 13; 98:9; Wis 12:12–13). Just judgment, as the Scriptures define it, involves condemning the guilty and exonerating the innocent (Gen 18:25; Exod 23:7). Paul knows no other god than the God who views judgment as just judgment and who defines justice in such a way that the unrighteous are condemned and punished. Paul's point, then, is simply that if God is to judge the world at all (and the Scriptures affirm that he will), he must judge it justly. For the one true God, no other option is available.[25]

3:7 But if the truthfulness of God abounded by means of my lie for his glory, why am I too still judged as a sinner? (εἰ δὲ ἡ ἀλήθεια τοῦ θεοῦ ἐν τῷ ἐμῷ ψεύσματι ἐπερίσσευσεν εἰς τὴν δόξαν αὐτοῦ, τί ἔτι κἀγὼ ὡς ἁμαρτωλὸς κρίνομαι;). Someone might raise the objection to Paul's teaching on God's wrath that God should not judge the liar to be a sinner because the liar's very deceptiveness enhances God's reputation as truthful.

Paul now repeats the misunderstanding of his teaching that he anticipated in 3:5, but shifts from the first-person plural to the first-person singular and tackles the same issue from a slightly different angle. In 3:5 the question was whether God was unjust, whereas here it is whether the liar is correctly judged to be a sinner.[26] To put it another way, in 3:5 the reputation of God was at stake, but here the reputation of the liar is at stake. The adverb "as" (ὡς) introduces an element of subjectivity into the idea that the questioner is a sinner, and this puts the subject up for debate.[27] He is being judged a sinner, but should he be judged that way? It is a matter of perspective, and from the questioner's perspective, he has done God the favor of enhancing his reputation (δόξα) as truthful. This good result, he thinks, should prevent him from being relegated to the camp of the "sinner" (ἁμαρτωλός)—the irreligious outsider (cf., e.g., 1 Macc 1:34; Matt 11:19; Mark 2:15; Luke 5:30; 6:32 [cf. Matt 5:46]; 15:1; Gal 2:15).[28]

24. BDF §456 (3); LSJ 613, s.v. ἐπεί B1; BDAG 360, s.v. ἐπεί 2.

25. Cf., e.g., Calvin, *Romans*, 120–21; Meyer, *Romans*, 117; Cranfield, *Romans*, 1:185; Hultgren, *Romans*, 138.

26. Sanday and Headlam, *Romans*, 73; Moo, *Romans*, 193.

27. BDAG 1104, s.v. ὡς 3 a; *CGELNT* 389, s.v. ὡς 2.

28. BDAG 52, s.v. ἁμαρτωλός b β.

The structure of the reasoning here and the structure of the reasoning behind the question in 3:5 are identical: Paul simply replaces the righteousness of God with the truthfulness of God, the unrighteousness of human beings generally with the lie of the individual, and the demonstration of God's righteousness with the abundance of God's truth. In both instances the fairness of God in condemning a wicked person comes into question because the act of condemning evil reveals that God is righteous. Because his or her actions have had this good result, the reasoning runs, the wicked person should not be punished.

3:8 And we should not do bad things that good things may come should we? As we are slandered and as some claim that we say. Their condemnation is just (καὶ μὴ καθὼς βλασφημούμεθα καὶ καθώς φασίν τινες ἡμᾶς λέγειν ὅτι Ποιήσωμεν τὰ κακά, ἵνα ἔλθῃ τὰ ἀγαθά; ὧν τὸ κρίμα ἔνδικόν ἐστιν). If God cannot punish the wicked because their wickedness enhances his glory, then, to be consistent, people should come to the unthinkable conclusion that they should do what is bad merely because such conduct, in the end, results in something good. Those who slander Paul with teaching such nonsense (although they argue their case in a different way) deserve condemnation.

The rhetorical questions in both 3:5 and 3:7 are based on the idea that when God's reputation is at stake in human ethics, the good result of one's evil behavior justifies the means by which it is attained. If human unrighteousness and deceit somehow promote God's reputation as righteous and truthful, then God should not punish the unrighteous. It is a short step from this sort of reasoning to the claim that one should intentionally do bad things in order to achieve good results. Paul assumes that his readers will be appropriately horrified at such a conclusion, and he frames the rhetorical question that articulates it so that it expects a resounding "no!" in answer.[29] Paul's argument runs like this: If the person who lies should not be condemned as a sinner because his or her lie enhances God's glory (3:7), then people should simply expand this principle and do bad things so that good things might happen as a result (3:8). The "and" (καί) that opens the verse links the two rhetorical questions together and shows that Paul intended the second question to be a logical extension of the first question. This second question draws such an absurd conclusion from the first question that it functions as Paul's brief response to that question, and this is all the response he felt it deserved.

As the complicated syntax of the sentence and the sudden reference to actual slanders against Paul indicate, however, Paul is doing more in this verse than simply rehearsing his objection to his fictional interlocutor's reasoning. The complicated syntax probably reflects the sudden merger in his thinking of his fictional discussion with a Jewish interlocutor and actual misrepresentations of Paul's teaching. As it turns out, the slogan "we should do bad things that good things might come" is more than a theoretical construct placed into the mouth of a fictional interlocutor to advance Paul's argument. Real people were saying he taught this. This misinterpretation of his teaching, moreover, was not an innocent misunderstanding of his complex theology but a nefarious attempt to slander Paul. The verb "slander" (βλασφημέω) could refer to putting the worst possible light on someone's actions or words in order to damage his or her reputation, and in the honor-shame society of the ancient

29. See Cranfield (*Romans*, 1:185–87) for a thorough discussion of possible ways of taking the syntax. The option adopted here is close to Cranfield's iii (a) on p. 187. Cf. Sanday and Headlam, *Romans*, 74.

Greco-Roman world this was an extraordinarily serious offense.[30]

Luke used this term to describe the opposition of unbelieving Jews in Pisidian Antioch to Paul's preaching (Acts 13:45), and it seems likely that the slander about which Paul had heard came from Jews who were opposed to him because of his approach to the Mosaic law. When Paul wrote Romans, he was concerned that unbelievers might harm him when he arrived in Judea (his next destination) and that believers in Judea might not accept the relief aid he had labored to collect and bring to them (15:31). When he arrived in Jerusalem, he discovered that his concerns were well founded. The apostle James met him with the news that the Jewish believers in the city were "all zealous for the law" and had heard that Paul taught "all the Jews who are among the Gentiles to forsake Moses, telling them not to circumcise their children or walk according to our customs" (Acts 21:20–21). Perhaps the unbelieving Judean opponents about whom Paul expresses concern in Rom 15:31 were the source of this misinformation.

The slander Paul mentions here in 3:8 probably claimed that Paul's teaching on God's gracious justification of the ungodly opened the door to sinful behavior. It is easy to see how an opponent of Paul could misrepresent in this way the sort of teaching he gives later in Romans. Paul will say in 5:20 that the law entered history so that violation of the law might increase and that where sin increased, God's grace increased that much more.[31] Paul then immediately guards against the idea that this teaching should lead to increased sinning by posing two deliberative rhetorical questions in the first-person plural, just as the slogan here is formulated (6:1; cf. 6:15). Paul takes this particular misrepresentation of his teaching seriously and devotes a long subsection of his letter to refuting it (6:1–8:17). Here in 3:8, however, Paul's argument is at such an early stage that this particular slander makes no sense. So far, Paul has only said that survival on the day of God's wrath requires people to do what is good by keeping the law (2:6, 11, 15–16, 26–27). This means that Paul probably only mentioned the actual slander against him here because the result to which it came (that we should do bad things to bring about good things) happened to be the same result at which his own fictional conversation with his Jewish interlocutor had also arrived. His own fictional dialogue and the actual reasoning of his opponents, however, traveled different roads to arrive at this result.[32]

Paul ends his brief reference to the actual slan-

30. See the glosses in *CGELNT* 72 and BDAG 178, both s.v. βλασφημέω. An example of what Greek-speaking Romans around the time of Paul meant by "being blasphemed" appears in the description of the speech of the consul Appius against the restless Roman populace in Dionysius of Halicarnassus, *Ant. rom.* 9.44–45. Dionysius says that Appius "withheld neither any bitter fact nor any opprobrious [βλασφήμου] word" (9.44.8) in his speech. When the tribune Gaius Laetorius responded to Appius, he called the people against whom Appius had spoken, "the poor whom Appius maligned [βλασφημούμενοι]" (9.46.1; Earnest Cary, *Dionysius of Halicarnassus: Roman Antiquities*, 7 vols., LCL [Cambridge: Harvard University Press, 1947]). This is rendered more colorfully by Edward Spelman (*The Roman Antiquities of Dionysius of Halicarnassus*, 4 vols. [London: Booksellers of London and Westminster, 1758], 4:84) as "the poor, whom Appius had loaded with injurious appellations." Dionysius wrote in the late first-century BC.

31. So Pelagius, *Romans*, 78.

32. For this approach to the passage, see Sanday and Headlam, *Romans*, 74. Paul's fictional dialogue partner in 2:1–29 was an unrepentant, unbelieving Jew (2:3–5), whereas the real opponents behind his rhetorical questions in 3:8, 6:1, and 6:15 were probably Christians who believed Paul's gospel was antinomian. On this, see especially Stuhlmacher, "Paul's Understanding of the Law," 88–89; idem, *Paul's Letter to the Romans: A Commentary*, trans. Scott J. Hafemann (Louisville: Westminster John Knox, 1994), 8–10, although it seems that some of the questions Paul asks and that Stuhlmacher identifies as coming from real opponents (e.g., 4:1) are only part of Paul's fictional dialogue with an opponent.

ders against his teaching with a statement that the condemnation of those who slander him is just. It is at first attractive to see the relative pronoun (ὧν) as neuter, referring back to the "bad things" (τὰ κακά) that people do rather than as masculine and referring to the "some" (τινες) who slander Paul. If that were correct, then this final phrase would form a conclusion to the whole passage (3:1–8) and Paul would simply be reemphasizing his response to the twisted logic of his interlocutor: God will condemn evil (cf. 3:6).[33] The Greek of this already difficult sentence is less confusing, however, if the relative pronoun refers to the one masculine possibility for an antecedent rather than, almost at random, one of the two neuter possibilities from the preceding clause.[34]

Assuming their conduct remains unchanged, then, those who are slandering Paul will receive "condemnation" (κρίμα). This term can simply mean judgment, but, as the context shows, it carries the negative overtones here that it also carried in 2:2–3. Interpreting the expression this way does not mean that Paul is indulging in a "vengeful curse."[35] This is instead a sober statement of fact that serves as a warning to any who might be tempted to believe this slander. It also serves as a denial of the slander itself. If Paul believes in a just judgment for slanderers, then he does not think that people should do evil to produce a good result.

Theology in Application

This passage affirms God's faithfulness to his people, whether to Israel or the church. It also raises the question of how God can be righteous and gracious to sinners at the same time.

God's Continuing Commitment to the Jewish People

God's commitment to his people Israel is massively important in the Old Testament and remains important in the New Testament, yet it often goes neglected in the church. The reason for this is not hard to find. The New Testament sees the multiethnic body of believers in Jesus Christ as the new people of God and the continuation of the story of God's people in the Old Testament. This is why Paul can say in 15:4 that "whatever was written beforehand was written for our instruction." His "our" refers to those who believe the gospel regardless of their ethnicity and implies that the Scriptures of the Jews belong to the newly configured body of believers. Elsewhere, in the same way Paul can instruct the predominantly gentile church in Corinth to heed the warning God gave to "our fathers," meaning the Jewish people described in the exodus narrative (1 Cor 10:1). It is easy, then, for Christians to slide into thinking that the Old Testament now belongs solely to them and not to the Jews.

In Romans 3:1–3, however, Paul issues a reminder that although Israel's heritage belongs to the church, it continues to belong to Israel: the two entities share this

33. Achtemeier, "Romans 3:1–8," 84–87. See also, Paul Achtemeier, *Romans*, IBC (Atlanta: John Knox, 1985), 57.

34. Cf. Légasse, *Romains*, 236n186.

35. Achtemeier, *Romans*, 57.

heritage. There is still an "advantage" in being a Jew, and so in 9:4–5 when Paul describes the privileges of unbelieving Israel he describes them as present realities, despite their unbelief: theirs "is the adoption as sons, and the glory, and the covenants, and the legislation, and the worship, and the promises," and "the fathers."

As Paul has made abundantly clear in 2:1–29, this advantage does not exempt Jews from the wrath of God on the final day and the need that all human beings have to embrace the good news of Jesus Christ for salvation. The advantage is, instead, the access that Jews have in their sacred Scriptures to the word of God and to the commitment that God has made to the Jewish people in his word (cf. 11:28–29; Eph 2:12; 2 Tim 3:14–15). Paul will show later, in 9:1–11:36, the precise sense in which God is presently working out his faithfulness to the Jews and will continue to work it out in the future. For now, however, he simply makes the point that although many Jews may not believe in God as he is presented in the gospel, God will not be unfaithful to them.

What this text teaches about God's ongoing commitment to unbelieving Jews is relevant to the present-day witness of the church to Jewish people. The horrific story of the slander and eventual violence levelled at the Jewish people by certain postapostolic church leaders through the time of the Holocaust serves as a shocking and sobering reminder of what can happen when this important theological truth falls into neglect in the church's teaching.

As early as the Epistle of Barnabas (written between AD 70 and 135), the Jews became in the minds of some Christians "those people" whose covenant with God was "lost . . . completely" since "they were not worthy to receive it because of their sins" (4.6; 14:1, 4).[36] To the author of Barnabas, God's covenant had instead come to Christians, who, it seems to be assumed, did not include anyone identifiably Jewish (14.4). Soon after this, influential Christians were blaming the entire nation of Israel for all time for the death of Jesus (with no reference to the involvement of the Romans) and claiming that the nation's suffering was God's punishment for this worst of all possible crimes (Melito of Sardis, *Peri Pascha* 72–99).[37]

In later years Christian bishops excused the burning of synagogues, claiming that they were "a shelter of madness under the damnation of God himself."[38] Eventually, Martin Luther would repeat this sort of rhetoric, and the Nazis would use it to promote their murderous policies toward the Jews of Europe.[39] It is true that the Holocaust arose primarily out of a complex mixture of irrational, paranoid at-

36. Trans. Michael W. Holmes, *The Apostolic Fathers: Greek Texts and English Translations*, 3rd ed. (Grand Rapids: Baker, 2007), 389, 425.

37. Melito flourished in the second half of the second century.

38. *Saint Ambrose: Letters*, trans. Sister Mary Melchior Beyenka; FC 26 (New York: Fathers of the Church, 1954), 12. This is from *Ep.* 40.14. Ambrose wrote the letter to the emperor Theodosius after the bishop of Callinicum in Mesopotamia had encouraged the burning of the local synagogue. (Sister Mary's suggestion [p. 10n9] that it was struck by lightning does not seem plausible.)

39. David M. Whitford, *Luther: A Guide for the Perplexed* (London: T&T Clark, 2011), 154–68.

titudes toward an identifiable social minority, not out of the theological mistakes made by church leaders.[40] Still, a long literary tradition of slander against the Jews was preserved and nurtured by church leaders and contributed to the anti-Semitic attitude, particularly in central Europe, that made the Holocaust possible.[41] If more Christians had taken passages such as Romans 3:1–3, 9:1–5, and 10:1 seriously prior to 1938, perhaps many lives would have been saved and the Christian witness to non-Christian Jewish people today would be much less complex and far more effective than it presently is.

God's Faithfulness to Believers Even When They Are Unfaithful to Him

This passage also serves as a rich affirmation to all Christians of the common biblical theme that God is reliable, truthful, and faithful to his people. Although his people are sometimes unfaithful (3:3) and untruthful (3:4), God is faithful to them. What prompts him to be good even to those among his people who are unfaithful to him? The answer can be found in the biblical story of God's relationship with his people during the period of the exodus. At precisely the time that Moses was receiving the Decalogue from God on Mount Sinai, Israel was at the foot of the mountain, breaking the Decalogue's first commandment by worshiping a golden calf under the leadership of their high priest Aaron. Although God was displeased with his people and seemed ready to abandon them, Moses interceded with God on their behalf, and God forgave them.

God himself supplied the reason for his willingness to forgive when he described himself to Moses as "a God merciful and gracious, slow to anger and abounding in steadfast love and faithfulness, keeping steadfast love for thousands, forgiving iniquity and transgression and sin" (Exod 34:6–7).[42] The Old Testament frequently recalls this description of God's character, especially when people appeal to him for forgiveness (Num 14:8; Neh 9:17; Ps 103:8–14; Joel 2:13; Jonah 4:2; cf. Pss 86:15; 145:8).

Those who are willing to turn from their sin and turn to God for mercy will find in him a loving father who is compassionate toward the weakness of his children and is willing to forget and forgive their transgression. After recalling the famous words from the exodus narrative about God's mercy, grace, and love, Psalm 103 puts it this way:

> He does not deal with us according to our sins, nor repay us according to our iniquities. For as high as the heavens are above the earth, so great is his steadfast love

40. Steven Beller, *Antisemitism: A Very Short Introduction* (Oxford: Oxford University Press, 2007).

41. Ibid., 20–21; cf. David P. Gushee, *Righteous Gentiles of the Holocaust: Genocide and Moral Obligation*, 2nd ed. (St. Paul, MN: Paragon House, 2003), 149–52.

42. See the comments of Stuart, *Exodus*, 715–16.

> toward those who fear him; as far as the east is from the west, so far does he remove our transgressions from us. As a father shows compassion to his children, so the Lord shows compassion to those who fear him. For he knows our frame; he remembers that we are dust. (Ps 103:10–14)

This aspect of God's character should comfort all those who understand that they have been unfaithful to God and who also understand the grave threat that their unfaithfulness poses to their relationship with him. Thankfully, God is gracious, kind, and ready to forgive those who come to him in repentance. As 1 John 1:9 puts it, "If we confess our sins, he is faithful and just to forgive us our sins and to cleanse us from all unrighteousness." Confession, repentance, and reliance upon God's faithfulness and steadfast love to his people, even when they sin, should be constant elements of the believer's relationship with God.

God's Justified Wrath against Sinners

When God's faithfulness and steadfast love are clearly taught, however, some people conclude that sinning against God does not matter or should even be encouraged in order to give God the opportunity to display his gracious character. Paul addressed two forms of this reasoning in this passage.

One form of reasoning claimed, strangely, that God would be unrighteous to show his wrath against sinners since they have allowed him the opportunity to show how righteous he is by condemning their sin. This claim contradicts itself since, on its terms, God is righteous to condemn sin but also unrighteous to condemn sin. The desperation of this form of reasoning seems to reveal a high level of discomfort with the idea that God can justly condemn sinners. Paul affirms with Psalm 51:4, however, that God's judgment of a sinful world is just.

Resistance to the notion that God will inflict wrath on people for their sins is not limited to Paul's time. Whenever the prevailing cultural winds tempt the church to abandon the concept of God's judgment, passages such as Romans 3:4–6 serve as a reminder that if God is a just judge and if a distinction is to be made between good and evil, then God must be free to punish sin. No one can justly complain if God does not show mercy to the unrepentant wicked.

The second form of this reasoning probably claimed that sin allowed God the opportunity to be gracious and should therefore be encouraged. Paul has already supplied one answer to this kind of thinking when he scolded his interlocutor for not realizing that God's kindness, forbearance, and patience were intended as an encouragement to turn from sin (2:4). He will give a second answer to this reasoning later when he says that those who have experienced God's abundant grace in Jesus Christ have left the dominion of sin behind them and now belong instead to God and to righteousness (6:1–23).

Although some people seemed to have actually reasoned this way on the basis of Paul's teaching (Jude 4; cf. 2 Pet 3:16), in this passage Paul was not refuting those who actually believed this line of thought but people who slandered Paul with teaching it. Calvin, in his 1539 commentary on 3:8 was aware of the same slander against "the pure Gospel of Christ" in his own time, and his advice is helpful:

> We can conceive of nothing more monstrous than that the charge, which we read of here, had been laid against Paul for the purpose of treating his preaching with contempt among the ignorant. Let us, therefore, bear the slanderous abuse by the ungodly of the truth which we preach, and let us not cease on this account to guard constantly the simple confession of it, since it has sufficient power to crush and disperse their falsehoods.[43]

The best defense against the misinterpretation of the gospel, whether designed to discredit it or to use it for one's own selfish purposes, is the winsome presentation of its correct form.[44] The gospel has pervasive ethical ramifications for all who embrace it, but those ethical implications arise from God's mercy, love, and grace.

43. Calvin, *Romans*, 64.

44. Cf. John Stott, *Romans: God's Good News for the World* (Downers Grove, IL: InterVarsity Press, 1994), 98.

CHAPTER 7

Romans 3:9–20

Literary Context

Paul now closes the first major part of his argument with an indictment, grounded in Scripture, of every human being. The passage both summarizes what Paul has just said in 1:18–3:8 and takes the argument further. In 1:18–3:8 Paul demonstrates two truths about human beings. First, the unrighteousness that characterizes them cuts across the boundaries that separate one social group from another. Whether the social group is Jewish or Greek, wise or unwise, makes no difference; unrighteousness is a characteristic of them all. Second, Paul shows the depths that unrighteousness can reach in these societies, and he makes a special effort to point out that it goes just as deep in Jewish society as it does among groups that are not Jewish.

As part of his effort to make this second point, Paul introduced two ideas that would have come as uncomfortable reminders to Paul's fictional Jewish interlocutor of what the Scripture says on this issue. First, God is impartial and therefore will judge gentile and Jew by the same criterion on the final day without taking into account the social group to which either belongs (2:3, 5, 9–12). Second, it is possible for a non-Jew to keep what he or she knows internally to be the will of God better than a Jew keeps the corresponding commandments of God in the Scriptures (2:14–16, 15–29; cf. 2:9–10). If we set aside a commandment like male circumcision—something that gentiles would not naturally know to do—and stick to common notions of fairness and propriety, then it is possible for a gentile actually to keep such standards of righteousness more faithfully than a Jew (2:26–27). Paul's point is that simply being a Jew or having access to the requirements of God in God's own words does not exempt one from the requirement of keeping God's commandments. If it did, then God would not be righteous, and the good news that Paul proclaims in Romans asserts that God is righteous (1:17).[1]

So far, however, Paul has demonstrated only that all social groups are under sin, taking both Jews and Greeks as representative of them all. He has not yet shown that

1. Here I am taking the term "righteous" (δίκαιος) in the common first-century sense of "fair," "equitable." On this see, "In Depth: Righteousness Language in Romans" in the comments on 1:8–17.

every individual is unrighteous. He has described sin's deep entrenchment among Jews as well as gentiles, but he has not yet shown that no one is exempt from the charge that he or she is a sinner. It might even be possible to misunderstand certain sections of the argument in 1:18–3:8 to mean that some people would be justified on the final day by their faithful adherence to the law's commands (2:6–10; cf. 2:14–16, 26–27). Probably to avoid this misunderstanding, in 3:9–20 Paul both summarizes his previous argument—that Jews are as unrighteous as gentiles—and takes the argument a step further to say that no one has kept God's requirements faithfully enough to merit justification before him on the final day.

With this concluding summary and intensification of his case in 1:18–3:8, Paul brings the first major part of his argument to a close. He has shown that God's righteousness means the fair distribution of his wrath across social boundaries and, apart from the gospel briefly explained in 1:16–17, the punishment of every individual for his or her sin. This prepares the way for his detailed explanation in 3:21–4:25 of how God's righteousness also means his saving power, distributed equally across social boundaries and to every individual on the basis of his or her faith.

V. God's Wrath against Human Sin Is a Demonstration of His Righteousness (1:18–32)

VI. Jews Are Also Subject to God's Wrath (2:1–3:20)

A. God as an Impartial Judge Not Merely of Gentiles but of Jews Also (2:1–16)

B. God as an Impartial Judge Even of Jews Who Teach the Law and Possess Circumcision (2:17–29)

C. Objections to Paul's Understanding of God's Impartial Judgment (3:1–8)

➡ **D. Scripture's Testimony That Everyone Is under Sin (3:9–20)**

VII. The Death of Christ Demonstrates God's Righteousness and Excludes Human Boasting (3:21–31)

Main Idea

The Scripture shows that everyone is under the power of sin and answerable to God for his or her unrighteous behavior. Sin cuts across all social boundaries and affects every aspect of individual human existence. The law does not release human beings from sin's power; it only shows that even Jews are sinful and, apart from the gospel, stand (like everyone else) condemned before God.

Translation

Romans 3:9–20

9a	Rhetorical Question	**What then?**
b	Rhetorical Question	**Are we surpassed?**
c	Exclamation	**Not at all!**
d	Explanation	For **we have charged beforehand that both Jews and Greeks— all— are under sin**
10a	Comparison OT Quotation Repetition	just as it is written, "There is no one righteous," not even one." (Eccl 7:20 LXX; Ps 14:1)
11a	Assertion	"There is no one who understands;
b	Assertion	there is no one who seeks after God.
12a	Assertion	All have steered clear;
b	Assertion	they have become useless together.
c	Assertion	There is no one who practices kindness;
d	Assertion	there is not even one." (Ps 14:2–3)
13a	Assertion	"Their throat is an open tomb;
b	Assertion	with their tongues they were speaking deceit." (Ps 5:9b)
c	Assertion	"The poison of cobras is under their lips." (Ps 140:3)
14	Assertion	"Whose mouth is full of cursing and bitterness." (Ps 10:7)
15	Assertion	"Their feet are quick to shed blood;
16	Assertion	destruction and misery are in their ways,
17	Assertion	and the way of peace they have not known." (Isa 59:7–8)
18	Assertion	"There is no fear of God before their eyes." (Ps 36:1)
19a	Assertion	**Now we know that whatever the law says it speaks to those who are in the law**
b	Purpose	so that every mouth might be stopped and
c	Repetition	all the world become answerable to God.
20a	Explanation of 19b–c	For **by works of the law no flesh will be justified** before him (Ps 143:2),
b	Explanation of 20a	for **through the law comes the knowledge of sin.**

Structure

A reasonable case can be made for taking 3:9 with the preceding section since the identical opening words in 3:1 and 3:9 ("What then . . .") would provide a neat introduction and conclusion (an *inclusio*) for the resulting paragraph.[2] Paul would then circle back in 3:9 to the question of a Jewish advantage (or disadvantage) that he had raised in 3:1. The rhetorical questions in 3:9, however, introduce Paul's claim that people from all ethnic groups are under sin, and he explains this claim, in turn, with the series of Scripture quotations that follow. It is probably best, then, to view 3:9 as transitional. It opens the new paragraph but does so in a way that looks backward to the issue of Jewish advantage that Paul raised and answered in 3:1–4.

Many interpreters think the series of quotations and paraphrases of Scripture that prove everyone to be under sin in 3:10–18 is a piece of preformed tradition that Paul slotted into place at this point in his argument. A roughly similar assembly of biblical allusions appears in the Damascus Document (CD 5:13–17; cf. 2 Esd 7:21–24). In addition, Justin Martyr either abbreviated and shuffled Paul's material, or both he and Paul relied on the same assembly of quotations but used it differently (*Dialogue with Trypho* 27).[3] Some interpreters have also detected signs in Romans 3:10–18 that the texts Paul lists do not precisely make the point Paul himself makes in 1:18–3:8. Keck argues that in 2:17–29 some gentiles observe the law, whereas in 3:10–12 no one is righteous, and in 3:9 and 19 Paul asserts the universality of sin, whereas the focus of 3:13–17 lies on sin's character rather than its universality.[4]

All this is certainly possible but is too speculative to form a sound foundation for exegesis. Justin, who wrote his *Dialogue with Trypho* about a century after Romans, could have remembered Paul's use of Scripture in Romans 3:10–18 and reused some of that material in his own composition. The parallels in the Damascus Document and 2 Esdras, moreover, are not striking. It seems best, then, to interpret the passage as Paul's own creation designed for this place in his argument and carefully crafted out of the biblical passages that he quotes and echoes. There is no need, on this theory, to think of Paul dictating this collection of quotations on the spot without much consideration. The composition of Romans was probably slow and deliberate, despite its oral dictation to Tertius (Rom 16:22).

Romans 3:9–20 can be divided into three sections. The first section introduces Paul's main point that no social group can claim any special privilege on the day of judgment because all are under sin (3:9). The second section proves this from Scripture, but takes the point even further by stating that no individual is free from the power of sin (3:10–12) and that sin pervades the existence of every individual

2. Fitzmyer, *Romans*, 326.

3. See, e.g., Käsemann, *Romans*, 86; Leander A. Keck, "The Function of Rom 3:10–18: Observations and Suggestions," in *God's Christ and His People: Studies in Honour of Nils Alstrup Dahl*, ed. Jacob Jervell and Wayne A. Meeks (Oslo: Universitetsforlaget, 1977), 147–51; Wilckens, *An die Römer (Röm 1–5)*, 171; Dunn, *Romans 1–8*, 145.

4. Keck, "Function of Romans 3:10–18," 146.

(3:13–18). Sin wells up from within (3:13a), affecting one's speech (3:13b–14) and the direction of one's life (3:15–18). The third section draws the inevitable conclusion from the Scripture quotations in 3:10–18—it is not possible to be declared just on the day of judgment by means of living morally, not even for a Jew who possesses the Mosaic law, since that law can only show one to be a sinner (3:19–20).

Exegetical Outline

VI. Jews Are Also Subject to God's Wrath (2:1–3:20)

A. God as an Impartial Judge Not Merely of Gentiles but of Jews Also (2:1–16)

B. God as an Impartial Judge Even of Jews Who Teach the Law and Possess Circumcision (2:17–29)

C. Objections to Paul's Understanding of God's Impartial Judgment (3:1–8)

➡ **D. Scripture's Testimony That Everyone Is under Sin (3:9–20)**

1. Everyone, Whatever Their Social Group, Is under the Power of Sin (3:9)
2. Scripture Shows This to Be Thoroughly True of Every Individual (3:10–18)
3. This Means That God Will Declare No One Righteous on the Final Day Because of His or Her Moral Effort, Not Even the Jew (3:19–20)

Explanation of the Text

3:9 What then? Are we surpassed? Not at all! For we have charged beforehand that both Jews and Greeks—all—are under sin (Τί οὖν; προεχόμεθα; οὐ πάντως· προῃτιασάμεθα γὰρ Ἰουδαίους τε καὶ Ἕλληνας πάντας ὑφ' ἁμαρτίαν εἶναι). Although it may seem from what Paul said at the end of chapter two that the gentile has an advantage over the Jew when it comes to the day of judgment, that is not correct. Paul's argument has instead charged everyone with being in the grip of sin, whatever their social location.

The term translated here "are we surpassed" (προεχόμεθα) is ambiguous. It appears only here in the Greek Bible, but is fairly common in Greek literature generally, starting with Homer.[5] When it is used transitively, it means to have something beforehand or to hold something out in front.[6] Xenophon could use it in the active voice, for example, to refer to a child instinctively putting his hands out in front to protect himself from blows (*Cyr.* 2.3.10). The term could also be used this way in the middle voice, although it needed a direct object to serve this role.[7] Spartans could *place* a grievance *before* Athenians in the middle voice (Thucydides, *History of the Peloponnesian War* 1.140.4); people could *bend forward* their heads to hear a singer (Apollonius of Rhodes, *Argon.* 513), and consuls could *put* persuasive reasons *before* the people in the middle voice (Dionysius of Halicarnassus, *Ant. rom.* 10.38.1), but some object needed to be present to receive the action of the verb.[8] The term could also be used intransitively to refer to a peninsula

5. The verb does appear in a variant reading of Job 27:6 LXX (BDAG 869, s.v. προέχω).

6. LSJ 1479, s.v. προέχω I.1.

7. Cf. Sanday and Headlam, *Romans*, 76; Cranfield, *Romans*, 1:188.

8. It is not clear that the thorough study of Nils Alstrup

that "protrudes" out into the ocean (Thucydides, *History of the Peloponnesian War* 4.109.1–2), to a runner who "surges forward" in a foot race to win by a head (Xenophon, *Cyr.* 4.3.16), or to the fly who "excels" gnats and midges in size (Lucian, *The Fly* 1).[9] At least once the verb is used this way in the passive voice, and apparently in a transitive sense, to refer to good people who were free to imitate the haughtiness of Zeus because "they are in no wise surpassed [προεχομένοις] by" him (Plutarch, *Stoic. rep.* 1038 D; [Harold Cherniss, LCL]).[10]

Two aspects of Paul's use of the verb in 3:9 are clear: it is either middle or passive in form and it has no direct object. These two elements of the verb already make it very unusual. It is either a rare passive ("Are we surpassed [by the gentiles]?") or an even rarer middle with an active meaning and no direct object ("Are we better than [the gentiles]?")."[11] Since some precedent exists for its use as a passive, meaning to be "surpassed" (Plutarch, *Stoic. rep.* 1038 D), and since no known precedent exists for its use in the middle with an active, intransitive meaning, it seems best to part company with virtually all the translations and render Paul's question as "Are we surpassed?"

If the question comes from Paul's Jewish interlocutor, it expresses a natural concern that Jews will not merely be treated impartially on the day of judgment but will actually be at a disadvantage. Paul argued in 2:25–29 that uncircumcised gentiles might surpass circumcised Jews at the day of judgment, and in 3:5–8 he has asserted that the desperate sophistries of the wicked will provide no escape for them on that day. As things stand at this point in the argument, it appears that only the law-abiding gentiles of 2:26–27 will survive God's righteous judgment. "What then? Are we [Jews] surpassed [by the gentiles]?" poses an understandable question on this reading.

Paul's answer to this question summarizes his argument so far (1:18–3:8). The term "charge beforehand" (προαιτιάομαι) appears nowhere else in extant Greek literature prior to Paul and nowhere else except in quotations from Romans for centuries afterward, but its meaning is reasonably clear from its two components. The verb "accuse, censure" (αἰτιάομαι) is common (e.g., Prov 19:3 LXX; Sir 29:5; 4 Macc 2:19) and also commonly appears, as it does here, with the people being accused named in the accusative case and the accusation against them described with an infinitive verb (e.g., Herodotus, *Histories* 5.27.2). The prefixed preposition "before" (πρό) refers to what Paul has said up to this point.

Simon Gathercole has perceptively pointed out that a precise translation of this verb is necessary for a correct understanding of Paul's argument in 1:18–3:20. Paul does not claim to have "demonstrated" that every person is under sin, but to have "charged" (-αἰτιάομαι) every person with being under sin.[12] He has certainly charged human beings with stifling "the truth in unrighteousness"

Dahl ("Romans 3:9: Text and Meaning," in *Paul and Paulinism: Essays in Honour of C. K. Barrett*, ed. M. D. Hooker and S. G. Wilson [London: SPCK, 1982], 184–204) has taken this into account. His own example (1 En. 99:3) also has a direct object.

9. LSJ 1480, s.v. προέχω II.3a; cf. Christian Maurer, "προέχομαι," *TDNT* 6:692. The example from Lucian is intransitive despite the presence of what looks like a direct object because what is surpassed is in the genitive case (functioning as a genitive of comparison) rather than in the accusative case.

10. It is unclear to me why Maurer (*TDNT* 6:692) counts this as an intransitive use since in the context "good people" (τοῖς ἀγαθοῖς) functions as the logical direct object of "surpassed" (προεχομένοις).

11. For the first option, see, e.g., *CGELNT*, 299, s.v. προέχω (cf. BDAG 869, s.v. προέχω 1), and for the second option see Tyndale, KJV, and virtually all other English, German, and French translations.

12. *Where Is Boasting?*, 212. Claims, therefore, that Paul's rhetoric in 3:9 has outpaced the logic of his actual argument in 1:18–3:20 (e.g., Jewett, *Romans*, 258; Légasse, *Romains*, 240) are not correct.

(1:18) and has shown that Jews are not exempt from the charge (2:1–29), but the full demonstration of his conviction that every human being without exception is a sinner awaits the witness of Scripture in 3:10–18.

Paul has charged everyone with being "under sin" (ὑφ' ἁμαρτίαν). Paul used the verb "sin" (ἁμαρτάνω) in 2:12 and the noun "sinner" (ἁμαρτωλός) in 3:7, but this is the first of many uses of the abstract noun "sin" (ἁμαρτία) in Romans.[13] It is a summary word that covers the host of specific evil activities and attitudes Paul mentioned in 1:18–2:29 and encapsulates what Paul meant by other general terms: "unrighteousness" (1:18, 29; 2:8; 3:5), "uncleanness" (1:24), "that which is bad" (2:9), "transgression of the law" (2:23; cf. 2:25, 27), "unfaithfulness" (3:3), and "bad things" (3:8). The preposition "under" (ὑφ' = ὑπο) with the accusative case could mean "under the control of" or "under the power of," and it often appeared in military and political contexts: soldiers were "under" their commanding officers and subjects were "under" their king (e.g., Matt 8:9; Luke 7:8; cf. Gal 3:25; 4:2).[14] To be "under sin," then, was to be under its authority (7:14; Gal 3:22; cf. Rom 5:21; 6:12), to be its slave (6:6–9, 14, 19–20; 7:25), and to have it dwelling within (7:20, 23), prompting and directing one's actions. Sin began with the disobedience of the first human being to God and has continued to dominate every human being since then (5:12).

3:10 just as it is written, "There is no one righteous, not even one" (καθὼς γέγραπται ὅτι Οὐκ ἔστιν δίκαιος οὐδὲ εἷς). The Scripture bears authoritative witness to the truth of Paul's charge that all are under sin since it too says that absolutely no one is righteous.

For the fourth time in the letter, Paul uses the introductory formula "just as it is written" (cf. 1:17; 2:24; 3:4) to show that the statement he has just made agrees with the witness of the Jewish Scriptures. This quotation, however, differs from the seventeen other places in his letters where Paul introduces a quotation with these words: it is much longer (3:10–18) and is drawn from seven different passages (Eccl 7:20; Ps 13:1–3 [LXX; Eng. and Heb. 14:1–3]; 5:10 [LXX; Eng. 5:9; Heb. 5:10]; 139:4 [LXX; Eng. 140:3; Heb. 140:4]; 9:28 [LXX; Eng. and Heb. 10:7]; Isa 59:7–8; and Ps 35:2 [LXX; Eng. 36:1; Heb. 36:2]). The reason for these unusual features is probably not that Paul is using a preformed collection of passages that early Christians used in other contexts.[15] Rather, this group of texts is probably his own creation, thoughtfully constructed for this letter and intended to draw the long first part of his argument to a close. It provides a definitive and authoritative demonstration of the point he has intended to make all along: God is just when he impartially condemns everyone for their sin since everyone, without exception, is a sinner.

The collection of Scripture passages can be divided into two parts. In 3:10–12 Paul emphasizes the universality of sin: every person falls under its power. In 3:13–18 he emphasizes the pervasively evil effect of sin on human existence: the mind was already covered in the first part ("there is no one who understands," 3:11), but the second part covers the mouth, the feet, and the eyes.

The first line of Paul's scriptural proof comes either from Ecclesiastes 7:20 LXX or from Psalm 14:1 (13:1 LXX) or from both.[16] Ecclesiastes 7:20 contains the crucial adjective "righteous" (δίκαιος),

13. The noun appears sixty-four times in the Pauline corpus, forty-eight of them in Romans.

14. BDAG 1036, s.v. ὑπό B 2. Cf. LSJ 1875, s.v. ὑπό C II and MGS 2214, s.v. ὑπό II C C.

15. E.g., Keck, "Function of Rom 3:10–18," 143–51; Wilckens, *An die Römer (Röm 1–5)*, 171; Jewett, *Romans*, 254, 259.

16. Ps 13 LXX and Ps 52 LXX (Heb. and Eng. Ps 14 and Ps 53) are almost identical, but where they differ from one another, Paul's text parallels Ps 13.

whose closely related terms, "righteousness" (δικαιοσύνη), "unrighteousness" (ἀδικία), "righteous decree" (δικαίωμα), "righteous judgment" (δικαιοκρισία), "justify" (δικαιόω), and "just" (ἔνδικος) have formed such a major element in Paul's argument to this point. The passage in which Ecclesiastes 7:20 is located, moreover, makes the same point Paul is making here:

> For as to humanity, there is not a just person [οὐκ ἔστιν δίκαιος] in the earth who will do good and will not sin. Indeed, to all the words that people will speak do not give your heart so that you do not hear your slave cursing you, for frequently he will do you evil and many times he will bring hurt to your heart as, indeed, you have cursed others. (Eccl 7:20–22 LXX)

The opening phrase "there is not" (οὐκ ἔστιν) appears four other times in 3:10–12, and twice it is Paul's addition to the text (3:11).[17] It signals the main point of 3:10–12—that there is absolutely no one who stands in a right relationship with God apart from the gospel. Paul's addition of the phrase "not even one" (οὐδὲ εἷς) to Ecclesiastes 7:20 is probably derived from the slightly different wording in Ps 14:1 and 3 (13:1, 3 LXX [οὐκ ἔστιν ἕως ἑνός]) and makes the same point. Paul had said in 2:13, for the sake of argument, that "it is not the hearers of the law who are righteous [δίκαιοι] before God, but the doers of the law will be justified [δικαιωθήσονται]." He had also entertained the possibility that an uncircumcised person might keep the law, be circumcised in heart, and receive praise from God (2:27, 29). It now becomes clear that whatever Paul meant in those places, he did not intend to say that it was possible to be righteous before God apart from the gospel as he has already briefly described it in 1:16–17. The powerful, saving activity of God is necessary for anyone to become righteous and "live" in the full, theological sense of that word.

3:11–12 "There is no one who understands; there is no one who seeks after God. All have steered clear; they have become useless together. There is no one who practices kindness; there is not even one" (οὐκ ἔστιν ὁ συνίων, οὐκ ἔστιν ὁ ἐκζητῶν τὸν θεόν. πάντες ἐξέκλιναν ἅμα ἠχρεώθησαν· οὐκ ἔστιν ὁ ποιῶν χρηστότητα, οὐκ ἔστιν ἕως ἑνός). Scripture testifies that human beings, one and all, have abandoned God and become morally corrupt in their dealings with each other.

Paul underlines the point of 3:10 with a paraphrase of Psalm 14:2–3 (13:2–3 LXX).[18] By adding the phrase "there is not" and placing the article before each of the three participles, Paul has made the passage more emphatic and paraphrased it in a way that places particular stress on the individual. There is absolutely no one who understands or seeks after God or practices kindness.[19] The two verses contrast the picture of seeking (ἐκζητῶν) from the heart to know and rely on God (cf. Deut 4:29 LXX; Ps 34:4 [33:5 LXX]; 69:32 [68:33 LXX]) with the picture of "steering around" God (ἐξέκλιναν) and of becoming useless to society because of moral corruption (ἠχρεώθησαν).[20] No one sincerely seeks after God, but everyone steers clear of him and his purposes for human society (cf. 1:18–32).

3:13–14 "Their throat is an open tomb; with their tongues they were speaking deceit." "The

17. It also appears in the closing line (3:18), ending the whole series of passages on the note with which it had started and re-emphasizing its main point. Cf. Keck, "The Function of Rom 3:10–18," 142–43.

18. Cf. Ps 53:2–3 (52:3–4 LXX; 53:3–4 Heb.).

19. I am indebted to the NETS for the translation "practices kindness" (ποιῶν χρηστότητα).

20. BDAG 302, s.v. ἐκζητέω 1; 304, s.v. ἐκκλίνω 1b; 160, s.v. ἀχρειόω 2.

poison of cobras is under their lips"; "whose mouth is full of cursing and bitterness" (τάφος ἀνεῳγμένος ὁ λάρυγξ αὐτῶν, ταῖς γλώσσαις αὐτῶν ἐδολιοῦσαν, ἰὸς ἀσπίδων ὑπὸ τὰ χείλη αὐτῶν· ὧν τὸ στόμα ἀρᾶς καὶ πικρίας γέμει). Scripture also testifies that human sinfulness extends to every aspect of human existence, to, for example, human speech, which people often use to harm others.

The second major section of the quotation collection begins here and emphasizes the far-reaching consequences of sin in the human being. The collection had already spoken of the mind in 3:10–12 ("There is no one who understands"), and now, in 3:13–18, it covers the throat, tongue, lips, feet, and eyes.

Here in 3:13–14 Paul focuses on the organs of speech, using Psalm 5:9b (5:10b LXX), Psalm 140:3 (139:4 LXX; 140:4 Heb.), and Psalm 10:7 (9:28 LXX) to make his point.[21] The first two clauses, both from Psalm 5:9b (10b LXX) depict the damage that deceitful speech can inflict. The image of the throat as an open tomb from which this speech emerges evokes the inner corruption that produces lying speech and the violence that it does to its victims.[22] For those, like Paul, who knew the Psalm well, the immediately preceding couplet might have also come to mind, further emphasizing the idea that deceitful speech emerges from inner corruption: "Because there is no truth in their mouths, their heart is vain" (Ps 5:10a LXX [Eng. 5:9a]).

The term translated "cobra" (ἀσπίς) normally refers to a "shield" in Greek but could also refer to the sort of snake that flares its shield-like hood when threatened. The LXX translators and Paul may have had in mind the "Egyptian cobra" (e.g., Aelian, *Nature of Animals* 10.31), but ancient Greek speakers knew that that there were various species of cobra (Pausanius, *Description of Greece* 9.21.6), some of which spat extremely poisonous venom at their victims (Nicander, *Ther.* 185).[23] Paul may have thought of a spitting cobra when he quoted Psalm 140:3 (139:4 LXX) here. The words that come from human lips are often like the venom that spews from the cobra's mouth: they are intended to harm those toward whom they are directed.

Paul ends his description of sinful human speech with a reference to the mouth from Psalm 10:7 (9:28 LXX). The term "bitterness" (πικρία) was used to refer to something with a bad taste, like gall (Deut 29:17 LXX; Lam 3:19; Acts 8:23), and metaphorically to "harshness," especially to the sort of harshness that accompanies violence. Josephus, for example, says that when Herod the Great knew he was about to die "he became quite savage and treated everyone with uncontrolled anger [ὀργῇ] and harshness [πικρίᾳ]" (*Ant.* 17.148 [R. Marcus and A. Wikgren, LCL]; cf. Eph 4:31; Philo, *Drunkenness* 223).[24] In Psalm 9 LXX (Pss 9 and 10 in Eng. and Heb.), the person "whose

21. The text of Ps 13 LXX in some ancient Greek witnesses includes the material found in Rom 3:13–18, but it is likely that this material is a Christian expansion derived from Rom 3:13–18. If so, it would be the longest of several other similar expansions. Origen indicated doubts about the presence of this material, and the Lucianic text omits it. Although a few Romans commentators think that it is original to the Psalm (e.g., Jewett, *Romans*, 261; Hultgren, *Romans*, 144), the Hebrew text does not include it, and it seems safest to follow the judgment of Alfred Rahlfs that it is a Christian addition. See Alfred Rahlfs, ed., *Psalmi cum Odis*, vol. 10 of *Septuaginta: Vetus Testamentum Graecum* (Göttingen: Vandenhoeck & Ruprecht, 1979), 30–31, 96.

22. Moo, *Romans*, 203–4.

23. The asp "has four fangs, their underside hollow, hooked, and long, rooted in its jaws, containing poison, and at their base a covering of membranes hides them. Thence it belches forth poison unassuageable on a body" (*Nicander: The Poems and Fragments*, trans. A. S. F. Gow and A. F. Scholfield [Cambridge: Cambridge University Press, 1953], 41). LSJ (259, s.v. ἀσπίς II), BDAG (144, s.v. ἀσπίς), *CGELNT* (58–59, s.v. ἀσπίς), and Jan N. Bremmer ("Snake," *BNPA* 13:554) all interpret the "asp" specifically as the Egyptian cobra.

24. BDAG 813, s.v. πικρός 2.

mouth is full of cursing and bitterness and deceit" treats the poor and needy with violence. "Under his tongue are grief and hardship"—the difficulties that he has inflicted on the poor. "He sits in ambush with the rich, in secret places to kill the innocent" (Ps 9:28–29 LXX; 10:7–8 Eng. and Heb.). The cursing and bitterness here, then, are not mere words but threats and schemes of violence against the poor. When this context is coupled with the references to burial (τάφος) and spewing cobra poison (ἰὸς ἀσπίδων) in 3:13, it becomes clear that Paul measures the depth of human sinfulness by describing speech that produces real suffering, especially among the weak and needy.

3:15–17 "Their feet are quick to shed blood; destruction and misery are in their ways, and the way of peace they have not known" (ὀξεῖς οἱ πόδες αὐτῶν ἐκχέαι αἷμα, σύντριμμα καὶ ταλαιπωρία ἐν ταῖς ὁδοῖς αὐτῶν, καὶ ὁδὸν εἰρήνης οὐκ ἔγνωσαν). Scripture continues its testimony to sin's influence over every element of human existence when it describes the violence and misery that people choose to inflict on other human beings as they make their way through life.

Paul borrows the language of Isaiah 59:7–8 LXX (cf. Prov 1:16) to move from the organs of speech to the feet and the metaphorical roads on which they walk. The antecedent of the pronoun "their" (αὐτῶν) is still the "all" (πάντες) of 3:12, which, in turn, refers to all human beings, Jews and Greeks alike (cf. 3:9). Paul replaced Isaiah's term for "swift" (ταχινοί) with a word that could mean both "sharp" in the sense of "having a keen edge for cutting" and "quick" with respect to motion (ὀξεῖς).[25] The picture of the violence of the wicked is even more emphatic, then, in Paul's rendering. In its original context, the "destruction" (σύντριμμα) and "misery" (ταλαιπωρία) found in the crooked ways of the wicked referred especially to the dishonesty of those who took advantage of the vulnerable in legal cases and to the general miscarriage of justice in society (Isa 59:1–8). Their multiple, chaotic "ways" (ὁδοί) of destruction and misery, says Paul, contrast with God's way (ὁδός) of peace. "Peace" is something that they have not known (ἔγνωσαν) but clearly need to know (cf. 5:1).

3:18 "There is no fear of God before their eyes" (οὐκ ἔστιν φόβος θεοῦ ἀπέναντι τῶν ὀφθαλμῶν αὐτῶν). Sinful humanity acts so viciously because they do not take into account the existence and character of God—that he is present, sees their actions, and comes to the defense of those who take refuge in him.

Paul brings his lengthy series of phrases from the Scriptures to a close with a summary statement taken from Psalm 36:1 (35:2 LXX). Many of the texts he has chosen come from contexts in which the wicked are wicked precisely because they do not take God into account in the way they live. Psalm 14, which Paul quotes in 3:11, begins, "The fool says in his heart, 'There is no God'" (Ps 14:1). The people whose "throat is an open grave" in Psalm 5:9, which Paul quotes in 3:13, have also "rebelled against" God (Ps 5:10). The one whose "mouth is filled with cursing" in Psalm 10:7, which Paul quotes in 3:14, also "renounces the Lord" and thinks, "There is no God" (Ps 10:3–4). Those who "run to evil" and leave "desolation and destruction" in their wake in Isaiah 59:7, which Paul quotes in 3:16, have separated themselves from God by their iniquities (Isa 59:2), denied the Lord, and turned back from following him (Isa 59:13). The transgressor of Psalm 36 (LXX 35) similarly plots against those who know God because he refuses to take into account God's steadfast love, faithfulness, righteousness, and judgments toward those who take refuge in him (Ps 36:5–6, 10–12).

25. BDAG 715, s.v. ὀξύς 2.

Since it was proverbial that "the fear of the Lord is the beginning of knowledge" (Prov 1:7; cf. Job 28:28; Ps 111:10; Prov 1:29; 9:10; 15:33), this quotation brings the series of quotations back to its beginning, where Paul had linked the lack of righteousness among human beings with their failure to "understand" or "seek after God" (3:11). This is, in turn, reminiscent of Paul's indictment against all humanity in 1:18–32 where he had identified the origins of the futility and foolishness of human thinking in a failure to glorify God as the creator or thank him for his creation (1:21–22).

3:19 Now we know that whatever the law says it speaks to those who are in the law so that every mouth might be stopped and all the world become answerable to God (Οἴδαμεν δὲ ὅτι ὅσα ὁ νόμος λέγει τοῖς ἐν τῷ νόμῳ λαλεῖ, ἵνα πᾶν στόμα φραγῇ καὶ ὑπόδικος γένηται πᾶς ὁ κόσμος τῷ θεῷ). As all Jews know, the Jewish Scriptures tell them that they, like everyone else, are answerable to God for their unrighteous conduct, and that no one, Jews included, has anything to say in his or her defense.

Paul used the phrase "now we know" (οἴδαμεν δέ) in 2:2 in dialogue with his fictional Jewish interlocutor to introduce a principle that he assumed they both believed, and he uses it here in the same way (cf. 7:14; 8:22, 28; 1 Cor 8:1, 4; 2 Cor 5:1; 1 Tim 1:8). Both he and his fictional interlocutor agree that the Jews are the object of the law's instruction: Jews were "hearers of the law" (2:13), "instructed from the law" (2:18), and had the advantage over gentiles of being "entrusted with the oracles of God" (3:2). They lived, then, in the sphere (ἐν) marked out by the law (cf. 2:12), and the law spoke its message to them rather than to gentiles.[26]

Since Paul has just quoted from the writings (Ecclesiastes and Psalms) and the prophets (Isaiah) rather than from the law proper, what he means by "the law" (ὁ νόμος) here is not the Mosaic legislation or the five books of Moses but the Jewish Scriptures generally (cf. 1 Cor 14:21). His point is that the Scriptures he has just quoted, with their claim that every human being is a sinner, are directed to the Jews.

The clause that follows (beginning with ἵνα) could either indicate the purpose for which the law speaks this message to the Jews, the result that its speech produces, or, since God is the one who speaks through the law, both the purpose and the result of the law's speech.[27] God's purposes always result in what he intended. The clause probably indicates the purpose for which God gave the law since elsewhere Paul emphasizes the important role that the law's demonstration of human sinfulness plays in God's overall plan to rescue his people from sin (5:20–21; 7:13; cf. 11:32; Gal 3:22). This is not the law's only purpose, as Paul makes clear elsewhere (e.g., Rom 4:23; 1 Cor 10:11), but it is an important purpose.

The language Paul uses to describe the law's indictment of humanity recalls the law court, the place where people gave formal account for their conduct to a judicial authority or to the person whom they had wronged. The term "answerable" (ὑπόδικος) appears only here in the Greek Bible but was commonly used in the Greco-Roman world of Paul's era for being "under indictment" (Plutarch, *Apoph. lac.* 217 B [F. C. Babbitt, LCL]) or legally "answerable" either to a wronged party or a judicial authority, with the party who must receive satisfaction expressed in the dative case (Dionysius of Halicarnassus, *Ant. rom.* 3.37.3; 7.58.1).[28] Here, as Moo perceptively observes, God

26. Cf. Légasse, *Romains*, 244.

27. See, respectively, Cranfield, *Romans*, 1:196; Fitzmyer, *Romans*, 337; BDAG 477, s.v. ἵνα 3.

28. For nonliterary examples, see MM 657 and LSJSupp 302, s.v. ὑπόδικος.

is both the wronged party and the judicial authority (ὑπόδικος . . . τῷ θεῷ).[29] Although everyone is answerable to God, according to the case Paul has made in 1:18–3:18, no one will have a defense to give on the day of judgment, and so "every mouth" will be "stopped."

Paul's primary point is certainly that people will have nothing to say in light of the law's indictment, but the imagery he uses here often appears in Scripture to describe how God will silence the mouths of the unjust who have used their words to oppress the poor and needy (Job 5:15–16; Ps 107:41–42; 63:11). In light of the prominent place Paul gave to the use of the mouth in his biblical indictment of sinful humanity (3:13–14), he may also have used this imagery here to express something of the hope of Job 5:16 LXX: "So may the powerless have hope, but the mouth of the unjust be shut" (εἴη δὲ ἀδυνάτῳ ἐλπίς ἀδίκου δὲ στόμα ἐμφραχθείη). A day will come when all the world, Jews as well as gentiles, will give account to God for their evil and unjust actions. On that day no one will be able to defend themselves as innocent, and on that day God will bring injustice to an end.

3:20 For by works of the law no flesh will be justified before him, for through the law comes the knowledge of sin (διότι ἐξ ἔργων νόμου οὐ δικαιωθήσεται πᾶσα σὰρξ ἐνώπιον αὐτοῦ, διὰ γὰρ νόμου ἐπίγνωσις ἁμαρτίας). The whole world is answerable to God because human beings, with their tendency to sin, are incapable of keeping God's requirements. The record of those requirements in the Jewish Scriptures does not provide the means to acquittal in God's eschatological court but only brings human disobedience to God into sharp relief.

The term "for" (διότι) joins a statement to an expression of the reason why that statement "can reasonably be considered valid" (cf. 1:19–20; 8:6–7).[30] In this verse, then, Paul gives the reason why he could say in 3:19 that all the world is answerable to God.

Paul's expression "no flesh will be justified before him" recalls the psalmist's prayer in Psalm 143:2, "Enter not into judgment with your servant, for *no one living is righteous before you*."[31] The Psalm portrays God's servant as the victim of an enemy who has isolated him so completely that the psalmist fears for his life. At what seems like the lowest point of his despair (143:3, 4, 7), he expresses his trust in the "steadfast love" (*khesed*) God has promised to show his people (143:8, 12). This trust has proven well placed in the past (143:5), and the psalmist appeals to it now, once again, for deliverance (143:12). Within the context of God's commitment to be merciful to his people, David expresses his heartfelt desire to learn and do God's will and for God's Spirit to lead him (143:10).

Elsewhere in the Psalter such a person can be called "righteous" (Ps 1:5–6; 5:11–12; 14:5–6; 32:10–11; 34:11–18; 37:1–40; 97:10–12; 146:8).[32] James P. Ware has shown, however, that in Psalm 143:2 the psalmist considers what would happen if God entered into judgment with him apart from the context of God's covenant mercy: no one living, he says, could be found "righteous" before God in such a situation. Within its own context, the statement highlights the psalmist's relief that God deals mercifully with those who trust him rather than passing judgment on them as they deserve.[33]

By alluding to this statement, Paul provides a clue to the strategy he has followed in the entire

29. *Romans*, 205.

30. BDAG 251, s.v. διότι 3. Cf. LSJ 435, s.v. διότι 1.

31. Paul's Greek (οὐ δικαιωθήσεται πᾶσα σὰρξ ἐνώπιον αὐτοῦ) is especially close to Ps 142:2 LXX (οὐ δικαιωθήσεται ἐνώπιόν σου πᾶς ζῶν).

32. James P. Ware, "Law, Christ, and Covenant: Paul's Theology of the Law in Romans 3:19–20," *JTS* 62 (2011): 532.

33. Ware, "Law, Christ, and Covenant," 531–33. Cf. Byrne, *Romans*, 58.

argument from 1:18 to this point. Like the psalmist in Psalm 143:2, Paul has been considering what the human situation looks like apart from the covenant mercy and love of God. Anyone who stands before God's eschatological judgment in what Paul will later call one's "own righteousness" (10:3; cf. Phil 3:9), that is, in one's righteousness considered apart from trust in God's promise to be gracious to his people, will inevitably fail to escape God's just punishment of the unrighteous.[34]

Righteousness as the psalmists most often conceive it is not what Paul would call "one's own righteousness." Thus, the author of Psalm 32 can say, "I acknowledged my sin to you, and I did not cover my iniquity; I said, 'I will confess my transgressions to the Lord,' and you forgave the iniquity of my sin'" (32:5), and then, a few verses later, "Be glad in the Lord, and rejoice, O righteous, and shout for joy, all you upright in heart" (32:11). The "righteous" and "upright" person is the person who relies on the steadfast love of the Lord both for direction in living one's life and for forgiveness when one fails to follow that direction (32:8–11). In Romans 3:20, however, Paul is thinking of justification by keeping the commands of the law without reference to the covenant mercy of God. On that basis, no one will be justified. His focus on the commands of the law is clear from his insertion of the phrase "the works of the law" (ἔργων νόμου) into Psalm 143:2.[35]

Paul also changed the Psalm's reference to "no one living" (*lo . . . kol-khay*; οὐ . . . πᾶς ζῶν) into a reference to "no flesh," or, more literally, "not . . . all flesh (οὐ . . . πᾶσα σάρξ). His use of the term "flesh" elsewhere in Romans to refer to circumcision and to the Jewish people (2:28; 4:1; 9:3, 5, 8; 11:14) might at first lend plausibility to the idea that the term refers to "the fleshly distinctiveness of which the loyal Jew makes boast, particularly his circumcision 'in the flesh.'"[36] This is unlikely, however, since Paul left intact the Psalm's reference to "all" flesh, and the phrase "all flesh" is parallel to the phrase "all the world" in the immediately preceding clause of 3:19. The emphasis, then, falls on all humanity, especially in its inability to comply with the will of God (e.g., 6:19; 7:18; 8:7–9; cf. Gal 2:16).

Paul concludes the sentence with a brief explanation (γάρ ["for"]) of why no one can escape God's just punishment on the final day by doing the law. God did not intend the law to provide a basis for justification. Its purpose was instead to provide knowledge of sin. Paul will explain how the law provides this knowledge in 7:7–12.

IN DEPTH: "The Works of the Law"

Paul uses the expression "the works of the law" (ἔργων νόμου) eight times in his letters (Gal 2:16 [3x]; 3:2, 5, 10; Rom 3:20, 28), and these are the only known occurrences of the phrase in Greek literature prior to or contemporaneous with Paul.[37] The eight instances of the phrase share several similarities. It always occurs in prepositional phrases, seven times in the phrase "by works of the law" (ἐξ ἔργων νόμου) and once in the expression "apart from works of the law" (χωρὶς ἔργων νόμου). It only appears in Galatians and Romans and only in polemical

34. Cf. Ware, "Law, Christ, and Covenant," 535–39.
35. Ware, "Law, Christ, and Covenant," 527–39.
36. Dunn, *Romans 1–8*, 155.
37. Cf. Jacqueline C. R. de Roo, *Works of the Law at Qumran and in Paul*, New Testament Monographs 13 (Sheffield: Sheffield Phoenix, 2007), 1.

discussions where "works of the law" stand in contrast to faith as the means by which justification takes place (Gal 2:16; 3:10; Rom 3:20, 28) or as the means by which people receive and experience the Spirit (Gal 3:2, 5). The scarcity of the phrase within Greek literature generally and the similarities among its various uses imply that it has basically the same meaning wherever it occurs, but that meaning has been the subject of intense debate.

The earliest commentators on Romans anticipated the two most common positions in recent interpretation.[38] Origen, in the earliest extant commentary, believed that the phrase in Romans 3:20 referred to the natural law common to all people. On the basis of this law, a human being might seem to be relatively free of fault when compared to other human beings, but not when compared to the purity and holiness of God.[39] "Works of the law," in other words, refer to what most human beings would recognize as good works, and Paul's point is that no one's record of doing these works merits God's declaration that he or she is just.

About a century after Origen, the anonymous commentator commonly called Ambrosiaster took a different position on the phrase, at least as it occurs in Romans 3:28. "Works of the law," he explained, meant those elements of the law that gentiles do not have to observe, "circumcision or new moons or the veneration of the sabbath."[40] Pelagius took a similar position a few years later, and a few decades later still Theodoret of Cyrus was even more explicit about the ethnic meaning of the phrase in Romans 3:20.[41] "Works of the law," he wrote, were not part of the "natural" moral "knowledge" of humanity but were "imposed on Jews for that particular time, like circumcision, Sabbath, sacrifices, washings, prescriptions about leprosy and menstruation, and things like that; they are symbols of other things, but their performance does not suffice to make the performer righteous."

The debate of more recent times is better informed historically and linguistically, and the positions are more finely nuanced, but they are basically the same. One group of interpreters sees the phrase as a reference to human obedience to the commands of God.[42] The other group takes it to mean the Mosaic law

38. Paul L. Owen ("The 'Works of the Law' in Romans and Galatians: A New Defense of the Subjective Genitive," *JBL* 126 [2007]: 553–77) offers a third approach: "works of the law" refers to the effects that the law produces. In 3:20, for example, Paul says that the law produces condemnation rather than justification. When Paul last connected the law with justification (2:13), however, the issue was not what the law did but whether people were "doers of the law" (ποιηταὶ νόμου). It is likely that Paul speaks of the law and justification in 3:20 in the same way. Cf. the references to doing (ποιῆσαι) the law in close proximity to the phrase "works of the law" in Gal 3:10–12.

39. Origen, *Romans, Books 1–5*, 207.

40. Ambrosiaster, *Romans*, 30. See also his division of the law into "three parts" in a short excursus on the law in his comments on 3:20. The third part of the law, he says, consists of "the deeds of the law, in other words, sabbaths, new moons, circumcision, et cetera" (*Romans*, 28).

41. Pelagius, *Romans*, 8; Theodoret of Cyrus, *Letters of St. Paul*, 1:63.

42. This group can be further divided in various ways. Some believe that the phrase refers to the Mosaic law (e.g., Calvin, *Romans*, 69–70; Meyer, *Romans*, 126–27; Moo, *Romans*,

viewed from the perspective of its role in defining the Jewish people as a distinct people, set apart from other people groups.[43]

There is much to be said for both positions. Proponents of the view that the phrase "works of the law" refers to the human effort to obey God point out that when Paul uses the phrase in Romans 3:20 it has a universal reference to "all flesh" (πᾶσα σάρξ). Before the phrase first occurs in 3:20, moreover, Paul uses similar language to speak of the moral requirements that God places on all humanity, whether Jew or Greek. The "works" that God will use as a criterion for his righteous judgment are specifically defined as either "endurance in good work" or disobedience to the truth and obedience to unrighteousness (2:6–8), and gentiles have "the work [singular] of the law written in their hearts" (2:15).[44] Shortly after speaking of "works of the law" in 3:20, moreover, Paul uses the term "works" without the qualifying phrase "of the law" in 4:1–8, a passage designed to explain further the main point of 3:9–31. In 4:1–8 Paul insists that neither Abraham nor David could be justified by "works" because they were impious, lawless, and in need of forgiveness like everyone else. The "works" that could not justify Abraham and David in this passage do not seem to be distinctively Jewish works but the opposite of impiety and "lawless deeds" (ἀνομίαι). This reading of 4:1–8 appears to be confirmed in Romans 9:11–12 where "works" appear again without the qualifier "of the law" and are specifically defined as doing either good or evil.[45]

Proponents of the view that "works of the law" refers to doing the law as a way of distinguishing Jews from gentiles point out that circumcision and dietary observance were particularly important in setting Jews apart from gentiles (as in, e.g., 1 Macc 1:60–63).[46] The observance of precisely these elements of the Mosaic law among gentile Christians prompted Paul to write his letter to the Galatians (Gal 2:11–14; 5:2–3, 6, 11–13, 15) where the phrase "works of the law" first

209), others that it refers to the natural law common to all people (e.g., Shedd, *Romans*, 72; cf. Jewett, *Romans*, 266). Some interpreters believe that the phrase refers to keeping the law as a foundation for human boasting (e.g., Leenhardt, *Romans*, 96–97, 111; cf. Longenecker, *Romans*, 369), and others that it refers simply to obeying the law, something that no one can adequately do (e.g., Cranfield, *Romans*, 1:198; Moo, *Romans*, 209–10; Schreiner, *Romans*, 173).

43. See especially Dunn (*Romans 1–8*, 153–55; idem, *New Perspective on Paul*, 99–140, 213–26, 381–94, 413–428) and Wright ("Romans," 459–61), but also E. P. Sanders, *Paul, the Law, and the Jewish People* (Philadelphia: Fortress, 1983), 46; Terence L. Donaldson, *Paul and the Gentiles: Remapping the Apostle's Convictional World* (Minneapolis: Fortress, 1997), 120–21, 171–72; Francis Watson, *Paul, Judaism, and the Gentiles: Beyond the New Perspective*, rev. and exp. ed. (Grand Rapids: Eerdmans, 2007), 121–31.

44. C. E. B. Cranfield, "'The Works of the Law' in the Epistle to the Romans," *JSNT* 43 (1991): 93–95; Thomas R. Schreiner, *The Law and Its Fulfillment: A Pauline Theology of Law* (Grand Rapids: Baker, 1993), 52, 55–57.

45. Douglas J. Moo, "'Law,' 'Works of the Law,' and Legalism in Paul," *WTJ* 45 (1983), 94–96; Cranfield, "'Works of the Law,'" 96–97; Schreiner, *Law and Its Fulfillment*, 52; Ware, "Law, Christ, and Covenant," 523–24.

46. Dunn, *New Perspective*, 123; Wright, "Romans," 461.

occurs and most often appears (Gal 2:16; 3:2, 5, 10).[47] In Romans, moreover, the phrase also appears in contexts where Paul seems concerned to deconstruct the notion among Jews that their possession of the law separated them from the gentiles and could therefore entitle them to preferential treatment (3:20, 28).[48]

This understanding of the phrase as a reference to the role of the law in defining Jewish identity receives some support from the appearance of what looks like the Hebrew equivalent of the phrase in 4QMMT, a letter written about the time of Paul by members of the Dead Sea community of southern Judea. The letter was intended to explain the distinctive ways in which the community observed the Mosaic law in comparison with other Jews, and near its conclusion gives this statement of its purpose: "We have written to you some of the works of the Torah [*ma'ase hatorah*] which we think are good for you and for your people."[49]

The best approach to Paul's use of the phrase recognizes the truth in each of the two main positions and tries to find a way of accommodating both emphases. Two elements of Paul's use of the phrase are important to keep in mind in the effort to understand it. First, although the exact phrase "works of the law" never appears in Greek prior to Paul (as far as we know), the phrase is perfectly intelligible Greek. The terms "work" and "law" appear together fairly frequently in Greek literature in phrases such as "the action was against the law" (ὄντος παρὰ τὸν νόμον τοῦ ἔργου) or "exemplifying the law of God through actions" (ἐκδιδάσκων διὰ τῶν ἔργῶν νόμον θεοῦ) or "men who fulfill the laws by their deeds" (τοὺς νόμους ἔργοις ἐπιτελούντων).[50] Whether Roman law or Jewish law is in view, the common way of using these words together in Greek communicates that a body of law exists that can be either obeyed or disobeyed. "Works of the law," then, most naturally refers to actions in conformity with some law, and the particular law in view is determined by the context. This means, in turn, that the phrase is probably not a technical term for "works of the [Jewish] Torah," despite the appearance of a Hebrew cousin to the Greek phrase in 4QMMT.

Second, Paul uses the phrase in contexts where the term "law" seems one

47. Dunn, *New Perspective*, 108–11, 127.

48. Ibid., 127–28.

49. Ibid., 339–45. N. T. Wright, "Paul and Qumran," *BR* 14.5 (October 1998): 18, 54, does not think that Paul and 4QMMT use the phrase in the same way since Paul uses it to distinguish Jews from gentiles and 4QMMT uses it to distinguish one Jewish group from another. Still, the Qumran document does use the phrase in the context of making social distinctions. The relevant text is 4Q398, frag. 14–17, column 2, line 3, as printed and translated in Florentino Garciá Martínez and Eibert J. C. Tigchelaar, *The Dead Sea Scrolls: Study Edition*, 2 vols. (Leiden: Brill/Grand Rapids: Eerdmans, 1996), 2:802–3. The text 4Q174, column 1, line 7 (also cited as 4QFlor 1:7) is sometimes brought into the discussion, but whether that text reads "the works of the law" (*ma'ase torah*) or "the works of thanksgiving" (*ma'ase todah*) is unclear and will probably never be determined with certainty. See the conflicting conclusions in Wright, "Romans," 460n94, and de Roo, *Works of the Law*, 11–16.

50. Demosthenes, *Against Leochares* 25 (A. T. Murray, LCL); T. Dan 6.9 (H. C. Kee, *OTP* 1:810); Philo, *Rewards* 126 (F. H. Colson, LCL).

minute to refer to something unique to Jews (Gal 3:2, 5, 10–14; Rom 3:28–30) and the next minute to something that gentiles could obey just as well as Jews (Rom 3:20). "Works of the law," in other words, seems sometimes to refer to the common moral standards of justice and fairness that foster good relationships between individuals and allow society to function well (Rom 3:20), and sometimes to refer primarily to those elements of the Mosaic law, such as circumcision and food laws, that distinguish Jews from gentiles (Gal 3:2, 5, 10–14; Rom 3:28–30). In Galatians 2:16, where he uses the phrase three times, Paul seems to move from one use to the other in a single sentence. The first two uses of the phrase seem to have in mind primarily the Jewish dietary laws that were the issue between Paul and Cephas in Antioch and that separated Jew from gentile, but the third use of the phrase claims that "by works of the law no one will be justified," using an expression (lit., "all flesh [πᾶσα σάρξ] shall not be justified") that emphasizes the applicability of the claim to every human being, whether Jewish or not (cf. πᾶσα σάρξ in Rom 3:20). No human being, whether Jew or gentile, will be able to stand before God's court on the final day and escape punishment on the basis of obedience to God's requirements. This is true whether that person is a gentile to whom God has revealed basic theological and ethical knowledge through creation (Rom 1:19–20, 32) or a Jew who has "the embodiment of knowledge and truth in the law" (Rom 2:20), including the knowledge that Jews should circumcise their male children (Rom 2:25).

In Romans 1:18–4:25 Paul is particularly interested in showing Jews that they need the gospel as much as gentiles. Paul targets both the Jew who believes himself to be morally superior to the gentile and therefore exempt from punishment on the day of judgment (2:1, 17–24) and the Jew who thinks that possession of the law and circumcision will prompt an otherwise impartial God to turn a blind eye to his sin (2:2–5, 27). Neither Jew will escape the judgment of God. This is not Paul's only interest, however. He also holds the conviction that no human effort at obedience to God's law, whether the natural law that God wove into the fabric of human society (1:19–20, 32; 2:14–16) or its perfect expression for Israel in the Jewish law (2:20; 3:2), will result in justification before God.[51]

The phrase "works of the law," then, refers primarily to the Jewish law, and because of this Paul uses it to exclude any ethnic boasting before God. Yet since the Jewish law contains requirements that any just society recognizes to be good, the phrase operates on a broader level that was also important to Paul:

51. Ware ("Law, Christ, and Covenant," 535–36) may be correct, then, when he says that the phrase reflects the theology of the Psalms, particularly Ps 143:2. There, expressions of the impossibility of righteousness by means of doing the law assume that the person seeking to be justified by the law is operating outside the context of God's covenant love and mercy toward Israel.

the exclusion of works from justification also means that no one can boast of his or her moral accomplishments in God's presence and expect to be justified on that basis.

Theology in Application

This passage calls on us to evaluate humanity, including ourselves, from God's standpoint. From his perspective every individual is unrighteous, and because of this every human society, even those with the fairest systems of justice, have a tendency to drift into inequity and the oppression of the vulnerable.

Excusing Ourselves from Paul's Sweeping Condemnation

Like Paul's interlocutor in chapter two, it is easy to fall into excusing both humanity generally and ourselves specifically from this sweeping condemnation. There were many decent people in the Roman Empire in Paul's time, we might think, just as there are many decent people across the world today, and we are among the decent people. One can see the glass half full or half empty: of course horrible events have happened and evil people exist, but many fair-minded, kind people have also fought against the bullies of the world, and everyone is not as evil as the abusive people Paul depicts in 3:10–18. Perhaps Paul was simply carried away by the rhetorical needs of his argument. Since he thought everyone should trust in the sufficiency of Christ's death to atone for sin, he argued that everyone was a sinner in need of Christ's atoning death.

Speech as a Spiritual Barometer

Accepting the perspective of this passage of Scripture on human nature, however, involves believing that, despite some successes, we often fail to deal fairly and kindly with people. The way we use speech is one of the areas in which this becomes most clearly evident, even for people who think of themselves as "decent." It is perhaps not accidental that Paul takes up so much space describing verbal sins in this part of his argument. He speaks of the throat, the tongue, the lips, and the mouth and how people often use them to wish harm on others and actually to do them harm (3:13–14). If we think about our own speech over the past day or week, it is likely that we will be less optimistic about our own basic decency and fairness. The image of the throat as an open grave implies that the harmful words we often use against others arise from hearts with a tendency toward sinfulness. "How can you speak good," Jesus asked his opponents, "when you are evil? For out of the abundance of the heart the mouth speaks" (Matt 12:34).

The Human Tendency to Support Societal Injustice

Accepting the perspective of Romans 3:9–20 on human nature also involves taking its perspective on violence and injustice in human societies. Human history is filled with examples of people and societies that seem to know what justice entails but also seem incapable of recognizing the injustices that they commit or support. Martial, writing in AD 80, could describe the grisly death of a convicted thief, forced to take part in a play in the Roman Colosseum for the entertainment of the spectators, as "the punishment he deserved" (Martial, *On the Spectacles* 9.7 [D. R. Shackleton Bailey, LCL]). Martial was apparently blind to what now seems an almost incomprehensible injustice.

Similarly, the nineteenth-century American theologian Robert Lewis Dabney knew both that God had created all human beings in his image, including Africans, and that the institution of slavery in the American South was fraught with physical, sexual, and emotional violence. Yet he could somehow publish a book in which he tried to argue that slaves, because of their African descent, were so inferior to other human beings that they needed the institution of slavery to guard them from hurting themselves. Such notions are now justly consigned, along with the *Rassenforschung* of the Third Reich, to the curiosity shop of intellectual and moral horrors. It is sobering to reflect, however, that not only did Dabney seem to believe sincerely that he was arguing for a just cause but that his argument was found by thousands of people in the late nineteenth and early twentieth centuries to be appealing.[52]

It is worth reflecting, in light of Romans 3:9–20, on how our tendency to make excuses for ourselves can blind us to our sin, and how the prevailing winds of our society may keep us from seeing institutional evil around us. This passage should urge the unbeliever and remind the believer to accept God's perspective on humanity. Human beings have rebelled against God and failed to show love to their neighbors, and they have no excuse for their behavior.

After a series of questions and answers that describe the Ten Commandments, the *Westminster Shorter Catechism* answers the question of whether anyone is able to keep them all. Everyone, it insists, "doth daily break them in thought, word, and deed" (Q&A 149). The *Catechism* then says that whereas not all sins are equally heinous, "every sin . . . deserveth [God's] wrath and curse, both in this life, and that which is to come." This is an insight derived from Paul's profound theology of human sin, articulated perhaps most clearly in Romans 3:9–20. Everyone richly deserves the wrath of God, and the study of this passage provides an opportunity to reflect on the depth of our own failure to do what God requires.

52. Robert Lewis Dabney, *A Defense of Virginia (and Through Her, of the South)* (New York: E. J. Hale, 1867), 293–94. For the inconsistency of Dabney's thought on the morality of slavery, see Sean Michael Lucas, *Robert Lewis Dabney: A Southern Presbyterian Life* (Phillipsburg, NJ: P&R, 2005), 122–28.

CHAPTER 8

Romans 3:21–31

Literary Context

Paul has been waiting for this moment since announcing the theme of the letter in 1:16–17. There he had said that he was not ashamed to announce the good news of what God has done in Christ even in Rome because this good news had the power to bring salvation to everyone who believed, whatever their social or ethnic location. It was not immediately clear from that succinct statement, however, why Paul thought people needed salvation. Paul spent a number of paragraphs, therefore, describing the final day of judgment and why everyone, Jews included, needed salvation from the outpouring of God's wrath on that day.

He first pointed out that the day of judgment had already started as God revealed his wrath from heaven against human idolatry and mistreatment of other people (1:18–32). In this section, Paul emphasized the fairness of God both in requiring people to know that they should worship him (1:19–21, 32) and in punishing them for failing to do so in a way that was commensurate with their rebellion against him (1:24, 26, 28). He also emphasized God's fairness in refusing to give special treatment on the day of judgment to one people group, specifically the Jews (2:1–29). God would judge people on that day according to exactly the same criterion: whether they had done what he required (2:1–16). If what God required were defined by his law, then gentiles could do this as well as Jews (2:14–16). On the final day God would not require gentiles to have a record of obedience to the specifically Jewish aspects of the Mosaic law but only to the law written on their hearts (2:17–29). The Jews did have an advantage over the gentiles in possessing the Scriptures (3:1–4), but this was not an advantage that, by any stretch of the imagination (3:5–8), could give them an advantage over the gentiles on the day of judgment. Nor did the gentiles have an advantage over the Jews (3:9). The sad truth was that absolutely no one, whether Jew or gentile, could claim that they deserved to escape God's punishment on the final day because they had done what the law required (3:10–20). This is why Paul could say in 1:16–17 that salvation could only come to anyone, whether Jew or Greek, if God gave it to them through his power and righteousness.

In 3:21–31 Paul returns to his definition of the gospel as the righteousness of God that powerfully saves those who believe and explains it in more detail. He focuses on two elements of the gospel. First, the gospel shows God's fairness and impartiality, although it entails God declaring sinful people to be right with him. Second, the gospel excludes any form of human pride, whether pride in one's performance or pride in one's social status.

In 4:1–25 Paul will illustrate this second element of the gospel—that it excludes boasting in achievement or status—from the story of Abraham. His account of Abraham's justification by faith will also illustrate how Paul could say in 3:21 that the "law and the prophets" testified to the righteousness of God that has now been revealed.

VI. Jews Are Also Subject to God's Wrath (2:1–3:20)

➡ **VII. The Death of Christ Demonstrates God's Righteousness and Excludes Human Boasting (3:21–31)**

A. The Death of Christ Demonstrates God's Righteousness (3:21–26)

B. God's Righteousness Excludes Human Boasting (3:27–31)

VIII. The Scriptures Show That Righteousness Comes by Faith Rather Than by Works (4:1–25)

Main Idea

The righteousness of God powerfully saves sinful people from God's wrath but maintains God's fairness and impartiality through the sacrificial and atoning death of Christ. Like the mercy seat in the biblical tabernacle, Christ's death on the cross was the "place" where God's necessary and justified wrath against human rebellion ceased, allowing reconciliation between God and his people. That God took the initiative in this atoning sacrifice leaves no room for human boasting either in one's achievements or in one's social status.

Translation

Romans 3:21–31

21a	Contrast	But now, **the righteousness of God is disclosed,**
b	Separation	apart from the law,
c	Concession	although it is attested by the law and the prophets
22a	Restatement	that is, the righteousness of God
b	Means	through faith in Jesus Christ
c	Reference	to all who believe.

d	Explanation of 22c	For **there is no distinction,**
23a	Explanation	for **all have sinned and**
b	Explanation	**lack the glory of God** and
24a	Explanation	are justified
b	Manner	freely,
c	Means	by his grace,
d	Means	through the deliverance
		that is in Christ Jesus,
25a	Expansion	whom God displayed publicly
b	Restatement	as the mercy seat,
c	Means	through faith,
d	Means	by his blood
e	Purpose of 25a–d	for a proof of his righteousness,
f	Explanation of 25e	on account of the dismissal of sins previously committed
26a	Explanation	because of the forbearance of God
b	Restatement	for the proof of his righteousness
c	Time	in the present time,
d	Purpose	in order that he might be just
e	Simultaneous	even while justifying the one who has faith in Jesus.
27a	Rhetorical Question	**Where,** then, **is boasting?**
b	Assertion (Inference)	**It has been shut out.**
c	Rhetorical Question	**Through what law?**
d	Rhetorical Question	**That of works?**
e	Assertion	**No, but through the law of faith.**
28a	Explanation	For **we hold that a human being is justified**
b	Manner	by faith
c	Manner	apart from works of the law.
29a	Rhetorical Question	**Or is God the God of the Jews only?**
	Rhetorical Question	**Is he not also God of the gentiles?**
	Assertion (Inference)	**Yes, also of the gentiles,**
30a	Basis	since God is one,
b	Contrast/Comparison	who will justify the circumcision by faith and the uncircumcision through that same faith.
31a	Rhetorical Question	**Do we cancel the law through this faith?**
b	Exclamation	**Certainly not!**
c	Assertion	**Rather, we uphold the law.**

Structure

The passage begins with an expression ("but now" [νυνὶ δέ]) that alerts Paul's readers and hearers of a dramatic switch in the course of the argument. He is now about to describe in detail the saving righteousness of God that he had briefly mentioned in 1:16–17 and that answers the human plight he has just described at length in 1:18–3:20. This contrasting section can be divided into two parts. The first part (3:21–26) consists of one long, complex sentence of high-sounding prose, a style that was fitting for the solemn announcement that God's saving righteousness was displayed in the atoning death of Christ Jesus (3:21–26). The second part (3:27–31) returns to the feisty give-and-take of the philosophical diatribe, a style that Paul had last used in 3:9.

The first, long sentence begins by returning to the theme of the righteousness of God and its availability to all people, regardless of the social group to which they belong (cf. 1:14–17). Paul is now able to fill out that brief description in two ways. First, he includes within it a summary of the argument he has just made in 1:18–3:20 that, apart from God's intervention, all human beings will face God's just condemnation on the final day (3:21–23). This explains why Paul linked faith so closely with God's saving righteousness in 1:16–17. Apart from faith in God there was no exit from the condemnation that Paul had just described. Second, he also describes the means by which God could be righteous and yet rescue from condemnation those who deserved it. The death of Christ substituted for the death of the sinner, allowing justice to remain intact and providing a place for God and humanity to be reconciled (3:24–26).

A number of scholars have thought that in this second part of the first paragraph (3:24–26) Paul quoted from an early Christian confession that he edited so that it conformed more closely (although not entirely) to his own theology. The two indicative verbs in 3:23 ("sinned" [ἥμαρτον]; "lack" [ὑστεροῦνται]) lead us to expect a third indicative verb at the beginning of 3:24, but instead we find a participle ("being justified" [δικαιούμενοι]). Some of the vocabulary and the theology expressed in the passage, moreover, is not typically Pauline. The terms "dismissal" (πάρεσις) and "previously committed" (προγίνομαι) appear nowhere else in the NT, and "mercy seat" (ἱλαστήριον) shows up only in Hebrews 9:5. Similarly, the idea of atonement through Jesus's sacrificial blood appears explicitly nowhere else in Paul, and the notion that God passed over sins in the past, articulated here, seems to some interpreters to be at odds with Paul's case in 1:18–3:20 that God has already been revealing his wrath against sinners (1:18).[1]

1. The bibliography here is immense, but the basic thesis appears in Rudolf Bultmann, *Theology of the New Testament*, 2 vols. (New York: Scribner's, 1951, 1955), 1:46–47, with further elaboration in Ernst Käsemann, *Exegetische Versuche und Besinnungen* (Göttingen: Vandenhoeck & Ruprecht, 1960), 96–100 (idem, *Romans*, 92–101); and some tweaking in, e.g, John

There is much in the passage, however, that is distinctively Pauline. If one is willing to admit Colossians and Ephesians to the Pauline corpus, with their fourfold use of the term "deliverance" (ἀπολύτρωσις), then nothing in the vocabulary or theology of 3:24 is un-Pauline (Col 1:14; Eph 1:7, 14; 4:30; cf. Rom 8:23; 1 Cor 1:30), and there are analogies elsewhere in Paul to the troublesome participle that begins the verse.[2] It is true that Paul does not elsewhere speak explicitly of Christ's death as an atoning sacrifice, but, he comes close to this in Rom 5:9 where he speaks of believers having been "justified by his blood" (δικαιωθέντες νῦν ἐν τῷ αἵματι αὐτοῦ). Once again, this language seems much more Pauline if Colossians and Ephesians are admitted to the Pauline corpus (Col 1:20; Eph 1:7; 2:13).

The one remaining oddity in the passage is what Käsemann called its "overladen style."[3] It does stand out from its context as an especially long, syntactically complex piece of prose. The supposed quotation, however, is part of an even longer sentence that begins in 3:21. The whole section, therefore, including parts that everyone acknowledges to be Pauline, is syntactically complex and unusual within its context. Douglas A. Campbell has argued persuasively that Greco-Roman rhetorical convention called for variation in the style of writing within a single discourse and has sensibly concluded that "3.21–26 may be no more than an attempt on Paul's part to craft this section in a more elevated style than the surrounding discourse, presumably because of its more elevated subject matter."[4] The exegesis below proceeds on the assumption that this cautiously phrased suggestion is correct.

The style shifts again in the second paragraph of the section (3:27–31) as Paul moves back into the diatribe mode of composition. He finds this to be an appropriate style for drawing two conclusions from what he has just said and rejecting a polemical objection to his position.

First, he concludes that no one can boast either in the social group to which they belong or in the works they perform. God has graciously justified people without distinction through the death of Christ, so no one has grounds for boasting in any human characteristic whether that is a matter of personal achievement or of group identity (3:27–28). Moreover, since God justifies people in this way he shows himself to be the Creator and Sovereign over all peoples, not merely the national god of the Jews (3:29–30).

Reumann, "The Gospel of the Righteousness of God: Pauline Reinterpretation of Romans 3:21–31," *Int* 20 (1966): 433–52; Ben F. Meyer, "The Pre-Pauline Formula in Rom. 3.25–26a," *NTS* 29 (1983): 198–208; and Wolfgang Kraus, *Der Tod Jesu als Heiligtumsweihe: Eine Untersuchung zum Umfeld der Sühnevorstellung in Römer 3,25–26a* (Neukirchen-Vluyn: Neukirchener Verlag, 1991), 15–20.

2. See the comments on verse 24 below and Meyer, "The Pre-Pauline Formula," 199.

3. Käsemann, *Exegetische Versuche*, 96. Cf. Benjamin J. Ribbens, "Forensic-Retributive Justification in Romans 3:21–26: Paul's Doctrine of Justification in Dialogue with Hebrews," *CBQ* 74 (2012): 554.

4. Douglas A. Campbell, *The Rhetoric of Righteousness in Romans 3.21–26*, JSNTSup 65 (Sheffield: Sheffield Academic Press, 1992), 83.

Second, Paul anticipates an objection from what he has said so far about the lack of any role for works or social identity in justification. Does this mean that faith in the gospel cancels the law (3:31a)? This was not the place for an extended answer to that question, but he briefly denies that its implication is true (3:31b–c) in anticipation of what he will say later in 7:7–8:17.

Exegetical Outline

➦ **VII. The Death of Christ Demonstrates God's Righteousness and Excludes Human Boasting (3:21–31)**
- **A. The Death of Christ Demonstrates God's Righteousness (3:21–26)**
  1. God's Righteousness as the Only Escape from God's Wrath (3:21–23)
  2. Free and Gracious Deliverance from God's Wrath through Christ's Death (3:24–26)
- **B. God's Righteousness Excludes Human Boasting (3:27–31)**
  1. It Excludes Boasting because of One's Social Group or Works (3:27–28)
  2. Its Exclusion of Boasting because of One's Social Group Implies the Sovereignty of God over All Humanity (3:29–30)
  3. Paul Briefly Rejects the False Conclusion That He Cancels the Mosaic Law (3:31)

Explanation of the Text

3:21 But now, apart from the law, the righteousness of God is disclosed, although it is attested by the law and the prophets (Νυνὶ δὲ χωρὶς νόμου δικαιοσύνη θεοῦ πεφανέρωται μαρτυρουμένη ὑπὸ τοῦ νόμου καὶ τῶν προφητῶν). God has not left human beings in the plight of sin. The gospel discloses his saving power, by which he freely releases human beings from punishment for their sin and yet remains impartial and fair in his role as judge. Moreover, the very Scriptures that condemn human beings for their sin anticipated the gospel's appearance.

The phrase "but now" (νυνὶ δέ) signals the turning point in the argument Paul has been developing since 1:16. He has shown that everyone is answerable to God for their impiety and unrighteousness and that this is true even for those who live within the boundaries marked out by the Mosaic law (3:19). Paul has explained in detail that because of this universal guilt before God no one can attain righteousness and life apart from the gospel as Paul has succinctly defined it in 1:16–17. Paul now returns to that definition of the gospel and explains in greater detail what he meant when he said that, by faith, the righteousness of God is revealed in the gospel. His return to 1:16–17 is clear from the similar phrasing both here and there of the concept that God's righteousness is revealed:

1:17
"the righteousness . . . of God . . . is revealed"
(δικαιοσύνη . . . θεοῦ . . . ἀποκαλύπτεται)

3:21
"the righteousness of God is disclosed"
(δικαιοσύνη θεοῦ πεφανέρωται)

Although the perfect tense verb "is disclosed" (πεφανέρωται) is slightly more emphatic than the present tense verb "is revealed" (ἀποκαλύπτεται), the concept of the present (νυνί) unveiling of the righteousness of God binds the two phrases together.[5]

Just as in 1:17 (see the comments on that passage), so here the phrase is polyvalent. Three meanings mingle together in the expression. First, the idea that God is impartial in judgment has been a dominant theme of 1:18–3:20, and since the term "righteousness" commonly referred to impartiality and fairness in the Greco-Roman world it seems likely that the term would carry those connotations here. Paul's description in 3:22–23 of the righteousness of God as coming to all who believe, without distinction, confirms the presence of this nuance.

Second, the present "disclosure" of God's righteousness recalls the parallelism of his saving power with the revelation of God's righteousness in 1:16–17, and this parallelism makes clear that the righteousness of God here is also his powerful saving work.

Third, the parallelism between the statement in 3:20 that "by works of the law no flesh will be justified before him" (ἐξ ἔργων νόμου οὐ δικαιωθήσεται πᾶσα σὰρξ ἐνώπιον αὐτοῦ) and the claim here in 3:21 that "apart from the law, the righteousness of God is disclosed" (χωρὶς νόμου δικαιοσύνη θεοῦ πεφανέρωται) shows that the righteousness of God is the righteousness that comes to the believer from God through God's justifying action. The righteousness of God is God's judicial release of the believer from any punishment, and that judicial acquittal now belongs to the believer as a gift from God.

Paul is especially concerned in this verse to describe the complex relationship between the Scriptures, which Paul calls "the law and the prophets," and the gospel of God's righteousness.[6] On one hand God's righteousness is disclosed to believers "apart from" (χωρίς) the law. This must mean that it comes to them separately from any effort on their part to keep the law since, as Paul has just said, "by works of the law shall no flesh be justified before" God (3:20), and, as he will say shortly, a human being "is justified apart from [χωρίς] works of the law" (3:28; cf. 4:6; 7:8–9).[7] On the other hand, the righteousness of God is not disclosed to believers "independently of law" (REB) since the "law and the prophets" continue to bear witness to it.[8] The term translated "is attested" (μαρτυρουμένη; cf. NRSV) is in the present tense and places emphasis on the idea that Paul's notion of justification apart from the law does not nullify the continuing role of the "law and the prophets" as Scripture (cf. 3:31). The "law" continues to speak to everyone within its hearing of God's character and of his just requirements for his people (3:19). It continues to bear witness to human sinfulness and therefore to the human need for God's saving power (3:20). The "prophets" bear witness to all three nuances of Paul's polyvalent expression "the righteousness of God." God works powerfully for the salvation of his people and of all peoples (e.g., Isa 45:24; 51:5–8; 61:10–11; 62:1), upholds impartiality and

5. "But now" (νυνὶ δέ) signals not only an advancement in the logic of Paul's argument (e.g., Meyer, *Romans*, 128; Jewett, *Romans*, 272), nor only a turn from one age to the next in salvation history (e.g., Lagrange, *Romains*, 73; Fitzmyer, *Romans*, 343), but both a logical contrast with 3:20 and a change from the age dominated by the law and condemnation to the age dominated by deliverance and righteousness (e.g., Wilckens, *An die Römer [Röm 1–5]*, 184; Hultgren, *Romans*, 154).

6. For "the law and the prophets" as a name for the Scriptures generally, see 2 Macc 15:9; 4 Macc 18:10; Matt 5:17; 7:12; 11:13; 22:40; Luke 16:16; John 1:45; Acts 13:15; 24:14; 28:23.

7. *Pace* Jewett's argument (*Romans*, 274) that Paul has in view "law" itself, abstractly conceived, rather than doing the Mosaic law.

8. *Pace* BDAG 1095, s.v. χωρίς 2bδ.

fairness for the poor and oppressed (e.g., Isa 59:15–16), and justifies the ungodly (e.g., Isa 53:11; cf. Isa 45:25; 56:12–13).

3:22a–c that is, the righteousness of God through faith in Jesus Christ to all who believe (δικαιοσύνη δὲ θεοῦ διὰ πίστεως Ἰησοῦ Χριστοῦ εἰς πάντας τοὺς πιστεύοντας). God powerfully saves people, and justly releases them from punishment for their sin, when they trust Jesus Christ. Because God acquits them by means of their faith, this acquittal is available to all people, not merely to Jews.

Paul begins this clause with the same conjunction (δέ) that he used at the beginning of 3:21. Here, however, instead of being used adversatively ("but"), it is used to indicate that Paul is about to explain further the phrase, "the righteousness of God" (cf. 9:30; 1 Cor 10:11; 15:56; Phil 2:8).[9]

This further explanation comes in two prepositional phrases. The first phrase tells how the righteousness of God is disclosed: it is revealed "through faith in Jesus Christ" (διὰ πίστεως Ἰησοῦ Χριστοῦ). Taken apart from its context, this is a doubly ambiguous expression: the term "faith" (πίστις) can mean "faithfulness, reliability" or "trust, confidence," and the genitive construction could mean either that Jesus Christ "believed" or "was faithful" (taking "Jesus Christ" as a subjective genitive) or that some unnamed person or people put their trust in Jesus Christ (taking "Jesus Christ" as an objective genitive).[10] Traditionally, interpreters have taken the construction as an objective genitive, that is, as a reference to the trust that human beings put in Jesus Christ in order to benefit from the righteousness of God.[11] Some interpreters, however, have understood this construction as a subjective genitive and so as a reference to the "faithfulness" or "reliability" of Jesus Christ. From a lexical and grammatical perspective, the phrase could easily carry either meaning.[12]

Taking the phrase as a subjective genitive allows the reader to see Christ's faithfulness as the solution to Israel's unfaithfulness (3:2–3).[13] It would also avoid the redundancy of speaking of God's righteousness coming "through faith in Christ to all who believe [in Christ]."[14] According to some interpreters, moreover, it is more intelligible to speak of Jesus Christ's faithfulness disclosing the righteousness of God than of human faith somehow disclosing the righteousness of God (cf. 3:21).[15]

This understanding of the phrase is, however, unlikely to be correct. As interpreters on both sides of the debate agree, Paul's language in 3:22 intentionally echoes 1:17 ("For the righteousness of God is revealed in [the gospel] from faith to faith, just as it is written, 'But the one who is righteous by faith will live'").[16] In 1:17 Paul took the phrase "by faith" in the quotation from Habakkuk 2:4 with the subject "the one who is righteous" and not with the verb "will live." This is confirmed by Paul's use of the expression "by faith" elsewhere to qualify "righteousness" language rather than "life" language: people are justified by faith (Rom 3:26, 30; 5:1; Gal 2:16; 3:8, 24), or await righteousness

9. BDAG 213, s.v. δέ 2.

10. BDAG 818–20, s.v. πίστις.

11. Although a few early interpreters took the phrase as a subjective genitive, most understood it as an objective genitive. The KJV's rendering ("faith of Jesus Christ") was probably intended as an objective genitive (cf. its rendering of Col 2:12; 2 Thess 2:13). See Hultgren, *Romans*, 654–55.

12. For the objective genitive, see, e.g., Mark 11:22; Acts 3:16; Col 2:12; 2 Thess 2:13. For the subjective genitive, see, e.g., Rom 1:5, 12; 3:3; 1 Cor 2:5; Phlm 6.

13. Wright, "Romans," 470; Longenecker, *Romans*, 412.

14. See, e.g., Campbell, *Rhetoric of Righteousness*, 62–63.

15. Campbell, *Rhetoric of Righteousness*, 63–64; idem, "The Faithfulness of Jesus Christ in Romans 3:22," in Bird and Sprinkle, *Faith of Jesus Christ*, 67–69. See also Preston M. Sprinkle, "Ἰησοῦ Χριστοῦ as an Eschatological Event," in Bird and Sprinkle, *Faith of Jesus Christ*, 166.

16. Campbell, "Faithfulness of Jesus Christ in Romans 3:22," 60; Watson, "By Faith (of Christ)," in Bird and Sprinkle, *Faith of Jesus Christ*, 153, 160–61.

by faith (Gal 5:5), or attain righteousness by faith (Rom 9:30; cf. 10:6), but they never "live" or have "life" by faith.[17] Although some interpreters have tried to argue that "the one who is righteous" in Habakkuk 2:4 is "the Righteous One," or Jesus himself, this is unlikely.[18] Not only is there no evidence that anyone in antiquity interpreted Habakkuk 2:4 as a reference to the Messiah but Paul's meaning would have to be that Jesus somehow made himself righteous by his own faithfulness, a thought that Paul never develops in Romans or anywhere else.[19] This means that "the one who is righteous by faith" in Romans 1:17 is the believer who experiences God's saving power, and this, in turn, means that in Romans 3:22 the phrase "the righteousness of God which is by faith of Jesus Christ" (KJV) refers to "the righteousness of God that comes to those who rely on Jesus Christ."

The second prepositional phrase that further defines "the righteousness of God" is the statement "to all who believe" (εἰς πάντας τοὺς πιστεύοντας). This is not merely a redundancy, as if Paul had written, "the righteousness of God comes through faith to those who have faith." Instead, Paul included "all" in the phrase, demonstrating his intention to emphasize the universal nature of the righteousness that comes by faith.[20] Righteousness by faith is available to "all" precisely because it is by faith and is not restricted to those who possess the Mosaic law (cf. 3:28–29).

3:22d–23b For there is no distinction, for all have sinned and lack the glory of God (οὐ γάρ ἐστιν διαστολή, πάντες γὰρ ἥμαρτον καὶ ὑστεροῦνται τῆς δόξης τοῦ θεοῦ). God's saving power and status of acquittal comes to anyone who believes because God, as a fair God, does not distinguish between social groups in administering his saving power. Everyone, without distinction, needs God's righteousness because everyone, without distinction, has sinned and experienced the corrupting effects of sin.

The first instance of the conjunction "for" (γάρ) introduces the reason why God's saving power and verdict of acquittal are available to "all." As Paul has shown in 2:1–29 and confirmed from Scripture in 3:9–20, God is an impartial judge who, in his eschatological judgment, makes no "distinction" (διαστολή) between Jew and Greek (cf. 10:12). The second instance of "for" (γάρ) introduces the reason why God makes no such distinction. As 1:18–3:20 has shown, all are sinners.

Paul adds to this the thought that all "lack" (ὑστεροῦνται) the glory of God." "Glory" (δόξα) for Paul was associated with incorruptibility and eternal life. It was the state in which Jesus and God the Father existed (1 Cor 2:8; Eph 1:17), and the destiny toward which believers were moving (Rom 5:2; 8:18, 21; 9:23; 2 Cor 4:17; Col 1:27; 3:4; 1 Thess 2:12; 2 Thess 2:14). Even now God was transforming believers from one degree of glory to another (2 Cor 3:18), and one day their bodies would be like Jesus's glorious, resurrected body (1 Cor 15:43; Phil 3:21). Here, in Romans 3:23, Paul implies that sin is the reason human beings do not naturally exist in this glorious condition in the present. It is, as Godet says, their "normal state," but because of sin they lack it.[21]

3:24 and are justified freely, by his grace, through the deliverance that is in Christ Jesus (δικαιούμενοι δωρεὰν τῇ αὐτοῦ χάριτι διὰ τῆς ἀπολυτρώσεως τῆς ἐν Χριστῷ Ἰησοῦ). God acquits believers and delivers them from the outpouring of

17. Watson, "By Faith (of Christ)," 159–62; Hultgren, *Romans*, 77n145, 652.

18. E.g., Campbell, "Faithfulness of Jesus Christ in Romans 3:22," 64–66.

19. On the lack of evidence for a messianic reading of Hab 2:4, see Watson, "By Faith (of Christ)," 155–59.

20. Hultgren, *Romans*, 155, 640.

21. Godet, *Romans*, 148.

his eschatological wrath apart from any "payment" in the form of their compliance with the law's commands. He follows this extraordinary principle because of the rescue operation he launched on behalf of believers through the work of Christ.

It is difficult to know how the participle translated here "are justified" (δικαιούμενοι) is connected to the rest of the long sentence that stretches from 3:21 to 3:26. It is in the nominative case and therefore at first seems to be subordinate to the expression "all have sinned and lack." This way of taking the participle, however, does not fit Paul's argument. In this context a claim that "all have sinned and lack the glory of God *since* they are justified freely by his grace" would border on the nonsensical. It is more likely that we should coordinate the participle with the two indicative verbs in the phrase "sinned and lack" (ἥμαρτον καὶ ὑστεροῦνται). We should understand it simply as a continuation of Paul's explanation for why there is no difference in the way God deals with human beings in his eschatological judgment of them. Paul frequently used nominative participles in this way to continue a sentence (cf., e.g., Rom 12:9–13; 2 Cor 8:18–19; Eph 1:18; 5:21; and 6:18).[22] The thought that all have sinned and lack God's glory, therefore, stands coordinate to the thought that all are justified in the same way, without taking social distinctions into account.

The qualifying phrase "freely, by his grace" (δωρεὰν τῇ αὐτοῦ χάριτι) emphasizes that when God declares believers righteous he does not do so as a response to any metaphorical payment they might give him. The adverb "freely" is a financial term meaning "without payment of money" (Exod 21:11 LXX; cf. Gen 29:15; 2 Cor 11:7; 2 Thess 3:8), and the metaphorical money to which it refers here is "the works of the law" in 3:20.[23] Since God will declare no one righteous because they have done the law's commandments, his declaration of righteousness must be free or without any contribution from them. The addition of the phrase "by his grace" emphasizes the generosity of God's acquittal of believers. He does not acquit them grudgingly but with unreserved generosity.

Paul describes the means by which this acquittal comes as "deliverance in Christ Jesus" (ἡ ἀπολύτρωσις ἡ ἐν Χριστῷ Ἰησοῦ). The term "deliverance" (ἀπολύτρωσις) is not common in ancient Greek, but where it does occur refers to the rescue of captives or the liberation of slaves (Let. Aris. 12, 33; Philo, *Good Person* 114), and the means of rescue or liberation is sometimes the payment of a ransom (Josephus, *Ant.* 12.27; Diodorus Siculus, *Bibliotheca historica* 37.5.3; Plutarch, *Pomp.* 24.4).[24] Origen, a native speaker of the language, defined the term as "that which is given to enemies for those whom they are keeping in captivity, in order that they might restore them to their original freedom."[25] Greek speakers could also use the term, however, without the financial connotations simply to mean deliverance from some difficult condition (Dan 4:34 LXX; Philo, *Prelim. Studies* 109; Luke 21:28; Rom 8:23; Eph 1:7, 14; 4:30; Heb 11:35). It is not surprising, then, that the verbal form of the word without the prefixed preposition (λυτρόω) frequently appears in the ancient Greek renderings of the Hebrew Scriptures to refer to God's rescue of his people from slavery in Egypt (e.g., Exod 6:6; Deut 13:6; 15:15; 21:8; 24:18).

Interpreters do not agree over how many of these possible connotations are relevant to Paul's

22. So Campbell (*The Rhetoric of Righteousness*, 91 [citing BDF §468]), and most translations.

23. On the financial connotations of the term translated "freely," see MM 174 and BDAG 266, s.v. δωρεάν 1.

24. Cf. the use of the verb (ἀπολυτρόω) in Exod 21:8 LXX and Plutarch, *Pomp.* 24.6 to mean "release for payment of ransom."

25. Origen, *Romans, Books 1–5*, 215. This is the precise sense in which Plutarch seems to use the term in *Pomp.* 24.4.

use of the word here. Did he mean to emphasize that the death of Christ, to which he refers in the next clause, was God's "redemption" (e.g., Tyndale, KJV, NRSV, ESV, NIV) or "ransom" (CEB) of believers, the price God paid for their justification?[26] Did he intend to compare God's redemption of believers through the death of Christ with the redemption of Israel from slavery in Egypt?[27] Paul's use of the financial term "freely" (δωρεάν) in this verse and his references elsewhere to the metaphorical purchase of believers (1 Cor 6:20; 7:23) make it hard to deny that he was thinking here of the death of Christ as the price of deliverance (cf. Matt 20:28; Mark 10:45; 1 Pet 1:18–19).[28] Similarly, the important place of the exodus narrative in Paul's theology elsewhere suggests that he could have had that narrative in mind here too (cf. 1 Cor 5:7; 10:1–11; 2 Cor 3:7–13). Still, Paul says nothing explicit about either of these concepts here, and the text makes good sense without resorting to them.[29]

Paul's other use of the term in Romans (8:23) refers to eschatological deliverance from metaphorical slavery (8:15, 23), but there is no mention of the payment of a price. Since neither slavery nor a price appears here, it seems most reasonable to understand the term simply in terms of deliverance.[30]

Paul's primary focus in this text is on the undeserved and completely gracious nature of God's deliverance of believers from their sin. He has just described at length the depth of the human plight (1:18–3:20) and the impeccable fairness with which God acts when he pours out his wrath on rebellious humanity (1:18; 2:5, 8; 3:5; cf. Eph 4:30; 1 Thess 1:10). In light of this situation Paul wants his readers to appreciate that God's free justification of believers was a remarkable act of generosity. With no contribution on their part, God delivered them from his justified wrath. Precisely how he accomplished this act of free deliverance "in Christ Jesus" is the subject of the relative clause that comes next.

3:25a–d whom God displayed publicly as the mercy seat, through faith, by his blood (ὃν προέθετο ὁ θεὸς ἱλαστήριον διὰ πίστεως ἐν τῷ αὐτοῦ αἵματι). God's rescue operation on behalf of believers entailed the death of Christ Jesus as the ultimate and final sacrifice for sin. For everyone who has faith in what God has done through it, Christ's sacrificial death terminates the justified wrath of God against sin. His death, therefore, is the place of reconciliation between God and human beings.

The term "displayed publicly" (προέθετο) could also mean "intended," a meaning that it carries in its only other uses in the Pauline corpus, one of them in Romans (1:13; cf. Eph 1:9). In a context that explains how God's righteousness "is disclosed" (πεφανέρωται; Rom 3:21) in the death of Christ Jesus, however, the term probably carries its common meaning of setting something forth or displaying something publicly. It could sometimes refer to displaying the remains of the dead (e.g., Plato, *Phaed.* 115e; Thucydides, *History of the Peloponnesian War* 2.34.2; Appian, *Bell. civ.* 3.26).[31]

26. See, e.g., Origen, *Romans, Books 1–5*, 215–16; Godet, *Romans*, 149; Lagrange, *Romains*, 74; Moo, *Romans*, 229–30; Schreiner, *Romans*, 190–91.

27. See, e.g., Dunn, *Romans 1–8*, 169; Schreiner, *Romans*, 189; Wright, "Romans," 471.

28. *Pace* Campbell, *Rhetoric of Righteousness*, 119–30.

29. Cf. Hermann Martin Friedrich Büchsel, "λύω, κτλ.," *TDNT* 4:355; Cranfield, *Romans*, 1:207.

30. As Campbell argues with particular force (*Rhetoric of Righteousness*, 126–27).

31. For the meaning "intended," see, e.g., Origen, *Romans, Books 1–5*, 216–217; Chrysostom, *Romans*, 93–94; Godet, *Romans*, 150–151; Cranfield, *Romans*, 1:208–210, and, among translations, the REB. For "publically displayed," or its equivalent, see, e.g., Sanday and Headlam (*Romans*, 87) and most translations (e.g., KJV, NASB, NAB, NIV, ESV, NRSV). Campbell, *Rhetoric of Righteousness*, 134–37, thinks the term carries both meanings, "a genuine instance of polysemy."

God displayed Christ Jesus as the "mercy seat" (ἱλαστήριον). Translators have often rendered this term "propitiation" (KJV, NASB, ESV, HCSB), a translation that emphasizes the role the death of Christ plays in the removal of God's justified wrath against human sin. They have also sometimes translated it "expiation" (RSV, NAB, REB) or "sacrifice of atonement" (NIV). This second set of translations leaves open the question of precisely how Christ's death dealt with human sin and whether its primary function was rescue from God's wrath.

It seems reasonably clear that, whatever the correct translation of this difficult word, Paul intended it to describe the means God used to answer the problem of his own wrath against human sin as Paul has so fully described it in 1:18–3:20. As the "In Depth" comments on this term explain, however, it is best to understand it as a metaphorical reference to the rectangular golden lid on the ark of the covenant, commonly called "the mercy seat" (Exod 25:17–22; 31:7; 35:12; 37:6–9; Lev 16:2, 13–15; Num 7:89; Heb 9:5; cf. Luther, Tyndale, NET).[32] This was the place where God met with Moses and Aaron, the representatives and intermediaries of his people Israel. It was also the place where God offered reconciliation to his people through the sacrificial blood sprinkled there on the Day of Atonement.

The next two prepositional phrases communicate the means by which Christ Jesus became the metaphorical mercy seat and therefore the place of reconciliation between God and human beings. The first phrase "through faith" (διὰ [τῆς] πίστεως) describes the human response to the righteousness of God displayed in the atoning death of Christ that is necessary for God's reconciling work to become effective. This response is simply trust that God has taken the initiative in Christ's death to reconcile himself to sinners. Paul will later describe this response as "receiv[ing] the abundance of grace and the gift of righteousness" (5:17).

The second phrase, "by his blood" (ἐν τῷ αὐτοῦ αἵματι) does not refer to the object of faith ("through faith in his blood," HCSB; cf. Luther, Tyndale, KJV). When the object of faith is clear in Paul's letters, it is always God (4:3, 17, 24; 9:33; 10:11; Gal 3:6, 22; 1 Thess 1:8; Titus 3:8), Christ (3:26; Gal 2:16; Phil 3:9; 1 Tim 1:16), God's word (Rom 10:16), God's power (1 Cor 2:5; Col 2:12), or a conviction (Rom 10:9; 14:2; 1 Cor 11:18; 1 Thess 4:14; 2 Tim 1:12) or testimony (2 Thess 1:10; 2:11; 2:12–13) about something, not a material object such as blood, even when used metaphorically. Paul, then, uses the term "blood" to refer to Christ's death and to communicate that the crucified Christ is "the mercy seat" and therefore the place of atonement (e.g., RSV, NAB, NRSV, ESV, NIV, NET).

The mention of blood in the context of the mercy seat recalls the Day of Atonement sacrifices of the bull and the goat whose blood Aaron sprinkled on the mercy seat (Lev 16:14–15). Just as God met Moses and the high priest "above" or "over" the mercy seat (Exod 25:22; Lev 16:2; Num 7:89), so Paul says that God meets every believer and becomes reconciled to him or her in the death of Christ. The death of Christ is the place, then, where access to the presence of God is open to all who have faith and where God has saved them from his wrath by reconciling them to himself (5:2, 10).

32. Daniel P. Bailey, "Jesus as the Mercy Seat: The Semantics and Theology of Paul's Use of *Hilasterion* in Romans 3:25" (PhD diss., University of Cambridge, 1999), chs. 1, 2, 3, and 5; idem, "Jesus as the Mercy Seat: The Semantics and Theology of Paul's Use of *Hilasterion* in Romans 3:25," *TynBul* 51 (2000): 155–58. References to Dr. Bailey's work are to the dissertation, cited by chapter and section numbers. Many thanks to Dr. Bailey for making his dissertation available to me.

IN DEPTH: Jesus as the Biblical "Mercy Seat" (ἱλαστήριον)

The Greek term that stands behind the translation "mercy seat" in 3:25 (ἱλαστήριον) is formed from two common elements: a stem that refers to appeasement or conciliation (ἱλασ-) and a suffix that refers to the location where something happens or the instrument by which something is accomplished (-τήριον).[33] A place where "work" (ἔργον) is done, for example, is a "workplace" (ἐργαστήριον), an instrument for "charming someone with magic" (θέλγω) is a "magical charm" (θελκτήριον), and a golden votive statue of the goddess "Victory" is "a thank-you gift" (χαριστήριον).[34] The basic meaning of Paul's term (ἱλαστήριον), therefore, is either the place where, or the instrument through which, forgiveness, atonement, or propitiation happens.

Daniel P. Bailey has shown, moreover, that in the extant evidence the term in itself never refers to an idea, such as propitiation, expiation, or atonement, nor does it refer directly to a sacrificial animal. Instead, it refers to the inanimate objects used as votive offerings in Greco-Roman religious contexts, or it refers in Hellenistic-Jewish literature to "the mercy seat," the golden lid on the ark of the covenant in the biblical temple.[35] A votive offering was always made of durable materials, such as a stele (IKosPH 81), a column (IKosPH 347), the Trojan horse (Dio Chrysostom, *Trojan Discourse* [*Or. 11*] 121), or a marble monument (Josephus, *Ant.* 16.182). It was never a slaughtered animal.[36]

Even in 4 Maccabees 17:22, where the author uses the term to describe the death of the Macabbean martyrs, he probably did not mean to say that their death was a "propitiation" or "sacrifice of atonement." Rather, he meant that their death was a metaphorical "propitiatory votive offering," to use Bailey's words, a perpetual memorial of their devotion to God.[37] The term could be used as an adjective to describe "propitiatory sacrifices to the gods" (τοῖς θεοῖς εἱλαστη[ρίο]υς θυσίας, P.Fay. 337, I, 3–5), but Paul would probably have actually written out the noun "sacrifice" (θυσία) if he had intended that meaning, and in the unlikely event that he expected his readers to supply the noun mentally,

33. On the meaning of the root, see the various entries under this root in LSJ 828. On the point made here, see Zahn (*An die Römer*, 186) and Alexander Weiss ("Christus Jesus als Weihegeschenk oder Sühnemal? Anmerkungen zu einer neueren Deutung von *hilasterion* [Röm 3,25] samt einer Liste der epigraphischen Belege," *ZNW* 105 [2014]: 294).

34. For the Nike statue, see Weiss, "Christus Jesus als Weihegeschenk oder Sühnemal?," 299.

35. "Jesus as the Mercy Seat," chs. 1, 2, 3, and 5. Cf. Lagrange, *Romains*, 75–76. For this use of the term, see, in addition to the LXX rendering of the biblical texts mentioned above, Heb 9:5 and Philo, *Cherubim* 25; *Heir* 166; *Flight* 100, 101; *Moses* 2.95, 97.

36. Bailey, "Jesus as the Mercy Seat," ch. 1§3.2 and chs. 2 and 3. The translation of the term in Josephus, *Ant.* 16.182 is disputed and could be taken as an adjective rather than a noun, but it is probably a noun. On this, see Bailey, "Jesus as the Mercy Seat," ch. 3§5.

37. Bailey, "Jesus as the Mercy Seat," ch. 5.

he would have used the feminine form of "propitiatory" (ἱλαστήρια), not the neuter form (ἱλαστήριον).[38]

It is likely, then, that when Paul used the term, he intended to compare Jesus, at the time of his death, to "the mercy seat." [39] This was the place where God met with Moses, his people's representative, and communicated to him the commandments he wanted to give to Israel (Exod 25:22; cf. Num 7:89). It was the place where God appeared on the Day of Atonement as Aaron, another representative of God's people, sacrificed two goats "for a sin offering" (περὶ ἁμαρτίας, Lev 16:5). He sprinkled the blood of one goat on the mercy seat and sent the other goat alive into the wilderness (Lev 16:2, 13–15) "that atonement may be made for the people of Israel . . . because of all their sins" (Lev 16:34). Like the mercy seat, Jesus was the "place" where God revealed himself to his people. Because his death was a "sin offering" (περὶ ἁμαρτίας, Rom 8:3), he was also "the place" where God reconciled himself to his people.

Would Paul's mainly non-Jewish audience in Rome have caught such an allusion from his use of this one word, a word that, after all, was reasonably common in their own culture and, in that culture, had the very different meaning of "a votive offering to the gods"? It is likely that they did catch the biblical allusion. Paul's argument up to this point has depended heavily on Israel's Scripture (1:3, 17; 2:6, 24; 3:4, 10–18), and he has just asserted that "the law and the prophets" testify to the righteousness of God as it is revealed in the death of Christ (3:21).[40] Moreover, as the introduction to the commentary tried to show, it is likely that Paul's gentile audience was quite familiar with Judaism and its sacred traditions since Judaism flourished in first-century Rome and Christianity had probably come to the city through Jewish Christians.

Even for those Roman readers who did not understand the allusion, however, the meaning of the text would have been reasonably clear. They could have understood Paul to be saying that God publicly set forth Christ Jesus as "an instrument of appeasement" by which God's wrath against sin (1:18; 2:5, 8; 3:5) was removed.[41] Josephus used the term this way when he referred to the expensive "propitiatory votive offering" (ἱλαστήριον) in the form of "a white marble monument" (μνῆμα) that Herod erected at the tomb of David in Jerusalem.[42] Herod had robbed the tomb, and he hoped his monument would ap-

38. Ibid., ch. 2§3.1–2.

39. Many commentators down through the centuries have taken the term this way. See, e.g., Origen, *Romans, Books 1–5*, 217–18; Theodoret of Cyrus, *Letters of St. Paul*, 1:64; Moo, *Romans*, 236; Hultgren, *Romans*, 157, 662–75; Schnabel, *An die Römer: Kapitel 1–5*, 397.

40. Bailey, "Jesus as the Mercy Seat," 4§3.3. Cf. Hultgren, *Romans*, 671; Campbell, *Rhetoric of Righteousness*, 131.

41. Cf. Weiss, "Christus Jesus als Weihegeschenk oder Sühnemal?," 298–302.

42. I have used the translation of Bailey, "Jesus as the Mercy Seat," 3§5.3.

pease the wrath of whatever deity (or deities) he had angered (*Ant.* 16.182). Dio Chrysostom, similarly, described the "votive offering" (ἀνάθημα) of the "most beautiful and large" Trojan horse as the Greeks' "propitiatory gift" (ἱλαστήριον) offered to Athena as the necessary "satisfaction" or "penalty" (δίκη) for their aggression against Troy (*Trojan Discourse* 121).[43]

There is probably even some precedent for seeing a person as an instrument of reconciliation in an important inscription found on an altar in Metropolis (just north of Ephesus) dating from the late first-century BC. On the front of the altar is the prominent inscription, "Of Caesar, instrument of reconciliation" (ΚΑΙΣΑΡΟΣ ΕΙΛΑΣΤΗΡΙΟΥ). Caesar here is Caesar Augustus, and the reconciliation that the altar refers to is the peace he brought to the region.[44]

Whether Paul's Roman audience picked up his allusion to the biblical "mercy seat" or not, therefore, they would have understood him to say that God had put Christ forward, or intended him to be, the instrument through which God reconciled his people to himself and solved the problem of his justified wrath against the rebellion of his people. Without the interpretive context of Leviticus 16, Paul's reference to Christ's blood may have seemed odd, but his basic point would have remained intact.

3:25e–26a for a proof of his righteousness, on account of the dismissal of sins previously committed because of the forbearance of God (εἰς ἔνδειξιν τῆς δικαιοσύνης αὐτοῦ διὰ τὴν πάρεσιν τῶν προγεγονότων ἁμαρτημάτων ἐν τῇ ἀνοχῇ τοῦ θεοῦ). God intended Christ's death to prove that, although he had kindly dismissed the sins of his people prior to the death of Christ, he had not ceased to be committed to the impartial and fair administration of justice.

The phrase "for a proof of his righteousness" (εἰς ἔνδειξιν τῆς δικαιοσύνης αὐτοῦ) explains why God publicly displayed Christ's death as the place of atonement for sin. "Proof" (ἔνδειξις) could also be translated "display, showing" and could refer to the "display" of God's righteousness in the sense of his "power for the salvation of everyone who believes" (1:16; cf. 1:17).[45] Plutarch uses the term this way to speak of Pericles making a policy decision "for the display of his power" (πρὸς ἔνδειξιν ἰσχύος; *Pericles* 31.1 [Bernadotte Perrin, LCL]), and in language that is closer to Paul's idiom Philo used the word to speak of God ordering creation "for the more visible demonstration of the might of his rule" (εἰς ἔνδειξιν ἐναργεστάτην κράτους ἀρχῆς, *Creation* 45, my transl.; cf. *Moses* 1.96). Philo could use the same expression, however, to speak of proving an argument (*Creation* 87), demonstrating a truth

43. I have followed the translation of Bailey, "Jesus as the Mercy Seat," 3§4.3.2 and of LSJ 430, s.v. δίκη IV.3.

44. See Boris Dreyer and Helmut Engelmann, "Augustus und Germanicus im ionischen Metropolis," *ZPE* 158 (2006): 174. Many thanks to Mark Wilson for bringing this inscription to my attention in his presentation, "*Hilasterion* and Imperial Rhetoric: A Possible New Reading of Romans 3:25," at the Annual Meeting of the Evangelical Theological Society on November 19, 2015.

45. W. G. Kümmel, "Πάρεσις and Ἔνδειξις: A Contribution to the Understanding of the Pauline Doctrine of Justification," *JTC* 3 (1967): 4–5.

(*Confusion* 173; *Heir* 200; *Spec. Laws* 1.286; cf. Phil 1:28), or showing one's good faith in the prosecution of a court case (*Spec. Laws* 3.55; cf. 2 Cor 8:24). Paul's next phrase makes it likely that he had this more legal sense in mind here.[46]

The next phrase, "on account of the dismissal of sins previously committed" (διὰ τὴν πάρεσιν τῶν προγεγονότων ἁμαρτημάτων) tells why God needed to prove his righteousness. Like "proof," the term "dismissal" (πάρεσις) sometimes appears in legal contexts to speak of the dismissal of charges against someone to avoid a trial (Dionysius of Halicarnassus, *Ant. rom.* 7.37.2).[47] Paul is concerned with God's justice in "dismissing" the sins of those who have disobeyed his law prior to the coming of the gospel. If God is an impartial, just judge as 1:18–3:20 has maintained, how could he come in Christ, not with judgment, wrath, and condemnation (as, for example, the Messiah does in Pss. Sol. 17:21–25) but in humility and offering reconciliation with himself? Paul sees the atoning death of Christ as the means by which God preserved his commitment both to impartial justice and to lavish mercy.

This understanding of the terms "proof" and "dismissal" entails taking Paul's reference to God's "righteousness" here in a more narrow way than in 3:21–22 where the phrase is polyvalent. Here Paul focuses on the fairness, impartiality, and justice of God, a focus that began when he used righteousness language in 3:24 to speak of God "justifying" sinners "freely" (δικαιούμενοι δωρεάν) and that became especially clear in 3:26 where he says that God proved his righteousness by publicly displaying Christ Jesus as the mercy seat "in order that he might be just" (δίκαιον).[48]

The "sins previously committed" (τῶν προγεγονότων ἁμαρτημάτων), then, are the sins committed before the death of Christ. Although God punished sinners during this period, he also justified ungodly people such as Abraham (4:5) and forgave wicked people such as David (4:7).

God dismissed these sins, Paul says, "because of" (ἐν) his "forbearance" (τῇ ἀνοχῇ). Paul uses the preposition at the beginning of this phrase in a causal sense, a slightly unusual usage, but not unprecedented in his letters (8:3; 1 Cor 4:4).[49] Just as God's "forbearance" (ἀνοχή) gave people time and opportunity to repent of their sins prior to the day of "wrath" (2:4–5), so God's forbearance led him to provide the means by which he could set aside sins and yet preserve his commitment to justice.

3:26b–e for the proof of his righteousness in the present time, in order that he might be just even while justifying the one who has faith in Jesus (πρὸς τὴν ἔνδειξιν τῆς δικαιοσύνης αὐτοῦ ἐν τῷ νῦν καιρῷ, εἰς τὸ εἶναι αὐτὸν δίκαιον καὶ δικαιοῦντα τὸν ἐκ πίστεως Ἰησοῦ). Christ's death was the critical moment in history when God proved himself to be just despite his willingness to release from punishment the sinner who trusts Jesus.

The phrase "for proof of his righteousness" (πρὸς τὴν ἔνδειξιν τῆς δικαιοσύνης αὐτοῦ), like its

46. *Pace* Kümmel ("Πάρεσις and Ἔνδειξις," 1–13), who seems to have missed the interpretive significance of the constellation of legal terms in 3:21–26.

47. The term is rare and can also refer to permitting someone to escape punishment (Plutarch, *Dion* 2.2), to "mercies" or "kindnesses" from God (πάρεσιν . . . ἐκ τοῦ θεοῦ; Dio Chrysostom, *Charidemus* [*Or. 30*] 19), or to "neglect" (Appian, *Concerning the Kings*, fragment 13). Even these instances, however, occur in governmental, judicial, or legal contexts. See LSJ 1337; BDAG 776, both s.v. πάρεσις; Ribbens, "Forensic-Retributive Justification," 561–63; and especially the careful analysis (*pace* Kümmel, "Πάρεσις and Ἔνδειξις," 3–4) of J. M. Creed, "ΠΑΡΕΣΙΣ in Dionysius of Halicarnassus and in St. Paul," *JTS* 41 (1940): 28–30.

48. Cf., e.g., Fitzmyer, *Romans*, 353; Schreiner, *Romans*, 197. *Pace* Kümmel, "Πάρεσις and ἔνδειξις," 8.

49. For this usage, see BDAG 329, s.v. ἐν 9.

nearly identical twin in 3:25, modifies the verb "displayed publicly" and repeats the reason why God "displayed" Jesus "publicly" as the mercy seat. This repetition shows how important Paul considered the preservation of God's fairness and impartiality even as he described God's grace in dismissing the offenses of human beings against the law's just requirements.

The phrase "in the present time" (ἐν τῷ νῦν καιρῷ) also repeats for emphasis a thought implicit in the phrase "sins previously committed" in 3:25. The atoning death of Christ is the climactic moment (καιρός) in salvation history, the hinge on which God's saving purposes for his people turns.[50] Sins committed beforehand may have been symbolically forgiven through the annual repetition of the Day of Atonement ritual, but Jesus's death is the reality to which that ritual pointed and the reality which obviates the need for any further sacrifice for sin.

The term "even" (καί) in the final clause appears in most translations as "and," but it is better to take it in an "intensive" sense and to render the participle temporally. God publicly displayed Jesus as the mercy seat to prove that he was "just *even while justifying* the one who has faith in Jesus" (δίκαιον καὶ δικαιοῦντα τὸν ἐκ πίστεως Ἰησοῦ).[51]

3:27 Where, then, is boasting? It has been shut out. Through what law? That of works? No, but through the law of faith (Ποῦ οὖν ἡ καύχησις; ἐξεκλείσθη. διὰ ποίου νόμου; τῶν ἔργων; οὐχί, ἀλλὰ διὰ νόμου πίστεως). Because human deliverance from sin and divine wrath is a matter of trust in God and his free gift of atonement in the death of Christ, no room is left for human boasting. Pride in one's social group and pride in one's obedience to the Mosaic law are both completely incompatible with God's demand for faith.

Paul now picks up again the fictional dialogue he had dropped in 3:9. His dialogue partner had been a Jew who had boasted in both possessing and obeying the Mosaic law (2:17, 23). He believed that his Jewish identity, defined by his possession of the law and his obedience to the law, would exempt him from God's judgment on the final day. In answer to this, Paul had emphasized both God's righteous impartiality (2:12–29) and the human inability, across the board, of escaping the law's indictment of sinners (3:9–18). "Works of the law" were a dead end as a path to justification (3:20). Paul has now described God's gracious solution to this problem (3:21–26) and is ready to draw an important conclusion from it that implies the unity of all humanity before God, whether Jew or gentile (cf. 1:16; 3:22). The gospel has excluded "boasting" (καύχησις) either in possessing the Mosaic law or in doing it.[52] Boasting is excluded not only by the common plight of humanity in its inability to keep God's law (3:10–20) but also by God's completely gracious solution to that plight in the atoning death of Christ.

The term "shut out" (ἐκκλείω) literally referred to shutting someone outside, as when Josephus recounts how the residents of Japha in Galilee locked the city gates against their own soldiers to prevent the Roman army, which was chasing them, from entering the city (Josephus, *J.W.* 3.293). Ancient Greek speakers could also use the term with a mixture of literal and figurative meanings, as when, according to Herodotus, the Dorians kept anyone among their own people who had broken their temple laws from entering their temple, an action that

50. For the use of καιρός with this nuance, see Dunn, *Romans 1–8*, 174–75 and BDAG 498, s.v. καιρός 3.

51. See Cranfield, *Romans*, 1:213, and cf. BDAG 495–96, s.v. καί 2 b.

52. Gathercole, *Where Is Boasting?*, 225–26.

also meant they were "excluded" from participating in temple ritual (*Histories* 1.144.1; cf. Plutarch, *Per.* 19.1–2). The only use of the term in the Greek Bible other than Romans 3:27 is in Galatians 4:17 where this mixture of literal and figurative meanings is also present: the Judaizers were probably excluding the Galatian Christians from table fellowship with them (cf. Gal 2:12), but this action was bound up with their conviction that the Galatian Christians were excluded from the people of God unless they conformed to the Mosaic law (cf. Gal 2:11–14). All of this means that here, the term was probably a live metaphor for Paul and was therefore emphatic. Human boasting is locked out—utterly out of the question—because of the display of God's grace in the atoning death of Christ.[53]

The term "what" (ποῖος) might mean "what kind of" (1 Cor 15:35), and the word "law" (νόμος) here might refer to the Mosaic law in both its uses, just as it does in its nine other uses in 3:19–31.[54] If this is correct, then Paul says that when the Mosaic law is viewed from the perspective of faith rather than works it excludes boasting.[55] The conjunction "therefore" (οὖν) at the beginning of the verse, however, makes this interpretation unlikely.[56] Boasting is excluded through the great act of deliverance that Paul has just described in 3:24–26 and to which his "therefore" points, not through the Mosaic law now considered from a new angle. Paul uses "law," then, in two senses in this verse, playing on the word, just as he does in 7:21–25.[57] The "law . . . of works" is the Mosaic law with its requirement of engaging in certain activities in order to receive life (cf. 10:5; Gal 3:10, 12). The "law of faith" is the gospel's requirement of reliance for deliverance from sin on the gracious activity of God who has freely reconciled his people to himself in the atoning death of Christ.[58]

3:28 For we hold that a human being is justified by faith apart from works of the law (λογιζόμεθα γὰρ δικαιοῦσθαι πίστει ἄνθρωπον χωρὶς ἔργων νόμου). God has closed the door on boasting in one's self or one's social group because he justifes those who simply rely on Jesus, not those who rely on their possession or performance of the law.

The conjunction "for" (γάρ) introduces a further explanation of what Paul meant when he distinguished between two "laws," one that does and one that does not exclude boasting. This explanation continues the antithetical nature of that statement but replaces boasting with justification. *Boasting* is excluded by the law of faith and not by the law of works because *justification* takes place by means of faith, and performing the law has nothing to do with it. The term "is justified" (δικαιοῦσθαι) means to be declared right "before God" (cf. 2:13), to receive a positive verdict when he sits in judgment (cf. 3:4; 8:33–34). Because justification comes to a human being freely, by God's grace (3:24) it must be a matter of trust (πίστις) and not of doing what the Mosaic law requires (ἔργα νόμου). Because God has fulfilled the requirement necessary for human justification before him and done this freely and graciously, all human boasting in doing what the Mosaic law requires is without foundation. Paul considered this approach to justification to be

53. For the translation "locked out," see Fitzmyer, *Romans*, 362–63.

54. A. Andrew Das, *Paul, the Law, and the Covenant* (Peabody, MA: Hendrickson, 2001), 193–94.

55. See, e.g., Cranfield, *Romans*, 1:220; Dunn, *Romans 1–8*, 185–86; Schreiner, *Romans*, 202.

56. Cf. Westerholm, *Perspectives Old and New on Paul*, 324.

57. So Chrysostom (*Romans*, 96), who was thoroughly familiar with ancient Greek rhetorical devices. See also Heikki Räisänen, *Jesus, Paul and Torah*, JSNTSup 43 (Sheffield: Sheffield Academic Press, 1992), 69–94; Westerholm, *Perspectives Old and New on Paul*, 322–25; Hultgren, *Romans*, 168–69.

58. Meyer, *Romans*, 142. Cf. Pelagius, *Romans*, 83; Theodoret of Cyrus, *Letters of St. Paul*, 1:65; Brian S. Rosner, *Paul and the Law: Keeping the Commandments of God*, NSBT 31 (Nottingham: Apollos, 2013), 119–20.

a common Christian conviction, and hence he framed it as something that "we hold" (λογιζόμεθα; cf. "we know" in Gal 2:16).[59]

3:29–30 Or is God the God of the Jews only? Is he not also God of the gentiles? Yes, also of the gentiles, since God is one, who will justify the circumcision by faith and the uncircumcision through that same faith (ἢ Ἰουδαίων ὁ θεὸς μόνον; οὐχὶ καὶ ἐθνῶν; ναὶ καὶ ἐθνῶν, εἴπερ εἷς ὁ θεὸς ὃς δικαιώσει περιτομὴν ἐκ πίστεως καὶ ἀκροβυστίαν διὰ τῆς πίστεως). God is not the god of a single ethnic group but the creator and judge of the universe. It makes sense, then, that he would justify the Jews and everyone else in the same way, by faith alone.

The particle "or" (ἤ) often occurs at the beginning of rhetorical questions, particularly when they attempt to refute an ill-considered opinion (cf., e.g., Matt 26:53; Rom 6:3; 7:1; 11:2). The idea Paul tosses aside here is that God is a national god, restricted in his sovereignty to one social group, the Jews. This is what would necessarily be true if justification came to people on the basis of doing the Mosaic law and if boasting in the possession and doing of that law were therefore appropriate. Yet such an idea would be inconsistent with the foundational Jewish conviction that "God is one" (εἷς ὁ θεός; cf. Deut 6:4), that he is, in other words, the creator of the universe and therefore sovereign over all other peoples (Deut 4:35, 39; 2 Kgs 19:15–19; Neh 9:6; Isa 37:16).[60]

Paul has already reminded his fictional Jewish interlocutor in 2:26–29 that the notion of God as merely the God of Israel was not true from the perspective of the Mosaic law itself. There he imagined a gentile who, although uncircumcised in a physical sense, was circumcised in heart and kept "the just requirements of the law." Any Jew who knew Deuteronomy and the prophets would have to admit that this gentile would justly condemn the Jew who possessed Scripture and physical circumcision but transgressed the law (2:26–27; cf. Deut 10:16; 30:6; Jer 4:4; 9:25–26).

Now Paul puts flesh and bones on this idea. Because faith leads to justification and because the physically circumcised as well as the physically uncircumcised can rely on Jesus and be justified, the importance of ethnicity drops away, just as it did in 2:26–29, and God is found to be the righteous judge of the whole world (cf. 3:6). Paul will pursue this concept in much greater detail and show its consistency with Scripture in chapter 4.

The translation "that same" in the final clause represents Paul's "anaphoric" use of the article (τῆς) to point back to the term "faith" in the preceding prepositional phrase and to emphasize that God will justify both circumcised and uncircumcised in exactly the same way.[61] It is unlikely, then, that Paul means anything different by "from faith" (ἐκ πίστεως) than he means by "through faith" (διὰ τῆς πίστεως). This is simply a stylistic variation that places the emphasis on the importance of faith rather than on the precise mechanism by which faith justifies the believer.

3:31 Do we cancel the law through this faith? Certainly not! Rather, we uphold the law (νόμον οὖν καταργοῦμεν διὰ τῆς πίστεως; μὴ γένοιτο, ἀλλὰ νόμον ἱστάνομεν). No one should interpret Paul's argument so far to mean that under the gospel no more room exists for the commandments of the law.

This rhetorical question prevents the reader

59. Cf. Dunn, *Romans 1–8*, 187. For the translation "we hold," see also the RSV, NRSV, and ESV.

60. On the OT concept of God's unity, see, e.g., Jeffrey H. Tigay, *Deuteronomy*, JPS Torah Commentary (Philadelphia: Jewish Publication Society, 1996), 76, and J. A. Thompson, *Deuteronomy*, Tyndale Old Testament Commentaries (Downers Grove, IL: InterVarsity Press, 1974), 109, 121–22.

61. On this use of the article, see Smyth, *Greek Grammar*, 287 (§1120 b).

from drawing a false conclusion about the law on the basis of what Paul has just said. The "law" (νόμος) here is not the Scriptures generally (cf. 3:19, 21), nor is it the Mosaic law understood to teach justification by faith (cf. 4:1–25).[62] The logical link Paul makes with "therefore" (οὖν) to the immediately preceding context (3:27–30) requires that by "law" Paul means the "law . . . of works" in 3:27. This is the only form of the law that Paul's argument could be accused of nullifying, and so only this form of the law is at issue here. "The law of works" is the law that tells people what God wants them to do, whether the Mosaic law in the case of Israel (2:12–14, 25, 27) or an innate understanding of God's requirements in the case of gentiles (1:12; 2:14–15, 26–27). It is, in other words, the law in its commanding role.[63] Paul was concerned that his readers might conclude from the negative comments he has made about this law that the "law of faith" entails the abolition of the law's commandments. Paul has said that Jews sometimes boast inappropriately because they possess the law in written form, and he has said that no one can be justified on the basis of doing the law. It might seem natural to conclude that by limiting the criterion for justification to faith and specifically excluding the performance of the law from any role in justification, his argument has stripped the law's commandments of their authority and idled them, making them irrelevant (καταργέω).[64]

Paul insists, to the contrary, that he upholds the law. The verb "uphold" (ἱστάνω) was used in the first century to refer to supporting tradition (1 Macc 2:27; Mark 7:9), and that is how Paul uses it here with respect to the law's requirements.[65] He does not explain at this point how he can make this claim in light of what he has said about the law so far. He has more to say about the Mosaic law that is relatively negative: that it is temporary (4:13–14), that it brings God's wrath (4:15), and that it has a close relationship with sin (5:13, 20). So this was not the place for a defense of the law's goodness or a discussion of its role in the believer's life (7:1–8:7; 13:8–10; 14:1–23). Paul was concerned about the misrepresentation of his teaching in an antinomian direction, however (3:8; cf. 6:1, 15), and he may have thought it advisable to anticipate his later, positive statements about the law at this early point with a brief denial that he considered the law irrelevant.[66]

Just as in 3:28, the first-person plurals ("we cancel . . . we uphold" [καταργοῦμεν, ἱστάνομεν]) indicate that Paul did not think of his position on the law in either its negative or positive elements to be his own, unique position. His understanding of the Mosaic law, although complex, was something that he shared with others who believed the gospel.

Theology in Application

Three themes dominate 3:21–31. Paul opens and closes the passage with references to the interplay between continuity and discontinuity in the two testaments on the subject of the righteousness of God (3:21, 31). Sandwiched between these two statements Paul twice expresses the implications of the gospel

62. For the first position, see, e.g., Légasse, *Romains*, 271, and Longenecker, *Romans*, 456–57, and for the second position, see, e.g., Meyer, *Romans*, 144–46, and Wilckens, *An die Römer (Röm 1–5)*, 250.

63. Schreiner, *Romans*, 207–8.

64. Cf. Paul's use of this term in 3:3; see BDAG 525–26 and MGS 1075, both s.v. καταργέω.

65. BDAG 482, s.v. ἵστημι A4.

66. Cf. Longenecker, *Romans*, 451.

for the unity of all people groups through faith in Jesus Christ (3:22–24c, 27–30). Right at the center of the passage Paul describes the significance of Christ's death (3:24d–26), the event from which reconciliation with God and humanity flows, and the event that supplies the answer to the theological and social problems Paul had discussed at length in 1:18–3:20. The passage, then, provides a clear, succinct presentation of the gospel and can serve as as a touchstone for how Christians should present the gospel to others.

The Unity of the Testaments on the Theme of God's Righteousness

Paul begins and ends the passage by raising the question of the compatibility of his definition of the righteousness of God with the Jewish Scriptures (3:21, 31). The righteousness of God, he says at the beginning, is revealed apart from the law and the prophets, although both law and prophets attest to it (3:21). At the end of the passage, Paul similarly rejects the notion that he cancels out or annuls the law through his case that the righteousness of God is appropriated by faith rather than by works (3:31).

Paul believed that the gospel contained an element of mystery, that it had aspects no one could have predicted on the basis of the Jewish Scriptures (16:25–26; 2 Cor 3:14; Eph 3:4–6). He also believed, however, that what Christians now call the Old Testament was the inspired, authoritative word of God that continued to be essential for the faith and practice of believers (Rom 4:23–24; 15:4; 1 Cor 10:11; 2 Tim 3:15–16). The gospel of God's righteousness, Paul says in 3:21, appears apart from the law and the prophets—it is new revelation from God—but the law and the prophets attest to it. They display God's righteous character so clearly that they lead the careful reader to expect something like the gospel to arrive and tie up the loose ends of the story. Believers who reason erroneously that because the gospel fulfills the law and the prophets the Old Testament is no longer necessary are left with an understanding of God so impoverished that it is a caricature of who God really is. As Romans 1:18–32 teaches, profound misunderstandings of God lead to horrific consequences for the mistreatment of other human beings.[67]

An example from the modern history of the church in Europe illustrates the point. Adolf von Harnack, one of the most influential German theologians of the early twentieth century, argued in a monograph published in 1921 that the Old Testament should no longer be considered part of the Christian canon. It contained some useful ethical teaching in the Psalms and prophets, but to place the Old Tes-

67. Paul R. House, "God's Character in God's World: God's Justice" (lecture presented at Beeson Divinity School, Birmingham, AL, 17 February 2012).

tament "on a fully equal footing with the New Testament had an unhealthy effect on dogmatics, on piety, and on the practice of the Christian life. In some groups it even produced an Islamic zeal, while in others it called forth a new kind of Judaism and promoted everywhere a legalistic entity." Harnack singled out the Huguenots, the theological descendents of John Calvin in France, as a particular example of a Christian group that took the Old Testament too seriously and so had succumbed to this legalistic and Judaistic spirit.[68]

Only twenty years later, during the harsh winter of 1940–41, a snow-covered, hollow-eyed Jewish woman from Harnack's native Germany knocked on the door of a Huguenot pastor's house in the mountains of Vichy-controlled southern France. She asked the pastor's wife to shelter her from the Nazis. "It was the evening," reported Magda Trocmé, "and she said she was a German Jew, coming from northern France, that she was in danger, and that she had heard that in Le Chambon somebody could help her. Could she come into my house? I said, 'Naturally, come in, and come in.'"[69] This was the first of hundreds of Jewish refugees that she, her husband André, and their church would feed, shelter, educate, and smuggle to safety during the horrific years of Hitler's "final solution" to "the Jewish question." In the end, the few thousand farmers and villagers of this predominantly Huguenot region of France would save from Hitler's death camps a population of Jews roughly equal to their own population.

When asked many years later why they were willing to put themselves in great danger and to share the little they had with the Jews, they often answered that their Bibles taught them to love their neighbors as themselves and to help those in need. They would have done what they did for anyone in need. But they felt a special kinship to these needy Jews. The Jews were the chosen people of God, and they shared with them a large part of their Scriptures.[70]

It is easy to see in hindsight that the theological instincts of these simple people who knew their Bibles well and had learned from their own hardships how important it was to help others were more profound than the rather complex theological and historical judgments of one of Europe's greatest theologians. The lesson should be clear for Christians today who are tempted to neglect the witness of the Old Testament to the character of God. In our personal study, teaching, and preaching of God's word, it is important to spend as much time in the Old Testament as in the New Testament. Focusing only on the New Testament can lead to an unbalanced

68. Adolf von Harnack, *Marcion: Das Evangelium vom Fremden Gott*, TUGAL 45.15 (Leipzig: J. C. Hinrichs, 1921), 252. In English see, idem, *Marcion: The Gospel of the Alien God*, trans. John E. Steely and Lyle D. Bierma (Durham, NC: Labyrinth, 1990), 136.

69. Philip P. Hallie, *Lest Innocent Blood Be Shed: The Story of the Village of Le Chambon and How Goodness Happened There* (New York: Harper & Row, 1979), 120.

70. See the documentary film, *Weapons of the Spirit*, 90 min., Los Angeles: Chambon Foundation, 1989, and, on the whole phenomenon, see Gushee, *Righteous Gentiles of the Holocaust*, 152–59.

understanding of God's character, of the nature of what he is doing in history, and of what he requires from his people.

The Anthropological and Social Implications of God's Free, Gracious Justification of Sinners

Paul also emphasizes the socially unifying nature of God's righteousness. It comes to all who believe without distinction. Since all without distinction have sinned, God in his righteousness has made justification freely available to all without distinction as well (3:22–24c, 27–30). This free, gracious justification of every human being who believes has both anthropological and social implications.

On the anthropological side, it means that no one can boast in his or her "works." Justification is given to those who rely on God to provide release from punishment and reconciliation as a free gift, not to those who work for it by means of obedience to the law. Paul has shown that justification by means of obedience to the law's requirements is impossible, whether the Mosaic law for Jews or the law written on the heart for gentiles (2:15; 3:20, 22).

In practical terms, this means that human beings cannot be in a proper relationship with God if they are trying to manipulate God into giving them eternal life. Membership in a particular social group, whether an ethnic group, a nation, a political party, or a particular religious group, including the visible church, does not convince God to give them eternal life. God is not persuaded to bless people when they take particular theological, social, or political positions. A human being stands in a right relationship with God (is "justified") when he or she relies upon God's promise to reconcile himself to human beings through the death of Christ Jesus. As Paul will explain later and as he hints in his comment on not canceling the law in 3:31, the good that believers do flows from a relationship with the triune God that begins with this trust in the gospel, but obedience to the law does not generate the relationship and therefore it provides no ground for boasting.

On the social side, justification by faith alone means that God's people will come from all ethnic groups and all walks of life. Within the church, any discrimination among people on the basis of their social status, their economic resources, or their ethnic origins, for example, emerges from a serious misunderstanding of the gospel. This was the problem in the Corinthian church, which was caught up in a competition of social one-upmanship based on the skills and knowledge of the Christian leaders that various groups claimed as their own (1 Cor 1:10–4:21). Although Paul's reply to the Corinthians is complex, it is summarized in 4:7: "What do you have that you did not receive? If then you received it, why do you boast as if you did not receive it?" The only boasting that was appropriate for them was boasting in the Lord, who had given them everything that really mattered in life (1 Cor 1:30–31). To the extent that churches today have become exclusive clubs for people of a certain income bracket, social group, or political persuasion they are not bearing faithful witness to Paul's teaching on justification by faith alone.

Paul also reminds believers in this passage that if they are boasting in their social group, they are failing to bear witness to the unity and sovereignty of God (3:29–30; cf. Deut 6:4). The implication of living as if one particular group has some ground for boasting before God is that God is the god only of that group, not the one God who created all the peoples of the earth and who looks forward to "that day" when "many nations shall join themselves to the LORD . . . and shall be my people" (Zech 2:11).

Churches today need to make sure that they make it easy for people of various economic brackets and ethnic groups to worship and work together. Cultivating an atmosphere within the church that welcomes social diversity is often complex and difficult, but it is also a necessary part of the church's witness to the gospel.

The Theological Implications of Christ's Death

One of the most important descriptions of God's character in the Old Testament affirms that he is both merciful and just, but not in equal measure. His mercy is more typical of God's character than his justice. He describes himself to Moses as

> Merciful and gracious, slow to anger, and abounding in steadfast love and faithfulness, keeping steadfast love for thousands, forgiving iniquity and transgression and sin, but who will by no means clear the guilty, visiting the iniquity of the fathers on the children and the children's children, to the third and the fourth generation. (Exod 34:6–7)[71]

How can God both forgive sin and refuse to clear the guilty? One answer might be that God forgives those who renounce their sin and turn away from it, just as he expects his people to forgive one another. This is certainly true, but we learn from Romans 3:24–26 that more is involved in the forgiveness of sin than a willingness to look past the wrong that has been done and to allow the sinner to make a fresh start. As 1:18–32 has demonstrated, the consequences of sin are profound, often affecting not just the sinner who repents but leading to generations of people who refuse to worship God and hate him (Exod 20:5; cf. Exod 34:7). For God to be both just in acknowledging the profound consequences of human evil and yet gracious in releasing those who have rebelled against him from the punishment they deserve, someone must bear the consequences of human sin.

Already in Exodus 34:6–7 there is a hint of the identity of this person. When God describes himself as "forgiving" iniquity he uses a Hebrew term (*nasa*) that can mean "carry" or "bear." The same term appears both in Leviticus 16 for the scapegoat who "bears" into a remote area "all the iniquities of the people of Israel, and all

71. On the significance of this passage in its own context and throughout the canon, see House, "God's Character."

their transgressions, all their sins" (16:21–22) and in Isaiah 53:12 for the suffering servant who "bore the sin of many."[72] The Old Testament implies, in other words, that God himself bears the punishment involved in preserving his righteous character while forgiving human transgression against him and against others. In Romans 3:24–26 Paul shows us precisely how God did this. Through the death of his Son, God demonstrated both his commitment to justice and his even greater commitment to mercy.

How can God bear the consequences of sin when it is his Son who dies? As Martin Hengel has said, "We can only talk about the saving significance of the death of Jesus in appropriate theological terms if we talk of him in a 'trinitarian context.'"[73] It is because of the unity of God the Father with God the Son that Paul can say, "God commends his own love to us because while we were still sinners Christ died for us" (Rom 5:8).[74]

The understanding of the atonement that Paul articulates in 3:24–26 should remind Christians of God's commitment to justice, of his great mercy, and of the serious consequences of human sin. Like God, Christians too should be committed to justice and should be characterized by mercy. In addition they should allow the implications of this passage about the seriousness of sin to give them pause before taking sin lightly.[75]

The Faithful Presentation of the Gospel to Others

This passage is one of the clearest expressions of the gospel in Scripture, and so it serves as a touchstone for authentic presentations of the gospel. In seeking to communicate the gospel to others, it is essential to stress both the individual and the corporate elements within it. The gospel begins with God's creation of the individual and with his just requirement that every human being worship and serve him as his creature. It insists that no human being has met these reasonable and just requirements and therefore everyone without exception deserves God's punishing wrath—part of which is already visible in the moral chaos of the present world. God's just and merciful offer to forgive every human being who trusts him to do so through the death of Christ reveals the basic unity of humanity in God's eyes and excludes any form of boasting in human social position or accomplishment.

The gospel, then, not only has an individual impact but has a social impact also. It places individuals into a right relationship with God and breaks down barriers between people: no one can boast either in what they have done or in the group to which they belong. Everyone who believes the gospel acknowledges that he or she is

72. Ibid.

73. Hengel, *The Atonement: The Origins of the Doctrine in the New Testament*, trans. John Bowden (Philadelphia: Fortress, 1981), 74.

74. Ibid.

75. Cf. Cranfield, *Romans*, 1:213–14.

equally deserving of God's wrath and thankful for forgiveness through Christ's death. Every human being who believes the gospel for personal salvation also becomes part of God's people, the church, and lives in community with other believers, whatever social differences they have with one another. In faithfully presenting the gospel to unbelievers, then, it is important to stress not only God's forgiveness but the implications of God's forgiveness for living in loving community with others in the church.

CHAPTER 9

Romans 4:1–12

Literary Context

In 4:1–12 Paul continues to ask rhetorical questions directed to a fictional, unpersuaded Jew (4:1, 3, 9–10; cf. 3:27, 29, 31). Just as in 3:27, the topic of the dialogue is the exclusion of boasting through faith in the gospel Paul has outlined in 3:21–26. In 3:27–30 Paul had implied that two types of boasting were excluded by faith in God's gracious provision of atonement for sin through the death of Christ.

First, boasting on the basis of "works" was excluded. The expressions "works" and "works of the law" at this point in the paragraph (3:27–28) recall the emphatically argued case in 3:9–20 that "by works of the law no flesh will be justified before him" (3:20).

Second, boasting on the basis of one's social group was also excluded (3:29–30). When Paul spoke of "works" and "works of the law" in 3:27–28 he had in mind not only good works in general but the good works specifically commanded in the Mosaic law, the law of the Jews. In 3:27–30, therefore, Paul excluded boasting both in doing what God required in a general sense and in possessing the Mosaic law. His point was both anthropological (no human being can fully do God's will) and ethnological (no particular ethnic group can boast that God will favor them in the judgment more than another group).

Paul was not content, however, to let these convictions rest on the foundation of his own opinion. He had said in 3:21 that the law and the prophets testified to his understanding of the righteousness of God. Now, in 4:1–12 he seeks to show that this claim of scriptural support for his gospel is true.[1] Here he takes the biblical account of God's relationship with the great Jewish patriarch Abraham as evidence both for his claim that justification by works in a general sense was impossible and for his claim that Jews could not boast of their right standing with God merely on the basis of their national affiliation and loyalty.

In 4:13–25 these observations about human nature and social groups give way to observations on the way in which God directed history along the path of the gospel to the fulfillment of God's promise that he would make Abraham "the father of many

1. Fitzmyer, *Romans*, 369–70.

nations" (4:17; Gen 17:5). This lengthy proof from Scripture of his claim that in the gospel God justifies sinners regardless of the ethnic group to which they belong brings the first major part of his argument in Romans to a close.

Main Idea

Abraham, the forefather of the Jewish people, proves Paul's point that the gospel of justification by faith excludes boasting, whether in one's works or in one's ethnic origins. God counted Abraham righteous not because of his works but because he trusted God to be gracious to him. Moreover, God graciously gave Abraham the blessing of forgiveness as a response to Abraham's faith, not as a response to his circumcision, which occurred after God had already counted Abraham righteous. Abraham, therefore, is the father of all who believe, not merely the father of those who have received physical circumcision.

Translation

(See pages 225–26.)

Structure

In 4:1–12 Paul develops his argument that the gospel excludes boasting before God in two steps. In 4:1–8 he demonstrates from Scripture that God counts the impious as righteous on the basis of their faith, entirely apart from their actions. His primary text comes from the biblical story of Abraham's relationship with God (Gen 11:27–25:18), and specifically from Genesis 15:6, which speaks of God counting Abraham righteous because Abraham trusted him. Paul states his thesis (4:1–2), then cites his text (4:3), then illustrates his understanding of the text with an analogy drawn from the world of labor and accounting (4:4–5).

Romans 4:1–12

1a	Rhetorical Question	**What, then, shall we say that Abraham,**
b	Apposition	**our forefather according to the flesh,**
		found to be the case?
2a	Explanation	For
	Condition	if Abraham was justified by works,
b	Inference	**he has a reason for boasting**—but
c	Contrast	not with God.
3a	Rhetorical Question	For **what does the Scripture say?**
	Verification (of 2c)	
b	Cause	"But Abraham believed God, and
c	Result	it was counted to him as righteousness." (Gen 15:6)
4	Illustration	**Now wages are not counted** as a favor to the one who works but
	Contrast/Comparison	as a debt;
5a	Explanation	but to the one who does not work but
b	Contrast/Comparison	believes on him who justifies the impious,
c	Assertion	**his faith is counted** as righteousness.
6	Verification (of 4–5)	**Just as David describes the happiness of the human being** for whom God counts righteousness apart from works
7a	Assertion	"Happy are those whose lawless acts are forgiven and
b	Restatement	whose sins are covered.
8	Restatement (of 7a–b)	Happy is the person whose sin the Lord will not count." (Ps 32:1–2a)

Continued on next page.

Continued from previous page.

9a	Rhetorical Question	**Is this happiness for the circumcision** or also
b	General	**for the uncircumcision?**
c	Explanation	For **we say faith was counted**
d		to Abraham
e		as righteousness.
10a	Restatement (of 9a) Specific	**How, then, was it counted?**
b	More specific	**When he was circumcised** or **when he was uncircumcised?**
c	Exclamation	**Not when he was circumcised** but
		when he was uncircumcised!
11a	Explanation	And **he received the sign of circumcision**
	Manner	as a seal of the righteousness
	Means	by faith
	Identification	that he had in his uncircumcised state,
b	Purpose	in order that he might be the father of all who believe
c	Circumstances	while uncircumcised,
d	Result	so that righteousness might be counted to them, and
12a	Parallel	the father of the circumcised
b	Advantange	for those who are not only from the circumcised but also
		follow
		in the footsteps
		of the faith of our father Abraham,
c	Description	faith that he had in his uncircumcised state.

He concludes this part of his argument with another citation of Scripture, this time from Psalm 32:1–2, which expresses the same principle in different terms and shows that God's gracious treatment of Abraham in Genesis 15:6 was not unique to Abraham but was a steady feature of God's character. The association between Genesis 15:6 and Psalm 32:1–2 is not merely based on the catchword "count" (λογίζομαι). Rather, Psalm 32:1–2 illustrates nicely the point Paul makes from Genesis 15:6 that God freely forgives sinners and that this gives them a peaceful relationship with him (cf. 5:1). In 4:1–8 Paul calls this peaceful relationship "righteousness" (4:5, 6) or "happiness" (4:6; cf. 4:7, 8, 9).

In 4:9–12 Paul shifts his focus from the subject of whether human effort can lead to righteousness and therefore boasting before God to the subject of whether one's social identification with the Jewish people forms a basis for a happy or right relationship with God. Paul does not mention the issue of boasting in this paragraph, but since its concern with ethnic identity echoes the statement of that concern in 3:27–30 where boasting was more prominent, boasting is probably also in the background here. Paul observes that the pronouncement of happiness over the person whose sins are forgiven in Psalm 32:1–2 is not limited to Jews but is also available to non-Jews since Abraham's justification occurred before he became a Jew in the physical sense through the rite of circumcision.

Exegetical Outline

VIII. The Scriptures Show That Righteousness Comes by Faith Rather Than by Works (4:1–25)

➦ **A. Abraham Was Justified neither by His Works nor by His Circumcision but by Faith (4:1–12)**

1. Abraham Was Counted Righteous by Faith rather than by Works and Therefore Had No Ground for Boasting (4:1–8)
    a. Genesis 15:6 proves Paul's point (4:1–3)
    b. What Genesis 15:6 means in accounting terms (4:4–5)
    c. The same principle from a different text, Psalm 32:1–2 (4:6–8)
2. Abraham Was Counted Righteous by Faith before He Was Circumcised and Therefore Had No Ground for Boasting in His Identity as a Jew (4:9–12)

Explanation of the Text

4:1 What, then, shall we say that Abraham, our forefather according to the flesh, found to be the case? (Τί οὖν ἐροῦμεν εὑρηκέναι Ἀβραὰμ τὸν προπάτορα ἡμῶν κατὰ σάρκα;). Abraham himself experienced the truth of Paul's claim that trust in God, particularly in his gracious character, excludes human boasting.

Paul continues his dialogue with a fictional Jewish debating partner from 3:27–31.[2] This is clear both from his use of rhetorical questions in the two paragraphs and from his description here of Abraham as "*our* forefather according to the flesh" (cf. 9:3, 5; 1 Cor 10:18). Later in chapter four Paul will make the case that Abraham was the father of both uncircumcised and circumcised believers (4:11–12), but here, in dialogue with another Jew, he acknowledges that Abraham is related to the Jewish people in a special sense.[3] The conjunction "then" (οὖν) ties what Paul is about to say back to the thesis of 3:27–30 that justification by faith apart from works of the law excludes boasting. If this is true, Paul asks, then in what way is it true of Abraham?

Paul articulates this question in a slightly ambiguous way since he supplies no clear object for the term "found" (εὑρηκέναι).[4] He could be asking what Abraham "found" to be true (NET, NIV), or he could be asking what object (such as "grace" or "justification") Abraham "found" or "gained" (ESV) for himself (cf., e.g., Matt 10:39; 11:29; 16:25; 2 Tim 1:18).[5] Interpreters often suggest that Paul had in the back of his mind the expression "to find grace before" (εὑρίσκειν χάριν ἐναντίον) someone, which shows up frequently in Greek renderings of the OT.[6] Paul never uses that expression elsewhere, however, and the subsequent argument focuses not on Abraham finding grace or justification (that seems to be assumed) but on how he found it.[7] Paul, then, is probably asking what Abraham found to be true or to be the case.[8]

4:2 For if Abraham was justified by works, he has a reason for boasting—but not with God (εἰ γὰρ Ἀβραὰμ ἐξ ἔργων ἐδικαιώθη, ἔχει καύχημα, ἀλλ' οὐ πρὸς θεόν). As the case of Abraham demonstrates, God rejects the possibility of justification by works, and therefore of boasting.

2. Cf. Joshua W. Jipp, "Rereading the Story of Abraham, Isaac, and 'Us' in Romans 4," *JSNT* 32 (2009): 217–42, and Paul A. Holloway, "Commendatio aliqua sui: Reading Romans with Pierre Bourdieu," *Early Christianity* 2 (2011): 365, but without adopting their idea that 4:1 comes from the interlocutor.

3. *Pace* Jewett (*Romans*, 308), who takes "according to the flesh" (κατὰ σάρκα) with "found" (εὑρηκέναι). Cf. TOB, Luther, and the Byzantine text, which shifts the verb closer to the end of the sentence and right next to the phrase "according to the flesh" (Τί οὖν ἐροῦμεν Ἀβραὰμ τὸν πατέρα ἡμῶν εὑρηκέναι κατὰ σάρκα;).

4. Manuscripts B, 6, and 1739 clarify the text by dropping the verb entirely. This yields the meaning, "What shall we say with respect to Abraham, our forefather according to the flesh?" Sanday and Headlam, *Romans*, 99, and BDF (§480 [5]) view this as the right reading, but the more difficult reading with the verb is likely to be correct.

5. See also Jan Lambrecht, "Romans 4: A Critique of N. T. Wright," *JSNT* 36 (2013): 193.

6. E.g., Gen 18:3, "And he [Abraham] said, 'Lord if I have then found grace before you, do not pass by your servant'" (καὶ εἶπεν κύριε εἰ ἄρα εὗρον χάριν ἐναντίον σου μὴ παρέλθῃς τὸν παῖδά σου; my transl.). See, e.g., Michel, *An die Römer*, 161; Cranfield, *Romans*, 1:227; Byrne, *Romans*, 145; Légasse, *Romains*, 288–89; Longenecker, *Romans*, 486–89.

7. Cf. Richard B. Hays, "'Have We Found Abraham to Be Our Forefather according to the Flesh?,'" *NovT* 27 (1985): 78; Michael Cranford, "Abraham in Romans 4: The Father of All Who Believe," *NTS* 41 (1995): 74; Jipp, "Rereading the Story of Abraham," 227. Hays, Cranford, and Jipp divide the single question of 4:1 into two questions and supply a subject for the infinitive from the first question's verb "shall we say" (ἐροῦμεν). It is much more likely, however, that Paul uses the infinitive in indirect discourse following a verb of saying than that he begins a question with an infinitive that just happens to follow another question ending with a verb of saying.

8. Moo, *Romans*, 259n13.

The "for" (γάρ) that begins this sentence shows that Paul knew his rhetorical question in the previous verse needed clarification. He now begins to explain precisely what Abraham found to be the case in the matter of works, boasting, and justification. Paul's conditional sentence is probably a "simple condition" rather than a "condition contrary to fact." A condition contrary to fact would have had a secondary tense in the second clause.[9] The first clause, then, imagines that the condition it states is true and the second clause gives the logical result. Assuming that Abraham was justified by works, Paul says, he has "a reason for boasting" (ἔχει καύχημα; cf. Gal 6:4). The further logical result of this, which Paul implies but does not state, is that what he has just said about the relationship between boasting, works, and justification would be wrong. Doing what the law required would provide a ground for boasting, and a human being would be justified by works rather than by faith (cf. 3:27–28).

It is true, as interpreters often comment, that Abraham was an appropriate choice for Paul's example of someone who would have a reason to boast if he were justified by works. Abraham was sometimes described in the Jewish literature of the period as perfect in his conduct and without sin (e.g., Jub. 23:10; Pr. Man. 8). It is easy to see how such a view of Abraham could slide into thinking that Abraham's justification and friendship with God resulted from his adherence to the law (e.g., 1 Macc 2:52; CD 3:2).[10]

Paul's primary interest in Abraham, however, comes not from Abraham's reputation as the pinnacle of piety, a reputation that Paul then wants to deny, but from his status as the "forefather" of the Jewish people (4:1) and from the explicit testimony of Scripture that he was justified by faith (4:3). The statement "but not with God" (ἀλλ' οὐ πρὸς θεόν), then, rejects the entire conditional sentence that precedes it and introduces the crucial proof from Scripture that justification by faith excludes boasting.

4:3 For what does the Scripture say? "But Abraham believed God, and it was counted to him as righteousness" (τί γὰρ ἡ γραφὴ λέγει; Ἐπίστευσεν δὲ Ἀβραὰμ τῷ θεῷ καὶ ἐλογίσθη αὐτῷ εἰς δικαιοσύνην). Paul can say with assurance that Abraham was not justified by his works and that he had no reason to boast, because Scripture affirms this. It says that Abraham's trust in God's promise to do him good led to his right standing with God, and this had nothing to do with Abraham's virtue.

Paul's use of "for" (γάρ) ties his quotation from Scripture closely to the preceding statement. He is about to prove from a text that he and his fictional interlocutor both consider authoritative Scripture that God justified Abraham by faith rather than by works and that any boast from Abraham is therefore excluded. The rhetorical question that introduces the scriptural quotation keeps the reader within the world of the fictional dialogue.

Both the original context and the precise wording of the quotation are important to Paul. In Genesis 15:1–6 God promises to Abram that he will be his reward and protection. Abram expresses his concern, however, that any reward the Lord could give him pales in comparison to the reward of having an heir of his own, something that Abram lacks

9. See Smyth, *Greek Grammar*, §§2297–301; Zerwick, *Biblical Greek* 103–104 (§ 306). *Pace* Jan Lambrecht (*Pauline Studies: Collected Essays*, BETL 115 [Leuven: Leuven University Press, 1994], 28–29) and Légasse (*Romains*, 289), who believe that Paul began to express a simple condition but then switched midstream to a condition contrary to fact.

10. See especially the discussions in Gathercole, *Where is Boasting?*, 232–42, and Jipp, "Rereading the Story of Abraham," 222–24.

and sees no prospect of ever having. God responds to this by promising him that his descendants will actually be more numerous than the stars in the night sky, a promise that echoes the previous promise of Genesis 12:2–3 that Abram would become "a great nation." The sentence that Paul quotes expresses Abram's response to God's reaffirmation of this promise in Genesis 15:4–5, and God's counterresponse.

This context is important because it helps the reader see how Paul took the expression "and he believed the Lord" in Genesis 15:6. Paul has altered the LXX text slightly.[11] First, he inserted the name "Abraham" into the text, although it is not really necessary for making sense of the quotation, and Abraham's name is "Abram" at this point in the Genesis narrative. He will not become "Abraham" until Genesis 17:5. Second, Paul has used the slightly more adversative term "but" (δέ) rather than "and" (καί), which is the more obvious rendering of the Hebrew (cf. LXX).[12]

It is hard to know how much significance to read into these changes, but they would make sense as an anticipation of Paul's fuller description of Abraham's faith in 4:17–22. There Paul recalls the place in the Genesis narrative where God changed Abram's name to Abraham, "for I have made you the father of a multitude of nations" (Gen 17:5; cf. Rom 4:17).[13] He also emphasizes the nature of Abraham's faith as trust in God despite the seeming physical impossibility that his wife Sarah could bear them a child (4:18–22). If these small changes to Genesis 15:6 are intentional pointers to the subsequent argument, then Paul seems to understand the first part of the sentence this way: Abraham saw nothing in his physical circumstances to give him hope that he could have any children, much less numerous descendants as the name "Abraham" implies, "but" he believed God's promise to do him good despite these circumstances.

The term "believed" (ἐπίστευσεν) translates a Hebrew verb (*he'emin*) that often refers in the OT to trust that God would sustain his people in the wilderness and bring them into the promised land, a trust that God desired from his people but that they typically lacked (Exod 14:31; Num 14:11; Deut 1:32; Ps 78:22).[14] The forefather of the Jewish people, however, displayed this type of trust in God.

God's response to Abraham's trust was important to Paul: "And it was counted [ἐλογίσθη] to him as [εἰς] righteousness." The expression "counted . . . as" is a metaphor drawn from the world of bookkeeping where it referred to being "charged for" (λογισθῆναι . . . εἰς) something (Plutarch, *Phoc.* 22.3) or having an amount of money "credited to" (λογιζομένων εἰς) someone (P.Fay. 21.9).[15] It was sometimes used in Hellenistic Judaism in a metaphorical sense for classifying one thing as another thing. The wording of Genesis 15:6 reappears in various contexts, for example, to describe how extraordinary zeal for God or obedience to God, or a marvelously pure trust in God is "counted as righteousness" (Ps 105:31 LXX [106:31, Heb. and Eng.]; 1 Macc 2:52; Jas 2:23; Philo, *Heir* 94–95). Sometimes the classification is surprising: silver was "counted as" (ἦν . . . λογιζόμενον . . . εἰς; my transl.) nothing in Solomon's day because, surprisingly, it was so plentiful that it was not worth all

11. Fitzmyer, *Romans*, 373; Marie-Jo Porcher, "Quelques considérations sur l'usage du Psaume 32 dans l'épître aux Romains (Rm 4,1–12)," *RevScRel* 77 (2003): 556–57.

12. The changes to "Abraham" (Ἀβραάμ) and "but" (δέ) also appear in Jas 2:23 and 1 Clem. 10:6, but these texts are probably dependent upon Paul's form of the quotation.

13. Cf. Porcher, "Quelques considérations," 557; N. T. Wright, "Paul and the Patriarch: The Role of Abraham in Romans 4," *JSNT* 35 (2013): 212.

14. *HALOT* 1:64. The LXX translates these instances of the term with "believe" (πιστεύω), except in Deut 1:32 where they render it with the closely related expression "trust in" (ἐμπιστεύω; cf. LSJ 545, s.v. ἐμπίστευσις).

15. For P.Fay. 219 (AD 135), see MM 377.

that much (2 Chr 9:20). The sons of Zion, once glorious, "were counted as" (ἐλογίσθησαν εἰς; my transl.) clay pots (Lam 4:2). Later in Romans the children of promise rather than the physical descendants of Abraham are "counted as" (λογίζεται εἰς) Abraham's offspring (9:8).

Here in Romans 4:3 Paul understands God's assignment of Abraham's faith to the category of righteousness as surprising. Abraham's faith was not an "act of justice" (δικαιοσύνης . . . ἔργον) as Paul's older contemporary Philo put it, nor an especially perfect "work of faith," as Origen thought, but the trust of an "impious" (ἀσεβῆ) man in God's gracious willingness to do him good.[16]

In terms that John M. G. Barclay has helpfully developed, the "incongruity" of God's grace is the great cultural surprise here. The gods often gave gifts to worthy recipients in antiquity, but Paul understands God's grace to Abraham to be completely "incongruous" with any "worth" that Abraham had in himself. Neither the works Abraham had done (4:2, 4–8) nor the ethnic group to which he belonged legitimated God's graciousness to him (4:9–12, 16–17).[17]

4:4–5 Now wages are not counted as a favor to the one who works but as a debt; but to the one who does not work but believes on him who justifies the impious, his faith is counted as righteousness (τῷ δὲ ἐργαζομένῳ ὁ μισθὸς οὐ λογίζεται κατὰ χάριν ἀλλὰ κατὰ ὀφείλημα, τῷ δὲ μὴ ἐργαζομένῳ πιστεύοντι δὲ ἐπὶ τὸν δικαιοῦντα τὸν ἀσεβῆ λογίζεται ἡ πίστις αὐτοῦ εἰς δικαιοσύνην). An employee's pay is not a gift but the discharge of a financial obligation. With Abraham in Genesis 15:6, however, there is no mention of work, only of reliance on the generosity of God and of God's willingness, surprisingly, to count that reliance as righteousness.

Paul now makes his understanding of Abraham's justification in Genesis 15:6 explicit with a further analogy from the world of bookkeeping.[18] The term translated "wages" (μισθός) referred to the payment a laborer received for work performed (Matt 20:8; Luke 10:7; 1 Tim 5:18; Jas 5:4), and the term "favor" (χάρις; cf. Tyndale, NASB) was what came naturally to mind when Greek speakers expressed the opposite of a "debt" (Thucydides, *History of the Peloponnesian War* 2.40.4). This term is appropriately translated "grace" in twenty-one out of its twenty-three other uses in Romans (the exceptions are 6:17 and 7:25), and a number of translators have chosen that rendering here (e.g., Luther, KJV, NET). Indeed, it is difficult to think Paul did not have the free grace of God from 3:24 in mind when he used the word, but the financial, bookkeeping imagery makes the translation "favor" slightly preferable.[19] In this sentence, then, Paul makes the mundane observation that the pay an employee receives is not "counted" (λογίζεται) as a "favor" (χάριν) but as a "debt" (ὀφείλημα).

Paul follows this observation with an application of it to the language of Genesis 15:6 that reveals the surprising nature of God's accounting system, at least with respect to Abraham. Normally, no record-keeping is necessary for the person who does no work since a lack of work leaves a zero balance in the ledger. Genesis 15:6, however, says that God "counted" something to Abraham although he had done no work. This is in itself odd, but even more surprising is that God credited "righteousness" to Abraham. Under normal circumstances, "righteousness" is counted to someone who has

16. Philo, *Heir* 95 (Colson and Whitaker, LCL); Origen, *Romans, Books 1–5*, 240–42.

17. Barclay, *Paul and the Gift*, 483–90.

18. The image of God at the final judgment consulting a written record of the good and evil deeds of those being judged may lie in the background here. See, e.g., Dan 7:10; Rev 20:12; Jub. 30:18–23.

19. Cf. Dunn, *Romans 1–8*, 203.

done righteous deeds (2:6–13; cf. Jub. 30:18–23), but Paul understands Genesis 15:6 to imply that God's action of counting Abraham righteous corresponded with no work of any type on Abraham's part.

Instead, God counted Abraham's "faith . . . as righteousness," and Abraham's faith is defined specifically as his reliance "on the one who justifies the impious." This confirms and intensifies the surprising nature of God's accounting practices. Paul does not say directly that Abraham was impious, but since Paul has already explained in 3:9–26 that everyone is sinful and that God justifies all who believe in Christ Jesus despite their sin, he implies here that Abraham joins all humanity in the category of the "impious" (ἀσεβής). This was a particularly strong term, used by Abraham himself for Sodom in Genesis 18:23 and 25 (LXX) and closely related to the term "impiety" (ἀσέβεια) that Paul used to summarize the wickedness of all humanity in 1:18.[20] The resulting picture of God shows him crediting righteousness to Abraham on the basis of Abraham's trust that God would do him good despite Abraham's impiety. It is precisely the picture of God that Paul has just painted in 3:9–26 where God justifies sinners as a gift on the basis of the atoning death of Christ and apart from any worth in themselves, whether that worth is calculated in ethnic terms or in terms of virtuous behavior.[21]

4:6 Just as David describes the happiness of the human being for whom God counts righteousness apart from works (καθάπερ καὶ Δαυὶδ λέγει τὸν μακαρισμὸν τοῦ ἀνθρώπου ᾧ ὁ θεὸς λογίζεται δικαιοσύνην χωρὶς ἔργων). The psalmist puts the same point in a slightly different way when he describes the inner contentment that comes to the person whom God counts right with himself without taking righteous deeds into account.

Paul now cites a new biblical text to support his claim that God justified Abraham by faith rather than works and that Abraham therefore has no ground for boasting. The introduction of his quotation with the conjunction "just as" (καθάπερ) and the repetition of the concept that "God counts righteousness apart from works" show that he intended the quotation not as a separate biblical witness to justification by faith but as a further explanation of his main text, Genesis 15:6.[22] He considered the forgiveness of sins in Psalm 32:1–2 to be equivalent to justification apart from works.

The term translated "happiness" here (μακαρισμός) could mean either "happiness" (Plato, *Republic* 491d; Aristotle, *Rhetoric* 1367b 34–35; Plutarch, *Tranq. an.* 11) or "the pronouncement or judgment that someone is happy" (Josephus, *J.W.* 6.213). Since Paul uses the verb "describes" (λέγει) and it would be redundant to speak of David describing the pronouncement of happiness, he probably intended the term here simply to mean "happiness."

The translation "happiness" (cf. REB, TOB ["bonheur"]) is an effort to communicate the idea of "inner contentment" that is present in Paul's use of the term but is obscured by the usual translations "blessed" and "blessedness." The term is rare in the Greek Bible, occurring only here, in 4:9, and in Galatians 4:15. Its use in Galatians 4:15, however, is particularly instructive. The wider context of that occurrence shows that we should understand it as the contentment and well-being people feel about their relationships with each other when those relationships are peaceful. That would also be a fair description of what the psalmist felt, according to Psalm 32:1–5, about his relationship with God now that he has confessed his sins and

20. Cf. his universalizing use of ἀσεβής again in 5:6.
21. Barclay, *Paul and the Gift*, 481.
22. Godet, *Romans*, 171–72; Dunn, *Romans 1–8*, 205.

God has forgiven them. Here, then, Paul probably used the term to interpret Psalm 32:1–2a as the psalmist's expression of happiness that God has counted him righteous despite his sin and apart from any good works, and so his relationship with God is now peaceful.

4:7–8 "Happy are those whose lawless acts are forgiven and whose sins are covered. Happy is the person whose sin the Lord will not count" (μακάριοι ὧν ἀφέθησαν αἱ ἀνομίαι καὶ ὧν ἐπεκαλύφθησαν αἱ ἁμαρτίαι· μακάριος ἀνὴρ οὗ οὐ μὴ λογίσηται κύριος ἁμαρτίαν). The inner contentment of which the psalmist speaks springs from God's willingness to put the sins of the forgiven out of his sight and to preserve no record of them.

Psalm 32:1–2a (31:1–2a LXX) pronounces "happy" (μακάριος) the one who, like the psalmist, confesses his or her sin and experiences God's forgiveness.[23] Although the psalm does use the critical term "count" (*khashab*; λογίζομαι; 32:2 [31:2 LXX]), and this must have been a consideration to Paul in choosing to cite it, he is not simply associating two texts by means of catchword and then using one text to explain the other.[24] Psalm 32 offers a plausible biblical confirmation for Paul's interpretation of Genesis 15:6.[25] There is no mention in the psalm of works of penitence: the "righteous" and "upright in heart" (32:11) are those who, like the psalmist, confess their sin to the Lord and receive his forgiveness (32:5).[26]

The terms "lawless acts" (ἀνομίαι) and "sins" (ἁμαρτίαι) appear frequently together in the LXX, and God is also frequently said to be willing to forgive them both (e.g., Exod 34:7; Num 14:18; Ps 85:2; Isa 6:7; 44:22; cf. Lev 16:21; Isa 53:5). The psalmist uses two metaphors to describe this forgiveness. First, God is willing to "cover" (ἐπικαλύπτω) sins, a term that appears in the LXX for flood waters covering the earth (Gen 7:19–20), a tablecloth covering an altar (Num 4:11, 13), or a head-covering covering the head (2 Sam 15:30). Here the metaphorical meaning is clear. God puts human sin out of his sight.

Second, the psalmist uses the same accounting metaphor that appeared in Genesis 15:6, but now uses it negatively, and Paul finds this use of the metaphor helpful in explaining Genesis 15:6. The psalmist pictures God as keeping no record of the sin he has forgiven.[27] When Paul says that God "counts righteousness apart from works" to the believer (Rom 4:6), therefore, he not only means that God releases those who believe the gospel from punishment but that he keeps no record of their former sins.[28]

4:9–10 Is this happiness for the circumcision or also for the uncircumcision? For we say faith was counted to Abraham as righteousness. How, then, was it counted? When he was circumcised or when he was uncircumcised? Not when he was circumcised but when he was uncircumcised! (ὁ μακαρισμὸς οὖν οὗτος ἐπὶ τὴν περιτομὴν ἢ καὶ ἐπὶ τὴν ἀκροβυστίαν; λέγομεν γάρ, ἐλογίσθη τῷ Ἀβραὰμ ἡ πίστις εἰς δικαιοσύνην. πῶς οὖν ἐλογίσθη; ἐν περιτομῇ ὄντι ἢ ἐν ἀκροβυστίᾳ; οὐκ ἐν περιτομῇ ἀλλ' ἐν ἀκροβυστίᾳ). God counted Abraham righteous when he was an uncircumcised gentile, and

23. Allen P. Ross, *A Commentary on the Psalms*, 3 vols., Kregel Exegetical Library (Grand Rapids: Kregel, 2011–16), 1:705–7.

24. As, e.g., Käsemann (*Romans*, 113); Fitzmyer (*Romans*, 376); Haacker (*An die Römer*, 103); and Hultgren (*Romans*, 182) think.

25. Cranfield, *Romans 1–8*, 1:233; Moo, *Romans*, 266; cf. Kraus, *Psalms 1–59*, 372.

26. Cf. Porcher, "Quelques considérations," 556, 562, 564.

27. Ross, *Psalms*, 1:710–11.

28. The expression "will not count" (οὐ μὴ λογίσηται) takes a form that is occasionally emphatic in classical Greek (Smyth, *Greek Grammar*, §919; cf. Wallace, *Greek Grammar*, 468), but is often unemphatic in the LXX and probably carries no special emphasis here (Zerwick, *Biblical Greek*, 149–50 [§444]).

so circumcision is irrelevant to the question of whether one is righteous in God's sight.

"Therefore" (οὖν) sometimes resumes a line of argument after a slight digression, such as a quotation, has intervened (e.g., Luke 3:7), and that is its function at the beginning of 4:9.[29] The "happiness" of which the psalm speaks comes to the forgiven person not only apart from works but apart from membership in the Jewish people. The rite of circumcision was so distinctive of Jewish identity in the first century that Jews such as Paul could speak of the Jewish people as simply the "circumcision" (περιτομή) and non-Jewish people as the "foreskin" (ἀκροβυστία), usually translated euphemistically as "the uncircumcision" (cf. Gal 2:7–9; Eph 2:11; Col 3:11).[30]

Paul, then, is leading his fictional Jewish debating partner to the realization that the happiness of a restored relationship with God that comes at God's initiative and through his forgiveness of sins is not limited to the Jewish people. He shows this by linking Psalm 32:1–2 back to Genesis 15:6 through a rhetorical question (4:10) and asking his audience to think about Abraham's circumstances at the time of his justification. The biblical story of Abraham describes his justification by faith (Gen 15:6) well before his circumcision (Gen 17:24), and so Abraham's circumcision could have played no role in his justification. God justified Abraham by faith as a gentile, not as a Jew, and this makes the literal rite of circumcision or one's membership in the Jewish people irrelevant to the question of one's standing with God (cf. 1 Cor 7:18–20; Gal 5:6; 6:15). Paul could understand Psalm 32:1–2 in the same way because it speaks not of the Israelite but generically of "the man" (*'adam*; ἀνήρ) whose sin the Lord did not count against him.[31]

4:11a And he received the sign of circumcision as a seal of the righteousness by faith that he had in his uncircumcised state (καὶ σημεῖον ἔλαβεν περιτομῆς σφραγῖδα τῆς δικαιοσύνης τῆς πίστεως τῆς ἐν τῇ ἀκροβυστίᾳ). God's purpose in instituting the rite of circumcision was to provide Abraham with a tangible reminder that God gave righteousness to him on the basis of his faith.

Paul's case in 4:9–10 that God counted Abraham righteous before he was circumcised naturally raises the question of the purpose of circumcision, and so the term "and" (καί) introduces the continued discussion that answers this question. Paul refers back to Genesis 17:11 where God instructs Abraham to accept the physical rite of circumcision for himself and every male in his household as "a sign of the covenant between me and you." Circumcision functioned as a sign in the sense that it was a "seal" on Abraham's right relationship with God, a relationship he received through faith. People in antiquity used seals on property and documents to prevent tampering and forgery and so to provide assurance of authenticity and completeness. Someone might seal a letter to show that it was authentic and to discourage anyone from tampering with its contents before its delivery (1 Kgs 21:8 [LXX]). A purse might have a seal so that its recipient would know whether anyone had opened it and stolen part of its contents (Tob 9:5). People might seal a tomb to discourage grave robbers (Matt 27:66).[32] The term lent itself naturally

29. *A Greek-English Lexicon of the New Testament, Being Grimm's Wilke's Clavis Novi Testamenti*, trans. and rev. John Henry Thayer, corr. ed. (New York: American Book Company, 1889), 463, s.v. οὖν b.δ. See also BDAG 736, s.v. οὖν 2a.

30. Luther's 1545 translation, however, rendered the term literally as "foreskin" (*Vorhaut*). On circumcision as a marker of Jewish identity in Greco-Roman antiquity, see Cohen, *Beginnings of Jewishness*, 39–49.

31. Porcher, "Quelques considérations," 564.

32. On the use of seals in the Greco-Roman world generally, see Gottfried Fitzer, "σφραγίς, κτλ.," *TDNT* 7:940–42.

to use as a metaphor, and so Paul could speak of believers in Corinth as the "seal [σφραγίς] of my apostleship in the Lord" (1 Cor 9:2). Here, then, circumcision is the outward, tangible sign that God had counted Abraham righteous on the basis of his faith. Although Abraham's righteousness might be in dispute since he was impious and could boast in no works before God, his circumcision served as a physical reminder that his righteousness before God was no delusion.

4:11b–12 in order that he might be the father of all who believe while uncircumcised, so that righteousness might be counted to them, and the father of the circumcised for those who are not only from the circumcised but also follow in the footsteps of the faith of our father Abraham, faith that he had in his uncircumcised state (εἰς τὸ εἶναι αὐτὸν πατέρα πάντων τῶν πιστευόντων δι' ἀκροβυστίας, εἰς τὸ λογισθῆναι αὐτοῖς δικαιοσύνην, καὶ πατέρα περιτομῆς τοῖς οὐκ ἐκ περιτομῆς μόνον ἀλλὰ καὶ τοῖς στοιχοῦσιν τοῖς ἴχνεσιν τῆς ἐν ἀκροβυστίᾳ πίστεως τοῦ πατρὸς ἡμῶν Ἀβραάμ). Because God counted Abraham righteous by faith before he was circumcised, Abraham unites believers in a single family of uncircumcised gentiles and circumcised Jews, all of whom, like Abraham, trust in the grace of God.

Paul now uses a lengthy purpose clause to describe God's design in placing Abraham's justification by faith chronologically prior to his circumcision. He does this in two parts. First, this ordering of events allowed Abraham to serve as the father of non-Jews who trust God to be gracious to them. Paul's way of expressing the idea of believing while being uncircumcised (lit., "through the foreskin" [δι' ἀκροβυστίας]) is unusual, but he is again using the term "foreskin" to refer to the state of uncircumcision and the expression "through" (δία + gen.) to refer to "attendant or prevailing circumstance" (cf. 2:27; 8:25; 14:20; Xenophon, *Cyr.* 4.6.6).[33] Although the next clause ("so that righteousness might be counted to them") is structured in the same way as the main purpose clause (εἰς τό + infinitive), it expresses the result of the faith of those who are uncircumcised rather than the purpose for which they believed.[34]

Second, God's ordering of Abraham's faith prior to his circumcision also allowed Abraham to serve as the father of Jews who are not only circumcised but also follow Abraham's example of trusting God. The Greek of this second part of Paul's statement is difficult because the article (τοῖς) before the word "follow" (στοιχοῦσιν) is what we would expect if Paul were speaking of two groups, those who practice circumcision and those who walk in the footsteps of Abraham during his uncircumcised phase. That this is not what Paul meant is clear from the flow of the argument, which emphasizes not Abraham's fatherhood of unbelieving Jews but his fatherhood of believing gentiles. It is also clear from the way Paul formulates the first part of his "not only . . . but also" clause. He does not say "not only for those who . . ." (οὐκ μόνον τοῖς . . .) but "for those who are not only . . ." (τοῖς οὐκ . . . μόνον). He would only have started his sentence this way if he had intended to describe those who, like Abraham after Genesis 17, both trusted in God and viewed circumcision as a sign and seal of their faith.[35]

The verb "follow" (στοιχέω) referred basically to being in a row, standing side by side in battle, or lining up in a certain order.[36] Greek speakers

33. BDAG 224, s.v. διά A3c.

34. On the construction, see Zerwick, *Biblical Greek*, 122 (§352), and Wallace, *Greek Grammar*, 592–93, and on the use of it here, see Cranfield, *Romans*, 1:236–37.

35. Cranfield, *Romans*, 1:237. Cf. Sanday and Headlam, *Romans*, 108; Lagrange, *Romains*, 91.

36. LSJ 1647–48 and MGS, both s.v. στοιχέω.

sometimes used it metaphorically of conduct that was "in line" with certain expectations (Gal 5:25; 6:16; Phil 3:16).[37] Similarly, the image of walking in someone's "footsteps" (τοῖς ἴχνεσιν) was sometimes used in ethical exhortations of imitating someone's example (1 Pet 2:21; cf. 2 Cor 12:18). Here, then, Paul speaks of people who value circumcision but who also walk in line with Abraham's example of putting faith in a gracious God. Paul emphasizes again that Abraham expressed this faith when he was uncircumcised, and Paul does this to prioritize faith over circumcision.

Theology in Application

This passage seeks to show that the principle of God's free and gracious forgiveness of sin apart from any human effort is not something newly revealed in the gospel but also sits at the theological center of the Old Testament. Paul has already made his basic point that God justifies people by faith apart from works of the law in 3:21–31, and now he makes that same point over again but does so out of the Old Testament narrative of God's dealings with Abraham.

Abraham as Old Testament Evidence for Justification by Faith

Paul's reasons for choosing the Abraham narrative are clear. Abraham was the great forefather of the Jewish people, and he was counted righteous not on the basis of what he did but on the basis of his trust in God. Moreover, if circumcision is the physical mark of those who belong to the nation of Israel, then Abraham was a gentile up to the point of his circumcision and then became a Jew in the physical sense when he was circumcised. God specifically ordered the course of history so that Abraham was counted righteous on the basis of his faith, in the gentile phase of his life. Abraham, then, provides an obvious illustration of Paul's point in 3:27–30 that no one can claim to be in a right relationship with God on the basis of what they have done or on the basis of the social group to which they belong. Believers, whether gentile or Jewish, find unity with one another not only in the gospel but in this critically important Old Testament narrative as well.

God's Pardoning Mercy as a Persistent Old Testament Theme

Paul was not proof texting his understanding of God's grace, however, when he demonstrated his point from the Abraham narrative. As we have already seen in the "Theology in Application" section above on 3:21–31, the Old Testament affirms and reaffirms that God is "merciful and gracious, slow to anger, and abounding in steadfast love and faithfulness" (Exod 34:6; cf. Num 14:18; 2 Chr 30:9; Neh 9:17, 31; Pss

37. BDAG 946, s.v. στοιχέω.

86:5, 15; 103:8–14; 111:4; 116:5–6; 145:8–9; Joel 2:12–13; Jonah 4:2).[38] The context in which this description of God's essential character first appears is instructive. Israel had just broken the first commandment of the Decalogue by worshiping a metal calf, and now, unaccountably from the perspective of strict justice, God renews his covenant with them. As Francis I. Andersen says,

> There was justification for his anger. There is no justification for his compassion and kindness, and his *hesed* [graciousness] is completely incomprehensible. The amazing thing is that he is much more eager to pardon than to judge, even if that pardon must flow from his sheer goodness.[39]

God's gracious willingness to justify the impious and forgive their sins is just as clear in the Old Testament as it is in the New Testament.

The Ethnically Unbounded Nature of God's Mercy

Similarly, God's willingness to show mercy across ethnic boundaries to those who are not Jews is also clear in the Old Testament. The covenant of circumcision itself included not only Abraham's physical relations but "any foreigner who is not of your offspring" (Gen 17:12). Likewise, the Mosaic law made provision for non-Israelites who lived in the land of Israel to observe the Sabbath and benefit from its refreshment (Exod 20:10; 23:12; cf. Lev 25:6) and to benefit from every aspect of the law's protection and direction: "There shall be one law for the native and for the stranger who sojourns among you" (Exod 12:49).[40] The Psalms envisioned a time when "all the ends of the earth shall remember and turn to the Lord, and all the families of the nations shall worship before you" (22:27), a time when the Lord's "saving power" will be known "among all nations" and they will praise him (67:2–3; cf. 145:10; see too Isa 2:2–3; Micah 4:1–2). Even in his own time, however, the psalmist knew that "the Lord is good to all, and his mercy is over all that he has made" (Ps 145:9). As Christopher J. H. Wright has demonstrated, the Old Testament often describes God's universal kindness in language and concepts that intentionally echo God's promise to Abraham in Genesis 12:1–3 to bless all the nations of the earth through him.[41]

The twin implications of God's grace in Romans 4:1–12, then, are found throughout Scripture. In a person's relationsip to God, no one has a legitimate ground for boasting, either in accomplishments or in social status. The critical element of a right relationship to God is trust. As the psalmist said in Psalm 32:1–5, happiness

38. House, "God's Character," 4–17; J. B. Green, "Grace," *New Dictionary of Biblical Theology*, ed. T. Desmond Alexander, Brian S. Rosner, D. A. Carson, Graeme Goldsworthy (Leicester: Inter-Varsity Press, 2000), 525.

39. Francis I. Andersen, "Yahweh, the Kind and Sensitive God," in *God Who Is Rich in Mercy: Essays Presented to D. B. Knox*, ed. Peter T. O'Brien and David G. Petersen (Homebush West, NSW, Australia: Lancer, 1986), 51.

40. Sarna, *Exodus*, 64, 246n76.

41. Wright, *Mission of God*, 222–43.

comes from facing up to one's sin, trusting in God's mercy, and experiencing God's forgiveness.

God's Mercy as an Incentive to Human Mercy

The Laura Waters Hinson documentary *As We Forgive* tells the story of a man only identified as Saveri, a Rwandan who himself had killed seven people during the Rwandan genocide of 1994 in which over eight-hundred thousand people were slaughtered.[42] A powerful social group, the Hutus, had targeted an oppressed minority, the Tutsis, for elimination because they regarded them falsely as violent enemies and perpetrated this myth among the wider population. Saveri, a Hutu, believed the myth, and in a cowardly act of self-preservation, killed others out of fear that unless he complied with the orders of the Hutu militia leader who had led him to the "rebels" in his neighborhood, he would himself be killed. The "rebels" turned out to be a defenseless family of six—a pregnant mother and her four children who had gone into hiding at a neighbor's house.

"After killing these people, my heart was shattered," he confessed. "From that point on, I had no peace in my heart. I could not understand how dark my heart had become . . . killing God's creature when I was one as well. Personally, I never believed that I deserved mercy. I'd put myself in a place where I thought God's mercy could not reach. . . . I thought death itself was not enough payment for all the wrong I had done."

But then, after twelve years, the Rev. Stephen Gahigi, himself a Tutsi who had lost 142 members of his extended family in the genocide, showed up at the prison where Saveri was being held. Rev. Gahigi explained how forgiveness was available through the gospel and worked out a way for Saveri to express his sorrow and regret to Rosaria, the sister of the woman he had killed. He also facilitated a way in which Saveri could work with a group of others to build this woman a new home in the village where they both had lived and to process her sorghum crop, something that she could only do with difficulty herself because of the injuries she had sustained during the genocide.

Rwanda was and is a heavily Christianized country, and, sadly, church leaders and institutions were far from guiltless in the genocide, just as in Germany under the Nazis. When the gospel was rightly understood and obeyed among both murderers and their victims after the genocide, however, healing and reconciliation could begin to happen, at least in some instances. Rosaria, herself a believer, commented on her own willingness to forgive Saveri, "How can I refuse to forgive when I am a forgiven sinner too?"

42. *As We Forgive* (Washington DC: Image Bearer Pictures, 2008), documentary, 54 mins.

On the other side of this horrible human tragedy, which a failure to obey the gospel had facilitated, the message that Romans 4:1–12 articulates brought a measure of healing and hope: all humanity is united both in its common guilt before God and under the free offer of God's forgiveness. This message can do something similar for all who are burdened by the weight of their own sin, are willing to receive God's forgiveness through the gospel, and are willing to live out the implications of these truths in their relationships with others. Romans 4:1–12 teaches that this is not merely the point of a paragraph or two in the Scriptures but a critical theme that runs throughout them.

CHAPTER 10

Romans 4:13–25

Literary Context

In 4:13–25 Paul continues his demonstration from the Scriptures that the righteousness of God excludes boasting. He is especially interested in excluding boasting of two types: boasting in doing what God requires and boasting in the possession of the Mosaic law (3:27–29). In 4:1–12 he introduced Abraham into the argument to show how God justifies people by faith instead of works (4:1–8; Gen 15:6) and to show that God even justifies uncircumcised people by faith (4:9–12; Gen 17:14).

These twin themes continue in 4:13–25, but now with an added emphasis on the role of Abraham's faith in salvation history. Paul still wants to use Abraham as an example of how any person is justified, and much of the passage is devoted to a careful examination of what Paul means by justifying faith (4:17b–22). Now, however, Paul adds to this theme the notion that from the perspective of salvation history, Abraham was not just any person. Because he was justified by faith in the God who gives life to the dead and gentiles are justified by faith in the God who raised the Lord Jesus from the dead, Abraham was the father of the multinational people of God.[1] That he would be the father of God's multiethnic people was the content of the promise that God gave to Abraham and that he believed. This promise is fulfilled through the gospel as gentiles flow into God's people through faith. The term "promise" (ἐπαγγελία; ἐπαγγέλλομαι), then, appears in 4:13 for the first time in the letter and not only remains important in this section (4:13, 14, 16, 20, 21) but becomes important again at critical turning points in the overall argument (9:4, 8, 9; 15:8).[2]

Paul's brief concluding paragraph to this section (4:23–25) applies all he has said in 4:1–25 to the present faith he and the Roman Christians have placed in God as the one who raised Jesus from the dead. This paragraph, and particularly its pithy,

1. N. T. Wright ("Paul and the Patriarch: The Role(s) of Abraham in Galatians and Romans," a paper written for the SNTS seminar on "Pauline Theology in Galatians and Romans," at the SNTS annual meeting, Leuven, Belgium, August 1–3, 2012) helpfully emphasizes this theme.

2. On the importance of the term in marking off 4:13–25 as a discrete unit, see Jewett, *Romans*, 323.

poetic final sentence (4:25), brings the first major section of his argument in the letter (1:16–4:25) to a close and opens the way to the next major section (5:1–8:39). The paragraph mentions the death of Christ for the trespasses of believers (4:25a–b) and so recalls the argument of 1:16–4:25. Its focus, however, is on the resurrection of Christ (4:24c, 25c–d), and, in a surprising move, Paul links the justification of believers to Christ's resurrection rather than to his death. This link anticipates the focus on "life" in 5:1–8:39 where the terms "life" (ζωή) and "live" (ζάω) dominate the discussion.[3]

VII. The Death of Christ Demonstrates God's Righteousness and Excludes Human Boasting (3:21–31)

VIII. The Scriptures Show That Righteousness Comes by Faith Rather Than by Works (4:1–25)

A. Abraham Was Justified neither by His Works nor by His Circumcision but by Faith (4:1–12)

➡ **B. The Link between Abraham's Faith and God's Faithfulness to His Promise to Abraham (4:13–25)**

IX. Justification by Faith Brings Peace and Reorients the Believer's Existence (5:1–8:39)

Main Idea

Abraham exercised the faith by which God justified him in the context of God's promise that Abraham would be the father of many nations. Both the quality and the content of this faith are important for understanding the gospel. The quality of Abraham's faith was important because it was the sort of trust in God that anyone, not merely the Jews, could have, and it was a trust that turned its back on the world and placed a confident hope in God. The content of Abraham's faith was also important because it was specifically faith that God could bring life out of death. The faith of those who believe the gospel is similar. God has raised the Lord Jesus from the dead and will raise them from the dead also.

Translation

(See pages 242–43.)

3. Together, the two terms appear thirty-seven times in Romans, twenty-four of them in chs. 5–8.

Romans 4:13–25

13a Basis (of 11b–12c)	For **it was not through the law that the promise came**
	to Abraham or
	to his offspring
Content of 13a	that he would be heir of the world, but
Contrast	through the righteousness of faith.
14a Explanation (of 13) Condition	For if the people of the law are heirs,
b Inference	**faith is rendered useless** and
	the promise invalidated.
15a Explanation (of 14b)	For **the law produces wrath**
b Expansion (of 15a)	**(indeed where there is no law, neither is there transgression).**
16a Result (of 13–15a)	Because of this,
b Assertion	**it is by faith,**
c Purpose (of 16a)	so that it might come as a gift,
d Purpose (of 16b)	in order that the promise might be confirmed to all his offspring, not only
e Description	to those of the law but also
f Expansion (of 16d)	to those of the faith of Abraham,
g Description	who is the father of us all.
17a Verification (of 16f)	Just as it is written, "I have made you the father of many nations" (Gen 17:5)
b Place (of 17a; metaphorical)	—in the sight of God,
c Description	whom he believed,
d Description	the one who makes the dead alive and
e Description (of God)	calls the things that do not exist as if they existed
18a Description (of Abraham)	who believed
	beyond hope
	on the basis of hope,

b	Purpose	so that he might
		become the father of many nations,
c	Reference	according to what is spoken,
		"So shall your offspring be." (Gen 15:5)
19a	Simultaneous (with 19b)	And not growing weak in faith,
b	Description (of "believed" in 18a)	**he looked carefully** at his own body,
c	Description	dead as it was
d	Explanation	(since he was about a hundred years old), and
e	Expansion (of 19b)	the deadness of Sarah's womb.
20a	Contrast/Comparison	But **he was not internally divided** toward the promise of God because of unbelief.
b		Rather, **he was empowered in faith** and
c	Expansion (of 20b)	gave glory to God and
21	Expansion (of 20c)	was fully convinced that what he had promised he was also able to do.
22	Result	Therefore, "It was counted to him as righteousness." (Gen 15:6)
23–24a	Contrast/Comparison	But **it was not written**
		only because of him
		that it was counted to him but also
		because of us,
b	Description	to whom it will be counted—
c	Description	to those
		who believe in the one
		who raised Jesus
		our Lord from the dead,
25a	Description	who was handed over
b	Cause	because of our trespasses and
c	Description	raised
d	Purpose	because of our justification.

Structure

The passage is organized around two themes, Abraham's faith in God's promise as the context of his justification and the correspondence between Abraham's justification by faith and those who believe the gospel in the present. Paul first describes Abraham's faith in God's promise by means of a negative comparison between Abraham's faith and the Mosaic law (4:13–15).[4] The Mosaic law could not have been the means through which God fulfilled his promise to Abraham, he argues, since the Jews experienced God's wrath as a result of their disobedience to the law. They did not experience obedience, righteousness, and blessing.

Paul then turns to a positive description of Abraham's faith, which he links with God's grace (4:16–17).[5] The righteousness, blessing, and fulfillment of the promise that were impossible through the law were available to Abraham through faith as a free gift. Because one did not need to be a Jew to have faith in God, Paul argues, God could fulfill his promise to Abraham through gentiles who believed the gospel in the same way that Abraham believed God's promise.

If this is so, then it was important for Paul to describe more precisely the quality and content of Abraham's faith and to demonstrate that those who believe the gospel have a faith that corresponds to Abraham's faith in both these areas. Paul, then, describes Abraham's faith in God's willingness and ability to bring life to the dead despite the human improbability that this could happen (4:18–22). Paul and the Roman Christians similarly trust that God raised from the dead the same Lord Jesus who died for their trespasses. This faith provides the context in which God accounts them righteous, just as he did with Abraham (4:23–25).

With this last, brief paragraph (4:23–25), Paul has brought his treatment of Abraham full circle, back to Genesis 15:6. Now, however, his readers understand how that statement allows Paul to say that the Scripture testifies to the manifestation of the righteousness of God in the gospel (3:21).

Exegetical Outline

VIII. The Scriptures Show That Righteousness Comes by Faith Rather Than by Works (4:1–25)

A. Abraham Was Justified neither by His Works nor by His Circumcision but by Faith (4:1–12)

➡ **B. The Link between Abraham's Faith and God's Faithfulness to His Promise to Abraham (4:13–25)**

1. Abraham's Faith and the Mosaic Law Negatively Compared (4:13–15)
2. Abraham's Faith and God's Grace (4:16–17)
3. Abraham's Faith as Reliance on God to Do What Seemed Impossible (4:18–22)
4. The Correspondence between Abraham's Faith and the Faith of Believers (4:23–25)

4. Jewett, *Romans*, 323.

5. Ibid.

Explanation of the Text

4:13 For it was not through the law that the promise came to Abraham or to his offspring that he would be heir of the world, but through the righteousness of faith (Οὐ γὰρ διὰ νόμου ἡ ἐπαγγελία τῷ Ἀβραὰμ ἢ τῷ σπέρματι αὐτοῦ, τὸ κληρονόμον αὐτὸν εἶναι κόσμου, ἀλλὰ διὰ δικαιοσύνης πίστεως). God did not make his promise to use Abraham and his family in the restoration of all creation because of Abraham's possession of or obedience to the Jewish law. Rather, God made this promise to Abraham because of the righteousness that God gave to him on the basis of his faith.

The "for" (γάρ) reaches back to 4:9–12 and introduces a second reason why Abraham is the father not so much of circumcised Jews as of all who believe, whether physically circumcised or not. God not only counted Abraham righteous by faith apart from his circumcision but also promised that Abraham would inherit the world on the basis of his faith rather than on the basis of the law. The concept of God's "promise" (ἐπαγγελία; ἐπαγγέλλομαι) is important in Paul's theology and refers primarily to the promise God gave to Abraham that he would be "the father of many nations," a promise he began to fulfill with the birth of Isaac (Rom 9:7–9; Gal 4:23, 28) and Jacob (Rom 9:10–13) and continues to fulfill through the inclusion of gentiles within the people of God by means of the gospel (Rom 4:16; 9:8; Gal 3:16–19, 29; 4:28). This theme binds 4:13–25 together as a discrete unit.

Paul's description of God's promise to Abraham as the commitment to make him "heir of the world" is a later way of speaking (e.g., Sir 44:21; Jub. 17:3; cf. Jub. 32:19; Philo, *Dreams* 1.175) not found in the Old Testament itself, although the concept is present (Gen 12:3; 18:18; 22:18; 26:4; 28:14). Paul probably used this language because he believed that the inclusion of gentiles within Abraham's family through the gospel was a further step toward God's restoration of creation to the condition it had prior to Adam's sin (cf. 8:19–21).[6]

The "law" (νόμος) here means the Mosaic law, the constitution of the Jewish nation through which God intended to set Israel apart from all the nations of the earth as his special people (cf. Exod 19:5–6). This becomes clear in 4:16–17 where Paul distinguishes between descendants of Abraham who possess the Mosaic law (and faith) and descendants of Abraham who have faith (but not the Mosaic law).[7]

Paul was not merely referring to the law as an ethnic marker of the Jewish people, however, but also as an object of Abraham's efforts to obey God. This element of Paul's argument will become more explicit in 4:15, where he says that the law produces wrath. Jewish thinkers in the Second Temple period sometimes claimed that God promised Abraham the world as his inheritance because of his obedience to the law (Sir 44:19–21). Paul holds the opposite position: Abraham was "ungodly" (4:5) and, like everyone else, deserved God's wrath, but God did not count his sin against him and instead graciously justified him on the basis of his faith. This gracious method of justifying Abraham allowed him to become the inheritor of the world and was the means by which God fulfilled his promise.

4:14 For if the people of the law are heirs, faith is rendered useless and the promise invalidated (εἰ

6. Meyer, *Romans*, 163; Dunn, *Romans 1–8*, 213; Wright, "Romans," 495–96; idem, "Paul and the Patriarch," 5n18; cf. Cranfield, *Romans*, 1:240.

7. Cranfield, *Romans*, 1:238.

γὰρ οἱ ἐκ νόμου κληρονόμοι, κεκένωται ἡ πίστις καὶ κατήργηται ἡ ἐπαγγελία). If only the Jewish people lived in God's new creation, Abraham's faith would be pointless and the promise he trusted God to perform could never reach fulfillment.

This is a first class conditional sentence: Paul assumes the "if" clause is true for the sake of argument, and this way of stating the sentence lends rhetorical liveliness to the discourse (cf. 8:9).[8] He asks his audience to imagine that Abraham and his descendants were heirs of the world but were also, by definition, "people of the law" (οἱ ἐκ νόμου). The term "of" (ἐκ) in this phrase is sometimes used with the article, as it is here (οἱ ἐκ . . .), to indicate group affiliation, as in the expressions, "those who belong to the synagogue" (οἱ ἐκ τῆς συναγωγῆς, Acts 6:9) or "those from the household of Aristobulus" (οἱ ἐκ τῶν Ἀριστοβούλου, Rom 16:10).[9] "The people of the law," then, are the Jewish people. The parallel between "faith" and "promise" means that "faith" is Abraham's faith and "the promise" is the promise that Abraham believed in Genesis 15:6.

This faith-promise sequence, Paul argues, is null and void if only the people of the law are heirs of the world. The implication of Paul's argument up to this point seems to be that if only the Jewish people were heirs of the world, then Abraham would be the father of only one nation, not many nations as the promise claimed (cf. 4:17). Thus, Abraham would have trusted God in error because God could not have fulfilled his promise to him. In addition to this ethnically oriented point, however, Paul adds another point in 4:15 that implies the law cannot be the source of the fulfillment of a promise of blessing simply because no one can keep it.

4:15 For the law produces wrath (indeed where there is no law, neither is there transgression) (ὁ γὰρ νόμος ὀργὴν κατεργάζεται· οὗ δὲ οὐκ ἔστιν νόμος οὐδὲ παράβασις). God's promise that Abraham would inherit the world could not be fulfilled in the Jewish people alone because they too are sinners and have fallen under the wrath of God for their disobedience to the law.

The "wrath" (ὀργή) Paul refers to is God's punishment of "impiety and unrighteousness" (1:18; cf. 3:5), of selfish ambition and disobedience to the truth (2:5, 8). The law "produces" wrath because wherever God expresses his will, those to whom he reveals it disobey his will and suffer his just punishment (1:18; 2:5, 8). This was true for gentiles who did not have the specific revelation of God's will in the Mosaic law but who disobeyed "the work of the law written in their hearts" (2:15). Here, however, Paul was thinking especially of the Jews, "the people of the law" to whom he had just referred in 4:14 (cf. 4:16). God's promise that Abraham would inherit the world could not mean that the Jewish people would inherit the world. The Jewish people, like everyone else, had experienced the wrath of God as a result of their disobedience to what they knew of the will of God. In their case what they knew was the law of God in its purest form (Ps 119:7–9; cf. Rom 3:2; 7:12). Rather than obeying the law and receiving God's blessing (Lev 26:3–13; Deut 28:1–14), however, they disobeyed it and experienced death and exile (Lev 26:14–39; Deut 28:15–68).

The Jews differed from other people groups in being the recipients of God's word, where God's will, the consequences for disobedience to it, and the reason for the human plight were clearly explained (3:2; 9:4; cf. Eph 2:12). "Transgression" (παράβασις) is a more specific term than "sin" (ἁμαρτία) and refers to the knowing violation of a clearly expressed law (Ps 100:3 LXX [101:3 Heb.,

8. Cranfield, *Romans*, 1:240n2. On this use of the first-class condition, see Wallace, *Greek Grammar*, 692–94.

9. BDAG 296, s.v. ἐκ 3b.

Eng.]; Heb 2:2) or oath (2 Macc 15:10; cf. Heb 9:15). Paul uses it elsewhere for the disobedience of Adam (Rom 5:14) and Eve (1 Tim 2:14) to the command God had given them not to eat of the tree of the knowledge of good and evil (Gen 2:17). When Paul says that where the law is absent transgression is absent, therefore, he does not mean that there is no sin in the law's absence but that, apart from the law's specificity and clarity, sin remains general and undefined (cf. Rom 5:13–14; Gal 3:19).

How does the statement "where there is no law, neither is there transgression" fit into Paul's argument? It is a parenthetical comment, in the form of a general maxim (cf. Jub. 33:15–16). Paul used it to support his claim that the law produces wrath. In the presence of the law, with its clear description of God's requirements and its sanctions for disobedience, an inevitably disobedient people can only become even more culpable and fall more fully under the curses that the law promises to the disobedient.[10]

4:16 Because of this, it is by faith, so that it might come as a gift, in order that the promise might be confirmed to all his offspring, not only to those of the law but also to those of the faith of Abraham, who is the father of us all (διὰ τοῦτο ἐκ πίστεως, ἵνα κατὰ χάριν, εἰς τὸ εἶναι βεβαίαν τὴν ἐπαγγελίαν παντὶ τῷ σπέρματι, οὐ τῷ ἐκ τοῦ νόμου μόνον ἀλλὰ καὶ τῷ ἐκ πίστεως Ἀβραάμ, ὅς ἐστιν πατὴρ πάντων ἡμῶν). Because exposure to God's law leads human beings into disobedience and God's wrath, God could only fulfill his promise to Abraham by means of graciously justifying him and his offspring by faith. In this way, God gave to Abraham numerous descendents, both from the Jews and from the gentiles.

"Because of this" (διὰ τοῦτο) does not point forward to what Paul is about to say. Rather, it points backward (cf. 1:26) beyond the parenthetical comment that there is no transgression in the absence of the law (4:15b) to the double-sided point Paul has just made in 4:13–15a. Because it takes many people groups to fulfill God's promise, not merely the Jewish people (Gen 17:5), and because the Jewish people have violated the law and deserve God's wrath rather than his blessing (Deut 28:15–68; 30:17–18), the promise must be fulfilled by means of faith and as a free gift. Gentiles as well as Jews can join Abraham's descendants if God defines Abraham's descendants as those who have faith. Those who have sinned apart from the law and experienced the forms of God's wrath that 1:18–32 describes, and those who have the Mosaic law and have experienced the curse it pronounces on the disobedient, can receive God's blessing if it comes to them as a free gift.

Even as he lumps the Jew and the believing gentile together here as descendents of Abraham, he also seems to draw a contrast ("but also") between them as if to say that one group is affiliated with the Mosaic law ("those of the law") whereas the other group is affiliated with Abraham's faith ("those of the faith of Abraham").[11] If this was Paul's intention, then he points forward to what he will say later about the important place the Jews continue to play in God's purposes as Jews (11:11–12, 15, 18, 20, 23, 26, 28–29, 31).

In light of the flow of Paul's argument up to this point, however, it is more likely that Abraham's "offspring" (σπέρματι) refers to those who have embraced the gospel, whether Jewish or gentile (cf. 4:11–12). Here, then, Paul does not distinguish between Jews (whether believers or not) who are Abraham's offspring and gentile believers who are Abraham's offspring because of their faith. Rather, he observes that some believing descendents of

10. Godet, *Romans*, 177.

11. E.g., Jewett, *Romans*, 328–29; Hultgren, *Romans*, 186.

Abraham come from the Jews, which is unsurprising (cf. 11:1; 2 Cor 11:22), "but" others "also" (ἀλλὰ καί) come from the gentiles. These gentiles are among Abraham's descendants only because of their faith (cf. Rom 9:6–9; Gal 3:29).

4:17 Just as it is written, "I have made you the father of many nations"—in the sight of God, whom he believed, the one who makes the dead alive and calls the things that do not exist as if they existed (καθὼς γέγραπται ὅτι Πατέρα πολλῶν ἐθνῶν τέθεικά σε, κατέναντι οὗ ἐπίστευσεν θεοῦ τοῦ ζῳοποιοῦντος τοὺς νεκροὺς καὶ καλοῦντος τὰ μὴ ὄντα ὡς ὄντα). God confirmed that he considered Abraham the father of all believers—Jews as well as gentiles—when he promised that Abraham would be the father of many nations. Abraham believed God when God promised him this, and Abraham's faith was not misplaced, because God is so powerful and reliable that he treats his plans for the future as if they had already happened.

Paul now shows that the point he has just made corresponds with God's promise to Abraham in Genesis 17:5. Abraham is the father of all Jewish and gentile believers in accord with God's promise that he would make Abraham the father of many "nations" (ἐθνῶν). Although the term "nations" refers to non-Jewish people groups in most of its other occurrences in Romans, it may include the Jewish nation here, as it probably did in Genesis 17:5. That reading of the term would fit nicely with Paul's claim in 4:11–12, 16 that Abraham is the father of both Jewish and gentile believers.[12]

The words translated here "in the sight of God, whom he believed" (κατέναντι οὗ ἐπίστευσεν θεοῦ) are difficult and have been understood to mean "in light of which [promise] he believed" or "in the presence of the God whom he believed."[13] The proper translation hangs on the meaning one gives to the preposition (κατέναντι), whether "in the sight of," "in light of," or "in the presence of." It also depends on the antecedent one chooses for the relative pronoun (οὗ), whether the promise of Genesis 17:5 in the previous clause or "God" in the following clause. It is very difficult to find a use of the preposition with the meaning "in light of," and the attraction of an antecedent (θεοῦ) into the case of the relative pronoun (οὗ) is reasonably common in Greek.[14] The most obvious reading of the phrase, then, according to the standard meaning of the terms and the rules of Greek grammar is that in the sight of God Abraham was the father of many nations, Jews as well as gentiles.[15]

The God in whose sight Abraham was the father of believers from many people groups (4:16c–17a), and the God in whom Abraham believed (4:17c), is the God who makes the dead alive. The broader context of this statement shows that Paul was thinking both of God giving life to Abraham and Sarah's "dead" child-bearing abilities (4:19c–e) and of God raising Jesus from the dead (4:24–25). Without both these life-giving miracles, God's promise to Abraham would have remained unfulfilled.

Paul further describes God as the one who speaks of what does not exist as though it existed (καλοῦντος τὰ μὴ ὄντα ὡς ὄντα). Again, the Greek is difficult since, on one hand, the phrase seems to recall a way of describing God's creation of the world out of nothing that was common in Paul's era (e.g., 2 Bar. 21:4; Philo, *Spec. Laws* 4.187; Jos. Asen. 8.10), and yet, on the other hand, the

12. Cf. Jewett, *Romans*, 332–33, although Jewett thinks that Paul refers to non-Christian Jews both here and in 4:16.

13. See, respectively, Douglas A. Campbell, *The Deliverance of God: An Apocalyptic Rereading of Justification in Paul* (Grand Rapids: Eerdmans, 2009), 741–42; Jewett, *Romans*, 333.

14. LSJ 923–24; BDAG 530–31; MGS 1095, all s.v. κατέναντι; Smyth, *Greek Grammar*, §2533.

15. Cranfield, *Romans*, 1:243.

most obvious reading of the phrase understands it to mean that God calls "the things that do not yet exist as though [ὡς] they already do" (NET; cf. Tyndale, Luther, KJV). Although almost no modern translations choose this second sense, the NET seems to be correct here.[16] The term translated "as though" (ὡς) can indicate result or purpose, but when it means this, an infinitive, not a participle, typically follows it. The idiom Paul uses here, moreover, occurs in writers close to Paul's era clearly to mean "as though existing" or "as though it were [the case]" (Philo, *Joseph* 126; *Flaccus* 164; Strabo, *Geogr.* 1.2.35).

Paul, then, describes God as one whose purposes and promises are so certain to happen that God speaks of them as if they already exist. This understanding of the phrase fits neatly into the context of Genesis 17:5 where God names Abraham the "father of a multitude" when he and Sarah remain childless, and also speaks definitively in the perfect tense of having made (τέθεικα) Abraham the father of many nations.

4:18 who believed beyond hope on the basis of hope, so that he might become the father of many nations, according to what is spoken, "So shall your offspring be" (ὅς παρ' ἐλπίδα ἐπ' ἐλπίδι ἐπίστευσεν εἰς τὸ γενέσθαι αὐτὸν πατέρα πολλῶν ἐθνῶν κατὰ τὸ εἰρημένον, Οὕτως ἔσται τὸ σπέρμα σου). Abraham based his faith on his hope in the God who gives life to the dead and always fulfills his word. Abraham's faith was also the means God used of fulfilling his promise to make Abraham the father of many nations.

The expression "beyond hope . . . on the basis of hope" (παρ' ἐλπίδα ἐπ' ἐλπίδι) contrasts natural human hope with hope in the God Paul has just described in 4:17.[17] Abraham could not reasonably hope for children from the human perspective, but he nevertheless based his faith on a hope that was grounded in the character of the God Paul has just described—the God who gives life to the dead and speaks of his future plans as if they have already happened.

From God's perspective, the purpose of Abraham's faith was that he might become (γενέσθαι) the father of many nations as Genesis 17:5 promised.[18] The Greek construction Paul uses here (εἰς τό + infinitive) could indicate the object of Abraham's faith (NJB) or its result (NIV, NET, HCSB) rather than its purpose (RSV, NASB, ESV).[19] Since 4:18–21 focuses on Abraham's time period and the quality of his faith, Paul is probably describing how Abraham's faith was part of God's plan to include within Abraham's family those from every nation who believed the gospel.[20]

Nothing in the context of Genesis 17:5 speaks of Abraham's faith, but Paul's introduction at the end of the verse of a phrase from Genesis 15:5 shows that he was reading Genesis 17:5 through the lens of Genesis 15:6, whose focal point is Abraham's faith that God would give him descendants as numerous as the stars. Genesis 17:5 simply clarified for Paul that these numerous descendants would come from many nations.

4:19 And not growing weak in faith, he looked carefully at his own body, dead as it was (since

16. See also Moo, *Romans*, 282.

17. Cf. Luther's 1545 translation: "Und er hat geglaubet auf Hoffnung, da nichts zu hoffen war" ("And he believed on hope since there was nothing to hope for"), and the comments of Cranfield, *Romans*, 1:245.

18. On the Greek construction, see Sanday and Headlam (*Romans*, 114), Cranfield (*Romans*, 1:246), and BDAG 290, s.v. εἰς 4e.

19. My translation's "so that he might" follows the NASB.

20. The use of this construction to indicate the content of Abraham's faith (NJB) would be very odd Greek and unprecedented within either the LXX or NT. On this, see Cranfield, *Romans*, 1:245–46.

he was about a hundred years old), and the deadness of Sarah's womb (καὶ μὴ ἀσθενήσας τῇ πίστει κατενόησεν τὸ ἑαυτοῦ σῶμα νενεκρωμένον, ἑκατονταετής που ὑπάρχων, καὶ τὴν νέκρωσιν τῆς μήτρας Σάρρας).[21] Abraham's trust lay in the word of God, and God is both powerful and reliable, so circumstances that would have been discouraging in another, totally human context, did not weaken his faith.

Paul's interpretation of Genesis 17 through the lens of Genesis 15:5–6 continues in this verse. The picture of Abraham not growing weak in faith when he "looked carefully at" (κατενόησεν; cf. Jas 1:23–24) the condition of his own body probably depends on Genesis 17:17, where Abraham questions God about his promise in light of his age and Sarah's age. Paul did not see this as a sign of unbelief but rather as Abraham's willingness to stare at the improbabilities of the fulfillment of God's promise from a human level and to believe anyway, as Genesis 15:6 says he did.

Paul's adverbial participle "growing weak" (ἀσθενήσας) is an ingressive or inceptive aorist, indicating the beginning of an action.[22] It appears before the main verb "looked carefully" (κατενόησεν) because it expresses Paul's main point despite its syntactically subordinate status.[23] It is normal, from a human perspective, for someone nearly a hundred years old to grow weak in faith when promised a child. Abraham's response, however, was not normal. His hope was placed on the God who gives life to the dead and speaks about what he will do in the future as if it has already happened (4:16).

4:20 But he was not internally divided toward the promise of God because of unbelief. Rather, he was empowered in faith and gave glory to God (εἰς δὲ τὴν ἐπαγγελίαν τοῦ θεοῦ οὐ διεκρίθη τῇ ἀπιστίᾳ ἀλλ' ἐνεδυναμώθη τῇ πίστει, δοὺς δόξαν τῷ θεῷ). In the face of his difficult physical circumstances Abraham responded with a divinely strengthened faith and trusted God's word. This, it turns out, was an act of worship—the sort of worship that God desires.

Paul's "but" (δέ) draws a contrast between the human circumstances of old age that Abraham faced and the undivided faith that Paul is about to describe. His description takes the form of a skillfully drawn contrast between how Abraham might have responded to his circumstances and how he did respond.[24] The balance of the contrast in Greek is lost in English translation. English cannot reproduce the play on words having to do with lack of faith (τῇ ἀπιστίᾳ) and faith (τῇ πίστει) or the breadth of meaning in the dative case of those words. Nor can it duplicate the correspondence in form between the words for "was internally divided" (διεκρίθη) and "was empowered" (ἐνεδυναμώθη).

Ancient Greek speakers commonly used the term translated "internally divided" (διεκρίθη) to mean "separate, distinguish, decide, judge, dispute, criticize" (e.g., Acts 11:2, 12; 15:9; 1 Cor 6:5; 11:29, 31; 14:29; Jude 9).[25] When it occurs in the NT, interpreters typically consider it a deponent verb meaning "doubt" or "waver" in the middle or passive voices. It never carries that meaning, however,

21. An impressive array of manuscripts (e.g., ℵ A C D Ψ 6 33 81) adds the adverb "already" (ἤδη) before the perfect participle "dead" (νενεκρωμένον). Witnesses to the omission of the term, however, are also early and geographically diverse (e.g., B F G 1739 1881). The adverb tends to soften the rather jarring (albeit figurative) notion that when Abraham took a close look at his body, it was simply dead.

22. See Ernest de Witt Burton, *Syntax of the Moods and Tenses in New Testament Greek*, 3rd ed. (Chicago: University of Chicago Press, 1898), §145, and Wallace, *Greek Grammar*, 558–59.

23. Cf. Zerwick, *Biblical Greek*, 130 (§376), and Moo, *Romans*, 283.

24. Cf. Dunn, *Romans 1–8*, 220–21.

25. LSJ 399; BDAG 231; MGS 492, all s.v. διακρίνω.

prior to the composition of the NT documents.[26] It is possible, then, that it carries the more common meaning "dispute, criticize" here and refers less to an inner disposition of Abraham than to Abraham's compliance with God's plan for his family.[27] The term, however, often refers in the passive voice to "being divided or separated" (e.g., Thucydides, *History of the Peloponnesian War* 1.105.5; 3.9.2), sometimes with respect to opinion about some matter (Josephus, *J.W.* 4.517), and it is easy to see how, in a context where a person's convictions are under discussion, the passive form of the verb could assume the meaning of "internal division" about some course of action.

The term translated "was empowered" (ἐνεδυναμώθη), like its negative counterpart "was internally divided" (διεκρίθη), was a religious term that appears first in the LXX, then in the NT, and usually in contexts where God or Christ Jesus give someone the ability to accomplish a difficult task (Judg 6:34 LXX; 1 Tim 1:12), defend one's self against spiritual opposition (Eph 6:10), or endure adversity (Phil 4:13; 2 Tim 4:17; cf. 2 Tim 2:1). Here, the passive probably means that God gave Abraham the inner strength to believe the promise despite the human improbability of its fulfillment. "In faith" (τῇ πίστει) is a "dative of sphere" describing the area in which God gave Abraham inner strength.[28]

The final phrase, "and gave glory to God," uses an aorist participle of attendant circumstance to express an action that happened at the same time as the strengthening (Tyndale, Luther, NAB, NIV). The notion of giving God glory is common in the OT and often refers to giving God the worship and praise that belong to him (LXX 2 Chr 30:8; Psa 67:35 [Heb. 68:35; Eng. 68:34]; Luke 17:18; Rev 11:13). Dunn and Moo are correct, then, to contrast Abraham's worship of God here with the failure of sinful human beings in 1:21 to glorify God as God.[29] Abraham's trust in God's promise, against all humanly conceived odds, was the appropriate act of worship for someone whose relationship with God was what it should be.

4:21 and was fully convinced that what he had promised he was also able to do (καὶ πληροφορηθεὶς ὅτι ὃ ἐπήγγελται δυνατός ἐστιν καὶ ποιῆσαι). Abraham was not indecisive about believing that God could perform his promise but gave himself completely over to God's word.

The expression "fully convinced" (πληροφορηθείς) translates a verb that occurs in literature prior to the NT only rarely.[30] Its pre-Christian and NT occurrences have something to do with completion or fullness: being completely filled with some inner quality, such as evil (Eccl 8:11 LXX) or conviction (Rom 14:5; Col 4:12), or fully accomplishing some course of action (Luke 1:1; 2 Tim 4:5, 17). Here Paul refers to Abraham being completely filled with the conviction that God was powerful enough to make Abraham the father of many nations despite his human limitations (cf. 14:5). The idea of completeness and integrity contained in the term forms a neat contrast with the divided mind pictured in 4:20.

4:22 Therefore, "It was counted to him as righteousness" (διὸ [καί] ἐλογίσθη αὐτῷ εἰς δικαιοσύνην).[31] God considered Abraham to be in a

26. BDAG 231, s.v. διακρίνω 6; Peter Spitaler, "Διακρίνεσθαι in Mt. 21:21, Mk. 11:23, Acts 10:20, Rom. 4:20, 14:23, Jas. 1:6, and Jude 22—the 'Semantic Shift' That Went Unnoticed by Patristic Authors," *NovT* 49 (2007): 1–39.

27. Benjamin Schliesser, "'Abraham Did Not "Doubt" in Unbelief' (Rom 4:20): Faith, Doubt, and Dispute in Paul's Letter to the Romans," *JTS* 63 (2012): 492–522.

28. On the dative of sphere, see Wallace, *Greek Grammar*, 153–55.

29. Dunn, *Romans 1–8*, 221; Moo, *Romans*, 286.

30. *TLNT* 3:120–23; BDAG 827, s.v. πληροωφορέω 2.

31. An impressive group of Alexandrian manuscripts (א, A, Ψ, 33, 1739) and a majority of Byzantine manuscripts have "and" (καί) right before "it was counted" (ἐλογίσθη). KJV and

right relationship with him because Abraham fully trusted his word.

Paul now returns explicitly to the biblical statement that has controlled the discussion since 4:3. Even when he has alluded to and quoted other elements of the Genesis account of God's dealings with Abraham (Gen 12:3; 17:5; 18:18; 22:18; 26:4; 28:14), he was thinking primarily of this text. The repetition of this climactic statement from Genesis 15:6 brings Paul's description of Abraham's justification by faith full circle. He has now carefully defined what he means by faith. It is reliance on God's promise that he is able to bring life to the dead, despite appearances to the contrary. Faith of this quality brings glory to God, and God graciously puts it down in the heavenly books as righteousness.[32] Although this faith is not a work, it is nevertheless the right approach to God. God accepts it and withholds his wrath from all whose lives are characterized by it.

4:23–24a But it was not written only because of him that it was counted to him but also because of us (Οὐκ ἐγράφη δὲ δι' αὐτὸν μόνον ὅτι ἐλογίσθη αὐτῷ ἀλλὰ καὶ δι' ἡμᾶς). Abraham's experience of trusting God prompted the composition of the account of his faith in Scripture, but that account was also written down because those who believe the gospel in the present need to benefit from what it says about the quality of Abraham's faith.

This statement begins a brief but critical paragraph in which the entire discourse on Abraham's justification by faith achieves its goal. Paul says in this section that the description of the object and quality of Abraham's faith in the scriptural narrative provides instruction to believers in the present about the object and quality of their faith in God.

What did Paul mean when he said that the account of Abraham's faith was not written "because of" (διά) Abraham "only" (μόνον)? Abraham was the "cause" of the account of his justification by faith in the sense that he experienced the events that prompted its composition. These events were not written simply to convey Abraham's story, however, but "because" they had significance for those who believe in the present (cf. 15:4; 1 Cor 10:6).[33]

4:24b–c to whom it will be counted—to those who believe in the one who raised Jesus our Lord from the dead (οἷς μέλλει λογίζεσθαι, τοῖς πιστεύουσιν ἐπὶ τὸν ἐγείραντα Ἰησοῦν τὸν κύριον ἡμῶν ἐκ νεκρῶν). Those who believe the gospel have a faith of the same quality as Abraham's faith since both Abraham and more recent believers trust God graciously to give life to the lifeless, something that seems impossible from a merely human perspective.

Paul puts the justification of believers in the future, but it is unclear whether he means the future from the perspective of Abraham and therefore his own present, or the future from his own perspective and therefore the final day of judgment.[34] Paul sometimes describes justification as a future event (2:13; 5:19; Gal 2:17; 5:5), but that is likely not his meaning here. Not only is his focus in 4:1–22 on Abraham's justification at the moment he trusted God rather than at some distant time but immediately after this brief concluding para-

NASB translate the text as if the "and" were present but too smoothly to reflect the rough nature of the resulting Greek. Cranfield's suggestion that scribes mistakenly assimilated the text to Gen 15:6 LXX and Rom 4:3 (which have the "and") is probably correct (*Romans*, 1:250n1).

32. See the comments on 4:3–5, and, for the imagery of a heavenly record by which people are judged, see Dan 7:10; Rev 20:12; Jub. 30:18–23.

33. Cf. Pelagius, *Romans*, 88; Calvin, *Romans*, 101; Michel, *An die Römer*, 174, and the analogous use of "on account of" (διά) with an accusative personal pronoun in Matt 27:19; John 6:57; 7:43; 12:30; Rom 2:24.

34. For the first perspective, see, e.g., Michel, *An die Römer*, 174n11, and Dunn, *Romans 1–8*, 222–23, and for the second perspective, see, e.g., Cranfield, *Romans*, 1:250; Moo, *Romans*, 287n3; and Jewett, *Romans*, 341.

graph (4:23–25) Paul will speak of believers "having been justified" (5:1).[35] It is likely, then, that here Paul speaks of the future faith of all believers viewed from the historical perspective of Genesis 15:6. His meaning here is close to his meaning in Galatians 3:8 where "the Scripture, foreseeing that God would justify the Gentiles by faith, preached the gospel beforehand to Abraham."

Since Paul and the Roman Christians believed in the God who raised Jesus from the dead, their faith closely paralleled the faith of Abraham who believed "the one who makes the dead alive" (4:17; cf. 4:19–21). Abraham and those who believe the gospel trust the same God, and they trust him to provide them with life when death appears to be the only option apart from God's intervention. Without God's power on their behalf, Abraham and Sarah would have died without an heir (4:19; cf. Gen 15:2–3; 17:17–18), and without the resurrection of Jesus from the dead believers would have suffered God's justified wrath with its penalty of spiritual and physical death. As Romans 5:10 says, they will "be saved by his life," a rescue that 5:9 has just described as salvation from the "wrath" of God (cf. 6:4; 8:11, 34; 10:9).

4:25 who was handed over because of our trespasses and raised because of our justification (ὃς παρεδόθη διὰ τὰ παραπτώματα ἡμῶν καὶ ἠγέρθη διὰ τὴν δικαίωσιν ἡμῶν). Christ's death atoned for the trespasses of Paul and the Roman Christians. Christ's resurrection provided a context in which they could exercise a faith like Abraham's and so, like him, be justified.

This relative clause is a neatly balanced combination of two coordinated clauses, each consisting of a verb in the aorist passive and an adverbial prepositional phrase indicating the cause of the verbal action. God stands in the background of the verb "he was handed over" (παρεδόθη). This becomes clear in 8:32 where Paul uses the same verb in the active voice and with God as the subject (8:31) to describe how emphatically God has come to our aid: "He who indeed did not spare his own Son but handed him over [παρέδωκεν] for us all, how will he not also, with him, graciously give us all things?" The use of the verb both here and in 8:32 probably goes back to the statement in Isaiah 53:5–6 (LXX), "The Lord gave him over [παρέδωκεν] to our sins" (cf. Isa 53:12 LXX).[36] The prepositional phrase, "because of our trespasses," probably also goes back to that passage, which describes the suffering servant as "wounded because of our acts of lawlessness [ἐτραυματίσθη διὰ τὰς ἀνομίας ἡμῶν]" and "weakened because of our sins [μεμαλάκισται διὰ τὰς ἁμαρτίας ἡμῶν]."[37] Just as in Isaiah 53:1–12, the one who is handed over suffers because of the sins of others, and for Paul this meant suffering to atone for their sins (Rom 3:25; 5:8–10).

Despite the otherwise neat balance between the first and second clauses, the prepositional phrase in the second clause ("because of our justification") is used in a different way than its counterpart in the first clause ("because of our trespasses"). It is unlikely that Paul would describe the justification of believers as the necessary precondition of Christ's resurrection.[38] It is also unlikely that the statement is an imprecise rhetorical flourish. Since the construction Paul uses here (διά + the accusative) indicates the "cause" or "reason why something happens" in a broad way, it can introduce the purpose for which something happens, and that makes

35. Cranfield, *Romans*, 1:250; Légasse, *Romains*, 329; Downing, "Justification as Acquittal?," 317–18.

36. See especially Gathercole, *Defending Substitution*, 63–64.

37. Bruce A. Lowe, "Oh διά! How is Romans 4:25 to Be Understood?," *JTS* 57 (2006): 151–52.

38. For a somewhat tortured argument to this effect, see Godet, *Romans*, 184–85.

the most sense in this second phrase.[39] The justification of Paul and his readers was the reason Christ was raised in the sense that it was the purpose for which his resurrection took place.

This is the only place in his extant corpus where Paul explicitly connects the justification of believers with the resurrection of Christ. Elsewhere, justification is a result of Christ's death, and Paul explains the connection lucidly in terms of Christ's role as a substitutionary, atoning sacrifice that shows God to be just in punishing sin at the same time that he justifies sinners, allowing them to go unpunished (3:24–26; 5:9, 18; cf. 8:3).[40] But how was Christ's resurrection necessary for the justification of believers? Did Paul think that believers shared in the acquittal that Christ experienced when he was raised from the dead?[41] Did he think that they could rest assured of their own justification in the future because the risen Christ was interceding for them at God's right hand?[42]

Bruce A. Lowe, in an important article on Romans 4:25, has provided the most likely explanation of the link between Christ's resurrection and the believer's justification.[43] Lowe ties the sentence closely to what Paul has just said about Abraham's faith in the God "who makes the dead alive" (4:17–22). The context of Abraham's justifying faith was a situation in which, against all human hope, Abraham trusted that God could enliven his and Sarah's ability to bear a child so that Abraham would become the father of many nations. In the same way, Paul and the Roman Christians have placed their trust, against all human hope, in the gospel's affirmation that God raised Christ from the dead and in the further conviction that Christ's resurrection is the first instance of the general resurrection of believers from the dead (8:11, 18–25; cf. 1 Cor 15:12–20; 2 Cor 4:13–14). The resurrection of Christ, then, provided the basis for the justification of believers because it gave a concrete, if unseen, object for their hope and for their trust in God. Christ's resurrection provided an opportunity analogous to the opportunity that God gave to Abraham in Genesis 15:1–6 for his people to put their faith in him and for him to count this trust as righteousness.

This reading receives confirmation from Paul's discussion of salvation in 8:24–25 and 10:9. In 8:24–25 hope is the instrument of salvation in the same way that Abraham's faith, which Paul explains in terms of his hope in 4:18, is the basis for Abraham's justification. Similarly, in 10:9 salvation comes in part from the heartfelt belief that God has raised Jesus from the dead.[44]

39. BDAG 225, s.v. διά B 2 a; Sanday and Headlam, *Romans*, 116.

40. See also Colin G. Kruse, *Paul's Letter to the Romans*, PNTC (Grand Rapids: Eerdmans, 2012), 223.

41. M. D. Hooker, "Raised for Our Acquittal (Rom 4,25)," in *Resurrection in the New Testament: Festschrift J. Lambrecht*, ed. R. Bieringer, V. Koperski, and B. Lataire (Leuven: Leuven University Press, 2002), 323–41.

42. Kruse, *Romans*, 223.

43. Lowe, "Oh διά!," 149–57.

44. Cf. also 1 Cor 15:17 ("And if Christ has not been raised, your faith is futile and you are still in your sins") and Ben C. Dunson, "Faith in Romans: The Salvation of the Individual or Life in Community," *JSNT* 34 (2011): 28–29.

Theology in Application

In this passage Paul demonstrates that God was already at work in the time of Abraham, gathering a people he had justified by faith and setting them free from from the oppression, injustice, and destruction of sin. Romans 4:13–25 demonstrates from the story of Abraham's justification that God has never intended his people to rescue themselves from sin nor has he ever intended to confine to one people group his work of making sinners right with himself.

The Law Cannot Lead to Righteousness

Whether one considers "the law" in 4:13–15 to be the embodiment of customs that define a certain ethnic group (cf. 2:17–20) or simply the universal code of conduct by which people of any ethnic group should live (cf. 2:14–15), Paul makes clear that "the law" cannot be the means through which human beings enter into a peaceful relationship with God. Viewed as the Jewish law, it is too socially restrictive to describe God's ultimate purposes for his people; viewed as a universal code of conduct, it can only bring God's wrath as the penalty for disobedience to it since no one can keep it fully.

If the church in our own time seems to be a place primarily where rules are made and kept and where only one type of person is welcome, then it is not living out the theological principle taught in Romanas 4:13–15. The church should be a vibrant community of people from many different backgrounds and abilities united not by the homogeneity of the personalities within it, nor by the ethnic group from which people come, nor by the stage of spiritual maturity at which they have arrived but by their common experience of a right relationship with God through faith in Jesus Christ.

Faith Leads to Righteousness

In 4:16–25 Paul describes in detail what he means by the faith that God counts as righteousness. His description has three elements. First, it is the faith not of the community but of the individual.[45] It is true that the promise Abraham believed was the promise that he would be the father of many nations, but Abraham believed this promise as an individual, and the benefits of his justification were first of all benefits for himself in his personal relationship with God. This is apparent in the way Paul describes Abraham's faith as something he exercised in the presence of God (4:17) and as confident hope that God would do for him personally what he had promised he would do despite Abraham's own physical limitations (4:17–21).

45. See also Dunson, "Faith in Romans," 19–46.

It is possible to emphasize the individual aspects of saving faith to the unbiblical neglect of its communal aspects, but it is also possible to do the reverse.[46] The church should never neglect its responsibility to call individuals to turn from their own individual sin and to trust God's promise that through the death and resurrection of Christ God will reconcile to himself those who trust him.

Second, 4:16–22 shows the quality of the faith that God counts as righteousness. It is not closing one's eyes to the obvious difficulties that life presents, an irrational belief in "what you know ain't so" as Mark Twain famously wrote.[47] Rather, it is a sober assessment of how difficult a particular situation would be apart from God's intervention and a trust that God is both willing and able to intervene with blessing in that situation. This is not irrational because, as John Stott has said, the reasonableness of one's faith "depends on the reliability of the person being trusted."[48] Abraham did not close his eyes to the difficulties God would have to overcome to give him a child (4:19–20; Gen 15:2–3; 17:17–18), but he trusted that God was both willing and able to do what he had promised.

Believers today, similarly, face calls to reject entirely the idea of God's existence, and these calls are supposedly supported by scientific evidence for the self-generating nature of the universe. Or they encounter admonitions to view all religions as equally valid strivings for a connection with the transcendent. Or they encounter suffering in their own lives and wonder if God could possibly love them in the way that the gospel describes his love for his people. When these kinds of challenges to faith arise, it is helpful to seek the encouragement of others who have known God to be faithful and, as Paul does here, to meditate on the word of God, which records God's faithfulness in times past.

Third, Paul also describes the content of the faith that God counts as righteousness, especially in 4:23–25. Abraham believed God's promise that he would inherit the world, a promise to which God was faithful when the gospel opened the floodgates of his people to the gentiles and suddenly Abraham became the father of many nations. As we have seen in the exegesis of 4:13, however, this reference to the world hints that Paul had in mind God's restoration of the world from the effects of sin. Paul will explain explicitly in the paragraphs to come that God's plan for his creation includes not only the gathering of a multiethnic community of humanity whom he has reconciled to himself but eventually the defeat of sin's supreme penalty, death itself. He has already started to defeat death in the resurrection of Jesus, and as we saw above in the exegesis of 4:25, Jesus's resurrection and the promise that it holds

46. So, correctly, Dunson, "Faith in Romans," 20–22.

47. Mark Twain (Samuel L. Clemens), *Following the Equator: A Journey around the World* (Hartford, CT: American, 1898), 132.

48. Stott, *Romans*, 133.

for the resurrection and eternal life of believers is precisely the object of the faith that God counts as righteousness.

There is perhaps no greater challenge to the believer's faith than death. How can the eternal God create people in his image with the capacity to know and serve him but then allow death to silence their praise? The psalmists sensed this: "What profit is there in my death, if I go down to the pit? Will the dust praise you? Will it tell of your faithfulness?" (Ps 30:9; cf. 88:10–12). Yet death appears from the earthly perspective to be absolutely final. "Dust" is an appropriate metaphor for the sense of loss that it engenders.

For those who have put their faith in "the one who raised Jesus our Lord from the dead," death still brings sadness, but it need not bring despair. God has defeated death through Jesus's sacrificial death for sin and through his resurrection from the dead. When believers trust God in faith, then, this is what they are believing—that God has defeated death in the death and resurrection of Jesus and will give eternal life to those who commit themselves to him (cf. Rom 10:8–10).

CHAPTER 11

Romans 5:1–11

Literary Context

In 1:18–4:25 Paul described the first phase of the good news that God has used his power to save his human creation. Everyone, whether Jewish or not, had knowingly, culpably rebelled against their creator (1:18–3:20). Possession of the Jewish law and circumcision made no difference in this rebellion (2:1–29). All alike were impious and unjust (3:9–20), deserving the outpouring of God's wrath both in the present (1:18) and at the future day of God's just judgment (2:5). Because of his gracious character, however, God was unwilling to leave his creatures in this condition and rescued them from it by means of the atoning sacrifice of Christ Jesus (3:21–26). Those who relied on Jesus for rescue from sin in this way were justified, that is, they escaped the just condemnation of God and the justified punishment of his wrath (3:24–26). God made no distinction between Jew and non-Jew in this regard (3:22, 29–30), nor should Jews who knew the story of Abraham have expected him to do so (4:1–25). Abraham was justified by faith, and God fulfilled the very promise that Abraham had faith he would fulfill (Abraham would be the father of many nations) when non-Jews (the "many nations") joined the people of God by faith in Christ Jesus.

Now, in 5:1–8:39 Paul describes a second phase of the gospel, namely, its impact on the lives of those who have been justified by faith. The ethnic concerns that so dominated 1:18–4:25 drop away here because Paul is describing the character of the lives of those who have entered the people of God by faith, whether Jewish or non-Jewish.[1] His concern in this new section is with the movement of the believer from "wrath" to "peace," from "death" to "life," from "slavery" to "freedom," and especially from the past and present ravages of sin to the future "glory" of God. His emphasis lies on the tension that characterizes the existence of the people of God in the period before God fully accomplishes his purposes for humanity. Although they have experienced God's love and need have no fear of his future wrath, they continue to

1. Cf. Fitzmyer, *Romans*, 97.

struggle against the tyranny of sin and to experience the suffering that comes from living within a world in rebellion against God.

In 5:1–11 the turn in Paul's argument from God's justification of the impious on the basis of their faith to the life that those justified by faith now live is evident in the sudden dominance of perfect- and present-tense verbs to describe the situation that now characterizes the existence of believers. They "have" (present tense) peace with God (5:1), "have" (perfect tense) access to his grace, and "stand" (perfect tense) in this grace (5:2). They "boast" (present tense) in the hope of God's glory (5:2), in afflictions (5:3), and in God (5:11). They remain "unashamed" (present tense) despite the as yet unrealized nature of their hope (5:5). God's love is "poured out" (perfect tense) in their hearts (5:5), and God "demonstrates" (present tense) his love for them (5:8).

The paragraph describes lives that are the mirror image of the wicked and impious people in 1:18–2:27.[2] The people described there failed to worship and glorify God as their creator (1:18–23, 25, 28) and produced suffering within the world by their violence toward each other (1:29–32). They also boasted in God but did not obey him (2:17). In contrast, God has transformed the believers whom Paul describes here from God's impious enemies into friends who stand in his grace (5:1), experience his love (5:5), and boast in what God is doing and will do for them (5:2–3, 11). Unlike the people of 1:18–2:27 who experience the outpouring of God's wrath now (1:18) and will experience it in the future (2:5, 8), God has changed the believers of 5:1–11 so that they are at peace with him (5:1, 10–11) and have assurance of salvation from his wrath in the future (5:9).

The paragraph also looks forward to the final section (8:18–39) of this second major part of the letter.[3] Although 8:18–39 is roughly twice as long as 5:1–11, it explores the same themes: hope for the glory of God in the midst of affliction (8:18–25; cf. 5:2–4), the assurance and aid that the Holy Spirit gives to believers in the midst of their present suffering (8:23, 26–27; cf. 5:5), Christ's initiative in dying for believers as a demonstration of God's love (8:31–34, 37–39; cf. 5:8), assurance that God will save believers from his future wrath (8:31–34; cf. 5:9–10), and finally Christ's resurrected and ascended life as assurance of God's care for believers in the present and in the future (8:34–39; cf. 5:10–11). The first and last sections of the second major part of Paul's argument, then, stand like bookends on either side of it, emphasizing its primary concerns.

2. Cf. Dunn, *Romans 1–8*, 242: "The climactic sequence of 5:6–10 (weak, ungodly, sinners, enemies) answers the reverse sequence of 1:19–32."

3. Cf. Nils Alstrup Dahl, *Studies in Paul: Theology for the Early Christian Mission* (Minneapolis: Augsburg, 1977), 88–90; Moo, *Romans*, 293.

VIII. The Scriptures Show That Righteousness Comes by Faith Rather Than by Works (4:1–25)

➡ **IX. Justification by Faith Brings Peace and Reorients the Believer's Existence (5:1–8:39)**

- **A. Justification by Faith Rescues Believers from God's Present and Future Wrath (5:1–11)**
- B. Christ's Obedience Overwhelms the Effects of Adam's Disobedience (5:12–21)
- C. Union with Christ's Death and Resurrection Initiates a New Life (6:1–23)
- D. Union with Christ's Death and Resurrection Frees Believers from the Law (7:1–6)
- E. The Goodness, Yet Inability, of the Law (7:7–25)
- F. God's Solution to the Human Plight (8:1–39)

X. Israel's Present Rejection of the Gospel Does Not Imply the Failure of God's Word (9:1–11:36)

Main Idea

In this paragraph, Paul makes two affirmations about the lives of those who have been justified by faith. First, he says that the love of God provides a firm foundation for the hope of believers that they will share in God's glory. God's love for them is clear from the presence of the Holy Spirit in their lives and from the sacrificial, atoning, and therefore justifying death of Christ. Second, Paul affirms that even in the present, with its inevitable experiences of suffering, believers can live in joyful confidence that God has reconciled them to himself. Although they were once his enemies, they are now at peace with him. He loves them, and they do not, and will not, fall under the wrath that he justifiably pours out on the wicked.

Translation

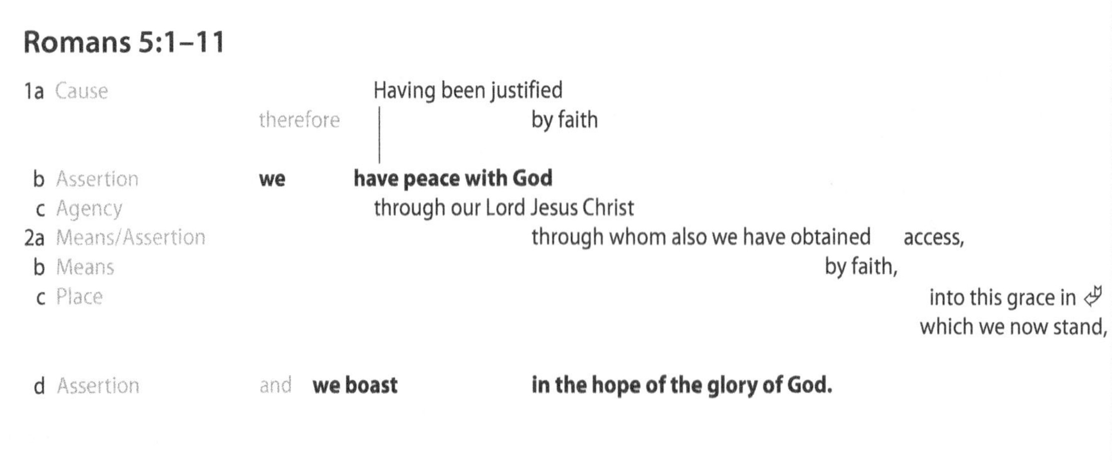

Romans 5:1–11

1a	Cause	therefore	Having been justified by faith
b	Assertion	we	**have peace with God**
c	Agency		through our Lord Jesus Christ
2a	Means/Assertion		through whom also we have obtained access,
b	Means		by faith,
c	Place		into this grace in which we now stand,
d	Assertion	and	**we boast in the hope of the glory of God.**

3a	Contrast	And not only so,
		but **we** also **boast** **in afflictions**
b	Cause	because we know
c	Content	that affliction produces endurance and
4a	Content	endurance character, and
b	Content	character hope.
5a	Assertion	**And hope does not bring shame**
b	Cause	because the love of God has been poured
c	Place	into our hearts
d	Means	through the Holy Spirit given to us.
6a	Time (Specific)	For while we were still weak,
b	Time (General)	at just the right time,
c	Basis (for 5a–b)	**Christ died for the impious.**
7a	Explanation (of 6c)	For only rarely
		will someone die
b		for a just person,
c	Advantage	
d	Contrast (with 7a)	but for a benefactor
		someone might even perhaps dare to die.
8a	Contrast (with 7a–b)	But **God demonstrates his own love for us**
b	Explanation (of 8a)	in that while we were still sinners Christ died for us.
9a	Comparison/Result	How much more,
		therefore,
b	Cause (of 9c)	having been justified now
	Means (of 9b)	by his blood
c	Promise	**shall we be saved**
d	Agency	through him
e	Separation	from God's wrath.
	Time	
10a	Restatement of 8b as Condition of 10d	For if, while we were enemies,
		we were reconciled to God
b	Means	through the death of his Son,
c	Comparison/Cause	how much more,
	Circumstances	having been reconciled,
	Exclamation	**shall we be saved**
d	Means	by his life.
11a	Contrast	And not only so, but
b		**we also boast**
c	Sphere	in God
d	Agency	through our Lord Jesus Christ,
e	Description	through whom we have now received the reconciliation.

Structure

The paragraph begins and ends with a declaration of the peace and reconciliation that believers presently have because of what the exalted Lord Jesus Christ has done for them (5:1–2a, 10–11). The hostility that believers had toward God prior to their justification by faith (1:18–3:20) is now at an end, and for them God has set aside the fully justified, impartial outpouring of his wrath in the present (1:18) and in the future (2:5, 9). They have peace with God, have permanent access to him, and stand firmly in his grace (5:1–2a). They have received reconciliation (5:10–11).

Although the "peace" (εἰρήνη) Paul announces at the beginning of the passage (5:1) and the "reconciliation" (καταλλαγή) he announces at its conclusion (5:11) are closely related to one another, the two terms are not identical. "Reconciliation" is a more specific term that implies a period of conflict before "peace" is obtained.[4] As the passage unfolds, it defines the "peace" with which it begins as reconciliation between God and his people who, at the time of their reconciliation, were weak, impious sinners and enemies deserving wrath rather than salvation (5:6–8).

Paul's primary interest in this paragraph is not how God accomplished reconciliation through the death of Christ, although in 5:6–10 he recalls his explanation of this in 3:21–26. Rather, his interest lies in the implications of that accomplishment for believers in the present and the future. As the passage moves, then, from peace to reconciliation, it describes these implications in various ways. When believers experience "affliction" (5:3; cf. 2:9), it is no longer a sign of God's wrath or a cause for shame but of his ability and willingness to create within the believer endurance, character, and hope (5:3–4).[5] Suffering is accompanied, moreover, by God's love, something which believers experience in the present because of the Holy Spirit's work in them, and something which Christ's death demonstrates to them (5:5–8). The justification and reconciliation that Christ's death and life accomplished for believers also assures them that they will not experience God's wrath in the future but that God will save them from it (5:9–10).

The paragraph concludes (5:11) by circling back to the affirmations of the opening line (5:1), but now having explained the "peace" mentioned there as "reconciliation" and having explained the reconciliation as something undertaken at God's initiative and as a clear demonstration of his love for believers. Because of what God has done for them through their "Lord Jesus Christ" they have grounds for boasting in God in the present and need have no fear that their boast will turn to shame in the future (5:11). They will share his glory (5:1).

4. J. Bersot, "La paix avec Dieu, passage de la justification à la reconciliation. Observations structurelles et narratives en Romains 5,1–11," *ScEs* 62 (2010): 132.

5. Cf. Bersot, "La paix avec Dieu," 127, 140.

Exegetical Outline

IX. Justification by Faith Brings Peace and Reorients the Believer's Existence (5:1–8:39)

➡ **A. Justification by Faith Rescues Believers from God's Present and Future Wrath (5:1–11)**

1. Justification by Faith Leads to Peace with God and Future Participation in God's Glory (5:1–2)
2. Peace with God Means Rescue from God's Wrath and Confidence in His Love Both in the Present and in the Future (5:3–9)
3. Rescue from God's Wrath Means Reconciliation with God and Assurance of Future Salvation (5:10–11)

Explanation of the Text

5:1 Having been justified therefore by faith we have peace with God through our Lord Jesus Christ (Δικαιωθέντες οὖν ἐκ πίστεως εἰρήνην ἔχομεν πρὸς τὸν θεὸν διὰ τοῦ κυρίου ἡμῶν Ἰησοῦ Χριστοῦ). Because they have relied on God to release them from the punishment they deserve for their violations of his law, and to do this through the death and resurrection of Jesus, the relationship of believers with God is free from both hostility and anxiety.

With the expression, "having been justified therefore by faith," Paul summarizes the argument of 3:21–4:25. He has used the verb "justify" (δικαιόω) in the previous argument to refer to recognizing that someone is in the right (3:4) or to deciding not to condemn someone (2:13; 3:20, 24, 26, 28, 30; 4:2, 5). In all but one of these uses (3:4), God is the one who decides not to condemn, and he bases his decision on the person's faith (ἐκ πίστεως, 3:26, 30; πίστει, 3:28; διὰ τῆς πίστεως, 3:30), not on their obedience to the law (ἐξ ἔργων νόμου, 3:20; ἐξ ἔργων, 4:2) or their possession of circumcision (3:30).[6] Paul has described the object of faith sometimes as Jesus (3:22, 26) and sometimes as God (4:24; cf. 4:3, 5, 17). He has described the content of faith as God's justification of the ungodly (4:5), presumably through the atoning death of Jesus (3:24–26; 4:24–25) and the resurrection of Jesus from the dead (4:24–25; cf. 1:4; 6:8; 10:9).

Paul has been describing the convictions he shares with his Roman readers about why this justifying faith is necessary and through much of the argument has been explaining the gospel to them as he would explain it to unbelieving Jews. Now references to faith and believing will drop away, reappearing only briefly in 6:8 until they reenter the argument at 9:30, and Paul's focus will be on the character of the lives of those who have become obedient to the call to believe the gospel as he has just proclaimed it (cf. 1:5). Now when Paul says "we," he does not mean "we Jews" but "we believers."

Justification by faith forms the basis for the first characteristic of the believer that Paul mentions in 5:1–8:39: "peace with God."[7] This "peace" is foremost a cessation of hostility between God and believers, as the emphasis on salvation from God's wrath and on reconciliation with God in 5:9–10 demonstrates (cf. 8:6–7), but Paul probably also intended to express a subjective understanding of peace with God. This is a peace stemming both

6. On the use of the verb "justify" to mean the decision not to condemn someone to punishment, see Downing, "Justification as Acquittal?," 298–318.

7. On the difficult textual problem in 5:1, see "In Depth: Did Paul Write 'Let Us Have Peace' in 5:1?".

from the happiness that comes to those whose lawless deeds God has forgiven (4:7–8; cf. Ps 32:1–2) and from the love that, as Paul will say shortly, God has poured into the hearts of believers (5:5; cf. 5:8). Calvin, then, was not incorrect to say that peace here means "serenity of conscience, which originates from the awareness of having God reconciled to oneself."[8] Paul means more than this, but not less.

Haacker helpfully points out that the concept of the gods pouring out their wrath on people in the form of disaster and plague and then relenting would have been familiar in Rome (Livy, *History of Rome* 3.5–8). For Paul, the basis for peace with God is not the desperate supplications of a ravaged people to "the angry gods to grant them pardon and to put an end to the plague" (Livy, *History of Rome* 3.7) but the initiative of God himself on behalf of his sinful people "through our Lord Jesus Christ."[9] Christ's death on the cross and his resurrection came at God's gracious initiative for the purpose of establishing and maintaining peace between himself and his people (3:21–26).

Paul has only rarely used the title "Lord" for Jesus up to this point (1:4, 7; 4:24), and if we interpret the title here through the lenses of 1:4 and 4:24 then Jesus's role as Lord is especially connected with his resurrection. The peace believers have with God, therefore, is due both to the death of Christ and to his resurrection (4:24–25; cf. 5:10). Exactly how the resurrection of Christ contributes to peace with God does not come out explicitly here, but in 8:34 Paul will say that since Jesus has been resurrected and exalted to God's right hand Jesus continues to intercede on behalf of believers and so they need never fear condemnation.

IN DEPTH: Did Paul Write "Let Us Have Peace" in 5:1?

One of the most difficult textual problems in Romans occurs at the main verb in 5:1. The weightiest manuscripts from a diversity of text types read the subjunctive "let us have" (ἔχωμεν) here rather than the indicative "we have" (ἔχομεν). The difference in spelling is slight, involving the substitution of an omicron (ο) for an omega (ω) or the reverse. The difference in pronunciation is even smaller, which is probably how the variation arose, whatever the correct reading. The difference in meaning, however, is significant. A present-tense subjunctive would most naturally mean something like "let us continue to have peace" and would be an exhortation for believers to hold onto or perhaps to enjoy the peace they had attained when they were justified by faith.[10] The indicative, however, would be an affirmation that because believers have been justified by faith they already exist in a state of peace with God.

The subjunctive has on its side a strong set of manuscript witnesses from the

8. Calvin, *Romans*, 104.

9. Haacker, *An die Römer*, 113. Livy, *The Early History of Rome*, trans. Aubrey de Sélincourt (London: Penguin, 2002), 202.

10. Sanday and Headlam, *Romans*, 118: "It becomes our duty to enjoy to the full the new state of peace with Him which we owe to our Lord Jesus Messiah." Cf. Stanley E. Porter, "The Argument of Romans 5: Can a Rhetorical Question Make a Difference?," *JBL* 110 (1991): 664; Longenecker, *Romans*, 555–56.

Alexandrian tradition (א B A C), the most conservative text type, as well as the impressive, confirming witness of the more independent Codex Claromontanus (D) and two important Byzantine manuscripts (K L).[11] One can also make a good case that this is the more difficult reading (and therefore less likely to represent a scribal improvement) because Paul has been engaged in theological argumentation up to this point in the letter, not in exhortation.[12]

Still, the subjunctive is not likely to be the correct reading. The manuscript evidence for the indicative is not as weak as is sometimes assumed. It has on its side the Wyman Fragment (0220), a parchment page from a third-century codex that contains Romans 4:23–5:3.[13] Although there is an unfortunate hole in the manuscript at precisely the place where the χο of εχομεν would have appeared, the small remnants of the letters and the size of the hole make it very unlikely that both a χ and an ω appeared there.[14] This manuscript is of the Alexandrian text type and is a witness to the text of 4:23–5:3 at least as weighty as the great Alexandrian uncials.

Significantly, correctors of both of the earliest Alexandrian uncials, א and B, working in the fourth–sixth centuries and the sixth–seventh centuries respectively, indicated that omegas in these manuscripts should be omicrons at this point. This reflects uncertainty about the subjunctive at an early date.

In addition to these strong witnesses, the witness of most Byzantine manuscripts to the indicative and two eighth-ninth century uncials with Alexandrian affinities (P Ψ) provide a measure of diversity.

On balance, the manuscript evidence for the subjunctive remains stronger than that for the indicative, but the evidence for the indicative is far from negligible.

It is the evidence from the flow of Paul's argument that tips the balance heavily in favor of the indicative. Prior to 5:1 Paul has not explicitly said that believers presently have peace with God. Rather, he is about to argue in the most emphatic terms in 5:1–11 that God has brought reconciliation and peace with himself to his people through their justification. This makes it very unlikely that at this point, before he has made his case, he would urge his readers to enjoy or hold onto a peace with God that they presently possess.[15]

11. On Codex Claromontanus and the ancient witness to the text that it represents, see D. C. Parker, *An Introduction to the New Testament Manuscripts and Their Texts* (Cambridge: Cambridge University Press, 2008), 259–60.

12. Although Porter ("Argument," 664) argues that the subjunctive becomes a plausible reading when the diatribal nature of Romans is taken into account.

13. Parker (*New Testament Manuscripts*, 259) thinks this early date needs reconsideration because the manuscript is parchment rather than papyrus.

14. William H. P. Hatch, "A Recently Discovered Fragment of the Epistle to the Romans," *HTR* 45 (1952): 83.

15. Cranfield, *Romans*, 1:257n1. Cf. Wallace, *Greek Grammar*, 464.

5:2 through whom also we have obtained access, by faith, into this grace in which we now stand, and we boast in the hope of the glory of God (δι᾽ οὗ καὶ τὴν προσαγωγὴν ἐσχήκαμεν τῇ πίστει εἰς τὴν χάριν ταύτην ἐν ᾗ ἑστήκαμεν καὶ καυχώμεθα ἐπ᾽ ἐλπίδι τῆς δόξης τοῦ θεοῦ). The risen Lord Jesus gives believers permanent access to the grace of God, and because of his own resurrection he gives them assurance that they too will share in God's incorruptible existence.

The term "access" (προσαγωγή) occurs only here and twice in Ephesians (2:18; 3:12) in biblical Greek, but it is a fairly common term outside the Bible. It could describe the "access" that ships might gain to a city through its good harbor (Polybius, *Histories* 10.1.6) or the "access" that the friends of a great ruler might provide for others to their powerful friend (Xenophon, *Cyr.* 7.5.45).[16] Since Paul has just spoken of Jesus as Lord and that title seems to be especially connected with his resurrection, he was probably thinking of access that believers have to God's favor because of his continued intercession for them at God's right hand (8:34). In addition, the term "grace" with the demonstrative pronoun (τὴν χάριν ταύτην) points back to the completely free nature of the justification and redemption that came through Jesus's death (3:24). The perfect-tense verbs "we have" (ἐσχήκαμεν) and "we stand" (ἑστήκαμεν) emphasize the continuation of this new, gracious situation for believers.[17]

Boasting often has negative connotations in Romans. Paul has spoken of people who boast in the law without doing it (2:23 [καυχάομαι]). He has excluded this sort of boasting on the basis of faith (3:27 [καύχησις]). He has denied that works provided Abraham any ground for boasting before God (4:2 [καύχημα]). He will instruct gentile believers in Rome not to boast that they have believed the gospel (11:18 [κατακαυχάομαι]). There is another sort of boasting, however, that Paul finds appropriate—boasting in what God has done for the believer. Paul, for example, is willing to boast in the work of taking the gospel to the gentiles because God gave this work to him (15:17–18 [καύχησις]).

The boasting here in 5:2 is this second type of boasting (cf. 5:11). God has given the believer a hope as certain as God is trustworthy (4:18) that believers, like the resurrected Jesus himself, will experience the incorruptible state of "glory" (τῆς δόξης) in which God himself dwells (cf. 1:23; 2:7). Prior to believing the gospel, Paul and his readers in Rome had no hope for this eschatological glory because of their sin (3:23), but because of the death and resurrection of Jesus they can be sure that they will share in Jesus's resurrection glory (8:17, 18, 21, 30).

5:3 And not only so, but we also boast in afflictions because we know that affliction produces endurance (οὐ μόνον δέ, ἀλλὰ καὶ καυχώμεθα ἐν ταῖς θλίψεσιν, εἰδότες ὅτι ἡ θλῖψις ὑπομονὴν κατεργάζεται). For the believer, suffering provides the basis for testifying joyfully to others about God's ability to bring good even out of the evil that is now so prevalent.

Paul often uses the phrase "and not only so, but also" (οὐ μόνον δέ, ἀλλὰ καί) to make a principle he has just applied to a specific situation applicable to a broader range of circumstances (5:11; 8:23; 9:10; 2 Cor 8:19). He has just said that believers boast in the hope of the glory of God, and now he applies this boasting even to suffering. "Afflictions" (θλίψεσιν) referred for Paul both to extraordinarily difficult, life-threatening circumstances such as

16. BDAG 876, s.v. προσαγωγή.

17. Cf. K. L. McKay, *A New Syntax of the Verb in New Testament Greek: An Aspectual Approach*, Studies in Biblical Greek 5 (New York: Peter Lang, 1994), 32–33; Moo, *Romans*, 300n31.

he faced in proclaiming the gospel and nurturing churches (e.g., Rom 8:35; 2 Cor 1:8; 2:4; 1 Thess 1:6) and to the everyday pressures that came, for example, to married couples (1 Cor 7:28). So far in Romans, he has used the term only to refer to the "affliction" that God would repay to those who do evil (2:9). For those who have peace with God, however, present affliction becomes a means of developing hope in the very "glory" that he had said in 2:10 God would give to those who do what is good (cf. 5:4).[18]

The expression "because we know" (εἰδότες) represents a perfect-tense adverbial participle of cause describing the reason why Paul is able to say something so counterintuitive.[19] "Afflictions" would normally be a cause for alarm and complaint, but for the believer they can form a reason for boasting because they initiate a chain of results—endurance, character, and hope—that does not end in shame (5:5a). The boasting of which Paul speaks here is not, therefore, pride in one's ability to endure hardship but a celebration of God's ability to bring good out of evil (cf. 8:17–28; 2 Cor 11:30; 12:5–9; 2 Thess 1:4). God uses affliction as an ingredient in producing (κατεργάζομαι) endurance (cf. 2 Cor 4:17; 7:10–11; Jas 1:2–4).

5:4 and endurance character, and character hope (ἡ δὲ ὑπομονὴ δοκιμήν, ἡ δὲ δοκιμὴ ἐλπίδα). Endurance of the suffering that results from the world's sinful rebellion against God tests the mettle of believers, and those who have this tested character hope for the future world that God has promised.

With this phrase it becomes clear that Paul is arranging his words in a rhetorically sophisticated way, repeating the final and climactic word of the previous clause at the beginning of the next clause ("climax" or "anadiplosis").[20] The effect communicates inevitable progression toward a particular goal (cf. 8:29–30; 10:14–15, 17; 2 Pet 1:5–7), and in this case the goal is "hope."

The endurance that affliction produces according to the previous clause (5:3) itself produces "character" (δοκιμή). Paul's letters are among the first extant texts to use this term, and it is unique to his writings in the NT. Its meaning here, however, is not in doubt. The LXX frequently used the verb "test, examine, put to the proof" (δοκιμάζω) metaphorically for testing someone in the fires of difficulty (e.g., LXX Ps 25:2 [Eng. 26:2]; 65:10 [Eng. 66:10]; Prov 17:3; Wis 3:5–6), and for Paul, "character" results from this process (cf. 2 Cor 2:9; Phil 2:22).[21]

The thought that the crucible of suffering tests and refines one's commitment to God is a traditional Jewish idea, and Paul may have joined other Christians in borrowing it from this tradition (cf., e.g., Prov 17:3; Sir 2:5; 1 Pet 1:7; Jas 1:3–5; T. Jos. 2:6).[22] If so, he has given the idea his own theologically distinctive stamp by indicating the paradox involved: the hardships that are the prerequisite of "endurance" and "character" are the means God uses to engender "hope" in the believer. This is probably not the "hope" that one's faith is genuine, as the traditional use of the metaphor might lead us to think, but the eschatological "hope" that Paul describes more fully in 8:20–25. When suffering has shaped the "character" of people, they hope for freedom from sin and the decay of mortality. The relationship between the suffering of believers and their hope matches Abraham's experience. His

18. Cf. Berot, "La paix avec Dieu," 127, 140.

19. The adverbial perfect participle almost always expresses cause (Wallace, *Greek Grammar*, 631).

20. BDF §493; Edward P. J. Corbett, *Classical Rhetoric for the Modern Student* (New York: Oxford University Press, 1971), 475.

21. On the term, see Walter Grundmann, "δόκιμος, κτλ.," *TDNT* 2:55–60 and *TLNT* 1:353–61.

22. Cf. Michel, *An die Römer*, 179–80, who thinks that both Paul and James reflect a common tradition.

childlessness was the crucible where his hope in the faithfulness of God was forged (4:18–22).

5:5 And hope does not bring shame because the love of God has been poured into our hearts through the Holy Spirit given to us (ἡ δὲ ἐλπὶς οὐ καταισχύνει, ὅτι ἡ ἀγάπη τοῦ θεοῦ ἐκκέχυται ἐν ταῖς καρδίαις ἡμῶν διὰ πνεύματος ἁγίου τοῦ δοθέντος ἡμῖν). The believer's hope is not a point of embarrassment because already in the present God's Spirit provides the believer with evidence of his love.

When Paul says that "hope does not bring shame," he is speaking of the humiliation that one feels when one's publicly expressed expectations are not realized. After Paul had boasted to Titus about the Corinthians (probably that they would receive him gladly), he was relieved that Titus found a welcome reception among them, "for whatever boasts I made to him about you, I was not put to shame [κατῃσχύνθην]. But just as everything we said to you was true, so also our boasting [καύχησις] before Titus has proved true" (2 Cor 7:14; 9:3–4).[23] In the same way, believers "boast in the hope of the glory of God" according to 5:2, and Paul now affirms that this hope does not result in their shame. The thought is similar to Psalm 119:116: "Uphold me according to your promise, that I may live, and let me not be put to shame in my hope!" (cf. Ps 22:5; 25:20; Isa 28:16 LXX).[24]

The common translation "hope does not disappoint" (RSV, NAB, NASB, NET, HCSB) for 5:5, then, is too weak. It fails to capture Paul's conviction that even in the midst of suffering the believer can trust God because God has proven himself to be faithful. As the present tense "does not bring shame" (οὐ καταισχύνει) affirms, moreover, this is not something that will only become clear in the future.[25]

Paul expresses the reason the believer has no cause for shame despite the suffering of the present in the causal clause (ὅτι . . .) that concludes the sentence. "The love of God" could refer either to the love that God has for believers (taking τοῦ θεοῦ as a subjective genitive) or to the love that believers have for God (taking τοῦ θεοῦ as an objective gentive), but since Paul speaks unambiguously in 5:8 of God demonstrating his love for believers through the death of Christ, it is likely that Paul also refers here to God's love.[26]

Hellenistic Jewish literature frequently refers to the practical effects of God's actions as the outpouring (ἐκχέω) of these effects on people, whether grace (Ps 45:2 [44:3 LXX; 45:3 Heb.]), mercy (Sir 18:11), or anger (Hos 5:10 LXX). Despite the frequent references in early Christian literature to the outpouring of God's Spirit on believers (Acts 2:17, 33; 10:45; Titus 3:6; Barn. 1:3; 1 Clem. 46:6), then, it is important to keep the focus of Paul's statement where he places it, on the outpouring of God's love. This in turn means, as Cranfield has said, that Paul's emphasis lies on the lavish nature of God's love. As Chrysostom comments, Paul does not merely say that God has *given* his love to believers but that God has *poured out* his love, clearly showing its abundance (τὸ δαψιλές).[27] The Holy Spirit gives believers an inward assurance that God loves them greatly (cf. Eph 2:4; 3:17, 19; 5:2; 2 Thess 3:5).

23. Murray J. Harris, *The Second Epistle to the Corinthians: A Commentary on the Greek Text*, NIGTC (Grand Rapids: Eerdmans, 2005), 551.

24. The Hebrew term for "hope" here (*seber*) is rendered with "expectation" (προσδοκία) in the LXX (Psa 118:116), but elsewhere is sometimes rendered "hope" (ἐλπίς) (Ps 146:5 Heb. and Eng. [145:5 LXX]; cf. Isa 38:18; Ps 119:166 [118:166 LXX]; 145:15 [144:15 LXX]).

25. On the use of the present tense here, see Meyer, *Romans*, 184; Dunn, *Romans 1–8*, 252; Wright, "Romans," 517; Jewett, *Romans*, 355–56.

26. So correctly Origen, *Romans, Books 1–5*, 292–93; Calvin, *Romans*, 108.

27. Cranfield, *Romans*, 1:263; cf. BDAG 312, s.v. ἐκχέω; Chrysostom, *Romans*, 141 (*PG* 60:470).

5:6 For while we were still weak, at just the right time, Christ died for the impious (ἔτι γὰρ Χριστὸς ὄντων ἡμῶν ἀσθενῶν ἔτι κατὰ καιρὸν ὑπὲρ ἀσεβῶν ἀπέθανεν). The inward assurance that the Holy Spirit gives to believers of God's lavish love corresponds to the concrete, historical reality of Christ's death for believers before and apart from their willingness to acknowledge him.

The conjunction "for" (γάρ) ties this sentence to what Paul has just said about God's love and introduces Christ's death as the concrete demonstration of that love. The unusual repetition of "still" (ἔτι) and the phrase "at the right time" (κατὰ καιρόν) reveals the emphasis that Paul places on the timing of Christ's death. Christ died for Paul and his readers when they were "weak" (ἀσθενής) and "impious" (ἀσεβής).[28] Paul often uses the term "weak" to mean "without adequate faith" (1 Cor 8:7, 9–12; 9:22; cf. 1 Thess 5:14) and will speak later in Romans of the believer who is "weak in faith" (14:1–2; cf. 15:1). Here the term refers not to those with inadequate faith but to those who, like the people that practice "impiety" (ἀσέβεια) in 1:18, have no faith at all. The people Paul described in 1:18–32 were without hope when left to themselves, moving in a downward spiral from bad to worse. The weakness to which Paul refers, then, is an inability for people to reconcile themselves to God (cf. Eph 2:1–3, 11–12; 4:17–19; Col 1:21; 2:13a; Titus 3:3).

The evidence of God's lavish love, says Paul, is Christ's death "for" (ὑπέρ) sinners while they were in this rebellious state. The brief formula "Christ . . . died for the impious" reaches back to Paul's more detailed description of the atoning death of Christ in 3:24–26 where the redemption that Christ brings comes through his role as the "mercy seat," the place where God initiated reconciliation with humanity through Christ's sacrificial death.

The notion that Christ died "for" the weak and impious, moreover, means not that he died out of loyalty to them in the same way, for example, that the Maccabean martyrs died "for" (ὑπέρ) God's laws (2 Macc 7:9) or "for" virtue (4 Macc 1:8). It means, rather, that he died both to benefit the weak and impious and to do so in their place, suffering the curse that they justly deserved (cf. Gal 3:13).[29] As Harris puts it, "Acting on behalf of a person often involves acting in their place."[30] Paul will illustrate this dual meaning of "for" (ὑπέρ) in the next verse.

5:7 For only rarely will someone die for a just person, but for a benefactor someone might even perhaps dare to die (μόλις γὰρ ὑπὲρ δικαίου τις ἀποθανεῖται· ὑπὲρ γὰρ τοῦ ἀγαθοῦ τάχα τις καὶ τολμᾷ ἀποθανεῖν). Christ's death for the impious is unique: it is not analogous to the death of someone for a particularly virtuous or politically important person.

The term "only rarely" (μόλις) probably refers here to what one does not ordinarily expect, just as it does in an early second-century BC papyrus that refers to people who will "hardly [i.e., not likely] depart until the 25th" (P.Tebt. I 19.10).[31] Paul matches it with the contrasting term "perhaps" (τάχα) in the next clause to emphasize the unlikely but possible need to qualify the first clause (cf. Heliodorus, *Aeth.* 5.13.1). The clauses are not, then, saying the same thing, as interpreters sometimes argue.[32]

28. For the phrase "at the right time" (κατὰ καιρόν), see, e.g., Herodotus, *Histories* 1.30.2; Num 9:7 LXX. It is unlikely to mean "at that time" (Dunn, *Romans 1–8*, 255; Jewett, *Romans*, 358).

29. Moo, *Romans*, 307n65.

30. Murray Harris, *Prepositions and Theology in the Greek New Testament: An Essential Reference Resource for Exegesis* (Grand Rapids: Zondervan, 2012), 215–16.

31. MM 416. Cf. BDAG 657, s.v. μόλις 2–3; *CGELNT* 236, s.v. μόλις.

32. E.g., Hultgren, *Romans*, 210–11.

The overall effect is a cautiously worded statement about the unprecedented nature of Christ's death for the impious. Justice, goodness, and piety all go together as highly admired virtues in the first-century Greco-Roman world. Paul's point is that for someone to die for a person who is virtuous in these ways is rare enough, but Christ's death for the impious is unique.

The nature of the contrast between the "righteous" person and "the good" or "the good person" is not entirely clear, and interpreters have proposed a number of different options for understanding where the contrast lies.[33] The solution that best fits the Greco-Roman context into which Paul was writing sees the contrast in the difference between a merely "just" person, who was impartial and honest in his or her dealings and judgments, and the civic benefactor who was often described in the literature and inscriptions of the first and second centuries as a "good man" (ἀνὴρ ἀγαθός). Dio Chrysostom, for example, chides the citizens of Rhodes for their lack of attention to their benefactors with this observation: "How very much worse it is to rob good men [τοὺς ἀγαθοὺς] of honours bestowed than to rob anyone else, and to injure your benefactors [εὐεργέτας] than to injure any chance person" (Dio Chrysostom, *To the People of Rhodes* [*Or. 31*] 65 [J. W. Cohoon and H. Lamar Crosby, LCL]).[34] Andrew Clarke has argued persuasively that people of lower social standing often incurred social obligations to such benefactors and might conceivably even die for a benefactor to whom they were obligated.[35]

5:8 But God demonstrates his own love for us in that while we were still sinners Christ died for us (συνίστησιν δὲ τὴν ἑαυτοῦ ἀγάπην εἰς ἡμᾶς ὁ θεός, ὅτι ἔτι ἁμαρτωλῶν ὄντων ἡμῶν Χριστὸς ὑπὲρ ἡμῶν ἀπέθανεν). Contrary to all normal expectations in the field of human relations, God loved those who had sinned against him to the point of death and did this before they had turned away from their sin.

Previously Paul had spoken of human unrighteousness "demonstrating" (συνίστημι) God's righteousness by means of the contrast between the two (3:5), and now he uses the same term to describe how God "demonstrates" his love by means of his own action in Christ. The term translated "in that" (ὅτι) often means simply "that," but here Paul uses it to introduce a further explanation of the first clause.[36] In contrast to the rare death of someone for a righteous person or benefactor, Christ died for sinners. The adverbial participle translated here "while we were" (ὄντων), moreover, emphasizes that Christ died, even more remarkably, for sinners before they had turned from their sins (cf. 2 Cor 5:21; Gal 3:13; 4:4–5).

Stories of one person substituting his or her own death "for" (ὑπέρ) another person out of love or some other emotional bond were not unknown in antiquity.[37] Paul is affirming much more than this, however, when he says that Christ "died for us" (ὑπὲρ ἡμῶν ἀπέθανεν). As 5:9 will demonstrate clearly, Christ's death was a sacrificial death that rescued believers from the eschatological wrath of God by putting them right with God.[38]

33. Andrew D. Clarke, "The Good and the Just in Romans 5," *TynB* 41 (1990): 128–42.

34. Cited in Clarke, "The Good and the Just," 140.

35. Clarke, "The Good and the Just." See also Cranfield, *Romans*, 1:264–65; Schreiner, *Romans*, 261–62; Haacker, *An die Römer*, 114–15.

36. Michel, *An die Römer*, 182. BDAG 732, s.v. ὅτι 2 b. Cf. "inasmuch as" as a gloss for the term in *CGELNT* 257, s.v. ὅτι 3.

37. Cilliers Breytenbach, "'Christus starb für uns.' Zur Tradition und paulinischen Rezeption der sogenannten 'Sterbeformeln,'" *NTS* 49 (2003): 447–75; Harris, *Prepositions and Theology*, 211. See, e.g., Euripides, *Alc.* (especially 155, 284, 700–701) and Xenophon, *Anab.* 7.4.9.

38. The blood of 5:9 recalls the atoning, sacrificial blood of 3:25, and this makes Breytenbach's position that no atonement is in view here ("Christus starb für uns," 447–75) improbable.

The demonstration of God's love through an action of Christ implies the unity between God and Christ in Paul's thinking. Not surprisingly, then, he moves easily between the notion of "the love of God" (5:5), "the love of Christ" (8:35; cf. 8:37), and "the love of God in Christ Jesus" (8:39) elsewhere in the letter, just as he does here.

5:9 How much more, therefore, having been justified now by his blood shall we be saved through him from God's wrath (πολλῷ οὖν μᾶλλον δικαιωθέντες νῦν ἐν τῷ αἵματι αὐτοῦ σωθησόμεθα δι' αὐτοῦ ἀπὸ τῆς ὀργῆς). Believers stand uncondemned by God because of the death of Christ, and so they can rest assured that the God who loved them enough to sacrifice Christ for them will rescue them from the outpouring of his wrath on the day of judgment.

The phrase "how much more" signals Paul's use of a common type of logical reasoning in Greco-Roman antiquity. Aristotle calls it an argument derived from "the more and the less" (Aristotle, *Rhetoric* 2.13.4 1397b), the principle that if evidence proves a less probable proposition it also proves a similar, more probable proposition.[39] Paul uses this style of argumentation often, particularly in Romans (5:10, 15, 17; 11:12, 24; cf. 2 Cor 3:7–11; Phlm 16).[40]

Here his point is that if God has made people right with himself by means of the blood of Christ, it is even more probable that he will rescue those same people from the punishment that he will justly give to the impious, unrighteous, impenitent, and disobedient (1:18; 2:5, 8; 3:5) on the future day of his righteous judgment (2:5, 16; cf. Eph 5:6; Col 3:6; 1 Thess 1:10; 5:9). Christ's death for the impious was the improbable event, as Paul has just shown in 5:6–8, as improbable as the childless Abraham becoming the father of many nations (4:17–22). It is relatively easy in light of this event to believe that God will rescue those whom he so clearly loves from the punishment that comes to the unrighteous.

The aorist participle "having been justified" (δικαιωθέντες) recalls 5:1, but Paul qualifies it in a different way. In 5:1 Paul spoke of the means of justification (ἐκ) as faith; here he speaks of the instrument of justification (ἐν) as the blood of Christ. Together the two phrases recall 3:25 where Paul speaks of God displaying Christ publicly as the mercy seat "through faith, by his blood" (διὰ [τῆς] πίστεως ἐν τῷ αὐτοῦ αἵματι). The death of Christ atoned for sin in a way that the Day of Atonement sacrifice anticipated since Aaron sprinkled the blood of that sacrifice on and in front of the mercy seat (Lev 16:14–15).

Because of Christ's atoning death, those who believe the gospel are "now" justified. Although God will punish in the future those whose hearts are hard and unchanged (2:5), the present justification of believers should assure them that they will not experience God's wrath on that day. God will save believers "through" Christ at that time, just as God has justified them in the present by his atoning death.[41]

5:10 For if, while we were enemies, we were reconciled to God through the death of his Son, how much more, having been reconciled, shall we be saved by his life (εἰ γὰρ ἐχθροὶ ὄντες κατηλλάγημεν τῷ θεῷ διὰ τοῦ θανάτου τοῦ υἱοῦ αὐτοῦ, πολλῷ μᾶλλον καταλλαγέντες σωθησόμεθα ἐν τῇ ζωῇ αὐτοῦ). Believers can also rest assured that God will save them on the day of judgment because, in a highly unusual move, he took the initiative to overcome their hostility to him by means of the costly death of his Son, even while they were still hostile.

39. LSJ 1076, s.v. μάλα, II 7.

40. M. Wolter, "μᾶλλον," *EDNT* 2:382; Jewett, *Romans*, 362.

41. Moo, *Romans*, 310–11.

This sentence is conceptually and rhetorically parallel to 5:9. Both sentences compare something that God has done through Christ for believers in the present age with the salvation God will give believers through Christ in the future. In 5:9 Paul uses the legal language of justification through Christ's death to describe what God did for us (he justified believers), how he did it (by the atoning death of Christ), and what this implies about the future judgment (believers will be saved through Christ). Here he uses the political and social language of reconciliation through Christ's death to say much the same thing.

The verb "reconcile" (καταλλάσσω) and the noun "reconciliation" (καταλλαγή) appear in the New Testament only in Paul's writings and are especially frequent in Romans (5:10–11; 11:15) and Second Corinthians (5:18–20; cf. 1 Cor 7:11).[42] In ancient Greek literature generally the terms refer to social and political relationships—the reconciliation of personal enemies with each other (Euripides, *Iphigeneia at Aulis* 1157; Aeschines, *Against Ctesiphon* 162), the reconciliation of husband and wife (Josephus, *Ant.* 5.137; 1 Cor 7:11), and frequently the achievement of peace between warring parties, sometimes through a mediator. Herodotus, for example, says that Periander, son of Cypselus, "reconciled" (κατήλλαξε) the Mytilenaeans and Athenians with each other by convincing each side simply to keep what they already had and not attempt to take what belonged to the other (*Histories* 5.95.2). Dionysius of Halicarnassus, similarly, describes how the Alban general Metius Fufetius invited the Romans to negotiate "reconciliation" (καταλλαγάς) with the Albans in light of a pending attack upon them both by a common enemy (*Ant. rom.* 3.5.4).[43] Later in the narrative, Dionysius calls this "reconciliation" a "cessation of hostilities" (διάλυσις, *Ant. rom.* 3.7.1).[44] Paul's use of the term "peace" in 5:1 and of "enemies" here in 5:10 shows that his use of the metaphor falls into this last category of reconciliation after a period of warfare.

On rare occasion Greek speakers used this terminology metaphorically, in a way similar to Paul's use of it here, to refer to the reconciliation of people to the gods or, by Jewish writers, to God (Sophocles, *Aj.* 744; Josephus, *Ant.* 3.315; 6.143).[45] When they used it in this sense, however, the desire for and efforts at reconciliation typically flowed from the human side to the gods or God, whether through sacrifices (Sophocles, *Aj.* 744), the pleas of a mediator (Josephus, *Ant.* 6.143), fervent prayers (2 Macc 1:5; 8:29; cf. Dionysius of Halicarnassus, *Ant. rom.* 8.50.4), or martyrdom (2 Macc 7:33, 37–38). In these passages God is angry, and those with whom he is angry are trying to find a way to assuage his anger.

Within this context, Paul's use of the concept stands out as extraordinary.[46] For Paul, reconciliation happens at God's initiative and expense and at a time when those who were warring against him had no intention of laying aside their rebellion, as Paul's focus on human impiety and sin within the context shows (5:6–8).[47] Mediators are involved,

42. A closely related term whose meaning is identical (ἀποκαταλλάσσω) appears in Eph 2:16 and Col 1:20, 22.

43. The plural was commonly used in the idiom "to make reconciliation." See LSJ 899, s.v. καταλλάγδην II 1.

44. For the meaning of this term, see LSJ 402, s.v. διάλυσις 2 and MGS 495–96, s.v. διάλυσις C.

45. Cilliers Breytenbach, "Salvation of the Reconciled (With a Note on the Background of Paul's Metaphor of Reconciliation," in *Salvation in the New Testament: Perspectives on Soteriology*, ed. Jan G. van der Watt, NovTSup 121 (Leiden: Brill, 2005), 271, 276.

46. I. H. Marshall, "The Meaning of 'Reconciliation,'" in *Unity and Diversity in New Testament Theology: Essays in Honor of George E. Ladd*, ed. Robert A. Guelich (Grand Rapids: Eerdmans, 1978), 127–31; Wilckens *An die Römer (Röm 1–5)*, 298–99; Harris, *Second Epistle to the Corinthians*, 436–39.

47. The debate among interpreters about whether Paul had in mind God's enmity toward human beings or their enmity toward God, then, should be decided in favor of the latter position.

whether Christ, whose death effects reconciliation (3:25; 5:9–10), or Paul who, in the role of ambassador, brings the message of reconciliation (2 Cor 5:19–20; cf. Eph 6:20), but the mediators are God's representatives, acting at his initiative.

Paul's point in using the language of reconciliation here, however, is not merely to say that God has taken the initiative in reconciling rebellious human beings to himself but to emphasize that this initiative was costly to God and that if he has engaged in this unusual and costly action on behalf of believers then they need not fear the future day of judgment. The costly nature of God's peace-making initiative is clear from Paul's use of the expression "his Son" for Jesus (cf. 8:3, 32). His emphasis on assurance about the future is clear, just as it was in 5:9, from the "how much more" clause that concludes the verse. As one of the earliest commentators on Romans put it, "The God who acts on behalf of his enemies will not be able to love his friends any less than that."[48] This salvation will take place, Paul says, through Christ's life, and this probably means that their union with the risen, victorious Christ will assure them of salvation from God's wrath (cf. 4:25; Eph 2:5–6).

5:11 And not only so, but we also boast in God through our Lord Jesus Christ, through whom we have now received the reconciliation (οὐ μόνον δέ, ἀλλὰ καὶ καυχώμενοι ἐν τῷ θεῷ διὰ τοῦ κυρίου ἡμῶν Ἰησοῦ Χριστοῦ δι' οὗ νῦν τὴν καταλλαγὴν ἐλάβομεν). As if future salvation from God's wrath were not enough, God's gracious gift of a peaceful, reconciled relationship with him provides believers with a reason to praise God in the present.

Paul now summarizes and concludes the whole paragraph.[49] The phrase "and not only so, but we also boast" repeats almost word for word the opening clause of 5:3 and sums up the important theme of present boasting from the beginning of the paragraph. The only difference is that instead of using a present indicative (καυχώμεθα), Paul uses a present participle (καυχώμενοι). As the parallelism suggests, however, he probably intended the participle to function as if it were an indicative (cf. Rom 12:6; 2 Cor 4:8; 5:6; 9:11).[50]

Instead of tying boasting to present afflictions as he did in 5:3 Paul now ties it to reconciliation, the theme that dominated 5:10 and that he foreshadowed in 5:1 when he described the "peace with God" that characterizes those who have been justified by faith. Believers boast in the present, then, not only because of their future hope of sharing in God's incorruptible state of glory (5:2) or because present suffering is instilling patience, character, and hope in them (5:3–5) but also because they presently possess reconciliation with God. This reconciliation comes at God's initiative, and therefore believers boast not in themselves or that they, and not others, are the ones reconciled (cf. 11:18) but in God who initiated and achieved the reconciliation (cf. 1 Cor 1:29–31). God did this "through our Lord Jesus Christ," that is, through his sacrificial, justifying death, as Paul has explained in 5:8–10.

The designation of Jesus as both Lord and Christ in this phrase also emphasizes, however, that boasting in God is not only possible because of what Jesus did in the past but because of "his life" (5:10) in the present. He is the living, reigning Lord and King, and, as Paul will soon explain, the union of believers with their living Lord has important implications for the way they live in the present and the way they will live in the future (cf. 4:25; 6:4–11; 7:4; 8:11, 17, 34).

48. Ambrosiaster, *Romans*, 39.
49. Dunn, *Romans 1–8*, 261.
50. On the use of a participle in an indicative sense, see Wallace, *Greek Grammar*, 653.

Theology in Application

This passage describes the joyful confidence that those who rely on the gospel should have in their relationship with God both in their present circumstances and in the future. Paul does this through emphasizing three principles.

The Firmness with Which Believers Stand under God's Favor

The present- and perfect-tense verbs in 5:1–2 describe the definitive nature of the believer's position before God. Believers "have" (present tense) peace with God and access (perfect tense) to his grace in the present. This access, moreover, is not an inert, passive route of access to God that believers must somehow now travel. Jesus Christ has already led believers through the way of access to God, and they stand in God's grace (perfect tenses). Believers can be so confident of their peaceful, grace-filled relationship with God that they can "boast" in the hope they have for its continuation in the future when God is revealed to everyone in all his glory (5:2).

As the comments on this section mention, Paul was speaking to people whose understanding of God may have been heavily influenced by the view that injury, sickness, war, poverty, and death occurred because the gods were unhappy with them. There were certainly exceptions to this view of the gods, but many people believed that to escape suffering they needed to appease the gods in various ways. Plutarch, for example, describes the lengths to which the person who feared the gods would go to avoid their wrath:

> He sits outside his house with sackcloth on and filthy rags about him; and oftentimes he rolls naked in the mire as he confesses divers sins and errors of his—eating this or drinking that, or walking in a path forbidden by his conscience. (Plutarch, *Superst.* 7, 168D [Frank Cole Babbitt, LCL])

Plutarch was critical of this approach to the gods, and his picture is a caricature, but it illustrates the practical theology of most people in Paul's world.

People of every age, including those who live in scientifically oriented, technologically sophisticated societies, often have a similar understanding of God. God is largely absent from their lives until things become difficult or they desperately need something, and then they plead with God to relieve their suffering or to give them what they want. Sometimes they try to persuade God to answer their prayers with the promise that they will, in return, give to God something they think he wants or needs. In Ernest Hemingway's 1929 novel, *A Farewell to Arms*, for example, the protagonist Frederic Henry is desperate that his lover Catherine Barkley not die after giving birth to their stillborn child. Although he has occasionally thought about God during the course of the story and has been friendly toward the priest assigned to his Italian military unit, God has played virtually no role in his life. When Catherine's condition becomes serious, however, he turns in desperation to God, begging him in prayer to save her life and promising he will do anything God wants if Catherine lives.[51]

In Romans 5:1–11 Paul announces the good news that this fearful and uncertain approach to God, so common in the modern world, reflects a wrong understanding of his character. The way to peace with God, access to his grace, and hope for a bright future lies not in trying to win this happy relationship through pleas and promises. It lies instead, as Paul says twice in 5:1–2, in trusting what God has already done through the death and resurrection of the Lord Jesus Christ.

Suffering and Love as the Contexts in Which Hope Is Nurtured

Paul recognized in 5:3–5 that trust in God does not exempt the believer from suffering. Had Frederic and Catherine believed the gospel and joined the local church in the little Swiss village where they passed that winter, nothing in Romans promises them Catherine would have had an easier labor or that Frederic would have suddenly had the resources for enduring the real pain of his situation without anguish. Paul does remind believers, however, that God will use their suffering to engender patience, "proven character" (NASB; cf. NAB), and hope for the coming world in which suffering and anguish have disappeared.

He also reminds them of the signs of God's love for them in the present and in the past, signs that point to a future in a world free from suffering and full of God's love. One sign of God's love is the assurance of the lavish nature of the love that the Holy Spirit gives to believers (5:5). Paul probably thought of this experience as similar to the experience of God's Spirit testifying "together with our spirit that we are the children of God" (8:16).[52] This is a subjective experience, and so it is not always present in the midst of suffering, but when it is present, "it not only mitigates our sorrow in adversity, but like a sweet seasoning gives a loveliness to our tribulations."[53]

Another sign of God's love is objective. Christ died for believers not while they were righteous and good but while they were impious and unrighteous (5:7–8; cf. 1:18). In the sacrificial death of Christ for sinners, God and Christ acted in concert with each other, and so Paul takes the action of Christ as a measure of the love of God. Moreover, the overwhelming greatness of God's love is clear from the timing of Christ's death. It occurred not when believers had made some movement toward reconciliation with God but when they were still in rebellion against him. This objective

51. Ernest Hemingway, *A Farewell to Arms* (New York: Charles Scribner's Sons, 1929), 330.

52. Stott, *Romans*, 143.

53. Calvin, *Romans*, 108.

proof of God's great love toward believers is a persistent theme in Paul's letters (Eph 2:1–5; 2 Tim 1:9–10; Titus 3:3–7) and is a fixed point of reference for believers who, in the midst of suffering, may not feel that God loves them.

The Assurance of Believers That They Will Be Saved from God's Wrath

The anger of God toward human beings who have rebelled against him and who have dealt unjustly and unkindly with each other has been a frequent theme of Paul's argument so far. God reveals his wrath against these people in the present as their impious and unjust behavior creates increasing levels of chaos in the world (1:18–32), and he will reveal it in the future on "the day of wrath" (2:5). Paul is not specific about precisely what form God's wrath will take on that final day, but from some of the words he uses to describe it (e.g., "affliction and distress," 2:9), it seems as if the suffering and anguish that presently afflict the world provide foretastes of what his wrath will be like. "Aside from Scripture there is no stronger proof for the existence of hell than the existence of this world, the world from whose misery the features of the [biblical] picture of hell are derived."[54] Paul is clear, in any case, that God's judgments on that day will be fair (2:5; 3:5; 2 Tim 4:8; cf. Acts 17:31) and that apart from the redemptive, atoning, reconciling death of Christ believers would justly fall under God's judgment on that day along with everyone else.

Both Christ's death and his life provide believers with the assurance that they are free from God's wrath. God has already decided not to punish believers because of the costly death of his Son, so it is certain that they will not become the objects of his wrath in the future. As if this were not enough, Christ is no longer dead but alive, and if his death was effective in reconciling them to God, his life can hardly be less effective for their future salvation. As 8:33–34 explains, God has justified us, so it would make no sense if he condemned us. Christ lives, victorious over all God's enemies, and this victor is the one who is an advocate on behalf of believers. Believers, then, can face suffering, death, and whatever else the future brings with confidence that they are and always will be at peace with God.

54. Herman Bavinck, *Holy Spirit, Church, and New Creation*, vol. 4 of *Reformed Dogmatics*, ed. John Bolt, trans. John Vriend (Grand Rapids: Baker, 2008), 712.

12 CHAPTER

Romans 5:12–21

Literary Context

Paul continues to describe the impact of the gospel on the lives of those who have been justified by faith, but now moves from a personal description of God's love for believers, cast throughout in the first-person plural (5:1–11), to a sweeping description of the impact of God's justifying work on all humanity expressed in the third person (5:12–21).[1]

The two paragraphs, however, are closely tied together logically and thematically. Logically, 5:12–21 advances the argument of 5:1–11 by explaining an important implication of the reconciliation that believers have experienced through the atoning death of Christ. "Because of this" costly act of reconciliation (5:12), the disaster of sin and death that Adam brought on all humanity has started to be reversed. Through the death of Christ (his "righteous act" or "obedience" [5:18, 19]), believers already experience the free gift of God's grace (5:15), justification (5:16, 18, 19), and life (5:18, 21), although through the use of the future tense in 5:17 ("will . . . reign in life") Paul shows that the reversal of the consequences of Adam's transgression is not yet complete.

Thematically, 5:12–21 continues to emphasize the generous nature of God's grace and love that played an important role in 5:1–11. In 5:5 Paul had spoken of God's love as "poured into" believers' hearts, emphasizing its lavish nature, and in 5:7–8 he had described God's love as so great that Christ died for believers while they were sinners. In the same way, Paul's qualification of his comparison between the universal effects of Adam's trespass and Christ's righteous act in 5:12–21 focuses on how God's grace does not simply meet the disastrous effects of Adam's sin measure for measure but overwhelms it with an abundance of grace (5:15–17, 20).

In 5:12–21 Paul not only advances the argument of 5:1–11 but also prepares the ground for the argument to come. He does this by personifying sin and death as powers that reign over humanity in its state of rebellion against God (5:12, 14, 17, 21). He had already hinted at this view of sin in 3:9 when he said that in 1:18–2:29 he

1. Cranfield, *Romans*, 1:269; Dunn, *Romans 1–8*, 271.

had shown all humanity, whether Jews or Greeks, to be "under sin," meaning under sin's domination.[2] Now he personifies not only sin but death also (5:14, 17), and he will continue to use this literary figure in 6:1–7:25 to show the strong grip that sin and death have on humanity (6:6, 9, 12–23; 7:6, 8, 11, 13).

Similarly, the discussion of the universal effects of sin and death in 5:12–21 prepares the reader for 8:18–25 where Paul puts the suffering of believers within the context of the suffering that the whole world presently experiences. This suffering will eventually come to an end when "creation also will be set free from slavery to decay for the freedom of the glory of the children of God" (8:21), or, as Paul puts it in 5:17, "those who receive the abundance of grace and the gift of righteousness will reign in life through the one person, Jesus Christ."

VIII. The Scriptures Show That Righteousness Comes by Faith Rather Than by Works (4:1–25)

IX. Justification by Faith Brings Peace and Reorients the Believer's Existence (5:1–8:39)

- A. Justification by Faith Rescues Believers from God's Present and Future Wrath (5:1–11)
- ➡ **B. Christ's Obedience Overwhelms the Effects of Adam's Disobedience (5:12–21)**
- C. Union with Christ's Death and Resurrection Initiates a New Life (6:1–23)
- D. Union with Christ's Death and Resurrection Frees Believers from the Law (7:1–6)
- E. The Goodness, Yet Inability, of the Law (7:7–25)
- F. God's Solution to the Human Plight (8:1–39)

X. Israel's Present Rejection of the Gospel Does Not Imply the Failure of God's Word (9:1–11:36)

Main Idea

In this paragraph Paul demonstrates an important consequence of God's gracious initiative to reconcile people to himself through the death of Christ. The atoning death of Christ has reversed Adam's introduction of sin and death into the world. This reversal, moreover, does not merely correct Adam's misstep and its consequences but overwhelms them with the lavish grace of God. God has decisively defeated the power of sin and death and brought the era of their reign to an end. Now the era of the eternal reign of God's grace has begun.

Translation

(See pages 279–80.)

2. Dunn, *Romans*, 148–49; idem, *Theology of Paul*, 111.

Romans 5:12–21

12a Result Because of this, just as **sin entered the world** **through** **one human being,** and
b **death** **through sin,** and
c so **death advanced to** **all human beings,**
d Result whereupon all sinned—.

13a Assertion For until the law **sin was in the world,**
b but **sin is not invoiced** when there is no law.
14a Contra-expectation Yet **death reigned from Adam until Moses,**
b even over those who had not sinned
c Manner in the likeness of the transgression of Adam
d Description who is a type of the coming one.

15a Contrast Yet **the trespass is not like the free gift,**

b Expansion for
if by the trespass of the one the many died,
c Contrast/Inference how much more
has **the grace of God** and
the gift given by grace abounded to the many
d Means by the one human being, Jesus Christ.

16a Contrast And **the gift is not like what happened through the one who sinned,**

b Expansion for **the judicial sentence** **arose out of one deed** and
brought condemnation,

c Contrast but **the free gift** **arose in the context of many trespasses**
for the purpose of justification.

17a Expansion For if death reigned by the trespass of the one person,
b Contrast/Inference how much more
c Assertion **will those ...**
d Identification who receive the abundance of grace and
the gift of righteousness **... reign in life**
e Means through the one person, Jesus Christ.

18a Comparison So then, as through the trespass of the one person
condemnation **came to all human beings,**

so also
b Inference/Means through the righteous act of the one person
c **life-giving justification** **came to all human beings.**

Continued on next page.

Continued from previous page.

19a	Expansion/ Comparison	For	just as through the disobedience of the one human being **the many were rendered sinners,**
b	Inference/Means		so also through the obedience of the one
c			**the many will be rendered righteous.**
20a		But	**the law slipped in**
b	Purpose		so that the trespass might increase;
c	Sphere	but	where sin increased,
d			**grace superabounded**
21a	Purpose/ Comparsion		in order that just as sin reigned in death, so also grace might reign
b	Means		through righteousness
c	Purpose		for eternal life
d	Means		through Jesus Christ our Lord.

Structure

Despite its initial sentence, which breaks off midstream, 5:12–21 displays a line of thought that is carefully constructed. The section can be divided into three main paragraphs, using three important transitional markers as dividing points: "because of this" (5:12), "yet" (5:15), and "so then" (5:18).[3]

First, Paul explains the devastation that Adam's sinful misstep brought to all humanity and states that Adam was merely an outline (or "type") of Christ (5:12–14). The "just as" near the beginning of this section (5:12) reveals immediately that Paul intends to compare Adam with Christ. The term "type" at the end of the section shows that this will not be a comparison of equals. Adam is merely a "type" of Christ, corresponding to him only in the sense that both were human and what both did affected all humanity.[4] The "just as . . . so also" form of the comparison breaks down as Paul emphasizes the universal impact of sin and death on all humanity, an impact that came equally to those with and without the law.

Second, in a section that begins with the strong adversative conjunction "yet" (ἀλλά), Paul explains the vast difference between the effect of Adam's trespass and the effect of God's gracious gift through Jesus Christ (5:15–17). He describes two

3. Otfried Hofius, "The Adam-Christ Antithesis and the Law: Reflections on Romans 5:12–21," in *Paul and the Mosaic Law*, ed. James D. G. Dunn, 2nd ed. (Grand Rapids: Eerdmans, 2001), 166–68.

4. Ibid., 168.

differences in 5:15–16, supporting each statement of difference with a sentence that begins with "for" (γάρ). The first difference is a contrast of certainties: if it is certain that Adam brought sin and death into the world, then it is much more certain that God has brought justification and redemption to the world through Jesus Christ (5:15). The second statement of difference contrasts Adam's ability to bring disaster on all humanity through a single sinful blunder and God's ability to bring lavish blessing to humanity despite the countless sins he had to overcome in order to do this (5:16). This second section concludes with 5:17, where Paul summarizes all that he has said about Adam and Jesus Christ since 5:14.

Third, with the important qualifications of 5:15–17 complete, Paul can finally proceed to a direct statement of the comparison between Adam and Christ (5:18–21).[5] What these two human beings did affected all humanity: the action of one brought sin, condemnation, and death to all people and the action of the other made grace, righteousness, and life available to everyone (5:18–19, 21).

Sandwiched between the two statements of this comparison in 5:18–19 and 21 Paul digressed briefly to address the obvious question of whether the law could do anything to repair the damage that Adam's trespass had wreaked on the world (5:20). Paul's answer is that the law by itself only made the damage worse, increasing rather than hindering sin. In God's purposes, however, the law's increase of sin provided the context in which God's grace flourished and so served the purpose of establishing the reign of God's grace through the Lord Jesus Christ.

Exegetical Outline

IX. Justification by Faith Brings Peace and Reorients the Believer's Existence (5:1–8:39)

- A. Justification by Faith Rescues Believers from God's Present and Future Wrath (5:1–11)
- ➦ **B. Christ's Obedience Overwhelms the Effects of Adam's Disobedience (5:12–21)**
    - 1. Adam's Sinful Misstep (5:12–14)
    - 2. The Differences between Adam and Christ (5:15–17)
        - a. Sin and death through Adam; justification and redemption through Christ (5:15)
        - b. Multiplied disaster through Adam; lavish blessing out of disaster through Christ (5:16)
        - c. A summary of 5:14–16 (5:17)
    - 3. The One Similarity between Adam and Christ, and a Digression on the Law's Role in Salvation History (5:18–21)

5. Ibid., 169–70.

Explanation of the Text

5:12 Because of this, just as sin entered the world through one human being, and death through sin, and so death advanced to all human beings, whereupon all sinned (Διὰ τοῦτο ὥσπερ δι᾿ ἑνὸς ἀνθρώπου ἡ ἁμαρτία εἰς τὸν κόσμον εἰσῆλθεν καὶ διὰ τῆς ἁμαρτίας ὁ θάνατος, καὶ οὕτως εἰς πάντας ἀνθρώπους ὁ θάνατος διῆλθεν, ἐφ᾿ ᾧ πάντες ἥμαρτον). Since God has reconciled believers to himself through the living, reigning Lord Jesus Christ, this same living Christ has started to reverse the curse of sin and death that Adam brought upon all humanity.

"Because of this" (διὰ τοῦτο) points backward to 5:1–11 (cf. 1:26; 4:16), and in particular to the statement in 5:10 that the salvation of believers through the life of God's Son is completely assured. Because Christ's life brings salvation, Paul was about to say, Christ has reversed the sin, condemnation, and death that came to all humanity as a result of Adam's trespass against God's command (5:12, 14, 16, 18–19). He expressed the first half of this thought in 5:12, but then digressed to explain the role of the law in God's dealings with humanity (5:13–14) and the vast difference between Adam and Jesus Christ (5:15–17), before expressing the thought's second half (5:18–19). The "even as" (ὥσπερ), which begins the comparison between Adam and Christ, is not completed by "so also" (οὕτως καί) until the second half of 5:18.

The term "human being" is not gender specific, but 5:14 makes clear that even here Paul had Adam in mind. This does not mean that Paul was unaware of Eve's part in the story (2 Cor 11:3; 1 Tim 2:13), but like other Jewish theologians of his period he identified Adam as primarily responsible for the first sin (e.g., 4 Ezra 7:48; 2 Bar 54:19; see "In Depth: Adam's Sin in Early Jewish Thought"). This faithfully reflects the tenor of the Genesis account: God communicates the command not to eat of the tree directly only to Adam (2:16–17) and, in the final scene of the passage, pronounces the climactic curse of death over Adam (3:17–19).

Paul had started to personify sin already in 3:9 where he said that his previous argument had charged all people with being "under sin." That trend continues and intensifies here in the description of sin entering (εἰσῆλθεν) the world through Adam. These references are the beginning of a picture of sin as an insidious power that, once allowed entry, multiplies until it dominates, enslaves, and kills everyone. Here, the chief agent of sin is death, which "advanced" (διῆλθεν; cf. 1 Macc 1:3 ESV) to humankind as a result of sin.

Death advanced to every human being, Paul says, "whereupon" (ἐφ᾿ ᾧ) all sinned. Ambrosiaster (in the late fourth century) and Augustine (in the early fifth century) used this phrase to support their teaching on original sin, which was already traditional in the Latin-speaking church. It was an interpretation that the Latin rendering "in whom" (*in quo*) facilitated but did not require.[6] This teaching, in Ambrosiaster's memorable words, claimed "that all sinned in Adam as though in a lump."[7] For Augustine, this teaching eventually took an unbiblical and particularly unfortunate turn when he identified the principal evidence of original sin with the sexual impulse and the means by which original sin was transmitted as sexual intimacy.[8]

6. Theodore de Bruyn, *Pelagius's Commentary on St Paul's Epistle to the Romans*, Oxford Early Christian Studies (Oxford: Oxford University Press, 1993), 92n22; "Original Sin," in *The Oxford Dictionary of the Christian Church*, ed. F. L. Cross, 3rd ed. (Oxford: Oxford University Press, 2005), 1202–3.

7. *Romans*, 40. Cf. Augustine, *Grat. Chr.* 2.34; *C. du. ep. Pelag.* 4.7.

8. Peter Brown, *Augustine of Hippo* (Berkeley: University of California Press, 1967), 387–93.

The mess that Augustine made of this passage has produced an unfortunate legacy of popular misunderstanding about Paul's teaching on Adam's sin and its effect on the rest of humanity. It is essential, then, to think clearly about precisely what Paul said and what he is likely to have meant.

First, the phrase Paul used (ἐφ' ᾧ) appears fairly often in ancient Greek and has a variety of meanings.[9] Greek speakers could use the phrase idiomatically as a conjunction meaning "on the condition that" or "for the purpose of" if they followed it with the infinitive or future indicative. They might use it to mean "with the result that" if they followed it with some past tense of the indicative.[10] The preposition and its dative object could also function simply as the separate elements of a prepositional phrase. When used in this second, more literal sense, the relative pronoun's antecedent could be either masculine or neuter. It could certainly mean "in whom" if modifying a verb of trusting or hoping (LXX Prov 21:22; Isa 25:9; 37:10; Jer 7:14). It could also mean "at which" in the sense of "whereupon," as, for example, when Dionysius of Halicarnassus says that a consul named Brutus condemned his sons to death in front of the gathered consuls, "whereupon [ἐφ' ᾧ] they all cried out" in horrified surprise at the strictness of his justice (Dionysius of Halicarnassus 5.8.3, *Ant. rom.* [Earnest Cary, LCL]; cf. 11.6.1; Josephus, *Ant.* 19.307; *J.W.* 1.484). This second, more literal sense comes very close to the use of the phrase as a conjunction meaning "with the result that."[11]

Second, it is unlikely that Paul used the phrase here to mean either "in whom" (Douay-Rheims) or "because" (e.g., RSV, NIV, ESV, NET, NASB, HCSB). "In whom" is unlikely because no verb of trusting or hoping is involved, and the antecedent of "whom" is too far from the pronoun to make this reading likely. "Because" is unlikely despite its current popularity, since a causal meaning for the phrase is rare before the tenth century, if it is present at all.[12]

Third, the most straightforward way of taking the phrase is as a reference back to the set of circumstances described in the first part of the sentence, back, that is, either to the entry of sin and universal death through one human being or simply to the advancement of death to all people. For Paul, death is the consequence of sin rather than the reverse (5:21; 6:23).[13] It is likely, then, that Paul means, "Adam introduced sin and death into the world, whereupon [or, as a result of which] all sinned." In some sense all human beings sinned with Adam and that is why all human beings share the penalty of death pronounced over Adam (cf. 5:19; 1 Cor 15:22).[14]

This means that although Augustine's exegesis was incorrect and the connection he drew between original sin and the sexual impulse was tragically misguided, his basic observation was on the right track. Paul seems to say in 5:12 that all subsequent humanity (except Christ) sinned with Adam, and this reading becomes more likely as Paul's argument progresses.[15]

9. Joseph A. Fitzmyer, "The Consecutive Meaning of ἐφ' ᾧ in Romans 5.12," *NTS* 39 (1993): 328–38.

10. Fitzmyer, "Consecutive Meaning," 329, 332–33. Paul uses the phrase three other times in his letters (2 Cor 5:4; Phil 3:12; 4:10), but those instances shed little light on the use here, since they too can be interpreted in various ways.

11. It is not accidental, then, that Fitzmyer, who opts for "with the result that" in Rom 5:12 also comments that "of the relative-pronoun understandings of ἐφ' ᾧ this one makes the best sense" ("Consecutive Meaning," 325).

12. Fitzmyer, "Consecutive Meaning," 329–32.

13. Augustine, *Against the Two Letters of the Pelagians* 4.7; Fitzmyer, *Romans*, 414.

14. C. E. B. Cranfield, "On Some of the Problems in the Interpretation of Romans 5.12," *SJT* 22 (1969): 335.

15. Cranfield, "Interpretation of Romans 5.12," 336. Cf. Calvin, *Romans*, 111–12.

IN DEPTH: Adam's Sin in Early Jewish Thought

Early Jewish thinkers frequently referred to Adam and his sin against God in their writings. At times they assumed that Adam freely chose to disobey God and that everyone else faces the same choice:

> [God] created mankind in the beginning, and he left him in the power of his own choice. If you desire, you will keep the commandments, and to act faithfully is a matter of choice. (Sir 15:14–15)

The account of Adam's sin in Genesis provided an object lesson in the principle that "God, as the universal Father and Lord who beholds all things, grants to such as follow Him a life of bliss, but involves in dire calamities those who step outside the path of virtue" (Josephus, *Ant.* 1.20 [H. St. J. Thackeray, LCL]; cf. 1.40–51).[16] Adam and Eve may have been the first human beings to disobey God, but there is no indication in these texts that Adam's sin plunged humanity into sin and death. Adam certainly sinned, but Wisdom "delivered him from his transgression and gave him strength to rule all things" (Wis 10:1–2).

A number of Jewish writers, however, made a connection between Adam's sin and the common human experience of death. Although Genesis 2:17 (cf. 3:3) and 3:19 only speak of the death of Adam for his sin, it was natural for ancient readers to assume that the curse of returning to the dust from which God had made Adam would be as common to humanity as pain in childbearing and the hard labor of farming (3:16–18). Writing at a time probably close to Paul's period, Pseudo-Philo says that after Adam sinned "death was ordained for the generations of men" (LAB 13:8).[17]

Some Jewish thinkers reflected more deeply on the nature of Adam's sin and its consequences. Philo associated Adam's sin with the human craving for pleasure and located "the beginning of a blameworthy life" for Adam in the sexual pleasure he experienced with Eve (*Creation* 151–52 [Colson and Whitaker, LCL). Once he and Eve had become slaves to pleasure, they immediately discovered its consequences: for Eve, pain in bearing and rearing children and subjection to her husband, and for Adam hard manual labor (*Creation* 167). Although Philo does not say so explicitly, he assumes that these conditions have affected humanity ever since. In another passage he lists the virtues that Adam rejected in favor of their corresponding vices and then comments that as "a natural consequence" (ἐφ' οἷς) Adam traded "mortality for immortality" (*Virtues* 205 [Colson, LCL]).[18]

16. John R. Levison, "Adam and Eve," *EDEJ* 301.

17. *OTP* 2:322 (trans. D. J. Harrington). On the date, see *OTP* 2:299.

18. Cf. Paul's use of "whereupon" (ἐφ' ᾧ) in 5:12.

After the Roman destruction of Jerusalem and its temple toward the end of the first Jewish revolt against Rome (AD 66–70), Jewish thinkers sometimes turned to Adam and the sinful nature that seemed to infect all humanity after Adam's sin to explain God's justice in allowing such disaster to befall his people. When Adam transgressed the commandment God had given him, God "appointed death for him and for his descendants" (4 Ezra 3:7 [*OTP* 1:528, trans. B. M. Metzger]; cf. 2 Bar 17:3; 48:42–43; 56:6), and the "evil heart" that was in Adam persisted in Adam's descendants, even in the Israelites who "in everything" did "as Adam and all his descendants had done" (4 Ezra 3:26 [*OTP* 1:529, Metzger]).

These writers express a sense of despair that anyone could keep God's commandments and live, "for an evil heart has grown up in us, which has alienated us from God, and has brought us into corruption and the ways of death" (4 Ezra 7:48 [*OTP* 1:538, Metzger]). In a pitiful lament, the author of 4 Ezra exclaims, "O Adam, what have you done? For though it was you who sinned, the fall was not yours alone, but ours also who are your descendants" (4 Ezra 7:48 [*OTP* 1:541, Metzger]). Similarly the author of 2 Baruch mourns, "O Adam, what did you do to all who were born after you?" (48:42 [*OTP* 1:637, trans. A. F. J. Klijn]).

Despite this pessimism about the human ability to keep God's commands and live, both authors also believed that people were responsible for their own sins. All people groups pursued their own will and were destroyed contrary to God's intention for their defilements and ingratitude to God (4 Ezra 3:8; 8:59–60 [*OTP* 1:528, 544]). Adam did not cause the destruction of others but, as 2 Baruch puts it, "each of us has become our own Adam" (2 Bar 54:19 [*OTP* 1:640, Klijn]).

5:13 For until the law sin was in the world, but sin is not invoiced when there is no law (ἄχρι γὰρ νόμου ἁμαρτία ἦν ἐν κόσμῳ, ἁμαρτία δὲ οὐκ ἐλλογεῖται μὴ ὄντος νόμου). Adam's sin, and the penalty of death that he received, continued to affect all humanity even before the appearance of the Mosaic law with its full account of sin and sin's penalty.

With this statement, Paul breaks off the comparison he had started to make between the one man who introduced sin and death to all humanity and the one man who brought justification and life to many (5:12, 18). The thought that everyone sinned and died when Adam sinned now leads Paul to comment briefly on the question of how sin has affected those who had no formal revelation of God's law.

The conjunction "for" (γάρ) connects this digression with what Paul has just said about everyone sinning and dying when the first human being sinned and died. Evidence for this is clear, he says, in the presence of sin even when the law was absent. Adam received a form of the law from God in the command not to eat of the tree in the midst of the garden, and Israel received the law of God in the form of the Mosaic law at Sinai, but even between these two periods when human beings lived in the absence of specific revelation from God they nevertheless sinned. Sin, in other words, is more than simply an imitation of Adam's disobedience; it has been integral to human existence since the time of Adam.[19]

The statement that "sin is not invoiced when there is no law" disrupts the flow of this argument slightly. If Paul is making the point that sin and death existed in the period between Adam and Moses, why would he introduce a statement that at first seems to imply there is no sin between Adam and Moses? The statement was probably a parenthetical comment that Paul hoped would highlight one of his important convictions about the Mosaic law's role in salvation history. The law came to shine the light of God's revelation on human sin and rebellion by showing specifically why sin was rebellion against God (3:20; 4:15; 5:20; 7:5, 7–25). Paul's primary point, however, is that in the period when people only had an internal and somewhat vague sense of what God required (2:14–15), and before anyone had been "entrusted with the oracles of God" (3:2), they still sinned against God and received the penalty of death.

The verb "invoice" (ἐλλογέω) is a rare term, showing up in ancient Greek mainly in inscriptions and papyri.[20] The only other extant use of the term prior to the second century comes from Paul himself in Philemon 18 where Paul asks Philemon to bill him for any damages that Onesimus owes Philemon. Here in Romans 5:13 Paul uses the verb in much the same way, although metaphorically. In the period between God's command to Adam and God's commandments to Israel, God presented no "invoice" to people for their sin. As Otfried Hofius has shown in a careful analysis of Paul's argument, Paul does not refer here to an account that God keeps (as is often thought) but to the details of a debt that God presents to the debtor.[21] During the period between Adam and Moses God had not yet presented people the "bill" for their sin in the form of the Mosaic law (cf. Col 2:14). People both sinned and received the penalty for sin during this period, but only with the Mosaic law did they receive a clear explanation of the nature of sin and its sanctions (cf. 3:19–20).[22]

5:14 Yet death reigned from Adam until Moses, even over those who had not sinned in the likeness of the transgression of Adam, who is a type of the coming one (ἀλλὰ ἐβασίλευσεν ὁ θάνατος ἀπὸ Ἀδὰμ μέχρι Μωϋσέως καὶ ἐπὶ τοὺς μὴ ἁμαρτήσαντας ἐπὶ τῷ ὁμοιώματι τῆς παραβάσεως Ἀδὰμ ὅς ἐστιν τύπος τοῦ μέλλοντος). The presence of death in the period between God's command to Adam and the revelation of the law to Moses shows that Adam's sin and its penalty of death affected all subsequent humanity, even those who lived apart from any knowledge of God's word.

The strong adversative conjunction "yet" (ἀλλά) introduces the description of a situation that one would not expect on the basis of what Paul has just said (cf., e.g., Luke 21:9; John 11:11).[23] Simply because God has not presented people with the details of their sin and of the punishment they deserve for it does not mean that they do not suffer sin's consequences. As Paul has already said in the first half of 5:13, sin was present even when the law was absent, and that explains the presence of death even in the absence of sin against specific commands such as Adam and Israel disobeyed. The law, then, defines sin more specifically as transgression, but

19. Sanday and Headlam, *Romans*, 134–35.

20. MM 204; Adolf Deissman, *Light from the Ancient East*, trans. Lionel R. M. Strachan (Grand Rapids: Baker, 1978), 84; Herbert Preisker, "ἐλλογέω," *TDNT* 2:516–17.

21. Hofius, "Adam-Christ Antithesis," 193–97.

22. Ibid., 196.

23. BDAG 45, s.v. ἀλλά 2.

it does not introduce sin into the human situation. In Stephen Westerholm's words, it "effects a change from sin to transgression, but hardly one from innocence to guilt."[24]

Paul personifies "death" here, just as he had personified "sin" in 5:12.[25] The device of personification facilitates his emphasis on the close link between sin and death and their enormous power over all humanity. Death reigns over humanity, and, within the sphere marked out by death, sin reigns (5:17, 21; cf. 6:9–12). The metaphor of death reigning over humanity also emphasizes the power of death in the human situation: no one is exempt from its destructive force.

A "type" (τύπος) was, most basically, a "stamp" such as a mint might use to stamp coins (Lucian, *How to Write History* 10).[26] Paul could use the term metaphorically to refer to an "example" of moral behavior (Phil 3:17; 1 Thess 1:7; 2 Thess 3:9; 1 Tim 4:12; Titus 2:7) or to events in Scripture that resembled and prefigured events in the life of the church (1 Cor 10:6; see 10:11).[27] Because a "stamp" was itself only an outline of the desired image and a reversed outline at that, Greek writers could use the term metaphorically to refer to a "vague indication" or "outline" of something more substantial.[28] Adam was a "type" of the one to come because he was both like, and massively unlike, Jesus Christ.[29] Like Adam, Jesus Christ affected all humanity that came after him, but the difference between the two figures is so vast that Paul must spend the next three sentences explaining it.

5:15 Yet the trespass is not like the free gift, for if by the trespass of the one the many died, how much more has the grace of God and the gift given by grace abounded to the many by the one human being, Jesus Christ (Ἀλλ᾽ οὐχ ὡς τὸ παράπτωμα, οὕτως καὶ τὸ χάρισμα· εἰ γὰρ τῷ τοῦ ἑνὸς παραπτώματι οἱ πολλοὶ ἀπέθανον, πολλῷ μᾶλλον ἡ χάρις τοῦ θεοῦ καὶ ἡ δωρεὰ ἐν χάριτι τῇ τοῦ ἑνὸς ἀνθρώπου Ἰησοῦ Χριστοῦ εἰς τοὺς πολλοὺς ἐπερίσσευσεν). Despite the similarity between Adam and Jesus Christ (what they did affected all humanity), there are significant differences between them. For one thing, the penalty of death that Adam brought upon everyone displayed God's character far less than the generous, merciful gift of justification that Christ has brought to many.

The strong contrastive term "yet" signals that Paul now begins to explain the vast difference between the "type" (Adam) and "the one to come" (Jesus Christ).[30] He describes two differences in 5:15–16 and constructs his description of each difference in a similar way. He first states the difference and then explains it in a clause beginning with the conjunction "for" (γάρ). In 5:17 he summarizes all that he has said about Adam and Jesus Christ since 5:14.

First, then, Paul describes the difference between what Adam did and what Jesus Christ did. Adam committed a "trespass" (παράπτωμα) but Christ bestowed a "free gift" (χάρισμα).[31] Paul had earlier referred to Adam's sin as a "transgression" (παράβασις), the violation of a specific command

24. *Perspectives Old and New on Paul*, 424.

25. Sanday and Headlam, *Romans*, 135.

26. LSJ 1835, s.v. τύπος II.1.

27. On Paul's use of the term in 1 Cor 10:6, see Légasse, *Romains*, 366.

28. LSJ 1835, s.v. τύπος VIII; *TLNT* 3:385, and, on the importance of the reversed image, see Dunn, *Romans 1–8*, 277.

29. Unless, as Ryan S. Schellenberg has argued ("Does Paul Call Adam a Type of Christ?," *ZNW* 105 [2014]: 54–63), Paul is speaking of violation of the Mosaic law as a type of Adam's transgression, taking the antecedent of the relative pronoun (ὅς) not to be Christ but transgression, and "that which is to come" (τοῦ μέλλοντος) not as Christ but as the transgression of the Mosaic law. Although fascinating, the position of the relative pronoun in the clause (τῆς παραβάσεως Ἀδὰμ ὅς ἐστιν τύπος τοῦ μέλλοντος) makes this reading unlikely.

30. "The type is similar in genus but contrary in species" (Origen, *Romans, Books 1–5*, 329).

31. On the meaning of παράπτωμα, see LSJ 1322.

or law (cf. 2:25, 27).[32] It is true, as many commentators observe, that Paul may have varied the term only for rhetorical reasons since he uses a series of nouns ending with a "ma" sound in 5:15–20 (παράπτωμα, χάρισμα, δώρημα, κρίμα, κατάκριμα, δικαίωμα).[33] Still, the term "trespass" emphasizes the thoughtless, foolish nature of Adam's action (cf. Wis 10:1) and therefore stands in sharp contrast to the purposeful nature of God's "free gift" involving Christ's obedience to God for the justification and redemption of his people (5:19; cf. 3:24–25).

This understanding of the two terms becomes more likely as Paul proceeds to his explanation (γάρ) of the difference between Adam's "trespass" and God's "free gift." The phrase "how much more" (see the comments on 5:9) applies a logical inference from the first half of Paul's explanation to its second half. His reasoning seems to run as follows: if it is certain that Adam's foolish and sinful misstep brought death to all humanity, then it is that much more certain that God's free gift of Christ's sacrificial death has succeeded abundantly in bringing justification and redemption to many.

Lying beneath this premise is Paul's conviction that God is not only just but that he is especially merciful (cf. 5:6–8). God was just in punishing Adam and his progeny for their sin, but since he is "merciful and gracious, slow to anger, and abounding in steadfast love and faithfulness" (Exod 34:6; cf. Rom 9:15), it is even more certain that he has been gracious to believers through the redemptive death of Jesus Christ. If he, as a gracious God, punished Adam's sinful misstep with death, believers can rest assured that God's free gift of Christ's sacrificial death has reconciled them to God (5:9–10).

5:16 And the gift is not like what happened through the one who sinned, for the judicial sentence arose out of one deed and brought condemnation, but the free gift arose in the context of many trespasses for the purpose of justification (καὶ οὐχ ὡς δι᾽ ἑνὸς ἁμαρτήσαντος τὸ δώρημα· τὸ μὲν γὰρ κρίμα ἐξ ἑνὸς εἰς κατάκριμα, τὸ δὲ χάρισμα ἐκ πολλῶν παραπτωμάτων εἰς δικαίωμα). Adam is also unlike Christ because the contexts and effects of their respective actions were so different: Adam's one thoughtless sin brought sin's devastating consequences to all humanity, but God brought out of this devastation the freely bestowed gift of justification through Christ's death and resurrection.

Paul expresses his second qualification of the analogy between Adam and Jesus Christ in unusually condensed Greek. No verbs appear in the entire sentence, and his summary statement of the qualification at the beginning seems to compare apples with oranges, placing Adam in parallel not with Christ but with what Christ accomplished. A literal translation would read, "And not as through the one who sinned the free gift."

The explanatory comment (γάρ) that follows this compressed phrase helps to disperse the syntactical fog. Paul explains that God's pronouncement of a judicial sentence (κρίμα) of condemnation (κατάκριμα) against Adam originated in "one" (ἐξ ἑνός), presumably one trespass, and then he contrasts this one sinful blunder and its result of condemnation to the "free gift" and its origins. That "free gift" originated out of many "trespasses." The essence of the contrast lies in the parallel between Adam's ability to bring disaster on all humanity through a single sinful blunder and God's ability to bring generous, lavish, and utterly free blessing to humanity despite the countless sins he had to overcome in order to do this. Paul is contrasting the weakness and incompetent ill will of human beings

32. Richard H. Bell, "Rom 5.18–19 and Universal Salvation," *NTS* 48 (2002): 420n16.

33. See, e.g., Fitzmyer, *Romans*, 418–19. Cf. BDF §488(3).

in their relationship to God to God's strength and generosity in relation to human beings.

The compressed first part of the sentence now makes better sense. When Paul says that the freely bestowed gift is not like what happened "through the one who sinned," he means that the circumstances prompting God's free justification and redemption of sinners through the atoning death and resurrection of Christ (3:24–25; 4:25; 5:10) are not comparable to the circumstances that followed Adam's transgression. God did not merely forgive the one transgression of Adam and reverse his sentence of death. That would have been a gracious response exactly equivalent to Adam's sinful behavior, but it also would have failed to address the sin-ravaged condition of humanity. Instead, God brought "justification" (δικαίωμα) to human beings despite the utter disaster that they had brought on themselves, beginning with Adam, and did so through the "free gift" (χάρισμα) of Jesus Christ's death and resurrection.[34]

5:17 For if death reigned by the trespass of the one person, how much more will those who receive the abundance of grace and the gift of righteousness reign in life through the one person, Jesus Christ (εἰ γὰρ τῷ τοῦ ἑνὸς παραπτώματι ὁ θάνατος ἐβασίλευσεν διὰ τοῦ ἑνός, πολλῷ μᾶλλον οἱ τὴν περισσείαν τῆς χάριτος καὶ τῆς δωρεᾶς τῆς δικαιοσύνης λαμβάνοντες ἐν ζωῇ βασιλεύσουσιν διὰ τοῦ ἑνὸς Ἰησοῦ Χριστοῦ). Paul puts the difference between Adam's curse and God's grace another way. The ability of God to secure the triumph of human beings over the death-dealing effects of Adam's sin is secure to the extent that God is more powerful than Adam and to the extent that God's actions are more intentional and gracious than the thoughtless, sinful misstep of a single human being.

Paul repeats his explanation of 5:16, but now speaking of death rather than sin as the effect of Adam's trespass.[35] By using the expression "how much more" (πολλῷ μᾶλλον) that he had used in 5:15 and by returning to the topic of death that he had mentioned there, he sums up his two qualifications of the analogy between Adam and Jesus Christ and circles back to his description in 5:12 of the universal presence of, and connection between, sin and death. This prepares the way for his return in 5:18 to the contrast between Adam and Christ that he had started to make before he digressed.[36]

In a way similar to its use in 5:15, the phrase "how much more" sets up a chain of reasoning based on the premise that God is more powerful than human beings and is a merciful, gracious God.[37] If Adam, in his human frailty, could bring death to humanity through one sinful blunder, then God, in his strength, intentionality, and gracious generosity can easily and overwhelmingly reverse Adam's curse. Paul speaks of the "abundance" of God's grace here just as he said that grace had "abounded" in 5:15, and he speaks of the "gift of righteousness" (ἡ δωρεὰ τῆς δικαιοσύνης) here just as he had spoken of "the gift given by grace" (ἡ δωρεὰ ἐν χάριτι) there. This language recalls both 3:24, where Paul said that sinners were "justified freely by [God's] grace" (δικαιούμενοι δωρεὰν τῇ αὐτοῦ χάριτι) and the lavish description of God's

34. The term translated "justification" (δικαίωμα) is not the usual word for this concept (δικαίωσις). The term Paul uses here (δικαίωμα) normally means "a regulation" (1:32; 2:26; 8:4) or "righteous deed" (5:18). Here, however, he uses the term to describe the result of the action of justifying, just as he used "condemnation" (κατάκριμα) in the immediately preceding clause to describe the result of the action of condemning. See Sanday and Headlam, *Romans*, 141; Cranfield, *Romans*, 1:287n2; and BDAG 249–50, s.v. δικαίωμα 3.

35. Wilckens, *An die Römer (Röm 1–5)*, 324–25.

36. Käsemann, *Romans*, 155.

37. Cf. Légasse, *Romains*, 370: "une opposition est ici établie entre deux pouvoirs" (an opposition is established here between two powers).

love in 5:5, 8. The "gift of righteousness," then, is the gift of freedom from punishment and of peace with God that comes through the atoning death of Christ.

Christ did not remain dead, however, and so, just as Paul had emphasized in 5:10 that Christ's life meant future salvation for believers, so here he says that the free gift of righteousness will lead to the eschatological reign of believers "in life through the one person, Jesus Christ" (cf. 1 Cor 6:9–10; 15:50; Gal 5:21; Eph 5:5; 1 Thess 2:12; 2 Thess 1:5; 2 Tim 2:12; 4:14). The implied order of events here is important. Believers first receive the free gift of righteousness through the atoning death of Christ, and then they reign in life through Jesus Christ. Just as the resurrected Christ is a king who has taken his position of authority at God's right hand (8:34; cf. Ps 110:1), so believers, through their union with him, will also reign in life.[38]

5:18 So then, as through the trespass of the one person condemnation came to all human beings, so also through the righteous act of the one person life-giving justification came to all human beings (Ἄρα οὖν ὡς δι' ἑνὸς παραπτώματος εἰς πάντας ἀνθρώπους εἰς κατάκριμα, οὕτως καὶ δι' ἑνὸς δικαιώματος εἰς πάντας ἀνθρώπους εἰς δικαίωσιν ζωῆς). Adam's sinful blunder with its consequence of death and Christ's righteous deed with its consequence of justification and life are alike in one important way: both affected all humanity.

With his two qualifications of the comparison between Adam and Jesus Christ in place, Paul now completes the analogy he started to express in 5:12. The expression "so then" (ἄρα οὖν) introduces an inference from something that comes before it.[39] Since Paul's inference repeats the language of "trespass" (παράπτωμα), "condemnation," (κατάκριμα), "justification" (δικαίωμα) and "life" (ζωή) from the previous paragraph (5:15–17), he is probably drawing this inference from those three sentences.[40] His style is highly compressed, and this has produced differences of opinion about whether he contrasts one trespass with one righteous act (Luther, NASB, NIV, ESV, HCSB, NAB) or one *person's* trespass with one *person's* righteous act (cf. Tyndale, KJV, RSV, NRSV, NJB, REB, CEB). Since the contrasting word "all" in each clause refers to people, however, it is likely that Paul has "one person" in mind in each clause also. The parallel expressions "disobedience of the one human being" and "obedience of the one" in 5:19 confirm this reading.[41] Paul contrasts not so much the two actions and their results as the two people who performed these actions with their all-encompassing results. Adam and Jesus Christ are alike because what they did affected "all human beings" and because each stands at the head of one of the two critical and overlapping eras of human history.

Paul's use of "all" in both sides of the comparison does not mean that every human being will experience the life that comes from justification

38. Cf. Eph 1:20–23; 2:6, and Col 3:1 where, however, the union of believers with the reigning Christ is portrayed as to some extent a present reality. There is no contradiction here, merely a difference in emphasis to meet the pastoral needs of the first readers of Ephesians and Colossians. In contexts where an overemphasis on the union of believers with the reigning Christ had led to triumphalism or where suffering believers needed encouragement from the glorious future awaiting the faithful, Paul stressed that this reign had not been fully realized (1 Cor 4:8) or that it would be realized in the future (2 Tim 2:12). See Kruse, *Romans*, 250.

39. J. D. Denniston, *The Greek Particles*, 2nd ed. (Oxford: Oxford University Press, 1950), 40–41 (on ἄρα).

40. The term translated "justification" in 5:16 (δικαίωμα) is translated "righteous act" here, which is a more usual meaning for it (cf. Aristotle, *Rhetoric* 1359a25; Bar 2:19; LSJ 429; BDAG 249, s.v. δικαίωμα 2) and seems demanded by the parallel references to Adam's trespass in 5:15a and to Christ's obedience in 5:19. Cf. Bell, "Rom 5.18–19," 421.

41. Hofius, "Adam-Christ Antithesis," 175n63.

just as every human being is subject to sin and death. This is clear from the role that human faith plays in Paul's description of the gospel throughout 1:16–5:11, most recently in 5:1–2 where faith is the necessary condition of justification and access to God's grace.[42]

What, then, did Paul mean when he described Jesus Christ's righteous act as bringing life-giving justification to all human beings? He meant that God had graciously offered the benefits of Christ's righteous act to every human being in the gospel. As Calvin put it, "Paul makes grace common to all men, not because it in fact extends to all, but because it is offered to all."[43]

5:19 For just as through the disobedience of the one human being the many were rendered sinners, so also through the obedience of the one the many will be rendered righteous (ὥσπερ γὰρ διὰ τῆς παρακοῆς τοῦ ἑνὸς ἀνθρώπου ἁμαρτωλοὶ κατεστάθησαν οἱ πολλοί, οὕτως καὶ διὰ τῆς ὑπακοῆς τοῦ ἑνὸς δίκαιοι κατασταθήσονται οἱ πολλοί). The one human being Adam rendered the mass of humanity sinful through his reckless failure to heed God's command, but Jesus Christ, through disciplined obedience to the will of God, offered the mass of humanity a right standing with God. Many of those to whom he makes the offer accept it.

Paul now restates the essence of the analogy between Adam and Jesus Christ in complete and more precise terms. He finally completes the "just as" (ὥσπερ) of 5:12 with its corresponding "so also" (οὕτως καί), and he is more precise about the nature of Adam's "trespass" (παράπτωμα), calling it "disobedience" (παρακοή). Although this noun is rare in surviving ancient Greek, its meaning is clear from its cognate verb (παρακούω), which can mean "ignore," "hear carelessly," "take no heed," and so, "disobey" (Matt 18:17).[44] The verb is used in Hellenistic-Jewish writings to describe disobedience to the commandments (ἐντολῶν) of God (Tob 3:4), and so the noun was an appropriate term for the nature of Adam's sin. God had commanded (LXX, ἐνετείλατο) Adam not to eat from the tree of the knowledge of good and evil (Gen 2:16–17), but Adam was unsubmissive to that command, taking no heed of it when Eve gave him the fruit.

In contrast, Jesus exercised "obedience" (ὑπακοή). Early Christians used this term especially for submission to God's will as he expressed it in his word, to Christ, or to Christ's apostles (e.g., Rom 1:5; 6:16; 15:18; 16:19; 2 Cor 7:15; 10:5–6). When early Christians wrote of Jesus's submission to God's will, they often referred specifically to his willingness to suffer and die on behalf of God's people (Heb 5:8; cf. Matt 26:39, 42; Mark 14:36; Luke 22:42; John 14:31). Paul too speaks of Jesus "becoming obedient [ὑπήκοος] to the point of death, even death on a cross" (Phil 2:8). Here in Romans 5:19, then, Paul contrasts Adam's willful disregard of God's command not to eat of the tree with Jesus's thoughtful, costly submission to God's will that he should die an atoning death for the justification of sinners (cf. 3:24–25; 5:9).

"The many were rendered" sinners by Adam's disobedience, and "the many will be rendered" righteous by Jesus Christ's obedience. The term "render" (καθίστημι) had a wide range of meanings

42. Cf. Moo, *Romans*, 344. It seems to me that neither Bell ("Rom 5.18–19," 417–32) nor Hofius ("Adam-Christ Antithesis," 189–91) sufficiently consider this element of the immediate context.

43. Calvin, *Romans*, 118.

44. The noun appears prior to Paul only in Plato's seventh letter, where it is used in the plural and means something like "hearsay" (341b). Paul also uses it in 2 Cor 10:6, again in contrast to "obedience" (ὑπακοή). In Heb 2:2 it is a synonym of "transgression" (παράβασις), and like the verb in Tob 3:4 refers to disobedience to God's law. See LSJ 1313, s.v. παρακοή 3; BDAG 766–67, s.v. παρακοή; MGS 1553, s.v. παρακοή; *TLNT* 3:28–29.

derived from the basic idea of setting something down or putting something in place.[45] It could mean "ordain," "appoint," "establish," "bring into a certain state," or, with a double accusative direct object, "make" or "render" something to be something else.[46] Socrates, in one of Plato's dialogues, for example, could say that a useful idea had fled from him and so rendered (κατέστησεν) him alone and helpless (*Phileb.* 16b). Diodorus Siculus could say that young men were made (κατεστάθησαν) athletes of the skills of warfare on account of their demanding training (*Bibliotheca historica* 12.75). In the same way, Adam rendered humanity sinners and Jesus Christ will render humanity "righteous" (δίκαιοι). This does not mean that former sinners become righteous in the moral sense but that they become "righteous" in the juridical sense. Having been justified (δικαιωθέντες) by faith (5:1) and by Christ's sacrificial blood (5:9), they have been released from the outpouring of his eschatological wrath (5:9, 17).[47] A judge committed, as God is, to "righteous judgment" (δικαιοκρισία, 2:5) normally releases people from punishment only if they are "righteous" (2:13), but in an extraordinary display of grace and as a free gift (2:15–17) God renders sinners righteous and therefore free from the punishment they deserve.[48]

Despite the eschatological overtones and the future tense ("will be rendered"), justification does not await the final day. Just as the ungodly and wicked have started to experience God's wrath in the present (1:18), so those who believe the gospel are rendered righteous when they believe it (4:5; 5:1, 9). The future tense, then, is a logical future, indicating what is true for "the many" that benefit from Christ's obedient, atoning death.[49]

5:20 But the law slipped in so that the trespass might increase; but where sin increased, grace superabounded (νόμος δὲ παρεισῆλθεν ἵνα πλεονάσῃ τὸ παράπτωμα· οὗ δὲ ἐπλεόνασεν ἡ ἁμαρτία, ὑπερεπερίσσευσεν ἡ χάρις). Contrary to expectation, the law was not the answer to the problem of human rebellion against God. The law only made that rebellion worse by providing an avenue for further rebellion. God, however, used precisely this situation as the opportunity for showing the extravagance of his grace to his rebellious human creatures.

Paul indicates a turn in the direction of his thought with the word "but" (cf. Luther, Tyndale, NRSV), and the turn is more adversative than most translations indicate. Many translators simply leave the word (δέ) untranslated (NASB, NIV, HCSB), and others render it "moreover" or "now" (KJV, ESV, NET). It would be natural for the Roman Christians to assume that the law, whether the Mosaic law or the justice systems of other societies, helped to restrain sin in the wake of Adam's sin and its disastrous consequences for humanity.[50] There is a sense in which, at the societal level, this is correct, and in other contexts Paul can affirm this principle (2:14–15, 26–27; 13:1–10; 1 Tim 1:8–11).

At the level of the individual's relationship to God, however, God's law, given to Israel in the form of the Mosaic law, not only fails to restrain sin but brings an "increase" in offenses against God. Paul is

45. Albrecht Oepke, "καθίστημι, κτλ.," *TDNT* 3:444.

46. LSJ 854–55; BDAG 492; MGS 1006, all s.v. καθίστημι.

47. Moo, *Romans*, 345–46; Bell, "Rom 5.18–19," 425; Westerholm, *Perspectives Old and New on Paul*, 275–76. On justification as release from punishment, see Downing, "Justification or Acquittal?," 298–318.

48. See Westerholm (*Perspectives Old and New on Paul*, 275–76), and on the "utter incongruity" of God's grace, "showing no correspondence with the worth of its recipients," see Barclay's argument on Romans (*Paul and the Gift*, 449–561 [quotation from 474]).

49. Bell, "Rom 5.18–19," 424.

50. Jewett, *Romans*, 387.

probably saying here that it was worse for people to violate a divinely given command that they knew to be God's will than a general principle of human society that they suspected came from God and that everyone should therefore observe. As Paul has shown in 1:18–32, all human beings, not just Jews, had enough information from observing the world around them to know that the Creator deserved their worship and that they should treat other people justly. In 5:13–14 Paul had implied that the Mosaic law provided a guide to God's will that, like the command to Adam, was both more reliable and more detailed than these observations. There he had again implied that although people sin against God even when they do not know his law, there is a qualitative difference between sinning against general principles derived from human observation of the surrounding world and sinning against a body of divinely revealed law (cf. 4:15). Paul's statement here about the "increase" of the "trespass," then, probably reflects this same notion: although it is evil to violate principles one suspects are right, it is worse, because it is a sign of active distrust and rebellion, to violate well-understood laws that are known to come from God himself.

Paul says that the law "slipped in" and, again, many translations do not communicate the negative connotations of this term, rendering it with innocuous expressions such as "came in" (NRSV, ESV) and "came along" (HCSB).[51] The term (παρεισέρχομαι) is widely used in Greek literature, however, to describe the secret entry of someone to a city or home, often for unwelcome or unwanted purposes (Polybius, *Histories* 1.7.3; 1.8.4; 2.55.3; Plutarch, *Cor.* 23.1), and this is the way Paul uses it in Galatians 2:4, its only other appearance in either the LXX or the NT.[52] At first this idea may seem to be in conflict with Paul's conviction, stated elsewhere, that God gave the Mosaic law to Israel (3:2) and that it is "holy . . . and just and good" (7:12; cf. 3:31; 9:4).[53] It is important, however, to pay close attention to Paul's language. He does not say, "God slipped the law in," but "the law slipped in." He is using a figure of speech, personifying the law in order to depict the unexpectedly negative consequences that the law has on people who are already in rebellion against God. For example, the commandment, "You shall not covet" (Exod 20:17; Deut 5:21) does not help people to avoid coveting but only makes the situation worse. Paul will explore exactly how this happens in 7:7–25.

Immediately after the main verb, however, Paul returns to God's purposes in giving the law. The effect that the toxic mixture of sin and law had on rebellious human beings did not lie outside the gracious purposes of God. God intended that the law should increase the trespass so that, precisely in this context, his grace might "superabound" (cf. 5:6–8, 10; Col 2:14–15).

It is hard not to think that Paul had in mind both the role that appeal to the Mosaic law played in the death of Christ (e.g., John 19:7) and the role that his own zeal for the law played in his persecution of Christians prior to his personal transformation from persecutor to apostle (Gal 1:13–14; Phil 3:5–6). It was precisely in such circumstances that the grace of God overflowed for Paul, for other Jews, and eventually for gentiles also (1 Tim 1:13–14).

51. Among commentators, see, e.g., Meyer, *Romans*, 218–19; Lagrange, *Romains*, 112 (who seems to have mistaken the term for παρέρχομαι); Cranfield, *Romans*, 1:292; Hofius, "Adam-Christ Antithesis," 198–99.

52. LSJ 1333, BDAG 774, and MGS 1576, all s.v. παρεισέρχομαι. Kari Kuula, *The Law, the Covenant, and God's Plan*, 2 vols., Publications of the Finnish Exegetical Society 85 (Göttingen: Vandenhoeck & Ruprecht, 2003), 2:197; Jewett, *Romans*, 387.

53. Kuula (*The Law, the Covenant, and God's Plan*, 2:190–204) leans in this direction.

5:21 in order that just as sin reigned in death, so also grace might reign through righteousness for eternal life through Jesus Christ our Lord (ἵνα ὥσπερ ἐβασίλευσεν ἡ ἁμαρτία ἐν τῷ θανάτῳ, οὕτως καὶ ἡ χάρις βασιλεύσῃ διὰ δικαιοσύνης εἰς ζωὴν αἰώνιον διὰ Ἰησοῦ Χριστοῦ τοῦ κυρίου ἡμῶν). The death and resurrection of Jesus Christ, by which God has freely and graciously released his people from the punishment they deserve for their sins, has undermined the power of sin and death and established the authority of God's grace over his creation forever.

Paul now summarizes his argument in 5:12–21 by stating its main point in the form of a purpose clause containing a final comparison (cf. 5:12, 18, 19). Because of the reconciliation God has accomplished "through Jesus Christ our Lord" (cf. 5:1, 11), the reign of sin in the sphere of death has ended and the eternal reign of grace and life has begun.

In the preceding argument Paul had explained that Adam's sin led to the reign of death (5:14, 17), but had also made clear that Adam's sin and the spread of death to everyone resulted in the sinfulness of all people (5:12, 19). He now summarizes this thought with the expression "sin reigned in death." This does not mean that sin reigned by means of death since death is the consequence of sin, not its cause or instrument (6:23).[54] Paul means instead that sin reigned in the sphere of death. Sin generates death and rules as a harsh taskmaster over the morbid kingdom it has created.

We might have expected Paul to balance the first half of his comparison with a second half that ran, "so grace might reign in life," and this is certainly the most basic meaning of the second half of the clause. Paul needed to say more than this, however, to summarize his careful statement of the imbalance between the lavishness of God's grace and the universal effects of human sin and to summarize the role of Jesus Christ in God's gracious purposes. Grace does not merely reign in life, then, but "through righteousness for eternal life." "Righteousness" refers to the release of sinners from the punishment of God's wrath that they deserve. It is the means through which grace reigns because it is the gift by which God shows the abundance of his grace to those under the reigning power of death (5:17; cf. 3:24). Because God has released them from punishment, the righteous can experience eternal life.

All this is possible because of the atoning death and resurrection of the Lord Jesus Christ (3:24–26; 4:25; 5:9–10). The designation of Jesus Christ as "Lord" is a reminder of the importance of his resurrection to the triumph of God's grace over sin and death (cf. 1:4; 4:25; 5:10).

Theology in Application

This passage teaches both the all-pervasive destructiveness of human sin and the generosity and love of God in providing a remedy for this plight. God's remedy is neither difficult to obtain nor stingy in its effects but is absolutely free, graciously given, and overwhelmingly effective. If there were ever good news, this is it.

54. Godet, *Romans*, 229.

The Destructiveness of Human Sin

To appreciate just how good this good news is, however, it is necessary to understand both what sin is and the havoc it has created in human existence. The passage makes the definition of sin clear. Sin is what Adam did when he refused to respect the boundaries God had placed around him in the garden (5:14, 19). It is what the generations of human beings after Adam did when they failed to acknowledge God and respect each other, knowing full well that what they were doing was wrong (5:14; cf. 1:32; 2:15). It is what Israel did when it repeated these failures despite having a detailed description of God's requirements in the Mosaic law (5:13–14, 20; cf. 3:2).

Sin, moreover, is often not merely self-centered thoughtlessness but open rebellion. This is Paul's point when he says that the law did not restrain sin when it appeared but caused sin to increase (5:20). When people discovered exactly what God required of them, their response was not to try harder to do what God required but to rebel against those requirements. Although they knew God's just requirement, they not only did the opposite themselves but applauded when others joined them in their rebellion (1:32). "Like a hunter who, in a little flare of self-assertion, fires at each letter of a No Hunting sign," says Cornelius Plantiga, "sinners sometimes draw pleasure from mere rebellion."[55]

Paul's teaching on sin in this passage goes even further. He affirms not only that sin is common to everyone and often takes a particularly rebellious form but that "through the disobedience of the one human being the many were rendered sinners" (5:19; cf. 5:12). Because of Adam's sin, then, every human being conceived in the normal way (Jesus's birth is an exception) is already a sinner, not through committing willfully sinful acts but through possessing an inclination to sin. This has nothing to do with sex (Augustine's error), nor with being human, since God created monogamous sexual intimacy and humanity without any hint of sinfulness. It is instead a consequence of descent from Adam who chose to rebel against God and so transmitted to all subsequent human beings the tendency to sin. Humanity, then, is fertile and fruitful because God created it that way, but as a result of Adam's sin it is also "fertile and fruitful" for the production of evil.[56]

Many people have rejected this notion of "original sin," whether implicitly or explicitly. Confucius's follower Mencius thought that Confucius's ideas about well-functioning societies could be enacted because people were born with a predisposition to virtue.[57] Paul's contemporary Seneca considered erroneous the idea that

55. Cornelius Plantinga Jr., *Not the Way It's Supposed to Be: A Breviary of Sin* (Grand Rapids: Eerdmans, 1995), 50. The library copy that I used was heavily underlined, providing a wonderful illustration of the book's thesis.

56. John Calvin, *Institutes of the Christian Religion*, trans. Ford Lewis Battles, 2 vols., Library of Christian Classics (Philadelphia: Westminster, 1960), 1:241–55 (2.1.1–11), esp. 252. Calvin relies extensively on Augustine in this section. See also Plantinga, *Not the Way It's Supposed to Be*, 52–77.

57. Alan Jacobs, *Original Sin: A Cultural History* (New York: HarperCollins, 2008), 12.

"vices are inborn in us." Instead, "they come upon us, they are imposed."[58] Pelagius believed that sin was a bad habit originating with Adam's bad "example . . . or pattern."[59] Yet the horrors that human beings inflict on one another at all levels from the kindergarten playground to the family to the workplace to the village, the nation, and the world belie these optimistic appraisals of human nature, as both traditional theologians and atheological scientists agree.[60]

Social scientists who factor God out of human existence have found some reason to be guardedly optimistic that reason, education, and well-run governments can curb the human tendency to violent domination of others.[61] In the words of Thomas Hobbes, "*justice, equity, modesty, mercy,* and, in sum, *doing to others, as we would be done to,* of themselves, without the terror of some power, to cause them to be observed, are contrary to our natural passions, that carry us to partiality, pride, revenge, and the like."[62] That is why, said Hobbes, it was necessary that a government in the form of a single man (such as a king) or an assembly of men (such as a parliament) was necessary for civil society to exist.[63] More recent social scientists agree, as would Paul himself (cf. Rom 13:1–7; 1 Tim 1:8–11).

As this passage reveals, however, Paul believed that the sort of human social chaos he realistically described in 1:18–32 was only symptomatic of a deeper, theological problem. As God himself intervened to solve that deeper problem in the lives of the individuals who made up his people, society would begin to improve in ways that were permanent. A world in which grace would reign through righteousness for eternal life through Jesus Christ would be a world where the effects of sin had subsided.

God's Loving and Generous Response to the Human Plight

The eternal solution to the endemic problem of human sin, then, comes in the form of a completely free, generously given gift from God, the gift of freedom from God's justified condemnation and punishment for sin against himself. This gift is possible because of Jesus Christ's willing submission to God's plan to consider Christ's death an atoning sacrifice for sin.

How can believers apply these theological truths in practical terms? They can adopt a realistic understanding of the human propensity to sin and therefore be on

58. As quoted in Herman Bavinck, *Sin and Salvation in Christ*, vol. 3 of *Reformed Dogmatics*, ed. John Bolt, trans. John Vriend (Grand Rapids: Baker, 2006), 87.

59. Pelagius, *Romans*, 92.

60. Plantinga, *Not the Way It's Supposed to Be*, 52–77; Steven Pinker, *The Blank Slate: The Modern Denial of Human Nature* (New York: Viking, 2002), 57–58. For Pinker's hostility to religious explanations for human behavior, see pp. 121–35. For Pinker's case that human viciousness has declined sharply in modern times thanks in part to the marginalization of religion, see *The Better Angels of Our Nature: Why Violence Has Declined* (New York: Viking, 2011), 676–78.

61. Pinker, *Blank Slate*, 58; idem, *Better Angels*, 680–92.

62. Thomas Hobbes, *Leviathan*, vol. 3 of *The English Works of Thomas Hobbes of Malmesbury*, ed. William Molesworth (London: Bohn, 1839–45), 153–54. Emphasis in the original.

63. Ibid., 157–58.

their guard both against their own tendency toward idolatry and the will to dominate others. They can recognize that the ultimate solution to these seemingly constant companions of human existence does not lie in any mechanism of human ingenuity but in trusting God's promise that he has put them in a right relationship with himself through the death of Christ. Embracing these truths forms the basis from which believers can then seek to live a life of righteousness in the often vicious human societies of this present, sinful world. That is the subject to which Paul turns in the next section of Romans.

CHAPTER 13

Romans 6:1–14

Literary Context

This passage continues Paul's description of the new life that those live who have been justified by faith. Paul had explained in 5:1–11 that justified believers live in the context of peace and reconciliation with God. They live this way, Paul reiterates, because of the gracious initiative of God in the death and resurrection of his Son. Paul had also explained in 5:12–21 that because of God's gracious initiative life can reign over human beings (in Jesus Christ) rather than death (in Adam).

As the future tense "will reign" in 5:17 hints, however, those who receive God's abundance of grace and the free gift of righteousness have not immediately entered an existence that is free from sin and death. They must choose to live in a way that is consistent with the new age Christ has introduced. The nature of the believer's existence in this overlap of ages is the subject of 6:1–8:39. In this section of the letter, Paul will discuss the tension of living in the period after Christ's death and resurrection but before the full redemption of believers' bodies (8:23) as a period of subjection to powerful overlords. Paul had already started to use the language of political power in 5:12–21 when he described sin's advancement (5:12), death's reign (5:14, 17), and especially sin's increase and reign (5:20–21), but now that language becomes dominant as Paul describes how believers, through their union with Christ, have the resources to break free from sin's dominion. Here too, death and sin rule (6:9, 14), and sin enslaves and reigns (6:6, 12), but believers through their union with Christ's death and resurrection are able to shift their physical, intellectual, and emotional capacities into God's service as "weapons of righteousness" (6:13).

Two controversial statements about the Mosaic law drive the first major section of this argument (6:1–23). In 5:20 Paul had said that the Mosaic law entered history "so that the trespass might increase," and in 6:14 he says that believers are "not under law but under grace." These statements imply that Israel's law no longer guides the conduct of believers. Paul understood that some people might conclude from this that believers had no basis for ethical behavior at all. In 6:1–23, then, he answers this concern, not by reinstating the Mosaic law as a basis for Christian ethics but by explaining how union with the death and resurrection of Christ breaks the power of sin over believers and moves them into the realm of God's powerful and righteous reign. In 6:1–14 political imagery dominates Paul's explanation, and the movement of the believer outside the power of sin and death is his primary concern. In 6:15–23 the imagery of slavery dominates, and Paul will dwell at greater length on the existence of believers under their new masters, obedience (6:16), righteousness (6:18, 19), and God (6:22).[1]

Paul's statements about the law in 5:20 and 6:14, however, also generated another question: Is the law on the side of sin (7:7; cf. Gal 3:21)? After a thorough restatement of the believer's freedom from the law in 7:1–6, Paul addresses that question in 7:7–25. In 8:1–39 he finishes the second major section of his argument by bringing the Spirit into his description of how the person who is justified by faith lives.[2]

Main Idea

God has united those who have been justified by faith with Christ's death of atonement for sin and will fully unite them in the future with the new, immortal life that he has as a result of his resurrection from the dead. Since believers now have this new identity, they should live in a way that is consistent with it. They should consider themselves delivered from the power of sin and death and alive to God. In practical terms, this means placing their capabilities not in the service of sin with its illicit cravings and injustices but in the service of God who fights for what is just.

1. Cf. Michel, *An die Römer*, 199.

2. Cranfield, *Romans*, 1:295–96.

Translation

Romans 6:1–14

1a	Rhetorical Question	**What, then, shall we say?**
b	Rhetorical Question	**Should we remain in sin that grace might increase?**
2a	Exclamation	**Certainly not!**
b	Rhetorical Question	**How will those of us who have died to sin continue to live in it still?**
3a	Rhetorical Question	Or **are you unaware**
b	Content	that as many of us as were plunged into Christ Jesus
c		were plunged into his death?
4a	Result (of 3)	Therefore **we were buried**
b	Association	with him
c	Means	through that plunge into death
d	Purpose (for 4a)	in order that just as Christ was raised from the dead through the glory of the Father,
e	Comparison (with 4b)	so also we might walk in the newness of life.
5a	Clarification (of 4c)	For if we are united with the likeness of his death,
b		**we shall certainly be united** with the likeness of his resurrection.
6a	Explanation (of 5a)	For this we know, that our old man has been co-crucified
b	Purpose (of 6a)	in order that the body of sin might be rendered powerless
c	Purpose (of 6b)	so that we might no longer be slaves to sin.
7	Explanation (of 6a–b)	For **the one who has died is released from sin.**
8a	Explanation (of 5b)	Now if we died together with Christ,
b		**we believe that we shall also live together with him.**
9a	Cause (of 8b)	Because we know that Christ, having been raised from the dead, no longer dies;
b	Restatement (of 9a)	death no longer rules over him.
10	Explanation (of 9a–b)	For that which he died, **he died** with respect to sin, once and for all time; but that which he lives, **he lives** to God.
11	Conclusion (to 2–10)	**So, you too count yourselves to be dead with respect to sin** but **alive with respect to God in Christ Jesus.**
12a	Exhortation	**Let not sin,** therefore, **reign in your mortal body**
b	Result	with the result that you obey its lusts.

13a Exhortation	**And do not**	**offer your members** to sin as weapons of unrighteousness,	
b Contrast (to 13a)	but	**offer yourselves** to God, as alive from the dead,	
c Contrast (continued)	and	**your members** as weapons of righteousness.	
14 Explanation (of 13b–c)	For **sin will not rule as lord over you,** for **you are not under law** but **under grace.**		

Structure

The passage falls into four parts. First, in 6:1–2 Paul asks two rhetorical questions that place the theme of the passage before his readers.[3] The first question presents the problem that the passage addresses. If God's grace multiplies when sin is present, as 5:20 has said, then it is difficult to see where the foundation for ethical behavior lies (6:1). The second question gives a pithy response to this problem. Believers have died with respect to sin and therefore cannot live in its power any longer (6:2). This brief response, however, leaves an important question unresolved. God displayed his grace to his people in Christ's death, which atoned for their sin, but it is not immediately obvious how this atoning death also implies that believers should no longer live in sin.

Second, then, Paul explains in 6:3–10 how Christ's death for sin and the believer's death to sin are connected with each other. Paul's explanation unfolds in a thesis statement (6:3–5) and two elaborations of that statement (6:6–7, 8–10).[4] He begins by asserting that all believers are united with Christ, plunged into and overwhelmed by him just as an object might be immersed in water (6:3a). This means they share both his death and the new life he received at his resurrection (6:3b–5). Paul then explores the meaning of union with Christ's death: this union has broken the power of sin to enslave the believer (6:6–7). Next he explains the meaning of union with Christ's new life: the believer looks forward to and lives in a way that is consistent with the life Christ now has in the presence of God (6:8–10).

Third, Paul summarizes what he said up to this point in terms designed to recall his initial, pithy answer in 6:2 to the question of 6:1. How does the experience that

3. Cf. Légasse, *Romains*, 390.

4. Moo, *Romans*, 354.

believers have of God's grace in the atoning death of Christ form a basis for ethics? Believers not only trust that God has graciously atoned for their sin but they also believe ("reckon") themselves to be united with the death and resurrection of Christ and therefore set free from the enslaving power of sin (6:11).

Fourth, Paul applies what he has said directly to the Christians in Rome (6:12–14). If the believer's union with Christ has broken sin's enslaving power and bound the believer to Christ, who lives in the presence of God, then believers should present all their faculties and abilities to God for use in the service of righteousness.

Exegetical Outline

IX. Justification by Faith Brings Peace and Reorients the Believer's Existence (5:1–8:39)

- A. Justification by Faith Rescues Believers from God's Present and Future Wrath (5:1–11)
- B. Christ's Obedience Overwhelms the Effects of Adam's Disobedience (5:12–21)
- **C. Union with Christ's Death and Resurrection Initiates a New Life (6:1–23)**
  - ➦ **1. Union with Christ as the Source of Righteous Living (6:1–14)**
    - a. The thesis: Christians no longer live "in" sin (6:1–2)
    - b. Paul explains his thesis (6:3–11)
      - (1) Believers are plunged into Christ's death and new life (6:3–10)
        - (a) Union with Christ's death has broken the power of sin (6:3–7)
        - (b) Union with Christ's life places believers in the presence of God (6:8–10)
      - (2) Summary: believers are dead to sin and alive to God (6:11)
    - c. Paul applies his thesis: believers should live in the power of God's grace (6:12–14)

Explanation of the Text

6:1 What, then, shall we say? Should we remain in sin that grace might increase? (Τί οὖν ἐροῦμεν; ἐπιμένωμεν τῇ ἁμαρτίᾳ, ἵνα ἡ χάρις πλεονάσῃ;). If the Mosaic law cannot form the basis for breaking the power of sin in the believer's life (5:20), then surely—with the law out of the picture—the believer has no basis for ethical behavior.

Paul poses as a Christian interlocutor asking a hostile question in order to move the argument forward (cf. 6:15; 7:7; 9:14). His strategy is directly parallel to that of his near contemporary Seneca in a famous letter on the humane treatment of slaves. Seneca has just recalled the good old days when Romans treated their slaves kindly, sometimes even eating together with them:

> "Do you mean to say," comes the retort, "that I'm to have each and every one of my slaves sitting at the table with me?" Not at all. . . . (*Ep.* 47.15)[5]

Here, however, Paul is not merely using a conventional rhetorical device to shape his argument.

5. Seneca, *Letters from a Stoic*, trans. Robin Campbell (Hammondsworth, UK: Penguin, 1969), 94. Cf. BDAG 1007, s.v. τίς 1.a.β.ℶ).

He must have also had in mind the objection that people sometimes placed against his gospel according to 3:8: "And should we not do bad things so that good things may come?"[6]

The repetition of the verb "might increase" (πλεονάσῃ) from 5:20 links the question back to Paul's claim that "the law slipped in so that the trespass might increase [πλεονάσῃ]; but where sin increased [ἐπλεόνασεν], grace superabounded." If the Mosaic law is not the basis for Christian ethics, then mustn't Christians simply remain in sin?

6:2 Certainly not! How will those of us who have died to sin continue to live in it still? (μὴ γένοιτο. οἵτινες ἀπεθάνομεν τῇ ἁμαρτίᾳ, πῶς ἔτι ζήσομεν ἐν αὐτῇ;). God has released those for whom Christ died from sin's power, and so they should not continue to live under its control.

Paul rejects the absurdity implied in the rhetorical question with his characteristic expression, "Certainly not!"[7] This expression usually opens the way to the topic Paul wants to discuss, in this case the movement of believers out of the sphere of sin's power and into the sphere of Christ's power.[8] In classical Greek, the expression translated here "those of us who" (οἵτινες) often denoted "a person or thing in general, or . . . the *class, character, quality,* or *capacity* of a person."[9] In Paul's time Greek speakers often used it simply as a relative pronoun, but it seems likely that here Paul uses its older, more specific sense.[10] Because they belong to the group of people who have died to sin, it is absurd for Paul's readers to think of themselves as still under sin's power.

The dative expression "to sin" (τῇ ἁμαρτίᾳ) is a "dative of respect" emphasizing the sense in which believers have died. They have not died in every sense, but they have died with respect to sin.[11] Paul explicitly says in 2 Corinthians 5:14–15 that the death of Christ for the sins of Christians means that Christians have, in a sense, died with Christ. They have died with him, he goes on to explain, in the sense that the focus of their lives is no longer on themselves but on Christ because of his death and resurrection on their behalf (cf. 1 Cor 15:31; Gal 2:19–20). Here in Romans 6:2, then, it is likely that the believer's death to sin is a death to a self-centered way of life, a death made possible by God's love, displayed in the atoning death of Christ (5:6, 8).[12]

If this is correct, then the meaning of the preposition "in" (ἐν) here becomes clear. Believers are no longer living in the sphere of sin, that is, in its power because Christ, through his atoning death, has delivered them from sin's overwhelming power (cf. Eph 2:1–6; Col 3:3).[13]

6:3 Or are you unaware that as many of us as were plunged into Christ Jesus were plunged into his death? (ἢ ἀγνοεῖτε ὅτι, ὅσοι ἐβαπτίσθημεν εἰς Χριστὸν Ἰησοῦν, εἰς τὸν θάνατον αὐτοῦ ἐβαπτίσθημεν;). At their conversion Christians moved into the realm of Christ's power, and this spelled the demise of a life centered on themselves.

The phrase "Or are you unaware . . . ?" (cf. 6:16; 7:1) assumes that Paul's hostile interlocutor is a Christian (cf. 3:8) and, like all Christians, knows the basic truth Paul is about to state (cf. 7:1).[14]

6. Käsemann, *Romans*, 165.

7. See the comments on 3:4.

8. Malherbe, "μὴ γένοιτο," 236–38.

9. Smyth, *Greek Grammar*, §2496.

10. Moule, *Idiom-Book*, 124; Cranfield, *Romans*, 1:298.

11. Cf. Wallace, *Greek Grammar*, 154.

12. Cranfield, *Romans*, 1:299; idem, "Romans 6:1–14 Revisited," *ExpTim* 106 (1994): 41.

13. On the possibility that "in" (ἐν) can mean "in the power of," see Constantine R. Campbell, *Paul and Union with Christ: An Exegetical and Theological Study* (Grand Rapids: Zondervan, 2012), 72–73.

14. See, already, Origen, *Romans, Books 1–5*, 357.

What was this basic truth? Identifying it hinges on what Paul meant by the phrase "were plunged into Christ Jesus." The term "plunged," typically translated "baptized," was a well-known term in the first century for the water ritual that John the Baptist used on those who wanted to turn from their sins and receive God's forgiveness (Mark 1:4; Acts 13:24; 19:3–4; cf. Justin, *Dialogue with Trypho* 88.7) and that Christians used for initiation into the Christian faith (John 3:22, 26; 4:1–2; Acts 2:41; 1 Cor 1:13–17). Elsewhere Paul implies that Christians described this ritual as baptism "into [εἰς] the name" of Christ, probably meaning that the ritual signaled the believer's new relationship with and worship of Christ (1 Cor 1:13, 15 [my transl.]; cf. Acts 8:16; 19:5; see too Matt 28:19).[15] All this means that when Paul speaks of being "plunged into Christ" here it is difficult to think that he did not have somewhere in mind the Christian ritual of baptism in the name of Jesus Christ.

Still, this ritual is not his primary concern, and because he goes on in this context to use other metaphors (service to a king and enslavement to a master) to describe the shift of the believer's existence from the sphere of one controlling power to another, it seems likely that here too his main concern is to describe the dramatic change that occurs in human existence when one is united to Christ by faith. The term "plunge" (βαπτίζω) referred at the literal level to the total immersion of something, such as a sinking ship or a drowning person, usually in water. The expression "plunge into" (βαπτίζω εἰς) was a normal way of describing the immersion or insertion of objects "into" something, for example, rings of rope into very salty water or a scalpel into a patient (Strabo, *Geography* 12.5.4; Soranus, *Gynaecology* 4.11.5; cf. Mark 1:9).[16] Greek speakers could use the same expression metaphorically to refer to the total control that something might have over someone, such as wine over someone who was drunk (Josephus, *Ant.* 10.169).[17] The most natural way to take Paul's phrase, then, is less as a reference to baptism (although that must be in the background) than as a metaphorical reference to the placement of the believer, at his or her conversion, into the sphere of Christ's power (cf. Gal 3:27).[18]

The believer who has entered into such a relationship with Christ, Paul continues, has been plunged into "his [Christ's] death." This phrase makes clearer the sense in which believers have "died to sin" (6:2). By uniting them with Christ's death God has not only atoned for their sins but dealt a fatal blow to the self-focused existence into which human beings since Adam are born (cf. 5:12–21; Matt 10:38–39; 16:24–26; 1 Cor 15:31; 2 Cor 4:7–12; Gal 2:19–20).

6:4 Therefore we were buried with him through that plunge into death in order that just as Christ was raised from the dead through the glory of the Father, so also we might walk in the newness of life (συνετάφημεν οὖν αὐτῷ διὰ τοῦ βαπτίσματος εἰς τὸν θάνατον, ἵνα ὥσπερ ἠγέρθη Χριστὸς ἐκ νεκρῶν διὰ τῆς δόξης τοῦ πατρός, οὕτως καὶ ἡμεῖς ἐν καινότητι ζωῆς περιπατήσωμεν). Believers are united with Christ's death so that God might empower them to live in a fresh, radically new way.

Since (οὖν) sharing someone's death means also sharing their burial, Paul is able to shift the metaphor slightly in order to prepare the way for the

15. BDAG 164, s.v. βαπτίζω 2.c; Everett Ferguson, *Baptism in the Early Church: History, Theology, and Liturgy in the First Five Centuries* (Grand Rapids: Eerdmans, 2009), 182–83.

16. Ferguson, *Baptism*, 49–50.

17. Ibid., 52–55.

18. Cf. Sorin Sabou, *Between Horror and Hope: Paul's Metaphorical Language of 'Death' in Romans 6:1–11*, Paternoster Biblical Monographs (Milton Keynes: Paternoster, 2005), 95–109; Campbell, *Paul and Union with Christ*, 335–36.

thought that in some sense God has raised believers with Christ. Paul makes no correlation between plunging beneath the water in baptism and Christ's burial beneath the earth. His focus is rather on Jesus's burial as the necessary first step for his resurrection, and this serves as the foundation for the main point of the sentence, the articulation of the purpose for which God has united believers with Christ in his death.[19]

Paul's next clause begins to describe this purpose clause (ἵνα . . .).[20] Death to sin through union with Christ's death is merely the necessary first step toward the more important goal of living in a qualitatively new way through the same divine power that raised Christ from the dead. The term "glory" in the phrase "the glory of the Father" refers to the outward manifestation of the power of God (cf. 9:22–23; Eph 3:16; Col 1:11), in this case the power that raised Christ from the dead (cf. Eph 1:19–20).[21]

The term "newness" (καινότης) connotes startling freshness, a quality in something that makes it unlike anything else of its type. This term could describe the grandeur of Solomon's temple, the beauty of Pericles's speeches, or the strategic cleverness of the siege engine (2 Kgs 8:53 LXX; Plutarch, *Per.* 13.3; 27:3). Paul's focus, then, lies on the qualitative break between the believer's old life under the reign of death and sin (Rom 5:17, 21) and the new life of union with Christ (cf. Rom 12:2; 2 Cor 5:17; Gal 6:15; Eph 2:15; 4:24).[22]

6:5 For if we are united with the likeness of his death, we shall certainly be united with the likeness of his resurrection (εἰ γὰρ σύμφυτοι γεγόναμεν τῷ ὁμοιώματι τοῦ θανάτου αὐτοῦ, ἀλλὰ καὶ τῆς ἀναστάσεως ἐσόμεθα). Paul now supports his statement that believers were united with the death of Christ for the purpose of living a new life. He does this by correlating the believer's existence not only with Christ's death but also with his resurrection.

The adjective "united" (σύμφοτος) appears only here in the NT but was not uncommon in the Greek of Paul's time. It was an organic term and described the visual effect of unity that individual items had on the observer when they grew close together, a thick forest, for example, or furniture with legs so finely wrought in the shape of animal legs that they appeared to grow naturally out of the furniture itself (LXX Amos 9:13; Zech 11:2; Josephus, *Ant.* 8.84).[23] In a metaphorical sense the adjective was often used to mean "inborn" or "innate" (Dionysius of Halicarnassus, *Ant. rom.* 2.3.7; Josephus, *Ag. Ap.* 1.42).

The perfect-tense indicative verb translated "we are" (γεγόναμεν) emphasizes the continuing effects of the past decision of Paul's readers to believe the gospel.[24] They continue to be united to the likeness of Jesus's death in the present. There is a contrast, then, between this past decision with its present results and the future that "will be." One day, believers will be united with Christ in the likeness of his resurrection (cf. 2 Cor 4:14). The expression "cer-

19. Godet, *Romans*, 240–41. On Christ's burial, see Légasse, *Romains*, 394. For the anaphoric use of the article here ("*that* plunge"), see Wallace, *Greek Grammar*, 219.

20. Ulrich Wilckens, *Der Brief an die Römer (Röm 6–11)*, EKKNT 6.2 (Zürich: Benziger, 1980), 12.

21. Cf. Sanday and Headlam, *Romans*, 157; Cranfield, *Romans*, 1:304–5.

22. Wilckens, *An die Römer (Röm 6–11)*, 12n31; Légasse, *Romains*, 395.

23. Cf. *TLNT* 3.321–22; Sabou, *Between Horror and Hope*, 109–16, although it is not clear that Sabou's concluding, highly nuanced definition is what Paul had in mind.

24. Jewett, *Romans*, 500. Cf. Tyndale's "For yf we be graft in deeth lyke vnto him." See the discussion of the "intensive" perfect in Smyth, *Greek Grammar*, §1947, and Wallace, *Greek Grammar*, 574–76, and the comment of McKay (*New Syntax of the Verb*, 32–33) that the perfect of stative verbs "can often be translated in the same way as the imperfective" (i.e., the present tense).

tainly" (ἀλλὰ καί) emphasizes that although it lies in the future, this outcome is not in doubt, and its certainty undergirds the implied imperative in the previous sentence. Since believers will be united with Christ's resurrection, they should live, even now, in a new way.

The term "likeness" (ὁμοιώματι) hints that the similarity between Jesus's death and resurrection and the believer's conversion and new life goes only so far. Jesus's historical death and resurrection were unique, epoch-changing events. Although the believer's conversion, new life, and eventual resurrection are analogous to them, then, they are events of a different order.[25]

6:6 For this we know, that our old man has been co-crucified in order that the body of sin might be rendered powerless so that we might no longer be slaves to sin (τοῦτο γινώσκοντες ὅτι ὁ παλαιὸς ἡμῶν ἄνθρωπος συνεσταυρώθη, ἵνα καταργηθῇ τὸ σῶμα τῆς ἁμαρτίας, τοῦ μηκέτι δουλεύειν ἡμᾶς τῇ ἁμαρτίᾳ). The participation of believers in Christ's atoning death on the cross means that although they live in a sinful world day-to-day, sin's grip on their own existence has been broken.

The expression, "For this we know, that . . ." (τοῦτο γινώσκοντες ὅτι) signals that Paul is about to give the reason for the certainty he expressed in 6:5 concerning the unity of believers with Christ's resurrection.[26] He assumes that his readers know, as he knows, that "the old man" to which believers used to belong has been co-crucified. Paul leaves it to his readers to supply the idea that believers have been crucified "with Christ" (cf. 6:4, 8). Elsewhere in his writings when he uses the expression "the old man," it forms a contrast with "the new man [τὸν καινὸν ἄνθρωπον] who has been created in God's image" (Eph 4:22–24 NET; cf. Col 3:8–10). Since Paul has just mentioned human solidarity with Adam in the previous passage (5:12–21), it seems likely that here too the expression "the old man" recalls the creation of the first man in God's image and then the disastrous consequences for all subsequent humanity of that first man's transgression.

The solidarity of believers with this "old man" was crucified together with Christ when Christ justified sinners by his blood (5:9) and in this way answered Adam's disobedience with his gracious act of obedience (5:19). Although Paul speaks here in general terms of what has happened to believing humanity, he certainly does not exclude from view the implications of what he says for the individual, as the closely parallel passage in Galatians 2:19–20, with its personal and confessional character, implies.

The crucifixion of believers with Christ in this sense happened for a purpose that Paul explains in the next clause (ἵνα . . .). Paul used the term "body" (σῶμα) in a rich variety of ways in his letters, but its basic meaning seems to be the person's "means of living in, of experiencing the environment," as James D. G. Dunn puts it.[27] In 6:12–13, then, Paul can speak of a person's body as his or her physical "members" that, in the present state of "mortal" existence, the believer can use in the service of "unrighteousness" or "righteousness."[28] The "body of sin" (Tyndale, KJV, NASB, ESV, NET) then, is not "the sinful body" (Luther, RSV, NAB) if one takes that to mean an existence that is sinful precisely because it is embodied.[29] It is instead the body in its susceptibility to sin, "the self which belonged to

25. Cf. Wilckens, *An die Römer (Röm 6–11)*, 14.

26. Cf. Sophocles, *Ant.* 187–89: "Nor could I take as friend my country's foe; For this I know that (τοῦτο γιγνώσκων ὅτι) there our safety lies . . . ." (*The Tragedies of Sophocles*, trans. E. H. Plumptre [London: Routledge, 1908]).

27. Dunn, *Theology of Paul*, 56. Cf. Moo, *Romans*, 376: "The person as the instrument of contact with the world."

28. Eduard Schweizer, "σῶμα, κτλ," *TDNT* 7:1064.

29. So correctly Godet (*Romans*, 245) and Schweizer ("σῶμα," 1060–62). Godet points to Paul's statement in 6:13

sin," in the rendering of the NJB. God has "rendered" this self "powerless" for believers through their crucifixion with Christ and so broken their bondage to sin.[30]

6:7 For the one who has died is released from sin (ὁ γὰρ ἀποθανὼν δεδικαίωται ἀπὸ τῆς ἁμαρτίας). The principle that physical death puts people beyond the reach of sin's power demonstrates the principle in effect in the union of the believer with Christ's death. This union, too, breaks sin's power over believers.

Paul now uses a generally understood maxim to support his statement in 6:6 that crucifixion with Christ has broken sin's power over the self. The force of the maxim was that when a human being died physically he or she was no longer subject to sin's power (cf. 1 Pet 4:1). So Paul is saying that metaphorical death with Christ on the cross breaks the power of sin over the existence of believers, just as when people die they are beyond the reach of sin's power to lead them astray.

The perfect tense verb "is released" (δεδικαίωται) would normally be translated "is justified" or "is acquitted" (e.g., 1 Cor 4:4), but the preposition that follows the verb and the epigrammatic nature of the statement hint that we should interpret it differently here. When other Jewish and Christian literature uses this verb with the preposition "from" (ἀπό), it sometimes means "released from." This is the case, for example, in Sirach 26:29 where the ability to "keep from wrongdoing" is equivalent to being "declared innocent of sin" (δικαιωθήσεται . . . ἀπὸ ἁμαρτίας) or, as the NAB puts it, "free from sin."[31]

6:8 Now if we died together with Christ, we believe that we shall also live together with him (εἰ δὲ ἀπεθάνομεν σὺν Χριστῷ, πιστεύομεν ὅτι καὶ συζήσομεν αὐτῷ). When people trust that Christ's death atoned for their sins, they also trust that one day they will rise from the dead and live forever with him.

Paul's expression "now" (δέ) does not signal a contrast with the principle he has just articulated ("but," REB, NRSV) but a specific application of that principle (NIV, ESV). If it is true that people who have died are no longer subject to the enticements of sin, then those who have died together with Christ ought to count themselves as dead with respect to sin (6:11). Before Paul draws that conclusion, however, he explains again (cf. 6:5) that death with Christ provides certainty of a future resurrection with Christ, a resurrection that ought to inform the way believers live in the present. The expression "we believe that" makes life with Christ in the future a matter of faith and therefore of eschatological existence (cf. 1 Thess 4:14).[32]

The expression "with Christ" (σὺν Χριστῷ) here refers to believers accompanying Christ in his death.[33] When he died on the cross, they, in a sense, also died on the cross since Christ died "for" (ὑπέρ) them (5:6, 8), and this became true of them when they were plunged into his death at the moment of their trust in the gospel, a trust that their baptism confirmed. Here again the preposition prefixed to the verb (συ-) expresses the idea of accompaniment. Believers will accompany Christ in his resurrection from the dead (cf. 2 Cor 4:14; 1 Thess 4:14).

that one can use "the mortal body" with its "members" in the service of righteousness.

30. For the translation "rendered powerless" (καταργηθῇ), see Sanday and Headlam, *Romans*, 71, 158, and cf. Luke 13:7; Rom 3:3, 31; 4:14; Gal 3:17 (BDAG 525, s.v. καταργέω 1–2).

31. Cf. T. Sim. 6.1 and perhaps Acts 13:38–39 (BDAG 249, s.v. δικαιόω 3).

32. Cf. Moo, *Romans*, 377; Légasse, *Romains*, 401–2.

33. Campbell, *Paul and Union with Christ*, 217–21; Harris, *Prepositions and Theology*, 199–200.

6:9 Because we know that Christ, having been raised from the dead, no longer dies; death no longer rules over him (εἰδότες ὅτι Χριστὸς ἐγερθεὶς ἐκ νεκρῶν οὐκέτι ἀποθνῄσκει, θάνατος αὐτοῦ οὐκέτι κυριεύει). Christians believe that God will one day raise them from the dead just as he raised Christ because they know that Christ's resurrected body was an immortal body and so his resurrection was the first of the resurrection of God's people during the last days.

Adverbial perfect participles, Wallace says, are "almost always" causal participles, and that understanding of Paul's opening expression in this verse makes good sense of the syntax.[34] Christians believe that they will live together with Christ (6:8) "because" they know that Christ was raised.

Christians will live with Christ, however, not only because he was raised but because he was raised to an eternal, embodied life. Stories sometimes circulated in the Greco-Roman world of people who had died and come back to life (e.g., Lucian, *The Lover of Lies* 26), and Christians would know of miraculous resurrections from their own traditions (1 Kgs 17:17–24; 2 Kgs 4:18–37; Mark 5:35–43; Luke 7:11–17; John 11:1–44; Acts 9:36–43; 20:7–12), but Christ's resurrection was unlike these other events. He was raised into a transformed and immortal body no longer susceptible to death (1 Cor 15:42–50; Phil 3:20–21), and therefore his resurrection was clearly the first of the general resurrection of God's people from death in the last days (Rom 8:29; 1 Cor 15:20–23, 49–50; Phil 3:21). This conviction about Christ's resurrection gave Christians confidence that they would also live eternally with him in a body like his (cf. Rom 6:5; 1 Cor 15:47–49; Phil 3:21).[35]

6:10 For that which he died, he died with respect to sin, once and for all time; but that which he lives, he lives to God (ὃ γὰρ ἀπέθανεν, τῇ ἁμαρτίᾳ ἀπέθανεν ἐφάπαξ· ὃ δὲ ζῇ, ζῇ τῷ θεῷ). Christ experienced death, but his death was a climactic, unrepeatable event that atoned for the sins of others. Christ's death stands in contrast to his eternal life with the eternal God.

This statement further explains what Paul meant ("for" [γάρ]) when he said that Christ will not die again and that death no longer rules over him (6:9). Paul's explanation contrasts the unrepeatable and definitive nature of Christ's death with the eternal nature of the life that he now lives in his resurrected existence in the presence of God.[36]

Paul expresses this contrast in two balanced phrases. Each phrase begins with a relative clause that stands for a noun corresponding to the main verb of the phrase ("that which he died [i.e., the death], he died . . . /that which he lives [i.e., the life], he lives . . ."), and each qualifies that main verb with a dative of respect ("with respect to sin"/"with respect to God").[37] The balance is broken, however, by the adverb translated here "once and for all time" (ἐφάπαξ). This is an emphatic adverb used rarely in ancient literature and only a few times elsewhere in the NT.[38] In all but one of these other occurrences (1 Cor 15:6) the term expresses the unique, definitive, and sacrificial nature of Christ's death (Heb 7:27; 9:12; 10:10).

That is also its meaning here. Christ did not die to sin in the same way that believers die to sin (Rom

34. Wallace, *Greek Grammar*, 631.

35. Cf. N. T. Wright, "Romans," 540; idem, *The Resurrection of the Son of God*, vol. 3 of *Christian Origins and the Question of God* (Minneapolis: Fortress, 2003), 360–61.

36. Cranfield, *Romans*, 1:314.

37. On the relative clauses, see BDF §154, and on the datives, see Stanley E. Porter, *Idioms of the Greek New Testament*, Biblical Languages: Greek (Sheffield: JSOT Press, 1992), 98; Wallace, *Greek Grammar*, 144–46.

38. LSJ 740, BDAG 417, and MGS, all s.v. ἐφάπαξ; *TLNT* 1:142.

6:2, 11). Unlike them he "knew no sin" (2 Cor 5:21; cf. Heb 7:27) and therefore had no need to die to it in that sense. Instead, his death with respect to sin was the climactic and final sacrifice for sin. This sacrifice accomplished two goals. It atoned for the sins of believers, making possible their reconciliation with God (Rom 3:25–26; 5:6–11, 18–19). It also opened a new era in which sin and death no longer dominated the lives of believers. Instead they became free to serve righteousness and God (5:17, 21; 6:6, 9, 16, 18–20, 22).[39]

6:11 So, you too count yourselves to be dead with respect to sin but alive with respect to God in Christ Jesus (οὕτως καὶ ὑμεῖς λογίζεσθε ἑαυτοὺς εἶναι νεκροὺς μὲν τῇ ἁμαρτίᾳ ζῶντας δὲ τῷ θεῷ ἐν Χριστῷ Ἰησοῦ). The union of believers with Christ has applied Christ's atoning death and defeat of sin to them, but their minds and hearts need constantly to attend to this truth so that they might live in a way that is consistent with it.

This sentence performs three functions in Paul's argument. First, it recalls the rhetorical question in 6:2, implying that Paul has now answered it fully. Second, it extends what Paul has just said in 6:10 in order to draw a comparison between believers and Christ. Third, it introduces a paragraph (6:11–14) that applies Paul's argument in 6:1–10 to his readers. The last two functions are visible in the expression "so . . . too." "So" (οὕτως) introduces the conclusion to 6:1–10 and "too" (καί) signals the comparison of Christ's death and life to the death and life of believers.[40]

Paul relies heavily on the two expressions "count" and "in Christ" to communicate the message of the sentence. He last used the term "count" (λογίζομαι) in chapter four where it took its basic meaning from Genesis 15:6 and Psalm 32:2. There God's method of counting was surprising. He counted Abraham's faith as righteousness and did not count the iniquity of people against them (Rom 4:3–9; cf. 2:26). Here too Paul asks his readers to draw conclusions that do not at first seem obvious. They have not experienced physical death as Christ did; they do not have immortal bodies as Christ does; and they still experience the effects of the sinful world around them, including its deceptive appeal. Nevertheless, because they are "in Christ" they are now in the realm that he rules.[41] Within this sphere, his death and resurrection have effectively atoned for their sin, reconciled them to God, and broken the power of sin (3:24–25; 5:1–6:11; cf. 8:1).[42] They can only live in a way that is consistent with these truths if they "count" (λογίζεσθε) them as true for themselves (cf. 2 Cor 5:14–15).[43]

Later, in 12:1 Paul will recall this language when he urges his readers to offer their bodies as a living sacrifice to God, an activity that he calls their "reasonable [λογικήν] worship." In light of the sinful nature of the visible world around them, they will need to make a conscious mental effort to reason from their identity in Christ to conduct that is consistent with this identity.[44]

This counting, moreover, should be an ongoing activity, as the present tense of the verb indicates.[45]

39. Cf. Theodoret of Cyrus, *Letters of St. Paul*, 1:76; Calvin, *Romans*, 126–27; Cranfield, *Romans*, 1:314; Kruse, *Romans*, 265–66.

40. Cranfield, *Romans*, 1:314–15. Cf. BDAG 742, s.v. οὕτω/οὕτως 1b.

41. Campbell, *Paul and Union with Christ*, 115–16.

42. Cf. Wilckens, *An die Römer (Röm 1–6)*, 19.

43. The concept, then, is virtually identical with "faith" (Michel, *An die Römer*, 208).

44. Teresa Kuo-Yu Tsui, "Reconsidering Pauline Juxtaposition of Indicative and Imperative (Romans 6:1–14) in Light of Pauline Apocalypticism," *CBQ* 75 (2013): 300–308.

45. On the "aspect" of the present imperative, see K. L. McKay, "Aspect in Imperatival Constructions in New Testament Greek," *NovT* 27 (1985): 201–26, and Wallace, *Greek Grammar*, 721–22. On the importance of the present tense here, see Tsui, "Reconsidering," 300, 314.

The nature of the world around and within believers, with its impulses of rebellion against God, makes their union with Christ less than obvious. Because of this they should adopt a way of life in which they frequently "do the math" and see for themselves that what is true of Christ is also true of them.

6:12 Let not sin, therefore, reign in your mortal body with the result that you obey its lusts (Μὴ οὖν βασιλευέτω ἡ ἁμαρτία ἐν τῷ θνητῷ ὑμῶν σώματι εἰς τὸ ὑπακούειν ταῖς ἐπιθυμίαις αὐτοῦ). Because believers are united with Christ's atoning death and immortal life, they must not permit sin to reign over them by submitting to the sinful impulses of their bodies. These impulses are still part of their existence despite their union with Christ, because God has not yet fully accomplished his goals for the salvation of his people.

Paul's "therefore" (οὖν) introduces a strong admonition on the basis of all that he has said in 6:1–11.[46] The use of the term "reign" (βασιλευέτω) echoes its use in 5:14, 17, and 21 to describe the "reign" of death and sin and implies that what Paul says here should be understood in the light of 5:12–21 as well as 6:1–11. Adam, by his trespass, introduced the reign of sin and death, and Jesus, by his righteous deed, introduced the reign of life, grace, and righteousness. Believers live at the overlap of these two ages, occupying bodies subject to sin and death, but united with Christ who has broken the power of sin by his death on the cross (cf. 6:6). Believers should not only understand and believe these truths (6:11) but now Paul says they should act on them.

Paul first describes what he urges them to do in negative terms, using two metaphors, one of a king reigning over his subjects and the other of soldiers fighting in a battle (6:12–13a). The present-tense imperative "let . . . reign" again (cf. "count" in 6:11) implies that believers must be constantly on guard against the tendency of sin to establish its rule.[47] Sin tends to do this "in" the "mortal body," that is, in the domain of the believer's existence that is still subject to death.[48]

How do believers forbid sin from reigning in them? Paul probably intended the result clause (εἰς τὸ + infinitive) that follows his imperative to answer this question.[49] If the result of sin's reign is that people obey the "lusts" prompted by their present existence in a fallen world, then they can avoid sin's reign by refusing to obey those cravings. It is a point on which both Augustine and Pelagius agree: "We still have desires," says Augustine, "but, by not obeying them . . . we do not allow sin to reign in us," and, according to Pelagius, "Sin reigns in the body . . . by obedience and consent."[50]

6:13 And do not offer your members to sin as weapons of unrighteousness, but offer yourselves to God, as alive from the dead, and your members as weapons of righteousness (μηδὲ παριστάνετε τὰ μέλη ὑμῶν ὅπλα ἀδικίας τῇ ἁμαρτίᾳ, ἀλλὰ παραστήσατε ἑαυτοὺς τῷ θεῷ ὡσεὶ ἐκ νεκρῶν ζῶντας καὶ τὰ μέλη ὑμῶν ὅπλα δικαιοσύνης τῷ θεῷ). Since believers are united with Christ's life and not with the sin that put him to death, their abilities and opportunities should not promote sin and injustice but should advance God's desire to establish justice and equity in the world through his people.

Paul continues to explain in negative terms how

46. BDAG 736, s.v. οὖν 1b.

47. On the present negative imperative, see McKay, "Aspect in Imperatival Constructions," 216–19.

48. Godet, *Romans*, 250. For this use of the preposition, see Harris, *Prepositions and Theology*, 118.

49. On the construction, see BDAG 290, s.v. εἰς 4e.

50. Pelagius, *Romans*, 98 (and see translator's note, 98n10); Augustine, *Exp. prop.* 13–18, in *Augustine on Romans*, trans. Paula Fredriksen Landes, SBLTT 23 (Chico, CA: Scholars Press, 1982), 7.

his readers should act on the truth that they are dead to sin and alive to Christ, now shifting to a military metaphor. Despite a long English tradition of translating the term rendered here as "weapons" (ὅπλα) with the less specific "instruments" (Tyndale, KJV, RSV, NIV, ESV), "weapons" is almost certainly correct (Luther, NAB, HCSB, CEB). Not only does the verb translated "offer" here (παρίστημι or παριστάνω) often appear in military contexts (Matt 26:53; Polybius, *Hist.* 3.109.9), sometimes with "weapons" as its object (Demosthenes, *On the Crown* 175), but when Paul uses the term elsewhere he uses it in military metaphors where it clearly means "weapons" (2 Cor 6:7; 10:4, and probably Rom 13:12).[51]

Paul, then, continues to view sin as a power, much like a king, that now commands an army, and he urges his readers not to place their "members" at the disposal of this powerful commander to use as his "weapons of unrighteousness." "Members" (μέλη) stands parallel both to "mortal body" in the previous clause (in 6:12) and to "yourselves" in the following clause. One's "mortal body," then, is one's self, and the members of that body are its various abilities, whether physical, emotional, or volitional (cf. 12:4–5; 1 Cor 12:12–27; Col 3:5).[52]

The imperative verb "offer" appears in the present tense in the first clause and in the aorist tense in the second clause (παριστάνετε/παραστήσατε). Although it is important not to read too much significance into this difference, the first imperative probably emphasizes an ongoing, habitual action and the second imperative a complete commitment.[53] The emphasis on vigilance against sin's tendency to dominate the believer is especially appropriate after Paul has just said that believers still live in a mortal body with a tendency toward illicit cravings (6:12).

The term "righteousness" refers not to freedom from God's wrath against those who sin (5:9) but, as the contrast with the term "unrighteousness" shows, to behavior that is the opposite of the impiety, injustice, and oppression that characterized "unrighteous" behavior in 1:18–3:20 (cf. 1:18, 29; 2:8; 3:5).[54] "Righteousness," then, is the ethical and societal righteousness that, according to Isaiah, characterizes God and should characterize his people (Isa 5:7; 33:15; 59:14–17 LXX).

6:14 For sin will not rule as lord over you, for you are not under law but under grace (ἁμαρτία γὰρ ὑμῶν οὐ κυριεύσει, οὐ γάρ ἐστε ὑπὸ νόμον ἀλλὰ ὑπὸ χάριν). Paul promises his readers that sin will not gain the upper hand and dominate their lives. This is true because God in his grace has broken the power of sin to enslave them and lead them to death.

The verb "rule as lord over you" (κυριεύω) was a synonym of the verb "reign" (βασιλεύω) that Paul had used earlier in the argument (5:14, 17, 21; 6:12), and so here Paul continues to use the metaphor of a powerful king ruling over his subjects.[55] The term frequently (although not always) had negative connotations of harsh domination, and Paul probably intended those connotations to come through at this point (cf. 6:9; Gen 3:16 LXX; 2 Cor 1:24). Sin is a domineering master seeking to control those under its power in ways that harm them. What Paul issued as a command in the imperative in 6:12, he states here as a promise in the future indicative. He says in 6:12 that his readers

51. Cf. Meyer, *Romans*, 241; Käsemann, *Romans*, 177.

52. Käsemann, *Romans*, 177.

53. On the difference between the present and the aorist imperative, see McKay, "Aspect in Imperatival Constructions," 206–7, 207–13, and especially the examples on 212–14.

54. Moo, *Romans*, 386n182.

55. See the parallelism between the two verbs in Gen 37:8 LXX and 1 Tim 6:15.

should not allow sin to reign over them, and here he assures them that sin will not be their harsh taskmaster.[56] Sin, in other words, will not win its war of rebellion against God and establish its cruel dominion over his people.

Paul explains that this is true because his readers have moved from existence under the power of the law to existence under the power of God's grace. The expression "to be under something" (ὑπό τινα εἶναι) in Greek meant to be under its power, control, or sway.[57] Thucydides, for example, could describe the result of Sicily falling to the military aggression of Syracuse as "being under their dominion" (ὑπ' αὐτους εἶναι).[58]

Paul's use of the phrase here, then, fits smoothly into his imagery of political power. If the law is imagined as a ruler over a realm in the same way that death and sin rule a realm (5:14, 17, 21; 6:12), then believers are no longer under the domination of that ruler. Here Paul looks back to his connection between the law and the increase of the trespass in 5:20 and anticipates his full description of the mire of disobedience that sin creates from the action of the law on the sinful self in 7:7–25.[59] God has empowered believers to move out of that fatal web by shifting them into the realm of his grace. This is why Paul could be confident that sin would not reign over his readers.

Theology in Application

Paul has made the case at length in 1:16–5:21 that God has justified sinners and reconciled them to himself as a wholly gracious act, apart from anything they have done. In the words of 4:7–8, he has forgiven their lawless deeds, covered their sins, and decided not to count their sin against them. In 6:1–14 he addresses the question that naturally arises from this argument of whether such an unusual approach to justice means that believers are, as a logical result, free from moral responsibility. Should the justified person paradoxically remain in sin so that God can be all the more gracious (6:1; cf. 3:8)?

God's Grace an Excuse for Sin in Early Christianity

The New Testament provides ample evidence that some people twisted early Christian teaching on God's grace in this direction. Jude speaks of those "who pervert the grace of our God into sensuality and deny our only Master and Lord, Jesus Christ" (Jude 4). James is aware that some people defined faith as intellectual assent to Christian doctrine (Jas 2:19) and then, parroting Paul, claimed that this "faith" justified them (Jas 2:24). They felt this freed them from, for example, any responsibility toward the poor in their midst (Jas 2:1–7). Matthew is aware that some within the Christian community called Jesus Lord but, as their deeds revealed, were actually unknown to Jesus (Matt 7:21–23; 13:24–30, 36–43; 25:11, 31–46). Against those who

56. Michel, *An die Römer*, 210.

57. BDAG 1036, s.v. ὑπό B(2); Harris, *Prepositions and Theology*, 221.

58. Thucydides, *History of the Peloponnesian War* 6.86.4 (Smith, LCL).

59. Cf. Wright, "Romans," 543.

focused on their progressive knowledge as the key to a right relationship with God, John had to say, "whoever does not practice righteousness is not of God, nor is the one who does not love his brother" (1 John 3:10).

The Nature of the Problem and Paul's Answer to It

The early eighteenth-century Scottish novelist James Hogg addressed the same problem in his disturbing but insightful work, *The Private Memoirs and Confessions of a Justified Sinner*. This is the story of a young man, Robert Colwan, whose father assured him, as Robert puts it, that he was "a justified person, adopted among the number of God's children . . . and that no bypast transgression, nor any future act of my own, or of other men, could be instrumental in altering the decree."[60] Despite any clear evidence that this pronouncement was true, Robert took it quite seriously and went on to live a life of cruelty to others, constantly justifying his actions as the product of religious zeal and comforted over and over again by the thought that even if his actions were evil Jesus's death had atoned for them, "let them be as heinous and atrocious as they may."[61] Robert's guide into this twisted world was an attractive and brilliant theologian who subtly distorted the Reformed doctrines of election and grace that were so well-known in the rural Scotland of the eighteenth and nineteenth century. This brilliant theologian, as it turns out, was Satan himself.

In Romans 6:1–14 Paul is as clear as Jude, James, Matthew, and John that those who have believed the gospel of Christ's atoning death and powerful resurrection and have been freed from punishment for their sins must begin to live outside sin's realm of power. Those whom God has declared righteous in a juridical sense must give themselves to the service of righteousness, now conceived in an ethical sense.[62] When believers are crucified together with Christ, they die to themselves and live for him (14:7–8; 2 Cor 5:15; Gal 2:20), and living in union with and for Christ has numerous practical, ethical ramifications in Paul's theology. Suffering becomes participation in Christ's suffering, with the promise of glorification and resurrection in the future (2 Cor 4:7–11). Avoiding pride, valuing the contribution of others, caring for and empathizing with others, and equipping others to do the loving work of ministry—all of these flow from membership in Christ's body (Rom 12:3–5; 1 Cor 12:24–27; Eph 4:11–16).[63] The focus of one's life becomes the advancement of the gospel and the good of others rather than self-justification and self-centeredness.

60. James Hogg, *The Private Memoirs and Confessions of a Justified Sinner*, ed. Peter Garside (Edinburgh: Edinburgh University Press, 2002), 79.

61. Ibid., 87.

62. The contrast between "unrighteousness" (ἀδικία) and "righteousness" (δικαιοσύνη) in 6:13 shows that Paul has started to use righteousness language in this passage in ethical rather than juridical ways.

63. Campbell, *Paul and Union with Christ*, 380–84.

In Hogg's novel, when Robert first meets Satan, Satan looks exactly like Robert himself. He wins Robert over not only because they share the same appearance but because Satan appeals to Robert's pride and desire to justify his cruelty to others. In the end Robert becomes so self-focused and, at the same time, so driven to do the will of this figure that he destroys those around him and eventually himself. Union with Christ's death and resurrection frees the believer from obsession with one's self to focus on love for God and love for one's neighbor. Paradoxically, this focus on others also helps to prevent the kind of self-destructive behavior that ruined Robert. "Whoever loses his life for my sake," Jesus said, "will find it" (Matt 16:25).

CHAPTER 14

Romans 6:15–23

Literary Context

As the opening set of rhetorical questions in 6:15–16 indicates, Paul's primary interest in this section is to continue to explain the theological basis for ethical behavior among believers. If the Mosaic law has functioned in salvation history to increase sin rather than to prevent it (5:20), and if believers are not under the sway of this powerful sin-law combination (6:1, 14–15), then what guides the believer's behavior? In 6:1–14 Paul had grounded the ethical conduct of believers in their union with the death and resurrection of Christ. Their union with Christ's death had broken the power of sin over them, and this meant that they were "no longer . . . slaves to sin" (6:6–7).

In 6:15–23 Paul focuses on the metaphor of slavery and explains two further consequences of the believer's freedom from sin. First, freedom from sin and the law entails the domination of other powers: grace (6:15), righteousness (6:18), and God (6:22). Serving one's self is not an option.[1] To serve one's self, as we just saw in the application of 6:1–14, is to serve sin, and as 6:16 and 18 make clear, one serves either sin or righteousness.

Second, Paul emphasizes the important role of the human will in living outside the power of sin. He started to address this second issue in the imperatival language of 6:11–14, but now his appeal to the human will becomes even more pronounced. Believers are not the helpless victims of powerful forces beyond their control, whether death (5:17), the law (5:20; 6:14–15), or sin (5:21; 6:6, 12–14). Instead, because God has freed them from these powers, they can place themselves at the disposal of righteousness and God (6:15–18), and they must do this if they are to live in a way that is consistent with the gift of righteousness that God has graciously bestowed on them in Christ (6:19–23).

Although Paul's jarring comments on the law in 5:20 and 6:14 generated this discussion, he has not so far discussed the law itself. In 7:1–6, then, he explains in greater detail his conviction that the believer's freedom from the law was a necessary corollary to the believer's freedom from sin. Then, in 7:7–25 he will address exactly

1. Cranfield, *Romans*, 1:321; Käsemann, *Romans*, 179–80; Moo, *Romans*, 397.

how sin has used the law to engender rebellion against God and why freedom from the law is necessary in order to live in a way that is pleasing to God. That explanation will set in motion Paul's discussion in 8:1–17 of the Spirit's role in enabling the believer to do what is pleasing to God.

Main Idea

People are either slaves of sin, which leads to death, or slaves of God, choosing to act in righteous ways and, in the end, receiving eternal life. God has broken the power of sin over believers, and they are now under the power of his grace. As believers choose to live in a way that is consistent with this truth, they live righteous lives that identify them as the people of God.

Translation

Romans 6:15–23

15a	Rhetorical Question	**What, then?**				
b	Rhetorical Question	**Should we sin** because we are not	under law but under grace?			
c	Exclamation	**Certainly not!**				
16a	Rhetorical Question	**Do you not know that**	to	whom you offer yourselves as slaves for obedience,		
b	Assertion	**you are slaves**				
			to the	one whom you obey,		whether
c	Alternative			of sin,	resulting in death,	or
				obedience,	resulting in righteousness?	

17a	Contrast	But **thanks be to God that you were slaves of sin**
b		but **you began to obey** from the heart the imprint of the teaching to which you were handed over.
18a	Explanation	That is,
b	Time	when you were freed from sin
c	Assertion	**you became enslaved to righteousness.**
19a	Assertion	**I am speaking in a merely human way**
	Cause	because of the weakness of your flesh.
b	Explanation	For just as **you once offered your members** to impurity and lawlessness to be their slaves,
c		with lawlessness as the result,
d	Comparison	so now **offer your members** to righteousness, to be its slave,
e		with sanctification as the result.
20	Explanation	For when you were slaves of sin
	Assertion	**you were free with respect to righteousness.**
21a	Rhetorical Question	**What fruit, then, did you use to have at that time?**
b	Assertion	**Things for which you are now ashamed!**
c	Explanation	For **the end of those things is death.**
22a	Cause	But now, freed from sin and enslaved to God,
b	Contrast	**you have your fruit** with sanctification as the result, and the end is eternal life.
23a	Explanation	For **the wages that sin pays is death,**
b	Contrast	but **the free gift that God gives is eternal life in Christ Jesus our Lord.**

Structure

The passage begins with a rhetorical question in 6:15 that Paul's potentially controversial statement about the law at the end of the previous section (6:14) prompted. If Christians are not under the law but under grace, then what guides their behavior?

This opening rhetorical question contains the term "grace" (χάρις), a term closely related to the "free gift" (χάρισμα) to which Paul refers in the passage's final clause. The two terms enclose the passage and emphasize the question it addresses: What relationship to sin do people have who have received God's free grace and live under its power?[2]

In 6:16 Paul states the basic principle on which he will base his answer. There is no option for human beings other than either slavery to sin or slavery to obedience to God's word. One sort of slavery leads to death, and the other sort of slavery leads to righteousness.[3]

In 6:17–18 Paul describes his Roman readers against the background provided by this principle. They moved from one type of slavery to another. Before they believed the gospel they were slaves of sin, but God changed their hearts in accordance with the gospel. This change set them free from sin and enslaved them to righteousness.

After a brief caveat in 6:19a alerting his readers not to apply certain elements of the slavery metaphor to their relationship with righteousness and with God, he states the central concern of the passage in 6:19b and d. As J.-C. Viard has shown, the repetition of the verb "offer" (παρίστημι) and the central place of 6:19 in the structure of the passage show how important the statement is to Paul.[4] His Roman readers should place themselves at the service of righteousness with the result that they become God's distinct people, reflecting his own righteous character.

Immediately after Paul's admonition in 6:19b–e, he returns in 6:20–22 to a description of the basis of that admonition, as the "for" in 6:20 indicates. Just as he did in 6:17–18, Paul focuses on the change that the gospel has produced in his readers' existence. At one time they were slaves of sin, free from righteousness (6:20; cf. 6:18), and bore shameful fruit with death as its result (6:20–21). Now, however, they are free from sin, enslaved to God and bear fruit that ends in sanctification and life (6:22). Paul's central admonition to his readers to offer themselves as slaves of righteousness (6:19b–e), then, stands sandwiched between these two descriptions of the change that the gospel has produced in his readers' existence.[5]

The pithy statement in 6:23 sums up the argument both of 6:21–22 and of the larger section 5:12–6:22. Sin leads to death (5:12–21), but God has freely given to believers the remedy to both sin and death in Jesus Christ's death and resurrection (6:1–14). As 6:15–22 has now explained in detail, believers should live in a way that is consistent with this truth.

2. Jean-Sébastien Viard, "Obéissance ou liberté? Redécouverte structurelle de Rm 6,15–23," *ScEs* 54 (2002): 359.

3. Ibid., 360.

4. Ibid., 358, 360, 361–62.

5. Cf. Moo, *Romans*, 397, 405.

Exegetical Outline

IX. Justification by Faith Brings Peace and Reorients the Believer's Existence (5:1–8:39)

A. Justification by Faith Rescues Believers from God's Present and Future Wrath (5:1–11)

B. Christ's Obedience Overwhelms the Effects of Adam's Disobedience (5:12–21)

C. Union with Christ's Death and Resurrection Initiates a New Life (6:1–23)

1. Union with Christ as the Source of Righteous Living (6:1–14)

➡ **2. Slavery to Righteousness and God Replaces Slavery to Sin (6:15–23)**

a. The thesis: people are enslaved either to sin or to God (6:15–16)

b. The basis for Paul's admonition: the gospel's reorientation of the believer's life (6:17–18)

c. A caveat: the inadequacy of the slave metaphor (6:19a)

d. Paul's admonition: offer one's self as a slave to righteousness (6:19b–e)

e. A restatement of the basis for Paul's admonition: the gospel's transformation of the fruit of one's life (6:20–22)

f. A summary: death as sin's wages and eternal life as God's free gift (6:23)

Explanation of the Text

6:15 What, then? Should we sin because we are not under law but under grace? Certainly not! (Τί οὖν; ἁμαρτήσωμεν, ὅτι οὐκ ἐσμὲν ὑπὸ νόμον ἀλλὰ ὑπὸ χάριν; μὴ γένοιτο). The freedom of believers *from* the power of sin and of sin's use of the law for its purposes does not imply that believers are free *to* sin.

Just as in 6:1, Paul introduces a false inference with a rhetorical question (cf. Xenophon, *Mem.* 4.2.17; Josephus, *J.W.* 2.364) and frames the false inference itself as a rhetorical question. The false inference here and its companion in 6:1 tackle the same subject from slightly different angles. Both here and in 6:1 Paul assumes that when law and sin come together in the sinful human being, the result is more, not less, sin. That is why in 6:14 Paul could assume that being under the power of the law ("under law") was equivalent to being under sin's authority ("sin will not rule as lord over you"). Both here and in 6:1 God's grace is the answer to this problem.

In 6:1 the false inference from this set of assumptions was that increased sinning (prompted by the law) should generate more grace from God, and since the fictional interlocutor assumes that more grace is good the assumption also follows that more sinning is good. In the words of Robert Colwan in James Hogg's novel, "The more heavily loaden with transgressions, the more welcome was the believer at the throne of grace."[6] Here, however, the false inference is slightly different. If the believer is free from the power of the law (6:14), the logic runs, then the believer must be free from the law's constraint, and as a result of this freedom, free to sin.[7]

Just as he did in 6:2, Paul rejects this false inference with his characteristic expression, "Certainly not!" This opens the way to his discussion of the nature of the believer's freedom from sin.

6. Hogg, *Private Memoirs and Confessions*, 78.

7. Wilckens, *An die Römer (Röm 6–11)*, 34; Moo, *Romans*, 398.

6:16 Do you not know that to whom you offer yourselves as slaves for obedience, you are slaves to the one whom you obey, whether of sin, resulting in death, or obedience, resulting in righteousness? (οὐκ οἴδατε ὅτι ᾧ παριστάνετε ἑαυτοὺς δούλους εἰς ὑπακοήν, δοῦλοί ἐστε ᾧ ὑπακούετε, ἤτοι ἁμαρτίας εἰς θάνατον ἢ ὑπακοῆς εἰς δικαιοσύνην;). Human beings serve either sin or obedience. There is no other option.

Paul uses the phrase "do you not know . . . ?" (οὐκ οἴδατε) in the same way that he used the similar expression "are you unaware . . . ?" (ἀγνοεῖτε) in 6:3, although here the assumption about what they know derives not from his readers' Christian convictions but from their knowledge of how the institution of slavery works.

In his magisterial study of early Roman Christianity, Peter Lampe makes a convincing case that the first Roman Christians belonged largely to the lower social classes and many lived in Trastevere, a densely populated area on the west bank of the Tiber and the least desirable neighborhood in the city. Those who lived there tended to be leather workers and dock workers and would have been intimately familiar with slavery.[8] Clement, writing from Rome a few decades after Paul's time, says that many Christians there had "sold themselves into slavery, and with the price received for themselves have fed others" (1 Clem. 55.2).[9] Clearly this group understood the notion of presenting one's self to someone as a slave and, as a result, being compelled to obey that person.

Perhaps it was precisely the well-known idea of selling one's self into slavery that prompted Paul to write such cumbersome Greek. Rather than simply saying, "Do you not know that . . . you are slaves to the one whom you obey . . . ," he has added a somewhat redundant relative clause, "Do you not know that *to whom you offer yourselves as slaves for obedience*, you are slaves to the one whom you obey . . . ?"[10] The relative clause, although awkward, adds the thought that one could become a slave by choosing to place one's self at another's service.

The second part of Paul's rhetorical question completes the analogy and drives home his primary point: no third way exists between slavery to sin or slavery to obedience. Paul will state explicitly what he means by slavery to obedience in the next sentence. Here he focuses on the result of serving sin or obedience. Sin results in death both naturally and theologically, naturally as injustice breeds violence (1:29) and theologically since death is God's just punishment for rebellion against him (1:32). Many interpreters think that obedience brings righteousness in the sense that the obedience of faith (cf. 1:5) brings God's declaration of acquittal on the final day of judgment.[11] It is more likely, however, that Paul uses "righteousness" here to mean justice, fairness, and uprightness, since this ethical sense of the term dominates the immediate context (6:18–20).[12]

6:17 But thanks be to God that you were slaves of sin but you began to obey from the heart the imprint of the teaching to which you were handed over (χάρις δὲ τῷ θεῷ ὅτι ἦτε δοῦλοι τῆς ἁμαρτίας ὑπηκούσατε δὲ ἐκ καρδίας εἰς ὃν παρεδόθητε τύπον διδαχῆς). The Roman Christians are no longer enslaved to sin but instead God has placed them under the power of Christian teaching.

The phrase "but thanks be to God" elsewhere in Paul's letters often signals God's reversal of a des-

8. Lampe, *From Paul to Valentinus*, 48–66, 153–83.

9. Ibid., 85–87. The translation belongs to Holmes, *Apostolic Fathers*, 117.

10. On the cumbersome nature of Paul's Greek here, see Cranfield, *Romans*, 1:322.

11. See, e.g., Wilckens, *An die Römer (Röm 6–11)*, 34.

12. BDAG 248, s.v. δικαιοσύνη 3a; Moo, *Romans*, 400.

perate situation (7:25; 1 Cor 15:57; 2 Cor 2:14).[13] Here that situation was the enslavement of Paul's readers to sin, thanks to Adam's disobedience and their own complicity in his original rebellion against God. "You began to obey" translates an aorist tense verb used "ingressively," that is, to indicate the beginning of a state.[14] The qualifying phrase "from the heart" was a natural expression in Greek for sincerely motivated behavior, as Aristophanes shows in his comic play *The Clouds*. There, a father tells his son to show by his obedience that his love is "from the heart" (ἐκ τῆς καρδίας).[15]

Paul may have been thinking more specifically of God's promise in Scripture to replace his people's heart of stone with a heart of flesh, causing them "to walk in my statutes and be careful to obey my rules" (Ezek 36:26–27). If this passage is somewhere in the background, then heartfelt obedience stands in contrast to obedience that is forced or merely for display (cf. 2:28–29) and flows from a heart that God's lavish love has changed (5:5).[16]

The idiom "to be handed over to" (παραδοθῆναι εἰς) was often used to refer to someone being handed over to the power of others or over to some personified force, such as death (Isa 53:12 LXX; 2 Cor 4:11; cf. Rom 1:24, 26, 28).[17] God stands behind the passive voice of the verb here.

The term "impression" (τύπος) referred most basically to the pattern a stamp left on the material into which someone pressed it, but it could also mean "example" (Phil 3:17; 1 Thess 1:7; 2 Thess 3:9; 1 Tim 4:12; Titus 2:7) or "type" in the sense of an outline or pattern (Rom 5:14). Exactly what Paul means by this metaphor here is unclear. He may refer to a particular "type" of teaching, such as Christian (rather than Jewish) or Pauline (rather than Jewish-Christian) teaching.[18] Or he might refer to the teaching implicit in Christ's example, or to a "standard" of teaching that new converts to the Christian faith learned.[19] In light of the ambiguities, however, it seems best to take the word in its most basic Greek sense of "impression," "stamp," or "imprint" and to understand Paul to be describing the inner impact of Christian teaching on the hearts of believers.[20]

6:18 That is, when you were freed from sin you became enslaved to righteousness (ἐλευθερωθέντες δὲ ἀπὸ τῆς ἁμαρτίας ἐδουλώθητε τῇ δικαιοσύνῃ). To summarize what Paul has just said, when his Roman audience became believers they moved from rebellion against God's moral standards to a commitment to what is right and good.

The term "that is" (δέ) introduces a summary of 6:15–17.[21] In 6:17 Paul had emphasized the timing of his readers' shift from one lordship to another, and so the participle he uses here (ἐλευθερωθέντες) is probably temporal: "When you were freed." Just as with the aorist "you began to obey" (ὑπηκούσατε) in 6:17, so here Paul used the aorist "became enslaved" (ἐδουλώθητε) "ingressively" to speak of the beginning of this new enslavement. The Roman believers *became* slaves of righteousness *when* they were set free from sin.

13. The exception is 2 Cor 8:16.

14. See Smyth, *Greek Grammar*, §§1924–25; McKay, *New Syntax*, 30; Wallace, *Greek Grammar*, 558–59.

15. Aristophanes, *Clouds* 85–87. On this, see BDAG 508, s.v. καρδία 1bα.

16. Cf. Dunn, *Romans 1–8*, 343.

17. Cf. Robert A. J. Gagnon, "Heart of Wax and A Teaching that Stamps: ΤΥΠΟΣ ΔΙΔΑΧΗΣ (Rom 6:17b) Once More," *JBL* 112 (1993): 669–70.

18. Meyer, *Romans*, 245–46.

19. See, respectively, Pelagius, *Romans*, 99, and Sanday and Headlam, *Romans*, 168.

20. Gagnon, "Heart of Wax," 667–87 (cf. Calvin, *Romans*, 133; Schreiner, *Romans*, 336).

21. See BDAG 213, s.v. δέ; Fitzmyer, *Romans*, 450.

Slavery and freedom were frequently viewed as polar opposites in Greco-Roman antiquity, and Paul often makes use of this polarity (1 Cor 12:13; Gal 3:28; 4:21–31; 5:1; Col 3:11).[22] He also recognized, however, that for the believer freedom in one sphere sometimes entailed slavery in another sphere. Although free from the constraints that other people might impose on him, Paul was nevertheless "a servant [ἐδούλωσα] to all" (1 Cor 9:19). Similarly, the Galatians should not use their freedom from the Mosaic law selfishly but to "serve [δουλεύετε] one another" through love (Gal 5:13). So here, Paul makes clear that freedom from sin does not entail "freedom" to please one's self but a commitment to what is just, right, and fair.

6:19 I am speaking in a merely human way because of the weakness of your flesh. For just as you once offered your members to impurity and lawlessness to be their slaves, with lawlessness as the result, so now offer your members to righteousness, to be its slave, with sanctification as the result (ἀνθρώπινον λέγω διὰ τὴν ἀσθένειαν τῆς σαρκὸς ὑμῶν. ὥσπερ γὰρ παρεστήσατε τὰ μέλη ὑμῶν δοῦλα τῇ ἀκαθαρσίᾳ καὶ τῇ ἀνομίᾳ εἰς τὴν ἀνομίαν, οὕτως νῦν παραστήσατε τὰ μέλη ὑμῶν δοῦλα τῇ δικαιοσύνῃ εἰς ἁγιασμόν). Slavery is a harsh institution and therefore an inadequate, albeit necessary, analogy to the believer's relationship to righteousness. Paul's readers once spent their energy in sexual immorality and socially destructive behavior, but now they have the responsibility of standing apart from that behavior and living as God's people, committed like God himself to fairness, justice, and equity.

Early interpreters of Romans from Origen to Calvin, with remarkable consistency, take the first sentence of this verse as Paul's claim that he does not demand too much of his readers when he merely asks them to give the same level of obedience to righteousness that they once gave to impurity and lawlessness.[23] As Meyer observed long ago, however, Paul's interest in 6:18–20 lies not in the relative degree of devotion that the Roman Christians have to their new master "righteousness" but in the dramatic change itself from one master to another.[24]

The first sentence, then, points backward to what Paul has just said and serves as an apology for having to use a metaphor as harsh as slavery to describe the relationship of the believer to righteousness.[25] As Paul will say in 8:15, the believers in Rome are not slaves cringing in fear of harsh masters but adopted children of God with all the affection and privilege that comes from this status. The expression "in a merely human way" refers to activity (in this case, speech) that is ordinary and therefore not ideal for an explanation of divine truth (cf. 1 Cor 2:13).[26] The fleshly weakness of Paul's Roman readers makes such inadequate analogies necessary not because their ability to grasp spiritual truths is less astute than that of others (cf. 15:14) but because even believers are still in the flesh and affected by its sinful tendencies.[27]

After this necessary caveat, Paul returns to the slavery metaphor again and, recalling the language

22. On the slave-free antithesis, see Murray J. Harris, *Slave of Christ: A New Testament Metaphor for Total Devotion to Christ*, NSBT 8 (Downers Grove, IL: InterVarsity Press, 1999), 69–70.

23. Origen, *Romans, Books 6–10*, 10–11; Ambrosiaster, *Romans*, 51; Chrysostom, *Romans*, 183–84; Pelagius, *Romans*, 99; Calvin, *Romans*, 134.

24. Meyer, *Romans*, 248.

25. Cranfield, *Romans*, 1:325.

26. LSJ 141, s.v. ἀνθρώπινος 3. For the human-divine contrast, see, e.g., Plato, *Republic* 497 C (cf. Meyer, *Romans*, 247) and, closer to the time of Paul, Dionysius of Halicarnassus, *Ant. rom.* 3.5.1; 10.2.2; 10.10.7.

27. Cf. Godet, *Romans*, 258.

of 6:13 and 6:16, urges his readers to act on the new reality that governs their lives. The expression "for just as" does not point back to the caveat of the immediately preceding sentence but to 6:18 and elaborates on what Paul said there. If his Roman readers are freed from sin and have become enslaved to righteousness, then they should devote their various abilities, whether physical, emotional, or volitional (their "members") to the service of "righteousness" rather than to the service of "impurity" and "lawlessness." The term "impurity" (ἀκαθαρσία) carries overtones of sexual immorality in Paul (1:24; 2 Cor 12:21; Gal 5:19; Eph 4:19; 5:3; Col 3:5; 1 Thess 4:7), and the term "lawlessness" (ἀνομία), a less distinctively Pauline word, had broader connotations of rebellion against God and his requirements (2 Cor 6:14; 2 Thess 2:3, 7; Titus 2:14).

Concrete acts of lawlessness resulted from his readers' former service to impurity and lawlessness, but now that they have believed the gospel, "sanctification" should be the result of their commitment to righteousness. "Sanctification" (ἁγιασμός) was a cultic term of Greek-speaking Judaism, used to describe the process of setting apart the temple, its priests, and its sacrifices for God's purposes (2 Macc 2:17; 14:36; 3 Macc 2:18; Sir 7:31; Ezek 45:4 LXX).[28] Paul may have used the term here to suggest that believers in Rome were, as a body, the eschatological temple of God and should therefore set themselves apart from the rest of the world by their righteous conduct (cf. 1 Cor 3:17; 2 Cor 6:14–7:1; 1 Thess 4:3, 4, 7).[29]

6:20 For when you were slaves of sin you were free with respect to righteousness (ὅτε γὰρ δοῦλοι ἦτε τῆς ἁμαρτίας, ἐλεύθεροι ἦτε τῇ δικαιοσύνῃ). The righteousness and sanctification that believers must pursue flow from lives that God has radically reoriented away from sin and toward righteousness.

The term "for" (γάρ) shows that Paul is about to provide the basis for his admonition to his readers to place their faculties and abilities at the disposal of righteousness (6:19). They should do this, he says here, because although they were once slaves of sin and free from the claims of righteousness, that is now no longer true. This is simply the other side of his assertion in 6:18 that his readers became enslaved to righteousness when they were freed from sin. Paul's ethical admonition in 6:19, then, is surrounded on both sides by the change in lordships on which it is based.[30] The gospel has freed them from bondage to sin and placed them under the authority of righteousness.

6:21 What fruit, then, did you use to have at that time? Things for which you are now ashamed! For the end of those things is death (τίνα οὖν καρπὸν εἴχετε τότε; ἐφ' οἷς νῦν ἐπαισχύνεσθε, τὸ γὰρ τέλος ἐκείνων θάνατος). The enslavement of Paul's readers to sin prior to their conversions led to vicious and shameful behavior that harmed others and would have ended in a just sentence of death on the day of judgment.

Most English translations place the question mark after "you are ashamed" and render the verse in a way similar to, for example, the NIV: "What benefit did you reap at that time from the things you are now ashamed of?" On this reading, Paul would have assumed the answer "none" to his question and then would have given the reason why their formerly sinful conduct produced nothing useful. Its end was death. It is more likely, however, that the question mark should be placed after "at

28. On the term's reference to a process, see Otto Procksch, "ἁγιάζω, κτλ.," *TDNT* 1:113.

29. Cf. Légasse (*Romains*, 425), who stresses the cooperation of human beings with God in the process of sanctification; see also Jewett, *Romans*, 421.

30. Moo, *Romans*, 405.

that time." This makes the rhetorical question more succinct and therefore more rhetorically effective, and it produces a question and answer with three parts that neatly match the three parts of 6:22. Paul first refers to his readers' condition (bearing sinful fruit/freed from sin), then to the result of that condition (shame/sanctification), and then to the ultimate end of that condition (death/eternal life) (cf. REB; NJB).[31]

"Fruit" was a common metaphor for the outcome of one's behavior. "In every dealing there is nothing worse than bad companions," says Eteocles in Aeschylus's play, *Seven Against Thebes* (600–601), "let that bitter fruit [καρπός] never be plucked. The field of folly yields death as its harvest [θάνατον ἐκκαρπίζεται]."[32] Paul's imperfect-tense verb "used to have" emphasizes the progressive nature of the action and so the consistency with which his readers lived sinful lives prior to their conversions.[33]

The appearance of "for which" (ἐφ' οἷς) at the beginning of a sentence and referring back to something in the previous sentence is not unusual (2 Macc 8:21; 4 Macc 4:21), and the clause that it introduces here refers back to the "fruit" of the rhetorical question, now viewing that "fruit" as discreet acts of evil.[34]

Just as in 6:16, "death" is both the natural outcome of vicious and therefore sinful behavior (1:29) and God's just penalty for rebellion against him (1:32). When Paul's readers recall their former way of life, they recognize the injustice and violence that it often involved. Now, on the other side of their conversions, they are ashamed of that behavior. Paul understood this type of shame because he too was ashamed of the violence that characterized his preconversion way of life (1 Cor 15:9; 1 Tim 1:13; Titus 3:3).[35]

6:22 But now, freed from sin and enslaved to God, you have your fruit with sanctification as the result, and the end is eternal life (νυνὶ δὲ ἐλευθερωθέντες ἀπὸ τῆς ἁμαρτίας δουλωθέντες δὲ τῷ θεῷ ἔχετε τὸν καρπὸν ὑμῶν εἰς ἁγιασμόν, τὸ δὲ τέλος ζωὴν αἰώνιον). Because God has freed Paul's readers from bondage to sin and placed them in his service, they now live in ways that display God's character and end in life with God himself.

The expression "but" (δέ) introduces a contrast to the way of life Paul's readers used to lead before they became believers (6:20–21), and the adverb "now" (νυνί) goes not with the two participles at the beginning of the sentence but with the main verb "you have" (ἔχετε).[36] Just as they had "at that time" fruit of which they are now ashamed, so "now" they have fruit that results in sanctification (cf. REB, NET, HCSB). The present tense "you have" emphasizes the progressive nature of the having, just as the imperfect tense "you used to have" in 6:21 expressed the ongoing nature of their shameful behavior. The two adverbial participles probably express cause (HCSB) and do so in a form that recalls Paul's statement in 6:18. Since it is true, as 6:18 says, that God has freed Paul's readers from sin and enslaved them to righteousness and to himself (6:21), they now live in new ways, bearing different "fruit." The result of this fruit is sanctification, and the "goal" of this way of living is eternal life. The expression "the end" (τὸ τέλος) suggests the image of a journey that has reached

31. Cranfield, *Romans*, 1:328; Moo, *Romans*, 407.

32. Aeschylus, *Persians, Seven against Thebes, and Suppliants* (trans., Aaron Poochigian; Baltimore, MD: Johns Hopkins University Press, 2011), 62.

33. On this element of the imperfect, see McKay, *New Syntax*, 42–43.

34. The relative pronoun is plural.

35. Cf. Jewett, *Romans*, 423–24, and, on the vicious nature of much ancient Roman life, see Toner, *Popular Culture*.

36. Cranfield, *Romans*, 1:328.

its goal (τέλος). This, in turn, implies that Paul has been speaking of a way of life that progresses in sanctification, with the people of God continuing to act in righteous ways that set them apart from unbelievers and, then, in the end, sharing God's life forever.[37]

6:23 For the wages that sin pays is death, but the free gift that God gives is eternal life in Christ Jesus our Lord (τὰ γὰρ ὀψώνια τῆς ἁμαρτίας θάνατος, τὸ δὲ χάρισμα τοῦ θεοῦ ζωὴ αἰώνιος ἐν Χριστῷ Ἰησοῦ τῷ κυρίῳ ἡμῶν). To summarize, human beings are sinful and so can only earn death. Eternal life comes as God's free gift, however, to those whom God has united to Jesus, their King and Lord.

This pithy statement with its neat set of contrasts (wages/free gift; sin/God; death/eternal life) sums up both 6:21–22 and the whole section from 5:12–6:22.[38] Death as the destiny of those under sin's control, and eternal life as the destiny of those who have been transformed by God's free gift, have been the subjects of both the shorter and the longer passage. The term "free gift" (χάρισμα) recalls Paul's reference to "grace" (χάρις) in 6:15 and provides a neat rhetorical conclusion to 6:15–23.[39]

The "wages" (ὀψώνια) in the first clause are earned. Although Greek speakers often used this term for the provisions soldiers received, they could also use it of the pay that soldiers earned (e.g., Luke 3:14).[40] Early interpreters of Romans often took it that way here, believing that Paul was continuing to use the metaphor of placing weapons at the service of a king, in this case "King Sin," as Origen memorably put it (cf. Rom 5:21; 6:12–13).[41] Although it is true that "sin" is a subjective genitive here and therefore personified (cf. 5:21; 6:6–7, 12, 14, 16–22), this understanding of the term "wages" is probably too specific. Paul uses the term with a nonmilitary meaning elsewhere (2 Cor 11:8), and here his interest lies less in the nature of service to sin than in the contrast between what is earned and what is freely given. Those who sin earn the death they receive (cf. 1:32).[42]

In contrast to the "wages" that sin pays, Paul tells his readers in the second clause that God gives eternal life as a "free gift." This expression recalls 5:15–16 where it referred to the justification of sinners through the death and resurrection of Christ. According to 5:17–18, God's "free gift" enabled those who had fallen under the sway of sin and death to "reign in life" instead. Here too, eternal life comes as God's freely bestowed gift to those whom God has united with Christ's death and resurrection (cf. 6:3–11). Just as in 4:4–5, life together with God is not something that one earns—sinful human beings can only earn death—but is a gift that God freely bestows.[43]

37. Cf. Godet, *Romans*, 261.

38. For the relationship of 6:23 to 6:21–22, see Käsemann, *Romans*, 185.

39. Viard, "Obéissance," 359.

40. The argument that the term means "provisions" here (Chrys Caragounis, "ΟΨΩΝΙΟΝ: A Reconsideration of Its Meaning," *NovT* 16 [1974]: 35–57) is not convincing because of the contrast with God's "free gift."

41. E.g., Origen, *Romans, Books 6–10*, 17; Pelagius, *Romans*, 100. Cf. Michel, *An die Römer*, 215–16; Wilckens, *An die Römer (Röm 6–11)*, 40; Fitzmyer, *Romans*, 452.

42. Godet, *Romans*, 262.

43. Jewett, *Romans*, 426.

Theology in Application

Paul wants to show in this passage that the freedom of believers from sin and from sin's use of the law does not mean that believers are now free to sin. Rather, the reverse is true. Believers are now obligated to God and capable of serving him by means of righteous behavior because sin's sway over them has ceased. As Paul's two-fold use of the term "sanctification" (6:19, 22) shows, moreover, this new obligation plays an important role in God's purposes for his people.

The Old Testament Roots of Paul's Teaching on Sanctification

The terms "sanctification" and "holiness" (ἁγιασμός, ἁγιωσύνη) applied in Paul's culture primarily to the temple, its priests, and its sacrifices. They were set apart from the world around them because of their devotion specifically to God's purposes. The Old Testament also expresses the view, however, that everyone among God's people is holy, that they were "a kingdom of priests and a holy nation" (Exod 19:6). Moses tells God, "We are distinct, I and your people, from every other people on the face of the earth" (Exod 33:16), and God tells his people, "I am the Lord your God. Consecrate yourselves therefore, and be holy, for I am holy" (Lev 11:44), and later, "I am the Lord your God, who has separated you from the peoples" (Lev 20:24). The primary purpose of the Mosaic law was to show Israel how to be holy, how to live in a way that reflected God's character and demonstrated to the world around Israel who God was:

> You shall not do as they do in the land of Egypt, where you lived, and you shall not do as they do in the land of Canaan, to which I am bringing you. You shall not walk in their statutes. You shall follow my rules and keep my statutes and walk in them. I am the Lord your God. (Lev 18:3–4)

Paul understood God's people, both as a group and as individuals, to be God's metaphorical temple because God lived together with them (1 Cor 3:16–17; 6:15–19; 2 Cor 6:16; Eph 2:20–22). He also believed that Christians stood in continuity with ancient Israel. He could describe the wilderness generation of Israelites as "our fathers," for example, to a group of Corinthian Christians who were predominantly gentile (1 Cor 10:1). It is not surprising, then, that Paul believed God had called all Christians "in holiness" (1 Thess 4:7) and that he urged believers to purify themselves "from everything that contaminates body and spirit, perfecting holiness [ἁγιωσύνη] out of reverence for God" (2 Cor 7:1 NIV). This close relationship to God through Christ and the Holy Spirit meant that like the priests, temple implements, and sacrifices, and like ancient Israel itself, they needed to be different from the world around them in ways that reflected the character of God.

What Sanctification Entailed for Paul and His Readers

Elsewhere Paul tells his readers specifically what "sanctification" means for them in their first-century, Greco-Roman contexts. They were to stand apart from their culture in their approach to sex, religious practice, property, money, alcohol use, and speech, for example (1 Cor 6:9–11; 1 Thess 4:3–7). Unlike so many of their neighbors in Thessalonica, Corinth, and Rome, they were not to use any honor or power they might have for their own selfish ends but were to practice cooperation, love, nonretaliation, submission, and self-control (e.g., Rom 12:1–2, 3–21; 1 Cor 6:1–4; 8:1–3; 10:23, 31–33; 13:1–13; 1 Thess 4:6, 9). When Paul spoke of being enslaved to "righteousness" (6:13, 16, 18–19), he probably used the term to summarize these virtues. The task of living this way must have seemed mammoth in the face of the habits and ways of life that the mostly gentile Christians to whom Paul wrote had absorbed since childhood (Rom 13:13–14; 1 Thess 4:3–8; Eph 4:17–19).

Later in Romans Paul will make clear that God has not left his people to live holy lives by their own power but has given them the Holy Spirit to help them (Rom 7:6; 8:1–17, 26–27).[44] Here in 6:15–23, however, he focuses on the important role that believers themselves play in willing to do what is right.

Paul has emphasized in previous sections of his argument that human beings apart from God's intervention are in bondage to sin. The tendency of their lives is to rebel against God (1:18–3:20; 5:12–14, 17a, 20a–c, 21a). In 6:15–23 he says that God has now broken the power of sin to enslave believers and that they are able to live righteously. Their minds, hearts, abilities, and opportunities belong to God, and so they should place themselves at God's disposal for him to use for his just, fair, compassionate purposes.

Sanctification Today

Systematic theologians in the Reformed tradition have often expressed concern about any separation of "sanctification" from God's grace and concern about any notion that human beings can achieve perfection in this life.[45] Even those who have been justified by faith remain too sinful to produce righteous works that might merit a reward from God, and they remain too sinful to expect great progress toward perfection in this life. Claims to perfection or near perfection are based on a failure to take the rigor of God's law seriously. These are helpful emphases, derived both from a close reading of Scripture and a perceptive understanding of the errors into which Christians have sometimes fallen when they have embraced a less-than-biblical view of God's grace. As the exegesis above has shown, 6:15–23 begins and ends with God's

44. Cranfield, *Romans*, 1:295–96.

45. See, e.g., G. C. Berkouwer, *Faith and Sanctification*, Studies in Dogmatics (Grand Rapids: Eerdmans, 1952), 101–13; Bavinck, *Holy Spirit, Church, and New Creation*, 230–32.

grace: the believer is under grace rather than law (6:15), and eternal life, which is the end of a fruitful life of obedience to God, is God's free gift (6:23).

Even so, it is important when applying Paul's teaching in 6:15–23 to the church to leave the emphasis where the apostle himself places it, and that is on the necessity that believers present themselves to God for the purpose of living righteous and holy lives. This obedience arises from grace and so should never be the cause of pride in the believer, but it nevertheless involves the believer's effort and will. In his letter to Titus, who was training church leaders in the rough culture of Crete, Paul tells his coworker that "the grace of God has appeared, bringing salvation for all people, training us to renounce ungodliness and worldly passions, and to live self-controlled, upright, and godly lives in the present age" (Titus 2:11–12). The term "training" here (παιδεύουσα) refers to teaching and education and so connotes discipline and effort for the one being taught. As Paul says only a few clauses later, Christ redeemed his people that they might be "zealous for good works" (Titus 2:14).

Christians, then, should certainly rest in God's grace if they are anxious about whether they are at peace with God, but they should also discipline themselves to do what is right toward people around them, tending to the needs of the poor and oppressed, proclaiming the gospel to the unevangelized, and worshiping God according to his word and with his people.

CHAPTER 15

Romans 7:1–6

Literary Context

Although Paul himself considered the Jewish Scriptures to be authoritative (1:2), he has made several surprising comments in his argument so far about a central part of those Scriptures, the Mosaic law. He has said that God disclosed his righteousness apart from the Mosaic law (3:20), that the Mosaic law brings God's wrath (4:15), that when it "slipped in" to history, it actually caused the violation of its own precepts to increase (5:20), and that believers are no longer "under law" just as they are no longer under the rule of sin (6:14–15). By the end of his discussion of the ethical consequences of the believer's union with Christ (6:1–23), a discussion generated by his comments in 5:20 and 6:14, the pressure on Paul to explain how he could say these things about the law has increased to the breaking point.

This is a pressure that Paul has placed on himself for purposes of making his understanding of the law clear, and as 7:1–25 shows, he never intended that his more radical statements should be taken on their own.[1] He always meant for them to be pedagogical preparation for the explanation of his understanding of the law that he gives in this important section of his argument. That the more radical descriptions of the law needed further explanation was already clear from 3:20 where Paul finished his statement about the disclosure of the gospel apart from the law with the caveat that the gospel was "attested by the law and the prophets." This statement hints that the Mosaic law played an important role in God's purposes that has now ended, but that it still continues to function as authoritative Scripture.

In 7:1–25 Paul will address why the believer is no longer "under law" (6:14–15) from the perspective both of the law's action on the individual sinner and from the perspective of God's purposes for the law in history. He will explain in 7:1–6 how the law causes the trespass to increase and state that the era of the Mosaic law has given way, in God's purposes, to the era of the Spirit's outpouring, just as the law and the prophets testified. Since the alliance of the law with sin has been so close in the era of the law's dominance, Paul naturally addresses in 7:7–12 the question of whether the

1. Dunn, *New Perspective*, 279.

law and sin are virtually identical to one another. Since he has coupled the law with death so often in his argument, he next answers in 7:13–25 the question of whether the law is itself responsible for the death that comes to those who violate it. The effect of 7:1–25, then, is to exonerate the law from blame for the sin and death that were so pervasive in the era of its dominance.

In light of this, it is unsurprising that in 8:1–17 Paul uses the term "law" in a positive sense.[2] Now, however, it is reasonably clear that this is not the Mosaic law, which has passed away, but a new law, which believers, empowered by the Spirit, are able to keep. That believers do not keep this law perfectly is clear from the admonitory tone of 8:12–17, but it is also clear that they have entered the era in which sin's use of the law to increase rebellion against God is coming to an end. Sin's use of the law has been so crippled by the death of Christ that Paul can speak of this powerful alliance as decisively broken.

This complex approach to the law continues in the rest of the letter. In 9:30–10:13 the Mosaic law has come to an end at the same time that it testifies to the gospel, but in 13:8–10 the law in its new form continues to provide ethical guidance to the believer.

Main Idea

Like a wife whose husband has died and who is now free from her legal obligation to remain faithful to her former husband, believers are free from the law. Their union with the crucified and risen Christ has released them from life "under law" in two senses. First, they are no longer under the power of the law, as sin used it to generate

2. Cf. ibid., 279–81.

even more sin in their lives, and, second, they are no longer under the Mosaic law because the new outpouring of the Spirit through the gospel has signaled that the Mosaic law's work is finished.

Translation

Romans 7:1–6

1	Rhetorical Question	Or **are you unaware,** brothers and sisters (for I speak to those who know the law),
	Content	that the law rules
	Manner	as lord over a human being
	Duration	as long as he or she lives?
2a	Explanation (of 1)	For **the married woman is bound**
		by law
		to her living husband,
b	Contrast	but if her husband should die,
		she is released
		from the law as it concerns her husband.
3a	Condition	So then, if she should become another man's while her husband is living,
	Inference (from 2a–b)	**she is styled an adulteress.**
b	Contrast	**But** if her husband should die,
		she is free from the law
c	Result	so that she is not an adulteress
	Concession	although she should become another man's.
4a	Inference (from 1–3)	So, my brothers and sisters, **you too have been put to death**
	Reference	with respect to the law
b	Means	through the body of Christ—
c	Restatement	the one who was raised from the dead—
d	Purpose (of 4a)	in order that you might become another's
e	Purpose (of 4d)	that we might bear fruit for God.
5a	Time (of 5b)	For when we were in the flesh,
b	Explanation (of 4)	**the sinful passions that were prompted through the law used to work in our members**
c	Result (of 5b)	so that we bore fruit for death.
6a	Contrast (to 5)	But **now we have been released from the law,**
b	Cause (of 6a)	having died to that by which we used to be held captive
c	Result (of 6a–b)	so that we serve in the newness of the Spirit and not
d	Contrast	in the oldness of the letter.

Structure

The passage unfolds in four steps.

First, in 7:1 Paul states a basic principle concerning the reach of the law that illustrates the main point of the passage. This principle is that a death has ended the power of the law over them.

Second, in 7:2–3 Paul uses an analogy that explains both how death brings an end to the law's power and how believers continue to live after the law's power over them has ended. The analogy features a married woman whose husband dies and who has married another husband. The death of her husband freed her from the law mandating that she not marry anyone else.

Third, in 7:4 Paul applies to his readers the principle in 7:1 as he has explained it through the analogy in 7:2–3.[3] This is clear from Paul's use of the conjunction "so" (ὥστε), a term for drawing an inference rather than for making a correlation.[4] In accord with the principle that people are only under the law's authority while they are alive (7:1), and just as in marriage law a widow does nothing wrong if she lives with a second husband (7:2–3), so the Roman Christians have been released from the law's power over them and empowered to live in ways that are pleasing to God. This has happened through their union with Christ who both died for their sins and was raised from the dead so that they might live productive lives in service to God.

At this point a number of interpreters down through the centuries have wondered if Paul's argument has somehow lost its way. If Paul intended to clarify the principle of 7:1 (that the law has no power over a dead person) with the marriage analogy of 7:2–3, then why, in the analogy, does the wife go on living?[5] Moreover, if the dead husband in the marriage analogy corresponds to the law, then why does Paul say that the believer is dead to the law rather than that the law itself is dead?[6] Dodd thought that Paul's argumentation here was simply inept, "confused from the outset" and "gone hopelessly astray."[7] Many ancient commentators on Romans thought that Paul did not want to offend his Jewish audience or add fuel to heretical fires by speaking of the death of the law, so he spoke more delicately of the death of believers to the law in 7:4.[8]

The key to understanding the illustration, however, lies in seeing 7:4 as an application to the believer of the principle articulated in 7:1 and clarified in 7:2–3.[9] In other words, the marriage analogy in 7:2–3 is not an allegory that Paul then explains

3. Cranfield, *Romans*, 1:335.

4. Meyer, *Romans*, 261; Cranfield, *Romans*, 1:335; Dunn, *Romans 1–8*, 361; BDAG 1107, s.v. ὥστε 1a.

5. Dodd, *Romans*, 119.

6. Ibid., 120.

7. Ibid., 119, 120. Cf. Heikki Räisänen, *Paul and the Law*, WUNT 29 (Tübingen: Mohr Siebeck, 1983), 46, 61–62.

8. Chrysostom, *Romans*, 187; Pelagius, *Romans*, 101; Theodoret of Cyrus, *Letters of St. Paul*, 1:80–81; John of Damascus, *PG* 95:491; cf. Räisänen, *Paul and the Law*, 62n95.

9. Cranfield, *Romans*, 1:331, 335; Dunn, *Romans 1–8*, 361.

in 7:4 but simply a clarification of the principle in 7:1 so that this principle now matches the situation of the believer. Because believers are united with Christ, like Christ they have both died and are alive in a new way (cf. 6:1–14). Their death with Christ has broken the law's power over them, and their new life in union with Christ and empowered by the Spirit enables them to serve God.

The fourth part of Paul's argument, 7:5–6, explains the application of 7:4 in greater detail by means of a contrast between existence before and after faith in Christ. Prior to faith in Christ, believers were at the mercy of sin's use of the law to shape them so that they sinned against God and were destined for death (7:5). Faith in Christ, however, released them from this fatal connection between themselves, the law, and sin. Faith did this because the Spirit, whose coming was predicted by the prophets, powerfully freed believers from their bondage (7:6).

Exegetical Outline

IX. Justification by Faith Brings Peace and Reorients the Believer's Existence (5:1–8:39)

- A. Justification by Faith Rescues Believers from God's Present and Future Wrath (5:1–11)
- B. Christ's Obedience Overwhelms the Effects of Adam's Disobedience (5:12–21)
- C. Union with Christ's Death and Resurrection Initiates a New Life (6:1–23)
- ➡ **D. Union with Christ's Death and Resurrection Frees Believer's from the Law (7:1–6)**
  1. The Law Has No Authority over a Dead Person (7:1).
  2. A Widow Is Free from the Law's Requirement That She Not Marry Another (7:2–3).
  3. The Believer Has Died with Christ to the Law (cf. 7:1) and Is Free to Belong to the Resurrected Christ (7:4; cf. 7:2–3).
  4. The Believer Is Free from Sin's Use of the Law and Serves God by the Spirit's Power (7:5–6).
     - a. The believer is free from sin's use of the law to generate more sin in the human being and bring death (7:5).
     - b. The believer serves God not under the authority of the Mosaic law but in the power of the Spirit (7:6).

Explanation of the Text

7:1 Or are you unaware, brothers and sisters (for I speak to those who know the law), that the law rules as lord over a human being as long as he or she lives? (Ἢ ἀγνοεῖτε, ἀδελφοί, γινώσκουσιν γὰρ νόμον λαλῶ, ὅτι ὁ νόμος κυριεύει τοῦ ἀνθρώπου ἐφ' ὅσον χρόνον ζῇ;). Because Paul's readers are familiar with the Mosaic law and because they accept the common-sense principle that no dead person is responsible to keep the law, they should understand that they are no longer under the law's power.

Ever since the flurry of rhetorical questions in 6:1–3 Paul has shifted his mode of discourse from a fictional dialogue with an unbelieving Jewish interlocutor to a dialogue with Christians. A series of rhetorical questions in 6:15–16, again part of this Christian dialogue, marked the beginning of the preceding paragraph, and now another rhetorical question, addressed unambiguously to Paul's Christian "brothers and sisters" in Rome, marks the beginning of another new section of the argument.

Paul's rhetorical question focuses on the Mosaic law and introduces a section (7:1–8:17) that will finally answer three important, closely related questions that have hovered in the background of Paul's statements about the law up to this point. First, how can Paul assume that the righteousness of God comes to believers apart from the law (3:21)? Second, in what sense are believers no longer "under law" (6:14–15)? Third, how does the law, counterintuitively, cause the trespass to increase (5:20)?

The phrase "or are you unaware, brothers and sisters," or its equivalent, appears six other times in Paul's letters and always introduces information that should be obvious to his audience and should therefore, by deduction, also make obvious to them the truth of some statement that Paul has previously uttered.[10] There is an implicit rebuke in the statement, but, here at least, it is the gentle rebuke of a teacher to his students. The previous statement that Paul is about to explain appears in 6:14–15.[11] Believers, Paul says there, are no longer "under law." As the comment on 6:14 demonstrated, the phrase "under law" (ὑπὸ νόμον) in Greek most naturally means "under the power of the law," and Paul continues to think of the law here as something that exercises power over people, like a political figure who "rules as lord" (κυριεύω) over others (cf. 6:9, 14). Paul had said in 6:9 that death no longer "rules as lord" over the risen Christ, nor does it rule, he implies, over those who are united by faith with the risen Christ. He had said in 6:14 that sin should not rule as Lord over believers because they are no longer "under law," and now he says clearly what 6:14 implied: the law also no longer rules as Lord over believers.

The "law" that Paul assumes his audience knows is the Mosaic law rather than general human custom or Roman law. This is clear from Paul's use of the word "law" up to this point. The law that "slipped in so that the trespass might increase" in 5:20 must be the Mosaic law (cf. 5:14), and this means that the law believers are no longer under in 6:14–15 must be the Mosaic law also. Since 7:1 introduces an explanation of that phrase in 6:14–15, Paul must be referring to the Mosaic law here as well. Paul's audience, although it included many gentiles (1:13; 11:13), was therefore familiar with the Mosaic law.[12]

Paul begins to explain how he can say that believers are no longer under the Mosaic law by illustrating his point from a commonly accepted principle about the reach of any law. People are only subject to the law, Paul observes, while they are alive. In the same way, those who are now believers are no longer subject to the Mosaic law because they have died a metaphorical death together with Christ (6:1–11).

7:2 For the married woman is bound by law to her living husband, but if her husband should die, she is released from the law as it concerns her husband (ἡ γὰρ ὕπανδρος γυνὴ τῷ ζῶντι ἀνδρὶ δέδεται νόμῳ· ἐὰν δὲ ἀποθάνῃ ὁ ἀνήρ, κατήργηται ἀπὸ τοῦ νόμου τοῦ ἀνδρός). Believers are no more under the power of the Mosaic law than a widow retains a responsibility to be faithful to her deceased husband.

Paul now offers a further explanation of the

10. Cranfield, *Romans*, 1:332. See 6:3; 1 Cor 6:2, 9, 16, 19.

11. Cf. Werner Georg Kümmel, *Römer 7 und das Bild des Menschen im Neuen Testament: Zwei Studien*, TB 53 (Munich: Kaiser, 1974), 7–8.

12. On the interest that many non-Jewish people in Rome had in Judaism, see Leon, *Jews of Ancient Rome*, 250–56, and Das, *Solving the Romans Debate*, 79–81, 85–87.

analogy between the law's lack of power over the dead person and the Mosaic law's lack of power over the believer. His explanation comes in the form of an analogy between the believer's freedom from the Mosaic law and the freedom of a widow from her marital responsibility to her former husband. The term "married" (ὕπανδρος) carried the nuance of subjection, by law or custom, to a man's power (ὑπό + ἀνδρός) and was often used in discussions of a husband's exclusive sexual rights to his wife (Prov 6:24, 29 [LXX]; Sir 9:9; 41:23; Polybius, *Histories* 10.26.3).[13] The notion of subjection that the term conveyed suited Paul's understanding of the law as a power that held people in subjection (cf. 7:6).

Paul's argument seems to assume the law of marriage as Jesus interpreted it in the Gospel tradition. In the Greco-Roman world, and in some Jewish thinking, either the husband or the wife could initiate divorce for many different reasons.[14] In contrast, Jesus viewed marriage as basically permanent and refused to allow Deuteronomy 24:1–4 to become the basis for a loose approach to divorce (Matt 19:1–9; Mark 10:1–12). This was also Paul's view (1 Cor 7:10, 39), and he probably assumed that his Christian audience in Rome followed this same approach to marriage.[15]

Both the present participle (ζῶντι ["living"]) and the perfect indicative (δέδεται ["is bound"]) communicate the permanence of the marriage bond for the woman while her husband is alive. In the same way, the perfect tense verb "released" (κατήργηται) stands in contrast to "is bound" (δέδεται) and indicates the permanent dissolution of the woman's responsibility to keep the marriage law with respect to her dead husband. The qualifying phrase "as it concerns her husband" indicates that the woman is not free from the constraints of the law generally but only from the law as it affects her relationship with her former husband (cf. 1 Cor 9:21).

7:3 So then, if she should become another man's while her husband is living, she is styled an adulteress. But if her husband should die, she is free from the law so that she is not an adulteress although she should become another man's (ἄρα οὖν ζῶντος τοῦ ἀνδρὸς μοιχαλὶς χρηματίσει ἐὰν γένηται ἀνδρὶ ἑτέρῳ· ἐὰν δὲ ἀποθάνῃ ὁ ἀνήρ, ἐλευθέρα ἐστὶν ἀπὸ τοῦ νόμου, τοῦ μὴ εἶναι αὐτὴν μοιχαλίδα γενομένην ἀνδρὶ ἑτέρῳ). Since death dissolves the marriage bond, a woman whose husband has died does nothing wrong when she marries someone else. Rather, a death has freed her from the law's insistence that she remain faithful to her former husband.

With the expression "so then" (ἄρα οὖν) Paul signals that he is about to draw an inference from what he has just said about a husband's death dissolving the law's restriction on the wife's marriage to another man.[16] Paul's two expressions "should become another man's" and "although she should become another man's" are derived from Deuteronomy 24:2 LXX (καὶ ἀπελθοῦσα γένηται ἀνδρὶ ἑτέρῳ ["and if, having gone out, she becomes another man's"]) and confirm that he was thinking about divorce and remarriage in the context of the basically Jewish teaching of Jesus.

The way Paul articulates the principle that a wife

13. See LSJ 1852; *CGELNT* 361, both s.v. ὕπανδρος.

14. On the Greco-Roman world, see Dunn, *Romans 1–8*, 360. Despite frequent statements to the contrary, it seems likely that Jewish women in the first century could also initiate divorce. On this, see David Instone Brewer, "Jewish Women Divorcing Their Husbands in Early Judaism: The Background to Papyrus Ṣe'elim 13," *HTR* 92 (1999): 353, 354.

15. Theodoret of Cyrus, *Letters of St. Paul*, 1:80; Peter J. Tomson, "What Did Paul Mean by 'Those Who Know the Law' (Rom 7.1)?," *NTS* 49 (2003): 575–79, 580.

16. BDAG 127, s.v. ἄρα 2b.

is free to remarry after the death of her husband shows that his thought has already moved toward the application of his analogy.[17] The verb "should die" (ἀποθάνῃ) recalls the use of the same verb in 6:7–10 to speak of death releasing a person from sin's lordship (6:7) and so of Christ's death releasing people from sin who are united with Christ by faith (6:9). The phrase "free . . . from the law" similarly recalls the language of freedom from enslavement to sin that Paul has just used in 6:17 and 22 (cf. 6:20). Paul already hints, then, at the sense in which believers are no longer under the law's power. They are free from sin's use of the law to increase transgression. In the words of 8:2, they have been "liberated . . . from the law of sin and death."

7:4 So, my brothers and sisters, you too have been put to death with respect to the law through the body of Christ in order that you might become another's—the one who was raised from the dead—that we might bear fruit for God (ὥστε, ἀδελφοί μου, καὶ ὑμεῖς ἐθανατώθητε τῷ νόμῳ διὰ τοῦ σώματος τοῦ Χριστοῦ, εἰς τὸ γενέσθαι ὑμᾶς ἑτέρῳ, τῷ ἐκ νεκρῶν ἐγερθέντι, ἵνα καρποφορήσωμεν τῷ θεῷ). Because of their union with the crucified and resurrected Christ, believers are both like the husband who died and like the living widow who is now free to live in marriage with another man. The freedom that believers have from the law means that they now have a relationship with Christ that leads to a way of life pleasing to God.

Paul now applies both the general principle that the law has no power over the dead person (7:1) and his further explanation that a widow is free from marriage law as it applies to her dead husband (7:2–3) to his audience of fellow believers in Rome. His use of "my brothers and sisters" recalls the use of "brothers and sisters" in 7:1 and brings his audience back to what he said there. The term "so" (ὥστε), therefore, draws an inference not merely from the marriage illustration but from 7:1 as that illustration has clarified it.[18] The believer, Paul argues, is both the person who dies and is beyond the reach of the law's power (7:1) and the widow who continues to live and now is married to another husband (7:2–3).

The passive-voice verb "you . . . have been put to death" emphasizes God's initiative in the conversion of Paul's audience, and the phrase "the body of Christ" indicates the means God used to put them to death with respect to the law.[19] When Christ died on the cross, he atoned for the sins that the law exposed (3:20; cf. 5:13), sins for which the law had mandated punishment (4:15), and he inaugurated a new era in which sin's use of the law to increase rebellion against God would eventually come to an end (5:20–21). When believers were united with the crucified Christ, the link between the law and sin was broken—the "old man" was "co-crucified," as Paul says in 6:6, "in order that the body of sin might be rendered powerless" (cf. Gal 2:19–20).[20]

Believers have not only been united with Christ's death but also with his resurrection (Rom 6:8, 11, 13), and so Paul describes their union with the risen Christ in marriage language appropriate to his analogy of the living, remarried widow. They have "become another's" (γενέσθαι . . . ἑτέρῳ; cf. γένηται ἀνδρὶ ἑτέρῳ; Deut 24:2 LXX). They belong to the risen Christ for the purpose of bearing fruit for God. The "fruit" imagery may be a continuation of the marriage imagery since marriage naturally yields the "fruit" of offspring, but in any case it certainly refers back to the ethical fruit of 6:22 that results in

17. Cf. Légasse, *Romains*, 436.

18. Meyer, *Romans*, 261; Cranfield, *Romans*, 1:335; Dunn, *Romans 1–8*, 361; BDAG 1107, s.v. ὥστε 1a.

19. Dunn, *Romans 1–8*, 361; Schreiner, *Romans*, 350; Légasse, *Romains*, 436.

20. Cf. Fitzmyer, *Romans*, 458; Wright, "Romans," 559.

"sanctification."[21] As believers, united with the risen Christ and freed from sin's use of the law to condemn them and engender further rebellion in them, Paul's audience is now free to live in the way that God intended his people to live—as Christ's sanctified, beautiful bride, without spot, wrinkle, or blemish (Eph 5:26–27; cf. 1 Cor 6:15–17; 2 Cor 11:2).

7:5 For when we were in the flesh, the sinful passions that were prompted through the law used to work in our members so that we bore fruit for death (ὅτε γὰρ ἦμεν ἐν τῇ σαρκί, τὰ παθήματα τῶν ἁμαρτιῶν τὰ διὰ τοῦ νόμου ἐνηργεῖτο ἐν τοῖς μέλεσιν ἡμῶν, εἰς τὸ καρποφορῆσαι τῷ θανάτῳ). When Paul speaks of the Roman believers' death to the law, he means that God has rescued them from the plight they were in because of the death-producing encounter within them of their sinful condition and the law's commandments.

Paul now explains in more detail ("for" [γάρ]) what he has just said about the death his audience has experienced with respect to the law. His explanation reaches all the way back to the period before they were united with Christ by faith and describes the way they lived at that time and its deadly result.

Paul can use the term "flesh" (σάρξ) to refer simply to physical existence (1:3; 4:1; cf. 2:28), but here he uses it to mean existence prior to union with Christ's death and resurrection. This is existence, then, before God has broken sin's dominion over the believer (3:20; 6:19). Although it will become clear in the admonitory language of 8:1–13 that present existence for believers continues to involve a struggle with their fleshly tendency to disobey God (cf. Gal 2:20; 5:16–23, 25–26), here Paul adopts the perspective of the sanctified believer (6:22) looking back on existence prior to union with Christ (cf. Gal 5:24).

The term "passions" (παθήματα) is difficult. Like other NT authors, Paul typically uses it to mean "sufferings" (e.g., Rom 8:18), but in one other place (Gal 5:24) he links it with sinful desires as he does here. In nonbiblical Greek it not only often meant "sufferings" or "misfortunes" but frequently referred to "experiences," such as the hard lessons of life, to troublesome medical symptoms, and to "conditions," such as animal characteristics.[22] The term, therefore, had a passive connotation that the common translation "passions," at least in modern English usage, does not quite capture. Sin and the law together form harmful impressions within people, shaping their impulses to respond in ways that are displeasing to God.

Paul will explain how sinful passions come into existence "through the law" in 7:7–8 and 11 when he says that sin used the commandment to deceive him. This perspective is reminiscent of the way the serpent used God's command not to eat from the tree of the knowledge of good and evil to deceive Eve both about God's motive in giving the command and the penalty of death that would follow violation of the command (Gen 2:16–17; 3:1–7). Paul seems to have thought that sin used the law in the same way when God gave the Mosaic law to Israel (5:13–14, 20), and that sin continues to work this way even for believers with respect to the gospel (2 Cor 11:3–4). Anytime people are faced

21. Theodoret of Cyrus, *Letters of St. Paul*, 1:81. The idea that the "fruit" metaphor continues the marriage imagery goes back at least as far as Origen (*Romans, Books 6–10*, 26).

22. See, respectively, Herodotus, *Histories* 1.207.1; Galen, *In Hippocratis librum de fracturis commentarii iii* (in Karl Gottlob Kühn, ed., *Claudii Galeni, Opera Omnia*, vol. 18, pt. 2 of *Medicorum Graecorum Opera quae Exstant*, ed. Karl Gottlob Kühn [Leipzig, 1830], 616); and Aristotle, *Generation of Animals* 778 a 16–18. See also the article in LSJ 1285. Plutarch, *Moralia* 1128 E (τὰ τῆς ψυχῆς παθήματα ["the disorders of the mind" (B. Einarson and P. H. De Lacy, LCL)]) is frequently cited as a parallel to Paul's negative and moral use of the term here and in Gal 5:24. This instance, however, is not very helpful since Plutarch is engaged at this point in a play on the medical meaning of the term.

with the will of God, whether in the law or the gospel, and decide to assert their independence from God instead of trusting his word, they are acting out the principle that Paul articulates here.

As with 5:20, it is possible that Paul included other, more complex notions of the law's connection to sin in the idea that the law prompts sinful passions.[23] He may have thought of the occasional human tendency to use the law of God to advance one's own selfish agenda by harming others, the very problem that led to Jesus's crucifixion (e.g., John 19:7). He may have also considered the more sincere but misguided attempts to keep the law by rejecting the gospel (Rom 9:30–10:4), especially by rejecting it violently, as in his own case prior to his conversion (Gal 1:13–14; Phil 3:5–6; cf. 1 Cor 15:9). Paul was aware that in the hands of sinful people the law could become not merely an occasion for rebellion but a justification for rejecting the gospel and even a tool of violence against others.

Although the passions that the law has impressed on people have a passive quality (they are the impressions left on people by their sinful experiences with the law), once they are present they take on a life of their own, going to work in the "members" (μέλεσιν) of unbelievers. Just as in 6:13 and 19, "members" refers to the human self from the perspective of its various abilities, whether physical, emotional, or volitional (cf. 1 Cor 12:12–31).[24] The expression "so that we bore fruit for death" explains the result, rather than the purpose, of the sinful passions' activity, as the parallel result clause in 7:6 indicates.[25] People do not intend to lead themselves into the realm of death through their sinful activity, any more than Eve intended to die when she disobeyed God, but death is nevertheless the result (Gen 3:3–6, 22).

7:6 But now we have been released from the law, having died to that by which we used to be held captive so that we serve in the newness of the Spirit and not in the oldness of the letter (νυνὶ δὲ κατηργήθημεν ἀπὸ τοῦ νόμου ἀποθανόντες ἐν ᾧ κατειχόμεθα, ὥστε δουλεύειν ἡμᾶς ἐν καινότητι πνεύματος καὶ οὐ παλαιότητι γράμματος). The Spirit has freed the believer from the oppressive effect the law has on sinful people. Now the Spirit has started empowering his people, newly constituted on the basis of the gospel, to serve him faithfully. This fulfills what the prophets said God would do for his people.

Paul continues to explain what he meant when he said in 7:4 that believers "have been put to death with respect to the law" so that "they might bear fruit for God." Here he presents the other side of his contrast between his audience's pre-Christian and Christian modes of existence. Just as the widow in his illustration was "released [κατήργηται] from the law as it concerns her husband" (7:2), and just as the sinful body of believers had been "rendered powerless" (καταργηθῇ) by their union with the crucified Christ (6:6), so here they have been "released [κατηργήθημεν] from the law" by their death to the law.[26]

In what sense have they been "released from the law"? Paul is probably thinking of the noxious mixture of sinful impulses with the law's commandments that he has just referred to in 7:5. They have been released, then, from sin's use of the law to generate even more rebellion against God than

23. See the variations on this approach in, e.g., Bultmann, *Theology of the New Testament*, 263–69 (cf. G. C. Berkouwer, *Sin* [Grand Rapids: Eerdmans, 1971], 176–77); Dunn, *Romans 1–8*, 364–65; idem, *Theology of Paul*, 160–61; Jewett, *Romans*, 436.

24. Cf. Käsemann, *Romans*, 177.

25. I. T. Beckwith, "The Articular Infinitive with εἰς," *JBL* 15 (1896): 164.

26. The expression "to be released from" (καταργηθῆναι ἀπό) is rare but seems to have meant "to be placed outside the sphere of influence, power, or benefit of" (Gal 5:4; Acts of John 84 ["excommunicated from"; see *PGL* 716, s.v. καταργέω 7]).

would have been the case had they never encountered the law (4:15; 5:13, 20).

This was the sense in which Paul could say they used to be "held captive" (κατειχόμεθα) by the law. The term "hold captive" (κατέχω) had a wide variety of meanings, but frequently referred to being held prisoner or in slavery (Gen 39:20 LXX; Josephus, *Ant.* 2.158).[27] Since Paul used the imagery of bondage and freedom with respect to the law in the marriage illustration of 7:2–3 and since he mentions slavery in this sentence's next clause, it is very likely that he refers here to release from the law's metaphorical captivity (Tyndale, Luther, RSV, NAB, NRSV, ESV; cf. Gal 3:23). Here, then, Paul speaks of the believer's release from the oppressive constraint that the law places on unbelievers when sin uses the law as a tool to engender further rebellion against God.

Just as he had argued in 6:15–23, however, Paul clarifies here that freedom from the law's oppression does not mean freedom from obligation to God. The result (ὥστε) of death to the law and release from its suppression is slavery "in the newness of the Spirit" rather than in the "oldness of the letter." For the first time since 5:5 Paul mentions the Spirit, and this is a reminder that his appeals to the human will in 6:11–13 and 19 are not complete by themselves. Believers are not left to their own resources to bear the fruit of obedience to God that results in their sanctification (6:22; 7:4). It is not unreasonable to conclude that the Spirit is the agent of the passive action behind the expressions "you too have been put to death with respect to the law" (7:4) and "we have been released from the law" here. Paul probably envisioned the Spirit of God as the divine person who broke the stranglehold the law had on believers prior to their union with Christ.

As the terms "newness" and "oldness" hint, Paul describes here not merely a contrast between two modes of existence, one before and one after conversion, but also a contrast between two periods in salvation history, the present period dominated by the lavish outpouring of God's Spirit on his people (cf. 5:5) and the prior period dominated by the rule of the Mosaic law among God's people.[28] Paul uses the term "letter" in 2 Corinthians 3:6–7 to refer to the Decalogue engraved on "stone tablets" and "written by the finger of God" (Exod 31:18 LXX; cf. 2 Cor 3:3). He explains in 2 Corinthians 3:7–18 that Moses's ministry of mediating a law that had condemned God's people was, even in Moses's own time, "being brought to an end" (καταργούμενον, v. 11; cf. vv. 7, 13). "The ministry of the Spirit" in which Paul and his coworkers were engaged (2 Cor 3:8; cf. 3:11) had now succeeded it. This is a development in salvation history that the prophets had anticipated (Jer 31:31–34; Ezek 11:19–20; 36:26–27) and that Paul had already hinted at in 2:28–29 in his comparison between the law-breaking Jew and the gentile who kept the law.

27. *TLNT* 2:287. The term could also simply refer to the law "constraining" people (*TLNT* 2:289), but in light of Paul's use of the slavery metaphor in the next phrase, he probably had a metaphorical use in mind.

28. See Stephen Westerholm, "Letter and Spirit: The Foundation of Pauline *Ethics*," *NTS* 30 (1984): 235–36, 239–41, 46, and, especially, Schreiner, *Romans*, 353–54.

Theology in Application

Paul makes two points in this passage, both of them about the Mosaic law. First, Christians now live in a new stage of salvation history in which the Mosaic law's rule over God's people has ended. This freedom has come to Christians through their union with Christ's death and resurrection. Second, the Spirit has freed Christians from the tendency of the law to increase human rebellion against God and has empowered them to live in ways that are productive and useful for the service of God.

A Change in the Shape of the Law's Authority

The first point, that the Mosaic law no longer rules over believers, has important implications for the Christian understanding of the Old Testament. Since the death of Christ, the commandments of the Mosaic law no longer govern the church in the same way they were intended to govern Israel (Rom 7:6; Gal 3:19, 23–25; Eph 2:15). So Paul can assume, for example, that believers no longer need to observe the commandment in the Mosaic law to circumcise their sons (Rom 4:11–12; 1 Cor 7:19; Gal 5:6; 6:15), to restrict their diet (Rom 14:1–4, 14; 1 Cor 9:21; 10:25; Gal 2:11–14), or keep the special days in the calendar of the Mosaic law (Rom 14:5–6; Gal 4:10). The Mosaic law has completed its God-given task of showing Israel how to live (Rom 2:17–20; 10:5), of condemning Israel's unwillingness to live in this way (2:21–24), and, in the process, condemning the entire world for joining Israel in this rebellion (3:19–20; 4:15; Gal 2:15–16; Col 2:14). Since the death and resurrection of Christ, God has set the Mosaic law aside, and God's people live in the power of his Spirit in ways that please God (Rom 7:6; cf. Eph 2:15).

This does not mean, however, either that the Mosaic law is no longer God's authoritative word for his people or that Christians receive no concrete ethical guidance from the teaching of Scripture. Paul himself, speaking of what we would call the Old Testament, said, "Whatever was written beforehand was written for our instruction, in order that through the endurance and the encouragement provided by the Scriptures we might have hope" (Rom 15:4; cf. 4:23–24; 1 Cor 10:1–11). The "whatever" (ὅσα), is all-inclusive and confirms that Christians should take Paul seriously when he says that faith establishes the law instead of overthrowing it (3:31). Paul will eventually speak of the Spirit enabling Christians to fulfill the just requirement of the law (8:4) and will imply that they should fulfill the law's commandment to love one's neighbor as one's self (Lev 19:18) because that commandment itself fulfills the Decalogue's instructions about how one should treat other people (Exod 20:13–17; Deut 5:17–21; Rom 13:8–10). Much of Paul's ethical teaching in his letters arises from the Mosaic law and reaffirms the continuing, direct authority of certain central commandments within it (e.g., Rom 13:8–10; 1 Cor 5:13; 9:8–9; 2 Cor 13:1; Gal 5:14;

Eph 6:2–3; 1 Tim 5:19). There is, in other words, much overlap between what Paul calls "the law of Christ" (Gal 6:2) and the law of Moses.[29]

How should Christians understand elements of the Mosaic law that do not receive clear reaffirmation in the New Testament? Often these elements provide illustrations, within a particular ancient Near Eastern context, of God's practical commitment to the flourishing of his creation, to kindness, and to justice, and these are eternal commitments of God, tied to his unchanging character, that the New Testament reaffirms. "If you go into your neighbor's vineyard," says Deuteronomy 23:24, "you may eat your fill of grapes, as many as you wish, but you shall not put any in your bag." This law helps believers today understand God's commitment to helping the needy and urges the needy not to exploit those who help them.[30] Although the New Testament never quotes or reaffirms this command, it is consistent with Paul's approach to hard work, generosity, and stealing in Ephesians 4:28. If people work hard rather than steal from others and if they share with those in need from the proceeds of their hard work, then, Paul implies, the needy will be able to survive without stealing (cf. Acts 20:35).

Christians no longer live in an ancient Near Eastern theocracy where the law of God is also the law of a particular political entity. Neither, thanks to the atoning death of Christ, do they live under the curse that the law justly pronounced on "anyone who does not confirm the words of this law by doing them" (Deut 27:26). Instead, they live after the rule of the Mosaic law over God's people has ended. They can continue to learn about God's character and desires for his people, however, even from the parts of the Mosaic law that the New Testament does not directly reaffirm.

Sin's Parasitic Use of the Law

Paul also maintains in this passage that believers live in a new era in which the Spirit has broken the power of the law to create sinful passions within them. He describes both how the law does this and how the Spirit breaks this power in much greater detail in 7:7–8:17, but he announces his basic approach here. It is astonishing to think that the law itself—the description of God's will, set down in writing before his people—could become a means of sin, but that it does so is a reminder both of how insidious sin can be and of how necessary the Spirit's power is for breaking its corrupting influence. Whether it is members of the clergy using their positions of authority and trust to take advantage of children or truly needy people using the generosity, tolerance, and acceptance of the church not merely to take what they need from the church but to swindle it out of the resources that it could use to help others,

29. Stuhlmacher, "Paul's Understanding of the Law," 98–104.

30. Cf. J. G. McConville, *Deuteronomy*, Apollos Old Testament Commentary (Downers Grove, IL: IVP Academic, 2002), 352–53.

what is good (i.e., God-given authority, trust, helping the needy) can often become the occasion for great evil. This is what Cornelius Plantinga calls the parasitic nature of sin. Having nothing good in itself and therefore nothing of lasting value, it attempts to survive and grow by attaching itself to the good.[31]

Romans 7:1–6 teaches believers to be wary of the ways that, as sinners, they are capable of using even the law of God in the service of sin. It also teaches, however, that as people in whom God's Spirit dwells they have the resources for discerning sin's subtle attempts to deceive them into distrust of and disobedience to God. Paul will have much more to say about this in the paragraphs that follow.

31. Plantinga, *Not the Way It's Supposed to Be*, 78–95.

CHAPTER 16

Romans 7:7–25

Literary Context

In 7:1–6 Paul had started to explain more fully than in his previous argument the relationship between the gospel and the Mosaic law. He had said in 5:20 that the coming of the Mosaic law to Israel had caused the trespass to increase and in 6:14–15 that believers were no longer under the law's power. Since both Paul and his Roman audience believed that the Mosaic law was part of Scripture and since the law itself urges people to obey its precepts and live, it was important for Paul to explain why believers were no longer under the law's power. In 7:1–6 he explained that the law generated sinful passions within them so that they bore the sort of ethical fruit that would lead to their death (7:5), and he also explained that the time of the law's rule over God's people had come to a close with the advent of the Spirit (7:5–6). This helped explain what he meant when he said that the law caused the trespass to increase and that believers were no longer under the law, but it did not answer the more pressing question of how Paul could link the law so closely with sin and death. Did he deny the divine origins of the law and even think of it as sinful?

In 7:7–25 Paul addresses these questions. In 7:7–12 he shows that sin, not the law, was at fault in causing the trespass to increase. In 7:13–25 he shows that the weak and fleshly self, not the law, led the individual to live in ways that brought death. One important function of 7:7–25, then, is to serve as an apology for the law.

The passage also performs another important function in the argument. It prepares for 8:1–17 by demonstrating the impotence of the law to give people life.[1] So, at the same time that it makes the case that the law is not responsible for sin, it also makes clear that the law cannot solve the human problem of enslavement to and captivity under sin's power. The law emerges from 7:7–25 as holy, just, and good (7:12), but also helpless to rescue humanity from its plight of sinfulness. In 8:1–17 Paul explains that this rescue must come from outside the human being. It comes from God himself, through the atoning death of his Son and through the empowerment of

1. On the twofold function of 7:7–25 in Paul's argument, see Dahl, *Studies in Paul*, 85.

God's Spirit. Paul then puts this rescue of humanity in cosmic perspective in 8:18–39 and in this way brings the second major part of his argument (5:1–8:39) to a close.

VIII. The Scriptures Show That Righteousness Comes by Faith Rather Than by Works (4:1–25)
IX. Justification by Faith Brings Peace and Reorients the Believer's Existence (5:1–8:39)
- A. Justification by Faith Rescues Believers from God's Present and Future Wrath (5:1–11)
- B. Christ's Obedience Overwhelms the Effects of Adam's Disobedience (5:12–21)
- C. Union with Christ's Death and Resurrection Initiates a New Life (6:1–23)
- D. Union with Christ's Death and Resurrection Frees Believers from the Law (7:1–6)
- ➦ **E. The Goodness, Yet Inability, of the Law (7:7–25)**
- F. God's Solution to the Human Plight (8:1–39)

X. Israel's Present Rejection of the Gospel Does Not Imply the Failure of God's Word (9:1–11:36)

Main Idea

The close association between the law, sin, and death in Paul's argument up to this point does not mean that the law, like sin and death, is evil. The law is God's word and therefore is completely good. However, the law has no power to overcome sin in the weak, sin-prone human being, and in the face of sin's power it becomes a tool by which sin deceives the human being into persistent disobedience to God.

Translation

Romans 7:7–25

7a Rhetorical Question — **What, then, shall we say?**
b Rhetorical Question — **Is the law sin?**
c Exclamation — **Certainly not!**
d Explanation — On the contrary, **I would not have known sin**
e Condition — except through the law.

f Illustration — Indeed, **I would not have known coveting**
g Condition — unless the law had said, "You shall not covet." (Exod 20:17; Deut 5:21)

8a Expansion — And **sin,** taking its opportunity, through the commandment
. . . produced in me all manner of coveting.

b Explanation/Separation — For apart from the law,
Assertion — **sin is dead.**

9a Explanation	And **I was once living**
b Separation	apart from the law,
c Sequence	but when the commandment came
	sin revived.
10a Simultaneous	But **I died,**
b Conclusion	and **the commandment** whose purpose was life—
	this, for me, **was found to result in death.**
11a Restatement (of 10a–b)	For **sin,** taking its opportunity,
	. . . deceived me through the commandment
b Assertion	and through it
	killed me.
12a Conclusion/Summary	So, **the law, for its part, is holy,**
b Restatement	and **the commandment is holy and**
c List	**just and**
d List	**good.**
13a Rhetorical Question	**Did that which is good, then, become death for me?**
b Exclamation	**Certainly not!**
c Explanation	On the contrary, **sin, so that it might be shown to be sin, was producing death in me**
d Means	through what is good
e Purpose	so that sin might become extremely sinful
f Means	through the commandment.
14a Basis	For **we know that the law is spiritual,**
b Contrast/Comparison	but **I am fleshy,**
c Restatement	**sold under sin.**
15a Explanation (of 14b–c)	For **I do not understand what I produce,**
b Explanation (of 15a)	for **it is not what I want that I accomplish,**
c	but **precisely what I hate that I do.**
16a Condition	But if I do precisely what I do not want,
b Assertion	**I concur**
c	with the law
d Content	that it is good.
17a Inference	And **now I no longer produce it,**
b	but **sin that dwells within me.**

Continued on next page.

Continued from previous page.

18a	Restatement (of 17a–b)	For **I know that good does not dwell in me,**
		that is, in my flesh,
b	Explanation (of 18a)	for **willing lies close at hand,**
c	Alternative	but **producing what is praiseworthy does not.**
19a	Restatement (of 18a–b)	For **I do not do the good that I will,**
b		but **I accomplish precisely the evil that I do not will.**
20a	Condition	But if I do precisely what I do not want,
b	Inference (cf. 17a)	**I no longer produce it**
c	(cf. 17b)	but **sin that dwells in me.**
21a	Summary	So **I discover the law**
b	Content	that when I want to do what is excellent, evil lies close at my hand.
22a	Explanation (of 21b)	For **I rejoice in the law of God**
b	Place	in the inner human being.
23a	Contrast/Comparison	But **I see another law in my members**
b	Result	warring against the law of my mind and
c	Result	taking me captive by the law
	Description	of sin
d	Place	that exists in my members.
24a	Exclamation	**I am a miserable human being!**
b	Question	**Who will deliver me from the body of this death?**
25a	Answer	But **thanks be to God through Jesus Christ our Lord!**
b	Summary	So then, **I myself serve the law of God**
		with my mind but
		with my flesh the law of sin.

Structure

Paul's argument is carefully structured and develops in two sections, both of them tightly knit together by the extensive use of the first-person singular pronoun. He sets the first section (7:7–12) in past time and presents his argument as an autobiography whose details are general enough to apply to any human being that encounters God's law. He begins with a set of rhetorical questions (7:7a–b) formulated to announce one of the main purposes of the passage, the explanation of the law's relationship to sin. He immediately rejects the notion that the law is sin (7:7c) and then grounds this rejection in an explanation of how sin used the law to increase rebellion and produce death in the individual sinner (7:7d–11). He concludes this first section with a succinct statement of what his argument has just demonstrated: the law is holy and just and good (7:12). This statement crisply answers the rhetorical question at the beginning of the section. The law is not sin (7:7) but something good. Sin, not the law, is the culprit.

The second section (7:13–25) is longer, and Paul sets it almost entirely in the present.[2] It can be divided into three paragraphs: (1) a transitional announcement of the extremely powerful nature of sin (7:13), (2) a central argument that demonstrates the power of sin in Paul himself (7:14–20), and (3) a summarizing conclusion to the entire discussion (7:21–25).[3]

The first paragraph (7:13) is a set of clauses whose form mimics the structure of the first section's beginning (7:7). As with 7:7, a rhetorical question draws a false inference from what Paul has just said in the previous section. Paul then rejects the false inference with "certainly not!" and explains the reason for the rejection with a sentence that begins with "on the contrary. . . ." This opening series of clauses provides a transition between the first two paragraphs. It echoes the themes of the paragraph Paul has just dictated (the relationship between the law, sin, and death). It also points forward to the theme in the next two paragraphs of sin's extreme sinfulness and its continuous production of death in the individual it holds captive.

The second paragraph (7:14–20) falls into two nearly identical subsections (7:14–17 and 7:18–20). Each subsection begins by stating something that "we" (7:14) or "I" (7:18a) know about the fleshly nature of the individual human being. Each subsection then continues with a brief description of Paul's inability to do the good that he wills (7:15–16/7:18b–20a). And each subsection ends with an identical summary statement about sin's powerful influence over Paul's actions (7:17/20b–c). Paul's brief statement in 7:16b that he accepts the excellence of the law and his strikingly precise repetition in 7:20 of sin's powerful influence over him (cf. 7:17) reveal the two main points of 7:7–25: first, that the law is good, but, second, that the law is impotent to deal with sin's power.

The third and final paragraph (7:21–25) begins with a statement of the principle Paul has discovered about the effect of sin on himself (7:21). It continues with an explanation of what this principle reveals about the relationship between God's good law and Paul's sinful self (7:24). It then concludes with a succinct, summarizing statement of Paul's inability, because of his sinful and fleshly nature, to obey the law of God (7:25b).

Briefly intruding into this final paragraph is the welcome exclamation, "But thanks be to God through Jesus Christ our Lord!" (7:25a). The placement of this interjection is surprising, since Paul immediately returns to the bleak tones of 7:7–25

2. The past tense in 7:13 is the only real exception to this. The future tense in 7:24 is part of a question set in the present.

3. Cf. Mark A. Seifrid, "The Subject of Rom 7:14–25," *NovT* 34 (1992): 327–30.

in his concluding summary at the end of the passage (7:25b). This odd rhetorical switchback does not represent confusion in the dictation or transmission of the text.[4] It is instead typical of the way Paul either begins or ends a section of his argument with themes that echo what has gone before or anticipate what comes next (cf., e.g., 5:1–11; 7:13; Eph 2:5, 8–10).[5] In 7:25a, then, Paul anticipates the joyful news of his deliverance, which he will describe in detail in 8:1–17, before he concludes the negative side of his presentation in 7:25b.

Exegetical Outline

IX. Justification by Faith Brings Peace and Reorients the Believer's Existence (5:1–8:39)

- A. Justification by Faith Rescues Believers from God's Present and Future Wrath (5:1–11)
- B. Christ's Obedience Overwhelms the Effects of Adam's Disobedience (5:12–21)
- C. Union with Christ's Death and Resurrection Initiates a New Life (6:1–23)
- D. Union with Christ's Death and Resurrection Frees Believers from the Law (7:1–6)
- ➦ **E. The Goodness, Yet Inability, of the Law (7:7–25)**
  - 1. The Law is Good (7:7–12)
    - a. The law makes sin known by defining sin as rebellion against God (7:7)
    - b. The law makes sin known by prompting rebellion against God (7:8)
    - c. The law's role in prompting sin is sin's fault, not the fault of the law (7:9–11)
    - d. Conclusion: the law is holy, just, and good (7:12)
  - 2. The Law is Unable to Break Sin's Power (7:13–25)
    - a. Sin is so powerful that it brings death through something good, such as the law (7:13)
    - b. The law is impotent to counteract sin's power (7:14–20)
    - c. Only God can rescue the fleshly self from sin's grasp (7:21–25)

Explanation of the Text

7:7 What, then, shall we say? Is the law sin? Certainly not! On the contrary, I would not have known sin except through the law. Indeed, I would not have known coveting unless the law had said, "You shall not covet" (Τί οὖν ἐροῦμεν; ὁ νόμος ἁμαρτία; μὴ γένοιτο· ἀλλὰ τὴν ἁμαρτίαν οὐκ ἔγνων εἰ μὴ διὰ νόμου· τήν τε γὰρ ἐπιθυμίαν οὐκ ᾔδειν εἰ μὴ ὁ νόμος ἔλεγεν, Οὐκ ἐπιθυμήσεις). When people who sin, and that includes everyone, understand what the law says, they continue to sin in the full knowledge that they are disobeying God.

The expression "what shall we say?" (3:5) or "what, then, shall we say . . . ?" (4:1; 6:1; 7:7; 8:31; 9:14; 9:30) is a characteristic feature of Romans, where it is part of the dialogical, question-answer style that carries the argument of the letter for-

4. For this surprisingly persistent view, which receives no support in the manuscript tradition, see, e.g., Troels Engberg-Pedersen ("The Reception of Graeco-Roman Culture in the New Testament: The Case of Romans 7.7–25," in *The New Testament as Reception*, ed. Mogens Müller and Henrik Tronier, JSNTSup 230 [London: Sheffield Academic, 2002], 53–54) and Jewett (*Romans*, 457–58).

5. Cf. Dahl, *Studies in Paul*, 85.

ward. Paul uses it three other times in the same way he uses it here, to introduce a false inference from the preceding argument, an inference that he then rejects with his characteristic expression, "certainly not!" (3:5–6; 6:1–2; 9:14).

Paul has aligned the law so closely with sin in 3:20, 4:15, 5:20, 6:14, and especially 7:5–6 that he must now reject the notion that the law is somehow sin. It is not, however, as if Paul has put himself into this quandary by accident. He has already shown in his positive statements about the law that he never intended his various alignments of the law with sin to be isolated and examined on their own (3:21, 31). Anyone among the Roman Christians who was attending carefully to the argument up to this point would be expecting a clearer explanation of those statements, especially 5:20 and 7:5, and Paul gives that explanation here.[6]

The term translated "on the contrary" (ἀλλά) shows that Paul emphatically rejects the notion that the law is sin (KJV, NASB, HCSB), not that he qualifies the statement slightly (NIV, NRSV, REB, ESV, NET). This is clear from his use of the same expression in 7:13 where the meaning is unambiguously "on the contrary" (cf. 3:31).[7] The law's function of defining sin demonstrates that it is not on the side of sin. Instead, the law tells the truth about sin (cf. 3:20; 4:15; 5:13), unlike sin's own deceptive approach to its true effect (7:11).

Paul's shift to the first-person singular here is a perspective that he famously maintains throughout 7:7–25. It is certainly a change from his style of argumentation so far in Romans, but it is not unique to this letter. The same mode of argumentation is also present in 1 Corinthians 6:12, 15; 12:31; 13:11; and Galatians 2:18–20.[8]

In Galatians 2:18–20 Paul uses the first-person singular in an argumentative context similar to his use of "I" here. Paul has just said that justification comes only by faith in Christ and not by works of the law, and he has just rejected with "certainly not!" the false inference, based on this statement, that Christ facilitates sin. He then explains why he rejects this inference by describing in the first-person singular how a reintroduction of his old approach to the law would involve him in the nullification of God's grace. The primary purpose of this first-person argument is to state what is true for anyone who has embraced the gospel, including Cephas, Barnabas, and "the rest of the Jews" (Gal 2:13–14), but there is also an autobiographical element to the passage since Paul extends to them what he regarded as true for himself.

In Romans 7:7–25 Paul uses the first-person singular in the same way to show both what he has found to be true in his own experience and what he believes to be true about the law's effect on anyone who takes it seriously.[9]

Paul's "indeed" (τε γάρ) shows that he is about to cite a particular example of the general principle he has just stated (cf. 1:26).[10] The effect of the commandment "you shall not covet" (Exod 20:17; Deut 5:21) demonstrates how the law brings the knowledge of sin to the individual. The commandment does not so much instruct the individual what coveting is (he or she already knows that) but reveals

6. Dunn, *New Perspective*, 279.

7. BDAG 44, s.v. ἀλλά 1a; Cranfield, *Romans*, 1:348; Wilckens, *An die Römer (Röm 6–11)*, 76n290; Jewett, *Romans*, 446. Otherwise Godet, *Romans*, 272; Moo, *Romans*, 432.

8. Jan Lambrecht, *The Wretched "I" and Its Liberation*, Louvain Theological & Pastoral Monographs 14 (Louvain: Peeters, 1992), 75–76, 80–81. Cf. Kümmel, *Römer 7*, 121.

9. For the use of the first-person singular in ways that are similar to Paul's use in 7:7–25, at least at the level of argumentative structure, see Jewett's analysis of Epictetus, *Diatr.* 1.10.7–9 and 1.12.10–12 (*Romans*, 443–44). Epictetus's use of the first-person singular in 1.12.12–15, however, actually seems a bit closer to the substance of Paul's usage.

10. Cf. Calvin, *Romans*, 142; BDAG 189, s.v. γάρ 1b.

that coveting is expressly forbidden by God.[11] As Paul has said in 5:13, sin was in the world before the law was given to Israel, but those who sinned did not understand the implications of what they were doing (cf. 4:15). The effect of the law on Israel was the same as the effect of God's commandment on Adam (5:14), but Paul mentions neither Adam nor Israel explicitly here. He probably simply thinks of the effect the law has on the individual and reflects an understanding of that effect informed by (1) Genesis 3:1–6, (2) the history of Israel as the Scriptures tell it, and (3) his own experience with the law prior to the transforming work of the Spirit in his life. Apart from the work of the Spirit, the law brings only the knowledge that one is in rebellion against God, not deliverance from that rebellion.

The meaning of the terms "coveting" and "covet" (ἐπιθυμία, ἐπιθυμέω) are molded by the context in which they appear. They could simply refer to strong desire and be used with no negative moral connotations (Phil 1:23; 1 Thess 2:17; Gal 5:17), or they could be used to refer to a strong desire for what is forbidden (Rom 6:12; Gal 5:17), especially for forbidden sexual relations (Rom 1:24; 13:14; 1 Thess 4:5).[12] Here the meaning comes from the Greek translation of the Decalogue's tenth commandment where the focus is on desire for what belongs to a neighbor, beginning with his wife (LXX Exod 20:17; Deut 5:21). The tenth commandment is the only commandment of the Decalogue that forbids a disposition and so focuses attention on one's inner life where the decisions take place that result in unloving actions toward others.[13] It is likely that Paul chose this commandment for this reason since so much of 7:7–25 examines the tensions in Paul's will, mind, and "inner human being" (7:22).

7:8 And sin, taking its opportunity, through the commandment produced in me all manner of coveting. For apart from the law, sin is dead (ἀφορμὴν δὲ λαβοῦσα ἡ ἁμαρτία διὰ τῆς ἐντολῆς κατειργάσατο ἐν ἐμοὶ πᾶσαν ἐπιθυμίαν· χωρὶς γὰρ νόμου ἁμαρτία νεκρά). Sin took advantage of the opportunity that God's word afforded to suggest to people that rather than trust God's word they should do what was in their own best interest according to their own judgment.

The expression translated "taking its opportunity" (ἀφορμὴν . . . λαβοῦσα) was common in ancient Greek for opportunistic behavior, sometimes, as here, with a negative connotation.[14] Philo used it within a few years of Paul's time to describe the fear of Jews in Alexandria that people in other parts of the empire might learn of the mob violence against Jewish institutions in Alexandria and "take their cue" (τὴν ἀφορμὴν . . . λαβόντες) from what was happening to attack Jewish synagogues and ancestral customs in their own cities (*Flaccus* 47 [F. H. Colson, LCL).[15] In the same way, sin, now personified (cf. Rom 3:9; 5:12; 6:12–23) jumped at the opportunity provided by the appearance of God's commandment against coveting to produce in the individual all kinds of illicit desires.[16]

The phrase "through the commandment" (διὰ τῆς ἐντολῆς) does not modify "taking its opportunity," as virtually all translations render it (e.g., KJV, RSV, NASB, NAB, NIV, REB, NET, ESV), but the verb "produced" (κατειργάσατο).[17] This is clear from the nearly identical construction in 7:13 where the prepositional phrase goes unambig-

11. Cf. Ambrosiaster, *Romans*, 54–55; Cranfield, *Romans*, 1:348–49; Fitzmyer, *Romans*, 466.

12. BDAG 371–72, s.v. ἐπιθυμία and ἐπιθυμέω; cf. LSJ 634–35, s.v. ἐπιθυμ-έω (-ία).

13. Cf. Cranfield, *Romans*, 1:349.

14. LSJ 292; BDAG 158; MGS 359, all s.v. ἀφορμή.

15. Philo was writing a few years after events that occurred in AD 38. On this, see Gregory R. Sterling, "Philo," *EDEJ* 1068.

16. Cranfield, *Romans*, 1:350.

17. So, correctly, the CEB.

uously with the verb "producing" (διὰ τοῦ ἀγαθοῦ μοι κατεργαζομένη θάνατον ["producing death in me through what is good"]).[18] Here, then, Paul explains in greater detail what he meant when he said in 7:5 that sinful passions were at work in believers' members through the law.

Paul says nothing explicit about Genesis 3:1–6, and there is certainly no need to assume that his argument depends on a Jewish notion that Adam somehow knew the Mosaic law.[19] Still, it is likely that Paul's understanding of how personified sin uses the law to generate rebellion against God came from Scripture, and from two biblical narratives in particular. In Genesis 3:1–6 Eve and Adam act on the serpent's advice and their own judgment and disobey God, demonstrating a lack of trust in him. Similarly, Israel often disobeyed God's command to worship him alone and refused to trust his word through the prophets (Neh 9:13–17, 26, 29–30; Dan 9:4–6; Bar 1:18–19, 21). God's word in each case provided the opportunity for lack of trust in and rebellion against God with disastrous consequences. Paul knew that this was also the way sin often used the word of God in the lives of individuals.

When Paul says that apart from the law sin lies dead, he does not mean that people only sin in the presence of the law. Rather, he means that sin does not have the opportunity to generate knowing, willful rebellion against God and his word apart from the law (cf. 4:15; 5:20).[20]

7:9 And I was once living apart from the law, but when the commandment came sin revived (ἐγὼ δὲ ἔζων χωρὶς νόμου ποτέ, ἐλθούσης δὲ τῆς ἐντολῆς ἡ ἁμαρτία ἀνέζησεν). Paul, like all people, understood at some point in his life that his sin was a violation of God's demand. Even when his sin was exposed as disobedience to God, however, he continued to disobey.

Paul now describes the existence of someone he calls "I" within a context where, for all practical purposes, there is no law and sin lies dormant. The "I" to whom he refers lived for an extended period of time in this situation as both the imperfect tense "was living" (ἔζων) and the adverb "once" (ποτέ) indicate.

Who is this "I"? It is probably anyone who encounters the demand of God, including Paul who experienced God's demand in the form of the Mosaic law. The notion of living apart from the law is probably metaphorical for living and sinning but being unaware that God has forbidden one's sin. Paul intended this statement to express the same situation he had described earlier when he said that where there is no law there is no transgression (4:15) and that when the law did not exist, sin was not "invoiced" (5:13). Applied to himself, it referred to the point in his life when he began to take the word of God and his responsibility to obey it seriously, but this "I" could describe the same situation in anyone's life.[21]

The verb translated "revived" (ἀνέζησεν) here is often rendered "came alive" or "sprang to life" with no connotation that what was now living had been alive before. This fits the theory that Paul was thinking of Adam, for whom sin was not

18. Cranfield, *Romans*, 1:350; Dunn, *Romans 1–8*, 380; Lambrecht, *The Wretched "I"*, 45–46. Otherwise, Wilckens, on the basis of the parallel in 7:11 (*An die Römer [Röm 6–11]*, 81n319). The phrase in 7:11, however, should be taken with the main verb "deceived" (ἐξηπάτησέν) just as "through it" (δι' αὐτῆς) in the next phrase must be taken with the verb "killed" (ἀπέκτεινεν).

19. The case for the relevance of this background appears in, e.g., Käsemann (*Romans*, 196) and Dunn (*Romans 1–8*, 379), but for a more persuasive approach, similar to that taken here, see Lambrecht, *The Wretched "I"*, 47, 82–84.

20. So many commentators, but see especially Fitzmyer (*Romans*, 467).

21. Cf. Sanday and Headlam, *Romans*, 180 (apart from their odd comments on early Greek art).

alive prior to his encounter with God's commandment.[22] There is, however, no known use of the verb to mean "come to life" for the first time. It always means "return to life."[23] The older translators, then, are correct with their rendering "revived" (Tyndale ["revyved"], KJV; cf. Luther's "ward . . . wieder lebendig").

Paul probably intended to communicate that sin works in the individual in the same way that it has worked in salvation history. Just as sin lay dormant between Adam and Moses but increased with the giving of the law, so it lies dormant in the individual until he or she becomes aware that their behavior violates a moral standard justly laid upon them. That realization often elicits rebellion from them. This is true for both non-Jews and Jews alike (1:32; 2:15; 3:20), and Paul knew it was true of himself, which is one reason he speaks in the first person here.

7:10 But I died, and the commandment whose purpose was life—this, for me, was found to result in death (ἐγὼ δὲ ἀπέθανον καὶ εὑρέθη μοι ἡ ἐντολὴ ἡ εἰς ζωήν, αὕτη εἰς θάνατον). The effect of God's demand on Paul, just as with all human beings, was to reveal sin as rebellion against God and to pronounce the penalty of death, a penalty that no one—certainly not Paul—could escape.

Paul has assumed from the first section of his argument in Romans that the just penalty for sin against God is death (1:32; 5:12, 14; 6:16, 21). He did not die in the sense that he experienced a subjective impression such as remorse for his sin but in the judicial and theological sense that when the commandment came it confirmed his disobedience to God's clearly expressed will and handed down the sentence of death.[24] To paraphrase 3:19, the commandment stopped Paul's mouth and held him accountable to God. Paul did not realize this at the time that he became aware of God's commandment (Phil 3:4–6) but understood it later through the lens of the gospel. This is the force of the passive verb "was found" (εὑρέθη), which means that the truth about his spiritual death was revealed to him by God in the gospel.[25]

What is the origin of this understanding of the relationship between the law, sin, and death? Once again, Paul probably reflected the pattern of the relationship between the law, sin, and death that he learned from Scripture, and particularly from the stories of Adam and Israel. The serpent used God's command to Adam to lead the first humans into disobedience against God and death (Gen 2:16–17; 3:1–24). Israel persistently disobeyed the Mosaic law and received death and exile as a result (e.g., Ps 78; Dan 9:4–15). Although Adam could have continued to live had he obeyed God (the implication of Gen 2:17), and although the law promised life to Israel if they obeyed it (e.g., Lev 18:5; Deut 4:40; 5:32–33; 8:1; 30:15–16, 19–20; Neh 9:29), the actual result in both cases was death. That is also the result of disobedience to God for every human being, including Paul.

7:11 For sin, taking its opportunity, deceived me through the commandment and through it killed me (ἡ γὰρ ἁμαρτία ἀφορμὴν λαβοῦσα διὰ τῆς ἐντολῆς ἐξηπάτησέν με καὶ δι᾽ αὐτῆς ἀπέκτεινεν).

22. See, e.g., Käsemann, *Romans*, 197; Dunn, *Romans 1–8*, 381–83.

23. Cf. Luke 15:24 and the examples listed in Deissman, *Light from the Ancient East*, 97–98, and LSJ 104, s.v. ἀναζάω, to which Chariton, *Chaereas and Callirhoe* 3.8.9 and 8.1.14 should be added. BDAG (62, s.v. ἀναζάω 2) thinks that the preposition has lost its force, but this is probably incorrect in light of the usage of the word elsewhere. Thayer (*Greek-English Lexicon* 37, s.v. ἀναζάω) is more reliable at this point.

24. For the idea that Paul refers to remorse, see Shedd, *Romans*, 185–86.

25. Leon Morris, *Romans*, PNTC (Grand Rapids: Eerdmans, 1988), 282.

Just as the serpent deceived Eve by cleverly using God's command to distort God's character and good intentions toward his creation, so sin uses God's command to generate human rebellion against God with its inevitable consequence of death.

The conjunction "for" (γάρ) introduces a more detailed explanation of Paul's statement in 7:9–10 that when the commandment came sin revived and he died.[26] He repeats the idea from 7:8 that when the commandment came sin saw its opportunity, but that statement is now part of the picture of sin lying dead and then reviving. The commandment provided the opportunity for sin's revivification. It is hard not to think of sin as lying dormant, waiting for its opportunity to strike and then finding the perfect moment to ambush its prey when the commandment came. This fits perfectly with the picture of the "crafty" (*arum*) serpent deceiving Eve in Genesis 3:1–6.[27]

The probability that Paul was thinking of Genesis 3 as he portrayed sin here increases with his use of the term "deceived."[28] Although in Genesis 3:13 LXX Eve describes the serpent's deception with the simple form of the verb (ἀπατάω) rather than the compound form that appears here (ἐξαπατάω), Paul uses the compounded form elsewhere when he alludes to Eve's words (2 Cor 11:3; 1 Tim 2:14). The term means to beguile or seduce someone and in Paul carries the connotation of clever theological deception involving a sinister mixture of truth and error (Rom 16:18; 2 Cor 11:3; 2 Thess 2:3; cf. Josephus, *Ant.* 10.111; Epictetus, *Diatr.* 2.20.7–8).[29] Paul may have had in mind, then, the development of the narrative in Genesis 3:1–6 where the serpent tells Eve correctly that eating from the tree will give her knowledge of good and evil, but then uses this truth to depict God falsely as jealous and miserly, trying to withhold from Eve something that he wants to keep for himself.[30]

When Eve and Adam disobeyed God, their death was assured (Gen 2:17; 3:19). So here Paul implies that in his own case, as with everyone else, sin kills those whom it deceives.

7:12 So, the law, for its part, is holy, and the commandment is holy and just and good (ὥστε ὁ μὲν νόμος ἅγιος καὶ ἡ ἐντολὴ ἁγία καὶ δικαία καὶ ἀγαθή). Paul now states the conclusion he has been driving at since the rhetorical questions in 7:7. The explanation of how sin uses the law to kill its prey through deception (7:7–11) has shown that the law is not sin but only sin's tool and that the law, because it defines sin clearly, is entirely on the side of a holy, just, and good God.

The conjunction "so" (ὥστε) introduces the conclusion that Paul draws from his discussion of the relationship between the law and sin in 7:7–11. He has explained in 7:8–11 why he could say "certainly not!" to the question, "Is the law sin?" Now he summarizes that discussion in positive terms.

The translation "for its part" represents a particle (μέν) that in a complete sentence would have an answering "but" (δέ) in 7:13. This "but" would introduce the statement that sin rather than the law was at fault in creating rebellion against God.[31] The adjective "good" (ἀγαθή) in 7:12, however, seems to have offered Paul an opportunity to shift blame even further from the law in 7:13. So in 7:13 he interrupts his contrast between the law and sin and

26. Légasse, *Romains*, 451.

27. LXX φρόνιμος. Cf. Matt 10:16: "Be wise [φρόνιμοι] as serpents and innocent as doves" (*HALOT* 1:883).

28. So already, Origen (*Romans, Books 6–10*, 34).

29. LSJ 586, BDAG 345, *CGELNT* 132, MGS 714–15, all s.v. ἐξαπατάω.

30. The LXX rendering of 3:1 makes more explicit than the Hebrew text the serpent's plan to question God's motives. Rather than "did God actually say . . . ?" it has "why is it that God said . . . ?"

31. Meyer, *Romans*, 273; Dunn, *Romans 1–8*, 385; Jewett, *Romans*, 453.

transforms it, by means of a rhetorical question, into a contrast between "what is good [τὸ ἀγαθόν]" and sin. The battle between the inner human being, which agrees with "the good" that the law articulates, and the flesh, which frustrates any intention to obey the law, will dominate 7:14–25.[32]

Meanwhile, Paul states clearly the implication of his discussion so far. The law is not sin, but, to the contrary, as a whole and in each of its commandments, it is "holy," "righteous," and "good." This affirmation reflects a traditional Jewish understanding of the law's divine origin (cf., e.g., Ps 19:7–9; Neh 9:13; 2 Macc 6:23, 28) and emphasizes that nothing about the law is immoral.[33] It is "holy" (ἁγία) in the sense that it shares the qualitative distinctiveness of God's moral purity (cf. Mark 6:20).[34] It is "just" (δικαία) in the sense that it is impartial and equitable (cf. Dionysius of Halicarnassus, *Ant. rom.* 11.59.3, 5). It is "good" (ἀγαθή) in the sense that it upholds what is best for society (cf. Aristotle, *Nicomachean Ethics* 1180b 25).[35] Sin used law as a tool and the coming of the law as an opportunity to accomplish its purpose of increasing human rebellion against God, but this is not the fault of the law.

7:13 Did that which is good, then, become death for me? Certainly not! On the contrary, sin, so that it might be shown to be sin, was producing death in me through what is good so that sin might become extremely sinful through the commandment (Τὸ οὖν ἀγαθὸν ἐμοὶ ἐγένετο θάνατος; μὴ γένοιτο· ἀλλὰ ἡ ἁμαρτία, ἵνα φανῇ ἁμαρτία, διὰ τοῦ ἀγαθοῦ μοι κατεργαζομένη θάνατον, ἵνα γένηται καθ' ὑπερβολὴν ἁμαρτωλὸς ἡ ἁμαρτία διὰ τῆς ἐντολῆς). Sin, not the law, causes the individual human being's death. God's law only reveals the extent of sin's powerful and insidious nature. Sin does not, however, have the last word since the revelation of sin's insidious nature was one of God's purposes in giving the law.

This verse repeats the rhetorical form of 7:7. It begins with a rhetorical question that draws a false inference from 7:9–12, just as 7:7 began with a rhetorical question that drew a false inference from 7:5. Following the pattern of 7:7 exactly, it then rejects the false inference with "certainly not!" and explains the reason for the rejection with a sentence that begins with "on the contrary."

The verse serves a transitional function between 7:7–12 and 7:14–25. Like 7:7–12 it is set in the past ("did that which is good . . . ?"), and the rhetorical question with which it begins arises naturally out of Paul's statement that sin "killed" him "through the commandment" (7:11). At the same time, however, its claim that sin became "extremely sinful" and its mention of the "death" that sin "produced" (κατεργαζομένη) in the individual anticipate the major themes and vocabulary of 7:14–25 (cf. especially 7:15, 17, 18, and 20).

Paul both explains his rejection of the notion that God's good commandment caused his death and announces the theme of what will follow in a lengthy sentence that contains no main verb. He probably intended his audience mentally to couple the main verb in his rhetorical question (ἐγένετο) with the participle (κατεργαζομένη) that appears here in the reply. In English this becomes "was producing" (HCSB) since the present participle emphasizes sin's continuous production of death.[36]

The substance of the sentence is that sin rather than the good commandment was the cause of the individual's death, and so the commandment is exonerated from blame for the death of the individual. With the two purpose clauses and the

32. Dunn, *Romans 1–8*, 386; Jewett, *Romans*, 453.

33. On the traditional nature of Paul's description of the law, see especially Kruse, *Romans*, 303.

34. Thayer, *Greek-English Lexicon* 7, s.v. ἅγιος 4.

35. BDAG 4, s.v. ἀγαθός 2aβ.

36. See also Cranfield, *Romans*, 1:340, 354.

passive-voice verbs they contain, however, Paul addresses the deeper question of how, in a world that God oversees, sin could get away with using the law this way. Paul answers this implied question with a principle he has already articulated in 3:20, 4:15, 5:13, and 5:20.[37] Sin did not steal the law from God and use it contrary to God's intentions. Instead, the close association between the law and sin fulfilled one of God's purposes in giving the law. When the law came into contact with human sin, it revealed sin's true nature as a deceptive force that tricks people into disobeying God and thus suffering the inevitable consequence of death (cf. Gen 3:1–6).

7:14 For we know that the law is spiritual, but I am fleshy, sold under sin (οἴδαμεν γὰρ ὅτι ὁ νόμος πνευματικός ἐστιν, ἐγὼ δὲ σάρκινός εἰμι πεπραμένος ὑπὸ τὴν ἁμαρτίαν). Paul can say with confidence that the law is not responsible for a person's spiritual death because the law is God's good gift. The individual, however, is weighed down by the tendency to disobey God.

"For" (γάρ) introduces a reason why Paul could say that sin rather than the commandment was responsible for the death of human beings. The reason comes in the form of a contrast not so much between the law and sin as between the law and the nature of the human being Paul is describing. He contrasts the "spiritual" nature of the law with the "fleshy" nature of the "I."

The first-person plural verb "we know" identifies Paul with his audience and prepares his audience to see themselves, along with Paul, in the "I" that appears in the second clause.[38] We should probably take its perfect tense seriously as a description of what Paul and his readers have come to know, and so as preparation for the vivid description of their own sinfulness in the present tenses that follow.[39]

Since Paul has just described the law and the commandment as "holy and just and good" (7:12), it is not surprising that he also considers it "spiritual" (πνευματικός). Elsewhere Paul uses this adjective to describe the gifts and blessings that God gives to people (1:11; 15:27; 1 Cor 10:3–4; 12:1; 14:1; Eph 1:3). He frequently uses it of people in whom God's Spirit dwells and who are therefore sensitive to God's guidance and concerns (1 Cor 2:13, 15; 14:37; Gal 6:1). The law, then, is God's good gift and appeals to the aspect of the inner person that is sensitive to God's will.

The contrast of the spiritual law with the "fleshy" "I" is reminiscent of the implied contrast between the "newness of the Spirit" and the former existence of the believer "in the flesh [σαρκί]" in 7:5–6. The term "fleshy" (σάρκινος) meant "made of physical, material flesh" and elsewhere Paul used it in contrast with "spiritual" to refer to immature believers. He told the Corinthians that he could not address them "as spiritual people [πνευματικοῖς], but as people of the flesh [σαρκίνοις], as infants in Christ" (1 Cor 3:1). In the same way, the "I" of this passage is disobedient to God's demand and so stands on the other side of the "spiritual" law.

Here in 7:14, then, the law has switched sides from its location in 7:5–6. There, the Mosaic law ("the letter") was associated with the flesh (7:5) and what was old (7:6) rather than with the Spirit's new creation of the individual. Here the law itself is spiritual, and Paul makes no mention of the Spirit's influence over the individual. He is clarifying what he said in 7:5, then, to show that the law as he

37. Cf. Cranfield, *Romans*, 1:354–55; Moo, *Romans*, 453.

38. Seifrid, "The Subject of Rom 7:14–25," 317–22.

39. "The shift in tense from vv. 7–13 to vv. 14–25 is one of perspective, not of time" (Mark A. Seifrid, "Romans 7: The Voice of the Law," in *Perspectives on Our Struggle with Sin: 3 Views of Romans 7*, ed. Terry L. Wilder [Nashville: B&H Academic, 2011], 153; cf. idem, "The Subject of Rom 7:14–25," 321–22).

described it there was not at fault. The "fleshy" self is at fault in the production of sinful passions, and the law was merely sin's tool (7:7–13).

Paul describes the self as "sold under sin." Since Greek speakers sometimes used the verb "sold" (πιπράσκω) to refer to the sale of human beings (e.g., Deut 21:14 LXX; Matt 18:25), and since Paul used slavery to sin as a metaphor for the condition of the unbeliever only a few paragraphs earlier (Rom 6:12–23), he probably refers here to the idea that, like a slave, the "fleshy" self is completely "under" the power of sin (cf. 3:9; Gal 3:22). Paul may have also intended to communicate the tone of betrayal and ruination that the verb could carry in anguished first-person expressions such as "alas! I am sold [πέπραμαι] and I am ruined!" (Sophocles, *Phil.* 978 [F. Storr, LCL]; cf. Euripides, *Daughters of Troy* 936).[40]

Since this sentence recalls 7:5 with its reference to a former existence in the flesh and 6:15–23 with its picture of a former existence in slavery to sin, it is very difficult to imagine that Paul intended it to be a statement about the believer's mode of existence.[41] Why, then, does he speak in the first person and in the present tense as if what he says is true of himself as a believer, in the present? The answer to this question becomes clear in the anguished cry of 7:24 with its desperate plea for a future rescue ("Who will deliver me . . . ?"). In 7:14–23 Paul describes in vivid present-tense language his plight (and anyone's plight) as an unbeliever who needs to be rescued but does not yet know when deliverance will come or who will bring it. As Origen already recognized, he adopts the "persona" of an unbeliever "in order that he might show clearly and demonstrate to the utmost from how many evils and from how many kinds of death Christ has rescued us."[42]

7:15 For I do not understand what I produce, for it is not what I want that I accomplish, but precisely what I hate that I do (ὃ γὰρ κατεργάζομαι οὐ γινώσκω· οὐ γὰρ ὃ θέλω τοῦτο πράσσω, ἀλλ᾽ ὃ μισῶ τοῦτο ποιῶ). The confusion that human beings experience about their own behavior illustrates what Paul means when he says that people are sold under sin. They often intend to do what is good, but in the end achieve only evil.

The "for" (γάρ) indicates that Paul is about to supply evidence for his assertion in 7:14 that he is sold under sin. Some translations render "understand" (γινώσκω [NIV, NRSV, ESV]) as "allow" (KJV) or "acknowledge" (REB), and in certain contexts it can mean "resolve."[43] If it had those connotations here, then Paul's meaning would be that he does not approve of or resolve to do what he actually accomplishes. When the word means "resolve," however, it precedes an infinitive describing the action one resolves to do (e.g., Polybius, *Hist.* 5.82.1; Josephus, *Ant.* 1.195; 14:352; 16:331), and "acknowledge" is not a common meaning for this term.[44] Paul, then, is saying that the sinful result of his actions makes no sense to him.

The second clause, with its "for" (γάρ), explains this statement further.[45] The term "accomplish" (πράσσω) always refers in Romans to moral conduct, whether good (2:25; 9:11) or evil (1:32; 2:1, 2, 3; 9:11; 13:4), and Paul uses it here to speak of

40. LSJ 1395, s.v. πέρνημι. Cf. BDAG 814–15, s.v. πιπράσκω.

41. Seifrid, "The Subject of Rom 7:14–25," 319; idem, "Romans 7," 143.

42. Origen, *Romans, Books 6–10*, 42. Cf. Stanley K. Stowers, "Romans 7.7–25 as a Speech-in-Character (προσωποποιία)," in *Paul in His Hellenistic Context*, ed. Troels Engberg-Pedersen (Minneapolis: Fortress, 1995), 193–98.

43. BDAG 200, s.v. γινώσκω 6.a.α; Cranfield, *Romans*, 1:258–59; Moo, *Romans*, 457.

44. Most of the references in BDAG, s.v. γινώσκω 7 are ambiguous.

45. Cf. Cranfield, *Romans*, 1:358.

doing the evil thing that he does not intend to do (cf. 7:19).[46] As the parallel in 7:19 shows, Paul probably did not intend to make a pronounced distinction between "accomplishing" and "doing" something. In 7:19 Paul says virtually the same thing he says here but reverses the places of the terms in the two clauses. Here, then, he explains what he means when he says that he is sold under sin (7:14) by saying that despite wanting to do what is right he achieves the opposite and does not understand why this happens.

Interpreters often mention at this point the parallels in ancient Greco-Roman literature to the kind of moral struggle that Paul seems to describe, particularly in the ancient story of Medea, a Colchian (and therefore barbarian) sorceress whose passions frequently overwhelmed her moral reasoning.[47] The literature and art of first-century Roman society told her story, and much of it takes place in Corinth, Paul's location as he wrote Romans 7. Ovid, writing in Rome a few decades before Paul, and Seneca, writing in Rome at almost the same time Paul was writing to Rome, used Medea to portray the inner struggle between doing what one knows to be right and the urge to follow one's illicit desire. The lovesick Medea wonders whether she should remain loyal to her father and homeland or give in to her passions and run away with Jason (Ovid, *Metam.* 7.11–71). When love goes wrong, she wonders whether to spare her innocent children or, in the ultimate act of revenge, murder them and Jason's lover, thus ruining his life forever (Seneca, *Medea* 926–66; cf. Euripides, *Medea* 1077–80; 1236–50).[48]

The parallel is useful because it reveals that the common people of first-century Rome understood well the issues Paul raises in 7:7–25. Paul's analysis of the human condition, however, was different than the plight described in the various retellings of Medea's story.

First, the portrait of Medea in Euripides, Ovid, and Seneca is heavily indebted to a stereotype of barbarian women current among Greeks and Romans in antiquity. This stereotype is completely missing from Paul's portrait of inner struggle.[49] Paul applies the inner struggle he describes here not to a certain group within humanity but "to the Jew first, and also to the Greek" (1:16; cf. 3:19–20). The Mosaic law is the moral standard against which the struggle takes place, and so the Jew is definitely in view, but the nature of the struggle is not specifically Jewish and certainly not limited to non-Greeks and women. This is a human struggle.[50]

Second, Medea and those around her understood the source of her struggle. Passion overwhelmed the loyalty she owed first to her father and siblings and then to her children (if not to Jason, who fares little better than Medea in the

46. Sanday and Headlam, *Romans*, 181.

47. See, e.g., Meyer, *Romans*, 277; Moo, *Romans*, 457; Klaus Haacker, *The Theology of Paul's Letter to the Romans*, New Testament Theology (Cambridge: Cambridge University Press, 2003), 127; Longenecker, *Romans*, 656–59.

48. Cf. Euripides, *Hipp.* 375–82; the popular attitudes reflected in Plato, *Prot.* 352d; Lesbonicus's explanation for his bad behavior in Plautus, *Trin.* 655–59; and Diodorus Siculus's idealized description of morality among ancient Egyptian kings in his *Bibliotheca historica* 1.71.3. On all these texts, see Hildebrecht Hommel, *Sebasmata: Studien zur antiken Religionsgeschichte und zum frühen Christentum*, 2 vols. (Tübingen: Mohr Siebeck, 1983–84), 2:157–63.

49. Stowers, "Romans 7.7–12 as a Speech-in-Character," 198.

50. Euripides may be closer to Paul on this point than interpreters typically recognize. In his version of the Medea legend, Jason also abandons duty for passion, and the chorus of Corinthian (and therefore civilized Greek) women support Medea's action in the moment of crisis. On this, see William Arrowsmith, "A Greek Theater of Ideas," in *Classical Tragedy: Greek and Roman*, ed. Robert W. Corrigan (New York: Applause Theater, 1990), 362–63.

struggle against evil). For Paul, however, the "I" fails to "understand" the actions that he does. Paul implies that the effects of sin on the human being run deeper than anything acknowledged in the Greco-Roman discussion of why people fail to do what they know is good.[51] In Paul's view, people sometimes intend to do what is good and think they are doing it when, in truth, they are disobeying God.

Later in Romans Paul will say that unbelieving Israel, despite its commendable pursuit of a law that showed the way to righteousness, did not reach the goal toward which the law was really pointing (9:31). The trouble was that although their zeal for God was commendable, it was not accompanied by an acknowledgement of the gospel (10:2).

This is probably the sort of plight Paul had in mind here in 7:15.[52] Human sin is so insidious that it can lead people to pursue obedience to God in the wrong way and so disobey him (cf. Jer 17:9; 1 Cor 4:3–4).

7:16 But if I do precisely what I do not want, I concur with the law that it is good (εἰ δὲ ὃ οὐ θέλω τοῦτο ποιῶ, σύμφημι τῷ νόμῳ ὅτι καλός). The tension in the self that Paul has just described demonstrates that the weak and sinful self is responsible for sin and that the law is good.

Paul now uses his description of the morally confused self as evidence for his statement that the law is good (7:12). This is a reminder that his analysis of the inner workings of the sinful human being serves the larger purpose of defending the goodness of the law.[53] He assumes that the conflicted self of 7:15 knows what is good through knowing God's law. The problem lies in carrying out what the good law commands, an effort that often ends in failure. Either illicit desire overwhelms the effort to do good (as with Medea) or the effort itself arises from a misunderstanding of what obedience to God actually entails (as, perhaps, with the pre-Christian Paul).[54] The very conflict within the human being between knowing the law and failing to do the law, then, reveals that the human being concurs with the law's own judgment that it is good (7:12; Deut 4:8).[55]

7:17 And now I no longer produce it, but sin that dwells within me (νυνὶ δὲ οὐκέτι ἐγὼ κατεργάζομαι αὐτὸ ἀλλὰ ἡ οἰκοῦσα ἐν ἐμοὶ ἁμαρτία). The conflict that Paul has described between willing what is good and actually doing it finds its origin in a strong human tendency to disobey God, a tendency that affects every part of a person's humanity.

Paul's "and now . . . no longer" (νυνὶ δὲ οὐκέτι) introduces a logical inference from 7:16.[56] If he and his audience can "now" agree that his argument so far is valid, then they can also agree that what he is about to say is a valid deduction from that argument. Paul has an "I" that produces disobedience to the law and an "I" that does not understand how this happens (7:15a). He has an "I" that hates and does not want to do what he does and an "I" that does it (7:15c). He has an "I" that concurs with the law's own witness to its goodness and does not want to violate its commands (7:16b), and an "I" that violates them anyway (7:16a). If all this is true, Paul argues, then some compulsion within Paul rather than Paul himself drives him to disobey God's law, and that compulsion is sin.

Does this mean that Paul excuses himself from culpability for disobeying the law on the grounds

51. Cf. Das, *Solving the Romans Debate*, 226.

52. Cf. Käsemann, *Romans*, 199–203; Seifrid, "The Subject of Rom 7:14–25," 329n47; idem, "Romans 7," 147–48; and Jewett, *Romans*, 462–64.

53. Dunn, *Romans 1–8*, 390.

54. On the pre-Christian Paul, see Jewett, *Romans*, 452–53 (on Rom 7:11).

55. Meyer, *Romans*, 278.

56. Ibid.

that some power outside himself forces him to sin?[57] The metaphorical nature of Paul's argument keeps it from moving in this direction. Although Paul has spoken of sin as a harsh and powerful person that conquerors territory (5:12), reigns over a kingdom (5:21; 6:12), holds slaves (6:6–7, 14–22), pays wages (6:23), and now settles down and makes its home in himself (cf. 7:20), this language is metaphorical. Sin was not actually a person in Paul's thinking but was both concrete acts of disobedience to God and a strong tendency—present in humanity since Adam's transgression—to commit these acts (e.g., 3:9 [summarizing 1:18–2:29]; 5:12–14).[58] Paul's flesh (7:18), members (7:23), and body (7:24) are complicit in sin, and they are all part of the "me" that sin takes captive (7:23). Even his understanding is involved, as 7:15 makes clear, so that although his inner human being and mind appear at one level to be on the side of God's law (7:22, 25), at another level they too are affected by the tendency to sin. Paul will make this explicit in 8:6 when he speaks of "the mindset of the flesh" (τὸ . . . φρόνημα τῆς σαρκός) that Christians must resist. Paul is not possessed by a demon who forces him to sin; rather, all facets of his humanity are affected by a tendency to disobey God, some more than others.[59]

7:18 For I know that good does not dwell in me, that is, in my flesh, for willing lies close at hand, but producing what is praiseworthy does not (οἶδα γὰρ ὅτι οὐκ οἰκεῖ ἐν ἐμοί, τοῦτ᾽ ἔστιν ἐν τῇ σαρκί μου, ἀγαθόν· τὸ γὰρ θέλειν παράκειταί μοι, τὸ δὲ κατεργάζεσθαι τὸ καλὸν οὔ). Paul's existence as a weak, sin-prone human being means that the law's good and praiseworthy principles cannot make their home in him no matter how much he wants to live by them.

Paul now begins to cover again in 7:18–20 the same basic territory he covered in 7:14–17, as the close correspondence between the structure of the two passages demonstrates, particularly their beginning and end.[60] His "for" introduces a restatement and clarification of what he has just said in 7:17 about indwelling sin. To say that sin dwells in him and prevents him from doing the law (7:17), which is good (7:12, 16), is to say that good does not dwell in him.

This does not mean that "nothing good dwells within me" as most translations put it (e.g., Tyndale, Luther, KJV, RSV, REB, NRSV, NET, ESV, HCSB). The verb "dwell" receives the negative particle in the sentence, not the subject "good" (so correctly NAB, NIV, CEB).[61] Paul is saying, therefore, that sin rather than good has settled down and made its home within him. This leaves room for what the passage makes clear—that some good does dwell within Paul. His agreement with the law (7:16) and desire to do what it commands (7:15), for example, are good. Precisely because these aspects of his being are oriented toward obedience to the good law, his will to do it "lies close at hand" (παράκειται).[62]

The problem lies in the fleshly nature of Paul's

57. Käsemann, *Romans*, 204. See Jewett's helpful criticism of this approach (*Romans*, 467).

58. Cf. Dunn, *Theology of Paul*, 111–12.

59. Cf. Herman Ridderbos, *Paul: An Outline of His Theology*, trans. John Richard De Witt (Grand Rapids: Eerdmans, 1975), 125. See also Eph 2:1–3 where Paul makes clear that there is a spiritual, diabolical element to the sin that naturally dominates every human being (2:2) but also that the will of every human being is culpable for following "the spirit that is now at work" within them (2:3).

60. Seifrid, "The Subject of Rom 7:14–25," 327.

61. Jewett, *Romans*, 467.

62. On the word, see LSJ 1312, s.v. παράκειμαι, and for Paul's choice between good and evil, both of which "lie before" him (7:18, 21), cf. Homer, *Odyssey* 22.65–66 ("Now it lies before [παράκειται] you to fight in open fight, or to flee" [A. T. Murray, LCL).

existence. The "me" of the passage is entirely "in the flesh," as the parallel with 7:14 makes clear ("I am fleshy, sold under sin").[63] His desire to do the good, therefore, is hindered by his fleshiness, an aspect of his existence that makes him especially weak and prone to sin (3:20; 6:19; 7:5; 8:3, 7–8; 13:14).

7:19 For I do not do the good that I will, but I accomplish precisely the evil that I do not will (οὐ γὰρ ὃ θέλω ποιῶ ἀγαθόν, ἀλλὰ ὃ οὐ θέλω κακὸν τοῦτο πράσσω). Instead of the good he wants to do, Paul only accomplishes evil, and this shows how far he stands from obeying God, despite his desire to obey him.

This sentence provides evidence (γάρ) that willing the good is within Paul's grasp, but doing the good is not (7:18). The statement almost duplicates 7:15b–c, simply making explicit what that earlier statement implied. Paul's struggle between what he wants to do and what he finds himself doing is a conflict between good and evil.[64] This struggle happens either because one's desire for what God forbids overwhelms one's acknowledgement that God is right to forbid it, or because one's desire to do the good expresses itself in evil ways and, in the end, accomplishes only evil.

7:20 But if I do precisely what I do not want, I no longer produce it but sin that dwells in me (εἰ δὲ ὃ οὐ θέλω ἐγὼ τοῦτο ποιῶ, οὐκέτι ἐγὼ κατεργάζομαι αὐτὸ ἀλλὰ ἡ οἰκοῦσα ἐν ἐμοὶ ἁμαρτία). Paul's tendency to disobey God is much stronger than his desire to do God's will.

Paul repeats the substance of 7:16–17 and draws this second paragraph of his description of the struggle of the "I" to the same conclusion as the first paragraph. Only three differences distinguish the two sentences: (1) Paul adds the pronoun "I" to the "if" clause, (2) he omits the reference to the law, and (3) he omits the introductory phrase "but now" in 7:16. This rephrasing concentrates the discourse on the main point. His flesh is so devoid of good, and sin has settled down so completely in his flesh, that if sin were a person and his human existence were a territory, sin would be fully in control, producing the evil that it wants rather than the good that Paul wants to accomplish.

7:21 So I discover the law that when I want to do what is excellent, evil lies close at my hand (εὑρίσκω ἄρα τὸν νόμον, τῷ θέλοντι ἐμοὶ ποιεῖν τὸ καλόν, ὅτι ἐμοὶ τὸ κακὸν παράκειται). Speaking of law, Paul formulates a law of his own based on what he has discovered about human experience with the law: whenever he seeks to walk the excellent and beautiful path of God's law, evil lurks close by.

Paul now begins a third paragraph within 7:14–25 whose purpose is to summarize 7:14–20 and to provide a "diagnosis" of the "I" on the basis of the symptoms he has described there.[65] The inferential particle "so" (ἄρα) introduces a conclusion that Paul will now draw from the previous discussion.[66] Up to this point in chapter seven, the term "law" has referred to God's law, containing, for example, the tenth commandment (7:7). Here, however, Paul must mean something different by this term. The verb "discover" (εὑρίσκω) with "law" as its direct object in the accusative case (νόμον) was normal Greek for the invention or formulation of a law (Demosthenes, *Against Timocrates* [24] 120; Di-

63. So correctly, Käsemann, *Romans*, 204–5; Fitzmyer, *Romans*, 475. George H. Van Kooten (*Paul's Anthropology in Context*, WUNT 232 [Tübingen: Mohr Siebeck, 2008], 381) says that 7:14 only speaks of a "'fleshly' level" in the now profoundly transformed human being, but this seems to read too much into Paul' statement. Cf. Dunn, *Romans 1–8*, 393–94.

64. See the helpful outline of the passage's structure in Seifrid, "The Subject of Rom 7:14–25," 327.

65. For this passage as a "diagnosis," see Stuhlmacher, *Romans*, 111. Cf. Lambrecht, *The Wretched "I"*, 39, 53.

66. BDAG 127, s.v. ἄρα 1.a.

odorus Siculus, *Bibliotheca historica* 13.26.3), and Paul cannot be saying that he invented or discovered the Mosaic law. Instead, he is playing on the word and now using it with the meaning "principle" (cf. Sophocles, *Ant.* 908, 914; Jer 38:37 LXX; Philo, *Prelim. Studies* 163).[67] The clause "when I want" (τῷ θέλοντι ἐμοί) is a dative of time expressing precisely when evil seems to lie so close, and the whole clause "when I want to do what is excellent" appears before the "that . . ." (ὅτι) clause (in the Greek text) for emphasis.[68] The observations Paul has just made about the tension in the sinful human being between willing and doing God's law Paul now formulates into a "law" of his own: when he wants to do what is excellent, evil lies before him.

7:22 For I rejoice in the law of God in the inner human being (συνήδομαι γὰρ τῷ νόμῳ τοῦ θεοῦ κατὰ τὸν ἔσω ἄνθρωπον). As far as his interior life is concerned, Paul joyfully embraces the excellence of God's law.

Paul now explains more fully (γάρ) the principle that he has discovered through experience according to 7:21. The term "rejoice" (συνήδομαι) usually referred to rejoicing together with someone or congratulating someone on their good fortune (Aristotle, *Rhetoric* 1381a; Josephus, *Ant.* 8.386). Paul probably uses it here in a slightly unusual way to refer to the joy he takes in the excellence and beauty of God's law, and the expression is reminiscent of the delight, love, and joy that the psalmists found in God's law according to Psalms 19 and 119.[69] If Paul uses the term in its more usual sense, then he thought of himself as delighting (-ήδομαι) together with (συν-) the personified law in its expression of what is good.[70] Although this interpretation is sometimes dismissed as unlikely, it is not too far distant from Psalm 119:24 where the psalmist personifies the "testimonies" of God, in which he takes "delight," as his "counselors."[71] Paul qualifies the law here as "the law of God" to distinguish it from his playful use of the term "law" in a different way in 7:21.[72]

Paul calls the aspect of his existence that delights in God's law "the inner human being" (ὁ ἔσω ἄνθρωπος), an expression close to one that Plato used in his discussion of the tripartite makeup of the soul. In Plato's account, "the human being within" (ὁ ἐντὸς ἄνθρωπος) referred to the divine human being inside the outer human being, and the outer human being could nurture this divine inner person by giving it control over the soul's more vicious, beastly parts (*Republic* 588b–590a; cf. *Symp.* 215a–b).[73] Philo, writing at roughly Paul's time, tried to find Plato's anthropology in the Scriptures (e.g., *Heir* 231; *Planting* 42), and Paul could use terminology similar to that of Plato and Philo in his own anthropological descriptions in, for example, 2 Corinthians 4:16.[74] Paul's description of

67. See Räisänen, *Jesus, Paul and Torah*, 82–85. Meyer (*Romans*, 281–82) and Jewett (*Romans*, 469) take the "that" clause (ὅτι . . .) rather than "the law" as the direct object of "discover," and Wright ("Romans," 569) takes "law" as an accusative of reference ("about the law"), but as the parallels in Demosthenes and Diodorus show, "law" should be understood simply as the direct object of "discover."

68. On the placement of the clause before "that," see Cranfield (*Romans*, 1:362), who draws attention to the parallel structure of the clause "what the Scripture says in the section on Elijah" in 11:2 (οὐκ οἴδατε ἐν Ἠλίᾳ τί λέγει ἡ γραφη).

69. E.g., Pss 19:8; 119:14, 24, 35, 47–48, 70, 77, 92, 97, 103, 119, 143, 162, 167, 174.

70. Meyer, *Romans*, 282.

71. For rejection of this interpretation, see Jewett, *Romans*, 469.

72. Cranfield, *Romans*, 1:363.

73. See the translation of G. M. A. Grube and C. D. C. Reeve (Plato, *Complete Works*, ed. John M. Cooper (Indianapolis: Hackett, 1977), 1196–97, cf. 497; Hans Dieter Betz, "The Concept of the 'Inner Human Being' (ὁ ἔσω ἄνθρωπος) in the Anthropology of Paul," *NTS* 49 (2000): 334; and Van Kooten, *Paul's Anthropology*, 362–63.

74. Van Kooten, *Paul's Anthropology*, 366–67, 370. Paul uses the phrase in a nonphilosophical context in Eph 3:16. Van Kooten does not, however, think that Paul wrote Ephesians

the makeup of the human being here, then, may have its origins in Greek and Hellenistic philosophical discussions, especially as Hellenistic Jewish thinkers of his time absorbed them.

If so, however, Paul does not reflect Plato's firm division between the outer and the inner human being (*Republic* 588d) or his view that the evil "body" enslaves the "soul" (*Phaedr.* 66b–67b).[75] Paul has a more integrated understanding of human existence, derived from the Scriptures. So, for example, in 6:11–14 the human will is in need of encouragement to resist sin, act righteously, and serve God, but in 7:15–25 it agrees with God's will and wants to do it. Similarly, in 7:14 and 18 Paul views himself as entirely flesh and therefore inclined to disobey God, but in 7:15–25 generally his will agrees with and wants to do God's law. Perhaps most revealing of all, the term "soul" never appears in the discussion, and in the following paragraphs the body becomes the object of God's eschatological work of redemption (8:11, 23).[76] Paul is miserable in his entire existence as a human being (7:24), and it is he himself, in his entirety, who serves the law of God with his mind and the law of sin with his flesh (7:25).[77]

Paul would agree with Plato, then, that every human being can be viewed from an exterior and an interior perspective. The anthropology Paul assumes here, moreover, applies to any human being, not merely to a Jew who has the written record of God's law and not merely to the believer, who has God's word and Spirit. Beyond this very limited agreement, however, it is difficult to see much overlap between Paul's anthropology and Plato's. By "the inner human being" Paul refers to his will (cf. 7:15, 16, 18–21) and his mind (7:23, 25). These are the elements of his person that want to obey God. These are also the elements of a person that, in unbelieving Jews, for example, would be the location of their commendable zeal for God (10:2).[78]

7:23 But I see another law in my members warring against the law of my mind and taking me captive by the law of sin that exists in my members (βλέπω δὲ ἕτερον νόμον ἐν τοῖς μέλεσίν μου ἀντιστρατευόμενον τῷ νόμῳ τοῦ νοός μου καὶ αἰχμαλωτίζοντά με ἐν τῷ νόμῳ τῆς ἁμαρτίας τῷ ὄντι ἐν τοῖς μέλεσίν μου). Paul's tendency to disobey God constantly overpowers his delight in God's will and his desire to obey it.

In contrast (δέ) to his inward delight in God's law stands the principle that Paul articulated in 7:21 and that he tries to explain in 7:22–23. Just as in 7:21, Paul engages here in a play on the various meanings of the term "law." The term (νόμος) could refer not only to a body of law, such as the law of God, that governs a particular people group (cf. 7:7) or to a "principle" of behavior, such as a "law" of nature (cf. 7:21), but to a set of typical characteristics, as in the expression, "according to women's custom" (Aeschylus, *Agamemnon* 594).[79] Here all three uses of the term fall into this third category.[80]

The other "law in my members," then, refers to something within Paul's members that tends to behave in a certain way. He makes clear what this is in the lengthier phrase, "the law of sin that exists in my members." Here Paul personifies sin again and assigns to it a particular "way" of behaving in

(George H. Van Kooten, *Cosmic Christology in Paul and the Pauline School*, WUNT 2.171 [Tübingen: Mohr Siebeck, 2003]).

75. On Plato's understanding of the body and the soul, see Eduard Schweizer, "σῶμα, κτλ.," *TDNT* 7:1028–29.

76. Betz, "Concept of the 'Inner Human Being,'" 337–39, 340.

77. Cf. ibid., 338.

78. Moo, *Romans*, 461.

79. Räisänen, *Jesus, Paul and Torah*, 78. The translation belongs to Alan H. Sommerstein, LCL.

80. Räisänen, *Jesus, Paul and Torah*, 89.

his members. He is recalling 7:5 where he said that prior to becoming believers he and his Roman audience were at the mercy of sinful passions at work in their members and prompted by the law.

"The law of my mind" refers to the characteristic tendency of Paul's mind, at least if we think of his mind as the location of his will. Throughout 7:14–22 Paul's mind has been on the side of God's law, desiring to do what the law commands. "The law of my mind," then, is not the law of God itself but the joy Paul takes in God's law and his desire to obey it.

The participles translated "warring against" (ἀντιστρατευόμενον) and "taking captive" (αἰχμαλωτίζοντά) are both present tense and refer to action that takes place continually in Paul. The resulting picture of Paul's existence is especially bleak: his delight in God's law and desire to obey it are in a constant struggle with the overpowering force of sin. Sin constantly wins this battle and takes Paul captive.

The metaphors of warfare and captivity were very much alive for Paul's readership, many of whom were Greek-speaking immigrants, slaves, and former slaves living among the narrow streets and crowded conditions across the Tiber and below the Janiculum Hill. Their parents and grandparents, in many cases, would have probably immigrated to Rome as wartime captives.[81] The vividness of Paul's language would have added to the dark picture Paul painted. As with the particularly bleak mercenary and power language of 7:14, it is difficult to think of Paul using this imagery to describe the normal existence of believers. As he says in 6:15–7:6, the Spirit (7:6) has released believers from sin's power.[82]

7:24 I am a miserable human being! Who will deliver me from the body of this death? (ταλαίπωρος ἐγὼ ἄνθρωπος· τίς με ῥύσεται ἐκ τοῦ σώματος τοῦ θανάτου τούτου;). Paul's rescue from defeat, capture, and certain death at the hands of sin must come from beyond himself, and so it must come from the Lord.

Greek speakers associated the adjective "miserable" (ταλαίπωρος) with extreme deprivation and suffering (cf. Rev 3:17) and could use it to describe the want and violence that captives experienced (Demosthenes, *Fals. leg.* 309; Tob 13:10). Ancient Greek philosophers used it for the sort of metaphorical deprivation that came to the human being without a proper relationship to or understanding of God (Plato, *Euthyd.* 302c; Epictetus, *Diatr.* 1.3.5). It was, therefore, an appropriate term for describing the sense of personal misery that Paul felt in the metaphorical state of military defeat and captivity that he has just described. He lives in the misery that comes from delighting in doing the will of God but being unable to do it.

It is difficult to know whether Paul pleads for rescue from "this body of death" (Tyndale, NAB, NIV, NRSV, NET, ESV) or from "the body of this death" (Luther, KJV, NASB; cf. REB). The decision is difficult because where Paul refers to the "body" in the broader context, he often connects it with death (6:12; 8:10, 11; cf. 7:4), but in the immediate context the "body" does not figure into the discussion. Instead, Paul describes how sin uses the commandment to produce "death" in him (7:13). Either translation, then, fits well within Paul's use of this vocabulary elsewhere.

In such a situation, the immediate context and the proximity of the demonstrative pronoun to "death" (θανάτου τούτου) should probably tip the balance in favor of the translation "the body of this death." "This death," then, refers both to the miserable tension between willing the good and being

81. Jewett, *Romans*, 471.

82. Moo, *Romans*, 465.

unable to accomplish it that Paul has just described, as well as to the eschatological death that comes to those who disobey God's law.

With this reference to "death," Paul circles back to the rhetorical question that started this part of his discussion, "Did that which is good, then, become death for me?" (7:13). "This death" that Paul experiences because of his disobedience to the law was not the law's fault. It was the fault of a weak, fleshly self with its tendency to sin despite knowing that the law was good and beautiful and deserved obedience.[83]

7:25 But thanks be to God through Jesus Christ our Lord! So then, I myself serve the law of God with my mind but with my flesh the law of sin (χάρις δὲ τῷ θεῷ διὰ Ἰησοῦ Χριστοῦ τοῦ κυρίου ἡμῶν. ἄρα οὖν αὐτὸς ἐγὼ τῷ μὲν νοῒ δουλεύω νόμῳ θεοῦ τῇ δὲ σαρκὶ νόμῳ ἁμαρτίας). Paul anticipates Romans 8:1–17 with a brief outburst of thanks to God but then immediately returns to the subject of 7:14–24. Despite his desire, at one level, to obey God by doing what God's law commands, Paul's weakness as a sinful creature ensures that he remains enslaved to sin.

The phrase "but thanks be to God" recalls Paul's use of the same expression in 6:17 where he had used it to thank God for rescuing the Roman Christians from slavery to sin and enabling them to obey the Christian teaching that had made an impact on their lives. Here too Paul speaks of the difference between a life of constant captivity to sin (7:23) and on the path to death (7:24) and a life of deliverance from this deadly situation.

This deliverance comes "through Jesus Christ our Lord" (διὰ Ἰησοῦ Χριστοῦ τοῦ κυρίου ἡμῶν), a phrase that Paul uses, with slight variation, at the beginning and end of 5:1–8:39 and at the end of each major subsection of this passage. In each of these uses it refers to the present rescue of believers from the plight of sin, whether the plight of hostile relations with God that sinful rebellion against him created (5:1, 11) or the plight of sin's reign and lordship over humanity through death (5:21; 6:23).[84] Here too then the phrase refers not to the future rescue of believers from the death throes described in 7:14–25 but to their present rescue from this situation through the death of Jesus Christ, their risen Lord (cf. 8:3, 11, 31–34). The shift to the first-person plural "our Lord" shows that the plight Paul describes in 7:14–24 and the rescue from that plight, which he announces here, do not apply only to himself. He has described in 7:14–24 the situation from which God has delivered all believers.

The next phrase (7:25b) makes clear that Paul's expression of thanks to God for deliverance in 7:25a was a brief outburst that only anticipated the fuller discussion of God's deliverance in 8:1–17. In Romans the phrase "so then" (ἄρα οὖν) sometimes puts the argument back on track after a digression (5:18; cf. Eph 2:19) and sometimes signals a summary of the foregoing discussion (8:12; 9:16, 18; 14:12, 19).

Paul's summary is a concise restatement of his primary point in 7:14–24, but formulated with an emphatic "I myself" (αὐτὸς ἐγώ) that emphasizes, on the other side of his thanks to God, that only God could rescue him. Epictetus thought that rescue from a similar miserable spiritual condition must come from within, from one's efforts at philosophical discipline (*Diatr.* 1.2.37). Paul, however, knew from the Scriptures that his deliverance could only come from the Lord (Isa 59:20 LXX; cf. Rom 11:26).[85] He had no resources within himself to accomplish his own deliverance, and that has been one of the primary points of 7:7–25.[86]

83. Cf. Moo, *Romans*, 466.
84. Cranfield, *Romans*, 1:258.
85. On Epictetus, cf. Lagrange (*Romains*, 179).
86. Cf. Jewett, *Romans*, 473.

IN DEPTH: The Identity of the "I" in Romans 7:7–25

Understanding the identity of the "I" in Romans 7 is one of the most difficult interpretive problems in the letter. Who is this person that once lived apart from the law but then encountered the law and died (7:9–12)? Who is the "miserable human being" presently "sold under sin" and unable to break out of captivity to it (7:14–25)?

At first the answer may seem obvious that Paul, writing in the first person, is speaking of his own experience with the Mosaic law in a way that shows the effect of the law on people generally. If so, then the first paragraph of the passage (7:7–12) narrates Paul's experience of awakening to the burden that the law places on the human being, or at least on the Jew, a burden to do what the law commands. The second paragraph (7:13–25) explores at greater depth the tension that this burden generated in Paul and therefore generates in others also. On this reading of the "I," whether Paul depicts himself as a believer, an unbeliever, or specifically as an unbelieving Jew whom sin has deceived by means of the law, he speaks of the law's effect on humanity generally but incorporates generous insights from his personal experience with the law.[87]

The problem with finding large amounts of Pauline autobiography in the "I" of 7:7–25 lies in the correspondingly large amount of speculation that it involves, particularly in understanding 7:9–11. Paul says elsewhere that he was circumcised on the eighth day of his life and, prior to his conversion, lived a blameless life according to the law's standards (Phil 3:4–6). It is not immediately clear how this statement can cohere with an autobiographical claim in Romans 7:9 that he once lived apart from the law, or in 7:13–25 that he was engaged in a constantly frustrated struggle to keep the law. The speculation comes into play, then, in the theory that Paul was, relatively speaking, alive during a period of "childlike innocence" before he understood the law's demands and then "died" afterwards when the burden of the law and the unsuccessful struggle to obey it bubbled beneath the surface of his visible and "blameless" life.[88]

The need for so much speculation in order to explain 7:7–25 as primarily an autobiographical reference has led many interpreters to conclude that although the passage may contain an element of autobiography, its "I" is primarily symbolic of something else. If the "I" in 7:7–12 could somehow be understood

87. See, e.g., Calvin (*Romans*, 141–56), who thinks that Paul describes the believer's new awareness that sinful human beings cannot keep the law; Meyer (*Romans*, 265–68, 275), who holds that Paul describes the unbeliever's experience of trying and failing to do what is right; and Jewett (*Romans*, 450–53), who argues that Paul refers to his youthful introduction to the law's burden and then to his wrongheaded attempts to persecute Christians on the basis of the law.

88. Meyer (*Romans*, 266, 270–71) compares Paul to "Luther . . . before the light of the gospel dawned upon him . . ." (266). Cf. Jewett (*Romans*, 440–73), whose very different theory nevertheless has a similar structure.

as Adam, this would explain how Paul could say that this "I" was once living apart from the law but died when sin used the commandment to deceive the "I." Only Adam among human beings once lived before God issued a commandment, and the serpent used the commandment to trick Eve and then Adam into disobeying God. As a result, both Adam and Eve, and all humanity afterward, lived under the curse of death. If this is correct, then 7:13–25 might describe the struggle of every "fleshly" human being after Adam, or at least every believer, to live in a way that is fully pleasing to God.[89]

This approach to the passage, however, also has problems. Paul clearly speaks of sin "reviving" (ἀναζάω, 7:9), not of sin coming to life for the first time as it did for Eve and Adam in their original act of disobedience (cf. 5:12).[90] The commandment through which sin deceived the "I" of Romans 7:7–13, moreover, was the commandment "you shall not covet" (7:7), and this commandment was given to Moses, not to the first couple in the garden.[91] In addition, Paul never mentions Eve and Adam in the passage, although he was not hesitant to mention one or the other of the first couple elsewhere when his argument called for it (5:14; 1 Cor 15:45; 2 Cor 11:3).[92] It seems improbable, then, that Paul expected his Roman audience to decode "I" as Adam or as human involvement in Adam.

Some of the problems with both the autobiographical and the Adamic interpretations disappear, however, if the "I" of the passage is a reference to Paul as an unbeliever in solidarity with the rest of Israel prior to, or apart from, the gospel. Only Israel received the Decalogue, from which Paul quotes in 7:7, and the pattern of the law's effect on the "I" in 7:7–13 is close to the pattern that Paul describes for the coming of the law to Israel in 5:13–14, 20. When the law came to Israel, the law defined sin more specifically and caused it to increase; in the same way, when the "I" heard God's command not to covet, it began coveting all the more (7:8). On this reading, then, there is no need to explain how Paul could say autobiographically that he was once alive apart from the law.[93]

Those who take this approach believe that in 7:14–25 Paul speaks more autobiographically but as a member of Israel. In this role he describes what happens when the Israelite outside of Christ encounters the law. He does this from a Christian perspective, however, and therefore with a heightened understanding of the human inability to keep the law.[94]

89. Richard N. Longenecker, *Paul, Apostle of Liberty: The Origin and Nature of Paul's Christianity* (Grand Rapids: Baker, 1976), 109–16 ("the human cry . . . of the spiritually sensitive," whether Christian or not [116]); Dunn, *Romans 1–8*, 374–412 ("The eschatological tension is itself a proof that identification with Christ in his death has begun" [412]).

90. Lambrecht, *Wretched "I"*, 63; Engberg-Pedersen, "Reception," 42–43.

91. Engberg-Pedersen, "Reception," 42.

92. Fitzmyer, *Romans*, 464.

93. Moo, *Romans*, 428–30, 435–37, 439; cf. Kruse, *Romans*, 299–304.

94. Moo, *Romans*, 431; cf. Kruse, *Romans*, 304–12.

This solution also encounters difficulties. Paul does not refer to Israel by name anywhere in the passage, and although the Scriptures imply that sin increased in Israel when it received the law, they do not say this explicitly, nor do they portray Israel as moving from "life" to "death" when it received the law (7:9).[95]

If none of the other solutions seems convincing, then it is worth asking whether Paul was using the first person in 7:7–25 simply as a rhetorical device to argue his point about the relationship between the law and sin. Paul could use a rhetorical "I" this way elsewhere, even elsewhere in Romans itself. In Romans 3:7 Paul asks the rhetorical question, "But if the truthfulness of God abounded by means of my lie for his glory, why am I too still judged as a sinner?" Here Paul's "my" and "I" do not refer in any real way to himself but simply frame an objection to his argument. In the same way, Paul can give ethical advice in the first-person plural, seemingly including himself in the admonition (1 Cor 10:8–9), but then immediately shift into the second person (1 Cor 10:10), making it clear that his first-person advice in the previous two sentences was really directed to his readers.[96]

Once again, however, this view is not entirely satisfactory. Paul's other uses of the first person as a rhetorical fiction are relatively brief and emerge naturally out of their contexts, whereas his use in 7:7–25 is both unexpected and sustained over a long passage.[97] In 7:7–25, moreover, Paul is explaining 7:5, which describes the action of the law on people who are in the flesh, and Paul includes himself in this group with a first-person plural that is not fictional ("for when *we* were in the flesh, the sinful passions that were prompted through the law used to work in *our* members . . .").[98] It would be odd, then, if his first-person singular references in 7:7–25 were entirely fictional and had no bearing on what he thought about the effect of the law on himself.

It seems reasonably clear, then, that Paul neither excludes himself from the "I" of the passage nor speaks strictly about himself, about Adam, or about Israel. As most interpreters recognize, even when they emphasize one approach over another, the "I" of the passage has a composite character. Since Paul often uses the first-person singular pronoun in his letters to refer to himself or as a rhetorical device to emphasize an argumentative point (e.g., 1 Cor 6:12–20; 10:29–11:1; Gal 2:18–21; Phil 3:4–15), it is likely that he uses the "I"

95. Cf. Meyer, *Romans*, 266; Lambrecht, *Wretched "I"*, 65.

96. Kümmel, *Römer 7*, 121–22. This was also a common approach among ancient interpreters of Romans and has been adopted by Stowers ("Romans 7.7–25 as a Speech-in-Character," 180–202) in the form of an argument that 7:7–25 uses the ancient rhetorical device of "speech-in-character" (προσωποποιία).

97. Seifrid, "The Subject of Rom 7:14–25," 314–15.

98. Ibid., 314.

in Romans 7:7–25 in one or both of these two ways.[99] Moreover, since Paul uses the first-person plural immediately before the passage (7:5–6), mixes the first-person plural and singular in a single sentence in the middle of the passage (7:14), and uses the first-person plural again near the end of the passage (7:25), it seems likely that he intended his first-person singular descriptions to be generally applicable both to himself and to his audience of Roman Christians.[100]

Two further considerations help to bring Paul's use of the first person in 7:7–25 into still sharper focus. First, although Paul's use of the first person is more extensive here than it is anywhere else, there is nevertheless a helpful parallel in Galatians 2:18–21.[101] The "I" of the Galatians passage follows a series of first-person plural references in Galatians 2:15–17, just as the "I" of Romans 7:7–25 follows the first-person plurals of 7:5–6. In the Galatians passage, Paul lays out a general principle applicable to a group that includes himself and uses the first-person plural. He then illustrates that principle with respect to himself in a more personal way, using the first-person singular. The "I" of Romans 7:7–25 works in a similar way. The sentences that precede the passage (7:5–6) use the first-person plural to say that the Spirit has released all believers from sin's ability to co-opt the law as its own tool of enslavement. Paul then uses the first-person singular in 7:7–25 to analyze the plight of any unbeliever under the power of sin, himself included.

Second, the Scriptures shaped Paul's understanding of how the law affects the sinful individual, whether himself or anyone else. That is why his description of sin's use of the law in 7:7–12 resembles what he has already said, on the basis of Scripture, about the effect of God's command on Adam (5:12–14; cf. 3:19–20; 4:15) and the effect of the Mosaic law on Israel (5:20). Thus, when the law came into Paul's life, it had a negative effect (7:9) just as it had a negative effect when it came into Israel (5:13, 20; cf. Exod 20:3–6; 32:1–35). Similarly, sin used God's commandment to deceive Paul (7:11) just as the serpent deceived Eve, using God's commandment not to eat of the tree of the knowledge of good and evil (5:11; cf. Gen 3:13). Paul gives no details about when the law came into his life or precisely how sin used the commandment to deceive him, but it is unlikely that he speaks merely in the abstract here.

In summary, the analogy of Galatians 2:18–21 indicates that Paul uses "I" both autobiographically and generally. In addition, the allusions to Scripture make it

99. Lambrecht, *Wretched "I"*, 74–80; Kümmel, *Römer 7*, 121.

100. Cf. Seifrid, "The Subject of Rom 7:14–25," 320–21.

101. Lambrecht, *Wretched "I"*, 76; Seifrid, "The Subject of Rom 7:14–25," 315.

likely that he analyzes his own experience with sin, and that of others, through a biblical lens.

In the second main part of the passage (7:13–25), Paul uses the "I" to show that sin rather than the law was responsible for the human being's inability to obey God and inevitable death as a result of this disobedience (7:13). Here too Paul speaks for all humanity, and so the ancient idea that Paul produces a "speech-in-character" (προσωποποιία) is probably correct.[102] Still, he probably thought of his speech not as entirely fictional but as a fair representation of his own pre-Christian struggle to do what he knew from the Mosaic law to be right.[103] This struggle has certainly been sharpened by his post-Christian perspective on the pervasiveness of human sin, but the sense of enslavement to sin that Paul depicts here would have been intelligible to Jews (e.g., Ps 143:2; Jer 2:22; 13:23; 17:1, 9; 1QH^a 1.21–23; 11.19–24). The problem of wanting to do good but instead doing evil, moreover, was well-known both at the popular level and among the educated elites in the Greco-Roman world generally (e.g., Plato, *Prot.* 352B–C; Plutarch, *Virt. mor.* 446D–448C).[104]

If this is correct, however, then what becomes of Paul's claim in Philippians 3:6 that he was "blameless" when measured by the law's standard of righteousness? How could he have been embroiled in the inner turmoil that 7:13–25 depicts but thought of himself as blameless? Philippians 3:6 probably describes Paul's perspective on how others viewed him rather than anything about his interior life. His record of law observance, when measured from a distance ("in the flesh"), was blameless, but Romans 7:13–25 reveals that Paul was more conflicted about his ability to keep God's commands than this brief assessment discloses.[105]

If this is correct, then it is unlikely that Paul portrays the struggle of a believer in 7:13–25. The paragraph is an important part of Paul's explanation of Romans 7:5 where Paul clearly says that the law's effect of prompting sinful passions lies in the past for believers.[106] The plight depicted in Romans 7:13–25, moreover, finds its resolution in the description of the Spirit's work in the believer's life in Romans 8:1–17. Paul is clear elsewhere in his letters that believers, who continue to live in the flesh (Gal 2:20) also continue to struggle, in the Spirit, against fleshly

102. Stowers, "Romans 7.7–25 as a Speech-in-Character," 198–202.

103. Stowers's idea ("Romans 7.7–25 as a Speech-in-Character," 198–202) that Paul excludes Jews from his characterization and speaks only of gentile slavery to passion, then, is incorrect. The first-person plural in 7:5 shows that Paul believed that prior to his conversion "sinful passions" were at work in his "members" through the law.

104. On the Greco-Roman material, see Engberg-Pedersen, "Reception," 54–56.

105. Meyer, *Romans*, 266; Hultgren, *Romans*, 687–88.

106. Cf. Jean Noël Aletti, "Romans 7,7–25: Rhetorical Criticism and Its Usefulness," *SEÅ* 61 (1996): 88.

temptations (Gal 5:16–25). With its lack of any reference to the Spirit, however, and its claim that human beings are sold under sin, continuously defeated by sin and in sin's perpetual captivity, it is best to understand Romans 7:13–25 as a description of the plight from which God's Spirit has freed, or is freeing, the believer. It is not likely to be a description of normal Christian existence.

Theology in Application

Paul has crafted his defense of the law's goodness in a way that demonstrates clearly the power, pervasiveness, and deceptiveness of sin. Sin disables human beings from pleasing God and therefore from living in the fully human way that God, their creator, designed them to live. The passage functions as preparation for Romans 8:1–17 where Paul will introduce the Spirit into the discussion and show how, for believers, God has started to solve the problem so vividly portrayed in 7:7–25. In 7:7–25 Paul offers a primer on the insidious nature of sin and particularly on how sin can even use God's word to generate both knowing and unknowing rebellion against God. Two elements of sin's nature are especially clear from the passage.

Sin's Deceitful Nature

According to 7:11, sin is deceptive. Just as the serpent suggested to Eve that God's command not to eat of the tree of the knowledge of good and evil was motivated by a spirit of competitiveness ("For God knows that when you eat of it . . . you will be like God," Gen 3:5), and just as Eve trusted the serpent and her own judgment more than God, sin is often a matter of failing to trust that God, in giving his commandments, has the best interests of his human creatures in mind. The basic ethical admonitions of Scripture—to honor one's parents, to respect human life, to keep sex within marriage, to respect the property of others, to speak truthfully about other people, and to avoid greed (Exod 20:12–17; Deut 5:16–21)—seem fine until one's parents become very expensive to care for, one's spouse becomes difficult, one never has quite enough money, telling the truth will lead to endless trouble, and a friend who works half as hard lives a life of luxury.

Sin knows when to make God's commands look like blunt instruments that do not fit the complexities involved in one's personal situation, and it knows how to work with the human tendency to "stifle the truth in unrighteousness" (1:18).[107]

107. On the whole theme, see Berkouwer, *Sin*, 152–54; Merold Westphal, "Taking St. Paul Seriously: Sin as an Epistemological Category," in *Christian Philosophy*, ed. Thomas Flint, University of Notre Dame Studies in the Philosophy of Religion 6 (Notre Dame: University of Notre Dame Press, 1990), 200–207.

When God's commands become inconvenient, human beings can quickly invent reasons why they should not obey them.

The deceptiveness of sin, however, goes deeper than this. As Paul suggests in 7:15, sin is so sinister that it can lead someone to oppose God and his purposes precisely when they believe themselves to be obeying God. Before he believed the gospel, Paul's zeal drove him not only to reject it but to persecute the church (1 Cor 15:9; Gal 1:13; Phil 3:6; 1 Tim 1:13).

Paul Althaus was a highly regarded Luther scholar and respected German university professor and minister from immediately after his military service in World War I until 1964. By all accounts, he was a decent and reasonable person. During the 1930s he also viewed the German people as threatened by the influence of the Jews in their midst and was one of eight signatories of the infamous *Ansbacher Ratschlag* with its expression of gratitude "to God our Lord that he has sent to our nation in its plight the *Führer* as 'pious and trustworthy ruler'" and its assertion "that the Lord wills to prepare in the National Socialistic order of the country a 'good government,' a government in 'decency and honor.'"[108]

Althaus probably became involved in the formulation of this statement because of his hope that the German "people" were now recovering their dignity and national pride after their humiliation at the end of World War I. The statement probably also arose out of his own theology, which held that the church needed to supplement God's revelation in Scripture with God's supposed revelation of his purposes in history and culture. He grew silent about the country's direction after 1937 and seems to have lost all faith in the war his country waged after a soldier who had attended one of his sermons in 1943 described to him the existence of certain "camps" and the murder of civilians, including women and children. Nevertheless, Althaus never spoke unambiguously against what was happening until after the war was over and even then thought of his own errors as mainly matters of bad timing.[109]

In retrospect, Althaus's error seems obvious, but it did not seem obvious to many people at the time, and he seems never to have come fully to grips with it himself. Yet no one, least of all other believers, should point fingers at Althaus without recognizing how blind people usually are to their own sins. The desire to feed one's pride, to wield power over others, and to live in luxury whatever the consequences for other people can lead people to cloak their real motives in pious language and even to deceive themselves into thinking that they are obeying God when, in fact, they are only being selfish. Paul understood well that Satan often "disguises himself as an angel of light" (2 Cor 11:14). He also understood that even as a believer indwelt by God's Spirit he could not always trust his own judgment about his actions. "I do not

108. From Hans Schwarz, "Paul Althaus (1888–1966)," *Lutheran Quarterly* 25 (2011): 38.

109. Robert P. Ericksen, *Theologians under Hitler: Gerhard Kittel, Paul Althaus, Emmanuel Hirsch* (New Haven: Yale University Press, 1985), 79–119; Schwarz, "Paul Althaus (1888–1966)," 34–39.

even judge myself," he tells the Corinthians, "for I am not aware of anything against myself, but I am not thereby acquitted. It is the Lord who judges me" (1 Cor 4:3–4).

Romans 7:7–25 explains why this is true and issues an implicit warning that zeal for God and trust in God are not identical. Zeal for God is commendable and important (Rom 10:2), but unlike trust in God sin can also infect it and use it for its own nefarious purposes.

An important part of the antidote to this sort of blindness is trust in God's word, and failure to trust God's word may have been a large part of Althaus's mistake. He could not resist identifying God's revelation of himself with an effective leader who seemed to be healing his nation. He added another voice to God's revelation of himself in Scripture.

After a description of the perfection and value of the law of the Lord, the psalmist asks, "Who can discern his errors? Declare me innocent from hidden faults. Keep back your servant also from presumptuous sins; let them not have dominion over me!" (Ps 19:12–13a). From the psalmist's perspective, the Lord answers this prayer, in part, through the guidance found in his word.

Sin's Powerful Nature

In 7:13–25 Paul describes himself as wanting at one level to obey God's law but at another level being unable to do so. He delights in the goodness and beauty of God's law (7:21–22), but sin overpowers his desire to obey it. Apart from the transforming and empowering work of God's Spirit on the human heart, people are unable to live in the way that God created them to live. Sin has damaged their thinking and appetites too severely to allow an existence that, outside of Christ, is human in the fullest and best sense.

This does not mean that only believers, who have experienced the transforming work of the Spirit, flourish as human beings whereas all unbelievers live miserable lives. Rather, God's Spirit only does his transforming work in believers, and that transforming work will eventually lead believers into an eternal existence that is fully human. According to 7:7–25, this must be entirely God's work: no human being can rescue himself or herself from entanglement with sin's chains. They weigh too heavily on us all for anyone to break them by moral effort. Only God can release the chains of sin, and he does this as a free gift, by his grace, as Romans 8 explains.

CHAPTER 17

Romans 8:1–17

Literary Context

Since 5:1 Paul has been explaining the impact of the gospel of justification by faith on the lives of believers. They have been reconciled to God (5:1–11) and are experiencing the reversal of the consequences of Adam's sinful misstep (5:12–21). God has released them from sin and death through union with Christ's death and resurrection (6:1–14), and they are now no longer enslaved to sin, which leads to death, but enslaved to righteousness and God, which leads to eternal life (6:15–23). Since up to this point in the argument Paul had briefly referred to the Mosaic law in various statements as part of the plight from which God had rescued believers (5:20–6:1; 6:14–15), he next described more fully what he meant by these controversial comments (7:1–6).

He then laid the blame for the law's tendency to increase rebellion against God at the feet of sin and the sinful human being rather than at the feet of the law itself (7:7–25). Paul's explanation of the entanglements of sin, the law, and the flesh not only exonerated the law from blame but also showed how grave the human plight had become. Even those who delighted in God's law found themselves often unable to obey its commands and moving inevitably toward the death that the disobedient deserved (7:13–24, 25b).

If sin was so insidious that it could dupe even those who delighted in God's law into rebellion against God (7:22–23; cf. 7:11; Gen 3:4–5), then the plight of sinful humanity was desperate indeed (Rom 7:24). There is no suspense at this point in the argument about whether humanity will find relief from this plight. Paul has already shown in 6:1–23 that union with Christ's death and resurrection has broken the stranglehold of sin on believers. That description of liberation from sin, however, was incomplete, and in 7:6 Paul had briefly hinted at another element of God's solution to human enslavement that needed to be described in more detail. There he spoke of service in the "newness of the Spirit." References to the Spirit, whether using the noun (πνεῦμα) or the adjective (πνευματικός), are infrequent in Romans up to this point (1:4, 11; 2:29; 5:5; 7:6, 14) and become relatively infrequent again after chapter eight (9:1; 12:11; 14:17; 15:13, 16, 19, 27, 30), but in 8:1–39 Paul refers to the Spirit nineteen times, fifteen of them in 8:1–17. This section of Paul's argument, then, is largely about the work of the Spirit in the lives of believers, empowering them to live in a way that is pleasing to God, despite the suffering that this may entail.

The mention of suffering toward the end of 8:1–17 then leads Paul to describe the eschatological hope of believers. Prior to the time when God will end all suffering and decay, he says, the Spirit is present with believers to help them through their difficulties, and God is working among believers for their good (8:18–30). Nothing, Paul concludes, will separate believers from the love of God as God has displayed it in the gospel. A moving expression of this conviction concludes the second major section of the letter and leads naturally to the question of whether God has rejected Israel, since the majority of Israelites have not believed the gospel. Did God not promise Israel his eternal love? Have they not been separated from that love by the rejection of the gospel? Does this not imply that God has been unfaithful to his promises to them? Paul will address these questions in 9:1–11:36 and then in 12:1–15:13 will conclude the main argument of the letter with ethical admonitions designed specifically for believers in Rome and based on the gospel he has just explained.

VIII. The Scriptures Show That Righteousness Comes by Faith Rather Than by Works (4:1–25)

IX. Justification by Faith Brings Peace and Reorients the Believer's Existence (5:1–8:39)

- A. Justification by Faith Rescues Believers from God's Present and Future Wrath (5:1–11)
- B. Christ's Obedience Overwhelms the Effects of Adam's Disobedience (5:12–21)
- C. Union with Christ's Death and Resurrection Initiates a New Life (6:1–23)
- D. Union with Christ's Death and Resurrection Frees Believers from the Law (7:1–6)
- E. The Goodness, Yet Inability, of the Law (7:7–25)
- ➡ **F. God's Solution to the Human Plight (8:1–39)**
    - **1. Christ's Work and the Spirit's Power Overcome the Sinful Flesh (8:1–17)**
    - 2. God's Spirit Helps Believers Cope with Suffering as They Await Future Immortality (8:18–30)
    - 3. The Gospel's Meaning: God Loves and Protects His People through his Son Jesus Christ (8:31–39)

X. Israel's Present Rejection of the Gospel Does Not Imply the Failure of God's Word (9:1–11:36)

Main Idea

The solution to the plight of the wretched human Paul depicted in 7:7–25 comes with the work of Christ and the indwelling Spirit. Christ's incarnation and death punished sin and thereby ended the desperate plight of sin, sin's use of the law, and death described in 7:7–25. Christ's incarnation and death also marked the new age of the Spirit. The Spirit now dwells within believers, enabling them to please God in the present and, in the future, to live with Christ in the presence of God.

Translation

Romans 8:1–17

	Function	Text
1a	Inference (from 7:6)	**No condemnation now comes,** therefore,
b		to those who are in Christ Jesus.
2a	Explanation (of 1a)	For **the law of the Spirit of life has liberated you**
b	Means (of 2a)	through Christ Jesus
c	Separation	from the law of sin and death.
3a	Explanation (of 2a–c)	For **[this is] the very thing the law found impossible**
b	Cause (of 3a)	because it was weakened by the flesh:
c	Identification (of 3a)	**God condemned sin in the flesh**
d	Means (of 3c)	by sending his own Son
e	Manner	in the likeness of sinful flesh and
f	Purpose (of 3d)	for sin
4a	Purpose (of 3c)	so that the righteous requirement of the law might be fulfilled in us
b	Description	who walk not according to the flesh but according to the Spirit.
5a	Explanation (of 4a)	For **those who exist according to the flesh agree with the flesh,**
b	Contrast (to 5a)	but **those who exist according to the Spirit agree with the Spirit.**
6a	Explanation (of 5a–b)	For **the mindset of the flesh is death,**
b	Contrast (to 6a)	but **the mindset of the Spirit is life and peace.**
7a	Basis (of 6a–b)	Because **the mindset of the flesh is hostility against God,**
b	Cause (of 7a)	for **it does not submit to the law of God,**
c	Cause (of 7b)	for **it is not able.**
8	Explanation (of 7b)	And **those who are in the flesh are not able to please God.**
9a	Contrast (to 8)	**You,** however, **are not in the flesh** but **in the Spirit,**
b	Verification (of 9a)	if indeed the Spirit of God dwells within you.
c	Verification (of 9d)	And if anyone does not have the Spirit of Christ,
d	Expansion (of 9a)	**this person is not his.**

Continued on next page.

Continued from previous page.

10a	Verification (of 10c)	But if Christ is in you,
b	Contrast (to 10c)	although the body is a dead thing because of sin,
c	Contrast (to 9c)	**the Spirit is life because of righteousness.**
11a	Verification (of 11b)	And if the Spirit ...
b		of the one who raised Jesus
c		from the dead
		... dwells in you,
d	Explanation (of 10c)	**the one who raised Christ from the dead will also give life**
e	Indirect Object	to your mortal bodies
f	Means	through his Spirit that indwells you.
12	Conclusion (from 1–11)	So then, **brothers and sisters, we are debtors not to the flesh to live according to the flesh.**
13a	Condition (of 13b)	For if you live according to the flesh,
b	Explanation (of 12)	**you are about to die,**
c	Condition	but if, by the Spirit, you put to death the deeds of the body,
d	Contrast (to 13b)	**you will live.**
14a	Basis (for 13d)	For **all**
b	Identification 1	**who are led by the Spirit of God,**
c	Description	
d	Identification 2	**these are sons of God.**
15a	Explanation (of 14)	For **you did not receive a spirit of reenslavement,**
		with fear as the result,
b	Contrast (to 15a)	but **you received the Spirit**
c	Description	of adoption as a son,
d	Agent	by which we cry, "'Abba,' that is, 'Father.'"
16a	Assertion	**The Spirit himself bears witness together**
b		with our spirit
c		that we are the children of God and
17a	Verification (of 17b)	if children, also
b	Inference (16, 17a)	heirs;
c	Restatement (of 17b)	heirs of God and
d	Restatement (of 17c)	fellow heirs of Christ,
e	Condition (of 17b)	if indeed we suffer
f	Association	with him
g	Result (of 17c)	so that we might be glorified with him.

Structure

The passage divides into three parts. In 8:1–8 Paul first says that Christ's work in his incarnation and death, and the Spirit's presence in the lives of believers, have dealt decisively with sin's power over the flesh (8:1–4). He then describes the division that these decisive events have created within the world. People align themselves either with the flesh or with the Spirit, either with life and peace or with hostility against God (8:5–8).

In 8:9–11 Paul turns directly to his readers ("you, however" [ὑμεῖς δέ]) and reminds them that they are on God's side in this ongoing conflict because the Spirit dwells within them (8:9) and because Christ has atoned for their sin through his death on the cross (8:10). This section implies that the Roman Christians should live in a way that is consistent with these truths. The section ends by pointing to the future when their full, bodily identification with the risen Christ will resolve the tension inherent in life before the general resurrection of the righteous (8:11).

In 8:12–17 Paul repeats the pattern of 8:9–11, moving from the present life of tension between a fleshly and a Spirit-led life to a description of the bright future that awaits those in whom the Spirit of God is at work. Paul argues that the Roman Christians are able to avoid sinful behavior because of the power and leading of the Spirit within them (8:12–13) and then interjects the new concept that those who have the Spirit belong to God's family and, as his children, share the status, the suffering, and the bright future of God's Son (8:14–17).

Exegetical Outline

IX. Justification by Faith Brings Peace and Reorients the Believer's Existence (5:1–8:39)

- A. Justification by Faith Rescues Believers from God's Present and Future Wrath (5:1–11)
- B. Christ's Obedience Overwhelms the Effects of Adam's Disobedience (5:12–21)
- C. Union with Christ's Death and Resurrection Initiates a New Life (6:1–23)
- D. Union with Christ's Death and Resurrection Frees Believers from the Law (7:1–6)
- E. The Goodness, Yet Inability, of the Law (7:7–25)
- **F. God's Solution to the Human Plight (8:1–39)**
  - ➡ **1. Christ's Work and the Spirit's Power Overcome the Sinful Flesh (8:1–17)**
    - a. Christ's work and the Spirit's power make obedience to God possible (8:1–8)
    - b. The Roman Christians should live by the Spirit's standards and have life (8:9–11)
    - c. The Roman Christians should live by the Spirit's standards and in the knowledge that they are children of God (8:12–17)

Explanation of the Text

8:1 No condemnation now comes, therefore, to those who are in Christ Jesus (Οὐδὲν ἄρα νῦν κατάκριμα τοῖς ἐν Χριστῷ Ἰησοῦ). God will not punish in any way people who are united to Christ Jesus by faith.

The inferential particle "therefore" (ἄρα) returns Paul's line of thought to 7:1–6 where Paul had described the release of believers from sin's use of the law to prompt even greater sin in human beings and keep them on the path toward death.[1] He has filled out the negative side of this description in 7:7–25 and now returns to its positive side. Since they have been released through the death of Christ from bondage to sin, sin's use of the law, and death, they are "now" under "no condemnation." The adjective "no" (οὐδὲν) appears first in the sentence for emphasis and is sweeping in its connotations. It qualifies the term "condemnation" (κατάκριμα), a judicial word that refers to a decision to punish someone for wrongdoing, for example, with a large fine (Dionysius of Halicarnassus, *Ant. rom.* 13.5.1).[2] Paul has used it in 5:16 and 18 to refer to the punishment itself, in this case God's punishment of Adam and all humanity for their disobedience.[3] There, it stands opposite "justification" (δικαίωμα, δικαίωσις), the judicial decision that one will not be punished. Paul is saying, then, that God has decided not to punish in any way those who are "in Christ Jesus." "In Christ Jesus" (ἐν Χριστῷ Ἰησοῦ) describes the realm in which believers live, the realm in which people experience "justification" and "redemption" (3:24), where they are dead to sin and alive to God (6:11), and where they receive God's free gift of life rather than sin's wages of death (6:23). These eschatological blessings have broken into the present, as the term "now" (νῦν) demonstrates (cf. 7:6).[4]

8:2 For the law of the Spirit of life has liberated you through Christ Jesus from the law of sin and death (ὁ γὰρ νόμος τοῦ πνεύματος τῆς ζωῆς ἐν Χριστῷ Ἰησοῦ ἠλευθέρωσέν σε ἀπὸ τοῦ νόμου τῆς ἁμαρτίας καὶ τοῦ θανάτου). Those who are in Christ Jesus will escape God's punishment because his Spirit sets them free, through the work of Christ Jesus, from the toxic link between the law, sin, and death and so brings them out of spiritual death into spiritual life.

Paul now supplies the reason why (γάρ) God releases those who are in Christ Jesus from punishment. The phrase "in Christ Jesus" (ἐν Χριστῷ Ἰησοῦ) could modify "life" (ζωῆς) and refer to the life that people have who are united with Christ (Tyndale, Luther, KJV, RSV, NRSV, NAB, CEB).[5] If Paul had intended "in Christ Jesus" to modify "life," however, he would probably have made this clear with an article in front of the phrase (τῆς ζωῆς τῆς ἐν Χριστῷ Ἰησοῦ) as he does when he speaks in 3:24 of "the deliverance that is in Christ Jesus" (τῆς ἀπολυτρώσεως τῆς ἐν Χριστῷ Ἰησου).[6] The phrase, then, probably modifies the verb and speaks of the means by which "the law of the Spirit of life" has freed individuals from "the law of sin and death"

1. Cranfield, *Romans*, 1:373; Wickens, *An die Römer (Röm 6–11)*, 121; Jewett, *Romans*, 479.

2. Cf. LSJ 896, BDAG 518, both s.v. κατάκριμα.

3. Cf. Friedrich Büchsel, "κατακρίνω, κτλ.," *TDNT* 3:952.

4. Wickens, *An die Römer (Röm 6–11)*, 121; Schreiner, *Romans*, 398; Jewett, *Romans*, 479.

5. Lagrange (*Romains*, 191) supports this rendering with a reference to 6:23. Godet (*Romans*, 296) thinks "in Christ Jesus" modifies "law."

6. Since Theodoret of Cyrus, who shared Paul's native tongue, seems to have construed "in Christ Jesus" with "Spirit of life" (*Letters of St. Paul*, 1:88 [*PG* 82:128]), caution on this point is appropriate.

(NIV, REB, ESV). God freed them from sin and death by means of Christ Jesus, or as 8:3 will explain more specifically, through his incarnation and death.[7]

"The law [νόμος] of the Spirit of life" is an ambiguous phrase. It could refer to the Mosaic law viewed as holy, just, good, and spiritual (7:12, cf. 7:13d, 14a, 16b) and now able to give the life that it intended (7:10b).[8] It might also refer to the "principle" or "authority" of the life-giving Holy Spirit, using the term "law" in an unusual way and therefore as a play on its customary use in the next clause.[9] Paul has already used the term in a playful way in 7:21, and that makes his use of it here in the same way likely. This becomes even more likely in light of the flow of the argument since 7:1. Paul has just shown that the law, although holy, just, good, and spiritual, is nevertheless powerless to rescue the individual from the plight of sin, and he will make this point explicitly in the next sentence (8:3).[10] "The law of the Spirit of life," then, is the power of God's Spirit that enables believers to break free from sin's use of the law for its own deadly purposes (cf. 7:5, 8–11) and experience eternal life (6:22).[11]

This "law of the Spirit of life" liberates the believer from "the law of sin and death." The meaning of "the law of sin and death" is clear from Paul's discussion of the law in 7:1–25. There, sin used the law to multiply itself and keep the "fleshy" human being in bondage to itself and on the path to death. Now Paul announces the good news of God's remedy to this terrible plight. God's Spirit, by means of Christ Jesus, has broken the stranglehold that sin had on the law and, through the law, on the sin-prone self. The language of liberation recalls Paul's use of slave imagery in the previous argument for the plight of human beings under the power of sin (6:16, 18, 20, 22; 7:14, 23). The Spirit has now freed them from this bondage and given them life (cf. 6:22–23).

Paul addresses the person liberated here as "you" (σε), and this use of the second-person singular is surprising after his sustained use of the first-person singular in 7:7–25.[12] The shift to the second person indicates that Paul intended his first-person discourse in 7:7–25 to be generally applicable to his readers.[13] Every believer, including Paul and each of his readers, has experienced the liberating power of the Spirit from the overwhelming power of sin as Paul has just described it in 7:7–25.

8:3–4 For [this is] the very thing the law found impossible because it was weakened by the flesh: God condemned sin in the flesh by sending his own Son in the likeness of sinful flesh and for

7. Meyer, *Romans*, 300; Cranfield, *Romans*, 1:374–75.

8. See, e.g., Wilckens (*An die Römer [Röm 6–11]*, 121–23), Dunn (*Romans 1–8*, 416–17), and Schreiner (*Romans*, 400).

9. See, e.g., Cranfield (*Romans* 1:375–76) and Räisänen (*Jesus, Paul and Torah*, 93–94).

10. Kruse, *Romans*, 324.

11. Cf. Fee (*God's Empowering Presence*, 521–27), who appropriately observes that Paul qualifies the liberating work of the Spirit with the phrase "through Christ Jesus" and thus shows that the Spirit does not work independently from Christ Jesus in freeing the believer from sin.

12. Instead of "you" (σε) a diverse group of manuscripts reads "me" (με) in 8:2, including representatives of the Alexandrian (A P 81 104 1175), Western (D), and Byzantine (K L) text types. Some translations, including Tyndale, Luther, the KJV, RSV, and TOB have followed this reading. It is possible that at some point in distant antiquity a scribe changed an original "me" (με) to "you" (σε), perhaps repeating the final syllable of "freed" (ἠλευθέρωσεν) without the moveable nu (-σε-) and then leaving out "me" (με) entirely. The manuscript evidence for "you" (σε), however, comes from an earlier date, and appears in both Alexandrian (א B 1739) and Western witnesses (F G Tertullian Ambrosiaster). In addition, it is easy to see how a scribe might change an unexpected second-person singular pronoun to a first-person singular on the heels of the prolific use of the first-person singular in 7:7–25. "You" (σε) is probably original, therefore, and most modern translations correctly follow this reading.

13. Schreiner, *Romans*, 410.

sin so that the righteous requirement of the law might be fulfilled in us who walk not according to the flesh but according to the Spirit (τὸ γὰρ ἀδύνατον τοῦ νόμου, ἐν ᾧ ἠσθένει διὰ τῆς σαρκός, ὁ θεὸς τὸν ἑαυτοῦ υἱὸν πέμψας ἐν ὁμοιώματι σαρκὸς ἁμαρτίας καὶ περὶ ἁμαρτίας κατέκρινεν τὴν ἁμαρτίαν ἐν τῇ σαρκί, ἵνα τὸ δικαίωμα τοῦ νόμου πληρωθῇ ἐν ἡμῖν τοῖς μὴ κατὰ σάρκα περιπατοῦσιν ἀλλὰ κατὰ πνεῦμα). The tendency of human beings to sin against God made it impossible for the law of God to function as the means of setting people free from sin and death. What the law failed to do, however, God accomplished by the atoning death of his Son, which breaks the stranglehold of sin on believers and allows them, by the power of the Spirit, to begin living lives of love. Their love for one another fulfills the law, although their love for others will not be perfect until they fully share Christ's resurrected life.

This sentence explains (γάρ) how God freed believers from sin's use of the law to exercise a deadly power over them and makes the point that in doing this, God accomplished something the law was unable to do. Although this meaning is relatively clear, Paul's syntax is compressed and ambiguous. The phrase "the very thing . . . found impossible" (τὸ . . . ἀδύνατον) consists of an adjective with the neuter article and so implies that Paul will focus on one specific "thing" that the law could not do.[14] Instead of saying immediately what this one thing is, however, Paul states why the law could not do it ("it was weakened by the flesh"). He then starts a new sentence whose relationship to what he has just said about the inability of the law is not clear.

Paul may have intended his hearers to supply "to do" in this opening phrase and the words "this God has done" in his restarted sentence ("For what the law, weakened by the flesh, was powerless to do, this God has done," NAB).[15] Alternatively, the opening phrase could stand in apposition to the rest of the sentence and simply identify God's condemnation of sin in the flesh as precisely what the Mosaic law could not accomplish ("For [this is] the very thing the law found impossible because it was weakened by the flesh: God condemned sin in the flesh . . ."). This second approach is best because it is less speculative.[16] Just as 7:13–25 described human beings as encumbered with the tendency of the flesh to disobey God's law, so Paul describes God's solution to this wretched condition as a condemnation of sin that takes place precisely in the flesh.

The expression "by sending" (πέμψας) represents a participle that modifies the indicative "condemned" (κατέκρινεν) and describes the means by which God was able to condemn sin in the flesh. He did this through the incarnation and death of Jesus.

A reference to the incarnation is clear in the phrase "in the likeness of sinful flesh." The term "likeness" (ὁμοίωμα) does not mean that God's Son was only approximately flesh. Since Paul has identified "flesh" as the battleground between the human desire to do God's law and sin's defeat of that desire (7:5, 14, 18, 25), God would have sent Christ to the wrong location had he not sent him in human "flesh" in the fullest sense. The term does carry a connotation of approximation, but the element of approximation must lie either in the connection between the flesh and sin or in something

14. Paul uses the adjective "kind" (χρηστόν) in the same way in 2:4. There he distinguishes the "kind [action]" (τὸ χρηστόν) of God from the "kindness" (χρηστότης) of God. This distinction between the substantival adjective and its corresponding noun shows that he means something slightly different by the two different forms. On this, see Henry Alford, *The Greek Testament*, 4 vols. (London: Rivingtons, 1857), 2:361; BDF §263 (2).

15. See also Fitzmyer, *Romans*, 483–84, 497.

16. See Alford (*Greek Testament*, 2:361), who labels this a "nominativus pendens." Cf. Schreiner, *Romans*, 397, 402.

about Christ's own nature, such as his divinity, that permanently differentiates him from human flesh.[17]

When Paul speaks about the way in which God rescued people from sin through Christ in 2 Corinthians 5:21, he shows a concern to avoid the misunderstanding that Christ himself somehow became a sinner: "For our sake he made him to be sin who knew no sin, so that in him we might become the righteousness of God." This tips the balance in favor of understanding the term "likeness" here in 8:3 as a way of distancing Christ from sin. God, then, sent his Son as a human being, subject to human flesh in its frailty but without ever succumbing to sin (cf. Gal 4:4).

A reference to the death of Christ is clear in the phrase "for sin" (περὶ ἁμαρτίας). In Greek-speaking Judaism and early Christianity, this phrase often appears in connection with sacrifices and offerings that deal with human sin (e.g., Lev 5:6–7; Isa 53:10; Heb 10:18; 1 Clem. 16:11; 41:2), and sometimes the phrase carries the technical sense of "sin offering" (e.g., Lev 7:37; Ps 39:7 [Eng. 40:6]; Heb 10:6, 8).[18] It is not certain that Paul uses the phrase in a technical way here, but his own deep familiarity with the Jewish Scriptures and his knowledge of the Jewish roots of even gentile Christianity in Rome (see the introduction) make it likely that he used the phrase to refer to Christ's death as an atonement "for sin" (cf. 3:25–26).[19] So, God "condemned sin in the flesh" in the incarnation of Christ, which culminated in his sacrificial death on the cross. "In the flesh" goes with "condemned" and describes the location of the condemnation. The verb "condemned" itself refers to judicial punishment (Sus 1:53; Pss. Sol. 4:2; Mark 10:33; 14:64; Josephus, *J.W.* 5.530), and this is what sin received when the fully human Christ was crucified.

Paul has now explained why "no condemnation [κατάκριμα] . . . comes . . . to those who are in Christ Jesus" (8:1). Those who are united with Christ are united with him in his death (6:6; 8:10; Gal 2:20) and therefore experience the reconciling effects of God's condemnation of sin in Christ's flesh when he died on the cross (cf. 3:25; 5:1, 9–10).

Paul next states the purpose for which God condemned sin in Christ's flesh. He did this "so that the righteous requirement of the law might be fulfilled in us who walk not according to the flesh but according to the Spirit." The term "righteous requirement" (δικαίωμα) normally referred in Greek to a legal right (e.g., Dionysius of Halicarnassus, *Ant. rom.* 3.10.4; 3.11.3; Jer 11:20 LXX), and in the LXX could refer to a particular statute (e.g., Num 27:11 LXX) or to a summary of a body of law (e.g., Num 35:29 LXX).[20] Paul uses it of God's law in Romans 1:32 when he claims that people know enough about God to know his "righteous decree" (δικαίωμα) that those who engage in impious and antisocial behavior deserve death. It is possible, then, that Paul intended to refer to the law's just penalty of death for the sinner here in 8:4 and to describe the purpose of Christ's sacrificial death "for sin" as the fulfillment of this "righteous decree" in those who are united to Christ.[21] Or he may have intended to refer, more positively, to Christ's perfect obedience to the law and to imply that God has transferred Christ's obedience to those who are

17. For the view that Paul is protecting Christ's divinity, see Cranfield, *Romans*, 1:381.

18. See, e.g., Dunn, *Romans 1–8*, 422; Harris, *Prepositions and Theology*, 182–83.

19. Cf. Gal 1:4 where, on the most likely reading, Paul refers to Christ giving himself "for [περί] our sins" (𝔓[46] א A D F G K L P Ψ, etc.). See also BDAG 798, s.v. περί 1g.

20. Cf. LSJ 429; Gottlob Schrenk, "δικαίωμα," *TDNT* 2:219–20.

21. Pierre Benoit, *Exégèse et théologie*, 2 vols. (Paris: Éditions du Cerf, 1961), 1:28–33.

in Christ, thus rescuing them from God's wrath against the disobedient (cf. 2 Cor 5:21).[22]

Since Paul goes on to describe believers as those "who walk not according to the flesh but according to the Spirit," however, it is likely that "the righteous requirement of the law" refers to the behavior that God requires of his people. Paul's implied claim that the law's requirement will be "fulfilled" (πληρωθῇ) in believers, moreover, provides a clue about the precise "requirement" he had in mind.[23] In Galatians 5:14 Paul had already said that "the whole law is fulfilled [πεπλήρωται] in one word: 'You shall love your neighbor as yourself'" (Lev 19:18), and had then immediately urged the Galatian Christians to "walk by the Spirit" and not to "gratify the desires of the flesh" (Gal 5:16). In Romans 13:8–10, moreover, he will again say that love for neighbor fulfills (πεπλήρωκεν, v. 8; πλήρωμα, v. 10) the law and quotes Leviticus 19:18 to demonstrate the point. The purpose for which God condemned sin in human flesh through the death of Christ, then, is that believers might fulfill the law of God through their love for others.

Paul does not imply, however, that this happens perfectly in the present. His purpose clause describes an ethical trajectory that ends at the resurrection when those whom God has united with Christ's death in the present will also be fully united with his resurrection. Now that God has broken the power of sin, as Paul described it in 7:7–25, believers begin to fulfill the law in the present. That fulfillment will not happen, however, until God gives life to the mortal bodies that continue to affect the present existence of believers (8:10–11).[24]

8:5 For those who exist according to the flesh agree with the flesh, but those who exist according to the Spirit agree with the Spirit (οἱ γὰρ κατὰ σάρκα ὄντες τὰ τῆς σαρκὸς φρονοῦσιν, οἱ δὲ κατὰ πνεῦμα τὰ τοῦ πνεύματος). The flesh and the Spirit work according to completely different norms, and those whose existence is determined by the norms of the Spirit will take the Spirit's side in the conflict between the flesh and the Spirit.

Paul now explains why (γάρ) he can say that those who walk according to the Spirit fulfill the just requirement of the law. The preposition translated "according to" (κατά) in 8:4–5 introduces the "norm which governs something," and so when Paul spoke in 8:4 of walking according to the flesh or Spirit, he referred to two different patterns of daily living, one shaped by the flesh and one shaped by the Spirit. Here in 8:5 he speaks more literally of "those who exist according to the flesh" and "those who exist according to the Spirit," describing two modes of existence with their respective norms or expected patterns of behavior.

The expression "agree with the flesh . . . agree with the Spirit" (τὰ τῆς σαρκὸς φρονοῦσιν . . . τὰ τοῦ πνεύματος) uses a well-known idiom in ancient Greek for favoring or siding with a particular political party or cause.[25] So, for example, the Syrian ruler Alexander Epiphanes, in a letter designed to woo Jonathan Maccabaeus away from loyalty to Alexander's rival Demetrius, asks him to "take our side [φρονεῖν τὰ ἡμῶν] and keep friendship with us" (1 Macc 10:20), and Josephus can describe those loyal to Herod the Great in a civil conflict in Galilee as "the partisans of Herod" (τοὺς τὰ Ἡρώδου φρονοῦντας, *Ant.* 14.450 [Ralph Marcus, LCL]).[26]

22. E.g., Calvin, *Romans*, 160; Moo, *Romans*, 481–85; Hultgren, *Romans*, 300.

23. Fee, *God's Empowering Presence*, 535–37; Kevin W. McFadden, "The Fulfillment of the Law's *Dikaiōma*: Another Look at Romans 8:1–4," *JETS* 52 (2009): 489–90; Kruse, *Romans*, 328–29.

24. McFadden, "Fulfillment of the Law's *Dikaiōma*," 491–96.

25. BDAG 1066, s.v. φρονέω 2b; Cranfield, *Romans*, 1:385–86; Haacker, *An die Römer*, 153.

26. Cf. Mark 8:33.

Paul probably intended, therefore, to communicate that the pattern of life dictated by the flesh and the pattern of life dictated by the Spirit are rivals grappling for influence over the person. In the language of Paul's letter to the Galatians, "the desires of the flesh are against the Spirit, and the desires of the Spirit are against the flesh, for these are opposed to each other, to keep you from doing the things you want to do" (Gal 5:17; cf. Rom 7:16, 19–20, 23). The cognitive element preserved in most translations and assumed by most commentators is not missing, however, as his use of the noun "mindset" (φρόνημα) in 8:6–7 shows (cf. 8:27).

The Spirit lives within believers (8:9), so the believer's life is governed by the Spirit's norms. These norms are expressed in "the righteous requirement of the law," which, as we saw in the comments on 8:3–4, is probably a reference to the love command as the summary of the law. The Spirit, then, frees believers from the domination of sin and the flesh and empowers believers to live in a new way, oriented toward love for others.

8:6 For the mindset of the flesh is death, but the mindset of the Spirit is life and peace (τὸ γὰρ φρόνημα τῆς σαρκὸς θάνατος, τὸ δὲ φρόνημα τοῦ πνεύματος ζωὴ καὶ εἰρήνη). The flesh and the Spirit are naturally disposed to lead those whom they dominate in two completely different directions: one leads them toward death, and the other toward life and peace.

The "for" (γάρ) Paul uses in this verse signals a continuation of the line of thought he began in 8:5.[27] This sentence explains the result of siding with the flesh on one hand or the Spirit on the other.[28]

The term "mindset" refers to a person's instinctive mental inclinations. Josephus could describe the young Herod as "energetic by nature" and then immediately illustrate this description by saying he "found material for his mindset" (ὕλην . . . εὑρίσκει τῷ φρονήματι) in the pursuit and capture of thieves that plagued the border between Syria and Galilee (*J.W.* 1.204 [Thackeray, LCL; modified]). Herod, in other words, had an active disposition (cf. *Ant.* 4.245; 14.13).[29]

Here Paul uses the term metaphorically to describe the natural, and opposing, dispositions of the flesh and the Spirit. The flesh tilts those whose existence belongs to it toward death, and the Spirit tilts those who belong to him toward life and peace. This mention of "peace" as something the Spirit brings recalls Paul's description in 5:1–11 of the peace that believers have with God after the outpouring of his love through the Holy Spirit and after the initiative he took in the death of Christ to reconcile himself to his enemies (5:1, 6–10). If the Spirit is naturally disposed to bring life and peace to God's people, Paul implies, then the Spirit empowers those in whom he dwells (8:9) to have the same disposition.

8:7 Because the mindset of the flesh is hostility against God, for it does not submit to the law of God, for it is not able (διότι τὸ φρόνημα τῆς σαρκὸς ἔχθρα εἰς θεόν, τῷ γὰρ νόμῳ τοῦ θεοῦ οὐχ ὑποτάσσεται, οὐδὲ γὰρ δύναται). Paul can say that the flesh pushes those whose existence it defines toward death because the flesh is under sin's sway and so is incapable of doing anything other than rejecting God's authority.

The term "because" (διότι) introduces the basis for a statement that has just been made (cf. 1:19; 3:20).[30] Each time Paul uses the term in Romans,

27. Calvin, *Romans*, 161–62; Meyer, *Romans*, 306.

28. Calvin, *Romans*, 161–62.

29. On Josephus's use of the term, see Georg Bertram, "φρήν, κτλ.," *TDNT* 9:229.

30. BDAG 251, s.v. διότι 3.

he explains the clause it introduces with two further "for" (γάρ) clauses (1:19–20; 3:20), just as he does here. The term, then, sets up a chain of reasoning that unfolds in three steps:

1. The natural disposition of the flesh leads those under its domination toward death because the flesh is naturally hostile toward God.
2. Paul can reasonably say that the flesh is hostile toward God because the flesh does not submit to God's law.
3. The flesh does not submit to God's law because it is not able to do so.

Paul is summarizing the argument of 7:1–25 where he had described himself (and other human beings with him) as unable to submit to God's law precisely because he was burdened with a fleshly weakness that rendered him powerless to shake sin's domination (7:5, 14, 22–23). The hostility against God that resulted from this situation stands in contrast to the "peace" with God that comes to those whose disposition the Spirit is transforming (cf. 8:6 and 5:1, 5, 10–11).[31]

8:8 And those who are in the flesh are not able to please God (οἱ δὲ ἐν σαρκὶ ὄντες θεῷ ἀρέσαι οὐ δύνανται). People whose existence the flesh defines, and who do not have the Spirit within them, are not able to please God by fulfilling the righteous requirement of God's law.

The word "and" (δέ) introduces a further explanation of Paul's statement that the mindset of the flesh is not able to submit to God's law. The problem is that those whose existence the flesh dominates are unable to "please" God. Since elsewhere Paul could instruct new believers in how they ought to live in order to "please" God (1 Thess 4:1), he probably has unbelievers in mind here.

The expression "in the flesh" and Paul's elaboration on that expression in the next sentence confirm this (8:9). Paul knew that believers had a physical and moral existence "in the flesh" and that this set up a tension within believers between living "in the flesh" and "in the Lord" (2 Cor 10:3; Gal 2:20; 5:13–18; Phlm 16).[32] Here, however, he affirms another sense in which living "in the flesh" is in the past for believers, and such an existence is incompatible with the Spirit's indwelling (cf. Rom 7:5, 18). How can these two ideas cohere? Probably Paul thought of unbelievers as living at the mercy of the flesh and sin's power over the flesh. The absence of the Spirit from their lives meant they could not please God because they had no means of resisting sin's use of their flesh.

The parallel Paul draws in 8:7–8 between submitting to God's law and pleasing God shows that he thought the two concepts overlapped with each other. Since Paul expected believers to live in a way that was pleasing to God, he probably understood the law of God as an outline of this way of life. As we have seen in the comments on 8:4, the law of God for Paul was probably a form of the Mosaic law reinterpreted through the lens of the love command (cf. 13:8–10).[33] When Paul describes believers as those who agree with the Spirit, have the Spirit's mindset, and "exist according to the Spirit," therefore, he is not merely describing the identity of believers but also implying that they should live in a way that is consistent with this identity.[34]

8:9 You, however, are not in the flesh but in the Spirit, if indeed the Spirit of God dwells within

31. Cf. Sanday and Headlam, *Romans*, 196.

32. Jan Lambrecht, "The Implied Exhortation in Romans 8,5–8," *Gregorianum* 81 (2000): 449–50.

33. Kruse, *Romans*, 331. Cf. Frank Thielman, *The Law and the New Testament: the Question of Continuity*, Companions to the New Testament (New York: Crossroad, 1999), 7–46.

34. The seemingly contrasting conclusions of Moo (*Romans*, 485–89) and Lambrecht ("Implied Exhortation," 441–51) on whether Paul describes or exhorts believers in 8:5–8, then, are actually both valuable in understanding the passage.

you. And if anyone does not have the Spirit of Christ, this person is not his (ὑμεῖς δὲ οὐκ ἐστὲ ἐν σαρκὶ ἀλλὰ ἐν πνεύματι, εἴπερ πνεῦμα θεοῦ οἰκεῖ ἐν ὑμῖν. εἰ δέ τις πνεῦμα Χριστοῦ οὐκ ἔχει, οὗτος οὐκ ἔστιν αὐτοῦ). Paul's audience of believers in Rome stands apart from the description he has just given of unbelievers. They exist in the sphere marked out by the Spirit, and the Spirit gives them both the desire and the ability to please God by fulfilling his law.

Paul now makes the exhortatory intentions of 8:3–8 clear by turning directly to his readers with second-person plural pronouns and verbs and by setting their existence in contrast ("however" [δέ]) to the bleak description of existence in the flesh in 8:6–8. Unlike those dominated by the flesh's mindset of hostility toward God and by an inability to please God, Paul's readers live in the Spirit and the Spirit lives in them. The expression "if indeed" (εἴπερ) does not call Paul's audience to self-examination by suggesting that the Spirit of God might "in fact" *not* dwell within them (RSV, ESV).[35] Rather, Paul used the expression in the same sense as "if" (εἰ) at the beginning of the next two sentences (8:10, 11). It asks them to recognize the implications of the truth that the Spirit of God does dwell within them: if God's Spirit makes his home within them (and he does), then they live in the sphere that the Spirit governs.[36]

When Paul speaks of the Spirit dwelling within believers elsewhere in his letters, the imagery typically has corporate dimensions and means that the Spirit dwells among the believing community (1 Cor 3:16; Eph 2:22).[37] Here, however, he refers to the dwelling of the Spirit within the individual believer, as the singular pronoun "anyone" (τις) in the next sentence indicates (cf. 1 Cor 6:19). Unlike the "me" of 7:17 and 20 that the flesh controlled and in whom nothing good had made its home (7:18), God's Spirit dwells within Paul's readers. Paul does not state the ethical implications of this language explicitly at this point, but since this comment comes on the heels of his claim in 8:4 that the righteous requirement of the law is fulfilled in believers as well as his description in 8:7–8 of unbelievers as those who can neither "submit" to God's law nor "please" God, the ethical implications of what he says here are clear. His audience in Rome has the Spirit (8:9b), so the Spirit has made its home within them, and they are "in the Spirit" rather than "in the flesh" (8:9a). They can, therefore, live in a way that pleases God (cf. 8:8) and are willing and able to submit to God's law (cf. 8:7). God has freed them from the bondage of the "wretched" individual in 7:7–25.

8:10 But if Christ is in you, although the body is a dead thing because of sin, the Spirit is life because of righteousness (εἰ δὲ Χριστὸς ἐν ὑμῖν, τὸ μὲν σῶμα νεκρὸν διὰ ἁμαρτίαν τὸ δὲ πνεῦμα ζωὴ διὰ δικαιοσύνην). The presence of the Spirit within believers means that Christ is present with them and that the Spirit will raise their bodies from the dead (although now their bodies are mortal and sinful). The Spirit will do this because God is at peace with them, having given them the gift of a right standing with him.

"If" (εἰ) does not imply that Christ might not dwell within Paul's readers (cf. "if indeed" in 8:9) but throws the emphasis in the sentence on the consequences of Christ's presence with them in the final

35. Alford, *Greek Testament*, 2:364; Meyer, *Romans*, 308; Dunn, *Romans 1–8*, 428. Correctly, Chrysostom (*Romans*, 226), whose native tongue was Greek and who was well equipped to understand the rhetoric of Paul's argument. See also Schreiner (*Romans*, 413), Jewett (*Romans*, 489), and Légasse (*Romains*, 488).

36. Cf. the use of the term in 3:30 to mean "since" and the useful note on the word in Sanday and Headlam (*Romans*, 96).

37. Second Timothy 1:14 is ambiguous.

clause. Christ is within them, and so the Spirit will give them life at the resurrection of the dead because God has given them the gift of righteousness.[38]

The expression "Christ is in you" stands parallel to the ideas that God's Spirit dwells within Paul's audience and that they have the Spirit of Christ in 8:9. This raises the question whether Paul distinguished between God's Spirit, Christ's Spirit, and the presence of Christ within believers.[39] The answer becomes clear in 8:11 where Paul distinguishes between the Spirit of God on one hand and Jesus, whom God's Spirit raised from the dead, on the other hand. Paul probably understood the Spirit of God as the means through which Christ was present with believers despite Christ's physical location in his resurrected body at God's right hand (8:34). The situation is analogous to Paul's description of his own spirit's presence with the Corinthians for the purpose of church discipline in 1 Corinthians 5:3–5:

> For though absent in body, I am present in spirit; and as if present, I have already pronounced judgment on the one who did such a thing. When you are assembled in the name of the Lord Jesus and my spirit is present, with the power of our Lord Jesus, you are to deliver this man to Satan.

The phrase "the body is a dead thing because of sin" could refer either to the metaphorical death of the body's sinful tendencies or to the literal death of the body as a penalty for sin. If the metaphorical understanding is correct, then Paul would be echoing 6:6–12 where he urged his audience to "count yourselves to be dead with respect to sin" (6:11) and exhorted them to "let not sin . . . reign in your mortal body" (6:12).[40] The convergence of the terms "body" (σῶμα) and "dead" (νεκρός) together in this passage lend weight to this understanding, but the literal understanding of the body's death here is more likely.

Paul probably echoes 5:12–14, 17, 21, and 6:21–23 where he describes death as the penalty for sin. Two considerations weigh heavily in favor of this understanding, one contextual and the other grammatical.[41]

First, Paul will suggest in his next sentence (8:11) a solution to the plight he has described here, and that solution is the resurrection of believers from the dead through their union with the risen Christ and the power of God's Spirit. This solution suggests that the plight Paul describes in 8:10 is the body's physical mortality.

Second, the phrase "because of sin" (διὰ ἁμαρτίαν) can only have a causal sense (cf. 4:25), but if Paul were arguing the same point here about the body that he was arguing in 6:10–11, he would have said that believers were dead "with respect to sin" (τῇ ἁμαρτίᾳ).[42] Here, then, Paul says that the body of the believer is "a dead thing" (νεκρόν) because believers are also sinners, and sin's penalty of physical death still affects them (cf. 1 Cor 15:56).[43]

Paul's emphasis does not lie on this negative statement, however, but on the sentence's final, positive assertion: "the Spirit is life because of righteousness." Here too Paul's meaning is ambiguous, although the ambiguity is hidden by English translations (including mine) that capitalize the word "spirit" (NIV, NET, NRSV, REB, ESV, HCSB, CEB). The parallel structure of Paul's sentence suggests that "spirit" correlates with "body" in the previous clause, and this, in turn, suggests that Paul is talking about the human spirit here.[44]

38. Cf. BDAG 277, s.v. εἰ 1a.α.

39. Cf. Jewett, *Romans*, 491.

40. See, e.g., Wilckens, *An die Römer (Röm 6–11)*, 132.

41. Cf. Schreiner, *Romans*, 414.

42. Cf. BDAG 225, s.v. διά B.2.a.

43. For the translation of the adjective "dead" as a noun ("dead thing"), see Sanday and Headlam, *Romans*, 198.

44. Sanday and Headlam, *Romans*, 198; Fitzmyer, *Romans*, 127, 491.

Again, however, the literary context and the grammar of the sentence weigh heavily against this understanding of the term. Paul has just spoken of God's Spirit indwelling the believer in 8:9, and he is about to describe the work of God's Spirit in raising Jesus and those united with him from the dead in 8:11, so it is unlikely that the same term here would have any other meaning.[45] Paul, moreover, does not say that the spirit is "alive" as the parallelism would demand if he were correlating the human spirit and the human body. Rather, he says that the Spirit is "life." This unusual expression is reminiscent of his statement in 8:7 that the mindset of the flesh is "hostility" (not "hostile") against God. That expression probably meant that the mindset of the flesh *produces* hostility against God. Similarly, here, Paul probably means that the "spirit" *produces* "life," and this thought is consistent with what he will say next about the Spirit of God raising Jesus and believers from the dead.

The Spirit produces life "because of righteousness" not in the sense that the Spirit empowers believers to live righteous lives but in the sense that the righteousness God has given to them as a free gift allows them to "reign in life," as Paul has said in 5:17–19, 21. This echo of the link between righteousness language and eschatological life in 5:12–21, moreover, supports the case that Paul's phrase "because of sin" in the preceding clause also reflects the argument of that earlier paragraph.

8:11 And if the Spirit of the one who raised Jesus from the dead dwells in you, the one who raised Christ from the dead will also give life to your mortal bodies through his Spirit that indwells you (εἰ δὲ τὸ πνεῦμα τοῦ ἐγείραντος τὸν Ἰησοῦν ἐκ νεκρῶν οἰκεῖ ἐν ὑμῖν, ὁ ἐγείρας Χριστὸν ἐκ νεκρῶν ζῳοποιήσει καὶ τὰ θνητὰ σώματα ὑμῶν διὰ τοῦ ἐνοικοῦντος αὐτοῦ πνεύματος ἐν ὑμῖν). At the resurrection of the dead, God will transform the mortal bodies of believers and make them immortal through the Spirit that lives within them, just as he did for Jesus when he raised him from the dead by the Spirit's power.

Here Paul explains further what he meant when he said in the immediately preceding sentence that if Christ is in his Roman audience, then despite having bodies that are subject to death, "the Spirit is life" (8:10). That statement was rhetorically balanced but so compressed that it was somewhat unclear.[46] Paul now clarifies his meaning and substantiates its implications for his readers with a reference to the powerful work of God's Spirit in raising Jesus from the dead. Just as Paul's audience possesses bodies that are subject to death, so Jesus was once among the dead; but just as God used the Spirit to raise Jesus from the dead, so this same Spirit, now dwelling within Paul's audience, will give life to their mortal bodies (cf. 2 Cor 5:4–5).[47]

The Roman believers, then, have a bright future in which they will one day inhabit bodies like Jesus's resurrected body (cf. 1 Cor 15:20–24, 48–56). This is the "eternal life" that, according to 2:7, God will give those who "seek glory and honor and immortality by endurance in good work" (2:7). It is the "hope of the glory of God" in which those who

45. Dunn, *Romans 1–8*, 431.

46. Jan Lambrecht, "Style and Content: A Note on Romans 8,10," *ETL* 86 (2010): 171–76.

47. The manuscript evidence for and against replacing "through his Spirit that indwells" (διὰ τοῦ ἐνοικοῦντος αὐτοῦ πνεύματος) with "because his Spirit indwells" (διὰ τὸ ἐνοικοῦν αὐτοῦ πνεῦμα) is about equally strong, with important witnesses to the Alexandrian, Western, and Byzantine traditions supporting both readings. This balance is reflected in the translations, with most adopting the genitive (e.g., NAB, REB, NRSV, ESV, CEB) but the NIV opting for the accusative (cf. Tyndale). A genitive object for the preposition is probably correct because it disturbs the parallelism with the immediately preceding uses of the preposition with the accusative (διὰ ἁμαρτίαν; διὰ δικαιοσύνην, 8:10), and it is difficult to imagine a scribe creating this disturbance (Cranfield, *Romans*, 1:392).

have been justified by faith can boast (5:2; cf. 5:5). This is also the sense in which we shall be saved "through" Christ and "by his life" (5:9–10).

8:12 So then, brothers and sisters, we are debtors not to the flesh to live according to the flesh (Ἄρα οὖν, ἀδελφοί, ὀφειλέται ἐσμέν οὐ τῇ σαρκὶ τοῦ κατὰ σάρκα ζῆν). Believers are now free from the overpowering influence of the flesh and need not cave in to the pressure to sin that the flesh places on them.

The expression "so then" (ἄρα οὖν) introduces a conclusion drawn from the preceding discussion (cf. 5:18; 7:3, 25), in this case the discussion in 8:1–11 of the believer's liberation from the overpowering influence of the flesh (cf. 7:14–25). If God has condemned sin in the flesh though the death of Christ (8:3) and believers do not walk according to the flesh (8:4), do not have the mindset of the flesh (8:5–7), and in some sense are not in the flesh (8:9), then they owe the flesh nothing.

The implied admonition here shows that Paul understood the danger that their fallen nature continued to present to believers.[48] His point is not that his audience will no longer have a problem with sin but that the death of Christ and the presence of the Spirit have freed them from the overwhelming nature of sin's power. They are now able to choose not to sin. This is probably the force of the term "debtors" (ὀφειλέται) here, which refers to those who are "obligated to do something."[49] Like Ajax who claimed that he did not have to do what the gods wanted him to do because he was no longer their debtor (Sophocles, *Aj.* 590), Paul's readers no longer have to follow the flesh as the "I" in 7:14–25 had to do. God has freed them from its grip.

8:13 For if you live according to the flesh, you are about to die, but if, by the Spirit, you put to death the deeds of the body, you will live (εἰ γὰρ κατὰ σάρκα ζῆτε, μέλλετε ἀποθνῄσκειν· εἰ δὲ πνεύματι τὰς πράξεις τοῦ σώματος θανατοῦτε, ζήσεσθε). Those who claim to be believers but who continue to live by the norms of the flesh, norms outlined in 1:18–3:20, are in reality on the brink of death. They should instead submit to the Spirit's power, resist evil, and live.

The position of the "not" (οὐ) in 8:12 probably led Paul's audience to expect him to complete that sentence with "but to the Spirit to live according to the Spirit."[50] Instead, he continued to examine the idea of living according to the flesh by describing its consequences (8:13a–b) and then produced a corresponding statement that describes how the Spirit helps believers to avoid these consequences (8:13c–d). His shift from the first-person plural in 8:12 to the second-person plural here gives these sentences an admonitory tone.

Paul probably did not intend his phrase "you are about to die" to place special emphasis on the necessity of death (NASB, REB), nor did he intend it to express a simple future (e.g., NAB, NIV, NRSV, ESV). He could easily have written "you must die" (δεῖ ἀποθνῄσκειν ὑμᾶς) or "you will die" (ἀποθανεῖσθε), but instead chose a common expression that referred to being close to an inevitable death (Xenophon, *Cyr.* 3.1.38; 2 Macc 7:18; Dionysius of Halicarnassus, *Ant. rom.* 5.29.1; John 12:33; 18:32; Rev 3:2; Epictetus, *Diatr.* 2.6.27).[51] There is, therefore, an urgency to the phrase Paul uses here. Those who live by the norms of the flesh are treading the brink of a precipice. The idea that his audience can avoid death, expressed in the conditional

48. Dunn, *Romans 1–8*, 447–48.

49. BDAG 742, s.v. ὀφειλέτης 2 b. Cf. LSJ 1277, s.v. ὀφειλέτης.

50. Cranfield, *Romans*, 1:394. Cf. Calvin, *Romans*, 166 ("Paul's sentence here is defective. . . . The meaning, however, is in no way obscure.")

51. Cf. Jewett, *Romans*, 494.

form of the sentence, makes clear that Paul had in mind not the physical death to which all, including believers (8:10) are subject, but the transcendent death that is God's just penalty for sin against his law (1:32; 5:12, 16, 18; 6:12, 21, 23; 7:6, 10).

The alternative to living by the norms of the flesh and dying as a result is putting to death the deeds of the body and living as a result. The term "deeds" (πράξεις) was often used in a pejorative sense to mean "evil deeds" (Acts 19:18; Col 3:9; cf. Polybius, *Histories* 2.7.9), and although Paul's use of "body" rather than "flesh" is unexpected, the expressions "body of sin," "lusts [of the body]," and "the body of this death" (6:6, 12; 7:24) have prepared the ground for this reference.[52] Putting to death the deeds of the body, then, involves refusing to allow sin to reign in one's body (6:12) or to use the faculties of one's body in the service of unrighteousness (6:13). This would at least include the social sins to which Paul referred in 1:18–3:20: sexual immorality, greed, malice, envy, murder, discord, deceit, gossiping, slandering others, pride, and ruthlessness.

The expression "by the Spirit" translates a dative of means (πνεύματι) and indicates the way in which believers are to put evil deeds to death.[53] This does not imply that believers control or wield the Spirit as a tool since in the next sentence Paul describes them as "led by the Spirit of God" (8:14). Instead Paul must mean that the Spirit enables believers to do the good that the "inner human being" and the "mind" of the "I" of 7:22–23, unaided by the Spirit, could not do (cf. Gal 5:16, 25).

8:14 For all who are led by the Spirit of God, these are sons of God (ὅσοι γὰρ πνεύματι θεοῦ ἄγονται, οὗτοι υἱοὶ θεοῦ εἰσιν). The presence of the Spirit of God within believers and within the believing community is evident in the change the Spirit effects in their desires. Their new desire to please God shows that they, like ancient Israel, are God's beloved people.

The "for" (γάρ) introduces the reason why Paul can say that his readers "will live" if they put to death the deeds of the body by means of the Spirit. If they do this, they show themselves to be among those who "are led by the Spirit of God" and are "sons of God." Paul has already said that no believer is without the indwelling Spirit of God, and now he makes clear that the Spirit is powerfully active within believers to reshape their desires and give them the ability to please God by submitting to his law (cf. 8:7–8).

The passive verb "led" (ἄγονται) is a forceful term that Paul could use elsewhere of people "led" to stray after idols (1 Cor 12:2) or to give in to sinful desires (2 Tim 3:6). It was sometimes used in antiquity to refer to the compulsion to act on a particular inner feeling such as desire or pleasure (Euripides, *Med.* 310; Plato, *Prot.* 355a).[54] This does not mean that those "led by the Spirit of God" were forced by God's Spirit to act in certain ways.[55] Paul could use the same term to speak of disobedient people being unaware that God was trying to lead them to repentance (2:4), and Plato, using the exact grammatical construction Paul uses here (the passive verb with a dative of means), could speak of desires that are "directed by calculation" (λογισμῷ ἄγονται).[56] Paul's meaning is that the Spirit helps those in whom he dwells to make decisions about their behavior that please God rather

52. Cf. Meyer, *Romans*, 314; Légasse, *Romains*, 492; BDAG 860, s.v. πρᾶξις 4.b.

53. Wallace, *Greek Grammar*, 162–66.

54. BDAG 16, s.v. ἄγω 3.

55. For this idea, see Robert Jewett, "The Question of the 'Apportioned Spirit' in Paul's Letters," in *The Holy Spirit and Christian Origins: Essays in Honor of James D. G. Dunn*, ed. by Graham N. Stanton, Bruce W. Longenecker, and Stephen C. Barton (Grand Rapids: Eerdmans, 2004), 198; idem, *Romans*, 496.

56. Plato, *Republic* 431c (Grube and Reeve). See LSJ 18, s.v. ἄγω II.3.

than decisions that give in to the sinful desires of the flesh (cf. Gal 5:17–18).

The phrase "sons of God" introduces a new theme intended to assure Paul's readers that if the Spirit is leading them to live in ways that are pleasing to God, then they belong to the people of God. The notion that God's people are his children comes from the Jewish Scriptures (e.g., Exod 4:22; Isa 1:2; Hos 11:1), and Paul asserts here that those in whom God's Spirit dwells may rest assured that they belong to this people (cf. Gal 3:26; 4:5–6).[57]

The title "sons of God" for believers also recalls the title Paul had given to Jesus at the letter's beginning and introduces into the discussion a theme that Paul will develop further in the sentences that follow. Believers are united with Christ in his suffering, but especially in his resurrection, the resurrection by which he was appointed Son of God in power (1:3–4).[58]

8:15 For you did not receive a spirit of reenslavement, with fear as the result, but you received the Spirit of adoption as a son, by which we cry, "'Abba,' that is, 'Father'" (οὐ γὰρ ἐλάβετε πνεῦμα δουλείας πάλιν εἰς φόβον ἀλλὰ ἐλάβετε πνεῦμα υἱοθεσίας ἐν ᾧ κράζομεν, Αββα ὁ πατήρ). Believers are now freed from the harsh conditions of slavery to sin and have become God's adopted sons through the power of the Spirit. This new status has given believers a relationship with God not unlike that of a king and his beloved son, indeed not unlike the relationship between Jesus himself and God.

The "for" (γάρ) in this new sentence probably introduces an explanation of what it means to be "sons of God." Many in Paul's Roman audience had probably experienced slavery. Christianity in Rome seems to have originated among the Jewish population of the city that grew after Pompey conquered Judea in the mid first-century BC and then brought many Jews to Rome as slaves. Slavery as an institution only worked because of an uneasy alliance between the slave's hope of manumission and fear of brutal punishment. Of these two emotions, the fear of angry, violent, and often sadistic punishment seems to have been the institution's strongest support. "Whips, the hook, the cross: these were the basis of the Roman slave system, as everyone knew."[59] Paul uses this image, then, to deny that the relationship between his Roman audience and God resembles in a fundamental way the anxiety-laden, fear-producing institution of slavery.[60]

The term "again" (πάλιν) indicates that Paul uses the image to refer to a condition that once characterized his audience. They once lived in fear, probably the fear that seems to have been a fairly common feature of ancient Greco-Roman religion. Plutarch, writing in Greece a few decades after Paul, devoted an entire tractate to "the dread of the gods," the belief that the gods were irascible and unkind, ready to inflict punishment on people.[61] "Of all kinds of fear [φόβων] the most impotent and helpless," he said, "is superstitious fear [δεισιδαιμονίας]" (*Superst.* 3 [F. C. Babbitt, LCL]).

In contrast, Paul's audience has now received "the Spirit of adoption as a son." The gender specificity of the expression "adoption as son" (υἱοθεσία) emphasized the similarity between Jesus and be-

57. Fitzmyer, *Romans*, 497–98.

58. James M. Scott, *Adoption as Sons of God: An Exegetical Investigation into the Background of* ΥΙΟΘΕΣΙΑ *in the Pauline Corpus*, WUNT 2.48 (Tübingen: Mohr Siebeck, 1992), 244–45, 260–61.

59. Harris, *Restraining Rage*, 322.

60. That there is some resemblance is clear from 6:22, but Paul's recognition of the limitations of the metaphor are also clear from 6:19 (cf. Cranfield, *Romans*, 1:325).

61. Plutarch did not believe that the Jews were free from such anxiety and took their famous unwillingness to defend themselves in wartime on the Sabbath as an example of their fear of angering God (*Superst.* 8).

lievers as God's children, but the use of "adoption" rather than merely "sons" preserved some difference between the unique status of Jesus as God's Son and the status of believers as his sons.[62]

Paul's emphasis, however, lies on the similarity. Just as the Spirit was involved in raising Jesus from the dead and revealing that he was Son of God in power (1:3–4), so the Spirit effected the adoption of believers as "sons of God."

In the Roman world, social elites often used adoption to procure successors to carry on the family name and cult.[63] The adoptee frequently received a higher social status and increased honor through the adoption.[64] Paul's audience in Rome, many of whom probably occupied the social status of slaves, freedmen, and foreigners, would have heard as good news indeed that they were the adoptive sons of the one true God. Only a few years prior to Paul's letter, in AD 50, the emperor Claudius had adopted eleven-year-old Nero, and Nero had been proclaimed across the empire as "son of the greatest of the gods, Tiberius Claudius."[65]

The Spirit enables believers to "cry" (κράζω) to God for help in the midst of difficulty, just as any child might appeal to a loving father for help, and just as Jesus appealed to God shortly before his arrest, torture, and execution (Mark 14:36; cf. Gal 4:6).[66] The use of Aramaic, which was Jesus's native tongue, and the immediate translation of the term into Greek imply that Jesus's use of "Abba" to address God was a widely known characteristic of his familiar relationship with God. Paul now says that believers have this same level of familiar access to God (cf. 5:2; Eph 2:18).

8:16 The Spirit himself bears witness together with our spirit that we are the children of God (αὐτὸ τὸ πνεῦμα συμμαρτυρεῖ τῷ πνεύματι ἡμῶν ὅτι ἐσμὲν τέκνα θεοῦ). The Spirit of God and the believer's own emotions both play a role in assuring the believer and the believing community that they belong to God's family.

No conjunction connects this brief statement with the preceding sentence. This makes the sentence more emphatic but renders the logical connection with what precedes it unclear. Is the cry "Abba!" itself the testimony that Paul describes here, as some commentators have thought from ancient times forward?[67] Or does Paul describe a broader testimony of which the ability to call God Father is simply one result? Without a connecting word spelling out the logical link with what precedes, it seems safest to conclude that the second option is correct and that Paul speaks generally about how believers know they are God's children.[68]

When Paul uses the term "spirit," he usually means God's Spirit, but he also believed that human beings had a "spirit" that was the location of thoughts (1 Cor 2:11), anxieties (2 Cor 2:13), inner peace (1 Cor 16:18; 2 Cor 7:13), and conviction (Rom 1:9).[69] Here Paul speaks both of God's

62. Greek had a gender-neutral term for adoption (τεκνοθεσία). On the various terms for adoption, see Scott, *Adoption as Sons of God*, 3–57.

63. For Roman adoption, see Scott, *Adoption as Sons of God*, 9–13; Adolf Berger, Barry Nicholas, and Susan M. Treggiari, "Adoption," *OCD* 12–13; Trevor J. Burke, *Adopted into God's Family: Exploring a Pauline Metaphor*, NSBT 22 (Nottingham, UK: Apollos, 2006), 60–70.

64. Burke, *Adopted into God's Family*, 153–54.

65. This is the description of Nero on a votive inscription from AD 50–54 in Magnesia in the Roman province of Asia, on which see Jewett (*Romans*, 497) and Deissmann (*Light from the Ancient East*, 347). On Nero's adoption, see Suetonius (*Nero* 7.1).

66. Burke, *Adopted into God's Family*, 94–96.

67. See, e.g., codex D, which begins the sentence with "so" (ὥστε), and Fitzmyer (*Romans*, 501).

68. Again, an explanation offered since ancient times. See, e.g., Theodoret of Cyrus (*Letters of St. Paul*, 1:91 [*PG* 82:136]), who follows a text reading "for the Spirit himself" (αὐτὸ γὰρ τὸ πνεῦμα), and Cranfield (*Romans*, 1:402–3).

69. BDAG 833, s.v. πνεῦμα 3 b. Cf. Fee, *God's Empowering Presence*, 568.

Spirit and the human spirit and says that both spirits bear a common witness that believers are children of God.[70] This dual testimony is ample assurance, he says, of the otherwise unbelievable idea that he and his Roman audience are related to God in a way that is closely similar to Jesus's relationship with God.

8:17 and if children, also heirs; heirs of God and fellow heirs of Christ, if indeed we suffer with him so that we might be glorified with him (εἰ δὲ τέκνα, καὶ κληρονόμοι· κληρονόμοι μὲν θεοῦ, συγκληρονόμοι δὲ Χριστοῦ, εἴπερ συμπάσχομεν ἵνα καὶ συνδοξασθῶμεν). Those in whom the Spirit of God lives belong to God's family and, on the other side of the suffering that following Christ inevitably entails, they have a bright future of social acceptance and release from physical pain.

Adopted children were heirs of those who adopted them, something that the people of Rome knew well because of the high-profile adoptions that took place within the imperial family. The second-century historian Appian, for example, says that after Julius Caesar's murder, his adopted son Octavius refused to give up his adoption as Caesar's son and the inheritance that went with it despite the possibility that public sentiment might also turn against him (*Civil Wars* 3.11, 13). Paul informs his Roman audience that their status is much higher than even this: they are heirs of God and fellow heirs of Christ. The term "Christ" may retain for Paul in this instance its royal connotations derived from the use of the term in Psalm 2:2 (LXX) and the subsequent use of this psalm to refer to God's anointed king, the Messiah, who would rule the earth (e.g., Pss. Sol. 17:32; 18:5, 7).[71]

By the expression "if indeed" Paul did not intend to raise doubts about whether the people in his audience really were "heirs of God" and "fellow heirs of Christ." The expression takes its nuance from the "if" clause in its context, in this case "if children," and describes a logical connection between suffering with Christ and being coheirs with Christ. A condition is implied (those who do not suffer with Christ are not his coheirs), but that is not where the emphasis lies. Instead Paul emphasized that those who, because of their commitment to the gospel, share the physical pain and public shame that Christ endured when he was crucified will also experience the vindication and release from pain that he experienced when he was raised from the dead (cf. 2 Cor 4:10–11; Phil 3:20–21). Paul had said earlier in the letter that all had sinned and lacked "the glory of God" (3:23). Now he shows that through their union with Christ this lack will be supplied. This is the "hope of glory" that Christian suffering instills in the believer according to 5:2–4.

70. The expression "witnesses together with" can mean simply "bears witness" or "bears witness to" (cf. 2:15; 9:1; see Wallace, *Greek Grammar*, 160–61), but since the context here speaks of two separate parties, the term probably has its frequent meaning of "bear witness with" (LSJ 1677; MM 610, s.v. συνμαρτυρέω). See also Fee, *God's Empowering Presence*, 568–69.

71. So, correctly, Wright, "Romans," 594.

Theology in Application

Romans 8:1–17 describes the change that comes to the person God has freed from the sort of slavery to sin Paul depicted in 7:7–25. Because God's Spirit has now made his home within Christians, he has reoriented their lives. This has practical results for their present existence, and these practical results can be described in four ways.

The Fulfillment of the Law

First, the Spirit enables Christians to fulfill God's law (8:1–4). This is not the Mosaic law, at least not in the sense that first-century Jews defined it. For Paul, God's law included neither circumcision nor Sabbath keeping, for example, and no Jew would have said that someone who neglected the observance of such important commands was keeping the Mosaic law. God's law did include, however, the principle articulated in Leviticus 19:18, a principle that Paul interprets as covering the seventh through tenth commands of the Decalogue (Rom 13:8–10; cf. Gal 5:14). Paul's teaching at this point coincides with Jesus's teaching on the two greatest commandments (Matt 22:36-40; Mark 12:28–34; cf. John 13:34).

The Spirit, then, enables Christians to make progress in loving others in the way that the ethical principles of the Old Testament and the teaching of Jesus defined love. The importance that Paul gives to the Christian's fulfillment of the law in this new sense is evident from the position of the purpose clause in Romans 8:4. God used the incarnation and death of Christ to make it possible for Christians to fulfill God's desire that they love others.[72] The Roman Christians needed to ponder the implications of this startling theological truth for their own attitudes toward one another (14:1, 3–4, 10–13, 19; 15:1–2), and Christians in every age need to do the same.

A New Alliance with the Spirit

Second, Paul argues that Christians have a new alliance with the Spirit rather than the flesh and that this new alliance comes from a new mindset (8:5–8). Just as rebellion against God began with suppression of the truth, futile thinking, darkened hearts, and a failure to acknowledge God (1:18, 21, 25, 28, 32; cf. Eph 4:17–18), and just as this mental rebellion bore fruit in twisted and vicious behavior toward others (Rom 1:26–27, 29–30; cf. Eph 4:19), so now the Spirit brings Christians a new mind whose focus is life and peace.

The "for" that begins Romans 8:5 is important for understanding the logical relationship between the Christian's mind and the Christian's behavior. Christians walk

72. Stott, *Romans*, 222.

according to the Spirit *because* they take the Spirit's side in the Spirit-flesh conflict and now think the way the Spirit wants them to think. Christians in ancient Rome were surrounded with messages, whether depicted on statuary and friezes or written in inscriptions, that proclaimed the eternality, power, and glory of Rome, its emperors, and its gods.[73] It would have been easy for this propaganda, sometimes conveyed through images of almost overwhelming size and beauty, to sway the Roman Christians toward thinking that its message was true. Paul tells his readers, however, that this mindset leads to death and that its opposing mindset—the mindset of the Spirit—leads to life and peace.

The cultures surrounding most Christians today proclaim a similarly persuasive and misleading message about the nature of human existence and the pathways to lasting happiness, to "life and peace" in Pauline terms. The message that comes through multiple media is often that consumption of goods and power over others leads to self-fulfillment and therefore to happiness. Paul's message in Romans 8:5–8 is that the Spirit enables Christians, despite such unrelenting propaganda ("the mindset of the flesh"), to opt out of this system and to have minds shaped instead by the word of God, what Paul calls "the law" in 8:4.

Hope for a Better Self and a Better World

Third, the Spirit's transforming power in the lives of believers does not mean that their lives will be completely free from sin or entirely peaceful. Believers still have bodies that are mortal, and "the flesh" with its sinful tendencies still affects these mortal bodies, urging them to rebel against God. Paul reminds his readers, then, that their future existence will be like Jesus's present existence. Just as God raised Jesus from the dead and gave him an immortal existence, so their bodies will one day leave behind the sin, suffering, and death that are an inevitable part of existence in the present world. If they follow the Spirit's leading and avoid succumbing to the persuasions of the unbelieving world around them, they will live in immortality and in sinless perfection with Christ in eternity. Similarly, Christians in the present can take comfort that the world is not now what it will always be, nor are they, as individuals, what God will one day make them. Perseverance in resisting the world's mindset is necessary, but Paul is optimistic that with the Spirit's enabling power believers can persevere through the spiritual dangers in the world around them and live eternally.

73. Paul Zanker, *The Power of Images in the Age of Augustus*, trans. Alan Shapiro (Ann Arbor: University of Michigan Press, 1988), 101–66, 336; James R. Harrison, "Augustan Rome and the Body of Christ: A Comparison of the Social Vision of the *Res Gestae* and Paul's Letter to the Romans," *HTR* 106 (2013): 1–36.

Acceptance from a Loving and Faithful Father

Fourth, Paul wants the Romans to understand that God has adopted them into his family, giving them the status of highly privileged children within it (8:15). Their status as sons and daughters of God is similar in important ways to Jesus's own status as God's Son. When they experience physical and emotional suffering, just as Jesus did before his passion, they too can cry out to God as their Father (Mark 14:36; cf. Rom 8:15). Their status as God's adoptive sons and daughters is a sign of God's love and permanent commitment to them, both now, in the midst of their suffering, and in eternity when they will share the family "inheritance" of a fully restored creation (8:17; cf. 8:23).

Like the first Christians, Christians often live today in societies that misunderstand, ostracize, and sometimes even punish them for their commitment to Christ. Paul's words to the Roman Christians, however, are true for believers of all times and places. Whatever the societies in which they live may think of them, Christians are nevertheless honored members of God's family. As their Father, God is concerned about their suffering and will bring all injustice, oppression, and suffering to an end.

CHAPTER 18

Romans 8:18–30

Literary Context

Prompted by his mention of sharing Christ's suffering and glory in the last sentence of the previous paragraph (8:17), Paul now returns to the themes that dominated the opening paragraphs of the second major section of the letter's argument (5:1–5, 12–14).[1] At the beginning of the section, Paul had said that those who have been justified by faith boast in the hope of the glory of God (5:1–2). They boast even in their experience of suffering because God assures them, through the Holy Spirit's presence, that God loves them and that their hope in him is not misplaced (5:3–5). In 8:18–30 Paul explains in greater detail what this means, using themes he has introduced into the argument in 8:1–17.

"The hope of the glory of God" (5:2) turns out to be more specifically the hope of resurrection from the dead, of sharing, that is, in the immortality in which Christ himself now exists after his own resurrection (8:21–23, 29). Paul had introduced this idea in 8:11 where he had stated that just as God, by his Spirit, had raised Christ from the dead so he will give life to the mortal bodies of those in whom his Spirit dwells. Now Paul says that the mortality the believer continues to experience in the present is part of the death and decay that afflicts all creation because of Adam's sin and God's subsequent curse (8:20–23). The future resurrection of believers' bodies, however, is part of a plan to end the suffering not just of believers but of all creation (8:23). The hope of the believer (8:24–25) includes the hope that all creation will be freed from the decay and death that Adam introduced and that sinful humanity after him perpetuated (8:20).

In 5:5 Paul had said that the believer can be certain of the hope of glory despite the suffering that he or she experiences, because God has poured his Holy Spirit into the hearts of believers and thus demonstrates his love for them. Now in 8:18–30 he revisits the theme of God's loving presence with his suffering people and becomes more specific about how the Spirit assures them that despite their suffering they have

1. Cf. Dunn, *Romans 1–8*, 467; Fee, *God's Empowering Presence*, 517–18; Moo, *Romans*, 508–10; Jewett, *Romans*, 506.

no cause for shame. Paul does not speak explicitly of God's "love" in this passage, but that idea is implicit in the language of adoptive sonship Paul introduced in 8:14–17.[2]

Now he clarifies his use of that concept to say that believers will only see and experience this status in its fullness in the future. The suffering of the present obscures the status of God's children that believers currently possess. In this period of suffering, however, believers can nevertheless be confident that they are God's adoptive children because of the presence of God's Spirit among them. The Spirit serves as the "firstfruit," or guarantee, of the glorious bodily resurrection, of the restoration of all creation, and of the status of believers as God's children (8:23, 29). The Spirit also helps believers in their weakness in various ways, but prominent among them is the Spirit's intercession in the midst of their suffering (8:26–27). Although believers will not fully experience the benefits of being children of God until the future resurrection, therefore, God's love is nevertheless evident to them in the troubled present through the assistance of God's Spirit.

Paul will bring to a close in the next paragraph (8:31–39) his reflections on how the crucified and risen Christ displays God's love. The substance of his argument from 5:1 forward, however, concludes here in 8:18–30. Those who have been justified by faith have started to live a new, eschatologically oriented life characterized by the presence of God's Spirit in and with them and by the hope the Spirit gives. The Spirit's presence assures believers of God's love and of the bright future that awaits them even as the suffering of the sinful world around them continues to trouble their existence.

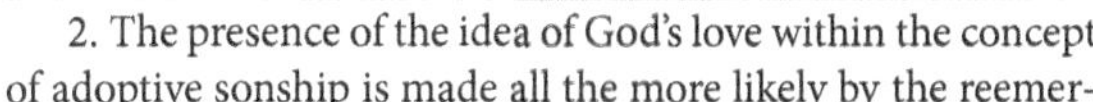

2. The presence of the idea of God's love within the concept of adoptive sonship is made all the more likely by the reemergence of explicit references to the love of Christ and of God in 8:35 and 39.

Main Idea

Although believers are united with the risen Christ and therefore, like him, are the beloved children of God, this status is not yet visible. The suffering of the world in which believers must live, and their own suffering within that world, obscure the reality of their adoptive sonship. Within this context of suffering, however, believers have hope that they will one day fully experience their status as God's children. This will happen when God gives them immortal bodies like the immortal body of God's resurrected Son and releases all creation from the suffering that human sin has brought to it. In the meantime, God has given his Spirit to his people. The Spirit assures them that their hope is not misplaced and helps them cope with the trouble they must face.

Translation

Romans 8:18–30

18a	Explanation (of 17b–c)	For **I reckon that the sufferings of the present time are not worth weighing against**
b	Comparison (to 18a)	**the glory about to be revealed in us.**
19	Basis (of 18)	For **the eager expectation of creation awaits the revelation of the sons of God.**
20a	Basis (of 19)	For **the creation was subjected to futility,**
b		not willingly, but
c	Contrast (to 20b)	because of the One who subjected it,
d	Sphere	in hope
21a	Basis (of 20d)	because the creation also will be set free
b		from slavery to decay
c		for the freedom of the glory of the children of God.
22a	Explanation (of 21b)	For **we know that the whole creation groans and suffers birth pangs**
b		in all its parts
c		up to the present time.
23a	Comparison (to 22a)	And not only so, but **we too ... we ourselves also groan,**
b	Concession	although we have the firstfruit of the Spirit,
c	Simultaneous	while we await adoption as sons,
d	Identification (of 23b)	the deliverance of our bodies.

24a	Basis (for 23c)	For **we were saved in hope.**
b		**Now hope that is seen is not hope,**
c	Basis (for 24b)	for **who hopes for what he or she sees?**
25a	Contrast (to 24c)	But if we do not see what we hope for,
b		**we wait for it** with endurance.
26a	Comparison (to 24b)	And likewise also, **the Spirit helps our weakness;**
b	Basis (for 26a)	for **we do not know**
c	Content	what it is necessary to pray,
d	Contrast (with 26b)	but **the Spirit himself intercedes**
e	Instrument	with wordless groans.
27a	Explanation (of 26)	And **the one who searches hearts knows**
b	Content	what the mindset of the Spirit is
c	Basis (for 27a)	because he intercedes on behalf of the saints according to God's will.
28a	Explanation (of 26a)	And **we know that for those who love God all things work together for good,**
b		for those who are called according to [God's] purpose.
29a	Basis (for 28a)	Because those whom he knew beforehand he also
b		decided beforehand would be similar in form to the image of his Son,
c	Purpose	in order that he might be the firstborn among many brothers and sisters.
30a	Explanation (of 29)	And those on whom he decided beforehand
b	Expansion (of 30a)	**these he also called;**
c		and those whom he called,
d	Expansion (of 30b–c)	**these also he justified;**
e		and those whom he justified,
f	Expansion (of 30d–e)	**these also he glorified.**

Structure

The passage begins and ends with a reference to the glorification of believers and explores the theme of the relationship between their glorification and the sufferings that they presently experience along with the rest of creation because of sin. The first sentence (8:18) announces the theme that will dominate the passage: "The sufferings of the present time are not worth weighing against the glory about to be revealed in us."[3] The argument of the passage then unfolds in four major steps, divided by the phrases "and not only" (8:23), "and likewise also" (8:26), and "and we know" (8:28).

In the first step Paul describes the entanglement of all creation in the suffering that Adam introduced into the world with his rebellion against God. This suffering is accompanied by an eagerness for the fulfillment of the hope that God held out to humanity even as he placed it under a curse for its disobedience (8:19–22). In the second step Paul describes the suffering that comes to believers as a result of their continued existence in this same plight and their hope for the immortal existence that they and all creation will have after God raises them from the dead (8:23–25). In the third step Paul describes how God has given his Spirit to his people in the difficulties they face prior to the realization of this hope. The Spirit helps them in many ways, but especially by joining them in intercession to God for the strength they need to cope with suffering (8:26–27). The fourth section assures believers of God's intention to glorify them in the end, just as he glorified Jesus, who also suffered (cf. 8:17). This section argues that all God has done for believers in the past makes their future glorification so certain that they can think of it as also in the past (8:28–30).

Exegetical Outline

IX. Justification by Faith Brings Peace and Reorients the Believer's Existence (5:1–8:39)

- A. Justification by Faith Rescues Believers from God's Present and Future Wrath (5:1–11)
- B. Christ's Obedience Overwhelms the Effects of Adam's Disobedience (5:12–21)
- C. Union with Christ's Death and Resurrection Initiates a New Life (6:1–23)
- D. Union with Christ's Death and Resurrection Frees Believers from the Law (7:1–6)
- E. The Goodness, Yet Inability, of the Law (7:7–25)
- **F. God's Solution to the Human Plight (8:1–39)**
  - 1. Christ's Work and the Spirit's Power Overcome the Sinful Flesh (8:1–17)
  - ➦ **2. God's Spirit Helps Believers Cope with Suffering as They Await Future Immortality (8:18–30)**
    - a. A summary of the section's theme (8:18)
    - b. Creation suffers as a result of Adam's sin, but does so in hope (8:19–22).
    - c. Believers share both the suffering and the hope of creation (8:23–25).
    - d. God's Spirit aids believers as they await the realization of their hope (8:26–27).
    - e. God's past work in the lives of believers assures them that their hope will not be disappointed (8:28–30).

3. Michel, *An die Römer*, 264; Moo, *Romans*, 510.

Explanation of the Text

8:18 For I reckon that the sufferings of the present time are not worth weighing against the glory about to be revealed in us (Λογίζομαι γὰρ ὅτι οὐκ ἄξια τὰ παθήματα τοῦ νῦν καιροῦ πρὸς τὴν μέλλουσαν δόξαν ἀποκαλυφθῆναι εἰς ἡμᾶς). The suffering that those who are united with Christ must endure is insignificant in comparison with the experience of God's splendor and power that awaits believers in the future because of their union with the risen Christ.

The "for" (γάρ) that begins this sentence is probably connected to an unexpressed concern based on what Paul has just said about suffering as the path to glory. Is the glory at the end of this path worth the trouble experienced along the way?[4] The adjective "worth" (ἄξια) implies a comparison, sometimes a metaphorical comparison of monetary worth. Speaking of "insight," Proverbs 3:13–15 LXX, for example, says that it is "far better to trade in her than in treasures of gold and silver . . . and nothing valuable is worth her [πᾶν δὲ τίμιον οὐκ ἄξιον αὐτῆς ἐστιν]."[5] The notion of calculation implicit in Paul's use of the term translated "reckon," then, is probably intentional (KJV, REB; cf. TOB). Paul is not merely saying that he "considers" or "believes" the present suffering of Christians to be outweighed by their future glorification (e.g., NIV, NRSV, ESV) but that a sober calculation of their relative weight yields this result (cf. 2 Cor 4:17).[6]

Paul has associated the term "glory" (δόξα) in Romans with God's splendor visible in creation (1:23), with the immortality of those to whom God gives eternal life (2:7), and with the power of God that raised Christ from the dead (6:4). In 5:2 he has said that believers have a firm hope of one day sharing in God's glory. Paul speaks here, then, of the believer's hope of becoming immortal like God himself and like the risen Christ (8:17). If this is correct, then the revelation of God's glory is not an unveiling of the glory that believers presently have (despite the past tense reference to the glorification of believers in 8:30) but the experience of sharing in God's glory for which they now hope (cf. 8:21).[7]

This glory will be revealed, Paul says, "in us." The term translated "in" here (εἰς) implies motion toward an object from the outside that then takes the motion "into" the object.[8] The future revelation of God's glory, therefore, will not merely be a revelation of something "to" God's people, but "in" them as well. It comes to them from the outside and transforms them (cf. 1 Cor 15:43; 2 Cor 3:18; Phil 3:21).[9]

8:19 For the eager expectation of creation awaits the revelation of the sons of God (ἡ γὰρ ἀποκαραδοκία τῆς κτίσεως τὴν ἀποκάλυψιν τῶν υἱῶν τοῦ θεοῦ ἀπεκδέχεται). Evidence of the glorious nature of the future that awaits believers is found in creation. Its disordered state cries out for restoration, and this restoration will take place when God's gracious purposes for his people are complete.

4. On this use of "for" (γάρ), see BDAG 189, s.v. γάρ 1e, and for this interpretation of what motivated Paul to make this comparison, see Calvin, *Romans*, 171.

5. My translation, which is a slightly modified version of NETS.

6. Godet, *Romans*, 312; Sanday and Headlam, *Romans*, 206; Lagrange, *Romains*, 204.

7. Meyer, *Romans*, 319; Dunn, *Romans 1–8*, 468. For the view that Paul speaks of the revelation of a glory that is now present but hidden, see Chrysostom, *Romans*, 243; Cranfield, *Romans*, 1:409; Jewett, *Romans*, 511.

8. Harris, *Prepositions and Theology*, 83–84.

9. Cranfield, *Romans*, 1:410; Wilckens, *An die Römer (Röm 6–11)*, 151–52n645. In Gal 1:16 Paul can speak of his conversion as the revelation of God's Son "in [ἐν] me" (NIV).

The "for" (γάρ) at the beginning of this sentence indicates that it serves as support for Paul's immediately preceding statement about the greatness of the glory that believers will experience in the future.[10] The "eager expectation" of creation in the present is evidence of the comparative greatness of the glory to come.

The expression "eager expectation" translates a Greek term (ἀποκαραδοκία) that appears here and in Philippians 1:20 for the first time in the known history of the Greek language, and for centuries later shows up only in quotations and allusions to these two texts. Its associated verb (ἀποκαραδοκέω) could refer to awaiting something in several different ways, whether simply waiting for an event to happen with no note of intensity intended (Polybius, *Histories* 18.48.4; 21.36.3), waiting for something harmful with anxiety (Josephus, *J.W.* 3.264; Plutarch, *Mor.* 310 E), or waiting for a desired outcome with hopeful anxiety (*Historia Alexandri Magni*, recension β, 3.32.1). Since Paul's use of the term in Philippians 1:20 matches this third use fairly closely and since here in Romans 8:19 Paul pictures creation awaiting deliverance, he probably intended this third nuance of hopeful tension (NASB, Luther).[11]

Waiting eagerly is something that people do, and so Paul has personified nonhuman creation in its suffering under the punishment that God gave to Adam after his sin in the garden. "Cursed is the ground because of you," God had told him (Gen 3:17). The long-standing debate over whether by "creation" Paul means the nonhuman elements of creation or all creation, including humans, should be decided in favor of creation apart from human beings since Paul's next sentence (8:20) recalls how God's curse on Adam involved a curse on the ground because of Adam's disobedience.[12] Paul pictures creation as an innocent bystander caught up in the consequences of Adam's rebellion and eagerly awaiting release from those consequences.

Jewett has plausibly argued that the understanding of creation as suffering the effects of human sin stood in sharp contrast to Roman imperial propaganda about a new golden age that was current in the mid first-century AD.[13] This myth pictured the peace Augustus had brought to the empire as extending to the natural order. The left side of the doorway of the massive Altar of Peace provides an example of how the Roman government projected this myth to the public. The altar walls show a woman, probably the earth goddess Tellus, with two children climbing on her, fruit in her lap, plants flourishing behind her, and healthy animals at her feet feeding and relaxing after a good meal.[14] On the opposite side of the doorway was the goddess Roma, sitting atop a mound of armor and communicating the message that under the rule of Augustus, Rome's military might had brought fertility and happiness to the earth, with all their associated benefits for Rome's people.[15]

This propaganda was experiencing a revival during the early years of Nero's reign and is visible in the poetry of Calpurnius Siculus, written in Rome in AD 55.[16] Calpurnius sings the praises of Nero as the author of a new "golden age" and as "that very god who is sovereign over nations and cities and toga-clad peace" (*Eclogues* 4.6–8).[17]

10. Cranfield, *Romans*, 1:410.

11. Cf. Chrysostom, *Romans*, 244 ("expecting intensely" [ἡ σφοδρὰ προσδοκία (*PG* 60.529)]).

12. Cf. Cranfield, *Romans*, 1:411; Dunn, *Romans 1–8*, 469.

13. Jewett, *Romans*, 511–12.

14. Giuseppe Moretti, *The Ara Pacis Augustae*, 4th ed., trans. Veronica Priestley, Itineraries of the Museums, Galleries and Monuments in Italy 67 (Rome: Istituto Poligrafico dello Stato, 1975), 10; Zanker, *Power of Images in the Age of Augustus*, 172–76.

15. Zanker, *Power of Images in the Age of Augustus*, 175.

16. Jewett, *Romans*, 509. On the date of the fourth *Eclogue*, see Beate Fey-Wickert, "C. Siculus, T.," *BNPA* 2:1004.

17. Trans. J. Wight Duff and Arnold M. Duff, *Minor Latin Poets*, 2 vols., LCL (Cambridge: Harvard University Press, 1934).

At the sound of Caesar's name, Calpurnius says, strong winds become silent, young lambs become energetic, their mothers produce an abundance of milk, and their fleece grows quickly and thickly (*Eclogues* 4.187–202).

Paul had not seen the Altar of Peace, nor had he read Calpurnius Siculus, but, writing from the Roman city of Corinth, he would have been aware of this kind of propaganda and would probably have understood how his sentence in 8:19 would be heard in Rome. Among the poor Christians living on the edges of the city and across the Tiber River in towering, dark, and smelly apartment complexes, the earth hardly appeared to be experiencing a golden age. Creation was instead waiting for the restoration that its true Creator and Sustainer would bring to it, and especially to "the sons of God," that is, his people, whose glorification with God's own Son would one day be complete (cf. 8:17, 23). This is the sense in which the "sons of God" will be revealed. When they are resurrected from the dead and fully redeemed, their status as sons of God will be unmistakable (cf. Col 3:4).[18]

8:20 For the creation was subjected to futility, not willingly, but because of the One who subjected it, in hope (τῇ γὰρ ματαιότητι ἡ κτίσις ὑπετάγη, οὐχ ἑκοῦσα ἀλλὰ διὰ τὸν ὑποτάξαντα, ἐφ' ἑλπίδι). When God punished Adam for his disobedience, creation itself was caught up in this curse and became unable, for the time being, to make progress toward the goal for which God had made it. God did not intend this situation of frustration to be a permanent condition.

The "for" (γάρ) introduces the reason why creation eagerly awaits the full glorification of God's people.[19] "Futility" (ματαιότης) marks creation's existence in the present.

Here this term refers to the inability of creation to accomplish the purpose for which it was created. It is the "vanity" of Ecclesiastes where, in the LXX, the term appears thirty-nine times and the futility of life without God is the theme of the book. "Everything is meaningless [ματαιότης]," says the Preacher. "What do people gain from all their labors at which they toil under the sun?" (Eccl 1:2–3 NIV). This was the condition to which God subjected creation because of Adam's sin (Gen 3:17–19; cf. Rom 5:12–19).[20] Yet Paul asserts that God did not do this in an unqualified way. Even as God subjected creation to futility, he provided people with "hope."

8:21 because the creation also will be set free from slavery to decay for the freedom of the glory of the children of God (ὅτι καὶ αὐτὴ ἡ κτίσις ἐλευθερωθήσεται ἀπὸ τῆς δουλείας τῆς φθορᾶς εἰς τὴν ἐλευθερίαν τῆς δόξης τῶν τέκνων τοῦ θεοῦ). When God restores his human creation to the glory that he originally intended for it, the rest of creation will also be restored to a condition in which there is no ruin or death.

The term rendered "because" (ὅτι [cf. Tyndale, Luther, KJV, RSV, TOB]) often appears in translations as "that" (NIV, REB, NRSV, ESV, HCSB, CEB). If this is correct, then the next phrase describes the content of the hope that accompanied God's subjection of creation to futility.[21] "Because" is more likely the meaning, however, since "in hope" qualifies the action of God, and when God gives hope

18. Cf. Harry Alan Hahne, *The Corruption and Redemption of Creation: Nature in Romans 8.19–22 and Jewish Apocalyptic Literature*, LNTS 336 (London: T&T Clark, 2006), 184–85.

19. Hahne, *Corruption and Redemption*, 186.

20. See, e.g., Sanday and Headlam, *Romans*, 208.

21. Some manuscripts clearly read "because" here (διότι), and this may be the right reading since it has early and geographically diverse support (א D F G 2127). A scribe's eye could easily have skipped from the final syllable of the previous word (ἐλπί-δι) directly to the last syllable of the next word (δι-ότι). On this, see Jewett, *Romans*, 504 note "d."

there is no uncertainty about whether or not it will come to pass (cf. 5:5).[22] This is not a hope "that" God will set creation free; it is a firmly grounded hope "because" God will certainly set creation free.

The term "also" (καί), although translations often leave it out (RSV, NAB, NIV, NRSV, ESV, CEB), is important because it illustrates the immensely glorious nature of "the revelation of the sons of God" (8:18–19). The time in which God's family experiences the glory of full union with Christ (cf. 8:17) will be so glorious that not only his children but all creation will be caught up in the transformation.

Paul explains what "glory" (δόξα) means in the phrases that follow. God will free both his creation and his children from "decay" (φθορά). When Greek speakers applied this term to living things, they referred to their tendency to become sick, tired, and die (LXX Ps 102:4 [Eng. 103:4]; Jonah 2:7). "Decay" was the process by which a seed fell apart when a farmer planted it in the earth (1 Cor 15:42). It was the tendency of flesh and blood to cease functioning normally (1 Cor 15:50; cf. Gal 6:8), or the inevitable process by which material objects collapsed and food spoiled (Col 2:22).

According to Roman propaganda preserved in an inscription from Priene in Roman Asia, Augustus had already set the world free from "decay."[23] It is probable that Paul and his readers were familiar with such propaganda, and if so, Paul's statement would have stood in clear contradiction to it. Paul asserts that the inevitable process of decay to which the world is so obviously enslaved (despite imperial mythologizing to the contrary) is not God's final intention for his creation, and one day he will set it free from this process.[24] Paul's perspective arises from Scripture, which spoke of God's eventual creation of "new heavens and a new earth" (Isa 65:17; 66:22; cf. 2 Cor 5:17; Gal 6:15).[25]

8:22 For we know that the whole creation groans and suffers birth pangs in all its parts up to the present time (οἴδαμεν γὰρ ὅτι πᾶσα ἡ κτίσις συστενάζει καὶ συνωδίνει ἄχρι τοῦ νῦν). God's subhuman creation continues to be caught up, in all its parts and as a whole, in the suffering that Adam introduced into the world when he sinned against God.

"For" (γάρ) introduces support for Paul's statement that the subhuman creation is in bondage to decay, and the expression "we know" (οἴδαμεν) refers to something that believers know because God has revealed it to them, whether in Scripture or in Christian teaching (2:2; 3:19; 7:14; 8:28).[26] An example of the traditional teaching Paul could have had in mind appears in Isaiah 24:4–13 where "the earth mourns" and "the world languishes" (24:4) because its inhabitants have "transgressed the laws, violated the statutes, broken the everlasting covenant" (24:5).[27]

The two terms "groan together" (συστενάζω) and "suffer birth pangs together" (συνωδίνω) are extraordinarily rare and, where they do occur, do not necessarily refer to childbirth (Aristotle,

22. Hultgren, *Romans*, 323.

23. MM 668.

24. The translation "slavery to decay" assumes that the genitive-case phrase (τῆς φθορᾶς) is a subjective genitive: decay enslaves the created order. Cf. Thucydides, *History of the Peloponnesian War* 1.8.3, where the weak are subject to "the dominion of the stronger" (τὴν τῶν κρεισσόνων δουλείαν) (*The Landmark Thucydides: A Comprehensive Guide to the Peloponnesian War*, trans. Richard Crawley and Robert B. Strassler [New York: Free Press, 1996], 7). On this, see Cranfield, *Romans*, 1:415.

25. This perspective also appears in Jewish apocalyptic literature from the first and early second century, indicating that the themes Paul treats in 8:19–22 were fairly widely discussed in his time (e.g., 1 En. 45:4–5; 72:1; 2 Bar 73–74). On this, see Hahne, *Corruption and Redemption*, 97–152.

26. Hahne, *Corruption and Redemption*, 199–200.

27. Ibid., 201.

Eudemian Ethics 1240a.36; Euripides, *Helen* 727; T. Iss. 7:5), but here the idea of birth pangs, with their mixture of pain and hope, is particularly appropriate to the context. The hope of glorification with the sons of God ameliorates the pain that creation experiences now, caught up as it is in the consequences of human sin.[28] Creation experiences this pain as a whole "together with" all its constituent parts, not "together with" believers, as the division between believers and creation implied in the next verse makes clear.[29] The REB captures the nuance precisely with its rendering, "the whole created universe in all its parts groans as if in the pangs of childbirth."

8:23 And not only so, but we too, although we have the firstfruit of the Spirit, we ourselves also groan while we await adoption as sons, the deliverance of our bodies (οὐ μόνον δέ, ἀλλὰ καὶ αὐτοὶ τὴν ἀπαρχὴν τοῦ πνεύματος ἔχοντες, ἡμεῖς καὶ αὐτοὶ ἐν ἑαυτοῖς στενάζομεν υἱοθεσίαν ἀπεκδεχόμενοι, τὴν ἀπολύτρωσιν τοῦ σώματος ἡμῶν). Despite the presence of the eschatological Spirit in their communities, believers nevertheless suffer alongside the rest of creation, but this suffering is infused with the hope that in the future God will deliver their bodies from degeneration, sickness, and death.

Paul's threefold use of intensifiers of the first-person plural subject of this sentence (αὐτοί, αὐτοί, ἡμεῖς) expresses a contrast between the created order generally and believers. Both creation and believers groan under the weight of sin's consequences, but the groaning of believers is more remarkable since they have the Spirit. Read this way, the participle "having" (ἔχοντες) should be understood concessively ("although we have") rather than causally ("because we have").[30] Even the Spirit does not rescue believers in the present time from the results of sin within God's creation (cf. 2 Cor 5:2, 4).

Nevertheless, the Spirit does provide believers with hope. This is the force of the metaphorical expression "firstfruit" that Paul uses to describe the Spirit. The LXX used this term (ἀπαρχή) for the harvest's first part, which was offered to the Lord (e.g., Lev 2:12; Num 18:12–13).[31] Here the term simply refers to the first part of something larger (cf. Rom 11:16; 16:5; 1 Cor 16:15; 2 Thess 2:13) and carries eschatological connotations that God's restoration of his creation has begun with the Spirit's work among believers but that much more will eventually follow (cf. 1 Cor 15:20, 23). Paul communicates the same idea elsewhere when he speaks of the "down payment" (ἀρραβών) of the Spirit (2 Cor 1:22; 5:5; Eph 1:14; HCSB; CEB).[32]

Paul describes the eschatological blessing to come as "adoption" (υἱοθεσία), the status that according to 8:15 the children of God have already received. Paul's statement in 8:19 that creation awaits "the revelation of the sons of God" easily resolves the surface discrepancy that this future adoption introduces into the text. Believers are adopted children of God in the present, as 8:15–17 implies, but God has not yet made their status as his sons and daughters publicly known.

28. Ibid., 202–5.

29. Cranfield, *Romans*, 1:416–17; Hahne, *Corruption and Redemption*, 205.

30. With, e.g., Meyer (*Romans*, 327) and Käsemann (*Romans*, 237) rather than Dunn (*Romans 1–8*, 473–74), Moo (*Romans*, 520), and Schreiner (*Romans*, 438).

31. Gerhard Delling, "ἀπαρχή," *TDNT* 1:485; Dunn, *Romans 1–8*, 473.

32. As Fee points out (*God's Empowering Presence*, 573), these parallels mean that the genitive "of the Spirit" (τοῦ πνεύματος) cannot be partitive, as if only a first portion of the Spirit has been given to believers with more to follow, but must be appositional: the first portion, like the down payment elsewhere, is the Spirit.

Paul further defines "adoption as son" with the phrase "the deliverance of our bodies." The term "deliverance" (ἀπολύτρωσις) sometimes referred to the rescue of someone from slavery (e.g., Philo, *Good Person* 114), and in this context where Paul has just spoken of the slavery of creation to decay (Rom 8:21), it clearly carries these connotations.[33] The deliverance of the bodies of believers from decay would come when God raised them from the dead (8:11; cf. 1 Cor 15:43, 53; Phil 3:20).

8:24 For we were saved in hope. Now hope that is seen is not hope, for who hopes for what he or she sees? (τῇ γὰρ ἐλπίδι ἐσώθημεν· ἐλπὶς δὲ βλεπομένη οὐκ ἔστιν ἐλπίς· ὃ γὰρ βλέπει τίς ἐλπίζει;). When people believe the gospel, they begin to base their lives on the confidence that one day God will deliver them from the results of sin. God's victory over sin is not obvious in the present, but they nevertheless are certain that it will happen.

Paul's "for" (γάρ) introduces the reason why believers await the full experience of their deliverance from creation's decay. Their existence is marked by waiting because they "were saved in hope," and "hope," by definition, involves waiting to "see" what one does not now experience. The expression "in hope" renders a dative of sphere (τῇ . . . ἐλπίδι), indicating the context in which the salvation of believers has taken place.[34] Just as Abraham expressed his faith in the context of the hope that God would make him the father of many nations, even if that meant giving life to the dead (4:17), so those who believe the gospel express their faith within the context of hope for the resurrection of the dead (8:11) and deliverance from slavery to decay (8:21).

This hope, moreover, is not a wavering wish that somehow things will work out for the best, but is confidence, based on the presence of God's Spirit and the love displayed in the atoning death of Christ, that God will rescue his people from the ravages of sin (5:2, 4). This confidence is so firm that Paul can speak here of salvation as if it had already taken place (cf. Eph 2:5, 8; 2 Tim 1:9; Titus 3:5), whereas elsewhere in Romans salvation lies in the future (Rom 5:9–10; 9:27; 10:9; 11:26).

8:25 But if we do not see what we hope for, we wait for it with endurance (εἰ δὲ ὃ οὐ βλέπομεν ἐλπίζομεν, δι᾽ ὑπομονῆς ἀπεκδεχόμεθα). The hope that believers have for the resurrection of the dead and the full experience of life in the family of God provides encouragement to persevere in their commitment to the gospel through the inevitable difficulties of existence in a sinful world.

The conjunction "but" (δέ) introduces a contrast to the absurd thought at the end of the previous sentence that someone might hope for something they already see and experience. If no one hopes for what they see, then hope implies waiting for what is unseen "with endurance." The term "endurance" (ὑπομονή) refers to patient persistence through various challenges and difficulties (5:3–4; see on 2:6), and the phrase "with endurance" (δι᾽ ὑπομονῆς) describes the circumstances in which the hopeful waiting of believers take place (cf. 2:27; 4:11; 14:20).[35]

Although Paul did not describe the circumstances of Abraham's hope in God back in 4:18–22 as "endurance," he probably thought of Abraham as exhibiting the sort of hopeful perseverance that he describes here. Abraham could only "see" his and Sarah's physically depleted bodies, but despite this he had faith and hope in God's ability to do what he had promised to make him the father of many

33. See the comments on this word, often translated "redemption" (e.g., KJV, NIV, NRSV, ESV), on 3:24.

34. Käsemann, *Romans*, 238.

35. BDAG 224, s.v. διά 3c.

nations. Paul makes the point that the Scriptures told this story to benefit believers in his own time (4:23–24). He could easily have been thinking of this part of the Abraham narrative when he wrote later in the letter that believers "have hope . . . through the endurance and the encouragement provided by the Scriptures" (15:4). Like Abraham, then, those who believe the gospel patiently persevere through the inevitable troubles of existence in a sinful world with the firm conviction that one day God will transform this existence into immortal life in God's family (cf. 4:24; 8:11, 15, 23).

8:26 And likewise also, the Spirit helps our weakness; for we do not know what it is necessary to pray, but the Spirit himself intercedes with wordless groans (Ὡσαύτως δὲ καὶ τὸ πνεῦμα συναντιλαμβάνεται τῇ ἀσθενείᾳ ἡμῶν· τὸ γὰρ τί προσευξώμεθα καθὸ δεῖ οὐκ οἴδαμεν, ἀλλὰ αὐτὸ τὸ πνεῦμα ὑπερεντυγχάνει στεναγμοῖς ἀλαλήτοις). The Spirit helps believers by entering their plight as they cope with existence in a sinful world and by articulating their suffering and their needs to God the Father. The Spirit does this in a more effective way than believers themselves are able to do in their own prayers.

The adverb "likewise" (ὡσαύτως) introduces a description of the similarity between the waiting of believers and the action of the Spirit.[36] The point of comparison is the involvement of both believers and the Spirit in the suffering that all creation has experienced since Adam's sin (5:12; 8:20). The Spirit does not remain aloof from the plight that believers experience along with the rest of creation but "helps" them in the midst of their troubles.

Luke 10:38–42 illustrates well the nuances of the term "helps" (συναντιλαμβάνεται) here. Martha, who had invited Jesus into her home, became "anxious and troubled about many things" related to showing Jesus hospitality. So she asked Jesus to urge her sister to stop sitting at Jesus's feet and instead "help" (συναντιλάβηται) her. Martha wanted someone to labor beside her to help relieve her stress and lighten her load. This is precisely the role that Paul gives to the Spirit here.

The Spirit gives a specific type of help to believers in their difficulties. Since they do not know what they should pray, given their limitations (cf. 11:33–34), the Spirit enters into their plight and intercedes with God on their behalf.[37]

The Spirit's wordless "groans" (στεναγμοί) recall the groaning ([συν-] στενάζω) of creation and believers (8:22–23) as a result of creation's subjection to futility after Adam's sin (8:20).[38] The term appears in the LXX description of how God heard the "groaning" of his people in slavery in Egypt (Exod 2:24; cf. Acts 7:34). It would be too speculative to say that Paul had this narrative in mind here, but the word's occurrence in that story demonstrates its appropriateness for describing the situation of metaphorical slavery from which believers are awaiting freedom and redemption (8:22–23).[39]

The term "wordless" (ἀλαλήτοις) does not refer to glossolalia (cf. 1 Cor 13:1; 14:9) or to the "inexpressible things" of paradise "that no one is permitted to tell" (2 Cor 12:4 NIV).[40] It simply emphasizes the inarticulate nature of the groans that characterize existence within a world subjected to futility (8:20). The Spirit enters into this existence

36. For the rendering of the first phrase as "and likewise also," see Godet, *Romans*, 320.

37. The Greek of this clause indicates that Paul speaks of what (τί) Christians should pray, and this should probably be understood both as the wording of their prayers (Sanday and Headlam, *Romans*, 213) and as the object of their prayers (Moo, *Romans*, 523). For the same view, see Alford, *Greek Testament*, 2:371.

38. Origen, *Romans, Books 6–10*, 80.

39. Cf. Légasse, *Romains*, 527.

40. See, respectively, e.g., Fee (*God's Empowering Presence*, 575–86) and Michel (*An die Römer*, 272).

in order to help believers and requests God's aid for believers in their plight.[41]

The term "intercedes" (ὑπερεντυγχάνω) refers to advocacy with a person in power on behalf of someone else. In his work *On Moses*, for example, Philo used a closely related word to refer to Moses's intercession with God in silent prayer (ἐνετύγχανεν ἀφανῶς τῷ θεῷ) for the Israelites who were trapped between the Red Sea and the vast Egyptian army on the hilltops above them (*Moses* 1.173).[42] In the same way, the Spirit intercedes with God on behalf of believers surrounded by a world suffering the effects of human rebellion against God.

8:27 And the one who searches hearts knows what the mindset of the Spirit is because he intercedes on behalf of the saints according to God's will (ὁ δὲ ἐραυνῶν τὰς καρδίας οἶδεν τί τὸ φρόνημα τοῦ πνεύματος, ὅτι κατὰ θεὸν ἐντυγχάνει ὑπὲρ ἁγίων). The Spirit is able to intercede effectively for believers because he not only knows what believers need in their distress but also because he knows, and is fully known by, God.

Paul continues to explain (δέ) how the Spirit's intercession on behalf of believers in their distress works. He has already said that the Spirit dwells within believers (8:9–11) and that there is mutual interaction between the spirit of believers and the indwelling Spirit of God (8:16). The Spirit, then, is able to communicate to God the needs that the inarticulate, distress-filled groaning of believers represents. The Spirit does this in a way that asks God not for what believers think they need (since they do not know either how to pray or what to pray for) but what they really need (8:26).

Now Paul explains that the Spirit is able to do this not only because he understands the human condition but because God fully understands the Spirit. God is "the one who searches hearts" (1 Chr 28:9; Jer 17:10; cf. 1 Thess 2:4), and so he knows the mindset of the Spirit. The clause that follows this description of God either gives the reason why Paul can say that God knows the mindset of the Spirit ("because" [ὅτι] the Spirit intercedes for the saints according to God's will), or it explains what the mindset of the Spirit is ("that" [ὅτι] the Spirit intercedes for the saints according to God's will).[43] The location of the prepositional phrase in the emphatic position in front of the verb (κατὰ θεόν ἐντυγχάνει) tilts the decision in favor of the causal rendering. God knows the mindset of the Spirit because the Spirit's intercession is "according to God," that is, according to the norm of God's own will.[44] As Paul puts it in 1 Corinthians 2:11, "no one comprehends the thoughts of God except the Spirit of God."

8:28 And we know that for those who love God all things work together for good, for those who are called according to [God's] purpose (οἴδαμεν δὲ ὅτι τοῖς ἀγαπῶσιν τὸν θεὸν πάντα συνεργεῖ εἰς ἀγαθόν, τοῖς κατὰ πρόθεσιν κλητοῖς οὖσιν). God orders the circumstances in which his people live so that these circumstances cooperate in bringing about his good purpose of delivering his people and creation from the effects of sin.

Paul's "and" (δέ), as with the conjunctions at the beginning of 8:26 and 27, shows that he continues to explain how God assists believers as they await deliverance from the suffering that sin has brought to the world (8:23, 25). This word of encouragement is something that Paul and his readers in

41. Cf. Moo, *Romans*, 526. Paul does not say that the Spirit prompts believers to pray with inarticulate groans, as Fee assumes throughout his discussion (*God's Empowering Presence*, 575–86) but that the Spirit "intercedes" for believers with wordless groans when believers pray.

42. *TLNT* 2:7.

43. See, respectively, e.g., Moo (*Romans*, 527) and Jewett (*Romans*, 525).

44. Alford, *Greek Testament*, 2:372; Moo, *Romans*, 527.

Rome already know, and many interpreters have pointed out that since Paul's statement has parallels elsewhere he was probably uttering a well-known truth.[45] Plato's Socrates claimed that if a just person experienced hardship it would turn out for the good, "either during his lifetime or afterwards, for the gods never neglect anyone who eagerly wishes to become just and who makes himself as much like a god as a human can by adopting a virtuous way of life" (*Republic* 613a [Grube and Reeve]).[46] Joseph makes clear to his brothers that although they intended to do him evil, "God meant it for good, to bring it about that many people should be kept alive, as they are today" (Gen 50:20).[47]

Neither of these parallels, however, expresses the essence of Paul's statement. It is true that he speaks of those who love God, but this love is a response to what God has already done, not, as in Plato, the effort to live a perfectly virtuous life. Joseph's statement is much closer to Paul's but is missing the specific focus on God's redemption of those who, at God's initiative, have entered a loving relationship with him (cf. Rom 1:7; 5:5, 8; 8:35, 37, 39). Moo, then, is correct to say that the mutual knowledge Paul and his readers share is probably not so much the traditional sentiments he is about to express but a shared knowledge and experience of God through his Son Jesus Christ.[48]

Although Paul often speaks of God's love for believers in Romans (1:7; 5:5, 8; 8:35, 37, 39), this is his only reference in the letter to their love for God.[49] The good that believers experience, then, is not a reward or repayment of their love. God is not like the sinners Jesus refers to in Luke 6:32–33 who only love and do good to those who first love and do good to them. The love that believers have for God is a response to the love that he first had for them while they were still sinners and enemies (5:8, 10). "Those who love God," then is a description of God's people, not a statement of the necessary requirement for God's blessing (cf., e.g., Exod 20:6; Deut 5:10; 6:5; 7:9; 30:6; cf. Matt 22:37; Mark 12:30; Luke 10:27).[50]

For God's people "all things work together for good." The Greek of this phrase is ambiguous since the relationship of the neuter plural term translated "all things" (πάντα) to the verb "work together" (συνεργεῖ) is unclear. "All things" could either be the subject of the verb ("all things work together for good," NRSV), the object of the verb, with God understood as the subject ("God causes all things to work together for good," NASB), or an adverbial modifier ("in all things God works for the good," NIV).[51]

It is probably not an adverbial modifier (an "accusative of respect") since this was a rare use of the accusative case in ancient Greek and other options make equally good sense of the sentence.[52] Similarly, there is no need to supply "God" as the subject of the sentence, since the sentence makes

45. Cf. 8:22 and the comments there.

46. Meyer (*Romans*, 333) regarded this as in some way parallel to Paul's statement.

47. See Dunn (*Romans 1–8*, 481), who also cites Eccl 8:12 and Sir 39:27, although Sir 39:27 seems only tangentially related to the idea that God brings good out of evil events.

48. Moo, *Romans*, 527.

49. He speaks of love for God in 1 Cor 2:9, 8:3, and possibly 2 Thess 3:5, and of love for the Lord Jesus in Eph 6:24 and Phlm 5.

50. Dunn, *Romans 1–8*, 481.

51. The REB takes the Spirit as the subject (cf. Fee, *God's Empowering Presence*, 589–90; Jewett, *Romans*, 526–27) and "all things" as an adverbial modifier ("and in everything, as we know, he [the Spirit] co-operates for good with those who love God").

52. Wallace, *Greek Grammar*, 203, although Wallace believes the category is possible in this instance. Josephus seems to use the construction this way in *J.W.* 1.505 (εἰς . . . τοῦτο πάντα τρόπον αὐτῷ συνεργήσειν ["for this purpose he would cooperate with him in every way," my transl.]). Still, the category is uncommon and should yield to more probable construals.

good sense with "all things" as the subject, and taking it that way obviates the need to supply anything. Virtually the same expression shows up twice in the botanical writings of the philosopher Theophrastus (ca. 371–287 BC) to describe how the properties of dust and certain characteristics of plants combine to yield a particular result. "All these things work together [πᾶντα . . . ταῦτα συνεργεῖ] for [πρός] both good feeding and concoction," he says in one place (*Caus. plant.* 3.16.4), and, in another place, "all these things work together [πάντα . . . ταῦτα συνεργεῖ] also for [πρός] an abundance of fruit" (*Caus. plant.* 4.8.3).[53] It is likely that Paul uses the expression in the same way here and intends to say that "all things work together [πάντα συνεργεῖ] for [εἰς] good."

Although the translation should be left ambiguous, just as the Greek is ambiguous, there is no doubt that Paul understood God's "purpose," and therefore his will and power, to be the force that causes everything to work together for good. The "good" that is the goal toward which all things are cooperating is the resurrection of the dead, which will result in the glorification of God's people with Christ and the redemption of their bodies from the decay that now plagues all creation because of sin (8:17–23).

Paul ends this word of encouragement with a further description of God's people as "those who are called according to purpose." The "purpose" here is God's (cf. 9:11; Eph 1:11; 3:11; 2 Tim 1:9), and it is a purpose for which God's people have been "called" (cf. Rom 1:6–7).[54] In 8:27 Paul had referred to God's people as "saints," and the language of calling echoes that designation (cf. 1:7; 1 Cor 1:2).[55] Their way of life and the goal toward which they are moving separate them from the unbelieving world around them, just as God separated Israel from the surrounding nations so that they might "be to me a kingdom of priests and a holy nation" (Exod 19:6).

8:29 Because those whom he knew beforehand he also decided beforehand would be similar in form to the image of his Son, in order that he might be the firstborn among many brothers and sisters (ὅτι οὓς προέγνω, καὶ προώρισεν συμμόρφους τῆς εἰκόνος τοῦ υἱοῦ αὐτοῦ, εἰς τὸ εἶναι αὐτὸν πρωτότοκον ἐν πολλοῖς ἀδελφοῖς). All things work together for the good of God's people because God planned both the existence of his people and the circumstances they would experience so that they might one day become what he created human beings to be. This destiny is already visible in the crucified and resurrected Christ.

Paul's "because" (ὅτι) indicates that he is about to state the reason why "all things work together for good" for God's people.[56] God has ordered the circumstances surrounding the lives of his people to accomplish his purpose for them. Paul communicates this by using two expressions: "knew beforehand" (προέγνω) and "decided beforehand" (προώρισεν). Together these terms refer to God's loving, purposeful choice of his people, with "knew beforehand" connoting the loving relationship God has with his people (cf. *yada* ["know"] in Hos 13:5 and Amos 3:2; and ἔγνω ["has come to know"] in Hos 12:1 LXX) and "decided beforehand" emphasizing the resolve with which he chose them for a particular purpose (cf. Eph 1:5, 11).[57] Here, in a way that is consistent with his focus on God's

53. Trans. Benedict Einarson and George K. K. Link, *Theophrastus: De Causis Plantarum*, 3 vols., LCL (Cambridge: Harvard University Press, 1976–90). I have modified the second passage to make the translation more literal.

54. On "purpose," see BDAG 869, s.v. πρόθεσις 2b, and on "called" (κλητός), see the comments above on 1:1.

55. Cf. Dunn, *Romans 1–8*, 482.

56. Sanday and Headlam, *Romans*, 217.

57. See especially Sanday and Headlam (*Romans*, 217), Cranfield (*Romans* 1:431), and Schreiner (*Romans*, 452).

"purpose" (πρόθεσιν, 8:28), Paul takes God's loving, intentional choice of his people back in time to a period before his people existed.

This good purpose Paul describes as the transformation of God's people so that they take a similar form to the image of God's resurrected Son. Paul uses the expression "similar in form" (σύμμορφος) in both its verbal and adjectival forms in Philippians, and the way he uses these terms there is instructive for his use of the adjective here. First, in Philippians 3:10, he describes his conformity to the death of Christ in his own life of suffering, and then in Philippians 3:21 he refers to the future transformation of the humble bodies of all believers so that they become like (σύμμορφον) the "glorious body" of Christ after his resurrection. Paul's thinking follows a similar pattern here in Romans 8:29. He envisions the transformation of believers' bodies from their union with Christ in his suffering to their union with the resurrected Christ in his glory (8:17), and from their "slavery to decay" to their "freedom" and "deliverance" from this situation when their status as God's children becomes obvious to all creation (8:21, 23).

When Paul speaks of the conformity of believers to the "image" (εἰκών) of God's Son, he recalls the theme of creation's restoration implicit in its eager longing for release from its bondage to corruption in 8:18–23. The term reaches back to the language of Genesis where God created humanity in his image (Gen 1:26–27; 5:1; 9:6) and hints that Paul thought of the resurrected Son of God as the archetype of a newly restored humanity (cf. 1 Cor 15:49; 2 Cor 3:18; 4:4; Col 1:15). Paul probably imagined this new humanity as the answer to the plight into which human beings plunged themselves according to 1:19–32 when they began to worship and serve the creature rather than the Creator.[58]

The purpose of (εἰς + infinitive) this conformity to the image of God's Son is the brotherhood of God's Son with believers, and this recalls the theme of adoption into God's family that dominated 8:12–17. At the resurrection of the dead the status of believers as the adopted children of God will become clear (8:18–19), and Christ will be the "firstborn" of the children in God's family. The term "firstborn" in this instance refers to Christ's status both as the first human being released from bondage to decay (cf. 1 Cor 15:20–23) and the first in importance among God's children.[59]

8:30 And those on whom he decided beforehand, these he also called; and those whom he called, these also he justified; and those whom he justified, these also he glorified (οὓς δὲ προώρισεν, τούτους καὶ ἐκάλεσεν· καὶ οὓς ἐκάλεσεν, τούτους καὶ ἐδικαίωσεν· οὓς δὲ ἐδικαίωσεν, τούτους καὶ ἐδόξασεν). The transformation of God's people from mortal to immortal human beings happens at God's initiative and direction from beginning to end, and its accomplishment is therefore certain.

Paul now backs up and fills the chronological gap between God's decision to gather a people whom he would love and that peoples' attainment of the glorious goal he had planned for them.[60] His decision to fashion this people for this purpose led to their creation through God's summons. He "called" them into being through Abraham's family (4:17; 9:7) and then from among the nations of the world through the gospel (4:16–17; 9:24–26). He also "justified" them, which in the context of the argument so far means that despite their sin, he put them right with himself through Christ's death and

58. Cf. Stephen Westerholm, *Justification Reconsidered: Rethinking a Pauline Theme* (Grand Rapids: Eerdmans, 2013), 90–93.

59. On "firstborn" as first in importance, see BDAG 894, s.v. πρωτότοκος 2a.

60. Sanday and Headlam, *Romans*, 218.

delivered them from the punishment their sins deserved (cf. 3:24–26; 4:2, 5; 5:9).

After their calling and justification, the process ends with their glorification. Surprisingly, however, Paul speaks of the glorification of believers as if it were in the past, using the aorist indicative (ἐδόξασεν) to describe the goal toward which God's prior decision about his people and his calling and justification of them were leading. It is possible that Paul thought believers were already glorified through their union with Christ (cf. Eph 2:6) or that they were in the process of glorification as they were being transformed into the image of Christ (2 Cor 3:18).[61] Within a context where Paul has just emphasized the contrast between the "sufferings of the present time" and "the glory about to be revealed in us" (Rom 8:18; cf. 5:2; 8:17, 21), however, neither of these interpretations is likely to be correct.

Rather, Paul probably spoke of the glorification of believers as a past event to emphasize the certainty of their future glorification. The great Greek grammarian Herbert Weir Smyth said that "the aorist may be substituted for the future when a future event is vividly represented as having actually occurred."[62] In the immediate context Paul has been focusing on the plight that believers must share with all creation since they are all caught up in the results of human rebellion against God. He has also been concerned with God's answer to this plight through the resurrection of the dead, first of Christ and then, in the future, of believers (8:17, 19–23). The resurrection of believers will be the moment when they are delivered from creation's decay and fully experience the freedom of their adoption into God's family (8:11, 23).

With this last phrase ("these also he glorified"), then, Paul has completed his description of the movement of believers from their union with Christ's suffering to their union, in the future, with Christ's glory (8:17). Paul has added to this thought the further encouragement that the Spirit aids believers as they struggle with the suffering sin has introduced into the world (8:26–27), and that their future glorification with Christ is as certain as the fulfillment of God's primordial choice of his people and direction of their lives (8:28, 29a, 30f).

With its movement from the justification to the glorification of God's people, this concluding sentence returns to the themes with which Paul began the second major section of his argument. Because of their justification by faith, believers can boast in the hope of the glory of God (5:1–2).

Theology in Application

The Capitoline Museum in Rome houses a large stone slab, once part of an early first-century AD funerary monument that stood beside a busy road outside the city boundaries. The inscription reads as follows:

> You see the funerary monument of Lucius Vettenius Musa Campester, place of rest for those who are tired of life; exhausted by a life conducted in many different re-

61. See, respectively, Godet (*Romans*, 327–28) and Jewett (*Romans*, 530). Cranfield (*Romans*, 1:433) wonders whether past glorification corresponds to sanctification, a step in the salvation process that is otherwise left out of Paul's list.

62. Smyth, *Greek Grammar*, §1934. For another Pauline example, see 1 Thess 2:16 (ἔφθασεν). See also Wallace, *Greek Grammar*, 564.

gions; tranquility welcomes him to a deathly abode. Death is release from wealth and poverty, for Nature forces both rich and poor to live in anxiety.[63]

Lucius might have just as easily lived in the twenty-first century. Like so many people today, whether they are wealthy or poor, he seems to have run himself ragged trying to survive life and free himself from its inevitable anxieties. Although wealthy enough to afford a beautifully engraved and public monument, he recognized that his wealth had bought him no more freedom from life's troubles than if he were poor. If he was like many others of his own time and culture, he was sure that death simply brought annihilation from existence and, with it, release from the sorrow and worry of life in an unfriendly world.[64] It was simply in the "nature" of things that life was difficult.

In this climate, it is no wonder that the gospel took root in Rome at an early date. The hope of the gospel that Paul explains so clearly in Romans 8:18–30 must have come as truly good news to people with Lucius's understanding of life, and its message has lost none of its power for suffering people around the world today. In this passage, Paul explains three elements of the gospel that help those who believe it to endure life's difficulties.

Realism about the Hardships of the Present Life

First, the gospel is realistic about the difficult nature of life for everyone, including believers. Everyone's life is burdened with "futility" (8:20) and "decay" (8:21), and at times the world itself seems to cry out with pain (8:22). Who has not spent effort or money on some project or product that, in the end, had no discernable redeeming value? Who has not noticed that even the healthiest person, the most well-built house, or the most cleverly designed machine eventually falls apart? What even modestly sensitive person has not grieved at the suffering of so many people at the hands of brutal criminals and crazed ideologues that somehow end up in charge of entire societies? Lucius's anxiety, and the anxiety of so many people down through the ages, is well founded.

Paul's gospel takes full account of these realities and explains, at least in general terms, why they exist. The world suffers because God's human creatures have rebelled against their creator. Rather than worshiping him and giving him thanks for the blessing of the good world he had created, they disobeyed him and went

63. *IGUR* 1291, found in 1954 on the Via Prenestina. The translation is from the museum label. The first sentence is in Latin and the second sentence is in Greek. I have modified the translation slightly to make it more literal.

64. Views on the afterlife were diverse, but the belief that death snuffed out existence was common enough to produce the often-used gravestone abbreviation "nf f ns nc." The abbreviation consists of the first letters of the Latin words for "I wasn't; I was; I'm not; I don't care" (trans. Mary Beard, John North, and Simon Price, *Religions of Rome*, 2 vols. [Cambridge: Cambridge University Press, 1998], 2:236).

their own way (1:19–22). The results were disastrous both for their relationship with God and for their relationships with one another (1:23–32). The world also suffers because God has actively handed over his rebellious human creatures to the consequences of their sin (1:24, 26, 28). He is a righteous God (1:1; 2:5; 3:4–5), and this is a fitting punishment for their rebellion (cf. 8:20).

Hope for Freedom from Sin and Its Effects

Second, the good news of the gospel is that God's just punishment is not his last word. When God subjected creation to futility, he did so "in hope" (8:20), and this hope characterizes Christian existence in the midst of a suffering world (8:20, 24–25; cf. 4:18; 5:2, 4–5; 12:12; 15:4, 13). It is not that Christians necessarily have any fewer practical problems than other people or experience less sadness, sickness, and disappointment. One only has to review the sordid history of the marginalization and outright persecution of Christians to discover that Christians may suffer more than others precisely because of their Christian commitments. In his next paragraph, Paul observes that it often seems as if Christians are lined up like sheep ready to be slaughtered for God's sake (8:36; cf. Ps 44:22). The gospel, however, gives believers hope that the suffering and injustice they and others experience will one day give way to God's re-created world. In that "new creation" they will no longer grow weak, fall apart, and die but will live in immortality. Moreover, God will also release the world around them from the effects of sin (Rom 8:21), and so both they and the world in which they live will be free from suffering. They will live in loving fellowship with God as his adoptive children (8:21, 23, 29; cf. 8:15–17; Gal 4:4–6), and their existence will be like that of Jesus himself, who presently lives in immortality and in a loving relationship with his Father (Rom 8:29; cf. 8:17).

All this gives believers a different perspective on life than Lucius had in first-century Rome and that many have today. Lucius may have thought that "Nature" was a force with a will of its own that "brings all things to destruction and recalls them to the state from which they sprang" (Seneca, *Polyb.* 1.1 [John W. Basore, LCL]). In more recent times, people have thought of "nature" as merely the material world moving in chaotic and random ways that sometimes create havoc for people.[65] In contrast, Paul affirms that God created and is sovereign over the natural world and the course of events in it, and he is so gracious that he will one day erase everything in nature that creates suffering for his people. This should give Christians a generally optimistic view of life and prompt them to work to alleviate suffering in the world around them. To do so is to cooperate with the ultimate purposes of God.

65. Although this conviction is not as unreligious as they may think. On this, see Charles Taylor, *A Secular Age* (Cambridge: Harvard University Press, 2007), 269–95.

Understanding the sovereignty of a gracious God over nature also provides believers with encouragement when efforts to alleviate suffering fail. God will eventually overwhelm all forms of suffering with a creation restored to his original design for it (Rom 8:18–19).

The Promise of God's Sympathy and Help

Third, the gospel affirms that God has not only given his people a forward-looking hope that sustains them in the midst of hardship, but the Spirit to aid them in the midst of their present suffering (8:26–27). The Spirit's groaning, reminiscent of the groaning of creation and of believers (8:22–23) assures them that God is not unaware of, or unconcerned about, their plight. Just as God heard the "groaning" (στεναγμός) of his people in slavery in Egypt (Exod 2:23–24; cf. 3:7, 9) and was sympathetic with their suffering, so he continues to sympathize with the suffering of his people in all times and places (cf. Rom 8:26). When believers experience trouble so profound that they do not know even how or what to pray, they should not add to their anxieties the notion that God fails to hear their unspoken, inner yearning for relief. God the Holy Spirit searches their hearts (8:27) and knows them fully, and God the Father also knows fully God the Spirit (8:27; cf. 1 Cor 2:10–12). This means that God understands the suffering of his people and is deeply concerned for them.

CHAPTER 19

Romans 8:31–39

Literary Context

This paragraph concludes the whole argument from 1:18–8:30. It opens in 8:31 with a rhetorical question that urges Paul's audience to stand on the summit they have reached in 8:18–30 and look back across the entire landscape they have just traversed together ("What, then, shall we say in view of these things?"). The rhetorical question that answers this question ("If God is for us, who is against us?") is itself a thinly disguised statement that summarizes 1:18–8:30.[1] Paul has shown in the preceding argument that God demonstrated his love for his people—that he is "for" them—by the death and resurrection of Christ (3:21–4:25; 5:1–21; 8:1–3, 11, 17, 23, 29), and therefore no enemy, whether sin, flesh, decay, death, or shame will be able to prevail over them (1:18–3:20; 5:12–8:30).

As the paragraph develops, Paul recalls in greater detail the movement of the preceding argument from the human plight, indeed the plight of all creation, to God's gracious response to it. The language of God not sparing his Son in 8:32a recalls 3:21–26, 4:25, 5:6–11, and 8:3. Similarly, the language of God giving his people "all things" recalls the theme of creation's restoration, beginning with the resurrection of Christ, that Paul developed in 8:18–30 (cf. 8:11, 17). The language of bringing charges against God's people, of God as the justifier, of the danger of condemnation, and of relief from that danger in the death of Christ in 8:33–34b recalls the argument of 1:18–3:26 with its portrait of unrighteous defendants standing silent before God (1:18–3:20) and then of God's justification of the ungodly through the death of Christ (3:21–26; cf. 5:6–10). The further reference in 8:34c–e to the present implications of Christ's resurrection, exaltation, and intercessory work for believers recalls Paul's argument in 5:10, 17, 6:1–11, and 7:4 that Christ's resurrection has implications for the day-to-day lives of believers in the period before God restores all creation.

As all this indicates, the paragraph primarily looks backward, but it would be a mistake to conclude that it does not also prepare for the second major part of the letter (9:1–16:27). This becomes evident in the turn the paragraph takes at 8:35 where Paul raises the issue of the marginalization and persecution of God's people. Paul will

1. Cf. Cranfield, *Romans*, 1:434.

have advice for his Roman audience in the letter's second major section about how to cope with their societal status as a misunderstood and despised minority (12:1–2, 14–21; 13:1–14). The second part of the paragraph (8:35–39), with its affirmation of Christ's love for God's people (8:35) and of God's love for his people through Christ (8:39), brings forward into the day-to-day existence of Paul's readers his affirmation of the vast extent of God's love for his people in 5:5–8. It also reminds them that God is not only "for" them in an abstract, theological sense but that he is "for" them in the difficulties that they face in the practical affairs of life.

The paragraph also prepares the reader for the next major step in Paul's argument (9:1–11:36). As Cranfield has observed, Paul's affirmation of God's love for and protection of his "chosen people" (8:33) in 8:31–39 raises poignantly the question of whether Paul's gospel implies that God has rejected Israel as his chosen people.[2] If God's promises in Scripture to love and protect Israel are not reliable, then Paul's claim that God will continue to love and protect those who believe the gospel rings hollow.[3] Romans 9:1–11:36 provides Paul's answer to this pressing problem, and Paul's question, "Who will bring charges against God's chosen people?" marks the point beyond which the argument cannot proceed without an answer to the question of Israel's place in salvation history. In addition, Paul's shift in 8:38 into the first-person singular, with its confessional and emphatic tone, prepares the way for his emotion-laden expression of personal grief over Israel's rejection of the gospel in 9:1–3. It also shows that 9:1–11:36 is no appendix to the letter but an integral and necessary part of the overall argument.

VIII. The Scriptures Show That Righteousness Comes by Faith Rather Than by Works (4:1–25)

IX. Justification by Faith Brings Peace and Reorients the Believer's Existence (5:1–8:39)

- A. Justification by Faith Rescues Believers from God's Present and Future Wrath (5:1–11)
- B. Christ's Obedience Overwhelms the Effects of Adam's Disobedience (5:12–21)
- C. Union with Christ's Death and Resurrection Initiates a New Life (6:1–23)
- D. Union with Christ's Death and Resurrection Frees Believers from the Law (7:1–6)
- E. The Goodness, Yet Inability, of the Law (7:7–25)
- **F. God's Solution to the Human Plight (8:1–39)**
  1. Christ's Work and the Spirit's Power Overcome the Sinful Flesh (8:1–17)
  2. God's Spirit Helps Believers Cope with Suffering as They Await Future Immortality (8:18–30)
  3. ➡ **The Gospel's Meaning: God Loves and Protects His People through his Son Jesus Christ (8:31–39)**

X. Israel's Present Rejection of the Gospel Does Not Imply the Failure of God's Word (9:1–11:36)

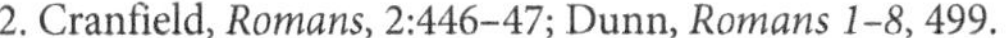

2. Cranfield, *Romans*, 2:446–47; Dunn, *Romans 1–8*, 499.

3. R. Michael Allen, *Justification and the Gospel: Understanding the Contexts and Controversies* (Grand Rapids: Baker, 2013), 4–5.

Main Idea

In this passage Paul summarizes the gospel as he has explained it in 1:18–8:30 and draws from his explanation the conclusion that God loves his chosen people, will protect them from all their enemies, and one day will give them eternal life in a restored creation. The proof of God's commitment to his people in these ways is the death of his own Son on their behalf and the present reign of his Son together with him over the universe. The death, resurrection, and heavenly session of Christ mean that, however difficult existence may become for God's people, they will always be the objects of his loving care.

Translation

Romans 8:31–39

31a	Rhetorical Question (Conclusion)	**What, then, shall we say in view of these things?**			
b	Rhetorical Question (Introduction)	If God is for us,			
		who is against us?			
32a	Identification	He who indeed did	not spare	his own Son but	
			handed	him over	
				for us all,	
b	Rhetorical Question (Expansion)	**how will he**	**not ...**		
				also,	
				with him,	
			... graciously give		
				to us	
				the whole created order?	
33a	Rhetorical Question (Series—no. 1)	**Who will bring charges against God's chosen people?**			
b	Exclamation	**God is**	**the one**	**who**	**justifies!**
34a	Rhetorical Question (Restatement of 33a)	**Who is**	**the one**	**who**	**condemns?**
b	Exclamation	**Christ is**	**the one**	**who**	**has died, and, even more,**
c	Sequence				**was raised,**
d	Sequence			**who also**	**is at the right hand of God,**
e	Sequence			**who also**	**intercedes for us!**
35a	Rhetorical Question (Series—no. 2)	**Who shall separate us from the love of Christ?**			

b	Rhetorical Question (List)	**Affliction or distress or persecution or famine or lack of clothing or danger or sword?**
36a	Verification	Just as **it is written** that,
		"For your sake we are being killed all day long;
b	Explanation	we are counted as sheep destined for slaughter." (Psa 44:22)
37a	Contra-expectation (Sphere)	But in all these things
b	Assertion	**we are winning a sweeping victory**
c	Agency	through the one who loved us.
38a	Basis (of 37b)	For **I am persuaded**
b	List (Contrast)	that neither death nor life,
c	List (Contrast?)	neither angels nor rulers,
d	List (Contrast)	neither things present nor things future,
e	List	nor powers,
39a	List (Contrast)	nor height nor depth,
b	List	nor any other created thing
c	Content (of 38a)	will be able to separate
d	Object	us
e	Separation	from the love
f	Subjective Genitive	of God
g	Sphere	in Christ Jesus our Lord.

Structure

Paul introduces the passage with a series of three rhetorical questions. The first question (8:31a) shows that he is about to draw an important conclusion from the preceding argument ("What, then, shall we say in view of these things?").[4] He then provides a pithy summary of that conclusion (8:31b) in a second rhetorical question ("If God is for us, who is against us?"). A third rhetorical question supplies the reason why he can say that God is on the side of believers: if God's Son died for his people, God is not likely to deny believers any other good thing (8:32). The rest of the passage explains this thesis in greater detail.

After this introduction, Paul illustrates his thesis by describing two threatening contexts that cannot overwhelm God's people (8:33–34, 35–37). First, he describes a judicial context in which charges are brought against them. Christ's death, resurrection, and continuing intercession on behalf of God's people mean that no charge against them can be successful (8:33–34). Second, he describes a situation of general

4. Wilckens, *An die Römer (Röm 6–11)*, 170.

social upheaval in which the love of Christ for his people might be obscured by their suffering. Here too, however, the display of Christ's love in his death for God's people (cf. 5:8; 8:32) gives them the resources they need to gain a decisive victory over these evils (8:35–37).

Paul concludes by shifting from the first-person plural to the more confessional first-person singular, a move that adds emphasis to what he is about to say (8:38–39).[5] His conclusion summarizes the paragraph in expansive terms and explains in a condensed form what makes the gospel good news: absolutely nothing will be able to frustrate the good intentions of God for those whom he loves (cf. 8:28).

Exegetical Outline

- **IX. Justification by Faith Brings Peace and Reorients the Believer's Existence (5:1–8:39)**
  - A. Justification by Faith Rescues Believers from God's Present and Future Wrath (5:1–11)
  - B. Christ's Obedience Overwhelms the Effects of Adam's Disobedience (5:12–21)
  - C. Union with Christ's Death and Resurrection Initiates a New Life (6:1–23)
  - D. Union with Christ's Death and Resurrection Frees Believers from the Law (7:1–6)
  - E. The Goodness, Yet Inability, of the Law (7:7–25)
  - **F. God's Solution to the Human Plight (8:1–39)**
    - 1. Christ's Work and the Spirit's Power Overcome the Sinful Flesh (8:1–17)
    - 2. God's Spirit Helps Believers Cope with Suffering as They Await Future Immortality (8:18–30)
    - ➡ **3. The Gospel's Meaning: God Loves and Protects His People through His Son Jesus Christ (8:31–39)**
      - a. Thesis: Christ's death shows that God has taken his people's side (8:31–32)
      - b. Two illustrations (8:33–36)
      - c. No judicial threat can succeed against God's people (8:33–34)
      - d. No amount of social upheaval can succeed against God's people (8:35–36)
      - e. Summary: Nothing in God's universe can block the love that God has for his people as he has shown it in the death and resurrection of Jesus Christ (8:37–39)

Explanation of the Text

8:31 What, then, shall we say in view of these things? If God is for us, who is against us? (τί οὖν ἐροῦμεν πρὸς ταῦτα; εἰ ὁ θεὸς ὑπὲρ ἡμῶν, τίς καθ' ἡμῶν;). Sin, decay, death, and shame are the enemies of God's people, but God has acted powerfully against these forces, and so the salvation of his people is secure.

The rhetorical question, "What, then, shall we say . . . ?" (sometimes with slight variation) is a stylistic feature of Romans, intended to carry for-

5. On the shift in grammatical person, see Cranfield, *Romans*, 1:434, 441.

ward the letter's instruction. It typically refers back to something Paul has said in the immediately preceding paragraph and introduces some inference from that discussion, whether true (9:30) or false (3:5; 4:1; 6:1; 7:7; 9:14). It is likely, then, that "in view of these things" refers most immediately back to 8:30, and especially to the last clause of that sentence, "those whom he justified, these also he glorified."[6] With its mention of justification and glorification, however, that clause echoes 5:1–2, which itself, through mention of justification and glory, points both backward to Paul's discussion of the need for and means of justification in 1:18–4:25 and forward to Paul's discussion of glorification in 8:17–30. Paul's "these things" (ταῦτα), then, surveys the entire landscape of the argument from 1:18 forward and asks the audience of the letter, "What conclusion should we draw from all this?"[7]

The second rhetorical question expresses the theme of 8:31–39 and the ultimate conclusion to the argument of 1:18–8:30. The phrases "for us" and "against us," juxtaposed to each other, assume that Paul and his audience of Roman believers exist in the midst of a conflict in which they can prevail only if they have help from outside themselves. This conflict is assumed throughout Paul's treatment of the justification of the believer in 1:18–4:25 where Paul explains how God makes it possible for his people to prevail in the final judgment despite their sin (3:21–25; 4:25). In 5:1–8:30 notions of conflict frequently dominate the discussion, whether the conflict between God and his sinful people (5:1, 10), between life and death (6:1–11), sin and righteousness (6:12–23), the flesh and the will to please God (7:1–25), or the flesh and the Spirit (8:1–17). Now, Paul says, in all these areas of conflict God's people will prevail because God has taken their side.

The question "who is against us?" then does not assume that God's people have no enemies (cf. 8:35–36, 38–39) but that these enemies cannot be victorious over them, however strong they may seem to be. Paul's rhetorical question comes out of the same understanding of God's saving power that prompted David's rhetorical question about Goliath: "For who is this uncircumcised Philistine, that he should defy the armies of the living God?" (1 Sam 17:26; cf. Pss 27:1; 118:6–7; Isa 50:9; 54:17).[8]

8:32 He who indeed did not spare his own Son but handed him over for us all, how will he not also, with him, graciously give to us the whole created order? (ὅς γε τοῦ ἰδίου υἱοῦ οὐκ ἐφείσατο ἀλλὰ ὑπὲρ ἡμῶν πάντων παρέδωκεν αὐτόν, πῶς οὐχὶ καὶ σὺν αὐτῷ τὰ πάντα ἡμῖν χαρίσεται;). Because God himself offered his own, beloved Son as an atoning sacrifice for the sins of his people, they can rest assured that he will also glorify them with Jesus and place them, like him, over his entire, restored creation.

The term "indeed" (γέ) often appears in combination with other words at the beginning of a clause to emphasize the entire clause.[9] Here it highlights just how dramatically God has shown himself to be "for" his people (8:31). The combination "who indeed" (ὅς γε), moreover, often has a causal force, and it probably carries that force here, infusing the entire rhetorical question with the nuance that "because" God did not spare his own Son, believers

6. The preposition translated "in view of" (πρός) typically means "to" (Tyndale: "unto"; Luther: "hiezu"; KJV, RSV, NASB, ESV: "to"), but here has the "transferred" sense of "concerning . . . in view of." See also Moule (*Idiom-Book*, 53), Cranfield (*Romans*, 1:435), and Légasse (*Romains*, 548).

7. Cf. Cranfield, *Romans*, 1:435; Dunn, *Romans 1–8*, 499; Kruse, *Romans*, 359–60.

8. Origen, *Romans, Books 6–10*, 93; Cranfield, *Romans*, 1:436; Dunn, *Romans 1–8*, 500.

9. Smyth, *Greek Grammar*, §2823.

can rest assured he will give them all things.[10] The basis of the hope for the redemption of the body and the deliverance of all creation from suffering that Paul described in 8:18–30 is the love that God displayed in the death of Christ (cf. 5:5).

Interpreters have often found an allusion to Abraham's near sacrifice of Isaac in the phrase "did not spare his own Son" (τοῦ ἰδίου υἱοῦ οὐκ ἐφείσατο).[11] In the LXX of Genesis 22 God commends Abraham (v. 12) and says that he will bless him (v. 16) because Abraham had "not spared" his "beloved son" (οὐκ ἐφείσω τοῦ υἱοῦ σου τοῦ ἀγαπητοῦ) but was willing to sacrifice him "for" God's "sake" (δι᾽ ἐμέ; vv. 12, 16). As Dunn says, Paul's familiarity with the language of the OT ran too deep for him to have been unaware of the echo of Genesis 22:16 in his language here.[12] This does not mean, however, that Paul's understanding of the atonement was derived from ancient Jewish interpretation of Genesis 22:1–18.[13] Jewish interpreters show no sign of understanding Isaac's sacrifice as atonement for sin until the second-century AD, and even then the idea probably emerged out of Christian interpretation of Genesis 22:1–18 in the late first century.[14] Paul merely wanted to express here the depth of God's commitment to his people and did so in language that probably presented itself readily to mind both because of his familiarity with Genesis 22:1–18 and because of the use he had just made in Romans 8:12–30 of the common Christian conviction that Jesus was God's Son (8:17, 29; cf. 5:10).

The verb "hand over" (παραδίδωμι) appears in the Gospels for Judas's betrayal of Jesus to the Jewish authorities (e.g., Mark 3:19; 14:10–11, 18, 21, 41–42, 44), for the Jewish authorities' action in delivering Jesus to Pilate (e.g., Mark 15:1, 10), and for Pilate handing Jesus over to be crucified (e.g., Mark 15:15). The earliest Christians, however, believed that ultimately none of this had happened because the Jewish and Roman authorities were able to frustrate the purposes of God. Rather, these hostile authorities did exactly what God's "hand" and "plan had predestined to take place" (Acts 4:27–28; cf. 1 Cor 2:7–8). In God's plan, Jesus "was handed over [παρεδόθη] because of our trespasses" (Rom 4:25), an idea that was probably facilitated by Isaiah 52:6, 12 LXX where the same verb appears in the description of God handing the servant over to death for the sins of God's people.[15] For Paul, moreover, this was not simply a matter of God handing over a passive Christ but, as he makes clear in Romans 8:35, 37, and 39 (cf. 5:5, 8), of Christ's own active love for God's people (cf. Gal 2:20; Eph 5:2, 25).[16]

The "all things" that God freely gives his people should be understood within the broader context of Romans 8:17–30. There Paul had said that after God's people had suffered with Christ they would be glorified with him (8:17) and had then explained that when believers were glorified "the creation" would also "be set free from slavery to decay" (8:21). It is likely, then, that when Paul speaks here of God graciously giving "all things" (τὰ πάντα) to believers "with" (σύν) Christ he refers to God's gift of a restored universe to his peo-

10. On the causal force of "who indeed" (ὅς γε), see Smyth, *Greek Grammar*, §2826, citing Xenophon, *Mem.* 2.3.15. Cf. Meyer (*Romans*, 338) and the example from AD 132 in MM 460: "Apart from the six arourae, which as a matter of fact [ἅς γε] you let to others, and with which I shall have nothing to do" (P.Flor. III.370.9).

11. Cf., e.g., Godet, *Romans*, 329–30; Sanday and Headlam, *Romans*, 220.

12. Dunn, *Romans 1–8*, 501.

13. Hans Joachim Schoeps, "The Sacrifice of Isaac in Paul's Theology," *JBL* 65 (1946): 391.

14. P. R. Davies and B. D. Chilton, "The Aqedah: A Revised Tradition History," *CBQ* 40 (1978): 514–46; Fitzmyer, *Romans*, 531–32.

15. See especially Gathercole, *Defending Substitution*, 63–64.

16. BDAG 762, s.v. παραδίδωμι 1b.

ple. This interpretation becomes even more likely in light of Paul's frequent use of the expression "all things" with the article (τὰ πάντα) to mean "the universe" (cf. 11:36; 1 Cor 8:6; Eph 3:9; 4:10; Col 1:16–17; and especially Phil 3:21).[17]

8:33 Who will bring charges against God's chosen people? God is the one who justifies! (τίς ἐγκαλέσει κατὰ ἐκλεκτῶν θεοῦ; θεὸς ὁ δικαιῶν). God's people need to fear neither the final day of judgment nor the accusations of their detractors in the present. God has accepted them and put them right with himself. His decision in their favor is final and trumps any other negative judgment against them.

The expression "bring charges" (ἐγκαλέω) translates a legal technical term, although normally the person charged was described in the dative case rather than, as here, within a prepositional phrase (κατὰ ἐκλεκτῶν).[18] The preposition may add a more personal and emphatic character to the imagery: charges are brought *against* God's chosen people.[19] The tribulation, persecution, and distress (8:35) that Paul and other believers, including those in Rome, experienced may lie in the background here. The suffering of the earliest Christians often took a personal form.

If this is right, then Paul has something more in view than the justification of the sinner in light of the future day of judgment, although that is certainly in view as well (cf. 2:5–16; 3:19–20; 5:9–10; 8:1).[20] He is also affirming that the marginalization and mistreatment of believers by the wider society is wrong and that God will not only declare them free from punishment when he sits as their judge on the final day but that even now, in the present, God declares all accusations against them unwarranted (8:35–36, 38–39). The present tense of the participle translated "the one who justifies" (ὁ δικαιῶν) supports this interpretation as does Paul's use of the expression "chosen people" (ἐκλεκτῶν), which often appears in descriptions of the persecution of God's people (e.g., Matt 24:22; Mark 13:20, 27; Luke 18:7; cf. 2 Esd 5:23–29; 1 En. 62:11–15).[21]

Both the question and its answer are closely tied to Paul's affirmation in 8:30 that "those whom [God] called, these also he justified." In Greek, the term translated "called" (ἐκάλεσεν) there is closely related to the term translated "will bring charges" (ἐγκαλέσει) here. Paul's statement here that God is the justifier of his chosen people reaffirms the expression of certainty in 8:30 that God has put them right with himself and destined them for glory. Because of this, they will prevail over all the forces ranged against them. This includes sin and death (5:21), their own lack of resolve (7:13–25), the flesh (8:1–17), and the suffering that comes to them through no fault of their own but simply through living in a world that is hostile to God (8:17–25).

The echo of Isaiah 50:8–9 LXX is too close to be accidental. Paul probably saw himself and other believers as walking the path of the servant who would not be put to shame because the Lord justifies him and helps him to prevail over his persecutors and accusers (Isa 50:4–10).[22]

17. BDAG 784, s.v. πᾶς 4dβ. Cf. Dunn, *Romans 1–8*, 502; Jewett, *Romans*, 538. Paul's use of "all things" (πάντα) in 1 Cor 3:21–22 (Schreiner, *Romans*, 461; Wright, "Romans," 612) is not a true parallel to this text since there Paul does not use the article.

18. LSJ 469; BDAG 273, both s.v. ἐγκαλέω. See Wis 12:12; Sir 46:19; Zech 1:4 LXX; Acts 19:38; 23:28.

19. Cf. Sophocles, *Phil.* 328, where Philoctetes says to Neoptolemus, "Now what is the reason that you have come complaining against them [κατ' αὐτῶν ἐγκαλῶν] with this fierce wrath?" (R. C. Jebb, LCL). No formal legal proceeding is under way. Neoptolemus has complained against the culprits that stole his father's armor.

20. The future tense "will bring charges" (ἐγκαλέσει), then, is "not eschatological . . . but logical" (Käsemann, *Romans*, 248; cf. Lagrange, *Romains*, 219).

21. Haacker, *An die Römer*, 175.

22. Cf. Wilckens, *An die Römer (Röm 6–11)*, 174.

8:34 Who is the one who condemns? Christ is the one who has died, and, even more, was raised, who also is at the right hand of God, who also intercedes for us! (τίς ὁ κατακρινῶν; Χριστὸς [Ἰησοῦς] ὁ ἀποθανών, μᾶλλον δὲ ἐγερθείς, ὅς καί ἐστιν ἐν δεξιᾷ τοῦ θεοῦ, ὃς καὶ ἐντυγχάνει ὑπὲρ ἡμῶν). No one will condemn God's people on the final day, and all condemnation of them now from those who are hostile to God will be ultimately unsuccessful. Paul can say this because Christ died for the sins of God's people and is now alive, using his power and authority over everything for their benefit.

The rhetorical question that begins this verse corresponds to the rhetorical question at the beginning of 8:33. Just as no one is able successfully to bring charges against God's chosen people, so no judge can legitimately condemn them. This question follows naturally from Paul's statement that "God is the one who justifies." In a legal setting justification, or release from punishment, is the opposite of condemnation, or the finding that one deserves punishment (cf. Josephus, *Ant.* 4.46). If God is the judge and he has decided to release his chosen people from punishment, then God's people are free from condemnation (cf. κατάκριμα in 8:1). His decision trumps that of any other judge.

The thought of God acting as a judge and releasing his people from punishment probably recalled to Paul the line of thought that he developed in 3:21–26 and the pressing question that he answered there (even if only implicitly). How can God be just and justify his sinful people? This happens through the death of Christ, which atoned for the sins of his people (3:26; 4:5; 5:6, 8–9). Now Paul makes clear that the justifying death of Christ not only atoned for the sins of believers prior to the time that they heard and believed the gospel but that it continues to atone for their sin in the present. Paul communicates this in an ascending series of affirmations. He begins with Christ's death, moves to Christ's resurrection, then to Christ's exaltation at God's right hand, and finally to his intercession in that position for believers (cf. 5:10).[23]

The image of Christ at God's right hand recalls Psalm 110:1 (109:1 LXX), which depicts Israel's king as the vice-regent of God and as victorious over his enemies through God's strength.[24] Paul now portrays Christ Jesus as the vice-regent of the psalm, having won the victory over his enemies and having taken his seat at God's right hand. The high point of this movement, however, is not Christ's own victory over death and his honored position but his use of that position for the benefit of God's chosen people. Greek speakers sometimes used the term translated "intercede" (ἐντυγχάνω) in judicial settings (cf., e.g., Acts 25:24 [ESV: "petitioned"]) and of appeals before a king on someone's behalf (Josephus, *Ant.* 12.18). Here Paul seems to imagine Christ, the "anointed" (χριστός) king, appealing to his coregent God on behalf of his people and on the basis of his atoning death.[25] The thought is close to Ephesians 1:20–23 where God gives the resurrected, enthroned, and victorious Christ "as head over all things to the church" (Eph 1:22).

Just as with the justification language in the pre-

23. Moo, *Romans*, 542.

24. Hans-Joachim Kraus, *Psalms 60–150: A Continental Commentary*, trans. Hilton C. Oswald (Minneapolis: Fortress, 1993), 348–49.

25. A number of ancient and diverse witnesses to the text (e.g., 𝔓[46vid] ℵ A C F G L Ψ 6 33 81 104 365 424[c] 436 1319 1505 1573 sy[h] lat bo) read "Christ Jesus" (Χριστὸς Ἰησοῦς) at this point rather than "Christ" (Χριστός). The witnesses that simply read "Christ," however, are also early and diverse (e.g., B D 263 424* 459 1175 1241 1506 1739 1881), and the simple term "Christ" is more likely to have been modified to the full name Christ Jesus than to be the result of a shortening of that name. If "Christ" is original, moreover, it focuses attention on Christ's role as anointed king, which seems to be Paul's emphasis in the text.

vious verse, here too the thought moves beyond assurance that there will be no condemnation for God's people on the final day of judgment. It also includes the notion that even now as they experience condemnation from a hostile culture, Christ intercedes for them (cf. 8:26).

8:35 Who shall separate us from the love of Christ? Affliction or distress or persecution or famine or lack of clothing or danger or sword? (τίς ἡμᾶς χωρίσει ἀπὸ τῆς ἀγάπης τοῦ Χριστοῦ; θλῖψις ἢ στενοχωρία ἢ διωγμὸς ἢ λιμὸς ἢ γυμνότης ἢ κίνδυνος ἢ μάχαιρα;). Disasters that normally separate people from the people who love and care for them are not able to distance believers from the sacrificial love of Christ who now lives and reigns with God.

In 5:8 Paul had already said that God demonstrated his love to his people clearly in the death of Christ on their behalf. Since Paul has just referred to Christ's death in 8:32 and 34, there can be little doubt that here too he has in mind Christ's demonstration of God's love through his death for the ungodly. It is significant that what he described before as a proof of God's love (5:8) he now describes as a proof of Christ's love. God and Christ acted in concert when Christ died for the ungodly, and the action of one demonstrated the love of both (cf. 8:39).[26]

It is not only Christ's death, however, that shows God's love for his people. His resurrection and present position of authority at God's right hand are also a demonstration of this love (8:34; cf. 5:10). The love of Christ comes as comfort to suffering believers not as a sentimental memory of a sacrificial act now long past. Rather, it comforts the believer because the one who loves them not only died for them but is now alive and enthroned as a victorious king.

The verb "separate" (χωρίζω) was a spatial term that often referred to relational separation (1 Cor 7:10–11, 15), and Paul could play on the literal and metaphorical uses of the word (Phlm 15).[27] The hardships Paul mentions here had often separated people from their loved ones, something that at least some Jewish Christians in Rome knew firsthand from their own experience of expulsion from the city under Claudius (Acts 18:2; cf. Suetonius, *Claud.* 25.4).[28] Paul himself had experienced all but the last of these hardships (2 Cor 6:4; 11:26–27; 12:10), although, if we should understand 2 Corinthians 1:9 literally, he had come close to that experience also (cf. Phil 1:20).[29] He knew what it meant to be "torn away" by persecution from those who loved him (1 Thess 2:17; cf. Acts 17:10), but here he affirms that nothing can separate the believer from Christ and his love. Refugees who are believers, although forced to flee all else that is familiar and everyone else who loves them, are never separated from Christ, together with whom they suffer (8:17), and who continues to love them.

8:36 Just as it is written that, "For your sake we are being killed all day long; we are counted as sheep destined for slaughter" (καθὼς γέγραπται ὅτι ἕνεκεν σοῦ θανατούμεθα ὅλην τὴν ἡμέραν, ἐλογίσθημεν ὡς πρόβατα σφαγῆς). Believers continue to endure suffering despite, and even because of, their faithfulness to God in the same way that God's people in ages past have suffered. Because of Christ's death and resurrection, however, God's response to the suffering of his people has now become clearer than it was to faithful Israel.

26. Cf. Chrysostom, *Romans*, 270.

27. LSJ 2016, BDAG 1095, MGS 2392, all s.v. χωρίζω.

28. Cf. Jewett (*Romans*, 547), but without following his speculation that the suffering of some Christians in Rome had led to disunity between those who had and those who had not suffered.

29. Cf. Haacker, *An die Römer*, 177.

Paul comments on the list of difficulties he has just mentioned with a quotation from Psalm 44:22 (43:23 LXX; 44:23 Heb.). Psalm 44 is an anguished complaint that God has allowed his people to suffer a devastating and humiliating military defeat at the hands of their enemies (44:9–16 [43:10–17 LXX; 44:10–17 Heb.]), and he has done this despite their faithfulness from the heart to the covenant he made with them (44:17–18 [43:18–19 LXX; 44:18–19 Heb.]).[30] God's inaction on behalf of his people puzzles the psalmist, and he urges God to "redeem" his people "for the sake of" his "steadfast love" (44:26).[31]

For purposes of Paul's argument, therefore, the quotation extends the thought of the second question in 8:35. Will the difficulties that believers face despite their faithfulness to the gospel separate them from God's love (cf. 8:35a, 39c–g)? Looking at the difficulties alone might lead one to wonder, like the psalmist, whether God has simply left his people for their enemies to slaughter like spotless sacrificial lambs.[32] What for the psalmist was a real question, however, has become a rhetorical question for Paul in light of the death, resurrection, and victorious rule of Christ. The innocent suffering of his people is not God's last word. God has answered the psalmist's prayer through the work of Christ. As Haacker has perceptively observed, Paul understood Christ to be both a metaphorical sacrificial lamb whom his oppressors killed (cf. 1 Cor 5:7) and the one whom God raised from the dead in a glorious, immortal body (8:17, 29). God will take the same action on behalf of believers by glorfying together with Christ those who suffer along with him (8:17, 23).[33]

8:37 But in all these things we are winning a sweeping victory through the one who loved us (ἀλλ' ἐν τούτοις πᾶσιν ὑπερνικῶμεν διὰ τοῦ ἀγαπήσαντος ἡμᾶς). The union of believers with Christ both in his suffering and in his victory over death and evil assures believers of his love and of their own victory, even as they suffer in the present.

"All these things" refers back to the seven forms of suffering Paul listed in 8:35b and to the summary description of those troubles as being "killed all day long" and being "sheep destined for slaughter" in the quotation of Psalm 44:22. Precisely in these sufferings believers "win a sweeping victory [ὑπερνικῶμεν]" (CEB). This rare expression refers not merely to overcoming an opponent nor to winning something in addition to victory ("more than conquerors," KJV, NIV, NRSV, NIV) but to winning by a long distance.[34] Diodorus Siculus's description of the superman Polydamas illustrates well the word's meaning. He could "slay lions with his bare hands as if they were sheep and easily outstrip [ὑπερνικῶν] swift-running chariots with winged feet" (*Bibliotheca historica* 9.15.1 [Oldfather, LCL]).[35]

The "sweeping victory" of believers over these evils happens not merely in spite of them but "in" (ἐν) the midst of them. This statement probably emerges out of Paul's complex set of convictions about the union of believers with Christ and the work of the Spirit on their behalf. Paul thought that God had united believers with Christ in his

30. Ross, *Psalms*, 2:40–42.

31. The LXX has "for the sake of your name" (43:27).

32. The genitive case of "slaughter" (σφαγῆς) is a "genitive of destination." On this, see Wallace (*Greek Grammar*, 100–101), and cf. Sanday and Headlam (*Romans*, 222).

33. Haacker, *An die Römer*, 177.

34. According to Cranfield (*Romans*, 1:441) "more than conquerors" is a "felicitous" rendering that goes back to the Geneva Bible. Luther ("überwinden wir weit") and Tyndale ("we overcome strongly") seem to have had better instincts about the word's meaning, however, than the Geneva and KJV translators.

35. Diodorus composed his history in Rome in the mid first-century BC. Cf. Chrysostom (*Romans*, 272): "They did not merely conquer, but in a wondrous way" (Οὐδὲ γὰρ ἁπλῶς ἐνίκων, ἀλλὰ μετὰ πολλοῦ τοῦ θαύματος, *PG* 60.545).

death, and as a result would also unite them with his glorified existence (8:17–18, 23–24, 29). The path to glory, then, leads through suffering. He also believed that suffering Christians, even in the present, experience the assistance of the Spirit (8:26–27) and have confidence that the evil around them will not frustrate God's good purposes for them (8:28). Because this victory is in some sense present now in the midst of suffering, Paul could say in 5:3 that believers boast "in afflictions" (ἐν ταῖς θλίψεσιν), and he can speak here of winning victory in the present tense (cf. 2 Cor 4:7–12; 12:9; Phil 4:11–13).[36]

8:38–39 For I am persuaded that neither death nor life, neither angels nor rulers, neither things present nor things future, nor powers, nor height nor depth, nor any other created thing will be able to separate us from the love of God in Christ Jesus our Lord (πέπεισμαι γὰρ ὅτι οὔτε θάνατος οὔτε ζωὴ οὔτε ἄγγελοι οὔτε ἀρχαὶ οὔτε ἐνεστῶτα οὔτε μέλλοντα οὔτε δυνάμεις οὔτε ὕψωμα οὔτε βάθος οὔτε τις κτίσις ἑτέρα δυνήσεται ἡμᾶς χωρίσαι ἀπὸ τῆς ἀγάπης τοῦ θεοῦ τῆς ἐν Χριστῷ Ἰησοῦ τῷ κυρίῳ ἡμῶν). No obstacle can prevent God from easily doing what he intends to do, in this case from showing his love to his people.

Paul's "for" (γάρ) points back to what he has just said about winning a sweeping victory in the present, in the midst of suffering, and Paul's perfect-tense expression "I am persuaded" (πέπεισμαι) refers to "giving in to reasons."[37] The victory of believers is less than evident on a superficial examination of the evidence; indeed, the evidence seems to indicate that a dramatic defeat is in progress (cf. 8:36). The case needs to be made, then, that what looks like defeat is actually victory, and for Paul God has made that case convincingly in the death, resurrection, and heavenly session of Christ.

Paul's list of possible limits to the reach of God's love extends the seven forms of suffering in 8:35 by including abstract and metaphorical terms. This has the effect of broadening Paul's claim beyond the category of suffering to include everything that exists (cf. 1 Cor 3:21–22). The first pair sets the tone. Everyone is either dead or alive, and so "death" and "life" cover all possible modes of existence. "Christ will be honored in my body, whether by life or by death," Paul says in Philippians 1:20–21, "for to me to live is Christ, and to die is gain." In either case, he experiences the love of God in Christ Jesus.

"Neither angels nor rulers" may refer to types of transcendent beings, whether good (2 Thess 1:7; 1 Tim 5:21) or evil (cf., e.g., 1 Cor 4:9; 6:3; Eph 6:12; Col 2:15), and that is certainly the assumption of virtually all interpreters from early times to the present.[38] Paul can, however, use the term "rulers" (ἀρχαί) unambiguously of visible, earthly governmental authorities (Titus 3:1), and if he uses it that way here, then the rhetorical pairing of opposites would be preserved. Angels would refer to invisible messengers, whether good or evil, and rulers would refer to governmental authorities, whether just (cf. Rom 13:3–4) or unjust (cf. 2 Cor 11:32–33).[39]

36. Cf. Wilckens (*An die Römer [Röm 6–11]*, 175), Haacker (*An die Römer*, 177–78), and Jewett (*Romans*, 549); for the connection to 2 Corinthians, see Meyer (*Romans*, 343).

37. *TLNT* 3:68, citing, e.g., Herodotus, *Histories* 6.100.3; 7.144.3; and Xenophon, *Anab.* 7.2.12, although only the last of these references uses the word in the perfect tense. Cf. Paul's use of the first-person perfect of this verb in Rom 14:14; 15:14; 2 Tim 1:5, 12.

38. E.g., Chrysostom, *Romans*, 273; Pelagius, *Romans*, 114; Theodoret of Cyrus, *Letters of St. Paul*, 1:97; Calvin, *Romans*, 189; Cranfield, *Romans*, 1:442; Wilckens, *An die Römer (Röm 6–11)*, 177; Schreiner, *Romans*, 465; Légasse, *Romains*, 556.

39. The notion that Titus is pseudonymous seems to have exercised significant influence over the decision to deny an earthly meaning for "rulers" (ἀρχαί). See, e.g., Légasse, *Romains*, 556. Jewett (*Romans*, 551–52) and Wright ("Romans," 615) are rare exceptions to the almost unquestioning approach to the meaning of this word here.

"Neither things present nor things future" broadens the dimensions of reality to which Paul refers beyond categories of consciousness and tangibility to the category of chronology. Nothing that believers presently are experiencing or anything that they will experience will separate them from God's love in Christ.

"Powers" (δυνάμεις) refers to transcendent beings or to those under their influence, who exercise authority over others through abilities given to them from beyond the earthly sphere (Acts 8:10; 1 Pet 3:22). Greek and Greco-Roman writers sometimes called the gods "powers" (e.g., Plato, *Crat.* 438c; Plutarch, *Is. Os.* 67 [377F–378A]; cf. 4 Macc 5:13), and where Paul uses the term elsewhere it probably refers to transcendent evil forces (Eph 1:20–21; cf. 6:12; 1 Cor 15:24–26).[40]

Notions of "height" and "depth," when used metaphorically and together in Scripture, tend to refer to difficulties that would easily defeat human beings but that for God pose no obstacle at all. The psalmist can go nowhere, whether heaven or Sheol, that God cannot easily be (Ps 139:8), and Ahaz can ask no sign of the Lord that the Lord cannot easily accomplish: "Let it be deep as Sheol or high as heaven" (Isa 7:11; LXX: "in depth [βαθός] or in height [ὕψος]"). This language fits the emphasis here on the limitless nature of God's love and is most likely the key to Paul's meaning despite Paul's use of the noun "height" (ὕψωμα) rather than the adjective "high" (ὕψος). No obstacle can successfully prevent God's love from reaching his people.

The phrase "any other created thing" covers any gaps Paul may have left in the preceding list and at the same time reminds believers in Rome that God is sovereign over all that exists. The entire world is God's creation (1:20), and so he governs all that exists and all that happens.

The final phrase of this long sentence returns to the language and thought of 8:35 and to the language of God's love demonstrated by the reconciling death of Christ in the first paragraph of the second major section of the letter (5:5–8). Absolutely nothing will be able to separate believers from the love that God has shown to them through the death of Christ. Unlike 8:35, however, where Paul spoke simply of "the love of Christ," he now speaks more fully of the love of God "in Christ Jesus our Lord," echoing the similar expressions at the beginning of the second major section of his overall argument (5:1) and at the end of the most significant steps within the argument of the section itself (5:21; 6:23; 7:25; cf. 5:11).[41] The result is an intensely christological description of God, and especially of his love.[42] God can only be fully known, and his love fully experienced, through Christ Jesus in his reconciling death and his glorious resurrection (5:5–8, 18–19; 8:3–4, 11, 17, 29).

IN DEPTH: Are "Height" and "Depth" in 8:39 Astrological Terms?

In Paul's time people commonly thought that the sun, the moon, the planets, and the stars controlled the fate of human beings, and astrological science was highly developed. Many people thought that the stars rose from a region below

40. Hans Dieter Betz, "Dynamis," *DDD* 267–70; BDAG 263, s.v. δύναμις 5.

41. Cranfield, *Romans*, 1:444.

42. Ibid.

the horizon and ascended into a region above the horizon, and the position of the various heavenly bodies at the time of one's birth dictated one's character and fate.[43]

Paul's list of forces that cannot separate believers from the love of God in Christ Jesus uses two terms that also appear in astrological discussions in antiquity, "height" (ὕψωμα) and "depth" (βάθος). The term "height" referred to the "elevation" or "exaltation" of a heavenly body above the horizon, and the term "depth" referred to the region below the horizon from which planetary bodies regularly ascended.[44] In the early twentieth century, the theory that Paul used these words in a technical astrological sense in Romans 8:39 began to appear in commentaries on Romans and in scholarly treatments of Paul's thought.[45]

Perhaps most significantly, this understanding of the terms showed up in Erwin Preuschen's Greek-German lexicon of 1910 and received support in 1928 from the publication of Walter Bauer's thorough revision of Preuschen's lexicon. Preuschen's approach to the meaning of the terms in Romans 8:39 had been inconsistent. In his article on "depth" (βάθος) he had said that the two terms simply referred to "heaven" and "earth" in Romans 8:39, but his article on "height" (ὕψωμα) called this term "an astronomical technical term" referring to "the highest approach of certain planets to the heavenly zenith" and implied that Paul used it, together with its opposite "depth," in this technical sense in Romans 8:39.[46] In Bauer's 1928 revision of Preuschen's work, the astrological interpretation appears in the first definition of both terms and cites Romans 8:39 as its only example of the use of the terms in this way in early Christian literature.[47]

This presentation of the meaning of the terms continues basically unchanged in BDAG (published in 2000). The first definition of ὕψωμα in BDAG calls it "an astronomical term," referring to "the domain of many transcendent forces" and cites Romans 8:39 as its only example of the use of the term in early Christian

43. Roger L. Beck, "Astrology," *OCD* 195. For an example of an astrological prescription written at the time of the birth of a child, see P.Lond. III.110 (from AD 138). This text uses the term ὑψώματι in line 14 (cf. BDAG 1046, s.v. ὕψωμα 1).

44. For "height" (ὕψωμα) see, e.g., Vettius Valens, *Anthologies*, 172–73 (4.13); Sextus Empiricus, *Against the Mathematicians* 5.35–36; and Claudius Ptolemy, *Tetrabiblos* 1.20 (1.19 in the LCL edition). For "depth," see, e.g., Vettius Valens, *Anthologies* 241.25 (6.1) (cited in LSJ 301, s.v. βάθος); *PGM* 4.575 (cited in BDAG 162, s.v. βάθος); and the liturgy of Mithras cited by Hans Lietzmann, *Der Brief des Apostels Paulus and die Römer*, 3rd ed., HNT 8 (Tübingen: Mohr Siebeck, 1928), 89. It has to be said, however, that only the Mithras liturgy clearly refers to heavenly bodies emerging "from the depth."

45. E.g., Lietzmann, *An die Römer*, 88–89; Martin Dibelius, *Die Geisterwelt im Glauben des Paulus* (Göttingen: Vandenhoeck & Ruprecht, 1909), 112; Wilfred L. Knox, *St Paul and the Church of the Gentiles* (1939; repr., Cambridge: Cambridge University Press, 1961), 106–7.

46. Erwin Preuschen, *Vollständiges Griechisch-Deutsches Handwörterbuch zu den Schriften des Neuen Testaments und der übrigen urchristlichen Literatur* (Gießen: Alfred Töpelmann, 1910), cols. 194, 1124, s.v. βάθος and ὕψωμα.

47. Walter Bauer, *Griechisch-Deutsches Wörterbuch zu den Schriften des Neuen Testaments und der übrigen urchristlichen Literatur* (Gießen: Alfred Töpelmann, 1928), cols. 205, 1358–59, s.v. βάθος and ὕψωμα.

literature.[48] Similarly, although BDAG recognizes that the term "depth" (βάθος) normally refers to "the distance beneath something," it claims that in Romans 8:39 the word, like its counterpart "height" (ὕψωμα), is an astronomical technical term and probably refers to "astral spirits."[49] It is perhaps from BDAG in its various editions that this interpretation of neither "height nor depth" in Romans 8:39 has exercised such wide influence among commentators on Romans.[50]

The foundation for this understanding of the terms "height" and "depth," however, is not at all secure. In the Greek of Paul's period, the term "height" meant "that which has been elevated—a lofty situation or position—elevation; exaltation."[51] It could refer to the "heavenly heights" (οὐρανίοις ὑψώμασι) that stand opposite the "earth" (χθών), for example, or to the exalted location of the air.[52] It was a natural term for astrologers or anyone else to use of the "height" or "elevation" of heavenly bodies above the horizon, but this meaning was derived from its more mundane uses.[53]

The word could refer in a metaphorical sense, for example, to the "exaltation" of someone or something to prominence or honor, and this use could have negative or positive connotations. It could also mean the "loftiness" that leads certain people to mistreat the needy (Job 24:24 LXX), or in the only other NT use of the term, to every "lofty thing" raised in opposition to God (2 Cor 10:5 NASB). Positively, it could refer to the proper recognition of some person or group as honorable and righteous, as when Judith's courage and cleverness in assassinating the wicked Holofernes led to the "exaltation" of Jerusalem (Jdt 10:8; 13:4; 15:9).

Uses of the term in the cultural contexts closest to Paul cluster around these nonspecialized meanings, whether literal or metaphorical, and refer to something that is high or exalted. It is far more likely that Paul would use the term in the way that it is used in Judith, the writings of Philo, the maxims of Pseudo-Phocylides, and elsewhere in his own writings than that he would use the term in the technical mode of astrologers who wrote a century or more after his death.

The only thing to be said for taking the term in an astrological or astronomical sense, then, is the immediate context in which it is found in Romans 8:39.

48. BDAG 1046, s.v. ὕψωμα.

49. BDAG 162, s.v. βάθος.

50. See, e.g., Dodd, *Romans*, 160, 194–95; Heinrich Schlier, *Der Römerbrief*, HTKNT 6 (Freiburg im Breisgau: Herder, 1977), 280–81; Käsemann, *Romans*, 261; Fitzmyer, *Romans*, 535; Jewett, *Romans*, 554.

51. James Donnegan, *A New Greek and English Lexicon* (Boston: Hilliard, Gray & Co., 1833), 1322, s.v. ὕψωμα.

52. LSJ 1910, s.v. ὕψωμα; Pseudo-Phocylides 73 (P. W. van der Horst, *OTP* 2:576); Philo, *Rewards* 2.

53. See, for example, Plutarch's use of the term in *Sept. sap. conv.* 3 [2.149] and *Princ. iner.* 782 D.

It stands opposite a term meaning "depth" (βάθος) that ancient Greek speakers used to describe the region below the horizon from which stars arose. Elsewhere in his list Paul also refers to invisible beings such as "angels" and "powers," increasing the likelihood that "height" and "depth" really should be understood as "powers of the height and of the depth," to quote C. H. Dodd.[54]

The astrological writers of antiquity, however, do not normally pair the "elevation" or "exaltation" (ὕψωμα) of a heavenly body with its "depth" (βάθος) but with its "depression" (ταπείνωμα).[55] Indeed, "not normally" is probably far too generous, since any pairing of "height" (ὕψωμα) with "depth" (βάθος) in the astrological literature is difficult to find. The example usually cited is Vettius Valens, *Anthologies* 241.25 (6.1).[56] Vettius, however, was writing about a century after Paul, and the relevant passage is not a true parallel to Paul's "height [ὕψωμα] nor depth [βάθος]." Vettius pairs "height" as a measurement (ὕψος) with "depth" (βάθος) as a measurement, not height in the sense of a high position (ὕψωμα) with depth as a measurement, as Paul does. Paul and Vettius, then, use two different terms for "height," and the terms have slightly different meanings.[57] Moreover, as the exegesis of Romans 8:38 has demonstrated, Paul refers to more than transcendent beings in his list. "Angels" and "powers" probably refer to heavenly beings, but the other items in the list could easily refer to earthly realities of everyday experience.

It is likely, then, that Paul did not intend "height" and "depth" in a technical astrological sense in 8:39. Instead, as the comments on 8:38–39 above argue, he used these terms metaphorically to say that no obstacle can prevent God from easily doing what he intends to do, in this case from showing his love to his people.

Theology in Application

This passage shows why the gospel is good news. The gospel is the announcement that in Christ God has acted so decisively and powerfully to save his people that no force seeking their harm can ultimately prevail. The sweep of the gospel's saving power is broad, as Paul shows with his opening question of defiance, "Who is against

54. Dodd, *Romans*, 194.

55. LSJ 1910, s.v. ὕψωμα; Dunn, *Romans 1–8*, 508; Jewett, *Romans*, 553–54.

56. Dunn, *Romans 1–8*, 508; Fitzmyer, *Romans*, 535. Cf. LSJ 301, s.v. βάθος.

57. When the pairing occurs, Vettius is in the middle of a defense of astrology against its naysayers and comments on how an astrologer can know all sorts of useful things about the heavens, including the height and depth of the moon. He seems to mean by this that an astrologer can predict the position of the moon in the night sky.

us?" (8:31a). He focuses in the passage, however, on two enemies in particular: sin and suffering.

Assurance of Deliverance from Sin

First, with regard to sin Paul repeats the essence of his argument from 5:1–8:30. God has delivered his own Son over to death on behalf of believers, and since his gracious generosity toward them has taken such a dramatic form already, it is clear that he intends to give them everything that enables them to flourish as human beings—the "all things" of 8:39. Human beings in their state of rebellion against God are their own worst enemy (1:18–32), and this rebellion is universal (2:1–3:20; 5:12–21). The good news of the gospel, however, is that this enemy no longer affects God's relationship with his people. At God's own initiative he has refused to pour out his wrath on them, has reconciled them to himself, and has entered a loving relationship with them. Anyone who doubts this has only to look at the cross of Christ and the love displayed there to see that God has overcome this enemy for his people (5:8; 8:35, 39). There is no charge left to bring against them, and there is no condemnation for them (8:33).

In case someone wonders whether sins committed after their initial justification might separate them from God's love, Paul answers that Christ not only died but was raised and seated at God's right hand. From this place of sympathy (he died, just as we do), victory (he conquered death, just as we will), and power (he reigns with God the Father), his continuing work on behalf of believers assures that they remain free from condemnation (8:34). For anyone who has accepted in faith Paul's description of sin's devastating consequences for all humanity (1:18–3:20; 5:12–21) and his bleak portrayal of sin's tight grip on even the most well-intentioned human being (7:5, 13–25), this assurance of Christ's love should come as good news indeed.

God's Compassion for His Suffering People

Second, Paul concludes that suffering, and especially persecution, cannot separate believers from God's love in Christ Jesus. Since the commitment of believers to the gospel involves turning away from the idolatrous and unloving behavior Paul has described in 1:18–3:20 at the same time that the unbelieving world continues within it, faithfulness to the gospel also sometimes involves suffering the pain of marginalization and mistreatment from the unbelieving world (cf. 12:14, 17). The earliest Christians, including Paul, were familiar with this experience. By the time Paul wrote Romans, John the Baptist had lost his head, Jesus had been crucified, Peter, John, and other apostles had been arrested, a mob had murdered Stephen, the pre-Christian Paul himself had "dragged off men and women and committed them to prison" (Acts

8:3), John's brother James had been killed (Acts 12:2), and the post-conversion Paul had experienced every trial he lists in Romans 8:35 except execution by the sword.[58]

It would be a mistake, however, to limit the suffering of which Paul speaks in this passage to persecution. Not all the tribulation, distress, famine, lack of clothing, danger, and death that Christians experience is a result of faithfulness to Christ. A careful look at Psalm 44 reveals that there too God's people were suffering despite their righteousness, not because of it. They have simply experienced defeat in battle, and nothing in the psalm indicates that this suffering was anything other than what millions before and since have experienced because of war. When believers suffer, whether for their faith or not, they sometimes ask like the psalmist, "O Lord . . . why do you hide your face?" (Ps 44:23–24).

In this passage Paul delivers the good news that God has not hidden his face from his people when they suffer. His face is found in the face of the crucified Jesus Christ. In the crucified Jesus Christ, who died because of his love for God's people (and Christ's love is also God's love), Christians can take confidence and courage that their suffering does not mean God has failed to care for them or to show up at the time of their distress. They were united with Christ in his death when they heard and believed the gospel (Eph 1:13), and their union with him in his suffering and death continues in the present (Rom 6:6; cf. 2 Cor 4:10; Gal 2:20; Phil 3:10). This union is, among other things, fellowship with the one "who loved me and gave himself for me" (Gal 2:20).

The living Christ who is seated in victory at God's right hand, interceding for his people (8:34), is at the same time the Christ with whose suffering believers are united (Rom 8:17). John depicts this victorious Christ at God's right hand as a lamb who has been slain and who therefore still bears the marks of his suffering on behalf of God's people (Rev 5:6). The marks of Christ's suffering, still there in his victorious, glorified existence, stand as a permanent reminder of his love for God's people and of God's identification with them in the midst of hardship.

This is the sense in which believers "win a sweeping victory through the one who loved us" (8:37). Their union with Christ in his death not only ensures their union with him in his immortal, incorruptible state of victory and glory (8:17) but also of his love for them even as they experience the tribulation and distress of life in a world alienated from its creator.

58. Marcus L. Loane, *The Hope of Glory: An Exposition of the Eighth Chapter in the Epistle to the Romans* (Waco, TX: Word, 1968), 150–51.

In Summary: The Good News That God Is Love

The gospel, then, is good news because it is a message of God's gracious reconciliation of himself to his human creation despite their sin and because, in the gospel, human beings discover that their creator is not unconcerned about their plight within a world wracked by suffering. In sum, the gospel is the good news that the only and all-powerful creator of the universe is, more than anything else, a God of love and that he has put his love into action on behalf of his human creatures.[59] He has done this through the death, resurrection, and present authority of his Son Jesus Christ.

59. On this, see Leon Morris, *Testaments of Love: A Study of Love in the Bible* (Grand Rapids: Eerdmans, 1981), 129–48.

CHAPTER 20

Romans 9:1–29

Literary Context

There is a sense in which 1:16–8:39 is a tightly structured, self-contained argumentative unit. Paul announces his definition of the gospel in compressed form in 1:16–17 and then explains it fully in 1:18–8:39, bringing his explanation to a close with a stirring affirmation of God's love for his people in 8:38–39. Paul has explained that the gospel announces not only God's righteous judgment on human sin (1:18–3:20) but also God's righteous salvation of sinful humanity (3:21–4:25) so that believers now live at peace with God and in the hope of inheriting a restored creation (5:1–8:39). God impartially gives sinners the wrath they deserve (1:18–3:20) and impartially justifies them through the atoning death of Christ and by faith rather than works, whether of the Mosaic law or any law (3:21–4:25). He then graciously gives them peace, life, and hope (5:1–8:39).

The argument is so well-balanced that someone in Paul's audience who had followed the letter at a superficial level up to this point might think that at the end of chapter eight Paul was finished. He had demonstrated the human plight and God's solution to it in Christ. He had shown that this message about Christ was the gospel of God's righteous, saving power for everyone, whether Jew or gentile. He had shown, moreover, that the law and the prophets had pointed forward to the gospel as he described it (3:21). They too portrayed God as an impartial judge (2:6) and hinted that God would fulfill his promise to Abraham by including the nations within Abraham's family through faith (4:1–25).

This superficial reading is inadequate, however, because it does not take into account the relationship between the gospel as Paul has described it so far and the actual results of the gospel's proclamation. By the time Paul wrote Romans, the gospel was having its greatest success among gentiles rather than Jews, and Jews, when they heard the gospel, had sometimes actively, even violently, opposed it (Acts 13:45, 50; 17:5–7, 13; 18:6, 12–13; 19:9; 1 Thess 2:14–16). The ethnic composition of Roman Christianity itself, at least at the time Paul wrote his letter, matched the lopsided results of Paul's own preaching. Paul wrote his letter to "all" of God's people in Rome (Rom 1:7), but the audience was predominantly gentile (1:13; 11:13; 15:15–16).

This historical reality called into question Paul's claim that the law and the prophets had laid the foundation for the gospel (1:2; 3:21) and especially that the gospel was the means by which God would fulfill his promise to Abraham (4:1–25). It may be true that the faith of gentiles in the gospel allows faithful Abraham to become the father of many nations, but if Abraham's own fleshly kinfolk form a minority within this group, how can Abraham, in the end, be "the father of us all" (4:16), and how can the gospel then be the fulfillment of God's promise to Abraham at this basic level? If members of the multiethnic group who are united with Christ and indwelt by the Spirit are now the adoptive children of God (8:14–15, 23, 16–17, 21), then has God renounced Israel's status as his children as it is described in the law and the prophets (Exod 4:22–23; Deut 14:1; Jer 31:9; Hos 11:1)?

In the exhilarating final paragraphs of his argument, Paul has said that no one can bring charges against God's chosen people (8:33) or separate them from God's love (8:39; cf. 8:35). Yet the balance between Jews and gentiles among those who had believed the gospel in Paul's time called this assurance into question.[1] If Paul's proclamation of the gospel has itself separated God from the very people he had chosen and promised to love in the Scriptures, then Paul's claim that his gospel was consistent with the Scriptures might seem empty or, worse yet, the God of Paul's gospel might seem unreliable. In the words of an anonymous Palestinian Jew of the first century urging God to be merciful to his people, "For even if you plant another vine, it will not trust you, because you destroyed the former one."[2]

In Romans 9:1–11:36 Paul acknowledges the tragedy of Israel's rejection of the gospel (9:1–5) but then explains why this response does not pose a threat to the claims he has made about the consistency of the gospel with Israel's Scriptures (9:6–11:32). The means by which God shows himself faithful to Israel despite its present rejection of the gospel are unexpected and complex, and so Paul concludes this section of his argument with a statement of his amazement at the depth of God's power and wisdom (11:33–36). Between its sorrowful introduction (9:1–5) and its awestruck conclusion (11:33–36), the argument proceeds in three steps.[3]

In 9:6–29 Paul explains two principles from the Scriptures that show that the current ethnic configuration of those who believe the gospel is not inconsistent with God's word. First, the Scriptures reveal that God's true people have always been a smaller group than the number of Abraham's physical descendants (9:6–23). Second,

1. According to Longenecker (*Romans*, 756, 769), Paul's use of the term "chosen people" (ἐκλεκτοί) for gentile as well as Jewish believers in 8:33 may have been particularly provocative. That expression was commonly used in Israel's Scriptures to refer to ethnic Israel as the people with whom God had a special, covenantal relationship (e.g., 1 Chr 16:13; Ps 89:3 [88:4 LXX]; 105:6 [104:6 LXX]).

2. LAB 12:9, quoted (and italicized) in J. Ross Wagner, *Heralds of the Good News: Isaiah and Paul "In Concert,"* NovTSup 101 (Leiden: Brill, 2002), 232n49.

3. Jean Noël Aletti (*God's Justice in Romans: Keys for Interpreting the Epistle to the Romans*, trans. Peggy Manning Meyer; Subsidia Biblica 37 [Rome: Gregorian and Biblical Press, 2010], 164) says that "almost every commentator divides the section" into these five parts (introduction, three intermediate steps, and conclusion).

the Scriptures also support the notion that as God works out his historical purposes there will be times when gentiles outnumber Jews within the true people of God (9:24–29).

In 9:30–10:21 Paul answers a question that naturally arises from what he has just said about gentiles outnumbering Jews in the true people of God. How, from a human perspective, could this happen in light of the advantage over the gentiles that access to God's law gives to Jews? Paul answers that their zeal for the law blinded unbelieving Jews to the righteousness that God offered them in the gospel.

In 11:1–32 Paul asks a question that naturally arises from the case he has just made that most Jews have rejected the righteousness of God in the gospel. Does this mean that God has also rejected them? Surprisingly, Paul says that this conclusion is not correct. Not only does a present remnant of Jewish believers exist (11:1–10) but eventually, when God has fully implemented his plan for history, vast numbers of Jews will be saved (11:11–32). Eventually, God will use Jewish rejection and gentile acceptance of the gospel (9:30–10:21) to save "all Israel" (11:11–32).[4]

IX. Justification by Faith Brings Peace and Reorients the Believer's Existence (5:1–8:39)

➡ **X. Israel's Present Rejection of the Gospel Does Not Imply the Failure of God's Word (9:1–11:36)**

A. Paul's Anguish over Israel's Rejection of the Gospel (9:1–5)

B. The Scriptures Describe God's Choice of His People as Free and Surprising (9:6–29)

C. Unbelieving Israel Is Culpable for Rejecting the Gospel (9:30–10:21)

D. Still, God Has Not Cast Off His People (11:1–32)

E. A Concluding Statement of Astonishment and Praise (11:33–36)

XI. Exhortation to Live in a Way That Is Consistent with the Gospel (12:1–15:13)

Main Idea

Although Paul was grieved over the relatively small number of Israelites who had believed the gospel in his own time, this sad situation did not impugn either the gospel in which he had just expressed such confidence or the Scriptures themselves. The word of God has not wrecked on the rocks of Israel's unbelief. Rather, the present ethnic configuration of the people of God is consistent with the portrait of God in Scripture. There God is free to choose who will belong to his people and who will be hardened in rebellion against him, and he is free to make what, from a human perspective, are unconventional choices about those to whom he will show mercy.

4. Cf. Aletti, *God's Justice in Romans*, 166–71.

Translation

Romans 9:1–29

1a Assertion	**I speak the truth**
b Sphere	in Christ,
c Assertion	**I am not lying,** and
d Confirmation	my conscience bears witness together
	with me
e Sphere	in the Holy Spirit
2 Content	that great sorrow is mine, and
	there is constant distress in my heart.
3a Explanation (of 2)	For **I could almost wish**
	that I myself were something cursed,
b Apposition	separated
	from Christ
	in place of my brothers and sisters,
c Apposition	my compatriots according to the flesh,
4a List	who indeed are Israelites,
b List	whose are the adoption as sons, and
c List	the glory, and
d List	the covenants, and
e List	the legislation, and
f List	the worship, and
g List	the promises,
5a List	whose are the fathers, and
b List	from whom is the Messiah,
c Description	as far as the flesh is concerned,
d Identification	who is God over all, blessed forever. Amen.
6a Assertion	But **that is not to say that the word of God has failed.**
b Basis	For **not all those from Israel are Israel;**

7a Expansion — nor because those from Israel are Abraham's offspring
are they all **children,**

b Contrast — but, "In Isaac will your offspring be called." (Gen 21:12)

8a Restatement — That is, **it is not the children of the flesh who are children of God,**
b Contrast — but **the children of the promise are counted as offspring.**

9 Basis — For **the word of promise is this:**
"At this season I will come and Sara will have a son." (Gen 18:10, 14)

10 Expansion/Concession — And not only so, but also **Rebecca,**
although becoming pregnant by one man, our forefather Isaac

11a Restatement (of 10) —for although they were not yet born or
had done anything good or evil,

b Purpose (of 12b) — in order that the chosen purpose of God might stand firm
12a Means (of 11b) — not by works but
by the one who calls—

b Contra-expectation (of 10) — **it was said to her,**
"The greater will serve the smaller," (Gen 25:23)

13 Verification (of 12b) — just as it is written,
"Jacob I have loved, but Esau I have hated." (Mal 1:2–3)

14a (False) Inference Assertion — **What, then, shall we say?**
There is no injustice with God is there?

b Exclamation — **Certainly not!**
15 Basis — For **to Moses he says,**
"I show mercy to whomever I show mercy, and
I will show compassion to whomever I show compassion." (Exod 33:19)

Continued on next page.

Continued from previous page.

16 Inference (from 15) So then, **it is not of the one who wills,**
nor of the one who runs, but
of God who shows mercy.

17 Verification (of 16) For **the Scripture says** to Pharaoh,
"For this very purpose I raised you up:
that I might show my power in you and
that my name might be proclaimed in all the earth." (Exod 9:16)

18 Inference (from 17) So then, **he shows mercy to whom he wills,**
and **he hardens whom he wills.**

19 (False) Inference **You will say to me, then,**
"Why does he still assign blame?
For who withstands what he plans?"

20a Contrast To the contrary, you mere human being,

Rhetorical Question **who are you to answer back to God?**

b Rhetorical Question **Will the thing formed say to the one who formed it, "Why did you make me this way?"**

21 Illustration/ Rhetorical Question Or **does the potter not have authority**
over the clay
to make from the same lump
one vessel for the purpose of receiving honor and
one for the purpose of receiving dishonor?

22a Rhetorical Question/ Explanation And **what if God endured**
b Manner with much patience
c Object vessels of wrath fitted out for destruction
d Cause (of 22a, c) because he wanted to show his wrath and
e Cause (of 22a, c) to make known his power, and

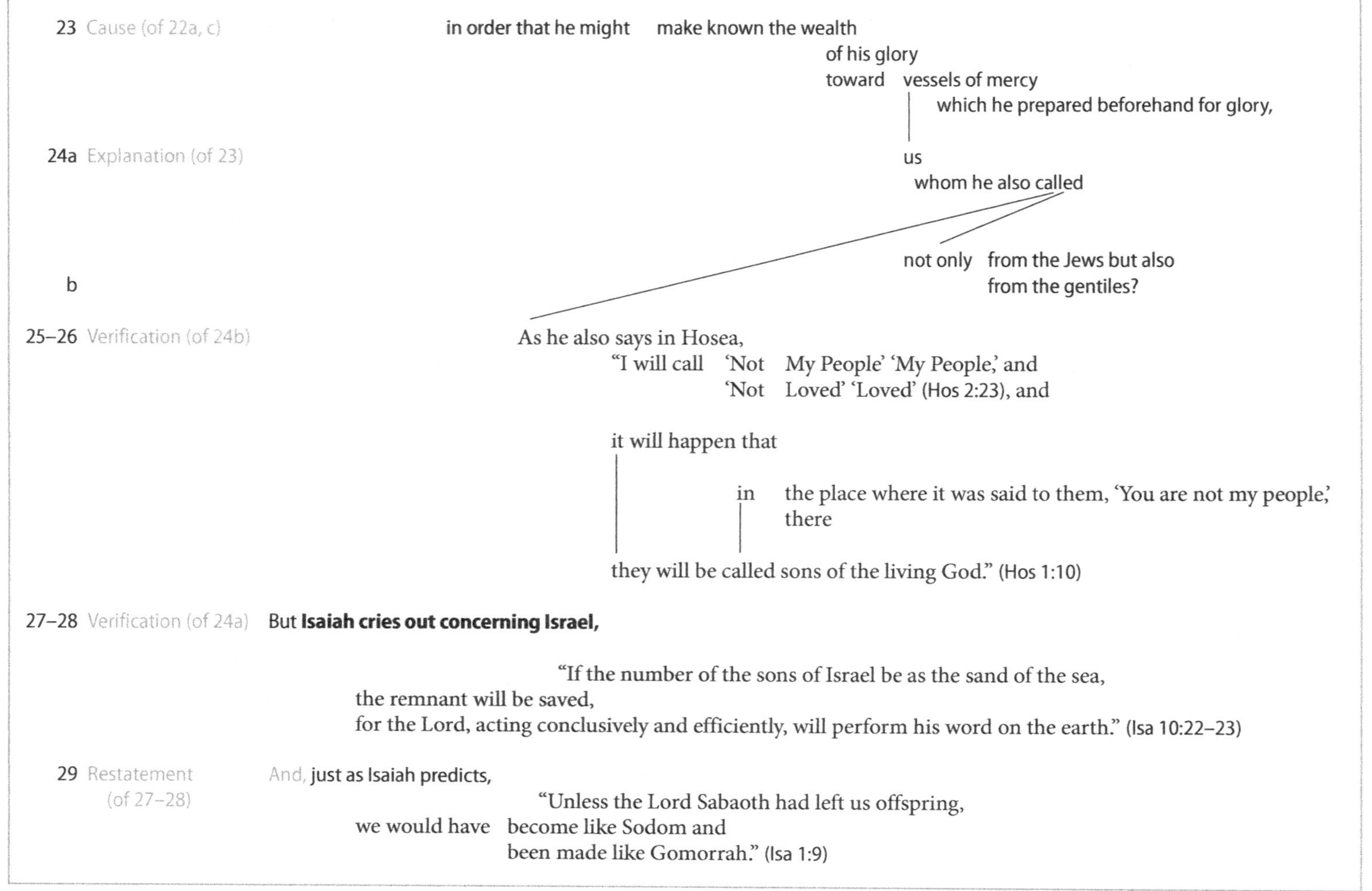

23 Cause (of 22a, c) in order that he might make known the wealth
of his glory
toward vessels of mercy
which he prepared beforehand for glory,

24a Explanation (of 23) us
whom he also called

not only from the Jews but also
b from the gentiles?

25–26 Verification (of 24b) As he also says in Hosea,
"I will call 'Not My People' 'My People,' and
'Not Loved' 'Loved' (Hos 2:23), and

it will happen that
in the place where it was said to them, 'You are not my people,'
there
they will be called sons of the living God." (Hos 1:10)

27–28 Verification (of 24a) But **Isaiah cries out concerning Israel,**

"If the number of the sons of Israel be as the sand of the sea,
the remnant will be saved,
for the Lord, acting conclusively and efficiently, will perform his word on the earth." (Isa 10:22–23)

29 Restatement (of 27–28) And, just as Isaiah predicts,
"Unless the Lord Sabaoth had left us offspring,
we would have become like Sodom and
been made like Gomorrah." (Isa 1:9)

Structure

The passage is carefully constructed and falls into five parts. First, in 9:1–5 Paul indicates that he is beginning a new, major section of the letter by formulating a sentence with no conjunction connecting it to the exalted language of 8:31–39. At the same time, the deeply personal, confessional style of 9:1–3 alerts the reader that Paul is as deeply moved by the problem he is about to articulate as he was by the joyful confidence he described in 8:31–39.[5] The problem is that the majority of God's people Israel who have heard the gospel have not believed it, and this calls into question the faithfulness of God to his promises to his people in his word. Paul does not say this explicitly, however, but leaves the reader slowly to apprehend the painful truth that constitutes the problem. His startling and solemn ascription of praise to the Messiah as God in 9:5 brings this opening paragraph to a close.

Second, in 9:6–13 Paul states the thesis he will develop in 9:7–11:32 and then begins to support this thesis from Scripture. Israelite unbelief does not mean that God's promises to be faithful to his people have failed (9:6). Scripture demonstrates that the children of God and the physical children of Abraham are overlapping but different groups (9:7–9) and that God freely chooses his children without regard to their relative virtues and vices or their family connections (9:10–13).

Third, in 9:14–18 Paul answers the question whether God can be just and, at the same time, can be as free in choosing his people as Paul has just portrayed him. Should not membership within God's people be the reward for having the right family connections or living more virtuously than those not chosen? Paul does not answer the question directly but instead appeals to Scripture again to show that it portrays God dealing with his own people and with Pharaoh during the period of the exodus in precisely the way Paul has just described. An important assumption lies beneath this section of Paul's argument. Since everyone is a sinner and deserves his condemnation, God has the right to choose those to whom he will be merciful and to harden in their rebellion against him those who have not received his mercy.

Fourth, in 9:19–23 Paul answers the question of whether God can rationally fault those whom he has hardened in rebellion for continuing their rebellion against him. In reply, Paul argues that God has the same relationship to human beings that a potter has to the clay from which he fashions various vessels. Just as the potter has the freedom to fashion vessels for different purposes, so God has the freedom to ready some people for destruction and to show mercy to others, and to do all this for his glory. Again, Paul assumes that all humanity is sinful and deserving of destruction. The purpose of the illustration is not to describe God's role as a creator (as if God creates some people for the purpose of destroying them) but his role as a shaper who determines the destinies of all human beings.

5. Ibid., 176.

Fifth, in 9:24–29 Paul circles back to the thought of 9:7–13 and articulates the concern of that passage more explicitly. The small success of the gospel among Jews and its greater success among the gentiles in Paul's time follow a pattern found in Scripture. Hosea spoke of God calling those who were not his people to be his people, and Isaiah spoke of God preserving only a remnant of Israel after he had punished them for their disobedience. The multiethnic people of God, then, has a surprising configuration from an ethnic perspective, but it is no more surprising than God's choice of Isaac over Ishmael or Jacob over Esau (9:7–13).

Exegetical Outline

- **X. Israel's Present Rejection of the Gospel Does Not Imply the Failure of God's Word (9:1–11:36)**
  - ➡ **A. Paul's Anguish over Israel's Rejection of the Gospel (9:1–5)**
  - **B. The Scriptures Describe God's Choice of His People as Free and Surprising (9:6–29)**
    1. Isaac and Jacob as Objects of God's Free and Surprising Choice (9:6–13)
    2. An Objection: Is God's Unconventional Choice Unjust? (9:14–18)
    3. Another Objection: Can God Justly Blame Those Whom He Has Hardened? (9:19–23)
    4. Hosea and Isaiah Confirm the Sometimes Surprising Composition of God's People (9:24–29)

Explanation of the Text

9:1 I speak the truth in Christ, I am not lying, and my conscience bears witness together with me in the Holy Spirit (Ἀλήθειαν λέγω ἐν Χριστῷ, οὐ ψεύδομαι, συμμαρτυρούσης μοι τῆς συνειδήσεώς μου ἐν πνεύματι ἁγίῳ). Whatever Paul's detractors may claim, he is certain that what he is about to say reflects his genuine feelings. This certainty comes not simply from his own self-examination but from Christ, with whom he is united, and from God's Spirit who dwells within him.

There is no connecting particle in this new sentence, and this is a sign that Paul is about to begin a new section of his argument. Still, the first-person singular speech here and Paul's focus on his inner life continue the personal, confessional tone to which he had already shifted in 8:38–39. These elements of the new section skillfully bind it to the preceding paragraph. Paul's personal persuasion that nothing will separate God's people from God's love (8:38–39) involves a corresponding, deeply felt grief at the rejection the gospel has received from many of Paul's own people (9:1–5; cf. 10:1).[6]

Paul often used truth claims for his speech when he was answering criticisms of the way he conducted his apostolic ministry (2 Cor 6:7; 7:14; 11:10; Gal 1:20; 1 Tim 2:7; cf. 2 Cor 2:17; 12:19), and many interpreters believe that here too he had critics of his gospel and his mission to the gentiles in mind.[7] The emphasis on the truthfulness of what he is about to say concerning his own sorrow

6. Cf. Godet, *Romans*, 338; Aletti, *God's Justice in Romans*, 176.

7. So already Calvin (*Romans*, 190–91), and see, e.g., Käsemann (*Romans*, 257) and James D. G. Dunn (*Romans 9–16*, WBC 38B [Dallas: Word, 1988], 523).

at the Jewish rejection of the gospel may reflect rumors that Paul advocated erasing the lines between Jew and gentile and showed disrespect for Jewish institutions such as the law and the temple (cf. Acts 21:20–21, 28).

Paul calls on two witnesses to the truthfulness of what he is about to say: himself and his conscience.[8] His appeal to himself is especially emphatic, using both a positive statement that he speaks the truth (cf. 2 Cor 4:2) and a negative statement that he does not lie (cf. Gal 1:20). His conscience can serve as a second witness since he conceived of it as an internal gauge of how well one's actions conformed to one's moral standards (cf., e.g., Rom 2:15; 2 Cor 1:12).[9] Paul had a robust understanding of the tendencies of people to deceive themselves about their own sinfulness, however, and he did not exclude himself from these tendencies (1 Cor 4:4).[10] Here, then, he qualifies both his own witness to the truthfulness of what he is about to say and the reliability of his conscience with the claims that his speech is "in Christ" and that the testimony of his conscience is "in the Holy Spirit."

9:2 that great sorrow is mine, and there is constant distress in my heart (ὅτι λύπη μοί ἐστιν μεγάλη καὶ ἀδιάλειπτος ὀδύνη τῇ καρδίᾳ μου). Paul feels profound anguish over the danger that threatens many of his own compatriots, the Jewish people.

Paul's "that" (ὅτι) introduces the content of the truth he speaks, and it is a statement about his emotional condition. His language is emphatic. The term "sorrow" (λύπη) describes an emotion that is the opposite of joy (2 Cor 2:3; Philo, *Embassy* 15), and, like joy, could lead to tears (Xenophon, *Hell.* 7.1.32).[11] The term was synonymous with "anxious thought" (σύννοια) and "dejection" (κατήφεια).[12] When it was excessive or "great" (μεγάλη), as it is here, "sorrow" could overwhelm a person and lead him or her to wish for death (2 Cor 2:7; Tob 3:6).[13]

The noun "distress" (ὀδύνη) could refer to constant physical pain, such as the torment that might come from an extremely swollen leg (Xenophon, *Hell.* 5.4.58). The related verb is used for the anguish of being burned with fire in Luke 16:24 (ὀδυνάω).[14] The word could also mean mental anguish (1 Tim 6:10) and appears in the NT twice in its verbal form to refer to the extreme anxiety that people feel when someone they love is in danger. Jesus's mother scolded her twelve-year-old for staying in Jerusalem after Passover without his parents' permission: "Your father and I have been anxiously [ὀδυνώμενοι] searching for you" (Luke 2:48 NIV). Similarly, the elders of the church at Ephesus, where Paul had worked for nearly three years, became "sorrowful" (ὀδυνώμενοι) when they heard the ominous report that his life was in danger and they would never see him again (Acts 20:38). In much the same way, Paul's heart, the seat of his desires (10:1), is in anguish because of the spiritual danger that threatens many of his fellow Jews.

9:3 For I could almost wish that I myself were something cursed, separated from Christ in place of my brothers and sisters, my compatriots according to the flesh (ηὐχόμην γὰρ ἀνάθεμα εἶναι αὐτὸς ἐγὼ ἀπὸ τοῦ Χριστοῦ ὑπὲρ τῶν ἀδελφῶν μου

8. Lagrange, *Romains*, 225; Michel, *An die Römer*, 291–92; Cranfield, *Romans*, 2:452.

9. See p. 139, "In Depth: Paul's Understanding of the 'Conscience.'"

10. Cranfield, *Romans*, 2:453n1.

11. See LSJ 1065–66, s.v. λύπη and BDAG 604–5, s.v. λύπη.

12. Philo, *Embassy* 15; LSJ 926, 1720, s.v. σύννοια and κατήφεια.

13. Cf. the Greek portion of the inscription on the early first-century A.D. funerary monument of Lucius Vettenius Musa Campester in the Capitoline Museums in Rome [*IGUR* 1291]: "Death renders us free of wealth and poverty; in fact, Nature forces us to spend our lives in anxiety [ἐν λύπαις]" (transl. from the museum plaque).

14. LSJ 1199, s.v. ὀδύνη; BDAG 692, s.v. ὀδυνάω and ὀδύνη.

τῶν συγγενῶν μου κατὰ σάρκα). Paul was so distraught over the rejection of the gospel among so many Jews that, like Moses in the wilderness, he almost wanted to be condemned instead of them.

Paul's "for" (γάρ) introduces a description of the reason why he was so distressed, although the description is allusive rather than explicit. It does not state the cause of Paul's anxiety directly but only that the cause concerns his "compatriots according to the flesh," leaving his audience to conclude that he is speaking of the rejection of the gospel among many Jews. It is true that this allusiveness probably aroused sympathy in the letter's first audience as the causes of Paul's distress slowly dawned on them.[15] This effect, however, was probably not calculated. The subject was probably so painful for Paul that talking about it explicitly was difficult. So he worked his way slowly toward an explicit description of Israel's rejection of the gospel in 9:6–10:4.

Paul's statement that he "could almost wish" himself (ηὐχόμην) to be separated from Christ uses the imperfect indicative with a verb of wanting or wishing to express a desire that cannot, and in this case should not, be fulfilled (the "desiderative" or "tendential" imperfect).[16] Paul did not mean, then, that at one time he wished to be separated from Christ (cf. Tyndale's "I have wysshed my selfe to be cursed") nor that he presently wishes for the impossible (cf. CEB's "I wish I could be accursed"), but that he almost wishes for something that he should not wish for and that cannot happen (NIV: "I could wish that I myself were cursed," and most others).[17]

The wish itself is reminiscent of Moses's desire that, instead of idolatrous Israel, God blot Moses off his list of those who belonged to his people (Exod 32:32).[18] The term translated "something cursed" (ἀνάθεμα) here often referred to a votive offering (e.g., 2 Macc 9:16; Philo, *Moses* 1.253; *Res gest. divi Aug.* 24.5–6, 10) and could be synonymous with "an instrument of divine reconciliation" (ἱλαστήριον).[19] Although Paul uses the term elsewhere simply to mean "something devoted to God for destruction" (1 Cor 12:3; 16:22; Gal 1:8–9; cf., e.g., LXX Num 21:3; Deut 13:16), it seems likely that here it has additional substitutionary and sacrificial connotations similar to the term "mercy seat" in 3:25. This would, at least, be consistent with Moses's offer to substitute his own destruction for that of God's people.[20] If this is correct, then Paul was almost willing to wish that God would accept his own eternal destruction as a sacrifice in the place of those Jews who had rejected the gospel.

9:4 who indeed are Israelites, whose are the adoption as sons, and the glory, and the covenants, and the legislation, and the worship, and the promises (οἵτινές εἰσιν Ἰσραηλῖται, ὧν ἡ υἱοθεσία καὶ ἡ δόξα καὶ αἱ διαθῆκαι καὶ ἡ νομοθεσία καὶ ἡ λατρεία καὶ αἱ ἐπαγγελίαι). God's people Israel have received numerous gifts from God as

15. Jewett, *Romans*, 559–60.

16. Cf. Smyth, *Greek Grammar*, §1782; Moule, *Idiom-Book*, 9; Wallace, *Greek Grammar*, 551–52; Cranfield, *Romans*, 2:454–57.

17. "Wish" (εὔχομαι) could mean "pray" (2 Cor 13:7, 9; Cranfield, *Romans*, 2:454), but since the desiderative imperfect is commonly used with verbs of wanting or wishing (e.g., ἐβουλόμην, ἤθελον), the term probably means "wish" here (cf. Gal 4:20; Phlm 13). See BDAG 417, s.v. εὔχομαι; *TLNT* 2:152.

18. As commentators since Origen (*Romans, Books 6–10*, 106–7) have observed.

19. Dio Chrysostom, *Trojan Discourse* (*Or. 11*) 121. See Haacker, *An die Römer*, 181–82. *Pace* Calvin (*Romans*, 193) the term could be spelled in two ways (ἀνάθημα, the older spelling, and ἀνάθεμα, the newer spelling). On this, see Johannes Behm, "ἀνάθεμα, κτλ.," *TDNT* 1:354.

20. Haacker, *An die Römer*, 181. Cf. also the Roman concept of *devotio*, the ritual battle suicide of a Roman commander to gain the favor of the gods and to save his people (Livy, *History of Rome* 8.6; Cicero, *Fin.* 19.60; Lucan, *Civil War* 304–13).

a sign of his love for them, but tragically they have rejected the gospel to which all these gifts point.

The indefinite relative pronoun, translated here "who indeed" (οἵτινες), often simply substitutes for the relative pronoun ("who"), but here it carries its older, classical sense that emphasizes "a characteristic quality, by which a preceding statement is to be confirmed."[21] The emphasis adds to the pathos of the situation: the very people who are Paul's compatriots and the recipients of the gifts he is about to list have stumbled over the righteousness of God in the gospel that Paul proclaims (9:32–33; 10:3) and so have failed to benefit from the greatest gift of all (9:31).

Paul has carefully constructed his list of God's gifts to Israel. It is arranged in a series of relative clauses, the first of which designates Paul's "compatriots according to the flesh" as "Israelites." The three relative clauses following this designation are dependent on it and explain its significance.[22]

"Israelite" (Ἰσραηλίτης) was a name that emphasized the historical origins of the Jews as the descendants of Abraham, Isaac, and Jacob, whom God renamed "Israel" (Gen 32:28; cf. 4 Macc 18:1; Rom 11:1). This was the name Paul's compatriots liked to call themselves. The name "Jews" was a more geographically and ethnically oriented designation and the name that non-Jews used to distinguish them from others.[23] Paul used the term "Jew" for his people prior to this point because his focus was on comparing Jew with gentile (e.g., Rom 1:16; 2:9–10; 3:29). In chapters 9–11, however, he will refer to them as "Israel" with only two exceptions, and the exceptions fall in places where he is again comparing Jews and non-Jews (9:24; 10:12).[24] Here in 9:4 and throughout chapters 9–11, then, Paul speaks as one of his own people and reminds his Roman audience of the privileges that Scripture assigned to Israel, privileges that Paul believed continued into the present.

The first of the three relative clauses that qualify "Israelites" is a carefully constructed list of six gifts God has given to his people. All six items are feminine nouns ending in an "a" sound, and if there was any distinction between "a" and "ai" in Paul's pronunciation, then he has punctuated the list halfway through and at the end with matching, slightly altered "a" sounds. The result, in any case, was a poetic list marked by euphony and balance.[25] Poetry in speech often signals emotion, and here it is likely that Paul is expressing a sense of tragedy that this list represents gifts which many Israelites have rejected, at least in the form the gifts have taken since the death and resurrection of Christ.[26]

"Adoption" (υἱοθεσία) recalls God's designation of Israel in Scripture as his "firstborn son [υἱός]" (Exod 4:22–23; cf. Deut 14:1; Jer 31:9; Hos 11:1; Jub. 1:24–25), a status that now belongs to believers whatever their ethnicity (Rom 8:15, 23). Unbelieving Israel does not have "adoption" in this sense be-

21. BDAG 729, s.v. ὅστις 2b. Cf. Smyth, *Greek Grammar*, §2496.

22. On the arrangement of 9:4–5, see especially Dunn (*Romans 9–16*, 522) and Jewett (*Romans*, 556). Cf. Cranfield, *Romans*, 2:460.

23. Walter Gutbrod, "Ἰουδαῖος, κτλ.," *TDNT* 3:371–72; Dunn, *Romans 9–16*, 526; Jewett, *Romans*, 561–62. On the use of the terms "Judean" and "Jew" in antiquity, see Cohen, *Beginnings of Jewishness*, 69–106. For "Israelite" as a name that Roman Jews used of themselves, see the tomb inscription of three and a half-year-old Eioudea found in the catacombs beneath Rome's Villa Torlonia that calls her an "Israelite." The inscription probably dates from several centuries after Romans. See BDAG 481, s.v. Ἰσραηλίτης, and Hermann Wolfgang Beyer and Hans Lietzmann, eds., *Die jüdische Katakombe der Villa Torlonia in Rom*, Studien zur spätantiken Kunstgeschichte 4 (Berlin: Walter de Gruyter, 1930), 37 (no. 44).

24. Dunn, *Romans 9–16*, 526.

25. Dunn, *Romans 9–16*, 522. On the pronunciation of vowels and diphthongs in Greek of the Roman period, see Geoffrey Horrocks, *Greek: A History of the Language and Its Speakers*, Longman Linguistics Library (London: Longman, 1997), 102–27.

26. Cf. Wright, "Romans," 629.

cause this form of adoption arises from union with God's Son (8:14–17). Paul's anguish over unbelieving Israel probably arose in part from this disparity.

"Glory" (δόξα) refers to the experience of God's presence and is reminiscent of God's meeting with his people at Sinai, in the tabernacle, in the temple, and at his coming at the restoration of all creation (e.g., Exod 24:16–17; 29:23; 33:18–22; 40:34–35; 1 Kgs 8:11; Ps 26:8; Isa 60:1–2). The hope for this glory, however, now belongs preeminently to those who have believed the gospel (5:2; 8:18, 21).[27]

"Covenants" (διαθῆκαι) probably refers to God's covenants with Abraham (Gen 15:8; 17:2–21), Isaac, and Jacob (Exod 6:3–5), to God's covenant with Israel at Sinai (Exod 19:5), and to the new covenant in the period of Israel's restoration (Jer 31:31, 33) since these are the covenants of greatest importance to Paul elsewhere (Rom 11:27; 1 Cor 11:25; 2 Cor 3:6, 14; Gal 3:17; 4:24). Here too, those who have believed the gospel have become the ultimate beneficiaries of these covenants.

"Legislation" (νομοθεσία) appears only here in the NT and is close in meaning to the much more common term "law" (νόμος). Paul may have chosen this more unusual term because, like the other words in this part of his list, it ends in an "a" sound. If so, its meaning was still appropriate for a list of Israel's privileges since this term viewed the law from the perspective of the thought and work that went into creating it. Greek speakers could use it for praising a people's laws as "good and useful" or "very philosophical and genuine."[28] Tragically, however, Israel did not reach the goal toward which its own "holy . . . and righteous and good" (7:12) law pointed (9:30–10:4).

"Worship" (λατρεία) referred in the OT to cultic ritual, such as the prescribed ritual for the observance of the Passover (e.g., Exod 12:25–26, 13:5 LXX). Paul must have been thinking of the rituals for worship prescribed in the Mosaic law (cf. Heb 9:1, 6), rituals that, like the other gifts he mentions, have taken a new form for those who believe the gospel (Rom 12:1; cf. Phil 3:3).

"The promises" (ἐπαγγελίαι) are "the promises given to the fathers" of the Jewish people (Rom 15:8), preeminently the promise that Abraham would be the father of many nations (4:13, 20; cf. Gen 17:5), but probably also the reiteration of that promise to Isaac (cf. Gen 26:3–5) and Jacob also (Rom 9:10; Gen 28:13–15).[29] Ironically, although Abraham is the father of Jews and gentiles who believe, gentiles have outpaced the Jews in becoming children of Abraham in this most important way despite the still important connection between Abraham and his physical descendants (Rom 9:6–8; 11:28).

9:5 whose are the fathers, and from whom is the Messiah, as far as the flesh is concerned, who is God over all, blessed forever. Amen (ὧν οἱ πατέρες καὶ ἐξ ὧν ὁ Χριστὸς τὸ κατὰ σάρκα, ὁ ὢν ἐπὶ πάντων θεὸς εὐλογητὸς εἰς τοὺς αἰῶνας, ἀμήν). God's gifts to Israel include the patriarchs Abraham, Isaac, Jacob, and the Messiah himself in all his significance both as Israel's king and Israel's God. Tragically, Israel has largely rejected the gospel toward which the gifts were all pointing.

Paul now modifies "Israelites" (9:4) with two more relative clauses, and each clause has only one element, "fathers" and "the Messiah." As the reference to "the promises" in the previous verse has just clarified, God made promises to "the fathers"

27. On Paul's use of this word, see *TLNT* 1:368–73.

28. Dionysius of Halicarnassus, *Ant. rom.* 2.24.1 (Earnest Cary, LCL); Let. Aris. 31 (R. J. H. Shutt, *OTP* 2:15; cf. Josephus, *Ant.* 12.37).

29. Cranfield, *Romans*, 2:464.

of the Jewish people (Abraham, Isaac, and Jacob). The physical connection between the Jews of Paul's day and their ancestors remained so important to God in Paul's view that Paul could say God loved unbelieving Jews "because of the fathers" (11:28). Still, this connection was not enough to make them children of Abraham in the most important sense (9:6–8), and paradoxically in that sense gentiles rather than Jews have outnumbered them in the family of Abraham.

Similarly, the Messiah was both an Israelite and Israel's God. Many Jews of Paul's time believed that a great king, a descendant of David, would arise among their people not only to rule Israel but to establish justice among all the nations of the earth (e.g., Pss. Sol. 17:21–46; Mark 12:35). In the letter's opening Paul affirmed his own agreement with this tradition and said that he thought Jesus fulfilled this expectation. Jesus, he said, was "born from David's offspring according to the flesh" (1:3). Just as he did in that opening statement, however, here too Paul balances Jesus's identity "according to the flesh" with a statement about Jesus's relationship to God (cf 1:4).[30]

When Paul affirms the unity of Jesus with Israel's God elsewhere in his letters, he calls Jesus "Lord" rather than "God" (e.g., 1 Cor 8:6), and so the idea that Paul calls the Jewish Messiah "God" here has led a number of interpreters to conclude we must read the grammar another way.[31] If we place a period after "according to the flesh" (RSV, NAB, REB) then the final phrase of the verse forms a complete sentence ascribing praise to God, perhaps as the source of the blessings Paul has just listed in 9:4–5 or as the God who is sovereign over all people, Jews as well as gentiles.[32]

This is not, however, the most likely understanding of the grammar, as a comparison between Romans 9:5 and 2 Corinthians 11:31 demonstrates. In both passages Paul uses the phrase "he who is" (with a participle of εἰμί) to describe further a previously named subject.[33] Here that previously named subject must be the Messiah.[34] Moreover, when ascriptions of praise to God using the term "blessed" (εὐλογητός) occur in Hellenistic Greek, "blessed" characteristically comes before, not after, "God" as it does here.[35] This means that "blessed" is likely to be a syntactically isolated expression of praise to Christ.

Paul, then, is affirming as the last in his list of gifts given to Israel that the Messiah too was an Israelite, but also much more. His identity was bound up with the identity of the one God, the God whom Israel worships as sovereign over all things and all peoples (cf. Rom 3:29–30). Again, this expression of praise to the God who is sovereign over the universe and whom Israel knows through its close relationship with him sharpens the tragedy that so many in Israel have refused to acknowledge Jesus "Lord" of all and to call upon him for salvation (10:9, 12–13).[36]

Although the emphasis in the passage lies on Israel's failure to realize the perfection of the gifts God has given to them because of their rejection of

30. Bruce M. Metzger, "The Punctuation of Rom. 9:5," in *Christ and Spirit in the New Testament: Studies in Honour of Charles Francis Digby Moule*, ed. Barnabas Lindars and Stephen S. Smalley (Cambridge: Cambridge University Press, 1973), 103–4.

31. See, e.g., Käsemann (*Romans*, 259), Wilckens (*An die Römer [Röm 6–11]*, 189), Dunn (*Romans 9–16*, 535–36), and Fee (*Pauline Christology*, 272–77).

32. See, respectively, Fee (*Pauline Christology*, 272–77) and Dunn (*Romans 9–16*, 536).

33. Cf. Jdt 12:11 and 14:13 where the author first identifies the personal assistant of Holofernes as "the eunuch who was in charge of all his things" (τῷ εὐνούχῳ ὃς ἦν ἐφεστηκὼς ἐπὶ πάντων τῶν αὐτου) and then later, using the participle, as "the one who was in charge of all his things" (τῷ ὄντι ἐπὶ πάντων τῶν αὐτου).

34. Metzger, "Punctuation," 105–6.

35. Ibid., 106–7.

36. Cf. Jewett, *Romans*, 568.

the gospel, it is significant that Paul describes these gifts as still the possession of unbelieving Israel. The church has not taken these gifts from Israel but only realized prior to Israel the eschatological direction in which they were pointing. Israel's continuing possession of these gifts points forward, then, to Paul's argument in 11:25–29 that eventually "all Israel will be saved" and that God's "gifts and calling" will then be seen as irrevocable.[37]

9:6a But that is not to say that the word of God has failed (Οὐχ οἷον δὲ ὅτι ἐκπέπτωκεν ὁ λόγος τοῦ θεοῦ). Israel's tragic rejection of the gospel and failure to realize the full significance of its privileges does not mean that God, who gave Israel these privileges in Scripture, promised more than he could deliver.

The opening phrase, "But that is not to say" (οὐχ οἷον δέ), uses an expression close to three other common idioms: "it is impossible that" (οὐχ οἷόν τε; cf. REB), "by no means" (οὐχ οἷον [without ὅτι]) and "it is not that" (οὐχ ὅτι).[38] The phrase does not duplicate any of these idioms exactly, however, and so Paul may have simply used the adverbial expression "that is to say" (οἷον) and negated it.[39] This seems to be the way that both Luther and Tyndale took the phrase in the sixteenth century.[40] The point is not unimportant since, if this is the right translation, the phrase points emphatically back to what Paul has just said and brings out the implication of his list of Israel's privileges, an implication that he never explicitly draws in the list itself. As a people, Israel has not experienced the full blessing of its privileges, and instead gentiles are in the process of inheriting them. Paul now gets to the heart of the matter. Israel's failure to benefit fully from its privileges does not mean that the word of God has failed.

The term "fail" (ἐκπίπτω) could refer to the breaking of an axe (Deut 19:5 LXX), the withering of a flower (Isa 28:1, 4; 40:7 LXX), and the wreck of a ship against the rocks (Acts 27:17, 26, 29). In each of these cases, something once strong and beautiful has come to grief, and here Paul denies that all the privileges he has listed, gloriously described in the Scriptures, have withered in the reality of Israelite rejection of the gospel (cf. Isa 40:7–8 LXX). The rest of Romans 9–11, with their intense engagement with Scripture, will demonstrate the truth of this assertion.[41]

9:6b–7 For not all those from Israel are Israel; nor because those from Israel are Abraham's offspring are they all children, but, "In Isaac will your offspring be called" (οὐ γὰρ πάντες οἱ ἐξ Ἰσραὴλ οὗτοι Ἰσραήλ· οὐδ' ὅτι εἰσὶν σπέρμα Ἀβραὰμ πάντες τέκνα, ἀλλ', Ἐν Ἰσαὰκ κληθήσεταί σοι σπέρμα). God has never determined the identity of the remnant within Israel merely through physical descent from Abraham.

Paul now begins to support his claim ("for" [γάρ]) that despite the rejection of the gospel by so many within Israel the word of God has not failed. He begins with a succinct thesis statement that he will explain in greater detail in 9:7–29. He formulates this statement using a common figure

37. Cf. Moo, *Romans*, 562; Richard H. Bell, *The Irrevocable Call of God*, WUNT 184 (Tübingen: Mohr Siebeck, 2005), 198–209.

38. See the full discussion in George Benedict Winer (*A Grammar of the Idiom of the New Testament*, ed. Gottlieb Lünemann, trans. E. Masson and J. H. Thayer, 7th ed. [Andover, MA: Warren F. Draper, 1881], 597–98 [§64.1.6]), and Cranfield (*Romans*, 2:472).

39. For this meaning of the term, see LSJ 1209, s.v. οἷος V.2.d (e.g., Plato, *Phaedr.* 278a; Diogenes Laertius, *Lives of the Philosophers* 9.69).

40. Luther: "aber nicht sage ich solches, daß . . ."; Tyndale: "I speake not these thinges as though. . . ."

41. Cranfield, *Romans*, 2:473 ("This half verse is . . . the sign and theme of the whole of chapters 9–11.")

of speech in which the same word appears twice but with two different meanings.[42]

It is not entirely clear at this distance, however, what either occurrence of "Israel" means. The first occurrence of the word could refer to the patriarch Jacob or to the nation Israel, and the second occurrence could refer to Israel as a nation, to Israel as the people of God across time, including Jewish and gentile believers in Paul's own time, or to faithful Israelites across time, including Jewish Christians of Paul's own time.[43] Later in 11:5–6 Paul will argue that there is a present "remnant" of believers who are Israelites, a remnant, he implies, that stands in continuity with the faithful remnant of biblical times (cf. 9:27–29). Here too, then, Paul probably refers to Israelites who have believed the gospel, like himself (11:1, 5–6).

His point is that membership in God's people has never been merely a matter of family ties. Whereas physical Israel maintains a unique relationship to God (9:1–5), those within Israel who believe the gospel have brought physical Israel's privileges to their eschatological goal and are, therefore, "Israel" in a separate, perfected sense.

Next, in v. 7 Paul illustrates his thesis statement from the biblical description of Abraham's family. The substantivized prepositional phrase "those from Israel" (οἱ ἐξ Ἰσραήλ) serves as the subject of the verb "are" (εἰσίν) in this new clause, and so the first part of Paul's illustration simply restates 9:6b in other words: Israelites are not "children" merely because they are Abraham's physical descendants.[44] Most translations throw in a gratuitous "his" or "Abraham's" at this point to make clear that the "children" of which Paul speaks are Abraham's children (e.g., ESV: "Not all are children of Abraham because they are *his* offspring").[45] Paul's Greek, however, has no such qualifier, and this is probably because he was already shifting the ground of the discussion slightly to imply that not even physical descent from Abraham was necessary for people to be "children of God." As he has shown in 8:16–17, God's "children" are those to whom God's Spirit bears witness, and as he will say in 9:24, God calls his people into existence from both gentiles and Jews.

Paul next proves his point with a statement that reproduces God's words to Abraham in Genesis 21:12 LXX exactly.[46] After tension arose between Hagar and Sarah over their sons by Abraham, God told Abraham he intended to "call" (καλέω) Abraham's offspring through Isaac rather than Ishmael. Paul probably saw significance in this use of the word to refer to God's choice of one child over another: God "calls" his people into existence elsewhere in Romans (8:30; cf. 1:6; 4:17; 8:28; 9:24), and he called a special people into existence from among Abraham's offspring. God's free decision, then, defines the identity of his people, not merely their physical relationship to the right patriarch.

42. Quintilian (writing in Rome a few decades after Paul) calls this the second of three types of "paronomasia" or "adnominatio" (9.3.66–67 [Donald A. Russell, LCL]).

43. See, respectively, Sanday and Headlam (*Romans*, 240), Susan Grove Eastman ("Israel and the Mercy of God: A Re-reading of Galatians 6.16 and Romans 9–11," *NTS* 56 [2010]: 380–85), Wright ("Romans," 635–36), and Moo (*Romans*, 573–74).

44. Meyer, *Romans*, 366; Sanday and Headlam, *Romans*, 241. "Because" (ὅτι) could be rendered "that" and "seed" given the consistent meaning of "chosen seed" (e.g., Schreiner, *Romans*, 495; Moo, *Romans*, 575n25; Jewett, *Romans*, 575), but it is more likely that 9:6b, 7a, and 8a have a parallel structure with the first reference to Abraham's family as the comprehensive reference, and the second reference as the restricted reference. On this, see Brendan Byrne, *'Sons of God'-'Seed of Abraham': A Study of the Idea of the Sonship of God and of All Christians in Paul against the Jewish Background*, AnBib 83 (Rome: Biblical Institute Press, 1979), 130n201.

45. Emphasis mine. The older (Luther, Tyndale, KJV) and more literal (NASB) translations are more accurate here.

46. The LXX at this point is a literal translation of the Hebrew.

9:8–9 That is, it is not the children of the flesh who are children of God, but the children of the promise are counted as offspring. For the word of promise is this: "At this season I will come and Sara will have a son" (τοῦτ' ἔστιν, οὐ τὰ τέκνα τῆς σαρκὸς ταῦτα τέκνα τοῦ θεοῦ ἀλλὰ τὰ τέκνα τῆς ἐπαγγελίας λογίζεται εἰς σπέρμα. ἐπαγγελίας γὰρ ὁ λόγος οὗτος, Κατὰ τὸν καιρὸν τοῦτον ἐλεύσομαι καὶ ἔσται τῇ Σάρρᾳ υἱός). Those who fulfill God's promise to Abraham are the branch of Abraham's family that are God's children, not those who are merely physical descendants of Abraham.

Paul uses the expression "that is" (τοῦτ' ἔστιν) when he wants to define more precisely something he has just said (7:18; 10:6–8; Phlm 12). Here he restates and makes more specific his general claim in 9:6b–7a that physical descent from Abraham was not sufficient to make people "children." His restatement comes first: "It is not the children of the flesh who are children of God." The expression "children of the flesh [σαρκός]" refers to biological descent, as in the expression "my compatriots according to the flesh" in 9:3 and "Messiah, as far as the flesh is concerned" in 9:5. The phrase "children of God" further defines the "children" to whom Paul referred in 9:7 and recalls Paul's claim in 8:14–17 that all who are "led by the Spirit of God" are adoptive "sons," "children," and "heirs" of God.

If physical descent from Abraham is not enough to make one a child of Abraham, what does define Abraham's children? They are, Paul says, "children of the promise." Paul will specify the promise to which he refers in his next sentence. Before doing so, however, he makes clear that only those who fulfill the promise he is about to quote "are counted as" Abraham's offspring. The expression "counted as" (λογίζεται εἰς) refers to the surprising consideration of one thing as something else, as, for example, when God "counted" Abraham's faith "as" righteousness (4:3).[47] Biological progeny are by definition one's children, but God surprisingly considers those who fulfill his promise to Abraham as Abraham's children and therefore God's children also.

Genesis 18:10 and 14 record and then repeat this promise in slightly different words, and Paul conflated the two occurrences of the promise into one statement: God would give Abraham and Sarah a son despite their advanced years. Although Abraham had another child, it was through this particular child, Isaac, that God would fulfill his promise to Abraham of numberless progeny and of being a blessing to the earth's various people groups (Gen 18:18; cf. 15:5; 17:5). The concepts of "counting" one thing "as" another and of the "promise" to Abraham must have recalled for Paul's audience his earlier argument that Abraham was the father of both circumcised and uncircumcised believers and that the multiethnic composition of those who believed the gospel fulfilled the promise God had made to Abraham (Rom 4:13–22; cf. Gen 15:5; 17:5; 18:18). Once again, the discussion shifts away from the question of who among Israelites is a true Israelite to the question of whether being an Israelite in the physical sense has anything to do with being a child of God in the most important sense.[48]

9:10 And not only so, but also Rebecca, although becoming pregnant by one man, our forefather Isaac (οὐ μόνον δέ, ἀλλὰ καὶ Ῥεβέκκα ἐξ ἑνὸς κοίτην ἔχουσα, Ἰσαὰκ τοῦ πατρὸς ἡμῶν). Paul now gives an even more convincing illustration of his point: God chose Jacob over Esau although they were twins, and so Jacob's physical relationship to his father could have had nothing to do with God's decision to choose him.

47. See the other examples of the expression from Hellenistic Jewish texts in the comments on 4:3 above.

48. Cf. Moo, *Romans*, 577.

Paul typically uses the phrase "and not only so, but also" to add a second, more emphatic statement to something he has just said (5:3, 11; 8:23) or to provide a second piece of evidence that clinches an argument he is making (2 Cor 8:19). His use of the phrase here falls into the second category. Someone might be able to object to the evidence he has just offered that since Ishmael was not Abraham's son by his wife but by his wife's slave, he was not a legitimate son on biological grounds. Physical descent could then still play a role in determining who belongs to the children of God.

Paul now fills this gap with an even more impressive piece of evidence, which he describes in a long, complex sentence whose main clause, "it was said to her" (ἐρρέθη αὐτῇ), does not appear until 9:12b. The participle translated "becoming" (ἔχουσα) here in 9:10 is used concessively to modify "it was said" (ἐρρέθη) in 9:12b, and the whole construction should be translated, "Rebecca, although becoming pregnant by one man, . . . Isaac . . . , it was said to her that the greater will serve the lesser."[49]

"Becoming pregnant" (κοίτην ἔχουσα) translates an expression that referred to "having" (ἔχουσα) sexual relations with someone, and in the LXX the term "bed" (κοίτη) could refer to a "seminal emission" (Num 5:20; cf. Lev 15:16, 32; 18:20).[50] Here, then, the phrase might be rendered "going to bed [κοίτην] with" except that Paul's argument depends on a pregnancy resulting from the sexual relations Rebecca had with Isaac.[51] For Paul's readers, who knew the story well, his point was clear. Rebecca's pregnancy was the result of a single instance of sexual intercourse with one man, her husband Isaac. In other words, Esau and Jacob were not half-brothers like Ishmael and Isaac but full brothers, and they were conceived at exactly the same time.

9:11–12a —for although they were not yet born or had done anything good or evil, in order that the chosen purpose of God might stand firm not by works but by the one who calls— (μήπω γὰρ γεννηθέντων μηδὲ πραξάντων τι ἀγαθὸν ἢ φαῦλον, ἵνα ἡ κατ' ἐκλογὴν πρόθεσις τοῦ θεοῦ μένῃ, οὐκ ἐξ ἔργων ἀλλ' ἐκ τοῦ καλοῦντος). God told Rebecca that he had chosen Jacob over Esau before either child possessed any qualification, whether by parentage or performance, that could serve as a basis within themselves for this choice. He did this so that his freedom to include within his people anyone whom he chose might remain uncompromised.

The "for" (γάρ) that begins this clause shows that Paul is about to support the general case he is making in 9:10–13. At the same time, however, the genitive-absolute construction and purpose clause show that he has left behind the sentence he began in 9:10 and started over with a new thought.[52] Like the participial expression "Rebecca, although becoming" (Ῥεβέκκα . . . ἔχουσα) in 9:10, the genitive absolute (γεννηθέντων . . . πραξάντων) and purpose clauses (ἵνα . . . μένῃ) here qualify the expression "it was said to her" (ἐρρέθη αὐτῇ) in 9:12a. The genitive-absolute construction broadens Paul's case that God chose Jacob over Esau apart from their physical relationship to Isaac and Rebecca. Now Paul includes the further thought that God chose Jacob over Esau without regard to the moral quality of their lives. The purpose clause states that God worked this way to preserve his sovereign freedom

49. The manuscript 𝔓[46] preserves a text that shows this was a possible way of reading the sentence. It omits "to her" (αὐτῇ), and this ommission clearly makes "Rebecca" (Ῥεβέκκα) the subject of "was told" (ἐρρέθη) and produces a sentence that is much easier to read: "Rebecca, although becoming pregnant by one man, Isaac . . . , was told that . . ." (Ῥεβέκκα ἐξ ἑνὸς κοίτην ἔχουσα, Ἰσαὰκ . . . ἐρρέθη ὅτι . . .).

50. See also Dunn (*Romans 9–16*, 542), although Dunn's translation is a bit confusing since Paul's "one" refers to the father rather than to "the one act of sexual intercourse."

51. Many thanks to ZECNT series editor Clinton E. Arnold for pointing this out to me.

52. Sanday and Headlam, *Romans*, 242; Cranfield, *Romans*, 2:477; Wilckens, *An die Römer (Röm 6–11)*, 194.

to determine the identity of those through whom he would accomplish his purposes.

The term "purpose" (πρόθεσις) could refer to the goal that people carefully planned to achieve, whether a wicked king plotting to steal the money in the temple treasury (2 Macc 3:8) or sailors calculating how to reach their destination (Acts 27:13).[53] Paul has used the term once before in Romans to speak of the good "purpose" God has for his people and that all things, under his direction, work together to achieve (Rom 8:28). "Purpose," then, refers to the goal that God has carefully thought through and wants to achieve. Paul qualifies the term with a prepositional phrase (κατ' ἐκλογήν) that we should understand adjectivally. Paul speaks of God's "chosen purpose."[54] At the same time the noun "choice" (ἐκλογή) that forms the object of the preposition echoes the adjective "called" (κλητός) and the verb "call" (καλέω) that Paul used to describe the way in which God puts his plan into effect for the good of his people in 8:28–30. The result emphasizes that God's choice of Jacob over Esau served his freely chosen and benevolent purpose. God chose Jacob so that this free and good purpose might "stand firm" (μένῃ).[55]

The phrase "not by works but by the one who calls" qualifies the verb "stand firm" and reiterates the freedom of God's choice by summarizing the clause "although they were not yet born or had done anything good or evil."[56] That Paul can summarize matters of birth and matters of moral virtue by the term "works" hints that he did not make a sharp distinction between ethnic affiliation and moral virtue as possible qualifications for a right standing with God (cf. 3:20, 27, 28; 4:2, 6; 11:6). In Paul's thinking, God's freedom was not bound by either form of human "works."

The phrase "not by works but by the one who calls" also shows that Paul's idea of God's freedom in choosing his people goes beyond the level of the group to comprehend the individuals who make up that group. Up to this point in the letter when Paul has denied that human works can function as a criterion for a right standing with God, he has had the individual primarily in view. "We hold that a human being [ἄνθρωπον] is justified by faith apart from works of the law," he says in 3:28, and again in 4:6, "David describes the happiness of the human being [τοῦ ἀνθρώπου] for whom God counts righteousness apart from works."

Similarly, the affirmation that membership within God's people originates with "the one who calls" (τοῦ καλοῦντος) picks up the language of 8:30 that God "called" (ἐκάλεσεν) those whom he justified. Since in the argument so far justification is a matter of faith, and faith is something that individuals rather than groups exercise (e.g., 3:28; 4:4), it is likely that here in 9:12 Paul assumes God calls his people into existence by calling certain individuals to have faith and to be justified by that faith (cf. 4:1–9, 18–25).[57] This approach is confirmed further in 9:14–18 where Paul consistently uses the singular to refer to the person who is the object either of God's mercy or his hardening.[58]

53. Cf. LSJ 1481, s.v. πρόθεσις II.1.; BDAG 869, s.v. πρόθεσις 2.a.

54. BDAG 513, s.v. κατά 7.c.

55. For the description of a purpose (πρόθεσις) as standing firm (μένω) see Polybius, *Hist.* 28.6.3 where Lycortas stood firm on the purpose he had from the beginning (ὁ . . . Λυκόρτας ἔμεινεν ἐπὶ τῆς ἐξ ἀρχῆς προθέσεως). This idiom makes unlikely the idea that the verb "stand firm" means "continue" and emphasizes the continuing purpose of God (e.g., Wilckens, *An die Römer [Röm 6–11]*, 194).

56. Cranfield, *Romans*, 2:478.

57. Thomas R. Schreiner, "Corporate and Individual Election in Romans 9: A Response to Brian Abasciano," *JETS* 49 (2006): 379–80.

58. Thomas R. Schreiner, "Does Romans 9 Teach Individual Election unto Salvation? Some Exegetical and Theological Reflections," *JETS* 36 (1993): 34.

9:12b it was said to her, "The greater will serve the smaller" (ἐρρέθη αὐτῇ ὅτι Ὁ μείζων δουλεύσει τῷ ἐλάσσονι). God's freedom to choose Jacob rather than Esau to accomplish his purposes stood firm because he told Rebecca which of the two children he had chosen before they were born or had done anything. God's freedom of choice is also evident in its surprising nature. Contrary to the customary and expected procedure, God chose to work through the younger rather than the older sibling.

Paul now completes the sentence that he started in 9:10 and restarted in 9:11. God's word about Rebecca's children came to her apart from any consideration of the identity of their father or their moral rectitude. In other words, his choice of Jacob over Esau was utterly free, unfettered by any human quality or performance.

The brief sentence, "the greater will serve the smaller," is an exact quotation of the last part of Genesis 25:23 LXX, itself a faithful rendering of the Hebrew. "Greater" (μείζων) and "smaller" (ἐλάσσων) mean "older" and "younger" and refer to the law of primogeniture whose violation forms an important leitmotif in the storyline of Genesis.[59] Paul began this passage in 9:1–5 by sounding a note of surprise that Israel, despite its many God-given privileges, had not believed the gospel. He may have quoted Genesis 25:23 here, therefore, to demonstrate that God's free choice to include gentiles within his people through the gospel, as surprising as it may seem, is not inconsistent with the character of God as it is described in Scripture. When God chose Isaac and Jacob, in each case he chose the younger rather than the older brother to carry forward his purposes.[60]

9:13 just as it is written, "Jacob I have loved, but Esau I have hated" (καθὼς γέγραπται, Τὸν Ἰακὼβ ἠγάπησα, τὸν δὲ Ἠσαῦ ἐμίσησα). The course of later history confirmed God's words to Rebecca. He continued his close relationship with the descendants of Jacob but rejected the descendants of Esau, who became his and his people's enemies.

This paraphrase of Malachi 1:2–3 LXX confirms that the word God spoke to Rebecca came to pass "just as" (καθώς) God had promised.[61] Malachi has just summed up the attitude toward God of a decimated and beleaguered Israel with the complaining question, "How have you loved us?" To this Malachi answers, "'Is not Esau Jacob's brother?' declares the Lord. 'Yet I have loved Jacob but Esau I have hated.'"[62] Paul must have known that this statement looked back over the history of God's relationship with the descendants of Jacob and the descendants of Esau and summed up in sharp, antithetical terms God's protection of Israel from enemies such as Esau and his descendants the Edomites. The statement was, then, a confirmation that God had carried out his freely decided purpose that began with the choice of Jacob over Esau. The term "hated" (ἐμίσησα) is both harsh and startling, but it is also hyperbole. Paul probably thought of it as clarifying his point that God freely chose one individual over another (cf. Luke 14:26).[63]

9:14 What, then, shall we say? There is no injustice with God is there? Certainly not! (Τί οὖν ἐροῦμεν; μὴ ἀδικία παρὰ τῷ θεῷ; μὴ γένοιτο). God's

59. Robert Alter, *The Art of Biblical Narrative* (New York: Basic Books, 1981), 6.

60. For more on this, see Frank Thielman, "Unexpected Mercy: Echoes of a Biblical Motif in Romans 9–11," *SJT* 47 (1994): 169–81.

61. Paul rearranged the LXX text (ἠγάπησα τὸν Ιακωβ τὸν δὲ Ησαυ ἐμίσησα) so that the names "Jacob" and "Esau" came first in each clause. He may have done this to make the contrast between Jacob and Esau more pointed (Jewett, *Romans*, 580).

62. On the original setting of Mal 1:2–3, see Douglas Stuart, "Malachi," in *The Minor Prophets: An Exegetical and Expository Commentary*, ed. Thomas Edward McComiskey (Grand Rapids: Baker, 2009), 1280–85.

63. Cf. Fitzmyer, *Romans*, 563.

refusal to allow any human quality to influence his choice of Isaac and Jacob over Ishmael and Esau may seem arbitrary and therefore unfair, but that impression cannot be right.

Paul signals a division in his argument with the rhetorical question, "What then shall we say?" This question often provides a transition into Paul's reply to a false conclusion from his argument (3:5; 6:1; 7:7), and it functions in that way here.

The term "injustice" (ἀδικία) sometimes carried the nuance of "unfairness" in ethical discussion in antiquity: "The unjust man and the unjust act are unfair or unequal," said Aristotle (*Nicomachean Ethics* 1131a10).[64] Paul used the term this way in 2 Corinthians 12:13 (cf. Rom 3:5), and elsewhere in his use of the term he contrasts "injustice" with "truth" (Rom 1:18; 2:8; 1 Cor 13:6; 2 Thess 2:10, 12; cf. Deut 32:4). Here, then, the accusation would be that Paul's explanation of the way God chose Isaac and Jacob was unfair and untruthful. According to the commonly accepted notions of justice in the ancient world, a person in power who acted justly chose or favored those whom longstanding custom dictated should be chosen, whether it be the elder brother or the most virtuous candidate.[65] According to the case Paul has made from Scripture, however, God did not follow the normal canons of justice and so seems to have been untruthful or unfair in his choice of Isaac and Jacob. Isaac was not better than Ishmael, nor was Jacob better than Esau from the perspective of family connections, social custom, or virtue.

Paul denies the charge with his usual "certainly not!"[66] The normal canons of justice do not apply to God because God sets the standard for justice (cf. 3:4), and the "normal canons" are, from his perspective, often unjust. God, for example, is impartial when it comes to distributing justice to human beings (cf. 2:11). He considers neither their family connections nor their birth order.

9:15 For to Moses he says, "I will show mercy to whomever I show mercy, and I will show compassion to whomever I show compassion" (τῷ Μωϋσεῖ γὰρ λέγει, Ἐλεήσω ὃν ἂν ἐλεῶ καὶ οἰκτιρήσω ὃν ἂν οἰκτίρω). God has revealed himself to no less an authority than Moses as abundantly merciful, but also as just in freely choosing those who will receive his mercy.

The "for" (γάρ) introduces scriptural support for Paul's dismissal of the idea that God acted unjustly in choosing Isaac over Ishmael and Jacob over Esau. The position of this conjunction after Moses's name rather than after the article (τῷ γὰρ Μωϋσεῖ λέγει) emphasizes that God revealed this supporting evidence to *Moses*, no less, and it should therefore carry special weight.[67]

The quotation comes word for word from Exodus 33:19b LXX, and both Paul and his audience must have known its wider context.[68] That context emphasizes mercy as a primary characteristic of God's nature (cf. Exod 3:14–15; 33:19a; 34:6–7), but also God's refusal to acquit the guilty (Exod 34:7) and his right to choose the objects of his mercy (Exod 33:19b).[69] Paul believed that God was abundantly merciful and extraordinarily patient with those who rebelled against him (Rom 9:22),

64. Aristotle, *Ethica Nicomachea*, trans. W. D. Ross (London: Oxford University Press, 1925), 1131a; J. O. Urmson, *The Greek Philosophical Vocabulary* (London: Duckworth, 1990), 10.

65. On injustice as violation of custom, see Heinrich Schlier, "ἄδικος," *TDNT* 1:150.

66. See the comments on 3:4 above.

67. Cranfield, *Romans*, 2:483.

68. Ibid., 2:483–84; Dunn, *Romans 9–16*, 552.

69. *Pace* Cranfield (*Romans*, 2:484), who restricts God's freedom to a freedom to show mercy to people apart from their works rather than a freedom to show either mercy or wrath according to his own decision. On the meaning of Exodus 33:19b in its context, see especially U. Cassuto, *A Commentary on the Book of Exodus*, trans. Israel Abrahams (Jerusalem: Magnes, 1967), 436.

desiring their repentance (2:4; 10:21). He also believed, however, that everyone who received God's wrath justly deserved it (1:18–3:20, 23) and that whereas mercy was a primary and critically important aspect of God's character, God was also just and would "by no means clear the guilty" (Exod 34:7). He is able to show mercy to some and remain a just God only because of the atoning death of Christ, as Paul has explained in 3:25–26.[70]

9:16 So then, it is not of the one who wills, nor of the one who runs, but of God who shows mercy (ἄρα οὖν οὐ τοῦ θέλοντος οὐδὲ τοῦ τρέχοντος ἀλλὰ τοῦ ἐλεῶντος θεοῦ). Nothing that originates from the human side, whether desire or effort, influences God's decision to show mercy to some and not others.

"So then" (ἄρα οὖν) draws an inference from something before it (cf. Rom 5:18; 7:3, 25; 8:12), in this case from the quotation Paul has just cited. Paul formulated the sentence that states the inference without an indicative verb and with no head noun to govern his string of genitives. Since the context emphasizes God's right to decide how to dispense his mercy, however, Paul must be denying, as an implication of that right, that anything within a particular human being or group of people impinges on it.[71]

The verb "will" (θέλω) refers here to formulating a goal that one resolves to attain (cf. 7:15–21; 1 Cor 7:36; Gal 5:17), and the verb "run" (τρέχω), used metaphorically, would then refer to the attempt to carry out that goal (cf. Gal 2:2; 5:7; Phil 2:16).[72] Apart from the rather pedestrian use of the verb "want" or "will" (θέλω) in Romans 1:13, the only other place Paul has used the term in the letter so far is in 7:15–21 where it occurs seven times and refers consistently to the bondage of the human will to sin: the human being without the Spirit of God finds doing the good to be impossible.[73] For those in Paul's audience who have carefully followed his argument up to this point, it would be clear that the person who wills and runs apart from the transforming work of God's Spirit (cf. 8:4–13) can only will and run in sinful ways that merit God's wrath rather than his mercy.

9:17 For the Scripture says to Pharaoh, "For this very purpose I raised you up: that I might show my power in you and that my name might be proclaimed in all the earth" (λέγει γὰρ ἡ γραφὴ τῷ Φαραὼ ὅτι Εἰς αὐτὸ τοῦτο ἐξήγειρά σε ὅπως ἐνδείξωμαι ἐν σοὶ τὴν δύναμίν μου, καὶ ὅπως διαγγελῇ τὸ ὄνομά μου ἐν πάσῃ τῇ γῇ). God's treatment of Pharaoh in Scripture supports the case Paul is making about God's right to show mercy to some people, but not to others.

"For" (γάρ) introduces evidence from Scripture to support the point Paul has just made about God's right to dispense mercy according to his own decision and not on the basis of any human activity.[74] The text he cites provides a negative example

70. The atoning death of Christ preserves God's righteousness in showing mercy to the wicked and prevents Paul's description of God in Romans 9–11 from descending into the sort of moral irrationality that John M. G. Barclay describes in "Unnerving Grace: Approaching Romans 9–11 from the Wisdom of Solomon," in *Between Gospel and Election*, ed. Florian Wilk, J. Ross Wagner, Frank Schleritt, WUNT 257 (Tübingen: Mohr Siebeck, 2010), 104–9.

71. Moo, *Romans*, 593.

72. BDAG 448, 1015 s.v. θέλω 2 and τρέχω 2. Paul often used "run" (τρέχω) in athletic metaphors (e.g., 1 Cor 9:24), and some interpreters suggest he did that here (e.g., Cranfield, *Romans*, 2:485). This seems unlikely, however, since there is no other athletic imagery in the immediate context, and the imagery of pursuit and stumbling in 9:30–32 seems too distant to be relevant.

73. Cf. Jewett, *Romans*, 582.

74. Cf. Meyer, *Romans*, 374; Sanday and Headlam, *Romans*, 255. It is possible that the parallel structure of 9:15–18 ("for," 9:15, 17; "so then," 9:16, 18) hints that both quotations support Paul's statement that God is not unjust (e.g., Cranfield, *Romans*, 2:485), but it is difficult to think of the second "for" as reaching all the way back to 9:14.

of God's right to withhold his mercy for his own purposes.

Paul's quotation comes from Exodus 9:16, but departs from the LXX in significant ways. Paul emphasizes more clearly than the LXX that God has determined the course of history for the accomplishment of his very specific purpose of displaying his power to everyone on earth. Whereas the LXX says that Pharaoh had "been spared" (διετηρήθης) from death in the recent plagues "for" the "reason" (ἕνεκεν) that God wanted to show his "power" (ἰσχύν) and proclaim his name in all the earth, Paul's rendering says that God "raised up" (ἐξήγειρα) Pharaoh "for this exact purpose" (εἰς αὐτὸ τοῦτο), and the purpose is the display of God's "power" (δύναμιν) and the proclamation of his name in all the earth.

Paul's rendering hints that Pharaoh's very existence as ruler of Egypt served the precise purpose of the display of God's willingness and ability to save his people.[75] Paul's description of God's might as his "power" (δύναμιν) recalls Paul's connection between God's righteousness and his "power" (δύναμις) in 1:16–17 as well as Paul's development of the theme of God's righteousness as both his saving power and his impartiality in judgment in the argument of 1:18–3:26.

9:18 So then, he shows mercy to whom he wills, and he hardens whom he wills (ἄρα οὖν ὃν θέλει ἐλεεῖ, ὃν δὲ θέλει σκληρύνει). It is God's right to show mercy to one person and to make another person more resistant than ever to obeying his commands.

Paul now sums up his response to the question of whether God is unjust to show mercy to some but not others. "So then" (ἄρα οὖν) points back not merely to 9:17 but as the reference to mercy in the next clause reveals, to the entire argument in 9:14–17.[76] The repetition of the relative clause "whom he wills" (ὃν θέλει) has the same effect as the repetition of the verbs "show mercy" and "show compassion" in the relative clauses in 9:15 (ἐλεήσω ὃν ἂν ἐλεῶ καὶ οἰκτιρήσω ὃν ἂν οἰκτίρω). In both instances, the emphasis falls on God's freedom to act in a way that no one else's actions can constrain.

The verb "hardens" (σκληρύνει), like the quotation of Scripture in the previous sentence, comes from the narrative of God's relationship with Pharaoh in Exodus 4–14.[77] Before the plagues descended on the Egyptians, God told Moses twice that he would "harden" Pharaoh's heart and that as a result Pharaoh would not grant Moses's request to let Israel go into the wilderness to sacrifice to God (Exod 4:21; 7:3). Throughout the subsequent narrative, we read either that Pharaoh "hardened" his heart (8:15, 32; 9:34), that Pharaoh's heart "was hardened" (7:13; 8:19; 9:7, 35), or that "the LORD hardened" the heart of Pharaoh (9:12; 10:20, 27; 11:10; 14:8; cf. 10:1; 14:4). The verb that the LXX uses most often for "harden" in this story is the verb Paul uses here (σκληρύνω).[78]

The interplay in Exodus 4–14 between God's initiative and Pharaoh's initiative is helpful in understanding what Paul meant when he said that God "hardens" certain people such as Pharaoh. Paul believed that God punished people for their own sin, not that God forced people to sin and then punished them for it. Otherwise, God would be acting nonsensically when he endured the rebellions of the wicked "with much patience" and

75. John Piper, *The Justification of God: An Exegetical and Theological Study of Romans 9:1–23* (Grand Rapids: Baker, 1983), 145–48. Piper suggests that Paul's language may have come from the tendency of the LXX to describe God as "raising up" (ἐξεγείρω) nations or kings to accomplish his purposes (e.g., Hab 1:6; Jer 27:41 [Heb. and Eng. 50:41]). Cf. Sanday and Headlam, *Romans*, 256.

76. Moo, *Romans*, 596.

77. See, e.g., Dunn, *Romans 9–16*, 554; Moo, *Romans*, 598.

78. Piper, *Justification of God*, 140–42.

stretched out his hands in appeal to disobedient Israel (Rom 9:22; 10:21).[79] No patience is necessary for enduring the behavior of people doing what one wants them to do, and a lengthy appeal to people not to do what one has designed them to do is obviously fruitless.

When Paul says here, then, that God "hardens" people he must mean that God justly punishes people who, like Pharaoh (Exod 8:15, 32; 9:34) and everyone else (Rom 1:18–3:20; 5:12–19), are already in rebellion against him. God punishes them by calcifying this rebellion, or, to put it another way, he further hardens resistant hearts. This second level of resistance, which God himself initiates, is Paul's concern here, and it corresponds exactly to God's judgment in 1:24, 26, and 28 when he hands people over to their lust, dishonorable passion, and worthless thoughts.[80]

9:19 You will say to me, then, "Why does he still assign blame? For who withstands what he plans?" (Ἐρεῖς μοι οὖν, Τί οὖν ἔτι μέμφεται; τῷ γὰρ βουλήματι αὐτοῦ τίς ἀνθέστηκεν;). If what Paul has just argued is correct and God makes some people resistant to obeying him in accordance with his carefully designed plan, then it seems illogical and unjust for God to hold them responsible. They are only doing what his planning has decided they should do.

Paul suddenly shifts into the second-person singular and assumes the presence of an interlocutor. When Paul used this device in 2:17–29, he addressed a fictional Jewish unbeliever who "claimed" that because Jews possessed the Mosaic law and circumcision, God would treat them more leniently than gentiles on the day of judgment. Here too Paul probably assumes that his fictional objector is an unbelieving Jew. This interlocutor recognizes that in Paul's argument he has played the role of Ishmael, Esau, and Pharaoh and so falls among those whom God has hardened.

The verb "assign blame" (μέμφομαι) assumes culpability (Sir 41:7) and that the person blamed deserves rebuke (Sir 11:7). Paul and his fictional interlocutor both assume that the hardened person was originally culpable, and the question now is how God can "still" (ἔτι) find this person culpable when God himself holds the person in a state of resistance to his will.

The perfect-tense verb "withstands" (ἀνθέστηκεν) does not refer to past resistance, as if the interlocutor asserts that no one has ever succeeded in resisting God's plan (KJV, NET, CEB), but to the presently valid principle that no one stands in the way of what God has decided should happen.[81] The expression "what he plans" (βούλημα) emphasizes the carefully considered nature of God's design for the future (cf. Josephus, *Ant.* 2.304).[82]

9:20 To the contrary, you mere human being, who are you to answer back to God? Will the thing formed say to the one who formed it, "Why did you make me this way?" (ὦ ἄνθρωπε, μενοῦνγε σὺ τίς εἶ ὁ ἀνταποκρινόμενος τῷ θεῷ; μὴ ἐρεῖ τὸ πλάσμα τῷ πλάσαντι, Τί με ἐποίησας οὕτως;). The opponent's question about how God can blame sin-

79. It is unlikely that Paul refers to God's "patience" (μακροθυμία) as an aspect of his wrath in 9:22 (Piper, *Justification of God*, 190–92). See Paul's positive use of God's "patience" (also μακροθυμία) in 2:4, the only other occurrence of this term in Romans. See also the comments below on 9:22.

80. See, e.g., Hodge (*Romans*, 315–17), Shedd (*Romans*, 291–93), and John Murray (*The Epistle to the Romans*, 2 vols., NICNT [Grand Rapids: Eerdmans, 1959–65], 2:28–30).

81. Cf. the use of the same verb in the perfect tense in Rom 13:2.

82. Sanday and Headlam, *Romans*, 259; Gottlob Schrenk, "βούλημα," *TDNT* 1:636–37; Dunn, *Romans 9–16*, 556. On nouns with the -μα suffix, see Smyth, *Greek Grammar*, §230.

ners whom God himself has hardened in sin is as absurd as a handcraft springing to life and questioning its maker about the function for which it was created.

The expression "human being" (ὦ ἄνθρωπε) could simply be a polite way to begin a discussion with someone (Strabo, *Geography* 14.2.21), but in philosophical or political debate it sometimes indicated the heated emotion involved in sharp disagreement or rebuke (Rom 2:1, 3; Jas 2:20; Plutarch, *Phil.* 17.3). It could also highlight the contrast between the divine nature of God and the human nature of a debating partner (Philo, *Moses* 2.199; cf. *Spec. Laws* 2.82). Both heightened emotion and the divine-human contrast are present here.

The term "answer back" (ἀνταποκρίνομαι) carries a tone of superiority and indignation, implying that the debating partner has assumed the moral high ground, like that of the fowler over the double-crossing partridge in the fable (Aesop, *Fables* 301) or like Job's friends over Job (Job 32:12 LXX). Paul, then, portrays a debating partner who has arrogantly assumed he is more righteous than God and is able, although a mere human being, to point out God's mistakes.

The absurd image of a handmade object talking back to the artisan who made it comes from Isaiah 29:16 and 45:9 where, as with Paul, the image portrays the folly of asserting one's independence from God's intentions for the unfolding of history.[83] Beyond that general correspondence, however, Paul uses the image in his own way. The question, "Why did you make me this way [οὕτως]?" focuses attention on the function of the thing that the artisan has made and betrays the questioner's dissatisfaction with the role God has assigned him or her. Since the questioner here represents Paul's fictional portrayal of an unbelieving Jew, the question expresses dissatisfaction with the idea that God has freely hardened unbelieving Jews in their unbelief for his own purposes.

9:21 Or does the potter not have authority over the clay to make from the same lump one vessel for the purpose of receiving honor and one for the purpose of receiving dishonor? (ἢ οὐκ ἔχει ἐξουσίαν ὁ κεραμεὺς τοῦ πηλοῦ ἐκ τοῦ αὐτοῦ φυράματος ποιῆσαι ὃ μὲν εἰς τιμὴν σκεῦος ὃ δὲ εἰς ἀτιμίαν;). God, like a potter working clay, has the right and the skill to shape some sinful people so that, in the end, they receive his mercy and honor and to shape other sinful people so that they eventually receive the dishonor they deserve for their rebellion against him.

The power of the potter to make whatever he wished from the lump of clay on his wheel was a common image in Hellenistic-Jewish literature (Wis 15:7–17) and frequently appears as an image of God's sovereignty over the human beings he had created (Isa 45:9; Jer 18:1–6; Sir 33:13; cf. Gen 2:7, 8, 15). The term "authority" (ἐξουσία) here means more than simply "power." It connotes rightful power (cf. Rom 13:1–3), and the illustration appeals to the commonsense notion that the potter has both the right and the skill to make of his own clay what he wants to make.[84]

The preposition "for" (εἰς) refers to the purpose for which the potter makes the two types of vessels. God intends some vessels for "honor" (τιμή) and some for "dishonor" (ἀτιμία). Within the context of the image Paul is using, it is natural to think of these two terms as references to the use for which the potter designed each vessel, whether for public display because of its beauty (τιμή) or to be hidden

83. The phrase "shall the thing formed say to the one who formed it" (μὴ ἐρεῖ τὸ πλάσμα τῷ πλάσαντι) in Isa 29:16 LXX reappears word for word in Paul's text. On the meaning of the imagery in Isaiah, see Edward J. Young, *The Book of Isaiah*, 3 vols. (Grand Rapids: Eerdmans, 1972), 2:323–25; 3:203–4.

84. Cf. Calvin, *Romans*, 210.

because of its menial use (ἀτιμία; cf. RSV, NIV, NRSV; 2 Tim 2:20). In light of Paul's application of the imagery in the next sentence, however, the terms probably also carry an eschatological nuance. Just as the potter makes some vessels for dishonor, so in the application some vessels are fitted out for destruction (Rom 9:22), and just as he makes some vessels for honor, so in the application he prepares some vessels for glory (9:22–23; cf. 2:7).

Interpreters of this passage often explain the image of God as a potter shaping clay as a reference to God's creation of human beings and his determination of their eternal destinies at creation.[85] It is true that Scripture and Hellenistic-Jewish literature sometimes depict God the Creator as a potter working with clay (e.g., Isa 45:9–12; Sir 33:13), but Scripture could also use the image more broadly to refer to God's creation of Israel as his people and to his sovereignty over the affairs of Israel and other nations (Isa 29:16; 41:25; 64:7; Jer 18:1–6).

Here Paul probably uses the image in a broader sense, without a specific reference to God's creation of human beings. He depicts God as sovereign over sinful humanity (the potter's clay) and as within his rights to show mercy to some sinners by preparing them for eschatological glory (the vessels of honor) and to punish other sinners by arranging for their eschatological destruction (the vessels of dishonor). Paul does not, therefore, picture God as creating people in order to destroy them but as dealing sovereignly with a body of human beings who, without exception, are sinful. He mercifully saves some but justly punishes others.[86]

9:22–23 And what if God endured with much patience vessels of wrath fitted out for destruction because he wanted to show his wrath and to make known his power, and in order that he might make known the wealth of his glory toward vessels of mercy which he prepared beforehand for glory (εἰ δὲ θέλων ὁ θεὸς ἐνδείξασθαι τὴν ὀργὴν καὶ γνωρίσαι τὸ δυνατὸν αὐτοῦ ἤνεγκεν ἐν πολλῇ μακροθυμίᾳ σκεύη ὀργῆς κατηρτισμένα εἰς ἀπώλειαν, καὶ ἵνα γνωρίσῃ τὸν πλοῦτον τῆς δόξης αὐτοῦ ἐπὶ σκεύη ἐλέους ἃ προητοίμασεν εἰς δόξαν). No logical objection can be offered against God for confirming certain people in their rebellion against him and preparing others to receive his mercy. He wanted to do this for two reasons: (1) to reveal his powerful yet mercifully restrained wrath against sin, and, more importantly, (2) to reveal the great good he has in store for those who, despite their sin, receive his mercy.

The conjunction "and" (δέ) does not set up a contrast between the potter analogy and God, as some commentators have thought, but introduces Paul's application of the analogy.[87] Paul's continued use of the vessel metaphor in what follows shows this clearly.[88]

Paul's application is expressed in a long rhetorical question that extends to the end of 9:24.[89] Since the time of Origen, interpreters have often commented on how "unpolished" the whole construction is.[90] As others have noticed, however, it is not without precedent (Acts 23:9) and corresponds almost exactly to the practice in English of starting a rhetorical question with "what if . . . ?"[91] In

85. E.g., Piper, *Justification of God*, 179; Schreiner, *Romans*, 516–17.

86. "In the sovereignty here asserted, it is God as moral governor, and not God as creator, who is brought to view. It is not the right of God to create sinful beings in order to punish them, but his right to deal with sinful beings according to his good pleasure, that is here, and elsewhere asserted" (Hodge, *Romans*, 319). Cf. Murray, *Romans*, 2:32–33.

87. Godet, *Romans*, 359. For the view that the conjunction introduces a contrast, see, e.g., Cranfield (*Romans*, 2:493), Dunn (*Romans 9–16*, 558), REB, and NET.

88. Meyer, *Romans*, 381.

89. See the punctuation in WH and the full discussion of Cranfield (*Romans*, 2:471, 492–93, 497–99).

90. Origen, *Romans, Books 6–10*, 122.

91. Cranfield, *Romans*, 2:492–93. Cf. Calvin, *Romans*, 211.

Greek, the hearer or reader must mentally supply the apodosis (the "then" clause) of the conditional sentence, which runs something like, ". . . then what reasonable objection can you make?"[92]

The expression "because he wanted" (cf. CEB) translates a participle (θέλων) that many interpreters have taken concessively ("although choosing," NIV) rather than causally.[93] In the context, Paul uses the verb "want" (θέλω) to describe what God plans to do and then accomplishes (9:18), not what God wants to do but patiently refrains from doing. Moreover, the thought of 9:22–23 closely parallels the thought of 9:17–18 where Pharaoh's rise to power and hardening fulfilled God's purpose of displaying his power and fame. In 9:22–23, then, God's patient endurance of vessels of wrath, like Pharaoh's rise to power, should facilitate the display of God's wrath and power. On a concessive reading, however, the desire of God to show his wrath and power would remain unfulfilled.[94]

Paul explains what God desires with three complementary expressions, the infinitives "to show" (ἐνδείξασθαι) and "to make known" (γνωρίσαι) in 9:22, and the purpose clause "in order that he might make known" (ἵνα γνωρίσῃ) at the beginning of 9:23.[95] The ponderous use in the purpose clause of a conjunction ("and" [καί]) and the subjunctive mood, as well as the qualification of this clause with two subordinate relative clauses ("which he prepared beforehand . . ." and "us whom he also called . . ."), all signal that this is where Paul's primary emphasis lies.[96] The display of God's wrath and the revelation of his power are subsidiary purposes to the revelation of "the wealth of his glory toward vessels of mercy."

To facilitate the revelation of God's wrath, power, and mercy, God "endured with much patience vessels of wrath fitted out for destruction." The term "patience" (μακροθυμία) could refer negatively to God's strategic patience, which waits until the sins of rebellious people are at their height so that he might punish them more severely.[97] Or it could refer positively to his "customary" loving patience by which he reveals his sorrow at having finally to pour out his wrath on people determined to resist him.[98]

The negative use of the term would correspond nicely to God's strategic use of Pharaoh according to Exodus 9:16 (cf. Rom 9:17), but it is unlikely that Paul would use the term in this negative way here. Not only does the only other occurrence of the term in Romans refer to God's kind and forbearing willingness to delay executing his wrath on sinners (Rom 2:4) but the reference here to God acting with "much" (πολλῇ) patience recalls the common refrain in the OT that, in addition to his mercy and grace, God is "slow to anger" (e.g., Exod 34:6; Num 14:18; Neh 9:17; Psa 86:15; 103:8).[99]

This does not mean, however, that the purpose of God's patience is to allow those whom he has hardened (Rom 9:18) time to repent of their sin.[100] He has fashioned them for a particular purpose (9:21) and fitted them out for destruction (9:22), and they cannot fill their intended role if they

92. Cf. Moo, *Romans*, 605.

93. Among commentators, see, e.g., Sanday and Headlam (*Romans*, 261) for the concessive view, and, e.g., Cranfield (*Romans*, 2:493–94) for the causal view.

94. Piper, *Justification of God*, 188–89.

95. As Piper points out (*Justification of God*, 188), the construction is very close to the pattern of 1 Cor 14:5 where Paul also uses the verb "want" (θέλω) with two complements, first the infinitive "to speak" (λαλεῖν) and then the purpose clause "that you might prophesy" (ἵνα προφητεύητε).

96. Cranfield, *Romans*, 2:496.

97. E.g., Pelagius, *Romans*, 119; Calvin, *Romans*, 211; Piper, *Justification of God*, 189–92. The corresponding verb (μακροθυμέω) is used this way in 2 Macc 6:14.

98. E.g., Ambrosiaster, *Romans*, 79; Theodoret of Cyrus, *Letters of St. Paul*, 1:103 (who uses the term "customary" [συνήθως]); Cranfield, *Romans*, 2:495.

99. Cf. Dunn, *Romans 9–16*, 558.

100. E.g., Origen, *Romans, Books 6–10*, 122; Chrysostom, *Romans*, 299; Cranfield, *Romans*, 2:495; Kruse, *Romans*, 387.

repent of their sin. Rather, his patience qualifies the wrath and power that he displays toward these "vessels of wrath." God's characteristic mercy and grace temper even the demonstration of this element of his righteousness.[101]

God is very patient with "vessels of wrath fitted out for destruction." The term "vessels" (σκεύη) recalls the analogy of the potter in 9:21 who shapes one "vessel" (σκεῦος) for an "honored" purpose and another for a "menial" purpose, and this means that the agent of the passive action implied in the term "fitted out" (κατηρτισμένα) must be God. The vessels of wrath did not equip themselves for destruction. God equipped them for this purpose just as a potter shapes a pot with particular features for menial use.

This does not mean that God creates certain people in order to destroy them. The term "fitted out" describes something, like a fishing net, that already exists but needs to be set in order before it can be used for its proper purpose (cf. Mark 1:19).[102] God confirmed already rebellious people in their rebellion, thus setting them in order for his purpose of displaying his wrath and power.

Moreover, the passive voice of the expression "fitted out" (κατηρτισμένα) is not insignificant. It stands in contrast to the active voice verb that Paul uses when he says that God "prepared beforehand [προητοίμασεν]" vessels of mercy for glory. God's punishment of sinners is not as characteristic of his nature and identity as his mercy and grace to the sinful, and so the passive voice in the expression "fitted out for destruction" contains an element of reserve, ambiguity, and mystery that is appropriate to this element of God's activity.[103]

9:24 us whom he also called not only from the Jews but also from the gentiles? (οὓς καὶ ἐκάλεσεν ἡμᾶς οὐ μόνον ἐξ Ἰουδαίων ἀλλὰ καὶ ἐξ ἐθνῶν). The group of those whom God mercifully prepared to share his glorious existence includes Paul and all those who have believed the gospel. Once again, just as with Isaac and Jacob, God has broken with convention and constituted this new body of believers not only from Israelites but from non-Israelites as well.

Although this is a relative clause describing the "vessels of mercy" in the immediately preceding clause, the coupling of the relative pronoun with the conjunction "and" (καί) gives it an independent quality similar to a new sentence.[104] In a way that is consistent with this form, the clause has a function independent of the rest of the complicated rhetorical question of which it is a part (9:22–24). It brings Paul's defense of God's righteousness in 9:14–23 back to the concern that launched it in 9:7–13 and picks up an important theme that Paul had only hinted at there.

In 9:7–13 Paul had argued from the biblical stories of Isaac and Ishmael and of Jacob and Esau that a person becomes part of God's people when "called" (κληθήσεται) by God (9:7), not as a result of physical birth into the family of Abraham (9:7–10) nor as a result of behavior, whether good or bad (9:11–13). The results of God's call are often surprising, as, for example, when he refuses to take the relative vices and virtues of people into account or to favor the elder brother in a family. This unwillingness of God to follow human convention had called into question his righteousness, and so Paul digressed to defend God's right to guide the destiny

101. Hodge, *Romans*, 320: "Even in the necessary punishment of the wicked, God does not proceed with any undue severity, but, on the contrary, deals with them with the greatest long-suffering and tenderness."

102. See *TLNT* 2:271–74. The term does sometimes appear in the context of God's creative work (*TLNT* 2:271–72; e.g., Ps 73:16 LXX [74:16 Eng. and Heb.]). Even there, however, it often seems to connote God's arrangement of what he has already created.

103. Cf. Hodge, *Romans*, 321.

104. BDAG 496, s.v. καί 2f.

of sinful human beings according to his own purposes rather than according to human expectations or standards (9:14–23).

Although Paul had intended this entire argument (9:7–23) primarily as a support to his statement that not every "Israelite" was an Israelite in the deepest sense (9:6; cf. 2:25), he had hinted at the subsidiary point that some who were not ethnic Israelites were true Israelites nevertheless (cf. 2:26–29). When he had said that not all Israelites are "children" (τέκνα) rather than "children of Abraham" (9:7), he had recalled the language of 8:16–17, which describes the inner work of the Spirit as the criterion for belonging to the "children" (τέκνα) of God. Similarly, when he had said that "the children of the promise are counted as offspring" (9:8), he recalled the argument of 4:13–17 that the fulfillment of God's promise to Abraham required the inclusion of gentiles within God's people. Now, here in 9:24, he picks up this theme, which was previously expressed in 9:7–23 only subtly, and brings it out into the open.

9:25–26 As he also says in Hosea, "I will call 'Not My People' 'My People,' and 'Not Loved' 'Loved,' and it will happen that in the place where it was said to them, 'You are not my people,' there they will be called sons of the living God" (ὡς καὶ ἐν τῷ Ὡσηὲ λέγει, Καλέσω τὸν οὐ λαόν μου λαόν μου καὶ τὴν οὐκ ἠγαπημένην ἠγαπημένην· καί, ἔσται ἐν τῷ τόπῳ οὗ ἐρρέθη αὐτοῖς, Οὐ λαός μου ὑμεῖς, ἐκεῖ κληθήσονται υἱοὶ θεοῦ ζῶντος). God's word in Hosea confirms the surprisingly multiethnic nature of God's people. Just as in Hosea's time God mercifully accepted an idolatrous and unjust Israel again as his people, so now he has turned gentiles into recipients of his mercy. In both cases, those who were not his people because of their rebellion against him have become his people.

In 9:25–29 Paul confirms what he has just said about God calling his people into existence not only from the Jews but also from the gentiles (9:24) with a series of quotations from Scripture. He first quotes from Hosea to show that God has called gentiles to belong to his people, and he then quotes from Isaiah to show that God has also included within his people a remnant of Jews.[105]

"As . . . also" (ὡς καί) often introduces authoritative support for some statement in an argument (e.g., Acts 17:28; 22:25; 25:10; Josephus, *Ant.* 14.255; *Ag. Ap.* 2.43).[106] Here it introduces a carefully crafted composite quotation from Hosea, confirming Paul's statement that God calls some "vessels of mercy . . . prepared beforehand for glory" from among the gentiles (9:24).

The first part of Paul's quotation is an altered form of Hosea 2:23 (2:25 LXX), and the second part of his quotation comes word for word from Hosea 1:10 (2:1 LXX). Paul's alterations of Hosea 2:23 (2:25 LXX and Heb.) are significant. He reverses Hosea's two clauses and changes their wording to fit the themes he has developed in Romans 9:6–25. Hosea's "I will say [ἐρῶ]" becomes "I will call [καλέσω]" to match the statement that God "called" (ἐκάλεσεν) vessels of mercy from among both Jews and gentiles in Romans 9:24 (cf. 9:7, 12). This change also allows Paul to form an inclusion with the verb "they will be called" (κληθήσονται) from Hosea 1:10 (2:1 LXX), which he uses in the second part of his quotation. In addition, Paul changes Hosea's "I will have pity on Not Pitied" to "[I will call] 'Not Loved' 'Loved' [ἠγαπημένην ἠγαπημένην]," and this echoes the line, "Jacob I have loved [ἠγάπησα]" from 9:13.

These changes highlight the twofold theme that (1) God has the right to show mercy to whomever he will and that (2) God's choice of those to

105. Sanday and Headlam, *Romans*, 265; Michel, *An die Römer*, 316; Moo, *Romans*, 611.

106. Cf. BDAG 1104, s.v. ὡς 2dα.

whom he will show mercy is often surprising from a human perspective. In this case, the surprise is that those who have received God's mercy are "not only . . . Jews but also . . . gentiles" (9:24).

At first it may seem that Paul has applied the wording of Hosea to his argument arbitrarily. After all, Hosea speaks of God's merciful willingness to accept "the house of Israel" (Hos 1:6) as his people once again after they had rebelled against him through their idolatry (2:13) and injustice (4:2). Paul speaks of God's acceptance of gentiles who had never been God's people.

"The house of Israel," as Hosea portrays it, however, had become so mixed up with the religious, cultural, and political systems of the surrounding nations that there was little difference between it and the gentiles. Paul, moreover, has already made the case in Romans that idolatry and injustice plagued the Jewish community just as it did the gentiles (2:1–29). He may have intended the Hosea quotation, then, to communicate that God's promises to Israel in Hosea could also apply to gentiles since their idolatry and injustice were actually no worse in God's sight than Israel's occasional lapses into the same sins.

9:27–28 But Isaiah cries out concerning Israel, "If the number of the sons of Israel be as the sand of the sea, the remnant will be saved, for the Lord, acting conclusively and efficiently, will perform his word on the earth" (Ἡσαΐας δὲ κράζει ὑπὲρ τοῦ Ἰσραήλ, Ἐὰν ᾖ ὁ ἀριθμὸς τῶν υἱῶν Ἰσραὴλ ὡς ἡ ἄμμος τῆς θαλάσσης, τὸ ὑπόλειμμα σωθήσεται· λόγον γὰρ συντελῶν καὶ συντέμνων ποιήσει κύριος ἐπὶ τῆς γῆς). Isaiah announced that God would both judge Israel through the invasion of Assyria and would, through a spared remnant, be faithful to his promise that his people would flourish. This bittersweet message corresponds to Israel's experience in the present. God has drawn some of his vessels of mercy from the Jews, but in the present their numbers are small.

Paul next provides scriptural support for his claim that God has also called Jews to belong to his people. The conjunction "but" (δέ) implies a contrast between what Hosea said about the calling of the gentiles and what Isaiah 10:22–23, which Paul is about to quote, says about the Jews.[107] It is the same contrast that Paul implied in 9:1–5 and that runs beneath the surface of the argument of 9:6–24. The proclamation of the gospel among the gentiles has had surprising success, whereas few believers have come from Israel itself. This is not what one might expect on the basis of God's promises to Abraham. Here in 9:27 Isaiah "cries out" (κράζει) his message with the same sense of sorrow and urgency that characterized Paul's description of this tragic irony in 9:1–5.

Paul's quotation changes the wording of Isaiah 10:22–23 LXX, which itself departs from the Hebrew, but the basic meaning of the passage remains consistent from the Hebrew text to its rendering in the LXX to its rewording and use in Paul.[108] Both Isaiah (whether in the Hebrew or the LXX) and Paul's rendering of Isaiah send a two-part message about the nature of God's judgment of Israel. On the positive side, God will save his people from destruction, but on the negative side, only a remnant

107. Cranfield, *Romans*, 2:501.

108. An essentially literal translation of the Hebrew text runs, "For though your people Israel be as the sand of the sea, only a remnant of them will return [*yashub*]. Destruction is decreed [*killayon kharuts*], overflowing with righteousness [*shotep tsedaqah*]. For the Lord God of hosts will make a full end, as decreed [*kalah wenekhratsah*], in the midst of all the earth" (ESV). The LXX has the somewhat different translation: "And if the people of Israel become like the sand of the sea, the remnant will be saved [σωθήσεται], for he is completing [συντελῶν] and cutting short [συντέμνων] a reckoning [λόγον] with righteousness [ἐν δικαιοσύνῃ], because God will perform a shortened reckoning [λόγον συντετμημένον] in the whole world" (NETS). Paul changes the LXX's "the people of Israel . . . like the sand of the sea" to "the number of the sons of Israel . . . as the sands of the sea," which exactly reproduces a phrase from

of them will be saved. In the original context the destruction would come from the Assyrians, who would sweep into Israel from the north as God's tool of judgment on his sinful people. God would nevertheless leave a remnant within Israel both to humble the Assyrians and to provide for the eventual fulfillment of his promise to Abraham to "multiply" his "offspring . . . as the sand that is on the seashore" (Gen 22:17).[109]

So in Paul's argument God has both been faithful to his promises to Abraham by calling some Jews to receive his mercy in the present time, and he has, in judgment for disbelief, preserved only a remnant. Although in the present God has reduced true Israel to a number less than those within Israel generally, this does not mean the word of God has failed (9:6) any more than the same procedure involved the failure of God's word in the time of Isaiah.

9:29 And, just as Isaiah predicts, "Unless the Lord Sabaoth had left us offspring, we would have become like Sodom and been made like Gomorrah" (καὶ καθὼς προείρηκεν Ἠσαΐας, Εἰ μὴ κύριος Σαβαὼθ ἐγκατέλιπεν ἡμῖν σπέρμα, ὡς Σόδομα ἂν ἐγενήθημεν καὶ ὡς Γόμορρα ἂν ὡμοιώθημεν). Isaiah said that God's judgment on eighth-century Judah had been devastating but had also left a surviving remnant. This statement laid down in advance the pattern of Israel's relationship to God that was in effect in Paul's own time. God's promises to Abraham had not failed, but their fulfillment rested, sadly, on a small group of Jews who had believed the gospel.

Paul now adds additional support from Isaiah for the idea that God has called some Jews in the present to receive his mercy. Once again, the quotation is double-edged both in its original context and in Paul's context. Paul's quotation reproduces Isaiah 1:9 LXX exactly, a passage whose larger context (Isa 1:2–20) admonishes Judah that its trust in its political alliance with the powerful and aggressive Assyrians (1:2–6) and its failure to tend to the needs of the oppressed, the orphan, and the widow (1:17) had produced the desolation everyone could see around them (1:7). Had it not been for "a few survivors," the destruction of God's judgment would have been as complete for Judah as it was for Sodom and Gomorrah (1:9; cf. Gen 19:24–25).

Despite this theme of Judah's resistance to God and God's subsequent judgment, Isaiah also sounds a note of hope when he cites the difference between Judah on one hand and Sodom and Gomorrah on the other. Like a disheveled and abandoned campsite for field workers, left behind once the crop has been harvested (1:8), a small group of survivors would remain after God's judgment (1:9).[110]

The LXX translates "a few survivors" (*sarid*) with "offspring" (σπέρμα), and this loose rendering probably recalled for Paul the bittersweet note of judgment and hope on which the argument of Romans 9:1–29 had started.[111] So far, few Israelites had believed the gospel (9:1–5), but those who had done so demonstrated that God's word had not failed (9:6). Through this believing remnant God was demonstrating his faithfulness to his promise to provide Abraham with "offspring" (σπέρμα) (9:7–8; cf. 4:13, 16, 18).

Hos 1:10 (2:1 LXX), part of which he has just quoted in 9:26. This makes it likely that although Paul did not reproduce the exact wording of Hos 1:10 (2:1 LXX) in 9:26, he nevertheless had the broader context and its original meaning in mind. Paul also changes the LXX's "God [ὁ θεὸς] will perform . . . in the whole world [ἐν τῇ οἰκουμένῃ ὅλῃ)" to "the Lord [κύριος] . . . will perform . . . on the earth [ἐπὶ τῆς γῆς]." It is not clear that this change is hermeneutically significant.

109. John N. Oswalt, *The Book of Isaiah: Chapters 1–39*, NICNT (Grand Rapids: Eerdmans, 1986), 268–73.

110. For this reading of Isa 1:2–20, see Oswalt (*Isaiah: Chapters 1–39*, 84–85, 90–93).

111. Moo, *Romans*, 616; Jewett, *Romans*, 604–5.

Theology in Application

This passage could easily encourage two interpretive errors. It might be tempting to rush past 9:1–6 and to lose energy when arriving at 9:24–29 with their concern for the problem of Israel's unbelief, and instead to camp on the philosophically interesting problem of the relationship between God's sovereignty and human responsibility that rises so sharply from 9:7–23. Or, it might be tempting to dwell on the fertile soil that 9:1–6 and 9:24–29 offer for Jewish-Christian dialogue and to become bored with the discussions of "predestination" found on the well-traveled path of 9:7–23. The passage, however, is about both Israel's unbelief and God's sovereignty over salvation, and the two subjects are woven together so tightly that it seems ill-advised to tease them apart and study them separately.

The passage would not exist apart from the historical datum that so few Jews had responded positively to the message of the gospel. This is a problem that the oppression of the Jewish people, often and sadly at the hands of people calling themselves Christians, has only made worse. Like all of 9:1–11:36, then, the passage has much to say about God's commitment to Israel. At the same time, the passage answers the question of this commitment in a way that reveals much about God's character, about the way he distributes his mercy and his wrath, and about why he distributes them in this way. For those who want to worship God as the Scriptures reveal him rather than as human imagination constructs him, this passage is crucially important.

God's Continuing Faithfulness to Unbelieving Israel

The passage could hardly be clearer that Paul continued to identify himself with unbelieving Israelites, whom he calls his brothers and sisters in 9:3 (οἱ ἀδελφοί μου). It is also clear that Paul's grief ran deep that so few Israelites had believed the gospel. In 9:1–5 he is already laying the groundwork for his conclusion in 11:25–29 that all Israel will be saved and that the gifts and the calling of God to his people Israel are irrevocable. The Jews and gentiles who believe the gospel have received the gifts and privileges Paul lists in 9:4–5 in their ultimate, eschatological form. Nevertheless, these gifts and privileges continue to belong in their unfulfilled condition to the Jews.[112] They are the spiritual blessings that gentile believers have come to share and for which they are indebted to the Jews (15:27; cf. 11:18). Thus, although Paul goes on to argue that physical descent from Abraham does not make one a child of God in the ultimate sense (9:7–13), he does not mean by this that Jews have lost their identity as God's people in light of the gospel (cf. 3:1–2).

None of this implies that Christians do not need to proclaim the gospel to unbe-

112. Cf. Bell, *Irrevocable Call*, 202–9.

lieving Jews.[113] Paul's anguish over the unbelief of the majority of his Jewish kinfolk is the dominant message of the passage and arises from his compassionate concern that so many of them are not benefitting from the gospel. The gospel is the wonderful news that God has broken the grip of sin and death on humanity through the death and resurrection of Christ Jesus. It is hardly a kindness to anyone, least of all the Jewish people, to withhold this message from them.

The long, horrific history of "Christian" oppression of the Jews certainly introduces an element of complexity into the way in which Christians should communicate the gospel to Jewish people.[114] A thorough knowledge of this history and a Spirit-transformed character of humility, kindness, empathy, and compassion are therefore essential accompaniments to any Christian effort in this direction. But unless one has lost faith in the gospel to transform human life in positive ways, the most compassionate response to the sad story of Jewish oppression is not to keep the message of the gospel from anyone simply because he or she is Jewish.[115]

God's Sovereignty over the Human Response to the Gospel

For Paul the problem was not whether to proclaim the gospel to the Jews. The gospel was for the Jew first (1:16). Instead, it was how to account for Jewish rejection of the gospel. How could one be a Jew, with all the privileges Paul lists in 9:4–5, and yet fail to receive the climactic resolution of those gifts in the gospel? It is significant that in answering this question Paul does not, in the first instance, blame those Jews who have rejected the gospel. He will do that later (9:30–10:21). Rather, he begins by entertaining the question of whether the fault could lie with God. God promised the Jews that they would be his people, but now because they have rejected the gospel, unbelieving Jews are only his people in a provisional sense. Given his promises, how could God have arranged things so that so many Jews did not believe in him? Behind this question lies the assumption that God decides who will believe the gospel and decides this down to the level of the relative numbers of individuals in each people group who will do so (9:12, 14–18). The problem Paul addresses is how God can be faithful to Israel and choose such a small number of Israelites to belong to the inner circle of his people.

113. As in, e.g., R. Kendall Soulen, "'They are Israelites': The Priority of the Present Tense for Jewish-Christian Relations," *Between Gospel and Election*, ed. Florian Wilk, J. Ross Wagner, Frank Schleritt, WUNT 257 (Tübingen: Mohr Siebeck, 2010), 498–501.

114. See, e.g., *A History of the Jewish People*, ed. H. H. Ben-Sasson (Cambridge: Harvard University Press, 1976). I place the term "Christian" in quotes because I do not think that everyone who claims to be a Christian is one (Matt 7:21–23; 25:1–13, 31–46), and the pride, jealousy, greed, and sheer cruelty so characteristic of "Christian" persecution of the Jews is incompatible with the way the Christian Scriptures define and describe Christianity (Matt 5:21–26, 38–42, 43–48; Gal 5:22–23; 6:9–10).

115. Bell, *Irrevocable Call*, 395–407, especially pp. 400 and 403.

For centuries students of Scripture have found this teaching to be particularly difficult, and it is easy to see why. First, this idea seems to remove all human responsibility for proclaiming or believing the gospel. What is the point of human involvement in the gospel with respect either to communicating it or accepting it if God has determined in advance which individuals belong to his people?

Second, one can describe the idea that God decides who will believe the gospel in a way that makes God not only responsible for the salvation of human beings but also for evil since he seemingly creates certain human beings in order that they might sin and that he might then destroy them for his glory. A variation on this idea depicts God as within his rights even to destroy innocent human beings, if any had existed, simply because he created them. One follower of Augustine in antiquity put it this way: "If the human race, which exists as originally created out of nothing, had not been born under the guilt of death and with original sin, and the omnipotent Creator had wanted to condemn some to eternal perdition, who could say to the omnipotent Creator: Why have you done this?"[116] This is the sort of thinking that George MacDonald probably had in mind when he said, "Of all evils, to misinterpret what God does, and then say the thing as interpreted must be right because God does it, is of the devil."[117]

To read Romans 9:7–23 in these ways, however, is to read the passage in a one-sided way, without the balance provided by the context. As Paul will say in 9:30–10:21 and as his own missionary efforts imply (1:5, 13; 15:14–21; 16:25–26), Christians were called to preach the gospel, and those who heard the gospel were responsible for responding to it with obedience (1:5; 16:26). Although those who believe the gospel do so because God predestined, called, justified, and glorified them (8:30), God uses those who proclaim the gospel and the spiritually transformed hearts of those who hear the gospel as the means by which he "shows mercy to whom he wills" (9:18; cf., e.g., Acts 2:39; 13:48; 18:9–10; Eph 1:3–14; 2:5–10). Scripture does not clarify how the human responsibility to believe and proclaim the gospel coheres logically with God's initiative and freedom in showing mercy to whom he will. The logical web that binds together these two sides of redemption may be beyond human understanding, but it is reasonably clear that Scripture affirms both.

The idea that this passage teaches God created people in order to destroy them, moreover, attributes conduct to God that God himself finds sinful in human beings. It depicts God as forcing people to sin and then condemning them for it or, worse, condemning the innocent. The idea that God is unrighteous but, thankfully, is on the side of the church cannot be the gospel.[118]

116. Quoted in Herman Bavinck, *God and Creation*, vol. 2 of *Reformed Dogmatics*, ed. John Bolt, trans. John Vriend (Grand Rapids: Baker, 2004), 395. The author's identity is uncertain. See Bolt's note (ibid., 395n157).

117. George MacDonald, *Unspoken Sermons, Series I, II, III* (1889; repr. Whitethorn, CA: Johannesen, 1997), 549.

118. Cf. MacDonald, *Unspoken Sermons*, 542–43: "Is there any gospel in telling me that God is unjust, but there is a way of

Again, however, this is not the picture of God that Paul paints in Romans 9:7–23. Paul certainly depicts God as sovereignly raising up Pharaoh and hardening him for the purpose of showing his power and proclaiming his name in the whole earth (9:17). He also illustrates God's sovereignty over salvation by picturing God as a potter making some vessels for honor followed by glory and others for dishonor followed by destruction (9:20–21). But he tempers the entire concept with the notion that God endured the vessels of wrath that he made with much patience and by speaking of the fitting out of these vessels in the passive voice (9:22). By doing this, he indicates that one must not misread the illustrations to make God the author of evil and sin.

Although Paul is not explicit, it is likely that he understood God's actions of raising up Pharaoh, hardening him, and shaping vessels for dishonor and destruction as God's judgment on already sinful human beings. This presupposition would be consistent at least with the interplay between God's hardening of Pharaoh and Pharaoh's hardening of himself in Exodus 4–14. It would also be consistent with Paul's conviction, expressed unambiguously in 5:12–19, that all human beings since Adam's disobedience have themselves been disobedient to God and deserving of his condemnation. Paul's illustration of the potter in 9:19–23, then, is not about God predestining certain people to sin, nor is it about the relationship between the entry of sin into God's creation and God's predestining will. It is instead about God's response to already sinful human beings.

This does not mean that human sin took God by surprise and was somehow outside the scope of God's original design for the universe. It simply means that the answer to such questions lies beyond human understanding. Herman Bavinck, reflecting on the biblical doctrine of reprobation fairly represents the theological implications of this passage (although he is not speaking specifically about Rom 9:19–23):

> Sin and its punishment can never as such, and for their own sake, have been willed by God. They are contrary to his nature. He is far removed from wickedness and does not willingly afflict anyone. When he does it, it is not because, deep down, he wants to. They can therefore have been willed by God only as a means to a different, better, and greater good. . . . Sin is not itself a good. It only becomes a good inasmuch as, contrary to its own nature, it is compelled by God's omnipotence to advance his honor. It is a good indirectly because, being subdued, constrained, and overcome, it brings out God's greatness, power, and justice.[119]

Ultimately, then, we must hold God's sovereignty over the response of human beings to the gospel and to their inclusion or exclusion from his people in tension with

---

deliverance from him?" This rhetorical question only points to theological truth, however, if one's understanding of justice has been shaped by Scripture rather than by cultural expectations, as the exegesis of 9:12 above has hopefully demonstrated.

119. Bavinck, *God and Creation*, 398.

the insistence of the Scriptures that God's people are responsible for proclaiming the gospel and that those who hear the gospel proclaimed are responsible for believing it.

J. I. Packer, in a wise treatment of the subject, urged Christians to accept the inconsistency that seems to be involved in this antinomy as only apparent and as reflective of a deficiency in human understanding rather than in God's word. Christians, he argued, should "be careful . . . not to set" God's sovereignty and human responsibility "at loggerheads, nor to make deductions from either that would cut across the other," but to "use each within the limits of its own sphere of reference."[120]

In practical terms, this means that believers should be active in evangelism, presenting the gospel in winsome ways through word and deed and recognizing that God is not willing "that any should perish, but that all should reach repentance" (2 Pet 3:9). At the same time their evangelistic efforts should be free from any hint of manipulation, coercion, or impatience, and they should not bear the burden of thinking that their own mistakes and failures have prevented someone from believing the gospel. God is sovereign and merciful, and so nothing can separate from his love those whom he has called to be his people (8:30, 38–39).[121]

These practical observations are helpful for understanding how Christians should approach explaining the gospel to Jewish friends. Whereas Christians need to remember that the gospel is for the Jew first, they also need to remember that God is sovereign over the response of Jewish people to the gospel. An impatient approach in evangelism to Jewish people that fails to recognize the complex history of Jewish-Christian interaction and the many barriers that history has constructed between Christians and Jews is likely only to erect further barriers and create greater misunderstanding. Because God is sovereign over evangelism, Christians can take comfort that the patience necessary for listening to, learning from, and becoming genuine friends with their Jewish neighbors is not jeopardizing their possible salvation but following the most loving and prudent path.

120. J. I. Packer, *Evangelism and the Sovereignty of God* (Downers Grove, IL: InterVarsity Press, 1961), 21.

121. Ibid., 40–41.

Romans 9:30–10:21

CHAPTER 21

Literary Context

In 9:1–11:36 Paul is engaged in an effort to show why the meager results of proclaiming the gospel among the Jews do not demonstrate that his gospel is wrong or at least incorrectly conceived. He had made the case that his gospel defines the basic problem confronting humanity (1:18–3:20) and had announced the good news that God graciously solved that problem through the death and resurrection of Christ and the coming of the Spirit (3:21–8:39).

A biblical perspective shaped the whole presentation, and because of this, Israel played a prominent role in defining both the problem and the solution. Despite having the Scriptures, Jewish humanity was as sinful as non-Jewish humanity, and the effect of God's law on the Jews was not to make them less sinful than the gentiles but to show how sinful all humanity actually was (2:1–3:20). Similarly, the good news that God had made redemption from sin available through Christ took a particularly biblical shape since Paul conceived of it as the fulfillment of God's promise to Abraham, whom Paul described as the father not only of believing Jews but also of believing gentiles (4:1–25).

This biblical shape of Paul's gospel, however, created a problem when measured against the actual effect of the gospel when it was preached. When Jews in synagogues around the eastern Mediterranean heard Paul's gospel, comparatively few believed it, some violently opposed it, and surprisingly its greatest success was among gentiles (e.g., Acts 13:45–48; 17:1–9; 28:23–28; 1 Thess 2:14–16). To an objective Jewish observer, looking in from the outside, it must have seemed that in the process of redefining Abraham's family on the basis of faith Paul had ignored the commitment of God to Abraham's physical descendants that was so clearly laid out in Scripture (e.g., Deut 4:37; 7:6–8; 10:14–15). If Paul's understanding of the gospel were accurate, then it seemed as if the word of God had failed, and since Paul had made the case that the benefits of the gospel were limited to those who believed it as God's word, this seeming failure loomed as a major, disqualifying problem.

Paul's first step in addressing this problem had demonstrated that Scripture itself does not identify physical Israel with true Israel (Rom 9:6–29). According to

Scripture, being an Israelite in the deepest sense had always involved more than simple physical descent from Abraham. True Israelites were "children of the promise" (9:6–8), which meant that their inclusion in God's people was God's decision and came at his initiative, not from anything in themselves, whether their personal virtue or their family of origin (9:9–23). Surprisingly, God had decided in recent times to include large numbers of gentiles within his people and only a remnant of Israelites, but Scripture had anticipated even this development (9:25–29).

In 9:30–10:21 Paul takes a second step in explaining how his understanding of the gospel can be correct when so many Israelites have rejected it. The rhetorical question that begins the section, "What, then, shall we say?" (9:30) refers back to the poignant contrast in 9:24–29, drawn from Scripture, between a clueless "no people" becoming God's people and God's beloved Israelites forming only a remnant of the saved. The question introduces this new section in which Paul will examine how this happened not from the perspective of God's choice but from the perspective of Israel's error in rejecting the gospel. Unbelieving Israel, Paul will argue, is fully culpable for its rejection of God's word in the gospel.

The initial rhetorical question also points back to Paul's thesis statement in this major part of his argument, "but that is not to say that the word of God has failed" (9:6). Throughout this new section Paul will continue to demonstrate that Israel's rejection of the gospel in recent times is consistent with the portrait Scripture draws of an Israel that has often disobeyed God's word. Just as God's surprising choice of many gentiles and few Israelites within his people is consistent with Scripture, this is also true of Israel's own rejection of the gospel.

In the third step in his argument (11:1–32), Paul will deny that this bleak perspective on physical Israel is God's final word. God will one day transform the zeal (cf. ζῆλον, 10:2; παραζηλώσω, 10:19) that unbelieving Israel has misdirected against the gospel, and especially against the gospel's inclusion of gentiles within God's people, into jealousy (παραζηλῶσαι, 11:11; παραζηλώσω, 11:14) of the blessings that God has given believing gentiles. This development will, in turn, lead to physical Israel's salvation (11:12, 14–15, 23–24, 26–27, 31). This hope, and the conviction that his own proclamation of the gospel to the gentiles might facilitate its realization (11:13–14), probably accounts for Paul's earnest prayer in the midst of his otherwise bleak account of Israel's rejection of the gospel in 9:30–10:21 that they might be saved (10:1).

IX. Justification by Faith Brings Peace and Reorients the Believer's Existence (5:1–8:39)

X. Israel's Present Rejection of the Gospel Does Not Imply the Failure of God's Word (9:1–11:36)

  A. Paul's Anguish over Israel's Rejection of the Gospel (9:1–5)

  B. The Scriptures Describe God's Choice of His People as Free and Surprising (9:6–29)

➡ **C. Unbelieving Israel Is Culpable for Rejecting the Gospel (9:30–10:21)**

  D. Still, God Has Not Cast Off His People (11:1–32)

  E. A Concluding Statement of Astonishment and Praise (11:33–36)

XI. Exhortation to Live in a Way That Is Consistent with the Gospel (12:1–15:13)

Main Idea

The many Israelites who have heard and rejected the gospel are fully responsible for their disobedience to God's word. They focused so energetically on the law of God that instead of continuing to listen to God's word in the gospel, they rejected it. Having rejected the gospel of Christ's atoning death, they were left only with an impossible attempt to live eternally by following the commands of the Mosaic law. Ironically, gentiles, who cared nothing about God or his word, often responded positively to the gospel and through faith received the right standing with God that leads to life. Israel's Scriptures anticipated both its rejection of the gospel and the gentiles' surprising acceptance of it.

Translation

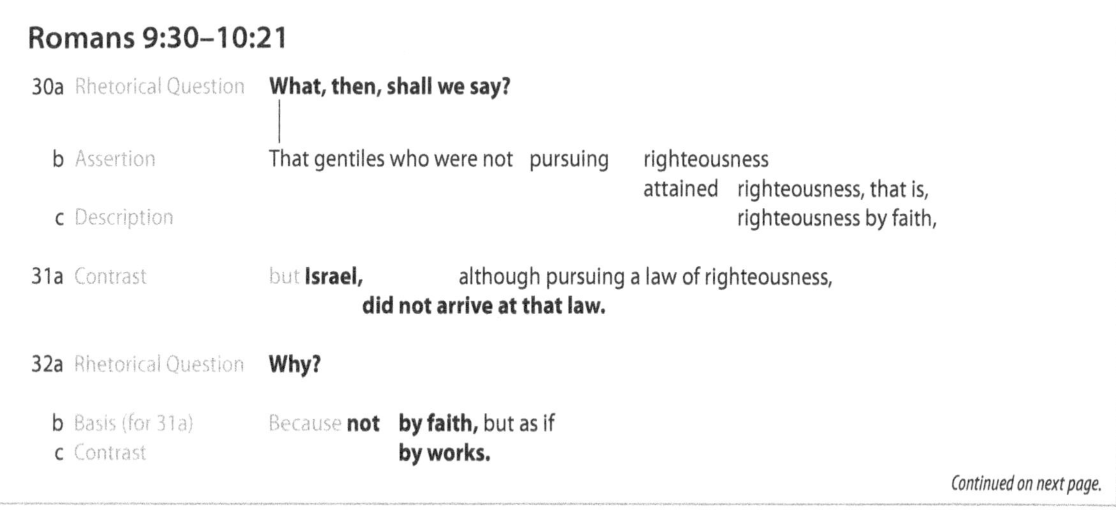

Romans 9:30–10:21

30a	Rhetorical Question	**What, then, shall we say?**
b	Assertion	That gentiles who were not pursuing righteousness attained righteousness, that is,
c	Description	righteousness by faith,
31a	Contrast	but **Israel,** although pursuing a law of righteousness, **did not arrive at that law.**
32a	Rhetorical Question	**Why?**
b	Basis (for 31a)	Because **not by faith,** but as if
c	Contrast	**by works.**

Continued on next page.

Continued from previous page.

d	Assertion	**They stumbled**
		on the stumbling stone,
33a	Verification	just as it is written,
		"Look! I put in Zion (Isa 28:16a) a stone of stumbling and
b		a rock of offense (Isa 8:14), and
c	Assertion	the one who believes on him will not be ashamed." (Isa 28:16b)
10:1a	Address	Brothers and sisters,
b	Assertion	**the desire of my heart and my petition to God for them is for their salvation.**
2a	Basis	For **I testify to them that they have** zeal for God, but
b	Contrast	not according to knowledge.
3a	Cause (of 3c)	For, being ignorant about the righteousness of God, and
b	Cause (of 3c)	seeking to establish their own righteousness,
c	Assertion	**they did not submit to the righteousness of God.**
4a	Basis (for 3c)	For **Christ is the goal of the law,**
b	Result (of 4a)	with the result of righteousness for everyone who believes.
5	Verification (of 4b)	For **Moses writes about the righteousness from the law,**
		"The human being who does them will live by them." (Lev 18:5)
6a	Contrast (to 5)	But **the righteousness from faith says this:**
		"Do not say in your heart, (Deut 9:4)
		'Who will go up to heaven?'" (Deut 30:12; Ps 107:26a)
b	Purpose	—that is, to bring Christ down
		or,
7a	Restatement (of 6a)	"Who will go down into the abyss?" (Deut 30:13; Ps 107:26b)
b	Purpose	—that is, to bring Christ up from the dead.
8a	Contrast (to 6a–7b)	But **what does it say?**
		"The word is near you, in your mouth and in your heart." (Deut 30:14)
b	Description	—That is, the word of faith that we preach.
9a	Basis (of 8a)/ Condition (of 9c)	Because if you confess with your mouth that the Lord is Jesus and
b	Condition (of 9c)	believe in your heart that God raised him from the dead
c	Assertion	**you will be saved.**
10a	Explanation (of 9b)	For with the heart
b		**it is believed,**
c	Result (of 10a)	resulting in righteousness,

d Explanation (of 9a) and with the mouth
it is confessed,
e Result (of 10c) resulting in salvation.

11 Inference (of 10) So **the Scripture says,**
"Everyone who believes on him will not be ashamed." (Isa 28:16b)

12a Inference (of 11) So **there is no distinction between Jew and Greek,**

b Basis (of 12a) for **the same Lord is over all,**
c Result (of 12b) being rich toward all who call upon him.

13 Verification For, "Everyone who calls upon the name of the Lord will be saved." (Joel 2:32)

14a Rhetorical Question **How,** then, **should they call upon him whom they have not believed?**

b Rhetorical Question And **how should they believe him whom they have not heard?**

c Rhetorical Question And **how should they hear without a preacher?**

15a Rhetorical Question And **how should they preach unless they are sent?**

b Verification (of 15a) Just as it is written,
"How beautiful are the feet of those who proclaim good news." (Isa 52:7)

16a Contrast (to 15b) But **not all have obeyed the gospel.**

b Verification (of 16a) For **Isaiah says,**
"Lord, who has believed our report?" (Isa 53:1)

17 Inference (of 16b) So, **faith comes**
from hearing, and
hearing
through the word of Christ.

18a Rhetorical Question But, **I say, they didn't fail to hear did they?**

b Assertion/Verification To the contrary!
"Their voice went out to all the earth and
c Restatement (of 18b) their words to the limits of civilization." (Ps 19:4)

19a Rhetorical Question But, **I say, Israel didn't fail to understand did it?**

b Assertion/Verification **First, Moses says,**
"I will make you jealous of those who are not a people, and
c I will make you resent a foolish people." (Deut 32:21)

Continued on next page.

Continued from previous page.

20a	Assertion/ Verification	And **Isaiah dares to say,** "I have been found among those who do not seek me,
b	Restatement	I have become visible to those who do not ask for me." (Isa 65:1)
21	Contrast (to 19b–20b)	But **to Israel he says,** "All day long I have stretched out my hands to a disobedient and oppositional people." (Isa 65:2)

Structure

Paul tightly structured this second major step in the argument of chapters 9–11. This step begins and ends with a statement of its main theme. Gentiles who neither pursued righteousness nor sought God have embraced the gospel in surprisingly great numbers, whereas Israel has, apart from a remnant, rejected it (9:30–32; 10:20–21).

Sandwiched between these two statements, Paul's argument unfolds in three steps (9:30–10:4; 10:5–13; 10:14–21), designed to show that unbelieving Israel is culpable for rejecting the gospel. First, Paul describes the basic problem and his explanation for it (9:30–10:4). The basic problem is that gentiles who do not pursue righteousness have attained it, but Israel, who pursues the law with its righteous precepts, has failed to keep the law and so failed to attain righteousness by this path (9:30–32). The reason they pursued this route to righteousness lies in their misguided zeal for the law, a notion that led them to reject Christ and, in the process, fail to attain the real goal of the law (9:32–10:4).

Second, Paul explains from Scripture why unbelieving Israel's elevation of the law over Christ as the way to righteousness and life is misguided (10:5–13). According to the law itself, one must "do" the law in order to gain righteousness and life by it (10:5; Lev 18:5), but this is something that Paul has shown earlier in the letter's argument to be impossible (Rom 3:19–20; 4:15; 5:20; 7:7–25; 8:7). According to the gospel, however, righteousness comes to those who simply trust in the effectiveness of what God has done for them through the death and resurrection of Christ. This is consistent with what the Scriptures say about the need for God to transform the hearts of his people to make them capable of obeying and calling upon him (Deut 30:11–14 [cf. Deut 29:4; 30:1–10]; Joel 2:32).

Third, Paul argues that unbelieving Israel is fully responsible for their rejection of the gospel (10:14–21). In a series of questions, Paul addresses three possible excuses for Israel's failure to obey the gospel. First, did God send them messengers with the gospel (10:14–15)? Second, did they hear the gospel message (10:16–18)? Finally, did they understand the gospel message (10:19–21)? Paul insists that God amply fulfilled all these conditions in a way that is consistent with the record of his interactions with Israel in Scripture. Israel, however, has so far largely rejected God's overtures and done this in a way that is again consistent with its behavior in Scripture. Instead, gentiles have responded with faith to the gospel in large numbers.

Exegetical Outline

X. Israel's Present Rejection of the Gospel Does Not Imply the Failure of God's Word (9:1–11:36)
- A. Paul's Anguish over Israel's Rejection of the Gospel (9:1–5)
- B. The Scriptures Describe God's Choice of His People as Free and Surprising (9:6–29)
- ➡ **C. Unbelieving Israel Is Culpable for Rejecting the Gospel (9:30–10:21)**
  - 1. Why Gentiles Attained Righteousness but Israel Fell Short (9:30–10:4)
    - a. The basic problem: Israel lacks righteousness (9:30–31)
    - b. An explanation for the problem: righteousness by works is impossible (9:32–10:4)
  - 2. Why Israel's Choice of Law over Faith Was Unwise (10:5–13)
  - 3. Why Israel Is Culpable for Its Rejection of the Gospel (10:14–21)

Explanation of the Text

9:30 What, then, shall we say? That gentiles who were not pursuing righteousness attained righteousness, that is, righteousness by faith (Τί οὖν ἐροῦμεν; ὅτι ἔθνη τὰ μὴ διώκοντα δικαιοσύνην κατέλαβεν δικαιοσύνην, δικαιοσύνην δὲ τὴν ἐκ πίστεως). Gentile Christians who made no effort to obtain a right standing with God have ironically received precisely this right standing through their faith in the gospel.

Just as he did in 9:14, Paul signals a division in his argument with the rhetorical question "what, then, shall we say?" In 9:14, however, Paul used the question to introduce a possible objection to his preceding argument (cf. 3:5; 6:1; 7:7), whereas here it introduces a new line of thought supporting Paul's main contention in 9:6 that the word of God has not failed (cf. 4:1; 8:31). Paul has just finished arguing that the word of God has not failed because it depicts God choosing the true children of Abraham on the basis of his own freely formed plans, not on the basis of anything from the human side, including a physical connection to Abraham's family. Now Paul shifts the ground of his main contention to say that the responsibility for the salvation of only a remnant within Israel lies with Israel's failure to respond appropriately to the word of God (9:30–10:4), not with the unavailability or difficulty of God's word (10:5–21). "What, then, shall we say?" launches this discussion by implicitly asking why Israel's participation in the true people of God has been reduced to that of a remnant (9:27–29).

Paul's "that" (ὅτι) introduces his thesis about why gentiles outnumber Jews in the present configuration of God's true people.[1] The language of pursuit (διώκοντα) and attainment (κατέλαβεν) is

1. This sentence, which extends to the end of 9:31, is probably not a second rhetorical question (NAB) despite Paul's use of a second question after "what, then, shall we say?" in 6:1; 7:7; 8:31; 9:14. As Sanday and Headlam (*Romans*, 279) point

metaphorical, recalling the sweaty, labor-intensive task of pursuing and overtaking someone in the arid, often hot climate of the eastern Mediterranean (e.g., Gen 31:23 LXX; Deut 19:6 LXX; 2 Kgs 25:5 LXX; Sir 11:10; Phil 3:12). The result is a deeply ironic, almost humorous, picture of a group of people who have reached a goal they were not even trying to attain.

The "righteousness" (δικαιοσύνη) that gentiles overtook without even trying is a right standing with God (Rom 3:22, 25–26; 4:6, 9, 11, 13, 22, 25). So far in Romans a right standing with God has been obtainable by flawlessly doing what is right (2:6–7, 10, 13, 25) or, since no one can reach that standard, by receiving it in faith as a free gift from God who through the death of his Son has atoned for human sin against him (3:9–26; 5:17, 21). Those gentiles who have attained a right standing with God ironically did not "pursue" it in either of these senses.

It was true, as Origen observed, that unbelieving gentiles engaged in ethical reasoning and moral conduct (cf. Rom 2:14–15).[2] Plato could even speak of pursuing righteousness (*Republic* 545b).[3] Here, however, Paul thinks in general terms, as he does in 1:18–32, and probably assumed that gentile polytheism and idolatry tainted even the best moments in non-Jewish moral discourse.

Gentile Christians attained righteousness, then, out of the blue as a result of God's call, promise, love, and mercy rather than by any exertion (cf. 9:11–12, 16). Their involvement in attaining righteousness was limited to their faith, but in Paul's thinking faith was not an activity or pursuit (cf. 3:20, 27–28; 4:1–6).

Paul signals that he knows this way of talking about righteousness is unusual with the phrase "that is [δέ)] righteousness by faith."[4] "Righteousness" (δικαιοσύνη) normally refers to the quality of fairness and upright behavior, and people typically "pursue" this behavior as a means of possessing "righteousness" (Prov 15:9 LXX; Isa 51:1 LXX; Sir 27:8; 1 Tim 6:11; 2 Tim 2:22). In the words of Stephen Westerholm, righteousness is "not simply what one ought to do but what one has . . . when one has done it."[5] To say that trust in God is the means by which (ἐκ) someone attains righteousness is to understand "righteousness" in an extraordinary way—as a right relationship with God based on God's willingness, through the atoning death of Christ, to give people the same relationship with him that they would have had if they had consistently done what was right.[6] This redefinition of righteousness has been a frequent characteristic of Paul's use of the concept in the argument up to this point (cf., e.g., Rom 3:22; 4:3–8).

9:31 but Israel, although pursuing a law of righteousness, did not arrive at that law (Ἰσραὴλ δὲ διώκων νόμον δικαιοσύνης εἰς νόμον οὐκ ἔφθασεν). In contrast to the gentiles, who made no effort to gain a right standing with God, Israel worked hard to fulfill the law's righteous requirements but failed (like everyone else) to reach its high standards.

The term "but" (δέ) introduces the other side

out, the phrase "that is, a righteousness by faith" asserts Paul's position and is not appropriate to the tone of debate and discussion that would be necessary if the sentence were a rhetorical question.

2. Origen, *Romans, Books 6–10*, 128.

3. At the beginning of book 8, Socrates and Glaucon are discussing the various character types of cities and individuals to find out which type produces the greatest happiness. In summing up a major section of the discussion, Socrates says to Glaucon, "We may either follow the counsel of Thrasymachus and pursue injustice [διώκωμεν ἀδικίαν] or the present argument and pursue justice [δικαιοσύνην]" (Paul Shorey, LCL). Cf. Meyer, *Romans*, 391.

4. For this use of the term translated "that is," see BDAG 213, s.v. δέ, 2.

5. Westerholm, *Perspectives Old and New on Paul*, 266 (cf. 272).

6. Ibid., 273–84.

of the contrast that Paul began developing in 9:30, and the name "Israel" recalls "Israelites" from 9:4 and the whole list of gifts and privileges that belong to Israel according to 9:4–5. Among those privileges was "the legislation" (νομοθεσία) that God gave to his people through Moses (9:4), a positive term that, as the comments on 9:4 mentioned, carried the nuance of a carefully crafted legal system. Here Paul also describes the Mosaic law in positive terms as "a law of righteousness" (νόμον δικαιοσύνης).

This relatively simple Greek phrase is unlikely to carry the more complex meanings that interpreters sometimes suggest for it, such as "a rule of life which would produce righteousness" or "the righteousness of the law" or "the law that points to righteousness by faith" (cf. 3:21).[7] These renderings are not only somewhat unnatural but are out of step with the way Paul connects "righteousness" (δικ-) language and "law" (νόμος) language elsewhere in the letter. Elsewhere this language simply implies that the Mosaic legislation is itself righteous (7:12) in the sense that it describes righteous conduct (2:13; 8:4; 10:5).[8] "A law of righteousness," then, is the Mosaic law, which is itself just and which describes the just conduct that leads to life (10:5).[9]

When Paul pictures Israel "pursing" (διώκων) but not "arriving at" (ἔφθασεν . . . εἰς) the law of righteousness, he is again using the live metaphor of hot pursuit. In the ancient Greek fable of "The Deer and the Hunters," for example, the deer discovered that his unimpressive legs were more useful than his showy antlers when a group of hunters surprised him. The hunters "began pursuing" (ἐδίωκον) him, "and as long as he was running on the open plain, he was staying ahead of his pursuers [διωκόντων], but when he arrived at [φθάσασα . . . εἰς] the marshland" his antlers became entangled in the branches of the vegetation there, and he was "overtaken by his pursuers" (ὑπὸ τῶν διωκόντων καταλαμβάνεται; cf. Rom 9:30).[10]

The image, then, of Israel pursuing (διώκων) the righteous law, but not arriving at (ἔφθασεν . . . εἰς) it pictures Israel running with great energy after the law's promise of righteousness and life to those who live by it (10:5) but failing to arrive at this goal. Like the gentiles, who did not even pursue righteousness prior to believing the gospel, Israel had also been sinful (2:1–3:20; 5:20–21; cf. 7:7–25) and was therefore unable to "arrive at" the law's fulfillment and therefore at the righteousness and life that the law promised.

The term "arrive" (φθάνω) often carried the connotation of arriving before someone else, just as the deer arrived at the marshland before the hunters (2 Cor 10:14; 1 Thess 4:15). It may have that connotation here and refer to the irony that Israel lags behind the gentiles in attaining righteousness (or the law that commands righteousness) because they are attempting the impossible task of doing all that the law commands.[11]

9:32a–c Why? Because not by faith, but as if by works (διὰ τί; ὅτι οὐκ ἐκ πίστεως ἀλλ' ὡς ἐξ ἔργων). Israel failed to arrive at the real significance of the

7. See, respectively, Sanday and Headlam (*Romans*, 279), Calvin (*Romans*, 217; cf. RSV, NRSV), and Cranfield (*Romans*, 2:508).

8. Lagrange, *Romains*, 249; Wilckens, *An die Römer (Röm 6–11)*, 212n944; Moo, *Romans*, 625–26; Légasse, *Romains*, 630. Cf. Philo, *Rewards* 162: "I have now described without any reservation the curses and penalties which they will deservedly suffer who disregard the holy laws of justice and piety [τοὺς τῶν ἱερῶν νόμων δικαιοσύνης καὶ εὐσεβείας]" (trans. F. H. Colson, LCL).

9. Cf. Moo, *Romans*, 624–25.

10. Aesop, *Fables* 15. I could not find a translation of this parable that was sufficiently literal, so here I have had to supply my own translation.

11. Cf. Haacker (*An die Römer*, 199), who, however, draws the different conclusion that "the word leaves open whether Israel will reach the goal in the future, after other people groups."

Mosaic law, with its righteous precepts, because it rejected the gospel's claim that all human beings are sinful and therefore incapable of attaining life by fully keeping the law.

Those who first heard the letter read aloud had to make sense of this brief rhetorical question and its answer by supplying them with verbs and objects from the immediately preceding sentence. Paul expected his hearers to complete the simple question "why?" with the immediately preceding thought ". . . did Israel not arrive at the law?" His answer to this question consisted basically of two adverbial phrases that required the mental addition of a verb and its object. Since Paul had just said that Israel did not "arrive at" the law, the only verb and object left to supply was "it pursued the law" (ἐδιώκεν νόμον).[12] Israel failed to "arrive at," or fulfill, the law, then, because it pursued the law in the wrong way, "as if" (ὡς) the law should be pursued "by works" rather than "by faith."

Interpreters have sometimes understood the contrast between faith and works here as a contrast between living as a Jew and believing the ethnically inclusive gospel. Ambrosiaster thought that when Paul spoke of "works" he had distinctively Jewish elements of the Mosaic law in mind—purity laws, dietary observances, Sabbath keeping, and circumcision.[13] Theodoret of Cyrus thought Paul was criticizing the Jews for their obsession with "their way of life" (πολιτείαν), which they believed was sufficient for attaining righteousness without conversion to Christianity.[14] More recent interpreters have understood the contrast as between a nationalistic, Israel-centered approach to the Mosaic law's promise of righteousness and an approach to the law that emphasizes the obedience of faith and therefore something that includes gentiles.[15]

It is not likely, however, that this approach to Paul's contrast captures Paul's meaning, at least in its entirety. In 9:7–31 the effortlessness with which those who belong to the people of God (whatever their ethnic identity) have attained their status as God's children has played an important role in Paul's argument that God's word has not failed. According to God's word, Paul has argued, one's mother, birth order, and relative virtue have nothing to do with whether one belongs to God's people, and this has happened "in order that the chosen purpose of God might stand firm not by works [οὐκ ἐξ ἔργων] but by the one who calls" (9:12). Although ethnic considerations are certainly not irrelevant (hence the mention of family and birth order), the notion of human effort also plays a role in the argument. Human zeal and energy do not form the basis for God's decision to show mercy (9:16), and as Paul has just said, righteousness comes not to those who pursue it but, surprisingly, to those who do not pursue it (9:30–31).

In light of this context, it is likely that the antinomy between pursuing the law "by faith" and pursuing it "as if by works" contrasts human faith, which, for Paul, does not involve work (4:4–5), with human effort. The "as if" (ὡς), moreover, adds to this thought the idea that one could not "arrive at" (9:31) or fulfill the law by human effort in any case.[16] This thought arises naturally out of Paul's thesis, developed earlier in the argument, that sinful human beings cannot keep the law well enough to receive righteousness and life by it (3:9–20; 7:7–25; 8:7–8).

12. Cf. Schreiner (*Romans*, 538) in answer to Wilckens's suggestion (*An die Römer [Röm 6–11]*, 212) that "arrived" (ἐφθάσεν) be supplied in this second clause.

13. Ambrosiaster, *Romans*, 81–82.

14. Theodoret of Cyrus, *Letters of St. Paul*, 1:106.

15. Dunn, *Romans 9–16*, 582–83; idem, *Theology of Paul*, 364–65; idem, *New Perspective*, 465–66; Wright, "Romans," 649.

16. For this use of "as" (ὡς), see 2 Thess 2:2 (Jewett, *Romans*, 610n36).

To summarize, Paul is saying that those within Israel who have rejected the gospel have done so because they focused on keeping the law, and this is something they could not accomplish. Paul is not accusing Jews generally of "cherishing the illusion that they could so fulfil [the law's] demands as to put God under an obligation to themselves."[17] He is simply saying that Israelites who had rejected the gospel implied, by this rejection, that they could keep the law and therefore did not need the Messiah to rescue them from their sins.

In contrast to pursuit of the law as if human effort could succeed in fully keeping its precepts, Paul places pursuit of the law "by faith" (ἐκ πίστεως). This is not a claim that the Scriptures generally point to Christ and to Christian faith but that the Mosaic law's promise of life actually comes to those who have faith.[18] Israel would not have failed in its pursuit of a righteous law if it had realized that righteousness and life do not come to those who work at the law's requirements but only to those who accept the condemnation that the law pronounces on all human beings because of their sin.[19]

It is not that doing the law is wrong (8:7–8 implies that doing the law is pleasing to God) but that rejecting the gospel and relying instead on doing the law in order to receive life is using the law in the wrong way. "Arriving at" the law "by faith," then, is paradoxically a matter of recognizing that the law pronounces a negative verdict on all attempts to attain life by doing it and so points away from itself to the gospel as the means to righteousness. Paul articulates these principles in compressed form here, but he will spell them out in greater detail in 10:5–13.

9:32d–33 They stumbled on the stumbling stone, just as it is written, "Look! I put in Zion a stone of stumbling and a rock of offense, and the one who believes on him will not be ashamed" (προσέκοψαν τῷ λίθῳ τοῦ προσκόμματος, καθὼς γέγραπται, Ἰδοὺ τίθημι ἐν Σιὼν λίθον προσκόμματος καὶ πέτραν σκανδάλου, καὶ ὁ πιστεύων ἐπ᾽ αὐτῷ οὐ καταισχυνθήσεται). The overzealous concern of Israel, especially its political and religious leaders, with the Mosaic law prevented them from recognizing that God was intervening in their affairs in the Messiah, Jesus. This misstep was both a result and a continuing cause of their failure to understand that the law underscores the universal human need for Christ's atoning death.

No particle connects this sentence with what Paul has just said about Israel's failure to arrive at "the law of righteousness" because they pursued it as if it were by works. This gives the sentence the quality of a grave pronouncement, but leaves ambiguous precisely how the pronouncement is connected to Israel's failure to attain the law.[20] The imagery of a foot pursuit that Paul has been using, however, suggests that he is about to describe the result and the cause of Israel's mistaken notion that people can fully keep the law and receive life by doing so.[21] Israel failed to arrive at the righteous law they were pursuing because they stumbled (προσέκοψαν) over a rock in their path.[22]

With the words "just as it is written" (καθὼς γέγραπται) Paul points out that the imagery of tripping over a rock comes from Scripture, and he probably made this explicit because the theology behind the passages he quotes and the theology behind his analysis of Israel's unbelief are the same.[23]

17. Cranfield, *Romans*, 2:510.

18. Westerholm, *Perspectives Old and New on Paul*, 329.

19. Cranfield (*Romans*, 2:510) says that pursuing the law by faith "must include accepting, without evasion or resentment, the law's criticism of one's life."

20. On the solemnity communicated by the sentence's asyndeton, see Godet (*Romans*, 369), Meyer (*Romans*, 392), and especially Cranfield (*Romans*, 2:510).

21. Moo, *Romans*, 628.

22. On the word's meaning, see Gustav Stählin, "προσκόπτω, κτλ.," *TDNT* 6:745–46.

23. Cf. Dunn, *Romans 9–16*, 584.

He combines slightly altered versions of Isaiah 28:16 and Isaiah 8:14.[24] In both these passages, Isaiah uses the metaphor of a stone in his description of two aspects of the Lord's intervention in the affairs of his people. The Lord's coming in Isa 8:14, pictured as the foundation he lays in Zion in Isa 28:16, will bring judgment to Israel's corrupt leaders who have defied the Lord by placing their trust in their own ability to negotiate alliances for their security with the surrounding nations (Isa 8:14–15; 28:14–15, 17–22). At the same time, the Lord's intervention will bring security and righteousness to the remnant who have trusted the Lord rather than these corrupt leaders (Isa 8:11–14; 28:16).[25]

In Isaiah 8:14 the stone metaphor appears on the negative side of this twofold intervention. It will be "a stone of stumbling" and "a rock of offense" to Israel's leaders who are defying the Lord. In Isaiah 28:16 the stone imagery appears on the positive side of the Lord's intervention. The one who trusts in the "stone" that the Lord lays as a foundation in Zion will have no need to run to and fro in an anxious attempt to make allies of the surrounding nations or, as the LXX has it (rather differently), "will not be put to shame" (οὐ μὴ καταισχυνθῇ).

Paul's composite quotation captures both the negative connotations of the stone metaphor in Isaiah 8:14 and its positive connotations in Isaiah 28:16. Christ is the "stone" and "rock" (cf. Rom 10:9, 11). He is the means by which God has intervened within the affairs of his people for judgment and salvation. He brings judgment to the part of Israel (particularly its leadership) that has rejected God's word and trusted their own ability to keep themselves safe (cf. Isa 8:6; 28:14–15; John 11:47–48) and blessing to the remnant who have placed their trust in God (cf. Isa 8:11–14; 28:5, 16; Rom 9:27–29; 11:5–6).

Paul is saying that Israel's focus on keeping the righteous decrees of the law prevented them from understanding one of the law's purposes—to show Israel how far short they had fallen from God's righteous standard (Rom 3:20).[26] They failed to realize that this was the law's purpose because when they encountered Christ either in his own ministry or in the gospel, they rejected him (see In Depth: The Origins of Paul's Understanding of Israel's Stumbling below). Had they seen Christ as the Lord himself rescuing his people from sin (cf. Rom 10:6–13), they would have understood this function of the law and not continued to be led astray by the idea that they could attain righteousness by doing it.

IN DEPTH: The Origins of Paul's Understanding of Israel's Stumbling

It is possible that Paul knew the tradition, handed down from Jesus himself, that compared Jesus to a stone valued by God but rejected by Israel's political and religious leaders. According to Mark 12:10–11 (cf. Matt 21:42; Luke 20:17), Jesus had applied Psalm 118:22–23, with its own double-sided stone imagery, to his

24. See the useful comparison charts in Barnabas Lindars (*New Testament Apologetic* [Philadelphia: Westminster, 1961], 177); Wagner (*Heralds of the Good News*, 128); and Jewett (*Romans*, 612).

25. Oswalt, *Isaiah, Chapters 1–39*, 234–35, 517–19. Wagner (*Heralds of the Good News*, 136–51) convincingly argues that the LXX translator(s) of Isaiah also interpreted Isa 8 and 28–29 in terms of each other.

26. Cf. Godet, *Romans*, 369; Jewett, *Romans*, 611.

rejection by "the chief priests and the scribes and the elders" (Mark 11:27; cf. Matt 21:45–46; Luke 20:19) and to his subsequent vindication by God in the resurrection.[27] "The stone that the builders rejected has become the cornerstone," Jesus said, "this was the Lord's doing, and it is marvelous in our eyes."

The early church continued to use the rejected stone image from Psalm 118:22 (Acts 4:10–11) and, at some point, connected the "stone" of that psalm with the costly foundation stone of Isaiah 28:16 and the stumbling stone of Isaiah 8:14. All three texts appear grouped together but without conflating their wording in 1 Peter 2:6–8.[28] This probably means that early Christians grouped all three texts together in a collection of biblical testimonies to Jesus and that Paul and Peter had access to this collection. Paul may well have taken Isaiah 28:16 and 8:14 from this collection and conflated them.[29]

The use of biblical stone imagery to describe the rejection of Jesus, then, was not original with Paul. It runs from Paul back through even earlier Christian interpretation of Jesus's rejection and, at least in the use of Psalm 118:22–23, back to Jesus himself. The theological contexts of both Jesus's and Paul's use of this imagery is also similar. Jesus had used the imagery in a context where the Jewish leadership had rejected him because they thought he posed a threat to such Jewish institutions as the Mosaic law and the temple (e.g., Mark 3:1–6; 11:15–18, 27–28; John 5:15; 11:48; 19:7). Paul also used the imagery in a context where Israel's approach to the law (Rom 9:32) had caused it to stumble over Christ (Rom 9:33).[30]

It is true that Jesus used the stone text from Psalm 118 whereas Paul uses the passages from Isaiah. Paul may have chosen the Isaianic passages, however, because they better suited his extended metaphor of an ill-fated foot pursuit (Rom 9:30–33a). The stone of Psalm 118:22, which is far off the ground at "the head of the corner" (κεφαλὴν γωνίας, RSV) would confuse Paul's imagery of runners encountering an impediment, whereas the stones on the ground in Isaiah 8:14 and 28:16 fit neatly into the mental picture of running that Paul had developed.[31]

It is also true that elsewhere Paul speaks of the cross rather than Jesus himself or Jesus's attitude to the law as a "stumbling block" (σκανδάλον) to Jews

27. Lindars, *New Testament Apologetic*, 170.

28. Peter's deviations from the LXX wording of Isa 28:16 and Isa 8:14 match Paul's deviations almost exactly, yet not in such a way as to suggest Peter's dependence on Paul. Cf. Lindars, *New Testament Apologetic*, 177–78; Jewett, *Romans*, 612.

29. Wagner, *Heralds of the Good News*, 133–35. Wagner wisely comments that this way of working does not imply that Paul was unaware of the larger contexts of the two passages.

30. Jewett (*Romans*, 611) writes that Paul was thinking of Israel's repudiation of Christ "as a Sabbath breaker and a companion of sinners," although he does not connect this with Jesus's use of Ps 118:22 in the synoptic tradition.

31. Cf. Dunn, *Romans 9–16*, 585.

(1 Cor 1:23; cf. Gal 5:11). But the crucified Jesus may lie in the background of Paul's stone imagery in Romans 9:33, just as the cross casts its shadow over Jesus's use of Psalm 118:22–23 (cf. Mark 12:6–8). The cross may have been offensive to the Jews Paul has in mind in Romans 9:32–33 precisely because accepting the positive role it played in Christian preaching meant admitting that Jesus's crucifixion for supposed violations of the Mosaic law was both a terrible miscarriage of justice (cf. Acts 4:10–11; 5:28) and an atonement for their own failure to keep the law (cf. Acts 3:17–18; 8:32–33; Isa 53:5–6, 10–12).[32]

It seems likely that Paul also had himself in mind as an example of a leader among the Jews who, prior to his conversion, violently persecuted Christians because they supposedly spoke against the temple and the law, saying that Jesus of Nazareth would "change the customs that Moses delivered to us" (Acts 6:13–14; cf. Acts 7:58; 8:1).[33] Paul had been a leader among a group of Greek-speaking Jews from the diaspora who had emigrated, probably for religious reasons, to Jerusalem.[34] His zeal for the law and "blameless" law observance (Phil 3:5–6) led him to preside over the death of the Greek-speaking, Jewish Christian Stephen (Acts 7:58; 8:1) and to persecute Christians as far away as Damascus (Acts 9:1–2). The same bodies of leaders who sought Jesus's death because of his attitude toward the law were involved in the accusations against Stephen and in the scheme the pre-Christian Paul had developed to arrest "any belonging to the Way" in Damascus (Acts 6:12; 9:1–2). Later, people in the same elite circles turned on their former ally Paul, forcing him to flee for his life from Judea (Acts 9:29–30; cf. 1 Thess 2:14–16).

Later still, Paul encountered this same level of violent opposition to the gospel's proclamation on the basis that it undermined the Mosaic law when he

32. Cf. Seyoon Kim, *The Origin of Paul's Gospel* (Grand Rapids: Eerdmans, 1981), 47; idem, *Paul and the New Perspective: Second Thoughts on the Origin of Paul's Gospel* (Grand Rapids: Eerdmans, 2002), 22. The common idea (e.g., Kim, *Origin*, 46–47) that Jesus's crucifixion was a stumbling block to the Jews because it implied that Jesus, as one who had been hanged on a tree, was under God's curse (Deut 21:23; cf. Gal 3:13) is less convincing. Despite Trypho's statement that "whosoever is crucified is said in the law to be accursed" (Justin, *Dialogue with Trypho* 89.1–90.1 [*ANF* 1:244]), it is unclear that most Jews would have thought this. Not only is Trypho a fictional Jew from a century after Paul's letter, but the Romans had crucified too many innocent Jews merely as a means of social control in the first century (e.g., Josephus, *J.W.* 2.308; 5.449–51) to make it likely that most Jews would have regarded crucifixion, by itself, as God's curse. The Jews hung on a tree and cursed by God in 11Q19 64.8–13 are wicked people on other grounds. Their crucifixion was a sign of God's curse, not its cause.

33. The extent to which these early Hellenistic Christians took a radical position on the Mosaic law is a matter of controversy, but there is agreement about the radical nature of their approach to the temple cult, and since the Mosaic law governed the temple cult it is difficult to see how a radical view on one would not have implied a radical view of the other. For the debate, see especially Martin Hengel (*Between Jesus and Paul: Studies in the Earliest History of Christianity*, trans. John Bowden [Philadelphia: Fortress, 1983], 1–29, 56–58); James D. G. Dunn (*The Partings of the Ways: Between Christianity and Judaism and Their Significance for the Character of Christianity* [London: SCM, 1991], 119–20); and Kim (*Paul and the New Perspective*, 23–24).

34. On Greek-speaking Judaism in early first-century Jerusalem, see Martin Hengel, *Between Jesus and Paul*, 18, 57.

preached the gospel in the diaspora and traveled with alms to Jerusalem. The accusation of the Corinthian Jews against Paul before the proconsul Gallio was that "this man is persuading people to worship God contrary to the law" (Acts 18:13).

Paul also encountered similar problems when he arrived in Jerusalem with his offering for Jewish Christians there. James the brother of the Lord informed him that even the believers in Jerusalem were "all zealous for the law" and consequently suspicious of Paul (Acts 21:20). On this same visit, Jews from Asia who were not believers but whose zeal for the law had led them to travel to Jerusalem for Pentecost, accused Paul of "teaching everyone everywhere against the people and the law and this place [the temple]" (Acts 21:28).

Only a few years later still, in AD 62, James himself was killed in Jerusalem despite the care he had taken earlier not to offend those who were zealous for the law. According to Josephus, the recently appointed high priest Ananus took advantage of the gap in Roman leadership between the death of the procurator Festus and the arrival of Albinus to convene "the judges of the Sanhedrin" (cf. Acts 6:12) and bring "before them a man named James, the brother of Jesus who was called the Christ, and certain others. He accused them of having transgressed the law [παρανομησάντων] and delivered them to be stoned" (*Ant.* 20.200 [L. H. Feldman, LCL]).

Paul wrote Romans in the thick of this kind of Jewish resistance to the gospel. He wrote from Corinth where only a few years earlier unbelieving Jews had accused him before Gallio of persuading people to abandon the Mosaic law (Acts 18:13). He also wrote on the eve of his journey to Jerusalem with his collection of famine-relief funds for Jewish Christians there (Rom 15:25–28). As he was writing to the Romans, he sensed the danger that awaited him in Jerusalem. "Fight alongside me in prayers to God on my behalf," he tells them, "in order that I might be rescued from the disobedient in Judea and my ministry to Jerusalem might be acceptable to the saints" (15:30–31).[35]

Paul's understanding of Israel's stumbling, therefore, probably originated in this context. He knew that the Jewish leadership in Jerusalem had crucified Jesus in large part on the basis of their claim that he violated the Mosaic law. He had himself persecuted the church because he thought of it as a group that advocated breaking the Mosaic law. And he often proclaimed the gospel in contexts where unbelieving Jews opposed him for teaching people to "worship God contrary to the law" (Acts 18:13).

Israel's narrow focus on the law had led it to reject the Messiah, to see the

35. Cf. Haacker, *An die Römer*, 204.

law as a path to future life instead of an indictment for past sin, and to carry on after God's intervention in their affairs through Jesus as if righteousness before God were attainable on the basis of the law. Paul is not claiming that every unbelieving Israelite approached the law in this overzealous way any more than in 1:18–32 he intended to say that every gentile was crazed with sexual lust or full of envy, murder, strife, deceit, and malice.[36] In 9:30–33 he describes an extreme position into which people can fall when they reject the gospel because of their commitment to the law.

10:1 Brothers and sisters, the desire of my heart and my petition to God for them is for their salvation (Ἀδελφοί, ἡ μὲν εὐδοκία τῆς ἐμῆς καρδίας καὶ ἡ δέησις πρὸς τὸν θεὸν ὑπὲρ αὐτῶν εἰς σωτηρίαν). Israel has stumbled over the Messiah, but Paul is hopeful that all is not lost. Israel's salvation would satisfy him at a deep level, and so he prays that this longing will be fulfilled.

Paul uses the vocative "brothers and sisters" (ἀδελφοί) at the beginning of a sentence when he wants to emphasize what he is about to say (1 Cor 14:20; Gal 3:15; 6:1; 1 Thess 5:25). Here the expression calls attention to the depth of Paul's hope that Israel's stumbling, described in 9:32–33, might not be permanent.

The Greek noun translated "desire" (εὐδοκία) occurs sparingly outside the LXX and NT, and its meaning here is not entirely clear. In the everyday Greek of Paul's time, the verb (εὐδοκέω) referred to meeting with approval, such as when a tax collector "approves" a merchant's estimate of a product's value.[37] In the LXX the noun refers most often to God and to his "benevolence," "goodness," "kindness," and "favor"—what is pleasing and acceptable to him (e.g., Ps 19:14 [18:15 LXX]; Sir 1:27).[38] Here, then, the noun refers to the outcome of Israel's situation that would give Paul inner peace and contentment, an outcome that would be satisfactory to him in the richest sense of that term.

The preposition "for" (εἰς) indicates purpose, and this implies that Paul held out hope for Israel.[39] Although they had stumbled, they had not yet fallen irretrievably (Rom 11:11), and Paul prays earnestly and specifically for their ultimate salvation (cf. 11:25–32). The unmistakable emphases in 9:7–29 on God's freedom to choose who will belong to his people and on his surprising choice in the present of only a remnant of Israel is balanced here with the urgent need for prayer that those (and especially those among Israel) who have rejected the gospel would turn from their rejection of it, believe it, and receive salvation.[40]

36. For examples of Jews who knew the early Christians and, while not accepting their views, believed they should be treated with tolerance, see, e.g., Acts 5:33–39; 22:12; Josephus, *Ant.* 20.201. I take Paul's comments in 1 Thess 2:14–16 as a description of the corrupt leaders of Judea, and those under their influence, who plotted Jesus's crucifixion (e.g., Mark 11:27; 12:1, 12) and drove Paul out of Jerusalem (Acts 9:29–30). On this, see Frank Thielman, "Paul's View of Israel's Misstep in Rom 9.32–33: Its Origins and Meaning," *NTS*, forthcoming.

37. *TLNT* 2:99, citing P.Rev. 29,8 ("If, on one hand, the tax collector should approve [εὐδοκῆι] . . ."). This text goes on to describe the procedure that should be followed "if, on the other hand, he should dispute [ἀ[ν]τιλέγηι] the price" that the merchant had placed on the goods (29,12).

38. Ibid., 2:104.

39. Cf. BDAG 290, s.v. εἰς 4f; Harris, *Prepositions and Theology*, 92.

40. Moo, *Romans*, 632; Schreiner, *Romans*, 542.

10:2 For I testify to them that they have zeal for God, but not according to knowledge (μαρτυρῶ γὰρ αὐτοῖς ὅτι ζῆλον θεοῦ ἔχουσιν ἀλλ' οὐ κατ' ἐπίγνωσιν). Paul yearns so deeply for the salvation of those in Israel who have rejected the gospel because they and he are equally devoted to the God who gives salvation. A true knowledge of God's ways, however, does not govern their enthusiasm for him.

Paul's "for" (γάρ) indicates that he is about to explain why his hope for Israel's salvation runs so deep. The phrase "I testify to them" (cf. Luther, Tyndale, KJV, ESV, NRSV) could perhaps mean "I testify about them" (NAB, NIV, HCSB, CEB), but elsewhere when Paul uses the verb "testify" (μαρτυρέω) followed by a dative personal pronoun and a "that" (ὅτι) clause giving the content of the testimony, the construction clearly refers to testimony directed to someone (Gal 4:15; Col 4:13).[41] The statement probably reflects Paul's firsthand discussions with Jews about the gospel, discussions such as the one he would eventually have with "the local leaders of the Jews" in Rome upon his arrival there (Acts 28:17, 23).

His heart yearns for the salvation of Israelites who are rejecting the gospel because he and they agree on an important theological truth: it is good to expend energy in the service of God. The translation "zeal for God" (ζῆλον θεοῦ) takes the genitive term "God" (θεοῦ) as an objective genitive since the LXX frequently uses the verb (ζηλόω) with God, the temple, or the law as its object to refer to acts of extraordinary devotion to God, his institutions, and his commandments (Num 25:11, 13; 1 Kgs 19:10, 14; Jdt 9:4; 1 Macc 2:26; cf. Ps 118:139 [119:139 Heb. and Eng.]).[42] Although Paul could speak of "zeal" (or "jealousy" in most English renderings) as a vice to be avoided (Rom 13:13; 1 Cor 3:3; 12:20; Gal 5:20), in the right cause it was a commendable quality (2 Cor 7:7, 11; 9:2; 11:2), and that is how he uses the term here.[43] Paul's strong adversative conjunction "but" (ἀλλ') indicates this clearly.[44]

The problem with Israel's zeal lay not in the energy expended in accomplishing it, nor with its object, but with the way Israel carried it out. It did not follow the standard laid down by "knowledge" (κατ' ἐπίγνωσιν). The term translated here as "knowledge" (ἐπίγνωσις) always refers to knowledge of God or of truth in the LXX and NT, and Paul probably used it without an object here because he could assume his audience would understand that it referred to knowledge from God's perspective (cf. Rom 1:28; 3:20).[45] Paul will, in any case, explain exactly what he means in the next sentence.

10:3 For, being ignorant about the righteousness of God, and seeking to establish their own righteousness, they did not submit to the righteousness of God (ἀγνοοῦντες γὰρ τὴν τοῦ θεοῦ δικαιοσύνην καὶ τὴν ἰδίαν [δικαιοσύνην] ζητοῦντες στῆσαι, τῇ δικαιοσύνῃ τοῦ θεοῦ οὐχ ὑπετάγησαν). When unbelievers within Israel encountered and rejected the gospel, they were left following their own way to righteousness and life via the law. This approach gives to the law a place of centrality it was never intended to occupy and fails to recognize

41. BDAG 618, s.v. μαρτυρέω 1.a.α.

42. Cranfield, *Romans*, 2:514; Dunn, *Partings*, 120–21 (emphasizing Israel's nationalistic zeal); Dane C. Ortlund, *Zeal without Knowledge: The Concept of Zeal in Romans 10, Galatians 1, and Philippians 3*, LNTS 472 (London: T&T Clark, 2012), 50–61, 110–14, 126.

43. Dunn, *Romans 9–16*, 586.

44. John M. G. Barclay, "Is It Good News That God is Impartial? A Response to Robert Jewett, *Romans: A Commentary*," *JSNT* 31 (2008): 104; Ortlund, *Zeal without Knowledge*, 126–27.

45. Ortlund (*Zeal without Knowledge*, 127–28) is correct to warn against distinguishing too sharply between "knowledge" (γνῶσις) and "transcendent knowledge" (ἐπίγνωσις), but the latter term does seem to have a narrower semantic range (BDAG 369, s.v. ἐπίγνωσις).

that righteousness and life by means of the law are impossible because the law cannot be fully kept.

"For" (γάρ) introduces Paul's explanation of Israel's misdirected zeal. The "ignorance" he describes here has a willful, culpable edge to it, as Paul will explain more fully in 10:18–21. It is not unlike the willful ignorance of all human beings, who "knew God" but "did not glorify or thank him as God" (1:21) and who "exchanged the truth that came from God for a lie" (1:25). This is the ignorance of God's requirements or purposes that leads people to disaster (Rom 1:24, 26, 28; 2:4–5; cf. Num 12:11 LXX; Acts 13:27; 1 Cor 2:8).[46]

Paul describes God's purposes as "the righteousness of God" (τὴν τοῦ θεοῦ δικαιοσύνην), an expression he last used in his explanation of the gospel in Romans 3:21–26.[47] There it summarized Paul's description of the way God remained fair in his dealings with humanity (δίκαιον) even as he released the guilty from the punishment they deserved (δικαιοῦντα) through the atoning death of Christ Jesus (3:26). Paul now says that unbelieving Israel has stumbled over Christ by rejecting his death as God's means of atonement for universal human sin against himself (cf. 9:33; 1 Cor 1:23; Gal 5:11). This rejection left them running energetically down the pathway of the law under the illusion that their rejection of Christ and focus on the law itself was conformity to the will of God.

Paul refers to this series of events as Israel "seeking to establish their own [ἰδίαν] righteousness." The adjective "own" (ἴδιος) emphasizes what belongs to one's self as opposed to another (cf., e.g., Rom 11:24; 14:4–5) and highlights Israel's tragic pursuit of its own way to righteousness via the law rather than God's way of righteousness, via faith (9:32; 10:5–6; cf. Phil 3:9; Titus 3:5). When they rejected the gospel, unbelieving Israelites made the law central to their lives, but they misunderstood the law as a viable path to life.

Some scholars have argued that when Paul spoke of Israel's attempt to establish their "own righteousness" he was referring to Israel's effort to set itself apart from other peoples and to keep their covenant relationship with God as their own (cf. Exod 19:5; Lev 18:3–4; Acts 11:3; 15:1, 5; 21:20–21; Let. Aris. 139).[48] The adjective "own," however, does not emphasize the righteousness that Israel possessed as a nation distinct from the gentiles. Rather it sets up a contrast between Israel's "own" way to righteousness with God's way to righteousness, and as Paul explains on either side of this passage (9:31–32; 10:4–5), that is a contrast between trying to attain righteousness by doing what the law commands and submitting, in faith, to God's way of justifying sinful people.[49]

Ethnic and national considerations are certainly in the background. Paul's unbelieving Jewish dialogue partner in 2:17–20 thought of himself as better informed than any gentile on God's definition of righteousness. But the primary focus here is on unbelieving Israel's rejection of Christ's atoning death in favor of attaining life through law observance (10:5), something that Paul has already shown to be impossible (3:9–20; 4:15; 5:20; 7:7–25; 8:7–8).

46. It is, however, an ignorance that is not beyond the reach of God's mercy according to 1 Tim 1:13. Paul's ignorance here does not offer an excuse for his conduct and therefore make him less culpable. It explains why Paul acted as he did and therefore why God's mercy was necessary. On this, see Luke Timothy Johnson (*The First and Second Letters to Timothy*, AB 35A [New York: Doubleday, 2001], 179).

47. The syntax of the phrase in 3:21–26 ([ἡ] δικαιοσύνη θεοῦ) differs slightly from its syntax here, but the two expressions are basically synonymous.

48. So Dunn, *Partings*, 121–22; idem, *New Perspective*, 203; Wright, *Paul and the Faithfulness of God*, 1169.

49. Ortlund, *Zeal without Knowledge*, 132–33; cf. Westerholm, *Perspectives Old and New on Paul*, 311–13.

10:4 For Christ is the goal of the law, with the result of righteousness for everyone who believes (τέλος γὰρ νόμου Χριστὸς εἰς δικαιοσύνην παντὶ τῷ πιστεύοντι). Paul can say that Israel did not submit to the righteousness of God when they rejected the gospel because the law's indictment of all humanity for its sin points to Christ. His atoning death is God's way of releasing both Jews and gentiles from the punishment they deserve and putting them in a right relationship with himself.

In 10:4 Paul supplies the basis for (γάρ) his argument in 9:31–10:3 that when Israel pursued the law by works rather than faith and stumbled over Christ they failed to submit to the righteousness of God. The term "goal" (τέλος) had a wide range of meanings in ancient Greek, falling into three broad categories: (1) coming to pass, performance, consummation; (2) state of completion or maturity; and (3) achievement, attainment. Within these three categories lay a variety of more specialized meanings such as "tax" (under category (1), as in Rom 13:7), "finish" (under category (2), as in "the project's finish"), and "goal" (under category (3), in the sense of purpose).[50] Although the word could certainly mean "termination," this meaning lay further from the center of its semantic range than the idea of purpose or goal.[51] Aristotle, for example, distinguishes between the "end" (τέλος) of something and its "termination" (ἔσχατον). It's "end" is its purpose, he says, whereas its "termination" is simply its last stage of existence (*Physics* 2.194 A).[52] Here, then, Paul could mean that Christ is the termination of the law, but the context would need to point fairly strongly in this direction for that meaning to be the most probable.[53]

The imagery of pursuit that Paul has been using in 9:30–10:3 weighs heavily in favor of taking the term to mean "goal" or "purpose" (cf. 6:21–22). Although he has not used the term "goal" before in 9:30–10:3, the idea of pursuit in order to reach a goal has nevertheless dominated the discussion. Gentiles reached the goal of righteousness without pursuing it (9:30). Israel pursued the law of righteousness but did not arrive at that law (9:31), and they failed to arrive at the law because they focused on works and stumbled over the immense significance of the atoning death of Christ (9:32–33). They pursued the law in the wrong way and therefore failed to arrive at the "goal" toward which the law should have led them. If instead of attempting to keep the law after being confronted with the gospel they had viewed the law through the lens of the gospel, they would have realized that the law points to Christ.

How does the law do this? It promises righteousness and life to those who keep its commands (10:5), but also indicts all humanity, Israel included, for not keeping those commands. Apart from the work of the Spirit in the lives of God's people (8:4), the law can, in practice, only bring knowledge of sin (3:20) and God's wrath (4:15). The law, then, describes the human plight and, by doing this, implicitly points to Christ. This is the sense in which Christ is the law's goal.

The prepositional phrase translated "with the result of righteousness" (εἰς δικαιοσύνην) is a bone of interpretive contention since it either could indicate the result of Christ's role as the goal of the law or it could indicate the sense in which Christ has brought the law to an end. Christ is either "the goal of the law, with the result of righteousness for everyone who believes" or "the end of the law

50. LSJ 1772–74, s.v. τέλος; Cranfield, *Romans*, 2:516.

51. Cf. Robert Badenas, *Christ the End of the Law: Romans 10.4 in Pauline Perspective*, JSNTSup 10 (Sheffield: JSOT Press, 1985), 79–80; Moo, *Romans*, 639; Jewett, *Romans*, 619.

52. Badenas, *Christ the End of the Law*, 45.

53. See, e.g., Godet (*Romans*, 370).

as a way of righteousness, for everyone who believes."[54] If Paul had intended to focus on Christ's termination of the law's misuse, however, he probably would have placed the prepositional phrase directly after the word "law."[55]

Christ is the goal of the Mosaic law, then, because the law demonstrates clearly the need for Christ and specifically for his atoning, reconciling death. Paul states the same principle in Galatians 2:21: "If righteousness were through the law, then Christ died for no purpose."

Righteousness comes "for everyone who believes," whether Jews or gentiles, because at the level of the law's indictment there is no distinction between these groups (3:9, 19, 22–23). The need for Christ's reconciling death is universal (cf. 3:24, 27–31).

10:5 For Moses writes about the righteousness from the law, "The human being who does them will live by them" (Μωϋσῆς γὰρ γράφει τὴν δικαιοσύνην τὴν ἐκ τοῦ νόμου ὅτι ὁ ποιήσας αὐτὰ ἄνθρωπος ζήσεται ἐν αὐτοῖς). Paul can say that the law points to Christ because no human being can receive the law's promise of life to those who keep it. This means that if life is to come to human beings at all, it must come by another means.

"For" (γάρ) introduces a theological exposition of Scripture supporting the statement Paul has just made that "Christ is the goal of the law, with the result of righteousness for everyone who believes." This exposition begins with a text from the law (Lev 18:5) that promises life to the person who "does" (ποιήσας) its "ordinances" (LXX, προστάγματα) and "judgments" (LXX, κρίματα).[56] In its original context, the statement summarizes how God expected Israel to live in the land of Canaan they were about to occupy after he had rescued them from slavery in Egypt. They were to establish a new society in Canaan that followed the laws and customs neither of the Egyptians nor of the Canaanites but the injunctions and judgments of the Lord their God. Clearly there is a concern here for keeping ethnic boundaries intact, but as the use of the verb "live" (ζάω) in the LXX of Leviticus shows (e.g., 14:4; 16:10; 18:18), there was also a concern simply to "live" rather than die.

By the Second Temple period, Jewish interpreters sometimes understood the life that this text promised as eternal life, which God gives "to those who live in the righteousness [δικαιοσύνη] of his commandments, in the Law [νόμῳ], which he has commanded for our life" (Pss. Sol. 14:2 [*OTP* 2:663, trans. R. B. Wright]). In contrast, "sinners" and "criminals" [παράνομοι] were consigned to "Hades, and darkness and destruction" (Pss. Sol. 14:6, 9 [*OTP* 2:663, 664, Wright]).[57] This is the understanding of Leviticus 18:5 that Paul reflects here with the critical difference that the author of Psalms

54. For the first position, see, e.g., Cranfield (*Romans*, 2:519–20n2) and Moo (*Romans*, 637). For the second position, see, e.g., Murray (*Romans*, 2:50), Schreiner (*Romans*, 547–48), and Dunn (*Romans 9–16*, 590). For Murray and Schreiner, the misuse of the law that Christ brings to an end is the attempt to be justified by the law. For Dunn it is the misuse of the law as a social barrier to the inclusion of Gentiles within God's people.

55. Das (*Paul, the Law, and the Covenant*, 252n76) observes, "Only 77 of the 1800 NT occurrences of εἰς modify a noun, and 56 of these instances immediately precede or come after the noun it modifies. Of the remaining twenty-two instances, the prepositional phrase is never separated from its noun by the subject of the sentence."

56. Paul's quotation alters the LXX text by turning the adverbial participle (ποιήσας) into a substantival participle (ὁ ποιήσας) and shifting the position of the pronoun "them" (αὐτά) slightly to make it the object of the participle. The meaning of the text, however, remains unchanged.

57. See also Preston M. Sprinkle, *Law and Life: The Interpretation of Leviticus 18:5 in Early Judaism and in Paul*, WUNT 2.241 (Tübingen: Mohr Siebeck, 2008), 93–96; idem, *Paul and Judaism Revisited: A Study of Divine and Human Agency in Salvation* (Downers Grove, IL: InterVarsity Press, 2013), 218–19.

of Solomon 14 thought doing the law was possible, but Paul thought that attaining life in this way was impossible.[58] Sin's impact on fleshly, unspiritual humanity had been too devastating for life to come to anyone through keeping God's commandments (Rom 3:20; 5:12–14, 18–21; 7:7–25; 8:7–8). It was true that any "doers of the law" would be "justified" (2:13), but since Adam's fatal act of disobedience no one could find life that way.[59]

10:6 But the righteousness from faith says this: "Do not say in your heart, 'Who will go up to heaven?'—that is, to bring Christ down" (ἡ δὲ ἐκ πίστεως δικαιοσύνη οὕτως λέγει, Μὴ εἴπῃς ἐν τῇ καρδίᾳ σου, Τίς ἀναβήσεται εἰς τὸν οὐρανόν; τοῦτ' ἔστιν Χριστὸν καταγαγεῖν). In contrast to the impossible task of fulfilling the law as a way of receiving righteousness and life, receiving righteousness and life by faith is easy. The difficult task has already been accomplished by Christ's descent from heaven to reconcile people to God through his death on the cross.

Paul's "but" (δέ) sets up a contrast between "the righteousness from the law" that Moses wrote about in Leviticus 18:5 and "the righteousness from faith" that speaks the message Paul is about to describe. There is little probability that this conjunction coordinates "the righteousness from the law" with "the righteousness from faith" and should be translated "and," as some interpreters have argued.[60] Paul's frequent contrast in the argument up to this point between doing the law and faith (Rom 3:20–22, 27–28; 4:5, 13–16; 9:32) makes anything but a contrast here unlikely (cf. Gal 3:12; Phil 3:9). His use of Leviticus 18:5 in Galatians 3:12 to show that "the law is not of faith [ἐκ πίστεως]," moreover, confirms this approach (cf. Phil 3:9).[61]

Paul personifies "the righteousness from faith" just as the psalmist personified "righteousness" and "peace" (Ps 85:10) and Jesus personified "wisdom" (Luke 11:49; cf. Prov 1:20).[62] "The righteousness from faith" speaks rather than writes (as Moses did in 10:5) because Paul had in mind the proclamation of the gospel (10:8).[63] The message of "the righteousness by faith," which Paul summarizes in 10:6–8, is a heavily reworked form of Deuteronomy 30:12–14. In its original context, that passage emphasized how easy the Mosaic law was for Israel to access, understand, and do, but in Paul's hands the passage becomes a witness to how easy God has made it for his people to attain righteousness through the gospel.

Paul's transformation of the passage begins with the phrase "do not say in your heart," which comes from Deuteronomy 9:4 LXX (cf. 8:17). In its own context these words introduced an admonition from Moses to Israel urging them not to think of their possession of Canaan as a reward for their own righteousness, "for you are a stubborn people"

58. On human ability to avoid sin in Paul and ancient Judaism generally, see Stephen Westerholm, "Paul's Anthropological 'Pessimism' in Its Jewish Context," in *Divine and Human Agency in Paul and His Cultural Environment*, ed. John M. G. Barclay and Simon J. Gathercole (London: T&T Clark, 2008), 71–98.

59. Cf. Calvin, *Romans*, 222–24; Westerholm, *Perspectives Old and New on Paul*, 310, 326–29; idem, "Paul's Anthropological 'Pessimism,'" 74–81; Sprinkle, *Paul and Judaism Revisited*, 128–32.

60. E.g., Badenas, *Christ, the End of the Law*, 123; Paul A. Barker, *The Triumph of Grace in Deuteronomy: Faithless Israel, Faithful Yahweh in Deuteronomy*, Paternoster Biblical Monographs (Carlisle: Paternoster, 2004), 194. Cf. Wagner (*Heralds of the Good News*, 159–68), who does not, however, base his argument on the conjunction.

61. Schreiner, *Romans*, 552–54; Sprinkle, *Law and Life*, 170–73.

62. Sanday and Headlam, *Romans*, 287; Jewett, *Romans*, 625n21.

63. Cf. Akio Ito, "The Written Torah and the Oral Gospel: Romans 10:5–13 in the Dynamic Tension between Orality and Literacy," *NovT* 48 (2006): 240.

(Deut 9:6).[64] Paul uses the line here, however, as an encouragement not to despair that the high standard Moses has set for receiving righteousness and life is too high for anyone to reach.

The phrase "in your heart" (ἐν τῇ καρδίᾳ σου) refers to the location of one's conviction about what leads to righteousness and salvation (Rom 10:8–10), and so Paul describes here what one's heartfelt conviction should *not* be. No one should despair that righteousness and life are available only to those who engage in such heroics as keeping the whole law or fetching the Messiah from the end of the world. It is true that human beings cannot reconcile themselves to God, but because of the gospel they need not "say in [their] heart" that reconciliation with God is impossible.

Paul begins to explain this with a phrase from Deuteronomy 30:12 that originally applied to the simplicity and accessibility of the "commandment" God had given to Israel in the form of the Mosaic law. "It is not in heaven, that you should say, 'Who will ascend to heaven [LXX, τίς ἀναβήσεται . . . εἰς τὸν οὐρανόν] for us and bring it to us, that we may hear it and do [LXX, ποιήσομεν] it?'" Paul omits any reference to "doing" since he is drawing a contrast between the Mosaic law's demand for doing as the path to life and the easy availability of righteousness (and therefore life) through faith. He applies these words, moreover, not to the law but to the message that the gospel proclaims about Christ. No human action is necessary to effect Christ's appearance, but instead Christ has come from heaven to earth at God's initiative.

10:7 or, "Who will go down into the abyss?"—that is, to bring Christ up from the dead (ἤ, Τίς καταβήσεται εἰς τὴν ἄβυσσον; τοῦτ' ἔστιν Χριστὸν ἐκ νεκρῶν ἀναγαγεῖν). Christ's resurrection from the dead was also part of the difficult task of gaining righteousness and life for the believer, but just as God sent Christ down from heaven that people might live, so he raised Christ from the dead for the same reason. Nothing is left for people to "do" in order to be reconciled to God and live with him eternally. God has already done it all for them.

Paul continues his description of the easy availability of righteousness through the gospel by matching an imaginary and impossible ascent to bring Christ down from heaven with a hypothetical and equally impossible descent into the abyss to lead Christ up from the dead. The impossibility of both tasks matches the impossibility of keeping the law well enough to receive life by doing it (10:5). Paul's point is that through the incarnation and resurrection of Christ God has already done everything necessary to provide righteousness and life for the believer.[65]

Greek speakers used "the abyss" (ἡ ἄβυσσος) not only to refer to a place of great depth (Gen 1:2 LXX; Strabo, *Geography* 4.6.6), and especially the ocean (Job 41:23 LXX), but on rare occasion to describe the place of the dead (Euripides, *Phoenician Maidens* 1605; Diogenes Laertius, *Lives of the Philosophers* 4.27), which is how Paul uses it here.[66] Paul borrowed the language of descent into the abyss from the description of desperate, storm-tossed sailors in Psalm 107:26 riding the waves up "as far as the heavens" and down "as far as the depths" (NETS; ἀναβαίνουσιν ἕως τῶν οὐρανῶν καὶ καταβαίνουσιν ἕως τῶν ἀβύσσων [Ps 106:26 LXX]). This language replaces the line in Deuteronomy 30:13 that describes how just as the Mosaic law is not far away in heaven, so also "neither is it beyond

64. Cranfield, *Romans*, 2:523; Dunn, *Romans 9–16*, 602; Moo, *Romans*, 651.

65. Fitzmyer, *Romans*, 590, as quoted in Kruse, *Romans*, 408.

66. Sanday and Headlam, *Romans*, 288; Joachim Jeremias, "ἄβυσσος," *TDNT* 1:9.

the sea, that you should say, 'Who will go over the sea for us and bring it to us, that we may hear it and do it?'" The replacement allowed Paul to interpret the new vertical imagery he has introduced from Psalm 107 as Christ's resurrection from the dead.

Treacherous and difficult journeys to the realm of the dead were well known in the mythology of the first-century Greco-Roman world, not least in Vergil's wildly popular *Aeneid* where, in book 6, Aeneas makes the arduous trek to the underworld to find his deceased father.[67] No such journey is necessary in the quest for righteousness. God himself has made righteousness and life readily available for those who believe, and he has done this by means of his own power in bringing Christ up from the dead (cf. Rom 8:11).

10:8 But what does it say? "The word is near you, in your mouth and in your heart."—That is, the word of faith that we preach (ἀλλὰ τί λέγει; Ἐγγύς σου τὸ ῥῆμά ἐστιν ἐν τῷ στόματί σου καὶ ἐν τῇ καρδίᾳ σου, τοῦτ᾽ ἔστιν τὸ ῥῆμα τῆς πίστεως ὃ κηρύσσομεν). In contrast to the impossibility of gaining righteousness and life through doing the law, receiving righteousness and life through the gospel is simply a matter of sincerely embracing the good news, proclaimed by the apostles, that God has already gained righteousness and life for people in Christ.

The subject of the verb "say" (λέγει) is "the righteousness from faith" (10:6), which speaks with the voice of Deuteronomy 30:14.[68] In its original context, the sentence emphasized the availability of God's "word" in the form of the Mosaic law and Israel's ability "to do" (LXX, ποιεῖν) it from the heart.[69] Again, Paul omits any reference to "doing" God's word since he has already assigned the notion of doing to "the righteousness from the law," and he interprets the meaning of God's "word" not as the Mosaic law but as "the word of faith that we preach." Paul's point is straightforward: in contrast to the impossibly difficult task of gaining righteousness and life by keeping the "ordinances" (LXX, προστάγματα) and "judgments" (LXX, κρίματα) of the Mosaic law (Lev 18:5), righteousness and life are easily available simply by believing the word that Paul and his coworkers preach. This is why gentiles could receive righteousness without even pursuing it and why unbelieving Israel could fail to attain righteousness although they sought it by means of God's "holy . . . just and good" law (Rom 7:12; 9:30–31).

IN DEPTH: Paul's Use of Deuteronomy 30:12–14 in Romans 10:6–8

The elephant in the room at this point in Paul's argument is the apostle's use of Deuteronomy 30:12–14 in a way that seems to contradict its original meaning. In its own context, the passage describes how simple the Mosaic law is to obey, but Paul uses it to support his own argument that no one can fully "do" the law

67. "School boys studied it, even in Roman Egypt . . . , and its opening words became a common graffito on the walls of Pompeii" (Don P. Fowler and Peta G. Fowler, "Vergil [Publius Vergilius Maro]," *OCD* 1603).

68. Cranfield, *Romans*, 2:525.

69. The notion of "doing" God's word is strengthened in the LXX, which expands "in your mouth and in your heart, so that you can do it" to "in your mouth and in your heart and in your hands [καὶ ἐν ταῖς χερσίν σου], to do it."

and that it is the gospel instead that is accessible and simple. What would lead Paul to use this, of all Scripture passages, to make his point?

It is unlikely that Paul has intentionally rewritten the passage on the basis of his eschatological convictions about Christ to make it say the opposite of what it originally intended.[70] Paul's argument began with the thesis that Israel's failure to believe the gospel did not mean that the word of God had failed (9:6), but contradicting the message of Deuteronomy 30:12–14 would show precisely that the word of God had failed. It also seems unlikely that Paul did not really intend to engage Deuteronomy 30:12–14 as Scripture but only used the language of this well-known passage to communicate his own message.[71] His three uses of "that is" (τοῦτ' ἔστιν; 10:6, 7, 8) reveal that he was interpreting Scripture here.[72]

The solution to this puzzle probably lies in Paul's belief that the theology of Deuteronomy generally, including Deuteronomy 30:11–14, was congenial to the overall argument he has been developing in Romans. The narrative setting of Deuteronomy assumes that Israel has already demonstrated its strong tendency to rebel against God: Israelites lack righteousness (9:4–5), are a stubborn people (9:6), and even as they stand assembled to hear Moses recite the commandments of the law, their hearts do not understand, their ears do not hear, and their eyes do not see because "to this day" the Lord had not given them the ability to obey him (29:4, quoted in Rom 11:8).[73] This pessimism about the ability of human beings to obey God without his empowerment parallels Paul's understanding of the pervasive, enslaving power of sin in Romans 1:18–3:20, 5:12–21, 7:7–25, and 8:7–8.

Deuteronomy also envisions a solution to this problem when, after Israel has suffered the punishment of exile for its continual disobedience, it awakens to the relationship between disobedience and curse and obedience and blessing and returns to the Lord (Deut 30:1–3). This awakening and return is apparently not something that Israel will generate within itself but is something that the Lord will accomplish as he circumcises Israel's heart, gives his people a heartfelt love for him, and grants them life (30:6).[74] The pattern of Paul's solution to human sin in Romans runs parallel to this: God takes the initiative to reconcile

70. For this view, see, e.g., Sprinkle (*Law and Life*, 180). Badenas (*Christ, the End of the Law*, 123) is right on this point.

71. E.g., Sanday and Headlam, *Romans*, 289.

72. Cf. Schreiner, *Romans*, 556.

73. See J. Gordon McConville, *Grace in the End: A Study in Deuteronomic Theology* (Grand Rapids: Zondervan, 1993), 135; idem, *Deuteronomy*, Apollos Old Testament Commentary 5 (Downers Grove, IL: InterVarsity Press, 2002), 414, 429.

74. McConville, *Grace in the End*, 136–37; idem, *Deuteronomy*, 427; Barker, *Triumph of Grace*, 164–65. McConville and Barker comment that Deut 30:6 solves the problem posed by Israel's inability to follow Moses's command in 10:16 to circumcise its own heart and "be no longer stubborn."

people to himself through the atoning death of Christ and gives them life by means of union with the resurrected Christ and the power of his Spirit (Rom 5:1–11; 8:1–17).

Deuteronomy 30:12–14 comes, in its original context, directly after Moses's prophecy that one day God would circumcise the heart of his stubborn people, would give them a heartfelt love for himself, and would give them life. Although the verbs of Deuteronomy 30:11–14 shift from the future tenses of 30:1–10 into the present tense, the passage is connected to the preceding prophecy by the conjunction "for" (*ki*; LXX: ὅτι) in 30:11.[75] The conjunction shows that 30:11–14 fills out the prophecy of Israel's eventual, divinely empowered obedience with a description of the commandments that Israel will obey. The commandments themselves, the passage says, are neither burdensome nor inaccessible. Israel's stubborn disobedience has never simply been an understandable reticence to obey difficult and inaccessible rules. God's commandments and statutes have always been good, and keeping them has always resulted in blessing. The problem, the passage implies, has been with Israel's stubborn nature. Once God has circumcised Israel's heart and instilled within his people a love for himself, however, Israel will experience his word for what it always has been in reality—anything but a burden, and as available as the impulses of Israel's own heart.

It is true that Paul's use of this passage in Romans 10:6–8 to describe "the righteousness from faith" and the message of the gospel that he and his co-workers preach removes from it any reference to "doing" God's commandments and therefore changes the theology of the passage slightly.[76] But Paul's use of the passage is not arbitrary, even by modern standards, nor is the passage itself, considered within its wider context, uncongenial to Paul's argument. Paul has taken a paragraph about obedience to the law and used its voice to describe God's gift of reconciliation to himself through the atoning death of Christ. In its own context in Deuteronomy, however, the passage describes an obedience to the law that will only occur after God takes the initiative in reconciliation through circumcising the hearts of his people and instilling a love for himself within them.[77]

Paul's use of the passage appears even less arbitrary in light of his own earlier claim that "the righteous requirement of the law" is "fulfilled in" believers, "who walk not according to the flesh but according to the Spirit" (8:4; cf. 13:8–10).

75. Barker, *Triumph of Grace*, 185–87. Cf. McConville, *Deuteronomy*, 429. Barker and McConville also point out the connection between the two passages provided by the repetition of the term "today" in 30:2, 8, and 11.

76. Rosner, *Paul and the Law*, 140–41.

77. Ibid., 141–42.

Although Paul is not talking about this fulfillment of the law in Romans 10:6–8, and Deuteronomy 30:12–14 does speak of the law's fulfillment, Paul affirms (albeit elsewhere) the principle articulated in Deuteronomy 30:12–14.

10:9 Because if you confess with your mouth that the Lord is Jesus and believe in your heart that God raised him from the dead you will be saved (ὅτι ἐὰν ὁμολογήσῃς ἐν τῷ στόματί σου κύριον Ἰησοῦν καὶ πιστεύσῃς ἐν τῇ καρδίᾳ σου ὅτι ὁ θεὸς αὐτὸν ἤγειρεν ἐκ νεκρῶν, σωθήσῃ). God has made avoiding his wrath simple. It merely involves accepting (in the fullest sense of that term) that Jesus is the creator and ruler of the universe and that through him God has reversed the curse of death that sin has brought to his creation.

The "because" (ὅτι) at the beginning of this clause could be translated "that" and introduce the content of the word of faith which Paul and his coworkers preach.[78] Since Paul's argument here is that the gospel makes righteousness and life easy to obtain, it is slightly more likely that this conjunction introduces the reason why "the righteousness from faith" says that the word is "near you" (10:8). It does this "because" or "in the sense that" the only human response the gospel requires is verbal confession and heartfelt conviction of its foundational claims.

The content of the verbal confession is that "the Lord is Jesus." The identification of Jesus with the Lord God of Israel who created and sustains the universe (1 Cor 8:5–6) did not originate with Paul. As Paul's use of μαράνα θά ("our Lord, come!") in 1 Cor 16:22 shows, worship of Jesus as Lord goes back to the earliest, Aramaic-speaking Christians (cf. Luke 5:8; John 20:28).[79] This identification of Jesus with Israel's God was what Paul preached (2 Cor 4:5).

It is difficult to think that the confession of Jesus as Lord did not also have a second meaning for Paul's audience in the church in Rome. At least since Augustus, the Roman public and imperial functionaries in the eastern empire had sometimes called the emperor "Lord" (Latin: *dominus*; κύριος), although emperors liked to make a show of refusing the title to avoid any appearance of acting as a monarch (Acts 25:26; Suetonius, *Aug.* 53; *Tib.* 27; Tacitus, *Ann.* 2.87). In such a cultural context, the confession "the Lord is Jesus" probably also meant that the ultimate loyalty of Christians lay with Jesus rather than with the emperor.[80]

The verb "confess" (ὁμολογέω) has a communal nuance. It does not merely refer to an internal intellectual acknowledgement that something is true but also to an identification of one's self with others who believe the same truth.[81] Paul's point, then, is not the importance of mouthing certain words but of throwing in one's lot with others who share the same conviction.

Along with this confession of Jesus's identity, Paul mentions heartfelt belief in God's resurrection of Jesus from the dead. This is not the willingness to believe in the improbable resuscitation of a dead man (e.g., Lucian, *The Lover of Lies* 26) but the conviction that with the resurrection of Jesus God had

78. E.g., Käsemann, *Romans*, 291; Murray, *Romans*, 2:55. Cf. KJV, NIV.

79. Bauckham, *Jesus and the God of Israel*, 128–30.

80. MM 365, s.v. κύριος 4; Barrett, *Acts*, 2:1147–48; Haacker, *An die Römer*, 212.

81. Cf. BDAG 708, s.v. ὁμολογέω 2 and 3.

begun to reverse the effects of sin and recreate the world (Rom 4:25; 8:11, 18–23).[82]

Confession of Jesus as the one Lord who is sovereign over the universe and the victor over sin and death through his own resurrection from the dead leads, Paul says, to salvation. Paul is speaking of salvation from the outpouring of God's wrath (cf. 5:9). God has already started revealing his wrath against sin in the present (1:18), and his just judgment will come to a climactic finish "on the day when God judges the hidden things of human beings according to my gospel, through Christ Jesus" (2:16).

To be rescued from this judgment, sinful human beings need to "do" nothing. Salvation is simply a matter of accepting what God has already done for his people in Jesus and of identifying one's self with others who have also received this good gift from God.

10:10 For with the heart it is believed, resulting in righteousness, and with the mouth it is confessed, resulting in salvation (καρδίᾳ γὰρ πιστεύεται εἰς δικαιοσύνην, στόματι δὲ ὁμολογεῖται εἰς σωτηρίαν). Righteousness and salvation come simply and easily to those who receive what God has accomplished for them in the resurrection and lordship of Jesus.

"For" (γάρ) introduces a further explanation of the two sides of 10:9, but now in reverse order.[83] This gives a poetic, A B B′ A′ arrangement to 10:9–10 and demonstrates that Paul's intention is not to compartmentalize heartfelt faith and verbal confession, nor to distinguish between righteousness and salvation, but to see these elements as mutually defining.[84] He does not conceive of a believer who fails to identify with other believers or of a righteousness that fails to lead to salvation, so he lumps them all together here.

Rather than making such distinctions, Paul's emphasis lies on the heart and the mouth, faculties that receive and agree with the word of God according to Deuteronomy 30:14 (cf. 10:8).[85] The word of God, in turn, is the gospel, and the gospel is the story of what God has done to save his people, not the conditions that his people must fulfill in order that they might be saved (cf. 10:5).

10:11 So the Scripture says, "Everyone who believes on him will not be ashamed" (λέγει γὰρ ἡ γραφή, Πᾶς ὁ πιστεύων ἐπ᾽ αὐτῷ οὐ καταισχυνθήσεται). Scripture supports the idea that trust in God is the means to vindication on the final day and that this means is open to anyone, whatever their social group.

The conjunction "so" (γάρ) is usually translated "for," as it is in the immediately preceding sentence, but the meaning "so" is also attested for this word (1 Pet 4:15; Diogenes Laertius, *Lives of the Philsophers* 6.46), and that is probably its nuance here.[86] Paul points out an implication of what he has just said about the means by which a person receives righteousness and salvation. If righteousness and salvation come through faith and confession, then anyone can receive them. Righteousness and salvation are not limited to Israel.

Paul states this implication in the words of Isaiah 28:16, which he had also quoted in Romans

82. Cranfield, *Romans*, 2:530.

83. On this use of "for" (γάρ), see BDAG 189, s.v. γάρ 2.

84. On the chiastic arrangement, see Michel, *An die Römer*, 331, and Schlier, *Römerbrief*, 314.

85. The subjects of the passive verbs "it is believed" (πιστεύεται) and "it is confessed" (ὁμολογεῖται) are not entirely clear, but probably Paul intended Jesus's resurrection and Jesus's lordship (10:9) respectively to serve as subjects. It is just possible that "the word of faith" (τὸ ῥῆμα τῆς πίστεως) in 10:8 plays this role. For discussion of these passives, but with a different conclusion, see Moo (*Romans*, 658n62) and Jewett (*Romans*, 631).

86. On this meaning, see BDAG 190, s.v. γάρ 3.

9:33 at the end of his contrast between gentile faith and Israelite unbelief in the gospel. Here, however, he has made one significant change to the quotation. Whereas in 9:33 he had written that "the one who believes" (ὁ πιστεύων) in Christ will not be ashamed, here he says that "everyone who believes" (πᾶς ὁ πιστευών) in him will not be ashamed. This slight change makes the text speak the language Paul has used elsewhere in Romans for the universality of the gospel (1:16; 3:22; 4:11; 10:4). It reveals that Paul had never lost sight of the ethnic concerns with which the section began in 9:30–32. The ease with which God makes righteousness available explains the irony that gentiles had attained righteousness without even seeking it, whereas unbelieving Israel, with their zeal for God's righteous law, had failed to attain it. If righteousness comes to those who merely believe and confess the gospel, then Greeks as well as Jews can receive it.[87] It does not involve, as a first step, becoming a Jew by adopting the Jewish law (cf. 4:9–17; cf. Acts 15:7–11; Gal 2:14–16).

The future expression "will not be ashamed" (οὐ καταισχυνθήσεται) looks forward to the future judgment when the hope of those who have trusted in the Lord will be vindicated. Ambrosiaster captured the meaning precisely in the late fourth century:

> On the day of judgment, when everything will be examined and all false opinions and teachings will be overthrown, then those who believe in Christ will rejoice, seeing it revealed to all that what they believed is true, and what was thought to be foolish was wise.[88]

10:12 So there is no distinction between Jew and Greek, for the same Lord is over all, being rich toward all who call upon him (οὐ γάρ ἐστιν διαστολὴ Ἰουδαίου τε καὶ Ἕλληνος, ὁ γὰρ αὐτὸς κύριος πάντων, πλουτῶν εἰς πάντας τοὺς ἐπικαλουμένους αὐτόν). Anyone who calls upon God alone for salvation, whatever their social standing or cultural background, can receive God's generosity.

Using "so" (γάρ) again, Paul explains that Isaiah 28:16 is consistent with the universality of the gospel. God makes no distinction between Jew and Greek when he judges people since he is a righteous, impartial judge (Rom 2:11), and the emphasis of Isaiah 28:16 on trust in God is consistent with this principle. Everyone, whatever their cultural heritage, can put faith in God. Or, as Paul puts it here, anyone can call upon him and experience his rich generosity.

The phrase "for there is no distinction" (οὐ γάρ ἐστιν διαστολή) reproduces precisely the wording of 3:22d; "between Jew and Greek" (Ἰουδαίου τε καὶ Ἕλληνος) recalls 1:16, 2:9–10, and 3:9; and "the same Lord is over all" recalls the thought, if not the wording of 3:31. Paul seems to be intentionally echoing the argument of 1:18–3:31 that all human beings alike are sinful, that righteousness is available to all alike through faith in the gospel, and that this arrangement is consistent with God's status as the only God, the God who created and rules the universe.[89] The only difference is that here "the Lord" is not God the Father but Jesus (cf. 10:9).

10:13 For, "Everyone who calls upon the name of the Lord will be saved" (Πᾶς γὰρ ὃς ἂν ἐπικαλέσηται τὸ ὄνομα κυρίου σωθήσεται). Salvation comes to the community of people who worship Jesus, and there are no ethnic or social limitations barring anyone's access to this community.

Paul supports ("for" [γάρ]) his claim of the availability of salvation to everyone regardless of their social standing by using the exact wording of Joel

87. Cf. Calvin, *Romans*, 228–29.

88. Ambrosiaster, *Romans*, 84.

89. Dunn, *Romans 9–16*, 610.

2:32 (3:5 LXX). In the OT, to call upon the name of the Lord was often to worship him exclusively in the midst of other people groups who called upon their own gods (cf., e.g., Ps 105:1; Isa 12:4; cf. Zech 13:9).[90]

Paul probably understood calling upon the Lord both here and in the previous sentence in the same way that he understood the idea of confession in Romans 10:9–10. Calling on the name of the Lord entails identifying with the community of those who trust him for salvation (cf. 1 Cor 1:2). Joel envisioned a time when a remnant of Israel would be saved from judgment because they were willing to call upon the name of the Lord in this sense. Paul now makes this idea more specific. The Lord on whom people call is the Lord Jesus of 10:9, and the people who call upon him includes both Jews and Greeks since "all" (πᾶς) who commit themselves to Jesus as Lord will be saved from God's wrath on the day of judgment (cf. 2:16).

10:14–15 How, then, should they call upon him whom they have not believed? And how should they believe him whom they have not heard? And how should they hear without a preacher? And how should they preach unless they are sent? Just as it is written, "How beautiful are the feet of those who proclaim good news" (Πῶς οὖν ἐπικαλέσωνται εἰς ὃν οὐκ ἐπίστευσαν; πῶς δὲ πιστεύσωσιν οὗ οὐκ ἤκουσαν; πῶς δὲ ἀκούσωσιν χωρὶς κηρύσσοντος; πῶς δὲ κηρύξωσιν ἐὰν μὴ ἀποσταλῶσιν; καθὼς γέγραπται, Ὡς ὡραῖοι οἱ πόδες τῶν εὐαγγελιζομένων [τὰ] ἀγαθά). The majority of those among Israel who have heard the gospel persist in their unbelief, despite hearing the good news of Israel's redemption from the messengers God has provided. God has sent people to proclaim the gospel in accord with Isaiah's prophecy that he would send messengers to proclaim Israel's eschatological redemption joyously.

Paul's formulation of a rhetorical question with "then" (οὖν) indicates a turn in the argument (cf. 9:14, 30; 11:1, 11).[91] The turn is not so drastic, however, that the main subject has changed. He continues to address the problem announced in 9:30–32 that although many within Israel have heard the gospel (10:19a) few have believed it, and instead gentiles, who were not even seeking God, have surprisingly found him (10:20).[92] The subject of Paul's third-person plural verbs in the first three questions, then, is "Israel" just as it was in 9:32 and 10:2–3 where he last used the third-person plural.[93]

Paul's series of questions traces the natural sequence of the transmission of an important message from its sender to its recipients, and does so backwards to form a link between his new train of thought and the immediately preceding sentence. In 10:13 he had spoken of the simplicity of receiving salvation: it was available to anyone, whether Jew or Greek, who called upon the name of the Lord. Now he raises the question of whether those Jews who have rejected the gospel have actually received a fair chance of hearing, understanding, and embracing it. With his questions, Paul admits that for the Jews to call upon the Lord, the Lord must send heralds out with news of who he is, and they must communicate their message to the Jews, who must, in turn, believe it.

His quotation of Isaiah 52:7 (cf. Nah 1:15 [2:1 Heb. and LXX]) shows that God has provided all

90. Hans Walter Wolff, *Joel and Amos*, trans. Waldemar Janzen, S. Dean McBride Jr., and Charles A. Muenchow, Hermeneia (Philadelphia: Fortress, 1977), 68.

91. Sanday and Headlam, *Romans*, 294.

92. Cranfield was therefore correct to treat this long section as a single unit rather than follow most commentators and divide it into two major sections at 10:14 (*Romans*, 2:503–42).

93. Cf. Cranfield (*Romans*, 2:533) and Chrysostom (*Romans*, 320). In 9:32 and 10:2–3 Paul views the singular "Israel" of 9:31 as a group of individuals and so uses plural verbs. On the grammar involved, see Wallace (*Greek Grammar*, 401).

these requirements to his people. In its original context the passage was about God's redemption of his people from the oppression of their enemies and the establishment of peace, happiness, and salvation through the reign of God himself over them (Isa 52:1–12). Isaiah had depicted a herald running across the mountains surrounding Jerusalem to bring the good news of victory over their enemies to God's people. Isaiah understandably described the feet of such a welcome messenger as "beautiful" (*na'wu*; cf. Song 1:10).[94]

Paul understood his own proclamation of the gospel, and that of the other apostles, to be the fulfillment of this prophecy.[95] He has made Isaiah's reference to a single messenger into a plural to account for the group of apostles who were proclaiming the gospel. In addition, his Greek term (ὡραῖοι) refers not to something that is well proportioned but to something at its chronological prime; for example, a young man "in the prime of life" (ὡραίου νεωστί) or "crops" (τῶν ὡραίων) ripe for harvest (Plato, *Republic* 574C; *Laws* 845E).[96] The term communicates that at just the right time and to the relief of all who recognized the significance of the messengers' message, the good news of salvation appeared (cf. 2 Cor 6:2; Gal 4:4). God, then, has more than adequately fulfilled the requirements for Israel to hear the good news of its redemption.

10:16 But not all have obeyed the gospel. For Isaiah says, "Lord, who has believed our report?" (Ἀλλ' οὐ πάντες ὑπήκουσαν τῷ εὐαγγελίῳ. Ἠσαΐας γὰρ λέγει, Κύριε, τίς ἐπίστευσεν τῇ ἀκοῇ ἡμῶν;). Very few within Israel have submitted to the gospel, but this is consistent with Isaiah's experience and message.

The strong adversative conjunction "but" (ἀλλά) introduces Paul's description of what actually happened despite God's provision for making the gospel known to Israel. They did not obey what they heard. The expression "not all obeyed" uses the common rhetorical device, called *litotes* (λιτότης) or *meiosis* (μείωσις) in antiquity, which deliberately understates the truth "not to deceive someone but to enhance the impressiveness of what we say."[97] (Another example in the NT is Acts 21:39: "I am . . . a citizen of no obscure city.") Here, then, Paul means that very few obeyed.

Paul's argument from Romans 9:30 up to this point has demonstrated that faith in the gospel is not a work but simply trust in God's word. Believing the gospel nevertheless involves submission to God, and this comes out clearly here when Paul speaks of obeying the gospel (ὑπήκουσαν τῷ εὐαγγελίῳ; cf. 1:5; 15:18; 2 Thess 1:8). Israel failed to submit to what the message of the gospel called on them to do. It urged them to identify themselves with others who claimed that Jesus expressed the identity of God himself and to believe that God had raised Jesus from the dead (Rom 10:9), thus vindicating Jesus's claims of authority and his message (cf. 1:4; Acts 4:10; 13:33; 17:31).

Paul's quotation of Isaiah 53:1 LXX demonstrates again that Israel's disobedient response to the gospel does not mean that the word of God has

94. Oswalt, *Isaiah, Chapters 40–66*, 367–69. Cf. Wagner, *Heralds of the Good News*, 174–75.

95. Cf. Wagner, *Heralds of the Good News*, 173–76. Wagner suggests (173n163) that the definite article (τά) added to "good things" (ἀγαθά) functions anaphorically to refer back to "the word of faith" that Paul and the other apostles preach.

96. These translations belong, respectively, to Chris Emlyn-Jones and William Preddy, LCL, and to R. G. Bury, LCL. See LSJ 2036, s.v. ὡραῖος I.1, III.2. The LXX text available to Paul may have read either "beauty" (an unusual meaning for ὥρα) or "beautiful" (ὡραῖοι), but probably read the latter. On this, see James Barr ("Paul and the LXX: A Note on Some Recent Work," *JTS* 45 [1994]: 600–601) and Wagner (*Heralds of the Good News*, 171–73).

97. Corbett, *Classical Rhetoric*, 487. See *Rhet. Her.* 4.38 and Harry Caplan's footnote "a" in the LCL edition, as well as Meyer, *Romans*, 414.

failed (Rom 9:6). Israel's rejection of the glad tidings that Paul and other apostles were preaching in his own time corresponded in the apostle's thinking to Israel's rejection of the beautiful news of God's redemption in Isaiah's time (Isa 52:7; 53:1).[98]

10:17 So, faith comes from hearing, and hearing through the word of Christ (ἄρα ἡ πίστις ἐξ ἀκοῆς, ἡ δὲ ἀκοὴ διὰ ῥήματος Χριστοῦ). Isaiah's testimony supports the principle that one has to hear the good news of God's deliverance before one believes it.

Paul's "so" indicates that he is about to draw a conclusion from his quotation of Isaiah 53:1 in the immediately preceding sentence. If Isaiah complains that no one has believed his account of God's redemption, then it is clear that faith in God arises from hearing and believing an account of that redemption that someone has preached. Paul had already stated this basic principle in Romans 10:14–15a, but now his statement has the backing of the prophet Isaiah. Here, then, Paul summarizes his newly supported statement, and he also prepares to make the case again in 10:18–21 that Israel has not obeyed the account of the gospel they heard through the messengers God provided them (cf. 10:15b–16).

In 10:16b "report" (ἀκοή) referred to the content of what Isaiah, Paul, and the other apostles preached, but the term could also refer to the activity of "hearing" something.[99] Since Paul is summarizing 10:14–15a, where he had used the verb "hear" (ἀκούω) twice, he shifted the meaning of the word slightly to bear this new connotation.

"The word of Christ" (ῥήματος Χριστοῦ) is an objective genitive construction describing the word that Paul and the other apostles preached about Christ.[100] It is identical to "the word of faith" that according to 10:8 Paul and his coworkers preach and that, like the word of God described in Deuteronomy 30:14, is easy to appropriate. Just as in Isaiah's time, however, many within Israel have failed to heed this lovely and easily obeyed message.

10:18 But, I say, they didn't fail to hear did they? To the contrary! "Their voice went out to all the earth and their words to the limits of civilization" (ἀλλὰ λέγω, μὴ οὐκ ἤκουσαν; μενοῦνγε, Εἰς πᾶσαν τὴν γῆν ἐξῆλθεν ὁ φθόγγος αὐτῶν καὶ εἰς τὰ πέρατα τῆς οἰκουμένης τὰ ῥήματα αὐτῶν). Jewish unbelievers have not failed to believe as a result of having no opportunity to hear the gospel.

Paul forestalls a possible objection to unbelieving Israel's culpability. The first-person expression "I say" shows that the objection comes not from a fictional, hostile interlocutor (as in 6:1, 15; 7:7, 13) but from Paul himself as he thinks this problem through. This is the agonized first-person singular of 9:2–3 and 10:2.[101] Paul's question (beginning with μή) expects a negative answer, but its verb is in turn negated (with οὐ), so the overall force of the question is an affirmation (cf. 1 Cor 9:4–5; 11:22): they did actually hear.[102] The expression "to the contrary" (μενοῦνγε; cf. 9:20) introduces Paul's counterproposal to any notion that they did not hear.

This counterproposal itself uses the voice of Psalm 19:4 (18:5 LXX; 19:5 Heb.), although Paul does not introduce it as a quotation of Scripture.[103] He is probably recalling the language of the psalm and its broad claim that God is not a hidden and mysterious being but has revealed himself to everyone (cf. Rom 1:19–20). What the psalm says

98. Sanday and Headlam, *Romans*, 297; Wagner, *Heralds of the Good News*, 179–80.

99. BDAG 36, s.v. ἀκοή 2. This is, admittedly, a rare use of the term (e.g., Isa 6:9 LXX; Ps 17:45 LXX; 2 Pet 2:8).

100. Sanday and Headlam, *Romans*, 298; Moo, *Romans*, 666.

101. Jewett, *Romans*, 642.

102. Smyth, *Greek Grammar*, §2651 d; BDF §427(2); BDR §427(4).

103. Cf. Zahn, *An die Römer*, 490.

about creation Paul says about the proclamation of the gospel. Both are God's revelation of himself, and both have made him known on a wide scale. Paul was under no delusion that every Israelite had heard the gospel. Like the psalm, he is speaking poetically rather than with scientific precision and is making his point by means of hyperbole.[104]

As Theodoret of Cyrus observed in the fifth century, Jesus himself had sent his apostles first to "the lost sheep of the house of Israel" (Matt 10:6), and Acts regularly shows Paul going first to the Jews (e.g., Acts 13:46).[105] Paul's point, then, is that in the wide proclamation of the gospel (cf. 15:19), the Jews have hardly been neglected.

10:19 But, I say, Israel didn't fail to understand did it? First, Moses says, "I will make you jealous of those who are not a people, and I will make you resent a foolish people" (ἀλλὰ λέγω, μὴ Ἰσραὴλ οὐκ ἔγνω; πρῶτος Μωϋσῆς λέγει, Ἐγὼ παραζηλώσω ὑμᾶς ἐπ' οὐκ ἔθνει, ἐπ' ἔθνει ἀσυνέτῳ παροργιῶ ὑμᾶς). Unbelieving Israel not only heard but understood the gospel that they rejected. If people groups outside Israel and without the benefit of Scripture could understand the gospel, surely Israel with all its advantages was able to understand it. Instead, they became jealous and angry at the proclamation of the gospel to the gentiles.

Paul now examines Israel's culpability for not believing the gospel from another angle. They have certainly heard the gospel (10:18), but people can hear something and still not be fully responsible for what they have heard because they have not understood it. Just as in 10:18, however, the complex double-negative question (μὴ . . . οὐκ) amounts to an affirmation, and in this case Paul affirms that they understood the gospel.

The term "understand" (γινώσκω) most often means simply "know about," but the slightly more precise meaning makes sense here (cf. Matt 24:39).[106] Paul has already affirmed that Israel "heard" the gospel, which implies that they "know about" it. This second question, then, asks whether they have understood what they have heard.[107]

Paul's claim that they have understood the gospel at first seems to stand in tension with his claim in 10:2–3 that Israel's zeal was not informed by knowledge and that they were ignorant of the righteousness of God.[108] But there too, Israel's ignorance had a willful edge to it. Unbelieving Israel was ignorant of the righteousness of God because they failed to trust God and sought to establish their own righteousness. This was something that they should have known from Scripture not to do (Deut 9:4–5; Isa 28:16). Here, then, Paul says that Israel understood "the word of Christ" (Rom 10:17) well enough to be held responsible for believing it.

Paul calls two witnesses from Scripture, Moses and Isaiah, to testify that Israel understood the universal nature of the gospel. Moses comes "first" (πρῶτος) because he appears first in the biblical canon, and although the words Paul quotes are obviously God's words, Paul describes Moses as their source because he is thinking of the biblical "song" of Moses where the words appear.[109] This empha-

104. Cf. Moo (*Romans*, 667) and the expansive language in Rom 1:8; 2 Cor 2:14; 3:2; 1 Thess 1:8 (Schlier, *Römerbrief*, 319).

105. Theodoret of Cyrus, *Letters of St. Paul*, 1:109.

106. On the use of the term without a direct object and with the meaning "understand," just as it is used here, see BDAG 200, s.v. γινώσκω 3.b.

107. So most translations. For this meaning of the word, see BDAG 200, s.v. γινώσκω 3 and Wilckens (*An die Römer [Röm 6–11]*, 230).

108. This has led some commentators to explain the double-negative question in 19a, against grammatical norms, as a denial of Israel's knowledge. See, e.g., Haacker (*An die Römer*, 217).

109. Cf. Hans Hübner (*Gottes Ich und Israel: Zum Schriftgebrauch des Paulus in Römer 9–11*, FRLANT 136 [Göttingen: Vandenhoeck & Ruprecht, 1984], 97): "Daß nämlich das Ich in dem Zitat 10,19 das *Ich Gottes* ist, nicht aber das Ich des Mose, ist evident."

sis on the witness of Israel's Scripture to the gospel supports Paul's view that God has given Israel ample opportunity to recognize how his purposes described in Scripture mesh with "the word of Christ." Israel had the "oracles," "covenants," "legislation," and "promises" that God had entrusted to them (Rom 3:2; 9:4) and so should have recognized "the word of Christ" as the word of God.

In its original context, Deuteronomy 32:21 describes how Israel will, in the future, provoke God to jealousy and anger "with their idols," and so God will provoke them to jealousy and anger "with those who are no people . . . with a foolish nation." As Jeffrey H. Tigay puts it, "God will punish Israel measure for measure, treating it as it treated Him," presumably by means of an invading army of foreigners.[110] The identity of this "no people" and "foolish nation" is not clear, allowing Paul to identify it with his understanding of the phrase "not my people" in Hosea 1:10 and 2:23 (Rom 9:25–26) and therefore with gentiles who have believed the gospel.[111]

Some interpreters have thought Paul used the quotation to criticize Israel for its failure to understand the universality of the gospel, but that is unlikely.[112] The universality of the gospel is not the chief point of 10:14–21a; rather, it is Israel's culpability for not believing the gospel that has been so clearly proclaimed to them. Paul uses Deuteronomy 32:21, then, to support his contention that the gospel was easy for Israel to understand. If "a foolish nation" could hear and understand it, surely Israel, with all its advantages, could do so.[113] Israel's leaders rejected the gospel not because they failed to understand it but because they were so zealously focused on the Mosaic law that when tax collectors, sinners, and the uncircumcised were invited into the people of God through the gospel, Israel's leaders became angry (Mark 2:16; Luke 5:29–30; 15:1–2; 19:3; Acts 21:21, 27–28; cf. Acts 11:2; 15:1).

The term "provoke to jealousy" (παραζηλόω) is a rare term that an LXX translator seems to have coined in an effort to render Deuteronomy 32:21.[114] It appears most often in the LXX in connection with God's jealous anger toward Israel when they worship other gods (1 Kgs 14:22; Ps 78:58 [77:58 LXX]; cf. 1 Cor 10:22), but it can also refer to envy (Ps 37:7, 8 [36:7, 8 LXX]; Sir 30:3).[115] Its corresponding noun, although extremely rare (Philo, *Rewards* 89 [F. H. Colson, LCL]), seems to mean "emulation," and it is likely that Paul uses the verb with this connotation in Romans 11:11 and 14.[116]

10:20 And Isaiah dares to say, "I have been found among those who do not seek me, I have become visible to those who do not ask for me" (Ἠσαΐας δὲ ἀποτολμᾷ καὶ λέγει, Εὑρέθην τοῖς ἐμὲ μὴ ζητοῦσιν, ἐμφανὴς ἐγενόμην τοῖς ἐμὲ μὴ ἐπερωτῶσιν). Testimony that Israel has understood the gospel comes not only from Moses but from Isaiah who speaks of God's willingness to make himself known even to those who are not seeking him. God has done this in the case of gentiles who have heard the gospel, and some of them have believed. If God makes the gospel clear even to gentiles, who know nothing of his ways, then surely unbelieving Israel, with its advantage of God's revelation in Scripture, has understood the gospel.

110. Tigay, *Deuteronomy*, 308.

111. Wagner, *Heralds of the Good News*, 197n227. In Deuteronomy God says he will use this godless and foolish nation as an instrument of judgment on Israel for their idolatry and their scorning of God (McConville, *Deuteronomy*, 457).

112. Godet, *Romans*, 388; Meyer, *Romans*, 417; Richard H. Bell, *Provoked to Jealousy: The Origin and Purpose of the Jealousy Motif in Romans 9–11*, WUNT 2.63 (Tübingen: Mohr Siebeck, 1994), 99–103.

113. Sanday and Headlam, *Romans*, 299–300.

114. Bell, *Provoked to Jealousy*, 27.

115. Cf. Albrecht Stumpff, "ζηλόω, κτλ.," *TDNT* 2:879.

116. Bell, *Provoked to Jealousy*, 34–35. Cf. LSJ 1309, s.v. παραζηλόω.

Paul now quotes Isaiah as his second biblical testimony that Israel understood the gospel. Once again, although the words clearly belong to God, Paul wants to emphasize the availability of God's words to Israel in Scripture, and so he attributes the words to the biblical prophet who wrote them down. He uses an early Greek rendering of Isaiah 65:1 that differs slightly from Codex Sinaiticus, but none of the various Greek versions of the text seriously alters the meaning of the underlying Hebrew.[117]

Interpreters often comment on the dramatic difference between the meaning of Isaiah's words in their original context and the meaning Paul assigns to them here. In Isaiah, the quotation is an answer to the complaint in 63:7–64:12 that God is distant from Israel, that instead of rescuing them in his zeal and might he has left them desolate (63:15; cf. 64:1–3, 8–12). God replies in 65:1–16 that he has always been available to Israel, but that there is a recalcitrant party within his people who think of themselves as pious when they are actually rebelling against him.[118] For his part, God "was ready to be sought by those who did not ask" for him and "to be found by those who did not seek" him (65:1a), and he was standing there answering the rebellious group with "here I am," but they never called (65:1b).

Paul turns this rebuke into a positive description of God's mercy to gentiles who were oblivious to God's presence. As a rule, gentiles neither seek nor ask for him (the verbs are in the present tense), and yet God has brought the word of Christ to them through the preaching of the apostles, and many of them have believed. The thought stands parallel to the statement at the beginning of this section of Paul's argument that "gentiles who were not pursuing righteousness attained righteousness, that is, righteousness by faith" (9:30). Paul hints by this return to the initial announcement of the section's theme that he is drawing the section to a close.

It is true that Paul's point is not "precisely" Isaiah's point, as one nineteenth-century Isaiah commentator put it.[119] It is also true, however, that Paul's quotation of Isaiah 65:1a is not intended merely as a celebration of God's grace to the gentiles. The quotation functions for Paul, as it did for Isaiah, as a rebuke to a recalcitrant element within Israel that has sought to establish its own righteousness rather than submit to God's righteousness (cf. Isa 63:15–64:12).[120] Paul's point is that if even non-Jewish peoples, who were neither seeking righteousness nor God, have submitted to the gospel, Israel has certainly understood the gospel they have heard but has simply refused to submit to it.

10:21 But to Israel he says, "All day long I have stretched out my hands to a disobedient and oppositional people" (πρὸς δὲ τὸν Ἰσραὴλ λέγει, Ὅλην τὴν ἡμέραν ἐξεπέτασα τὰς χεῖράς μου πρὸς λαὸν ἀπειθοῦντα καὶ ἀντιλέγοντα). Just as God's merciful appeal to recalcitrant Israelites provides an analogy to his merciful approach to foolish gentiles, so Israel's stubborn refusal to obey God in Isaiah's time provides an analogy to their unbelief and opposition to the gospel in Paul's experience.

The conjunction "but" (δέ), translated "and" in the previous sentence, here introduces a contrast between what Isaiah said about the gentiles and what he said about Israel. In its own context, the passage Paul quotes (Isa 65:2a) simply extends the rebuke to Israel that Paul had quoted in Romans 10:20. It continues the theme of God's availability to the recalcitrant group described in Isaiah 63:7–

117. See the full discussions in Wagner (*Heralds of the Good News*, 206–11) and Jewett (*Romans*, 647–48).

118. Oswalt, *Isaiah: Chapters 40–66*, 635.

119. Joseph Addison Alexander, *The Later Prophecies of Isaiah* (New York: Wiley and Putnam, 1847), 445.

120. Cf. Wagner, *Heralds of the Good News*, 211–16.

64:12 who consider themselves pious but actually are walking "in a way that is not good, following their own devices" (65:2b), or as the LXX puts it, "after their own sins" (ὀπίσω τῶν ἁμαρτιῶν αὐτῶν). This is also Paul's understanding of the position of unbelieving Israel. They are willfully ignorant of the righteousness of God provided in the atoning death of Christ and continue the vain attempt to establish their own righteousness by doing the requirements of the Mosaic law (Rom 10:3).

Paul has relocated the phrase "all day long" to the front of his sentence to emphasize God's patience with Israel.[121] This emphasis sounds a note of hope that anticipates Romans 11:25–32 where Paul affirms that one day "all Israel will be saved" (11:26).

In the OT, people often spread out their open hands to the Lord in prayer (Exod 9:29, 33; 1 Kgs 8:22, 38, 54; Ezra 9:5; Ps 88:9; Isa 1:15), but here God has spread out his hands to unbelieving Israel in appeal to them.[122] He has done this despite their "disobedient" (ἀπειθοῦντα) and "oppositional" (ἀντιλέγοντα) attitude toward the gospel.[123] Paul will pick up this language again in Romans 11:30–32 where he describes how God has been using the disobedience (ἀπείθεια) of Israel for his own merciful purposes to the gentiles and how one day these merciful purposes will also extend to Israel.

In 10:20–21, then, Paul returns to the picture with which he began in 9:30–31. Gentiles who neither pursued righteousness nor sought after God have found God and the righteousness he gives. Many within Israel, however, despite having the Scriptures and a zeal for God, have not submitted to God's righteousness and remain disobedient to the gospel. By the time Paul reaches the end of this section, he has demonstrated that Israel's own Scriptures anticipated this turn of events, however surprising it might be.

Theology in Application

This passage teaches that salvation from God's justified wrath against human sin is easy, involving merely trust in God and embracing what he has done for sinners through the gospel. Because salvation is not difficult, many different kinds of people can experience it, and sometimes the identity of those who respond to it is surprising. The irreligious may respond to it more readily than the religious, and there is a form of religious zeal that leads to rejection of the gospel.

The Effortlessness of Reconciliation with God

In 9:30–10:21, Paul emphasizes how easy it is to have a peaceful relationship with God. It is a matter of listening to God, and alongside others who have done the same, of accepting what one hears. The process is so easy that Paul does not even want to

121. The LXX reads, "I stretched out my hands all day long" (ἐξεπέτασα τὰς χεῖράς μου ὅλην τὴν ἡμέραν). See Jewett, *Romans*, 649.

122. John D. W. Watts, *Isaiah 34–66*, WBC 25 (Waco, TX: Word, 1987), 342–43.

123. For the use of this vocabulary to describe Jewish opposition to Christianity, see Acts 13:45; 28:19; Rom 11:30–31; 15:31.

say one "does" it. The emphasis has to lie squarely on what God has done to put his people right with himself, not on their cleverness in finding out the gospel or their efforts in applying it. Christ died on the cross to atone for human sin, God raised him from the dead to break sin's stranglehold on humanity, and God sent the apostles to the ends of the earth with this beautiful message. God's people themselves simply stand in place together and receive this outpouring of God's love (cf. 5:5). The belief in one's heart and the confession of one's mouth that Paul describes in this passage refer to the sincere and open acceptance of what God has already graciously done for his people through the death and resurrection of Christ. As Calvin put it in his comments on 10:10, "We obtain righteousness by embracing the goodness of God offered to us in the Gospel . . . , by believing that God is gracious to us in Christ."[124]

The Universal Outreach of the Gospel

Paul teases from the easy nature of reconciliation with God the crucial ancillary truth that the gospel is for everyone. The point is so important to him that he adds an "everyone" to his quotation of Isaiah 28:16 in 10:11 and explains in no uncertain terms what this means: "There is no distinction between Jew and Greek," he says, "for the same Lord is over all, being rich toward all who call upon him" (10:12). Being in a right relationship with God, then, is God's work, and since God accomplishes it, this work can benefit anyone: from mentally handicapped infants in whom God's Spirit can engender faith to the most celebrated scholars and athletes; from powerful elites in the world's most economically resourced countries to the illiterate poor in its most undeveloped societies; and from those deeply invested in the oldest and most sophisticated religious traditions to those who have never given God a second thought. As the Westminster Confession of Faith puts it, "the Spirit . . . worketh when, and where, and how he pleaseth" to form God's people (10.3).

The Gentiles' Suprising Response to God

Paul's concern in 9:30–10:21 is chiefly with this last contrast and the irony that in the race for righteousness, it was not Israel, despite all their theological privileges and zealous exertions, but a motley crew of clueless gentiles who attained the goal. The problem lay in Israel's stumbling over Christ and especially his attitude to the Mosaic law. The Jewish leadership of Christ's time disagreed with his loose approach to the law, and failed to recognize his authority to interpret it, and so they rejected him. They preferred instead to continue down the road of their own ideas about how people should keep the Mosaic law. They heard and understood the gospel, but they rejected it in favor of their own notion about what would lead to a right relationship

124. Calvin, *Romans*, 227–28.

with God. Their theological sophistication had hindered rather than helped them understand God and his word.

Paul certainly does not speak here of all unbelieving Israelites. Many unbelieving Jews were appalled at the miscarriage of justice involved in the persecution of Christians by their more zealous compatriots (John 7:50–52; Acts 5:34–39; Josephus, *Ant.* 20.201). Paul is instead describing Jews who, like himself prior to his conversion, were so focused on protecting their vision of Jewish society that they were willing to kill people to accomplish their goals. The chief priests and the scribes who brought Jesus to Pilate accused him, among other things, of "misleading our nation" (Luke 23:2), a charge that also emerges in John's Gospel when the ruling elites who had decided that Jesus must die told Pilate, "We have a law, and according to that law he ought to die" (John 19:7). Some of these Jewish leaders may have thought they were serving God by sending Jesus to the cross. They were certainly careful to avoid ritual impurity so that they might keep the Passover even as they engaged in their miscarriage of justice (John 18:28; cf. 16:2).[125]

A Warning against a Certain Form of Religious Zeal

There is a warning here for all religious people, and Paul is aware that Christians need it as much as anyone (11:17–21; 12:3; 14:4, 10–12). It is possible to become so entrenched in one's understanding of God that even God's word itself is not allowed to correct that understanding. The societal elites who engineered the death of Jesus were offended by his approach to the Mosaic law, but Paul insists in this passage that it is they who failed to understand that the law pointed to Christ by its indictment of sinful humanity. The Jewish leadership of Jesus's time refused to accept his correction of their approach to the law as the prophetic word of God and, instead, plotted his death.

In much the same way, Martin Luther was capable of turning his zeal for the truth of the gospel into an unbiblical animosity toward the Jewish people. Luther clearly knew what attitude toward the Jews a biblically informed Christian should adopt. In his second set of lectures on the Psalms (1519–1521) he condemned mistreatment of the Jews by "certain Christians (if they can be called Christians)" and urged the church to extend to the Jews "all kindness, patience, prayers, and care," citing Paul's example of compassion in Romans 9:1 and his admonition to humility in Romans 11:18 and 20.[126] In later years, however, Luther returned to the unbiblical notions and disgusting rhetoric that he had used of the Jews in his first lectures on the Psalms (1513–1515), just before working through Romans (1515–1516).[127] His ill-informed

125. Craig S. Keener, *The Gospel of John: A Commentary*, 2 vols. (Peabody, MA: Hendrickson, 2003), 2:1100.

126. Brooks Schramm and Kirsi I. Stjerna, eds., *Martin Luther, the Bible, and the Jewish People: A Reader* (Minneapolis: Fortress, 2012), 68–69.

127. Ibid., 48–49.

paranoia about the small and heavily oppressed minority of Jews living in sixteenth-century Germany led him to call for the destruction of their homes, synagogues, and way of life.[128] These publications made life even more difficult for the Jews in Luther's own time and later contributed significantly to the atmosphere that made possible the societal horrors of Germany under National Socialism.[129]

The reasons for Luther's anti-Jewish rhetoric are complex, but one prominent motivation was the idea that Jews might lead Christians astray from the gospel and persuade them to become Jews.[130] In a way that was puzzlingly inconsistent with his own deepest theological insights about the sovereignty and the grace of God, expressed not least in his comments on Romans 9:30–10:4, he advocated that human beings violently take the advancement of the gospel into their own hands.[131] The result was disaster for countless human beings who were beloved of God (11:28) and to whom God continued to stretch out his hands of appeal (10:21).

Romans 9:30–10:21 calls upon all humanity, unbelievers as well as believers, to embrace the word of God in faith in its totality, to receive the mercy and grace of God offered there, and to recognize that the gospel is about human flourishing under God's mercy and grace. It does not advance any particular social or ethnic group within humanity over another. God's word in its totality is two-sided. It announces the disturbing news that every human being, even the religiously zealous person (including the person zealously committed to God's grace!), is profoundly affected by a tendency toward pride and fear and, as a consequence, rebellion against God. It also announces the joyful news that God has freely reconciled sinful human beings to himself through Christ and cut the chains of their bondage to sin through the power of the Holy Spirit. No social or ethnic group within humanity is less affected by the tendency to sin than any other group, and no group is excluded from the offer of God's love in Christ.

128. Ibid., 164–80.

129. David M. Whitford, *Luther: A Guide for the Perplexed* (London: T&T Clark, 2011), 154–68; Schramm and Stjerna, *Martin Luther, the Bible, and the Jewish People*, 9.

130. Whitford, *Luther*, 156; Schramm and Stjerna, *Martin Luther, the Bible, and the Jewish People*, 178–79.

131. Whitford, *Luther*, 168. For confirmation of this, see Luther's comment on Rom 10:2 ("They have a zeal for God, but it is not enlightened"), which concludes with "the man who knows that he does not know is gentle, teachable, unresisting, ready to give his hand to all men" (*Romans*, 405).

CHAPTER 22

Romans 11:1–10

Literary Context

So far in Romans 9–11 Paul has argued that Israel's rejection of the gospel does not mean the failure of God's word for two reasons. First, Scripture itself shows that God has always decided who would belong to his people. If more gentiles than Jews currently fill their ranks, then this only shows that salvation comes to people at God's initiative (9:1–29). Second, he has demonstrated that despite God's sovereignty over who belongs to his people, Israel itself bears responsibility for rejecting the gospel, and their disobedience is consistent with the disobedience of Israel so often described in Scripture (9:30–10:21). So far, then, Paul has shown that God's relationship to the Israelites who have rejected him is not inconsistent with the portrait of God's relationship to his people in Scripture, and he has gone a long way toward successfully defending his thesis that "the word of God has not failed" (9:6).

Still, the argument so far has not demonstrated how the current situation of Israelite unbelief can be consistent with God's promises of faithfulness to Abraham's physical descendants.[1] God may be justified in placing within his people anyone he chooses, and he may be just in punishing those who have rebelled against him, and all this may be consistent with his approach to Israel in Scripture. Yet in Scripture God promised to be faithful to the Israel defined not merely in spiritual terms but in physical terms also, and in Scripture he is merciful to this particular ethnic group even when they rebel against him.

The final step in Paul's argument, then, shows that God is both merciful to physical Israel in the present (11:1–10) and in the future will continue to be merciful to them (11:11–32). Each of the two sections begins the same way rhetorically.[2] A rhetorical question suggests an idea that Paul emphatically rejects and then follows with a thesis statement describing the essence of what he is about to argue:

1. Cf. Aletti, *God's Justice in Romans*, 216.

2. Moo, *Romans*, 671. As Aletti observes, however, Paul's initial rhetorical question in 11:1a is the all-encompassing thesis of 11:1–32 that the subsequent paragraphs explain (*God's Justice in Romans*, 216).

11:1	11:11
I say, then,	I say, then,
God did not cast off his people did he?	they did not stumble so as to fall did they?
Certainly not!	Certainly not!
For even I am an Israelite, from the offspring of Abraham, from the tribe of Benjamin.	Rather, by their trespass salvation has come to the gentiles, in order to provoke the rest of Israel to jealousy.

In 11:1–10 Paul shows that in the present there is a remnant of Israelites whom God has graciously chosen to attain righteousness through faith in the gospel (11:1–6) despite God's hardening of the rest of Israel (11:7–10). The section explores the idea of the salvation of a "remnant" (λεῖμμα, v. 5; cf. ὑπελείφθην, v. 3) that Paul had mentioned in passing in the set of scriptural quotations that ended the first major section of his argument (9:27, ὑπόλειμμα; 9:29, ἐγκατέλιπεν). Then, in 11:11–32 Paul shows that even this hardened majority will receive God's mercy in the future. Here Paul explores the concept of Israel's jealousy of gentile believers mentioned briefly in the scriptural quotations that ended the second major section of his argument (10:19). Israel's present hardened state may appear to be inconsistent with God's merciful character, but in reality it is part of God's plan to show mercy to the non-Israelite nations of the earth and eventually to the majority of Israel also.

God's arrangement of history so that he shows mercy to all (11:32) prompts the expression of amazement at God's power and wisdom that concludes the argument of chapters 9–11 (11:33–36). It also prepares the way for Paul's ethical admonitions in 12:1–15:13, whose foundation is the merciful character of God (12:1).

I. Justification by Faith Brings Peace and Reorients the Believer's Existence (5:1–8:39)
II. Israel's Present Rejection of the Gospel Does Not Imply the Failure of God's Word (9:1–11:36)
  A. Paul's Anguish over Israel's Rejection of the Gospel (9:1–5)
  B. The Scriptures Describe God's Choice of His People as Free and Surprising (9:6–29)
  C. Unbelieving Israel Is Culpable for Rejecting the Gospel (9:30–10:21)
➦ **D. Still, God Has Not Cast Off His People (11:1–32)**
    1. Paul States His Thesis (11:1a)
    2. God Has Graciously Chosen a Remnant within Israel (11:1b–10)
    3. Eventually, Many Israelites Will Be Saved (11:11–32)
  E. A Concluding Statement of Astonishment and Praise (11:33–36)
III. Exhortation to Live in a Way That Is Consistent with the Gospel (12:1–15:13)

Main Idea

Paul argues that the remnant of those within physical Israel who have received God's grace and attained righteousness demonstrates that even in the present situation God has not rejected his people. The imbalance between Israelite believers and unbelievers in the present differs little from the situation described in Scripture. In Elijah's time a remnant existed who had not abandoned God to worship Baal, and in David's time there were unjust Israelites, like those who in more recent days had rejected Jesus and persecuted his followers. Once again Paul shows that God's word has not failed (9:6) because the present situation is consistent with what Scripture says about God's approach to physical Israel.

Translation

Romans 11:1–10

1a	Rhetorical Question	**I say,** then, **God did not cast off his people did he?**
b	Exclamation	**Certainly not!**
c	Basis	For **even I am an Israelite,**
d	Description	from the offspring of Abraham,
e	Identification	from the tribe of Benjamin.
2a	Restatement (of 1a–b)	**God did not cast off his people** whom he foreknew.
b	Rhetorical Question	Or **do you not know what the Scripture says** in the section on Elijah?
2c–3	Explanation (of 2b)	How he appeals to God against Israel, "Lord, they have killed your prophets and torn down your altars, and only I am left, and they are seeking my life." (1 Kgs 19:10, 14)
4a	Rhetorical Question	But **what does the divine reply say** to him?
b	Explanation (of 2b)	"I have left for myself seven thousand men, those who did not bow the knee to Baal." (1 Kgs 19:18)

Continued on next page.

Continued from previous page.

5 Inference (from 4b) So, then also, in the present time,
a remnant exists
by gracious choice

6a and
Condition (of 6b) if by grace,
b Inference (from 5) no longer from works,
c Basis (of 6b) since grace would no longer be grace.

7a Rhetorical Question **What then?**

b Assertion That which Israel seeks,
this it has not attained;
c Contrast/Comparison but **the chosen have attained it,**
d Explanation (of 7b) and **the rest were hardened.**
8 Verification (of 7b) Just as **it is written,**
"God gave them a spirit of stupor, (cf. Isa 29:4)
eyes that do not see and
ears that do not hear until this very day." (Deut 29:4)

9–10 Verification (of 7b) And **David says,**
"Let their table become a bird trap and a net and (cf. Ps 35:8)
a stumbling block and a repayment to them.

Let their eyes be darkened
that they may not see and bend their back continually." (Ps 69:22–23)

Structure

The section falls into three parts. The first part is simply the rhetorical question and Paul's rejection of its implications in 11:1a ("I say, then, God did not cast off his people did he? Certainly not!"). This brief part of the passage stands over both 11:1b–10 and 11:11–32 as the primary thesis that Paul is about to prove in both sections.[3]

The second and third parts speak first positively and then negatively about physical Israel, and Paul proves his point in both parts from Scripture.[4] The second part (11:1b–6) supplies one reason why Paul can claim that God has not rejected his people: Paul himself is an Israelite, and God has not rejected him (11:1b). Paul then demonstrates this thesis from Scripture (11:2b–4; cf. 1 Sam 12:22 LXX; 1 Kgs 19:10,

3. Cf. Aletti, *God's Justice in Romans*, 216.

4. Michel, *An die Römer*, 337.

14, 18 LXX) and concludes his case with a reference to the present remnant of physical Israel that God has chosen by grace (11:5–6).

The argument recalls 9:6b–29 in two ways. First, at the beginning and end of that argument Paul had referred briefly to an Israel within Israel (9:6b) and to a faithful remnant within physical Israel that God would save (9:27–29, ὑπόλειμμα; ἐγκατέλιπεν; cf. 11:3, ὑπελείφθην; 11:5, λεῖμμα). Second, Paul's primary goal in 9:6b–26 was to show that the God of Scripture is sovereign over who belongs to his people and so has the right to include gentiles within his people as well as physical descendants of Abraham. His overall point in 11:1–10 is similar, except that now he limits the discussion to physical Israelites (11:1) and claims that God in his grace has the right to choose from rebellious Israel a remnant who are faithful to him (11:5–6) and to harden the rest of Israel in their rebellion against him (11:7–10).

The third part of 11:1–10 turns to the negative side of this idea and follows the same pattern of stating a thesis and then proving the thesis from Scripture. Here the thesis is that whereas the elect within Israel attained righteousness through the gospel, the rest were hardened (11:7). Paul then demonstrates his thesis using a composite quotation drawn from the law (Deut 29:3 LXX), the prophets (Isa 29:10 LXX), and the writings (Ps 35:8 and 68:23 LXX).[5] Here too Paul's argument recalls 9:6b–29, but now echoes the negatively oriented end of that chapter where he demonstrated that the present recalcitrance of Israel is consistent with its stubbornness against God's overtures to them in biblical history (9:27–29).[6]

Exegetical Outline

- **I. Israel's Present Rejection of the Gospel Does Not Imply the Failure of God's Word (9:1–11:36)**
  - A. Paul's Anguish over Israel's Rejection of the Gospel (9:1–5)
  - B. The Scriptures Describe God's Choice of His People as Free and Surprising (9:6–29)
  - C. Unbelieving Israel Is Culpable for Rejecting the Gospel (9:30–10:21)
  - **D. Still, God Has Not Cast Off His People (11:1–32)**
    - ➡ **1. Paul States His Thesis (11:1a)**
    - **2. God Has Graciously Chosen a Remnant within Israel (11:1b–10)**
      - a. Paul as an example of God's faithfulness to Israel (11:1b)
      - b. Biblical precedent for God's election of a remnant within Israel (11:2–6)
      - c. God's hardening of the rest of Israel (11:7)
      - d. Biblical precedent for God's hardening of recalcitrant Israel (11:8–10)

5. Dunn, *Romans 9–16*, 634.

6. Michel, *An die Römer*, 337.

Explanation of the Text

11:1 I say, then, God did not cast off his people did he? Certainly not! For even I am an Israelite, from the offspring of Abraham, from the tribe of Benjamin (Λέγω οὖν, μὴ ἀπώσατο ὁ θεὸς τὸν λαὸν αὐτοῦ; μὴ γένοιτο· καὶ γὰρ ἐγὼ Ἰσραηλίτης εἰμί, ἐκ σπέρματος Ἀβραάμ, φυλῆς Βενιαμίν). The argument up to this point has laid the blame for Israel's rejection of the gospel squarely at Israel's feet and painted a portrait of Israel's relationship to the gospel that is bleak. Nothing of what Paul has said, however, should be understood to mean that God has rejected Israel and turned instead to the gentiles. Even Paul himself, the apostle to the gentiles, is an Israelite and is therefore evidence that God's hands remain outstretched toward Israel.

The repetition of "I say" (λέγω; cf. 10:18, 19) and the conjunction "then" (οὖν) together connect what Paul is about to say to what he has just said in 10:18–21.[7] If Israel has heard and understood the gospel but rejected it (10:18–20), and if they continue to reject God's offer of conciliation (10:21), that does not mean, does it, that God has cast his people away? The question is formulated in such a way (with μή) that it expects a negative answer, but that negative answer is also implied by the question itself, which is reminiscent of denials in the LXX that the Lord has "cast off" (ἀποθέω) his people (1 Sam 12:22; Ps 94:14 [93:14 LXX]; Lam 3:31; cf. Pss. Sol. 7:8).[8]

Paul may have especially had in mind the context of 1 Samuel 12:22 where, after Israel had "rejected . . . God" by asking for a king (1 Sam 10:19), they worried that God would punish them with death (1 Sam 12:19) and asked Samuel to intercede for them with God. Samuel responds, "Do not be afraid. . . . For the Lord will not cast away [ἀπώσεται] his people for his great name's sake, because the Lord graciously took you to him for a people" (1 Sam 12:20, 22 LXX).[9]

Paul proves his strong denial by offering himself as evidence ("for" [γάρ]). The ascensive force of "even" (καί) probably means that he is saying something more than simply that he is at least one Jew who remains within the people of God, although exactly what about himself he wants to emphasize is unclear. Since a few paragraphs later he highlights his role as "apostle of the gentiles" (11:13), he may well mean that even he, as concerned as he is with proclaiming the gospel to the gentiles, is not a gentile but an Israelite.[10]

His further description of himself as "from the offspring of Abraham" recalls his inclusion of believing gentiles among Abraham's offspring in 4:13–18 and 9:7–8 and belies the notion that Paul had reconfigured the people of God in his thought to the extent that no place remained for physical Israel. Believing gentiles are "Abraham's offspring," but Paul could still apply the name "offspring of Abraham" to the Jews.

He intended both this reference and his even more precise description of himself as "from the tribe of Benjamin" to show the impeccable nature of his credentials. He came from a long-established Jewish family (cf. 2 Cor 11:22; Phil 3:5).[11]

11:2–3 God did not cast off his people whom he foreknew. Or do you not know what the Scripture says in the section on Elijah? How he appeals to God against Israel, "Lord, they have

7. Godet, *Romans*, 391; Cranfield, *Romans*, 2:543; Moo, *Romans*, 672.

8. Sanday and Headlam, *Romans*, 309; Cranfield, *Romans*, 2:543; Wagner, *Heralds of the Good News*, 227–28.

9. Cf. Schreiner, *Romans*, 579–80.

10. Ibid., 544; cf. Chrysostom, *Romans*, 327.

11. Cf. Pelagius, *Romans*, 124: "Not from the class of proselytes."

killed your prophets and torn down your altars, and only I am left, and they are seeking my life" (οὐκ ἀπώσατο ὁ θεὸς τὸν λαὸν αὐτοῦ ὃν προέγνω. ἢ οὐκ οἴδατε ἐν Ἠλίᾳ τί λέγει ἡ γραφή, ὡς ἐντυγχάνει τῷ θεῷ κατὰ τοῦ Ἰσραήλ; Κύριε, τοὺς προφήτας σου ἀπέκτειναν, τὰ θυσιαστήριά σου κατέσκαψαν, κἀγὼ ὑπελείφθην μόνος καὶ ζητοῦσιν τὴν ψυχήν μου). God's character, as it is revealed in Scripture, shows him to have an unwavering commitment to his people Israel despite their own rebellion against him. This is clear from the account of Israel's rebellion against God in the time of Elijah.

Paul now restates his denial in 11:1 and does so in language that alludes even more clearly to 1 Sam 12:22 ("the Lord will not cast away his people" [οὐκ ἀπώσεται κύριος τὸν λαὸν αὐτοῦ]; cf. Ps 94:14 [93:14 LXX]). Paul has changed the tense of the verb from the future to the present to indicate that God's promise not to cast off his people still stands, and he has added the phrase "whom he foreknew [προέγνω]" to emphasize God's prior choice of his people (cf. Rom 11:28–29).[12] The result of all this is an emphatic denial that God has failed to fulfill his promises to Israel, his chosen people (cf. 9:6).

The phrase "do you not know" assumes that Paul's audience knows the OT well (cf. 7:1), well enough to understand that the subsequent references in 11:3–4 bring out in explicit terms what the allusion to 1 Samuel 12:22 had implied. Paul moves forward in the narrative of Israel's history to "the section on Elijah" (ἐν Ἠλίᾳ; cf. Mark 12:26; Luke 20:37; Philo, *Agriculture* 107) where Elijah complains to the Lord that he alone has stood firm in his commitment to the covenant whereas other Israelites have "thrown down your altars, and killed your prophets with the sword" (1 Kgs 19:10, 14).[13] Paul shifts the reference to killing the prophets to the beginning of the quotation and leaves out the reference to the sword probably in order to emphasize the correspondence between what happened in Elijah's time and the persecution of Jesus and the apostles in his own time (cf. Rom 9:32–33; 10:2–3; 1 Thess 2:16).[14]

11:4 But what does the divine reply say to him? "I have left for myself seven thousand men, those who did not bow the knee to Baal" (ἀλλὰ τί λέγει αὐτῷ ὁ χρηματισμός; Κατέλιπον ἐμαυτῷ ἑπτακισχιλίους ἄνδρας, οἵτινες οὐκ ἔκαμψαν γόνυ τῇ Βάαλ). God corrected Elijah's misimpression with the news that he was not, in fact, the only faithful Israelite left. God had graciously preserved a large remnant of seven thousand Israelites who had not been unfaithful to him.

The unusual term "divine reply" (χρηματισμός), which only appears here in the NT, could refer in a context like this either to an authoritative response to some official communication (e.g., 2 Macc 11:17; Josephus, *Ant.* 14.231) or to a message of divine guidance (e.g., 2 Macc 2:4; Artemidorus Daldianus, *Onir.* 1.2 [5]). Here it certainly refers to God's authoritative response to Elijah's despondent complaint (1 Kgs 19:14), but it also refers to the prophetic, oracular quality of that response (1 Kgs 19:15–18).[15]

12. Cf. the use of "foreknow" (προγινώσκω) in Rom 8:29 and the idea of God's "knowledge" of his people in, for example, Hos 11:12 (12:1 LXX: "Now God has come to know [ἔγνω] them, and the holy people shall be called God's"). On this, see BDAG 200–201, s.v. γινώσκω 7. For the connection between this foreknowledge and 11:28–29, see Godet, *Romans*, 392.

13. On the method of citation, see Sanday and Headlam (*Romans*, 310–11) and Cranfield (*Romans*, 2:545–46).

14. See Jewett (*Romans*, 655–56), who relies on Dietrich-Alexander Koch (*Die Schrift als Zeuge des Evangeliums: Untersuchungen zur Verwendung und zum Verständnis der Schrift bei Paulus*, BHT 69 [Tübingen: Mohr Siebeck, 1986], 74).

15. LSJ 2005, s.v. χρηματισμός I.5; Bo Reicke, "χρηματισμός," *TDNT* 9:482; G. H. R. Horsley, ed., *New Documents Illustrating Early Christianity*, vol. 4 (Sydney: Macquarie University, 1987), 176. For the reference in Artemidorus, see Daniel E. Harris-McCoy, *Artemidorus'* Oneirocritica: *Text, Translation, and Commentary* (Oxford: Oxford University Press, 2012), 50.

In its original context, God's response to Elijah simply assumes that Elijah is wrong, that his despondency arises from misinformation, and that God's ongoing plan for his people is far from collapsing. Elijah is to get busy with his work of anointing kings to govern Syria and Israel and with anointing a prophet to succeed Elijah himself when his work is finished. These figures will deal out justice to the apostates within Israel, but, God says, "I will leave seven thousand in Israel, all the knees that have not bowed to Baal, and every mouth that has not kissed him" (1 Kgs 19:18).[16] Paul has shifted the future expression into the past and added the emphatic personal-reflexive pronoun "for myself" (ἐμαυτῷ). As a result, the emphasis falls on God's foreknowledge of who belongs to his people (cf. "whom he foreknew" in 11:2) and the value he places on them as "his people" (11:1, 2). The addition of "for myself" also implies that the seven thousand are God's people because God took the initiative in making them his people (cf. 11:6).[17]

11:5 So, then also, in the present time, a remnant exists by gracious choice (οὕτως οὖν καὶ ἐν τῷ νῦν καιρῷ λεῖμμα κατ᾽ ἐκλογὴν χάριτος γέγονεν). What happened in Elijah's time provides an analogy to what was happening in Paul's time. It might seem to Paul's fictional interlocutor that God's promise always to bless his people has failed because so few Israelites have embraced the gospel. In fact, however, Paul and other Jewish believers form a remnant of faithful Israelites, and this remnant demonstrates by its existence that God's gracious choice of Israel has never been in question.

The phrase "so then" (οὕτως οὖν) introduces the application of an analogy (cf. Matt 6:9; Luke 14:33), and Paul makes it slightly more emphatic by adding "also" (καί). Just as God had retained for himself a remnant of faithful Israelites in Elijah's time, so in Paul's time Paul himself and other Jewish believers form a remnant that demonstrates God's faithfulness to physical Israel.

The phrase "in the present time" (ἐν τῷ νῦν καιρῷ) does not necessarily carry special theological connotations (Gen 29:34; 30:20; Exod 9:14; 2 Cor 8:14), but elsewhere in Romans Paul uses it with one eye on the present advancement of God's saving purposes (3:26; 8:18; cf. 2 Cor 6:2). Here, existence in "the present time" (ἐν τῷ νῦν καιρῷ) of a remnant of Abraham's "offspring" (cf. Rom 9:27, 29; 11:1) demonstrates that God's word of promise to his people has not failed (cf. 9:6–13). In a way that is consistent with the salvation-historical connotations of the phrase in 3:26 and 8:18, however, its occurrence here also implies that the small number presently contained in the remnant is only temporary. It will one day expand to include "all Israel" (11:25), in the same way that "the sufferings of the present time [τοῦ νῦν καιροῦ]" in 8:18 will yield to a glorious existence for God's people.

This present remnant "exists" (γέγονεν) because God chose to be gracious to them: the phrase "by gracious choice" (κατ᾽ ἐκλογὴν χάριτος) has a causal quality to it.[18] God's gracious choice of Paul

Artemidorus (mid-second or early third-century AD) places the "oracle" (χρηματισμός) in the same category as a dream or vision that tells the future. Macrobius (fourth-century AD) defines the term more specifically as the appearance in a vision of some notable person who gives one direction (Harris-McCoy, *Artemidorus'* Oneirocritica, 14, 423, citing Macrobius, *In Somn.* 1.3.8). Although Macrobius's definition comes from a time much later than Paul, it does describe precisely what Elijah experienced when "the Lord passed by" and spoke to him in a "low whisper" (1 Kgs 19:11–12).

16. The Hebrew and the Antiochene revision of the Old Greek text use the future expression "I will leave" (*hisharti*; καταλείψω). The Old Greek has "you will leave" (καταλείψεις), assuming that Elijah is the means through which God will punish the apostates within Israel. On this, see Wagner (*Heralds of the Good News*, 235n60), Jewett (*Romans*, 657), and Légasse (*Romains*, 682, 689n26).

17. Chrysostom, *Romans*, 331; Cranfield, *Romans*, 2:547–48.

18. BDAG 512–13, s.v. κατά 5.a.δ.

and other believing Jews is the reason why this remnant exists. In his greetings at the end of the letter, Paul specifically points out that Andronicus, Junia, Herodion, Lucius, Jason, and Sosipater are his "compatriots" (συγγενεῖς, 16:7, 11, 21; cf. 9:3). He must have taken special encouragement from such fellow Jewish Christians that God had not cast off his people (cf. Col 4:11).

11:6 and if by grace, no longer from works, since grace would no longer be grace (εἰ δὲ χάριτι, οὐκέτι ἐξ ἔργων, ἐπεὶ ἡ χάρις οὐκέτι γίνεται χάρις). God chose Paul and other Jewish believers to form the remnant of his faithful people as a completely free gift to them.

"And" (δέ) joins what Paul has just said about God's "gracious choice" of an Israelite remnant to an important implication of that statement. The gracious nature of God's choice logically implies that nothing these believing Israelites did prompted God to choose them. In Elijah's time, God did not reserve the seven thousand for himself because they refused to "bow the knee to Baal" (as the expression "those who" [οἵτινες] might otherwise imply), nor in Paul's time did God choose a remnant of Israelites because they did anything that prompted him to be gracious to them. Paul's "no longer" (οὐκέτι) is logical rather than temporal as its clear use in a logical way in the second clause reveals.

In 9:11–12 Paul had demonstrated that God was free to choose gentiles as well as Jews to belong to Abraham's family by referring back to God's choice of Jacob rather than Esau apart from their birth order or the character they would develop later in life (their "works"). Paul had shown there that God was not unfaithful to his word (9:6) by exercising his freedom to choose some people rather than others. Here he echoes that sequence of thought, but this time he applies the principle to Israelites rather than to gentiles.

The gracious nature of his choice of an Israelite remnant means that it is a free choice, uncompelled by the "works" of the chosen party. In Paul's thought God is gracious not in the ways so common among human beings—to those who show some moral promise (Seneca, *Ben.* 4.11.1) or have the right family connections (Seneca, *Ben.* 4.31.1–4.32.4)—but freely and unconditionally (cf. Rom 3:24; 4:4).[19]

11:7 What then? That which Israel seeks, this it has not attained; but the chosen have attained it, and the rest were hardened (τί οὖν; ὃ ἐπιζητεῖ Ἰσραήλ, τοῦτο οὐκ ἐπέτυχεν, ἡ δὲ ἐκλογὴ ἐπέτυχεν· οἱ δὲ λοιποὶ ἐπωρώθησαν). Despite the existence of a remnant of Israelite believers, most of Israel continues to seek for righteousness without attaining it. Attaining righteousness is only possible through faith in Christ, and God has made most of Israel ever more resistant to the gospel as a punishment for their rebellion against him.

The rhetorical question "what then?" (τί οὖν) is reminiscent of "what, then, shall we say?" (Τί οὖν ἐροῦμεν;) in 9:30 and introduces a summary of Paul's argument that echoes 9:30–31. Just as the question in 9:30 arose from Paul's argument that God had included only a "remnant" (ὑπόλειμμα) of physical Israel among his vessels of mercy prepared for glory (9:27–29), so here Paul's question grows out of his argument that God's faithfulness to Israel is demonstrated in the "remnant" (λεῖμμα, 11:5) of physical Israel that has trusted the gospel (11:1–6). In a similar way, both here and in 9:30–31, Paul compares those who sought for something but did not attain it with those who did attain it. Since the object of the search in 9:30–31 was "righteousness,"

19. On the whole subject, see Barclay, *Paul and the Gift*.

it is likely that the unnamed object of Israel's search here is also righteousness.

Paul uses a natural pair of verbs for "seeking" (ζητεῖν) and "obtaining" (τυγχάνειν) an object. Epictetus could criticize the person who thinks that happiness depends on being Caesar's friend "because, when he has succeeded in being Caesar's friend, he has none the less failed to get what he was seeking [οὐδὲν ἧττον τοῦ ζητουμένου οὐ τέτευχεν]."[20] Paul, however, modifies these two verbs slightly with a prefixed preposition (ἐπί), a move that, in this case, "seems to fix the verb upon a definite object."[21] If so, then the nuance of the two verbs may be that the very thing Israel sought—righteousness—they did not attain, a clear echo of the tragedy expressed in 9:31 and 10:2. Israel "seeks" (ἐπιζητεῖ) the right goal but has not attained it.

"The chosen" (ἡ . . . ἐκλογή), Paul says, attained it instead. Paul normally uses this noun in an active sense to refer to God's sovereignty in selecting certain individuals to belong to his people (9:11; 11:5; cf. 11:28).[22] Here, however, he uses it in a passive sense, and the emphasis falls on the nature of the group as the chosen subset of a larger body.[23] Within the context of 11:1–10 where Paul is concerned with physical Israel, both the larger body and the "chosen" subset must refer to physical Israelites. The "chosen," then, are not the multiethnic people of God whether Jewish or gentile but a small group of Jewish Christians whom God chose for salvation from his wrath against sin.

In contrast (δέ) to "the chosen" among Israel who have believed the gospel and attained righteousness are "the rest" (οἱ . . . λοιποί) whom God "has hardened" (ἐπωρώθησαν). Paul was probably thinking here of the early Christian teaching that "hardness" (πώρωσις) of heart prompted some Jewish leaders to plot Jesus's death (Mark 3:5–6), and the further teaching that just as in the time of Isaiah, God had "hardened [ἐπωρώσεν] their heart" as a punishment for their rebellion against him (John 12:40; cf. Isa 6:10).[24]

Although Paul uses a different verb here than he did in 9:18 (where the verb is σκληρύνω), the idea is similar. Behind the passive voice "were hardened" (ἐπωρώθησαν) lies the punishing action of God who has hardened the rest because of their rebellion against him.[25] The difference between God's judicial hardening of Pharaoh in Romans 9:18 and his judicial hardening of Israel here is that the hardening of Pharaoh clearly implies that God sometimes hardens individuals in their sin and in such a way that they do not recover from it, whereas here, Paul describes the hardening of a group (unbelieving Israel), but in such a way that the hardening may, at some point, be removed (cf. 11:25).[26]

20. Epictetus, *Diatr.* 4.1.45 (trans. W. A. Oldfather, *Epictetus: Discourses, Books 3–4, Fragments, the Encheiridion*, LCL [Cambridge: Harvard University Press, 1928]).

21. J. Armitage Robinson, *St. Paul's Epistle to the Ephesians*, 2nd ed. (London: Macmillan, 1904), 249. Cf. Davies and Allison, *Matthew*, 1:658, and Meyer, *Romans*, 431.

22. BDAG 306, s.v. ἐκλογή 1.

23. For the translation "the chosen," see Jewett (*Romans*, 650, 661). Cf. Polybius, *Hist.* 1.47.9 where the historian attributes a military loss to "the selection of men" (διὰ τὴν ἐκλογὴν τῶν ἀνδρῶν) in the enemy's ranks. This "selection" was a specially chosen group of elite, particularly capable soldiers (*Hist.* 1.47.9). See BDAG 306, s.v. ἐκλογή 2.

24. John's "hardened" (ἐπωρώσεν) stands in place of "grown fat" (ἐπαχύνθη) in Isa 6:10 LXX (cf. Matt 13:15; Acts 28:27) and probably represents an independent translation of the underlying Hebrew term (*hashmen*). On this, see Wagner (*Heralds of the Good News*, 244–52). On the interplay between divine sovereignty and human responsibility as it appears in Isa 6:10, see Young, *Isaiah*, 1:259–61.

25. Cf. Origen, *Romans, Books 6–10*, 160; Sandy and Headlam, *Romans*, 313.

26. Kruse, *Romans*, 425.

11:8 Just as it is written, "God gave them a spirit of stupor, eyes that do not see and ears that do not hear until this very day" (καθὼς γέγραπται, Ἔδωκεν αὐτοῖς ὁ θεὸς πνεῦμα κατανύξεως, ὀφθαλμοὺς τοῦ μὴ βλέπειν καὶ ὦτα τοῦ μὴ ἀκούειν, ἕως τῆς σήμερον ἡμέρας). God's action of punishing those who reject him by making them insensible to his revelation of himself is not unprecedented. God worked this way with the disobedient among his people in the time of Isaiah.

Paul provides precedent from Scripture for God's punishment of his people by blocking their ability to understand his revelation of himself. His quotation comes basically from Deuteronomy 29:4 (29:3 LXX), but with a phrase added from Isaiah 29:10 LXX ("a spirit of stupor" [πνεύμα{τι} κατανύξεως]) and a few other minor changes. The changes have the effect of emphasizing God's initiative in causing the insensibility of unbelieving Israel to the gospel. Whereas in Deuteronomy God passively does not give Israel a heart to know, eyes to see, and ears to hear, Paul portrays God as actively giving to Israel "a spirit of stupor," which is further defined in terms of God giving them eyes that do not see and ears that do not hear.[27]

Paul's "to this present day" (ἕως τῆς σήμερον ἡμέρας) stands in place of the LXX's "to this day" (ἕως τῆς ἡμέρας ταύτης), and although the two phrases mean virtually the same thing, Paul's slight change probably signals his conviction that the condition Deuteronomy and Isaiah describe continued into his own time and accounted for the resistance of unbelieving Israel to the gospel.[28] Just as within the wider context of Deuteronomy 29:4 (29:3 LXX) and Isaiah 29:10 (i.e., Deut 30:1–10; Isa 29:17–24), however, God's judgment on recalcitrant Israel is not his last word to them. The hardness that characterizes unbelieving Israel in the present serves God's merciful purposes of extending the gospel to the gentiles, and when the full number of gentiles has entered God's people, then "all Israel" will also be saved (11:25–26).[29]

11:9–10 And David says, "Let their table become a bird trap and a net and a stumbling block and a repayment to them. Let their eyes be darkened that they may not see and bend their back continually" (καὶ Δαυὶδ λέγει, Γενηθήτω ἡ τράπεζα αὐτῶν εἰς παγίδα καὶ εἰς θήραν καὶ εἰς σκάνδαλον καὶ εἰς ἀνταπόδομα αὐτοῖς, σκοτισθήτωσαν οἱ ὀφθαλμοὶ αὐτῶν τοῦ μὴ βλέπειν καὶ τὸν νῶτον αὐτῶν διὰ παντὸς σύγκαμψον). David, in the Psalms, also demonstrates that God sometimes punishes the disobedient among his people by blinding them to the danger of their sin. Israel's rejection of Jesus was as unjust as the mistreatment of David at the hands of his enemies.

Paul identifies his next quotation with "and David says," hinting that he has the personal setting of the psalm in mind. Psalm 69 (68 LXX) is an "individual lament" in which the psalmist appeals to God out of the distress that "those who hate" him "without cause" have created for him (69:4 [68:5 LXX; 69:5 Heb.]).[30] Although the psalmist is certainly not perfect (69:5 [68:6 LXX; 69:6 Heb.), in the present case he is not only innocent of wrongdoing but is persecuted because "zeal for" God's "house has consumed" him (69:9a [68:10a LXX; 69:10a Heb.]), and the "reproaches of those who reproach" God "have fallen on" him (69:9b [68:10b

27. Paul's use of the infinitive with the genitive article (whereas the LXX has the simple infinitive) may strengthen the idea of God's purpose (cf. "let their eyes be darkened that they may not see" [σκοτισθήτωσαν οἱ ὀφθαλμοὶ αὐτῶν τοῦ μὴ βλέπειν] in Rom 11:10). See BDF §400, especially 400(2).

28. For the virtually identical meaning of the two phrases, compare the underlying Hebrew of Gen 19:37–38 and Gen 26:33 with the LXX rendering of these passages.

29. Cranfield, *Romans*, 2:550; Wagner, *Heralds of the Good News*, 252–57.

30. Ross, *Psalms*, 2:488.

LXX; 69:10b Heb.]). This reproach has made him miserable. People who should have offered him comfort instead gave him "poison for food" and "sour wine to drink" (69:20–21 [68:21–22 LXX; 69:21–22 Heb.]).

In light of all this, he appeals to God to punish his enemies. Just as their treachery was like comforting someone with poison food and sour wine, so he asks God, as just recompense (εἰς ἀνταπόδοσιν), to make their own table "a trap" (εἰς παγίδα) and "a stumbling block" (εἰς σκάνδαλον) and to darken their eyes and bend their backs continually (69:22–23 NETS [68:23–24 LXX; 69:23–24 Heb.]).[31]

Paul's quotation comes from this appeal of the Psalmist to God against his enemies with a few small changes. The significance of some of these changes is not clear, but the importance of others is more certain.[32] His addition of the term "net" (θήραν) probably comes from Ps 35:8 (34:8 LXX), which uses this term in the same highly unusual way and in a psalm of David that is also an individual lament with imprecations against those who have dealt unjustly with the psalmist.[33] These connections between Psalm 35 (34 LXX), Psalm 69 (68 LXX), and Romans 11:8 make it that much more likely that Paul was thinking of the broader context of Psalm 69:23 (68:23 LXX; 69:22 Heb.) when he quoted it.[34]

In addition, Paul places "stumbling block" (εἰς σκάνδαλον) before "repayment" (εἰς ἀνταπόδομα), and this reverses the order of the two terms in Psalm 69:23 (68:23 LXX; 69:22 Heb.) This reversal may have originated in Paul's interest in the expression "a rock of offense" (πέτραν σκανδάλου) as a description of the reason why unbelieving Israel did not submit to God's righteousness (9:32–33).[35] If so, then Paul hints here that the stumbling of Israel over Jesus, and especially his approach to the Mosaic law, was part of God's judgment against them. Their blindness with respect to the gospel, expressed in 11:10 in terms of darkened eyes and a stooped posture (which keeps their gaze on the ground), then, is part of God's judgment. Although this judgment in Paul's time was continual (διά παντός), it was not permanent, as Paul will make clear in the next section of his argument (11:11–32).

What suggested Psalm 69 to Paul at this point in his argument? Paul's use of the psalm in Romans 15:3 to refer to Jesus's rejection and death (cf. 69:9 [68:10 LXX; 69:10 Heb.]) shows that like other early Christians, he believed the experience David described in the psalm paralleled in significant ways Jesus's experience of rejection (cf. John 2:17; 15:25; Acts 1:20). Here, then, Paul probably thought of the words of the psalm as expressing Jesus's own pronouncement of judgment on those who had rejected and punished him unjustly.

31. The NETS translates "continually" (διὰ παντός) with "permanently," but the phrase is more likely to mean "continually" (e.g., Matt 18:10; Mark 5:5; Luke 24:53). See BDAG 224, s.v. διά 2.a.

32. Paul drops "before them" (ἐνώπιον αὐτῶν) from the Psalm and adds "to them" (αὐτοῖς). He also changes the ending on the term "retribution" (ἀνταπόδοσιν, literally "a requiting") to make it the slightly more concrete term "repayment" (ἀνταπόδομα; LSJ 150). On all this, see Wagner, *Heralds of the Good News*, 257–59.

33. The term (θήρα) almost always means "hunt" or "prey" elsewhere, but clearly means "net" in Ps 34:8, where it renders the Hebrew term for "net" (*reshet*) and stands parallel to "snare" (παγίδι). See LSJ 799, s.v. θήρα; LSJSupp 151, s.v. θήρα; LEH 275, s.v. θήρα. On the form and setting of the psalm, see Ross, *Psalms*, 1:763–64.

34. Cf. Wagner, *Heralds of the Good News*, 259–61.

35. Cf. Wagner, *Heralds of the Good News*, 262–65.

Theology in Application

In 11:1–10 Paul explains again why he believes God has not rejected his people but remains faithful to his promises to them. His explanation raises the question of how the church can work to preserve the Jewish identity of Jewish Christians, and it also reminds Paul's readers, and the church of every age, not to presume that God will always refrain from judgment.

The Jewish Christian Community as Evidence That God Is Faithful

Paul begins this paragraph in 11:1–6 with a caution to his audience not to conclude on the basis of 9:30–10:21 that because Israel has rejected God, God has also rejected them (11:1). They do not experience salvation apart from faith in Christ, as Paul has just made clear and as he will repeat in 11:7–10.[36] But they are, nevertheless, God's "people whom he foreknew" (11:2). This reference to God's foreknowledge of his people recalls the chain of reasoning in 8:29–30 where Paul describes God's faithfulness to those who have believed the gospel and in whom God's Spirit is at work. For this reason, sweeping statements to the effect that "the community of believers has in all respects replaced carnal, national Israel" need to be carefully qualified.[37] That God had preserved a remnant of Israelites who believed the gospel in the present and that in the future many more Israelites would be saved were theologically necessary convictions for Paul.[38] These convictions provided critical evidence for Paul's claim in 9:6a that God's word had not failed.

Paul did not think that Jewish Christians formed a separate people of God in addition to gentile Christians, but he nevertheless believed that within the one church of Jews and gentiles, the continuing identity of Jews as Jews was an important witness to God's faithfulness. Explaining this is the primary point of 11:1b–6: Paul himself was a Jewish believer, and just as in Elijah's time, more Jewish believers existed in Paul's time than might at first be apparent. God has not been unfaithful to physical Israel in the present, Paul argues, any more than he was unfaithful to physical Israel in the time of Elijah.

Similarly, in Romans 15:7–13 Paul envisions a future in which Christian Jews will see the promises to the patriarchs confirmed as they praise God "among the gentiles," and gentiles, under the righteous rule of David's descendent Jesus Christ, will praise God for his mercy to them.[39] Paul believed that God would continue to work through Israel in salvation history even as he showed mercy to all his human

36. See the definitive case for this conclusion in Das, *Paul and the Jews*, 78–113.

37. Bavinck, *Holy Spirit, Church, and New Creation*, 667; cf. 279.

38. As Bavinck agrees (ibid., 671).

39. Scott J. Hafemann, "The Redemption of Israel for the Sake of the Gentiles," in *Introduction to Messianic Judaism: Its Ecclesial Context and Biblical Foundations*, ed. David Rudolph and Joel Willitts (Grand Rapids: Zondervan, 2013), 206–13.

creation. Neither Jew nor gentile is subordinate to the other, but Paul acknowledges their separate roles in God's saving plan. It is a vision that Paul repeats in Ephesians 2:11–3:10 where both Jewish and gentile believers are critical to the mission of the church as it proclaims to the inimical forces of the universe "the wisdom of God in its rich variety" (3:10 NRSV).

Jewish Christians within a Predominantly Gentile Church

How is it possible for Jewish people who embrace the gospel to maintain their Jewish identity within the predominantly gentile Christian church? This question has been a matter of considerable debate both in ancient and more recent times. In places where Judaism was numerically strong in antiquity, Jewish Christians often made efforts to keep the Mosaic law and to maintain ties with the Temple and with synagogues. Those efforts frequently led to theological mistakes and social tensions. Jewish Christians sometimes tried to compel gentile Christians to adopt Jewish practices (Acts 15:1, 5; Gal 2:3–5, 14; 6:12; cf. Titus 1:10), and unbelieving Jews sometimes disciplined Jewish Christians because of their Christian beliefs or expelled them from participation in the Jewish community (John 9:22, 35; 16:2; Acts 26:11; 2 Cor 11:24).

On the gentile side, as Romans itself shows, gentile Christians could develop haughty attitudes toward Jews that needed apostolic correction (Rom 11:18). In later centuries this sort of thinking seems to have aided the intellectual elites who from the early second century onward developed a polemic against the Jews as Jews in order to rein in Christian fascination with the synagogue.[40] The hysterical slander in John Chrysostom's eight sermons *Against the Jews*, for example, seems to assume that friendly relations between Christians and Jews were the inevitable precursor to apostasy.[41] This lamentable tradition demonstrates that despite the negative attitudes of certain Christian leaders toward Judaism, Christians continued to attend synagogues and to turn out for Jewish festivals into the Middle Ages.[42] In this complicated social environment, it is probably safe to assume that some Christians were also Jews and continued to practice elements of Judaism after their conversions.

In more recent times, a movement has gained popularity among some Christians that rejects the tendency to view Christianity and Judaism as separate, unrelated religions and encourages Jewish Christians to remain identifiably Jewish. Exactly how to do this is not clear. Some Christians advocate the establishment of separate Jewish congregations that Jewish Christians should join in order to maintain loyalty

40. Paula Fredriksen, "What 'Parting of the Ways'? Jews, Gentiles, and the Ancient Mediterranean City," in *The Ways that Never Parted: Jews and Christians in Late Antiquity and the Early Middle Ages*, ed. Adam H. Becker and Annette Yoshiko Reed (Minneapolis: Fortress, 2007), 35–63.

41. See, e.g., Saint John Chrysostom, *Discourses Against Judaizing Christians*, trans. Paul W. Harkins, FC 68 (Washington, DC: Catholic University of America Press, 1979), 15–18, 30 (1.4.3–10; 1.7.9).

42. Fredriksen, "What 'Parting of the Ways'?" 60n79, 62.

both to the Mosaic law and faith in Jesus as Messiah.[43] Other Christians respond that the New Testament never envisions Jewish Christians and gentile Christians going their separate ways in corporate worship, however friendly the parting might be.[44]

In light of Ephesians 2:11–3:10, it is difficult to imagine Paul approving of the intentional separation of the worshiping church in a given location into culturally homogenous units. The cross of Christ has destroyed the wall that divides Jews from gentiles, and Christ is now the cornerstone of a temple whose members, whether Jewish or gentile, are tightly joined together to form the temple's structure. In Romans 14:1–15:6 Paul encourages gentile and Jewish believers in Rome to be tolerant of each other's distinctive observances (or lack thereof) and to glorify God "with one heart and voice" (ὁμοθυμαδὸν ἐν ἑνὶ στόματι δοξάζητε, 15:6). This struggle to maintain unity seems to assume that Jewish and gentile Christians are meeting together and should work hard at the give-and-take necessary for maintaining their unity despite their different customs and convictions.

It is equally clear, however, that Paul would not have approved of Christians who considered themselves free from the law imposing their freedoms on others. Paul did not require Jewish Christians to abandon their ancestral customs in order to become Christians (Acts 21:20–26; Rom 4:11; 14:1–15:6; cf. 1 Cor 9:20). That would have been a reverse form of the Judaizing error Paul encountered in Galatia.[45] At a minimum, it seems that Christian churches should demonstrate in their teaching that they value the Old Testament as of equal canonical authority with the New Testament and should find ways to affirm and accommodate Jewish Christians in their midst who wish to observe Jewish dietary customs and festivals (Rom 14:5–6, 23; 15:1, 7). They should also cultivate friendly relations and mutual understanding with unbelieving Jewish neighbors.[46]

A Warning Not to Presume upon God's Mercy

Romans 11:1–10 not only affirms the theological importance of the Jewish-Christian remnant but also comments in sobering terms on the blindness that God can give to people who continue to rebel against him (11:7–10). Paul speaks in this passage of Jewish unbelievers who have heard, understood, and rejected the gospel, but the same principle informs Paul's description of God's judgment of all humanity in 1:24, 26, and 28. There God hands recalcitrant sinners over to their "lusts," "passions," and a "worthless mind."

43. Mark S. Kinzer, *Post-Missionary Messianic Judaism: Redefining Christian Engagement with the Jewish People* (Grand Rapids: Brazos, 2005), 151–79.

44. Eckhard J. Schnabel, "The Identity and the Mission of Believers in Jesus Messiah," *Mishkan: A Forum on the Gospel and the Jewish People* 48 (2006): 42–47.

45. Craig Keener, "Interdependence and Mutual Blessing in the Church," in Rudolph and Willitts, *Messianic Judaism*, 190.

46. Cf. William S. Campbell, "The Relationship between Israel and the Church," in Rudolph and Willitts, *Messianic Judaism*, 202.

In all these cases, God has revealed himself clearly to people who know full well that he is God and what he requires of them, but they willfully reject his authority. In Romans Paul portrays God as kind, gracious, merciful, and patient with those who oppose him. He delays showing his wrath in order to give people time to change their minds about him, and he takes the initiative in reconciling his enemies to himself at great cost to himself. Eventually, however, judgment comes, and it often comes in the form of God veiling the truth from those who would benefit from it but who continue to reject him. He gives them "a spirit of stupor, eyes that do not see, and ears that do not hear" (11:8). All who hear and understand the gospel but do not accept it stand in danger of this form of God's judgment.

Those who think of themselves as Christians, however, also need to pay attention to Paul's implicit warning here against a hard heart. A few paragraphs further down in chapter eleven, Paul will encourage gentile Christians in his audience in Rome not to become arrogant when they consider that many Jews have rejected the gospel but they have accepted it. Now, it may seem, gentile believers have taken the place within God's people that Jewish unbelievers would have occupied (11:18–20). This sort of pride, however, is so incompatible with the gospel of God's grace that Paul suggests those who display it may not continue to experience God's kindness but instead find themselves outside God's people after all (11:22). An attitude of self-satisfied pride at membership within God's people may be symptomatic of a heart that God is hardening in judgment.

The hardening Paul describes in 11:7–10, as we have seen in the comments on that passage, is different than God's hardening of Pharaoh in 9:18. The hardening of Pharaoh was a final judgment from which there was no recovery, but the hardening of 11:7–10 has not yet arrived at that point. Some of the hardened in 11:7–10 would eventually be among "all Israel" that God will save in the end (11:26). Those who realize they have become unresponsive, disobedient, and even opposed to God still have time to turn from their rebellion to the God whose arms remain outstretched to them "all day long" (10:21).

CHAPTER 23

Romans 11:11–36

Literary Context

Paul now brings the complex argument of Romans 9–11 to a conclusion. He began with an emotional description of his personal sorrow that so many of his fellow Israelites had not believed the gospel (9:1–5). In 9:6–29 he explained that the exclusion of physical Israelites from God's people did not mean the failure of God's word (9:6). Rather, God's word indicates that he is sovereign over the boundaries of his people, and that contrary to what one might expect, not all his children are physical children of Abraham (9:7). Throughout biblical history, God has made surprising choices about who would belong to his people, and the surprising success of the gospel among gentiles and its rejection among Jews continue this pattern (9:7b–24). Paul had ended that passage with quotations from Hosea and Isaiah that affirmed both the overall point he was making about God's acceptance of gentiles and sounded a note of hope that a remnant of Abraham's seed would be saved (9:25–29).

Rather than explore that note of hope more fully in his next step, Paul explained in greater detail the topic of the rejection of the gospel among the majority of Israelites who had heard it. If this situation reflects God's sovereign choice, Paul argues, it also reflects Israel's disobedience and opposition to God (9:30–10:21). Here the focus shifts from God to Israel.[1] Paul explains that Israel has no excuse for failing to believe the gospel. The gospel is easy to obey (9:30–10:13) and has been widely and clearly proclaimed to Israel (10:14–21). Instead of believing and confessing the gospel when they heard its message, however, Israel refused to submit to God's offer of righteousness through the atoning death of Christ and pursued righteousness in their own way. They failed to see that zealous obedience to God should have ended with faith in Christ (9:30–10:4). Although this picture is bleak, just as with 9:6–29, it contains a hopeful note, expressed at the end. God's hands remain outstretched to his disobedient and oppositional people (10:21).

Paul brings the argument of chapters 9–11 to a conclusion by picking up this element of hope and explaining that it is not misplaced. Using a rhetorical question,

1. Aletti, *God's Justice in Romans*, 167–68.

he states the thesis that will occupy him in 11:1b–32: despite their rejection of the gospel, God has not cast off his people (11:1a; cf. 11:2a). He pursues this thesis in two parts. First, he argues in 11:1b–10 that God's faithfulness to his word has already been demonstrated in the remnant of Israelite Christians who have believed the gospel (cf. 9:27–29). Second, he reveals in 11:11–32 that even the rest of Israel, who were hardened, will experience God's acceptance and salvation in full numbers (11:12, 15, 25–26).

This second part of 11:1–32 (11:11–32) does not merely assert that hardened Israel will one day be saved but explains why, from God's perspective, so many within Israel opposed the gospel in the first place (9:30–10:21). This was part of a complex plan of God to enclose "all people within disobedience in order that he might have mercy upon all people" (11:32). God used "disobedient" (ἀπειθοῦντα) Israel (10:21; 11:30–31) to shift the focus of the gospel's proclamation to non-Israelite people groups. This shift in focus, however, will eventually benefit Israel. As Israel sees gentiles receiving the blessings meant for them, they will emulate the gentile's faith and receive God's mercy also. In the future, vast numbers of Israelites will be saved, and God will stand vindicated as both impartial in his dealings with all humanity and yet faithful to his promises to Israel. In 11:11–32, then, Paul completes his answer to the question he raised in 9:6 about the failure of the word of God by placing God's faithfulness to Israel on a firm footing. Anyone who might doubt the credibility of Paul's claim that nothing in all creation can separate the people of God from the love of God (8:39) should be confident that when history is finished, God will be found faithful to Israel.

The power and wisdom of God, evident in his guidance of history to accomplish his saving purposes for both Israel and the gentiles, led Paul to a final expression of astonishment that ends in praise to God (11:33–36). This awestruck description of God's greatness answers the mournful lament with which chapter 9–11 began (9:1–5). The sorrow that characterized Paul in 9:1–5 was still an appropriate expression of his sadness at his experience of the resistance of so many within Israel to the gospel. The high note of praise on which the argument ends, however, affirms that God is able to use even Israel's rebellion against him for his merciful intention to save vast numbers of Israelites.

The argument of 11:11–36 also plays an important role in preparing for Paul's instruction in the next section (12:1–15:13). The humility that Paul urges the Roman Christians to exercise toward one another, and the surprising mercy that he wants them to show toward unbelievers who would harm them, find their theological foundation in the actions of God in 11:11–32. God has been patient and generous with both Jews and gentiles who were in rebellion against him (11:22–23, 32). This action on God's part requires his people, similarly, not to repay evil with evil but to bless those who persecute them (12:14–21). It also requires them not to be haughty (12:3,

16) or to sit in judgment on other Christians but to welcome them on behalf of God, who has welcomed every believer in Christ (14:3–4, 10–13, 18–19; 15:1–7).

IX. Justification by Faith Brings Peace and Reorients the Believer's Existence (5:1–8:39)
X. Israel's Present Rejection of the Gospel Does Not Imply the Failure of God's Word (9:1–11:36)
A. Paul's Anguish over Israel's Rejection of the Gospel (9:1–5)
B. The Scriptures Describe God's Choice of His People as Free and Surprising (9:6–29)
C. Unbelieving Israel Is Culpable for Rejecting the Gospel (9:30–10:21)
D. Still, God Has Not Cast Off His People (11:1–32)
1. Paul States His Thesis (11:1a)
2. God Has Graciously Chosen a Remnant within Israel (11:1b–10)
➡ **3. Eventually, Many Israelites Will Be Saved (11:11–32)**
E. A Concluding Statement of Astonishment and Praise (11:33–36)
XI. Exhortation to Live in a Way That Is Consistent with the Gospel (12:1–15:13)

Main Idea

The rejection of the gospel among many Israelites does not mean that God's promise to bless all Israel has failed. The present situation in which Israelite believers are a remnant within Israel and gentile Christians are growing in number will one day change. Once the number of gentiles within the people of God has reached its climax, many Israelite unbelievers will see the blessings that have come to the gentiles and seek to emulate their faith in the gospel. In the end, vast numbers of both gentiles and Israelites will populate the people of God in an amazing display of God's power and wisdom.

Translation

(See pages 528–31.)

Structure

Just as with the previous section (11:1–10), Paul begins this new section with a thesis statement formulated as a rhetorical question (11:11; cf. 11:1). He can say that God has not cast off his people not only because a remnant of believers currently exists (11:1–10) but because even the part of Israel that has stumbled over the gospel has not fallen irretrievably (11:11).

Romans 11:11–36

11a	Rhetorical Question	**I say, then, they did not stumble so as to fall did they?**
b	Exclamation	**Certainly not!**
c	Means	Rather, by their trespass
	Contrast (to 11a)	**salvation has come to the gentiles,**
d	Purpose (of 11c)	in order to provoke the rest of Israel to jealousy.
12a	Restatement (of 11c)	Now if their transgression is wealth for the world and
b	Restatement (of 11c)	their defeat is wealth for the gentiles,
c	Inference (from 11a–c)	**how much more their fullness!**
13a	Assertion	Now **to you gentiles I speak.**
b	Condition (of 13c)	To the degree that I am an apostle to the gentiles,
c	Assertion	**I glorify my ministry**
14	Basis (for 13c)	in the hope that perhaps I might somehow provoke my kinfolk to emulation and save some of them.
15	Basis (for 14)	For if their casting away is the reconciliation of the world, **what will their acceptance be except life from the dead?**
16a	Restatement (of 15)	And if the first fruit is holy, **the dough is also.**
b	Introduction (to 17–24)	And if the root is holy, **the branches are also.**
17a	Contrast (to 16b) Condition (of 18a)	But if some of the branches have been broken off, and
b	Contra-expectation	you, although a wild olive branch, have been grafted in among them and
c	Condition (of 18a)	have become a sharer of the oiliness of the root of the olive tree …
18a	Exhortation	**Do not boast over the branches.**

b	Warning	But if you boast … **you do not support the root,** but the root you.
19a	Assertion	**You will say, then,** “Branches were broken off
b	Purpose (of 19a)	that I might be grafted in.”
20a	Assertion	Very well. **They were broken off** because of unbelief,
b	Contrast	and **you stand because of faith.**
c	Exhortation	**Do not think haughty things,** but **fear.**
21	Basis (for 20c)	For if God did not spare the natural branches, perhaps **he will not spare you either.**
22a	Exhortation	**Note** then the kindness and strictness of God:
b	Explanation (of 22a)	toward those who fell, strictness,
c	Contrast (with 22b)	but toward you, the kindness of God
	Condition (of 22c)	—if you remain within that kindness,
d	Warning	since otherwise you will be cut off.
23a	Assertion	And **those** too, if they do not remain in their unbelief, **will be grafted in,**
b	Basis (of 23a)	for **God is able to graft them in again.**
24a	Explanation (of 23b)	For if you were, according to your nature, cut from a wild olive tree and contrary to nature were grafted into a cultivated olive tree,
b	Inference (from 24a)	how much more **will these, the natural branches, be grafted** into their own tree.

Continued on next page.

Continued from previous page.

25a	Explanation (of 24b)	For **I do not want you to be ignorant,** brothers and sisters, about this mystery
b	Purpose (of 25a)	so that you might not be wise in your own estimation:
c	Content (of 25a)	**a partial hardening has happened**
		to Israel
		until the fullness of the gentiles should come in.
26a	Means/Sequence	And so, **all Israel will be saved,**
26b–27	Verification (of 26a)	just as **it is written,**
		“The deliverer will come from Zion;
		he will turn impiety away from Jacob;
		and this will be my covenant with them (Isa 59:20–21a)
		when I do away with their sins.” (Isa 27:9a)
28a	Summary (of 11–27)	According to the gospel,
b	Assertion	**they are enemies**
c	Cause	because of you,
d	Contrast	but according to election
e	Assertion	**they are beloved**
f	Cause	because of the fathers.
29	Basis (for 28)	For **God has no misgivings about his gifts and calling.**
30a	Explanation (of 29)	For just as you once disobeyed God,
b	Contrast (to 30a)	but **now you were shown mercy**
c	Cause	because of the disobedience of these,
31a	Inference (from 30)	so also **these disobeyed now**
b	Cause	because of the mercy shown to you
c	Purpose (of 31a)	in order that they also might now be shown mercy.
32a	Summary (of 30–31)	For **God has enclosed all people within disobedience**
b	Purpose of 32a	in order that he might have mercy upon all people.

33a	Exclamation	**How deep is the wealth and wisdom and knowledge of God!**
b	Exclamation	**How undiscoverable his judgments** and **untraceable his ways!**
34a	Rhetorical Question	For, "Who has known the mind of the Lord?
b	Rhetorical Question	Or who has become his adviser?" (Isa 40:13)
35	Rhetorical Question	Or "who has advanced him a sum and will be repaid by him?" (Job 41:11)
36a	Basis (for 35)	Because **all things are from him** and
b	Agency	**through him and**
c	Advantage	**for him.**
d	Exclamation	**Glory belongs to him** as age gives way to age.
e	Conclusion	**Amen.**

After announcing his thesis, Paul briefly and allusively explains it, setting down the parameters of the discussion before filling in the details (11:11–16). The stumbling of Israel served God's purpose of focusing the gospel on the gentiles, but this would, in its turn, result in Israel's "fullness," in God's "acceptance" of them, and in the end "wealth, "reconciliation," and "life" for the world (11:11–16). Paul inserts into this brief and allusive statement of his thesis a reference to his own role in these significant events. He is an apostle to the gentiles, and so God is using him indirectly and partially to accomplish these salutary results for hardened Israel (11:13–14).

The allegory of the olive tree in the next section (11:16b–24) not only emphasizes the overall theme of God's unwillingness to give up on Israel despite their unbelief (11:23–24) but issues a pastoral admonition directed to the predominantly gentile Christians in Rome (11:17–22). The reason for Paul's reference to his role as an apostle to the gentiles in the introductory section (11:13–14) now becomes clear. It laid the groundwork for the admonition in this section by reminding Paul's readers of his authority to give it. Shifting into the second-person singular form that he had used earlier with a fictional unbelieving interlocutor who was Jewish (2:1–29; 9:19–20), Paul now argues with a fictional believer who is a gentile. He establishes with this gentile believer the same point that he had established at the beginning of the letter with his Jewish unbeliever (2:1–29). God shows no partiality, and authentic membership within his people comes by trust in his generosity, not through privileges won by associating with a certain social group.

Paul next says clearly what he had referred to allusively in the previous two sections (11:25–27). Unbelieving Israel will be saved after the gentiles have reached their full number and prior to the return of "the deliverer," Christ Jesus. Paul has already clarified how this will happen. Israelites will emulate the acceptance of the gospel among gentile believers in order to receive the same blessings they have received (11:11, 14–15; cf. 10:19).

Paul's next section (11:28–32) recapitulates the argument of 11:11–27 and ends with a statement that summarizes the argument of the entire letter to this point (11:32). God has planned history to accomplish his merciful purpose of salvation for both Jews and gentiles.

The concluding statement of astonishment and praise (11:33–36) looks back over the argument from 9:1–11:32 and expresses amazement at the power and wisdom of God to which it bears witness. God has accomplished his purposes in surprising ways. He has included gentiles among his people to the surprise of the Jews, and in the end he will include vast numbers of Israelites within his people to the surprise of some gentile Christians. Despite these surprises of mercy, he has remained faithful to his promises and to his righteous character.

Exegetical Outline

- X. Israel's Present Rejection of the Gospel Does Not Imply the Failure of God's Word (9:1–11:36)
  - A. Paul's Anguish over Israel's Rejection of the Gospel (9:1–5)
  - B. The Scriptures Describe God's Choice of His People as Free and Surprising (9:6–29)
  - C. Unbelieving Israel Is Culpable for Rejecting the Gospel (9:30–10:21)
  - **D. Still, God Has Not Cast Off His People (11:1–32)**
    - 1. Paul States His Thesis (11:1a)
    - 2. God Has Graciously Chosen a Remnant within Israel (11:1b–10)
    - ➦ **3. Eventually, Many Israelites Will Be Saved (11:11–32)**
      - a. Paul's thesis: Israel's present disobedience to the gospel is not permanent (11:11)
      - b. Paul's thesis allusively summarized: Israelite rejection leads to gentile salvation and, in time, Israelite salvation (11:11–16a)
      - c. An allegorical admonition directed at gentile Christians and advancing Paul's thesis (11:16b–24)
      - d. Paul's thesis clearly stated: in time, all Israel will be saved (11:25–27)
      - e. A summary of 11:11–27 and of 1:18–11:31 (11:28–32)
  - **E. A Concluding Statement of Astonishment and Praise (11:33–36)**

Explanation of the Text

11:11 I say, then, they did not stumble so as to fall did they? Certainly not! Rather, by their trespass salvation has come to the gentiles, in order to provoke the rest of Israel to jealousy (Λέγω οὖν, μὴ ἔπταισαν ἵνα πέσωσιν; μὴ γένοιτο· ἀλλὰ τῷ αὐτῶν παραπτώματι ἡ σωτηρία τοῖς ἔθνεσιν εἰς τὸ παραζηλῶσαι αὐτούς). Even the large group of Israelites who have heard and rejected the gospel have not been left out of God's saving purposes. Their refusal to believe in the present has focused Paul's immediate efforts on the gentiles, but as gentiles participate in God's newly reconfigured people, Israelite unbelievers, in their zeal for God, will want to participate also.

"I say, then" (λέγω οὖν) recalls the same phrase in 11:1. Just as in 11:1, here it introduces Paul's rejection of a false inference from the bleak picture he has just painted of Israel's rejection of the gospel. In 11:1 this rhetorical pattern expresses the overall thesis of 11:1–32 that God has not cast off his people. Here it expresses the corollary truth that God's hardening of part of Israel is temporary (11:7).

"Stumbling" (πταίω) was common imagery for making a mistake (Plato, *Theaet.* 160d) or for sinning (Deut 7:25 LXX; Jas 2:10; 3:2; Arrian, *Anab.* 4.9.6), and the metaphorical element in the imagery was still alive in Paul's time.[2] A popular adage, for example, urged people not to "stumble [πταίειν] twice on the same stone [λίθον]," meaning that one should learn from one's mistakes (Polybius, *Hist.* 31.11.5 [Jeffrey Henderson, LCL]).[3] Since Paul has already presented the rejection of

2. BDAG 894, s.v. πταίω.

3. Cf. Meyer, *Romans*, 434. For the popularity of the saying in antiquity, see Desiderius Erasmus, *Adages I.i.1–I.v.100*, vol. 31 of *Collected Works of Erasmus*, trans. Margaret Mann Phillips (Toronto: University of Toronto Press, 1982), 392.

Jesus among Israel's political elites as "tripping" (προσκόμματος) or "stumbling" (σκάνδαλον) over a rock in their path (9:32–33), and since he has just recalled that thought with his reference to the "stumbling" (σκάνδαλον) of unbelieving Israel in 11:9, it is likely that his reference here to stumbling refers to Israelites who have rejected the gospel and who make up "the rest" that, according to 11:7, God has hardened. Among those Israelites who have heard the gospel, the majority have not believed it, and in rejecting it they have lost their theological footing.

Paul is not thinking of individuals here, as he was in 9:18, but of unbelieving Israel as a group.[4] Thus, unlike Pharaoh and the vessels "fitted out for destruction" in 9:22, the hardening of this group is reversible, and Paul can answer the question of whether they have stumbled "so as to fall" with a resounding "certainly not!" (μὴ γένοιτο). The clause "so as to fall" (ἵνα πέσωσιν), indicates the result of the stumbling (NASB, NRSV, NIV), not its purpose ("in order to fall," HCSB, ESV).[5] Paul is using an extended metaphor, and since people do not stumble with the intention of falling, he imagines the more realistic picture of stumbling with the result of falling.[6] Israel, then, has stumbled on a stone in its path that has knocked it off balance, but not so badly that they "fall" (πέσωσιν).[7]

Paul continues the metaphor of stumbling in the next clause with the noun "trespass" (παράπτωμα), which is closely related etymologically to the verbs "stumble" (πταίω) and "fall" (πίπτω). Some translations try to show the connection by translating the term "fall" (Tyndale, Luther, KJV) or "stumbling" (NRSV, HCSB), but it clearly carries the connotation of culpable disobedience elsewhere in Romans (4:25; 5:15–20). As Israel's stumbling over Christ in 9:32–33 makes clear, their rejection of the gospel was not simply a mistake.

In Paul's view, however, God was already bringing good out of Israel's disobedience (cf. 8:28), since it provided the opportunity for the gospel to go to the gentiles. The prepositional construction with the infinitive indicates purpose (εἰς τὸ παραζηλῶσαι αὐτούς), and here, although Paul does not explicitly mention God, he is clearly talking about God's purpose.

The term "provoke to . . . jealousy" (παραζηλῶσαι) recalls Paul's quotation of Deuteronomy 32:21 in 10:19. There too God provokes unbelieving Israel to jealousy by means of non-Israelites who, with respect to the things of God, are foolish. At that point in the argument, the accent lay on God's punishment of Israel for its disobedience as the parallel sentence, "I will make you resent a foolish people" (10:19c), showed. Here, however, Paul hints that this negative aspect of Deuteronomy 32:21 did not exhaust its meaning. Since the term "provoke to . . . jealousy" can also mean "provoke to emulation," now Israel's jealousy bears the positive connotation of striving after the good that another is already attaining.[8] Although he uses a cognate of Paul's term, Aristotle's positive definition of "emulation" (ζῆλος) fits Paul's use of the term "provoke to . . . jealousy" here:

> Emulation [ζῆλος] is a feeling of pain at the evident presence of highly valued goods, which are possible for us to attain, in the possession of those who naturally resemble us—pain not due to the fact that another possesses them, but to the fact

4. Moo, *Romans*, 681.

5. So, correctly, e.g., Origen, *Romans, Books 6–10*, 168–69; Sanday and Headlam, *Romans*, 321; Lagrange, *Romains*, 275.

6. Cf. Sanday and Headlam, *Romans*, 321.

7. The fallen branches of 11:22, therefore, are equivalent to Israel's stumbling in 11:11 (not to its falling) and, once again, a metaphorical use of "fall" (πίπτω) dictates the meaning of the term. For the idea of fallen branches (ἔπεσαν οἱ κλάδοι), see Ezek 31:12 LXX.

8. Bell, *Provoked to Jealousy*, 39–43; idem, *Irrevocable Call*, 249–50; Wagner, *Heralds of the Good News*, 265–67.

that we ourselves do not. Emulation therefore is virtuous . . . whereas envy [φθονεῖν] is base. (Aristotle, *Rhetoric* 2.11.1 [1388a; J. H. Freese, LCL])[9]

Paul may have envisioned the multiethnic church of Jews and gentiles, the product of God's "multifaceted wisdom" (Eph 3:10 NET), as steadily maturing into a newly created humanity (Eph 2:19–22; 4:11–16). As Jews who were zealous for God but not yet convinced of the truth of the gospel understood this vision and saw its realization in the church, they would seek to be included.[10]

11:12 Now if their transgression is wealth for the world and their defeat is wealth for the gentiles, how much more their fullness! (εἰ δὲ τὸ παράπτωμα αὐτῶν πλοῦτος κόσμου καὶ τὸ ἥττημα αὐτῶν πλοῦτος ἐθνῶν, πόσῳ μᾶλλον τὸ πλήρωμα αὐτῶν). The refusal of most Israelites to believe the gospel is only temporary, and when God has finished removing their "hardness" (11:25), a vast number of both Israelites and non-Israelites will belong to his newly constituted, eschatologically formed people.

The conjunction "now" (δέ) takes the line of argument up one level and introduces the main discussion of the subsection (11:12–32) to which 11:11 was the opening remark.[11] Paul argues from the lesser to the greater, a common rhetorical device in antiquity, and one that he uses often (5:10, 15, 17; 11:12, 24; cf. 2 Cor 3:7–11; Philm 16). The hinge on which the argument swings is God's unfailing commitment to Israel and sovereignty over their history. If God loves Israel but has brought a significant blessing to the world through hardening them to the gospel, then God's blessing for the world will be that much greater when he shows his love to Israel by softening their hearts to the gospel. As Wright has argued, the pattern is not unlike God's method of using the death of Christ for the justification and redemption of sinners, although how much to make of this for understanding Paul's theology is not clear.[12]

The phrase "wealth for the world" (πλοῦτος κόσμου) refers to gentiles hearing and believing the gospel. In Paul's thinking, God was enormously rich (11:33), particularly in kindness (2:4; cf. Eph 1:7; 2:7) and glory (Rom 9:23; cf. Eph 1:18; 3:16; Phil 4:9; Col 1:27), and believers shared in these riches (1 Cor 1:5; 2 Cor 6:10; 8:9; 9:11; Eph 3:16; Phil 4:19). When Paul preached the gospel to the Jews first in the various cities to which he traveled and they rejected it, he then focused on the gentiles, many of whom believed the gospel and received a share in God's wealth (Acts 13:44–49; 18:5–8; 19:8–10; 28:17–28).

The term "defeat" (ἥττημα) is extremely rare, showing up in only two other places in known Greek literature prior to Romans (Isa 31:8 LXX; 1 Cor 6:7).[13] Closely related terms, however, are common. The cognate verb (ἡττάομαι/ἡσσάομαι) often means "be defeated" in the passive voice and seems to carry that meaning in its two NT uses (2 Pet 2:19, 20).[14] Since nouns ending in the sound "-ma" (-μα) typically indicate the result of their corresponding verb in Greek, "defeat" makes sense here, just as it does in its other two

9. Cf. Bell, *Provoked to Jealousy*, 40n185.

10. Wagner, *Heralds of the Good News*, 267: "The sight of Gentiles crossing the finish line will be what inspires Israel to regain their feet and run with renewed zeal toward the goal—the righteousness of God revealed in Christ."

11. Godet, *Romans*, 400; Meyer, *Romans*, 434; cf. Denniston, *Greek Particles*, 171.

12. Wright, *Paul and the Faithfulness of God*, 1206–11. One obvious difference is that "the redemptive effects of Israel's casting aside are due to her disobedience. . . . The Messiah on the other hand works redemption through his obedience (Rom. 5.18)" (Bell, *Irrevocable Call*, 248).

13. BDAG 441, s.v. ἥττημα.

14. LSJ 779, s.v. ἡσσάομαι; BDAG 441, s.v. ἡττάομαι. Cf., e.g., Sanday and Headlam, *Romans*, 322.

appearances.[15] The translations "diminishing" (KJV) or "diminished number" (NAB), although they attempt to preserve some parallelism with "fullness" (πλήρωμα), are not well supported by the actual evidence of the word's meaning.[16] Israel's trespass, then, was also its defeat in the sense that because they rejected the gospel, they did not attain the righteousness of God (Rom 9:30; 11:7).

The meaning of "their fullness" (τὸ πλήρωμα αὐτῶν) is not entirely clear. It could mean Israel's "fulfillment" of God's demand (cf. 13:10) or the full number of Israelites destined to believe the gospel.[17] The same term in the same construction in 11:25 refers to the full number of the gentiles destined to belong to God's people, and so that is likely to be its meaning here (cf. 11:26). The idea was common in first-century Judaism that the day of judgment would not come until God's people had reached a predetermined number (e.g., 4 Ezra 4:35–37; Rev 6:11).[18]

11:13–14 Now to you gentiles I speak. To the degree that I am an apostle to the gentiles, I glorify my ministry in the hope that perhaps I might somehow provoke my kinfolk to emulation and save some of them (Ὑμῖν δὲ λέγω τοῖς ἔθνεσιν· ἐφ' ὅσον μὲν οὖν εἰμι ἐγὼ ἐθνῶν ἀπόστολος, τὴν διακονίαν μου δοξάζω, εἴ πως παραζηλώσω μου τὴν σάρκα καὶ σώσω τινὰς ἐξ αὐτῶν). Paul has an important pastoral admonition for his gentile readers in Rome. As a foundation for this admonition, he reminds them that he is their apostle and informs them that part of the great significance of his apostleship to the gentiles lies in the saving implications that it has for the Jews.

It is possible to understand these sentences as a parenthetical and somewhat apologetic comment to Paul's gentile audience in Rome, designed to explain how what he is saying about Israel is relevant to them also. His concern for Israel leads him to embrace his proclamation of the gospel to the gentiles because this will lead to the conversion of some Jews and, after the full number of Jewish believers has come to faith, to the consummation of God's good purposes for the whole world.[19]

It is best, however, to see the statement as the beginning of an important pastoral point that Paul will continue to make through 11:24. God had assigned Paul to call the gentiles to obey the gospel (1:5), and here Paul engages in that task. Later in his argument he will urge gentile believers in Rome not to "boast" over unbelieving Jews who, because they have rejected the gospel, do not have a place in God's newly formed, multiethnic people (11:18). Later still, he will admonish gentile believers to accept and not despise Jewish believers who continue to observe the Mosaic law (14:1–2, 10). As Paul's "now" (δέ) indicates, he begins this pastoral theme here by describing the sense in which his own ministry to the gentiles plays a critical role in taking the gospel to "the rest" of Israel who have not believed it (cf. 11:7). Far from adopting an arrogant attitude toward Jews (cf. 11:18), gentile Christians in Rome ought, like Paul, to appreciate the important role that physical Israel has played and will play in God's saving purposes for all peoples of the world.

The phrase "to the degree that" (ἐφ' ὅσον) focuses on the extent to which Paul's ministry to the gentiles is also a ministry to unbelieving Israel. The two go hand in hand, just as in Matthew 25:40 and

15. Smyth, *Greek Grammar*, §841.2; Robertson, *Grammar*, 153.

16. Cf., e.g., Cranfield, *Romans*, 2:557. Ancient Greek-speaking theologians who used the term similarly gave it the sense "defeat" or "defect" (*PGL* 610, s.v. ἥττημα) rather than a numerical meaning.

17. See respectively, e.g., Tholuck (*Romans*, 378) and Jewett (*Romans*, 677–78).

18. Jewett, *Romans*, 678.

19. Sanday and Headlam, *Romans*, 323–24. Cf., e.g., Barrett (*Romans*, 199); Byrne (*Romans*, 337, 338–39).

45 where the same phrase appears (kindness to the poor goes hand in hand with a warm reception for Jesus). Paul's "therefore" (οὖν) connects his apostleship to the gentiles with the statement he has just made about speaking to the gentiles in Rome. It is on the basis of his authority as apostle to the gentiles that he can legitimately issue the admonitions that follow. Somewhat counterintuitively (μέν), his ministry to the gentiles is at the same time ministry to unbelieving Jews.[20]

Tyndale translated the term "glorify" (δοξάζω) as "magnify," and English translations have often left it this way (KJV, RSV, ESV), or toned it down even further to something like "publicize" (CEB). The term means "praise, honor, extol," however, and probably has this more common meaning here (cf. the NRSV's "glorify" and the NAB's "glory in").[21] Paul is certainly not boasting in himself, but he is attaching great significance to the "ministry" (διακονίαν) God has given him to preach the gospel to the gentiles (cf. 15:20; 2 Cor 3:11–18).[22]

The reason for the great weight Paul gives to his ministry lies in part with the contribution it makes to the scenario described in 11:12 where the figurative "wealth" (πλοῦτος; cf. 10:12) that comes to the gentiles as they respond to the gospel and receive salvation prompts unbelieving Jews to emulate the gentiles' response to the gospel. Despite the significance Paul gave to his own role in these events (ἐγώ; cf. Eph 3:4–10), he knew that he would only make a partial contribution to a larger and longer process (cf. 11:26), and so he spoke with reserve of "perhaps" (εἴ πως) saving "some" (τινάς) of Israel.[23] Only later will "all Israel" be saved (11:26).[24]

11:15 For if their casting away is the reconciliation of the world, what will their acceptance be except life from the dead? (εἰ γὰρ ἡ ἀποβολὴ αὐτῶν καταλλαγὴ κόσμου, τίς ἡ πρόσλημψις εἰ μὴ ζωὴ ἐκ νεκρῶν;). Paul's seemingly mundane ministry of proclaiming the gospel to gentiles and hoping that some Jews will follow the example of those who believe is actually contributing to something that, in the end, will be of worldwide and eschatological significance.

Paul's "for" (γάρ) introduces an explanation of his desire to see as many unbelieving Israelites as possible emulate the faith of gentiles who have accepted the gospel, and this explanation echoes his description of the same scenario in 11:12. Now, however, Paul is more specific about what "wealth for the gentiles" entails, and what he meant by his vague "how much more their fullness." The gentiles' wealth is their reconciliation to God, and Israel's fullness refers to Israel's experience of eschatological life in the final day when the dead are raised to immortality.

The expression "their casting away" (ἡ ἀποβολὴ αὐτῶν) is difficult.[25] "Their" (αὐτῶν) could refer to Israel's action of "casting away" the gospel (a subjective genitive), and a number of interpreters have taken it this way.[26] It could also refer to God's action of "casting away" Israel (an objective

20. On the use of μέν here, see BDAG 630, s.v. μέν 2b.

21. On the term's meaning, see BDAG 258, s.v. δοξάζω 1.

22. Cf. Zahn, *An die Römer*, 510n39. On the word "ministry" (διακονία), see the comments below on 12:7.

23. So, correctly, e.g., Cranfield, *Romans*, 2:561; Moo, *Romans*, 692. On Paul's intensifying "I" (ἐγώ), see Meyer (*Romans*, 436), and for the translation "in the hope that perhaps I might somehow" (εἴ πως), see Zerwick and Grosvenor, *Grammatical Analysis*, 484.

24. *Pace*, e.g., Dunn, *Romans 9–16*, 657.

25. The term "casting away" (ἀποβολή) can have the passive meaning "loss" (e.g., Acts 27:22; Aristotle, *Physics* 229b line 13; 245b lines 8 and 22–23; 247a line 5; *Metaphysics* 1055a line 37), but the meaning "casting away" is also attested (e.g., Plato, *Laws* 943e). See LSJ 193, s.v. ἀποβολή. Jewett is correct (*Romans*, 680) that the common translation "rejection" is not well attested, although see the translation of *Metaphysics* 1018a, lines 34–35 by Hugh Tredennick (LCL).

26. Theodoret of Cyrus, *Letters of St. Paul*, 1:112–13; Fitzmyer, *Romans*, 612; Légasse, *Romains*, 707; Jewett, *Romans*, 680–81.

genitive), and this more common interpretation is probably correct because of the way Paul uses the noun "acceptance" (πρόσλημψις) in the next clause. "Acceptance" probably refers to God's acceptance of Israel, just as Paul's use of its verbal form (προσλαμβάνω) in 14:3 and 15:7 refers to God's or Christ's acceptance of both Jewish and gentile Christians. If God initiates the "acceptance" in 11:15b, then he probably also initiates the "casting away" in 11:15a. This "casting away" of Israel does not contradict Paul's statement that "God did not cast off [ἀπώσατο] his people" in 11:1 because that statement referred to "casting off" Israel permanently, whereas this statement parallels the temporary hardening of Israel in 11:7–10, which will be removed on the final day (11:25–26).[27]

"Reconciliation" (καταλλαγή) recalls 5:9–11 where Paul described God's reconciliation of his enemies to himself through the atoning death of his Son and the promise that this holds for their future salvation through the Son's resurrection from the dead. His argument here takes the "how much more" form of the argument there. If God can bring something good out of something bad, he is able to bring something extraordinarily good out of something good.

Commentators have sometimes explained "life from the dead" (ζωὴ ἐκ νεκρῶν) as a metaphorical reference to the inner transformation that takes place in the human being when he or she believes the gospel.[28] It is more likely, however, that Paul refers to the final resurrection of the dead. He can certainly use life-from-death language metaphorically to refer to the new existence of believers prior to the final day (6:4, 11, 13), but the last time he used this language (8:10–11) it referred to the resurrection. Paul's present argument, moreover, is building toward an eschatological climax in 11:25–27 that makes a reference to the resurrection from the dead here likely.[29]

11:16a And if the first fruit is holy, the dough is also (εἰ δὲ ἡ ἀπαρχὴ ἁγία, καὶ τὸ φύραμα). When Jews in Paul's time prepared their daily bread for cooking, they set aside a small piece of dough as an offering to God and believed that God sanctified the rest of the dough and blessed their house. In the same way, when all Israel believes the gospel, death will be defeated and the final day will come.

"And" (δέ) signals a continuation of the line of thought that Paul expressed in the immediately preceding rhetorical question and follows the same "if x, how much more y" logic. This new sentence uses a figure whose imagery is borrowed from the Mosaic law's description of a common domestic offering. According to Numbers 15:19–21, when Israelites made bread, they were to set aside a choice piece, or "first fruit" (ἀπαρχή), of their "dough" (φύραμα) as an offering for the Lord. Paul's imagery assumes what most Israelites of his time probably also assumed, that this sacrifice made the rest of the dough holy in the sense that the large portion of the dough left for bread after the offering reflected the devotion to the Lord of the person who mixed it.[30] Paul's interest lay not in the details of what was probably a common custom among Jews

27. See, e.g., Byrne (*Romans*, 345–46); Moo (*Romans*, 693); and Schreiner (*Romans*, 597–98).

28. E.g., Ambrosiaster, *Romans*, 90; Pelagius, *Romans*, 127; Calvin, *Romans*, 248; Godet, *Romans*, 403–4; Légasse, *Romains*, 708.

29. E.g., Origen, *Romans, Books 6–10*, 175; Theodoret of Cyrus, *Letters of St. Paul*, 1:113; Käsemann, *Romans*, 307; Byrne, *Romans*, 339–40; Moo, *Romans*, 695–96.

30. Ezek 44:30 says, "You shall also give to the priests the first of your dough, that a blessing may rest on your house." The small offering of the piece of dough sanctified the larger context from which it came by conferring blessing on it. Cf. Jacob Milgrom, *Numbers*, JPS Torah Commentary (Philadelphia: Jewish Publication Society, 1990), 121.

of his own time but in the theology he wanted to illustrate by referring to it.

Most interpreters think that the imagery represents a shift in the direction of Paul's argument from the concerns of 11:15 (God's acceptance of Israel after the reconciliation of the gentiles) to the concern Paul expresses in 11:28 (God's election of and love for Israel "because of the fathers"). The "first fruit" in 11:16a, on this reading, is the patriarchs, and Paul claims that because the patriarchs were holy in God's eyes, all Israel, even those Israelites who have rejected the gospel, are holy also. In 11:16b Paul repeats this thought, but now using the imagery of "root" and "branches" that he will take up in the subsequent allegory of the olive tree.[31]

A number of interpreters, however, have noticed that this explanation does not fit the preceding argument where Paul was concerned with the relationship between "the remnant" and "the rest" (11:1–10) and between his mission to the gentiles and the salvation of "the rest" (11:11–15).[32] Various ideas have been proposed for fitting 11:16a more successfully into the preceding context, but it is best to adopt a simple reading of the phrase that matches the structure of the preceding rhetorical question.[33] The homey image of a holy piece of dough leading to the sanctification of the whole batch of dough fits well with what Paul has just said about God's acceptance of Israel leading to life from the dead. A small beginning that is good leads to a very good conclusion. The "first fruit," then, does not refer to the patriarchs, the Jewish-Christian remnant, Christ himself, or the elect, whether Jewish or gentile, but to the time when unbelieving Israel accepts the gospel and ushers in the final day.[34] The sanctified "dough" represents the "wealth" and "life" that come to the whole world on the final day when the full number of gentiles has entered God's people and a vast number of formerly hardened Israelites have believed the gospel and been saved (11:25–26).

11:16b And if the root is holy, the branches are also (καὶ εἰ ἡ ῥίζα ἁγία, καὶ οἱ κλάδοι). Israel's rich heritage as the recipient of God's revelation, promises, and blessings sets it apart from the world's other nations and prepares them to embrace the gospel.

The thought now shifts from the future to the present, and Paul prepares his audience in Rome for the allegory of the olive tree that will follow immediately in 11:17–24. In the allegory, the tree's natural branches are the Israel of Paul's time viewed from the perspective of the gospel. Israelites who have rejected the gospel, although naturally part of the tree, have been broken from it, and by implication Israelites who have believed the gospel are branches that have grown naturally from the tree and remain connected to it.

The identity of the root is unclear both in the allegory and here in the transitional introduction to the allegory. According to what Paul says here, the root supplies holiness to all Israel, whether believers or not. According to the allegory that follows, it supplies nourishment (11:17) and physical support to the branches that have not been broken off as well as to the new branches that have been grafted

31. E.g., Ambrosiaster, *Romans*, 90; Chrysostom, *Romans*, 346; Calvin, *Romans*, 249; Sanday and Headlam, *Romans*, 326; Byrne, *Romans*, 346; Schreiner, *Romans*, 600–601.

32. E.g., Barrett, *Romans*, 200; Dunn, *Romans 9–16*, 659; Hultgren, *Romans*, 409. Less explicitly, Cranfield, *Romans*, 2:564; Wright, *Paul and the Faithfulness of God*, 1212.

33. The most common alternative to identifying "first fruit" with "the patriarchs" is identifying the term with the Jewish-Christian remnant (e.g., Cranfield, *Romans*, 2:564; Barrett, *Romans*, 200; Fitzmyer, *Romans*, 614; Bell, *Irrevocable Call*, 274–75; Wright, *Paul and the Faithfulness of God*, 1212).

34. Cf. Hultgren, *Romans*, 409–10. For the first fruit as Christ, see, e.g., Origen (*Romans, Books 6–10*, 178–79) and Theodoret of Cyrus (*Letters of St. Paul*, 1:113); for the first fruit as Jewish and gentile believers, see Dunn (*Romans 9–16*, 659).

into the tree (11:18). It is possible that the root refers to the "remnant" of Jewish Christians (cf. 9:27, 29; 11:5; Sir 47:22; 1 Esd 8:87).[35] In the allegory that follows, however, Jewish Christians play a specific (if implied) role as natural branches that derive nourishment and support from the root (Rom 11:17), so they cannot also be the tree's root.[36] The vast majority of interpreters, then, identify the root with the patriarchs, and many identify the root even more specifically with Abraham himself (11:28; cf. 4:1, 11–12).[37] Since Paul is not specific, however, all that can be said with confidence at this point in the argument is that the root represents the rich heritage of Israel that Paul described in 9:4–5: "The adoption as sons, and the glory, and the covenants, and the legislation, and the worship, and the promises," including "the fathers and ... the Messiah, as far as the flesh is concerned.[38]

If the branches are Israel, whether believers or not, and the root is Israel's heritage, including the patriarchs, then Paul is saying that Israel's rich heritage sanctifies not only the remnant who has believed the gospel (11:5) but also the rest who were hardened (11:7). "The rest" are sanctified in the sense that their heritage has prepared them to understand and accept the gospel and has therefore made their eventual salvation more likely (cf. 1 Cor 7:14).

11:17 But if some of the branches have been broken off, and you, although a wild olive branch, have been grafted in among them and have become a sharer of the oiliness of the root of the olive tree . . . (Εἰ δέ τινες τῶν κλάδων ἐξεκλάσθησαν, σὺ δὲ ἀγριέλαιος ὢν ἐνεκεντρίσθης ἐν αὐτοῖς καὶ συγκοινωνὸς τῆς ῥίζης τῆς πιότητος τῆς ἐλαίας ἐγένου . . .). In the present, some Israelites have rejected the gospel and failed to realize the goal of their rich heritage, whereas some gentiles have begun to share with Jewish Christians the richness of Israel's heritage and to benefit from it.

Paul now develops the theme of a tree with root and branches from 11:16 into an allegory involving cultivated and wild olive trees. He begins with a conditional sentence whose "if" clause (protasis) describes God's judgment on unbelieving Israel and his acceptance of gentile believers in Rome ("you" [σύ]) into his people (cf. 9:22–29; 9:30–10:4; 10:19–21). Paul shifts into the second-person singular in order to address a fictional interlocutor and will sustain this fictional dialogue until the end of the allegory in 11:24.[39] When Paul has done this before in his argument, the interlocutor has been a Jew (9:19–20), but now, with a sense of evenhandedness, Paul makes his interlocutor a gentile (cf. 11:13).

Israel's Scriptures sometimes depict Israel as an olive tree (Jer 11:16; Hos 14:5–6) and God's judgment as felling a forest or lopping branches from a tree (Isa 10:33–34; cf. 11:1; Jer 11:16; John 15:2, 6).[40] Here "branches ... broken off" refers to the part of Israel that has rejected the gospel and whom God, in judgment, has made insensitive to his word (Rom 11:7–10).

Paul uses the proper horticultural terms for "wild olive" (ἀγριέλαιος), for "grafting" (ἐγκεντρίζειν) the branch of one tree onto another (Theophrastus, *Hist. plant.* 2.2.5), and for the "oiliness" (πιότης) of the olive tree itself (Theophrastus, *Hist. plant.* 9.1.3; *Caus. plant.* 6.11.6–7; Judg 9:9 LXX).[41] In the

35. Barrett, *Romans*, 200; cf. Dunn, *Romans 9–16*, 660.

36. Kruse, *Romans*, 434.

37. E.g., Chrysostom, *Romans*, 346; Pelagius, *Romans*, 127; Theodoret of Cyrus, *Letters of St. Paul*, 1:113; Calvin, *Romans*, 249; Wilckens, *An die Römer (Röm 6–11)*, 246; Fitzmyer, *Romans*, 614; Moo, *Romans*, 700.

38. Cf. 2:17–20; 3:2.

39. Dunn, *Romans 9–16*, 652; Jewett, *Romans*, 683–84.

40. Cf. Sanday and Headlam, *Romans*, 326–27.

41. Cf. BDAG 15, 273, 814, s.vv. ἀγριέλαιος, ἐγκεντρίζω, and πιότης.

eastern Mediterranean where Paul lived and traveled, grafting the branches of a wild olive tree onto a cultivated olive tree would have been unusual.[42] The philosopher and agricultural writer Theophrastus, for example, thought the benefits ran the other way: an olive grove owner might coax a wild olive tree into producing ripe olives if he grafted the branches of a cultivated tree into it.[43] Paul, who was probably well aware of such practices, has reversed the normal procedure in his allegory for a pastoral reason. He wanted to portray gentile believers in Rome, who seem to have been tempted to arrogance in their attitudes toward Jews, as the wild and unfruitful element in his allegory. Contrary to expectation and solely as a matter of God's grace, God had brought them into the sphere of Israel and enabled them to derive rich spiritual benefits from Israel's heritage (Rom 9:4–5; 15:27; cf. Eph 2:11–13, 19; 3:6).[44]

11:18 Do not boast over the branches. But if you boast . . . you do not support the root, but the root you (μὴ κατακαυχῶ τῶν κλάδων· εἰ δὲ κατακαυχᾶσαι οὐ σὺ τὴν ῥίζαν βαστάζεις ἀλλὰ ἡ ῥίζα σέ). Gentile believers who have benefited from Israel's rejection of the gospel must understand that they have been reconciled to the God of Abraham, Isaac, and Jacob and that God's promises to these patriarchs still stand.

The word "boast over" (κατακαυχάομαι) is an unusual term that Paul uses only here. It carried connotations of boasting in triumph over an adversary, as when the Chaldeans "boasted" in triumph over Judah as they plundered it (Jer 27:11 LXX; Heb. and Eng. 50:11) or when, in a grave inscription from Asia Minor, a gladiator "boasts" in triumph over his slain opponent.[45] It might seem natural for gentile believers in Rome to gloat in triumph over the irony that they had actually attained what Israel's heritage should have led Israel to attain (cf. Rom 9:30–10:4), or that God had hardened Israel so that the gospel might go to the gentiles (11:11). Here Paul forbids any such triumphalism by pointing out the fundamental theological misunderstanding that such an attitude would represent. Gentile believers have only attained the rightousness of God through their attachment to Israel's heritage, and that heritage contains God's unbreakable promises to Israel (11:28–29).

11:19 You will say, then, "Branches were broken off that I might be grafted in" (ἐρεῖς οὖν, Ἐξεκλάσθησαν κλάδοι ἵνα ἐγὼ ἐγκεντρισθῶ). Someone might arrogantly object to Paul's claim that gentile Christians share a common heritage with Israel by observing that a vast difference separates Israelites from gentiles in the people of God. Gentiles have taken the place in God's eschatological people once occupied by Israelites.

Paul keeps the debate going with his fictional interlocutor by using the expression, "You [sing.] will say . . ." (ἐρεῖς; cf. 9:19), and formulating an objection that is technically correct but whose haughty tone reflects serious theological misunderstanding (11:7–10). The haughty tone is clear from the chiastic form of the objection, which English cannot reproduce. The verbs "broken off" (ἐξεκλάσθησαν) and "grafted in" (ἐγκεντρισθῶ) stand in antithesis

42. Philip F. Esler, "Ancient Oleiculture and Ethnic Differentiation: The Meaning of the Olive-Tree Image in Romans 11," *JSNT* 26 (2003): 116. Columella, *Rust.* 5.9.16, which is sometimes thought to describe the grafting of a wild olive branch onto a cultivated tree to increase fruit production may not refer to grafting at all, and in any case refers to procedures followed in the western part of the Mediterranean rather than in the east (ibid., 118–20).

43. Ibid., 114–115, citing Theophrastus, *Caus. plant.* 1.6.10 and 1.15.3–4.

44. Cf. Barclay, *Paul and the Gift*, 552. Barclay identifies the root as "the unconditional favor of God on which Israel's existence depends" (ibid., 550). Although perhaps slightly too abstract, this definition usefully stresses the gift character of Israel's heritage.

45. BDAG 517, s.v. κατακαυχάομαι.

to one another at the beginning and end of the sentence, and the subjects of the verbs, "branches" (κλάδοι) and "I" (ἐγώ), stand next to one another in the center of the sentence, separated only by a conjunction. Whereas Paul stressed the dependency and connectedness of gentile Christians with the heritage of Israel in 11:18, the interlocutor wants to describe in a haughty way the vast chasm that supposedly exists between the two groups.

11:20 Very well. They were broken off because of unbelief, and you stand because of faith. Do not think haughty things, but fear (καλῶς· τῇ ἀπιστίᾳ ἐξεκλάσθησαν, σὺ δὲ τῇ πίστει ἕστηκας. μὴ ὑψηλὰ φρόνει ἀλλὰ φοβοῦ). The right response to justification by faith is humility, not pride that arises from winning some imagined competition. A haughty response to God's grace should engender fear in the one who has it.

With the expression "very well" (REB; καλῶς) Paul concedes the technical accuracy of the point his fictional debating partner has just made, but only to show that the point itself neglects a crucial element of the situation (cf., e.g., Demosthenes, *1 Against Boeotos* 39.15).[46] The interlocutor's statement is true as it stands. "Branches were broken off that I might be grafted in" could serve as a gentile's neat summary of the problem that generated the entire argument of chapters 9–11. Against all expectations, God has excluded the majority of Israel from his newly constituted, eschatological people and included gentiles.

The interlocutor's statement is wrongheaded not because of what it says but because of what it implies about the interlocutor's attitude. Unlike Paul, the interlocutor sees the breaking off of Israelite branches and the grafting in of gentile branches not as a problem but as a competitive advantage.[47] After accepting the technical accuracy of his interlocutor's statement, therefore, Paul explains its inadequacy.

The interlocutor, Paul says, has failed to recognize the cause of the surprising situation he or she has so neatly summarized.[48] Gentile believers belong to God's newly configured people not as a result of their pursuit of righteousness but strictly as a result of God's gracious gift of righteousness to them through the death of Christ and their reliance on that gracious gift (9:30). Israelite unbelievers have only been excluded from God's eschatological people in the present because, relying on their own works, they stumbled over Christ and refused to receive God's gracious gift of righteousness (9:31–10:4). The proper response to inclusion within God's people, then, is not thinking haughty thoughts (ὑψηλὰ φρόνει; cf. 12:3, 16). The gracious character of justification by faith excludes boasting (3:27), and this is true not merely for the Jew (3:29) but now, Paul says, also for the gentile.[49] The person who responds to inclusion within God's people with pride should stop thinking this way and instead be afraid.

11:21 For if God did not spare the natural branches, perhaps he will not spare you either (εἰ γὰρ ὁ θεὸς τῶν κατὰ φύσιν κλάδων οὐκ ἐφείσατο, [μή πως] οὐδὲ σοῦ φείσεται). If anyone could lay claim to God's mercy, it would be an Israelite. Yet God has not spared Israelites who have rejected the gospel. It is hardly likely, then, that he will spare gentile Christians who, by their haughty attitudes, show that they too have rejected the gospel.

46. LSJ 870, s.v. κάλος IV.c.6.

47. See Jewett's insightful comments on this passage (*Romans*, 688).

48. The two dative nouns (ἀπιστίᾳ, πίστει) are causal datives. See BDF §196 and cf. Rom 4:20 and 11:30–31.

49. Jewett, *Romans*, 688. Cf. the comments of Dunn on 11:18 (*Romans 9–16*, 662).

Here Paul gives the reason why ("for" [γάρ]) his interlocutor should be afraid. The "natural branches" are Israelites who by nature (κατὰ φύσιν) belong on the domesticated olive tree of God's people (cf. 11:24). God had adopted them, made covenants with them, and given them promises (9:4), and they for their part were zealous for God (10:2). Yet, despite all this God did not spare them when they refused to believe the gospel and pruned them from his new, eschatological people. God's relationship with Paul's gentile interlocutor carries with it no such complications. Compared to the Israelite, it is easy to see that the gentile who belongs to God's people is there only by trust in God's gracious offer of reconciliation through the death of Christ. The gentile who has adopted a haughty attitude toward Israel should fear God's judgment because this attitude betrays a lack of faith. It hints that the gentile believer imagines God is somehow obligated to him or her. If this is not true for the Jew, Paul says here, it is hardly true for the gentile.[50]

11:22 Note then the kindness and strictness of God: toward those who fell, strictness, but toward you, the kindness of God—if you remain within that kindness, since otherwise you will be cut off (ἴδε οὖν χρηστότητα καὶ ἀποτομίαν θεοῦ· ἐπὶ μὲν τοὺς πεσόντας ἀποτομία, ἐπὶ δὲ σὲ χρηστότης θεοῦ, ἐὰν ἐπιμένης τῇ χρηστότητι, ἐπεὶ καὶ σὺ ἐκκοπήσῃ). To put what Paul has just said another way, the only recourse for anyone on the final day of judgment is the kindness God has shown to sinners through the atoning death of Jesus Christ. If gentile Christians take pride that they have triumphed where unbelieving Jews have failed, then they demonstrate they are not actually living within the sphere of God's kindness.

The phrase, "note then" (RSV, ESV, NRSV; ἴδε οὖν) introduces a summary of the point Paul wanted to make in the preceding sentence (11:17–21).[51] "Kindness" (χρηστότης) is a relational term. A lover could use a closely related word to say of his "sweetie" (μέλι), "I remember you often because of your kindness [χρηστοσύνης]."[52] God's "kindness" is associated in Jewish and early Christian tradition with his forebearance, patience (Rom 2:4), generosity (Pss. Sol. 5:14; Eph 2:17), mercy (Pss. Sol. 8:28), and love (Titus 3:4). The term "strictness" (ἀποτομία) was used in legal contexts to refer to the unyielding enforcement of the law.[53] Applied to people, it could describe someone who enforced the law with "inexorable sternness"

50. Editors of the Greek text and translators differ on whether to follow the set of manuscripts that reads "if God did not spare the natural branches, neither [οὐδέ] will he spare you" (ESV; cf. RSV, NIV, REB; NA[26, 27, 28]) or "if God did not spare the natural branches, perhaps [μή πως οὐδέ] he will not spare you" (NRSV; cf. Tyndale, NAB, NET; WH, NA[25]). Although an impressive set of Alexandrian witnesses has the shorter, more straightforward reading (ℵ A B P 6 81), the longer reading has in its favor both its grammatical difficulty (μή πως should be followed by the subjunctive rather than the future indicative [Bruce M. Metzger, *A Textual Commentary on the Greek New Testament*, 2nd ed. (Stuttgart: German Bible Society, 1994), 465]) and a substantial set of more geographically diverse witnesses (𝔓[46] Ψ 33 104 1175 [Alexandrian], D F G [Western], L [and most other Byzantine manuscripts]). Some interpreters resist what they see as the softening of Paul's point with a "perhaps" (e.g., Murray, *Romans*, 2:88n38; Dunn, *Romans 9–16*, 651), but in Paul's fictional debate with his interlocutor this "perhaps" may well be ironic. There is, then, no softening of the idea that God will not spare the gentile whose haughty attitude betrays a lack of faith.

51. Cf. Philo (*Alleg. Interp.* 1.28), who sums up an allegorical interpretation of Gen 2:6 by beginning, "See then" (ἴδε οὖν [F. H. Colson and C. H. Whitaker, LCL]).

52. For the lover's inscription, see *TLNT* 3:512n4, and for the full text and description, see Louis Robert, *Noms Indigènes dans L'Asie-Mineure Grèco-Romaine*, Part 1 (Paris: Librairie Adrien Maisonneuve, 1963), 232. The translation is mine.

53. Helmut Köster, "τέμνω, κτλ.," *TDNT* 8:107. See, e.g., Diodorus Siculus, *Bibliotheca historica* 12.16.3: "The lawgiver also preserved the laws he made by means of their severity [ἀποτομίας]. That is, he commanded that under every circumstance obedience should be rendered to the law even if it had been altogether wrongly conceived" (C. H. Oldfather, LCL).

(ἀπαράπειστος).[54] It was, therefore, precisely the opposite of the "kindness" that was willing to overlook faults generously and patiently.[55]

Paul has already explained in Romans 3:21–26 how God's kindness and legal strictness have met in the atoning death of Christ. God graciously took the initiative in reconciling sinful people to himself by means of Christ's sacrifical death. In this way he was able both to dismiss the sins of his people, which he had previously disregarded in his forbearance, and to prove his righteousness (3:25–26). Anyone who trusted this gracious provision would be free from any punishment on the final day (3:24, 26). Hardened Israel's refusal to trust this gracious gift led to its "fall" from the tree, and only by remaining within the sphere of this demonstration of God's kindness are gentile Christians able to avoid being cut off from the tree themselves.[56]

Paul's claim that Israel "did not stumble so as to fall" in 11:11 refers to a permanent fall, which, as Paul will explain in 11:25–27 and 31–32, Israel has not experienced. The fall he has in mind here is the fall that led them to be cut off from the tree of God's eschatological people in the present. As Paul will explain in the next sentence, that condition can be reversed.

11:23 And those too, if they do not remain in their unbelief, will be grafted in, for God is able to graft them in again (κἀκεῖνοι δέ, ἐὰν μὴ ἐπιμένωσιν τῇ ἀπιστίᾳ, ἐγκεντρισθήσονται· δυνατὸς γάρ ἐστιν ὁ θεὸς πάλιν ἐγκεντρίσαι αὐτούς). God is an impartial and powerful God. He is both willing and able to accept into his people Israelites who once rejected the gospel if they will receive his kindness.

The expression "those too," with its emphatic use of the pronoun (ἐκεῖνοι), places special emphasis on God's impartiality in showing kindness (cf. 2:11). Just as Paul's gentile Christian interlocutor "stands" (ἵστημι, 11:20) within God's people merely by "remaining" (ἐπιμένω, 11:22) within God's kindness, so too unbelieving Israelites who begin to trust the gospel will be grafted back into the olive tree of God's people.

Paul assumes that not remaining in unbelief parallels remaining in the sphere of God's kindness. Faith, therefore, is a matter simply of accepting the kindness that God has shown to his people by sparing them from his wrath through the death of his Son. As Paul's admonition to his gentile Christian interlocutor in 11:19–22 shows, however, this faith is no mere formality but an understanding of one's relationship to God and his grace that produces humility in one's relationships with others.[57]

The shift from the passive to the active voice of the verb "graft in" (ἐγκεντρίζω) in this sentence shows clearly that God was the agent of the action passively described in the verbs "graft in" and "break off" (ἐκκλάω) in 11:17–22. He has grafted believing gentiles into his people, and he has cut off unbelieving Israelites from his people. Because God is behind these actions, he is able to do what seems surprising or impossible (cf. 4:21; 14:4).[58]

11:24 For if you were, according to your nature, cut from a wild olive tree and contrary to nature were grafted into a cultivated olive tree,

54. Dionysius of Halicarnassus, *Ant. rom.* 8.61.2 (E. Cary, LCL). See also Helmut Köster, "τέμνω, κτλ.," *TDNT* 8:107.

55. Cf. "Plutarch," *Lib. ed.* 18: fathers should "temper the keenness [ἀποτομίαν] of their reproofs with lenity [πραότητι]" (W. W. Goodwin, ed., *Plutarch's Morals* [Medford, MA: Little, Brown, and Company, 1874], 30).

56. "Within that kindness" (τῇ χρηστότητι) translates the article as anaphoric (Smyth, *Greek Grammar*, §1120b; Wallace, *Greek Grammar*, 217–20) and the noun as a dative of sphere (Wallace, *Greek Grammar*, 153–55).

57. See especially the comments of Jewett (*Romans*, 688, 691).

58. Cf. Chrysostom, *Romans*, 350–51; Moo, *Romans*, 707.

how much more will these, the natural branches, be grafted into their own tree (εἰ γὰρ σὺ ἐκ τῆς κατὰ φύσιν ἐξεκόπης ἀγριελαίου καὶ παρὰ φύσιν ἐνεκεντρίσθης εἰς καλλιέλαιον, πόσῳ μᾶλλον οὗτοι οἱ κατὰ φύσιν ἐγκεντρισθήσονται τῇ ἰδίᾳ ἐλαίᾳ). It is clear that God is able to reincorporate Israelites who have rejected the gospel into his people since he has already accomplished the harder, less natural, feat of incorporating gentiles into his people.

"For" (γάρ) introduces an explanation of how Paul's gentile interlocutor can be sure that God is able to graft branches he has previously broken from the tree back into it. The gentile interlocutor only needs to consider how unlikely it was that he or she would become part of the olive tree of God's people to see that God is certainly able to graft presently unbelieving Israelites back into that tree.

The gentile Christian interlocutor was "according to . . . nature" (κατὰ φύσιν) a branch "from a wild olive tree" (ἀγριελαίου). Paul's Greek here is difficult. The phrase "according to . . . nature" could describe either the wild olive tree (e.g., Tyndale, KJV, RSV, NRSV, ESV, NIV) or the gentile interlocutor (e.g., REB, HCSB, CEB). As a number of commentators have observed, since it is obvious that a wild olive tree is wild by nature, it is more likely that Paul intended to describe the gentile interlocutor as "by nature" a wild olive tree.[59] As Paul puts it elsewhere, gentiles were "separated from Christ, alienated from the commonwealth of Israel and strangers to the covenants of promise, having no hope and without God in the world" (Eph 2:12). Despite this and against all expectations (παρὰ φύσιν), they were grafted into "a cultivated olive tree."

The term "cultivated olive tree" (καλλιέλαιον) is a rare term that does not show up in ancient Greek botanical literature, but it does appear, used as an adjective, in a mid-third century BC letter from the high-ranking Egyptian official Apollonius to Zeno, the overseer of his estate.[60] Zeno apparently did the right thing to order the planting of "the cultivated olive tree" (τῆς καλλιελαίου ἐλαίας) in Apollonius' "park" (παράδεισον).[61] Paul, then, has used a term that emphasizes God's election of and love for Israel and perhaps alludes to the figure in Scripture of Israel as a carefully cultivated planting (Isa 5:1–2; 60:21; 61:3). The term "cultivated olive tree" now prepares the way for Paul's conclusion: God is eager and able to graft the missing branches from his cultivated tree back into that tree.

11:25 For I do not want you to be ignorant, brothers and sisters, about this mystery so that you might not be wise in your own estimation: a partial hardening has happened to Israel until the fullness of the gentiles should come in (Οὐ γὰρ θέλω ὑμᾶς ἀγνοεῖν, ἀδελφοί, τὸ μυστήριον τοῦτο, ἵνα μὴ ἦτε ἑαυτοῖς[62] φρόνιμοι, ὅτι πώρωσις ἀπὸ μέρους τῷ Ἰσραὴλ γέγονεν ἄχρις οὗ τὸ πλήρωμα τῶν ἐθνῶν εἰσέλθῃ). Any gentile Christian arrogance about

59. E.g., Zahn, *An die Römer*, 520n61; Cranfield, *Romans*, 2:571.

60. The masculine form of the term, which Paul uses here, appears in "Aristotle," *Plants* 820b 40 (Meyer, *Romans*, 445; BDAG 504, s.v. καλλιέλαιος; Moo, *Romans*, 708n64; Légasse, *Romains*, 724n96), but the extant Greek text of this spurious work is "a somewhat poor translation of the mediaeval Latin copy, which was itself an inferior translation of the Arabic" (W. S. Hett, LCL).

61. P.Cair.Zen. 125.3 (third-century BC). For the reference, see LSJ 867, s.v. καλλιελαία, and for the text and an English summary, see http://papyri.info/ddbdp/p.cair.zen;1;59125. For Apollonius, see Dorothy J. Thompson, "Apollonius," *OCD* 127.

62. The difficulty of the Greek is probably what led some early scribes to clarify the phrase so that it explicitly said "in yourselves" (ἐν ἑαυτοῖς [e.g., A B]) or "in your own view" (παρ' ἑαυτοῖς [e.g., ℵ C D]; cf. Prov 3:7; 12:16). The reading without a preposition is found in, e.g., 𝔓[46] F G and Ψ. On this, see Lagrange, *Romains*, 284. For the expression with the simple dative, cf. Xenophon, *Cyr.* 1.6.21: "For people are only too glad to obey the man who they believe takes wiser thought for their interests [ἑαυτοῖς φρονιμώτερον] than they themselves do" (W. Miller, LCL).

gentiles replacing unbelieving Israelites in the people of God is based on an erroneous understanding of God's future plan for Israel. Paul now reveals to his readers what God has revealed to him. Many in Israel will believe the gospel and be saved once the gospel has been fully proclaimed to the gentiles.

Paul's "for" (γάρ) introduces a further explanation of his claim that if Israel does not continue to reject the gospel, God will graft them back into the olive tree of his people (11:23–24). What he had just described as a possibility he now reveals to his readers as a certainty. The phrase "I [we] do not want you to be ignorant, brothers and sisters" (οὐ . . . θέλω [-ομεν] ὑμᾶς ἀγνοεῖν, ἀδελφοί) often introduces a piece of information that backs up an admonition Paul wants to give to his audience (1 Cor 10:1; 12:1; 1 Thess 4:13).

Here Paul backs up his admonition to humility by revealing a "mystery" (μυστήριον) to the Christians in Rome. Although he uses this term in Romans only here and in 16:25, it is a characteristically Pauline word, appearing far more often in his writings than elsewhere in early Christian literature. Elsewhere Paul connects the term with prophecy (1 Cor 13:2; Eph 3:4–5) and with God's revelation to people of how the final stage of history is unfolding (1 Cor 2:7) and will unfold (1 Cor 15:51; Eph 1:9–10; 2 Thess 2:7). He also implies that "mysteries" contain information that would remain unknown had not God graciously revealed it to his people (Rom 16:25; 1 Cor 2:7; Eph 3:9; Col 1:26; cf. 1 Cor 14:2) through his messengers (1 Cor 4:1; Eph 3:3–4). The mystery Paul reveals here describes the order of events before "the deliverer" comes "from Zion" (11:26).

Before Paul reveals this order of events, however, he tells the Roman Christians why he wants them to know it. Understanding what God will do with unbelieving Israel in the future, he says, will encourage them not to be "wise in" their "own estimation" (ἑαυτοῖς φρόνιμοι). This phrase is difficult since it could easily have the positive connotation of being "wise with respect to yourselves," that is, conducting one's self wisely. In this context, however, where Paul has just engaged in a fictional dialogue with a gentile Christian who tends to "boast over" Israel's rejection of the gospel (11:18–19) and "think [φρονεῖν] haughty things" (11:20), it clearly refers to people thinking that they are wiser than they are (cf. 12:3, 16).

The mystery, Paul says, concerns the temporary nature of Israel's "partial hardening" (πώρωσις ἀπὸ μέρους). The language of hardening and the description of it as partial recalls 11:5–7 where Paul divided Israel into a "hardened" (ἐπωρώθησαν) part so large that he could simply designate it as "Israel" (11:7) and a graciously chosen remnant of Israelite believers (11:5). This hardening, Paul now explains, will only last "until [ἄχρι οὗ] the fullness of the gentiles should come in."[63] "Fullness" (τὸ πλήρωμα) refers to the full number of gentiles whom God has determined would belong to his people.[64] Together with the notion of "entering in" (εἰσελθεῖν), this sounds an apocalyptic note reminiscent of Jesus's teaching on entering life or the kingdom of God (cf., e.g., Mark 9:43, 45, 47; 10:15, 23–25).[65] Paul's mention of "the fullness of the gentiles," moreover, is reminiscent of his reference to the "fullness" of Israel in 11:12 and the hint there that a large number of Israelites would have a place in his people.

The picture Paul draws of the course the gospel will take from his own time to the final day, then, is relatively clear up to this point in the argument.

63. "Until" (ἄχρι οὗ) is shorthand for "until the time at which" (ἄχρι χρόνου ᾧ). On this, see BDAG 160, s.v. ἄχρι 1.b.α.

64. Jewett, *Romans*, 700.

65. See also, e.g., 4 Ezra 4:35–37; Schreiner, *Romans*, 617; Jewett, *Romans*, 700.

The gospel will find an important but limited response among Israelites in Paul's time (11:5–7), but will have more success among gentiles (11:11, 15a). As the gospel is preached to the gentiles, even in Paul's own time, some Jews will also continue to believe (11:14), and presumably that number will grow with the passing of time as some Jews whose "minds were hardened" (ἐπωρώθη) turn to the Lord and have the veil covering their spiritual sight lifted (2 Cor 3:14–16).[66] Israel will continue to be divided into believing and unbelieving parts, however, until the mission to the gentiles is complete, and all those gentiles destined to believe the gospel have done so (11:25). Paul will say next what the argument has now made obvious.

11:26a And so, all Israel will be saved (καὶ οὕτως πᾶς Ἰσραὴλ σωθήσεται). Many presently unbelieving Israelites will be spared God's wrath on the final day because, after the gospel has been fully proclaimed to the gentiles, the full number of Israelites destined to be saved will also believe the gospel.

Paul's "and so" (καὶ οὕτως) refers both to the timing of all Israel's salvation and to the means by which it will happen. Paul would probably have written "and then" (καὶ τότε) if he had intended simply to indicate the sequence of events (cf. 1 Cor 4:5), and he could certainly use "and so" (καὶ οὕτως) with both sequence and means in mind (1 Thess 4:17).[67] Interpreters have sometimes understood "Israel" here to refer to the multiethnic group of believers in Christ. Elsewhere, Paul assumes continuity between ancient Israel and Christians, regardless of their ethnicity (cf. Rom 4:1; 1 Cor 10:1; Gal 6:16; Phil 3:3).[68] But the term "Israel" as Paul uses it here must refer to the same group that he identifies in 11:28 as both "enemies" and "beloved," and that group must be unbelieving Israel.[69]

Here, then, Paul is saying that after the gospel has been fully proclaimed to the gentiles and the full number of gentiles destined for salvation has been completed, Israelite unbelievers will also believe the gospel, presumably in larger numbers than up to this point (cf. Matt 24:14; Mark 13:10).[70] Since "and so" also refers to the means by which all Israel is saved, Paul probably expected that a desire to emulate (παραζηλόω) gentile believers would prompt this large number of Israelites to enter the kingdom of God (10:19; 11:11, 14). "All Israel" (πᾶς Ἰσραήλ) does not mean every single Israelite but, as with the use of the expression elsewhere in Scripture, to a group of Israelites large enough that they can represent the whole people (e.g., Deut 27:9; Josh 3:17; 1 Sam 3:20; Dan 9:11).[71]

In the OT, when gentiles feature positively in the eschatological restoration of Israel, the order of events is often simpler than the scenario Paul describes and sometimes looks like the reverse of it: Israel's law and worship draw gentiles to God, and they make their way to Jerusalem to worship him (Isa 49:5–6; Zech 8:23).[72] Paul's more complex

66. Wright, *Paul and the Faithfulness of God*, 1236.

67. Cf. Lagrange, *Romains*, 284; Dunn, *Romans 9–16*, 681; Byrne, *Romans*, 354; Hultgren, *Romans*, 414. For extensive evidence of the use of the phrase in ancient Greek with a temporal reference, see Das, *Solving the Romans Debate*, 251n195.

68. E.g., Calvin, *Romans*, 255; Wright, *Paul and the Faithfulness of God*, 1239–52.

69. Schreiner, *Romans*, 615 (citing Scott Hafemann, "The Salvation of Israel in Romans 11:25–32: A Response to Krister Stendahl," *ExAud* 4 [1988]: 53); Das, *Solving the Romans Debate*, 238.

70. Wagner, *Heralds of the Good News*, 277n187.

71. Das, *Solving the Romans Debate*, 256–57. Cf. Longenecker, *Romans*, 897–98.

72. The two visions of Israel's restoration are not ultimately incompatible with one another. Gentiles were attracted to the gospel first through the witness of Israelites who believed it, and from the perspective of the earliest Christians, this is the point at which the restoration of Israel began. Paul has added two steps after this: (1) the numbers of gentiles will increase to the point that they actually outnumber Israelites within the people of God, and (2) through the mechanism of Israel's

outline of Israel's restoration probably accounts for his description of it in 11:25 as a "mystery."[73] It would have remained unknown had God not revealed it to his people.

11:26b–27 just as it is written, "The deliverer will come from Zion; he will turn impiety away from Jacob; and this will be my covenant with them when I do away with their sins" (καθὼς γέγραπται, Ἥξει ἐκ Σιὼν ὁ ῥυόμενος, ἀποστρέψει ἀσεβείας ἀπὸ Ἰακώβ. καὶ αὕτη αὐτοῖς ἡ παρ᾽ ἐμοῦ διαθήκη, ὅταν ἀφέλωμαι τὰς ἁμαρτίας αὐτῶν). The salvation of Israel will happen in close proximity to the time when Jesus, the Son of David and Israel's Messiah, comes again. He will deliver Israel from the wrath of God against sin and transform it into a society of justice and peace.

Paul supports his claim that all Israel will be saved with a composite quotation from Isaiah 59:20–21a and 27:9a. Isaiah 59 is part of an indictment against Israel for its sins, "which have made a separation between" Israel and God (59:2). The first section of the chapter details Israel's sins, especially the violence, deceit, and legal injustice that characterized Israelite society (59:1–8). The second section is a confession that these charges are true (59:9–15a). The final section describes how God will come to establish the justice he had sought from his people and how he will do this, in part, by turning his people away from their impiety (59:15b–21).[74]

For Paul, "the deliverer" (ὁ ῥυόμενος) who accomplishes this is Christ himself at his second coming (cf. 1 Thess 1:10). In the Hebrew text of Isaiah 59:20, he will come "to" (*le*) Zion, and in the LXX text he will come "for the sake of" (ἕνεκεν) Zion, but in Paul's text he will come "from" (ἐκ) Zion. Paul may have intended by this change to emphasize the Jewishness of Jesus: that, for example, he came "from [ἐκ] David's offspring" (Rom 1:3) and "from" (ἐξ) Israel (Rom 9:5).[75]

The deliverance Christ will bring to Israel involves not only salvation from the wrath of God (Rom 11:26a; cf. 1 Thess 1:10), but a transformation of society so that violence, deceit, and injustice no longer characterize it.[76] According to Isaiah, this transformation will be accompanied by a covenant between God and his people that involves God enabling his people, by means of his Spirit, to communicate his revelation of himself to future generations (Isa 59:21b).

Immediately after citing Isaiah's reference to "this . . . covenant" and before the prophet describes God's covenant with Israel this way, Paul switches his attention to another part of Isaiah that allows him to describe God's future covenant with Israel as one that takes away Israel's various sins (Isa 27:9a). Paul may especially have had in mind the sinful behavior he attributed to Israel in 3:10–18, where he quoted Isaiah 59:7–8 (see Rom 3:15–16). He may also have been thinking of the sort of violence and injustice that some Jews used against

emulation of believing gentiles, all Israel will be saved. Cf. G. K. Beale and Benjamin L. Gladd, who believe that Paul's understanding of the pattern may have originated with "the entire context of Deuteronomy 27–32" (*Hidden But Now Revealed: A Biblical Theology of Mystery* [Downers Grove, IL: InterVarsity Press, 2014], 90). It seems possible that Paul's pattern originated with Isa 2:1–5 where, after the gentiles "go up to the mountain of the Lord" (2:3), Isaiah makes the appeal, "O house of Jacob, come, let us walk in the light of the Lord" (2:5). On this, see Wagner, *Heralds of the Good News*, 292n226.

73. Wagner, *Heralds of the Good News*, 276–77; Beale and Gladd, *Hidden But Now Revealed*, 91. The pattern of Israel's restoration, followed by gentile attraction to Israel's God, was also common in the Second Temple period. See, e.g., Tob 13:11, 14:5–7, and the discussion in Donaldson, *Paul and the Gentiles*, 69–74.

74. Oswalt, *Isaiah Chapters 40–66*, 512.

75. Jewett, *Romans*, 703–4. It is also possible that, either intentionally or unintentionally (Meyer, *Romans*, 450), Paul simply recalled the language of Pss 14:7 and 53:6 (13:7 and 52:7 LXX).

76. Jewett, *Romans*, 704–5.

the proclamation of the gospel (1 Thess 2:14–16; cf. Rom 11:3).[77] Rather than a place where such "transgressions are multiplied" (Isa 59:12), Paul envisions a future Israel that will cultivate peace and justice (cf. 59:8).

11:28 According to the gospel, they are enemies because of you, but according to election they are beloved because of the fathers (κατὰ μὲν τὸ εὐαγγέλιον ἐχθροὶ δι᾽ ὑμᾶς, κατὰ δὲ τὴν ἐκλογὴν ἀγαπητοὶ διὰ τοὺς πατέρας). It is true that unbelieving Israel is, at the moment, God's enemy, but two qualifications temper the enmity between them. This enmity has a saving purpose, and it will one day yield to the fulfillment of God's loving commitment to Israel's forebears.

The lack of a conjunction connecting this sentence with the preceding sentence signals the beginning of a new section (11:28–32), which turns out to be a summary of 11:11–27.[78] This first sentence is itself a compact statement of the problem that generated chapters 9–11. From the perspective of the gospel, the majority of God's beloved people, to whom God has promised his unfailing love, are his enemies.

The substantive adjective "enemies" (ἐχθροί) refers to God's hostility toward Israel rather than Israel's hostility toward God.[79] This is clear from the parallel term "beloved" (ἀγαπητοί), which must refer to God's love for Israel. God's hostility toward unbelieving Israel originates in their rejection of the peace initiative God had undertaken toward them through the reconciling death of Christ (5:1, 8–11). They were God's enemies, then, in the same sense that all human beings were God's enemies according to 5:1–11. The relational breech between God and Israel, however, had a saving purpose. It facilitated the communication of the gospel to non-Israelites, as Paul has explained in the immediately preceding argument (11:11–12, 15, 16, 22, and 25). This is the force of Paul's "because of you" (δι᾽ ὑμᾶς) here.

In 5:1–11 Paul had implied that God could be hostile toward sinners at the same time that he loved them: "But God demonstrates his own love for us in that while we were still sinners Christ died for us" (5:8). God loved believers prior to their acceptance of the gospel and therefore while they were still his enemies (5:10). Here too God's hostility toward unbelieving Israel is accompanied by a love for them that eventually will rescue them from his wrath. Here Paul supplies the reason why God continues to love this group despite their continued rejection of the Messiah. By God's own choice (κατὰ . . . τὴν ἐκλογήν) he had promised their forebears, particularly Abraham, Isaac, and Jacob, that he would bless their descendants (4:13, 16–22; 9:4, 7–8, 13).

Paul had argued in 9:11 that God's "chosen purpose" (ἡ κατ᾽ ἐκλογὴν πρόθεσις τοῦ θεοῦ) was not somehow limited by the ethnicity or moral virtue of those whom he chose, and in 11:5 he had argued that God's "gracious choice" (κατ᾽ ἐκλογὴν χάριτος) had nevertheless included a remnant of ethnic Israelites. Here he reveals that, in the end, God's free choice will include the vast majority of Israel. As 9:11 and 11:5 have made clear, however, this large number of Israelites will be saved not because they are Israelites but by God's grace (9:11) and through the same faith in Christ that the Israelite remnant before them had exercised (11:5).

11:29 For God has no misgivings about his gifts and calling (ἀμεταμέλητα γὰρ τὰ χαρίσματα καὶ ἡ

77. Ibid., 706.

78. Cf., e.g., Godet, *Romans*, 412; Meyer, *Romans*, 452; Sanday and Headlam, *Romans*, 337.

79. Godet, *Romans*, 412; Meyer, *Romans*, 452; Cranfield, *Romans*, 2:580. For the reverse view, see, e.g., Zahn, *An die Römer*, 526; Lagrange, *Romains*, 287; Jewett, *Romans*, 707.

κλῆσις τοῦ θεοῦ). The reason why God continues to love rebellious Israel is that he is not unstable or unreliable. When he decides to choose and bless people, he never regrets that decision.

Paul now introduces the basis ("for" [γάρ]) for the statement he has just made about God's continued love for Israel despite his hostility toward them for rejecting the gospel. The "calling" (κλῆσις) of God is tied closely with God's "chosen purpose" (ἡ κατ' ἐκλογὴν πρόθεσις τοῦ θεοῦ) for his people in 9:11–12.[80] There Paul referred to God's formation of his people on the basis of his sovereign choice rather than on the basis of their family ties or moral virtue, but here he speaks of God's "calling" of ethnic Israel, Paul's "compatriots according to the flesh" (9:3) to whom God had given the gifts and promises described in 9:4–5.[81] Despite God's gracious and impartial extension of the boundaries of his people to all kinds of human beings, he was not finished with Israel. He had "called" them into existence and made commitments to them, and when God summons people into existence and blesses them with his gifts, he never regrets his decision. The term rendered "no misgivings" (ἀμεταμέλητα) is a plural, passive adjective that literally means "without regret."[82] It was a natural expression for not being sorry about one's major commitments, whether political (Polybius, *Hist.* 23.16.11) or religious (Dionysius of Halicarnassus, *Ant. rom.* 8.56.1; 2 Cor 7:10).

11:30–31 For just as you once disobeyed God, but now you were shown mercy because of the disobedience of these, so also these disobeyed now because of the mercy shown to you in order that they also might now be shown mercy (ὥσπερ γὰρ ὑμεῖς ποτε ἠπειθήσατε τῷ θεῷ, νῦν δὲ ἠλεήθητε τῇ τούτων ἀπειθείᾳ, οὕτως καὶ οὗτοι νῦν ἠπείθησαν τῷ ὑμετέρῳ ἐλέει, ἵνα καὶ αὐτοὶ νῦν ἐλεηθῶσιν). God will actually use Israel's disobedience as the means by which he will, in the end, be faithful to his promises to them. Their disobedience has opened a door of opportunity for gentiles to hear and believe the gospel, but this influx of gentiles into God's people will eventually result in God's mercy flowing to all Israel as well.

Paul's "for" (γάρ) introduces a rhetorically balanced explanation of how God can be faithful to his promises to Israel (11:29) despite the large number of Israelites who remain disobedient to the gospel. The "just as . . . so also" structure is reminiscent of 5:12, 19, and 21 and of the similarly sweeping review of salvation history in 5:12–21, although it is not clear that the passages are linked thematically.[83] The terms "disobeyed" (ἠπειθήσατε, ἠπείθησαν) and "disobedience" (ἀπειθείᾳ) recall not so much the disobedience (παρακοή) of Adam in 5:19 as God's impartiality in distributing justice to those who "are disobedient" (ἀπειθοῦσιν) to the truth in 2:8–9, and, even more clearly, the "disobedient" (ἀπειθοῦντα) within Israel in 10:21. Paul recalls this theme in order to summarize one side of his two-sided argument in 11:11–29. He has just made the case that Israel's disobedience has a merciful divine purpose. While God's hands are stretched out in appeal to disobedient Israel (10:21), a large group of formerly disobedient gentiles has flooded into his people.

The threefold use of "mercy" terms (ἐλεέω, ἔλεος) recalls the argument of 9:15–18, where Paul had used the concept as part of his argument that God was free to show his mercy in any way he pleased, even if this meant, surprisingly, showing

80. Paul uses the verb "call" (καλέω) rather than the noun "calling" (κλῆσις) in 9:12 (cf. 9:7).

81. Cf. Sanday and Headlam, *Romans*, 338.

82. BDAG 53, s.v. ἀμεταμέλητος. Although the term can have a legal sense, it is difficult to see why Spicq (*TLNT* 1:94) insists on it here.

83. Dunn, *Romans 9–16*, 687–88.

it to gentiles. Now "mercy" summarizes the other side of the two-sided argument in 11:11–29, and this reintroduction of the concept reveals that God is also free to show mercy to Israelites who once rejected the gospel. The element of surprise now shifts to gentile believers in Rome, some of whom, Paul suspects, have been harboring haughty attitudes about their replacement of unbelieving Jews within the people of God (cf. 11:13–24).

Translations and commentators are divided on how to take the phrase "because of the mercy shown to you" (τῷ ὑμετέρῳ ἐλέει) immediately before the purpose clause "that they also might now be shown mercy" (ἵνα καὶ αὐτοὶ νῦν ἐλεηθῶσιν). Some take the expression as an instrumental dative modifying the verb "shown mercy" (ἐλεηθῶσιν) and translate the phrase something like "in order that, by the mercy shown to you, they too may now receive mercy" (NRSV; cf. KJV, ESV, NAB, NET).[84] It is unlikely, however, that the verb would be modified by a phrase outside its clause. The dative, then, is probably causal, and the expression modifies the immediately preceding verb, exactly like its companion clause in the first part of the comparison (cf. REB, CEB):

you were shown mercy	because of the disobedience of these
these disobeyed	because of the mercy shown to you.[85]

The "now" (νῦν) in the final clause is at first confusing since Paul has spoken of Israel's salvation, acceptance, and ingrafting in the future tense throughout 11:13–29. This superficial difficulty probably explains why the term is missing in a broad range of early manuscripts and is replaced by the more intelligible "later" (ὕστερον) in a few witnesses to the text. Paul, however, understood the time of the gospel's proclamation as a late stage in salvation history. It would be followed by the day of judgment (2:5), the release of creation from its bondage (8:21), and the redemption of God's people (8:23). He could tell the Romans in 13:11, "Our salvation is nearer now [νῦν] than when we first believed." His "now" here in 11:31, therefore, refers to the closing period of history in which he understood himself to be living, a period that included both the proclamation of the gospel to the gentiles and, eventually, Israel's salvation.[86]

11:32 For God has enclosed all people within disobedience in order that he might have mercy upon all people (συνέκλεισεν γὰρ ὁ θεὸς τοὺς πάντας εἰς ἀπείθειαν, ἵνα τοὺς πάντας ἐλεήσῃ). In the gospel, God has demonstrated definitively that both Jews and gentiles have been disobedient to him, and he has demonstrated this so that Jews and gentiles alike might receive his merciful forgiveness for their disobedience.

"For" (γάρ) introduces a summary of what Paul has just said in 11:30–31. Indeed, this pithy sentence summarizes the sweep of the letter's argument up to this point.[87] As Byrne memorably puts it, "The wheel that began turning at 1:18 has now come full circle."[88]

The expression "enclose . . . within" (συγκλείω εἰς) often appears in military contexts to refer to surrounding or beseiging an opposing army so that it had no way of escape (cf. 1 Macc 5:5; Polybius, *Hist.* 3.40.30; 3.117.11; 4.48.11). Paul's use of the expression here recalls his use of the verb in Galatians to say that "the Scripture imprisoned [συνέκλεισεν]

84. Among interpreters, see, e.g., Zahn (*An die Römer*, 528n75), Cranfield (*Romans*, 2:572, 582–85), Fitzmyer (*Romans*, 627), Bell (*Irrevocable Call*, 282) and Wright (*Paul and the Faithfulness of God*, 1255).

85. On the causal dative, see Smyth, *Greek Grammar*, §1517–20, and Wallace, *Greek Grammar*, 167–68.

86. Cf. Cranfield, *Romans*, 2:586; Dunn, *Romans 9–16*, 687.

87. Cf. Godet, *Romans*, 415–16.

88. Byrne, *Romans*, 353.

everything under sin" (3:22; cf. 3:23), and this use, in turn, recalls Paul's long string of biblical quotations in Romans 3:10–18, which demonstrated the disobedience of every human being to God. Paul is, therefore, using the expression "enclosed within" here in a metaphorical and almost legal sense to mean that God has demonstrated in the gospel that everyone has disobeyed him, and he has done this in such a way that the charge is inescapable. He has also done this, however, for a specific and happy purpose: "that he might have mercy upon all people" (cf. 10:12).[89] Since Paul's "all" occurs in a context where the discussion has focused on the different roles that various people groups have played and will play in God's historical purposes, it refers not to every individual but to all kinds of people, whether Israelites or non-Israelites.[90]

11:33 How deep is the wealth and wisdom and knowledge of God! How undiscoverable his judgments and untraceable his ways! (Ὦ βάθος πλούτου καὶ σοφίας καὶ γνώσεως θεοῦ· ὡς ἀνεξεραύνητα τὰ κρίματα αὐτοῦ καὶ ἀνεξιχνίαστοι αἱ ὁδοὶ αὐτοῦ). God's plan of reconciling the world to himself and, at the same time, of remaining faithful to his promises to Israel demonstrates that the power and intelligence of God are far beyond human comprehension.

Paul now draws the argument of 9:1–11:32 to a close with a description of the magnificence of God's power and insight in 11:33–36. The passage has a carefully designed three-part structure.[91] It begins with an expression of amazement that describes three attributes of God (11:33). It then reflects on the vast difference between God's greatness and humanity's weakness, using three rhetorical questions. These three questions stand parallel to the three divine attributes, which are considered in reverse order (11:34–35). The passage ends with an expression of praise to God in light of his sovereignty that includes three identically structured prepositional phrases (11:36). Such features have led a number of interpreters to speak of the passage as a hymn, perhaps one that Paul took over and modified for his own purposes.[92]

It is more likely, however, that the passage was Paul's own carefully composed expression of amazement at the complex way in which God had demonstrated and would demonstrate his faithfulness to his promises to Israel.[93] God's method of saving fallen and hardened Israel by first saving a large number of gentiles whom Israel would then emulate was not something that any human would have predicted, even on the basis of the Scriptures. It was a "mystery" (11:25) that bore witness to the utterly transcendent nature of God's power and wisdom. The passage, then, did not originate in Paul's inability to explain how the various parts of his argument in chapters 9–11 fit together. It is certainly not Paul's way of "throwing up his hands in despair" at sorting out the logic of his argument.[94] It is rather an expression of wonder at what Paul

89. Lagrange, *Romains*, 289.

90. On this, see especially Calvin (*Romans*, 258), Godet (*Romans*, 415–16), Murray (*Romans*, 2:103), Schreiner (*Romans*, 629), and Bell (*Irrevocable Call*, 285–86). *Pace* Jewett (*Romans*, 712): "The expectation of universal salvation in this verse is indisputable, regardless of the logical problems it poses for systematic theologians."

91. See Eduard Norden, *Agnostos Theos: Untersuchungen zur Formengeschichte religiöser Rede* (Leipzig: Teubner, 1923), 241. Cf. Reinhard Deichgräber, *Gotteshymnus und Christushymnus in der frühen Christenheit: Untersuchungen zu Form, Sprache und Stil der frühchristlichen Hymnen*, SUNT 5 (Göttingen: Vandenhoeck & Ruprecht, 1967), 62, and Dunn, *Romans 9–16*, 698.

92. E.g., Ulrich Wilckens, "σοφία, κτλ.," *TDNT* 7:518; Deichgräber, *Gotteshymnus*, 61–64; Jewett, *Romans*, 713–15.

93. Cf. Dunn (*Romans 9–16*, 698) and Hultgren (*Romans*, 430), who do not deny the hymnic (Dunn) or poetic (Hultgren) qualities of the passage but believe that Paul probably composed it.

94. Edward Kessler, *An Introduction to Jewish-Christians Relations* (Cambridge: Cambridge University Press, 2010), 41.

does understand of God's ways now that God has revealed the complex path of salvation history to him.

Paul opens the passage with an exclamation that falls into two parts. The first word of the first part (ὦ) does not introduce a statement directed to God, as we might expect in a hymn (e.g., Marcus Aurelius, *Meditations* 4.23), but an expression of astonishment at what Paul has just described in 9:1–11:32, and especially in 11:11–32.[95] Chrysostom, who spoke the language in which Paul writes and who understood Greek rhetoric, captured the amazement expressed in these opening lines:

> Here after going back to former times, and looking back to God's original dispensation of things whereby the world hath existed up to the present time, and having considered what special provision He had made for all occurrences, he is stricken with awe, and cries aloud.[96]

Paul is amazed at the depth of God's wealth, wisdom, and knowledge (RSV, NAB, REB, ESV, NET, CEB), not at the depth of the wealth of God's wisdom and knowledge (Luther, Tyndale, KJV, HCSB, NIV).[97] This is clear from the series of rhetorical questions that follow in 11:34–35 and that touch on God's wealth, wisdom, and knowledge in reverse order.[98] God's "wealth" (πλοῦτος) here probably refers to his immense power, just as Paul aligns God's "power" (τὸ δυνατός) with "the wealth of his glory" (τὸν πλοῦτον τῆς δόξης αὐτοῦ) in 9:22–23.[99] God's "wisdom" (σωφία) probably refers to his ability to structure history in a way that accomplishes his saving purposes for his people (cf. 1 Cor 1:21; 2:6–7; Eph 3:10; 2 Bar. 14:9), and his "knowledge" (γνῶσις) probably refers to his prior knowledge of who would belong to his people (Rom 8:29; 11:2; cf. 9:6–29).[100] Together the three terms communicate that God has more than enough power and intelligence to save his chosen people, whether Jews or gentiles, and to be faithful to his promises to Israel in the process.

The opening word of the second part of Paul's exclamation, like the opening word of the first part, expresses amazement (ὡς). Now, however, the thought advances to amazement at the greatness of God's wisdom and power in comparison to human abilities. Paul expresses the thought skillfully with two rare terms that begin with the same two syllables (ἀνεξ-) and mean roughly the same thing. The term "undiscoverable" (ἀνεξεραύνητα) shows up in descriptions of "innumerable" wartime casualties (Josephus, *J.W.* 5.569; Cassius Dio, *Roman History* 69.14.1). It refers not to something that is illogical or chaotic but to something highly regular that is simply beyond the ability of human beings fully to grasp.

The term "untraceable" (ἀνεξιχνίαστοι) is slightly more common and is connected in Scripture with the inability of human beings fully to comprehend the greatness of God's power or to see in advance that what happens in the world actually serves God's commitment to justice (LXX Job 5:9; 9:10; cf. Wis 17:1–3). Paul uses it that way here also. He expresses amazement at how God has accomplished his purposes for the salvation of both Jews and gentiles and at the same time has remained faithful to his promises to Israel. Without God's help, no one could map the path God has walked as

95. So correctly, Romano Penna, "Il Dio inconcepibile secondo san Paolo: una immagine inimmaginabile," *Liber Annuus Studii Biblici Franciscani* 62 (2012): 148. Cf., e.g., Sophocles, *Aj.* 981, and see LSJ 2029, s.v. ὦ I; BDAG 1101, s.v. ὦ 2a.

96. Chrysostom, *Romans*, 354.

97. Among commentators who think that "wealth" describes "wisdom" and "knowledge," see especially Schreiner (*Romans*, 632–33).

98. Deichgräber, *Gotteshymnus*, 62; Wilckens, "σοφία," 518.

99. Cf. Meyer, *Romans*, 456; Zahn, *An die Römer*, 530.

100. Cranfield, *Romans*, 2:589–90; Moo, *Romans*, 741.

he has produced the course of history (Rom 11:25; cf. Eph 3:8).

11:34–35 For, "Who has known the mind of the Lord? Or who has become his adviser?" Or "who has advanced him a sum and will be repaid by him?" (Τίς γὰρ ἔγνω νοῦν κυρίου; ἢ τίς σύμβουλος αὐτοῦ ἐγένετο; ἢ τίς προέδωκεν αὐτῷ, καὶ ἀνταποδοθήσεται αὐτῷ;). Paul can say that God's judgments are undiscoverable and his ways untraceable because no one can match God in wisdom and power.

Paul now gives the reason why ("for" [γάρ]) humans are unable to discover or trace God's ways in all their complexity. He uses three rhetorical questions that recall first Isaiah 40:13 LXX and then Job 41:11 (41:3 LXX and Heb.) and correspond to the three attributes of God that Paul mentioned in 11:33, but in reverse order.[101]

The first and second questions, with their use of the terms "mind" (νοῦς) and "counselor" (σύμβουλος), recall Paul's astonishment at the depth of God's "knowledge" (γνῶσις) and "wisdom" (σοφία) in the preceding verse, and they repeat the first part of Isaiah 40:13 LXX almost word for word.[102] Isaiah is answering the skepticism of Israelites about the "good tidings" of Israel's coming restoration (40:9–11 NETS), a skepticism based on their observation that God had withdrawn from them and failed to give them justice (40:27).[103] Isaiah responds by recalling the vastness and complexity of God's creation (40:12) and by reminding the skeptics that their inability to understand God's method of being faithful to Israel points only to their own weakness in comparison with God, not to God's unfaithfulness to his commitments (4:13–17). Although Paul makes the point in a less polemical setting, it is nevertheless the same point.

Paul's third rhetorical question recalls his reference to the depth of God's "wealth" (πλοῦτος) in the preceding verse and echoes Job 41:11 (41:3 LXX and Heb.), this time in a version closer to the Hebrew than to the LXX.[104] Here too the context in Job matches the context of Paul's argument. Job has questioned God's justice in allowing him to suffer since he has been faultless in his relationships with others (Job 31), and God answers Job with a lengthy description of his great power and wisdom (Job 38–41). In the passage that Paul quotes, God tells Job that no one is able to make God his debtor because all creation belongs to him. Paul also focuses on the vastness of God's power and wisdom in comparison to that of Job and all other human beings.[105]

The conclusion that Paul wishes his readers to draw from these rhetorical questions is similar to the point these questions made in the Scripture passages from which they come. Hasty assessments of God's injustice or unfaithfulness because of present circumstances are ill advised. History has not yet fully traveled the course God has plotted for it, and he is powerful and wise enough to include even the present circumstances within his just and faithful purposes.

11:36 Because all things are from him and through him and for him. Glory belongs to him as age gives way to age. Amen. (ὅτι ἐξ αὐτοῦ καὶ δι' αὐτοῦ καὶ εἰς αὐτὸν τὰ πάντα· αὐτῷ ἡ δόξα εἰς τοὺς αἰῶνας, ἀμήν). No one can require repayment

101. E.g., Meyer, *Romans*, 456; Zahn, *An die Römer*, 530.

102. Paul only adds the conjunction "for" (γάρ) and changes Isaiah's "and" (καί) to "or" (ἤ). Cf. 1 Cor 2:16.

103. Wagner, *Heralds of the Good News*, 302–3.

104. The Hebrew reads, "Who has confronted me [*hiqdimani*] that I should repay [*wa'ashallem*]?" (NET), whereas the LXX reads, "Who will withstand me [ἀντιστήσεταί μοι] and survive [ὑπομενεῖ]?"

105. Cf. Schreiner, *Romans*, 637; Wagner, *Heralds of the Good News*, 302.

from God because he created all things and directs the course of history for his own purposes. He is, and always will be, deserving of the deepest honor.

Paul now gives the reason why ("because" [ὅτι]) no one can demand repayment from God. Everything originates with God (is "from him"); everything happens through God's agency (is "through him"); and everything works together to accomplish his purposes (is "for him"). It is true that Paul's language resembles Stoic descriptions of an omnipresent divine force that animates the universe and nature (Marcus Aurelius, *Meditations* 4.23).[106] For the Stoic, however, God was "all that you see, all that you do not see" (Seneca, *Nat.* I praef. 13 [Thomas H. Corcoran, LCL]) or the force of "Creative Reason" that permeates the natural world (Seneca, *Ep.* 68.13 [Richard M. Gummere, LCL]). For Paul, God was not a force but a person who created and continues to guide the universe for his own faithful and just purposes (1 Cor 8:6; Eph 1:23; 4:6; Col 1:16). Paul has built the argument of 9:6–11:32 on this premise.

Paul's reasoning, then, resembles the reasoning of God himself in the passage from Job Paul has just echoed in 11:35: "Who has confronted me that I should repay? *Everything under heaven belongs to me!*" (Job 41:11 NET, emphasis added). If all things are from God and happen through his power and for his purposes, then all things—including the course of history—belong to him. In view of their relative weakness, human beings should only trust, not question, God's faithfulness and justice.

Paul's final line of praise with its concluding "amen" is an expression of this trust. It also parallels the expression of praise, with its own "amen," at the end of the opening paragraph of 9:1–11:36 (9:5).

Theology in Application

Paul's system of thought is intensely antitribal. It addresses human beings at the level of their common humanity, describing them as people who owe their existence and essential nature to the God who created them in his image and offering them all God's free gift of reconciliation through Christ. This offer of reconciliation, however, came at a real time and place and in the form of a human being, Jesus Christ, who was himself a member of a particular group of people with a particular history. He was "born from David's offspring," as Paul puts it in Romans 1:3, or, as he writes in Galatians 4:4–5, "when the fullness of time had come, God sent forth his Son, born of woman, born under the law, to redeem those who were under the law, so that we might receive adoption as sons."

As these texts imply, God made preparations for the reconciliation of all humanity to himself many centuries in advance by beginning his work of redemption in the particular people through whom the fully human Messiah would be born. The origins of the gospel and of Christianity within Judaism and God's continuing commitment to the Jewish people are persistent features of Paul's theology. The church can only neglect these themes to its own theological peril.

106. E.g., Meyer, *Romans*, 458; Norden, *Agnostos Theos*, 240–50.

Israel in Paul's Theology

Paul has already explained in 4:1–25 that Abraham, the forefather of the Jewish people, was the means by which God intended to unite people from many nations of the world into one group of people through faith. He articulates the same idea more succinctly in Galatians: "The Scripture, foreseeing that God would justify the Gentiles by faith, preached the gospel beforehand to Abraham, saying, 'In you shall all the nations be blessed'" (3:8; cf., e.g., Gen 12:3; 18:18).

In Romans, it is clearer than anywhere else in Paul's letters that although Abraham is the father of all believers, God continued to work through Abraham's physical descendents through Isaac in a special way. God revealed himself to the world, Paul implies, through the Jews. Christ Jesus, God's Son, was not only "born from David's offspring" (1:3) but Jews know the will of God (2:18) because they have "the embodiment of knowledge and truth in the law" (2:20). "Circumcision is beneficial" to the Jew who is obedient to God (2:25), functioning as a "sign" and "seal" of "righteousness by faith" (4:11). The "advantage of the Jew" and "the benefit of circumcision" are "much in every way" because God revealed himself to Israel in the Scriptures (3:1–2).

In Romans 9:4–5 Paul takes this idea of God's special relationship with Israel even further by implying that it remains in effect even for unbelieving Israel. They retain "the adoption as sons, and the glory, and the covenants, and the legislation, and the worship, and the promises." Paul's sorrow in 9:1–5 originates in the tension that exists between the historical reality that most Jews have rejected the gospel and yet they remain God's people.

Paul has already resolved that tension to some extent by focusing in 11:1b–10 on the minority within Israel who have believed the gospel. Just as in Elijah's time, the faithful remnant who continues to trust God in the present through believing the gospel shows God's faithfulness to the promises he made to the patriarchs. Paul was not content, however, to describe God's mercy to this relatively small group of Israelites, and in 11:11–32 he explains that the future is bright for "all Israel." As the end of this age approaches, Israelites in great numbers will seek to emulate the gentiles who through faith in the Messiah are experiencing the blessings promised to Israel, and they will also be saved by believing the gospel (11:25).

Interpreters have sometimes wondered whether this description of Israel's salvation contradicts positions Paul took on unbelieving Jews in earlier letters, and even his own position on the impartiality of God and the essential equality of all humanity before him in Romans. In 1 Thessalonians 2:14–16 Paul described the persecution of Jewish Christians in Judea by their unbelieving Jewish compatriots in an effort to encourage the persecuted Thessalonian church to remain firm despite suffering at the hands of their own fellow citizens. He describes the persecutors of Christians in Judea as "the Jews who killed the Lord Jesus and the prophets and also drove us out. They displease God and are hostile to everyone in their effort to keep us from speaking to the Gentiles so that they may be saved. In this way they always heap up their sins to the limit" (NIV). He concludes with the grim statement that "the wrath of God has come upon them at last" (NIV).

These are harsh words, but it is important not to take them out of their literary and historical context. "The Jews" is probably not a reference to the Jewish people generally but to the powerful Jewish leaders in Jerusalem, and those in their circle, who plotted Jesus's death (e.g., Mark 11:27; 12:1, 12), persecuted the early Jewish Christians (e.g., Acts 4:1–7), and drove Paul out of Judea (Acts 9:29–30).[107]

The division of humanity with which he works in 1 Thessalonians 2:14–16, then, is not a division between Jews and gentiles, and certainly not a division between Jews and Christians, but rather a division between those who have believed the gospel and those who have rejected it with violence, whatever their ethnicity. One group will be rescued from God's wrath (1 Thess 1:10; 5:9), and the other group will experience God's wrath, and this is the case wherever believers might emerge in the world, whether Thessalonica or Judea.[108] Paul's point about Jesus and the prophets is as much praise of Jewish Christians in Judea in light of the noble lineage of faithful Jews in which they stand (including Paul himself) as it is criticism of an unbelieving Jewish leadership that has violently resisted God. Its critical element, moreover, is inner-Jewish polemic, akin to the polemic of the writing prophets in Israel's own Scriptures, not an indictment of Jewish people as Jews.[109]

Something similar is happening in Galatians 4:21–31 and 2 Corinthians 3:12–18. Galatians 4:21–31 explains the story of Hagar and Sarah and their two children allegorically, comparing "the present Jerusalem" with the enslaved Hagar and her son Ishmael and those who have believed the gospel with the "free woman," Sarah, and her son Isaac (4:22–26). This description of "the present Jerusalem . . . in slavery with her children" (4:25) certainly implies that unbelieving Jews are slaves to sin and need to believe the gospel, but Paul describes the pre-Christian existence of the gentile Galatians in exactly the same way: "Formerly, when you did not know God," he tells them, "you were enslaved to those that by nature are not gods" (4:8; cf. 4:3; Rom 6:17, 20; 7:6, 14, 23; 8:20–21).

Paul's application of his allegory, with its description of Ishmael as a persecutor of Isaac and its instruction to "cast out the slave woman and her son" (4:29–30), specifically targets Christian false teachers who were trying to force the gentile Galatian Christians to observe the Mosaic law. It says nothing about Paul's approach to Judaism generally.

In 2 Corinthians 3:12–18 Paul describes his unbelieving Jewish contemporaries as reading Moses with veiled minds and hearts (3:14–15) and says that only when

107. Cf. Frank D. Gilliard, "The Problem of the Antisemitic Comma between 1 Thessalonians 2.14 and 15," *NTS* 35 (1989): 481–502.

108. Das, *Paul and the Jews*, 138–39.

109. Ibid., 138.

"one turns to the Lord" is "the veil . . . removed" (3:16). Again, it is true that this implies unbelieving Jews are blind to the truth about the gospel, but Paul describes all of unbelieving humanity as having a "foolish" and "darkened" heart (Rom 1:21) and a "worthless mind" (Rom 1:28).[110] There is no special criticism of unbelieving Judaism here.

Since Paul does not criticize Jews as Jews elsewhere in his letters, it is not surprising that within Romans he identifies himself with his people and expresses his heartfelt affection for them (4:1; 9:1–5; 10:1). He is so insistent on God's continued love for Israel that some have thought that, at least in 11:11–32, he has contradicted his argument elsewhere in the letter that God is impartial in his treatment of humanity.[111] If God is not the God of the Jews only but also of the gentiles (3:29–30) and if Abraham is the father of all who believe without regard to their ethnicity (4:10–12), then why is there any need for "all Israel to be saved" in some special way (11:26)? Is it true, as Dodd said, that "Paul tries to have it both ways" and that "his emotional interest in his own people, rather than strict logic, has determined his forecast"?[112]

Throughout the letter Paul has made clear that everyone within the boundaries of God's people is there by God's choice and at his gracious initiative. God's choice, moreover, has often turned out to be surprising. Who would expect the gospel to be for "barbarians" and "foolish" people (Rom 1:14)? What right-thinking, essentially moral person would imagine God choosing the deceitful, idolatrous, sexually immoral, and violent rabble described in 1:18–32 (2:1)? The "miserable human being" of 7:24 is not the obvious choice to become God's adoptive child and coheir with the Messiah in 8:15–17. It was surprising that God chose Isaac and Jacob, the younger of Abraham and Isaac's children, rather than their older brothers (9:7–13), and that he chose gentiles who were not his people to be included within his people (9:25).

Paul is being consistent with this persistent theme throughout the letter, then, when he reveals the surprising content of the mystery that "all Israel will be saved" (11:26). They will be saved neither on the basis of their ethnicity nor on the basis of their obedience. Rather, their salvation will result from the commitments that God freely and graciously made to them long ago in his promises to their ancestors (11:28). It will also come to them through the faith they will place in the Messiah, Jesus, when he comes to deliver them from their sins (11:27; cf. 4:12).

There is, therefore, not only no ground for theological anti-Judaism in Paul's letters but Romans 11:11–32 shows that Paul had integrated into his gospel of God's impartiality the conviction that God would also be faithful to the commitments he made to ethnic Israel. He seems to bring this out in Romans because already among his predominantly gentile audience an unfortunate attitude of self-congratulation

110. Cf. Eph 2:1–3; 4:17–19; Col 1:21.

111. E.g., Dodd, *Romans*, 192; W. D. Davies, *Jewish and Pauline Studies* (Philadelphia: Fortress, 1984), 147–49.

112. Dodd, *Romans*, 192.

had started to take root, arising from the notion that they, as gentile Christians, had taken over the heritage of unbelieving Jews (11:18–19).

Paul's argument implies instead that gentile Christians should respect unbelieving Israel. The "root" of Israel's traditions supports the faith of gentile Christians (11:16). God continues to love unbelieving Israel (11:28), and will be merciful to them in the future (11:26, 31).

The Church's Failure to Heed Paul's Warning

Sadly, within a few decades of the time Paul wrote Romans, Christians began to adopt precisely the attitude toward unbelieving Jews that Paul forbids in 11:17–22. The author of the Epistle of Barnabas, for example, appeals, like Paul in Romans 9:12, to the motif of God's choice of the younger rather than the older brother in Genesis, but he uses it to argue that God has rejected Israel and has instead chosen Christians as his people (Barn. 13:1–6). Similarly, Abraham is not the father of both the circumcised and the uncircumcised who have faith in Christ but only of uncircumcised believers (13:7). "Barnabas's" answer to the question of whether God was unfaithful to his promises to the patriarchs, moreover, is that Israel's sin against God made it unworthy of receiving the fulfillment of those promises (14:1) and so their fulfillment passed instead to Christians (14:4). Israel was left behind "that they might fill up the measure of their sins and we might receive the covenant" (14:5), says "Barnabas," possibly echoing a decontextualized form of 1 Thessalonians 2:16.[113]

Only a few decades later still, Justin Martyr claimed that God gave the Jews circumcision to distinguish them "from other nations and from us Christians" so that the emperor Hadrian would know who to punish for the Bar Kokhba rebellion against Rome (AD 132–36). "The purpose" of circumcision, Justin tells his fictional Jewish dialogue partner, "was that you and only you might suffer the afflictions that are now justly yours; that only your land be desolate, and your cities ruined by fire; that the fruits of your land be eaten by strangers before your very eyes; that not one of you be permitted to enter Jerusalem."[114] Rather than considering circumcision as something of value (Rom 2:25) or as a possible seal on the faith of Jewish Christians (Rom 4:11–12), Justin ominously thinks of it as a way to single out Jews from everyone else for especially harsh treatment by the governing authorities (*Dialogue with Trypho* 16.2–28; cf. 19.2). Rather than adopting a humble posture that recognizes the sinfulness of all human beings, Justin adopts a triumphalist attitude toward unbelieving Israel that Paul had already exposed as incompatible with justification by faith (Rom 11:20).

113. Trans. Holmes, *Apostolic Fathers*, 425.

114. Justin Martyr, *The First Apology, the Second Apology, Dialogue with Trypho, Exhortation to the Greeks, Discourse to the Greeks, The Monarchy or the Rule of God*, trans. Thomas B. Falls, FC 6 (Washington, DC: Catholic University of America Press, 2010), 172.

Only a few decades later still the whole sordid tradition of patristic slander against the Jewish people was in full swing in the *Paschal Homily* of Melito of Sardis, where rhetorical display has overwhelmed historical and theological accuracy on the issue of human responsibility for the death of Jesus. Melito completely ignores the role of the Roman prefect and the Roman army in Jesus's crucifixion and pictures the entire nation of Israel scourging Jesus, placing the crown of thorns on his head, and nailing him to the cross (76, 79).

It is hard to identify the motivation for portraying the entire people of Israel as it existed many years after the death of Christ as somehow responsible for Christ's death. Perhaps it was the fear that Christians would convert to Judaism or the need to establish a clearer Christian identity.[115] Whatever the motivation, this unbiblical and theologically erroneous rhetoric contributed to the tragic history of oppression and violence toward Jews, especially in the years after Christians and Jews ceased to have close contact with each other in the cities of the Roman Empire.[116] The whole *contra Ioudaeos* tradition within the church stands as a grim reminder of how important it is for Christians to listen to the apostolic witness to the gospel found in Scripture, particularly to its witness concerning the impartiality of God toward all humanity and the abiding love of God for the Jewish people.

Listening to the Scriptures as One Reason for Brave Resistance to Anti-Judaism

Although the Holocaust emerged from a combination of political and social factors that included far more than the church's *contra Ioudaeos* tradition, that tradition helped to create and sustain an atmosphere, particularly in Central Europe, that facilitated Hitler's murderous policies.[117] There were sadly few places in Europe during the Nazi era where Christians were willing to hide and help their Jewish neighbors, but among Christians who did sometimes help Jews a significant number were people who valued the entire Bible, both Old and New Testaments, and who sought to live their day-to-day lives by its teachings. Reflecting on the reasons why the villagers of Le Chambon, France, were willing to put their own lives at risk to protect thousands of Jews, Holocaust researcher Pierre Sauvage, who was born in Le Chambon, has observed that many of the common people in this unusual village took the whole Bible and the Jewish roots of their Christian faith seriously. He quotes a couple of

115. Paul W. Harkins, introduction to *Saint John Chrysostom: Discourses against Judaizing Christians*, FC 68 (Washington, DC: Catholic University of America Press, 1979), xxvi–xxvii; Judith Lieu, *Image and Reality: The Jews in the World of the Christians in the Second Century* (Edinburgh: T&T Clark, 1996), 284–85; Geoffrey D. Dunn, *Tertullian*, The Early Church Fathers (New York: Routledge, 2004), 48–50.

116. On the close contact between Jews and Christians in urban centers through the coming of Islam, see Fredriksen, "'What Parting of the Ways'?" 35–63. On the tragic legacy of this tradition, see Steven Beller, *Antisemitism: A Very Short Introduction* (Oxford: Oxford University Press, 2007), 10–21.

117. Beller, *Antisemitism*, 20–21; cf. the attitudes assembled in Gushee, *Righteous Gentiles of the Holocaust*, 149–52.

sentences that he finds telling from a letter that their newly arrived pastor, André Trocmé, wrote to an American friend before all the trouble started:

> The old Huguenot spirit is still alive. The humblest peasant home has its Bible and the father reads it every day. So these people who do not read the papers but the Scriptures do not stand on the moving soil of opinion but on the rock of the Word of God.[118]

The Christians of Le Chambon had learned to test the surrounding culture and prevailing opinion by the touchstone of the Scriptures, and this, Sauvage seems to suggest, played an important role in their willingness to make the right but difficult choice to protect people during the Holocaust. Much the same can be said for some of the Christians in the Netherlands who protected Jews during this period. One Dutch rescuer speaks for many when he reports that at least part of the reason he sheltered Jews was that he imagined not helping and then trying to answer the Lord on the day of judgment when asked, "What did you do . . . when the Nazis were tormenting My people?"[119]

Romans 11:11–36 stands like a sentinel over any attempt to introduce notions of social discrimination or social privilege into the church. The Christians in France and the Netherlands who remained true to the teaching of this truth despite the prevailing political winds of the time serve as an example to the church of all times and places to base its life and worship on the Scriptures alone.

118. Pierre Sauvage, "Ten Things I Would Like to Know about Righteous Conduct in Le Chambon and Elsewhere during the Holocaust," *Humboldt Journal of Social Relations* 13 (1985–86): 253.

119. André Stein, *Quiet Heroes: True Stories of the Rescue of Jews by Christians in Nazi-Occupied Holland* (New York: New York University Press, 1988), 20.

CHAPTER 24

Romans 12:1–8

Literary Context

Paul's argument has brought his Roman audience from the justified wrath of God against all humanity because of their failure to glorify God (1:18–3:20) to God's gracious and merciful salvation of a socially diverse group within humanity who brings glory to God and is destined to share the glory of his Son, Jesus Christ (3:21–11:36). In the course of this argument Paul has described God's forgiveness of human sin through the death of Christ (3:21–26; 4:7; 5:1–11; 8:1–3), an action that God performs as a completely free and gracious gift received by faith (3:22–25, 28; 4:1–25; 5:12–21). When people trust that God has put them right with himself, or justified them, they are united with the risen, living Christ (6:1–14), and this union has a powerful impact on the way people live, an impact that Paul has so far described in abstract, theoretical terms. The believer has moved from death to life (6:1–11, 13, 21–23; 7:1–5, 8–11, 24–25a; 8:1–13), from sin's enslavement to the dominion of righteousness (6:9, 12–20; 7:6, 14–23, 25b; 8:15), from captivity within the nexus of the law and sin to freedom from the law and the eschatological possibility of freedom from sin (7:23; 8:2). He has also demonstrated how all this can be true and God still be faithful to his promises to Israel (9:1–11:36).

Now, in 12:1–15:13 Paul moves from these abstract principles to a concrete appeal to his Roman readers based on these principles about how they should live with each other and within the wider Roman culture in which they were located. The unity of all believers as those transformed by the gospel across ethnic lines has already been a primary theme of the argument up to this point, especially of 9:1–11:36. The contrast between the quality of the lives of believers (5:1–8:39) and the quality of the lives of the unbelievers among whom they lived (1:18–32) has also been a theme in the preceding argument, although somewhat less obvious. Now, at this point in his argument Paul was ready to speak specifically about the virtues that should characterize those whose minds and wills God's Spirit had transformed.

The character of the good life, and the relative usefulness of foundational principles on one hand and concrete precepts on the other hand, were topics of debate in mid first-century Rome, especially among Stoic philosophers and those under their influence.[1] The Stoic philosopher Seneca, who was a powerful advisor to Nero when Paul was writing Romans, advocated a balanced approach that recognized the importance of understanding the foundational philosophical reasons for one's conduct.[2] "Virtue is divided into two parts," said Seneca, "into contemplation of truth, and conduct" (*Ep.* 94.45 [Richard M. Gummere, LCL]). The Roman philosopher Musonius Rufus, also active during Nero's time, advocated the value of practice over theory. "Isn't being self-controlled and prudent about all one's actions," said Musonius, "much better than being able to say what is involved in prudence or self-mastery?" (Lecture 5§4 [Cynthia King]).[3] The differences between Paul's theology and Stoic philosophy are great, but the instructional method of providing concrete advice about behavior that is consistent with one's core convictions is similar in Paul and the sort of Stoicism that Seneca represents.[4] Even among the illiterate members of Paul's Roman audience, this educational method was probably familiar.[5]

In a way that is consistent with this method, Paul exhorts his readers to make decisions about their day-to-day conduct on the basis of God's transformation of their minds through the gospel (Rom 12:1–2). They should carry out their roles within the community of believers (12:3–8, 10, 13a, 16) and among their unbelieving neighbors (12:9, 11–12, 13b, 14–15, 17–21) with a humility and love that reflects God's sincere and unconditional love for them. They should not respond to the marginalization they are experiencing within their society with an attitude of revenge seeking and rebellion. Rather, they should respond with love, recognizing that God is in control of events around them even when his ways are difficult to discern. One day his justice would obviously prevail. In the way they handle social tensions within their own believing community, they should work for peace and they should build up one another, accepting one another as Christ accepted them (14:1–15:13).

1. On "the good life" in Greek philosophical discussion, see Philip F. Esler ("Social Identity, the Virtues, and the Good Life: A New Approach to Romans 12:1–15:13," *BTB* 33 [2003]: 55–58). On the debate over the relative importance of basic principles and practical wisdom in philosophical instruction, see Troels Engberg-Pedersen, "The Concept of Paraenesis," in *Early Christian Paraenesis in Context*, ed. James Starr and Troels Engberg-Pedersen, BZNW 125 (Berlin: Walter de Gruyter, 2004), 54–59.

2. *Ep.* 94–95. On Seneca's life, see Leighton Durham Reynolds, Mirian T. Griffin, and Elaine Fantham, "Annaeus Seneca, Lucius," *OCD* 96.

3. On his life, in addition to King's introduction (*Musonius Rufus*, 13–19), see Runar M. Thorsteinsson, *Roman Christianity and Roman Stoicism: A Comparative Study of Ancient Morality* (Oxford: Oxford University Press, 2010), 40–43.

4. Among the differences is Paul's robust understanding of human sin as a problem solvable only by means of divine transformation over against Stoicism's understanding of human nature as basically good and correctable through education (e.g., Seneca, *Ep.* 94.55–58, 68; Musonius Rufus, Lecture 2 [Cynthia King]).

5. Thorsteinsson, *Roman Christianity*, 85.

Main Idea

Through the gospel God has mercifully transformed believers from enemies in rebellion against him into sons and daughters at peace with him. In light of this transformation, the thinking and behavior of God's people stands in stark contrast to the world in which they live their day-to-day lives. Each member of the believing community now pursues whatever role God has given him or her with humility and enthusiasm. This humble service to others is one of the primary ways in which believers stand apart from the larger unbelieving society in which they live.

Translation

(See next page.)

Structure

Romans 12:1–8 falls into two parts, an introduction to the next major section of the argument (12:1–15:13) in 12:1–2 and the first step in that argument in 12:3–8. In 12:1–2 Paul announces that he will deliver concrete instruction to his Roman readers about how they should live day to day in a way that is consistent with the gospel he has just explained at length in 1:16–11:36. God has started to renew their minds, equipping them to be transformed from living in rebellion against him (1:18–32) to living in a way that is pleasing to God.

In 12:3–8 Paul begins to describe this new life in detail by instructing the Roman believers to engage with humility and enthusiasm in the roles God has assigned them in the community. These instructions fall into three parts: a thesis statement in 12:3, an illustration of what the thesis statement means in 12:4–5, and then an application of the illustrated thesis in 12:6–8. Paul's thesis statement is itself an example (γάρ) of what he meant when he spoke of the renewed "mind" (νοῦς) of believers in 12:2. Believers were now equipped to think with humility and sound judgment about the

Romans 12:1–8

1a Exhortation — **I appeal to you,** therefore, brothers and sisters,
 through God's compassionate actions,
 to offer your bodies as a sacrifice
b Description — that is living, holy, and pleasing to God,
c Apposition — which is your reasonable worship.

2a Exhortation — And **do not be conformed** to this age,
b Contrast — but **be transformed** by the renewal of your mind
c Result (of 2b) — so that you might approve what the will of God is
d Apposition (to 2c) — —that [you may approve, in other words, that] which is good and pleasing and perfect.

3a Expansion (of 1–2) — For **I say**
 to everyone among you,
 through the grace given to me,
 not to think too highly,
b Description — beyond what one ought to think, but
c Contrast — to think sensibly,
d Description — each one just as God has apportioned them a measure of faith.

4 Description (of 3) — For just as we have many members in one body, and all the members do not have the same function.
5 Comparison (to 4) — So, we the many are one body in Christ, and each one members of one another.

6a Slight contrast (to 5) — But, having different gifts according to the grace given to us, **[let us use them sensibly,]**
b List (1) — whether prophecy — in proportion to faith,
7a List (2) — whether ministering, — in ministry,
b List (3) — whether the one who teaches, — in teaching,
8a List (4) — whether the one who exhorts, — in exhortation,
b List (5) — the one who shares, — in sincerity,
c List (6) — the one who leads, — with diligence,
d List (7) — the one who shows mercy, — with cheerfulness.

role that God had given them in the community of believers, an approach to community that stood in dramatic contrast to the competitive spirit pervading Roman society at all levels.[6]

He then illustrates what he means with an analogy between the community and

6. Philip F. Esler, *Conflict and Identity in Romans: The Social Setting of Paul's Letter* (Minneapolis: Fortress, 2003), 77–84; Toner, *Popular Culture*, 92–122.

the human body (12:4–5). The analogy describes a diversely gifted group of people who are, despite their diversity, connected to one another through their common relationship to Christ.

The list of gifts that follows in the third part of the paragraph (12:6–8) emphasizes the humility and heartfelt enthusiasm with which each different member of the body should do the particular work it was designed to do. The list is carefully constructed of seven elements. The first six gifts focus on Christian instruction: prophecy, ministry (probably, ministry of the word), teaching, exhortation, sharing (again, probably, sharing a verbal message), and leading (also associated with teaching in 1 Thess 5:12 and 1 Tim 5:17). The last gift, showing mercy (ἐλεῶν), probably describes a role given to all believers, since all have received God's compassion (οἰκτιρμός) and should live in a way that is consistent with this (12:1). This seventh gift forms a bridge to Paul's description of the unusual, sacrificial nature of Christian love in 12:9–21.

Exegetical Outline

XI. Exhortation to Live in a Way That Is Consistent with the Gospel (12:1–15:13)

➡ **A. A Mind Transformed and Renewed by God (12:1–2)**

1. Worship That Is Logically Consistent with God's Mercy (12:1)
2. A Renewed Mind and a Transformed Life (12:2)

B. Community without Competition (12:3–8)

1. Humility about One's Role in the Believing Community (12:3)
2. Analogy of the Human Body (12:4)
3. Application of the Analogy: Diversity of Roles and Unity in Relationships (12:5)
4. Humility and Enthusiasm in Pursuing One's Role in the Believing Community (12:6–8)
   - a. Special roles involving community instruction (12:6–8c)
     - (1) prophesying (12:6b)
     - (2) ministering (12:7a)
     - (3) teaching (12:7b)
     - (4) exhorting (12:8a)
     - (5) sharing (12:8b)
     - (6) leading (12:8c)
   - b. Everyone's role: showing mercy (12:8d)

Explanation of the Text

12:1 I appeal to you, therefore, brothers and sisters, through God's compassionate actions, to offer your bodies as a sacrifice that is living, holy, and pleasing to God, which is your reasonable worship (Παρακαλῶ οὖν ὑμᾶς, ἀδελφοί, διὰ τῶν οἰκτιρμῶν τοῦ θεοῦ παραστῆσαι τὰ σώματα ὑμῶν θυσίαν ζῶσαν ἁγίαν εὐάρεστον τῷ θεῷ, τὴν λογικὴν λατρείαν ὑμῶν). The gospel as Paul has explained it in 1:16–11:36 has demonstrated that God's kindness, love, and mercy are evident in the justification of sinners through the death of Christ and through their release from bondage to sin. Believers should conduct their day-to-day affairs in edifying and loving ways because this is the most appropriate way to worship the loving God who has freed them to love others.

The phrase "I appeal to you, therefore . . ." (παρακαλῶ οὖν ὑμᾶς) signals the beginning of a new major section of the letter in which Paul will describe the kind of behavior that should characterize the day-to-day lives of his Roman Christian audience (cf. Gal 5:1, 13; Phil 4:1; Eph 4:1).[7] The appeal to live in the way Paul is about to describe comes "through" (διά + genitive) God's "compassionate actions" (τῶν οἰκτιρμῶν) in the sense that God's pity, expressed in the gospel Paul has just described in 1:16–11:36, provides the basis for the appeal, fueling it and sending it forward (cf. 2 Cor 10:1).[8] The expression "I appeal to you" carries nuances of both authority and affection. Paul's use of this expression in 1 Corinthians to depict himself as the Corinthians' attentive father provides a helpful analogy to his use of it here:

> I do not write these things to make you ashamed, but to admonish you as my beloved children. For though you have countless guides in Christ, you do not have many fathers. For I became your father in Christ Jesus through the gospel. I urge you, then [παρακαλῶ οὖν ὑμᾶς], be imitators of me. (1 Cor 4:14–16; cf. Phlm 8–10)[9]

The same concepts are present in Romans 12:1. Paul speaks to his "brothers and sisters" (ἀδελφοί) in Rome as members of his family, but he also exhorts them in the role of an apostle to the gentiles, whom God has charged to call the gentiles to "the obedience of faith" (1:5–6; 11:13).

The term "offer" (παραστῆσαι) was commonly used of slaughtering animals in a religious ritual intended to please God (e.g., Josephus, *Ant.* 4.113; Lucian, *Sacrifices* 13).[10] Here, however, Paul envisions sacrifices that are "living" (ζῶσαν), recalling his earlier description of the believer's transformation from the realm of death because of sin to the realm of life through union with the risen Christ (Rom 5:10, 17–18, 21). The term "living" also recalls the case he has already made that the transforming effect of the gospel on believers influences their conduct: "How will those of us who have died to sin continue to live [ζήσομεν] in it still?" (6:2; cf. 6:4, 11; 7:4; 8:2, 5–6, 10, 13).

The terms "holy" (ἁγίαν) and "pleasing" (εὐάρεστον) both recall sacrificial ritual (e.g., Gen

7. On this, see Engberg-Pedersen ("Concept of Paraenesis," 63).

8. See BDAG 225, s.v. διά A.3.f.

9. The term translated "appeal" here (παρακαλέω) appears in diplomatic contexts (Jewett, *Romans*, 726), such as when a king addresses his subjects (e.g., 2 Macc 9:26), but even there it seems to be part of a convention of addressing subjects as friends. See C. J. Bjerkelund, *PARAKALÔ: Form, Funktion und Sinn der parakalô-Sätze in den paulinischen Briefen*, Bibliotheca Theologica Norvegica 1 (Oslo: Universitetsforlaget, 1967), 62–65. Paul's use of "brothers and sisters" gives his language a friendly rather than a diplomatic tone.

10. BDAG 778, s.v. παρίστημι 1d.

8:21; 1 Sam 21:4; Phil 4:18), but Paul has given these words a metaphorical and ethical connotation.[11] Earlier in the letter Paul had appealed to his readers to "offer" (παρεστήσατε) their "members to righteousness, to be its slave, with sanctification [ἁγιασμόν] as the result" (6:19; cf. 6:12–13, 16, 22).[12] Similarly, Paul could use the term "pleasing" (εὐάρεστον) elsewhere to refer to conduct that pleases God (14:18; 2 Cor 5:9; Eph 5:10; Col 3:20).

Paul calls this "reasonable worship" (τὴν λογικὴν λατρείαν) not because it arises from within the human spirit (RSV, NAB, REB, NRSV, ESV, HCSB) but because it is the fitting response to the gospel as he has explained it in 1:16–11:36 (Luther ["vernünftiger"], Tyndale, KJV, NIV, CEB). The term "reasonable" (λογικός) was used in religious speculation during Paul's time to refer to the part of the human being that was most like God (Philo, *Alleg. Interp.* 2.23), and from at least the early second-century AD to the sort of worship that human beings should give to God since they are rational creatures and God is a rational God (Epictetus, *Diatr.* 1.16.15–21; *Corp. herm.* 13.18, 19).[13]

Paul also thinks that the believer's worship should match the nature of God, but he is not interested in rationality as the bridge between the human and divine. Instead, the offering of the believer's "body" (σῶμα) refers to the offering of the entire self to God, particularly in the kinds of edifying and loving attitudes and actions toward others that Paul will describe in 12:3–21.[14]

This is "reasonable worship" because it makes sense—it matches God's own merciful character as it is displayed in the good news that God has redeemed his people from slavery to sin.[15] This worship also stands in contrast to, and rectifies, the human condition as Paul described it in 1:24–25 where people were "dishonoring . . . their bodies [ἀτιμάζεσθαι τὰ σώματα αὐτῶν]" and "served the creature [ἐλάτρευσαν τῇ κτίσει] rather than the Creator."[16]

12:2 And do not be conformed to this age, but be transformed by the renewal of your mind so that you might approve what the will of God is—that [you may approve, in other words, that] which is good and pleasing and perfect (καὶ μὴ συσχηματίζεσθε τῷ αἰῶνι τούτῳ, ἀλλὰ μεταμορφοῦσθε τῇ ἀνακαινώσει τοῦ νοός εἰς τὸ δοκιμάζειν ὑμᾶς τί τὸ θέλημα τοῦ θεοῦ, τὸ ἀγαθὸν καὶ εὐάρεστον καὶ τέλειον). Paul continues to describe the content of his appeal to his Roman audience. They are not only to present their bodies as a sacrifice to God but are to avoid patterning their lives after this age and instead allow God to transform them from the inside out so that they both approve and engage in the good works that God desires.

As the "In Depth" look at the terms "be conformed" and "transformed" explains below, these

11. Otto Procksch, "ἅγιος, κτλ.," *TDNT* 1:90; Hodge, *Romans*, 384; Godet, *Romans*, 426.

12. Cf. Theodoret of Cyrus, *Letters of St. Paul*, 1:118.

13. Everett Ferguson, "Spiritual Sacrifice in Early Christianity and Its Environment," *ANRW* 23.2:1153–56; BDAG 598, s.v. λογικός. This idea seems to stand somewhere in the background of the very old claim that Paul implies a contrast here between "offering rams and goats and calves to the immortal and incorporeal God" and the more fitting offering of a "rational human being" to God (Origen, *Romans, Books 6–10*, 192–93; cf. Chrysostom, *Romans*, 360; Theodoret of Cyrus, *Letters of St. Paul*, 1:118).

14. Cf. Dunn (*Theology of Paul*, 544), who sees Paul's use of "body" (σῶμα) here as an indication that the apostle has in mind the believer's day-to-day life as it touches on the day-to-day lives of others.

15. See Lagrange (*Romains*, 293), Cranfield (*Romans 9–16*, 605), Schreiner (*Romans*, 645), Longenecker (*Romans*, 921), and LSJ 1056, s.v. λογικός II.2, citing Aristotle, *Rhetoric* 1355a13 (1.1.11), which refers to "logical syllogisms" (τοὺς λογικοὺς συλλογισμούς [J. H. Freese, LCL]).

16. Dunn, *Romans 9–16*, 708.

words had a similar, but not quite identical, meaning. Paul's "be conformed" (συσχηματίζεσθε) encourages believers in Rome not to adapt themselves to the pattern marked out by "this age," a pattern that is ephemeral and will soon pass away (cf. 13:13–14; 1 Cor 2:6). "Be transformed" (μεταμορφοῦσθε) recalls Paul's statement that God predestined believers "to be similar in form to the image of his Son" (8:29) and implies that believers should cooperate in this transforming work of God.[17] "This age" (τῷ αἰῶνι τούτῳ) refers to the evil values and systems of a world so blinded by Satan that they could crucify "the Lord of glory" (1 Cor 2:8; see 1 Cor 1:20; 2:6; 3:18; 2 Cor 4:4; Gal 1:4; Eph 2:2–3).

The transformation Paul describes happens through a renewal of the way believers think about the world. This is the reverse of the process Paul had outlined in Romans 1:28 where human beings did not "deem it worthwhile" (ἐδοκίμασαν) to acknowledge God, and so God "handed them over to a worthless mind [ἀδόκιμον νοῦν]."[18] A "worthless mind" is a mind unaffected by the transforming Spirit of God, a mind that may be able to acknowledge the goodness of God's law (7:12, 16; cf. 1:32), but is unable to obey it because the flesh overpowers its will to do good (7:18–25). Now, however, the renewal of the mind results in believers "approving" (δοκιμάζειν) the will of God so that they are actually able to present their bodies as living sacrifices to God and couple the approval of God's will with obedience.[19] Paul does not mention the Spirit of God here, but he has already explained that this movement from acknowledging the good to actually doing it comes to believers through the transforming work of the Spirit (8:2–9, 12–13).

IN DEPTH: Are "Be Conformed" and "Be Transformed" Synonymous?

An old interpretation of Romans 12:2a found a profound difference between the terms "be conformed" (συσχηματίζεσθε) and "be transformed" (μεταμορφοῦσθε), with the first term referring to fleeting fashion and the second term referring to permanent form. Paul, then, would be urging his Roman audience, in the words of J. B. Lightfoot, "not to follow the fleeting *fashion* of this world, but to undergo a complete change, assume a new *form*, in the renewal of the mind."[20] This interpretation goes back at least as far as Origen (writing in AD 246), John Chrysostom (writing ca. 381–98), and Theodoret of Cyrus (writing in the mid 440s), but Lightfoot's careful study seemed to place it on a firm academic

17. On what I have called cooperation here, see the balanced comments of Bavinck, *Holy Spirit, Church, and New Creation*, 252–56.

18. Dunn, *Romans 9–16*, 708, 714.

19. Zahn (*An die Römer*, 540) observes that the phrase translated here as "which is good and pleasing and perfect" must stand in apposition to "the will of God" rather than apply these three attributes to God's will (as in the KJV, NIV, and CSB) since Paul characteristically uses the term "pleasing" or "acceptable" (εὐάρεστον) to refer to what is acceptable to God (cf., e.g., Rom 12:1; 14:18). It would be odd to speak of the will of God as something acceptable to God. Cf. Jewett, *Romans*, 734.

20. J. B. Lightfoot, *Saint Paul's Epistle to the Philippians*, 4th ed. with additions and alterations (London: Macmillan, 1896), 131 (emphasis original). Cf. Tyndale: "And fassion not youre selves lyke vnto this worlde: But be ye chaunged in youre shape."

footing.[21] He influenced a number of late nineteenth and early twentieth-century commentators on Romans to take this view.[22]

Many more recent interpreters, however, have regarded this as an overinterpretation of the terms and seen the two words as essentially synonymous.[23] These interpreters tend to sum up the view they are rejecting as a claim that "be conformed" (συνσχηματίζεσθε) refers to "something external and superficial" and "be transformed" (μεταμορφοῦσθε) refers to "a profound transformation."[24] Paul would never regard conformity to this age as a superficial matter, it is said, and he seems to use cognates of the two terms synonymously (2 Cor 3:18; Phil 3:21).[25]

At issue is whether Paul usually distinguished between the words σχῆμα and μορφή and their various cognates and how likely it is that he intended a distinction here. BDAG glosses σχῆμα with "outward appearance, form, shape" and μορφή with "form, outward appearance, shape . . . way of life."[26] According to BDAG, then, "outward appearance" should first jump to mind when encountering σχῆμα and "form" when encountering μορφή, but the terms also have large amounts of semantic overlap.

LSJ analyzes the words in a similar way. It defines σχῆμα as "form, shape, figure" but then further defines it in terms of that which is easily changed, such as something's appearance (Plutarch, *Dion* 16.1), a friendly gesture (Plato, *Republic* 576a), or the phases of the moon (Vettius Valens, *Anthologies* 106.28).[27] The word μορφή is "form, shape . . . fashion, appearance, kind, sort," but with less emphasis in the examples on the changeable nature of the form. In Euripides's *Ion*, the old servant can ask Creusa what the monster Gorgon looked like with the question, "What was the fashion [σχῆμ'] of its grisly form [μορφῆς]?" [Arthur S. Way, LCL]. The difference between "fashion" and "form" here is not entirely

21. Origen: "If there are those who love the present world and the things that are in this world, they are being adapted to the form of the present world. But those who do not look to what is seen, but to what is unseen and eternal, are being transformed and renewed unto the form of the future world" (*Romans, Books 6–10*, 195). Chrysostom: "If, then, thou throwest the fashion [σχῆμα] aside, thou wilt speedily come to the *form* [μορφήν]" (*Romans*, 363 [*PG* 60:598]); Theodoret of Cyrus: "Form [μορφή] betrays things in reality, whereas figure [σχῆμα] is something easily lost" (*Letters of St. Paul*, 1:118 [*PG* 82:188]). Caution is required. Origen is only preserved at this point in Rufinus's Latin translation, and Rufinus was clearly meddling with Origen's text here (*Romans, Books 6–10*, 195n29). Chrysostom and Theodoret, moreover, were writing in a period when christological controversy had influenced the interpretation of μορφή and σχῆμα in Phil 2:6–7 (Lightfoot, *Philippians*, 133n1).

22. E.g., Sanday and Headlam, *Romans*, 353; Lagrange, *Romains*, 294; Zahn, *An die Römer*, 539; Johannes Behm, "μεταμορφόω," *TDNT* 4:759n22; Murray, *Romans*, 2:114 (all citing Lightfoot).

23. E.g., Barrett, *Romans*, 214; Cranfield, *Romans*, 2:605–7; Moo, *Romans*, 756; Schreiner, *Romans*, 646–47; Wright, "Romans," 705n489; Légasse, *Romains*, 761.

24. Cranfield, *Romans*, 2:605.

25. Barrett, *Romans*, 214. Cf. Légasse, *Romains*, 761.

26. BDAG 981, s.v. σχῆμα; 659, s.v. μορφή.

27. LSJ 1745, s.v. σχῆμα.

clear, but the question seems to assume that Gorgon's unchangingly monstrous nature might appear in a variety of possible ways.

Similarly, when Plutarch says that God gave definition to chaotic matter at the creation of the world he explains what he means this way:

> For shape [μορφή] or arrangement [σχῆμα] is always a limit imposed on the material that is shaped [μεμορφωμένου] or arranged [ἐσχηματισμένου]. Without this process it was, by itself, shapeless [ἄμορφος] and disorganized [ἀσχημάτιστος]. (*Quaest. conv.* 719 D)[28]

This statement shows how close the two terms and their respective cognates were in meaning, but also that they had slightly different nuances. There would be no need to use both terms unless each contributed something slightly different to the explanation of what happened when God created the world.

Paul's use of these terms and their cognates is consistent with their dictionary definitions. Cognates of σχῆμα most often describe change, such as adopting a disguise (μετασχηματιζόμενοι; 2 Cor 11:13–15) or the ephemeral "form" (σχῆμα) of the present world (1 Cor 7:31). Cognates of μορφή most often focus on something's essential nature, even when the subject is a change into a different nature. Believers are "predestined to be similar in form [συμμόρφους]" to God's Son (8:29); they are "transformed" (μεταμορφούμεθα) into the image of the Lord (2 Cor 3:18); Christ "is formed" (μορφωθῇ) in them (Gal 4:19), and Paul is "becoming like [συμμορφιζόμενος]" Christ "in his death" (Phil 3:10). Although the example is controversial, a distinction between the two terms also holds reasonably well in Philippians 2:7. When Paul says that Jesus took "the form [μορφήν] of a servant" and then in the next breath says that Jesus was "found in human form [σχήματι]," he seems to use σχῆμα because he is speaking of the way in which people viewed Jesus, of the form in which they "found" (εὑρεθείς) him.[29]

It is certainly true, as Cranfield especially has argued, that it is hard to maintain a clear distinction between the two terms in Philippians 3:21.[30] There Paul says that the Lord Jesus Christ "will transform [μετασχηματίσει] our lowly body to be like [σύμμορφον] his glorious body," and if he had distinguished between a changeable σχῆμα and a more durable μορφή in this instance, he should have written a cognate of μορφή for the verb "transform" (i.e., μεταμορφώσει) since it

28. Trans. Edwin L. Minar Jr., F. H. Sandback, and W. C. Helmbold, *Plutarch: Moralia, Volume IX*, LCL (Cambridge: Harvard University Press, 1961).

29. Johannes Schneider, "σχῆμα," *TDNT* 7:956; Ralph P. Martin, *A Hymn of Christ: Philippians 2:5–11 in Recent Interpretation and in the Setting of Early Christian Worship* (Downers Grove, IL: InterVarsity Press, 1997), 207.

30. Cranfield, *Romans*, 2:606.

is the "form" (μορφή) of the bodies of believers that is being changed (cf. 2 Cor 3:18).

This last example, however, only shows that the distinction does not always hold for Paul, not that it never holds, and the other examples show that Paul did sometimes distinguish between σχῆμα and μορφή and their cognates. In interpreting "be conformed" (συνσχηματίζεσθε) and "be transformed" (μεταμορφοῦσθε) in 12:2, then, it is important to ask whether these particular words within this particular context were likely to carry somewhat different nuances. In Plutarch, writing a few decades after Paul, the verb "conform" (συσχηματίζω) could refer unambiguously to adapting to the way one's surroundings appear in a given moment: the wicked person allows his thoughts to run wild at night, but during the day he is busy "conforming" (συσχηματιζομένη) his conduct to societal norms and popular opinion (*Virt. vit.* 100F–101A). Similarly, the flatterer constantly "changes his shape" (συσχηματιζόμενος), chameleon-like, to conform to the attitudes of the person whose favor he seeks to win (*Adul. am.* 52B [Frank Cole Babbitt, LCL]).[31] Since there is no indication in Romans 12:2 that Paul would want to say anything different than this, and since the term σχῆμα often connotes change, it seems likely that Paul intended to communicate in Romans 12:2 that the present position of "this age" would soon pass away (cf. 13:11–14; 1 Cor 7:31). He appeals to his Roman audience, then, not to adopt the same posture as the less-than-permanent culture around them.

The verb "be transformed" (μεταμορφοῦσθε) does not stand in sharp contrast to "be conformed" (συνσχηματίζεσθε), but it is distinguishable from it. It too carries connotations of change, but of change in a positive direction since Paul has already said that God is predestining believers "to be similar in form [συμμόρφους] to the image of his Son" (8:29).[32]

In light of this evidence, Lightfoot's interpretation of Romans 12:2 is not as far off the mark as many recent interpreters have thought. He laid too much stress on the idea of the world's "fleeting fashion" and saw too much contrast between the two verbs "be conformed" (συνσχηματίζεσθε) and "be transformed" (μεταμορφοῦσθε), but his basic linguistic instincts seem to be confirmed by the evidence. Paul does hint that conformity to this age involves adopting a framework for living that is prone to change and destined for failure, and he encourages his audience, in light of this, to cooperate with the transformation into the image of Christ that God has already started within them.

31. The occurrence of the term in 1 Pet 1:14 carries the same ambiguities as it does in Rom 12:2.

32. Cf. 2 Cor 3:18; Gal 4:19; Phil 3:10, 21 where cognates of μορφή are all associated with the concept of union with Christ.

12:3 For I say to everyone among you, through the grace given to me, not to think too highly, beyond what one ought to think, but to think sensibly, each one just as God has apportioned them a measure of faith (Λέγω γὰρ διὰ τῆς χάριτος τῆς δοθείσης μοι παντὶ τῷ ὄντι ἐν ὑμῖν μὴ ὑπερφρονεῖν παρ' ὃ δεῖ φρονεῖν ἀλλὰ φρονεῖν εἰς τὸ σωφρονεῖν, ἑκάστῳ ὡς ὁ θεὸς ἐμέρισεν μέτρον πίστεως). The transformed minds of believers should produce in them a humility based on the knowledge that faith, and all that goes with it, are gifts of God. The faith God has given to each believer is sufficient to sustain that believer's role in the community, and believers need to think clearly and realistically about their particular role.

Paul's "for" (γάρ) shows that he is about to explain the transformation of mind to which he has just referred in greater detail. The "grace given" to Paul is his vocation from God to be an apostle of the gospel to the gentiles (Rom 1:5; 11:13; 15:15). This vocation involved instructing the predominantly gentile believers in Rome on the implications of the gospel for the way they were to live, including the attitudes they were to adopt toward others. Paul had already urged them not to "think haughty thoughts" (μὴ ὑψηλὰ φρόνει) about Israelites who had not believed the gospel, as if their faith somehow provided them with a ground for boasting (11:20). Now he urges them not to have such attitudes in their interactions with other believers.

His play on the verb "think" (ὑπερφρονεῖν, φρονεῖν, σωφρονεῖν) links his admonition back to his command to "be transformed by the renewal of your mind" in 12:2 and introduces an illustration of how his readers can obey this command.[33] The verb "to be sensible" (σωφρονεῖν) and its cognates are, as Spicq says, "strictly speaking, untranslatable."[34] They signaled the virtue of using good moral judgment (Titus 1:8; 2:2–6, 12) and often stood opposite descriptions of insane, irrational, passion-driven behavior (Mark 5:15; 2 Cor 5:13).[35] Josephus, for example, says that the men of Sodom were "bent only on violence [βίαν] and outrage [ὕβριν]" against Lot's three visitors, but Lot urged them "to restrain their passions [σωφρονεῖν]" (*Ant.* 1.200–201 [H. St. J. Thackeray, LCL]). Similarly, Reuben tried to convince his brothers "to desist from their mad intent" to kill Joseph and yield "to penitence and sober reflexion" (σωφρονεῖν; *Ant.* 2.23; [H. St. J. Thackeray, LCL]). Here, then, Paul counsels against fantasies about one's own importance. Believers should assess themselves soberly and modestly in light of the humbling realities of human sinfulness and God's grace described in the gospel (Rom 11:18, 20).[36]

Believers should assess themselves, Paul continues, in light of the "measure of faith" (μέτρον πίστεως) God has apportioned them. We could understand the genitive "of faith" (πίστεως) in this expression appositionally so that the "measure" God apportions each believer is simply the believer's trust in God, with no thought of each person receiving a certain amount or type of faith.[37] If this is a correct reading of the phrase, then the Roman Christians were to think soberly about themselves in light of the gift of faith God had given them. "Of faith" might also refer loosely to the moment of conversion, and Paul might be saying that God has measured out a certain gift to each believer when that person first believed the gospel.[38] Neither of

33. On the wordplay, see BDF §488(1)(b), and Thorsteinsson, *Roman Christianity*, 94.

34. *TLNT* 3:359.

35. BDAG 986, s.v. σωφρονέω.

36. Cf. Philip F. Esler, "Paul and Stoicism: Romans 12 as a Test Case," *NTS* 50 (2004): 116.

37. Cf. the NIV's "in accordance with the faith God has distributed to each of you," and the detailed argument for this position in C. E. B. Cranfield, "ΜΕΤΡΟΝ ΠΙΣΤΕΩΣ in Romans XII.3," *NTS* 8 (1961–62): 345–51.

38. Byrne, *Romans*, 371.

these explanations, however, works very well, the first because it does not fit the context, and the second because it is not the most straightforward understanding of Paul's Greek.

Paul's emphasis in the context falls on the varying roles that each person plays in the believing community and the need for sound judgment about where one fits in the community in order to avoid haughtiness and the division that it brings (cf. 1 Cor 7:17; 2 Cor 10:13). The expression "apportion a measure of x," moreover, refers more naturally to measuring out a certain quantity of something than to measuring out something at a certain moment. Although the notion of varying degrees of faith is an unusual concept within Paul's letters, this was most likely what he meant (cf. Rom 12:6).[39]

12:4 For just as we have many members in one body, and all the members do not have the same function (καθάπερ γὰρ ἐν ἑνὶ σώματι πολλὰ μέλη ἔχομεν, τὰ δὲ μέλη πάντα οὐ τὴν αὐτὴν ἔχει πρᾶξιν). A properly working body has a diverse set of parts that perform a diverse set of functions.

The "for" (γάρ) once again shows Paul is about to explain the comment he has just made that believers should think sensibly about themselves by considering how God has apportioned each member of the community a suitable measure of faith. He does this with the help of an analogy between the community and a human body that was common in the political discourse of his time and was particularly well known in Rome.[40] Paul had used it extensively in a letter to Corinth (his location when he wrote Romans) and would use it again in letters to Colossae and Ephesus (1 Cor 10:16–17; 12:12–30; Col 2:19; 3:15; Eph 4:4–16).[41] Here, just as in 1 Corinthians 12:12–30 and Ephesians 4:4–16, Paul used the analogy to emphasize the need for a diversely gifted group of believers to work together for the common good.

Paul's "even as" (καθάπερ) introduces his description of the characteristics of the human body that he wants to compare to the church "body" (cf. 1 Cor 12:12).[42] The emphasis here, just as in 1 Corinthians 12:14–20 and 29–30, lies on denying that the body can function properly if all its parts perform the same task.

12:5 So, we the many are one body in Christ, and each one members of one another (οὕτως οἱ πολλοὶ ἓν σῶμά ἐσμεν ἐν Χριστῷ, τὸ δὲ καθ' εἷς ἀλλήλων μέλη). Because everyone who believes the gospel is united to Christ, he or she is also united to other believers and works together with them to accomplish the goals of the group.

"So" (οὕτως) introduces the application of Paul's description of the human body to those who are in Christ.[43] The first-person plural emphasizes the universality of the analogy to all believers everywhere, whether Paul's Roman audience or Paul himself. At one level this group is a company of in-

39. See especially Schreiner, *Romans*, 652–53.

40. See, e.g., Livy, *History of Rome* 2.32; Dionysius of Halicarnassus, *Ant. rom.* 6.86; Seneca, *Ira* 2.31.7–8; Josephus, *J.W.* 1.507; 2.264; 4.406–7; 5.279, and the discussion in Margaret M. Mitchell, *Paul and the Rhetoric of Reconciliation*, HUT 28 (Tübingen: Mohr Siebeck, 1991), 157–61; Dunn, *Theology of Paul*, 150–51; Thorsteinsson, *Roman Christianity*, 33.

41. Each time Paul uses the analogy, he uses it somewhat differently. In 1 Cor 12:12, 27 the church is the body of Christ, and in Col 1:18, 2:19 and Eph 4:15–16, 5:23 Christ is the head of his body, which is the church. Here in Romans, however, the "many" believers in Rome are like a body and are one body in Christ, but they are not identified explicitly with Christ's body (see Barrett, *Romans*, 217–18; Cranfield, *Romans*, 2:617).

42. Cf. Dionysius of Halicarnassus, *Ant. rom.* 6.86.5 ("just as in our bodies," καθάπερ ἐν τοῖς σώμασιν ἡμῶν [Earnest Cary, LCL]).

43. Cf. Dionysius of Halicarnassus, *Ant. rom.* 6.86.5 ("so in the commonwealths," οὕτως ἐν ταῖς πόλεσιν [Earnest Cary, LCL]).

dividuals as the phrase "each one" (τὸ . . . καθ' εἷς) emphasizes (cf. Mark 14:19; John 8:9).[44] At another level, it is a single body since each individual is "in Christ." Every believer, then, is united to every other believer by means of his or her common relationship to Christ.

12:6 But, having different gifts according to the grace given to us, [let us use them sensibly,] whether prophecy in proportion to faith (ἔχοντες δὲ χαρίσματα κατὰ τὴν χάριν τὴν δοθεῖσαν ἡμῖν διάφορα, εἴτε προφητείαν κατὰ τὴν ἀναλογίαν τῆς πίστεως). God's grace has equipped people to help the whole body of believers in different ways, and believers should fill the role God has assigned them in a humble way, recognizing that these roles originate with God, not with their own ability or cleverness.

It is possible that the participle "having" (ἔχοντες) at the beginning of this sentence should be attached syntactically to the main verb "we . . . are" (ἐσμεν) in the immediately preceding sentence. The seven gifts in 12:6b–8 would then simply explain what the body of believers looks like in all its diversity: "We all are one body in Christ . . . having charisms which differ in accordance with the grace given to us."[45] The syntax of 12:4–5, however, is tidy as it stands, without any hint that another clause needs to be added to it, and the expression "but having" (ἔχοντες δέ), with a nominative participle followed by a conjunction, is a normal way of beginning a new sentence in Greek (cf. 2 Cor 4:13).[46] In addition, the last three clauses in the list ("the one who shares, in sincerity; the one who leads, with diligence; the one who shows mercy, with cheerfulness," 12:8b–d) clearly adopt the stance of exhortations and require some verbal idea to be supplied to complete the thought ("*Let* the one who shares *do so* with sincerity").[47] The list both emphasizes the diverse (διάφορα) nature of the gifts in the one body and admonishes the Roman Christians to use their gifts humbly and sensibly (cf. 12:3).

The gift of prophecy enabled people to encourage, edify, and comfort the church (1 Cor 14:3–4) and to speak so incisively to outsiders who were present that they might "worship God and declare that God is really among you" (1 Cor 14:24–25; cf. Acts 15:32). Prophets commissioned people for certain tasks (Acts 13:1–3; 1 Tim 4:14), predicted future events (Acts 11:27–30), and directed the church's mission on the basis of this knowledge (Acts 21:10–11).[48]

The term "proportion" (ἀναλογία) refers to a mathematical ratio, and in a context where Paul has already spoken of God apportioning to each member of the body a "measure of faith" (12:3), it likely refers to the level of trust the prophet has that he or she is speaking for God.[49] Paul implies

44. MM 322, s.v. κατά I.5 (cf. BDF §305) report that the phrase (τὸ καθ' ἕν) appears at the head of a list of items in P.Tebt I.47[34] (from 113 BC). Paul probably considered the expression a single word (cf. καθείς in modern Greek), which would explain why it has the article (τό) and why the preposition (κατά) is followed by the nominative (εἷς) rather than the accusative (ἕνα). On this, see BDF §305; Lietzmann (*An die Römer*, 109) and Lagrange (*Romains*, 297).

45. Dunn's translation (*Romans 9–16*, 719). See also, e.g., Byrne (*Romans*, 372), Jewett (*Romans*, 744), and especially Kenneth Berding, "Romans 12.4–8: One Sentence or Two," *NTS* 52 (2006): 433–39.

46. The use of the same conjunction (τὸ δέ) at the end of the immediately preceding clause makes it very likely that the construction at the beginning of 12:6 (ἔχοντες δέ) signals a new sentence (Meyer, *Romans*, 472; Lagrange, *Romains*, 298; Michel, *An die Römer*, 374, 376; Cranfield, *Romans*, 2:618).

47. Meyer, *Romans*, 472.

48. David E. Aune, *Prophecy in Early Chistianity and the Ancient Mediterranean World* (Grand Rapids: Eerdmans, 1983), 192.

49. On the meaning of "proportion," see LSJ 111 and BDAG 67, both s.v. ἀναλογία. The term can mean "correspondence" (LSJ 111, s.v. ἀναλογία IV), but this meaning is rare, so it is unlikely that Paul speaks here of prophesying "in accord with the faith" (Tyndale, TOB; Fitzmyer, *Romans*, 647).

that the prophet should not go beyond the insight God has given but should modestly stay within these bounds when speaking a word of edification or direction (12:3).[50]

12:7 whether ministering, in ministry, whether the one who teaches, in teaching (εἴτε διακονίαν ἐν τῇ διακονίᾳ, εἴτε ὁ διδάσκων ἐν τῇ διδασκαλίᾳ). Those who mediate God's word to others and those who teach the Christian tradition should fill these roles humbly and without competing with others to whom God has assigned different roles.

"Ministering" (διακονία) is an ambiguous term that referred basically to acting as a go-between or courier who performed a task for someone else (e.g., Thucydides, *History of the Peloponnesian War* 1.133; Plato, *Republic* 371c; cf. Josephus, *Ant.* 19.41–42). The related term "minister" (διάκονος) could refer to a "messenger" of the deity (e.g., Aeschylus, *Prometheus Bound* 942; Josephus, *J.W.* 3.354).[51] In the Gospels and Acts "ministry" frequently refers to the sort of running around required to prepare and serve meals to others (e.g., Luke 10:40; Acts 6:1–2) or to the work of conveying an important message to others on God's behalf (e.g., Acts 6:4; 2 Cor 3:7–9). Paul uses the term in these basic senses in Romans 11:13 and 15:31 respectively where he speaks of conveying the gospel to the gentiles and of conveying to the "saints" in Jerusalem the relief aid he has collected from churches in Macedonia and Achaia (cf. διακονῶν in 15:25). Since "ministering" here is grouped with "prophecy," "teaching," and "exhortation," it seems likely that it refers to the work of relaying a message from God to other believers—to what Luke would call "the ministry of the word" (Acts 6:4).[52] Since the term also frequently referred to the work of people who served others (e.g., Luke 10:40; Acts 6:1–2), and Jesus had used its verbal form (διακονέω) to refer to his own ministry as humble service (Mark 10:45; cf. Matt 20:28; Luke 22:27), the term as Paul uses it here probably also carried connotations of humble service to God and others.[53]

With the expression "the one who teaches" (ὁ διδάσκων) Paul shifts from describing various activities that God has given believers to perform within the body to describing the people who perform them, although the focus remains on the activity as a gift and on the attitude with which it is performed. The attempt to find anything more than stylistic variation in this shift is too speculative to be convincing.[54] The content of the teaching is probably the foundational, unvarying principles of the Scriptures (Rom 15:4) and the gospel (1 Cor 4:17; Eph 4:21; Col 2:6–7) that are essential for Christian maturity (Col 1:28; Eph 4:11–13) and for avoiding false teaching (Eph 4:14–16; 2 Thess 2:15). There was a sense in which all believers should teach each other (Col 3:16), but another sense in which not all were "teachers" (1 Cor 12:29; cf. 1 Tim 3:2; 2 Tim 2:2, 24), and Paul has this more specialized role in mind here.

When Paul says that those whom God has given the ability to minister the word should use that ability "in ministry" (ἐν τῇ διακονίᾳ) and that teachers should use the gift God has given them "in teaching" (ἐν τῇ διδασκαλίᾳ) he probably means

50. See also, e.g., Sanday and Headlam (*Romans*, 256–57), Zahn (*An die Römer*, 544–45), Dunn (*Romans 9–16*, 727–28), and Schreiner (*Romans*, 655–56).

51. John N. Collins, *Diakonia: Re-Interpreting the Ancient Sources* (New York: Oxford University Press, 1990), 77–95, 141; LSJ 398, s.v. διακονία; BDAG 230–31, s.vv. διακονία, διάκονος.

52. Theodoret of Cyrus, *Letters of St. Paul*, 1:119; Collins, *Diakonia*, 233.

53. Andrew D. Clarke, *Serve the Community of the Church: Christians as Leaders and Ministers* (Grand Rapids: Eerdmans, 2000), 233–45; idem, *A Pauline Theology of Church Leadership*, LNTS 362 (London: T&T Clark, 2008), 65–67.

54. As in, e.g., Dunn, *Romans 9–16*, 729. Cf. Jewett, *Romans*, 750.

that they should be satisfied to use the abilities God has graciously given them rather than entering into a divisive spirit of comparison and competition with others (cf. Rom 12:3).[55]

12:8 whether the one who exhorts, in exhortation, the one who shares, in sincerity, the one who leads, with diligence, the one who shows mercy, with cheerfulness (εἴτε ὁ παρακαλῶν ἐν τῇ παρακλήσει· ὁ μεταδιδοὺς ἐν ἁπλότητι, ὁ προϊστάμενος ἐν σπουδῇ, ὁ ἐλεῶν ἐν ἱλαρότητι). Those who urge people to live in a way that is consistent with the gospel, those who impart the gospel to others, those who lead and support the community of believers, and those who show undeserved kindness to others should pursue these tasks with humility, attentiveness, and an open, joyful heart.

The distinction between teaching philosophical principles on one hand and advising people how to behave and live in particular situations on the other hand was a topic of discussion among philosophers of Paul's period.[56] "Virtue depends partly upon training and partly upon practice," said Seneca, "you must learn first, and then strengthen your learning by action. If this be true, not only do the doctrines of wisdom help us, but the precepts also, which check and banish our emotions by a sort of official decree" (*Ep.* 94.37 [Richard M. Gummere, LCL]).

Paul may have distinguished between "teaching" and "exhortation" in a similar way. The structure of Romans provides an example of this distinction, with 1:18–11:36 corresponding to "teaching" the gospel and 12:1–15:13 corresponding to "exhortation" (cf. 12:1; Eph 4:1; 1 Thess 4:1; 1 Tim 4:13; Titus 1:9).

When he describes the final four gifts, Paul shifts from naming a role and the activity specific to that role (e.g., "the one who exhorts, in exhortation") to naming the person who performs a particular role and the conviction with which that person should perform it (e.g., "the one who shares, in sincerity"). The emphasis shifts, then, from humility in exercising a particular gift to exercising it with enthusaism.

The verb "share" (μεταδίδωμι) could refer to "imparting" a message (Tob 7:10; 2 Macc 8:12; 1 Thess 2:8) or wisdom (Wis 7:13), to "giving" gifts (2 Macc 1:35; Rom 1:11), or "sharing" possessions (Job 31:17 LXX; Prov 11:26; Ep Jer 27; Luke 3:11; Eph 4:28). Interpreters have dismissed too quickly the argument of W. C. van Unnik that Paul refers to sharing the gospel here. Instead they tend to take the view that Paul refers to the generous sharing of one's possessions with others.[57] Elsewhere Paul could use the verb "share" (μεταδίδωμι) to mean "share . . . the gospel" (1 Thess 2:8) and the term usually translated "generosity" here (ἁπλότητι) to mean "sincerity" (2 Cor 1:12; 11:3; Eph 6:5; Col 3:22). The preceding four activities (prophecy, ministry, teaching, and exhorting), moreover, all describe instructional activities. It is not at all unlikely, therefore, that Paul refers here to sharing instruction sincerely with one's hearers (cf. Wis 7:13; 1 Thess 2:8).

"The leader" (ὁ προϊστάμενος) seems to have been both an instructor (1 Thess 5:12; 1 Tim 5:17) and a benefactor of the believing community.[58] The leader was to pursue such activities as teaching

55. Meyer, *Romans*, 473; Sanday and Headlam, *Romans*, 357.

56. Engberg-Pedersen, "The Concept of Paraenesis," 54–59.

57. W. C. van Unnik, "The Interpretation of Romans 12:8: ὁ μεταδιδοὺς ἐν ἁπλότητι," in *On Language, Culture, and Religion: In Honor of Eugene A. Nida*, ed. Matthew Black and William A. Smalley (The Hague: Mouton, 1974), 168–83. Unmentioned by most and dismissed by Jewett (*Romans*, 752n187) and Ulrich Wilckens (*Der Brief an die Römer [Röm 12–16]*, EKKNT 6.3 [Zürich: Benziger, 1982], 15n75).

58. Cf. Epictetus, *Diatr.* 3.24.3. Paul uses the noun (προστάτις) to refer to Phoebe as a "benefactor" in 16:2.

and benevolence "with diligence" (ἐν σπουδῇ), that is, with a sincere, attentive concern for the good of others (cf. 2 Cor 8:16).[59]

The final gift, showing "mercy" (ἐλεῶν), forms a bridge to the next paragraph, which describes genuine love (Rom 12:9–21). It also reaches back into the preceding argument that all believers have been the objects of God's "mercy" (9:15, 18; 11:30–32; cf. 12:1). In the preceding section of the argument, "showing mercy" (ἐλεέω) and "showing compassion" (οἰκτερμέω) meant rescuing not merely those who did not deserve it but showing grace to the "disobedient" (11:30–31). It meant loving the sinner and reaching out to the enemy in reconciliation (5:6–11; cf. 12:17–21). In light of Paul's use of the concept of mercy in this way in the preceding argument, it is difficult to avoid the impression that this is a gift God has given all believers because of their own experience of it from God (cf. 2 Cor 8:7–9; 9:7).

Theology in Application

In Romans 12:1–8 Paul returns to the language of Romans 1:18–32 and implies that the remedy to that situation of distorted worship, futile thinking, and violence toward others is found in the transforming power of the gospel. The gospel begins to transform both the individual believer and the church, and its transforming power leads to a community where people serve rather than compete with one another.

The Integration of the Person through the Gospel

In the long explanation of the gospel that has preceded Romans 12:1–8, Paul has occasionally described the disintegrated character of those who do not have faith in God. These are people who know what is just and that God's commands are just but nevertheless both do and applaud injustice (1:32). They are people who do the very same things they teach others not to do on the basis of God's word (2:21–23). They are like the miserable person who knows God's command and wants to do it but always finds evil close at hand, ready to take him captive (7:13–25). For this person, even zeal for God gets in the way of submitting to God (10:2–3).

Paul now describes the gospel as the solution to this problem. The gospel announces that through union with Christ and through the indwelling power of the Holy Spirit, the believer's mind is renewed, the whole orientation of the believer's life is transformed, and the believer is able not only to discern the will of God in the complexities of everyday existence but to act in accord with God's will (12:1–2). Wolfgang Schrage writes:

> According to Paul, the liberation and new being that comes through Christ is an all-encompassing event, a fundamental transformation, a "metamorphosis" (Rom. 12:2;

59. For the meaning of this term and the translation "diligence," see Jewett (*Romans*, 753), and cf. BDAG 939, s.v. σπουδή 2.

> 2 Cor. 3:18). The human contradiction (Rom. 7:14ff.), the dichotomy and division within the self, is a thing of the past. The radical nature of this new being implies an undivided integrity of God's claim upon us.[60]

God enables those who believe the gospel to live in the way he created human beings to live. In the church, the downward spiral of personal and societal disintegration described in 1:18–32 begins to be reversed. Rather than failing to honor God or give him thanks, believers present him their bodies as living, holy, and pleasing sacrifices. Rather than laboring under a futile and foolish worldview in slavery to evil, their renewed minds are able to understand what is good and perfect and their bodies are able to do it. The presentation of their bodies to God and renewal of their minds have set them on a path toward a new creation—a place unaffected by Adam's original and disastrous disobedience against God's command.

This understanding and application of 12:1–2 needs to be nuanced, however, in two ways. First, although a "fundamental transformation" has taken place in the believer, it is not yet complete, and, second, Paul's description of transformation and renewal in Romans 12:1–2 is addressed to the church, as the second-person plurals throughout the passage demonstrate.

A Transformation in Process

Elsewhere Paul describes the believer's renewal as an ongoing process: "Though our outer self is wasting away," he says in 2 Corinthians 4:16, "our inner self is being renewed [ἀνακαινοῦται] day by day" (cf. Col 3:10; Eph 4:23). The wasting away of Paul's outer self in this passage is the suffering that Paul endures in the course of work as an apostle. Paul views these difficulties as exterior to himself because his inner person is in a constant state of renewal that will one day be complete (2 Cor 4:17–18). The believer who continues to experience something like the struggle described in Romans 7:13–25, therefore, should not be discouraged. The offering of one's existence to God as a holy and acceptable sacrifice and the renewal of one's mind so that it approves and obeys what is good and perfect become more and more natural to the believer as the renewal of the believer's thinking and way of life proceeds.

The Corporate Dimensions of Gospel Transformation

As Richard B. Hays says, "The metaphor of 'living sacrifice' describes the vocation of the community: the addressees of the letter are called to present their bodies together as a single collective sacrifice of obedience to God."[61] Unlike Stoic philosophy,

60. Wolfgang Schrage, *The Ethics of the New Testament*, trans. David E. Green (Philadelphia: Fortress, 1988), 186–87.

61. Richard B. Hays, *The Moral Vision of the New Testament: Community, Cross, New Creation* (New York: HarperCollins, 1996), 36.

which was so prevalent in Rome at the time Paul wrote Romans, and unlike more contemporary emphases on the fulfillment of the individual, the gospel spoke of the transformation of entire groups of people so that their interactions with one another and with the wider societies of which they were a part became less self-centered and more loving toward others.[62]

This does not mean that the transformation of the individual was absent from Paul's moral vision for the church. In 2 Corinthians 4:26 the inner transformation of which Paul speaks is certainly the transformation of an individual—Paul himself. Whatever else the "I" of Romans 7:13–25 refers to, moreover, it would be extraordinarily odd if it did not refer to the existence of an individual human being.

Still, it would be easy simply to think of Paul as describing in Romans 12:1–2 the transformation of individuals so that they personally become more obedient to God. Paul's vision is broader, however, and encompasses the church. He envisions a new society of transformed individuals that function as God's prototype for what human society will look like when his restoration of the world is complete.

God's Gifts to the Church as Instruments of Service Rather Than of Competition

This focus on the church as a transformed society explains why Paul moves immediately from his introduction in 12:1–2 into a description of the way believers should live in community with one another in 12:3–8 by using the gifts God has given them.[63] The point of this paragraph does not lie in the precise definition of the seven gifts Paul lists in 12:6–8. The differences between the various lists of gifts in Paul's letters (cf. 1 Cor 12:8–10, 28–29; Eph 4:11) hint that none of the lists, including this one, is exhaustive.

Rather, Paul's emphasis lies on the humility and sincere inner conviction with which believers should fulfill the role within the church that God has assigned to them (Rom 12:3). The church is not the place for comparison between individuals to determine whose role is more important, nor for competition among individuals for supposedly more prestigious roles. It should instead be a place where the sort of competitiveness that dominated ancient Rome is turned upside down.[64] As Paul says in the next paragraph, the church should be a place where people "lead one another forth with respect to honor" (12:10). They should, in other words, provide examples to one another of honoring not themselves but others. Competition and seeking honor for one's self are no less a part of modern human societies than they were of

62. On the difference between Stoicism and Paul's theology in Rom 12:1–15:13, see especially Esler, "Paul and Stoicism," 106–24.

63. Hays, *Moral Vision*, 36.

64. On this, see the especially perceptive analysis of Barclay, *Paul and the Gift*, 432–39.

ancient Roman society. Paul's call upon believers to be vigilant against allowing this spirit to infect the church is as relevant now as it was in his own time.

A critical component in the transformed existence of both the individual believer and the church is a spirit of humility and an enthusiasm for doing good to others. Paul calls this love, and that forms the topic of his next exhortation (12:9–21).[65]

65. Cf. Paul's description of the unity of the church within its diversity in 1 Cor 12:1–31 followed by a description of love in 1 Cor 13:1–13 (Sanday and Headlam, *Romans*, 360).

CHAPTER 25

Romans 12:9–21

Literary Context

Paul signals the beginning of a new section of his exhortation with a sentence that contains no conjunction to coordinate what follows with what has come before. The style of his exhortation also changes. He now speaks in brief, syntactically compressed maxims reminiscent of ancient collections of wise sayings.[1] The change in style accompanies a shift in focus also. Whereas in 12:3–8 Paul was concerned with the smooth functioning of the body of believers as it carried out its assigned tasks of proclamation, exhortation, and service to others, in 12:9–21 he is more concerned with the interface between believers and the unbelieving societies in which they lived day-to-day. The passage is dominated by the contrast between good and evil (12:9b–c, 17, 21), and the stress falls on the love, hope, endurance, and unity that must characterize the tiny group of believers if they are to conquer rather than be conquered by the evil that surrounded them (12:9a, 10, 12, 16, 21).

Despite this change in emphasis, however, Paul has not lost sight of the thesis he announced in 12:1–2 that the conduct he describes in 12:3–15:7 should arise from within the believer as the result of a transformed and renewed mind. Just as sincerity, diligence, and cheerfulness should characterize those who use their gifts in the body of believers (12:8), so their day-to-day practical expressions of love should be sincere, reflecting their new heartfelt convictions (v. 9a).[2] They should not merely stay away from evil, but loathe it (v. 9b). They should not merely do what is good, but cling to it (v. 9c). Their love for one another should well up from within, like the instinctive love of a mother in the animal world for its young (v. 10a). Their commitment to the life of faith should be marked by enthusiasm, ardor, heartfelt service, joy, endurance,

1. See, e.g., Pseudo-Phocylides, *Sentences*, and the sayings gathered in H. Diels and W. Kranz, *Die Fragmente der Vorsokratiker*, 6th ed. (Berlin: Weidmann, 1951), 63–66. Cf. also 1 Thess 5:12–22. On the whole subject, see Walter T. Wilson, *Love without Pretense: Romans 12.9–21 and Hellenistic-Jewish Wisdom Literature*, WUNT 2.46 (Tübingen: Mohr Siebeck, 1991).

2. Cf. Troels Engberg-Pedersen ("Paul's Stoicizing Politics in Romans 12–13: The Role of 13.1–10 in the Argument," *JSNT* 29 [2006], 165). I do not agree, however, that 12:9a is the climactic conclusion to 12:6–8.

and devotion (vv. 11–12). These terms describe conduct that is not imposed from without by an external authority but arises from a transformed mind and a will that is now released from the wretched bondage to sin described in 7:13–25.

Several times in the passage, Paul's language implies that the community to which he writes is experiencing persecution from those outside its boundaries. Believers are to "remain firm in affliction" (12:12), "bless those who persecute" them (v. 14), "repay no one evil for evil" (v. 17), "live at peace with all human beings" if at all possible (v. 18), and not take justice into their own hands (v. 19) but rather treat their enemies kindly (vv. 20–21).

Paul wrote Romans during the early years of Nero's rule and a time of relative calm for Jews living in Rome, at least compared to the turbulence the Jewish community had experienced under Tiberius and Claudius (Tacitus, *Ann.* 2.85; Suetonius, *Claud.* 25.4; Acts 18:2). This tranquility may have extended to Christians with their deep connection to Judaism, at least as far as their relationship with the governing authorities was concerned. At the level of their everyday interactions with neighbors and family members, however, life must have been as difficult as ever. When Paul met with a group of local leaders in Rome's Jewish community several years after writing Romans, they informed him that the "sect" which he represented was "everywhere . . . spoken against" (Acts 28:22). Peter, writing from Rome probably a few years after Romans, commented that Christians were surrounded by a society surprised by their unwillingness to participate in the prevailing immorality of the culture and that these shocked unbelievers "maligned" Christians as a result (1 Pet 4:4).

It would not be long until Nero was able to pin the blame for the fire that devastated Rome in AD 64 on "a class hated for their abominations, called Christians by the populace" (Tacitus, *Ann.* 15.44).[3] From his friendship with Aquila and Priscilla who had been among the Jews Claudius exiled from Rome, Paul also would have understood how quickly officials in the city of Rome could turn against adherents to eastern religions such as Judaism, Isis worship, and now Christianity (Acts 18:2; Tacitus, *Ann.* 2.85 [cf. Josephus, *Ant.* 18.65–84]; Suetonius, *Claud.* 24.4).[4]

This tenuous relationship between the relatively small group of believers and the society in which they lived probably formed the background for Paul's emphasis in Romans 12:9–21 on elements of OT ethical instruction and the teaching of Jesus

3. Tacitus, *The Annals and the Histories*, 327 (Church and Brodribb). Cf. Suetonius, *Nero* 16.2. Tacitus was probably a young boy living in Gaul when these events occurred, and he published his account over fifty years later, but his description of the popular attitude toward Christians in Rome in the mid first century A.D. gives a plausible explanation for why Nero thought he could blame the Christians as part of a public relations strategy.

4. On the relationship between the government and the Jews in the first century, see Leon, *Jews of Ancient Rome*, 16–28; Wolfgang Wiefel, "The Jewish Community in Ancient Rome and the Origins of Roman Christianity," in *The Romans Debate*, rev. and exp. ed., ed. Karl Paul Donfried (Peabody, MA: Hendrickson, 1991), 88.

that advocated nonretaliation, deferring justice to God's judgment, and kindness toward enemies. As 7:7–25 shows, Paul had a robust understanding of sin's insidious ability to establish a beachhead in a person's life by means of something that seemed good, such as the command not to covet, and then lead them into further transgression. What better opportunity for sin to mire the Christian community in a cycle of revenge than for the community to preempt God's judgment by taking vengeance against their persecutors into their own hands? This same background and the same kinds of concerns probably also lie beneath Paul's admonitions in the next section (13:1–14) that believers in Rome submit to the governing authorities, pay their taxes, and not fall into the sinful way of life that characterized most people in the neighborhoods where they lived.

X. Israel's Present Rejection of the Gospel Does Not Imply the Failure of God's Word (9:1–11:36)

XI. Exhortation to Live in a Way That Is Consistent with the Gospel (12:1–15:13)

- A. A Mind Transformed and Renewed by God (12:1–2)
- B. Community without Competition (12:3–8)
- ➦ **C. Loving One Another and Remaining Steadfast in a Hostile Environment (12:9–13:14)**
  - **1. Heartfelt Love for One Another and Service to the Lord in Thirteen Areas (12:9–13)**
  - **2. Overcoming Evil and Maintaining Harmony (12:14–21)**
  - 3. The Necessity of Submission to Government Authorities (13:1–7)
  - 4. The Critical Importance of Loving Others (13:8–14)
- D. The Strong Should Show Love for the Weak (and the Weak for the Strong) (14:1–15:13)

XII. The Purpose of Paul's Letter in the Context of His Apostolic Vocation (15:14–33)

Main Idea

Believers should have a love for others and the Lord that arises from within them and shows itself in practical ways such as preserving the dignity of one another, sharing resources with the needy, and showing hospitality to one another and to strangers. When they face marginalization, bullying, and ostracism, believers should not respond harshly but with an unusual kindness that can sometimes transform persecutors into people who also want to do what is good.

Translation

Romans 12:9–21

9a	Exhortation	**Let love be without pretense.**
b	Exhortation	**Loathe what is evil.**
c	Exhortation	**Cling to what is good.**
10a	Exhortation	**Be authentically loving** toward one another
b		with familial affection;
c	Exhortation	**lead one another forth**
d		with respect to honor.
11a	Exhortation	**Do not be lazy**
b		in enthusiasm;
c	Exhortation	**be ardent**
d		in spirit;
e	Exhortation	**serve**
f		the Lord.
12a	Exhortation	**Rejoice**
b		in hope;
c	Exhortation	**remain firm**
d		in affliction;
e	Exhortation	**be stubbornly devoted**
f		to prayer.
13a	Exhortation	**Share**
b		in the needs of the saints;
c	Exhortation	**pursue**
d		hospitality.
14a	Exhortation	**Bless** those who persecute;
b	Exhortation	**bless** and **do not curse.**
15a	Exhortation	**Rejoice** with those who rejoice;
b	Exhortation	**weep** with those who weep.

Continued on next page.

Continued from previous page.

16a	Exhortation	**Think the same way** toward one another;
b	Exhortation	**do not think haughty thoughts,**
c	Exhortation (contrast)	but **be carried away with humble concerns.**
d	Exhortation	**Do not be wise in your own estimation.**
17a	Exhortation	**Repay no one evil for evil;**
b	Exhortation	**take into consideration what is good in the sight of all human beings.**
18a	Condition	If possible, to the extent that it is up to you,
b	Exhortation	**live at peace with all human beings.**
19a	Exhortation	**Do not give out justice yourselves,** beloved,
b	Exhortation (contrast)	but **give place to God's wrath,**
c	Basis (for 19a–b)	for it is written, "'It is for me to give out justice, I will repay,' says the Lord." (Deut 32:35)
20a	Exhortation	But, "if your enemy is hungry, give him something to eat;
b	Exhortation	if he is thirsty, given him something to drink.
c	Basis (for 20a–b)	For, if you do this, you will pile fiery coals on his head." (Prov 25:21–22)
21a	Exhortation	**Do not be conquered** by evil,
b	Exhortation (contrast)	but **conquer evil** by good.

Structure

The grammatical structure of this passage continues the syntactically ambiguous style that began in 12:6. Just as he had done in 12:6–8, Paul often leaves out finite verbs in this passage and counts on his audience to fill out the syntactical details of his pithy maxims. He primarily uses adjectives (12:9a, 10a, 11a), infinitives (v. 15), and especially participles (vv. 9b–c, 10b, 11b–13, 16a–c, 17–19a) to convey the substance of his exhortations. Only 12:14, 16d, and 19b–21 adopt a more normal prose style using finite verbs. Despite this stylistic similarity to the long concluding sentence of 12:3–8 (vv. 6–8), 12:9–21 is a separate section dominated by the contrast between good and evil that is announced at its beginning (v. 9b–c) and end (v. 21).[5]

Many interpreters have thought that the first sentence of the section, "let love be without pretense," describes the section's theme.[6] It is difficult, however, to see how everything in the section fits under this rubric. Instead it is best to see 12:9–21 as a body of practical advice for living as a mutually supportive community within a predominantly hostile culture. Love for one another (12:9a–10, 13a, 15–16), for the stranger (v. 13b), and even for the enemy (vv. 14, 17, 19–20) are important, but so are inward conviction, hope, steadfastness, peacemaking, and the principle that good will triumph over evil (vv. 9b–c, 11–12, 18, and 21).[7]

The passage falls into two parts. The first part (12:9–13) focuses on loving relationships and steadfastness within the community and issues thirteen maxims describing the attitude that believers should adopt toward one another and the difficult times in which they live. The use of the imperative mood in 12:14 signals the opening of the second part, which focuses on the relationship of the community with the wider society.[8] The division between these two sections, however, is not watertight: the hope and affliction mentioned in 12:12a–b are applicable to a community experiencing persecution from the outside, and the harmony and humility that Paul advocates in 12:15–16 are pertinent to inner-community relations.

Despite their proverbial form, these exhortations were not chosen at random. Little is known about the Roman church of the first century, but it is likely that it experienced persecution. It makes sense that in such a situation Paul would provide the community with a strategy for supporting one another and responding to harsh treatment out of the wisdom that the Scriptures and the gospel provided.[9]

5. This inclusion makes it unlikely that 12:9a is the conclusion to 12:6–8 (Engberg-Pedersen, "Paul's Stoicizing Politics," 164–65).

6. E.g., Godet, *Romans*, 434; Lagrange, *Romains*, 301; Wilson, *Love without Pretense*, 150; Haacker, *An die Römer*, 257; Jewett, *Romans*, 756; Hultgren, *Romans*, 454.

7. Cf. Käsemann, *Romans*, 343.

8. Cranfield, *Romans*, 2:629; Dunn, *Romans 9–16*, 738; Jewett, *Romans*, 757.

9. Cf. 1 Thess 5:15, undoubtedly written to a persecuted church (1 Thess 1:6; 2:14–16; 3:3) and also emphasizing nonretaliation.

Exegetical Outline

- **XI. Exhortation to Live in a Way That Is Consistent with the Gospel (12:1–15:13)**
  - A. A Mind Transformed and Renewed by God (12:1–2)
  - B. Community without Competition (12:3–8)
  - **C. Loving One Another and Remaining Steadfast in a Hostile Environment (12:9–13:14)**
    - ➦ **1. Heartfelt Love for One Another and Service to the Lord in Thirteen Areas (12:9–13)**
      - a. love
      - b. loathing evil
      - c. good
      - d. brotherly and sisterly love
      - e. honor
      - f. enthusiasm
      - g. ardor
      - h. service
      - i. hope
      - j. affliction
      - k. prayer
      - l. the needy
      - m. hospitality
    - **2. Overcoming Evil and Maintaining Harmony (12:14–21)**
      - a. The stance of believers toward persecutors (12:14)
      - b. Empathy and harmony with other believers (12:15–16)
      - c. Gaining victory over evil in the midst of persecution (12:17–21)

Explanation of the Text

12:9 Let love be without pretense. Loathe what is evil. Cling to what is good (Ἡ ἀγάπη ἀνυπόκριτος. ἀποστυγοῦντες τὸ πονηρόν, κολλώμενοι τῷ ἀγαθῷ). The inner transformation described in 12:1–2 reveals itself in love that is heartfelt rather than mere display, an inner revulsion at what is evil, and a desire to align one's self with what is good.

The epigrammatic nature of Paul's statement, "Let love be without pretense," has often puzzled interpreters. It contains neither a conjunction connecting it to what has gone before nor a verb to indicate exactly how the adjective "without pretense" (ἀνυπόκριτος) should be related to the noun "love" (ἡ ἀγάπη). The syntax of the brief statement is similar, however, to other ethical maxims from antiquity: "a middle course is best" (μέτρον ἄριστον); "come under a pledge, and mischief is at hand" (ἐγγύα, πάρα δ'ἄτα); "let nothing be too much" (μηδὲν ἄγαν).[10] Paul was certainly familiar with various Greek maxims (1 Cor 15:32; Titus

10. Clement of Alexandria (*Miscellanies* 1.14.61 [*ANF* 2:314]), quoting Cleobulus, tyrant of Rhodes (ca. 600 BC). On Cleobulus, see Diogenes Laertius, *Lives of the Philosophers* 1.89–93. Cf. Wilson, *Love without Pretense*, 151.

1:12), and it seems likely that the terse style he adopted here simply reflects the form of epigrams with which he was familiar.[11]

The term Paul uses for "love" (ἀγάπη) referred to esteem and affection demonstrated in practical ways.[12] In the preceding argument, God has demonstrated his love for believers by providing them with the sustaining presence of the Holy Spirit (Rom 5:5) and with reconciliation to himself through the death of Christ (5:8; 8:32, 35, 37, 39). In a way that is consistent with his exhortation to sincere service to the body of believers in 12:8b–d, then, Paul urges the Romans not merely to demonstrate their love in practical ways but to do so without insincerity (cf. 2 Cor 6:6).[13]

The next two statements are again syntactically and grammatically puzzling. Do they explain what Paul means by "love without pretense," or are they separate exhortations? Why do the statements use participles rather than imperatives? Did Paul expect the reader to supply an imperatival form of the verb "to be" (ἔστω)?[14] The epigrammatic nature of the first statement ("let love be without pretense") makes it likely that Paul intended the next two statements also to have an epigrammatic nature. They are not, then, intended to explain what Paul means by sincere love but to give separate pieces of advice.[15] The exhortatory context (Rom 12:1–3, 8, 14, 16, 19–21), moreover, makes it likely that these participles should be construed as imperatives. This seems to be confirmed by 12:17 where Paul uses a participle in the same way he has used them in 12:9–13 and 16 but is clearly relying on Proverbs 3:4 LXX, which uses an imperative.[16]

The verb "loathe" (ἀποστυγέω) refers to a strong feeling of revulsion, for example at the thought of having a drunken fool for a son-in-law (Herodotus, *Histories* 6.129.4) or remaining childless (Euripides, *Ion* 488).[17] The verb "cling to" (κολλάω), which Paul opposes to "loathe," could refer to dust "clinging" to feet (Luke 10:11), to "joining" or "associating" with a group or person (Acts 5:13; 8:29; 9:26; 10:28; 17:34; cf. Luke 15:15), or to "uniting" with someone in a sexual sense (1 Cor 6:16). Both terms, then, emphasize alignments that arise from one's basic commitments and inner feelings, and this idea unites these two admonitions with the maxim about sincere love and also with the implied admonitions in Romans 12:8b–d. The believer's renewed mind and transformed existence (12:2) should reveal itself in love that is not mere display, in a genuine inner revulsion at what is evil, and in a heartfelt alignment with what is good.

12:10 Be authentically loving toward one another with familial affection; lead one another forth with respect to honor (τῇ φιλαδελφίᾳ εἰς ἀλλήλους φιλόστοργοι, τῇ τιμῇ ἀλλήλους προηγούμενοι). Like a close family that shows each other sincere love, believers in Rome should nurture one another and put the same energy into respecting others that the culture around them puts into ensuring that their own dignity is recognized.

Paul once again speaks in maxims, the first one

11. On Paul's knowledge of Greek wisdom, see the still useful comments of Clement of Alexandria (*Miscellanies* 1.14).

12. *TLNT* 1:12.

13. BDAG 91, s.v. ἀνυπόκριτος.

14. Jeffrey S. Lamp, "An Alternative Explanation for the Alleged 'Imperatival' Participles of Romans 12:9–21," *TynBul* 61 (2010): 213–14.

15. See, e.g., Sanday and Headlam, *Romans*, 360; Cranfield, *Romans*, 2:631. For the view that 12:9b–13 explains 12:9a, see, e.g., Dunn (*Romans 9–16*, 738–39); Wilson (*Love without Pretense*, 150); Moo (*Romans*, 774); Esler (*Conflict and Identity*, 316–17).

16. Wilson, *Love without Pretense*, 157. "Take into consideration [προνοοῦ] what is right in the sight of the Lord and of human beings" (Prov 3:4 LXX, my transl.). "Take into consideration [προνοούμενοι] what is right in the sight of all human beings" (Rom 12:17). Cf. BDF §468 (2).

17. LSJ 220, s.v. ἀποστυγέω. For the translation "loathe" here, see the REB.

using an adjective to communicate its exhortation (cf. 12:9a–b), and the second one using a participle (cf. 12:9c–d). Paul expected his audience to supply an imperatival sense to both maxims. The first maxim imagines the believing community as a close family and urges believers to show the same affection and nurture for one another that they would show to their siblings or children. Greek speakers typically used the expression "familial affection" (φιλαδελφία) in a literal sense for the close affection that brothers and sisters might have for one another (4 Macc 13:23, 26; 14:1). The early Christians, however, used it metaphorically for the familial kindness they should have for one another (1 Thess 4:9; Heb 13:1; 1 Pet 1:22).[18] The adjective "authentically loving" (φιλόστοργος) refers to the sort of nurturing love that parents have for their children.[19] The term was used for the instinctive nurture that animals gave to their offspring, and so it could carry the connotation of instinctive love (Plutarch, *Am. prol.*).[20] Just as in 12:8–9, Paul seems to emphasize the inwardness and authenticity of the virtues that he admonishes the Roman believers to display.

Interpreters of Romans have often understood the verb "lead . . . forth" (προηγέομαι) to mean "esteem . . . more highly" (REB) because when the verb occurs elsewhere in a transitive sense its object is typically in the genitive or dative rather than the accusative, which Paul uses here. In addition, Paul uses a closely related verb (ἡγέομαι) to mean "esteem" in 1 Thessalonians 5:13 and Philippians 2:3.[21] The meaning "esteem," however, is not attested for the verb with the prefixed preposition (προηγέομαι), which Paul uses here. Moreover, this verb with its normal meaning "lead forth" can be used with an accusative object (although this construction is admittedly rare).[22] Thus, Josephus, can speak of Agrippa "leading an expedition to the Bosporus [εἰς Βόσπορον . . . στρατείαν προηγούμενον]" (*Ant.* 16.16 [Ralph Marcus and Allen Wikgren, LCL]). Paul speaks here, therefore, of "leading one another forth with respect to honor."

Jerry Toner says of Roman nonelite people, "Most of them saw their neighbours as competitors not comrades in the harsh struggle for scarce resources. To have nothing was to be nothing in the Roman world. Theirs was a culture where people strove to look down on their neighbours with something of the same disdain that the elite looked down on them."[23] Here Paul insists that believers, whose thinking God has refashioned (12:1–2), must live by a radically different standard. They must renounce the vicious competition for honor that dominated Roman society, and instead make sure that others receive honor.[24]

12:11 Do not be lazy in enthusiasm; be ardent in spirit; serve the Lord (τῇ σπουδῇ μὴ ὀκνηροί, τῷ πνεύματι ζέοντες, τῷ κυρίῳ δουλεύοντες). Believers should obey the will of God with an excitement born from their inward transformation.

To do something with "enthusiasm" (σπουδή) was the opposite of being "lazy" (ὀκνηρός) about it (Josephus, *Ant.* 1.115), and in a way typical of his epigrammatic style in this passage Paul combines the two ideas. One's zeal should have no hint of negligence or hesitance.

18. BDAG 1055, s.v. φιλαδελφία.

19. *TLNT* 3:462–64. The translation "authentically loving" belongs to Spicq (and to Spicq's translator, James D. Ernest).

20. Ibid., 462n3.

21. E.g., Sanday and Headlam, *Romans*, 361; BDF §150; Wilckens, *An die Römer (Röm 12–16)*, 20; Cranfield, *Romans*, 2:632–33.

22. Cf. LSJ 1480, s.v. προηγέομαι 2.

23. Toner, *Popular Culture*, 2.

24. Jewett, *Romans*, 759–60; Barclay, *Paul and the Gift*, 432–39, 509–10.

This maxim should guide the understanding of the term "spirit" in the next clause. It probably does not refer to God's Spirit (e.g., REB: "aglow with the Spirit") but to the human spirit (e.g., ESV: "fervent in spirit").[25] The term "be ardent" (ζέοντες) was used in a literal sense to refer to boiling, bubbling, or fermenting, and not uncommonly in a metaphorical sense to refer to seething emotions (e.g., Sophocles, *Oed. col.* 434; Plato, *Republic* 440c).[26] Since the dative expression "with enthusiasm" (τῇ σπουδῇ) refers to inner convictions in the immediately preceding clause, the dative expression "in spirit" (τῷ πνεύματι) here probably also refers to one's inner convictions (cf. Acts 18:25).[27] The meaning, then, is that believers should obey the sort of exhortation Paul gives in Romans 12:3–15:7 with an ardor that bubbles up from within.

Paul's reference to "serving" (δουλεύοντες) the Lord recalls his positive use of this verb in 6:14–23 for "serving as a slave" (δουλεύω) to "obedience," to "righteousness," and to "God" (6:16, 18–19, 22; cf. 7:6). As Paul emphasized there, this service is "from the heart" (6:17), which is also his point here.

12:12 Rejoice in hope; remain firm in affliction; be stubbornly devoted to prayer (τῇ ἐλπίδι χαίροντες, τῇ θλίψει ὑπομένοντες, τῇ προσευχῇ προσκαρτεροῦντες). In the suffering that continues prior to God's full salvation of his people and restoration of the universe, believers should be happy that God will rescue them, should remain faithful to their commitment to the gospel, and should never give up communicating with God.

These three exhortations recall the argument of 5:1–5 and 8:18–30 where Paul describes the object of the believer's hope as salvation from suffering and sin and the re-creation of a world presently dominated by the effects of human rebellion against God. This hope was an appropriate object of boasting (καυχώμεθα) for the believer, Paul had argued (5:2), and now, using a different word (χαίροντες) but with a similar meaning, he urges his readers to adopt an attitude of joy in light of this hope.

Hope goes naturally together with "remaining firm [ὑπομένοντες]" (5:3–4; 8:25; cf. 1 Cor 13:7) since suffering continues until hope's goal is fulfilled (Rom 5:3–4; 8:20, 25). Indeed, endurance in the midst of this suffering is itself a cause for boasting, because it engenders hope for God's rescue of his creation from sin and suffering (5:3–4).

Paul had also argued in 8:26–27 that as believers persevere in this hope and continue to experience the weakness and ignorance of the sin-ravaged world in which they live, God's Spirit both enables them to pray and prays for them. Paul now urges his readers to "be devoted" (προσκαρτεροῦντες) to prayer, a term that carried connotations of stubbornness and even obstinacy and therefore neatly paralleled the idea of "endurance" in affliction.[28] Persistence in prayer (Acts 1:14; 6:4; Eph 6:18; Col 4:2), even to the point of seeming impertinence (Luke 18:1–9), was a common theme in early Christian teaching and practice.[29]

12:13 Share in the needs of the saints; pursue hospitality (ταῖς χρείαις τῶν ἁγίων κοινωνοῦντες, τὴν φιλοξενίαν διώκοντες). Believers should

25. Meyer, *Romans*, 476; Fitzmyer, *Romans*, 654. Many commentators find here a reference to the Holy Spirit's work in the human spirit (e.g., Origen, *Romans, Books 6–10*, 213; Chrysostom, *Romans*, 376; Calvin, *Romans*, 272; Sanday and Headlam, *Romans*, 361; Lagrange, *Romains*, 302; Michel, *An die Römer*, 384; Dunn, *Romans 9–16*, 742; Moo, *Romans*, 778).

26. LSJ 755, s.v. ζέω 3b.

27. As Fitzmyer (*Romans*, 654) and Byrne (*Romans*, 379) observe, at Acts 18:25 Apollos had only received the baptism of John and cannot, therefore, have been "fervent [ζέων] in [the Holy] Spirit [τῷ πνεύματι]."

28. *TLNT* 3:193.

29. Ibid.

contribute in practical ways to helping other believers who are facing difficult circumstances. They should also look for opportunities to be kind to strangers and travelers in their midst.

"Saints" (ἁγίων) refers to all believers (cf. 1:7), not only to the poor "saints" in Jerusalem for whom Paul had organized a relief offering (15:25, 26, 31). That offering, however, provides an illustration of the sort of practical participation in helping the needy to which Paul refers here. The term "share" (κοινωνοῦντες) carries connotations of deep involvement and participation in the lives of others.[30] Such involvement in "the needs" of other believers could only mean helping in practical ways to relieve those needs (cf. Eph 4:28; Phil 2:25; 4:14–16; Titus 3:14).

"Hospitality" (τὴν φιλοξενίαν) also refers to helping those in need and helping them in practical ways, but refers more specifically to protecting and caring for the traveler or stranger (ξένος).[31] It was a commonly valued virtue in antiquity (e.g., Homer, *Odyssey* 6.207–8, 9.270–71), and the idea that Zeus was the protector of strangers circulated in the Rome of Paul's time as proverbial wisdom (Musonius Rufus, Lecture 15 A [Cynthia King]). Advice about giving hospitality, however, was also frequently attended by caveats. Cicero advised giving the stranger "what it costs us nothing to give," specifically water, fire, and honest counsel. He advised further that "since the resources of individuals are limited and the number of the needy is infinite, this spirit of universal liberality must be regulated" by the principle that we should only give what does not diminish our own resources (*Off.* 1.52).[32] Paul is not discussing hospitality here at a philosophical level, but in light of what he says about helping the needy elsewhere, he must have envisioned something more gracious than Cicero had in mind (cf. 2 Cor 8:1–2, 9–15). The surprising use of the verb "pursue" (διώκοντες) certainly does not leave the occasion for showing hospitality to chance but speaks of actively looking for opportunities to meet the needs of others.[33]

12:14 Bless those who persecute; bless and do not curse (εὐλογεῖτε τοὺς διώκοντας, εὐλογεῖτε καὶ μὴ καταρᾶσθε). Believers should not respond with a vengeful spirit to those who bully them because of their faith but should speak to and treat them kindly instead.

Paul now adopts a slightly less compressed style, shifting from exhortatory participles and adjectives to the more normal imperative mood. The participial expression "those who persecute" (τοὺς διώκοντας) echoes the participle "pursue" (διώκοντες) at the end of the previous sentence.[34] Now, however, the tables are turned, and Paul depicts believers as the object of hostile pursuit.[35] In such a situation, he says, believers should respond in a radically unnatural way and wish their persecutors well with kind words rather than wishing their

30. Jewett, *Romans*, 764; cf. Paul's use of the related term "sharer" (συγκοινωνός) in Rom 11:17 to refer to the profound involvement of gentile Christians in the rich heritage of the Jews.

31. See *TLNT* 3:454–57; Beate Wagner-Hasel, "Hospitality," *BNPA* 6:529–31; Walter T. Wilson, *The Sentences of Pseudo-Phocylides*, CEJL (Berlin: Walter de Gruyter, 2005), 106.

32. Trans. Walter Miller, *Cicero: On Duties*, LCL (Cambridge: Harvard University Press, 1913).

33. So already Origen (*Romans, Books 6–10*, 214–15) and Chrysostom (*Romans*, 377).

34. Sanday and Headlam, *Romans*, 363; Lagrange, *Romains*, 305.

35. The "you" (ὑμᾶς) supplied in a number of early and geographically diverse manuscripts (e.g., ℵ A D L P Ψ 81 104 365 1175) should probably be omitted. The omission of the pronoun, although admittedly limited primarily to the Alexandrian text type ($\mathfrak{P}^{46}$ B 6 1739), is very early and conforms with Paul's compressed style elsewhere in the passage. The addition of the pronoun is easily explained as an attempt to make the text easier to read and perhaps, as Cranfield says, arose from scribal memory of Matt 5:44 (*Romans*, 2:640).

destruction with words of abuse.[36] As the quotation of Proverbs 25:21–22 in Romans 12:20 shows, this approach to those who actively seek one's harm arises from the OT (Exod 23:4–5; Job 31:29–30; Prov 24:17–18), probably as it was reformulated in the teaching of Jesus (Matt 5:43–48; Luke 6:27–29, 31–35).[37] Paul acted on this principle himself (Acts 16:25–33; 1 Cor 4:13), and it was a consistent feature of his ethical teaching (1 Thess 5:15).[38]

12:15 Rejoice with those who rejoice; weep with those who weep (χαίρειν μετὰ χαιρόντων, κλαίειν μετὰ κλαιόντων). Believers should not be self-absorbed but empathetic with the joys and sorrows of others.

Paul uses two infinitives here where we would expect imperatives. He may simply be using the infinitive as an imperative, something that was common in older Greek, or he may expect his audience mentally to supply the little word for "it is necessary" (δεῖ) with the infinitive.[39] Either way, the two infinitives have imperatival force. Paul was perhaps already thinking of the unity and humility that he would advocate in the next sentence. To share in the joy and sadness of others requires regarding their circumstances as more urgently in need of attention than one's own circumstances and seeing others as more important than one's self (cf. 1 Cor 12:26).[40]

12:16 Think the same way toward one another; do not think haughty thoughts, but be carried away with humble concerns. Do not be wise in your own estimation (τὸ αὐτὸ εἰς ἀλλήλους φρονοῦντες, μὴ τὰ ὑψηλὰ φρονοῦντες ἀλλὰ τοῖς ταπεινοῖς συναπαγόμενοι. μὴ γίνεσθε φρόνιμοι παρ' ἑαυτοῖς). Believers should not view themselves as better than others but should instead identify with the plight of the poor and dispossessed.

The use of the prepositional phrase "toward one another" (εἰς ἀλλήλους) takes the expression "think the same way toward one another" (τὸ αὐτὸ εἰς ἀλλήλους φρονοῦντες) in a different direction than the similar language in the commonly cited parallels (Rom 15:5; 2 Cor 13:11; Phil 2:2).[41] Paul refers here not so much to agreeing with one another as to thinking in the same way about each other, or as the CEB puts it, considering "everyone as equal."[42]

The next two clauses explain this meaning in greater detail. Thinking "haughty thoughts" (τὰ ὑψηλὰ φρονοῦντες) refers to an inappropriate pride that fails to recognize one's own failures and reliance on God's grace (cf. Rom 11:17–20).[43] The verb "carried away with" (συναπάγω) is uncommon in Greek. Elsewhere, it is used literally to mean "led away together with" someone (Josephus, *J.W.* 1.493), or figuratively to refer to becoming caught up with and

36. "Bless" (εὐλογέω) stands opposite "revile" (λοιδορέω) in 1 Cor 4:12, and "cursing" (καταρώμενοι) leads to destruction (ἀπολοῦνται) in T. Levi 4:6. See also BDAG 408, s.v. εὐλογέω 2.

37. Wilson (*Love without Pretense*, 165–71) and Gordon M. Zerbe (*Non-Retaliation in Early Jewish and New Testament Texts: Ethical Themes in Social Contexts* [Sheffield: JSOT Press, 1993], 232–40) seem too skeptical about the connection between Jesus and Paul at this point. The form and wording of Paul's admonition seem closer to Luke 6:28 than to the other early-Jewish parallels they cite in their discussions. Didache 1.3b, although very close to Luke 6:28, is probably later than Luke and itself dependent on the Jesus saying.

38. Cf. Origen, *Romans, Books 6–10*, 215. Interpreters occasionally suggest that the persecution Paul has in mind here is hostility from other Christians (e.g., Kent L. Yinger, "Romans 12:14–21 and Non-Retaliation in Second Temple Judaism: Addressing Persecution within the Community," *CBQ* 60 [1998]: 74–96), but when Paul uses the term "persecute" (διώκω) in a hostile sense, he typically has in mind the hostility of unbelievers toward believers (1 Cor 15:9; Gal 1:13, 23; Phil 3:6).

39. See Smyth, *Greek Grammar*, §2013; BDF §389; and the form of the wise sayings of Cleobulus in Diels and Kranz, *Die Fragmente der Vorsokratiker*, 1:63.

40. Godet, *Romans*, 436.

41. E.g., Sanday and Headlam, *Romans*, 363.

42. On the meaning of "toward" (εἰς) here, see BDAG 290, s.v. εἰς 4bβ.

43. Cf. Lucian (*The Dream* 23) who compares the rich to Icarus and the poor to Daedalus and claims that the poor, like Daedalus, "have not let their ambitions soar high in the air" (ὑψηλὰ ἐφρόνησαν [A. M. Harmon, LCL]).

carried away by something (Gal 2:13; 2 Pet 3:17). The common translations "condescend to" (KJV) or "associate with" (NIV, NRSV, ESV) represent an unattested meaning. Here, then, the dative expression translated "humble concerns" (τοῖς ταπεινοῖς) should be understood as a neuter, matching "haughty thoughts" (τὰ ὑψηλά), and Paul is saying that people should forget about climbing the social ladder and make the concerns of humble people their own concerns. He summarizes all this in the final clause with an echo of Proverbs 3:7 LXX.[44]

12:17 Repay no one evil for evil; take into consideration what is good in the sight of all human beings (μηδενὶ κακὸν ἀντὶ κακοῦ ἀποδιδόντες, προνοούμενοι καλὰ ἐνώπιον πάντων ἀνθρώπων). Believers should not harbor a vengeful spirit against those who wrong them, and they should affirm what is noble and good in the cultures in which they live.

Paul recalls the ethical principle of 12:14, but in broader terms that are not limited to the relationship of believers to their unbelieving persecutors. Just as with 12:14, the principle of nonretaliation was already present in the OT. Leviticus 19:17–18, for example, instructs an injured party not to resent his or her adversary but instead to "reason frankly" with and love that person (cf. Prov 20:22; 24:28–29).[45] It was a principle that reappeared in Hellenistic Judaism (e.g., Ps. Phoc. 32–34, 77–78; Jos. Asen. 28:10, 14), that Jesus affirmed and sharpened (Matt 5:43–47; Luke 6:27–36), and that Paul and other early Christians conveyed to their readers, making clear that it applied to the Christian's relationship with everyone, whether believer or unbeliever (1 Thess 5:15; 1 Pet 3:9).[46]

In the next clause, Paul focuses specifically on the relationship between believers and the wider society in which they live. His admonition recalls Proverbs 3:4 LXX, but leaves out the reference to taking thought for what is good before "the Lord" and adds "all" before "human beings."[47] This stands in contrast to 2 Corinthians 8:21, where he also alludes to Proverbs 3:4 but uses its wording more precisely. The variation in his procedure here probably means that he wanted to focus attention on the need to give careful consideration to the things that all people consider noble, right, and good (καλά).[48] Paul is not saying that believers should march to the ethical drum of the surrounding culture, an idea that would radically contradict Romans 12:1–2, but that they should give careful thought to the ethical principles of the prevailing culture and affirm what is good within it (cf. Phil 4:8; 1 Tim 3:7; Titus 2:1–10; 3:1–2).[49] Presumably this exercise involves the sort of divinely guided discernment he described in Romans 12:2.[50]

12:18 If possible, to the extent that it is up to you, live at peace with all human beings (εἰ δυνατόν τὸ ἐξ ὑμῶν, μετὰ πάντων ἀνθρώπων εἰρηνεύοντες). Believers must stay true to the gospel and to what is right, but if these are not at stake, they should make every effort to avoid conflict and encourage the well-being of everyone in their society.

This brief statement summarizes what Paul has said in 12:14–17. Blessing one's persecutors, empathizing with others, thinking humbly about one's

44. Prov 3:7 LXX: "Be not clever in your own eyes" (μὴ ἴσθι φρόνιμος παρὰ σεαυτῷ).

45. Yinger, "Romans 12:14–21 and Non-Retaliation," 77.

46. On the wide currency of the ethic of nonretaliation, see Zerbe (*Non-Retaliation*, 34–173), Yinger ("Romans 12:14–21 and Non-Retaliation," 78–85), Wilson (*Pseudo-Phocylides*, 129–31), and Jewett (*Romans*, 771).

47. Prov 3:4 LXX: "And think of what is good in the sight of the Lord and of human beings" (καὶ προνοοῦ καλὰ ἐνώπιον κυρίου καὶ ἀνθρώπων; my transl.).

48. Jewett, *Romans*, 772.

49. Cf. Moo, *Romans*, 785; Jewett, *Romans*, 772–73.

50. Moo, *Romans*, 785.

self in relation to others, refusing to repay wrongs, and thinking hard about areas of moral agreement with the wider culture are all ways of living at peace with as many people as possible.[51] The importance Paul places on seeking peace with everyone (cf. 12:14, 17) probably reflects his knowledge of Jesus's reformulation of OT teaching (Ps 34:14; Matt 9:5; Mark 9:50; 2 Cor 13:11; 1 Thess 5:13).[52]

The caveat that believers should do this "if possible" and "to the extent that it is up to you" recognizes that some people refuse to live at peace with others until everyone under their power has become complicit in their wickedness. In this situation, Paul implies, the believer must forgo peace and remain faithful to the "good and pleasing and perfect" will of God (12:2).

12:19 Do not give out justice yourselves, beloved, but give place to God's wrath, for it is written, "'It is for me to give out justice, I will repay,' says the Lord" (μὴ ἑαυτοὺς ἐκδικοῦντες, ἀγαπητοί, ἀλλὰ δότε τόπον τῇ ὀργῇ, γέγραπται γάρ, Ἐμοὶ ἐκδίκησις, ἐγὼ ἀνταποδώσω, λέγει κύριος). Although it is a difficult principle to follow, believers in Rome should not attempt to avenge themselves against those who hurt them, for the Scriptures teach that avenging wrongdoing is God's prerogative.

The verb "give out justice" (ἐκδικέω) had a judicial sense, and Paul believed that such judicial punishment, if deserved and the result of proper procedure, was appropriate (13:4).[53] With the reflexive pronoun, however, the verb refers to "taking justice into one's own hands" or seeking revenge.[54] The passive adjective "beloved" (ἀγαπητοί) in this context probably does not imply that Paul's audience is loved by God and therefore should show love to others. Rather, it means that Paul loves them and is giving them ethical guidance that, although difficult to follow, is for their own good and the gospel's progress (cf. 1 Cor 4:14; 2 Cor 12:19).[55] The expression "give place" (δότε τόπον) means to provide an opportunity (cf. Eph 4:27), and the use of the article with "wrath" (τῇ ὀργῇ) implies a specific wrath. The quotation of Deuteronomy 32:35 makes clear that this specific wrath is the wrath of the Lord. Paul's admonition and the reasoning behind it, therefore, is clear: believers in Rome should not impatiently take justice into their own hands when they are wronged but wait for the Lord to render justice.

Paul backs up his reasoning with the authority of Scripture, paraphrasing Deuteronomy 32:35.[56] The principle of leaving justice to God was common in the OT and Jewish tradition (cf., e.g., Ps 37:7–9, 12–13; Prov 20:22; T. Gad 6:7; 7:4–6; Jos. Asen. 28:10).[57]

12:20 But, "if your enemy is hungry, give him something to eat; if he is thirsty, give him something to drink. For, if you do this, you will pile fiery coals on his head" (ἀλλ' ἐὰν πεινᾷ ὁ ἐχθρός σου, ψώμιζε αὐτόν· ἐὰν διψᾷ, πότιζε αὐτόν· τοῦτο

51. *TLNT* 1:435.

52. For discussion of these parallels, see Wilson (*Love without Pretense*, 191).

53. Cf. Sanday and Headlam, *Romans*, 366; F. F. Bruce, "Paul and 'The Powers that Be,'" *BJRL* 66 (1983–84): 81.

54. MM 192, s.v. ἐκδικέω; LSJ 504, s.v. ἐκδικέω II; BDAG 300, s.v. ἐκδικέω 1. See especially P.Oxy. 6.937.5–8 and Aesop, *Fables* 279b.

55. Cf. Cranfield, *Romans*, 2:646. For the view that Paul reminds his readers that they are the objects of God's love, see, e.g., Moo (*Romans*, 786).

56. "Vengence is mine" (ἐμοὶ ἐκδίκησις) is a word-for-word rendering of the Hebrew into Greek, but is quite unlike the LXX's "in the day of vengeance" (ἐν ἡμέρᾳ ἐκδικήσεως). The expression "I will repay" (ἀνταποδώσω), however, parallels the LXX's departure from the Hebrew "and recompense" (*weshillem*). Paul's "says the Lord" (λέγει κύριος) follows neither the Hebrew nor the LXX.

57. Zerbe, *Non-Retaliation*, 167.

γὰρ ποιῶν ἄνθρακας πυρὸς σωρεύσεις ἐπὶ τὴν κεφαλὴν αὐτοῦ). The believer should treat an enemy with kindness because the unusual action of not merely refusing to retaliate but actually meeting an enemy's needs will help him see how wrongheaded his actions are and perhaps bring about a change in his character.

The conjunction "but" (ἀλλ') reaches back to 12:19a and to the notion of believers taking justice into their own hands. Rather than doing this, they should, in the words of Proverbs 25:21–22 LXX, lovingly meet the needs of their enemies.[58]

The enigmatic imagery of heaping coals of fire on the enemy's head supplies the reason why (γάρ) believers should show kindness to their enemies. The most straightforward reading of the statement is that one actually harms one's enemies by "lovingly" meeting their needs.[59] It is difficult to imagine, however, that this is the right meaning of this maxim either in Proverbs or in Paul. "The book of Proverbs," says Bruce Waltke, "rejects any form of personal revenge (17:13; 20:22; 24:17, 18)," leaving it instead to God.[60] Paul, for his part, started the ethical admonitions of 12:9–21 with the unambiguous command, "Let love be without pretense" (v. 9), and then urged his readers to "bless" their persecutors (v. 14). It would be odd indeed if Paul now brought this section to a close by advising believers to use pretension of love as a means of luring their enemies into a fiery trap of eschatological judgment.

Perhaps, then, Paul is simply nuancing slightly the idea of 12:19 by encouraging believers to leave the judgment of their enemies' evil deeds to God. This interpretation has the great advantage of taking "fiery coals on [the] head" as an image of God's judgment, which is the way the expression tends to be used in other ancient Jewish literature (e.g., Ps 140:9–10; 2 Esd 16:53).[61] Here in 12:20, however, it is not God who piles fiery coals on the enemy's head but the believer who does this by means of kindness.

It seems likely, then, that Paul refers not to the eschatological judgment of God but to the present effect of the believer's kindness on an enemy.[62] Precisely what effect Paul has in mind is not clear from the image. A number of interpreters down through the centuries have understood the statement as a reference to the burning shame an enemy feels when treated with kindness by those whom he or she has mistreated.[63] It is unnecessary, however, to be so specific, and it may be best to admit that we do not know precisely what the imagery means.[64] Paul's basic point, however, is clear, and Lagrange has described it succinctly: "'To have burning coals on the head' constitutes a most painful situation, and a situation that is easy to exit, if one wants to. The idea is that the enemy would feel de-

58. Paul's quotation differs from the LXX only in replacing the word for "feed" (τρέφε) with the word for "give something to eat" (ψώμιζε) and omitting the final clause, "and the Lord will reward you with good things" (ὁ δὲ κύριος ἀνταποδώσει σοι ἀγαθά).

59. Krister Stendahl ("Hate, Non-Retaliation, and Love: I QS X, 17–20 and Rom. 12:19–21," *HTR* 95 [1962]: 343–55) seems to imply this interpretation. Cf. Matthew Black, *Romans*, 2nd ed., New Century Bible Commentary (Grand Rapids: Eerdmans, 1989), 178, and the discussion of this position, with bibliography, in Zerbe (*Non-Retaliation*, 218).

60. Bruce K. Waltke, *The Book of Proverbs: Chapters 15–31*, NICOT (Grand Rapids: Eerdmans, 2005), 331.

61. Zerbe, *Non-Retaliation*, 254–55; Schreiner, *Romans*, 674–75; Légasse, *Romains*, 797–98. Cf. Stendahl, "Hate," 347.

62. The notion that Paul's future tense points to the eschatological judgment toward which the enemy is "storing up" evidence for God's wrath (Stendahl, "Hate," 348, 353) is read into the text.

63. E.g., Origen, *Romans, Books 6–10*, 220 (Stendahl ["Hate," 346] mischaracterizes Origen's view); Meyer, *Romans*, 481; Sanday and Headlam, *Romans*, 365.

64. Dunn, *Romans 9–16*, 751.

feated by such generosity and disposed to better sentiments."[65]

12:21 Do not be conquered by evil, but conquer evil by good (μὴ νικῶ ὑπὸ τοῦ κακοῦ ἀλλὰ νίκα ἐν τῷ ἀγαθῷ τὸ κακόν). To join the fray of retaliation against one's enemy is to succumb not to the enemy himself but to something worse—the evil that drives him. Responding to one's enemy with practical deeds of love, however, deprives evil of a place to grow and eventually defeats it.

Lagrange's understanding of 12:20 receives confirmation from this brief, summarizing statement. The statement does not envision conquering the evil *person* through good deeds, as a retributive reading of 12:20 would require, but conquering *evil itself*, embodied in the hostile deeds of the enemy. The two occurrences of "evil" (τοῦ κακοῦ and τὸ κακόν) are neuter, as the second occurrence shows. Retaliating against the enemy himself would involve usurping the role of God (12:9), who alone knows the intentions of the human heart and who alone can judge justly (2:16; 14:4, 10–12; 1 Cor 4:3–5). It would also involve entering the endless, ever deepening cycle of revenge. To respond to evil with good, however, is to live in a way that is consistent with the "sweeping victory" God has won for us (ὑπερνικῶμεν) over the evil within and outside of us through the death, resurrection, and heavenly session of Christ (Rom 8:37; cf. 5:8).

Theology in Application

This passage teaches Christians that the love God expects them to show to others arises from God's transforming work within them, not from outward coercion. It also contributes to Christian teaching on nonretaliation and provides a strategy for practicing a kind of love for the church's enemies that does not excuse or perpetuate injustice.

Love That Arises from an Inner Transformation

In 12:9–21 Paul describes the important role that simple acts of kindness and faithfulness to others, performed from the heart, should play in the lives of believers. They should love and honor each other, serve the Lord, adopt a prayerful attitude of hope and steadfastness in their commitment to the gospel, and share what they have with other believers who are in need (12:9–13). Paul is careful to communicate along with these admonitions, however, that obeying them should be the free choice of the believer acting from the transformed mind Paul has described in 12:1–2. Expressions such as "without pretense," "loathe," "cling," "enthusiasm," "ardent," and "rejoice" were intended to remind Paul's audience that their new way of life as Christians was not

65. Lagrange, *Romains*, 309. Cf. Pelagius (*Romans*, 136), who envisions the enemy shaking off the coals of fire that have amassed on his head simply by repenting. This interpretation does not require the common but dubious procedure of appealing to a third-century BC Egyptian ritual of repentance and shaming involving coals of fire carried on the head (e.g., Cranfield, *Romans*, 2:650; Käsemann, *Romans*, 349). It is best to admit that the precise way in which the imagery functions is simply not known.

something imposed on them from outside themselves but was the fruit of the new way of thinking God had given to them when he transformed and renewed their minds.

This is a steady feature of Paul's ethical instruction. In 14:20–23 he will appeal to those in Rome who disagree with each other over the observance of the Mosaic law simply to let the disagreement stand since the really important issue is not whether one does or does not observe the Mosaic law but whether one acts in a way that is consistent with one's inner conviction about the truth of the gospel. Similarly, Paul wanted the Corinthians to contribute to his collection for needy believers in Jerusalem because, like the Macedonians, their desire to do so welled up from within as a result of their prior commitment to the Lord (2 Cor 8:2, 5; cf. 9:7). He hoped that Philemon would release Onesimus from slavery so that Onesimus could work with Paul for the gospel's progress, but he refused to pull rank on Philemon and order him to do this. The reason for such an approach, Paul tells Philemon, is so that his "goodness might not be by compulsion but of [his] own accord" (Phlm 14; cf. 8–9).

Does this mean that believers should only do good when they "want" and "feel" able to do it? Clearly this is not the case, since Paul will later emphasize that doing what is good involves "not pleasing" one's self but pleasing one's neighbor (15:1–2) and will point out that Jesus did not please himself when he suffered in the place of others (15:3). The inner enthusiasm for obedience that Paul talks about here must operate at a deeper level than some surface feeling. Rather, it must refer to a basic desire to do God's will, even when doing so is costly and runs against the current of one's surface feelings.

The theological principle that obedience to Christian ethical instruction should arise from within the person who obeys is as applicable to those who are giving Christian instruction as it is to those receiving it. Paul's focus on inner convictions implies that no believer should ever coerce the obedience of another believer, much less those outside the church. Large amounts of ethical instruction are necessary for forming the character of believers, as Paul demonstrates in 12:1–15:7, but Christians who instruct others must also follow Paul's example in patiently leaving the inner change that produces obedience to the work of God.

Nonretaliation

There is perhaps no more costly form of Christian obedience and no requirement of Christian ethics that runs more powerfully against human intuition than the principle of nonretaliation that Paul develops in 12:14 and 17–21. "It is a difficult sacrifice which Christ demands of us when he demands that we abandon our attempts at vengeance," said Dietrich Bonhoeffer, "perhaps it is the most difficult sacrifice of all. For it is entirely natural for humans to seek vengeance against their enemies."[66] Bonhoeffer made this comment in a sermon he preached on 12:16–21 in late January, 1938. This was only a few months after the Gestapo had closed the small Confessing Church seminary he led at Finkenwalde and less than two weeks after the Gestapo had arrested him and twenty-nine other believers at a church meeting and then interrogated them for seven hours.[67] Eventually Bonhoeffer would become a key player in a military plot to kill Hitler, but this was an effort to defend others against the horrors of the Third Reich, not an act of personal revenge.[68]

Because much is sometimes at stake in following Paul's advice, it is important to be clear about what he is saying. When Paul speaks of blessing one's persecutor (12:14) and living in peace with everyone (12:18), he is not implying that believers should capitulate to the demands of bullies or that conciliation is more important than addressing injustice. In a context where blessing is contrasted with cursing, both terms refer to something that one is asking God to do for or to someone else, whether good or evil. Paul, then, is instructing believers to ask God to bring good to those who are doing them harm. Since it is not in the best interest of the wicked that they continue their rebellion against God and hatred of others, the blessing that Paul refers to must include the prayer that they turn from injustice and seek God's mercy. This understanding of 12:14 seems to be confirmed by 12:20 where, on the most likely understanding of the believer's role in heaping coals of fire on the enemy's head, the believer's kindness is a way of encouraging the enemy's repentance.

The teaching of Jesus on the same subject provides a reason why Jesus's disciples and hearers should do good to those who hate them: God is kind and merciful to those who are themselves ungrateful and evil, and Jesus's followers should imitate God. They are "to be merciful [οἰκτίρμονες], even as [their] Father is merciful [οἰκτίρμων]" (Luke 6:35–36). In other words, their willingness to treat their enemies better than they deserve is an active witness to an essential aspect of the character of God and of the gospel. It is difficult to think that Paul's advice, coming on the heels of his reference in 12:1 to God's compassionate actions (τῶν οἰκτιρμῶν) in the gospel, is not also grounded in this idea of bearing witness to the merciful nature of God as he is revealed in the gospel. Believers were themselves once God's enemies, and while they were still hostile to him, he took the initiative in seeking reconciliation

66. Evan Drake Howard, trans., "Loving Our Enemies: Dietrich Bonhoeffer's Sermon on Romans 12:16–21," *The Reformed Journal* 35 (1985): 20. Information on the sermon's context comes from the translator's note on p. 18. See also Esabel Best, ed., *The Collected Sermons of Dietrich Bonhoeffer* (Minneapolis: Fortress, 2012), 193. For the chronology, see Eberhard Bethge, *Dietrich Bonhoeffer: Man of Vision, Man of Courage*, trans. Eric Mosbacher, Peter and Betty Ross, Frank Clarke, William Geln-Doepel, ed. Edwin Robertson (New York: Harper & Row, 1970), 489–91.

67. On the arrest and interrogation, see Eric Metaxas, *Bonhoeffer: Pastor, Martyr, Prophet, Spy* (Nashville: Thomas Nelson, 2010), 302.

68. Bethge dates Bonhoeffer's active political resistance from early 1938 (*Dietrich Bonhoeffer*, 526), again, within months of Bonhoeffer's sermon on Rom 12:16–21.

with them and provided the costly means by which they could be at peace with him through the death of his Son (5:6–10).[69]

Leaving Punishment to God

Just as God did not seek retribution against believers while they were his enemies but made peace with them, so Paul says in this passage that believers are not to take justice into their own hands and avenge themselves against their enemies. Instead they are to work at peace with all people, including their persecutors. His statement that they are to do this "if possible, to the extent that it is up to you," however, implies that the just peace believers seek with their enemies may not be possible. Their adversaries may have hearts so hard that they never respond to the loving overtures of believers. In this situation Paul continues to call on Christians not to retaliate, but now the reason for their nonretaliation shifts to the principle that God's people cannot usurp God's authority over the judgment and punishment of sin.

According to William V. Harris, this is a matter of "the Christian authorities . . . telling the faithful to avoid anger" but encouraging them "to think that God would annihilate their enemies."[70] This, he argues, sent an ambiguous message about anger and whether it was permissible.[71] When Paul speaks of the "wrath" (ὀργή) of God in 12:19, however, he is speaking of the perfectly just punishment meted out by an omniscient being. This, at least, is how Paul defines God's "wrath" in 1:18–32. Far from being a problematic concept, the concept solves a massive problem. Christians may not take the law into their own hands, exacting "just" punishment upon their enemies, because the sinful tendencies that still operate within them almost guarantee that their revenge will be unjust. Does this mean that justice can never be served? That evil has triumphed over good? The eschatological wrath of God demonstrates that this is not the case. Since God is merciful and wants the wicked to repent, his justice may come slowly from the perspective of the victims, but it will come, and when it comes it will confirm that God has not turned a blind eye to evil but remains committed to the triumph of the good.

69. A point that Bonhoeffer emphasizes throughout his sermon.

70. Harris, *Restraining Rage*, 394.

71. Ibid., 395–97.

CHAPTER 26

Romans 13:1–14

Literary Context

The lack of any conjunction in 13:1 connecting it to the previous paragraph and the change of style from pithy maxims to Paul's more normal mode of reasoned argumentation signal a switch to the topic of the relationship of believers to the governing authorities in 13:1–7. Some interpreters have thought that the appearance of this topic at this point is strange and have pointed out that 12:9–21 could move seamlessly into 13:8–14 if 13:1–7 were removed.[1] Perhaps, then, 13:1–7 is an interpolation into the letter reflecting the concerns of the church of a later era, or if that seems too extreme, a piece of traditional advice derived from Judaism and not fully integrated into Paul's normal eschatological and christological convictions.[2]

This approach to the passage, however, is unconvincing. Thematically it makes sense for Paul to describe how his believing audience in Rome should think about the governing authorities, and to do so at this point in the letter. Paul was concerned throughout 12:3–21 to show in practical terms how his audience in Rome could avoid conformity to the present age and instead think and make decisions on the basis of God's will (12:2). In 12:9–21 Paul had turned his attention especially to how believers should conduct their day-to-day lives as a tiny, often misunderstood minority before their unbelieving neighbors. He had emphasized the need for sincere love, abhorrence of evil, attachment to what is good (v. 9), nonretaliation (vv. 14, 17, 19–21), and living at peace, as far as possible, with everyone (v. 18). Within this context, and especially in a letter to Rome, the seat of authority for the vast empire in which both Paul and his Roman audience lived, it was natural for Paul to address how the believing community should think about the rulers of their city and its many subject peoples.

The paragraph not only fits well within its context thematically, but also advances the argument of 12:9–21. One way Paul's audience can live at peace with all (12:18), avoid dealing out justice (ἐκδικοῦντες) themselves, and give place to God's wrath (τῇ

1. James Kallas, "Romans XIII.1–7: An Interpolation," *NTS* 11 (1964): 366.

2. See, respectively, Kallas, "Romans XIII.1–7," 365–74; and Ernst Käsemann, *New Testament Questions of Today*, trans. W. J. Montague (Philadelphia: Fortress, 1969), 196–216; idem, *Romans*, 350–55.

ὀργῇ) (12:19) is to submit to the governing authorities who are God's agents for dealing out justice (ἔκδικος εἰς ὀργήν) (13:4). One way they can overcome evil with good (τῷ ἀγαθῷ) (12:21) is by submitting to God's divinely appointed means of upholding the good (τὸ ἀγαθόν) through government (13:3–4).[3] Repaying (ἀποδιδόντες) no one evil for evil on the negative side is balanced on the positive side by repaying (ἀπόδοτε) tribute, tax, fear, and honor to those who should have them (12:17; 13:7).[4]

Paul used the idea of obligation to move from the theme of submission to the government (13:1–7) to the theme of acting in loving rather than self-indulgent ways (13:8–14). This theme, in turn, laid the foundation for his pastoral advice about the relationship between the weak and the strong in 14:1–15:13. The government, and indeed all people, should receive the formal payment and respect they are due, but others are always due the debt of love (13:7–8, τὰ ὀφειλάς . . . ὀφείλετε). The notion of loving others, Paul concludes, involves avoiding "contention and envy" (13:13) and putting on the Lord Jesus Christ (13:14). The two ideas of avoiding contention and union with Christ lead naturally into the next major section of the letter. That section begins with an admonition for the strong to welcome the weak without arguing (14:1) and ends with an admonition for everyone to welcome one another and so to imitate the unselfish love of Christ (15:3, 7–9a).

3. See, respectively, Erwin Ochsenmeier ("Romans 12,17–13,7 and the Justice of God: Two Neglected Features of Paul's Argument," *ETL* 89 [2013]: 362–66) and Engberg-Pedersen ("Paul's Stoicizing Politics," 168).

4. Cf. Bruce, "Paul and 'The Powers that Be,'" 81–82.

Main Idea

As part of their renewed way of thinking about the world around them, believers should consider the government of Rome under which they live as an agent of God to promote good and keep evil at bay. Insurrection is not only ill advised because it is likely to lead to judicial punishment, but also because it attempts to overthrow God's appointed means of ruling society. Submission to the government, then, including the payment of tribute, taxes, fear, and honor to those who legitimately require them, is a necessary part of obedience to God's will. Loving others, however, is a more important responsibility: it is a debt that is never repaid and fulfills the aim of the Mosaic law. Believers live at a critical moment in salvation history, and so loving others rather than living self-indulgently should be the hallmark of those who are united with Christ by faith.

Translation

(See pages 604–05.)

Structure

The passage is thoughtfully composed, consisting of two major parts. In 13:1–7 Paul focuses on the relationship of the believing community to the governing authorities, and in 13:8–14 he focuses on the critical importance of acting with love toward everyone.

Paul's treatment of the governing authorities (13:1–7) begins with a thesis statement in 13:1a claiming that every person should submit to the functionaries that maintain societal order. He then explains this thesis in two steps, one that engages in an abstract discussion of the relationship between God and government (13:1b–5) and another that applies this abstract discussion to the very practical issue of rendering one's obligations to the government (13:6–7).

Paul begins by giving two reasons why submission to government is necessary. First, God is the source of governmental authority (13:1b–2), and, second, the people in charge of government are God's agents for upholding what is good and just and punishing evil (13:3–4). He neatly summarizes his thesis and these two reasons in a pithy sentence that concludes his abstract discussion (13:5):

Thesis: "It is necessary to submit"
Reason 1: "Because of God's wrath"
Reason 2: "Because of conscience"

Paul then applies this theoretical discussion to the practical issue of paying the

Romans 13:1–14

1a	Exhortation	**Let every person submit** themselves to the ruling authorities.
b	Basis 1 (of 1a)	For **no authority exists except by God,**
c	Restatement	and **those that do exist are set in place by God.**
2a	Inference	So, **the one who opposes authority has become rebellious**
		against the ordinance of God,
b	Result Disadvantage	and **those who are in rebellion will receive judgment**
		against themselves.
3a	Basis 2 (of 1a)	For **officials are not a threat** to what is good, but
		to what is evil.
b	Rhetorical Question	**Do you want to be free from fearing governmental authority?**
c	Means	**Do what is good,**
		and **you will have praise from it.**
4a	Basis (of 3c)	For **she is the agent of God** **for good,**
		for your benefit.
b	Condition	But
		if you do evil,
		fear.
c	Basis (of 4b)	For **she does not wear the sword in vain,**
d	Explanation	for **she is** **the agent of God,**
		one who distributes justice,
e	Result (of 4d)	resulting in wrath for the one who does evil.
5a	Summary (of 1b–4)	Therefore, **to submit one's self is a necessity,**
b		not only because of that wrath
c		but also because of the conscience.
6a	Basis (of 5)	For because of this **you pay tribute,**
b	Basis (of 6a)	for **they are servants of God,**
c		devoted to this very purpose.
7a	Exhortation	**Repay your obligations to everyone,**
b	List	tribute to whom tribute is due,
c	List	tax to whom tax is due,
d	List	fear to whom fear is due,
e	List	honor to whom honor is due.

8a Exhortation **Owe**
no one anything
except to love one another,

b Basis (of 8a) for **the one who loves the other has fulfilled the law.**

9a Explanation (8) For **the list,**
"You shall not commit adultery; (Exod 20:14; Deut 5:18)
you shall not murder; (Exod 20:13; Deut 5:17)
you shall not steal; (Exod 20:15; Deut 5:19)
you shall not covet" (Exod 20:17; Deut 5:21) (and if there is any other commandment)
is summarized in this statement:

b Summary (of 9a) "You shall love your neighbor as yourself." (Lev 19:18)

10a Restatement (of 9) **Love does nothing wrong to a neighbor;**

b Inference (from 10a) therefore **love is the fulfillment of the law.**

11a Basis (of 8a) And this, because you know the time—
b Expansion (of 8a) that it is already the hour for you to wake up from sleep,

c Basis (for 11b) for **our salvation is nearer now than when we first believed.**

12a Assertion **The night has advanced,**

b Restatement (of 12a) and **the day has drawn near.**

c Exhortation/Inference **Let us throw off,** then, **the works of darkness**

d Restatement (of 12c) and **put on the weapons of light.**

13a Exhortation/Inference **Let us go around**
b Expansion (of 13a) presentably, as if it were day,
c Contrast not in orgies and drinking bouts,
d not in sexual liaisons and self-abandonment,
e not in contention and envy.

14a Contrast (to 13b–d) But **put on the Lord Jesus Christ,**

b Contrast (to 14a) and **do not make provision for the flesh**
c for the purpose of sinful desires.

obligations that the government rightfully places on those who benefit from the social order it provides (13:6–7). He summarizes these obligations in terms relevant to the Roman Empire of the mid-first century (tribute, tax, fear, and honor) and urges his Roman audience to render them to the relevant authorities.

Paul moves to the second major section of the passage by skillfully using the concept of obligation as a transition: believers should render to the government the "obligations" that it deserves, but the obligation to love others is never fulfilled (13:8a). He then explains this thesis in two major steps. The first part (13:8–10) emphasizes the critical importance of love by showing that loving actions bring the people of God to the goal toward which the Mosaic law's second table pointed (13:8b–10).

The second part (13:11–14) is connected to the first part by the phrase "and this" (καὶ τοῦτο, 13:11a), which points back to the command not to owe anyone anything except the debt of love (13:8a). Loving others is important not only because it fulfills the law but because Paul and his audience of Roman believers are living at a critical moment in salvation history: the night is nearly over, and Paul's readers need to be up and busily preparing for that eschatological day that is about to break upon the whole world. Loving others as a result of their union with Jesus Christ is one of the most important ways they can prepare for that day (13:11–14).

Exegetical Outline

XI. Exhortation to Live in a Way That Is Consistent with the Gospel (12:1–15:13)

- A. A Mind Transformed and Renewed by God (12:1–2)
- B. Community without Competition (12:3–8)
- **C. Loving One Another and Remaining Steadfast in a Hostile Environment (12:9–13:14)**
    - 1. Heartfelt Love for One Another and Service to the Lord in Thirteen Areas (12:9–13)
    - 2. Overcoming Evil and Maintaining Harmony (12:14–21)
    - ➡ **3. The Necessity of Submission to Government Authorities (13:1–7)**
        - a. Paul's thesis statement: submission to government is necessary (13:1a)
        - b. Two reasons why submission is necessary and a summary (13:1b–5)
            - (1) Government originates with God (13:1b–2)
            - (2) Government functionaries are necessary for upholding what is good and just in society (13:3–4)
            - (3) Paul summarizes the abstract part of his exhortation (13:5)
        - c. A practical application of Paul's abstract thesis: payment of obligations (13:6–7)
    - **4. The Critical Importance of Loving Others (13:8–14)**
        - a. Paul's thesis statement: loving others is the most important obligation of believers (13:8a)
        - b. Two reasons why loving others is so important (13:8b–14)
            - (1) Love fulfills the law (13:8b–10)
            - (2) God's saving purposes are about to be fulfilled (13:11–14)

Explanation of the Text

13:1 Let every person submit themselves to the ruling authorities. For no authority exists except by God, and those that do exist are set in place by God (Πᾶσα ψυχὴ ἐξουσίαις ὑπερεχούσαις ὑποτασσέσθω. οὐ γὰρ ἔστιν ἐξουσία εἰ μὴ ὑπὸ θεοῦ, αἱ δὲ οὖσαι ὑπὸ θεοῦ τεταγμέναι εἰσίν). God placed the governing authorities in Rome in their positions, and so believers should voluntarily place themselves under their authority.

Just as with 12:9 and 12:14, the lack of any coordinating conjunction signals a shift to a new topic. The style of Paul's discourse also changes: he moves from the second-person singular in 12:20–21 to the third-person singular, and his pithy maxims give way to instructions accompanied by argumentation explaining the reasons for the instruction (cf. 12:3–5).[5]

The expression "every person" (πᾶσα ψυχή) is reminiscent of the LXX version of the Mosaic law, where it appears in important dietary and Sabbath commands and emphasizes that every individual is responsible for keeping these regulations (e.g., Lev 7:27; 17:12, 15; 23:29–30).[6] Here the expression sets a biblical tone for what follows, alerting Paul's audience that he is operating in the conceptual world of the Jewish Scriptures.

The term "authority" (ἐξουσία) was a natural term to use for an "office" or "magistracy" that carried with it the exercise of political or judicial power (e.g., Dan 7:27 LXX).[7] Paul could use the term to refer to invisible "authorities" in the heavenly places (e.g., Eph 6:12), to refer to visible, earthly authorities (Titus 3:1), and to both at the same time (e.g., 1 Cor 15:24). Here, as the talk of submission and payment of taxes shows (Rom 13:5–7), he has in mind the earthly magistrates who presided over the Roman system of justice.[8]

These are not really the "higher" magistrates (cf. KJV, NAB) in comparison to lower level officials, although the expression translated "ruling" (ὑπερεχούσαις) here could refer to persons of eminence.[9] In what follows, however, Paul does not pursue a line of reasoning that distinguishes between lower and higher authorities but speaks simply of "those who rule" (οἱ ... ἄρχοντες, 13:3). It is unlikely, then, that he means to counsel submission only to the most important authorities.

Paul explains why ("for" [γάρ]) his audience in Rome should submit to their local magistrates by emphasizing that their authority was derived from God and that they served at God's pleasure.[10] They would not exist in their positions "except by God," and they had been "set in place by God" to occupy those positions. This is a thoroughly Jewish and biblical approach to the relationship between the people of God and the non-Jewish governments under which they often found themselves living (cf. Prov 8:15–16; Dan 4:25; 5:21; Sir 10:4; 17:17).[11] It was not, however, a view unique to Judaism. In an essay written in Rome at virtually the same time that Paul wrote Romans, Seneca, the advisor to the young Nero, took the same position with the significant difference that Paul held the governing authorities to be agents not of "the gods" but of the one true God.[12]

Paul probably intended to echo the term "submit" (ὑποτασσέσθω) by using the perfect participle

5. Cf. Wilckens, *An die Römer (Röm 12–16)*, 29–30.

6. Cf. Rom 2:9 and the comments of Jewett, *Romans*, 787.

7. LSJ 599, s.v. ἐξουςία II.

8. Cranfield, *Romans*, 2:658–59; Bruce, "'The Powers That Be,'" 88.

9. LSJ 1863, s.v. ὑπερέχω II.4.c.

10. Jewett, *Romans*, 789–90.

11. Lagrange, *Romains*, 310; Wilckens, *An die Römer (Röm 12–16)*, 33; James D. G. Dunn, "Romans 13.1–7: A Charter for Political Quietism?," *ExAud* 2 (1986): 64.

12. Seneca, *Clem.* 1.1–4, discussed in Engberg-Pedersen ("Paul's Stoicizing Politics," 167–69).

of its cognate verb (τεταγμέναι, from τάσσω), which describes the authorities as "set in place by God." This wordplay would have communicated that Paul's audience should voluntarily submit to the government not because of any intrinsic worth that the authorities themselves possessed but because God used them to provide social order, and this social order was a good thing that God desired (cf. Rom 13:3–4).

13:2 So, the one who opposes authority has become rebellious against the ordinance of God, and those who are in rebellion will receive judgment against themselves (ὥστε ὁ ἀντιτασσόμενος τῇ ἐξουσίᾳ τῇ τοῦ θεοῦ διαταγῇ ἀνθέστηκεν, οἱ δὲ ἀνθεστηκότες ἑαυτοῖς κρίμα λήμψονται). The subordination of governmental authority to divine authority implies that settled rebellion against the societal order government provides will come under God's eschatological judgment.

Paul's "so" (ὥστε) introduces his description of one consequence of not submitting to the authorities. The verb "oppose" (ἀντιτάσσω) was the opposite of its cognate "submit" (ὑποτάσσω) and related to the noun "ordinance" (διαταγή). Paul seems to be intentionally playing on words that express order (ὑποτάσσω, τάσσω, ἀντιτάσσω, διαταγή) to emphasize that the governmental order in place in mid-first century Rome was there because God had willed it as a means of providing social order.[13] The wordplay was rhetorically effective, but the term "oppose" (ἀντιτάσσω) needed greater precision. Paul provides this precision with his twofold use of the verb "rebel" (ἀνθίστημι), a term that often refers to armed resistance or insurgency (Esth 9:2 LXX; 3 Macc 6:19; Eph 6:13; Josephus, *Ant.* 18.100).[14]

It is unlikely that the "judgment" of those who resist this order is the punishment that the authorities mete out to the guilty in the ordinary course of their work. Elsewhere in Romans "judgment" (κρίμα) is always the judgment of God (Rom 2:2–3; 3:8; 5:16; cf. 11:33), and the overall point of these two clauses is that those who organize violent resistance against governmental order are responsible for their actions before God.[15]

13:3 For officials are not a threat to what is good, but to what is evil. Do you want to be free from fearing governmental authority? Do what is good, and you will have praise from it (οἱ γὰρ ἄρχοντες οὐκ εἰσὶν φόβος τῷ ἀγαθῷ ἔργῳ ἀλλὰ τῷ κακῷ. θέλεις δὲ μὴ φοβεῖσθαι τὴν ἐξουσίαν· τὸ ἀγαθὸν ποίει, καὶ ἕξεις ἔπαινον ἐξ αὐτῆς). Not only has God put societal government in place, but ideally government officials punish bad behavior and encourage good behavior.

Paul now provides a second reason (γάρ), in addition to 13:1bc–2, why believers should submit to the government.[16] The expression "officials" (οἱ . . . ἄρχοντες) refers generally to those in charge of the government and who therefore have the duty of keeping societal order (cf. Acts 16:19). "Threat" (φόβος, cf. NAB) normally refers to fear itself rather than its cause (e.g., Rom 3:18; 8:15; 13:7), but it could also refer to something that is intimidating (Appian, *Civil Wars* 2.135) or inspires fear, such as the spectacle of an execution (Polybius, *Hist.* 11.30.2).[17]

13. Michel, *An die Römer*, 398.

14. On the meaning of this term and for the reference to Josephus's significant use of the substantival participle, see Ernst Bammel, "Romans 13," in *Jesus and the Politics of His Day*, ed. Ernst Bammel and C. F. D. Moule (Cambridge: Cambridge University Press, 1984), 370–71.

15. Cf. Moo, *Romans*, 799. For the expression "will receive judgment against themselves" (ἑαυτοῖς κρίμα λήμψονται), cf. 1 Cor 11:29 (Wilckens, *An die Römer [Röm 12–16]*, 33n157).

16. Moo, *Romans*, 800; cf. Dunn, *Romans 9–16*, 763.

17. BDAG 1062, s.v. φόβος 1b. John Carter's translation of Appian's *The Civil Wars* (London: Penguin, 1996), however, takes the relevant sentence in 2.135 as a reference to Antonius's own "fear" rather than his "intimidation" of the Senate.

When Paul says that officials are not a threat to what is good, he is not describing what always happens but what should happen according to the general principle he is discussing.[18] He knew that "the rulers [τῶν ἀρχόντων] of this age" had, for example, "crucified the Lord of glory" (1 Cor 2:8), but he must have seen this as a profound deviation from the general principle that he describes here.

The contrast between "what is good" and "what is evil" is reminiscent of 12:9–21, which started and finished with a similar contrast, and the articles in front of these abstract nouns give specificity to the concepts the nouns represent.[19] This is "good" and "evil" viewed from God's perspective.[20]

The second half of the verse, directed in the second-person singular to a fictional interlocutor (cf. 2:1–29; 9:19–20; 11:17–24), again assumes an ideal system of governmental authority.[21] Government, Paul says, poses no threat to those who live in the way that 12:9–21 describes but instead encourages this behavior with praise.

13:4 For she is the agent of God for good, for your benefit. But if you do evil, fear. For she does not wear the sword in vain, for she is the agent of God, one who distributes justice, resulting in wrath for the one who does evil (θεοῦ γὰρ διάκονός ἐστιν σοὶ εἰς τὸ ἀγαθόν. ἐὰν δὲ τὸ κακὸν ποιῇς, φοβοῦ· οὐ γὰρ εἰκῇ τὴν μάχαιραν φορεῖ· θεοῦ γὰρ διάκονός ἐστιν, ἔκδικος εἰς ὀργὴν τῷ τὸ κακὸν πράσσοντι). Paul now explains why (γάρ) government supports good rather than evil: it is God's tool, and the judicial power given to its officials preserves societal order.

The term "agent" (διάκονος) probably carries connotations less of humble service than of functional agency (e.g., Esth 1:10 LXX; Epictetus, *Diatr.* 3.24.65).[22] Paul now takes advantage of the feminine gender of the term, and of the word "authority" (ἐξουσία) in 13:3, to personify the Roman governmental system as a sword-bearing woman.[23] She is merely a functionary of God, who is far superior to her in rank. The dative singular pronoun "you" (σοί) continues the conversation with a fictional interlocutor, and now Paul instructs his dialogue partner that the governmental system in place in Rome is for his interlocutor's personal benefit: the dative is a "dative of advantage."

A caveat (δέ), however, is needed. If Paul's interlocutor does wrong, then the system of government, as God's agent of justice (διάκονος . . . ἔκδικος), will punish those who deserve it. At least in the second-century BC, even the youngest Roman soldiers were "ordered to carry a sword [μάχαιραν φορεῖν]."[24] When Paul says that the governmental authority does not "wear the sword [μάχαιραν φορεῖ] in vain," then, he is probably referring to a Roman prefect's or provincial governor's

18. Sanday and Headlam, *Romans*, 367.

19. Jewett, *Romans*, 792. On the use of the article with abstract nouns, see Wallace, *Greek Grammar*, 226–27.

20. Hodge, *Romans*, 407; Sanday and Headlam, *Romans*, 367.

21. It is possible to punctuate the sentence so that Paul makes a statement ("But you do not want to fear authority. Do what is good . . ." [cf. NA[28]; UBS[5]]) rather than asks a rhetorical question. Paul's normal mode of argumentation, especially in Romans, however, is not to state what his audience wants and then tell them how to get it, but rather to assume what they want in a rhetorical question and then draw a conclusion based on the obvious reply to the question.

22. Cf. Collins, *Diakonia*, 171–75.

23. BDAG 230, s.v. διάκονος 1. The goddess Roma is depicted on coins from the time of Nero with her left hand on the hilt of her scabbarded sword. The same portrayal of Roma was probably found on the right panel of the east side of the Ara Pacis, which, during Nero's time, faced one of the main highways leading into Rome from the north, the Via Flaminia. On this, see Orietta Rossini, *Ara Pacis: Guide* , 3rd ed. (Milan: Electa, 2012), 6–13, 24–25, 46–47, and Daniele Leoni, *Nerone*, vol. 2 of *Le Monete di Roma* (Verona: Dielle, 2010), 34–36 (figs. 58–62, 65–66).

24. Polybius, *Hist.* 6.22.1 (W. R. Paton, LCL).

use of groups of soldiers to quell disturbances and restore order.[25]

To the Romans, the Christian community looked like a "private association" (*collegium*), and governing authorities had often repressed such associations in Rome, considering them a threat to the social order (e.g., Suetonius, *Aug.* 32.1; Josephus, *Ant.* 14.215; cf. Livy, *History of Rome* 39.8.1–19.7).[26] Paul may have been concerned that individual Christians not attract the attention of the governing authorities by criminal activity, bringing disrepute on the gospel and suffering to the entire community (cf. 1 Pet 4:15).

Only a few decades earlier, in AD 19, Tiberius had banished Roman Jews from the city because four Jewish criminals had swindled a woman of high standing out of a considerable sum of money (Josephus, *Ant.* 18.81–84).[27] Thirty years later, Claudius ordered the Jews to leave Rome (Acts 18:2), and Suetonius says that he took this drastic step because "the Jews . . . persisted in rioting at the instigation of Chrestus" (*Claud.* 25.4).[28] If Christians were involved in this social unrest, Paul would have known about it from Prisca and Aquila (Rom 16:3–5; cf. Acts 18:1–3), and here he may have been trying to avoid a recurrence of similar problems.

13:5 Therefore, to submit one's self is a necessity, not only because of that wrath but also because of the conscience (διὸ ἀνάγκη ὑποτάσσεσθαι, οὐ μόνον διὰ τὴν ὀργὴν ἀλλὰ καὶ διὰ τὴν συνείδησιν). It is important to avoid socially disruptive activity that will bring trouble to the community not merely to escape punishment but also because it is the right thing to do.

Paul now brings the theoretical part of his discussion of the relationship between believers and the government to a close and signals this with a repetition of the verb "submit one's self" (ὑποτάσσεσθαι) with which he began in 13:1. The statement is a brief summary of the reasons he has just given for submitting to the government.[29] "Wrath" (ὀργή) is preceded by the article to identify it as the wrath to which Paul has just referred in 13:4.[30] This, then, is not the same as the "judgment" of 13:2, which was God's eschatological judgment, but is the temporal, immediate wrath that the criminal will receive from the government, which acts as God's "agent" (διάκονος, 13:4) for keeping societal order. "Conscience" (συνείδησιν) is an internal awareness that one's actions are morally wrong or right, and it can bear witness to an alignment or misalignment between one's convictions and one's actions (2:15; 9:1).[31] Here Paul's meaning is clear: he wants his readers to avoid the kind of socially disruptive behavior that will bring soldiers into their neighborhoods, and to do this not only to escape whatever judicial penalty they

25. No police force existed in Rome. Rather, as disturbances arose, the authorities sent soldiers to deal with them. On methods of keeping public order in the Roman Empire, see Wilfried Nippel, *Public Order in Ancient Rome*, Key Themes in Ancient History (Cambridge: Cambridge University Press, 1995), 1–3, 85–112.

26. Cf. Robert L. Wilken, *The Christians as the Romans Saw Them* (New Haven: Yale University Press, 1984), 31–47; Bruce Winter, "Roman Law and Society in Romans 12–15," in *Rome in the Bible and the Early Church*, ed. Peter Oakes (Grand Rapids: Baker, 2002), 69–75.

27. On the Jewish synagogues as *collegia*, see Romano Penna (*Paul the Apostle: A Theological and Exegetical Study*, 2 vols., trans. Thomas P. Wahl [Collegeville, MN: Michael Glazier, 1996], 1:31–32), and on the expulsion of Jews under Tiberius, see Leon (*Jews of Ancient Rome*, 16–20).

28. This translation is from Leon, *Jews of Ancient Rome*, 23.

29. So most commentators (e.g., Murray, *Romans*, 2:154; Schlier, *Römerbrief*, 391; Cranfield, *Romans*, 2:667; Dunn, *Romans 11–16*, 765; Moo, *Romans*, 802).

30. On the anaphoric use of the article, see Smyth, *Greek Grammar*, §1120b; BDF §252; and Wallace, *Greek Grammar*, 217–20.

31. See above at 2:15, "In Depth: Paul's Understanding of the 'Conscience.'"

might receive but because they recognize that to do otherwise would mean disobeying God.

13:6 For because of this you pay tribute, for they are servants of God, devoted to this very purpose (διὰ τοῦτο γὰρ καὶ φόρους τελεῖτε, λειτουργοὶ γὰρ θεοῦ εἰσιν εἰς αὐτὸ τοῦτο προσκαρτεροῦντες). Satisfying those who collect tribute helps to pay for the work of civil servants who are accomplishing God's purposes by providing an orderly society.

Paul's "for" (γάρ) introduces further support for his statement that submission to the government is necessary both to avoid punishment and because it is right. His audience in Rome already implicitly agrees with his reasoning in 13:1–5 because they do, in fact, pay tribute to the Roman government.[32] The phrase "to pay tribute" (φόρους τελεῖν) was a common expression for the payment of a special tax placed on militarily subjugated people groups (e.g., Diodorus Siculus, *Bibliotheca historica* 13.104.4; 16.2.2).[33] Roman citizens living within the city boundaries during this period were not required to pay this sort of tribute, but the precise tax situation for Greek-speaking immigrants and descendants of immigrants is not clear. Many of them probably lived across the Tiber and south of the Porta Capena along the Via Appia and therefore outside Rome's religious boundary (the *pomerium*).[34] It is easy to imagine that Paul's Greek-speaking, Christian readers were required to pay something like tribute to the government if they were not Roman citizens.[35]

In the provinces, at least, failing to pay such taxes could bring severe punishment (Philo, *Spec. Laws* 3.159–60), and if a particular people group did this in large enough numbers, it could be considered a declaration of war (Josephus, *J. W.* 2.402–6).[36] Paul may have been urging his audience to comply with any taxes of this sort to avoid arrest and to keep the social order undisturbed. His advice follows the same general pattern as Jesus's advice to Peter with regard to the Jewish temple tax (Matt 17:24–27), although Jesus's advice is more obviously based on practical considerations whereas Paul emphasizes the role of the conscience and God's sovereignty.

The term "servants" (λειτουργοί) could be used of soldiers or of any group who performed civil service (e.g., Polybius, *Hist.* 3.93.5; Plutarch, *Rom.* 26.4).[37] Paul uses the term here in a way that is synonymous with the word "agent" (διάκονος) in 13:4. Tax collectors of the period were infamous for their violent, extortionist behavior (e.g., Philo, *Spec. Laws* 1.143; Matt 18:17; 21:31–32; Luke 19:7–8), but the "servants" to whom Paul refers are probably the government officials of 13:1, 3, and 4 who, at least in abstract and ideal terms, were "devoted" to keeping the social order (cf. 13:4) and whose work was funded by tax revenues.[38]

13:7 Repay your obligations to everyone, tribute to whom tribute is due, tax to whom tax is due,

32. Paul's "because of this" (διὰ τοῦτο) refers back to what Paul has said in the preceding paragraph (cf. 1:26; 4:16; 5:12).

33. Thomas M. Coleman, "Binding Obligations in Romans 13:7: A Semantic Field and Social Context," *TynBul* 48 (1997): 311. The passages I have cited from Diodorus Siculus were located with the *TLG* and use the plural (φόρους).

34. Only sometime after AD 69, under Vespasian, was the *pomerium* extended to include part of Trastevere. On this, see Filippo Coarelli, *Rome and Environs: An Archaeological Guide*, updated ed. (Berkeley: University of California Press, 2014), 339.

35. Brent D. Shaw, "Roman Taxation," in *Civilization of the Ancient Mediterranean: Greece and Rome*, 3 vols., ed. Michael Grant and Rachel Kitzinger (New York: Charles Scribner's Sons, 1988), 2:811: "Ethnic origins . . . affected tax assessments; Jews, for instance, had to pay special poll taxes."

36. Shaw, "Roman Taxation," 2:809 (citing Cicero, *Leg. man.* 2.4–7 and 7.17); Coleman, "Binding Obligations," 311.

37. LSJ 1037, s.v. λειτουργός II.

38. On the ruthless nature of tax collection, see Shaw ("Roman Taxation," 2:815–17). At least some tax collectors, however, were presumably people of integrity (cf. Luke 3:13; 19:8).

fear to whom fear is due, honor to whom honor is due (ἀπόδοτε πᾶσιν τὰς ὀφειλάς, τῷ τὸν φόρον τὸν φόρον, τῷ τὸ τέλος τὸ τέλος, τῷ τὸν φόβον τὸν φόβον, τῷ τὴν τιμὴν τὴν τιμήν). Paul urges his readers to fulfill the financial and honorific burdens the government places on them.

Paul speaks of four obligations to "everyone" (πᾶσιν), although the context shows that he is talking about all civil authorities (13:1, 3–4, 6).[39] His list distinguishes between the tribute (φόρος) paid by subject peoples and the wide variety of taxes (τέλη) on property, merchandise, and activities in the Roman world.[40] The language of obligation was common in descriptions of such payments.[41] Paul also reflects the cultural context of Rome in speaking of an obligation to repay with "fear" (φόβος) and "honor" (τιμή) the various officials who supervised the social order. The functionaries of Roman government from the emperor down viewed the honor they were accorded as a critical part of their compensation for serving.[42] "The duty of respect," said Cicero, "requires us to reverence and cherish those outstanding because of age or wisdom or office, or any other claim to prestige."[43]

13:8 Owe no one anything except to love one another, for the one who loves the other has fulfilled the law (Μηδενὶ μηδὲν ὀφείλετε εἰ μὴ τὸ ἀλλήλους ἀγαπᾶν· ὁ γὰρ ἀγαπῶν τὸν ἕτερον νόμον πεπλήρωκεν). If another person has a legitimate claim to something that belongs to the believer, then the believer should repay that claim promptly and become free from the obligation. The obligation to love others is constant, however, as the Mosaic law demonstrates with its focus on showing justice and kindness to others.

Paul now shifts from the specific case of obligation to "everyone" (πᾶσιν) who is a governmental authority to a description of the Roman believers' obligation to "anyone" (μηδενί) without qualification.[44] "One another" (ἀλλήλους), then, does not refer merely to fellow believers but, as Paul will clarify in the next clause, "the other" (τὸν ἕτερον) person, whoever that person might be.

Paul last mentioned the law's fulfilment in 8:4 where he had described it as one of the purposes for Christ's sacrificial death and had said that the Spirit empowers believers to fulfill the law (see the comments on 8:3–4). Now he adds greater specificity to this description: when believers love other people, they fulfill the law's requirement. The perfect tense "has fulfilled" (πεπλήρωκεν) implies that love is related to the law teleologically: the second table of the Mosaic law aims at love for others, and therefore to love others accomplishes its goal.[45]

Paul's Greek could be rendered, "for the person who loves has fulfilled the other law" since "other" (ἕτερον) could be an adjective describing law rather than the object of the participle "loves" (ἀγαπῶν).[46] He would then be referring to civil law as distinct from the Mosaic law, or to the second table of the Mosaic law, or to a sort of eschatological law.[47] But

39. Meyer, *Romans*, 493.

40. See Shaw ("Roman Taxation," 2:809), who speaks of "a vast array of compulsory duties, services, and payments made under the threat, and indeed the actual use, of force."

41. For "tribute" (φόρος), see, e.g., Philo, *Spec. Laws* 3.159; Josephus, *Ant.* 13.143, and for "tax" (τέλος), see, e.g., Josephus, *Ant.* 16.170. See also Coleman, "Binding Obligations," 309.

42. J. E. Lendon, *Empire of Honour: The Art of Government in the Roman World* (Oxford: Clarendon, 1997), 1–29, 176–222. "Deference to officials was not optional. Failure was punished" (ibid., 208).

43. Cicero, *Inv.* 2.66, as quoted in Lendon (*Empire of Honour*, 23).

44. The language of obligation was often used when speaking of love in ancient Greek (e.g., Eph 5:27; 1 John 4:11; Dio Chrysostom, *Distrust* [*Or. 74*] 12).

45. Cf. Sanday and Headlam, *Romans*, 373.

46. Byrne, *Romans*, 394–95, 396.

47. See, respectively, Leenhardt (*Romans*, 337–38); Byrne (*Romans*, 394–95, 396); Johnson (*Reading Romans*, 204–5).

he uses a verbal form of love with a direct object referring to other people twice elsewhere in 13:8–9 ("to love *one another*," "love *your neighbor*"), and so it is likely that he also speaks here of loving "the other" person.

13:9 For the list, "You shall not commit adultery; you shall not murder; you shall not steal; you shall not covet" (and if there is any other commandment) is summarized in this statement: "You shall love your neighbor as yourself" (τὸ γάρ Οὐ μοιχεύσεις, Οὐ φονεύσεις, Οὐ κλέψεις, Οὐκ ἐπιθυμήσεις, καὶ εἴ τις ἑτέρα ἐντολή, ἐν τῷ λόγῳ τούτῳ ἀνακεφαλαιοῦται ἐν τῷ Ἀγαπήσεις τὸν πλησίον σου ὡς σεαυτόν). Love fulfills the law because the second table of the Decalogue, and other Mosaic laws related to it, simply spell out the practical details of what is involved in loving others.

Paul now explains ("for" [γάρ]) how he can make the surprising statement that the seemingly simple act of loving others fulfills the law in all its complexity. His use of the article (τό) before the list of commandments was a common device for signaling some well-known issue, idea, or quotation (Josephus, *Ant.* 10.205; Epictetus, *Diatr.* 4.1.45).[48] Jesus uses the article in precisely the same way to refer to the well-known commandments of the Decalogue's second table in Matthew's version of Jesus's encounter with the rich young man (19:18). Later in Matthew's Gospel (22:37–40) Jesus summarizes "all the Law and the Prophets" in terms of the commandments to love God (Deut 6:5) and to love one's neighbor (Lev 19:18). In light of these similarities, Paul's summary of the second part of the Decalogue here in terms of loving one's neighbor may reflect a knowledge of Jesus's teaching about the Mosaic law.[49]

It is not clear why Paul reverses the order of the commandments about adultery and murder (Exod 20:13–14; Deut 5:17–18) or why he leaves out the commandment about bearing false witness (Exod 20:16; Deut 5:20). In Luke's telling of Jesus's encounter with the rich ruler, however, Jesus also reverses the order of the commandments about adultery and murder (18:20; cf. Jas 2:11; Philo, *Decalogue* 121–31), and Paul has mentioned adultery, murder, robbery, and coveting elsewhere in the argument of Romans (1:29; 2:22; 7:7), but not bearing false witness. He may, then, be reflecting a common alternative order for the commandments and only listing the commandments from the second table of the law that have played a role in his previous argument.

The verb "summarize" (ἀνακεφαλαιόω) refers to providing a final, elegant summation of all the disparate pieces that have gone before (e.g., Dionysius of Halicarnassus, *Lys.* 9).[50] It carries a teleological nuance of bringing previous events or elements to the fitting end toward which they were all pointing (e.g., Eph 1:10; Barn. 5:11).

13:10 Love does nothing wrong to a neighbor; therefore love is the fulfillment of the law (ἡ ἀγάπη τῷ πλησίον κακὸν οὐκ ἐργάζεται· πλήρωμα οὖν νόμου ἡ ἀγάπη). The Decalogue's second set of commands forbids treating others unjustly, and loving others is incompatible with intentionally harming them. This means that those who love others, in the very process of acting with love toward them, accomplish the intention of the Mosaic law's commands relating to other people.

The commandments of the Decalogue's second table that Paul just listed (Exod 20:13–15, 17; Deut 5:17–19, 21) were all formulated nega-

48. BDAG 689, s.v. ὁ, ἡ, τό, 2.h.α; cf. BDF §267(1). As the NET makes clear with parentheses, the list of commandments is conceived as a single entity, which serves as the subject of the singular verb "is summarized" (ἀνακεφαλαιοῦται).

49. Cf. Stuhlmacher, "Paul's Understanding of the Law," 95–104.

50. Cf. Chrysostom, *Romans*, 400.

tively to describe the harm that God's people must avoid inflicting on one another. Paul now proves his thesis about the all-encompassing nature of love from the negative formulation of those commands.[51] Love, by definition, resists harming others (cf. Rom 12:17, 19–20; 1 Cor 13:4–6), so those who love others will, in the process, keep these commandments.[52]

The term "fulfillment" (πλήρωμα), like the perfect-tense verb "has fulfilled" (πεπλήρωκεν) in 13:8 and the verb "is summarized" (ἀνακεφαλαιοῦται) in 13:9, adopts a perspective on the law's fulfillment from the end of the process.[53] If someone has fully loved those around them, then that person has also avoided injuring them through adultery, murder, theft, and greed. Love is a positive and active term that is not limited to avoiding certain vices, but since loving another is incompatible with those vices, it avoids them as it works for the good of others.

13:11 And this, because you know the time—that it is already the hour for you to wake up from sleep, for our salvation is nearer now that when we first believed (Καὶ τοῦτο εἰδότες τὸν καιρόν, ὅτι ὥρα ἤδη ὑμᾶς ἐξ ὕπνου ἐγερθῆναι, νῦν γὰρ ἐγγύτερον ἡμῶν ἡ σωτηρία ἢ ὅτε ἐπιστεύσαμεν). Believers should be particularly urgent about showing love to others because God has called his people to this task, and a limited amount of time remains for doing it. It is, metaphorically speaking, just before the dawn of a new day and time to get out of bed.

The phrase "and this" (καὶ τοῦτο) reaches back to the command "owe no one anything except to love one another" in 13:8 and introduces a second, more emphatic reason for obeying that command beyond what Paul has just explained about love's fulfillment of the law.[54] The reason is something that Paul is certain his audience already knows: "because you know" renders a perfect participle (εἰδότες).[55] Paul describes this common knowledge with an extended analogy in 13:11–14 that compares the present, critical place of his audience in God's unfolding historical purposes to the routine of getting ready for the day in the early morning hours while it is still dark.

People in ancient Roman cities rose early, before daybreak, to take advantage of the daylight:

> The habit of getting up at dawn was so deeply ingrained that even if a person lay abed late he still woke before daybreak and took up the thread of his normal occupations in his bed by the flickering and indifferent light of the wick of tow and wax.[56]

Eight or nine a.m. was considered "late morning."[57] Here, Paul compares his and his readers' position in the chronology of God's saving purposes to the hour of the morning after waking and before dawn. The time to get out of bed and to spring into action has arrived.

Paul can speak of salvation from God's eschato-

51. Cf. Cranfield, *Romans*, 2:678.

52. Cf. Cicero, *Off.* 3.5.21: "Injustice is fatal to social life and fellowship between man and man" (Walter Miller, LCL) and the whole section 3.5.21–6.27. Cf. Haacker, *An die Römer*, 273. Paul's focus on love as the law's teleological fulfillment distinguishes his account from Cicero's.

53. See, e.g., Sanday and Headlam (*Romans*, 374); Byrne (*Romans*, 396).

54. For this understanding of "and this" (καὶ τοῦτο), cf. 1 Cor 6:6, 8, and see BDAG 741, s.v. οὗτος, αὕτη, τοῦτο, 1.b.γ; BDF §290(5); Meyer (*Romans*, 496); Murray (*Romans*, 2:165); and Cranfield (*Romans*, 2:680).

55. Cf. 1 Thess 5:1–2 where Paul also assumes that his readers "are fully aware [ἀκριβῶς οἴδατε] that the day of the Lord will come like a thief in the night" (cf. Matt 24:43; Mark 13:35; Luke 12:39).

56. Jérôme Carcopino, *Daily Life in Ancient Rome: The People and the City at the Height of the Empire*, trans. Henry T. Rowell (New Haven: Yale University Press, 1940), 152 (citing Martial, *Epigrams* 12.57 and Pliny, *Ep.* 3.5, both writing a few decades after Paul's letter).

57. Ibid., 151–52.

logical wrath as an event that for believers is both in the past (Rom 8:24; 11:11) and in the future (5:9–10; 10:9–10, 13; 11:26). He can speak this way because both God's wrath against unrighteousness and his salvation of believers through the death and resurrection of Christ are processes that have started but not yet reached their conclusion (1:18; 8:23–25; cf. 1 Cor 1:18; 2 Cor 2:15). Paul has this conclusion in mind here, and he simply reminds his audience that, like the dawning of a new day, it is constantly drawing closer.

13:12 The night has advanced, and the day has drawn near. Let us throw off, then, the works of darkness and put on the weapons of light (ἡ νὺξ προέκοψεν, ἡ δὲ ἡμέρα ἤγγικεν. [ἀποβαλώμεθα][58] οὖν τὰ ἔργα τοῦ σκότους, ἐνδυσώμεθα δὲ τὰ ὅπλα τοῦ φωτός). Those who have believed the gospel and become God's people live at a critical moment in salvation history, just before God himself comes to restore justice and peace to the earth. God's people should anticipate this future restoration in the way they live in the present. To continue the metaphor, it is time to throw the covers off the bed, pull on some clothes, and pick up the weapons of justice, peace, and love with which to fight for the purposes of God.

Paul continues his analogy by describing the night as not quite over but "advanced" (προέκοψεν), and the day as not quite arrived, but "drawn near" (ἤγγικεν).[59] It was at this point in the morning—shortly before sunrise—that people in the Roman world got up from sleep. "There was practically no interval between leaping out of bed and leaving the house. Getting up was a simple, speedy, instantaneous process" because bedrooms were small and unadorned, special clothes for sleeping nonexistent, and beds themselves plain.[60] The verb "throw off [of one's self]" (ἀποβάλλομαι) reflects the image of flinging off blankets in the morning. The verb "put on" (ἐνδύω) would at first bring to mind putting on the long shirt (the *tunica* or χιτών) that people in Roman antiquity wore over the loincloth that they both slept in and wore beneath their clothes during the day.[61]

Paul changes the metaphor suddenly and dramatically, however, to speak of putting on "weapons" (ὅπλα). This is an allusion to Isaiah 59:17–18 where the Lord "put on [LXX: ἐνεδύσατο] righteousness as a breastplate, and a helmet of salvation on his head."[62] In Isaiah, this event is set in the time just before "a Redeemer will come to Zion, to those in Jacob who turn from transgression" (59:20; cf. Rom 11:26). The Lord takes up the weaponry of righteousness and salvation because his people have refused to act in these ways toward others. They have instead pursued violence, lies, and oppression (Isa 59:1–15a; cf. Rom 3:15–17). Here, then, Paul wants the newly restored and configured people of God to act in a way that is consistent with God's own eschatological purpose of bringing justice and peace to his creation. God's people do this by loving others as themselves (13:8–10), and by behaving in the ways that Paul is about to describe in the next sentence (13:13–14).

58. The reading "let us throw off of ourselves" (ἀποβαλώμεθα) appears in the early Alexandrian manuscript 𝔓[46] and in the Western manuscripts D F G. This is Paul's only use of the verb, and Fitzmyer calls it "strange" (*Romans*, 683). This strangeness probably accounts for the appearance of "let us lay aside" (ἀποθώμεθα; cf. Col 3:8–10; Eph 4:22–25; 1 Pet 2:1) in the large majority of manuscripts, including the great Alexandrian uncials א A and B. On this, see especially Cranfield (*Romans*, 2:685n3) and Jewett (*Romans*, 816).

59. Paul uses common language for the advancement of the night and the nearness of the day (cf., e.g., Josephus, *J.W.* 4.298; Ezek 7:4; 12:23 LXX). On this, see BDAG 871, s.v. προκόπτω 1, and BDAG 270, s.v. ἐγγίζω 2.

60. Carcopino, *Daily Life*, 152.

61. Ibid., 153–54; BDAG 1085, s.v. χιτών.

62. Cf. 1 Thess 5:8; Eph 6:11–17.

13:13 Let us go around presentably, as if it were day, not in orgies and drinking bouts, not in sexual liaisons and self-abandonment, not in contention and envy (ὡς ἐν ἡμέρᾳ εὐσχημόνως περιπατήσωμεν, μὴ κώμοις καὶ μέθαις, μὴ κοίταις καὶ ἀσελγείαις, μὴ ἔριδι καὶ ζήλῳ). Believers live during a period of critical importance in salvation history and need to focus their energy on showing love toward others, as God has called his people to do, not in foolish, evil behavior. Although it is still night, it is the last part of the night, and believers need to be awake, properly dressed, and ready to greet the new day.

Paul continues with his analogy between the existence of believers in the present, critical period of salvation history and the common experience of getting up and ready for a new day. Because "the night has advanced, and the day has drawn near," believers need to be out of bed, dressed, and walking around in appropriate attire. Paul could use the expression "go around presentably" (εὐσχημόνως περιπατεῖν) in a general moral sense to mean "behave appropriately" (1 Thess 4:12 CEB), but here, in addition to carrying that meaning, it fits neatly into his extended metaphor of getting up and ready for the day. Paul pictures believers as out of bed, properly dressed, and behaving with decorum (εὐσχημόνως) in preparation for the early part of the day when people worked at their trades, conducted business, or tended to their households.

Debauchery of the sort described by the terms "orgies and drinking bouts . . . sexual liaisons and self-abandonment" took place in the night-time hours in Roman cities, and the leadership of Rome itself at the time Paul wrote Romans was notorious for debauchery so extreme that these terms describe it precisely.[63] The existence of believers, Paul implies, corresponds to the part of a typical and metaphorical day when such activities are out of place. Just as no Roman with any sense would party at mid-morning when survival often depended on mental focus and hard labor, so believers should live all day, every day engaged in the important "morning" work of loving others.[64] For Paul, drunkenness and debauchery were always incompatible with union with Christ (cf., e.g., 1 Cor 6:12–20; Gal 5:19, 21; Eph 5:3–14), but his point here is that part of the urgency in avoiding such behavior and acting in loving ways comes from the period of divinely ordered time in which he and his readers were living.

With the terms "contention" (ἔρις) and "envy" (ζῆλος) Paul begins pulling out of his extended metaphor about the dawn of a new day and looks ahead to the argument of Romans 14:1–15:7.[65] There he will urge believers in Rome, who are divided over how much of the Mosaic law to observe, to seek unity with each other. This too will be a practical expression of the love for others he has urged on them in 13:8–10.

13:14 But put on the Lord Jesus Christ, and do not make provision for the flesh for the

63. See, e.g., Tacitus, *Ann.* 13.12, writing of events in AD 55, and for the bizarre behavior of Nero and his companions in public at night during the year AD 56, see Tacitus, *Ann.* 13.25. Drunkenness, cruelty, and sexual misbehavior were not merely vices of social elites (Toner, *Popular Culture*, 92–122). For evening as the usual time for banqueting, whether civil or otherwise, see Carcopino (*Daily Life*, 263–76), and for the worries of Roman moralists about debauched banqueting, see George Paul, "Symposia and Deipna in Plutarch's Lives and in Other Historical Writings," in *Dining in a Classical Context*, ed. William J. Slater (Ann Arbor: University of Michigan Press, 1991), 157–69. For Paul's terminology, see, e.g., Cicero's description of Mark Anthony's early life in Cassius Dio, *Roman History* 45.26.1–3, which speaks of "orgies" (κώμους), "drinking bouts" (μέθας), and "self-abandonment" (ἀσελγείᾳ) in close proximity.

64. Tacitus's claim that Nero customarily feasted at midday (*Ann.* 14.2) implies the emperor's foolishness and immorality. Cf. Carcopino, *Daily Life*, 264.

65. Cf. Moo, *Romans*, 825; Jewett, *Romans*, 827.

purpose of sinful desires (ἀλλὰ ἐνδύσασθε τὸν κύριον Ἰησοῦν Χριστόν καὶ τῆς σαρκὸς πρόνοιαν μὴ ποιεῖσθε εἰς ἐπιθυμίας). Believers should live out their union with Christ in practical ways. They should, for example, recognize that they still have some tendency to sin against God, and they should not make it easy for this tendency to lead them into sinful indulgence or divisiveness.

In contrast to debauchery and competitiveness (13:13), Paul's audience should "put on [ἐνδύσασθε] the Lord Jesus Christ." To describe cultivating personal virtue metaphorically as putting on or wearing, say, excellence, righteousness, or justice was common in ancient moral discourse (e.g., Plato, *Republic* 5.457a; Job 29:14; Eph 6:11, 14; 1 Thess 5:8).[66] Here, however, Paul speaks of putting on a person, and this must refer to his idea of union with the crucified and living Christ (Rom 6:1–11; Gal 2:20–21; 3:27; cf. Eph 4:24; Col 3:12). This was something that, in a sense, had already happened when Paul's audience believed the gospel (cf. Gal 3:27), but because its implications still have to be worked out, Paul could also speak of it as something that his audience needed to do.

In 13:14b Paul explains what this means in practical terms. The expression "to make provision for something" (πρόνοιαν ποιεῖσθαί τινος) was idiomatic for having regard for (Demosthenes, *Against Meidias* 97) or making preparations for (Dan 6:19 LXX) something or someone.[67] Here it probably refers to placing one's self in situations that might lead to the debauchery and divisiveness he has just mentioned in 13:13.

Theology in Application

Paul's unqualified endorsement of governmental authority as God's agent for good and for the benefit of God's people has posed a hermeneutical problem for the church for centuries. How is it possible to be obedient to this part of God's word and yet recognize that governmental officials often enact unjust policies at cross purposes with God's moral standards and the church's witness to them? In hermeneutical situations like this, it is often helpful to sit at the feet of Christians from ages past whose thought about how to apply these passages was clarified in the crucible of suffering.

The Perennial Problem of Romans 13:1–7

Origen begins his third-century commentary on Romans 13:1–7 this way: "Perhaps someone will say: What then? Is even that authority that persecutes God's servants, attacks the faith, and subverts religion, from God?"[68] Origen had grown up in a church familiar with Roman persecution, and a few years after writing his commentary on Romans he would be arrested, imprisoned, and tortured under the anti-Christian policies of the emperor Decius. His questions, then, are not merely academic.[69]

66. P. W. van der Horst, "Observations on a Pauline Expression," *NTS* 19 (1973): 182.

67. LSJ 1491, s.v. πρόνοια II; BDAG 872–73, s.v. πρόνοια b.

68. Origen, *Romans, Books 6–10*, 223.

69. On Origen's life, see Joseph Wilson Trigg, *Origen: The Bible and Philosophy in the Third-Century Church* (Atlanta: John Knox, 1983), 20–25, 241–43.

The same can be said about the exegetical work on Romans 13:1–7 of Ernst Käsemann many centuries later. The governing authorities in the Germany of the late 1930s told Käsemann and other members of the Confessing Church to confine their preaching to the heavenly realm, not to comment on politics, and to avoid any ecclesial action that members of the Nazi party in their churches might interpret as a threat.[70] Violation of these instructions had severe consequences. The Gestapo arrested Käsemann three days after he preached a sermon on Isaiah 26:13 at a prayer meeting in the west German town of Gelsenkirchen.[71] He had suggested that God, not the Führer, was the church's Lord and that the German people were not the chosen people of God.[72] To excuse their mistreatment of pastors like Käsemann, the Gestapo appealed to the idea that such people were disruptive to "public safety and order."[73] Not surprisingly Käsemann, like Origen, had questions about 13:1: "What does ἀνάγκη ὑποτάσσεσθαι [to submit is a necessity] mean? What is the real aim of the apostolic argument for it? Is there any limit to the obedience which is here being demanded?"[74]

Compliance until the Government Makes Bearing Witness to the Gospel in Deed and Word Impossible

Both Origen and Käsemann have something to teach the church about the theological application of 13:1–7. Origen observes that when Paul speaks of obedience to the government, he is speaking of government in a general sense and assumes that, in this sense, it is a gift from God intended to punish evil and praise what is good. Like the God-given faculties of sight, hearing, and thought, however, government can be used for good or ill, and God will judge impious governments just as he will judge those who use their sight, hearing, and reasoning power for impiety and injustice. Where governments persecute the faith, reasons Origen (recalling Acts 5:29), "one must say, 'It is necessary to obey God rather than men.'"[75] Where government allows Christians to live as Christians, however, the church "should not oppose secular rulers and authorities," but "through the quietness and tranquility of life it should practice the work of righteousness and piety."[76]

In other words, Christians in totalitarian regimes such as the Roman Empire of the mid-third century should leave the judgment of the government to God. This means complying with the government's requirements as long as these requirements

70. "Predigt Ernst Käsemann im Bittgottesdienst am 15. 8. 1937 in Gelsenkirchen-Rotthausen," *Transparent: Zeitschrift für die kritische Masse in der rheinischen Kirche* 52 (1998): 6.

71. Ibid., 8.

72. Ibid., 6.

73. In 1937 the Gestapo in Koblenz gave endangerment of "public safety and order" as its reason for arresting the Confessing Church pastor Paul Schneider. For the text of the letter, see Rudolf Wentorf, *Paul Schneider: Witness of Buchenwald*, trans. Daniel Bloesch (Vancouver, BC: Regent College, 2008), 259.

74. Käsemann, *New Testament Questions of Today*, 207.

75. Origen, *Romans, Books 6–10*, 223.

76. Ibid., 226.

do not interfere with the ability of Christians to live out their faith with integrity. Origen's reference to "righteousness" refers to Christian ethics and his reference to "piety" refers to Christian worship.

Käsemann's view of 13:1–7 is more complex but follows the same basic pattern. He observes that Paul's admonition to submit to the governing authorities helpfully prevents Christians from living in a world of their own, detached from the circumstances of everyday life. God is the creator of the world, and he has given these circumstances to his people so that they can stake his claim in the world and announce his lordship over it.[77] When Paul says in 13:5, however, that submission to the government is necessary not only because of wrath but also because of "conscience" (συνείδησις), he makes clear that "Christian obedience is never blind; and, indeed, open-eyed obedience, directed by συνείδησις, must even be critical."[78]

Käsemann then interprets 13:5 through the lens of Philippians 1:9 where Paul prays that the Philippian believers' love "may abound more and more, with knowledge and discernment" (αἴσθησις). With respect to submission to the government, Käsemann says, "discernment" requires that the church draw the boundary of its obedience at the place where the government prevents Christians from living out their identity and task as Christians. In practical terms, this means that when the government forbids the Christian from bearing faithful witness to Christ's lordship over the world and engaging in humble service to others, the Christian must disobey the government.[79] In these circumstances the "conscience" of the believer that Paul refers to in 13:5 should lead him or her not to submission but to resistance.

Sometimes, says Käsemann, the government may narrow down "the Church's room for manoeuvre even into the compass of a prison cell or a grave," but also "sometimes the Lord of the world speaks more audibly out of prison cells and graves than out of the life of churches which congratulate themselves on their concordat with the State."[80] It is difficult not to imagine that with this last line Käsemann was thinking, in particular, of all those church bodies that compromised with the government of the Third Reich between 1933 and 1945.

The Brave Example of a Country Pastor

Paul Schneider was one faithful Christian who did not compromise with the Nazis and through whom the Lord spoke, first from his prison cell and then from his grave. Schneider was a Reformed German pastor of two churches in the small neighboring towns of Dickenschied and Womrath in the Rhineland of west-central Germany. Simply because he did not allow the tiny Nazi minority within these churches to act on their ideology in matters that concerned the Church, the Gestapo arrested

77. Käsemann, *New Testament Questions of Today*, 212–13.
78. Ibid., 213.
79. Ibid., 214.
80. Ibid., 215.

him on May 31, 1937 and kept him in prison without charge for eight weeks. When they finally released him, they gave him a "deportation order" that prohibited his return to his congregations, an order that he promptly tore to pieces in the presence of the Gestapo officials.

As he explained in a letter, written, incredibly, to the Reich chancellery in Berlin, the charges of injustice and rebellion leveled against him were unproven in a court of law and were untrue. Therefore, he would not obey the Gestapo order to stay away from his churches. God had placed him in charge of these congregations, and they wanted and needed him to return to them. He had made solemn vows to them before God at his installation, and he had no intention of breaking those vows. "The word of Holy Scripture applies to this joint assignment: 'What God has joined together, let man not separate,' just as much as it applies to Christian marriage."[81]

Schneider knew that the course of disobedience he had undertaken was very dangerous, and he lists in his letter the consequences of "threats . . . fines . . . arrest . . . detention" that he could face as a result of his actions.[82] He was also fully aware of Romans 13:1, a verse that had been thrown in his face by the Gestapo. His reply to their use of this verse follows the same pattern that Origen outlined almost seventeen centuries earlier:

> Even if the punishments are applied, I still know that God will establish justice for all who suffer injustice, and that he will also judge between me and my government on his Day of Judgment as to the obedience we owe according to God's Word in Romans 13:1, a verse they held against me during my deportation, and as to the disobedience that is commanded according to God's Word in Acts 5:29: "We must obey God rather than men," a verse to which I also appealed when I refused to accept my deportation.[83]

He concludes his letter by reminding the Reich chancellery that the Lord of the church is also the Lord of the government, and that his decision to obey his Lord and theirs, rather than their instructions is the right course. "He has given the government the worldly sword to punish the wicked and to protect the righteous, but he has given the church the spiritual sword of his holy and eternal Word until God's Kingdom comes in eternal and perfect righteousness when our Lord and Savior Jesus Christ himself will be both priest and king."[84]

On the Sunday that Schneider returned to his church in Dickenschied, and only a few weeks after Käsemann's release from prison, he was arrested and imprisoned.[85] Eventually he was sent to the concentration camp at Buchenwald where he insisted

81. See the full text of Schneider's letter in Wentorf, *Paul Schneider*, 270–74.

82. Ibid., 272.

83. Ibid.

84. Wentorf, *Paul Schneider*, 274.

85. See the moving and courageous letter of appeal on Schneider's behalf by pastor Fritz Langensiepen to a highly placed government official in Berlin (Wentorf, *Paul Schneider*, 297). Langensiepen gives the date of Schneider's arrest as October 3, 1937.

on preaching the gospel through his cell window, refused to salute the Nazi flag, and on Hitler's birthday would not remove his cap in honor of the Führer. This was not a refusal to repay the obligation of honor to government officials (Rom 13:7), because no real obligation existed in this case: despite their murderously enforced claims to the contrary, Hitler and the National Socialists were due no honor.

Schneider's courage and integrity were repaid with brutal beatings, torture, and finally, on July 18, 1939, death by lethal injection, a means of execution designed to hide his murder behind the mask of medical treatment. At any point during his detention he could have been released and returned to his wife and four small children, whom he dearly loved, had he simply agreed to abide by the Gestapo's orders not to pastor the two little country churches where God had placed him.

Schneider had a clear and exegetically sound understanding of Romans 13:1–7. The church should leave to God the judgment of the governing authorities and obey them as far as possible. "If possible," Paul says in 12:18, "to the extent that it is up to you, live at peace with all human beings." But, as both Origen and Käsemann argued, disobedience is the only path for the church when government policies and officials perversely require Christians to abandon their witness to God's lordship over the entire earth and to abandon their calling of showing love to others.

Good Government as a Facilitator of the Gospel's Advancement

The importance and nonnegotiable nature of this calling is the subject of the second major part of 13:1–14. When the government functions as a facilitator of what is good (13:3–4), it creates an environment in which the church can freely pursue its urgent task of engaging in loving service to others (13:8–14).

Elsewhere, in 1 Timothy, Paul urges Christians to pray "for kings and all who are in high positions" in the hope that Christians might "lead a peaceful and quiet life, godly and dignified in every way" (1 Tim 2:2). The purpose of such a life is not simply the comfort of the church but the untroubled spread of the gospel of Christ's mediation between God and humanity, a gospel that offers the only way to salvation (1 Tim 2:1–5). In a similar vein, in Titus, Paul can follow up his counsel of submission to rulers and authorities with the admonition to engage in good works and then with a description of the Holy Spirit's power to save and transform people through the gospel (Titus 3:1–8).

God's gift of good government, then, is not intended merely as a blessing for his own people but as a means for creating a well ordered society in which the church can freely and lovingly live out its witness to the transforming power of the gospel.

CHAPTER 27

Romans 14:1–12

Literary Context

In 14:1–15:13 Paul applies his general description of the transformation that has taken place in the way believers think (12:1–2) and his general instructions about believers treating each other with humility (12:3, 16), sincere love (12:9; 13:8–10), and empathy across social boundaries (12:15–16) to a specific problem of disunity within the Roman community. Paul's "now" (δέ) at the beginning of 14:1 signals both the beginning of a new section and a connection to what has gone before.

This initial "now" may even imply an element of contrast between the scene Paul has just described in 13:13–14 and the instructions he is about to give in 14:1–15:13. His instructions in 13:13–14 seem to picture a setting of lavish Roman feasting with its debauchery, contention, and envy, and the setting for 14:1–15:13 seems to be a common meal among believers in Rome. This common meal, Paul will argue, ought not to be a place where those in power hold the weak in contempt (14:3, 10) but where the strong bear with "the weaknesses of the weak" and seek to please their neighbors rather than themselves in order to build up the community (15:1–2).

As Paul's use of the technical term "ceremonially impure" (κοινός) in 14:14 shows, the problem arose because of different convictions among Roman believers on the extent to which they ought to continue to observe Jewish dietary and calendrical customs (see "In Depth: Who Are the 'Strong' and 'Weak' in 14:1–15:13?"). One group, whom Paul identifies as "the weak" (ὁ . . . ἀσθενῶν, 14:1–2) or "the powerless" (οἱ ἀδύνατοι, 15:1), continued to observe these customs. The other group, whom Paul identifies as "the strong" (οἱ δυνατοί, 15:1), did not observe them. Paul himself agrees with the theoretical position of the strong (14:14) but warns them against acting on their untraditional convictions in ways that fail to consider the vulnerable nature of the weak in faith (14:15b, 20a).[1]

As Wilckens comments, "the train of thought" in 14:1–15:13 "is quite tight and has no major turning points."[2] Throughout the section Paul wants to communicate

1. Cf. 1 Cor 8:4–13; 10:28, 33, and, on the issue of the weakness of the weak as their vulnerability, see John M. G. Barclay, "Faith and Self-Detachment from Cultural Norms: A Study in Romans 14–15," *ZNW* 104 (2013): 202.

2. Wilckens, *An die Römer (Röm 12–16)*, 79–80.

the importance of acting on questions of dietary and calendar observance in ways that are consistent with the impulses of one's own conscience. He also desires to communicate the importance of not applying social pressure to anyone else to act against these conscientiously held convictions. Paul maintains throughout the section that people can express genuine faith in Christ in both traditional and untraditional ways (at least with respect to the faith's connection with Judaism). It is crucial, then, for those who have chosen the untraditional path to recognize the vulnerable position of the traditionalists and to protect them against damaging their faith.

Paul provides rhetorical indicators that he treats this single topic in four steps. The first step (14:1–12) begins with "now" (δέ) and introduces the thesis of mutual tolerance at common meals on the basis of deferring any judgment of others to God. The second step (14:13–23) begins with "therefore" (οὖν) and focuses on the responsibility of the nontraditionalists to avoid behavior that damages the faith of traditionalists and creates division within the community. The third step (15:1–6) begins with "now" (δέ) and first summarizes Paul's exhortation to the strong in 14:13–23 (15:1) and then urges the whole community to work sacrificially for unity with one another from the example of Christ and the teaching of Scripture (15:2–6). The fourth step (15:7–13) begins with "therefore" (διό) and sums up both the argument of 14:1–15:6 and the important emphasis of the entire letter on the unity of Jews and gentiles who now, because of their common faith in Christ, belong equally to the people of God.

X. Israel's Present Rejection of the Gospel Does Not Imply the Failure of God's Word (9:1–11:36)

XI. Exhortation to Live in a Way That Is Consistent with the Gospel (12:1–15:13)

- A. A Mind Transformed and Renewed by God (12:1–2)
- B. Community without Competition (12:3–8)
- C. Loving One Another and Remaining Steadfast in a Hostile Environment (12:9–13:14)
- ➡ **D. The Strong Should Show Love for the Weak (and the Weak for the Strong) (14:1–15:13)**
  1. **Refraining from Contempt and Leaving Judgment to God (14:1–12)**
  2. Thoughtfulness toward the Vulnerable Faith of the Weak (14:13–23)
  3. The Christological and Scriptural Basis for Unity (15:1–6)
  4. A Summary and Conclusion Both to 14:1–15:6 and to the Letter So Far (15:7–13)

XII. The Purpose of Paul's Letter in the Context of His Apostolic Vocation (15:14–33)

Main Idea

The nontraditionalist who eats anything and considers every day equally special should welcome and not despise the traditionalists who carefully abstain from ritually impure food and observe the Jewish calendar. The traditionalists should, in turn, avoid judging the nontraditionalists. To the extent that either group adopts a contemptuous or judgmental attitude toward the other, that group has tried to usurp God's role as judge.

Translation

Romans 14:1–12

1a	Exhortation	**Now welcome the one who is weak in faith,** but
b	Expansion (of 1a)	not with the result of divisions caused by arguments.
2a	Description	**One person believes in such a way that he or she eats everything,**
b	Contrast (to 2a)	but **the weak person eats vegetables.**
3a	Exhortation	**Let the one who eats not hold the one who does not eat** in contempt,
b	Exhortation	and **let the one who does not eat not judge the one who eats,**
c	Basis (of 3a–b)	for **God has welcomed him or her.**
4a	Rhetorical Question	**Who are you, you who judge another's household servant?**
b	Assertion	**He or she stands or falls with respect to their own master,**
c	Assertion	and **that person will stand,**
d	Basis (for 4c)	for **the Master is able to make them stand.**
5a	Assertion	**One person chooses one day over another,**
b	Contrast (to 5a)	but **another person esteems every day.**
c	Exhortation	**Let each person be fully convinced in his or her own mind.**
6a	Assertion	**The one who gives special regard to a particular day does so for the Lord;**
b	Assertion	and **the one who eats does so for the Lord,**
c	Basis (same as 6e)	for **he or she gives thanks to God;**
d	Contrast (with 6b)	and **the one who does not eat does so for the Lord,**
e	Basis (same as 6c)	and **he or she gives thanks to God.**
7	Basis (for 6)	For **no one lives to oneself,** and **no one dies to oneself.**

8a	Basis (for 7)	For **just as we live to the Lord**
b	Condition	if we live,
c	Correlation	**so also we die to the Lord**
d	Condition	if we die.
e	Inference (from 8a)	So, then,
f	Condition/Alternative	if we live and if we die,
g	Assertion	**we are the Lord's.**
9	Basis (for 8b)	For **this is the reason Christ died and lived:** that he might rule as lord over both the dead and the living.
10a	Rhetorical Question	But you, **why do you judge your brother or sister?**
b	Rhetorical Question	Or you too, **why do you hold your brother or sister in contempt?**
c	Basis (for 10a–b)	For **we will all stand**
	Location	before the tribunal of God.
11a	Verification (of 10c)	For **it is written,** "'As I live,' says the Lord, 'every knee will bow to me and every tongue will praise God.'" (Isa 45:23)
12	Inference (from 11a)	So, **each of us will give an account**
	Content	of himself or herself to God.

Structure

The passage can be divided into an initial, one-sentence announcement of the entire larger section's theme (14:1), followed by four short paragraphs (14:2–4, 5–6, 7–9, and 10–12). Paul addresses the initial announcement of the section's theme to the strong, urging them to "welcome" (προσλαμβάνειν) the weak, and this anticipates the dominant concern of the section with "welcoming" others and particularly with the strong welcoming the weak.

The next two paragraphs each begin with a brief description of the situation in Rome that has generated the division: the first description focuses on food (14:2) and the second description focuses on days (14:5a–b). Both paragraphs then have third-person commands urging members of each side to worry more about their own position on Jewish observances than about the position others take on these observances (14:3a–b, 5c). Both paragraphs then supply a reason for this admonition that focuses on the impropriety of dwelling on a matter that is really only the business of God and the individual (14:3c, 6).

The passage's final two paragraphs (14:7–9 and 10–12) back up the idea that observance or nonobservance of Jewish customs is a matter that concerns only God and the responsible individual. In the first paragraph (14:7–9) Paul reflects on this idea from a christological perspective, and in the second paragraph (14:10–12) he reflects on it from a theological perspective. For those who are in Christ, he argues in the first paragraph that day-to-day life and even the experience of death happen under the lordship of Christ. Every believer, he says in the second paragraph, will stand as an individual before God's tribunal and account for the way he or she has lived.

Exegetical Outline

- **I. Exhortation to Live in a Way That Is Consistent with the Gospel (12:1–15:13)**
  - A. A Mind Transformed and Renewed by God (12:1–2)
  - B. Community without Competition (12:3–8)
  - C. Loving One Another and Remaining Steadfast in a Hostile Environment (12:9–13:14)
  - **D. The Strong Should Show Love for the Weak (and the Weak for the Strong) (14:1–15:13)**
    - ➡ **1. Refraining from Contempt and Leaving Judgment to God (14:1–12)**
      - a. Announcement of the theme of 14:1–15:13: welcoming the weak (14:1)
      - b. The problem of dietary observances (14:2–4)
      - c. The problem of calendrical observances (14:5–6)
      - d. The lordship of Christ (14:7–9)
      - e. God's role as judge (14:10–12)

Explanation of the Text

14:1 Now welcome the one who is weak in faith, but not with the result of divisions caused by arguments (Τὸν δὲ ἀσθενοῦντα τῇ πίστει προσλαμβάνεσθε, μὴ εἰς διακρίσεις διαλογισμῶν). Believers who see no need to observe Jewish customs should warmly welcome into their fellowship those who differ from them on this issue, but not with the result that, after welcoming them, they then segregate themselves into discrete groups on the basis of their disagreements.

"Now" (δέ) signals the beginning of a new section in which Paul will address primarily "the strong" (15:1) in the Roman community who do not feel compelled by their consciences to observe Jewish dietary laws and the Jewish calendar (see "In Depth: Who Are the 'Strong' and 'Weak' in Romans 14:1–15:13?").[3]

The term translated "welcome" (προσλαμβάνεσθε) has a wide range of meanings from "take [someone] aside" (Matt 16:22) to "gather [people together]" (Acts 17:5) to "take in [food]" (Acts 27:36), but Paul uses it here to refer to the warm, hospitable "wel-

3. On the use of δέ here, see Meyer (*Romans*, 507); Cranfield (*Romans*, 2:699); Légasse (*Romains*, 857); and see the NASB and NET.

come" that believers should give one another despite their differences (Rom 15:7; Phlm 17; cf. Acts 28:2). It is a welcome that imitates God's willingness to welcome those who belong to his covenant people (Rom 14:3; Ps 27:10 [26:10 LXX]; 65:4 [64:5 LXX; 65:5 Heb.]).

The expression "divisions caused by arguments" is difficult and is usually translated somewhat differently to refer to "quarreling over opinions" (NRSV; cf. NIV, Luther, ESV, TOB, CEB). The term "division" (διάκρισις), however, typically refers not to quarreling but to placing something into its proper category by making judgments about it (Job 37:16 LXX; 1 Cor 12:10; Heb 5:14; Josephus, *J.W.* 4.654) and means "separation," "segregation," "discrimination," and "differentiation."[4] Here Paul expresses his concern that the strong among the Roman believers not welcome the weak into their fellowship only then to segregate themselves from the weak as a result of (εἰς) arguing over whether one should continue to observe Jewish customs.[5]

IN DEPTH: Who Are the "Strong" and "Weak" in Romans 14:1–15:13?

In 14:1–15:13 Paul encourages two groups of Roman believers, "the weak" (οἱ ἀσθενοῦντες; οἱ ἀδύνατοι) and "the strong" (οἱ δυνατοί), to live in harmony with each other.[6] He does not specifically name the second group until 15:1 because his exhortation is primarily aimed at them, and so throughout chapter 14 he simply speaks to them directly in the second person (14:1, 15–16, 20, 22). In 15:1 he makes clear that he considered himself to be among "the strong," something that he had already implied in 14:14 and 20.

The verb "be weak" (ἀσθενέω) and terms related to it (ἀσθένεια, ἀσθένημα, ἀσθενής) refer to some inability or incapacity, whether a physical illness (1 Tim 5:23; 2 Tim 4:20) or a deficiency of some needed quality or ability (Rom 5:6; 6:19), such as the ability to believe that some truth is actually true (cf. 4:19; 8:26). Paul uses these terms in 14:1–2 and 15:1 in basically the same way that he had used them in 1 Corinthians 8:7–12 and 9:22. They describe people who believe the gospel but who, nevertheless, do not "believe" (πιστεύω, Rom 14:2; cf. 14:22–23) or are not "persuaded" (πέπεισμαι, 14:14), that some element of personal conduct actually permitted to followers of Christ is, in fact, permissible.

In Corinth the weak were not persuaded that eating meat previously used in idolatrous religious rituals was permissible (1 Cor 8:1, 4, 7–10). The weak in Rome were not only weak because their convictions about permissible foods failed to correspond with reality but also, and perhaps even more importantly,

4. LSJ 399. Cf. Käsemann, *Romans*, 367; Wilckens, *An die Römer (Röm 12–16)*, 81.

5. On the use of εἰς to indicate result here, see Meyer (*Romans*, 508).

6. Paul uses the singular "the weak person" (τὸν . . . ἀσθενοῦντα and ὁ . . . ἀσθενῶν) in 14:1–2 and the plural "the weak" or "the powerless" (τῶν ἀδυνάτων) in 15:1.

because they were vulnerable.[7] Since their dietary practices were such an important way of expressing their faith, their faith could be destroyed if they compromised their convictions and under pressure from "the strong" failed to live it out through these observances (Rom 14:13, 15, 20–23; cf. 1 Cor 8:7–13).

"The strong" (οἱ δυνατοί) were strong primarily because their convictions about diet and food corresponded to what was true theologically, and this theological truth had freed them from feeling any necessity to express their faith through dietary restrictions or the observance of certain days as special (Rom 14:5–6, 14). Moreover, Greek speakers could refer to powerful and influential people within society as "the strong" (οἱ δυνατοί), and so "the strong" in Rome might also be those who were capable of exerting social pressure on "the weak" (οἱ ἀδύνατοι).[8] In the same way, "weak" could have social connotations, referring, for example, to the oppressed poor (Job 24:6; 31:16; 31:20).[9] If these terms carried both an ideological and a social nuance for Paul and his Roman audience, then Paul's concern that the strong might influence the weak to act in a way that violated their deeply held convictions is understandable.

It is reasonably clear from the way Paul describes the practices that divided the weak from the strong that the weak were observing Jewish customs. The term normally translated "common" (κοινός) was a technical term within Judaism for food that was "ceremonially impure." In a Jewish context it was synonymous with the term "unclean" (ἀκάθαρτος; cf. Acts 10:14–15). This is the language Paul uses to describe the dietary restrictions of the weak group and the differences that they had with the strong group. They consider certain food "ceremonially impure [κοινός]" (14:14), but Paul and other members of the strong group know that "all things are clean [καθαρά]" (14:20).[10] When the difference between the two groups on the observance of certain days is added to this consideration, it seems very likely that the weak were those who followed the dietary restrictions and calendrical observances that were distinctive to Judaism.

It is true that vegetarianism and abstention from wine were not a normal part of Jewish dietary observance, whereas the weak restricted their diet to "vegetables [λάχανα]" (14:2) and probably abstained from wine also (14:21). Jews did abstain from meat and wine, however, in contexts where non-Jews

7. Barclay, "Faith and Self-Detachment," 201–2.

8. See, e.g., Josephus, *J.W.* 1.242; cf. 1 Cor 1:26.

9. See LSJ 25, s.v. ἀδύνατος I 2; MGS 34, s.v. ἀδύνατος; LSJ 453, s.v. δυνατός I 3; BDAG 264, s.v. δυνατός 1aβ, MGS 558, s.v. δυνατός A. Cf. Mark Reasoner, *The Strong and the Weak: Romans 14.1–15.13 in Context*, SNTSMS 103 (Cambridge: Cambridge University Press, 1999), 61–63.

10. See, already, e.g., Origen (*Romans, Books 6–10*, 248–49) and Theodoret of Cyrus (*Letters of St. Paul*, 1:127), and, more recently, Friedrich Hauck, "κοινός, κτλ.," *TDNT* 3:791; BDAG 552, s.v. κοινός 2b; and John M. G. Barclay, "'Do We Undermine the Law?' A Study of Romans 14.1–15.6," in *Paul and the Mosaic Law*, ed. James D. G. Dunn, 2nd ed. (Grand Rapids: Eerdmans, 1996), 290.

had supplied the food and they could not be sure how the meat had been butchered or whether it had been previously used in non-Jewish religious rituals (e.g., Dan 1:8, 12, 16; Add Esth 14:17; Jdt 10:5; 12:1–2, 19; Jos. Asen. 8:5; Josephus, *Life* 14).[11] There is, therefore, no need to think of the weak as following anything other than Jewish customs in their dietary practices, nor is there any need to imagine a situation in which ceremonially pure food was unavailable to Jewish Christians because of the crisis created by Claudius's expulsion of Jews from Rome in AD 49 (Acts 18:2; Suetonius, *Claud.* 25.4).[12] It is only necessary to imagine that at the common meal that seems to have been a regular practice in early Christianity (Acts 2:46; 20:7; 1 Cor 11:20–34; Jude 12), "weak" believers in Rome avoided much of the food because they assumed that the meat had not been butchered and the wine preserved according to the requirements of the Mosaic law and Jewish custom.[13]

Somewhat counterintuitively, none of this means that "the weak" were necessarily Jews and "the strong" were necessarily gentiles. The situation in mid first-century Rome was more complex than this simple division allows. Paul was himself a Jew but belonged to "the strong" who knew that "nothing is ceremonially impure in itself" (14:14; cf. 14:20; 15:1). The same could probably be said for his close coworkers Prisca and Aquila (16:3). "The weak" also could easily include people who had not been born into a Jewish family but were interested in and attracted to Judaism and its practices.[14] When Tiberius banished the Jews from Rome in AD 19, he also banished those who, although not ethnically Jewish, held "similar beliefs" (Suetonius, *Tib.* 36.1 [J. C. Rolfe, LCL]). Petronius, writing under Nero and within a few years of the time Paul wrote Romans, satirizes those who abstained from pork and observed the Sabbath but failed to comply with the Jewish requirement of circumcision (poem 24).[15] Nero's wife Poppaea seems to have had at least an interest in Judaism (Josephus, *Ant.* 20.195; *Life* 16), although there is no clear evidence that she was Jewish.[16]

11. E. P. Sanders, *Judaism: Practice and Belief 63 BCE–66CE* (London: SCM, 1992), 214–17, 520n13.

12. Either because law-observant Christians were not welcome in Jewish neighborhoods after causing the unrest that led to the expulsion (Francis Watson, "The Two Roman Congregations: Romans 14:1–15:13," in *The Romans Debate*, ed. Karl P. Donfried, rev. ed. [Peabody, MA: Hendrickson, 1991], 204; Das, *Solving the Romans Debate*, 114), or because the Jewish population of Rome was so decimated by the expulsion that it was difficult for any law-observant person to find ritually acceptable meat (Dunn, *Romans 9–16*, 801–2; cf. Jewett, *Romans*, 838).

13. On the common meal in early Christian practice, see Richard J. Bauckham (*Jude, 2 Peter*, WBC 50 [Waco, TX: Word, 1983], 84–85), and on the weak avoiding meat and wine at this meal, see Barclay, "'Do We Undermine the Law?,'" 291.

14. See the detailed discussion of the following texts, and others, in Das (*Solving the Romans Debate*, 77–82).

15. Cf. Juvenal, *Satires* 14.96–106; Epictetus, *Diatr.* 2.9.19–21, and the discussion in Das (*Solving the Romans Debate*, 80).

16. On this, see also Rosaria Ciardiello, "Beryllos, the Jews and the Villa of Poppaea in Oplontis," in *Contested Spaces: Houses and Temples in Roman Antiquity and the New Testament*, ed. David L. Balch and Annette Weissenrieder (Tübingen: Mohr Siebeck, 2012), 268.

The case that Paul's audience was entirely gentile is difficult to make since his argument in 15:7–8 about the two groups welcoming one another presupposes that at least some of the weak are Jews.[17] The reason they should welcome each other, Paul explains, is that Christ became a servant of "the circumcision" to confirm what God had promised the Jewish patriarchs and so that the gentiles might glorify God (Rom 15:8–9a). The harmonious voice raised in praise of God in 15:6, then, consists of both Jews and gentiles.[18]

Even so, "the weak" were probably a mixed group of people, some fully Jewish and others who simply observed some Jewish customs, but all of whom expressed their faith in traditional ways or, as Ambrosiaster put it in his fourth-century commentary, kept "the law by confessing Christ."[19]

14:2 One person believes in such a way that he or she eats everything, but the weak person eats vegetables (ὃς μὲν πιστεύει φαγεῖν πάντα, ὁ δὲ ἀσθενῶν λάχανα ἐσθίει). The Roman believers have among them both people who live out their faith by eating anything offered at the common meal and those who live out their faith by eating only what they can be sure is ritually pure according to the standards of the Mosaic law.

The term "believes" (πιστεύει), when it is followed by an infinitive (φαγεῖν) as it is here, can refer to a sense of confidence about some action (cf. Demosthenes, *1 Onet.* 7.6; Acts 15:11), and that nuance is probably present here.[20] The person Paul has in mind is confident that God permits his people to eat anything (cf. Mark 7:19; Acts 10:11–15; 11:1–9; 1 Cor 10:25–26). Since "faith" (πίστις) and "believe" (πιστεύω) are such critical terms throughout the letter, however, and since the concept of faith is carefully defined in 4:18–22 in terms that anticipate this passage ("growing weak in faith" [ἀσθενήσας τῇ πίστει], "empowered in faith" [ἐνεδυναμώθη τῇ πίστει], "fully convinced" [πληροφορηθείς]), Paul's use of the concept here must refer not merely to confidence but also to a particular way of living out one's faith. The "strong" (15:1), then, are not only confident in their position on food, but they express their faith in a way that is indifferent to food.[21]

The "one who is weak" (ὁ . . . ἀσθενῶν) does not agree with the conviction of the strong about food, and so, like Daniel, Esther (LXX), and Judith, chooses to eat only vegetables when sharing a meal with gentiles (Dan 1:8, 12, 16; Esth 4:17 LXX; Jdt 12:1–4). The problem was probably not that ritually pure meat was unavailable to Christians in Rome after the disturbances that led to the expulsion of Jews under Claudius (Acts 18:2; Suetonius, *Claud.* 25.4).[22] It is more likely that the weak restricted themselves to vegetables simply because they were unsure of the origin of the meat at the church's common meals.[23]

17. For an attempt to make this case, see Das, *Solving the Romans Debate*.

18. Cf., e.g., Esler, *Conflict and Identity*, 342–43.

19. Ambrosiaster, *Romans*, 1.

20. LSJ 1408, s.v. πιστεύω, I 3; BDF §397 (2); Dunn, *Romans 9–16*, 799.

21. Barclay, "Faith and Self-Detachment from Cultural Norms," 195, 203–5.

22. Watson, "The Two Roman Congregations," 204; Dunn, *Romans 9–16*, 801–2; Das, *Solving the Romans Debate*, 114.

23. Barclay, "'Do We Undermine the Law?'," 291; Watson, *Paul, Judaism and the Gentiles* (rev. ed.), 176.

14:3 Let the one who eats not hold the one who does not eat in contempt, and let the one who does not eat not judge the one who eats, for God has welcomed him or her (ὁ ἐσθίων τὸν μὴ ἐσθίοντα μὴ ἐξουθενείτω, ὁ δὲ μὴ ἐσθίων τὸν ἐσθίοντα μὴ κρινέτω, ὁ θεὸς γὰρ αὐτὸν προσελάβετο). In matters of diet, Roman believers should adopt neither a contemptuous nor a judgmental attitude toward those who disagree with their personal practices.

Paul evenhandedly addresses first those who feel free to eat anything offered at a common meal and then those who restrict their diet on these occasions to vegetables. The verb "hold in contempt" (ἐξουθενέω) was used to describe the assumption of an attitude of religious superiority. In AD 41 the emperor Claudius used a closely related word when he issued an edict that said the Jews deserved the freedom to observe their customs unhindered, but that they too should "not set at nought [ἐξουθενίζειν] the beliefs about the gods held by other peoples" (Josephus, *Ant.* 19.290 [L. H. Feldman, LCL]).[24] Luke also spoke of those who viewed themselves as righteous and "treated others with contempt [ἐξουθενοῦντας τοὺς λοιπούς]" (Luke 18:9). It is easy to imagine "the strong" among the Roman believers looking down on those who, in their view, were benighted traditionalists (cf. 1 Cor 8:1–13).[25]

Those who do not eat everything offered at the common meal, for their part, should not "judge" (κρίνω) those who feel free to eat anything. Again, it is easy to imagine the traditionalists assuming that those who eat anything have flagrantly violated God's law and so stand under his judgment (cf. Rom 2:3). Paul's final sentence is not directed at both groups.[26] The continuation of concern with those who observe the law and "judge" others in 14:4 shows that Paul intends 14:3c as an admonition to the traditionalists.[27] They need to be reminded that the one whom God "has welcomed" (προσελάβετο, cf. 14:1), no one else should condemn.

14:4 Who are you, you who judge another's household servant? He or she stands or falls with respect to their own master, and that person will stand, for the Master is able to make them stand (σὺ τίς εἶ ὁ κρίνων ἀλλότριον οἰκέτην; τῷ ἰδίῳ κυρίῳ στήκει ἢ πίπτει· σταθήσεται δέ, δυνατεῖ γὰρ ὁ κύριος στῆσαι αὐτόν). Believers in Rome who keep the dietary restrictions of the Jewish law should not judge those who disagree with them and consume any food or drink. Only God has the right to judge less scrupulous believers, and when God judges them, he will acquit them.

Paul once again asks a rhetorical question of a fictional interlocutor (cf. 13:3) and implies that this debating partner has adopted the foolish and untenable position of questioning the judgment of God (cf. 9:20; Job 35:2 LXX). As Paul's reference to judging (cf. Rom 14:3b) shows, those who are "weak in faith" (14:1) and eat only vegetables at the common meal (14:2) stand behind this fictional opponent.

A "household servant" (οἰκέτης) was a special slave who served within the house, mingling with the family and therefore working closely with the master (e.g., Plato, *Laws* 763a; Philo, *Flight* 212; Acts 10:7). Reference to such a slave works well within the metaphor Paul is developing because outside interference between a master and this more personal kind of servant would be especially inappropriate.[28] The metaphor of standing or

24. On the date of this edict, see E. Mary Smallwood, *The Jews under Roman Rule from Pompey to Diocletian: A Study in Political Relations*, Studies in Judaism in Late Antiquity 20 (Leiden: Brill, 1981), 195.

25. Cf. Moo, *Romans*, 838; Jewett, *Romans*, 839.

26. Calvin, *Romans*, 290; Jewett, *Romans*, 841.

27. Godet, *Romans*, 455; Dunn, *Romans 9–16*, 803.

28. Dunn, *Romans 9–16*, 803.

falling probably refers not to the issue of whether the person who eats anything on offer will continue in the faith (Rom 11:20; 1 Cor 10:12; 2 Cor 1:24; 1 Thess 3:8), but whether God will condemn that person on the day of judgment (Rom 14:7–12; Ps 1:5).[29] Paul's point is simply that the authority to judge whether his people have obeyed his will belongs to God alone and that the gospel Paul has explained in Romans 1:18–4:25 has made it possible for God to be both just and the justifier of those who stand before him on that day (3:26).

14:5 One person chooses one day over another, but another person esteems every day. Let each person be fully convinced in his or her own mind (ὃς μὲν [γὰρ][30] κρίνει ἡμέραν παρ' ἡμέραν, ὃς δὲ κρίνει πᾶσαν ἡμέραν· ἕκαστος ἐν τῷ ἰδίῳ νοῒ πληροφορείσθω). With respect to the calendar, the precise method of observance is not important but rather the observance itself. It should be a wholly sincere expression of one's devotion to the Lord Jesus Christ.

The topic now changes from the observance of dietary restrictions to the observance of certain days as special. Jews in Rome were well known as early as the late first-century BC for closing their shops on Saturday and taking it as a day of rest, and the custom had spread to non-Jews, whether from conviction or convenience (Ovid, *Ars* 1.413–16; cf. Horace, *Satires* 1.9.60–78).[31] "Weak" believers among the Roman Christians observed the Sabbath and probably other special days in the Jewish calendar also because of religious conviction. They were convinced this was the right way to honor the Lord Jesus Christ (Rom 14:5c–6). Paul is not concerned with the absolute correctness of this position or its opposite, although he would agree with "the strong" that distinguishing between days is unnecessary (cf. 14:14; Gal 4:10; Col 2:16). Rather, he admonishes both weak and strong to be sure that their practice with respect to the calendar is a heartfelt expression of their faith in Christ (νοῒ πληροφορείσθω; cf. Rom 4:21).

In the first two clauses (14:5a–b), Paul plays on the verb "judge" (κρίνω) from 14:3–4 and now uses it to mean "choose, pick out" in the first clause (14:5a) and "prefer, esteem" in the second clause (14:5b).[32] The Roman believers who observe the Mosaic law distinguish certain days from others, and those who do not observe the Mosaic law treat every day as special. The difference between the two groups is not that the calendar provides a form of honoring the Lord for one group but not the other. Rather, both groups consider the calendar an important way of honoring the Lord, but one group does this by selecting particular days out of the calendar and the other group does this by understanding every day in the calendar as special.

14:6 The one who gives special regard to a particular day does so for the Lord; and the one who eats does so for the Lord, for he or she gives thanks to God; and the one who does not eat does so for the Lord, and he or she gives thanks

29. See especially Schreiner, *Romans*, 718–19.

30. The term "for" (γάρ), which appears at the beginning of this sentence in some manuscripts (א A P 104 326 365 1506) and in the entire Latin tradition (cf. NAB, TOB), and which supplies a clear connection between 14:4 and 14:5, is probably not original. Manuscripts from the Alexandrian (𝔓[46] B Ψ 048 33 81 1175 1739), Western (D F G), and Byzantine (L) traditions do not include the conjunction, and it is difficult to understand why a scribe would have omitted it had it been present in the original text. Metzger's idea (*Textual Commentary*, 468) that scribes may have omitted the conjunction because they were unused to seeing Paul use it simply to continue the dialogue rather than to indicate the cause of a previous statement is too subtle to be convincing.

31. See the texts in Menahem Stern, *Greek and Latin Authors on Jews and Judaism*, 3 vols. (Jerusalem: The Israel Academy of Sciences and Humanities, 1974), 1:348–49, 324–25, and the analysis in Barclay, "'Do We Undermine the Law?'," 297–98.

32. See LSJ 996, s.v. κρίνω II.1, 7; BDAG 567, s.v. κρίνω 1.

to God (ὁ φρονῶν τὴν ἡμέραν κυρίῳ φρονεῖ· καὶ ὁ ἐσθίων κυρίῳ ἐσθίει, εὐχαριστεῖ γὰρ τῷ θεῷ· καὶ ὁ μὴ ἐσθίων κυρίῳ οὐκ ἐσθίει καὶ εὐχαριστεῖ τῷ θεῷ). Those who observe the particularly Jewish elements of the Mosaic law and those who do not observe them both express their faith in ways that show they are on the Lord's side.

Paul now explains further the reason why he advocated tolerance on the observance or nonobservance of the Mosaic law in 14:5. As long as each group uses their approach to the Mosaic law to express their trust in the Lord, and does so with full conviction (14:5) and no misgivings (14:22–23), then each group should feel free to continue the pattern of life they have adopted.[33]

Greek speakers often used the verb "has special regard for" (φρονέω) to describe support for one side or another in some political cause.[34] Something of that nuance probably lies beneath Paul's use of the term here. Those who favor the Sabbath day are also on the side of the Lord.

Paul next shifts back to the issue of diet and advocates an even-handed position that he clearly intends to apply to the observance of the Sabbath also. Both those who eat everything and those who do not eat everything at the common meal are on the Lord's side. This is obvious because both groups thank God for their food, whatever it is. Paul's reference to giving thanks to God here reflects the Jewish and early Christian custom of saying grace before meals (Mark 8:6; 14:23; John 6:11, 23; Acts 27:35; 1 Cor 11:24; 1 Tim 4:4).[35]

14:7–9 For no one lives to oneself, and no one dies to oneself. For just as we live to the Lord if we live, so also we die to the Lord if we die. So, then, if we live and if we die, we are the Lord's. For this is the reason Christ died and lived: that he might rule as lord over both the dead and the living (οὐδεὶς γὰρ ἡμῶν ἑαυτῷ ζῇ καὶ οὐδεὶς ἑαυτῷ ἀποθνήσκει· ἐάν τε γὰρ ζῶμεν, τῷ κυρίῳ ζῶμεν, ἐάν τε ἀποθνήσκωμεν, τῷ κυρίῳ ἀποθνήσκομεν. ἐάν τε οὖν ζῶμεν ἐάν τε ἀποθνήσκωμεν, τοῦ κυρίου ἐσμέν. εἰς τοῦτο γὰρ Χριστὸς ἀπέθανεν καὶ ἔζησεν, ἵνα καὶ νεκρῶν καὶ ζώντων κυριεύσῃ). The whole existence of the believer, both life and death, is focused on the Lord. To the extent that observance or nonobservance of the Mosaic law is an expression of this focus, both are acceptable to God.

In 14:7–9 Paul grounds the argument of 14:6 ("for" [γάρ]) that both believers who observe Jewish customs and those who do not observe them belong equally to the Lord. The passage is divided into three interdependent parts. First, Paul gives a negative description of the believer's Christ-centered existence: no believer lives or dies with reference to himself or herself (14:7). Second, he expresses the same principle from a positive perspective (14:8): believers live and die in a way that is consistent with their obedience to the Lord to whom they belong. Third, Paul describes the reason why he can assume these principles are correct (14:9): Christ's death and resurrection gave Christ authority over all things, including the life and death of believers.

The language of life and death, of belonging and lordship, recalls 6:1–23 and 8:34–39.[36] In 6:1–23 Paul had first described the Roman believers as united with Christ's death and destined for union with his resurrected life (6:1–14) and then had described believers as slaves of righteousness and of God (6:15–23). Here Paul does not use life and

33. Cf. Barclay, "Faith and Self-Detachment from Cultural Norms," 200–205.

34. LSJ 1956 s.v. φρονέω II.2.c. Cf. the comments above on Rom 8:5 and see, e.g., Josephus, *Ant.* 7.202; 8.10; *J.W.* 3.455.

35. Zahn, *An die Römer*, 574; Dunn, *Romans 9–16*, 807.

36. On the connection to chapter six, see Jewett (*Romans*, 847–48).

death as metaphors, as he had done in 6:1–14, but as literal experiences that sum up the believer's existence. Still, in 14:8–9 the death and life of Christ put him in a position of authority over all things, and this implies his authority over believers, just as in 6:1–23. Similarly, in 8:34–39 the death and resurrection of Christ implies Christ's authority over everything, including the life, suffering, and death of the believer. Paul seems to recall these themes when he grounds the authority of Christ over the literal life and death of the believer in Christ's death and resurrection.

Paul's point in 14:7–9, then, is that the believer faces every facet of existence in reference to the Lord (τῷ κυρίῳ), from the mundane question of whether to eat meat at a common meal to the momentous question of how to face death. If that is true, then it is possible to live as one who belongs to the Lord (τοῦ κυρίου ἐσμέν) and is under the Lord's authority (ἵνα καὶ νεκρῶν καὶ ζώντων κυριεύσῃ) in various ways. The critical thing is to observe Jewish customs, or remain free from them, as an expression of devotion to the Lord.[37]

14:10 But you, why do you judge your brother or sister? Or you too, why do you hold your brother or sister in contempt? For we will all stand before the tribunal of God (σὺ δὲ τί κρίνεις τὸν ἀδελφόν σου; ἢ καὶ σὺ τί ἐξουθενεῖς τὸν ἀδελφόν σου; πάντες γὰρ παραστησόμεθα τῷ βήματι τοῦ θεοῦ). No believer has the right to usurp God's role as the judge of every believer.

Paul here applies the theological reasoning of 14:7–9 to the division between weak and strong believers by reverting to rhetorical questions in the second-person singular (cf. 14:4). He has one question for a fictional member of each of the two sides in the dispute, both a weak believer who "judges" (κρίνω) the strong and a strong believer who "holds" the weak "in contempt" (ἐξουθενέω; cf. 14:3). Each is the other's "brother" (ἀδελφόν), a term that emphasizes the equality of status of both parties in God's family (cf. "household servant" in 14:4).[38] The rhetorical nature of the questions shows that Paul considers both attitudes equally absurd for the reason he has just given in 14:7–9. Because both weak and strong are believers, every area of their existence, whether life or death, is lived before Christ and so he alone is their judge.

Paul makes this reasoning even more explicit in 14:10c. The "for" (γάρ) introduces the reason why judging or despising a fellow believer is absurd. The expression "to stand before the tribunal" (παριστᾶν τῷ βήματι) was a common way of describing the appearance of a Roman subject before a magistrate to account for some behavior. Josephus, for example, uses it to describe the leaders of Jerusalem presenting themselves before the procurator Gessius Florus to account for a public insult that a few rabble-rousers had given to the procurator on his arrival in the city (Josephus, *J.W.* 2.301). Paul's point, then, is that since all believers will eventually have to explain to Christ how they have lived out their faith (cf. 2 Cor 5:10), human judgments in the present usurp his authority.[39]

14:11 For it is written, "'As I live,' says the Lord, 'every knee will bow to me and every tongue will praise God'" (γέγραπται γάρ, Ζῶ ἐγώ, λέγει κύριος, ὅτι ἐμοὶ κάμψει πᾶν γόνυ καὶ πᾶσα γλῶσσα ἐξομολογήσεται τῷ θεῷ). Paul can say with assurance that every believer, regardless of the social group to which he or she belongs, will stand before God's tribunal because Scripture affirms that peo-

37. Cf. Barclay, "Faith and Self-Detachment from Cultural Norms," 198.

38. Jewett, *Romans*, 850.

39. Cf. Origen, *Romans, Books 6–10*, 242, and Calvin, *Romans*, 295.

ple from every nation will acknowledge the God of Israel as the only God.

Paul next explains why (γάρ) he can say that "all" (πάντες) will appear before God's tribunal, leaving human "judges" with no one to judge. He says this on the authority of Scripture, in this case, Isaiah 45:23, with slight modifications to the LXX. Paul begins the quotation not with the LXX's "by myself I swear" (κατ' ἐμαυτοῦ ὀμνύω) but with the more common and synonymous "as I live, says the Lord" (e.g., Num 14:28; Isa 49:18; Jer 22:24; 46:18; Ezek 5:11; 18:3; 35:11; Zeph 2:9). He then skips the next two clauses ("verily righteousness shall go forth from my mouth; my words shall not be turned back") and reproduces the next two clauses with only a slight change in the LXX's word order.[40] This change has the effect of producing a couplet with a chiastic structure, at the center of which lies a repeated expression of the ethnic diversity of those who acknowledge God's supremacy ("to me will bow *every knee*, and *every tongue* will praise God").

Within its own context in Isaiah, this statement comes directly after the Lord calls on the idolatrous nations to "turn to" him and "be saved" (Isa 45:22).[41] Paul, then, probably understood Isaiah 45:23 as a reference to the multiethnic group who, on the final day, would acknowledge God as the only God.[42] God was beginning to assemble that group in Rome, as believers who followed Jewish customs and those who did not follow them came together through the gospel (15:9). If the weak among the Roman believers have a tendency to usurp God's role and "judge" the strong for not following Jewish customs, Paul argues, then they need a reminder that God will judge all nations on the final day. He has invited them to turn to him and be saved, and on that day many people from various social groups will acknowledge him as the one God.

14:12 So, each of us will give an account of himself or herself to God (ἄρα [οὖν][43] ἕκαστος ἡμῶν περὶ ἑαυτοῦ λόγον δώσει τῷ θεῷ). Each believer will describe to God on the final day how he or she has lived out the faith, not how someone else has done this, and so one believer should not sit in judgment on another believer in the present.

Paul now makes the inference explicit that he wants his Roman audience to draw from his quotation. The expression "give an account" (λόγον δοῦναι) could mean "pay the penalty for misdeeds" (Herodotus, *Histories* 8.100.3; Josephus, *Ant.* 16.120), but could also have a more neutral sense of giving a verbal description or account of something (1 Cor 14:9; Plutarch, *Cato the Younger* 43.2).[44] It has a neutral sense here. Each believer in Rome will one day stand before God and give an account of the way in which he or she has lived out the faith they profess. It is God's business to hear this account and to judge its authenticity. As Origen observed long ago, to fail to recognize this and to judge one's brother or sister in God's place and prior to that day is to fall into "a great crime of arrogance."[45]

40. In the final clause the LXX places the verb first just as in the Hebrew text (ἐξομολογήσεται πᾶσα γλῶσσα), whereas Paul places the subject before the verb (πᾶσα γλῶσσα ἐξομολογήσεται; cf. Phil 2:11).

41. Oswalt, *Isaiah, Chapters 40–66*, 223–24.

42. Tob 14:6–7 shows that this belief was not uncommon among Jews in the Second Temple period.

43. Cf. the use of "so" (ἄρα) in 10:17. It is unlikely that Paul followed "so" (ἄρα) here with "then" (οὖν) as in many ancient manuscripts (א A C L Ψ 33 81) and, apparently, many English translations (e.g., NIV, NRSV, ESV). Not only does a broad geographic spread of early manuscripts omit the word (B D F G P 6 630 1739), but in Paul's ten other uses of "so" (ἄρα) in Romans he omits to follow it with "then" (οὖν) in only two other places (7:21 and 10:17). It is likely that a scribe added the word, therefore, in accord with Paul's usual custom.

44. Cf. BDAG 600–601, s.v. λόγος 2a.

45. Origen, *Romans, Books 6–10*, 242.

Theology in Application

Paul began his pastoral instruction to believers in Rome by referring to the important transformation that needed to take place in their thinking as a result of their trust in the gospel. They were to engage in "reasonable" worship (12:1), to "be transformed by the renewal" of their "mind" (12:2), and "not to think too highly, beyond what one ought to think, but to think sensibly" (12:3). Here in 14:1–12 he takes those general precepts down to the level of the day-to-day interactions of Roman believers with one another at their gatherings. What was eaten at the common meals that accompanied those gatherings (14:2, 6; cf. 1 Cor 11:17–22; 2 Pet 2:13; Jude 12), and the day of the week on which those gatherings occurred (Rom 14:5; cf. 1 Cor 16:2), were issues that had created divisions among these believers. These divisions had originated in the ways that believers who differed on these matters thought about each other: the judgment and contemptuousness of which Paul speaks (Rom 14:3, 5, 10) were attitudes, and Paul's instructions urge his audience to reshape these attitudes toward one another.

Avoiding Judgmental Attitudes toward Others

This reshaping should take place, Paul argues, on the basis of an important theological truth. Every believer lives (and dies) under the lordship of no one else but Christ (14:7–9), and it is the role of God, and no one else, to render judgment about the authenticity of a particular believer's faith (14:10–12). Paul himself had been on the receiving end of judgmental and contemptuous attitudes. He wrote Romans from Corinth, where not long before some Corinthian believers had held him in contempt, questioning his qualifications to be an apostle because of the "weakness" (ἀσθένεια) with which he conducted his ministry when he was among them (1 Cor 2:3; 4:1–5). Paul had responded to this by saying that

> with me it is a very small thing that I should be judged by you or by any human court. In fact, I do not even judge myself. For I am not aware of anything against myself, but I am not thereby acquitted. It is the Lord who judges me. Therefore do not pronounce judgment before the time, before the Lord comes, who will bring to light the things now hidden in darkness and will disclose the purposes of the heart. Then each one will receive his commendation from God. (1 Cor 4:3–5)

Believers cannot even judge themselves correctly, Paul argues, and so sitting in judgment on whether a particular expression of another's faith or calling is authentic would not likely be accurate either.

This does not mean that the church has no responsibility to exercise discipline among its membership. Only a few paragraphs after 1 Corinthians 4:3–5, Paul impressed on the Corinthians how important it was "to judge" (κρίνειν, 5:12) a member of their community involved in flagrant sexual sin (5:1–14). At issue in Romans 14:1–12 and in 1 Corinthians 4:1–5 was the particular way in which believers sought to obey God as an expression of their faith, not the question of whether obedience to God really matters after all.

Seeking Practical Unity despite Differences

Romans 14:1–12 is instead an admonition to Christians to seek practical unity with other believers despite differences in the use, for example, of ritual, liturgy, music, the arts, the sacraments, and church organizational structure. Some ways of worshiping God are certainly more theologically sound than others, just as the theological position of "the strong" in Rome was more theologically sound than the position of the weak (14:14, 20). But especially where the customs of a group whose faith is vulnerable are concerned, the message of Romans 14:1–12 is clear. As long as no fundamental theological truth is at stake, extending to them the same welcome that God extends to them (14:1, 3) must take priority over the assertion even of a correct theological position.

What criterion decides whether a particular practice stands within the bounds of acceptable diversity or whether it has crossed a line and become unfaithful to the gospel? Since Paul's letter to the Romans is itself a full explanation of the gospel, it is a reliable resource for answering this question. The basics of the gospel, as Romans explains it, are straightforward. God created the universe and all the people within it, and he deserves both thanks for these good gifts and obedience to his command that his human creatures should love one another (1:18–32). The failure of every human being either to thank God or to treat others lovingly has led to a break in their relationship with God and with one another (2:1–3:18). These failures deserve God's punishment (1:18, 32; 2:2, 6–11; 3:19). God has taken the initiative, however, to reconcile humanity with himself and to transform human beings into loving people through the death and resurrection of the Jewish Messiah, Jesus, and through the power of the Holy Spirit (3:21–26; 8:1–11). Trust in this work of God—a trust that is not mere intellectual assent but is the reorientation of one's life to God—is all that God requires for reconciliation to and peace with him (4:1–25; 6:1–23; 12:1–2).

These elements should form the basis of Christian unity. Paul never mentions the Lord's Supper in Romans, and although he does speak briefly about baptism (6:1–4) his language is primarily metaphorical. He never touches on the authority structure of the church. Clearly, the diverse ways in which Christians have thought about these issues over the centuries should not prevent Christians from praying, evangelizing, and working together to help the poor and to educate church leaders.

In their biography of the Quechua church leader and martyr Rómulo Sauñe, W. Terry Shalin and Chris Woehr describe how the Presbyterian missionaries who first brought the gospel to the Andean village where Rómulo's grandfather lived did not fully understand Quechua social customs.[46] Although many of the village's inhabitants happily responded to the gospel with faith, the Presbyterian missionaries had proclaimed a highly individualized form of the gospel and discouraged the Quechuas in the village from participation in their community (or *ayllu*). They probably did this because some of the elements of that participation involved practicing traditional religious rituals.[47] It was unnecessary, however, to disregard every element of this essentially Quechua institution; indeed, some of the communal values that it expressed were fully compatible with Christian teaching.[48] It took Rómulo's uncle, Fernando Quicaña, to realize that it was possible both to affirm this central cultural tradition and to remain faithful to the gospel, to be fully Quechua and fully Christian.

Something similar happened with respect to Quechua hymns: missionaries sometimes resisted the composition and singing of hymns in the traditional Quechua mode because non-Christian versions of the same music seemed to advocate behavior incompatible with a Christian way of life. Here again, Fernando Quicaña and the hymn writer Florencio Segura advocated preserving Quechua musical traditions in the hymns written for their people.[49]

The case of evangelical Christianity among the Quechuas illustrates how important it is for believers of every culture to know the essence of the gospel well and to allow that gospel to flourish within the cultural particularity of the various human societies where it takes root. Whether we sing hymns by Isaac Watts and Charles Wesley in English or hymns by Florencio Segura in Quechua, we should welcome one another in the same way that Christ has welcomed us.

46. W. Terry Whalin and Chris Woehr, *One Bright Shining Path* (Wheaton, IL: Crossway, 1993), 58–59.

47. On the *ayllu* in Quechua tradition and its interface with Christianity, see Deborah Herath Chapman, "Florencio Segura: Communicating Quechua Evangelical Theology via Hymnody in Southern Peru" (Ph.D. diss., University of Edinburgh, 2006), 42.

48. See the description of the *ayllu* by pastor Luis Minaya in Chapman, "Florencio Segura," 42.

49. Chapman, "Florencio Segura," 149.

28 CHAPTER

Romans 14:13–23

Literary Context

There is no major break between the argument of 14:1–12 and the argument of 14:13–23, but there is a slight change of focus. Paul signals this shift with the conjunction "therefore" (οὖν) and the clever play on the verb "judge"/"decide" (κρίνω) in 14:13. Paul has just explained in 14:1–12 that neither the weak nor the strong should "judge" one another, and now he shows specifically what this means for the strong and why it means this. The strong must "decide" not to damage the faith of the weak with respect to their traditional dietary practices by putting social pressure on them to eat food they consider forbidden. If the strong, by their contempt and example, lead the weak to eat food they consider ceremonially impure, they will at least create distress (λυπεῖται, 14:15) for the weak and at worst destroy (ἀπόλλυε, v. 15) and tear down (κατάλυε, v. 20) their faith.

For the strong to "walk in love" with respect to the weak in this delicate situation, they need to do what is "good" (vv. 15, 21). Without changing their own convictions, but also without putting their convictions on public display, they should refrain from consuming food that the weak consider ceremonially impure during the meal that believers share together.

Paul's reasoning in this passage arises from the description of the believer's character that he developed in 12:1–21. There Paul had considered the thinking of believers, transformed by the gospel and renewed by God, to be the basis out of which they discerned the will of God and decided how to live out the gospel of 1:18–11:36 (12:1–2). This would involve thinking humbly about one's own place within the community (12:3). It would also involve treating others, including strangers (12:13), with sincere love (12:9), affection (12:10), and empathy (12:15). It would involve approaching others with humility (12:16) and a desire for peace (12:18).

Here too, then, Paul protects the need of the weak to think through how they will express their faith (14:14, 20, 23), even if the practical result of their thinking differs from that of the strong. The strong should not interfere with this process but should show love for the weak (14:15) and pursue their edification and the community's peace (14:17, 19) by deferring to them (14:21). At the same time, Paul urges the strong to continue to be "happy" in their own convictions (14:22–23). He is not trying to rein in their own use of their transformed minds to think through God's will (12:1–2; cf. 14:22), but only their use of those convictions in ways that damage the faith of others.

In 15:1–6 Paul will summarize 14:13–23 (15:1) and then support his admonitions to both the strong and the weak from the example of Christ and the teaching of Scripture (15:2–4). Then, in the first of five prayers that appear near the end of the letter, he will ask God to give them the resources to love one another sacrificially and to praise God with one heart and voice (15:5–6). In 15:7–13 he will connect his admonitions in 14:1–15:6 to the argument of the entire letter and bring that argument to a close.

X. Israel's Present Rejection of the Gospel Does Not Imply the Failure of God's Word (9:1–11:36)

XI. Exhortation to Live in a Way That Is Consistent with the Gospel (12:1–15:13)

- A. A Mind Transformed and Renewed by God (12:1–2)
- B. Community without Competition (12:3–8)
- C. Loving One Another and Remaining Steadfast in a Hostile Environment (12:9–13:14)
- **D. The Strong Should Show Love for the Weak (and the Weak for the Strong) (14:1–15:13)**
  1. Refraining from Contempt and Leaving Judgment to God (14:1–12)
  2. ➡ **Thoughtfulness toward the Vulnerable Faith of the Weak (14:13–23)**
  3. The Christological and Scriptural Basis for Unity (15:1–6)
  4. A Summary and Conclusion Both to 14:1–15:6 and to the Letter So Far (15:7–13)

XII. The Purpose of Paul's Letter in the Context of His Apostolic Vocation (15:14–33)

Main Idea

Those who see no need to avoid ceremonially impure food at the common meal of believers should not hold those who refrain from such food in contempt, nor should they put their own, less scrupulous convictions on display at these meals. The faith of the weak is vulnerable because they could be shamed into eating certain foods against their own convictions, and doing this could tear down their faith. The strong, then, should show love and a willingness to preserve the peace of the community by keeping their own convictions to themselves when the community meets together to eat.

Translation

Romans 14:13–23

13a	Exhortation	Therefore **let us no longer judge one another.**
b	Contrast (to 13a)	But instead, **decide this:**
c	Content	not to place an obstacle or
d		a stumbling block in the way of a brother or sister.
14a	Assertion	**I know** and
b		**am persuaded** in the Lord Jesus
c	Content	that nothing is ceremonially impure in itself,
d	Concession (to 14a)	but
e	Identification	to the one who reckons something to be ceremonially impure,
f	Restatement	to that one
g	Assertion	**it is impure.**
15a	Condition	For if, on account of food, your brother or sister is distressed,
b	Assertion	**you are no longer walking in love.**
c	Exhortation	**Do not destroy that person**
		for whom Christ died
		in preference to your food.
16	Exhortation	**Do not,** therefore, **let the good thing that is yours become the object of slander.**
17a	Explanation	For **the kingdom of God is not eating** and
		drinking but
b	Contrast	**righteousness** and **peace** and **joy** in the Holy Spirit.
18a	Explanation (of 17)	For **the one who serves Christ in this is pleasing to God** and
b	Contrast	**respected among human beings.**
19	Summary (of 13–18)	So then, **let us pursue peaceful things** and
		things that edify one another.
20a	Exhortation	**Do not tear down the work of God**
b		for the sake of food.
c	Explanation (of 20a)	**Everything is clean,**
d	Contrast (to 20c)	but to the person who eats as a result of stumbling,
		it is evil.

Continued on next page.

Continued from previous page.

21a Assertion	**It is good**
b List	not to eat meat or
c List	to drink wine or
d List	to do anything by which your brother or sister stumbles.
22a Exhortation	As for you, **hold the faith that you hold**
b	to yourself
c	before God.
d Basis (of 22a)	**Happy is the one who does not judge oneself**
Cause	because of what he or she approves.
23a Contrast (to 22b)	But **the one who doubts is condemned**
b Condition	if he or she eats,
c Basis (for 23a)	because that action is not from faith.
d Basis (for 23a–b)	And **everything that is not from faith is sin.**

Structure

The passage falls into three paragraphs, whose boundaries are marked by the logical conjunctions "therefore" (οὖν, 14:16) and "so then" (ἄρα οὖν, 14:19). In the first paragraph (14:13–15), Paul explains precisely how the strong can live according to the principles he has just outlined in 14:10–12 about leaving the judgment of a fellow believer to God. Despite the theological correctness of their position (14:14a), the strong should not act on the freedom that this position gives them with respect to food because this might contribute to the destruction of the weak (14:13b, 15). This paragraph concludes and the next paragraph opens with the transitional admonition, "Do not, therefore [οὖν], let the good thing that is yours become the object of slander" (14:16).

The second paragraph (14:17–18) explains in two sentences (14:17, 18), each introduced with "for" (γάρ), why it is more important for the strong to avoid damaging the faith of the weak than it is for them to express their theological freedom from dietary constraints. To restrain themselves in this way shows an understanding of what is most important to God, how one can best serve Christ, and the importance of bearing an attractive witness to the unbelieving world. This second paragraph concludes and the third paragraph opens with the transitional admonition, "So then [ἄρα οὖν], let us pursue peaceful things and things that edify one another" (14:19).

The third paragraph (14:20–23) returns to the themes of the first paragraph but states them in more specific terms. Snubbing the weak is not merely a matter of distressing and destroying them but of tearing down God's work (14:20). Deferring to the weak is not merely a matter of avoiding certain food but the particular foods at issue in Rome, meat and wine (14:21). Paul also describes more specifically the way in which thoughtless eating by the strong destroys the weak. The example of the strong might lead the weak to violate their sincerely held convictions about foods they consider forbidden, and so to sin (14:20b, 23).

Exegetical Outline

XI. Exhortation to Live in a Way That Is Consistent with the Gospel (12:1–15:13)
- A. A Mind Transformed and Renewed by God (12:1–2)
- B. Community without Competition (12:3–8)
- C. Loving One Another and Remaining Steadfast in a Hostile Environment (12:9–13:14)
- **D. The Strong Should Show Love for the Weak (and the Weak for the Strong) (14:1–15:13)**
  - 1. Refraining from Contempt and Leaving Judgment to God (14:1–12)
  - ➦ **2. Thoughtfulness toward the Vulnerable Faith of the Weak (14:13–23)**
    - a. How the strong should care for the weak (14:13–15)
    - b. Transitional admonition: do not open yourself to slander from outsiders (14:16)
    - c. The reason why caring for the weak is important (14:17–18)
    - d. Transitional admonition: pursue peace and edification of one another (14:19)
    - e. How the strong should care for the weak (14:20–23)

Explanation of the Text

14:13 Therefore let us no longer judge one another. But instead, decide this: not to place an obstacle or a stumbling block in the way of a brother or sister (Μηκέτι οὖν ἀλλήλους κρίνωμεν· ἀλλὰ τοῦτο κρίνατε μᾶλλον, τὸ μὴ τιθέναι πρόσκομμα τῷ ἀδελφῷ ἢ σκάνδαλον). Rather than examining others, believers should examine themselves to be sure they are not damaging the faith of fellow believers who live out their trust in God in different ways.

Paul's "therefore" (οὖν) introduces the practical effect each person's responsibility before God (14:10–12) should have on divisiveness among believers in Rome. His "no longer" (μηκέτι) implies that he was aware such divisions existed in Rome and wrote Romans, in part, to help heal these wounds (cf. 1:11; 15:15–16).[1]

As Paul's reference to "one another" (ἀλλήλους) shows, he directs the first part of the sentence to both weak and strong despite his use of the verb "judge" (κρίνω) to refer to the attitude of the weak earlier in the argument (14:3–4, 10). His argument that neither weak nor strong should usurp God's role as judge in 14:10–12 has paved the way for the admonition to each group not to "judge" the other.[2] The second part of the sentence is addressed to the strong and skillfully shifts the meaning of the word translated "judge" in the first part so that it now means "decide" (cf. 1 Cor 2:2; 7:37; 2 Cor 2:1;

1. Cf. Zahn, *An die Römer*, 577.

2. Murray, *Romans*, 2:187.

Titus 3:12).[3] Paul's use of the second-person plural (κρίνατε) means that he has dropped the dialogue with his fictional debating partner (14:10) and speaks directly to his audience in Rome.

Greek speakers could use the expression "to place a stumbling block" (τιθέναι σκάνδαλον) literally of putting up a barricade to prevent an enemy from traveling along a road (Jdt 5:1) or figuratively of laying a trap for someone (Ps 140:5 [139:6 LXX; 140:6 Heb.]).[4] Paul will explain what he means by this figure in the next three sentences. The weak may feel pressured by the contemptuous attitude of the strong to compromise their convictions about eating food forbidden in the Mosaic law, and if they cave in to the pressure their faith will be damaged (Rom 14:14–15). Paul does not mean to say that the strong laid such a trap for the weak intentionally, but that their thoughtlessness has injured the weak nevertheless.

14:14 I know and am persuaded in the Lord Jesus that nothing is ceremonially impure in itself, but to the one who reckons something to be ceremonially impure, to that one it is impure (οἶδα καὶ πέπεισμαι ἐν κυρίῳ Ἰησοῦ ὅτι οὐδὲν κοινὸν δι' ἑαυτοῦ, εἰ μὴ τῷ λογιζομένῳ τι κοινὸν εἶναι, ἐκείνῳ κοινόν). Paul's relationship with Christ has led him to the conviction, which the "strong" in Rome also held, that nothing intrinsic to food itself makes it improper for consumption. Consuming a particular food can only become improper if one is fully convinced that it is improper.

The perfect-tense, first-person verb translated "I am persuaded" (πέπεισμαι) was common in expressions of an opinion that was strongly held (e.g., Acts 26:26; 2 Tim 1:5; cf. Phil 1:6; Heb 13:18).[5] Paul intensifies it further by coupling it with "I know" (οἶδα). He is convinced of his position either because he knows and believes the teaching of Jesus on clean and unclean foods (Mark 7:15, 18b–19), or in a more general sense because the resurrected and exalted Lord had revealed to him that the Mosaic dietary laws no longer needed to be observed.[6] Paul's references elsewhere to being persuaded of something "in the Lord" make this general sense more probable (cf. Gal 5:10; Phil 2:24; 2 Thess 3:4; cf. Phil 1:14).

The Lord has shown Paul that nothing is "ceremonially impure" (κοινόν). This word most often meant "common" in ancient Greek, but it was used occasionally in Jewish texts to refer to ceremonially impure food (1 Macc 1:47; Acts 10:14; 11:8; Josephus, *Ant.* 11.346).[7] Paul's use of this term, more than anything else in 14:1–15:13, reveals that the divisions among believers in Rome centered on the observance of Jewish customs. In 1 Corinthians 10:26 he derives his view that nothing is ceremonially impure in itself from Psalm 24:1: "The earth is the LORD's and the fullness thereof." Paul's "in itself" is an important qualification, because, as he goes on to say, something can effectively become impure for a particular person if that person reckons it to be impure.

14:15 For if, on account of food, your brother or sister is distressed, you are no longer walking in love. Do not destroy that person, for whom Christ died, in preference to your food (εἰ γὰρ διὰ βρῶμα ὁ ἀδελφός σου λυπεῖται, οὐκέτι κατὰ ἀγάπην περιπατεῖς· μὴ τῷ βρώματί σου ἐκεῖνον ἀπόλλυε

3. BDAG 567–68, s.v. κρίνω 2b, 4.

4. BDAG 926, s.v. σκάνδαλον 2. Used with the verb "place" (τίθημι), the nouns "stumbling block" (σκάνδαλον) and "something that trips" (πρόσκομμα) were very close in meaning (cf. Isa 8:14; 28:16 LXX; 1 Cor 8:9, 13; 1 Pet 2:6, 8). On this, see Meyer (*Romans*, 515).

5. *TLNT* 3:76.

6. See, respectively, e.g., Jewett, *Romans*, 859, and Moo, *Romans*, 852–53.

7. Already recognized by Origen, *Romans, Books 6–10*, 248–49. See also Friedrich Hauck, "κοινός, κτλ.," *TDNT* 3:791; BDAG 552, s.v. κοινός 2b.

ὑπὲρ οὗ Χριστὸς ἀπέθανεν). To disregard a fellow believer's crisis of conscience is to make light of the profound and costly nature of Christ's love as it is expressed in his death for sinners.

The statement Paul has just made about how real the distinction between pure and impure foods can be to some believers forms the basis (γάρ) for the statement he is about to make and the command he is about to give to the strong believers in Rome.[8] Paul had started to personalize the argument in 14:14 by speaking in the singular of himself and of "the one who reckons something to be ceremonially impure," and now he speaks to the strong in the more personal tones of the second-person singular (σου, περιπατεῖς, ἀπόλλυε).

The verb "is distressed" (λυπεῖται) refers not merely to being "upset" (CEB) but to the sort of severe inner turmoil that one might experience from the death of a loved one (1 Thess 4:13) or a broken relationship (2 Cor 2:4).[9] Here the cause of the emotional pain is not the result of the weak person's indignant self-righteousness at the conduct of the strong. Rather, it comes from feeling pressured by the strong to compromise one's convictions.[10] This is clear from the language of destruction in 14:15c. To force the weak brother or sister into a corner on the issue of food by exuding an attitude of contempt for that person (14:3, 10) is to fail to live according to (κατά) the all-encompassing standard of sincere love that fulfills the law and should characterize the day-to-day life of every believer (12:9; 13:10).

Paul probably intended the strong to picture the ironic contrast between the self-giving love of Christ, dying the shameful death of crucifixion to save those who were "weak" (ἀσθενῶν; 5:6), and the astonishing selfishness of a strong believer who would flippantly overturn this profound and costly act for the sake of a food preference.[11]

14:16 Do not, therefore, let the good thing that is yours become the object of slander (μὴ βλασφημείσθω οὖν ὑμῶν τὸ ἀγαθόν). If the strong in Rome insist on putting their theological convictions into practice in a way that damages the faith of the weak, the resulting divisiveness will bring justified criticism from unbelievers and hinder the progress of the gospel.

It is possible that the shift from the singular "you" in 14:15 to the plural "you" here signals that Paul addresses both the strong and the weak in this brief command.[12] It is more likely, however, that the shift from singular to plural simply signals that Paul drops the fiction of speaking to an interlocutor and addresses the strong in Rome as a group. "The good thing that is yours" (ὑμῶν τὸ ἀγαθόν), then, is the freedom of the strong to eat whatever they like (cf. 14:14a, 22b). Those who might slander this freedom are probably the unbelievers in view in 14:17–18 who, if the strong do not take Paul's advice, will not see the believing community as a place of righteousness, peace, and joy but of power plays, strife, and relational pain.[13]

14:17 For the kingdom of God is not eating and drinking but righteousness and peace and joy in the Holy Spirit (οὐ γάρ ἐστιν ἡ βασιλεία τοῦ θεοῦ βρῶσις καὶ πόσις ἀλλὰ δικαιοσύνη καὶ εἰρήνη καὶ χαρὰ ἐν πνεύματι ἁγίῳ). The strong should avoid damaging the faith of the weak because living in a way that is consistent with the justice, peace, and

8. Cf. Barrett, *Romans*, 242. It seems less likely that "for" (γάρ) reaches back to 14:13 (e.g., Zahn, *An die Römer*, 580; Cranfield, *Romans*, 2:714; Dunn, *Romans 9–16*, 820).

9. See LSJ 1065, s.v. λυπέω II.

10. Käsemann, *Romans*, 376; Moo, *Romans*, 854; Jewett, *Romans*, 861.

11. Cf. Wilckens, *An die Römer (Röm 12–16)*, 92.

12. So, e.g., Meyer, *Romans*, 518.

13. Cf., e.g., Chrysostom, *Romans*, 434; Meyer, *Romans*, 517; Cranfield, *Romans*, 2:717; Dunn, *Romans 9–16*, 821–22; Schreiner, *Romans*, 740; and the concern for the reputation of believers among outsiders in 12:17–18.

happiness that characterize the reign of God is far more important than asserting one's correct position with respect to food.

Here Paul states the reason why (γάρ) the strong should "walk in love" by taking care not to damage the faith of the weak and the reputation of the gospel. For Paul, "the kingdom of God" was God's eschatological reign (1 Cor 6:9; 15:24, 50; Gal 5:21; Eph 5:5; 2 Tim 4:1), which God was establishing in the present in a powerful, visible way (1 Cor 4:20; 1 Thess 2:12). As in the prophets, when it was fully in place God's kingdom would bring justice, peace, and happiness (e.g., Isa 32:1–2, 16–20; cf. T. Jud. 22:2).[14] Paul argues here that these qualities should also characterize the gathered community of believers who, as the newly formed people of God, represent the beginning of God's eschatological reign over all creation. From Paul's perspective, tearing the community apart over an issue as unimportant as what food to eat could hardly have been more incompatible with the real identity of the believing community.

The phrase "in the Holy Spirit" (ἐν πνεύματι ἁγίῳ) describes the cause or source of the "joy."[15] Elsewhere, when the Holy Spirit is associated with joy, he is the source of a surprising happiness despite the experience of suffering (cf. Acts 13:52; 1 Thess 1:6).

14:18 For the one who serves Christ in this is pleasing to God and respected among human beings (ὁ γὰρ ἐν τούτῳ δουλεύων τῷ χριστῷ εὐάρεστος τῷ θεῷ καὶ δόκιμος τοῖς ἀνθρώποις). If the strong use their strength to live out the principles of righteousness and peace in their relationships with the weak, they will be presenting their bodies as living sacrifices to God and providing an attractively peaceable character to everyone, including their unbelieving neighbors.

Paul provides support (γάρ) for the preceding sentence with its description of God's kingdom. The antecedent of the singular "this" (τούτῳ) is not entirely clear.[16] It probably does not refer specifically to "righteousness, peace, and joy" but to the idea implied in 14:17 of prioritizing these three kingdom qualities over the relatively trivial matter of what to eat and drink.[17] The expressions "pleasing to God" (εὐάρεστος τῷ θεῷ) and "respected among human beings" (δόκιμος τοῖς ἀνθρώποις) recall the language of 12:1–2 and 12:18. The general principles of presenting one's body to God as a "pleasing" sacrifice, of doing the "pleasing" will of God, and of living "at peace" with others find their practical application among Roman believers when the strong do not take advantage of their positions of power but instead walk in love with respect to the weak (cf. 14:15; 1 Cor 9:19–23; 10:31–33; Phil 2:2–8). The unselfish character of this behavior will be winsome to unbelievers.

14:19 So then, let us pursue peaceful things and things that edify one another (ἄρα οὖν τὰ

14. Cf. Haacker (*An die Römer*, 288), who also notes the prevalence of imperial propaganda in the Rome of Paul's time portraying Rome as a place of exemplary justice and peace (e.g., Valerius Maximus, *Nine Books of Memorable Deeds and Sayings*, 6.5, preface; Calpurnius, *Eclogues* 4.127). Since Paul relates these three virtues to the reign of God, this interpretation seems more likely than either the idea that they are all "inward" virtues (e.g., Hodge, *Romans*, 425; cf. Calvin, *Romans*, 298–99) or an echo of Rom 5:1–2 (Lagrange, *Romains*, 331; Cranfield, *Romans*, 2:718–19).

15. Not the source of all three virtues (e.g., Godet, *Romans*, 462; Käsemann, *Romans*, 377). On this, see, e.g., Meyer (*Romans*, 518), Zahn (*An die Römer*, 582n32), and Cranfield (*Romans*, 2:718).

16. Origen (*Romans, Books 6–10*, 256) thought that the antecedent was "the Holy Spirit," while some interpreters (e.g., Godet, *Romans*, 462) despair of making sense of the singular and adopt the plural, primarily Byzantine, reading (τούτοις), which definitely refers back to "righteousness, peace, and joy."

17. A "disposition," as Lagrange (*Romains*, 331) puts it. Cf. Alford, *Greek Testament*, 2:429; Cranfield, *Romans*, 2:719–20; Jewett, *Romans*, 864.

τῆς εἰρήνης διώκωμεν καὶ τὰ τῆς οἰκοδομῆς τῆς εἰς ἀλλήλους). All believers, and particularly the strong and the weak in Rome, should live at peace with one another and build one another up. This will often require the powerful members to resist the urge to use their power for their own advancement at the expense of the weak.

Paul's "so then" (ἄρα οὖν) introduces a summary of the argument of 14:13–18 in the form of an exhortation.[18] Earlier Paul had urged his audience "if possible" to "live at peace with all human beings" (12:18), and he has just argued that God's kingdom places a high priority on "peace" (14:17). He now applies these principles to the specific divisions among believers in Rome, and especially to the strong who could use their power at the expense of the weak or lovingly decide to protect the weak at their own expense (14:15).

"Edification" (οἰκοδομή) was an important metaphor for Paul. He could summarize his own apostolic vocation as building the community of believers on the foundation of Christ and the gospel (Rom 15:20; 1 Cor 3:9–10; cf. Eph 2:19–3:13), and he admonished other believers to participate in this work of building up one another and the church generally (1 Cor 3:10–17; 8:1; 14:3–5, 12, 17, 26; Eph 4:12, 16, 29; 1 Thess 5:11).

14:20 Do not tear down the work of God for the sake of food. Everything is clean, but to the person who eats as a result of stumbling, it is evil (μὴ ἕνεκεν βρώματος κατάλυε τὸ ἔργον τοῦ θεοῦ. πάντα μὲν καθαρά, ἀλλὰ κακὸν τῷ ἀνθρώπῳ τῷ διὰ προσκόμματος ἐσθίοντι). The strong can destroy the work that God has done in the weak by pressuring them to do something that they believe is wrong.

Paul shifts back to the more personal tone of the second-person singular (κατάλυε; cf. 14:15) and continues to use the live architectural metaphor of a building (cf. Mark 14:58; 15:29), although now he envisions the destruction of a building that God has built (cf. 1 Cor 3:9, 17). For the first time in the argument he begins to explain exactly how the strong can injure and even ruin the faith of the weak by consuming food that the weak consider ceremonially impure (cf. Rom 14:14–15).

The Greek phrase translated here "the person who eats as a result of stumbling" (τῷ ἀνθρώπῳ τῷ διὰ προσκόμματος ἐσθίοντι) could just as easily mean "the person who causes stumbling by eating" and refer to the strong who, if they eat, might cause the weak to stumble.[19] If that is correct, then the sentence flows smoothly into 14:21, which is clearly directed to the strong.[20] Here in 14:20, however, Paul seems to be repeating the thought of 14:14 that what is permitted to one person may not be permitted "to" (dative) another person, depending on how that person thinks through (λογιζομένῳ) their decision not to eat ceremonially impure food (cf. 14:5). This is a thought that resurfaces in 14:23

18. Cf. 14:13 where a hortatory subjunctive, "let us no longer judge [κρίνωμεν] one another" summarizes the action that should follow from Paul's argument that only God can judge others. This pattern makes it unlikely that the indicative, "we are pursuing" (διώκομεν) is the correct reading here in 14:19, despite its superior manuscript support (א A B F G L P 048 0150 0209 6, etc.). The manuscript evidence for the hortatory subjunctive, although not as early as the alternative, also includes representatives of the Alexandrian (33 81 104 1175 1739), Western (D 1912), and Byzantine traditions. Chrys C. Caragounis (*The Development of Greek and the New Testament: Morphology, Syntax, Phonology, and Textual Transmission* [Grand Rapids: Baker, 2006], 544) does not think it is possible to know which reading is correct here, but he does observe that when pronunciation obscured the difference between ο and ω, a scribe would have been more likely to guess at an ο.

19. Modern translations and most commentators (e.g., Sanday and Headlam, *Romans*, 393) take this approach or think Paul could have intended both interpretations (e.g., Dunn, *Romans 9–16*, 826; Légasse, *Romains*, 879; Jewett, *Romans*, 867). Older translations (Luther, Tyndale, KJV) and a few other interpreters (e.g., Meyer, *Romans*, 519–20) adopt the approach argued for here.

20. See, e.g., Käsemann, *Romans*, 378.

where the term "evil" (κακόν) is replaced with "sin" (ἁμαρτία) and the whole statement describes the weak who eat ceremonially unclean food despite their conviction that they should not do so. The broader context of the argument, then, makes it probable that Paul refers to a weak person who might violate his or her dietary convictions under pressure from the contempt of the strong (14:3, 10).

14:21 It is good not to eat meat or to drink wine or to do anything by which your brother or sister stumbles (καλὸν τὸ μὴ φαγεῖν κρέα μηδὲ πιεῖν οἶνον μηδὲ ἐν ᾧ ὁ ἀδελφός σου προσκόπτει). The strong will do well if they are careful not to exert pressure on the weak to feel ashamed of expressing their faith by observing Jewish customs.

In contrast to the "evil" (κακόν) thing the weak would do if they violated their convictions about food, the strong will do a "good" (καλόν) thing if they avoid pressuring the weak to violate their principles. Paul had already hinted in 14:15 that he wanted the strong in Rome to abstain from eating food that the weak found objectionable, but now he is more specific. He mentions "meat" (κρέα) and "wine" (οἶνον) explicitly for the first time (cf. 14:2, 17). Someone following the Jewish dietary laws might avoid meat at the common meal of Christians since it might not have been properly drained of blood or might have been used in an idolatrous ritual prior to arriving for sale in the market (Acts 15:20, 29; Jos. Asen. 8:5). "Wine" too could have been tainted by the custom of tipping part of it onto the ground as a libation to the gods (Jdt 10:5; 12:1–2, 19; Add Esth 14:17; Jos. Asen. 8:5).[21]

Paul's phrase "by which" (ἐν ᾧ) assumes his audience will supply "to do anything" (ποιεῖν τι), and this thought would cover Jewish customs beyond dietary rules, including the calendrical observances he had mentioned earlier (14:5–6).[22] The phrase is not specific, however, because Paul wants to communicate that the edification of the community should take precedence over all sorts of relatively unimportant matters on which the strong can easily give way.

14:22 As for you, hold the faith that you hold to yourself before God. Happy is the one who does not judge oneself because of what he or she approves (σὺ πίστιν ἣν ἔχεις κατὰ σεαυτὸν ἔχε ἐνώπιον τοῦ θεοῦ. μακάριος ὁ μὴ κρίνων ἑαυτὸν ἐν ᾧ δοκιμάζει). The strong should not put their convictions about food on display at the common meals of the believing community, but neither should they feel they are acting in bad faith if they eat anything they like at home.

Paul continues to focus on the deference that the strong should show to the weak in matters of food, but now he shifts from the outward behavior of the strong (not eating meat, drinking wine, etc.) to the thought process that should lie behind this behavior. The somewhat awkward phrase "hold the faith [πίστιν] that you hold" shows that the term "faith" here has the nuance of "conviction" (cf. REB). It is important to continue to translate the term as "faith" to demonstrate that Paul is simply shading this theologically important word in a way that is different from his usual usage, but here he implies that the weak and the strong hold different "faiths," and this must mean different "convictions" about how to express their common faith.[23]

21. Sanders, *Judaism: Practice and Belief*, 214–17, 520n13.

22. On Paul's ellipsis here, see Meyer (*Romans*, 520), Lagrange (*Romains*, 333), and BDF §480 (1).

23. "That" (ἥν) appears in the earliest manuscripts (א A B C 048), but most manuscripts do not have it (e.g., D F G L P Ψ 81 104 365). Without the pronoun, the sentence's first three words (σὺ πίστιν ἔχεις) can be interpreted either as a question, "Do you have faith?" (cf. Luther, Tyndale, KJV) or as a statement, "You have faith" (cf. Jas 1:18). This produces a less complex sentence but loses Paul's point, which does not have to do with whether the strong have faith but with how they express their faith.

Paul uses the phrase "before God" (ἐνώπιον τοῦ θεοῦ) elsewhere to emphasize the importance of sincerity and truthfulness before God, who has an infallible knowledge of everyone's thoughts and intentions (e.g., 2 Cor 4:2; 7:12; Gal 1:20; 2 Tim 4:1), and that is also the emphasis here. Paul's point is that it is enough for the strong to know in all sincerity that their position on the matter of observing Jewish customs is correct (Rom 14:14). They do not have to express their position at the expense of other believers by eating food forbidden by the Mosaic law at the believing community's common meals. The strong can happily eat anything at home since the gospel has equipped them with renewed minds capable of exercising discernment and of approving (δοκιμάζειν) their own actions as God's will (12:2).

14:23 But the one who doubts is condemned if he or she eats, because that action is not from faith. And everything that is not from faith is sin (ὁ δὲ διακρινόμενος ἐὰν φάγῃ κατακέκριται, ὅτι οὐκ ἐκ πίστεως· πᾶν δὲ ὃ οὐκ ἐκ πίστεως ἁμαρτία ἐστίν). On the issue of whether to observe the Jewish food laws, one's actions matter less than one's convictions about whether eating a certain food is right or wrong. This is true because in the area of one's relationship with God, doing anything that one thinks might be wrong is in fact wrong.

The "but" (δέ) that introduces this sentence shows that what follows stands in contrast to the beatitude preceding it, and the contrast comes out clearly in Paul's verbal wordplays. Whereas the person is happy who does not judge (κρίνων) himself or herself for acting in accord with what he or she has discerned to be God's will, the person is condemned (κατακέκριται) who eats food forbidden by Jewish custom but "doubts" (διακρινόμενος) that eating it is the right thing to do.

Once again, the term "faith" (πίστεως) here has the nuance of "conviction." The term retains its connection to the important concept of "faith" as the letter's preceding argument has defined it (e.g., 4:20), but the emphasis in 14:22–23 falls on the process of thinking through the practical implications of one's faith (cf. 14:5, 14, 20). Paul is concerned that the weak might do something they think could be wrong, and, in one's relationship with God, doing that is in fact wrong. Paul describes here in specific terms what he was talking about when he spoke of the weak becoming "distressed" or being "destroyed" and "torn down" (14:15, 20). All this can happen when the weak act contrary to their convictions about how they should express their faith in God (cf. 14:5). They might begin to do this under pressure from the contemptuous eye of the strong (14:3, 10).

Theology in Application

In 14:13–23 Paul does something that from a modern, Western perspective, is quite countercultural. He advocates refraining from the exercise of one's own rights and power in order to help another who is weaker. Christians are to "pursue peaceful things and things that edify one another" (14:19).

The Spirit of the Times

The nineteenth-century German philosopher Friedrich Nietzsche thought of himself as far ahead of his time. "Only the day after tomorrow belongs to me," he said, and then, somewhat plaintively, "some are born posthumously."[24] In many ways he was right. Nietzsche thought that science had shown human beings to be just sophisticated mechanisms and that humanity only stood apart from the rest of the animal world because it was the most interesting of animal species. In such a situation, life was best lived by realizing that truth claims were a crutch and "convictions" simply a distraction from cool, rational thought.[25] Instead of relying on truth, those who wanted to rise above common human existence should embrace chaos and change and find strength and joy in the tensions this produces.[26]

Christianity claimed to tell the truth, thought Nietzsche, but it actually lied to people to control them, calling "sin" the basic human instinct "for growth, for durability, for an accumulation of forces, for *power*."[27] If one must be religious, Nietzsche said, far better to be a Buddhist than a Christian. Buddhism had no use for God and urged people to avoid suffering rather than sin, and especially to avoid "*worry* either for oneself or for others."[28] It would be difficult to find a more accurate prediction of the zeitgeist of the next century, at least in the Western world.

It is not clear that Nietzsche really understood biblical Christianity.[29] He did, however, understand at least one of its elements and unambiguously rejected it: Christianity sides with the weak rather than the strong and takes pity on the infirm, on those trampled by the seeming chaos of life. Pity, complained Nietzsche, "preserves what is ripe for destruction; it defends those who have been disinherited and condemned by life" and so "gives life a gloomy and questionable aspect." This democratic, anarchist impulse to give power to the weak and pitiable, he opined, "in every *noble* ethic . . . is considered a weakness," especially, for example, in the ethic displayed in the power of the Roman Empire, which Paul and other Christians ruined.[30] To embrace life, one needed to be more concerned with one's self and especially with one's freedom than the Christian ethic allowed. "The man of faith, the 'believer' of every kind," said Nietzsche, "was necessarily a dependent man—one who cannot posit *himself* as an end. . . . The believer does not belong to *himself*, he can only be a means, he must be *used up*, he requires somebody to use him up."[31] To follow Christianity is to smother the human "instinct for growth" and "power."[32]

Paul's Perspective

Paul would say that the "instinct" of the strong person to insist on his or her freedom to grow and become ever more powerful is always tainted by the sinful

24. Friedrich Nietzsche, "The Antichrist," in *The Portable Nietzsche*, ed. and trans. Walter Kaufman, Viking Portable Library (New York: Viking, 1954), 568 (preface).

25. Nietzsche, "The Antichrist," 638 (§54): "Convictions are prisons."

26. Lucy Huskinson, *Nietzsche: His Religious Thought* (London: SPCK, 2009), 3–8.

27. Nietzsche, "The Antichrist," 572 (§6).

28. Ibid., 587 (§20).

29. See, e.g., his description of Christianity in "The Antichrist," 633, 642–43 (§§51, 56).

30. Ibid., 573 (§7), 648 (§58).

31. Ibid., 638–39 (§54).

32. Ibid., 572 (§6).

tendency toward self-preservation at the expense of others. It is this instinct that the believer, whose mind God has transformed and renewed, must resist. Instead of using one's power to enhance his or her own enjoyment of life, the believer must be willing to sacrifice even a legitimately possessed freedom and authority, an authority based on truth, to help the weak.

Paul had himself experienced this sort of transformation. Prior to his conversion he had been "a blasphemer, persecutor, and insolent opponent [ὑβριστήν]" of his Christian enemies, a bully who tried to force people to conform to his ideas (1 Tim 1:13). God had dramatically changed his way of thinking, however, so that he could advise his coworker Timothy in his last letter that "the Lord's servant must not be quarrelsome but kind to everyone, able to teach, patiently enduring evil, correcting his opponents with gentleness" (2 Tim 2:24–25). Even when heretical opponents were creating problems for the community, as they were in Ephesus where Timothy was located, it was important to rein in one's authority and use it only with gentleness in the hope that "God may perhaps grant" these opponents "repentance leading to a knowledge of the truth" (2 Tim 2:25).

This idea that what the gospel says about God is true, that it is good for people to believe this truth, and that God calls on people to rein in their own authority and liberty to speak and act on the truth in order patiently to urge others to believe it often baffles unbelievers in the post-Nietzschean West. If you have the power to dominate others with your worldview, why not do it? Why not do this particularly when you have no doubt that your worldview is right?

In Romans 14:13–23 Paul helps us to understand that the priority of building up the strength of the other person's trust in God must take precedence over our own freedom of expression. It may certainly be necessary for another person's edification to speak to him or her a truth that challenges them in uncomfortable ways, but even in these moments believers should speak the truth in love (Eph 4:15). The goal of this truthful, edifying speech should always be building up rather than tearing down the other person's faith in God.

Whether the issue is admission to the Lord's Supper, who should be bapitized, the method of baptizing, what constitutes ordination, who can be ordained, divorce and remarriage, the relationship between Scripture and church tradition, or a host of other ecclesial bones of contention, this passage teaches that decision makers in the church should conduct themselves with charity and patience toward believers who differ from them. As they teach the truth, they should refuse to engage in unloving and coercive tactics that damage the faith of others and should instead, as Paul puts it in Ephesians, be "eager to maintain the unity of the Spirit in the bond of peace" (Eph 4:3).

CHAPTER 29

Romans 15:1–6

Literary Context

Paul has been arguing in 14:1–23 that the strong and the weak among the believers in Rome should be considerate and tolerant of one another. He has spent most of his energy on the strong, urging them to consider the vulnerable condition of the faith of the weak (14:15, 20, 23). They should walk in love toward the weak (14:15) by refraining from any behavior at the community's common meals that might pressure them to eat food they are convinced God had forbidden (14:21).

Now Paul summarizes his argument, addressing the strong directly (15:1), but also speaking to "each" member of the community (15:2, 5) and urging both groups to follow the example of Christ and of the psalmist in Psalm 69:9 (Rom 15:2–4). He concludes this paragraph with a prayer that asks God to give the Roman believers the strength and conviction to follow the example of Christ and the psalmist (15:5–6).

The prayer is the first of five prayers scattered throughout the closing portion of the letter (cf. 15:13, 33; 16:20, 25–27), and with its echoes of the prayer report at the letter's beginning (1:8–10) probably hinted to Paul's original audience that he was beginning to draw the letter to a close. This hint will become stronger as Paul moves into the next paragraph (15:7–13) where he will tie the pastoral admonitions in 14:1–15:6 to the preceding argument of the entire letter (1:16–15:6).

Main Idea

Both the strong and the weak believers in Rome should repay the debt of love they owe one another by agreeing to worship together and work for the common good of the community. To do this is to follow the example of Christ and of the author of Psalm 69, both of whom took up the cause of another rather than pleasing themselves.

Translation

(See page 654.)

Structure

The paragraph consists of three parts. In 15:1 Paul summarizes his exhortation to the strong in 14:13–23 and ties it back to the love command, discussed in 13:8–10. In 15:2–4 he provides Christ and the psalmist as examples of unselfish behavior in the service of someone else. In 15:5–6 he asks God to give the Romans the resources they need to praise him with a united heart and voice.

Romans 15:1–6

1a	Exhortation	Now **we who are strong have an obligation** to bear the frailties of the weak, and
b	Contrast	not to please ourselves.
2a	Exhortation	**Each of us must please our neighbor** for the common good,
b	Explanation	for edification.
3a	Basis (of 1–2)	For **even Christ did not please himself.**
b	Verification (of 3a)	Rather, **just as it is written,** "The reproaches of those who reproach you fell on me." (Ps 69:9b)
4a	Inference	For **whatever was written**
b		beforehand
c		**was written**
d	Advantage	for our instruction,
e	Purpose	in order that …
f	Means	through the endurance and
g		the encouragement provided by ↵
h		the Scriptures
		… we might have hope.
5a	Desire	Now **may the God of endurance and**
b		**encouragement grant you**
c	Object	the same way
d		of thinking
e		toward one another,
f	Measure	according to the pattern of Christ Jesus
6a	Purpose (of 5a)	in order that …
b	Manner	with one heart and voice
c		… you might glorify the God and
d		Father
e	Identification	of our Lord ↵
		Jesus Christ.

Exegetical Outline

- **XI. Exhortation to Live in a Way That Is Consistent with the Gospel (12:1–15:13)**
  - A. A Mind Transformed and Renewed by God (12:1–2)
  - B. Community without Competition (12:3–8)
  - C. Loving One Another and Remaining Steadfast in a Hostile Environment (12:9–13:14)
  - **D. The Strong Should Show Love for the Weak (and the Weak for the Strong) (14:1–15:13)**
    - 1. Refraining from Contempt and Leaving Judgment to God (14:1–12)
    - 2. Thoughtfulness Toward the Vulnerable Faith of the Weak (14:13–23)
    - ➦ **3. The Christological and Scriptural Basis for Unity (15:1–6)**
      - a. A summary of the obligation of "the strong" (15:1)
      - b. The obligation of both weak and strong not to please themselves, illustrated from the life of Christ and the words of Psalm 69:9 (15:2–4)
      - c. A prayer that God would provide the resources necessary for the strong and weak to worship God in unity (15:5–6)

Explanation of the Text

15:1 Now we who are strong have an obligation to bear the frailties of the weak, and not to please ourselves (Ὀφείλομεν δὲ ἡμεῖς οἱ δυνατοὶ τὰ ἀσθενήματα τῶν ἀδυνάτων βαστάζειν καὶ μὴ ἑαυτοῖς ἀρέσκειν). "Strong" believers are obligated by the law of love to refrain from any activity, especially at the community's common meals, that might undermine the faith of "the weak."

Paul's "now" (δέ) signals the beginning of his summary of 14:1–23. He has used the metaphor of "debt" often in the letter, most recently in 13:8 where he admonished his audience to owe (ὀφείλετε) no one anything except the debt of love. Here, then, he gives a practical example of what it means to pay this debt. Love "does not insist on its own way" (1 Cor 13:5), and so here Paul urges "the strong" not to insist on pleasing themselves at the expense of the weak.

For the first time, Paul gives a name to the strong and includes himself within this group. The phrase "the strong" (οἱ δυνατοί) could refer to society's "powerful" or "influential" members (1 Cor 1:26; Josephus, *J.W.* 1.242), and the term may carry something of that connotation here.[1] Its clearest reference, however, is to the strength of conviction with which this group feels free to ignore Jewish dietary customs. The strong person "believes in such a way that he eats everything" (14:2), and Paul agrees with this position (14:14, 20). Similarly, "the weak" (οἱ ἀδύνατοι) could refer to "the impotent," "the poor," and "persons of no importance" (cf. Job 31:20 LXX), but its primary reference here is to the vulnerability of the group's faith because it is expressed through dietary observances that are actually no longer in force (14:14, 22).

The mixture of theological and social elements within the two groups may explain why Paul was concerned that "the strong" not influence "the weak"

1. LSJ 453, s.v. δυνατός I.3; BDAG, s.v. δυνατός 1aβ; MGS 558, s.v. δυνατός A.

to violate their convictions about dietary and calendar observances and so tear down their faith (14:15, 20, 23). If "the strong" were accustomed to having their own way and giving little thought to the needs of society's "weak," then they could easily, and perhaps unthinkingly, make it difficult for the weak to express their faith at the community's common meals by observing Jewish dietary customs according to their convictions. Rather than make trouble, the weak might conform to the expectations of the strong against their convictions and so fall into sinful patterns that could ruin them spiritually (cf. 14:15, 20, 23).

The strong, then, from their position of power, should "bear the frailties of the weak." The term "bear" (βαστάζω) does not mean merely to "tolerate" but, much more actively, to "bear a burden," either literally (Matt 3:11; 14:13) or metaphorically (Matt 8:17).[2] Here it refers to becoming weak to the weak, as Paul puts it in 1 Corinthians 9:22.[3] In Rome this involved not eating meat, drinking wine, or doing anything else that might lead a brother or sister to stumble (14:21).

15:2 Each of us must please our neighbor for the common good, for edification (ἕκαστος ἡμῶν τῷ πλησίον ἀρεσκέτω εἰς τὸ ἀγαθὸν πρὸς οἰκοδομήν). Every believer, whether strong or weak, should play a part in showing practical, sacrificial love to other individuals within the body of believers for the good of the whole community.

Paul has used the term "each" (ἕκαστος) in the argument of the wider context to emphasize the responsibility of individual believers, whether strong or weak, to the community as a whole (12:3; 14:5, 12). Here too "each" believer has an obligation to please his or her neighbor, but this is not for the good of the individuals involved but for "edification" (οἰκοδομή), an expression that in 14:19 referred to the peace and faithfulness of the believing community.[4]

The term "neighbor" (πλησίον) recalls 13:8–10 with its quotation of Leviticus 19:18 as a summary of the part of the Decalogue dealing with human relations and its echo of the teaching of Jesus.[5] Paul is therefore giving specific directions to the believing community in Rome about how they can love one another with sincerity (Rom 12:9; 14:15).

15:3 For even Christ did not please himself. Rather, just as it is written, "The reproaches of those who reproach you fell on me" (καὶ γὰρ ὁ Χριστὸς οὐχ ἑαυτῷ ἤρεσεν· ἀλλὰ καθὼς γέγραπται, Οἱ ὀνειδισμοὶ τῶν ὀνειδιζόντων σε ἐπέπεσαν ἐπ᾽ ἐμέ). The weak and the strong should act unselfishly because Christ's own unselfish actions, demonstrated in his willingness to suffer in defense of another, set the pattern for Christ's followers. This is also the pattern set for the people of God in the Scriptures, as Psalm 69:9 shows.

Paul now grounds the preceding exhortation in the example of Christ and the authority of Scripture. His "even" (καί) implies that had anyone been entitled to please himself, it would have been Christ, the "anointed" (χριστός) king of God's people.[6] The Messiah, however, was the sort of king who did not exploit his power for his own advantage but, instead, was willing to suffer in order to help others (cf. Phil 2:6–8).[7] This essential unselfishness should also characterize believers in their relationships with one another (Eph 4:32–5:2; Phil 2:4; cf. 1 Cor 10:33–11:1; 2 Cor 8:9).

2. Cf. Paul's usage in 11:18. So, correctly, e.g., Moo (*Romans*, 866) and Jewett (*Romans*, 877). For the idea that the term refers to tolerance, see, e.g., Origen (*Romans, Books 6–10*, 264) and Hodge (*Romans*, 432).

3. Origen, *Romans, Books 6–10*, 264; Pelagius, *Romans*, 144.

4. Michel, *An die Römer*, 444; Dunn, *Romans 9–16*, 838; Moo, *Romans*, 867; Jewett, *Romans*, 878–79.

5. Michel, *An die Römer*, 444.

6. Cf. Moo, *Romans*, 868.

7. Cf. Origen, *Romans, Books 6–10*, 267.

Paul's quotation from Psalm 69:9b (68:10b LXX; 69:10b Heb.) is somewhat unusual for two reasons. First, Paul's audience might reasonably expect a quotation of something Christ said to illustrate the claim that he did not please himself (cf. 1 Cor 7:10; 9:14). Instead Paul quotes words that the psalmist addressed to God. Is Paul somehow attributing the psalmist's words to Jesus?[8] Second, in its original context the "you" (σε) of Paul's quotation refers to God, but Paul's argument seems to require an illustration of Christ's unselfishness with respect to other human beings.[9]

Both problems can be solved by thinking of Paul's quotation as an illustration of how the unselfish pattern of Christ's conduct followed a pattern laid down in Scripture. Christ did not please himself "even as" (καθώς) the Scriptures show that the psalmist also did not please himself, and the words of the psalmist are evidence of his unselfish attitude. This is a point that does not change if the "you" in the psalmist's statement refers to God. Both Christ and the psalmist acted unselfishly in their willingness to identify themselves with the cause of God and absorb the abuse of God's opponents. This unselfish willingness to suffer in defense of someone else should characterize the relationships between the weak and the strong in Rome, and particularly the relationship of the strong to the weak.

15:4 For whatever was written beforehand was written for our instruction, in order that through the endurance and the encouragement provided by the Scriptures we might have hope (ὅσα γὰρ προεγράφη, εἰς τὴν ἡμετέραν διδασκαλίαν ἐγράφη, ἵνα διὰ τῆς ὑπομονῆς καὶ διὰ τῆς παρακλήσεως τῶν γραφῶν τὴν ἐλπίδα ἔχωμεν). The Scriptures provide a resource for the Roman believers by urging them to remain steadfast as they suffer for their commitment to God and by offering them the comfort that other believers before them, such as the psalmist, have shared their experience. Their patient commitment to work for unity with one another leads to the hope that one day they will praise God together despite their differences.

Paul now explains further (γάρ) the implication of his quotation. It is not simply the example of Christ's unselfishness that instructs believers how to live as the people of God, but the Scriptures of Israel also offer instruction, as the quotation from Psalm 69 has demonstrated (cf. Rom 4:23–25; cf. 1 Cor 9:8–10; 10:6–11; 2 Tim 3:15–17). Christ and the Scriptures work in tandem, exhibiting the same pattern of life for God's people and urging them to follow it.

Many commentators and translators take the two prepositional phrases in the purpose clause in different ways so that the first prepositional phrase (διὰ τῆς ὑπομονῆς) refers in a general way to the endurance of believers and the second prepositional phrase (διὰ τῆς παρακλήσεως τῶν γραφῶν) refers specifically to the encouragement that the Scriptures provide.[10] For Paul to speak generally of endurance here, however, would be off topic since the point of the overall statement is that the Scriptures instruct believers and in this way provide them with resources to support their "hope."[11] It is

8. See, e.g., Hultgren, *Romans*, 526.

9. Sanday and Headlam, *Romans*, 395; Wilckens, *An die Römer (Röm 12–16)*, 101–2.

10. E.g., Zahn, *An die Römer*, 593n13; Cranfield, *Romans*, 2:735; Dunn, *Romans 9–16*, 839; Byrne, *Romans*, 427; NASB, NAB, NRSV, ESV, NET, CSB, CEB.

11. Alford, *Greek Testament*, 2:432. Meyer (*Romans*, 539) also uses this argument, but his analysis is slightly flawed because he was working with a text that did not have the second occurrence of "through" (διά; cf. D F G P Ψ 6 33 81 104 365 630 1175 1505 1506 1881). Cf. Godet (*Romans*, 469) and Jewett (*Romans*, 882), who are working with a text that has both prepositions. Among translations, see the NIV and REB.

more likely, then, that Paul intends to describe the Scriptures as the source of both the "endurance" and the "comfort" of believers. This understanding of the two clauses receives confirmation in the next sentence (Rom 15:5) when Paul speaks of God as the source of the "endurance" and "comfort" that Paul prays will characterize his audience.

The goal of the endurance and encouragement the Scriptures provide is "hope" (ἐλπίς). Elsewhere Paul connects endurance in the faith despite suffering with the hope of salvation from God's eschatological wrath (5:3–5, 9). Here in 15:4, however, Paul was probably thinking of the hope that those who believed the gospel had in a future time when all nations, both Jews and non-Jews, would join together in praise of God (15:13).[12]

15:5 Now may the God of endurance and encouragement grant you the same way of thinking toward one another, according to the pattern of Christ Jesus (ὁ δὲ θεὸς τῆς ὑπομονῆς καὶ τῆς παρακλήσεως δῴη ὑμῖν τὸ αὐτὸ φρονεῖν ἐν ἀλλήλοις κατὰ Χριστὸν Ἰησοῦν). Paul prays that God might give the Roman believers the resources to overcome any judgmental and contemptuous attitudes toward each other and so follow the example of Jesus, who, rather than pleasing himself, endured suffering for the purposes of God.

Paul's "now" (δέ) signals that he is about to draw 15:1–6 to a close, and the optative form translated "may . . . grant" (δῴη) signals that 15:5–6 is a prayer (cf. Eph 1:17; 2 Thess 3:16; 2 Tim 1:16, 18; 2:25). This is the first of five prayers that punctuate the concluding paragraphs of this long letter (cf. Rom 15:13, 33; 16:20, 25–27). The Scriptures were the source of "endurance" (ἡ ὑπομονή) and "encouragement" (ἡ παράκλησις) in the preceding sentence (15:4), so the God who inspired the Scriptures (2 Tim 3:16) is the ultimate source of the believer's endurance and encouragement.[13]

Paul prays that God will provide these resources to the whole believing community in Rome so that they might have "the same way of thinking toward one another" (τὸ αὐτὸ φρονεῖν ἐν ἀλλήλοις).[14] Since Paul has been arguing in 14:1–15:4 that the weak and the strong should neither judge nor despise each other (14:3, 10) and especially that the strong should accommodate the weak in their convictions on refraining from ceremonially impure food (14:15, 20), he does not mean here that the two groups should think the same way on this particular issue. Rather, he prays that they might follow the example of Christ (κατὰ Χριστὸν Ἰησοῦν) to which he just referred in 15:3. This means not pleasing themselves but working for harmony with each other despite their differences.[15]

15:6 in order that with one heart and voice you might glorify the God and Father of our Lord Jesus Christ (ἵνα ὁμοθυμαδὸν ἐν ἑνὶ στόματι δοξάζητε τὸν θεὸν καὶ πατέρα τοῦ κυρίου ἡμῶν Ἰησοῦ Χριστοῦ). The goal of Paul's prayer that "the strong" and "the weak" in Rome might drop their judgmental attitudes and love each other sacrificially is that they might give heartfelt praise to the God who has made them, like Jesus, his sons and daughters.

Paul indicates the purpose of the harmony for which he prays. Greek speakers could use the adverbial expression "with one heart" (ὁμοθυμαδόν) to describe a group of people united in a common cause raising their voices to express their feel-

12. Wilckens, *An die Römer (Röm 12–16)*, 102; Jewett, *Romans*, 883.

13. Cf. Calvin, *Romans*, 305; Schreiner, *Romans*, 749.

14. Cf. Rom 12:16; 2 Cor 13:11; Phil 2:2; 4:2; Appian, *Civil Wars* 1.65 (where a group of Roman senators who made common cause with Cinna [οἳ τὰ αὐτὰ ἐφρόνουν] aid his attempt to rise to power in Rome); BDAG 1065, s.v. φρονέω 1.

15. Meyer, *Romans*, 540; Sanday and Headlam, *Romans*, 396; Jewett, *Romans*, 884.

ings, whether of dismay (Acts 7:57; Josephus, *Ant.* 15.277) or enthusiasm (Jdt 15:9). It was especially appropriate for communicating the unity of feeling and purpose of people united in prayer (Jdt 4:12; 13:17; Acts 1:14; 4:24).[16] Here, then, it expresses the heartfelt harmony that Paul hopes will lie behind the one "voice" that both the weak and the strong in the Roman community use in their common worship of God.

The thought of the believing community in Rome glorifying "the God and Father of our Lord Jesus Christ" together recalls the letter's opening greeting: "Grace to you and peace from God our Father and the Lord Jesus Christ" (1:7). This echo of the letter's opening may have alerted Paul's audience that he was beginning to close his discourse, perhaps emphasizing that one important result of the gospel should be the peaceful coexistence of the believing community expressed in its common worship. The slight change in the description of God from "our Father" in 1:7 to the "Father of our Lord Jesus Christ" here may reflect the idea implied in 8:15–17 that God's Spirit has made believers children of God and therefore able to call God their Father, just as Jesus called God "'Abba,' that is, 'Father'" (8:15; cf. Mark 14:36).

Theology in Application

Romans 15:1–6 reminds believers that they should bear the scorn involved in unpopular associations with other believers in order to build those believers up and offer praise to God with a united voice. It is a reminder that recalls Jesus's own deepest concern for his followers.

The Imitation of Christ's Sacrificial Death

The imitation of the unselfish love of Christ is an important theme in Paul's letters. He encourages the Galatians to "bear one another's burdens, and so fulfill the law of Christ" (Gal 6:2), an admonition that probably owes something to the example of Christ's willingness to redeem us "from the curse of the law by becoming a curse for us" (Gal 3:13). He urges the Corinthians not to insist on their own preferences but to imitate Christ, as Paul himself has done for the salvation of unbelievers and the edification of the church (1 Cor 11:1). In another letter to Corinth he urges them to help needy believers in Jerusalem in imitation of the grace of the Lord Jesus Christ who "though he was rich, yet for your sake he became poor, so that you by his poverty might become rich" (2 Cor 8:9). He tells the Ephesians to be tenderhearted, forgiving, and loving toward each other "as Christ loved us and gave himself up for us" (Eph 4:32–5:2).

Where Paul is specific about which part of Christ's life believers should imitate, he refers either to his incarnation (2 Cor 8:9) or his death (Eph 5:2). In Romans 15:3 Paul may be thinking of Christ's death when he interprets Christ's unselfishness

16. *TLNT* 2:581.

through the lens of the "reproaches" (ὀνειδισμοί) that the psalmist endured on behalf of God. The Synoptic passion narrative uses the same language to describe the "reviling" (ὀνειδίζω) that Jesus endured from the chief priests, the scribes, and the criminals crucified with him (Matt 27:44; Mark 15:32).

The Imitation of Christ's Hospitality to Outcasts

In addition, it seems at least as likely that the idea of imitating Christ in Romans 15:3 arises from Paul's knowledge of Christ's willingness to cross social boundaries and eat with outcasts. This was behavior that brought the ire of Pharisees and scribes down on his head (e.g., Luke 5:30; 7:34; 15:1–2; 19:7). Origen, who wrote the earliest extant commentary on Romans, thought that Paul's quotation of Psalm 69:9 "will become clearer if we call to mind what is written in the Gospels how, in order that he might help men and save them, he was eating and drinking with sinners and tax collectors and the Jews were insulting these things."[17] Certainly in 1 Corinthians 10:31–11:1 where Paul urges the Corinthians to imitate his unselfish behavior, just as he imitates the unselfish behavior of Christ, Paul is urging the Corinthians to work for the salvation of others by treating them kindly around a common meal. That is also the issue here in Romans (cf. Acts 11:3; Gal 2:12).[18]

This passage of Scripture, then, calls on the church together, and individuals within it, to extend friendship and hospitality in practical ways to other believers who are not like them, especially those who would qualify as "weak" because their convictions on certain theological issues are less than ideal. As Romans 14:1–15:6 demonstrates, there is room for doctrinal disagreement among believers who confess with their mouths that Jesus is Lord and believe in their hearts that God raised him from the dead (10:8–10; cf. 15:6).[19] Christians from many different confessional and cultural backgrounds can agree on the authority of Christ over all his creation ("Jesus is Lord") and on God's desire, through Christ, to repair the damage that rebellion against God has done to his creation ("God has raised him from the dead"). Romans 15:1–6 teaches the importance of associating with others who believe these broad and basic elements of the Christian faith and giving them a place at the table of our church fellowships, whether literally or figuratively.

The Unity of the Church and Its Witness to the Gospel

In John's Gospel, after urging his disciples to keep his most basic commandment, "love one another as I have loved you" (John 15:12), Jesus prays that those whom God had given him from the world would be united with each other so that the

17. Origen, *Romans, Books 6–10*, 267.

18. Cf. the comments of Dunn (*Romans 9–16*, 839), which move in a similar direction.

19. Dunn (*Romans 9–16*, 840–41) comments on the correlation between the verbal confession of 10:8–9 and the "one voice" of 15:6.

world might believe God had sent him (John 17:21). The witness of the church to its united confession that Jesus is Lord and that God raised Jesus from the dead becomes credible to the world only when believers demonstrate their love for one another in concrete ways. As precise a theologian as Herman Bavinck could say that

> the endless divisions of the confessors of Christ offer the world an occasion for pleasure and scorn and give it a reason for its nonbelief in the One sent by the Father, inasmuch as it does not see the unity of believers in Christ (John 17:21). As Christians we cannot humble ourselves deeply enough over the schisms and discord that have existed all through the centuries in the church of Christ. It is a sin against God, and in conflict with Christ's [high-priestly] prayer [for unity], and caused by the darkness of our minds and the lovelessness of our hearts.[20]

20. Bavinck, *Holy Spirit, Church, and New Creation*, 316.

CHAPTER 30

Romans 15:7–13

Literary Context

This small paragraph plays a large role in the argument of Romans. It not only concludes the argument of 14:1–15:6, one of the primary steps in Paul's argument, but it attaches that section to the argument of the entire letter and brings the argument to a fitting close. Thus, the opening lines (15:7–9a) recall the opening lines of the main section (14:1–3) by reusing the term "welcome" (προσλαμβάνεσθε) and recalling the concept of imitating the welcome God has given all kinds of people across the social barriers that otherwise divide them from one another. In 15:3 Paul had extended the idea of imitating the welcome of God from 14:3 to include the imitation of Christ's unselfishness. When Paul recalls this theme in 15:7–9a, it is again Christ who provides the example.

Now, however, Paul uses Christ's example not merely to demonstrate to the weak and strong in Rome how they ought to act toward one another but also to make a point about the significance of Christ for all history. This is the move that ties 14:1–15:6 into the argument of the letter from 1:1 forward. Paul argues that Christ's welcome of both the weak and strong in Rome accomplished on a small scale something that God was doing in Christ on the much larger scale of salvation history. Non-observant believers in Rome should not hold law-observant believers in contempt or ignore their scruples because at the gospel's center stands the Jewish Messiah, born of the seed of David, promised beforehand in the prophets (1:2–3). The gospel is for the Jew first (1:16), and the Jewish people form the cultivated olive tree onto which gentile believers have been grafted and from whose privileges gentile believers derive nourishment (11:17–24). The balance between Jew and gentile in 15:7–13, then, reflects the balance between Jew and gentile in the argument of Romans from the first sentence forward (1:2–5, 16–17; 1:18–4:25; 9:1–11:36; 14:1–15:6).

Paul's argument in 15:7–13 also lays the groundwork for the description of his own plans for the future in the next section of the letter (15:14–33). Paul's proclamation of the gospel to the gentiles serves the larger goal of bringing them as an offering to God (15:16), an offering of non-Jewish peoples who understand the theological significance of the Jewish people and who, like Christ (διάκονος, 15:8) and

Paul (διακονέω, 15:25; διακονία, 15:31), seek to serve the Jewish people, especially the needy among them (15:26–27).

X. Israel's Present Rejection of the Gospel Does Not Imply the Failure of God's Word (9:1–11:36)

XI. Exhortation to Live in a Way That Is Consistent with the Gospel (12:1–15:13)

A. A Mind Transformed and Renewed by God (12:1–2)

B. Community without Competition (12:3–8)

C. Loving One Another and Remaining Steadfast in a Hostile Environment (12:9–13:14)

D. The Strong Should Show Love for the Weak (and the Weak for the Strong) (14:1–15:13)

1. Refraining from Contempt and Leaving Judgment to God (14:1–12)
2. Thoughtfulness toward the Vulnerable Faith of the Weak (14:13–23)
3. The Christological and Scriptural Basis for Unity (15:1–6)
4. **A Summary and Conclusion Both to 14:1–15:6 and to the Letter So Far (15:7–13)**

XII. The Purpose of Paul's Letter in the Context of His Apostolic Vocation (15:14–33)

Main Idea

When the strong and the weak in Rome welcome each other despite their differences over observance of Jewish customs, they not only follow the example of Christ but play a practical role in the fulfillment of God's promises to Israel in the Scriptures. God had promised Israel he would restore them to full fellowship with himself, and he had described their restoration as part of bringing all the nations of the earth together to worship him. The united worship of Jews and gentiles in Rome, orchestrated by Christ himself, is part of the fulfillment of this universal divine plan.[1]

Translation

(See page 664.)

Structure

The passage falls into four basic parts. It begins with a transitional sentence that summarizes 14:1–15:6 and especially 15:1–6 with its repetition of the idea of following Christ's example in welcoming all kinds of people into God's kingdom (15:7).

The notion of Christ welcoming both weak and strong in Rome then leads to a

1. For the image of Christ as the "choirmaster" in 15:9, see Byrne (*Romans*, 432).

Romans 15:7–13

7a	Summary	Therefore, **welcome one another,**
b	Comparison	just as Christ welcomed you
c	Purpose	for the glory of God.
8a	Basis (for 7a)	For **I maintain that Christ has become a servant of the circumcision**
b	Purpose 1 (of 8a)	for the sake of the truthfulness of God
c	Restatement (of 8b)	to confirm the promises given to the fathers, and
9a	Purpose 2 (of 8a)	that the gentiles might glorify God for the sake of his mercy.
b	Verification (of 8–9a) 1	Just as **it is written,** "Because of this I confess you among the gentiles, and to your name I will sing praise." (2 Sam 22:50/Ps 18:49)
10	Verification (of 8–9a) 2	And **again he says,** "Rejoice, O nations, with his people." (Deut 32:43)
11	Verification (of 8–9a) 3	And **again,** "Praise the Lord, all nations, and let all the peoples extol him." (Ps 117:1)
12a	Verification (of 8–9a) 4	And **again, Isaiah says,** "The root of Jesse will come, that is,
b	Restatement	the one who rises to rule the gentiles.
c	Clarification (of 12b)	In him the gentiles shall hope." (Isa 11:10)
13a	Desire	**Now may the God of hope fill you with all joy and peace**
b	Sphere (of 13a)	in believing
c	Purpose (of 13a)	in order that you might be rich in hope
d	Means (of 13c)	by the power of the Holy Spirit.

statement of the main subject of the passage, the connection between Christ's Jewishness and the new, multiethnic people of God (15:8–9a). That statement itself falls into three brief sections: an overarching statement that Christ became a servant to the Jews (15:8a) and then two purpose statements that explain why Christ did this (15:8b, 9a). He did it to fulfill the promises God had made to Israel in the Scriptures (15:8b) and to bring the gentiles into the worshiping people of God (15:9a).

Paul then demonstrates that the pattern he has just outlined of Christ serving the Jews in order to bring Jews and gentiles together in the worship of God is a pattern (καθώς) found in Scripture (15:9b–12). He demonstrates this with four quotations, all of which support the notion that Jews and gentiles will worship God together, and the first and last of which support Paul's claim that Christ, in his role as the Jewish Messiah, will orchestrate this unified praise (15:9b, 12). The last and most important of Paul's quotations (15:12) describes gentiles placing their hope in a descendant of David who will rise to rule over them.

Paul's concluding prayer asks God, who is able to supply the eschatologically oriented hope described in the final quotation, to give that hope in abundance to the Jews and gentiles in Rome who believe the gospel (15:13).

Exegetical Outline

XI. Exhortation to Live in a Way That Is Consistent with the Gospel (12:1–15:13)

- A. A Mind Transformed and Renewed by God (12:1–2)
- B. Community without Competition (12:3–8)
- C. Loving One Another and Remaining Steadfast in a Hostile Environment (12:9–13:14)
- **D. The Strong Should Show Love for the Weak (and the Weak for the Strong) (14:1–15:13)**
  - 1. Refraining from Contempt and Leaving Judgment to God (14:1–12)
  - 2. Thoughtfulness toward the Vulnerable Faith of the Weak (14:13–23)
  - 3. The Christological and Scriptural Basis for Unity (15:1–6)
  - ➡ **4. A Summary and Conclusion Both to 14:1–15:6 and to the Letter So Far (15:7–13)**
    - a. A transitional admonition for the strong and the weak to welcome each other (15:7)
    - b. An explanation of the necessity of welcoming each other (15:8–9a)
      - (1) Christ's service to the Jews (15:8a)
      - (2) The first purpose of this service: establishing God's truthfulness (15:8b–c)
      - (3) The second purpose of this service: bringing the gentiles into God's people (15:9a)
    - c. The scriptural basis for the unified worship of Jews and gentiles (15:9b–12)
    - d. A concluding prayer that God would give both Jewish and gentile believers in Rome abundant hope for the fulfillment of this scriptural vision (15:13)

Explanation of the Text

15:7 Therefore, welcome one another, just as Christ welcomed you for the glory of God (Διὸ προσλαμβάνεσθε ἀλλήλους, καθὼς καὶ ὁ Χριστὸς προσελάβετο ὑμᾶς εἰς δόξαν τοῦ θεοῦ). The entire community of Roman believers, whether strong or weak, should warmly accept each other, despite their differences, and so follow the pattern laid down by Christ's work of reconciling sinners to God.

Paul's "therefore" (διό) introduces a summary of his whole exhortation to the strong and the weak (14:1–15:6).[2] His double use of the verb "welcome"

2. Cf. his use of "therefore" (διό) in 13:5, where it introduces a summary of 13:1–4.

(προσλαμβάνω) recalls its double use in 14:1–3 to compare the welcome the Romans should give one another despite their differences to the welcome God has given them. Now, however, he refers to the welcome of Christ rather than to the welcome of God, a transformation that is consistent with his use of Christ as an example of welcoming others in 15:3.[3] This easy movement from the reconciling action of God to the reconciling action of Christ with its consequences for all God's people recalls 5:8: "God demonstrates his own love for us in that while we were still sinners Christ died for us." Paul uses "just as" (καθώς), then, in its normal comparative sense, again recalling the use of Christ as an example in 15:3 and 5.[4] His "you" (ὑμᾶς) covers all believers in Rome, whether strong or weak, just as the prayer in 15:5–6 uses the second-person plural to urge both groups to glorify God with one heart and voice.[5]

"For the glory of God" (εἰς δόξαν τοῦ θεοῦ) goes with "Christ welcomed you" (ὁ Χριστὸς προσελάβετο ὑμᾶς) rather than with "welcome one another" (προσλαμβάνεσθε ἀλλήλους).[6] Not only does the phrase "as Christ welcomed you" immediately precede the phrase "for the glory of God," but the lengthy sentence that follows in 15:8–9 shows how Christ's action resulted in the gentiles "glorifying" God.[7]

15:8–9a For I maintain that Christ has become a servant of the circumcision for the sake of the truthfulness of God to confirm the promises given to the fathers, and that the gentiles might glorify God for the sake of his mercy (λέγω γὰρ Χριστὸν διάκονον γεγενῆσθαι περιτομῆς ὑπὲρ ἀληθείας θεοῦ, εἰς τὸ βεβαιῶσαι τὰς ἐπαγγελίας τῶν πατέρων, τὰ δὲ ἔθνη ὑπὲρ ἐλέους δοξάσαι τὸν θεόν). Christ's welcome of both weak and strong, of both Jewish and gentile believers, becomes clear in the way that Christ has prompted gentile believers to praise God for his mercy and has done this through fulfilling God's promises to Israel.

The phrase "for I maintain" (λέγω γάρ) has a solemn, authoritative ring (cf. 12:3) appropriate to the summary statement of a considered argument.[8] Paul's "for" (γάρ) connects this summary statement tightly to the immediately preceding admonition to the Roman believers to follow Christ's example in welcoming one another. The complex series of clauses that follows these opening words recalls the argument of 1:16–8:39 with its emphasis on God's impartiality in the judgment and redemption of all human beings across the spectrum of ethnic identities. It also recalls the argument of 9:1–11:36 that God's impartiality does not involve him in unfaithfulness to his promises to Israel.

Paul had used the term translated "servant" here

3. Origen, *Romans, Books 6–10*, 271.

4. Not in a causal sense, as some commentators have argued (e.g., Cranfield, *Romans*, 2:739; Moo, *Romans*, 875; Schreiner, *Romans*, 754). The causal use of this conjunction is relatively rare (BDAG 494, s.v. καθώς 3). It is not even listed as a possibility in LSJ (857, s.v. καθώς) and MGS (1009, s.v. καθώς).

5. Most modern editions and translations accept the reading "you" (ὑμᾶς) here (e.g., NA[28] RSV NIV NAB NRSV ESV), but there is some learned dissent from this consensus based on the evidence of two early witnesses (B D) and some later manuscripts with Alexandrian affinities (048 104 1506). WH considered the reading "us" (ἡμᾶς) to be of equal value with "you" (ὑμᾶς), and NA[25] preferred it (cf. Godet, *Romans*, 470; Michel, *An die Römer*, 447n19 ["possibly original"]; REB). "You" (ὑμᾶς), however, has strong and diverse manuscript support (א A C F G L Ψ 33 81 365 630 1175 1241 1505 1739 1881), and the second-person plurals in 15:5–6 and 13 seem to require a second person plural here. "Us" (ἡμᾶς) probably arose from confusing the sound of ὑ with the indistinguishable sound of ἡ in ancient Greek (Caragounis, *Development of Greek*, 521–22).

6. As in, e.g., Cranfield (*Romans*, 2:739–40); Wilckens (*An die Römer [Röm 12–16]*, 105n500); Jewett (*Romans*, 889); Hultgren (*Romans*, 530); and RSV, NIV, NAB, TOB, ESV, and CEB.

7. See, e.g., Origen (*Romans, Books 6–10*, 271), Meyer (*Romans*, 540–41), Sanday and Headlam (*Romans*, 397), and the NASB.

8. BDAG 590, s.v. λέγω 2e; Cranfield, *Romans*, 2:740. On the summarizing character of 15:7–12, see especially Wagner, *Heralds of the Good News*, 307–10.

(διάκονος) to refer to a Roman governmental official as an "agent" or "functionary" of God in 13:4, and there the emphasis lay on the representative nature of the official's authority. Here, however, the emphasis lies on the idea that this person works in the interest of another.[9] Paul's use of "circumcision" (περιτομή) to designate the Jewish people, his reference to "the truthfulness of God" (ἀληθείας θεοῦ), and his mention of God's purpose of confirming (βεβαιῶσαι) his promises to the patriarchs all recall the earlier argument in 3:1–8 and 3:27–4:25. There Paul had made the case that the unbelief of most Jews did not threaten God's faithfulness to his word (3:3–4, 7; cf. 9:6) and that God's unity (3:30), as well as his promise to bless all nations through Abraham, required him to justify Jews and non-Jews by faith rather than by adherence to the Jewish law (4:11–12, 16–17).

Here in 15:8 the accent falls on the necessity of physical Israel's involvement in God's plan to bless all the nations of the earth. God had promised Abraham, Isaac, and Jacob that he would bless the nations through them (Gen 17:5; 26:3–5; 28:13–15; cf. Rom 4:13, 20; 9:4, 10), and the Jewish Messiah became a servant of the Jewish people to fulfill that promise (cf. 1:3–5; Gal 4:4).[10] Paul's perfect tense "has become" (γεγενῆσθαι) implies, moreover, that Christ's service to Israel continues into the present time, and this idea recalls the argument of 11:25–31 that even unbelieving Israel remains in some sense God's chosen people, "beloved because of the fathers" (11:28).[11]

The accusative and infinitive construction translated "that the gentiles might glorify God" (τὰ . . . ἔθνη . . . δοξάσαι τὸν θεόν) is difficult. It could stand parallel either with "Christ has become a servant" (Χριστὸν διάκονον γεγενῆσθαι) or with "to confirm the promises" (βεβαιῶσαι τὰς ἐπαγγελίας) in 15:8. If it parallels "Christ has become a servant," then Paul says that he maintains two convictions: (1) that Christ became a servant of the Jewish people to show that God keeps his commitments to Israel and (2) that the gentiles praise God for his mercy.[12] If it parallels "to confirm the promises," then Paul says that he maintains one main idea with two parts: Christ became a servant of the Jewish people, and he did this for two purposes: (1) to show that God keeps his commitments to Israel and (2) so that the gentiles might praise him for his mercy.[13]

This second approach to the syntax fits Paul's purpose in 15:7–13 better. As we have seen, this paragraph not only summarizes Paul's admonitions to the strong and the weak in 14:1–15:6, but it also summarizes the argument of the whole letter, including chapters 9–11. In chapter 11 Paul had argued for the complex idea that Israel's rejection of the Messiah led to mercy for the gentiles and that God's mercy to the gentiles would eventually result in the salvation of all Israel (11:11–12, 25–26, 30–32; cf. 9:15, 18, 24). This complex plan for the salvation of Jews and gentiles demonstrated that God's word, and in particular his promises to the patriarchs, had not failed (9:6; cf. 4:11–17). The

9. Cf. the use of the noun "service" (διακονία) in 15:31 and the use of the verb "serve" (διακονέω) in Matt 20:28, Mark 10:45, and Luke 22:27, a parallel noticed (although in the Latin version) as early as Pelagius (*Romans*, 146).

10. See, e.g., Sanday and Headlam (*Romans*, 398), Jewett (*Romans*, 892), and especially Schreiner (*Romans*, 755).

11. Cranfield, *Romans*, 2:741; Barrett, *Romans*, 249; Moo, *Romans*, 877; Légasse, *Romains*, 899; Hultgren, *Romans*, 531.

12. See, e.g., Alford, *Greek Testament*, 2:432–33; Hodge, *Romans*, 435; Lagrange, *Romains*, 347; Godet, *Romans*, 471; Cranfield, *Romans*, 2:742–44; Byrne, *Romans*, 431–32; Légasse, *Romains*, 899–900.

13. Meyer, *Romans*, 542; Sanday and Headlam, *Romans*, 398; Moo, *Romans*, 876–77; Hultgren, *Romans*, 531–32.

second approach to the syntax provides a compressed summary of this argument and is, then, more likely to be what Paul intended.[14]

When gentile believers in Rome glorify God alongside Jewish believers, this unified group testifies, on one hand, to God's faithfulness to his promises to Israel and, on the other hand, to his merciful character in sparing from his judgment even gentiles to whom he had made no promises. Their unified worship of God is one of the primary purposes for which Christ welcomed them both into his people (15:7) and should be a powerful incentive to them to welcome each other.

15:9b Just as it is written, "Because of this I confess you among the gentiles, and to your name I will sing praise" (καθὼς γέγραπται, Διὰ τοῦτο ἐξομολογήσομαί σοι ἐν ἔθνεσιν καὶ τῷ ὀνοματί σου ψαλῶ). The welcome into God's people that Christ has extended to the gentiles is consistent with the expectation, voiced in Psalm 18, that the nations would become obedient to King David and to his royal offspring.

Paul confirms Christ's welcome of both Jews and gentiles "for the glory of God" (15:7–9a) with a series of four quotations (15:9b–12) taken from the three major parts of the Jewish canon, the Writings (Ps 18:49 [17:50 LXX; 18:50 Heb.]; 117:1 [116:1 LXX]), the Law (Deut 32:43), and the Prophets (Isa 11:10). The first three quotations, taken together, envision Jews and gentiles worshiping God together. The final quotation, the only one whose source Paul designates ("Isaiah"), serves as a climactic, prophetic comment on the eschatological significance of Jews and gentiles joining together in praise of God.[15]

The first quotation comes from either 2 Samuel 22:50 or Psalm 18:49 (17:50 LXX; 18:50 Heb.). Paul often quotes the Psalms in Romans, and so it is likely he was thinking of Psalm 18:49 (17:50 LXX) here.[16] It is also likely, however, that he knew the historical setting of the Psalm that 2 Samuel 22 provided and understood the "I" of his quotation in its original context to be David, who "spoke to the Lord the words of this song on the day when the Lord delivered him from the hand of all his enemies, and from the hand of Saul" (2 Sam 22:1; cf. Ps 18 superscription [17:1 LXX; 18:1 Heb.]).

Psalm 18 is a prayer of thanksgiving to God for delivering David from his enemies and from the aggressive surrounding nations. Rather than posing a threat to him, these nations are now subdued underneath his power and obedient to him (18:43–47 [17:44–48 LXX]). Paul quotes the first part of the final, climactic sentence of the psalm, which continues, after Paul's quotation, "magnifying the acts of deliverance of his king and doing mercy to his anointed (τῷ χριστῷ), to David and his offspring forever" (17:51 LXX [18:50 Eng., 18:51 Heb.]).[17] It is difficult not to think that Paul had this context in mind when he used the psalm. For him, "the Christ" (ὁ Χριστός) of Romans 15:7–8 was "David's offspring" (1:3), and "the obedience of faith" that the gentiles rendered to him as the gospel was proclaimed from one people group to the next was in accord with (καθώς) this psalm's vision of a Davidic king ruling over the gentiles (Rom 1:5).[18]

15:10 And again he says, "Rejoice, O nations, with his people" (καὶ πάλιν λέγει, Εὐφράνθητε, ἔθνη, μετὰ τοῦ λαοῦ αὐτοῦ). Christ's welcome of weak and strong, Jew and gentile, in Rome is also consistent with the vision in the Song of Moses of gentiles acknowledging God together with Israel.

14. Theodoret of Cyrus, commenting on the passage in his native Greek, took it this way (*Letters of St. Paul*, 1:131 [*PG* 82.209, 211]).

15. Cf. Wagner, *Heralds of the Good News*, 317–18.

16. Moo, *Romans*, 878n36.

17. I have slightly modified the NETS.

18. Wagner, *Heralds of the Good News*, 311–13.

Paul quotes from the conclusion to the Septuagint version of the Song of Moses (Deut 32:1–43), Deuteronomy 32:43 LXX, which urges "the nations" or "gentiles" (ἔθνη) to join with God's people in happy praise to God. The phrase "his people" (τοῦ λαοῦ αὐτοῦ) refers to Israel and recalls Paul's insistence in 11:1–2 that the Israelite remnant of believers proves that "God did not cast off his people [τὸν λαόν αὐτοῦ]." Paul's quotation from the Song of Moses, moreover, recalls his use of another part of the Song (Deut 32:21) in Romans 10:19 and 11:11–14 to show that the influx of gentiles into God's people was part of God's plan to save many within Israel through faith in the gospel. Here we find the joyful conclusion to Paul's reading of Moses's Song.[19]

15:11 And again, "Praise the Lord, all nations, and let all the peoples extol him" (καὶ πάλιν, Αἰνεῖτε, πάντα τὰ ἔθνη, τὸν κύριον καὶ ἐπαινεσάτωσαν αὐτὸν πάντες οἱ λαοί). Christ urges all the people groups of the earth to worship God.

Paul's next quotation is a slight rearrangement of Psalm 117:1 (116:1 LXX). He shifts the reference to "all the nations" (πάντα τὰ ἔθνη) forward in the sentence, perhaps for emphasis, and attaches the sentence's two clauses to each other with an "and" (καί) that is not present in the original. Here the angle of vision changes, however, to become even broader as Israel is included among "all nations" and "all the peoples." The peoples of the earth are not pictured in two categories, Jews and gentiles, but as a multiethnic assembly in which all are equal before the God whom they worship (cf. Rom 2:11; 3:29; 4:11–12, 16–17; 11:30–32).

15:12 And again, Isaiah says, "The root of Jesse will come, that is, the one who rises to rule the gentiles. In him the gentiles shall hope" (καὶ πάλιν Ἠσαίας λέγει, Ἔσται ἡ ῥίζα τοῦ Ἰεσσαί καὶ ὁ ἀνιστάμενος ἄρχειν ἐθνῶν, ἐπ' αὐτῷ ἔθνη ἐλπιοῦσιν). Christ has welcomed both Jews and gentiles into God's people through the gospel as the fulfillment of Isaiah's prophecy, that through a descendant of David God would restore the whole world to a condition of righteousness and peace.

Paul's fourth and final quotation, from Isaiah 11:10, returns to the theme of the first quotation (15:9) and again pictures Christ as the descendent of David standing among the nations whom he rules. Now, however, Paul explicitly identifies the quotation's source as "Isaiah." Paul probably did this because he considered it the climactic statement in the series of quotations and because he wanted his audience to recall the Isaianic context from which the quotation comes.

Isaiah 10:5–12:6 prophesies God's judgment on Israel for its godlessness (10:5–6), God's mercy on a remnant (10:20–23; cf. Rom 9:27), and finally the restoration not only of Israel but of the whole earth under the reign of King David's descendant. This "shoot from the stump of Jesse" (11:1; cf. 1 Sam 16:1–13; Acts 13:22) will provide righteousness and equity for the poor and meek, and the peoples of the earth will live in peace under his reign (11:1–9).

Apart from one significant exception, Paul's quotation basically follows the LXX, which itself captures the meaning of the Hebrew text.[20] The exception is Paul's omission of the phrase "in that day" (ἐν τῇ ἡμέρᾳ ἐκείνῃ), perhaps because he

19. Wagner, *Heralds of the Good News*, 315–17.

20. Isaiah's description of Jesse's descendant as a "signal flag" (Heb. *nes*) for the nations (NET; cf. *HALOT* 1:701–2, s.v. 2 נֵס) becomes in the LXX "the one who stands up to rule" (ὁ ἀνιστάμενος ἄρχειν) the nations, and Isaiah's prophecy that the nations will "inquire" or "look . . . for guidance" (*yidroshu*; ESV, NET) from him becomes a prophecy that "nations shall hope [ἐλπιοῦσιν] in him."

considered the fulfillment of Isaiah's prophecy already to be under way.[21] As gentiles believed the gospel that Paul preached, the peaceful rule of Jesse's son was being established.[22]

15:13 Now may the God of hope fill you with all joy and peace in believing in order that you might be rich in hope by the power of the Holy Spirit (ὁ δὲ θεὸς τῆς ἐλπίδος πληρώσαι ὑμᾶς πάσης χαρᾶς καὶ εἰρήνης ἐν τῷ πιστεύειν, εἰς τὸ περισσεύειν ὑμᾶς ἐν τῇ ἐλπίδι ἐν δυνάμει πνεύματος ἁγίου). Paul prays that the Roman believers might have a joyful, peaceful existence even in the difficulties of the present time. This joy and peace, he prays, will come from the confidence they have in God to be faithful to his promise to bring peace and righteousness to the world.

Paul's "now" (δέ) shifts the discourse to a prayer that closes the section (cf. 15:5, 33) and provides a fitting conclusion to the entire letter up to this point.[23] This is the second of five prayers scattered through the final paragraphs of the letter (cf. 15:5–6, 33; 16:20, 25–27). Just as with 15:5–6, Paul describes a quality of life that God produces in his people. In 15:5–6, he was the God of the "endurance" and "encouragement" that, according to the preceding sentence, the Scriptures provided for God's people so that they "might have hope" (15:4). Here, he is the God of the "hope" that Paul has just described using Isaiah 11:10. The hope that Paul refers to both in 15:4 and here, then, is the hope that encourages the gentiles to join the Jewish people (15:10) in the praise of the one true God. It is the hope for a world where all the nations of the earth live in righteousness, equity, and peace under the Messiah's rule (Isa 11:3–9; cf. Rom 4:18; 8:20).

The phrase "by the power of the Holy Spirit" (ἐν δυνάμει πνεύματος ἁγίου) describes the means by which God produces this hope within believers in lavish quantities (περισσεύειν). This thought echoes the argument of 8:23–27 where Paul says that God's Spirit aids believers, in the midst of the suffering that sin has brought to all creation (8:18–22), to hope patiently for the time when God will free his people and his creation from this suffering.[24] Paul prays here that this time of waiting might not be characterized by grim endurance, but that the quality of his audience's confidence in God might give them "joy and peace."

Theology in Application

In Romans 15:7–13 Paul encourages Christians to step across ethnic boundaries and worship God together as a testimony to God's desire to receive praise from "all nations" and "all the peoples" (15:11; Ps 117:1). As his climactic quotation from Isaiah 11:10 shows, he understood this unified worship of God as part of God's plan to bring fairness, justice, faithfulness, and peace to the earth (Isa 11:1–9).

21. Wagner, *Heralds of the Good News*, 318. Cf. Schreiner, *Romans*, 758.

22. Cf. Matthew V. Novenson, "The Jewish Messiahs, the Pauline Christ, and the Gentile Question," *JBL* 128 (2009): 357–73.

23. See especially Jewett, *Romans*, 897–99.

24. Cf. Cranfield, *Romans*, 2:748.

Solidarity with the Weak in First-Century Rome

In mid first-century Rome, this meant that those who did not practice Jewish customs and would not have been identified as Jews by the wider society should "welcome" believers who were practicing Jews into their friendship and fellowship. Jews were often the object of stereotyping, ridicule, and fear in mid first-century Rome. Seneca viewed them as an "accursed race" and pondered conversion to Judaism with alarm: "The vanquished have given laws to their victors."[25] Petronius claimed that Jews worshiped pigs.[26] If the comments of Juvenal and Martial in the early second-century AD are an indication of earlier attitudes, Jews were sometimes identified as beggars and charlatans.[27] The "weak" believers in Rome, then, may also have been "powerless" (ἀδύνατοι) in a social sense, and there may have been a cost for the strong in associating with them. The church, however, was to reflect the vision of God for a just and peaceful world, expressed in Isaiah 11, and not the fears and prejudices of Roman society. Jews and non-Jews were to welcome one another as Christ had welcomed them, and as Paul had just said in the preceding paragraph, that meant acting unselfishly (15:3).

Solidarity with the Weak in Pre-Genocide Rwanda

In his carefully researched study, *Christianity and Genocide in Rwanda*, Timothy Longman describes the contrasting approaches to the poor and the prevailing power structures of two Presbyterian churches just before the 1994 genocide in which nearly a million people perceived to belong to the Tutsi ethnic group and their sympathizers were murdered. Both the church in Kirinda and the church in Biguhu engaged in various social programs to help the poor, but whereas in Kirinda church-leadership positions and jobs were filled by people of privilege in the area, in Biguhu there was a decided effort to be a church of the poor that sought to help all people equally and not to favor any particular group over another. This church tried to avoid corruption, to put people of integrity in charge of aid programs, and to disregard ethnic differences.[28] Fourteen months before the genocide began, the pastor of the church in Biguhu proclaimed from the pulpit that "God has not created all these ethnicities. God created a single person. People created ethnicity later. God does not teach us to divide from one another."[29]

When the genocide erupted, leaders in the church-sponsored programs of Kirinda facilitated the murder of Tutsis within their midst, rounding up Tutsis in church buildings so that they could be more efficiently killed there. The Tutsis of

25. Preserved in Augustine, *The City of God* 6.11 and quoted by Isaac, *Invention of Racism*, 459.

26. Petronius, *Fragment* 37. See Isaac, *Invention of Racism*, 470.

27. Isaac, *Invention of Racism*, 464–65.

28. Longman, *Christianity and Genocide in Rwanda*, 203–300.

29. Ibid., 278.

Biguhu, however, were not killed in the village, and the regional governmental officials who organized the genocide apparently did not feel they could be successful in motivating the local population to kill their neighbors.[30] As Longman puts it, "Biguhu's Tutsi were of course killed nevertheless, but they were killed in spite of the church not with the assistance of the church."[31] Longman believes that it was to a large extent the incorporation of the poor themselves into the work of the church, and a studied commitment among the church leaders to help the poor rather than to seek social advancement for themselves, that explains why the village of Biguhu resisted the genocide.

The approach of the church in Biguhu to the poor faithfully exemplifies the concern for the weak in Romans 14:1–15:13. The church should be a place where the weak receive understanding, empathy, and aid and where they are part of the fabric of the church. They should not be the distant "other," who lies largely out of sight if not out of mind.

Solidarity with Jewish Christians

The vision of Isaiah 11:1–16 and Romans 15:7–13 is not simply for multiethnic unity in a peaceful world but specifically for a world that shows God's faithfulness to his ancient promises to Israel. Isaiah envisions the root of Jesse raising "a signal for the nations" and assembling, at the same time, "the banished of Israel . . . , the dispersed of Judah" (11:12). In Romans Paul envisions harmonious relations between Jewish and gentile believers in Rome, as gentiles worship together with God's people Israel (15:9).

This means that as the church works to reach out sacrificially to all people groups, taking special care to nurture those who are especially vulnerable, it must not lose sight of its special obligation to nurture and encourage Jewish Christians. As Paul has already said in 11:17–18 and will say again in 15:25–27, the relationship of non-Jewish believers to Jews, whether believers or not, is unlike their relationship to any other people group. They owe the Jews a debt for sharing with them the spiritual resources God gave them (cf. 9:4–5), and according to 15:25–27 this debt should lead them to pay special attention to helping Jews and Jewish Christians who are in need.

30. Ibid., 268–300.

31. Ibid., 298.

CHAPTER 31

Romans 15:14–33

Literary Context

The stirring picture of Israel's great Davidic king leading the gentiles in a hymn of praise to God in the company of Israel (15:7–13) had brought Paul's explanation of the gospel to a close. He had shaped his treatment to highlight the goal of the gospel in uniting all nations, Jews as well as gentiles, in the common praise of God through Jesus Christ (3:29–30; 4:9–12, 17–18; 9:24; 11:11–36; 15:8–13). Now, with this understanding of the gospel before his Roman audience, he was ready to return to the subject of his apostolic calling and his impending visit to Rome, matters he had discussed in outline at the beginning of the letter (1:1, 5–6, 10–15). Here, however, he will cover them in much greater detail.[1] This more detailed description of his plans to come to Rome will reveal why he wrote a lengthy letter to the believers there instead of simply and immediately visiting them to strengthen their faith (1:11; 15:14–22, 25–29). It will also describe specifically how the Romans can provide Paul with encouragement (1:12) both before he arrives in Rome (15:30–31) and after he gets there (15:24, 28, 32).

It was necessary for Paul to write to the Roman believers because God had called him to proclaim the gospel to the gentiles and urge them to the "obedience of faith" (1:5; cf. 15:18). The Romans, as a mainly gentile group of believers, fell within the boundaries of this responsibility (1:6), but Paul had been so fully occupied fulfilling his mandate between Jerusalem and Illyricum that he had been unable to come to Rome (1:13; 15:22). His letter provided a solution to this problem by essentially allowing him to be in two places at one time:

> I have written very boldly in part as a reminder to you because of the grace given to me by God in order that I might be a minister of Christ Jesus to the gentiles, working as a priest with respect to the gospel of God, so that the offering of the gentiles might be acceptable, sanctified by the Holy Spirit (15:15–16).[2]

1. See Dunn's useful chart of parallels between 1:8–14 and 15:14–33 (*Romans 9–16*, 857).

2. Longenecker (*Introducing Romans*, 441), calls this "one of the clearest statements in Romans regarding his purpose in writing."

The tensions that plagued the Roman church originated in the same tensions Paul had sometimes encountered when proclaiming the gospel in the east. The gospel envisioned God's people as a multiethnic group not defined by the customs of Judaism but rather by the worship of Israel's God, recognition of Israel's Messiah, and obedience to Israel's Scriptures. For Paul to encourage the Roman believers to be at peace with one another in the midst of this tension, and so to become an acceptable and sanctified offering to God, it was necessary to show them how the gospel implies the peaceful resolution of this tension (1:3–4; 3:1–2; 7:12; 9:3–5; 11:17–24; 14:1–15:13).

It was precisely on this point, however, that the Roman believers could also provide Paul with encouragement (1:12). As Paul wrote Romans, he was in the final stages of conveying relief aid from his predominantly gentile churches to needy Jewish Christians in Jerusalem (15:25–27). This collection was a practical demonstration of the theological debt that gentile believers owed to Jewish Christians and a way of cementing the partnership between gentile and Jewish Christians in the one people of God. Paul needed believers in Rome to "fight alongside" him in prayer that this practical demonstration of mutual support among gentile and Jewish believers would be successful (15:30–31). The peace that would hopefully prevail between Jewish and gentile believers both in Rome and in the eastern Mediterranean would give the mutual rest that Paul and the Romans would enjoy once Paul had delivered this gift (15:29, 32–33).

The encouragement that the Romans would offer Paul (1:12), however, would not end there. Despite his strong desire to come to Rome (1:11, 13, 15; 15:23) and despite finally moving beyond the many hindrances that had prevented his coming so far (1:13; 15:22), his apostolic vocation to proclaim the gospel to gentiles would prevent a lengthy stay in Rome. Instead, Rome would be an important preparatory stop on Paul's way to Spain (15:24, 28). The same gospel that he had preached from Jerusalem to Illyricum and that he had just explained to the Romans would now go to the far west, to what Paul perhaps considered "the end of the earth" (Isa 49:6).

The purpose of 15:14–33, then, was to describe the multilayered purpose of the letter itself. The letter was an effort to preach the gospel to the gentiles, but to believing gentiles who needed the apostle's sometimes bold word of exhortation so that they too might be an acceptable offering to God, sanctified by the Holy Spirit (15:16). The letter explained the theological basis for Paul's request that the Roman Christians support his diplomatic relief mission to Jerusalem (15:30–32). The letter was also an effort to gain support for the gospel that Paul would proclaim in Spain (15:24, 28). The element that tied these layers together was Paul's call "to be an apostle, set apart for the gospel of God . . . for the obedience of faith among all the gentiles" (1:1, 5; cf. 15:15–18).

Main Idea

Paul's letter to the Christians in Rome had two primary purposes. First, it was Paul's effort to exercise his God-given responsibility to proclaim the gospel to the gentiles in Rome and encourage their obedience to its implications. For the Romans, this meant preaching the gospel to them in a way that showed how important their unity with one another was despite their different convictions on the way in which Christianity was related to Judaism. Second, it was Paul's request to the Romans for their help in fulfilling his apostolic vocation. He hoped they would support both his ministry to the needy Jewish Christians in Jerusalem and his future work in Spain.

Translation

(See pages 676–78.)

Structure

The argument of 15:14–33 unfolds in four steps.[3] The "now" (δέ) with which 15:14 begins signals the start of a new major section, just as it did in 14:1, and introduces the first step in the new section (15:14–16). Here Paul tells his Roman audience why he felt compelled to write the letter and particularly the "very bold" section of 14:1–15:13, in which he has given straightforward advice on their internal affairs. He begins this section apologetically with a strong statement of his confidence in their own goodness, knowledge, and ability to instruct one another (15:14), but then defends his decision to write as a reminder to them of what they already know (15:15). His authority to do this among gentile believers, he tells them, comes not from himself but from God (15:16).

The next section (15:17–21) continues to describe the shape that God's apostolic

3. Longenecker, *Introducing Romans*, 440.

Romans 15:14–33

14a	Assertion	Now **I myself am persuaded about you, my brothers and sisters,**
b		that you yourselves are full of goodness,
c		filled with all knowledge, and
d		able to admonish one another.
15a	Contrast (with 14)	But **I have written**
b		very boldly
c		in part
d		as a reminder to you
e		because of the grace given to me by God
16a	Purpose (of 15e)	**in order that I might be a minister of Christ Jesus to the gentiles,**
b		working as a priest with respect to the gospel of God,
c		so that the offering of the gentiles might be acceptable,
d		sanctified by the Holy Spirit.
17a	Expansion (of 16)	**I have,** therefore, **this reason for boasting**
b	Relationship	in Christ Jesus
c	Reference	with respect to the things that pertain to God.
18a	Explanation (of 17)	For **I will not dare to say anything about that which Christ did not accomplish**
b		through me
c		for the obedience of the gentiles,
d		by word and work
19a		in the power of signs and wonders,
b		in the power of the Spirit,
c	Result (of 18a–19b)	so that from Jerusalem and
		all around to Illyricum
		I have completed the preaching of the gospel of Christ
20a	Explanation (of 19c)	And
		in this way
		been eager to preach the gospel
b		where Christ has not been named,
c	Purpose (of 20b)	in order that I might not build on another's foundation.

21a	Verification (of 20)	But **even as it is writtten,**
b		"Those to whom the message about him was not disclosed will see,
c		and those who have not heard will understand." (Isa 52:15b)
22a	Result (of 19c)	For this reason, **I was hindered**
b		time and again
c		from coming to you.
23a	Contrast (to 19c, 22)	But now,
		since I no longer have a place in these regions, and
b		since I have a longing to come to you that goes back many years
24a		As soon as I go to Spain ....
		[unexpressed main verb]
b	Explanation (of 24a)	For **I hope** to see you as I pass through and
		to be sent on there by you
c		if I am able first to enjoy your company for a while.
25a	Contrast (to 24b)	But now
b		**I am going**
c		to Jerusalem
d		in order to serve the saints.
26a	Explanation (of 25)	For **Macedonia and Achaia were pleased to enter into a certain partnership**
b		with the poor among the saints in Jerusalem.
27a	Expansion (of 26a)	For **they were pleased,**
b		and **they are their debtors,**
c	Explanation (of 27a)	for if the gentiles have shared in their spiritual things,
d		**they also are indebted to serve**
e		them
f		in fleshly things.

Continued on next page.

Continued from previous page.

28a	Summary (of 25-27)	Having therefore completed this obligation and
b		sealed for them this fruit,
c		**I will depart for Spain via you.**
29a	Assertion	And **I know**
b	Content	that when I come to you, I will come bringing Christ's total blessing.
30a	Entreaty	Now **I appeal to you, brothers and sisters,**
b	Basis 1 (of 30a)	through our Lord Jesus Christ and
c	Basis 2 (of 30a)	through the love of the Spirit
d	Content (of 30a)	to fight alongside me in prayers to God on my behalf
31a	Purpose 1 (of 30d)	in order that I might be rescued from the disobedient in Judea and
b	Purpose 2 (of 30d)	my ministry to Jerusalem might be acceptable to the saints
32a	Result (of 31b)	with the result that I will come to you in joy,
b	Means (of 32a)	by the will of God, and
c	Restatement (of 32a)	will rest together with you.
33	Desire	**May the God of peace be with you all. Amen.**

call has given to Paul's ministry, but shifts from the present letter to Paul's past work. "Therefore" (οὖν) in the first sentence signals a transition to the new section, and this first sentence is itself transitional, pointing back to Paul's general description of his call in 15:16 and forward to the examples he will give in 15:18–21 of what Christ has accomplished through him among the gentiles in the past. The last part of this section ends with a general principle that Paul observes in all his work and explains why his past work had stretched over such a large area. He was "eager to preach the gospel where Christ has not been named" so that he "might not build on another's foundation" (15:20–21). This provides an effective transition to a discussion of his future work in the next section, which will include the surprising news that he will not stay in Rome for long but will quickly press on to Spain, where Christ has not been named.

"For this reason" (διό) signals the beginning of the third section (15:22–29), where Paul will discuss his future plans and how a visit to Rome fits into them. After a transitional statement (15:22), Paul first describes his eventual plan to go to Spain via Rome (15:23–24) and then his more immediate plan to complete his ministry to poor believers in Jerusalem before coming to Rome (15:25–29).

"Now I appeal to you" (παρακαλῶ δὲ ὑμᾶς) opens the final section (15:30–33). Here Paul issues an urgent personal request to the Romans to come alongside him in prayer to support his relief ministry to the Jerusalem church. The goal of that effort, like the goal of Paul's effort in Rome through the letter, was "peace," and so Paul closes this section of the letter with a prayer that the God of peace would be with the Roman Christians (15:33).

Exegetical Outline

➡ **XII. The Purpose of Paul's Letter in the Context of His Apostolic Vocation (15:14–15:33)**

- **A. Paul's Purpose in Writing the Letter, Especially 12:1–15:13 (15:14–16)**
- **B. Paul's Past Apostolic Labors (15:17–21)**
- **C. Paul's Future Plans (15:22–29)**
- **D. Paul's Appeal to the Romans to Pray for His Ministry in Jerusalem (15:30–33)**
    1. Peace in Jerusalem and in Rome (15:30–32)
    2. A Closing Prayer for Peace in Rome (15:33)

Explanation of the Text

15:14 Now I myself am persuaded about you, my brothers and sisters, that you yourselves are full of goodness, filled with all knowledge, and able to admonish one another (Πέπεισμαι δέ, ἀδελφοί μου, καὶ αὐτὸς ἐγὼ περὶ ὑμῶν ὅτι καὶ αὐτοὶ μεστοί ἐστε ἀγαθωσύνης, πεπληρωμένοι πάσης τῆς γνώσεως, δυνάμενοι καὶ ἀλλήλους νουθετεῖν). Paul did not write the admonitions of 12:1–15:13 because he thought the Roman believers were ignorant of the principles he articulated there or were unwilling to hold one another accountable for following them. To the contrary, he believed they were completely competent in these areas.

Paul's "now" (δέ) begins a new major section of the letter (cf. 14:1), and his vocative-case reference to his Roman audience as his "brothers and sisters" (ἀδελφοί) recalls the last use of this term in 12:1 where his concentrated section of ethical admonitions to his Roman audience began.[4] These ethical admonitions form the subject of this first sentence of the new section (15:14–24), and the purpose of the sentence is to assure his audience of his love and respect for them. The phrase "I myself" (καὶ αὐτὸς ἐγώ) is emphatic and is followed by an equally emphatic and contrasting "you yourselves" (καὶ αὐτοί). In AD 22, on December 11, an Alexandrian named Serapion, who was in legal trouble, wrote to his brother Dorion, desperate for some information he could put into the hand of the local governor. "Please write a reply to me about these things," he told Dorion, "that I myself [καὶ ἐγὼ αὐτός] might deliver a petition to the governor" (P.Oxy. 2.294, l.13).[5] Was Paul so desperate that he lapsed into "gentle flattery" or even "obsequiousness"?[6] Or was he trying to spur them to greater heights by praising them "so that they might blush for not being the sort of people they were believed to be by the apostle"?[7]

There is some hyperbole here, probably designed to assure the Romans that he had no intention of overstepping the bounds of his authority as an apostle who had never visited their city (cf. 1:11–12), but his statement about their "goodness," "knowledge," and ability to admonish one another is sincere.[8] Paul articulates here a conviction that he expresses in various ways throughout his correspondence: God aids believers to discern his will, and so believers do not need instruction from the outside on every matter (1 Cor 7:35–38; 1 Thess 4:9; Phlm 8–9, 14, 21; cf. Rom 12:2; Phil 1:9–10).[9] If "goodness" (ἀγαθωσύνη) is a gift the Holy Spirit gives to believers (Gal 5:22; cf. 2 Thess 1:11), then there is nothing surprising about the Romans having a full measure of it, and there is nothing insincere or manipulative about Paul pointing this out.

15:15 But I have written very boldly in part as a reminder to you because of the grace given to me by God (τολμηρότερον δὲ ἔγραψα ὑμῖν ἀπὸ μέρους ὡς ἐπαναμιμνήσκων ὑμᾶς διὰ τὴν χάριν τὴν δοθεῖσάν μοι ὑπὸ τοῦ θεοῦ). Paul issued a straightforward set of ethical admonitions to the Romans

4. Paul had certainly described how his readers should behave prior to this in the letter (6:1–23; 8:3–17), but in 12:1–15:13 he admonishes them at greater length and more concretely.

5. BDAG 152, s.v. αὐτός 1aβ. My translation, aided by that of Régis Burnet, *L'Égypte ancienne á travers les papyrus: Vie quotidienne* (Paris: Pygmalion, 2003), 258.

6. See respectively, Calvin (*Romans*, 309) and E. Trocmé ("L'épître aux Romains et la méthode missionnaire de l'apôtre Paul," *NTS* 7 [1960]: 148), as quoted in Légasse (*Romains*, 918n2).

7. Pelagius, *Romans*, 147; cf. Ambrosiaster, *Romans*, 111.

8. Schlier, *Der Römerbrief*, 427–28; Käsemann, *Romans*, 391; Jewett, *Romans*, 904.

9. For more on this, see Frank Thielman, "Law and Liberty in the Ethics of Paul," *ExAud* 11 (1995): 63–75.

in 12:1–15:13 and emphasized what they already knew, because urging gentile believers to persevere in their commitment to the gospel was an important part of the assignment God had given him.

The conjunction "but" (δέ) introduces a contrast with the immediately preceding sentence. Paul sets the confidence he has in his Roman audience against his boldness in writing to them. The precise contours of the contrast, however, are ambiguous because the prepositional phrase (ἀπὸ μέρους) can be understood in various ways. Did Paul write to the Romans "*somewhat* too boldly" (τολμηρότερον . . . ἀπὸ μέρους), or "very boldly *in places*" (ἔγραψα . . . ἀπὸ μέρους), or "*in part* to remind" them (ἀπὸ μέρους ὡς ἐπαναμιμνῄσκων) of what they already knew?[10] The position of the phrase directly after the main verb and its object favors taking it with that verb (cf. 2 Cor 2:14), and so Paul probably intended to say that he had written part of his letter with particular boldness. This was a reference not to the whole letter (still less to its emphasis on justification by faith apart from the law) but simply to the "part" of his argument that he had just finished, 12:1–15:13.[11] In that section, his ethical admonitions, particularly in 14:1–15:13, had targeted specific problems in the believing community in Rome.[12]

The term "remind" (ἐπαναμιμνῄσκω) is rare, but in the few places that it does occur it often carries the nuance of "reminding again" (Plato, *Laws* 688a 3; Aristotle, *Mem. rem.* 451a 12–13).[13] Demosthenes could use it to speak of reminding (ἐπαναμνῆσαι) each member of his audience, "however clearly he knows it," that Philip II of Macedon was a self-serving trickster who should not be trusted again (*2 Philip.* 35 [J. H. Vince, LCL]). Paul used the term here in a similar way to describe his letter as an effort to remind his audience of what, according to 15:14, they already knew.

Paul went to this trouble because of the "grace given to [him] by God," a phrase that echoes almost exactly his self-description in 12:3 where his concentrated section of ethical admonitions, and thus his "very bold" reminder, had begun.[14] Just as it did there, "grace" (χάρις) here refers to the vocation God had given to Paul of calling the gentiles to believe the gospel (1:5, 16–17). This does not mean, however, that Paul was only referring to 12:1–15:13 as a product of his apostolic vocation. The argument of that section is integrally related to the entire preceding letter and makes no theological sense without it. Although Paul describes only 12:1–15:13 as "very boldly" written, then, he implies that the entire letter was the product of his apostolic authority.

15:16 in order that I might be a minister of Christ Jesus to the gentiles, working as a priest with respect to the gospel of God, so that the offering of the gentiles might be acceptable, sanctified by the Holy Spirit (εἰς τὸ εἶναί με λειτουργὸν Χριστοῦ Ἰησοῦ εἰς τὰ ἔθνη, ἱερουργοῦντα τὸ εὐαγγέλιον τοῦ θεοῦ, ἵνα γένηται ἡ προσφορὰ τῶν ἐθνῶν εὐπρόσδεκτος, ἡγιασμένη ἐν πνεύματι ἁγίῳ). God gave Paul the role of apostle to the gentiles so that he might bring them the gospel and they

10. See, respectively, Hodge, *Romans*, 438 (cf. Chrysostom, *Romans*, 462 [*PG* 60:654]); Origen, *Romans, Books 6–10*, 277–78 (cf. Meyer, *Romans*, 546); and Godet, *Romans*, 476–77 (cf. Jewett, *Romans*, 905).

11. For the idea that Paul speaks of specific sections scattered throughout the letter, see Meyer (*Romans*, 546), and for the idea that Paul referred to his emphasis on justification by faith apart from the law, see Käsemann (*Romans*, 392).

12. Cf. Cranfield, *Romans*, 2:753.

13. LSJ 607, s.v. ἐπαναμιμνῄσκω.

14. In 12:3 Paul admonishes the Roman believers "through the grace given to me" (διὰ τῆς χάριτος τῆς δοθείσης μοι), and here he has reminded them of what they already know "because of the grace given to me [διὰ τὴν χάριν τὴν δοθεῖσάν μοι] by God."

might become part of God's people, set apart by God's own power for his use.

Paul states the purpose for which God gave him the role of apostle to the gentiles and therefore the ultimate reason why he was compelled to write very boldly to the Romans in 12:1–15:13. The word "minister" (λειτουργός) could simply mean "servant" and refer to a public official (cf. 13:6) or a personal "attendant" (2 Sam 13:18 LXX; cf. Phil 2:25), or it could refer to those who performed rituals for the gods (Dionysius of Halicarnassus, *Ant. rom.* 2.22.3).[15] Greek-speaking Jews often used the term for those performing religious service in the temple (LXX Ezra 7:24; Neh 10:40; Let. Arist. 95).[16] It is possible that Paul refers to himself here simply as a "servant" of Christ Jesus with special responsibility for the gentiles, just as in 3 Maccabees 5:5 Ptolemy IV Philopater had special "servants in charge of the Jews" (οἱ . . . πρὸς τούτοις [τοῖς Ἰουδαίοις] λειτουργοί), but since Paul goes on immediately to use language that refers to the work of a priest in offering sacrifice, it is clear that the term "minister" already carries religious connotations.[17]

The meaning of the phrase "the offering of the gentiles" (ἡ προσφορὰ τῶν ἐθνῶν) is also slightly ambiguous since it could refer either to the gentiles as a metaphorical offering that Paul gives to God or to the gentiles as a group who are themselves making an offering to God. If it refers to the offering that the gentiles make, then Paul is speaking either of gentile believers in Rome offering themselves as a living sacrifice (12:1) or gentile believers in Macedonia and Achaia offering their money to poor believers in Jerusalem (15:25–27) in order "to serve" (λειτουργῆσαι) them.[18] Within the context Paul's focus is on his role as one who offers sacrifice to God, and a secondary reference to the gentiles also offering something to God would complicate the imagery.[19] Paul, then, speaks metaphorically of himself as a priest offering the gentile believers to God.[20]

Paul describes these gentiles as an offering that has been "sanctified [ἡγιασμένη] by the Holy Spirit." In the LXX, offerings were sometimes "sanctified," or set apart, for God's use (Exod 13:2; Deut 15:19; cf. Matt 23:17, 19), and here Paul imagines God himself setting gentile believers apart, like an offering, for his purposes.[21] Paul thinks of his own work in evangelizing and instructing non-Jewish people as the means by which God does this. His letter to the Romans, and especially the "very bold" section 12:1–15:13, was part of that work.

15:17 I have, therefore, this reason for boasting in Christ Jesus with respect to the things that pertain to God (ἔχω οὖν τὴν καύχησιν ἐν Χριστῷ Ἰησοῦ τὰ πρὸς τὸν θεόν). God has given Paul a responsibility to the believers in Rome and the ability to carry it out. Even the bolder parts of his letter, therefore, were appropriate.

15. MGS 1223; cf. LSJ 1036–37; BDAG 591–92, all s.v. λειτουργός.

16. *TLNT* 381n11.

17. Cf. the language of Isa 66:20 where a group of people (probably Jews) are brought to God (probably by gentiles) as an offering in the sense that they are led to join with others in the worship of God. For the meaning of the passage, see Oswalt (*Book of Isaiah: Chapters 40–66*, 689–90), and for an argument that Isa 66:19–20 significantly influenced Paul's missionary strategy, see Rainer Riesner (*Paul's Early Period: Chronology, Mission Strategy, Theology*, trans. Doug Scott [Grand Rapids: Eerdmans, 1998], 245–52).

18. See, respectively, Dunn (*Romans 9–16*, 860), who is tentative about this reading and thinks that, if correct, it is only partially what Paul means, and David J. Downs ("'The Offering of the Gentiles' in Romans 15.16," *JSNT* 29 [2006]: 173–86). Cf. Donaldson, *Paul and the Gentiles*, 257.

19. Schreiner, *Romans*, 767.

20. Paul may have thought of the primarily gentile delegates who accompanied him to Jerusalem with the collection (Acts 20:4; Rom 15:25–26) as a sample of this metaphorical offering. On this, see Harris, *Second Epistle to the Corinthians*, 97–98.

21. BDAG 9–10, s.v. ἁγιάζω 1–2.

"Therefore" (οὖν) introduces a brief, transitional statement that summarizes Paul's defense of his bold approach to the Romans in 12:1–15:13 and introduces the broader discussion of his ministry among the gentiles in 15:18–21. The article (τήν) points back to 15:15–16 and shows that the "boast" Paul refers to is his call to evangelize and instruct the gentiles and to present them, as a priest might, to God.[22] He points out that he only has this boast because he is "in Christ Jesus" and that the boast itself consists only of "the things that pertain to God." It is, therefore, qualitatively different than either ethnic boasting (3:27; 11:18) or boasting in one's own works (4:2), both of which the gospel excludes. Nevertheless, the boast is only possible because Paul possessed a certain role and competence that qualified him to speak boldly, even to gentile believers in a city that he had never visited.

15:18 For I will not dare to say anything about that which Christ did not accomplish through me for the obedience of the gentiles, by word and work (οὐ γὰρ τολμήσω τι λαλεῖν ὧν οὐ κατειργάσατο Χριστὸς δι᾽ ἐμοῦ εἰς ὑπακοὴν ἐθνῶν, λόγῳ καὶ ἔργῳ). Paul's boast is in no way a claim to special status or power for himself, but only an explanation of why he claims apostolic authority among the gentiles.

Paul offers a further explanation (γάρ) of the claim that his boasting is "in Christ" and pertains only to "the things of God." The phrase "I will not dare" expresses Paul's deep concern not to overstep appropriate boundaries in his claims of apostolic authority and slip into self-commendation (cf. 2 Cor 10:8, 13, 15–18; 11:16–23, 30; 12:6–10).[23] God had given him the gift of his apostolic vocation (Rom 15:15), and none of the responsibility or power that went with it belonged in any ultimate sense to Paul. This deep concern probably explains why Paul put the sentence in the negative when it would have been simpler to communicate his meaning positively ("I will dare to speak only of those things which Christ has accomplished through me."). "See how violently he tries to shew that the whole is God's doing, and nothing his own," says Chrysostom.[24]

The obedience that Paul speaks of here probably includes both believing the gospel (1:5; 10:16) and living in a way that is pleasing to God (6:16), and the "word" and "work" that brought about this obedience is probably the preaching of the gospel (cf. 10:17) and the signs and wonders that accompanied this preaching (15:19; cf. 2 Cor 12:12; Gal 3:5).[25]

15:19 in the power of signs and wonders, in the power of the Spirit, so that from Jerusalem and all around to Illyricum I have completed the preaching of the gospel of Christ (ἐν δυνάμει σημείων καὶ τεράτων, ἐν δυνάμει πνεύματος [θεοῦ]·[26] ὥστε με ἀπὸ Ἰερουσαλὴμ καὶ κύκλῳ μέχρι τοῦ Ἰλλυρικοῦ πεπληρωκέναι τὸ εὐαγγέλιον τοῦ Χριστοῦ). Paul provides further evidence that his apostolic vocation was a God-given gift (15:15),

22. Lagrange, *Romains*, 351; Michel, *An die Römer*, 459; Cranfield, *Romans*, 2:757.

23. Cf. Dunn, *Romans 9–16*, 862.

24. Chrysostom, *Romans*, 465.

25. On taking "work" (ἔργῳ) here as a reference to miracles that occurred when Paul preached the gospel, see Graham H. Twelftree, *Paul and the Miraculous: A Historical Reconstruction* (Grand Rapids: Baker, 2013), 207–23.

26. Codex Vaticanus (B) is the only ancient manuscript of Romans that does not qualify "the Spirit" (πνεύματος) with either "of God" (θεοῦ [e.g., 𝔓[46] ℵ L P Ψ 1175 124 1505 1506]) or "holy" (ἁγίου [e.g., A D F G 33 81 104 365 630 1739 1881]). Acceptance of a reading that appears in only one manuscript is usually ill-advised, but since the other two readings are best explained as very ancient attempts to fill out the phrase "in the power of the Spirit" (ἐν δυνάμει πνεύματος) in slightly different ways, the shorter, more difficult reading of Vaticanus is probably original. See Metzger, *Textual Commentary*, 473; Jewett, *Romans*, 901.

and that his "boasting" must therefore be limited to what God has done through him (15:18). God's miraculous power, reminiscent of the exodus, had accompanied Paul's preaching all over the area between Jerusalem and Illyricum.

The phrase "signs and wonders" (σημεῖα καὶ τέρατα) was a well understood expression for divinely produced, unusual events that occurred at critical points in a nation's history (Josephus, *J.W.* 1.28; Polybius *Histories* 3.112).[27] The phrase appears often in the LXX to describe the miracles that God performed at the time of Israel's exodus from Egypt (Deut 6:22; 34:10–11; Ps 134:8–9 [135:8–9, Eng. and Heb.]; Jer 39:20–21). Such portents could be falsely claimed (Josephus, *Ant.* 20.168) or faked to gain a following (Mark 13:22; 2 Thess 2:9; cf. Rev 13:13–15), but here Paul refers to unusual events that accompanied his ministry and authenticated it as both from God and part of the beginning of a new epoch in salvation history (cf. Acts 14:3; 15:12). The phrase "in the power of the Spirit" explains both the source of Paul's preaching and the source of the miracles that accompanied his preaching (cf. 1 Thess 1:5).

The expression "so that" (ὥστε) introduces the result of Christ's accomplishment (κατειργάσατο, 15:18) through Paul, and Paul describes that result as completing (πεπληρωκέναι) the gospel of Christ. This is an unusual expression since, taken on its own, it might suggest that the gospel message itself needed completion. The noun "gospel" (εὐαγγέλιον), however, implies the activity of proclaiming good news, and together with the geographic references in the context must refer to the activity of proclaiming the gospel message in a certain region (cf. Col 1:25).[28] Some commentators have expressed astonishment that Paul would claim to have "completed the preaching of the gospel" in the region he describes.[29] His focus, however, is on the fulfillment of his own part ("I" [με]) in preaching the gospel in this region, not on the gospel's progress in the region in an absolute sense.

That region stretched from Jerusalem to Illyricum, but whether the adverb translated "all around" (κύκλῳ) refers (1) to the region "around" Jerusalem, (2) to a "circle" of nations surrounding Jerusalem, (3) to a geographical arc stretching from Jerusalem northeastward and then back to the northwest until it ends in Illyricum, or (4) to an indirect, meandering route from Jerusalem to Illyricum is unclear.[30] Ancient Greek commentators tended to take the expression in the fourth sense, and it is probably best, in matters of ancient Greek, to trust their judgment.[31]

Acts contains no record of Paul preaching either to gentiles in Jerusalem or to anyone in Illyricum, but that does not mean he was speaking symbolically or less than precisely here. He had in view neither the chronology of his travels nor the ethnicity of those to whom he preached but simply his role in taking the gospel at various times to various locations between the two geographical endpoints of Jerusalem in the east and Illyricum in the west. The southern part of Illyricum was a short

27. They seem often to have been events that occurred contrary to nature, such as pieces of wood sprouting or sweating (Theophrastus, *Caus. plant.* 5.4.3–4), but this was not absolutely necessary (e.g., Isa 20:3).

28. BDAG 828, s.v. πληρόω 3.

29. E.g., Dunn, *Romans 9–16*, 864.

30. For (1), see Godet (*Romans*, 480); for (2), see James M. Scott, *Paul and the Nations: The Old Testament and Jewish Background of Paul's Mission to the Nations with Special Reference to the Destination of Galatians*, WUNT 84 (Tübingen: Mohr Siebeck, 1995), 138–39; for (3), see Dunn (*Romans 9–16*, 863); and for (4), see Sanday and Headlam (*Romans*, 407).

31. Sanday and Headlam, *Romans*, 407. See, e.g., Theodoret of Cyrus (*Letters of St. Paul*, 1:132–33 [*PG* 82.213]): "Not only the nations situated on the direct route but also . . . the eastern and Pontic regions, and in addition . . . Asia and Thrace (*right around* suggesting this [τοῦτο γὰρ δηλοῖ τὸ, κύκλῳ])."

journey across the Adriatic Sea from Italy, and by Paul's time was heavily Romanized.[32] An otherwise unknown Pauline mission there, perhaps around the time Paul was in Macedonia shortly before the composition of Romans (Acts 20:2), would make sense as the apostle began to turn his attention to Rome and Spain in the Latin-speaking west.[33] Perhaps Paul later sent Titus to Dalmatia, the southern part of this region, to tend to churches established during Paul's work there (2 Tim 4:10).

15:20 And in this way been eager to preach the gospel where Christ has not been named, in order that I might not build on another's foundation (οὕτως δὲ φιλοτιμούμενον εὐαγγελίζεσθαι οὐχ ὅπου ὠνομάσθη Χριστός, ἵνα μὴ ἐπ' ἀλλότριον θεμέλιον οἰκοδομῶ). Paul preached the gospel in the Spirit's power in various places from Jerusalem to Illyricum because of his eagerness to establish Christ-worshiping communities in places where those communities did not currently exist.

Paul's "in this way" (οὕτως) points backward to what he has just said rather than forward to the infinitive "to preach the gospel" (εὐαγγελίζεσθαι). He is not starting a new thought in which he describes his method of preaching as not building on another's foundation ("but making it my ambition so to preach . . . that I do not build on another's foundation"). Rather, he carries forward and qualifies the previous description of his evangelistic strategy. He has preached the gospel in word and deed all over the region between Jerusalem and Illyricum because of his eagerness to preach where Christ has not been named. This way of reading the statement fits neatly with the claim in 15:23 that he no longer has "a place in these regions." He no longer had a place in Achaia, Macedonia, and Asia not because the work there was finished but because his strategy was to preach the gospel where others had never before taken it.[34]

The participle translated "been eager" (φιλοτιμούμενον) often carried a note of competition, and the competition could be either friendly or unfriendly (e.g., Josephus, *Ant.* 9.163; 12.3). Since Paul offers an implicit comparison of his own work in preaching the gospel with the work of others, it is possible that he used the term here with a hint of friendly competition in the good cause of advancing the gospel (cf. Rom 12:10; 2 Cor 9:2), or even of not-so-friendly competition with those who built flimsy structures on the foundation he had carefully laid (cf. 1 Cor 3:10–15; 2 Cor 10:13–18).[35]

The term, however, could also simply mean "be eager" (Josephus, *Ant.* 8.395), especially when coupled with an infinitive, as it is here.[36] Since Paul's only other uses of the word fall into this category (2 Cor 5:9; 1 Thess 4:11), his use of it here probably refers simply to his own eager endeavor.

15:21 But even as it is writtten, "Those to whom the message about him was not disclosed will see,

32. Paul used the Latinized form "Illyricum" (Ἰλλυρικόν) rather than Greek form "Illyria" (Ἰλλυρία) and therefore referred to the Roman province rather than to the area occupied by the Illyrian people (Allan Chapple, "Paul and Illyricum," *RTR* 72 [2013]: 20–21). By the time of Vespasian (AD 69–79), the Romans had divided Greater Illyricum into two provinces, Pannonia in the north, which they viewed primarily as a military buffer against the regions they had not subjugated north of the Danube, and Dalmatia in the south, which was more thoroughly Romanized and provided Italy with precious metals (Daniel Dzino, *Illyricum in Roman Politics: 229 BC–AD 68* [Cambridge: Cambridge University Press, 2010], 156–76; Franz A. W. Schehl and John Joseph Wilkes, "Dalmatia," *OCD* 426).

33. F. F. Bruce, *Paul, Apostle of the Heart Set Free* (Grand Rapids: Eerdmans, 1977), 316, 317; Chapple, "Paul and Illyricum," 20–35. Cf. Schnabel, *Paul and the Early Church*, 1250–51. Perhaps Paul had Illyricum in mind when he wrote from Macedonia to the Corinthians that he hoped to "preach the gospel in lands beyond you" (2 Cor 10:15–16). On this, see Bruce (*Paul*, 316).

34. Dunn, *Romans 9–16*, 865.

35. Cf. Dunn, *Romans 9–16*, 865.

36. LSJ 1941, s.v. φιλοτιμέομαι II; MGS 2287, s.v. φιλοτιμέομαι B; cf. BDAG 1059, s.v. φιλοτιμέομαι.

and those who have not heard will understand" (ἀλλὰ καθὼς γέγραπται, ὄψονται[37] οἷς οὐκ ἀνηγγέλη περὶ αὐτοῦ καὶ οἳ οὐκ ἀκηκόασιν συνήσουσιν). Paul's strategy of proclaiming the gospel in places where there were no communities that worshiped Christ agreed with Isaiah's prophecy that non-Israelite nations would hear about and understand the purpose of the suffering of the Lord's Servant.

Paul claims that his eagerness to preach the gospel in places where Christ has not been named agrees with the vision of Isaiah 52:15b. In its original context, the quotation refers to the response of the kings of various non-Israelite nations to the Servant of the Lord. The Servant's suffering will parallel the suffering of Israel, suffering so intense that "many were astonished" at it. One day, however, the nations and their leaders will see the Servant and understand the vicarious purpose of his suffering, described in Isaiah 53:1–12.[38] In Isaiah 52:15b LXX, the pronoun in the phrase "about him" (περὶ αὐτοῦ) refers back to God's "Servant" in Isaiah 52:13, and in Paul's sentence it refers to "Christ" in 15:20. Clearly Paul thought that Isaiah's Servant in this passage was the Christ whom he had preached in places scattered between Jerusalem and Illyricum where no communities existed that called on Christ's name (cf. Rom 10:13; 1 Cor 1:2; 2 Tim 2:19).[39]

15:22 For this reason, I was hindered time and again from coming to you (Διὸ καὶ ἐνεκοπτόμην τὰ πολλὰ τοῦ ἐλθεῖν πρὸς ὑμᾶς). Paul's large and complex task of proclaiming the gospel and establishing worshiping Christian communities from Jerusalem to Illyricum had kept him from coming to Rome.

"For this reason" (διὸ καί) does not point back to Paul's policy of preaching the gospel where Christ had not been named (15:20–21). Paul is not saying that he had delayed a visit to Rome because it would be inconsistent with this policy.[40] Rather, it points back to the end of 15:19 and the proclamation of the gospel from Jerusalem to Illyricum. This understanding of the argument becomes clear in Paul's next sentence where he says there is no more room for his pioneering work "in these regions" (15:23).[41] Despite his strong desire to come to Rome (cf. 1:13; 15:23), he had not been able to go there because of his dedication to establishing Christ-worshiping communties between Jerusalem and Illyricum.

Greek speakers sometimes followed verbs of hindering or preventing with an infinitive with the genitive article to indicate the action thwarted.[42] An inflated sheepskin, for example, could prevent a soldier from sinking (ἕξει τοῦ μὴ καταδῦναι) into a deep river (Xenophon, *Anab.* 3.5.11).[43]

37. Paul's quotation agrees almost exactly with the LXX, which is itself an almost word-for-word translation of the Hebrew. Paul brought forward the expression "will see" (ὄψονται) from the end to the beginning of the first clause and created a well-balanced chiasm that emphasizes the seeing and understanding of the gospel. Although most ancient manuscripts place "will see" (ὄψονται) at the end of the clause ($\mathfrak{P}^{46}$ א A C D F G, etc.), this form of the text probably represents an unconscious harmonization of Paul's quotation with the word order in the LXX. The word order adopted here agrees with the reading in B 69 330 and 1243 (Jewett, *Romans*, 902 note "x") and adopted by WH and NA[25]. See also, e.g., Cranfield (*Romans*, 2:765); Dunn (*Romans 9–16*, 856); and Jewett (*Romans*, 902).

38. Cf. Oswalt, *Isaiah: Chapters 40–66*, 380–81, and on Paul's use of Isaiah 53 generally, see Gathercole, *Defending Substitution*, 63–64.

39. Schreiner, *Romans*, 770; Wagner, *Heralds of the Good News*, 332–35. The unambiguous equation with the Servant and Christ here undermines arguments, such as those by Dunn (*Romans 9–16*, 866) and Haacker (*An die Römer*, 299), that Paul identifies himself as the Servant in this passage.

40. Cf. the use of these two conjunctions together in, e.g., 2 Cor 1:20; 5:9; Phil 2:9 and the comments of Légasse, *Romains*, 328n40.

41. Dunn, *Romans 9–16*, 871.

42. For the meaning of the term, see BDAG 274, s.v. ἐγκόπτω, and Paul's other uses in Gal 5:7 and 1 Thess 2:18.

43. BDF §400.

Paul uses the same construction here in the expression translated "hindered . . . from coming" (ἐνεκοπτόμην . . . τοῦ ἐλθεῖν). The neuter plural of the adjective commonly translated "much" (πολύς) could sometimes mean "often," such as when the philosopher Epictetus illustrates a point with reference to the typical senator, who was often away from home (τὰ πολλὰ . . . ἀποδημεῖν).[44] Combined with the imperfect tense (ἐνεκοπτόμην), "often" communicates the notion of regular, frequent action. Paul, then, is repeating with slightly more emphasis what he had said in 1:13 about having "often planned to come" (πολλάκις προεθέμην ἐλθεῖν) to Rome but having been "hindered" (ἐκωλύθην) from doing so. Now he explains that those plans had never materialized because time and again one thing or another kept preventing him from fulfilling them.

What were those hindrances? Paul probably thought especially of the physical suffering he had endured as he proclaimed the gospel and instructed new believers in various places (1 Cor 4:9–13; 2 Cor 4:7–12; 6:4–10; 11:23–33; 12:10; 1 Thess 2:2).[45] Since he was writing from Corinth just before taking his relief collection to Jerusalem (15:25–28), he may also have had especially in mind his recent, turbulent relationship with the Corinthian church (1 Cor 4:18–20; 2 Cor 1:23–2:13; 6:11–12; 7:2–16; 10:1–13:10), not least in connection with persuading the Corinthians to follow through on their original commitment to contribute to that collection (2 Cor 8:10–11).[46]

15:23 But now, since I no longer have a place in these regions, and since I have a longing to come to you that goes back many years (νυνὶ δὲ μηκέτι τόπον ἔχων ἐν τοῖς κλίμασι τούτοις, ἐπιποθίαν δὲ ἔχων τοῦ ἐλθεῖν πρὸς ὑμᾶς ἀπὸ πολλῶν ἐτῶν). Paul had planted and nurtured believing communities in enough places between Jerusalem and Illyricum that he now felt he must go to new, uncharted territory. Moreover, at least since meeting Prisca and Aquila in Corinth six years earlier, he had wanted to visit the Christians in Rome.

"But now" (νυνὶ δέ) changes the perspective from Paul's past work among the gentiles to his present plans for the future (cf. 3:21; 6:22; 7:6, 17). Paul begins to describe his future itinerary with two clauses that indicate the reasons why he is "now" ready to make a strategic change in the geographical location of his ministry.

First, it is because he does not "have a place in these regions." The expression "to have no place" (μὴ ἔχειν τόπον) in ancient Greek, just as in modern English, could be taken in either a negative or a neutral sense. Someone might have no place somewhere either because they are not welcome or because that place is not a good fit.[47] Paul is unlikely to be using the expression here to mean that he has worn out his welcome in the east and has been relegated to work in the west.[48] This would hardly encourage the Romans to support his work in Spain (15:24).[49] Rather, he means that in light of his special assignment to take the gospel where Christ has not been named, the regions stretching

44. MGS 1714, s.v. Πολύς 2.C.

45. Cf. Wilckens, *An die Römer (Röm 12–16)*, 124; Jewett, *Romans*, 922.

46. See Douglas A. Campbell's plausible argument (*Framing Paul: An Epistolary Biography* [Grand Rapids: Eerdmans, 2014], 52–55) that Paul wrote Romans with the knowledge that the Corinthians would overhear it before it was sent to Rome.

47. See, e.g., Plutarch, *Quaest. conv.* 646 A, where only invited guests and natural appetites have a place (τόπον ἔχουσιν) at a dinner party, and Dionysius of Halicarnassus, *Dem.* 23, where Dionysius says that Plato's *Apology of Socrates* (through no fault of its own) has no place (οὔτε . . . τόπον ἔχων) in the genre of either oratory or dialogue (LSJ 1806, s.v. τόπος 2).

48. Haacker (*An die Römer*, 309) mentions this possibility (referring to P. Vielhauer, *Geschichte der urchristlichen Literatur* [Berlin: de Gruyter, 1975], 184), but correctly rejects it.

49. Cf. Haacker, *An die Römer*, 310.

northwest from Corinth to Illyricum and southeast to Jerusalem are no longer a good "fit" for him.

Second, Paul is ready to make a strategic change in the location of his service to the gentiles because of a long-held desire to visit God's beloved and holy people in Rome (cf. 1:7, 10–11). The term translated "longing" (ἐπιποθία) appears only here in extant ancient Greek from Paul's time and before, but it seems to be identical in meaning with another, relatively common word (ἐπιπόθησις) that Paul uses elsewhere (2 Cor 7:7, 11). Both terms are closely related to the verb to "long for, desire" (ἐπιποθέω) that described Paul's desire to visit Rome in 1:11. Paul often used that verb to describe his longing to see people about whom he cared deeply (Phil 1:8; 1 Thess 3:6; 2 Tim 1:4; cf. Phil 2:26). The long list of greetings to specific people in 16:3–16 probably explains why he felt this way.

Paul says that he had wanted to visit believers in Rome for "many years" (ἀπὸ πολλῶν ἐτῶν). Beginning apparently with the scribe who first changed "many" (πολλῶν) to "quite a few" (ἱκανῶν), some have thought Paul was exaggerating at least slightly, perhaps to flatter the Romans and win their support.[50] If Paul had set his sights on visiting believers in Rome shortly after meeting the Romans Prisca and Aquila in AD 51, however, then the six or so years between that time and the composition of Romans in AD 57 could reasonably count as "many years" (Acts 18:2–3).[51]

15:24 As soon as I go to Spain. . . . For I hope to see you as I pass through and to be sent on there by you if I am able first to enjoy your company for a while (ὡς ἂν πορεύωμαι εἰς τὴν Σπανίαν· ἐλπίζω γὰρ διαπορευόμενος θεάσασθαι ὑμᾶς καὶ ὑφ' ὑμῶν προπεμφθῆναι ἐκεῖ ἐὰν ὑμῶν πρῶτον ἀπὸ μέρους ἐμπλησθῶ). Paul politely introduces for the first time in the letter his plan to visit the Roman believers on his way to somewhere else. He is heading to the western end of the world as he knew it, in accord with the principle of proclaiming the gospel primarily where there were no believers. He hopes for the Romans' support in this endeavor.

The sentence Paul started in 15:23 continues with the temporal clause "as soon as I go to Spain" (ὡς ἂν πορεύωμαι εἰς τὴν Σπανίαν) but then abruptly stops (cf. TOB).[52] What happened?

Paul probably realized as soon as he mentioned Spain that he needed to explain why his visit to believers in Rome was not his final destination despite his longing to go there (1:10–11; 15:23). Ancient Greek commentators on Romans, who were attuned to the cultural situation Paul faced, seem to have picked up on this instinctively. Origen says that Paul's mention of seeing the Romans on his way to Spain "should not be understood as if Paul was bearing so little love for the Romans that he had decided only to see them in passing while traveling in another direction."[53] Origen then spends a long paragraph explaining that Paul soft-

50. The earliest evidence for the change is Codex Vaticanus (B), but the reading is also found in, e.g., C P 81 326 365 1175 1506. The difficulty of reading "many" (πολλῶν) as well as the antiquity ($\mathfrak{P}^{46}$ ℵ A) and geographical distribution (e.g., D [F] G L) of the manuscript witnesses to it, favor it as genuine (cf. Jewett, *Romans*, 918nc, citing Bruce M. Metzger, *A Textual Commentary on the Greek New Testament* [London: UBS, 1975], 537). Since the variant (ἱκανῶν) is a more refined term, the change could also simply have been motivated by stylistic considerations (e.g., Cranfield, *Romans*, 2:768). On Paul's possible use of diplomatic flattery here, see, e.g., Jewett (*Romans*, 923) and Hultgren (*Romans*, 551).

51. Sanday and Headlam, *Romans*, 410–11; Zahn, *An die Römer*, 602.

52. Some late manuscripts (e.g., ℵ² L 33 104 365 630 1175 1241 1505) finish Paul's sentence for him to tidy up the syntax. They insert ". . . I will come to you" (ἐλεύσομαι πρὸς ὑμᾶς) after "when I go to Spain" (ὡς ἂν πορεύωμαι εἰς τὴν Σπανίαν). Cf. the KJV ("Whensoever I take my journey into Spain, I will come to you").

53. Origen, *Romans, Books 6–10*, 282.

ens the blow of his potentially insulting comment by assuring the Romans he will only leave for Spain when they are ready for him to go. Paul puts the length of his stay in Rome, says Origen, "under their power" and "at their discretion."[54] Paul's broken syntax probably reflects the delicate nature of a cultural situation in which giving and receiving hospitality were extremely important. In this case, however, cultural convention might conflict with the mission God had given him to proclaim the gospel where Christ had not been named.[55] He could not stay in Rome too long and still be faithful to that mission.

Paul says nothing about why he chose to go to Spain rather than to the many other places where there were no Christian communities. Allan Chapple has made the sensible suggestion that areas to the south and east, such as Cyrene, Egypt, and Mesopotamia, already had Christian communities at this stage and that Paul would have expected Roman Christians to extend the gospel into Italy and Narbonensis (between today's northwestern Italy and northeastern Spain). That left Gaul to the north and Spain to the west, and he may have intended to head north into Gaul himself after establishing churches in Spain.[56]

Paul often used the first part of Isaiah 49 as a framework for understanding the theological significance of his apostolic work (2 Cor 6:2 [cf. Isa 49:8]; Gal 1:15 [cf. Isa 49:1]; Phil 2:16 [Isa 49:4]), and it is easy to imagine him interpreting his pioneering ministry to the gentiles as bringing the "light" of God's "salvation . . . to the end of the earth" (Isa 49:6; cf. Acts 13:47).[57] The ancient geographer Strabo (who died in the early first century) thought of the western extreme of the inhabited world as "the promontory of Iberia which they call the Sacred Cape" (*Geography* 2.5.14 [Horace Leonard Jones, LCL]; cf. 3.1.4).[58] This was just northwest of Gades, an island city with a large population, a number of prestigious families, and well-established connections to Ostia and Rome (*Geography* 3.5.3).[59] At the western end of the world, then, lay a well-connected urban center not unlike the cities in which Paul had regularly worked in the east.[60] A number of other cities further east on the Iberian Peninsula, however, had connections with Rome and would have provided fertile ground for the proclamation of the gospel to the "barbarians" that Paul mentions in 1:14.[61] Roman people had been in the region of Tarraco on the east coast of Spain at least since the

54. Ibid., 282, 283. Cf. Chrysostom (*Romans*, 467–68), who explains Paul's reference to seeing the Romans only in passing as an attempt to keep the Romans from being haughty. He also sees Paul's references to needing their help in getting to Rome and enjoying their company for a while as attempts to keep them from being distressed. Theodoret of Cyrus, similarly, thinks that Paul's reference to seeing the Romans "first," before going to Spain, was an effort to smooth feathers ruffled by his revelation that Spain, not Rome, was his destination (*Letters of St. Paul*, 1:133).

55. Cf. Lagrange, *Romains*, 357.

56. Allan Chapple, "Why Spain? Paul and His Mission Plans," *Journal for the Study of Paul and His Letters* 1 (2011): 206–12.

57. Ibid., 204–6.

58. Ibid., 206. Cf. Schnabel, *Paul and the Early Church*, 1281.

59. "The Sacred Cape" is today's Cape St. Vincent, Portugal, and "Gades" is Cádiz, Spain. On mid first-century Gades, or Gadeira in Greek, see E. Earle Ellis, "'The End of the Earth' (Acts 1:8)," *BBR* 1 (1991): 127, 131–32, and Roy D. Kotansky, "Jesus and Heracles in Cádiz (τὰ Γάδειρα): Death, Myth, and Monsters at the 'Straits of Gibraltar' (Mark 4:35–5:43)," in *Ancient and Modern Perspectives on the Bible and Culture: Essays in Honor of Hans Dieter Betz*, ed. Adela Yarbro Collins (Atlanta: Scholars Press, 1998), 190–92.

60. Diodorus Siculus (writing in the first-century BC) describes Gades as "at the farthest extremity of the inhabited world, on the very ocean" (*Bibliotheca historica* 25.10.1 [Francis R. Walton, LCL]).

61. Jewett, *Romans*, 79.

third-century BC, and the influential first-century Romans Seneca the Younger, Martial, and Quintilian all came from cities in Spain.[62]

Paul hopes that after an enjoyable and substantial visit with the Roman believers, they will "send" him "on" (προπέμπω) to Spain. This expression could mean anything from sending him off "with prayers and good wishes" to outfitting him with "companions, food, money, and perhaps a means for travel by sea."[63] In a context like this, the term typically meant to send someone on their way in safety and with emotional support. This might involve, for example, letters of introduction, native companions for travel, or simply a supportive crowd of well-wishers at the dock (e.g., 1 Macc 12:4; Jdt 10:15; Acts 21:5; Josephus, *Ant.* 5.99). When Paul uses the term elsewhere, he seems to mean something more than a warm send-off: spending an entire winter in Corinth will prepare the Corinthians to send him on to Judea (1 Cor 16:6; 2 Cor 1:16), and when Titus sends Zenas and Apollos on their way, this involves seeing "that they lack nothing" (Titus 3:13). Paul himself may not have been entirely sure what the Romans would do to aid his Spanish venture, but the term communicates that he hopes at least for their heartfelt support of his journey and work there.

15:25 But now I am going to Jerusalem in order to serve the saints (νυνὶ δὲ πορεύομαι εἰς Ἰερουσαλὴμ διακονῶν τοῖς ἁγίοις). Before Paul goes to Rome and then to Spain, he must complete the task that lies directly before him. He intends to deliver relief aid to a needy group of believers in Jerusalem. This was aid he had collected among the churches he had established as he proclaimed the gospel from Jerusalem to Illyricum.

Paul's "but now" (νυνὶ δέ) introduces a complication into the plans he has just described (cf. 15:23). Before going to Rome on his way to Spain, he will travel to Jerusalem in service to God's people there. His use of the present tense (πορεύομαι . . . διακονῶν) indicates the imminence of his journey, and the participle is more likely to describe the purpose of the journey than to stress that the journey itself is part of the service he is performing.[64]

Grammatically, there is no reason that "the saints" (οἱ ἅγιοι) could not be "the saints" in Macedonia and Achaia. Paul's service to the saints, then, would be his work as a courier who would convey the charitable contribution of God's people in Macedonia and Achaia to its destination.[65] This reading brings out a significant nuance of the term Paul uses for his service (διακονῶν): he is acting as a go-between in taking the collection from mainly gentile believers in the west to Jewish believers in the east.[66] But since Paul defines "the saints" in his next sentence specifically as "the saints in Jerusalem" (15:26), it is very unlikely that "the saints" here refers to Macedonian and Achaian believers.[67]

62. Seneca: Corduba; Martial: Bilbilis; Quintilian: Calagurris. See Schnabel, *Paul and the Early Church*, 1277–78, 1280.

63. The first quotation comes from Sanday and Headlam (*Romans*, 411), and the second quotation comes from Hultgren (*Romans*, 552). See also LSJ 1494 and BDAG 873, both s.v. προπέμπω.

64. On the "present of anticipation," see Smyth, *Greek Grammar*, §1879. For the idea that the journey itself is service, see, e.g., Meyer (*Romans*, 554) and Godet (*Romans*, 484). For the participle as an indicator of purpose, see, e.g., Cranfield (*Romans*, 2:771) and Wilckens (*An die Römer [Röm 12–16]*, 124n601).

65. Schlatter, *Romans*, 267–68; Collins, *Diakonia*, 220–21. See the interaction with these scholars on this point in Cranfield (*Romans*, 2:771) and Stephan Joubert (*Paul as Benefactor: Reciprocity, Strategy and Theological Reflection in Paul's Collection*, WUNT 2.124 [Tübingen: Mohr Siebeck, 2000], 208).

66. Collins, *Diakonia*, 220.

67. Cf. Rom 15:31; 1 Cor 16:1; 2 Cor 8:4; 9:1, 12. "The saints" is probably not, therefore, a technical term for the early Jewish community, as in, e.g., Lietzmann (*An die Römer*, 121–23) and Käsemann (*Romans*, 398). On this, see Harris, *Second Epistle to the Corinthians*, 567.

IN DEPTH: Paul's Ministry to the Poor among the Saints in Jerusalem

In three letters, written in close chronological proximity to one another, Paul mentions a collection of funds among his churches in Galatia, Achaia, and Macedonia that he intended to convey, according to Romans 15:26, to "the poor among the saints in Jerusalem" (see 1 Cor 16:1–4; 2 Cor 8:1–9:15; Rom 15:25–32).[68] In addition, Luke alludes to the collection in Paul's defense speech before Felix, procurator of Judea, after Paul's arrest just outside the temple in Jerusalem. A riot had broken out because, according to Paul's accusers, he "brought Greeks into the temple and . . . defiled" it (Acts 21:28). In describing the events that led to this disturbance, Paul told Felix he had come to Jerusalem after several years' absence "to bring alms [ἐλεημοσύνας] to my nation and to present offerings [προσφοράς]" (Acts 24:17).

The terms Paul uses to describe the collection provide a window onto its purposes. In 1 Corinthians 16:1–2 he refers to it as a "collection" (λογεία), a rare and nonliterary term designating collections of various sorts, particularly the collection of money for religious purposes.[69] Around AD 58 in Egypt, for example, Psenamunis, a priest of Isis, issued a receipt to a laborer for money he had given in support of "the collection [λογίαν] of Isis on behalf of the public works."[70]

In 2 Corinthians 8:4 he calls the collection "this ministry [διακονίας] to the saints" (NRSV), emphasizing the humble nature of the collection as an errand of mediation between two parties (cf. Rom 15:31; 2 Cor 9:1, 13; cf. Rom 15:25; 2 Cor 8:19–20).[71] In 2 Corinthians 9:12 he adds a specifically religious nuance to this ordinary word by describing the collection as "the ministry of this service" (ἡ διακονία τῆς λειτουργίας ταύτης) and saying that it will overflow "in many thanksgivings to God." The term "service" (λειτουργία) here not only bears connotations of practical civil service for the common good (e.g., Aristotle, *Politics* 1309a 18–20; cf. Rom 15:27) but also of religious service such as a priest might perform when working in a temple (e.g., Luke 1:23; cf. Rom 15:16).[72]

68. Gal 2:10 is probably not a reference to the collection (e.g., Theodoret, *Letters of St. Paul*, 1:133–34), but a general reference to the continued observance of an important duty to care for the poor in the Jewish and early Christian tradition. On this, see Bruce W. Longenecker (*Remember the Poor: Paul, Poverty and the Greco-Roman World* [Grand Rapids: Eerdmans, 2010], 157–206) and the acceptance of Longenecker's case in Moo (*Galatians*, BECNT [Grand Rapids: Baker, 2013], 139).

69. Deissmann, *Light from the Ancient East*, 104–7; MM 377; LSJ 1055; BDAG 597, all s.v. λογεία.

70. Deissmann, *Light from the Ancient East*, 105, 106n14. Deissmann dates this ostracon to August, AD 63, but PSI 3.262 dates it, with a question mark, to AD 58, just over a year after Paul would have delivered the collection to Jerusalem in the spring of AD 57.

71. If the expression "in this undertaking" (NRSV; cf. CEB) correctly translates the Greek lying beneath 2 Cor 9:4 (ἐν τῇ ὑποστάσει ταύτῃ), then Paul also emphasizes the planning involved in the project (cf., e.g., Diodorus Siculus, *Bibliotheca historica* 15.70.2; BDAG 1040, s.v. ὑπόστασις 2).

72. *TLNT* 2:281–82. On "service" (λειτουργία), see Rudolf Meyer ("λειτουργέω, κτλ.," *TDNT* 4:216); MM 373; LSJ 1036;

Paul also calls the offering a "benefaction" (χάρις) (1 Cor 16:3; 2 Cor 8:6–7, 19; cf. 2 Cor 8:4, 19).[73] It was, then, a gift given as part of a relationship in which gifts were expected to produce a generous response in the recipient. Just as the Roman Senate expected people on whom they had conferred the "favour" (χάριτι) of citizenship to be more faithful and unwavering in their commitment to Rome than ever before (Appian, *Civil Wars* 1.49 [Horace White, LCL]), so Paul expected the Corinthians to give generously to the collection because they knew "the grace [χάριν] of our Lord Jesus Christ, that though he was rich, yet for your sake he became poor, so that you by his poverty might become rich" (2 Cor 8:9; cf. 8:1; 9:14–15).[74] The same idea is probably present when Paul calls the offering a generous "gift" or "blessing" (εὐλογία; 2 Cor 9:5; cf. 9:8), a term that recalls God's generosity toward people in, for example, giving them seed for sowing and bread for food (2 Cor 9:10; cf. 9:6).

When Paul uses the term "partnership" (κοινωνία) to describe the collection (Rom 15:26; 2 Cor 8:4; 9:13; cf. Rom 15:27), his focus is on the mutually beneficial relationship between the givers and the recipients of this "benefaction" (χάρις).[75] The term "partnership" (κοινωνία) was fairly commonly used in social and political settings to describe a friendly alliance in which each party received assistance from the other (e.g., Plato, *Republic* 371b; Isocrates, *Nic.* 40; Demosthenes, *3 Philippic* 28; Polybius, *Histories* 5.35.1).[76]

From this terminology, then, it seems that the collection was a practical, religiously motivated effort to raise money among the churches Paul had established in at least Galatia, Achaia, and Macedonia. This effort had three purposes: to bring relief to the poor, to express the gratitude of gentile Christians to Jewish Christians in Jerusalem for the blessings they had inherited from Israel, and to solidify the partnership already established between gentile and Jewish Christians because of the gentiles' theological indebtedness to the Jews.

The purpose of providing material relief for those in need is already clear from Paul's description of the beneficiaries of the collection as "the poor" (οἱ πτωχοί) in Jerusalem (Rom 15:26). This is not a title of dignity for the earliest

and MGS 1223, all s.v. λειτουργία; and Barclay (*Paul and the Gift*, 32–35).

73. For this translation, see David J. Downs (*The Offering of the Gentiles: Paul's Collection for Jerusalem in Its Chronological, Cultural, and Cultic Contexts*, WUNT 2.248 [Tübingen: Mohr Siebeck, 2008], 131), and cf. Harris (*Second Epistle to the Corinthians*, 572, 604).

74. BDAG 1079, s.v. χάρις 2a. On the connection between 2 Cor 8:1 and 8:6, and on the meaning of "benefaction" (χάρις) here, see Downs, *Offering of the Gentiles*, 131–32, 134–35. On gift-giving in Greco-Roman antiquity, see especially Barclay (*Paul and the Gift*, 24–32), and on the application of this concept to Paul's collection, see G. W. Peterman ("Romans 15.26: Make a Contribution or Establish Fellowship?," *NTS* 40 [1994]: 459–61).

75. See the discussion in Downs, *Offering of the Gentiles*, 15–19.

76. MGS 1149, s.v. κοινωνία A; cf. Peterman, "Romans 15:26," 459, 463; Downs, *Offering of the Gentiles*, 17n55.

Jewish Christian community, as some scholars have argued.[77] Paul's explicit references to the collection as "relief" (NRSV; ἄνεσις) and the designations of those receiving it as having "need" (ὑστέρημα) or as "needy" (πένητες) make it likely that "the poor" refers in an uncomplicated way to people who were struggling to find food, clothing, and shelter (2 Cor 8:13–15; 9:9, 12; cf. Rom 12:13).[78] As Harris has pointed out, this purpose for the collection probably explains why, in Paul's speech before the Ephesian elders on his way to Jerusalem, he touched on the importance of coming to the aid of the weak (Acts 20:35).[79]

As that speech also shows, giving to the poor in Jewish and early Christian thinking was an important act of obedience to God (e.g., Hos 6:6; Tob 4:11; Matt 12:7).[80] It is not surprising, then, to find Paul describing the collection as an appropriate response to Jesus's own greater act of charitable giving in his incarnation and atonement (2 Cor 8:9) and to the material blessings that God has given to the Corinthians (2 Cor 9:6–14).[81] This element of the collection also explains why Paul emphasizes that contributions to it should not arise from any feeling of coercion but from a cheerful, willing heart that is grateful to God "for his inexpressible gift" (2 Cor 9:15; cf. 8:1–5, 8, 12; 9:7; Rom 15:26–27). It is an example of "the obedience of faith" that God had called Paul to bring into existence through the proclamation of the gospel (1:5; cf. 15:18).[82]

In Romans 15:27 Paul describes the collection as the repayment of a debt of gratitude to the Jewish people for the "spiritual" (πνευματικοῖς) elements that the Jewish tradition handed down to gentile believers. He was probably thinking of the Jewish privileges he had mentioned at various points in the letter's preceding argument (3:2; 9:4–5) and that were a source of nourishment and support for gentile believers (11:17–18; cf. 4:23–25; 15:4; Eph 2:11–16, 19–20). These spiritual gifts had made gentile believers "debtors" (ὀφειλέται) to Jewish fellow believers (15:27). It would be a mistake, however, to take this expression of indebtedness as the introduction of an element of coercion into the

77. E.g., Ernst Bammel, "πτωχός," *TDNT* 6:909; Byrne, *Romans*, 444. Cf. Michel (*An die Römer*, 465) and Dunn (*Romans 9–16*, 875), who view this as a possibility, and Dieter Georgi (*Remembering the Poor: The History of Paul's Collection for Jerusalem*, trans. Ingrid Racz [Nashville: Abingdon, 1992], 37), who defines "the poor" this way only in Gal 2:20. Georgi recognizes that in Rom 15:26 "the poor among the saints in Jerusalem" is more an economic than a religious description (ibid., 114).

78. For the reference to Rom 12:13, I am indebted to Ernst Bammel ("πτωχός," *TDNT* 6:909), who cites Michel (*An die Römer*, 386).

79. Harris, *Second Epistle to the Corinthians*, 91.

80. Keith F. Nickle, *The Collection: A Study in Paul's Strategy*, Studies in Biblical Theology 48 (London: SCM, 1966), 101; Gary A. Anderson, *Charity: The Place of the Poor in the Biblical Tradition* (New Haven: Yale University Press, 2013), 104–10.

81. On Jesus's impoverishment according to 2 Cor 8:9, see Harris (*Second Epistle to the Corinthians*, 577–81).

82. Reimund Bieringer, "The Jerusalem Collection and Paul's Missionary Project: Collection and Mission in Romans 15.14–32," in *The Last Years of Paul: Essays from the Tarragona Conference, June 2013*, ed. Armand Puig i Tàrrech, John M. G. Barclay, and Jörg Frey, WUNT 352 (Tübingen: Mohr Siebeck, 2015), 24–25, 30.

collection.[83] Paul makes clear in Romans 15:26–27 that those who gave to the collection did so because they "were pleased" (ηὐδόκησαν) to contribute to it.

It is more likely that the language of indebtedness forms part of the idea of partnership that was also an important motivation for the collection. In Romans 11:17 Paul had said to his fictional gentile dialogue partner that he had become a "sharer" (συγκοινωνός) in Israel's spiritually nourishing traditions. Since in Romans 15:26 the language of "partnership" (κοινωνία) hints at a mutually beneficial alliance with useful contributions to the common welfare from both sides, it seems likely that Paul understood the collection as an opportunity to strengthen the bonds of friendship between his predominantly gentile churches in Galatia, Achaia, Macedonia, and Asia and the predominantly Jewish believers in Jerusalem. Paul was already eager to remember the poor before the Jerusalem apostles ever mentioned it to him (Gal 2:10) because it was simply a crucial element of obedience to God for Jews and Christians.[84] Still, meeting the needs of poor Jewish believers in Jerusalem had the added benefit of clearly showing the partnership, across ethnic and social lines, of gentile and Jewish Christians. Paul's request that the Roman believers join him in prayer that his "ministry to Jerusalem" might be "acceptable" to the saints there (Rom 15:31) shows how intensely he hoped the Jewish Christians in Jerusalem felt the same way.

Paul's ministry to "the poor among the saints in Jerusalem," then, was hardly just a pesky delay in his effort to get to Rome and on to Spain. It was a practical expression of a primary theme of the gospel as Paul has explained it in the letter (e.g., 1:16; 3:22–23, 29–30; 4:11–12; 9:4–5; 11:17–18). This same theme also needed appropriation among believers in Rome in the midst of their own divisions over the relationship between gentile and Jewish Christianity (14:1–15:13). Paul must have hoped that as the Romans fought alongside him in prayer for the success of this ministry (15:30–31), they would pray for and work toward the healing of their own divisions.

15:26 For Macedonia and Achaia were pleased to enter into a certain partnership with the poor among the saints in Jerusalem (εὐδόκησαν γὰρ Μακεδονία καὶ Ἀχαΐα κοινωνίαν τινὰ ποιήσασθαι εἰς τοὺς πτωχοὺς τῶν ἁγίων τῶν ἐν Ἰερουσαλήμ). Paul explains further that his practical service to believers in Jerusalem involved conveying relief aid to the needy among the believers there from believers in Macedonia and Achaia who were in a mutually beneficial partnership with the Jerusalem church.

Paul's compressed reference to his impending journey to Jerusalem in the service of the saints (15:25) required further explanation since he could

83. Bieringer, "Jerusalem Collection," 28.

84. Moo, *Galatians*, 139.

not assume his Roman audience knew about this relief project. "For" (γάρ) introduces this further explanation. The voluntary nature of the collection is clear from the verb "were pleased" (εὐδόκησαν) and is consistent with Paul's emphasis on giving joyfully and voluntarily to the collection in 2 Corinthians (2 Cor 8:2–5, 8, 11–12; 9:5, 7). Paul's language of obligation in the next sentence (Rom 15:27), then, should not be understood to mean that the collection was a formal requirement or a burden.

The phrase "to enter into . . . a partnership" (κοινωνίαν . . . ποιήσασθαι) was often used of entering a mutually beneficial social or political relationship such as a marriage, the formation of a state, or an alliance of mutual support among political leaders.[85] As Chrysostom comments, Paul speaks of facilitating a "partnership" (κοινωνίαν), not of carrying "alms" (ἐλεημοσύνην ἀποφέρων).[86] In both his world and in Paul's there was a difference between the two ideas, with "partnership" (κοινωνίαν) indicating mutuality. The Macedonians and Achaians, then, were not merely making a contribution or sharing their resources with the needy people in Jerusalem, as most English translations put it, but doing their part in a mutually beneficial social relationship (15:27).[87]

"The poor" (οἱ πτωχοί) is not an honorific title for the early Jewish Christian community in Jerusalem, as scholars have sometimes thought, but a reference to people in economic distress.[88] This is clear from Paul's emphasis on the need for economic equality among believers in his appeal to the Corinthians to contribute to the collection and in his claim, in that same context, that the collection will provide relief for those in need (2 Cor 8:13–15; 9:12).[89]

Paul mentions the contributions of Macedonia and Achaia to the collection, but makes no mention of Galatia despite having raised funds for the collection there (1 Cor 16:1). Similarly, Luke names delegates from Macedonia, Galatia, and Asia, but no one from Achaia (Acts 20:4). When Paul wrote to the Romans from Corinth in Achaia (16:1–2), he had just been to Macedonia (Acts 20:1–2), and so he may have only mentioned the most recent and geographically closest contributors at the time of writing. The absence of anyone from Corinth in Luke's list is more of a mystery, but it is possible that the Corinthians decided not to send a delegate with Paul despite contributing to the collection.[90]

15:27 For they were pleased, and they are their debtors, for if the gentiles have shared in their spiritual things, they also are indebted to serve them in fleshly things (εὐδόκησαν γάρ καὶ ὀφειλέται εἰσὶν αὐτῶν· εἰ γὰρ τοῖς πνευματικοῖς αὐτῶν ἐκοινώνησαν τὰ ἔθνη, ὀφείλουσιν καὶ ἐν τοῖς σαρκικοῖς λειτουργῆσαι αὐτοῖς). The practical, material help that gentile believers in Macedonia and Achaia were sending to needy believers in Jerusalem was a willing effort to bring balance to their partnership in light of the spiritual blessings they had received through their incorporation into God's people.

85. E.g., respectively, Isocrates, *Nic.* 40; Plato, *Republic* 371b; Demosthenes, *3 Philippic* 28; Polybius, *Histories* 5.35.1. Cf. MGS 1149–50, s.v. κοινωνία A, and cf. Downs, *Offering of the Gentiles*, 17n55.

86. Chrysostom, *Romans*, 474 (*PG* 60:661).

87. The French TOB comes close to this idea with its rendering "Macédoine et l'Achaïe ont décidé de manifester leur solidarité à l'égard des saints de Jérusalem" ("Macedonia and Achaia have decided to show their solidarity with the saints in Jerusalem").

88. For the idea that "the poor" is a technical term for the early Jewish Christian community in Jerusalem, see, e.g., Lietzmann (*An die Römer*, 123) and Ernst Bammel, "πτωχός," *TDNT* 6:909.

89. Leander Keck, "The Poor among the Saints in the New Testament," *ZNW* 56 (1965): 120–23.

90. In 1 Cor 16:3–4 Paul seems to leave the matter of sending a delegate to the Corinthians' discretion.

The first "for" (γάρ) in this verse introduces a qualification of Paul's statement that the Macedonians and Achaians "were pleased" to partner with the Jerusalem believers. These mainly gentile churches certainly gave freely, but they also owed what they gave to their Jerusalem partners as the fulfillment of their side of the mutually beneficial relationship they had with them.

The second "for" (γάρ) begins an explanation of that relationship. The gentile believers in Macedonia and Achaia had "shared" (ἐκοινώνησαν) in the spiritual benefits (τοῖς πνευματικοῖς) of the Jerusalem believers, and now the gentiles were responding with practically and religiously oriented material help. The verb "serve" (λειτουργέω) was commonly used of practical, material assistance in performing a religious duty of some type (e.g., Sir 45:15; Dionysius of Halicarnassus, *Ant. rom.* 2.22.2; *SIG* 717.29).[91] The "spiritual things" (τὰ πνευματικά) that the Jerusalem church had given the gentile believers in Macedonia and Achaia were probably the blessings of Israel in which these gentiles now shared because of their faith in Israel's Messiah (cf. Rom 3:2; 4:23–25; 9:4–5; 11:17–18; 15:4; cf. Eph 2:11–16, 19–20).[92]

15:28 Having therefore completed this obligation and sealed for them this fruit, I will depart for Spain via you (τοῦτο οὖν ἐπιτελέσας καὶ σφραγισάμενος αὐτοῖς τὸν καρπὸν τοῦτον, ἀπελεύσομαι δι' ὑμῶν εἰς Σπανίαν). In summary, once Paul has fulfilled the important task of safely delivering the gentiles' relief aid to Jerusalem, he will set out for Spain and visit Rome along the way.

"Therefore" (οὖν) introduces a summary (15:28–29) of the reason for his trip to Jerusalem and the place that it occupies in his future itinerary. The verb "complete" (ἐπιτελέω) could refer to bringing a particular project to its planned conclusion (2 Cor 8:6, 11), the fulfillment of a duty (Heb 9:6), or the payment of some monetary obligation, such as tribute (Herodotus, *Histories* 2.109; 5.49, 82, 84).[93] Since Paul has just used words that refer to a financial obligation (ὀφειλέται, ὀφείλουσιν; 15:27), the neuter pronoun "this" (τοῦτο) might stand for the implied neuter word for "debt" or "obligation" (ὀφείλημα). If so, then Paul may have intended the expression "having . . . completed" (ἐπιτελέσας) to carry connotations of fulfilling a financial responsibility.

"Fruit" (καρπός) is a natural metaphor for the completed collection. Paul had told the Corinthians at an earlier stage of the project, when he was still urging them to contribute to it, that the God who "supplies seed to the sower and bread for food" would "supply and multiply" their "seed for sowing and increase the harvest of" their "righteousness" (2 Cor 9:10). The completed collection is part of that fruitful harvest. "Fruit" was also an appropriate metaphor for the payment of a financial obligation, a payment that in an agrarian context was often part of a farmer's harvest (Matt 21:33–44).

Containers holding goods for shipment, including agricultural products such as seed, were often "sealed" (cf. σφραγισάμενος) to make any tampering evident and to insure an intact delivery.[94] Since Paul has used so much commercial language in this context, it is likely that this metaphor follows that pattern and refers to the safe delivery of the collection.[95]

91. Hermann Strathmann, "λειτουργεω, κτλ.," *TDNT* 4:218; *TLNT* 2:380–81, s.v. λειτουργέω. Cf. the comments on "servant" (λειτουργός) in 15:16 above.

92. See also Chrysostom (*Romans*, 474–75), Pelagius (*Romans*, 150), and Theodoret of Cyrus (*Letters of St. Paul*, 1:134).

93. LSJ 665, s.v. ἐπιτελέω III; MM 247, s.v. ἐπιτελέω.

94. MM 617, s.v. σφραγίζω.

95. BDAG 980, s.v. σφραγίζω 5; Dunn, *Romans 9–16*, 877; Jewett, *Romans*, 931–32.

15:29 And I know that when I come to you, I will come bringing Christ's total blessing (οἶδα δὲ ὅτι ἐρχόμενος πρὸς ὑμᾶς ἐν πληρώματι εὐλογίας Χριστοῦ ἐλεύσομαι). After Paul has safely delivered the collection to the Jewish believers in Jerusalem, he is certain that Christ will also go with him to Rome and enable him, by the Spirit's power, to strengthen the believers there in their faith.

Paul's "and" (δέ) shifts the thought back to the description of his route to Rome in 15:24, and the perfect tense "I know" (οἶδα) describes his settled confidence that he will bring with him the blessing of Christ. That "blessing" (εὐλογία) was probably a "spiritual gift" (χάρισμα . . . πνευματικόν) of "some" sort (τι) that he hoped to share with the Roman believers when he finally arrived and by which he hoped they would be strengthened (1:11). Paul may speak of the fullness or totality (πληρώματι) of that blessing because he was thinking of the joy he would feel when the collection project was complete (cf. 15:32).[96]

15:30 Now I appeal to you, brothers and sisters, through our Lord Jesus Christ and through the love of the Spirit to fight alongside me in prayers to God on my behalf (Παρακαλῶ δὲ ὑμᾶς, ἀδελφοί, διὰ τοῦ κυρίου ἡμῶν Ἰησοῦ Χριστοῦ καὶ διὰ τῆς ἀγάπης τοῦ πνεύματος συναγωνίσασθαί μοι ἐν ταῖς προσευχαῖς ὑπὲρ ἐμοῦ πρὸς τὸν θεόν). Paul appeals to his Roman audience to join him in the prayer battle he is waging against any forces in Jerusalem that might try to frustrate his plan to aid his gentile churches in showing solidarity with their Jewish Christian brothers and sisters and in fulfilling their theological obligation to them.

"Now" (δέ) signals the beginning of a new paragraph (cf., e.g., 16:17; 1 Cor 1:10), and the expression "I appeal" (παρακαλῶ) introduces a personal request based on a common bond of love (cf. 2 Cor 10:1–2; Phlm 8–10).[97] The two prepositional phrases beginning with "through" (διά) give the basis for the appeal (cf. Rom 12:1; 1 Cor 1:10; 2 Cor 10:1). Although Paul would have been unknown to many within the Christian community at Rome, he could make such a personal request on the basis of their common acknowledgement of the authority of the Lord Jesus Christ and on the basis of the love that the Spirit effects in the lives of believers (cf. Rom 5:5; Gal 5:22).

Paul requests that they might "fight alongside" (συναγωνίσασθαι) him in prayer for himself. This middle-voice term could simply mean "assist," such as when Josephus used it to describe King David's request that the people "assist" Solomon in building the temple (Josephus, *Ant.* 7.376 [Ralph Marcus, LCL]), but it was also often used in the context of war.[98] Diodorus Siculus, writing in the first-century BC, for example, could use the term in an expression similar to Paul's to describe sending Greek ambassadors to various neutral Greek cities in order "to urge [παρακαλέσοντας] them to join in the struggle [συναγωνίζεσθαι]" against the Persian invasion (Diodorus Siculus, *Bibliotheca historica* 11.3.3 [C. H. Oldfather, LCL]). In light of the conflict Paul hopes to avoid in Jerusalem (Rom 15:31), he probably meant to use a live metaphor for the formation of an alliance in the context of a conflict. The stakes were so high because the collection for the poor in Jerusalem was both the fulfillment of a theological debt that gentile believers owed to

96. Cf. Moo, *Romans*, 907.

97. This term can introduce an authoritative exhortation about how one ought to live (e.g., Rom 12:1; 1 Cor 4:16; Eph 4:1; Heb 13:22), and many commentators (e.g., Käsemann, *Romans*, 407; Dunn, *Romans 9–16*, 878; Schreiner, *Romans*, 781) take it that way here. Paul's request here, however, is for himself, and this makes the usage more like that in Phlm 8–10. Cf. Cranfield (*Romans*, 2:776).

98. LSJ 1692; BDAG 963–64, both s.v. συναγωνίζομαι. The translation "fight alongside" comes from MGS 2018, s.v. συναγωνίζω B. Cf. Origen, *Romans, Books 6–10*, 288–89.

the Jews and a sign of the practical partnership in the gospel that gentile and Jewish Christians had with each other (15:27; cf. 3:22–23, 29–30; 4:11–12; 9:4–5; 11:17–18).

15:31 in order that I might be rescued from the disobedient in Judea and my ministry to Jerusalem might be acceptable to the saints (ἵνα ῥυσθῶ ἀπὸ τῶν ἀπειθούντων ἐν τῇ Ἰουδαίᾳ καὶ ἡ διακονία μου ἡ εἰς Ἰερουσαλὴμ εὐπρόσδεκτος τοῖς ἁγίοις γένηται). Paul hopes that the prayer battle he wants the Romans to wage with him will have two results. He hopes he will not encounter physical violence at the hands of Judeans opposed to the gospel and that believers in Judea will accept his efforts in conveying the collection to them as a sign of the solidarity that gentile and Jewish believers have with each other.

Paul now describes the purpose (ἵνα) of the prayers he has just requested. The term "rescue" (ῥύομαι) is a strong expression appropriate for describing deliverance from deadly peril (2 Cor 1:10; cf. Matt 27:43; 2 Tim 3:11; 4:17), and that is probably what Paul has in mind here. "The disobedient [ἀπειθούντων] in Judea" are not merely nonbelieving Jews but Jews who, like Paul himself prior to his conversion, actively oppose the gospel (2:8; 11:30–31; cf. Acts 14:2).[99]

Paul's "ministry [διακονία] to Jerusalem" was Paul's work of conveying the collection from Macedonia and Achaia to Jerusalem (cf. 2 Cor 8:4; 9:1, 12–13).[100] The scribe who replaced the term translated "ministry" (διακονία) with a later and less ambiguous expression meaning "bringing of presents" (δωροφορία) captured the nuance that Paul probably intended to communicate about his role in the collection.[101] He was a courier—a go-between—on an important "errand" (REB) for his predominantly gentile churches in the Aegean area.

The term "acceptable" (εὐπρόσδεκτος) could be used to describe something "acceptable" to God, such as an attitude (2 Cor 8:12) or sacrifices (1 Pet 2:5), and Paul has just used it that way in Romans 15:16. He did not simply hope, then, that the believers in Jerusalem would appreciate the monetary gift he was bringing, but that they would understand and accept the theological implications of the collection. The collection was a demonstration that gentile and Jewish believers in Christ were unified with, and supportive of, one another as members of the people of God.

Luke's account of Paul's visit to Jerusalem reveals that God answered Paul's prayers. It is true, as many interpreters have pointed out, that Paul faced some Jewish Christian resistance on his arrival (Acts 21:20b–22), but "the brothers" who met him "received [him] gladly" (ἀσμένως ἀπεδέξαντο) and "James, and all the elders" "glorified God" when Paul described his ministry (διακονία) among the gentiles (Acts 21:17–20a).[102] It is also true that unbelieving Jews tried to kill Paul in Jerusalem (21:27–36; 22:32; 23:12–22), but God protected him and his life was spared (23:11).

99. BDAG 99, s.v. ἀπειθέω; Dunn, *Romans 9–16*, 878–89.

100. See on 12:7 above. See also BDAG 230, s.v. διακονία 1 and Collins (*Diakonia*, 217–21).

101. See LSJ 465, s.v. δωροφορία. This early textual variant appears in both the Alexandrian (B) and Western traditions (D F G) about a century and a half after the term begins to show up in the extant Greek literature of the second century (Pollux, *Onom.* 4.47; Aelian, *Nature of Animals* 10.48; Alciphron, *Epistulae* 6.3; 28.4).

102. Against the tendency among some scholars to question Luke's veracity here (e.g., Georgi, *Remembering the Poor*, 125), Craig S. Keener points out that "Luke's 'we' is present for this session (Acts 21:18); whatever his slant, his is an eyewitness report of the meeting and the only one available to us." Keener also produces a persuasive argument that Luke's picture of James as a peace maker fits what is known about James from other evidence about him (*Acts: An Exegetical Commentary*, 4 vols. [Grand Rapids: Baker, 2014], 3:3114).

15:32 with the result that I will come to you in joy, by the will of God, and will rest together with you (ἵνα ἐν χαρᾷ ἐλθὼν πρὸς ὑμᾶς διὰ θελήματος θεοῦ συναναπαύσωμαι ὑμῖν). Paul wants his delivery of the collection to be successful in the two ways he has just described because he wants to experience the happiness that comes from the peace and reconciliation God gives to his people across the social barriers that would otherwise divide them. He hopes to arrive in Rome in that frame of mind and to continue to experience that kind of rest during his visit with the Romans themselves. He knows that all this is possible only if God wills it.

Paul next describes the result (ἵνα) of a successful delivery of the collection for his visit to Rome.[103] He often associated "joy" with peace (14:17; 15:13; cf. Gal 5:22) and spoke of joy in his own life especially in contexts where he and the churches he had founded had experienced reconciliation with each other and were living in unity (2 Cor 2:3; 7:4, 13; Phil 2:2). Paul probably mentioned "joy" here, then, because he hoped the collection would create unity between the gentile believers who gave it and the Jewish believers who received it. He hopes to arrive in Rome in a joyful frame of mind because of this unity.

He may have also hoped this joy would spill over into the Roman church and heal some of the social divisions he had just addressed in 14:1–15:13 (cf. 14:17; 15:13). This would explain why Paul used the very odd verb "rest together with you" (συναναπαύσωμαι ὑμῖν) at this point. This term normally means to "sleep with" someone, an idea that is puzzlingly ill-suited to its context here. The only other appearance of this word in either the LXX or the NT, however, is Isaiah 11:6 where it refers to the reconciliation between formerly warring parties that will characterize the messianic age: when "the root from the stump of Jesse" comes, says Isaiah, he will bring peace to the world and "the leopard shall rest with [συναναπαύσεται] the kid."[104] It seems likely that Paul used the term here because it carried connotations of the peace between people groups that the gospel of the Messiah brings. The enjoyment of this peace, which he hopes will be evident both in Jerusalem and in Rome when he arrives, will bring Paul joy and refreshment.

15:33 May the God of peace be with you all. Amen (ὁ δὲ θεὸς τῆς εἰρήνης μετὰ πάντων ὑμῶν, ἀμήν). Paul prays that God will reconcile believers to one another across the ethnic and theological boundaries that divide them, whether in Jerusalem or in Rome.

Paul frequently refers to God as "the God of peace," especially near a letter's conclusion (16:20; 2 Cor 13:11; 1 Thess 5:23; cf. 2 Thess 3:16). Here, the reference flows naturally out of his appeal to the Roman Christians to be at peace with one another (14:1–15:13), his request that they pray for a peaceful outcome to his collection project (15:30–32), and the allusion he has just made to the eschatological experience of peace that God gives to his diverse people (15:32).[105]

103. On this clause (ἵνα . . .) as a result rather than a purpose clause, see Légasse (*Romains*, 930, 937n91), who cites BDF §391(5).

104. Cf. Jewett (*Romans*, 938), although a reference to Roman unity for the purpose of supporting Paul's Spanish mission seems to read too much into the context.

105. Cf. Theodoret of Cyrus (*Letters of St. Paul*, 1:135): "He also prayed for it [peace] for them in view of the arguments they were having with one another over the observances of the Law," and Calvin (*Romans*, 319), who writes: "The words *of peace* refer, I think, to their circumstances at the time, and is a prayer that God, who is the author of peace, may hold them all together."

Theology in Application

In this section, Paul explains how his calling to "be a minister of Christ Jesus to the gentiles" (15:16) prompted the letter to the Romans and continues to guide the course of his life. These comments teach us something about the continuing authority of the letter as Christian Scripture and about the nature of the gospel that Romans explains.

Romans as Christian Scripture

When Paul says that he has "written very boldly in part as a reminder to" the Roman Christians "because of the grace given to me by God" (15:15), he grounds the authority of the letter in the divine character of his apostolic vocation, just as he had done in the letter's opening paragraph (1:1, 5). Although the phrase "very boldly in part" refers to 12:1–15:13, the argument preceding that section (1:16–11:36) provides the necessary theological foundation for the admonitions it contains. This implies that Paul viewed the entire letter as a product of his apostolic authority. As an apostolic witness to the nature of the gospel, then, the letter carries canonical authority for the church.[106]

As Paul explains elsewhere in his letters, he did not confer this apostolic status on himself. Rather God conferred it upon him and gave ample testimony to Paul's calling in three ways. First, the risen Christ had appeared to him (Gal 1:1, 12, 16), and this was a necessary qualification for an apostle (1 Cor 15:3–11; cf. Acts 1:22). Second, other believers confirmed the appearance of Christ to Paul and his calling to be an apostle (Gal 1:2; 1:18–2:2). Third, the miracles that accompanied Paul's preaching of the gospel testified to his apostolic authority (Rom 15:19; 2 Cor 12:12; Gal 3:5).[107] The divine origin of his apostleship explains why Paul could consider his priestly work of bringing the offering of the gentiles to God as a point of pride (καύχησις, 15:17). This was not personal pride in his own accomplishments but pride in what God was doing through him (δι᾽ ἐμοῦ) to bring about the obedience of the gentiles (15:18). Wherever in the church Paul's letter to the Romans is faithfully explained and applied, Paul's work as the apostle to the gentiles continues.

Neither the church nor the individual believer, therefore, gives to Romans its canonical authority. God called Paul at a particular point in history to take the good news of salvation through Christ to the nations, and Paul executed his commission not only by orally proclaiming this message but by setting it down in written form

106. See the "Theology in Application" section on 1:1–7 above and the argument of Herman N. Ridderbos, *Redemptive History and the New Testament Scriptures*, trans. H. De Jongste and Richard B. Gaffin, 2nd ed. (Phillipsburg, NJ: Presbyterian and Reformed, 1988), 12–15.

107. Cf. Stott, *Romans*, 381.

in Romans. The church certainly calls upon people to recognize this authority, but it does not confer this authority on texts such as Romans.[108]

Similarly, the authority of the Scriptures may resonate with the feelings of the individual believer, but such feelings are far from an infallible guide to what is actually authoritative. Only God is able to appoint an apostle, and only a text that is in close touch historically with the apostolic tradition can qualify as authoritative Scripture.[109] Romans, therefore, is an invaluable canonical touchstone. Here an apostle, certified by both God and the earliest Christian community, explains the gospel and applies it to the life of God's people in a particular time and place.

The Gospel's Universal Outreach

Paul's comments on his past missionary labors and future plans demonstrate both the gospel's universal and multiethnic scope on one hand and, on the other hand, its historical, even ethnic, particularity. Its multiethnic scope has been evident throughout the letter, from Paul's introduction of himself to the Romans as one who had "received grace and apostleship for the obedience of faith among all the gentiles on behalf of his name" (1:5) to his concluding claim that he has just written them so boldly because God had graciously made him "a priest with respect to the gospel of God, so that the offering of the gentiles might be acceptable, sanctified by the Holy Spirit" (15:15).

In this passage it becomes clear that God's impartiality (cf. 2:11; 10:12–13) and his authority over all peoples as the one God of the universe (cf. 3:29–30; 4:11–12, 16) are not merely abstract theological principles. Nor are they simply ethical principles that generate unity among those who are already believers. In addition, the universal scope of the gospel implies that the church needs to be vigorously engaged in taking the good news of reconciliation to God through Jesus Christ to all human beings everywhere.

This missionary mandate is not the product of a single command to evangelize given somewhere in the course of the letter but is implicit in the nature of the gospel itself.[110] God is not merely the national God of Israel in the same way that Roma was the personification of Roman power.[111] The gospel claims that God is the one God of all creation and that although he has used the nation of Israel for his saving purposes, he is the God of all nations (3:30; 8:19–23).

Just as Paul's apostolic authority infuses Romans and makes it authoritative for all Christians, so Paul's eagerness to recruit the Roman Christians to aid him in taking

108. Herman Bavinck, *Prolegomena*, vol. 1 of *Reformed Dogmatics*, ed. John Bolt, trans. John Vriend (Grand Rapids: Baker, 2003), 456–57.

109. Ridderbos, *Redemptive History*, 30–38.

110. Wright, *Mission of God*, 522–30, 531–32.

111. Beard, North, and Price, *Religions of Rome*, 1:158–60.

the gospel to Spain is an implicit call to all Christians to join in the work of taking the gospel to the nations. The work of establishing communities of people around the world who worship God through Christ and live as God's people in the power of the Spirit (15:16) is far from complete.

The Gospel's Indebtedness to Israel's Traditions

At the same time that this passage calls upon all believers to bear witness to the worldwide character of the gospel, it also reminds the church of its indebtedness to the traditions of Israel and of the need to acknowledge this indebtedness in practical ways (15:27; cf. 11:17–18). The passage implies that non-Jewish Christians should be especially supportive of Jewish Christians. This may mean, as it did for Paul, being aware of the physical and material needs of poor Jewish Christians elsewhere in the world, but it is more likely, given the centuries of tension between Judaism and Christianity, that the practical help the church can give to Jewish Christians will come in the form of dialogue and empathy. Jewish Christians who seek to continue to live as Jews often face misunderstanding both from non-Christian Jews and from non-Jewish Christians.[112] Their efforts to live as Jews who believe the gospel as Paul explains it in Romans involve thinking through complex theological questions that have been raised for them by the church's tragic history of Jewish persecution. Patience, understanding, and help from their gentile Christian brothers and sisters as they work through these issues may be one way in which the majority gentile Christian church of more recent times can acknowledge the debt they have to Israel.[113]

The Gospel's Commitment to the Poor

Paul's ministry to the poor among the saints in Jerusalem also has broader implications for the mission of the church. As we saw in the "In Depth" section above on Paul's ministry to the poor among the saints in Jerusalem, Paul was concerned for needy Jewish Christians not only because they were Jewish but because they were poor, and God is deeply concerned for the needs of the poor.

Paul's concern for the poor reminds us that as the church advances through the world with the message of the gospel, it also needs to reach out to the world in compassion for the needy. As Paul hints in 15:26, and as he explains more fully in 2 Corinthians 8:1–5, 8, 12; 9:5, and especially 9:7, this giving should arise from a joyful, inner generosity that origninates in one's own experience of "the grace of our Lord Jesus Christ." It may also involve some trouble and even risk. Paul had to interrupt

112. For a concise chronicle of these difficulties, see David Rudolph, "Messianic Judaism in Antiquity and in the Modern Era," in Rudolph and Willitts, *Messianic Judaism*, 24–35.

113. Cf. Keener, "Interdependence and Mutual Blessing," in Rudolph and Willitts, *Messianic Judaism*, 193.

his long-term plans to travel west to Rome and Spain in order to go east to Jerusalem with his gift (Rom 15:24–25, 28), and he was sure neither that his gift would be accepted nor that he would avoid physical harm (15:31). Despite the sacrifice that meeting the needs of the poor entails, like Paul and the churches of Macedonia, Achaia, and Galatia the church today needs to couple its preaching of the good news about Jesus with practical help for the needy.

Romans 15:14–33, therefore, demonstrates both the broad implications of the gospel and the basis of the church's authority to call all people to believe it. If God raised Jesus from the dead and then established him as king over the universe (1:3–4), and if this same God called Paul to bring to the entire world a message about the significance of these events (1:5), and if Paul left that message in written form in his letter to the Romans, then the church also has the authority and the mandate to take this gospel to the world. As it does this, it needs to be as mindful as Isaiah, Jesus, and Paul that the gospel is "good news to the poor" (Isa 61:1; Luke 4:18).

CHAPTER 32

Romans 16:1–16

Literary Context

Paul closed the immediately preceding section of the letter (15:14–33) with a prayer that "the God of peace" would be with the Roman believers (15:33). Such a reference is not unique or even unusual for the end of a Pauline letter (cf. 2 Cor 13:11; Phil 4:9; 1 Thess 5:23), but in Romans it has a special, summarizing function. It comes at the end of Paul's extensive argument that the strong and the weak in Rome should welcome one another (Rom 15:7; cf. 14:1; 15:1), and after the discussion of his project to draw Jewish and gentile Christians together through the collection for needy believers in Jerusalem (15:25–29). That Paul intended the prayer of 15:33 to conclude this section is clear from the "amen" at its end.[1]

His letter, however, was far from finished. Before releasing his audience, he observed two epistolary customs. He commended the letter's courier, and he urged his audience to greet people in their midst that he knew either personally or by reputation. This sounds rather humdrum at the formal level, but the unusual features of these standard epistolary elements demonstrate that they were intended to advance one of the primary purposes of the letter in an important, practical way. They promote the mutual, familial love that Paul has been encouraging explicitly within the Roman community since 12:1.

Paul does not typically follow the custom of commending the letter courier in his letters, and in the two other places that such commendations appear at the end of a letter (Eph 4:21–22; Col 4:7–8), these commendations are brief. Here, however, Paul commends Phoebe at greater length and urges the Romans to "welcome her in the Lord in a way worthy of the saints" (16:2). He wants them to put into practice with Phoebe the principles of love, humility, harmony, and hospitality that he has urged them to practice with one another in 12:9–16 and 14:1–15:13.

In the same way, although sending personal greetings to one's relatives and friends was a common practice in ancient letters, and Paul observes this practice

1. The "amen" distinguishes this concluding prayer for peace from those found in 1 Thess 5:23, 2 Thess 3:16, and Phil 4:9 (*pace* Longenecker, *Introducing Romans*, 446).

occasionally in other places (Col 4:15; 2 Tim 4:15), nothing elsewhere in his letters compares to the lengthy list of greetings in Romans 16:3–16. Paul urges his audience to greet twenty-four named individuals, two others who are not named, and six discreet groups of individuals (including the letter's audience itself). Why Paul did this is not clear, and interpreters have often made guesses. Perhaps he wanted to support local leaders and point out righteous people for imitation, or prepare the way for Phoebe's visit and his own eventual visit by providing a list of supporters, or show the whole Roman church that he had a sizeable group of supporters, or bring his supporters in contact with the rest of the church.[2]

It is probably impossible at this distance to know why Paul wanted to greet so many specific people in this particular letter, but the effect of the greetings would have been to bring a socially diverse group of individuals together, urge them to show publicly their affection for one another, and publicly honor a number of people of the lower social classes. Since this effect of the list fits neatly with the theological argument of 1:16–11:36 and with the practical, pastoral advice in 12:1–15:13, it seems likely that encouraging unity was one of the list's purposes.[3]

Paul does not seem to have personally known many of the people he greets since he provides no descriptive phrase for some names and only identifies others by the group to which they belong (16:10c, 11d, 14–15). It is unlikely that drawing attention to them would do anything for Paul or Phoebe, but it would demonstrate to the whole church that Paul knew of their reputation and would probably communicate that he wanted to honor them. Many of those whom he greets, moreover, had names that were common among slaves, freedmen, and immigrants from the east.[4] A number of those whom he commends most highly are women.[5] Whatever lay behind Paul's choice of people to greet, the list certainly demonstrates that the gospel generates a socially diverse group of people who are not valued because of their powerful connections within human culture and society but simply because they are human and part of God's people. The instruction to "greet one another with a holy kiss," moreover, shows that Paul wanted this diverse group to rid itself of any social boundaries in its midst that encouraged pride and divisiveness and to treat one another as loving members of the same family. The Jews in the group (Aquila, Andronicus, Junia, Herodion, and probably Prisca and Miriam) will need to embrace gentiles and be embraced, in turn, by them.

Social division is not, however, the only source of division among believers, and

2. See, respectively, Calvin (*Romans*, 321), Dunn (*Romans 9–16*, 890), Byrne (*Romans*, 450), and Wilckens (*An die Römer [Röm 12–16]*, 133).

3. Jewett, *Romans*, 952.

4. Two-thirds of the names are Greek, and those with Greek names in Rome typically had slavery in their background (Lampe, *From Paul to Valentinus*, 171).

5. Paul greets nine women and seventeen men, but only two of the women, Julia and Nereus's sister (whom Paul probably did not know personally [16:15]), fail to receive a strong commendation for significant service to the Christian community (cf. Lampe, *From Paul to Valentinus*, 165–67). It is unclear to me why Lampe counts eight women (ibid., 165).

so in the next paragraph of his letter (16:17–20) Paul warns his audience against those who may attempt to divide believers in Rome from one another by teaching something other than the traditional gospel they now believe. Paul will then send greetings to the Romans from those who are with him in Corinth as he writes (16:21–23) and conclude the letter with a stirring ascription of praise to God, who has recently revealed in the gospel his purpose of unifying all people groups through their common faith in Jesus Christ (16:25–27).

Main Idea

Paul urges the Romans to put into practice the sort of familial love, humility, and mutual respect that believers should have for one another according to 12:1–15:33. He wants the Roman Christians to do this by showing the sort of hospitality to the letter's carrier, Phoebe, that should characterize God's people generally because of the close ties they have to one another in Christ. He also wants them to do this by honoring a socially diverse group of Christians in Rome whom Paul knows either personally or by reputation. This honor will come in the form of a greeting they give to each other from Paul.

Translation

(See pages 707–08.)

Structure

The passage falls into two parts of unequal length, the commendation of Phoebe (16:1–2) and the greetings (16:3–16). Phoebe's commendation begins with a statement of recommendation (16:1a), followed by Phoebe's name and title (16:1b) and a description of two ways the Roman Christians can help her (16:2).

The much longer greeting section (16:3–16) does not appear to be intricately organized. It uses the second-person plural verb "greet" (ἀσπάσασθε) sixteen times to

Romans 16:1–16

1a Assertion **Now I commend our sister Phoebe to you,**
b who is a deacon in the assembly in Cenchreae,

2a Purpose 1 in order that you might welcome her in the Lord in a way worthy of the saints and
b Purpose 2 might assist her in whatever she needs for [her] undertaking,

c Basis (for 2b) for **she also became a benefactor** of many and especially of me.

3a Exhortation **Greet Prisca and Aquila,**
b my coworkers in Christ Jesus,
4a who laid down their own neck for my life,
b to whom not only I give thanks, but
all the churches of the gentiles
5a Exhortation and
the church in their house.

b Exhortation **Greet my beloved Epaenetus,**
c who is the first fruit of Asia for Christ.

6a Exhortation **Greet Miriam,**
b who has labored hard for you.

7a Exhortation **Greet Andronicus** and
Junia,
b Apposition my compatriots and fellow prisoners,
c who are prominent among the apostles, and
d who were also in Christ before me.

8a Exhortation **Greet Ampliatus,**
b Apposition my beloved in the Lord.

9a Exhortation **Greet Urbanus,**
b Apposition/Description our coworker in Christ,

9c Exhortation and
my beloved Stachys.

10a Exhortation **Greet Apelles,**
b Description tried and true in Christ.

c Exhortation **Greet those from the household of Aristobulus.**

11a Exhortation **Greet Herodion,**
b Apposition my compatriot.

Continued on next page.

Continued from previous page.

c	Exhortation	**Greet those**
d		from the household of Narcissus
e		who are in the Lord.
12a	Exhortation	**Greet Tryphena** and
		Tryphosa,
b	Apposition/ Description	those hard workers in the Lord.
c	Exhortation	**Greet beloved Persis,**
d		who has worked very hard in the Lord.
13a	Exhortation	**Greet Rufus,**
b		chosen in the Lord,
c	Exhortation	also
		his mother—and
d		mine.
14a	Exhortation	**Greet Asyncritus,**
b	List	**Phlegon,**
c		**Hermes,**
d		**Patrobas,**
e		**Hermas, and**
f		**the brothers and sisters with them.**
15a	Exhortation	**Greet Philologus and**
b	List	**Julia,**
c		**Nereus and**
d		**his sister, and**
e		**Olympas, and**
f		**all the saints with them.**
16a	Exhortation	**Greet one another with a holy kiss.**
b	Assertion	**All the assemblies of Christ greet you.**

ask the Roman believers to convey Paul's sense of friendship with sixteen individuals whom he knows personally as well as ten other individuals and five groups of people that he wants to acknowledge. The section begins with Prisca and Aquila, probably because Paul knew them best (16:3–5a).

In addition to this couple, Paul greets the whole assembly of believers that gathered in their house (16:5a). This is the first of five such groups in the list, although Paul does not use the word "assembly, church" (ἐκκλησία) to describe the other four groups (16:10c, 11, 14, and 15).

He then greets eight people whom he describes with various phrases, indicating that he knows them personally (16:5b–10b). Next, he greets two separate groups of people from whom he only seems to know one person, Herodion (16:10c–11). He then greets five people and describes them with phrases showing that he knew them personally (16:12–13).

Paul's personal greetings close with two groups of five individuals each and the "brothers and sisters" (ἀδελφοί) or "saints" (ἅγιοι) who are with each group (16:14–15). Since he includes no description of any of the people named in these two groups, Paul probably did not know them personally but only by reputation.

The greeting list ends with a general request that all the Roman believers greet one another with a holy kiss and then with greetings to the Romans from "all the assemblies of Christ" (16:16). Thus no one within the hearing of the letter, whether known to Paul or not, remains without a welcome, and everyone learns that they are connected with every other Christian assembly, wherever it might be. This closing set of general greetings underlines the theme of unity that runs throughout 12:1–16:27.

Exegetical Outline

XIII. Paul's Concluding Greetings, Warnings, and Ascription of Praise to God (16:1–27)

➡ **A. Paul's Commendation of Phoebe (16:1–2)**

B. Paul's Greetings to Friends in Rome and Others Whom He Knows by Reputation (16:3–16)

1. Prisca, Aquila, and Their Assembly (16:3–5a)
2. Paul's Friends in Rome (16:5b–10b)
3. Two More Assemblies and a Friend of Paul Who Belongs to One of Them (16:10c–11)
4. Five More Friends (16:12–13)
5. Two Assemblies and Five People within Each Assembly Known to Paul by Reputation (16:14–15)
6. Greetings to Every Believer and from Every Believer (16:16)

Explanation of the Text

16:1 Now I commend our sister Phoebe to you, who is a deacon in the assembly in Cenchreae (Συνίστημι δὲ ὑμῖν Φοίβην τὴν ἀδελφὴν ἡμῶν, οὖσαν διάκονον τῆς ἐκκλησίας τῆς ἐν Κεγχρεαῖς). Phoebe carried Paul's letter to Rome, and Paul affectionately recommends her to the Roman Christians as an indispensable envoy of the Christian assembly in a busy, cosmopolitan port city just southeast of Corinth.

"Now" (δέ) signals the start of a new section of the letter, and this first paragraph of the section commends the letter's carrier to its Roman audience. Although Paul does not say explicitly that Phoebe will take the letter to Rome, it is very likely that this is why he mentions her here. Greek speakers commonly used the term "commend" (συνίστημι) to introduce one person to another, and it appears often in letters of recommendation, as in this letter from AD 25:

> Theon to his esteemed Tyrannos many greetings. Herakleides, who carries this letter to you, is my brother. Wherefore, I entreat you with all my power to regard him recommended [συνεσταμένον].[6]

Phoebe is not only Paul's sister in the faith, and a sister in the faith to the Roman believers (ἡμῶν), but also "a deacon in the assembly in Cenchreae." It is difficult to know precisely what role Phoebe filled in the local assembly of Christians in this city.[7] In Romans Paul has used the word translated here as "deacon" (διάκονος) to describe Christ as "a *servant* of the circumcision" (15:8) and the Roman government as "the *agent* of God for good" (13:4). It basically referred to a go-between or intermediary (Josephus, *Ant.* 1.298) and could be used of workers who bustled around and got things done (John 2:5, 9).

The term was also often used of a king's messenger or assistant (Matt 22:13; Sophocles, *Phil.* 497; Chariton, *Chaereas and Callirhoe* 6.9.7), and sometimes by analogy it referred to a "messenger" of the gods (Aeschylus, *Prometheus Bound* 942; Josephus, *J.W.* 3.354; SEG 30.326.8).[8] It is not surprising, then, to find Paul describing himself as a "minister" of God (2 Cor 6:4), of Christ (2 Cor 11:23), of the new covenant (2 Cor 3:6), of the gospel (Eph 3:7; Col 1:23), or of the church (Col 1:25), and using the term in similar ways of his associates (1 Cor 3:5; 2 Cor 3:6; 1 Tim 4:6).

It is sometimes difficult to know whether Paul used the word in its religious or more common sense. Was Tychicus, for example, simply Paul's "courier" for the letters to the Ephesians and Colossians, or did he function, like Paul, as God's "minister" (Eph 6:21; Col 4:7)?

From an early date, the term described a group of people who functioned alongside "overseers" (ἐπίσκοποι) as "assistants" or "deacons" in Christian assemblies (Phil 1:1; 1 Tim 3:8, 12). Paul's use of the present participle (οὖσαν) in his description of Phoebe's function seems to indicate that she held this position. Just as the recipients of the letter in 1:7 "are in Rome" (οὖσιν ἐν Ῥώμῃ), that is, they live there, so Phoebe is also a "deacon" (οὖσαν διάκονον): this is the position she occupies.[9] She was probably not, then, simply appointed as a messenger from the church in Cenchreae to the Roman Christians in the same way that someone could be appointed a "deacon" from the church in Philadelphia to serve "as God's ambassador" to the church in Syrian Antioch (Ign. *Phld.* 10.1).[10]

Her role as deacon must have involved some sort of practical service to the Christian assembly in Cenchreae and may well have entailed a lot of running around, since a deacon was most basically a go-between, messenger, or courier. Part of her duties, then, may have been to act as a human connection between her own assembly in Cenchreae and other groups of Christians, such as the various assemblies of believers in Rome.[11]

Cenchreae was "the port of Corinth" (Philo, *Against Flaccus* 155 [F. H. Colson, LCL]), located,

6. White, *Light from Ancient Letters*, 118 (no. 79, P.Oxy. 292). Cf. 2 Cor 3:1 and LSJ 1719, s.v. συνίστημι IV; BDAG 972, s.v. συνίστημι 2; and MGS 2046, s.v. συνίστημι 1.D; Peter M. Head, "Named Letter Carriers among the Oxyrhynchus Papyri," *JSNT* 31 (2009): 285–87.

7. The variation in English translations illustrates the problem: "servant" (KJV, NASB, ESV, CEB), "minister" (Tyndale, NAB, REB), "deaconess" (RSV), "deacon" (NRSV, NIV).

8. LSJ 398; LSJSupp 88; BDAG 230–31; MGS 491, all s.v. διάκονος.

9. Jewett, *Romans*, 944. Cf. Origen, *Romans, Books 6–10*, 290; Chrysostom, *Romans*, 477; Theodoret of Cyrus, *Letters of St. Paul*, 1:135; Calvin, *Romans*, 321.

10. Carolyn Osiek, Margaret Y. MacDonald, and Janet H. Tulloch, *A Woman's Place: House Churches in Earliest Christianity* (Minneapolis: Fortress, 2006), 215. The translation of Ignatius belongs to Holmes, *Apostolic Fathers*, 245.

11. Osiek, MacDonald, and Tulloch, *Woman's Place*, 215. Cf. Collins, *Diakonia*, 225–26.

like Corinth, on the isthmus that connected the Peloponnesian peninsula with the Greek mainland and was eleven kilometers (a little less than seven miles) to the southeast of its larger neighbor.[12] Excavations have revealed that Julius Caesar rebuilt Cenchreae in the mid first-century BC and that a century later, when Paul wrote Romans from Corinth, it was a busy, deep-water port with warehouses lining its waterfront.[13] Although they are difficult to date precisely to the first century, archaeologists have uncovered evidence of small shops, storage tanks for live fish, and the foundations of ancient dwellings on the hills north of the commercial district with "magnificent" views of the city and ocean below.[14]

Pausanias, writing about a century after Paul, says that the city contained "a temple and a stone statue of Aphrodite," and a coin minted under Nero confirms this for Paul's time. It features Nero's head on one side, and on the other side the misspelled name of the city (CENCRHEAE) and Aphrodite's head hovering above a galley-style ship like the ships that must have often docked there.[15] Pausanius claims further that there was "on the mole running into the sea a bronze image of Poseidon, and at the other end of the harbour sanctuaries of Asclepius and of Isis" (*Description of Greece* 2.3 [W. H. S. Jones, LCL]). In the time of Paul and Phoebe, then, Cenchreae was probably a fast-paced, commercially oriented city with some wealthy residents and a wide variety of religious options.

16:2 in order that you might welcome her in the Lord in a way worthy of the saints and might assist her in whatever she needs for [her] undertaking, for she also became a benefactor of many and especially of me (ἵνα αὐτὴν προσδέξησθε ἐν κυρίῳ ἀξίως τῶν ἁγίων καὶ παραστῆτε αὐτῇ ἐν ᾧ ἂν ὑμῶν χρῄζῃ πράγματι· καὶ γὰρ αὐτὴ προστάτις πολλῶν ἐγενήθη καὶ ἐμοῦ αὐτοῦ). Paul recommended Phoebe to the Roman Christians in the hope that they would treat her with the love and honor that all Christians deserve from one another. She was especially deserving because of her generosity to Paul and many others.

Paul now gives the two purposes (ἵνα) of his commendation for Phoebe.[16] First, he wants the Roman believers to "welcome" (προσδέξησθε) her, a term commonly used for receiving an envoy.[17] The phrases "in the Lord" and "worthy of the saints" refer to the way those who have been united with the Lord Jesus Christ should treat others who, like themselves, have been set apart by this union as the people of God. Paul has already described what such a welcome would involve in 12:10–13. It would mean showing Phoebe the sort of sincere, instinctive love that family members should have for one another, taking the lead in showing her respect and honor, sharing in her needs, and eagerly giving her hospitality.

12. BDAG 537, s.v. Κεγχρεαί; Robert L. Hohfelder, "Cenchreae," *ABD* 1:881; Yves Lafond, "Cenchreae," *BNPA* 3:101–2; Clyde E. Fant and Mitchell G. Reddish, *A Guide to Biblical Sites in Greece and Turkey* (Oxford: Oxford University Press, 2003), 41–42; John B. Salmon, "Cenchreae," *OCD* 307.

13. See the carefully drawn artist's conception of the southwest section of the harbor of first-century Cenchreae in *Topography and Architecture*, ed. Robert Scranton, Joseph W. Shaw, and Leila Ibrahim, vol. 1 of *Kenchreai, Eastern Port of Corinth: Results of Investigations by the University of Chicago and Indiana University for the American School of Classical Studies at Athens*, 6 vols. (Leiden: Brill, 1978–2007), frontispiece, 148–49.

14. Hohfelder, "Kenchreai on the Saronic Gulf: Aspects of Its Imperial History," *CJ* 71 (1976): 222.

15. Ibid., 223. See Barclay Vincent Head, *A Catalogue of the Greek Coins in the British Museum: Corinth, Colonies of Corinth, Etc.*, ed. Reginald Stuart Poole (London: The Trustees of the British Museum, 1889), 68, no. 556 (not 566, as Hohfelder has it), plate 17, no. 13.

16. Cranfield, *Romans*, 2:781.

17. Margaret Mitchell, "New Testament Envoys in the Context of Greco-Roman Diplomatic Conventions: The Example of Timothy and Titus," *JBL* 111 (1992): 647.

Second, Paul wants the Romans to respond appropriately to the benefaction Phoebe has given to him and many others. The term "benefactor" (προστάτις) typically referred to a person, usually a man, of high social status that received clients, did them favors, and expected favors in return, especially displays of honor. Women sometimes played this role.[18] For example, at almost exactly the time that Paul wrote Romans from Corinth, a woman living in Corinth named Iunia Theodora was well known and publicly honored by the people of Lycia for the generous hospitality that she showed to expatriate Lycians, whom she welcomed "in her own house [τῇ ἰδίᾳ οἰκίᾳ] . . . displaying her patronage [προστασίαν]."[19] Historians only know of her existence because of the inscriptions written on monuments erected in her honor that "testify to her according to her deserts" and sought to satisfy "her own love of fame and assiduousness," as the inscriptions put it.[20]

It is easy to imagine Phoebe as a woman of wealth and high social status, like Iunia Theodora, who accommodated the assembly of Christians in Cenchreae in her house and provided practical help to Paul and his coworkers during their ministry in the area. In response, Paul hopes that the Roman Christians will assist Phoebe either in "whatever she may need from you" (ESV; cf. NIV, NRSV) or "in whatever she needs for [her] undertaking." Paul's use of the term "undertaking" (πράγματι) seems to entertain the possibility that Phoebe is pursuing some specific project in Rome for which she could use some help. In any case, Paul believes that the Roman Christians should respond to the help Phoebe has generously given to the Christian community by generously helping her in return.[21]

There is no mention of honor here. Indeed, Phoebe's role as a "deacon" in the church in Cenchreae involved lowly service by Greco-Roman standards and contrasts with her ability to serve as a "patron" to others.[22] This may reflect the transforming effect that the gospel had on the systems of honor and status that were so prevalent in the cultures where it first flourished.[23]

16:3 Greet Prisca and Aquila, my coworkers in Christ Jesus (Ἀσπάσασθε Πρίσκαν καὶ Ἀκύλαν τοὺς συνεργούς μου ἐν Χριστῷ Ἰησοῦ). Paul follows a common custom in letters from antiquity and greets some of the recipients by name, beginning with a married couple he had known well for several years and who had helped him advance the gospel in Corinth and Ephesus.

During the time of Augustus, letters in the Greco-Roman world began to include the request that the recipient "greet" various third parties for the letter's sender.[24] Paul often followed this custom, but usually urged his audience generically to "greet one another" (1 Cor 16:20; 2 Cor 13:12) or "every saint" (Phil 4:21; cf. 1 Thess 5:26; Titus 3:15). Only rarely in his extant letters does Paul urge his audience to greet named individuals (Col 4:15; 2 Tim 4:19). In Romans, in a highly uncharacteristic move, Paul urges his audience to greet

18. Osiek, MacDonald, and Tulloch, *Woman's Place*, 195–209.

19. R. A. Kearsley, "Women in Public Life in the Roman East: Iunia Theodora, Claudia Metrodora and Phoebe, Benefactress of Paul," *TynBul* 50 (1999): 191–98, 207–8.

20. Ibid., 208.

21. Asking the recipients of a letter to help its carrier was also common practice in antiquity (Head, "Named Letter Carriers," 285–87).

22. See Clarke's persuasive argument (*Pauline Theology of Church Leadership*, 65–67) that the term continued to carry connotations of lowly service in certain contexts, despite the argument of Collins (*Diakonia*) to the contrary.

23. Bruce W. Winter, *Roman Wives, Romans Widows: The Appearance of New Women and the Pauline Communities* (Grand Rapids: Eerdmans, 2003), 196.

24. White, *Light from Ancient Letters*, 202.

twenty-four named individuals, two others who are not named, and six discreet groups of individuals (including the audience itself), but without naming the individuals in each group (16:3–16).[25]

Why Paul did this is unclear. It is likely that it had the effect of publicly honoring both the named individuals and the entire audience of the letter together. This effect would be consistent with the message of Romans that the gospel is for everyone across all kinds of social boundaries (1:14–16), undermining haughtiness and promoting loving service among those who respond to the gospel in faith (3:27; 11:18; 12:3; 12:9–10, 13; 14:1–15:13).[26]

Prisca and Aquila receive the first and longest greeting probably because Paul knew them best and owed them the greatest personal debt (16:4). They were his "coworkers" (συνεργούς), a term that Paul often used for those who helped him advance the gospel (e.g., Phil 4:3; Col 4:11). Theodoret of Cyrus says that Paul added the tag "in Christ Jesus" to "coworkers" to avoid the impression that he was speaking "of a professional association, they being tent makers like him."[27]

IN DEPTH: Prisca, Aquila, and the Church in Their Roman House

Prisca and Aquila appear six times in the New Testament and always together as a married couple (Acts 18:2, 18, 26; Rom 16:3; 1 Cor 16:19; 2 Tim 4:19). Paul uses the formal name Prisca, and Luke uses the less formal, diminutive form Priscilla.[28] In the two other places where they show up in Paul's letters, he associates them with Ephesus (1 Cor 16:19; 2 Tim 4:19), where a church met in their house (1 Cor 16:19), just as it did in Rome (Rom 16:5).

Paul first met Prisca and Aquila in Corinth where they discovered they had four things in common. First, they had a common connection to Judaism since Aquila, at least, was a Jew (Acts 18:2). Second, they shared the same trade skills in manufacturing, probably producing the linen awnings used to protect the open areas of private houses, market stalls, and certain streets and public places from the hot Mediterranean sun (18:3).[29] Third, they all had recently arrived in Corinth: Paul, fresh from a journey through eastern Macedonia and northern Achaia, establishing churches (16:9–17:34), and Prisca and Aquila as exiles from Italy "because Claudius had commanded all the Jews to leave Rome" (18:2).

25. Paul is sometimes said to greet twenty-six named individuals, but his greetings to "those who belong to" Aristobulus (16:10) and Narcissus (16:11) probably only include the households of these two people, not Aristobulus and Narcissus themselves (Lampe, *From Paul to Valentinus*, 164–65).

26. Jewett, *Romans*, 951–53.

27. Theodoret of Cyrus, *Letters of St. Paul*, 1:136.

28. BDAG 863–64, s.v. Πρίσκα. Some manuscripts have "Priscilla" (Πρίσκιλλα) in both Rom 16:3 and 1 Cor 16:19, but in both cases the witness to "Prisca" (Πρίσκα) carries greater weight.

29. Lampe, *From Paul to Valentinus*, 187–89. Cf. BDAG 928–29, s.v. σκηνοποιός. The first-century herbalist Dioscorides Pedanius used the verbal form of the word in the middle voice (σκηνοποιεῖσθαι) to describe how the asparagus plant, if allowed to grow tall enough, forms a canopy with its leaves (*De materia medica* 2.146). See LSJ 1608, s.v. σκηνοποιέω.

Fourth, they were all Christians. Luke does not say in so many words that Aquila and Priscilla were believers when Paul met them. He simply says that he "found" them, "went to see them," and "stayed with them and worked" (Acts 18:2–3), but it is very likely that they were already Christians when they arrived in Corinth from Italy. When Paul lists the people he baptized in Corinth (1 Cor 1:14–17), he says nothing about Prisca and Aquila. Suetonius, moreover, ascribes the reason for Claudius's expulsion of the Jews to "disturbances at the instigation of Chrestus" (*Claud.* 25.4 [J. C. Rolfe, LCL]).[30] Since the expulsion affected mainly those involved in the disturbances and since it is safe to assume that Prisca and Aquila would not riot against Christians in Rome and then support a Christian missionary in Corinth, it is very likely that they were believers before ever leaving Rome.[31]

Paul lived and worked with Prisca and Aquila in Corinth for a year and a half (Acts 18:11), and all three of them left Corinth together sometime after "the Jews made a united attack on Paul and brought him before the tribunal" of the proconsul Gallio (Acts 18:12–17). They traveled next to Ephesus (Acts 18:18–19) where Prisca and Aquila stayed and taught "the way of God" (Acts 18:26) as Paul pressed on to Caesarea, Jerusalem, and Antioch, eventually to return to Ephesus to live and work for the next three years (Acts 18:21–20:1, 31). It is clear that Prisca and Aquila joined forces with Paul for part of these three years in Ephesus (1 Cor 16:19), but at this point they drop out of Luke's narrative.

When they returned to Rome remains unknown. It is commonly assumed that they had to wait until Claudius died and his expulsion edict died with him (AD 54), but this assumption is probably mistaken. Erich S. Gruen has made a learned and persuasive case that beginning in the second-century BC the senate, and later the early emperors of Rome, often passed laws that were only lightly enforced but gave the appearance of resisting the threat that foreign groups in Rome supposedly posed to traditional Roman religion and ways of life.[32] Claudius's edict was probably one of these measures, "a public polishing of the imperial image" that was more propaganda than substance and not rigorously enforced.[33] In other words, Claudius certainly "commanded all the Jews to leave Rome," as Luke says (Acts 18:2), but this should lead neither to the conclusion that all Jews actually left Rome nor to the conclusion that those who did leave, like Prisca and Aquila, were unable to return until after learning

30. On the reason for Claudius's expulsion of Jews, see the Introduction at the beginning of the commentary.

31. Lampe, *From Paul to Valentinus*, 11–13.

32. Gruen, *Diaspora*, 15–41.

33. Ibid., 36–41. Cf. Das, *Solving the Romans Debate*, 164–65.

of Claudius's death on October 13, AD 54.[34] When Paul wrote Romans, they must have had time to travel from Ephesus to Rome, obtain a place to live in the city, and establish an assembly of Christians in their house. Time would also be needed for a report of this house church to reach Paul in Corinth. If Prisca and Aquila left Rome shortly after Claudius's edict in AD 49 and then moved back to Rome in AD 53 or early in AD 54, they would have lived in their house for three or four years before Paul wrote Romans in AD 57 or 58.

What sort of space was their house? Without public transportation to provide an easy way to travel from one part of an ancient city to another, people had to work, shop, eat, and assemble in their clubs within a manageable walking distance of where they slept at night. As a result, cities like Rome were very densely populated, and the vast majority of people lived in apartment buildings, some of which reached five stories.[35] It is easy to imagine tradespeople like Prisca and Aquila renting a ground-floor workshop in the apartment building where they lived with sleeping space either behind or above the workshop.[36] A space like this, accommodating perhaps thirty people, could easily have been where "the church in their house" met.[37] With time, believers may have started to live together in the same apartment block, perhaps using its common spaces for places of assembly, and this would allow many more people to assemble together at once.[38]

If Prisca and Aquila were affluent, they may have owned the block, or part of it, and facilitated its development into a Christian neighborhood through "social networking."[39] If so, rich and poor, slave and free would have lived together cheek by jowl, just as they seem to have done elsewhere in Rome.[40] They would have been united by their common worship of the one true God and his Son,

34. Hans Förster, "Der Aufenthalt von Priska und Aquila in Ephesus und die juristischen Rahmenbedingungen ihrer Rückkehr nach Rom," *ZNW* 105 (2014): 189–227.

35. Bradly S. Billings, "From House Church to Tenement Church: Domestic Space and the Development of Early Urban Christianity—The Example of Ephesus," *JTS* 62 (2011): 559. On the five-story *insula*, see John R. Clarke, *The Houses of Roman Italy 100 B.C.—A.D. 250* (Berkeley: University of California Press, 1991), 26.

36. Cf. Oakes, *Reading Romans in Pompeii*, 15–33; David G. Horrell, "Domestic Space and Christian Meetings at Corinth: Imagining New Contexts and the Buildings East of the Theatre," *NTS* 50 (2004): 367.

37. Oakes, *Reading Romans in Pompeii*, 93–95. On the broad meaning of the term "house" (οἶκος), see Adams, *Earliest Christian Meeting Places*, 19–20.

38. Cf. David L. Balch, "Rich Pompeiian Houses, Shops for Rent, and the Huge Apartment Building in Herculaneum as Typical Spaces for Pauline House Churches," *JSNT* 27 (2004): 27–46.

39. See the application of social-networking theory to early urban Christianity in Billings, "From House Church to Tenement Church," 551–67. For the debate over how affluent Prisca and Aquila were, see, e.g., Lampe (*From Paul to Valentinus*, 187–95), who believes they were people of very modest means, and Jewett (*Romans*, 954–58), who believes they were wealthy.

40. Wallace-Hadrill, "*Domus* and *Insulae* in Rome," 10–18. Wallace-Hadrill makes the case that large houses in Rome seem to have often functioned socially in the same way as large apartment blocks. They had their own versions of rental property, social diversity, and shared public spaces.

Jesus Christ, through the power of the Spirit and perhaps by their involvement in the awning-making business, just as associations of bakers, carpenters, bath workers, and catchers and sellers of fish banded together and sometimes purchased property together to promote their business interests.[41] If something like this was the arrangement, it is easy to see how tensions over diet and the observance of certain days could develop (Rom 14:1–15:13). These may well have been everyday tensions, not simply problems that emerged each week as people came together from disparate parts of the city.

This is all simply informed speculation. It does not provide a foundation firm enough to answer the sort of detailed exegetical questions that Romans often raises. The speculation is helpful more for excluding a certain reading of Romans than for providing a clear exegesis of any particular passage. Romans cannot merely be a theological treatise for a socially homogenous church without serious implications for the day-to-day relationships of its diverse recipients. Paul wrote Romans for people who, like Prisca and Aquila, were living out their commitment to Christ in the morally and socially complex world of first-century Rome, balancing their need to survive economically with their willingness to make large sacrifices for the progress of the gospel (16:4). Readers of Romans today can know very little about Prisca, Aquila, and the church that met in their house, but they can certainly know enough to appreciate their selfless commitment to Christ and to other believers amid the stresses of the social and commercial world of the early Roman Empire.

16:4 who laid down their own neck for my life, to whom not only I give thanks, but all the churches of the gentiles (οἵτινες ὑπὲρ τῆς ψυχῆς μου τὸν ἑαυτῶν τράχηλον ὑπέθηκαν, οἷς οὐκ ἐγὼ μόνος εὐχαριστῶ ἀλλὰ καὶ πᾶσαι αἱ ἐκκλησίαι τῶν ἐθνῶν). Paul is grateful to Prisca and Aquila for going to great trouble to save his life, and many gentile believers share his gratitude to them.

Interpreters commonly understand the phrase "laid down their own neck for my life" to mean that Prisca and Aquila had risked their lives for Paul, perhaps in Ephesus, where Paul encountered much social and political opposition (Acts 19:23–41; 1 Cor 16:9; 2 Cor 1:8). This may well be correct, but the examples interpreters often give of the use of the phrase in this way are not an exact match to Paul's phrase.[42] "To lay down one's neck" (ὑποτιθέναι τὸν τράχηλον) typically referred simply to placing one's self under a burden or submitting one's self to some duty (1 Clem. 63:1; Epictetus, *Diatr.* 4.1.77). Whether Prisca and Aquila risked their own lives for Paul or not, their

41. Cf. Billings ("From House Church to Tenement Church," 554–55), especially his example of "the Tyrian merchants of Puteoli" (ibid., 555).

42. The Herculaneum text often cited from Deissmann (*Light from the Ancient East*, 117–18), for example, uses a different verb (παραβάλλω) that means "to endanger, put at risk" (MGS 1542, s.v. παραβάλλω, 2 B): "[For (?)] the most beloved of his relatives or friends he would readily stake his neck (παραβάλοι ἄν . . . τὸν τράχλον)" (transl. Deissmann). See BDAG 1014, s.v. τράχηλος.

efforts involved great personal sacrifice and, from Paul's perspective, saved his life.

Paul's gratitude to them is understandable, but exactly what he meant by the gratitude of "all the churches of the gentiles" is unclear. He meant either that they helped many gentile believers in places such as Corinth, Ephesus, and Rome, or that, by saving Paul's life, they allowed him to continue his ministry of proclaiming the gospel and establishing Christian communities among the gentiles (Rom 15:16).[43]

16:5a and the church in their house (καὶ τὴν κατ' οἶκον αὐτῶν ἐκκλησίαν). In addition to urging all the Christians in Rome to greet Prisca and Aquila, he urges them to greet the assembly of believers that met in their house.

The earliest assemblies of Christians often met in homes (Acts 5:42; 12:12–16; 18:20), and Paul uses the formula that appears here three other times in his letters (1 Cor 16:19; Col 4:15; Phlm 2) to refer to these house churches (ἡ κατ' οἶκον ... ἐκκλησία).[44] Some of them may have met in large houses built in the classic Roman style with an entryway and an atrium open to the sky surrounded by various rooms.[45] In urban settings such as Rome, however, it is more likely that these "houses" were apartments or workshops in some of the city's many apartment blocks or an area in a large atrium-style house, whose owner rented living and workshop space to people like Prisca and Aquila.[46] As the "In Depth" look at Prisca, Aquila, and their Roman house explains, this couple may well have hosted the church in a workshop where they made and sold awnings. This workshop may have either doubled as a living space or been attached to another room where they slept.[47]

16:5b–c Greet my beloved Epaenetus, who is the first fruit of Asia for Christ (ἀσπάσασθε Ἐπαίνετον τὸν ἀγαπητόν μου, ὅς ἐστιν ἀπαρχὴ τῆς Ἀσίας εἰς Χριστόν). Paul urges the Roman Christians to greet a dear friend who was one of the first people to believe the gospel after Paul moved to the Roman province of Asia and began to work with Prisca and Aquila in Ephesus, Asia's largest city.

"Epaenetus" (Επαίνετος) was a fairly common Greek name. It shows up, for example, in Polybius as the name of an ambassador from Boeotia in central Greece (*Histories* 23.16.4–5), in Diodorus Siculus as the name of a naval commander in Ptolemaic Egypt (*Bibliotheca historica* 19.79.2), and in inscriptions from Corcyra (an island in the Adriatic Sea off the coast of Epirus), Hermopolis in Egypt, and the province of Asia.[48] One first-century inscription from Rome refers to an Epaenetus from Ephesus, the largest city in Asia.[49]

The phrase "my beloved" (τὸν ἀγαπητόν μου) expresses an affection for Epaenetus that shows he was well known to Paul (cf. Rom 16:8, 9). His status as the "first fruit" (ἀπαρχή) of Asia means that he was either the first person, or one of the first people, in Asia to believe the gospel (cf. Rom 8:23; 11:16; 1 Cor 16:15; 2 Thess 2:13).[50] He was almost certainly therefore from Ephesus where Paul, Prisca, and Aquila had worked for several years (Acts 18:26; 19:10; 20:31; 1 Cor 16:19). "First fruit" was cultic imagery (Num 15:17–21) that fit neatly with

43. See, on one side, e.g., Origen (*Romans, Books 6–10*, 292), and, on the other side, e.g., Meyer (*Romans*, 566).

44. See the texts listed in White, *Texts and Monuments*, 36.

45. Clarke, *Houses of Roman Italy*, 3.

46. Wallace-Hadrill, "*Domus* and *Insulae* in Rome," 10–18. Cf. Richard Last, "The Neighborhood (*vicus*) of the Corinthian *ekklēsia*: Beyond Family-Based Descriptions of the First Urban Christ-Believers," *JSNT* 38 (2016): 408–19.

47. See especially Balch, "Rich Pompeiian Houses," 34–35, 41–42; Horrell, "Domestic Space and Christian Meetings at Corinth," 360–68.

48. For the inscriptional evidence, see Sanday and Headlam (*Romans*, 421) and MM 227, s.v. Ἐπαίνετος.

49. Sanday and Headlam, *Romans*, 421.

50. BDAG 98, s.v. ἀπαρχή 1.

Paul's concept of himself as performing the work of a metaphorical priest who brought the gentiles to God as an acceptable and holy offering (Rom 15:16).

16:6 Greet Miriam, who has labored hard for you (ἀσπάσασθε [Μαριάν], ἥτις πολλὰ ἐκοπίασεν εἰς ὑμᾶς). Paul urges the Roman Christians to greet a Jewish Christian woman who worked hard to advance the gospel in Rome.

Ancient manuscripts of Romans are divided over whether the person Paul greets in this sentence is named "Maria" (Μαρία, often rendered "Mary") or "Miriam" (Μαριάμ).[51] "Maria" was a common Italian name for women, derived from the family name "Marius." The name "Miriam," however, was an indeclinable Hebrew name, derived from the name of the sister of Moses and Aaron (Exod 15:20; Num 12:1–16). The manuscript evidence slightly favors taking "Miriam" as the correct name, and if so, then this woman must have been a Jewish Christian.[52] When Paul uses the term "labor" (κοπίαω) in his extant letters, he most often refers to work specifically in the service of the gospel and the church (e.g., 1 Cor 15:10; 16:16; Gal 4:11; Phil 2:16; 1 Thess 5:12), and so the hard labor that Miriam devoted to Christians in Rome was probably this same kind of work.[53]

16:7 Greet Andronicus and Junia, my compatriots and fellow prisoners, who are prominent among the apostles, and who were also in Christ before me (ἀσπάσασθε Ἀνδρόνικον καὶ Ἰουνίαν τοὺς συγγενεῖς μου καὶ συναιχμαλώτους μου, οἵτινές εἰσιν ἐπίσημοι ἐν τοῖς ἀποστόλοις, οἳ καὶ πρὸ ἐμοῦ γέγοναν ἐν Χριστῷ). Paul instructs the Roman Christians to greet two fellow Jewish Christians who, like him, had suffered imprisonment for the gospel. They were also highly esteemed eye and ear witnesses to Jesus's ministry and teaching who, like Paul, took the gospel to others.

"Andronicus" (Ἀνδρόνικος) is another common Greek name. It shows up as the name of an important official in the Syrian government (2 Macc 4:31–38; 5:23) and as the name of a powerful Jewish figure with influence in Ptolemaic affairs in the second-century BC (Josephus, *Ant.* 13.75, 78–79).[54] It was also reasonably common in the Rome of Paul's time where it appears in inscriptions that name members of the imperial household.[55]

For hundreds of years interpreters of Romans accented "Junia" (Ἰουνίαν) with a circumflex on the last syllable (Ἰουνιᾶν) and took it to be a man's name, "Junias" (Ἰουνίας), which was sometimes said to be a shortened form of the name "Junianus" (e.g., RSV).[56] There are no examples of the masculine name "Junias" from Greco-Roman antiquity, however, making it certain that patristic commentators prior to the Middle Ages and recent interpreters are correct in identifying "Junia" as a woman.[57] This name was common in the Roman

51. The Zondervan Greek text, printed above, accepts "Maria" (Μαριάν) as the correct reading.

52. Légasse, *Romains*, 950; Jewett, *Romans*, 949. The witnesses to "Miriam" have on their side greater antiquity and geographical diversity (𝔓46 ℵ [Alexandrian]; D F G [Western] L [Byzantine]) than the heavily Alexandrian witnesses to "Maria" (A B P Ψ 104 1739). Haacker (*An die Römer*, 317n2) observes helpfully that the scribes who copied Romans would be more likely to conform a Hebrew name to a familiar Greek name than vice versa.

53. Jewett, *Romans*, 961. Cf. already Chrysostom, *Romans*, 488.

54. BDAG 76, s.v. Ἀνδρόνικος; Fitzmyer, *Romans*, 737.

55. Sanday and Headlam, *Romans*, 422; Lampe, *From Paul to Valentinus*, 169.

56. For a review of the history of interpretation, see Fitzmyer, *Romans*, 737–38; Eldon Jay Epp, *Junia: The First Woman Apostle* (Minneapolis: Fortress, 2005), 32–39. For Junias as a shortened form of Junianus, see, e.g., Godet, *Romans*, 491; Meyer, *Romans*, 567.

57. See especially Lampe, *From Paul to Valentinus*, 166–67n39; Epp, *Junia*, 23–31, 40–44.

west where it was, for example, the name of Junia Tertia, the wife of Julius Caesar's assassin Cassius.[58]

Paul describes Andronicus and Junia with four phrases. First, they were Paul's "compatriots" (συγγενεῖς) in the sense that they too were Jews (see Rom 9:3; cf. 16:11, 21). Some interpreters have thought that they were Paul's "relatives" (e.g., NAB, NRSV, CEB) since other Jews in the list, such as Aquila (cf. Acts 18:2), do not receive this designation and it is a natural meaning of the term (e.g., Mark 6:4).[59] It seems unlikely, however, that Paul would have three believing relatives in Rome (cf. 16:11) and three more relatives with him in Corinth (16:21).[60]

Second, Paul refers to Andronicus and Junia as his "fellow prisoners" (συναιχμαλώτους), a term that he also uses of Aristarchus (Col 4:10) and Epaphras (Phlm 23). This probably means that at some point Andronicus and Junia, like Paul, had experienced imprisonment because of their commitment to the gospel. It need not mean that they shared a particular imprisonment.[61]

Third, Paul describes them as "prominent among the apostles" (ἐπίσημοι ἐν τοῖς ἀποστόλοις). The adjective in the phrase (ἐπίσημοι) clearly means "notable, prominent" when it is applied to people, but a vigorous debate on the use of this adjective in constructions similar to the one here has yielded disagreement over whether Andronicus and Junia were prominent apostles or simply "noteworthy in the eyes of the apostles" (HCSB; cf. ESV, NET).[62] All parties to the debate agree that either meaning is possible.

In situations like this, it seems prudent to turn to the oldest Greek commentators on Romans, who spoke as their native tongue the language in which Paul was writing. All who comment on the passage assume without debate that Andronicus and Junia were apostles. Origen seems to have thought they were among the seventy-two whom Jesus sent out (ἀπέστειλεν) "two by two" according to Luke 10:1.[63] Theodoret of Cyrus comments on the high praise Paul gives the pair by calling them apostles: "He says they were not among the disciples but among the teachers—not any sort of teachers but the apostles."[64] Chrysostom's comments are particularly valuable because he expresses surprise that Junia would be called an apostle. "Oh! how great is the devotion of this woman," he says, "that she should be even counted worthy of the appellation of apostle!"[65] If the grammar of the text most naturally meant that Andronicus and Junia were "well known to the apostles," Chrysostom would probably have taken it that way.[66]

What kind of apostles were Andronicus and Junia? As Richard Bauckham says, Paul uses the

58. She lived to an advanced age and died in AD 22 (Tacitus, *Ann.* 3.76). See Theodore John Cadoux and Robin J. Seager ("Cassius Longinus, Gaius," *OCD* 300), and Lampe (*From Paul to Valentinus*, 169).

59. Meyer, *Romans*, 567–68.

60. Sanday and Headlam, *Romans*, 423.

61. Ibid.; Fitzmyer, *Romans*, 739.

62. On the meaning of the term, see LSJ 656, s.v. ἐπίσημος II.3; BDAG 378, s.v. ἐπίσημος. On the grammatical debate and for many examples of the use of the term, see Michael H. Burer and Daniel B. Wallace ("Was Junia Really an Apostle? A Re-examination of Rom 16.7," *NTS* 47 [2001]: 76–91) and Michael Burer ("'ΕΠΙΣΗΜΟΙ 'ΕΝ ΤΟΙΣ 'ΑΠΟΣΤΟΛΟΙΣ in Rom 16:7 as 'Well Known to the Apostles': Further Defense and New Evidence," *JETS* 58 [2015]: 731–55). For response to Wallace and Burer, see Richard Bauckham (*Gospel Women: Studies of the Named Women in the Gospels* [Grand Rapids: Eerdmans, 2002], 172–80); Linda Belleville ("'Ιουνιαν . . . ἐπίσημοι ἐν τοῖς ἀποστόλοις: A Re-examination of Romans 16.7 in Light of Primary Source Materials," *NTS* 51 [2005]: 231–49); and Epp, *Junia*, 69–78.

63. See Origen, *Romans, Books 6–10*, 293–94, and the translator's reference to Luke 10:1 in note 257. Origen is preserved at this point, however, only in Rufinus's early fifth-century Latin abridgment.

64. Theodoret of Cyrus, *Letters of St. Paul*, 1:136 (*PG* 82.220).

65. Chrysostom, *Romans*, 489 (*PG* 60.670).

66. Bauckham, *Gospel Women*, 179.

term "apostle" twice simply to mean "messenger" (2 Cor 8:23; Phil 2:25), but when he uses the term that way he qualifies it to say specifically who sent the messenger.[67] Without further qualification, "the apostles" most likely means the group of people who, like Paul himself, had seen the risen Christ and received a commission from him to take the good news about Christ to others (Rom 1:1; 11:13; 1 Cor 9:1; 15:5–11). Paul included within this group more than himself and Jesus's twelve primary disciples.[68] He definitely included James, the brother of the Lord (Gal 1:19), who was not one of the Twelve (Matt 10:2–4; Mark 3:14–19; Luke 6:13–16; Acts 1:13) and was apparently not a follower of Jesus prior to the resurrection (John 7:5; cf. 1 Cor 15:7). Paul may have also included Barnabas, Silvanus, and Apollos (1 Cor 4:6, 9; 9:5–6; 1 Thess 2:6–7).[69] There is nothing improbable, then, about the inclusion of Andronicus and Junia with the group of apostles, perhaps as a husband-and-wife team who functioned in a way similar to Prisca and Aquila.

Fourth, Paul says that this couple was "in Christ before me." This means that they were among the earliest Christians and, like Paul, could have seen the risen Lord (1 Cor 15:5–9), an experience that Paul probably considered an important apostolic qualification (1 Cor 9:1; cf. Acts 1:22).

16:8 Greet Ampliatus, my beloved in the Lord (ἀσπάσασθε Ἀμπλιᾶτον τὸν ἀγαπητόν μου ἐν κυρίῳ). Paul urges the Roman Christians to greet his close friend Ampliatus, whom he met and grew to love because of their mutual commitment to Christ. Ampliatus was probably a slave or freedman, but as tempting as it is to speculate further, nothing else is known about him.

"Ampliatus" was a common slave name, well attested from the time of Augustus and occurring frequently in Roman inscriptions.[70] Like Epaenetus and Stachys (16:5, 9; cf. 16:12), Paul calls Ampliatus "my beloved," indicating that Paul knew him well. The added phrase "in the Lord" refers to the sphere or realm in which Paul's love operated (cf. 16:2, 12, 13, 22) and implies that the origin of Paul's affection for Ampliatus lay in their common Christian faith.

After the late nineteenth-century publication of an article on "The Room of Ampliatus in the Cemetery of Domitilla" by the great catacomb archaeologist Giovanni Battista de Rossi (1822–1894), commentators began to mention the appearance of the name "Ampliatus" in two inscriptions from an underground cemetery outside Rome now known as the Catacomb of Domitilla.[71] Rossi connected this cemetery with Flavia Domitilla, a name that from ancient times was attached to a woman in the emperor Domitian's family who may have been a Christian (Eusebius, *Ecclesiastical History* 3.18.4; cf. Cassius Dio, *Roman History* 67.14.1–2; Suetonius, *Dom.* 15.1).[72] The earliest of the two "Ampliatus" inscriptions stands alone without the additional Latin names that would indicate someone whose status was above that of a slave. The ornamentation around the inscription and the style of its lettering are compatible with an early imperial date, perhaps as early as the late first century. Perhaps, the theory goes, Ampliatus became highly respected in

67. Ibid., 180.
68. Ibid.
69. Ibid.
70. Lampe, *From Paul to Valentinus*, 173.
71. Giovanni Battista de Rossi, "Il Cubicolo di Ampliato nel Cimitero di Domitilla," *Bullettino di Archeologia Cristiana* 3.6 (1881): 57–74. Antonio Bosio, who rediscovered the catacomb in the sixteenth century, calls it "the cemetery of Saints Petronilla, Flavia Domitilla, Nereus, and Achilleus on the Via Ardeatina" (*Roma Sotterranea* [Rome: Gugliolmo Facciotti, 1632], 192). On the rediscovery of the Domitilla catacomb, see L. V. Rutgers, *Subterranean Rome* (Leuven: Peeters, 2000), 15–18, 130–33.
72. Lampe, *From Paul to Valentinus*, 33, 198–205.

the Roman church and was honored with an elaborately decorated resting place under land owned by the Christian Flavia Domitilla.[73]

This idea is far too speculative, however, to carry conviction. It cannot be correct, moreover, if, as seems likely, the earliest parts of the Domitilla catacomb date to the late second century, at least a century too late for Paul's beloved friend.[74]

16:9 Greet Urbanus, our coworker in Christ, and my beloved Stachys (ἀσπάσασθε Οὐρβανὸν τὸν συνεργὸν ἡμῶν ἐν Χριστῷ καὶ Στάχυν τὸν ἀγαπητόν μου). Paul tells the Roman Christians to greet Urbanus who helped him in his proclamation of the gospel among the gentiles, and Stachys who was a dear friend and who may have immigrated to Rome from the east.

"Urbanus" (Οὐρβανός) was a Latin name meaning "refined in manner." This kind of name, which modern scholars sometimes categorize as a "wish name," was frequently used for slaves and expressed the hope of the slave's owner that the slave might exhibit the character described in the name.[75] Paul calls Urbanus a "coworker," a term that he uses for close associates in his work of advancing the gospel among the gentiles (e.g., 16:3 [Prisca and Aquila], 21 [Timothy]). This may mean that if Urbanus had slavery somewhere in his background he was free by the time he joined Paul in his work in the east.[76] Since Paul uses the plural pronoun "our," he was known to other coworkers of Paul, perhaps Prisca, Aquila, and Timothy.

"Stachys" (Στάχυς) is an uncommon Greek name, but it does occur several times in Roman inscriptions from about the time that Paul wrote Romans.[77] The name means "ear of grain" and was also the name of a star in the constellation Virgo. Greek speakers could use it figuratively to mean "offspring, progeny."[78] It is easy to see how either of these latter two uses might lead to a proper name for a child, especially one born under the constellation Virgo.

Stachys's Greek name may mean that he was an immigrant from the east.[79] He had, in any case, been with Paul in the east and, like Epaenetus and Ampliatus (16:5, 8; cf. Persis in 16:12), became his dear friend (τὸν ἀγαπητόν μου).

16:10a–b Greet Apelles, tried and true in Christ (ἀσπάσασθε Ἀπελλῆν τὸν δόκιμον ἐν Χριστῷ). Paul urges the Roman believers to greet a believer with the Greek name Apelles, who has endured some trial for his faith in Christ.

"Apelles" was the name of antiquity's most famous painter, the fourth-century BC Apelles of Colophon and Ephesus, and of a tragic actor who was an advisor to Emperor Caligula.[80] The name is fairly well attested in Rome during Paul's era, and a few of those who held it are known to have been slaves.[81] Since the name is Greek, Apelles may have been an immigrant from the east. The expression "tried and true [δόκιμον] in Christ" probably means he had endured some hardship because of his commitment to Christ (cf. Rom 5:4 [δοκιμή]; Jas 1:12).[82]

73. See, e.g., Sanday and Headlam, *Romans*, 424; Lagrange, *Romains*, 366–67; Cranfield, *Romans*, 2:790; Wilckens, *An die Römer (12–16)*, 136; Dunn, *Romans 9–16*, 895; Jewett, *Romans*, 964. Cf. Orazio Marucchi, *Le Catacombe Romane* (n.p.: La Libreria dello Stato, 1933 ["Anno XI E F"]), 168.

74. On the date of the catacomb, see, e.g., Lampe (*From Paul to Valentinus*, 32), and Coarelli (*Rome*, 386–87).

75. Lampe, *From Paul to Valentinus*, 181; Jewett, *Romans*, 965.

76. Lampe, *From Paul to Valentinus*, 183; Jewett, *Romans*, 965.

77. Lightfoot, *Philippians*, 174; Lampe, *From Paul to Valentinus*, 180.

78. LSJ 1635, s.v. "στάχυς."

79. Lampe, *From Paul to Valentinus*, 168.

80. On the artist, see Karim W. Arafat ("Apelles," *OCD* 118–19), and on Caligula's advisor, see Philo (*Embassy* 204–6).

81. Lampe, *From Paul to Valentinus*, 169, 179.

82. Jewett, *Romans*, 966.

16:10c Greet those from the household of Aristobulus (ἀσπάσασθε τοὺς ἐκ τῶν Ἀριστοβούλου). Paul urges the Roman Christians to greet a group of believers whom he probably knew only by reputation. They may have been Jewish Christian slaves belonging to a descendent of Herod the Great and the Hasmonean princess Mariamne.

Paul does not ask the Roman Christians to greet Aristobulus himself, but only certain members of or "from" (ἐκ) his household. This implies that Aristobulus was not a believer, but was someone wealthy enough to have household members, probably slaves, who were believers.[83] Paul may have known some of them through contact in the east, although since he gives them only a greeting and no further description or commendation, it seems more likely that he knew them by reputation.[84] It is easy to imagine them living with non-Christian members of the household of Aristobulus in a single apartment block in Rome where their regular meetings, perhaps in common areas, were tolerated.[85]

The Greek name "Aristobulus" was fairly common in Greek-speaking areas, but not in Rome.[86] It was, however, the name of several important figures of Jewish and Hasmonean descent in the circles of the emperors Claudius and Nero in the mid-first century.[87] The brother of Herod Agrippa I was named Aristobulus, and after their grandfather Herod the Great had executed their father, also named Aristobulus, the brothers seem to have been raised together in Roman imperial circles (Josephus, *Ant.* 18.133–34, 143). Agrippa, at least, was a close friend of Claudius, who claims to have "brought" him "up" (ἔθρεψα), and it is reasonable to think of Aristobulus as having close ties to Claudius also (Josephus, *Ant.* 20.12 [L. H. Feldman, LCL]).

References to Aristobulus in Josephus place him in the east, where he married Jotape, a princess of Emesa (*Ant.* 18.135), persuaded the proconsul of Syria not to trust his brother Agrippa (*Ant.* 18.151–54), and pled with Petronius, the legate of Syria, on behalf of the Jews when the emperor Caligula insisted in AD 40 on placing a statue of himself in the temple in Jerusalem (*Ant.* 18.273–77).[88] He died after his brother Agrippa passed away in AD 44, and although Josephus gives no indication of exactly when or where he died, he comments that at his death he was a private citizen (*J.W.* 2.219–21).

Did he finish his days in Rome where he had been raised? If so, did he bequeath his household slaves to the emperor, as was the custom among the political elite? Did they retain the name of their original owner, something that was also usual? J. B. Lightfoot thought so and has himself bequeathed this theory to most commentators after him.[89]

The theory seems plausible, although it is important not to make the field of people named Aristobulus connected with first-century Rome too narrow.[90] Aristobulus, the grandson of Herod, also had a nephew named Aristobulus, whom Nero made sovereign over Lesser Armenia in AD 55, and this Aristobulus also had a son named Aris-

83. Lampe, *From Paul to Valentinus*, 164–65.

84. Origen (*Romans, Books 6–10*, 295) and Chrysostom (*Romans*, 491) thought that Paul withheld a commendation from these believers because they were undeserving of praise.

85. Cf. Jewett, *Romans*, 966. For an example of the sort of living situation they may have occupied, see Wallace-Hadrill, "*Domus* and *Insulae* in Rome," 10–14.

86. Lampe, *From Paul to Valentinus*, 165; Scott T. Carroll, "Aristobulus," *ABD* 1:382; Jewett, *Romans*, 966.

87. Carroll, "Aristobulus," 1:383.

88. For the chronology, see Anthony A. Barrett, *Caligula: The Corruption of Power* (New Haven: Yale University Press, 1990), 188.

89. See Lightfoot (*Philippians*, 174–75), and, e.g., Sanday and Headlam (*Romans*, 425), Michel (*An die Römer*, 477), Cranfield (*Romans*, 2:791–92), Dunn (*Romans 9–16*, 896), and Jewett (*Romans*, 966).

90. As Lagrange (*Romains*, 367–68) seems to recognize.

tobulus (Josephus, *Ant.* 20.158). The father and nephew had, in Claudius's own words, "many ties of friendship" with the emperor and were deeply devoted to him (*Ant.* 20.13 [L. H. Feldman, LCL]). It seems possible that the nephew Aristobulus, and perhaps his son Aristobulus, could also have had household members in Rome when Paul wrote Romans in AD 57. Whether the precise details of Lightfoot's influential theory are correct or not, his idea usefully highlights the probability that the believers Paul greets here had some connection to this socially elite Jewish family and may well have been Jewish Christians.

16:11a–b Greet Herodion, my compatriot (ἀσπάσασθε Ἡρῳδίωνα τὸν συγγενῆ μου). Having greeted all the Christians in Aristobulus's household, Paul greets one of them by name, perhaps someone he knew through contact with him in the east.

It is likely that the syllable "-on" (-ων) attached to the end of "Herodion" is simply the Greek equivalent of "-anus," the suffix often attached to the names of slaves sold or bequeathed to someone other than their original master.[91] "Herodion," therefore, had been the slave or freedman of somone named Herod and then become attached to some other household. Although the Latin name "Herodianus" appears in seven inscriptions from ancient Rome, this is the only example of the Greek form of the name from Rome's early imperial period, and so it is likely that "Herodion" had come to Rome from the east. Since Paul has just greeted a group of Christians with a probable connection to Herod the Great's family, it is reasonable to conclude that Herodion belonged to "those from the household of Aristobulus" (16:10b).[92] Paul identified him as his "compatriot" (συγγενῆ), probably meaning not that he was a direct relative (e.g., NAB, NRSV, CEB), but simply a "fellow Jew" (NIV; cf. REB, ESV).

16:11c–e Greet those from the household of Narcissus who are in the Lord (ἀσπάσασθε τοὺς ἐκ τῶν Ναρκίσσου τοὺς ὄντας ἐν κυρίῳ). Paul wants the Roman Christians to greet the slaves and freedmen of Narcissus's household, perhaps people once attached to the powerful secretary of the emperor Claudius and, at the time Paul wrote Romans, attached to Nero.

Again Paul does not greet Narcissus himself but the subgroup of his household slaves who were believers (cf. 16:10c).[93] "Narcissus" was a common name for slaves and freedmen in Rome, and it was well-known in the Greek-speaking east.[94] It was also the name of a powerful and wealthy advisor to the emperor Claudius—so powerful, says Suetonius, that Claudius "played the part, not of a prince but of a servant" to him (*Claud.* 29.1 [J. C. Rolfe, LCL]). Lightfoot argued that Paul's greeting went to a group of Christian household slaves of this powerful figure, and many interpreters have expressed cautious optimism that Lightfoot was right.[95]

Agrippina, Nero's mother, had forced Narcissus to commit suicide by a cruel imprisonment shortly after Nero became emperor in AD 54 (Tacitus, *Ann.* 13.1). This happened only a few years before Paul wrote Romans, argued Lightfoot. After their master's death, the slaves and freedmen of Narcissus would have become attached to Nero's

91. On "Herodion," see Peter Lampe, "Herodion," *ABD* 3:176, and, idem, *From Paul to Valentinus*, 177–78.

92. Lightfoot, *Philippians*, 175; Sanday and Headlam, *Romans*, 425.

93. Lampe, *From Paul to Valentinus*, 164–65.

94. Ibid., 165; MM 422, s.v. Νάρκισσος.

95. Lightfoot, *Philippians*, 175. See, e.g., Sanday and Headlam's "very possibly" (*Romans*, 425), Cranfield's "quite probable" (*Romans*, 2:793), and Jewett's "most likely" (*Romans*, 967).

household but would have retained their original master's name.

As with "those from the household of Aristobulus" (16:10c), Paul seems to know this group of Christians only by reputation since he only greets them and gives them no further description. Perhaps their reputation was widely known because of their connection to households at the center of Roman imperial power.

16:12 Greet Tryphena and Tryphosa, those hard workers in the Lord. Greet beloved Persis, who has worked very hard in the Lord (ἀσπάσασθε Τρύφαιναν καὶ Τρυφῶσαν τὰς κοπιώσας ἐν κυρίῳ. ἀσπάσασθε Περσίδα τὴν ἀγαπητήν, ἥτις πολλὰ ἐκοπίασεν ἐν κυρίῳ). Paul greets three women, perhaps from the east and with slave backgrounds, whose hard work in their Christian communities has been valuable.

Tryphena and Tryphosa were Greek names that occur fairly frequently in Roman contexts contemporaneous with Paul. Over forty percent of the contemporary occurrences of both names indicate fairly clearly that they belong to slaves.[96] Since the first two syllables of the names alliterate and they are mentioned together, it seems reasonable to imagine them as sisters. "Persis," a name meaning "from Persia," was common among female slaves and occurs only four times in contexts from Rome contemporary with Paul.[97] It seems likely that "Persis," then, was from the east and had slavery in her background, although her freedom to devote much labor to the work of the church may indicate that she was a freedwoman. Paul may have only known Tryphena and Tryphosa by reputation, but he knew Persis personally and considered her a "beloved" friend. She was perhaps not quite as close to him as Epaenetus, Ampliatus, and Stachys, all of whom he calls "*my* beloved."

Like Miriam in 16:6, Trypena, Tryphosa, and Persis have all "worked hard" (κοπιάω), an expression that refers to particularly taxing, often manual, labor (cf. Matt 6:28; 11:28; John 4:6; Acts 20:34–35; 1 Cor 4:12; Eph 4:28). Paul uses this term of hard work in the service of the gospel, whether his own work as an apostle (1 Cor 15:10; Gal 4:11; Phil 2:16; Col 1:28–29) or the work of various Christian leaders for the wider Christian community (1 Cor 16:16; 1 Thess 5:12; 1 Tim 5:17). Since Paul describes the work of all three women as "in the Lord," it is likely that Paul knew them by reputation as people who contributed in valuable ways to their Christian communities, perhaps in leadership positions.

16:13 Greet Rufus, chosen in the Lord, also his mother—and mine (ἀσπάσασθε Ῥοῦφον τὸν ἐκλεκτὸν ἐν κυρίῳ καὶ τὴν μητέρα αὐτοῦ καὶ ἐμοῦ). Paul urges all the Roman Christians to greet Rufus, a believer with special standing in the Roman church and who, together with his mother, had helped Paul in the east before moving to Rome.

"Rufus" was a common Latin name ("red, ruddy") and could refer to people across the social classes from slaves to consuls.[98] Its only other occurrence in the New Testament is in Mark 15:21 where, among the three Synoptic gospels, Mark alone describes Simon of Cyrene, who was forced to carry Jesus's cross, as "the father of Alexander and Rufus." It is unclear why Mark would describe Simon this way unless his two sons were well-known to Mark's readers.[99] Since the Mark

96. BDAG 1018, s.vv. Τρύφαινα, Τρυφῶσα; Lampe, *From Paul to Valentinus*, 179–80.

97. MGS 1654, s.v. Περσίς (citing, e.g., Aeschylus, *Persians* 59, 135); BDAG 808, s.v. Περσίς; Lampe, *From Paul to Valentinus*, 174–75.

98. Lampe, *From Paul to Valentinus*, 181–82.

99. Robert H. Gundry, *Mark: A Commentary on His Apology for the Cross* (Grand Rapids: Eerdmans, 1993), 944.

to whom this Gospel was attributed from an early date was also closely associated with Rome (2 Tim 4:11; 1 Pet 5:13; Irenaeus, *Against Heresies* 3.1.1), it is not unreasonable to speculate that the Rufus here and the Rufus of Mark 15:21 are the same person.[100]

The term "chosen" (ἐκλεκτός) appears in the singular only here in Paul, and so he probably did not use it here the way he used it elsewhere to refer to God's choice of his people (cf. Rom 8:33). Rather, it means that Rufus had some special status as a Christian. It is easy to imagine that his ties, through his father, to the events surrounding Jesus's death gave him some special standing among Roman Christians. All of this, however, is uncertain.

It is clear in any case that Paul knew Rufus and his mother well, so well that Rufus's mother had "mothered" Paul. They had all therefore been together at some point in the eastern Mediterranean area before Rufus and his mother had traveled west to Rome, where Rufus played a special role among Roman Christians.

16:14 Greet Asyncritus, Phlegon, Hermes, Patrobas, Hermas, and the brothers and sisters with them (ἀσπάσασθε Ἀσύγκριτον, Φλέγοντα, Ἑρμῆν, Πατροβᾶν, Ἑρμᾶν καὶ τοὺς σὺν αὐτοῖς ἀδελφούς). Paul urges the Roman Christians to greet five believers who were either slaves or freedmen and probably belonged to the lower social classes. They were part of a larger group of Christians who may have lived close to one another and met together in a nearby common space.

The five people Paul names were probably all slaves or freedmen. "Asyncritus" is from a Greek adjective (ἀσύγκριτος) meaning "incomparable" and like "Urbanus" in 16:9 was probably a "wish name" expressing a slave master's hope that the slave would give unparalleled service. Similarly, "Phlegon" ("Blazer") is derived from a Greek verb meaning "burn" (φλέγω), was a name sometimes given to dogs, and shows up in Roman inscriptions of the first century as a slave name.[101] "Hermes" was an extraordinarily common slave name in first-century Rome for obvious reasons: "Above all, [the god Hermes] is a messenger god, who carries out the orders of Zeus with due respect."[102] "Patrobas" (cf. Martial, *Epigrams* 2.32.3) is probably a shortened form of the more common "Patrobius," which was the name of a freedman attached to Nero (Pliny, *Natural History* 35.47.13).[103] It is possible that Patrobas was this freedman's slave, but in any case since the name was used for slaves and freedmen and is here associated with other slaves or freedmen, Patrobas probably fell into one of those categories himself. "Hermas," like "Hermes," had a name reminiscent of the Greek god Hermes, but spelled a bit differently probably because the name reflects a different Greek dialect.[104] Since "Hermes" was such a common slave name, "Hermas" was probably also a slave or freedman.

Paul indicates that these five men were part of a larger group of metaphorical "brothers and sisters," whom he also urges the Roman Christians to greet. It seems likely that the entire group lived in close proximity to one another, whether in the

100. On Mark and Rome, see Martin Hengel (*The Four Gospels and the One Gospel of Jesus Christ* [Harrisburg, PA: Trinity Press International, 2000], 34–38, 65–68, 78–96). The interpretation of Rom 16:13 through the lens of Mark 15:21 seems to have begun with Lightfoot (*Philippians*, 176).

101. BDAG 1060, s.v. Φλέγων; MGS 2292, s.v. Φλέγων; Lampe, *From Paul to Valentinus*, 180.

102. On the frequent occurrence of the name as a slave name, see Lampe (*From Paul to Valentinus*, 169, 173–74). The quoted description of Hermes is from Madeleine Jost, "Hermes," *OCD* 690.

103. Lightfoot, *Philippians*, 176–77; Lampe, *From Paul to Valentinus*, 178.

104. MGS 821, s.v. Ἑρμᾶς, call this spelling Doric. Cf. Cranfield, *Romans*, 2:795.

same large house, apartment block, or neighborhood. It also seems likely that they supported one another in the faith and gathered periodically for instruction and worship.[105]

16:15 Greet Philologus and Julia, Nereus and his sister, and Olympas, and all the saints with them (ἀσπάσασθε Φιλόλογον καὶ Ἰουλίαν, Νηρέα καὶ τὴν ἀδελφὴν αὐτοῦ, καὶ Ὀλυμπᾶν καὶ τοὺς σὺν αὐτοῖς πάντας ἁγίους). Paul urges the Roman Christians to greet five more individuals and the group of believers to which they belonged. This was probably another house or neighborhood church (cf. 16:14).

"Philologus," meaning either "talkative" or "learned" in Greek, was a common name among slaves and freedmen in first-century Rome.[106] The "and" connecting Philologus to Julia implies a family connection, just as it does with Nereus and his sister in the next clause, although whether they were married or were brother and sister is unclear. "Julia" was one of the most common of all Latin names for women in ancient Rome and appears in a wide range of social classes, from the most noble women in the households of the Julian emperors to enslaved and formerly enslaved women attached to some member of the Julian family.[107] Since Paul speaks of Philologus and Julia in the same breath, and since Philologus's Greek name probably indicates that he was a slave or freedman from the east, Julia was probably also a slave or freedwoman.

"Nereus," too, may well have been a slave or freedman; more than half of the name's occurrences in material from ancient Rome indicate slave status for its holders.[108] The names of gods, moreover, were commonly used as slave names, and Nereus was a Greek god of the sea.[109]

The two syllables "Olymp-" could terminate in several different ways (e.g., Olympiodorus, Olympianus, Olympicus), and any of the masculine forms of these names could be shortened to "Olympas." As with so many of the names in Romans 16:3–15, "Olympas" was very common among slaves and freedmen.[110] It also shows up only twice in inscriptions and literature related to the city of Rome in antiquity, making it likely that Olympas had come to Rome from the east.[111]

Just as in 16:15, so here, Paul urges the Roman church to greet five people individually and then a group of Christians associated with them. The entire group was probably made up of believers from a particular neighborhood that supported one another in their faith in Christ and gathered periodically in a workshop, apartment, or house in Rome for mutual instruction and worship.

16:16 Greet one another with a holy kiss. All the assemblies of Christ greet you. (Ἀσπάσασθε ἀλλήλους ἐν φιλήματι ἁγίῳ. Ἀσπάζονται ὑμᾶς αἱ ἐκκλησίαι πᾶσαι τοῦ Χριστοῦ). Paul exhorts the Roman believers gathered from their various neighborhoods for hearing his letter to greet one another. They were to do this across the customary social boundaries and in a way that conveyed both love and respect for one another. He reciprocates by conveying a greeting to the Romans from every other assembly of those who worship Christ.

Just as he does in three other letters, Paul en-

105. For the possibilities, see Billings, "From House Church to Tenement Church," 558–67; Last, "The Neighborhood (*vicus*) of the Corinthian *ekklēsia*," 408–19.

106. *TLNT* 3:452–53.

107. Lampe, *From Paul to Valentinus*, 175.

108. Lampe, *From Paul to Valentinus*, 169, 174; Jewett, *Romans*, 972.

109. Lampe, *From Paul to Valentinus*, 173, 174.

110. Ibid., 179.

111. Peter Lampe, "Olympas," *ABD* 5:15; Jewett, *Romans*, 972.

courages all those assembled for hearing the letter to greet one another with a kiss (cf. 1 Cor 16:20; 2 Cor 13:12; 1 Thess 5:26).[112] Kisses were signs of affection for family members, of salutation between members of the same social class, and of respect for those in positions of authority in both the Jewish and the Greco-Roman world generally.[113] Jesus expected a kiss of greeting from Simon the Pharisee, probably as a customary sign of respect for a rabbi (Luke 7:45), and the author of Joseph and Aseneth pictured Joseph as telling Aseneth that "a man who worships God" kisses his family members who also worship God, and that "a woman who worships God" does not kiss a strange man "because this is an abomination before the Lord God" (8:6–7 [C. Burchard, *OTP* 2:212).[114]

On the Greco-Roman side, Pliny the Elder identified the source of an infectious skin disease in Italy in the mid-first century as the kiss of salutation that upper-class people gave to each other. "Women were not liable to the disease, or slaves and the lower and middle classes," he says, "but the nobles were very much infected through the momentary contact of a kiss" (*Natural History* 26.3.3 [W. H. S. Jones, LCL]).

Paul's exhortation that the Roman Christians should give one another this salutation irrespective of physical family ties or class distinctions was an expression of the gospel's insistence on treating everyone equally (Rom 3:27–30; 10:12; cf. 1 Cor 8:13–15; 12:13; Gal 3:28; Col 3:11).[115] The kiss was "holy" (ἅγιος) because it was exchanged among God's people, who effectively had formed a new family of brothers and sisters (cf., e.g., Rom 12:10a; 16:1, 14–15, 17).

In a move that is consistent with this spirit of equality and reciprocity across social boundaries, Paul next does for the Romans Christians what he has asked them to do for one another.[116] He conveys greetings to them from "all the assemblies of Christ" (αἱ ἐκκλησίαι πᾶσαι τοῦ Χριστοῦ), a unique phrase in the Pauline corpus.[117] Paul typically either leaves the word "assembly" (or "assemblies") unqualified (e.g., 1 Cor 7:17) or qualifies it with a place name (e.g., Macedonia [2 Cor 8:1], Judea [Gal 1:22], Thessalonica [1 Thess 1:1]). Sometimes he adds the phrase "of God" (e.g., 1 Cor 11:16, 22). Here Paul not only speaks generally of "all the assemblies," presumably in every place, but calls them assemblies "of Christ." Paul's precise motivation for doing this is unclear, but the effect was certainly to emphasize the unity of the Roman Christians with all other Christians as well as Paul's apostolic authority to convey greetings from everyone who worships Christ to Christians in a particular place (cf. Rom 1:1, 5; 15:14–21).

112. Peter, writing from Rome, also admonishes the audience of his letter to "greet one another with the kiss of love [φιλήματι ἀγάπης]" (1 Pet 5:14). A century after Paul's letter, the custom was still in place among Roman Christians (Justin, *First Apology* 65.2).

113. Gustav Stählin, "φιλέω, κτλ.," *TDNT* 9:119–24.

114. For discussion of the Joseph and Asenath passage, see William Klassen, "The Sacred Kiss in the New Testament: An Example of Social Boundary Lines," *NTS* 39 (1993): 124–26.

115. Chrysostom, *Romans*, 492; Cf. Klassen, "Sacred Kiss," 132–35; Jewett, *Romans*, 974; Hultgren, *Romans*, 579.

116. Cf. Chrysostom, *Romans*, 492.

117. Sanday and Headlam, *Romans*, 428; Cranfield, *Romans*, 2:796.

Theology in Application

The diverse list of people to whom Paul sends greetings in 16:1–16 illustrates the principle that reconciliation to God, at God's initiative, must lead to reconciliation between human beings. The church should lead the way in destroying the barriers that sinful human culture has put in place to divide people groups and to keep certain groups in power at the expense of others.

The Countercultural Nature of Early Christian Society

Paul names slaves and freedmen (e.g., Ampliatus, Hermes, Nereus, Persis), Jews (Aquila, Miriam, Andronicus, Junia, Herodion, Rufus and his mother) and gentiles, and probably some people who did not have slavery in their background and may have been relatively affluent (e.g., Prisca). He praises women for their contribution to the advancement of the gospel alongside men (e.g., Prisca, Junia, Miriam, Persis) and greets people with both Greek (e.g., Apelles, Nereus) and Latin names (e.g., Ampliatus, Rufus). He elevates women who had no real name of their own but only the name of their family (Julia), and slaves whose names bear witness to their cultural status as "living tools" in Aristotle's terms, valued by the culture simply for what their masters could get out of them (Urbanus, Asyncritus). To all of them, across the various societal barriers, Paul extends a familial and respectful greeting and hints throughout that he and they are all part of the same family, the people of God. Phoebe is everyone's sister (16:1), Rufus's mother is Paul's "mother" (16:13), the group of believers to which Asyncritus, Phlegon, Hermes, Patrobas, and Hermas belong are everyone's brothers and sisters (16:14), and everyone is a "saint" (16:2, 15).

This characteristic of Christianity brought great offense in the ancient Roman world, which depended in part upon strictly observed social barriers to maintain its coherence and keep the already powerful in power. In Rome itself, seating in the theater was according to social class with "noncitizens, women, and slaves, when they were permitted to attend theater at all," directed into seats in the highest sections at the rear.[118] Those invited to dinner were sometimes provided various menus according to their rank in society.[119] Even in the baths, where all were welcome and little clothing was worn, the wealthy displayed their social standing by the quality of their bath towels and the size of their slave entourage.[120] It is not that rich and poor did not mingle—they often lived in the same apartment buildings, went to the same baths, and watched the same spectacle entertainments—but that within this mingling everyone had an inviolable place. Celsus, writing in the late second century but probably reflecting earlier attitudes, was only acting predictably, then, when he

118. Zanker, *Power of Images in the Age of Augustus*, 149. See also Elizabeth Rawson, *Roman Culture and Society: Collected Papers* (Oxford: Clarendon, 1991), 508–45.

119. Stambaugh, *Ancient Roman City*, 207.

120. Ibid., 205.

expressed disgust at the appeal of Christians to the "illiterate country bumpkins" who met in "private houses" and were the "wool workers, cobblers, laundry workers" of society.[121] Indeed, "the Christians postulate that everyone is a sinner, so that they are able to extend their appeal to the public at large."[122] Celsus seems to be alarmed at the leveling tendency of Christianity.

Despite the offense this element of the gospel must have caused even in Paul's own time, he insisted on breaking down the boundaries that provided a structure for the oppression of the weak. He insisted that the church should expose the lie that some people were better than others. He publicly greeted and praised his friends in Rome and those about whom he had only heard, regardless of their social class or gender. Everyone was to greet everyone else with a holy kiss (16:16), because all belonged to God's family and were brothers and sisters of one another.

Paul seemed to recognize that this radical flattening of societal walls was not a normal human impulse but must happen among Christians because of the common bond that their faith in the gospel had created. Over and over again in his list of greetings, he emphasizes that those whom he greets are united with Christ by faith. They are "in the Lord" (16:2, 8, 11, 12, 13), "in Christ" (16:7, 9, 10; cf. 16:3, 16), and "for Christ" (16:5). This common union with Christ is the fountain from which their mutual honor, respect, and love flows. The gospel-transformed minds of Romans 12:1–2 provide the fuel that powers the ethical instructions in 12:15–16:

> Rejoice with those who rejoice; weep with those who weep. Think the same way toward one another; do not think haughty thoughts, but be carried away with humble concerns. Do not be wise in your own estimation. (12:15–16)

The Danger of Neglecting This Element of the Gospel

Martin Luther King Jr.'s "Letter from Birmingham Jail" is a justly famous document in the political and social history of the United States, and it makes a strong philosophical case for the moral goodness of civil disobedience in resisting the effect of unjust laws. It is also, however, a richly theological document. In it King expresses his disappointment that socially privileged church leaders have not supported more enthusiastically his efforts to end the institutionalized oppression of African Americans in the American South. King writes as a minister of the gospel to other ministers and as a Christian to others who claim to be Christians, and he expresses frustration at the unwillingness of his fellow Christians to empathize with the plight of their brothers and sisters in Christ laboring under oppression. "Shallow understanding from people of good will," he writes, "is more frustrating than

121. Celsus, *On the True Doctrine: A Discourse Against the Christians*, ed. and trans. R. Joseph Hoffmann (New York: Oxford, 1987), 73.

122. Ibid., 74.

absolute misunderstanding from people of ill will."[123] A little later in his argument he contrasts the courage of the early Christians with the complacency of the "the contemporary Church" in the American South in the face of massive injustice:

> In those days the church was not merely a thermometer that recorded the ideas and principles of popular opinion; it was a thermostat that transformed the mores of society. . . . Things are different now. So often the contemporary Church is a weak, ineffectual voice with an uncertain sound. So often it is an arch-defender of the status quo. Far from being disturbed by the presence of the Church, the power structure of the average community is consoled by the Church's silent—and often even vocal—sanction of things as they are.[124]

It is difficult to escape the impression that if more socially privileged Christians had been in regular contact in their neighborhood churches with the socially oppressed community that King represented, the religious leaders of the time, and the communities they represented, would have had a less "shallow" understanding of the deep injustices that affected so many of their brothers and sisters in Christ. If they had sipped the same communion cup during the worship service or sat down at dinner on the grounds afterward with African American families from their communities, King might not have had to explain to them in an open letter why the Alabama Christian Movement for Human Rights could not wait to help the needy until their complaint had somehow made its way through a profoundly unfair legal system.

In his letter, King warned the socially privileged church of his time that if it did not "recapture the sacrificial spirit of the early Church," it would "lose its authenticity" and that its witness to the watching world would suffer as a result. King had already observed, in 1963, the damage that the refusal of white Southern Christians to resist societal injustice had done to the cause of the gospel: "Every day I meet young people whose disappointment with the Church has turned into outright disgust."[125]

The church of every age must work hard to overcome the social barriers between people groups that sinful societies have put in place to keep certain people in power at the expense of others. It should not lag behind society in upholding the principles of fairness and human decency that God has implanted in the human heart. Instead, the social integration of neighborhood churches and the understanding of the plight of the poor and needy that comes with embracing all kinds of people ought to be an example of societal righteousness, peace, and joy to the wider unbelieving societies in which Christians live. Christians should be at the cutting edge of showing how well a society functions where kindness, respect, love, and justice are equally distributed to all.

123. Martin Luther King Jr., *The Autobiography of Martin Luther King, Jr.*, ed. Clayborne Carson (New York: Warner, 1998), 195.

124. Ibid., 200–201.

125. Ibid., 201.

CHAPTER 33

Romans 16:17–27

Literary Context

In the preceding commendation of Phoebe and lengthy set of greetings Paul had emphasized the gospel's effect of generating love and humility in relationships with one another and in this way tearing down the sinful social barriers that often divided various people groups in Greco-Roman society (16:1–16). Now he draws the letter to a close in a way that balances the positive expressions of social unity in 16:1–16 with a warning against doctrinal disunity (16:17–20) and then moves back to expressions of social unity in a series of closing greetings from third parties with him in Corinth (16:21–23).

A final doxology praises God for the gospel he has recently revealed, the gospel whose explanation has been the central focus of the letter (16:25–27). It also praises Jesus Christ, who stands at the center of that good news. The doxology returns to the letter's opening themes: the movement of the gospel to the gentiles so that they might obediently believe it, the strengthening of the Romans' faith, and the testimony of the Scriptures to the revelation of God's righteousness through the gospel (1:5, 11, 16–17).

This way of concluding Romans stands apart from any of Paul's other letter closings. Nowhere else does Paul end a letter with a doxology, and the "grace benediction" (16:20) with which he typically concludes (e.g., 1 Cor 16:23; 2 Cor 13:13; Gal 6:18) appears two paragraphs before the letter actually ends (16:21–23). Here in Romans, moreover, Paul interrupts his greeting section with a lengthy warning against false teachers (16:17–20), a unique move among his extant letters.

These unusual features of the final paragraphs of Romans have prompted a number of interpreters over the years to question whether the warning and the doxology were added to the letter later by someone other than Paul.[1] If they were removed, the letter would end in normal fashion, with a seamless section of greetings and a grace benediction.[2] In the view of these scholars, the style of the warning and the

1. E.g., Byrne, *Romans*, 455–56, 461–62; Jewett, *Romans*, 985–1014.

2. Byrne, *Romans*, 457; Jewett, *Romans*, 1012–14.

doxology is too different from Paul's usual diction, and the placement of the grace benediction too unusual, for the Pauline authorship of these elements to be likely. At least with the doxology, moreover, the uncertainty goes back over many centuries. A few manuscripts omit it entirely, and in others it wanders among ten different locations in the letter's concluding chapters, sometimes appearing in two different places in the same manuscript.[3]

Yet, the case for viewing both the warning and the doxology as part of the original letter is stronger. No Pauline letter ending follows precisely the same pattern as the others in its conclusion. Even the grace benediction, which almost always appears as the last sentence of Paul's letters, appears next to last in 1 Cor 16:23 and is followed by a unique concluding expression of Paul's affection for the Corinthians (1 Cor 16:24).[4] The warning (16:17–20), although it certainly contains some expressions that Paul does not use elsewhere (e.g., "fine speech" [χρηστολογία], "the unsuspecting" [οἱ ἄκακοι]) follows his regular pattern of issuing a concluding exhortation and warning, sometimes in rather harsh terms (1 Cor 16:22; 1 Thess 5:27), at the end of his letters (1 Cor 16:13–16; 2 Cor 13:11; Gal 6:11–13; Col 4:17; 2 Thess 3:14–15; 1 Tim 6:20–21; 2 Tim 4:14–15; Titus 3:14). It also contains the typical Pauline reference to peace near the end of a letter (Rom 16:20; cf. 2 Cor 13:11; Gal 6:16; Eph 6:23; Phil 4:23; 1 Thess 5:23; 2 Thess 3:16).

The doxology is more difficult since it appears in a number of different locations among the witnesses to the text of Romans and is actually missing in a few ancient manuscripts. Paul never concludes a letter with a doxology, moreover, and this particular doxology is unusual. It is the longest doxology in the New Testament and contains a grammatical conundrum in the final relative clause that is virtually unsolvable.

Here too, however, it is best to accept the doxology as Pauline. The manuscripts that omit it altogether are late, coming from the ninth (F G) and fourteenth centuries (629), and although it does move around in the manuscript tradition, this is probably because of the chaos created early in the textual history of Romans when the text was edited to make it more universally applicable. This universalizing effort removed references to Rome in 1:7 and 15, cut out chapters fifteen and sixteen, and probably salvaged 16:25–27 to provide a more fitting end to a letter that would otherwise have concluded with "everything that is not from faith is sin" (14:23).[5]

It is true, moreover, that Paul never closes another letter with a doxology, but he does utter a brief doxology near the end of Philippians (Phil 4:20), and Romans in any case is an unusual letter. It is Paul's longest extant letter and was written to

3. Raymond F. Collins, "The Case of A Wandering Doxology (Rom 16,25–27)," in *New Testament Textual Criticism and Exegesis*, ed. A. Denaux, BETL 161 (Leuven: Leuven University Press, 2002), 295–96.

4. Longenecker, *Introducing Romans*, 37.

5. Hurtado, "The Doxology at the End of Romans," 192.

a Christian community he had never visited at a critical turning point in his missionary career. These characteristics of the letter help explain its long introduction (1:1–7), the longest in the Pauline corpus, and make the doxology of 16:25–27 a less unexpected conclusion.

It is consistent with this explanation for the doxology that it returns to some of the key theological themes of the letter, especially those that Paul covers in the opening steps of his argument. It mentions the strengthening of the Roman Christians with his gospel (16:25; cf. 1:11), the revelation of the gospel in the present time (16:25–26; cf. 1:17–18; 3:21), the consistency of the gospel with Israel's Scriptures (16:26; cf. 1:2–3; 3:10–21), and the inclusive nature of the gospel as a demonstration of God's unity (16:26; 1:5; 3:29–30).

Although the doxology is a long, grammatically complex sentence, its style is not out of step with some of the complex sentences in Ephesians (cf. Eph 1:3–14, 15–23; 2:1–7; 3:1–7; 4:11–16; 6:14–20), and if that letter is accepted as genuine, there is no reason to deny 16:15–27 to Paul on stylistic grounds.[6] It is, instead, a fitting conclusion to Paul's most sustained and profound presentation of the gospel.[7]

XII. The Purpose of Paul's Letter in the Context of His Apostolic Vocation (15:14–33)

XIII. Paul's Concluding Greetings, Warnings, and Ascription of Praise to God (16:1–27)

A. Paul's Commendation of Phoebe (16:1–2)

B. Paul's Greetings to Friends in Rome and Others Whom He Knows by Reputation (16:3–16)

➡ **C. Paul's Warning, Greetings from Third Parties, and Concluding Doxology (16:17–27)**

Main Idea

Paul concludes his long exposition and application of the gospel with a straightforward warning to the Roman Christians not to be deceived by any form of the gospel that takes the focus off serving Christ and puts it instead on serving evil human desires. He then passes along greetings from those engaged in the work of the gospel with him in Corinth and utters a prayer of praise to the only God, who, according to the gospel Paul has just explained, is known not only through Israel's Scriptures but through Jesus Christ and is able both to bring people to faith in himself and strengthen them in that faith.

6. On the genuineness of Ephesians and the complexity of its style, see Frank Thielman, *Ephesians*, BECNT (Grand Rapids: Baker, 2010), 1–11.

7. Cf. I. Howard Marshall, "Romans 16:25–27—An Apt Conclusion," in *Romans and the People of God*, ed. Sven K. Soderlund and N. T. Wright (Grand Rapids: Eerdmans, 1999), 170–84.

Translation

Romans 16:17–27

17a	Warning	**Now I appeal to you, brothers and sisters,**
b		to look out for those who create dissensions and stumbling blocks
c		contrary to the teaching that you learned, and
d		steer clear of them.
18a	Basis (of 17)	For **such people are not slaves** to our Lord Christ but
b	Contrast (to 18a)	to their own belly,
c	Means	and through fine speech and blessing
d	Basis (of 17)	**they deceive the hearts of the unsuspecting.**
19a	Basis (of 17)	For **[the report of] your obedience has reached everyone.**
b	Result	So **I rejoice because of you,**
c	Exhortation	but **I want you to be wise with reference to what is good but**
d	Contrast (to 19c)	**pure with reference to what is evil.**
20a	Promise	But **the God of peace will quickly crush Satan under your feet.**
b	Desire	**The grace of our Lord Jesus be with you.**
21a	Assertion	**Timothy my coworker greets you, and also**
b	List	**Lucius,**
c		**Jason, and**
d		**Sosipater,**
e	Apposition	**my compatriots.**
22	Assertion	**I, Tertius, the one who has written this letter in the Lord, greet you.**
23a	Assertion	**Gaius, host to me and to the whole church, greets you.**
b	Assertion	**Erastus, the treasurer of the city greets you, and Quartus, the brother.**

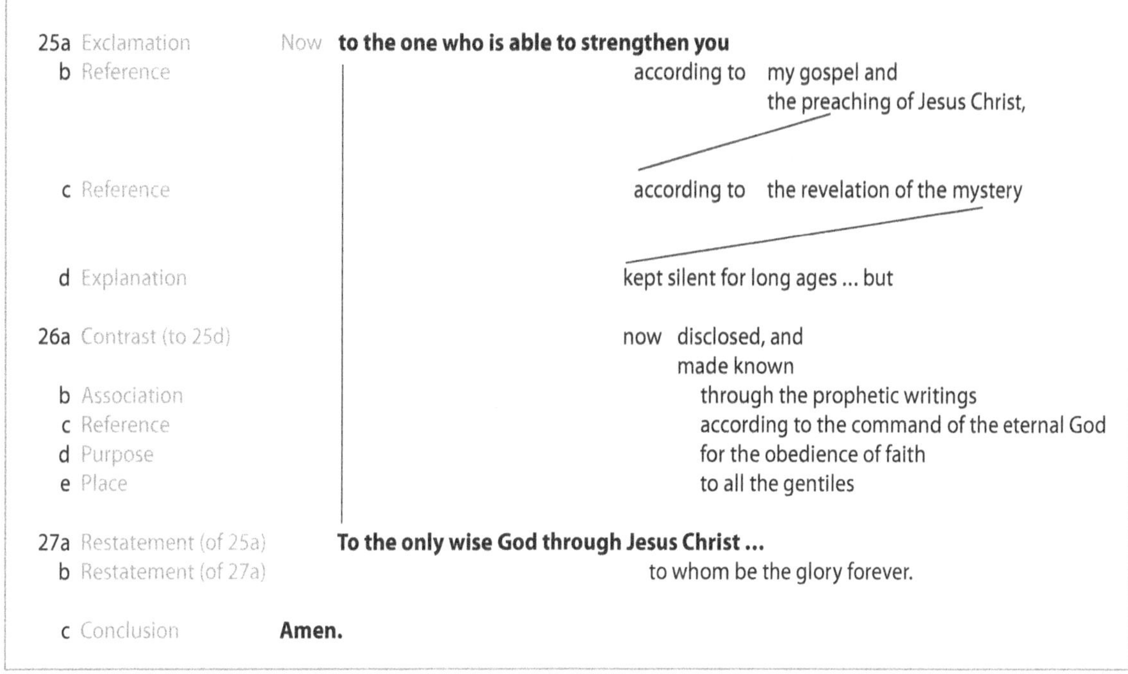
25a Exclamation Now **to the one who is able to strengthen you**
b Reference according to my gospel and
the preaching of Jesus Christ,
c Reference according to the revelation of the mystery
d Explanation kept silent for long ages ... but
26a Contrast (to 25d) now disclosed, and
made known
b Association through the prophetic writings
c Reference according to the command of the eternal God
d Purpose for the obedience of faith
e Place to all the gentiles
27a Restatement (of 25a) **To the only wise God through Jesus Christ ...**
b Restatement (of 27a) to whom be the glory forever.
c Conclusion **Amen.**

Structure

This final passage falls into four parts of uneven length, but each one fulfilling a discrete purpose appropriate to the close of such a complex letter. The first section (16:17–20), whose beginning Paul signals with "now" (δέ), is a warning against those who teach a different form of the gospel than the one Paul has just explained. This first section also unfolds in four steps. It begins with a description of these teachers (v. 17), explains why they are so dangerous (v. 18), explains that the warning was necessary only because the witness of the Roman Christians to the wider Christian world was so important (v. 19), and ends with a statement of confidence that God will be victorious over evil (v. 20).

The second section (16:20b) is the shortest discrete part of the conclusion. It is simply a grace benediction similar to those that almost always appear as the last sentence in Paul's letters.[8] Why it appears at this point, before Paul sends greetings from his associates and before the doxology, is not clear, but Paul may simply have added the next paragraph of greetings (16:21–23) as an afterthought and then viewed the doxology (16:25–27) as a substitute for the grace benediction.[9]

8. The only exception is 1 Cor 16:23 where the grace benediction is followed by "my love be with you all in Christ Jesus. Amen."

9. Michel, *An die Römer*, 483.

The third section conveys greetings from Paul's friends with him in Corinth to the Roman Christians (16:21–23), including an unusual first-person reference to the secretary who took down Paul's dictation (v. 22). Such greetings appear at the end of eight Pauline letters, but the list of names of people sending greetings here is longer by one than in any of the other letters (cf. Col 4:10–14).

The fourth section is the concluding doxology, which consists of one long, syntactically broken sentence in Greek (Rom 16:25–27). Although unique as a conclusion for a Pauline letter, it is not entirely unprecedented. Paul has already ended a major section of his argument with a doxology (11:33–36; cf. Eph 3:20–21), and other early Christian letters sometimes end this way (e.g., 2 Pet 3:18; Jude 24–25; 1 Clem. 65.2; 2 Clem. 20.5).[10]

The threefold reference to the one who is praised ("to the one who is able . . . to the only wise God . . . to whom . . .") dominates its syntactical structure, with the expression of praise only appearing climactically at the end (". . . be glory . . .").[11] Within this framework, the emphasis lies on a full description of the gospel that forms the standard "according to" which God is able to strengthen Paul's audience (16:25–26). That description, in turn, focuses on the contrast between the silence that dominated the period prior to the revelation of the gospel and the open proclamation of the gospel that dominates the present period. This contrast then leads to a climactic expression of praise to God, through Jesus Christ, for his wisdom (16:27).

Exegetical Outline

- **I. Paul's Concluding Greetings, Warnings, and Ascription of Praise to God (16:1–27)**
  - A. Paul's Commendation of Phoebe (16:1–2)
  - B. Paul's Greetings to Friends in Rome and Others Whom He Knows by Reputation (16:3–16)
  - ➡ **C. Paul's Warning, Greetings from Third Parties, and Concluding Doxology (16:17–27)**
    - 1. A Warning against Persuasive False Teachers (16:17–20)
      - a. A description of the false teachers (16:17)
      - b. Why they are so dangerous (16:18)
      - c. Why a warning against them is necessary (16:19)
      - d. An expression of confidence in God's victory over evil (16:20)
    - 2. Greetings from Eight Friends with Paul in Corinth (16:21–23)

10. Cf. Marshall, "Romans 16:25–27," 177–78.

11. See the diagram in Marshall, "Romans 16:25–27," 173.

3. A Prayer of Praise to the God Who Revealed the Gospel and Strengthens Those Who Believe It (16:25–27)
   a. Praise to God who can strengthen the faith of those who believe the gospel about Jesus Christ (16:25–26)
      (1) The details of the gospel were kept secret for ages past (16:25)
      (2) Now the gospel has been fully revealed in a way that is consistent with the ancient Scriptures (16:26)
   b. Praise to the God whose wisdom is displayed in the gospel (16:27)
      (1) Praise also to Jesus Christ (16:27a–b)
      (2) The concluding "amen" (16:27c)

Explanation of the Text

16:17 Now I appeal to you, brothers and sisters, to look out for those who create dissensions and stumbling blocks contrary to the teaching that you learned, and steer clear of them (Παρακαλῶ δὲ ὑμᾶς, ἀδελφοί, σκοπεῖν τοὺς τὰς διχοστασίας καὶ τὰ σκάνδαλα παρὰ τὴν διδαχὴν ἣν ὑμεῖς ἐμάθετε ποιοῦντας, καὶ ἐκκλίνετε ἀπ' αὐτῶν). Paul warns the Roman Christians against teaching that deviates from the gospel tradition they and he both believe.

"Now I appeal to you, brothers and sisters" echoes Paul's urgent request for prayer in 15:30 and uses the term "now" (δέ) to signal a new paragraph, just as it did there (cf. 12:1). Here, "brothers and sisters" (ἀδελφοί) picks up the family language throughout the greeting section and especially in Paul's instructions to "greet one another with a holy kiss" at the conclusion of that section (16:16b). The expression "look out" (σκοπεῖν) is not uncommon in Paul's letters, especially in instructions about how believers should behave, and he could use it either positively of watching someone as an example (Phil 3:17), or negatively, as he does here, of watching out for some error (Gal 6:1).

Paul's warning is against people who create two types of problems for the community, "dissensions" and "stumbling blocks contrary to the teaching that you learned." The term "dissensions" (διχοστασίας) could refer to political division over a body of law (Dionysius of Halicarnassus, *Ant. rom.* 8.72.4; 1 Macc 3:29), and elsewhere Paul sandwiches the term between "rivalries" (ἐριθεῖαι) and "divisions" (αἱρέσεις) (Gal 5:20). "Stumbling blocks" (σκάνδαλα) refers to ideas, teachings, or practices that prevent progress (cf. Rom 9:33) and send people down the path to destruction (cf. Rom 14:13, 20). The two types of problems are connected: Paul warns against people who create division and prevent progress in the faith by injecting erroneous ideas and practices into the Christian community.

The hallmark of these false teachers is their deviation from the gospel that Paul has just explained and that he believes he and the Roman Christians, and all right-thinking believers, hold in common (1:8, 12; 15:14; cf. 1 Cor 15:1–3).[12] It is the "teaching to which" they "were handed over" (6:17) when they first believed the gospel.[13]

If people emerge in Rome who teach in a way that is contrary to this commonly acknowledged

12. Sanday and Headlam, *Romans*, 430.

13. Cf. Wilckens, *An die Römer (Röm 12–16)*, 141.

teaching, the Roman believers should "steer clear" (ἐκκλίνετε) of them. This warning probably does not refer to false teaching that was already present in Rome. Paul was too confident in the soundness of the Romans' commitment to the faith for that to be likely (16:19; cf. 15:14).

16:18 For such people are not slaves to our Lord Christ but to their own belly, and through fine speech and blessing they deceive the hearts of the unsuspecting (οἱ γὰρ τοιοῦτοι τῷ κυρίῳ ἡμῶν Χριστῷ οὐ δουλεύουσιν ἀλλὰ τῇ ἑαυτῶν κοιλίᾳ, καὶ διὰ τῆς χρηστολογίας καὶ εὐλογίας ἐξαπατῶσιν τὰς καρδίας τῶν ἀκάκων). The Roman Christians should stay away from those who create divisions by their deceptive teaching because such people can use their rhetorical skill to convince others with little theological training to serve the immoral interests of the false teachers themselves.

Paul now gives the reason why (γάρ) his Roman audience should "steer clear" of people like those he has just described in 16:17. He has used the verb "be slaves to" (δουλεύω) several times in Romans to describe the stranglehold of sin (6:6; 7:25) on the human being and also to describe service to "the Lord" (12:11) and to "Christ" (14:18). Here he describes serving "the Lord Christ" and the "belly" (κοιλίᾳ) in a way that recalls the contrast of serving "the law of God" and the "law of sin" in 7:25 and the contrast of enslavement either to sin or to obedience to the Christian tradition, righteousness, and God in 6:15–23. It is likely, then, that enslavement to the belly here refers to nothing as specific as the Jewish food laws (cf. 14:1–15:6) but more generally to the appetites, or as Titus 3:3 puts it, being "slaves to various passions and pleasures."[14]

The kind of excesses that frequently took place at banquets in the ancient Roman world might well be in view. Paul has already urged the Romans once in the letter to avoid them (13:13), and he was writing from Corinth where these kinds of excesses had created problems for the church in the past (1 Cor 6:12–20).[15] That such excesses could be grounded in a specious theoretical rationale is clear from Corinthian sloganeering ("all things are lawful"; 1 Cor 6:12; 10:23).[16]

Here Paul characterizes the articulation of this special rationale as "fine speech [χρηστολογία] and blessing [εὐλογία]," an odd way of describing speech that is morally wrong. The first term appears here for the first time in extant Greek, and Paul probably coined it, so its meaning is not entirely clear.[17] The common adjective "fine" (χρηστός), however, typically pertains to what is "morally good and benevolent," and so Paul's neologism most naturally refers to "swete preachinges," as Tyndale memorably put it, or to what the KJV more blandly called "good words."[18] The second term, similarly, is a positive word for "good or fine language . . . praise," "lovely words."[19]

Why does Paul use such positive terms here to describe the deceptive speech of "those who create divisions and stumbling blocks"? He is probably describing people who use language that on the surface seems theologically correct but who draw incorrect conclusions from that language about

14. Cf. Philo, *Alleg. Interp.* 3.115: "To the lustful portion of the soul [they assign] the area around the abdomen and the belly [κοιλίαν], for there desire dwells, an irrational impulse" (transl. Jewett, *Romans*, 991). The same is probably also true of the reference to the "belly" in Phil 3:19.

15. Cf. Dunn, *Romans 9–16*, 904.

16. Cf. also 2 Pet 2:3, 18–19; 3:3–4; Jude 16.

17. J. Lionel North, "'Good Wordes and Faire Speeches' (Rom 16.18 AV): More Materials and a Pauline Pun," *NTS* 42 (1996): 602–6, 610.

18. See BDAG 1090, s.v. χρηστός 3.

19. Respectively, LSJ 720; MGS 853, both s.v. εὐλογία. It is sometimes said to have a negative connotation in Aesop, *Fables* 160, but North ("'Good Wordes and Fair Speeches,'" 600n1) has shown this to be incorrect.

how believers should live.[20] They may have, for example, waxed eloquent on the topics of "grace" and "faith," but then perverted "the grace of our God into sensuality" (Jude 4) and failed to recognize that "faith by itself, if it does not have works, is dead" (Jas 2:17).

"The unsuspecting" (οἱ ἄκακοι) could be "the innocent" in a praiseworthy sense (Prov 2:21; 13:6 LXX), but the context implies that they are instead those who are gullible and could use some instruction (cf. Prov 1:4; 8:5; 14:15; 21:11).

16:19 For [the report of] your obedience has reached everyone. So I rejoice because of you, but I want you to be wise with reference to what is good but pure with reference to what is evil (ἡ γὰρ ὑμῶν ὑπακοὴ εἰς πάντας ἀφίκετο· ἐφ᾽ ὑμῖν οὖν χαίρω, θέλω δὲ ὑμᾶς σοφοὺς εἶναι εἰς τὸ ἀγαθόν, ἀκεραίους δὲ εἰς τὸ κακόν). The reason for Paul's warning to the Romans lies in the example of obedience to the gospel that they have provided all other believers and his reflection on how important their continued obedience is to the gospel's progress.

Paul's "for" (γάρ) probably goes back to 16:17 and to the admonition both to look out for false teachers and stay away from them. The Romans' worldwide reputation for obedience to the gospel (1:8) means that if they succumbed to false teaching they would damage their example to others and hinder the gospel's progress. Paul occasionally urged the churches over which he exercised apostolic authority to pay attention to the example that they set for others (2 Cor 8:24; 9:31; 1 Thess 1:7–10), and that theme is also present here.[21]

"Therefore" (οὖν) in the second clause refers not to the fame of the Romans but to their obedience. As Paul had already emphasized in 15:14, and even further back in 1:12, he did not write his letter because he thought the Roman believers defective in their understanding of the gospel. They were instead a cause for rejoicing (cf. 2 Cor 2:3; 7:4; Phil 2:2; 4:1; 1 Thess 2:19–20). In the same way, he did not write the warning of 16:17–18 because he thought they were on the verge of apostasy but to add wisdom to their knowledge and hopefully prevent deception.

16:20a But the God of peace will quickly crush Satan under your feet (ὁ δὲ θεὸς τῆς εἰρήνης συντρίψει τὸν Σατανᾶν ὑπὸ τοὺς πόδας ὑμῶν ἐν τάχει). Paul promises that God will ultimately defeat the transcendent being who uses false teachers to nurture theological and moral chaos among Christians.

In contast (δέ) to the struggle between good and evil Paul has just mentioned in the previous clause, he holds out to his readers the promise of complete victory over evil in the future. His description of God as "the God of peace" recalls his prayer for peace in the Roman community in 15:33, but not because he identified the group that creates divisions and stumbling blocks in 16:17–18 with either party in that dispute. The path to peace in that local problem of division lay in each group welcoming the other; here the path to peace comes only through God's defeat of Satan. That problem of division was solved through negotiation and understanding in the give-and-take of everyday life; here the problem is solved only through metaphorical military action taken by God himself in the invisible, spiritual world at some point in the future.

The verb "will crush" (συντρίψει) was used in military contexts to refer to the rout of an enemy (e.g., Polybius, *Histories* 5.47.1), and imagery from the early empire often depicted Roman emperors

20. Cf. the texts cited in North ("'Good Wordes and Fair Speeches,'" 602n6).

21. Cranfield, *Romans*, 2:802.

or armies standing over conquered peoples.[22] The violent idea of crushing an enemy under foot, therefore, would have been familiar to Paul's audience. The enemy that God will crush, however, is not the false teachers of Romans 16:17–18 but Satan, the clever and deceptive opponent of God and his people (2 Cor 2:11; 1 Thess 2:18; 2 Thess 2:9), who stands behind false teaching in the church (2 Cor 11:13–15; 1 Tim 5:15). Paul often depicted God's future defeat of evil by using military imagery drawn from the Scriptures (2 Cor 10:3–6; Eph 6:10–17), and that is also his procedure here.

The Scripture lying in the background is not primarily Genesis 3:15, despite a long tradition of interpreting Paul's sentence as an echo of God's curse upon the deceiving serpent of Genesis 3:1–19.[23] Rather, Paul's language is more directly indebted to Psalms 8:6 and 110:1 (8:7 and 109:1 LXX), a combination early Christians often used to describe Christ's victory over God's enemies (e.g., 1 Pet 3:22; Heb 1:3, 13; 2:6–8; cf. Rom 8:34; 1 Cor 15:25–27).[24]

Paul also uses this combination in Ephesians 1:20–23 to make much the same point that he makes here. In Ephesians, however, the victory is depicted explicitly as something won through Christ's resurrection and ascension and is placed in the past, whereas here it is simplified as God's victory and is projected into the future. In both texts God gives the victory he has won over Satan to the church for its benefit.

16:20b The grace of our Lord Jesus be with you (ἡ χάρις τοῦ κυρίου ἡμῶν Ἰησοῦ μεθ' ὑμῶν). Paul prays that his audience might experience the generously given gifts of God.

At the end of all thirteen of his extant letters, Paul places a brief benedictory prayer that God's grace would be with his audience. Sometimes that prayer is worded almost exactly as it is here (1 Cor 16:23; 1 Thess 5:28; 2 Thess 3:18). Sometimes Paul expanded it slightly to become a prayer that God would be with the "spirit" (πνεῦμα) of his audience (Gal 6:18; Phil 4:23; Phlm 25), or more elaborately to assign grace to Christ, love to God, and fellowship to the Spirit (2 Cor 13:13), or to limit the prayer to those who love the Lord Jesus (Eph 6:24). Sometimes Paul simplifies the benediction to "grace be with you" (Col 4:18; 1 Tim 6:21; 2 Tim 4:22) or "grace be with you all" (Titus 3:15).

The consistency with which Paul uses this prayer to conclude his letters demonstrates the importance of God's grace to Paul's theology. God showed grace to people through the redemptive, reconciling death of Jesus (e.g., Rom 3:24–25), through providing them with victory over evil in Christ's resurrection (e.g., Rom 6:14), and through giving them resources to live in loving fellowship with one another (e.g., Rom 12:6).

With only one other exception in the Pauline corpus (1 Cor 16:24), the grace benediction is Paul's final sentence, but here in Romans two paragraphs follow.[25] The first paragraph is a set of greetings to the Roman Christians from those with Paul as he writes the letter (16:21–23), and the second paragraph is a concluding doxology (16:25–27). The unusual placement of the grace benediction here probably explains why manuscripts that omit the doxology after 16:23 replace it with a grace benediction (F G 629) and why some manuscripts that have the doxology follow it with

22. Zanker, *Power of Images in the Age of Augustus*, 183 (fig. 142), 231 (fig. 182), 303 (fig. 234); Jewett, *Romans*, 994.

23. See, e.g., Alford, *Greek Testament*, 2:442; Godet, *Romans*, 499; Zahn, *An die Römer*, 613n73; Fitzmyer, *Romans*, 746; Wright, "Romans," 765.

24. Derek R. Brown, "'The God of Peace Will Shortly Crush Satan under Your Feet': Paul's Eschatological Reminder in Romans 16:20a," *Neot* 44 (2010): 5–13.

25. Longenecker, *Introducing Romans*, 37.

a grace benediction (P 33 104). Both procedures locate the grace benediction at the end of the letter, in its usual position.[26]

16:21 Timothy my coworker greets you, and also Lucius, Jason, and Sosipater, my compatriots (Ἀσπάζεται ὑμᾶς Τιμόθεος ὁ συνεργός μου, καὶ Λούκιος καὶ Ἰάσων καὶ Σωσίπατρος οἱ συγγενεῖς μου). Paul conveys greetings from Timothy to the Roman Christians, and perhaps especially to Prisca and Aquila. He also sends greetings from three fellow Jewish Christians, part of God's graciously chosen Israelite remnant and perhaps also part of the delegation traveling with Paul to Jerusalem to convey the collection for the poor among the saints there.

Paul often conveyed greetings to his letters' recipients for friends and coworkers who were with him at the time of writing (1 Cor 16:19–20; Phil 4:21–22; Col 4:10–14; Titus 3:15; Phlm 23), and this was a common practice in letters of the period.[27] Paul's "coworker" (συνεργός) Timothy was perhaps unfamiliar to many in Paul's Roman audience.[28] He would have known Paul's other "coworkers" Prisca and Aquila well (Rom 16:3), however, since they were all together in both Corinth and Ephesus (Acts 18:5, 19; 19:22; 1 Cor 4:17; 16:19).[29]

Luke says that Timothy was with Paul during his three-month stay in Corinth prior to Paul's journey to Jerusalem (Acts 19:21; 20:4), and this was almost certainly the time at which Paul wrote Romans. According to Acts 20:4, Timothy was part of the group that assembled in Corinth from Macedonia, Asia, and Galatia and that traveled with Paul to Jerusalem, a journey that Paul's correspondence indicates was for the purpose of conveying the collection for the poor among the Jewish Christians in Jerusalem (Rom 15:25–27; 1 Cor 16:3–4; 2 Cor 8:19–21; cf. Acts 24:17).

"Lucius" (Λούκιος) may have also been part of this group, although nothing is known of him other than what Paul says here. He was not "Luke" (Λουκᾶς) the evangelist.[30] When Paul refers to "Luke," he spells his name the way it appears in the title to the Gospel (Col 4:14; 2 Tim 4:11; Phlm 24). Acts 20:5, moreover, implies that the author of Acts joined Paul in Philippi after Paul had finished his three months in Corinth.[31] He could not, therefore, have been with Paul at the time he was writing Romans. Perhaps the Lucius here was Lucius of Cyrene (Acts 13:1), but since "Lucius" was a common name, there is no way to know this.[32]

There is a good probability that "Jason" was the same person who hosted Paul in Thessalonica and bailed him out of custody when he got into trouble with "the city authorities" (Acts 17:5–9).[33] He may well have been one of the Thessalonians, in

26. Manuscripts that place the doxology (16:25–27) after 14:23 (e.g., L Ψ 181 326) tend to have a grace benediction both at the end of 16:20 and after 16:23, and manuscripts that omit the doxology from the letter altogether (e.g., F G 629) tend to have a grace benediction only after 16:23. Manuscripts that have the doxology both after 14:23 and after 16:23 (e.g., P 33 104) tend to have a grace benediction both at the end of 16:20 and after the doxology. In all these cases, the impulse was to conclude the letter with a grace benediction in accord with Paul's usual practice. See Gamble, *Textual History*, 130–31, and Metzger, *Textual Commentary*, 476.

27. Hans-Josef Klauck, *Ancient Letters and the New Testament: A Guide to Context and Exegesis*, trans. Daniel P. Bailey (Waco, TX: Baylor University Press, 2006), 11, 15, 24.

28. A common observation, usually attributed to H. W. Schmidt. See, e.g., Schlier (*Der Römerbrief*, 450); Dunn (*Romans 9–16*, 909), and Jewett (*Romans*, 977).

29. Cf. Jewett, *Romans*, 977; Hultgren, *Romans*, 597.

30. Origen (*Romans, Books 6–10*, 304), writing in AD 246, says that interpreters before him thought this, and Dunn (*Romans 9–16*, 909) finds the suggestion attractive.

31. Fitzmyer, *Romans*, 748.

32. For the suggestion, see, e.g., Lagrange (*Romains*, 376), and for the cautionary note, see, e.g., Hultgren (*Romans*, 597).

33. Origen, *Romans, Books 6–10*, 304.

addition to Aristarchus and Secundus, who functioned as delegates from Macedonia for conveying the collection to Jerusalem.[34] Similarly, "Sosipater" (Σωσίπατρος) is probably the same person as "Sopater the Berean, son of Pyrrhus" who accompanied Paul as part of the delegation from Macedonia (Acts 20:4). "Sopater" could easily be a shortened form of "Sosipater."[35]

Lucius, Jason, and Sosipater were all Paul's "compatriots" (συγγενεῖς) or fellow Jews (cf. Rom 9:3; 16:7, 11). Like Andronicus, Junia, and Herodion (16:7, 11), then, they were Jewish Christians and part of God's graciously chosen remnant. Paul may have pointed out that they were Jewish Christians because they served as proof to him that God's promises to Israel had not failed (9:6) and that God had not cast off his people (11:1–7).

16:22 I, Tertius, the one who has written this letter in the Lord, greet you (ἀσπάζομαι ὑμᾶς ἐγὼ Τέρτιος ὁ γράψας τὴν ἐπιστολὴν ἐν κυρίῳ). Paul's secretary, who took down the letter at the apostle's dictation, contributed his skills to the project of getting the letter to the Romans because he too was a believer. Both he and Paul felt that it was fitting for him to send his own greetings to the Roman believers in his own voice, and this in turn indicates the tendency of the gospel to overcome social barriers.

Paul seems to have frequently employed secretaries to assist him in taking down his letters since he occasionally took the pen from the person to whom he dictated a letter to make a comment in his own hand (1 Cor 16:21; Gal 6:11; Col 4:18; 2 Thess 3:17; Phlm 19). Only here, however, does a secretary suddenly walk onto the stage, announce his name, and speak in his own voice.

Professional secretaries, who were often slaves, did sometimes record the use of their services in letters as a legal way of explaining why the author had not actually written the letter: "I, the aforesaid Aphrodisios specified before, have written for him, Herakles, because he does not know letters."[36] Tertius's sudden appearance in Romans, however, is different. He placed his secretarial skills at Paul's disposal because he was a believer, just as Tryphena, Tryphosa, and Persis labored hard "in the Lord" (16:12).[37] Both he and Paul considered his labor to be such an integral part of the composition and conveyance of the letter to Rome that they both agreed he should send his own greetings to the community. As Jewett aptly writes, "Whether he was an independent secretary or a slave, the self-introduction of Tertius reveals the remarkable equality 'in Christ' that was characteristic for the first generation of Pauline Christianity."[38]

16:23a Gaius, host to me and to the whole church, greets you (ἀσπάζεται ὑμᾶς Γάϊος ὁ ξένος μου καὶ ὅλης τῆς ἐκκλησίας). Paul conveys greetings from Gaius, a believer whom he had baptized on his first visit to Corinth and who generously provided a safe place in his home for Paul and other foreigners in Corinth who were Christians.

Paul now continues his dictation and sends greetings from his "host" (ξένος) Gaius. The term translated "host" was used to refer both to a foreigner (e.g., Eph 2:19) and to someone willing to

34. E.g., Cranfield, *Romans*, 2:805–6; Jewett, *Romans*, 977–78.

35. Cranfield, *Romans 9–16*, 806; Jewett, *Romans*, 978.

36. P.Ryl. 94.14–16 (AD 14–37). English translation from Klauck, *Ancient Letters*, 57. For the role of secretaries in composing letters, see ibid., 55–60.

37. Most modern translations (e.g., NIV, NRSV, NET, ESV, CSB) take "in the Lord" (ἐν κυρίῳ) with the verb "greet" (ἀσπάζομαι), but the proximity of the phrase to the participle "has written" (γράψας) and the analogy of laboring "in the Lord" in 16:12 make the older rendering of Origen (*Romans, Books 6–10*, 306), Luther, and Tyndale, now also adopted by the CEB, more likely. Cf. Jewett, *Romans*, 979.

38. Jewett, *Romans*, 980. Cf. Lagrange, *Romains*, 376–77.

extend hospitality to a foreigner. Plato, for example, could describe the custom by which a distinguished person might travel to another country, present himself to people of similar social standing there, and "believing himself to be a proper guest [ξένος] for such a host [ξένῳ]" expect to receive a warm welcome (*Laws* 953d [G. Bury, LCL]).[39]

Gaius, however, was not merely a host to the foreigner Paul but to "the whole church" (ὅλης τῆς ἐκκλησίας). This phrase probably does not mean that Gaius accommodated in his supposedly large house an occasional, plenary assembly of all the different, smaller house churches in Corinth.[40] Since the term "host" indicates that he was hospitable to foreigners, "the whole church" describes the wide extent of his hospitality to believing foreigners.[41] Paul may have especially had in mind the delegates from Macedonia, Asia, and Galatia who had assembled in Corinth to go with Paul and the collection to Jerusalem (cf. Acts 20:4).[42] The term "church" (ἐκκλησία), therefore, has the sense here of the worldwide fellowship of believers (cf. 1 Cor 10:32; Gal 1:13) rather than, as in Romans 16:1, 4, 5, and 16, the local "assembly" of believers.[43]

Who was Gaius? He had a common Latin name of the period (cf. Acts 19:29; 20:4; 3 John 1), and so certainty is not possible. Probably, however, he was the person that Paul remembered baptizing in Corinth according to 1 Corinthians 1:14.[44]

16:23b Erastus, the treasurer of the city greets you, and Quartus, the brother (ἀσπάζεται ὑμᾶς Ἔραστος ὁ οἰκονόμος τῆς πόλεως καὶ Κούαρτος ὁ ἀδελφός). The wealthy and powerful city treasurer of Corinth along with an othewise unknown member of the family of Christ send greetings to the Roman Christians.

The name "Erastus" shows up two other times in the the New Testament and refers both times to an associate of Paul. Not long before Paul wrote Romans, Paul sent Timothy and someone named Erastus, both identified as "his helpers" (τῶν διακονούντων αὐτῷ), ahead of him to Macedonia, and presumably then on to Achaia while he stayed behind in Ephesus a little while longer (Acts 19:22; cf. 20:1–3). About a decade later, writing to Timothy in Ephesus, Paul informed Timothy that "Erastus remained at Corinth" (2 Tim 4:20). According to H. J. Cadbury, "The name Erastus belongs neither to the commonest nor to the most uncommon of names of the Hellenistic world."[45] It is possible, therefore, that the Erastus Paul refers to here in Romans was a different person than these other Erasti, but this seems unlikely. All three occurrences of the name refer to a close associate of Paul and place him in or near Corinth. It is reasonable to infer from the references in Acts, moreover, that he was with Paul in Corinth at the time Paul wrote Romans.[46]

Would a busy "treasurer" (οἰκονόμος) of a city the size of Corinth have had the freedom to travel with Paul this way?[47] Pelagius seems to have assumed that he once held this position and retained the title but no longer carried out the responsibilities associated with it.[48] Erastus may well have been

39. MGS 1415, s.v. ξένος A.

40. E.g., Jerome Murphy-O'Connor, *Paul: A Critical Life* (Oxford: Clarendon, 1996), 267.

41. Adams, *Earliest Christian Meeting Places*, 28.

42. Jewett, *Romans*, 981.

43. Adams, *Earliest Christian Meeting Places*, 28–29.

44. BDAG 186, s.v. Γάϊος.

45. Henry J. Cadbury, "Erastus of Corinth," *JBL* 50 (1931): 56. MM 252, s.v. Ἔραστος, calls it a "common name," and Andrew D. Clarke ("Another Corinthian Erastus," *TynB* 42 [1991]: 146–51) has drawn attention to an Erastus inscription from second-century Corinth in addition to the more famous inscription described below. Cf. Justin J. Meggitt, "The Social Status of Erastus," *NovT* 38 (1996): 222.

46. Cf. Zahn, *An die Römer*, 615; Fitzmyer, *Romans*, 750.

47. Meyer, *Romans*, 575. Cf. Wilckens, *An die Römer (Röm 12–16)*, 146.

48. Cadbury, "Erastus," 58. Cf. Pelagius, *Romans*, 153; Meyer, *Romans*, 575.

a person of great wealth and high social standing, moreover, and his resources of money and honor could have given him the freedom to travel with and support Paul. The Greek term translated "treasurer" here could refer to various offices from a low-level functionary that helped administrate the city's financial affairs (an *arcarius*) to a wealthy and socially powerful financial officer for the city (or *quaestor*).[49] It is hard to know why Paul would mention Erastus's office at all if it were not something unusual, and this makes it possible that he had been a *quaestor*, "a high-ranking, honourable, and costly municipal position within the civic hierarchy."[50]

If so, then he may have been the Erastus named in an honorific inscription uncovered in Corinth in 1929 and dated by some scholars, although not without controversy, to the middle of the first century.[51] The Erastus in the inscription is called an *aedile*, a lofty civic office reserved for the wealthy and socially powerful and to which the office of *quaestor* would be a natural stepping stone.[52] If the Erastus here in Romans and the Erastus of the inscription are the same person, then he would be a Christian of unusually high social and political standing within the Pauline circle.

Quartus, a Latin name meaning "fourth" (cf. Tertius in Rom 16:22, meaning "third"), appears nowhere else in the New Testament, and Paul describes him only as "the brother" (ἀδελφός). Despite Jewett's strong argument to the contrary, he was probably not Erastus's brother, since Paul would probably have used a possessive pronoun if he had intended to indicate that the two were siblings of each other (cf. 16:15: Νηρέα καὶ τὴν ἀδελφὴν αὐτοῦ).[53] Quartus was, then, a member of the metaphorical family of Christ and wanted to send greetings to his Roman "brothers and sisters," but beyond that, we can say nothing else about him.[54]

16:25 Now to the one who is able to strengthen you according to my gospel and the preaching of Jesus Christ, according to the revelation of the mystery kept silent for long ages (Τῷ δὲ δυναμένῳ ὑμᾶς στηρίξαι κατὰ τὸ εὐαγγέλιόν μου

49. Gerd Theissen, *The Social Setting of Pauline Christianity: Essays on Corinth*, trans. and ed. John H. Schütz (Philadelphia: Fortress, 1982), 76–79, 82–83; John K. Goodrich, "Erastus, *Quaestor* of Corinth: The Administrative Rank of ὁ οἰκονόμος τῆς πόλεως (Rom 16.23) in an Achaean Colony," *NTS* 56 (2009): 95, 108–14; idem, "Erastus of Corinth (Romans 16.23): Responding to Recent Proposals on His Rank, Status, and Faith," *NTS* 57 (2010): 583–93.

50. Goodrich, "Erastus, *Quaestor*," 114. Cf. Theissen, *Social Setting*, 82–83.

51. The inscription may come from as late as the second century. See, e.g., Meggitt, "Social Status," 220–21, and the discussions in Goodrich, "Erastus of Corinth," 587, 592, and Steven J. Friesen, "The Wrong Erastus: Ideology, Archaeology, and Exegesis," in *Corinth in Context: Comparative Studies on Religion and Society*, ed. Steven J. Friesen, Daniel N. Schowalter, and James C. Walters, NovTSup 134 (Leiden: Brill, 2010), 236–45.

52. A. N. Sherwin-White and Andrew William Lintott, "Aediles," *OCD* 15–16; Theissen, *Social Setting*, 81–83.

53. Meyer, *Romans*, 575. Cf. Jewett, *Romans*, 983–84.

54. A number of Western and Byzantine witnesses (e.g., D F G L 629) follow 16:23 with a grace benediction that runs, with occasional modifications, "The grace of our Lord Jesus Christ be with you all. Amen" (ἡ χάρις τοῦ κυρίου ἡμῶν Ἰησοῦ Χριστοῦ μετὰ πάντων ὑμῶν. ἀμήν). In some manuscripts (e.g., G 629), this is the letter's only grace benediction, and in other manuscripts two grace benedictions appear, one at 16:20b and one either after 16:23 (e.g., L Ψ) or after the doxology (P 33 104). Early western European versions of the Bible (e.g., Luther, Tyndale, the Clementine Vulgate, KJV) used the form of the text with benedictions both here and at 16:20b. When the text was eventually versified, this second benediction became 16:24. The earliest manuscripts of Romans, however, have a benediction only at 16:20b (e.g., 𝔓[46] 𝔓[61] א A B C). It seems likely that a form of the grace benediction at 16:20b was moved either to 16:24 or to a position after the doxology ("16:28") to avoid the appearance that the second set of greetings (16:21–23) was a haphazard appendage (Metzger, *Textual Commentary*, 476). These modifications resulted eventually in a form of the text with a grace benediction in two places, one of them in the place where Paul put it (16:20b) and the other in a less unexpected location (Sanday and Headlam, *Romans*, 431).

καὶ τὸ κήρυγμα Ἰησοῦ Χριστοῦ, κατὰ ἀποκάλυψιν μυστηρίου χρόνοις αἰωνίοις σεσιγημένου). Paul praises God who can empower the Roman Christians to remain faithful to the gospel he has just explained in the letter. This, the only gospel, is centered on Jesus Christ, and God graciously revealed it after a long period during which Christ was not known.

Paul's "now" (δέ) signals a shift to the lengthy sentence that forms the letter's concluding doxology. This is the only Pauline letter that ends this way, although it is not unusual for Paul to end a paragraph (Gal 1:5; 1 Tim 1:17), and sometimes a major section (Rom 11:36; Eph 3:21) of a letter, with a doxology. Occasionally this happens near the letter's conclusion (Phil 4:20; 1 Tim 6:16; 2 Tim 4:18).

Doxologies are expressions of praise to God that describe his glory, honor, or might, and their origin probably lay in the temple worship of Israel (1 Chr 16:28–29; Ps 29:1–2; 96:7). They sometimes appear in Hellenistic Jewish literature (Pr Man 15; 4 Macc 18:24) and are common enough in early Christian literature (1 Pet 4:11; 5:11; Heb 13:21; 1 Clem. 64; Mart. Pol. 20.2) that it seems likely early Christians used them in worship.[55] Since Paul probably intended Romans to be read aloud to large groups of believers, including those gathered from the household and neighborhood churches he has just greeted in 16:3–16, it probably seemed natural to conclude the letter with a well-known liturgical formula molded to fit the concerns of the letter.

Doxologies typically began with a pronoun or phrase in the dative case describing God, or Christ, "to" whom praise should be given, and Paul follows this pattern here by describing God as "the one who is able [τῷ . . . δυναμένῳ] to strengthen [στηρίξαι] you" (cf., e.g., Eph 3:20; Jude 24).[56] God's "power" (δύναμις) to save his people and Paul's desire to see the Roman Christians strengthened (στηριχθῆναι) through his gospel were important themes at the letter's beginning (Rom 1:11, 16). Paul recalls those themes here at the letter's end to encourage the Romans that God is willing and able to keep them faithful to him despite the challenges of false teaching (16:17–20), internal division (14:1–15:6), and persecution (12:14, 17–21).

The first instance of the preposition translated "according to" (κατά) does not modify "the one who is able" (τῷ . . . δυναμένῳ) but to "strengthen" (στηρίξαι).[57] Paul is not saying that his gospel *teaches* God's ability to strengthen Christians. Rather, he is praising God for his ability to strengthen the Roman Christians in a way that *agrees* with the gospel. Paul viewed his gospel as the standard against which God would judge people (2:16), and so it could also serve as the standard for determining whether one was or was not strong in the faith (cf. 2 Tim 2:8). Paul's "my" (μου) probably refers to the gospel as he has explained it in Romans. It does not refer to a peculiar angle on the gospel that he considers his own as the explanatory phrase "and the preaching of Jesus Christ" makes clear.[58] Paul's gospel is the gospel that has Jesus Christ at the center of its proclamation (cf. 10:8–10), and that makes it the gospel of many others also, including, Paul assumed, the Roman Christians to whom he was writing.[59]

The second "according to" (κατά) modifies "preaching" (κήρυγμα), and the phrase this preposition governs describes the norm in conformity with which the preaching of Jesus Christ takes

55. Gerhard Delling, *Worship in the New Testament*, trans. Percy Scott (Philadelphia: Westminster, 1962), 64.

56. Deichgräber, *Gotteshymnus*, 25.

57. Cranfield, *Romans*, 2:869.

58. Meyer, *Romans*, 576–77.

59. Cf. Godet, *Romans*, 503; Sanday and Headlam, *Romans*, 433; Cranfield, *Romans*, 2:809–10.

place.[60] It was not merely the idea of Paul or any other human being to preach Jesus Christ, but this preaching originated in a "revelation" (ἀποκάλυψις) from God (Gal 1:12). This revelation was a "mystery" (μυστήριον) in the sense that no one would have known it had God not graciously revealed it to his people (cf. Rom 11:25; cf. Dan 2:27–30; Eph 1:7–10). It was a mystery kept silent for long ages because it was revealed after many generations of God's work among his people and when the right moment for making it known had arrived (cf. 1 Cor 2:7; Gal 3:23; 4:4; Eph 3:5, 9).

16:26 but now disclosed, and made known through the prophetic writings according to the command of the eternal God for the obedience of faith to all the gentiles (φανερωθέντος δὲ νῦν διά τε γραφῶν προφητικῶν κατ' ἐπιταγὴν τοῦ αἰωνίου θεοῦ εἰς ὑπακοὴν πίστεως εἰς πάντα τὰ ἔθνη γνωρισθέντος). The previously unknown elements of the gospel have now been revealed not just to the Jews but to all people groups at God's initiative and in a way that shows the gospel to be consistent with the Jewish Scriptures.

Paul continues to describe "the mystery" that was the object of "the revelation" that takes place in the open proclamation of Jesus Christ. In contrast (δέ) to the long period of silence, in which God's purposes for the salvation of his people and the creation were unknown, God has "now" (νῦν) disclosed his purposes in the gospel.

Paul explains the means of this revelation more specifically in the next clause. The particle translated "and" (τε) shows that the participles rendered "disclosed" (φανερωθέντος) and "made known" (γνωρισθέντος) stand grammatically parallel to each other, and both modify the term translated "mystery" (μυστηρίου) in 16:25.[61] The open revelation of God's saving purposes that takes place in the public proclamation of Jesus Christ has four characteristics. It happens (1) through the prophetic writings, that is, in harmony with the witness of the Jewish Scriptures (cf. 1:2; 3:21), (2) in obedience to God's command that it should happen (1:1, 14–15; 15:15–21), (3) for the purpose that people might trust the gospel and respond to it with obedience to God (cf. 1:5; 15:18), and (4) to all the gentiles, not in the sense that they are the revelation's only object (1:16) but in the sense that their inclusion receives special emphasis (1:5, 14, 16; 3:29; 4:16–17; 10:12–13; 11:12, 32; 15:9–12, 16, 18).

16:27 To the only wise God through Jesus Christ . . . to whom be the glory forever. Amen (μόνῳ σοφῷ θεῷ, διὰ Ἰησοῦ Χριστοῦ, ᾧ ἡ δόξα εἰς τοὺς αἰῶνας, ἀμήν). Paul praises not only the God who is able to strengthen the Roman Christians in their commitment to the gospel, and whose unsurpassed wisdom is evident in the gospel, but Jesus Christ, whose sacrificial life, reconciling death, and victorious resurrection stand at the center of the gospel as Paul has explained it.

After his extensive description of the gospel with respect to which God will strengthen the Roman Christians, Paul returns to a description of the God whom he praises.[62] God is not only able to strengthen the Romans according to Paul's gospel (16:25–26), but he alone is wise (16:27). The phrase "only wise God" (μόνῳ σοφῷ θεῷ) echoes the world of ancient Greek philosophy, where, for example, Socrates could tell Phaedrus that even Lysias, Homer, and Solon should not be called "wise" (σοφόν) since "the epithet 'wise' is too great and befits God alone [θεῷ μόνῳ]" (*Phaedr.* 278d [Har-

60. Godet, *Romans*, 503; Sanday and Headlam, *Romans*, 434; Cranfield, *Romans*, 2:810.

61. Godet, *Romans*, 504; Sanday and Headlam, *Romans*, 434.

62. Cf. Eph 3:20–21: "Now to him who is able [τῷ δὲ δυναμένῳ] . . . to him be glory [αὐτῷ ἡ δόξα]."

old North Fowler, LCL]).[63] This was a notion that Hellenistic Judaism could readily adopt to support the conviction that not only was the God of Israel the only wise God, but he was the only God (e.g., Sir 1:8; Philo, *Migration* 134; Ps.-Phoc. 54).[64] Paul probably tapped into this traditional language to echo his own emphasis on the oneness of God (Rom 3:30; cf. Deut 6:4) and the wisdom of God (Rom 11:33) as both are displayed in God's ability, through the gospel, to unite Jews and gentiles into one people at peace with himself.

The final two clauses of the doxology are grammatically difficult. First, it is not clear where the phrase "through Jesus Christ" (διὰ Ἰησοῦ Χριστοῦ) fits into the thought Paul is developing: Does God show his wisdom through Jesus Christ (taking the phrase with the preceding reference to "the only wise God") or does Paul ascribe glory to God through Jesus Christ (taking the phrase with the following relative clause)?[65] Second, it is not clear whether God or Jesus Christ is the antecedent of the relative pronoun "whom" that opens the final clause of the doxology. Does Paul praise God, who has been the subject of the doxology to this point, or does he suddenly shift his attention to Jesus Christ, who is at the center of God's revelation?[66]

The solution to these difficulties probably lies in the close relationship between God and Jesus Christ in Paul's understanding of the gospel. After mentioning "the only wise God," Paul probably intended to ascribe glory to him through Jesus Christ (cf. Rom 5:11; 7:25; Jude 25; Did. 9.3; 1 Clem. 58.2), but his reference to Jesus Christ caused him to shift his attention to Christ himself and to end the doxology by ascribing glory to him.[67] In light of the centrality of Jesus Christ to the gospel God had recently revealed (Rom 1:3–4; 3:21–26; 5:1–21; 6:23; 7:25; 8:1–2, 31–39), the grammatical ambiguity that Paul's difficult syntax introduced was probably an ambiguity he was happy not to clarify.[68]

Theology in Application

Two theological themes dominate this final section of Paul's letter. First, Paul speaks of the importance of preserving the unity of God's people by staying grounded in the historically reliable apostolic tradition about the Christian faith. Second, he describes the importance of joining together with other believers to worship God, who strengthens his people to believe and obey this faith.

The Importance of Orthodoxy

The first part of the passage (16:17–20) focuses on remaining unified around the body of teaching that all Christians have learned. It begins with a warning against

63. Cf. Plato, *Apology of Socrates* 23a; Meyer, *Romans*, 580; Cranfield, *Romans*, 2:814; Légasse, *Romains*, 978.

64. Cranfield, *Romans*, 2:814; Dunn, *Romans 9–16*, 916; Légasse, *Romains*, 978.

65. For the first position, see, e.g., Meyer (*Romans*, 27), and for the second position, see, e.g., Lagrange (*Romains*, 380).

66. For the first position, see, e.g., Lagrange (*Romains*, 380), and for the second position, see, e.g., Friedrich Adolph Philippi (*Commentary on St. Paul's Epistle to the Romans*, trans. J. S. Banks, 2 vols. [Edinburgh: T&T Clark, 1878–79], 2:426–27).

67. See also Barrett (*Romans*, 263). This is a minority position among commentators, most of whom view the antecedent of "to whom" (ᾧ) as God, but it is difficult to read the pronoun any other way than as reference to the immediately preceding "Jesus Christ." For a similar ambiguity in the ascription of praise to either God or Jesus Christ, see 1 Pet 4:11, and for a Pauline doxology ascribing glory to Christ, see 2 Tim 4:18.

68. Wright, "Romans," 769.

a form of false teaching that creates division and hinders progress in the faith by insisting that some new form of the faith is better than the ancient form (v. 17). When Paul speaks of "the teaching that you learned," he implies that both he and the Roman Christians, many of whom he had never met, agreed on what the gospel was and that the teaching they had received and believed was the teaching that all Christians follow.

This teaching had made its way acrosss the Mediterranean Sea to Rome, and not only had the Roman Christians become famous for embracing it (1:8; 6:17; cf. 16:19), but Paul was confident that they could encourage one another (15:14), and himself also (1:12), to remain committed to this faith. Clearly Paul thought that the gospel he had just outlined at length in the letter, and the ethical principles he had articulated on the basis of it, were not merely his ideas about the gospel and its implications but a widely accepted understanding of what all Christians should believe. They were a summary of the Christian faith.

Articulating the content of the gospel in the way he had just done did not divide Christians from one another but brought them together. As Paul would say a few years later, in a letter written from Rome, Christ "himself is our peace, who has made us both one and has broken down in his flesh the dividing wall of hostility" (Eph 2:14). The gospel, with its message of God's reconciling grace, pulls people together instead of dividing them from one another.

In contrast, the false teachers that Paul warns against in 16:17 divided Christians from one another. The divisive tendency of their false teaching stemmed from their advocacy of some new form of the faith that hindered a Christian community's progress in the commonly held, traditional form of Christian belief. They were not outsiders expressing an interest in the Christian faith and asking sincere questions, nor were they fringe members of the traditional group who were expressing real doubts and occasionally registering dissenting opinions. Paul's welcoming approach to outsiders and the weak in faith is clearly visible elsewhere in his correspondence (Rom 14:1; 1 Cor 14:16–17, 23–25). Rather, these false teachers were disingenuous people with sophisticated rhetorical and analytical skills, who were using those abilities to serve their own greedy impulses—"their own belly"—as Paul memorably puts it (16:18). They must have been people with talent and experience in leading social groups. They were people who had enough power and influence to lure large numbers of Christians away from the gospel. In short, the false teachers of 16:17–20 were divisive, novel, self-serving, and persuasive.

Warnings against false teachers in the church with these four traits are not uncommon in the New Testament. The apostle John wrote three letters to Christian assemblies within his own sphere of responsibility in the wake of the kind of disruption that Paul was trying to avoid at Rome. A heretical group had broken fellowship with the main, orthodox group (1 John 2:19) because they were advocating some new "progressive" form of the gospel that had abandoned the apostolic witness to Jesus's life and teaching (2 John 9; cf. 1 John 1:1–5). They had apparently also left behind certain Christian ethical principles (1 John 3:4–10), including such basics as offering practical assistance to the poor (3:17), and they were making headway in their efforts to convince the larger group they had left, and to whom John was writing, that their knowledge of the truth was defective (2:20–21). The same pattern reappears in Jude and 2 Peter where apostles warn against rhetorically persuasive and immoral false teachers who have left "the faith that was once for all delivered to the saints" (Jude 3–4, 16; cf. 2 Pet 1:16; 2:1–3).

The church needs to heed this apostolic warning. People who fit secular notions of leadership ability and possess impressive rhetorical skill should not be quickly ushered into leadership positions in the church simply because they seem to be effective in attracting a following and getting things done. Rather than smoothing the way for such people, the church should examine them even more carefully than others before giving them responsibilities in the church. If they have a history of fomenting division, especially if their divisiveness is fueled by novel teaching and talking more about themselves and their ideas than practicing humble service to Christ, then they clearly fall within the boundaries of Paul's warning in this passage no matter how much their language is tinged with "fine speech and blessing."

It was probably not Paul's intention to set up a contrast when he followed his warning against false teachers with a paragraph of greetings from his associates. The eight people that appear in the letter's next paragraph (16:21–23), however, provide helpful examples of good church leaders. Paul's "coworker" Timothy was indispensible to the apostle because, as Paul describes him to believers in Philippi, he was genuinely concerned with the welfare of other believers and served with Paul as a "kindred spirit" (ἰσόψυχον) in the cause of the gospel (Phil 2:19–22 NASB). Little is known about Paul's fellow Jews Lucius, Jason, and Sosipater, but here too, if they were delegates from Paul's mainly gentile churches traveling with Paul on the risky famine relief mission to Jerusalem, they were certainly people more interested in service than in self-aggrandizement. Tertius worked hard with Paul because of his commitment to "the Lord" when he took down this long letter at the apostle's dictation. Gaius had shown Paul and other believers hospitality. We can say nothing specific about the work of Erastus and Quartus, but it is unlikely that their names would be found in the same paragraph with Timothy, Tertius, and Gaius if they had not helped Paul to advance the gospel in some practical way.

This group of eight coworkers and friends of the apostle illustrates the humble way believers should work together as "one body in Christ . . . each one members of one another" (12:5). In Ephesians, Paul explains that when the church works together in this way, with each part of the body playing its God-given role, the church grows in maturity and is not fooled by the kind of trickery that false teachers can use on spiritually immature and gullible followers, "tossed to and fro by the waves and carried about by every wind of doctrine" (Eph 4:11–14). Instead, "speaking the truth in love, we are to grow up in every way into him who is the head, into Christ, from whom the whole body, joined and held together by every joint with which it is equipped, when each part is working properly, makes the body grow so that it builds itself up in love" (Eph 4:15–16). A helpful antidote to the kind of false teaching that Paul describes in 16:17–20, therefore, is the kind of teamwork that Paul and the eight people in 16:21–23 seem to have demonstrated in Corinth.

Romans 16:17–23, then, provides both a warning and a positive example that will help those involved in selecting leaders for the church do so with discernment. John Stott usefully summarizes 16:17–20 as implying three tests, "biblical, Christological and moral," for any system of doctrine or ethics, and we can apply the same tests to people who seek to help lead the church.[69] Does this person affirm the apostolic witness to the Christian faith found in the Scriptures? Is this person interested in serving Christ more than self? Does this person promote what is good? Based on what Paul says about divisiveness in 16:17, we can also add a fourth question: Does this person seek the unity and peace of the church?

Praising the God Who Strengthens Believers

The second theological theme that Paul emphasizes here at the letter's conclusion is the praise that rightfully belongs to God because of his ability and willingness "to strengthen" (στηρίξαι) believers in their commitment to the gospel (16:25–27; cf. 1:11). The term "strengthen" appears elsewhere only in Paul's Thessalonian letters. Paul wrote these letters to a persecuted and theologically confused community in need of strength and encouragement to persevere in the faith despite the suffering and doctrinal deviation that surrounded them (1 Thess 3:2, 13; 2 Thess 2:17; 3:3).[70] The Roman Christians, too, needed strengthening and encouragement (1:11–12), and Paul probably envisioned Romans itself as a means to that end.

There is a sense, then, in which this concluding note of praise gives thanks to God for the letter itself with its full and lucid explanation of Paul's gospel. There is perhaps no more appropriate way in which to apply this doxology to the church of every age than to follow a study of Romans with praise to God for the gift of the letter itself with its bracing reminder of the gospel.

69. Stott, *Romans*, 400.

70. Cf. Erwin Ochsenmeier, "Romans 1,11–12: A Clue to the Purpose of Romans," *ETL* 83 (2007): 396–98.

Theology of Romans

Paul wrote Romans at an important turning point in his evangelistic efforts and to a group consisting mainly of people he had never met (1:9–13). His long-standing project of collecting money for the poor among the Jewish Christians in Jerusalem was nearing an end (15:25–28), and he felt that his pioneering evangelistic ministry in the east was complete (15:19–20, 23). Spain lay before him as did, hopefully, the support of the Roman Christians for his journey west (15:24). He must have devoted much of the three months that he spent in Greece to composing this long, well-organized explanation of the gospel and its implications (Acts 20:2–3). The result is one of the most profoundly theological texts in the New Testament.[1] "If we have gained a true understanding of this Epistle," said John Calvin, "we have an open door to all the most profound treasures of Scripture."[2] It is surely no accident that Calvin completely restructured his *Institutes of the Christian Religion* in the same year (1539) that he wrote these words.[3]

Fundamentally, Romans is about who God is and how his character explains the relationship he has with the universe he created and especially the human creatures within it. The God of Romans is not only the creator of the universe but a personal God, who is both righteous and gracious in his relationship with his human creatures. God displays these two qualities with the greatest clarity in his response to the rebellion of his human creatures against him. That response appears both in the justified wrath of God against human unrighteousness and in the deliverance God offers from his wrath in the death and resurrection of Jesus. Romans emphasizes that the various assemblies of God's people, meeting around the Mediterranean basin and including the assemblies in Rome, represent the beginnings of this work of deliverance and restoration.

1. Cf. Dunn, *Theology of Paul the Apostle*, 25.
2. Calvin, *Romans*, 5.
3. Cf. Barclay, *Paul and the Gift*, 117.

God and His Character

God Creates

Paul emphasizes God's role as creator of the universe perhaps more in Romans than anywhere else in his letters (cf. 1 Cor 8:6; 10:26; Eph 2:10; 3:9; 4:24; Col 1:16; 3:10; 1 Tim 4:3). For Paul, God made (ποιέω) the entire universe and has sovereignty over what he has made (Rom 1:20). Preeminent among his creation was humanity, listed first among God's creatures and made, Paul implies, in God's image and to reflect his glory (1:23; 3:23). In 8:18–23 Paul implies further that God created everything, both human and otherwise, to acknowledge him and reflect his glory (cf. 1:21). Thus, all creation joins believers in an eager longing for its restoration and perfection into what God intended it to be (8:19, 22–23).

This picture of God the creator comes from Israel's Scriptures, the first line of which states that "God created the heavens and the earth" (Gen 1:1). Like the story of creation in Genesis, Paul speaks of God creating "birds" (πετεινά, Gen 1:20–23 LXX), "quadrupeds" (τετράποδα, Gen 1:24 LXX), and "creeping things" (ἑρπετά, Gen 1:24 LXX), and also the first man, Adam (Gen 2:16 LXX). Paul insists in agreement with Israel's Scriptures, moreover, that the God who created all things is the one true God (Rom 3:30; 16:27; cf. Deut 4:35, 39; 6:4).

These affirmations about God as creator play important roles in Paul's argument. Because God created all things, he is not unjust in pouring out his wrath on human beings who fail to glorify and thank him for who he is and for his good gifts (Rom 1:21; 9:20–21). One of the primary effects of humanity's alienation from the God of all creation is its division into competing camps, such as Jews and gentiles, and its resulting failure to reflect God's oneness (3:30; 10:12). The suffering that believers see around them, and which they experience, is a sign of the alienation from its creator into which human sin has plunged the world (8:19, 22–23).

God Reveals

Paul also emphasizes in Romans that God has revealed himself to human beings, and that with the passage of time this revelation has become increasingly specific. He assumes that God's revelation of himself to people has come in four contexts: in nature, in Scripture, in Jesus Christ, and in the gospel.

In Nature

Paul maintains in Romans 1–2 that God had revealed his character and his will to all human beings. Since God is invisible to human beings, he had to take the initiative to make his "eternal power" and "divinity" visible to them, and he did this "from the time of the world's creation" by the things he made (1:19–20). Before God called his people into existence through Abraham (4:1, 12, 13, 16; 9:6–13; 11:1) and gave them the law through Moses (10:5), God was revealing himself to his human creatures and through this revelation calling upon them to worship him in acknowledgment and thanksgiving (1:21; cf. 5:14).

He not only revealed to them that he existed, was powerful, and deserved their worship but also made known to them how he wanted human beings to treat each other. This is clear from the implication that God held human beings responsible not only for their idolatry but also for their societal violence (1:23–31). They knew his "righteous decree" (δικαίωμα) that those who violently mistreated each other deserved death (1:32). It is also clear that Paul thought God had revealed his requirements to everyone from Paul's description of the law that God had written on gentile hearts (2:15–16). Gentiles, he argued, understood enough of the law's basic precepts that on the day of judgment God could justly hold them responsible for disobeying it, and in the end some of them may have obeyed it better than those who had God's fuller revelation of himself in Scripture (2:25–29).

Paul expresses his understanding of God's revelation of himself as part of his argument that God is a just judge. He does not hold people to a standard they could not know. Rather, he has revealed something of his character and will apart from Scripture to all human beings, and he rightfully holds them accountable for doing what they know to be good (1:20; 2:12, 14–16). Paul also uses the idea that God has revealed himself in nature to argue for God's impartiality (2:11). Jews cannot claim a special exemption from God's condemnation for their own disobedience simply because they possess the law. Everyone, both Jew and gentile, possesses enough of the law to demonstrate that no one in either camp is righteous in God's eyes (2:14–16, 25–29; 3:9).

In Scripture

God has not left humanity to figure out who he is and what he requires merely from nature and conscience. To and through his people Israel God has given humanity his written word, the Scriptures. Paul calls the Scriptures "holy" (1:2; 7:12), meaning that they are set apart from all other writings as God's word (3:2). One of Israel's great privileges is that God gave them these "oracles," especially his law (3:2; 9:4), which is "the embodiment of knowledge and truth" (2:20). The Scriptures contain "the covenants" God initiated with Israel and "the promises" he made to them (9:4). They contain "the word of God," which God has not failed to keep (9:6), and in the form of "the law and the prophets" the Scriptures testify to the gospel (3:21; 16:26). They offer "instruction," "endurance," and "encouragement" (15:4; cf. 2:18). They are the final arbiter of any dispute about who God is and how he relates to humanity. So when Paul wants to make a definitive case for his position, he asks his fictional interlocutor, "What does the Scripture say?" (4:3; 11:2) as if what Scripture says will settle the matter. In the same way, Paul can clinch an argument by introducing a biblical quotation with, "for the Scripture says" (9:17; 10:11).

Paul implies, moreover, that God did not give the Scriptures to Israel for them to keep to themselves. Rather he "entrusted" the Scriptures to them (3:2) so that they might be "a light to those in darkness" (2:17–23). The problem Paul "finds" with his fictional interlocutor in 2:17–24 is not the interlocutor's activity of instructing gentiles but the inconsistency between what he claims about God's requirements on the basis of the Scriptures and his own behavior. It is this inconsistency that lies at the center of the failure of this fictional debating partner and is the reason why "the name of God is blasphemed among the gentiles" (2:24).

God's revelation of himself in Scripture was so important to Paul in Romans because he wanted to demonstrate that there was no inconsistency between the gospel he proclaimed and the Scriptures he and his fellow Jews believed to be authoritative. It was true that the gospel was something lately revealed apart from the law (3:21; 16:25–26), but the law and the prophets promised it beforehand and testified to it (3:21).

In Jesus Christ

God's most important revelation of himself, however, was in Jesus Christ, the long-expected king prophesied in Scripture as a descendant of David, and now, because of his resurrection from the dead, seated at God's right hand (1:3; 8:34; cf., e.g., 2 Sam 7:12–14; Ps 2:7; 89:26–27; 110:1). He was the "goal" toward which the Mosaic law was leading God's people (10:4). He was now establishing a kingdom of righteousness, peace, and joy through the power and presence of the Holy Spirit (14:17). Jesus's human, messianic identity was important to Paul's argument in Romans as an affirmation that the central figure of the gospel stood in full continuity with Israel's Scriptures.

Jesus's human identity was also important to Paul's argument because, as a human being, he shared the "fleshly" existence of all human beings (1:3; 9:5) and therefore shared their weakness, although without sin (8:3). It was precisely because he came in the "flesh," with its tendency toward sin (7:5, 18, 25), that he was able to rescue human beings from slavery to this tendency (8:3). He came to the place where human rebellion against God was most intense—humanity in its sinful and therefore mortal existence—in order to bring human beings out of the plight of sin and death into which Adam had plunged them (5:12–19). He came to bring them from that plight of enmity with God into God's family where they, like him, were God's children (8:15–17).

In addition to Jesus's human nature, it is important to Paul that Jesus was God (9:5). Jesus was the embodiment of the "mercy seat" (ἱλαστήριον) of Exodus 25:17–22 and Leviticus 16:2, 13–15. He was, then, the "place" where God focused his presence among his people and where God atoned for their sins. He was also the person in whom God would deliver his people according to Isaiah's prophecy that a just God would one day step into history and rescue God's people from their transgressions (Rom 11:26; Isa 59:20–21).

In the Gospel

In Romans, Paul is especially concerned to show that God has revealed himself in "the gospel" (1:15–16), the good news about the coming of Christ and what God has done for all humanity in him. Romans itself is an explanation of the content of this message and of its implications for the Roman Christians. Since God "set" Paul "apart" (ἀφωρισμένος) as his messenger (1:1; cf. 1:5, 9) and gave him the obligation of proclaiming the gospel to everyone (1:14–15; cf. 15:15–21), Paul and his gospel message were themselves a means by which God revealed himself to all humanity (1:14–15). Paul, therefore, would have considered Romans itself part of God's gracious revelation to his human creatures.

This element of Romans explains why Paul speaks so forthrightly in the letter of his own importance and the importance of the letter. He felt free to write "very boldly" to the Christians in Rome (15:15); he emphasized that he was not ashamed of the gospel (1:16); and says that he glorifies his ministry (11:13; cf. 10:15). These are not statements of pride but, from Paul's perspective, reflect the weight of the responsibility God had given him. God was using Paul's proclamation of the good news about Jesus's defeat of sin to reveal himself to those who needed to know him or to know him better.

God Is Righteous

One of the most important characteristics that the gospel reveals about God is his "righteousness" (1:17), meaning that he is just and fair. He has not expected his human creatures to know who he is or honor or thank him for what he has done for them without revealing himself to them (1:2; cf. 1:32). The punishments he hands out to those who do not acknowledge him, moreover, are appropriate to their willful neglect of this reasonable duty (1:18–32). He is truthful in his judgments, justifying only those who are just as measured by a law available to both Jews and gentiles (2:5–6, 13, 14–16). He is also impartial in his judgments, not holding one group of people to a lower standard than another group, but judging everyone honestly and by the same standard (2:11; 14:10–12; cf. 3:30; 9:14). He does not fail to condemn wrongdoing just because a group he favors in other ways is doing it (3:3), nor does he lie about what is right even when everyone else claims it is wrong (3:4). He does not exonerate the guilty because they have threatened him with slander (3:5), nor does he fail to deal out justice to those who are evil (12:19; cf. 16:20).

God Is Gracious

Perhaps the most surprising and significant aspect of Paul's picture of God in Romans is the way he explains the righteousness of God in terms of God's grace. At the heart of the gospel stands the affirmation that God's righteousness comes to believers not in the form of God's just condemnation of the wicked but as "the power of God for salvation" (1:16). God's graciousness is the aspect of God's character that led him to express his righteousness as salvation rather than condemnation to anyone who would believe and receive this gift (3:24). Within the boundaries of the gospel, God's righteousness continues to be understood as God's commitment to do what is right and just. Now, however, this justice is expressed in God's faithfulness to fulfill the promises he had made to his people to save them from destruction (1:16–17; cf. Ps 98:2–3).

For God to remain just and yet release the unjust from the punishment they deserved (Rom 3:26), it was necessary for "his own Son" (8:32; cf. 5:20) to die the death they deserved (5:6–8), a "righteous act" (5:18) that Christ willingly undertook (15:3). This justification of sinners through the death of Christ was a free gift of God's grace (3:24), an intensely countercultural move that, to quote John M. G. Barclay, was "a gift of utter incongruity" with the worth of its recipients. God did not give this gift to deserving recipients, either from the perspective of work they had performed (4:4–5), in which case the "gift" would not have been a gift at all but a contractual obligation (11:5–6), or from the perspective of some social standing that the recipients possessed with the giver (1:14–16; 3:22, 29; 4:16; 10:12–13; 11:32).[4] Christ's justifying death was a completely "free gift" (5:15–16), prompted by no previous movement toward the giver on the part of its recipients. Shockingly, God gave them the gift of justification while they were not only weak (5:6) but his enemies (5:10a), and at the enormous cost of the death of his Son (5:10b). In this amazing display of love (5:8), those who believe the gospel experience the "abundance" (5:17), indeed superabundance (5:20), of God's grace.

In Paul's thinking, the graciousness of God's character was not a late development or a characteristic that became obvious for the first time in the gospel, nor did it briefly burst on the scene in Christ only to fall into the shadows afterward. It was a steady, persistent feature of God's character through all time. It was already evident in the gifts he gave to humanity at creation, gifts for which human beings should have thanked him (ηὐχαρίστησαν [1:21]).[5] It persisted throughout the period of his interactions with sinful human beings up to the coming of the gospel in the forms,

4. Barclay, *Paul and the Gift*, 474.

5. On the connection between "grace" (χάρις) and "thanksgiving" (εὐχαριστία) as the proper response to grace among ancient Greek speakers, see Barclay (*Paul and the Gift*, 577–78), who draws attention, for example, to 1 Cor 1:4; 2 Cor 1:11; 4:15; 9:11–12.

for example, of his "kindness and forbearance and patience" (2:4; cf. 3:25) and the "gifts" he gave to Israel (11:29; cf. 3:2; 9:4–5).

Moreover, it continues to be evident in the lives of believers and in the church through the presence of the Holy Spirit. The Spirit shows believers God's love, assures them they are included in his family, guarantees their future resurrection, and aids them in their prayers (5:5; 8:14–17, 23, 26–27). God's graciousness is also evident through the various abilities and vocations that God gives to people within the church so that they might work together to make it a loving, peaceable society (12:6; cf. 1:1, 5; 12:3; 15:14–21).

The graciousness of God plays a critical role in Paul's explanation of the gospel, both at the level of what the gospel is and at the level of the gospel's effect on how believers should live together. The "good news" (εὐ-αγγέλλιον) is only "good" because God is gracious and has shown his grace through the just forgiveness of believers provided in the death and resurrection of Jesus Christ and in the sustaining, comforting presence of the Holy Spirit in their lives (e.g., 3:24; 5:5). God's grace also implies something of critical importance about human beings and affects the way they live in community. Because God's grace belongs to God and he is sovereign over those to whom he shows it, the community of believers does not decide on its own membership (9:11, 15–16, 18, 11–24; 11:5–6, 22, 26). God sets the boundaries of his people, and often his choice of whom to include within those boundaries is surprising (9:12, 24, 30–31; 11:23, 25–27).[6] This means that the believing community, in all its diversity, must live in loving harmony with one another (12:3–13, 15–18; 14:1–15:13), imitating the welcome that God and Christ have given to each believer in the welcome that each believer gives to the other (14:3; 15:7; 16:3–16).

Humanity in Rebellion against God

Paul begins his explanation of the gospel with a description of the heights from which humanity has fallen. God revealed himself to human beings at creation in order that they might glorify him as God and thank him for the good gifts he had given to them (1:20–21). He wanted them to live and work together in loving harmony with one another, to obey his will (2:14–16, 25–29; 8:7–8) and to praise him and Jesus Christ together with one voice (15:5–6).

Instead of following this path, however, humanity, beginning with Adam, revolted against God. Adam made the serious, intentional misstep of disobeying God's command (5:15–19), and this misstep plunged all humanity into disobedience and death (5:12). Paul describes the downward spiral of human existence in two stages. First, human beings refused to glorify and thank God for who he was and what he

6. On this, see Thielman, "Unexpected Mercy," 169–81.

had given to them. This was such an irrational move that it led them into a seriously perverse understanding of God. As a result of this misunderstanding, they began to worship images of God's creatures rather than God himself (1:21, 23, 25). Paul communicates a sense of the deepening shadow of their thinking with the increasingly irrational objects of their worship: mortal human beings, birds, quadrupeds, and finally reptiles (1:23).

Second, this perverse response to what creation had revealed about God led to an equally disoriented understanding of their own identity as God's creatures. God had created human beings to enjoy their sexuality in monogamous, heterosexual intimacy, but confusion about the nature of God led to confusion about their own nature, and this led to sexual behavior that was futile and dishonoring to humanity (1:24–27). God had also created them to live in harmony (cf. 15:5), but instead, in their state of rebellion against him, society spiraled downward into ever more violent and socially chaotic behavior (1:28–32; cf. 12:14, 17, 19–21; 13:3–4, 13). Rather than realizing their plight and earnestly seeking a way out of it, moreover, their rebellion against God was so total, and human rationality so darkened, that they not only did what they knew deserved death but applauded those who followed their example (1:32).

This indictment covered Jews as well as non-Jews since Jews, despite having the clear revelation of God's will in the Mosaic law and even teaching the law to others, failed to obey the law (2:1–29; 3:2). Although Israel had many God-given privileges and promises (9:4–5), and had a certain zeal for God, they nevertheless failed to keep God's law and stumbled over the proclamation of the gospel toward which the law was pointing (9:30–10:4). "There is no one righteous," says Paul, "not even one" (3:10).

This plight of disobedience to God was so dire in Paul's thinking that he could describe humanity's relationship to sin as "slavery" (6:6, 17, 19–20) and could speak of sin as holding people "captive" (7:6). Sin's grip on humanity was tight enough that even God's holy, righteous, and good law (7:12) could not pry it loose. Instead, in an insidious move, sin co-opted the law for its own purposes, using it to engender not less but more rebellion against God (7:5, 7–12; cf. 3:20; 4:15; 5:20). Even when people recognized that the law's commands were beneficial, they discovered that they could not consistently obey them (7:14–24). Thus, Jews who rejected Paul's gospel believed they were acting within the bounds of the Mosaic law (9:30–31) and were zealous for God (10:2), but in fact they were stumbling over the very stone that God had laid in Zion (9:32–33) and failing to reach the goal toward which the law itself pointed (10:4).

The nature of the human plight appears clearly in the way Paul uses the term "flesh" (σάρξ) throughout his argument. On one hand, "flesh" simply refers to the physicality of life. Jesus was a descendent of David as far as the "flesh" goes (1:3; cf.

4:1; 9:3, 5, 8; 11:14), and giving money to the poor is serving "them in fleshly things [σαρκικοῖς]" (15:27). On the other hand, Paul can employ the term to refer to humanity considered from the perspective of the merely physical, without reference to God (2:28). It is this second use that allows the term to take on especially negative connotations in Romans. The "flesh" is humanity in its weakness over against sin and in its persistent tendency to live in a way that is disobedient to God's will (6:19; 7:5, 14, 18, 25; 8:3–13).

The bleak description of human wickedness in 1:18–3:20 did not cover the behavior of every person at every minute of the day. Occasionally people obeyed the revelation God had given them (2:14–15), and government officials with little or no understanding of God could act as God's agents to accomplish what was good and beneficial for society (13:4, 6). In their best moments (2:14–16), human beings knew that their own rebellion would not lead to their own happiness (7:22), that it deserved the penalty of death (1:32), and that it was still possible to have a zeal for God, however misguided (10:2).

Still, Paul's perspective on the human capacity to choose and do what was good was very dark, even compared to other very dark assessments of his own time. The author of 4 Ezra came close to Paul's pessimism with talk of "the first Adam, burdened with an evil heart" being "overcome, as were also all who were descended from him" (4 Ezra 3:21; cf. 4 Ezra 4:30; 7:68, 46–61).[7] Even this author, however, articulated the view that a few people would win the contest against sin and experience salvation because they had successfully kept the law (7:57–61; 8:1–3). The deeply humble author of the Prayer of Manasseh seems to have thought something similar. "You . . . did not appoint grace for the righteous ones such as Abraham, and Isaac and Jacob, those who did not sin against you," he prays (8).[8] He knows that he is not among the righteous and desperately needs God's mercy, but he seems to have thought that a few people were good enough to escape condemnation without appealing to God's grace.

Some interpreters have, in fact, thought that Paul's bleak assessment of the human condition in Romans 1:18–3:20 was too unrelenting, that it was "exaggerated" for rhetorical effect, as one scholar puts it, and as contradictions within it show (2:14–15, 25–29), not actually what Paul thought.[9] It is unlikely, however, that Paul involved himself in such substantive contradiction within the space of a few paragraphs. It is more likely instead that he did hold, as his settled view, the idea that God required perfect obedience to the law in order that humanity might receive life but that human beings were enslaved to sin. With the modern proliferation of knowledge about the extent of human violence and oppression, it is becoming increasingly difficult for

7. B. M. Metzger, *OTP* 1:529.

8. J. H. Charlesworth, *OTP* 2:636.

9. Dodd, *Romans*, 62; Sanders, *Paul, the Law, and the Jewish People*, 123–32; Räisänen, *Paul and the Law*, 97–109.

anyone who seriously reflects on the human condition to maintain a much more optimistic view of human nature.[10]

After reeling off a lengthy series of bleak assessments of human nature by basically secular philosophers, Herman Bavinck made this perceptive comment:

> It is truly not Scripture alone that judges humans harshly. It is human beings who have pronounced the harshest and most severe judgment on themselves. And it is always better to fall into the hands of the Lord than into those of people, for his mercy is great. For when God condemns us, he at the same time offers his forgiving love in Christ, but when people condemn people, they frequently cast them out and make them the object of scorn.[11]

This gracious willingness of God not only to tell the unvarnished truth about human beings but to extend redemption to them through Jesus Christ is what makes the gospel, as Paul explains it in Romans, "good news."

God's Gracious Deliverance of Humanity in Christ

The Motive and Means of Deliverance

God's motive for delivering human beings from slavery to sin was simply his own gracious and merciful character, as Paul's generous use of terms for grace demonstrates. Whenever people have turned away from their disobedience to God, it has always been because God's "kindness" has led them to do this (2:4). "The deliverance that is in Christ Jesus," Paul says in 3:24, came to believers "freely" by God's "grace" (δωρεὰν τῇ αὐτοῦ χάριτι). God demonstrated his "love" when Christ died for people while they "were still sinners" (5:8; 8:32, 39). This unprecedented effort at reconciliation arose out of the superabundant "grace" of God and of Jesus Christ himself (5:15, 17, 20–21), and those who, by faith, receive this offer of reconciliation live under the reign of God's grace (6:14; cf. 5:17, 21). Their new life is a response to the mercy and "compassion" God has shown them (12:1; cf. 9:15; 11:30–32) and to the "welcome" God has given them (14:3; 15:7).

The means of this deliverance was the death and resurrection of Jesus Christ, God's Son and the king of God's people Israel. Christ's death both preserved God's commitment to justice and effected the forgiveness of sins necessary for reconciliation between God and human beings (3:26). His resurrection was the first step in the general resurrection of the dead (6:5; 8:11), which would reverse the effects of human mortality (5:10, 17–18), God's just penalty for sin (1:32; 5:12). Through their union

10. Räisänen acknowledges this ("it is easy for us, with all the introspective Christian insights from Augustine onwards at our disposal, to agree that no man comes close to moral perfection"), but believes that "Paul's mind is divided" on the issue (*Paul and the Law*, 107).

11. Bavinck, *Sin and Salvation in Christ*, 124.

with Christ by faith, human beings, Paul argues, can share in this resurrected life despite their continued existence in the flesh and their own experience of suffering and death (6:4, 8–12; 8:4, 9–11, 18–23).

God began his gracious work of deliverance at least as early as Abraham, the forefather of God's people Israel (4:1), through whom the Messiah would come to deliver not only Israel but all humanity from sin (9:5; cf. 1:3–4). God entered into a peaceful relationship with Abraham despite his former impiety and based this relationship on Abraham's trust rather than any worth Abraham had to offer (4:1–5; cf. Gen 15:6).[12] This gracious act of God set in motion the means by which God would "justify the circumcision by faith and the uncircumcision through that same faith" (Rom 3:30). God gave Abraham and his descendants through Isaac and Jacob (9:7–13) the physical marker of circumcision as a "sign" and "seal" of the completely gracious relationship he had established with Abraham (4:11). This demonstrated that God would solve the problem of human impiety by means of graciously justifying those who trusted him and that he would do this both for Israelites, who carried the physical mark of circumcision, and for everyone else (4:9–12). God's gracious offer of justification by faith, therefore, not only rescued people from their sin but fulfilled God's promise to make Abraham "the father of many nations" (4:13–18; cf. Gen 17:5).

Israel, the descendants of Abraham through Isaac and Jacob (Rom 9:7–13), were the recipients of the Mosaic law (9:4), and the law was a trust they were given (3:2) and by which they would both know and be able to teach others the holy, righteous, and good will of God (2:17–20; 7:12). The Mosaic law not only contained specific teaching about God's identity as the only God and about the loving relationships he required of his human creation (2:21–22; 13:8–10). It also revealed that God is a gracious God, willing to forgive human sin against himself and generously provide the means of reconciliation with his human creatures (2:4; 3:25; cf. Exod 25:17–22; Lev 16:2, 13–15).

The effect of the law within Israel, however, was similar to the effect of the command God gave to Adam not to eat of the tree in the midst of the garden (Rom 5:18a; Gen 3:11). Sin took advantage of the law to create even more rebellion against God (Rom 2:17–24; 5:20–21; 7:5, 7–24, 25b). Rather than embracing the Messiah when he came as the goal of the law, many within Israel rejected him, driven by a misguided zeal for God that focused on the law (9:30–10:4). In doing this, Israel was neither more nor less culpable than non-Israelites, who also rejected God's revelation of himself to them. Israel was merely doing "the same things" as everyone else (2:1).

None of this, however, lay outside of God's plan for delivering his human creatures from their own destructive behavior. God gave the law "so that the trespass

12. Barclay, *Paul and the Gift*, 481, 485–86.

might increase" (5:20) and to demonstrate in this way how powerful and harmful sin against him actually was (7:13).

It was at this point—"at just the right time"—that Israel's Messiah, Jesus, "died for the impious" (5:6). By his death Jesus endured the penalty of death that all violators of God's law, whether Jew or gentile, deserved (1:32; 2:5, 8–9, 12). According to Paul, this category of people included everyone from the time of Adam forward (3:10–20), with the one exception of Jesus Christ himself (8:3). Paul could compare the crucified Jesus to "the mercy seat" (ἱλαστήριον) in Israel's temple (3:25). He was the "place" where God revealed himself most intensely to humanity and where God graciously reconciled to himself all who would receive this reconciliation (5:17).

Paul can refer to this reconciling, justifying action on God's part as "the righteousness of God" (3:21–22, 25–26) for two reasons. First, it was a means of rescuing human beings from their sin that allowed God to remain "just" and yet "justify," or release from punishment, those who deserved to be punished (3:26). It could do this because Jesus's death was a vicarious, substitutionary death (8:3), willingly undertaken (15:3, 7), and as costly to the Father as it was to the Son (5:10; 8:32). Second, it was a means of remaining faithful to his promises to Abraham and to his people Israel, both to make Abraham the father of many nations (4:17–18) and not to reject Israel (11:2, 29; 15:8). The abundantly gracious gift of salvation for Jews and gentiles through the atoning death of Christ, therefore, was a demonstration of "the righteousness of God" because it showed God to be faithful to his word (cf. 9:6).

As important as the death of Christ was for the forgiveness of humanity's disobedience to God (3:24; 4:6–9), however, it was far from the only element of Christ's existence that was important in the deliverance of human beings from sin. The superabundant grace that God showed in the death of Christ for people that were still his enemies (5:6–8, 10) set up a situation in which grace powerfully reigns over believers (5:21) and in which their existence is now "under grace" (ὑπὸ χάριν [6:14–15]).[13] They are united with Christ in his death and resurrection, and this union has broken sin's death-dealing stranglehold over them (6:3–7). It has also provided them access to the life-giving power of the living and ascended Christ (6:8–11; 7:5–6; 8:33–34). They are no longer slaves of sin but of righteousness, and by the power of the Holy Spirit are able to submit to God's law, resist the sinful tendencies of the "flesh," and live in ways that are pleasing to God (6:17; 7:6; 8:4, 6–8).

The compassion that God has shown to humanity in delivering both Jewish and gentile believers from sin empowers them to offer their transformed minds and lives to God in humble, loving service to others within the church (12:3–13). It also empowers them to seek reconciliation with those outside the church who persecute them (12:14, 17–21; 13:8–10) and provides an example of welcoming rather than

13. Barclay, *Paul and the Gift*, 494–500.

condemning and despising those who are different from them (14:1, 3; 15:3, 7). The justification and forgiveness that God has graciously given his people in the death of Christ, therefore, do not conclude God's gracious work among his people but open the door to an existence of "life and peace" (8:6).

The Goal of Deliverance

This existence of life and peace does not appear in its fullness immediately. Rather, in the present time, before God's wrath and salvation arrive on the final day, believers experience their new life within an existence not yet completely free from the tendency to sin (8:12–13, 17) and in the midst of suffering and persecution (8:17, 35–36; 12:14, 17–21). Paul must remind his audience to offer their bodies to God as pleasing sacrifices, to avoid patterning their lives after this age, and to allow God to transform them by renewing their thinking (12:1–2). The present time was, for Paul, a period of tension between the new life of the believing community and an existence still marked by sin, suffering, and death (8:18–23).

It was also a period in which the fulfillment of God's promises to Israel still lay in the future. Although God's promise that Abraham would be "the father of many nations" (4:17–18) was in the process of fulfillment as gentiles in an ever widening area believed the gospel (1:5, 8, 14–15; 15:19–20, 23–24), many Jewish people who had heard the gospel had rejected its message (9:2–3; 10:1–3, 21; 11:7–10). This meant that at least one important element of God's promise to make a new covenant with his people (Jer 31:31–34) remained unfulfilled (Rom 11:27). Many gentiles had experienced the Spirit's empowerment to fulfill God's law (8:4, 8–9), but many Jews had not yet experienced the fulfillment of a promise that, in the first instance, was directed to them. Yet, "God has no misgivings about his gifts and calling" to Israel (11:29).

Paul was careful to point out that the situation prevailing in his own day, in which most of Israel had not believed the gospel, did not imply the failure of God's word even if it never changed. Spiritual Israel had always been a subset of physical Israel (9:6–13), and there was in fact a remnant of Jewish believers, including Paul himself (11:1–10). Still, such a small benefit from the gospel for the people whom God had specially gifted and called would not be consistent with the unparalleled nature of God's graciousness (11:30–32).

How could the puzzle of Israel's rejection of their Messiah be explained in a way that was consistent with God's gracious character? Paul maintained that despite present appearances God's plan for the advancement of the gospel would eventually unfold in a way that would demonstrate his great grace and mercy. Israel's present rejection of the gospel had allowed it to flow to the gentiles, but this movement of the gospel to the gentiles would play an important role in the eventual salvation of Israel (11:11–12, 15–16, 25–32; cf. 8:18–19). When Israel saw gentiles receiving many of the blessings God had promised them (9:4–5), they would eventually emulate the gentiles and embrace the gospel also. "And so," Paul says, "all Israel will be saved" (11:26).

This final step in the fulfillment of his promises to his people would also signal the reconciliation of the created order to God (11:12, 15–16). The "eager expectation of creation" for "the revelation of the sons of God" (8:19) would be fulfilled as the Jewish Messiah came to establish in all its fullness his kingdom of righteousness, peace, and joy in the Holy Spirit (11:26; 14:17). Jews and gentiles together would sing harmonious praise to God as the Messiah established a new society of life and peace (15:7–13). In effect, by the time Paul's audience arrived at the closing paragraphs of his main argument (15:7–13), the apostle had succeeded in reversing the horrific picture of irrational idolatry and social discord that dominated the main argument's opening paragraphs (1:18–32). This dramatic reversal, motivated simply and entirely by the superabundant grace of God, is what makes the gospel as Paul envisioned it in Romans such good news.

Scripture Index

Genesis

Exodus

Leviticus

Numbers

Deuteronomy

Joshua

Judges

Ruth

1 Samuel

2 Samuel

1 Kings

2 Kings

Ezra

Nehemiah

Job

Psalms

Proverbs

Ecclesiastes

Song of Solomon

Isaiah

Jonah

Micah

Habakkuk

Zephaniah

Zechariah

Malachi

Matthew

Mark

Luke

John

Acts

Romans

1 Corinthians

2 Corinthians

Galatians

Ephesians

Philippians

Colossians

1 Thessalonians

2 Thessalonians

1 Timothy

2 Timothy

2 John

3 John

Jude

Revelation

Other Ancient Literature Index

Apocrypha

Tobit

Judith

Additions to Esther

Wisdom of Solomon

Sirach

Old Testament Pseudepigrapha

Philo

On Rewards and Punishments

On the Cherubim

On the Confusion of Tongues

On the Creation of the World

On the Decalogue

On the Embassy to Gaius

On the Life of Abraham

On the Life of Joseph

On the Life of Moses 1, 2

On the Migration of Abraham

On the Preliminary Studies

On the Special Laws 1, 2, 3, 4

On the Virtues

That Every Good Person is Free

Who is the Heir?

Josephus

Against Apion

Jewish Antiquities

Subject Index

Author Index